Phillip Miller Augustus Fleming Agnes Chase

The Gardeners Dictionary

Containing the best and newest methods of cultivating and improving the kitchen, fruit,

flower garden, and nursery, as also for performing the practical parts of agriculture :

including the management of vineyards, with the

Phillip Miller Augustus Fleming Agnes Chase

The Gardeners Dictionary
*Containing the best and newest methods of cultivating and improving the kitchen, fruit,
flower garden, and nursery, as also for performing the practical parts of agriculture :
including the management of vineyards, with the*

ISBN/EAN: 9783743308817

Manufactured in Europe, USA, Canada, Australia, Japa

Cover: Foto ©Thomas Meinert / pixelio.de

Manufactured and distributed by brebook publishing software (www.brebook.com)

Phillip Miller Augustus Fleming Agnes Chase

The Gardeners Dictionary

fruitful; and another thing should be observed in planting of the succeeding crops, which is, to make choice of moist strong land for the later crops; for if they are planted on dry ground, they rarely produce a crop.

These after-crops should be planted at about a fortnight distance from each other, from the middle of February to the middle of May; after which time it is generally too late to plant, unless the land is very strong and moist; for in warm dry light land all the late crops of Beans are generally attacked by the black insects, which cover all the upper part of their stems, and soon cause them to decay.

Where the seeds of these Beans are designed to be saved, a sufficient number of rows should be set apart for that purpose, according to the quantity desired; these should be managed in the same way as those which are designed for the table; but none of the Beans should be gathered, though there are some covetous persons, who will gather all the first ripe for the table, and are contented to save the after-crop for seed, but these are never so large and fair as the first; so that if these are for sale, they will not bring near the price as the other; therefore, what is gained to the table is lost in the value of the seed; but those who are desirous to preserve the several varieties as pure as possible, should never suffer two of the varieties to grow for seeds in the same place; for by their farina mixing with each other they will not continue so pure, but be apt to vary; and in order to keep the early kinds perfect, those which come the earliest should be saved for seeds; but this is what few people chuse to do, because they are then the most valuable.

When the seed is ripe, the stalks should be pulled up, and set upright against a hedge to dry, observing to turn them every third day, that they may dry equally; then they may be threshed out, and cleaned for use, or otherwise stacked up in a barn, till there is more leisure for threshing them out; and afterward the seed should be drawn over to take out all those that are not fair, preserving the best for use or sale.

It is a very good method to change the seeds of all sorts of Beans, and not to sow and save the seeds long in the same ground, for they do not succeed so well; therefore, if the land is strong where they are to be planted, it will be the best way to procure the seeds from a lighter ground, and so vice versa; and by this method the crops will be larger, and the Beans fairer, and not so liable to degenerate.

Having given directions for the culture of the Garden Beans, I shall next proceed to that of the Horse Bean, which is cultivated in the fields: there are two or three varieties of these Beans, which differ in their size and colour; but that which is now in the greatest esteem, is called the Tick Bean; this doth not grow so high as the other, is a more plentiful bearer, and succeeds better on light land than the common Horse Bean, so preferred to it.

The Horse Bean delights in a strong moist soil, and an open exposure, for they never thrive well on dry warm land, or in small inclosures, where they are very subject to blight, and are frequently attacked by a black insect, which the farmers call the black dolphin; these insects are often in such quantities as to cover the stems of the Beans entirely, especially all the upper part of them; and whenever this happens, the Beans seldom come to good; but in the open fields, where the soil is strong, this rarely happens.

These Beans are usually sown on land which is fresh broken up, because they are of use to break and pulverize the ground, as also to destroy weeds; so that the land is rendered much better for corn, after a crop of Beans, than it would have been before, especially if they are sown and managed according to the new husbandry, with a drill plough, and the horse hoe, used to stir the ground between the rows of Beans, which will prevent the growth of weeds, and pulverize the ground, whereby a much greater crop

of Beans may, with more certainty, be expected, and the land will be better prepared for whatever crop it is designed for after.

The season for sowing of these Beans is from the middle of February to the end of March, according to the nature of the soil; the strongest and wet land should always be last sown; the usual quantity of Beans sown on an acre of land is about three bushels; but this is double the quantity which need be sown, especially according to the new husbandry; but I shall first set down the practice according to the old husbandry, and then give directions for their management according to the new. The method of sowing is after the plough, in the bottom of the furrows; but then the furrows should not be more than five, or at most six inches deep. If the land is new broken up, it is usual to plough it early in autumn, and let it lie in ridges till after Christmas; then plough it in small furrows, and lay the ground smooth; these two ploughings will break the ground fine enough for Beans; and the third ploughing is to sow the Beans; when the furrows should be made shallow, as was before mentioned.

Most people set their Beans too close; for, as some lay the Beans in the furrows after the plough, and others lay them before the plough, and plough them in; so, by both methods the Beans are set as close as the furrows are made, which is much too near; for when they are on strong good land, they generally are drawn up to a very great height, and are not so apt to pod as when they have more room, and are of lower growth; therefore I am convinced by many late trials, that the better way is to make the furrows two feet and a half asunder, or more; which will cause them to branch out into many stalks, and bear in greater plenty than when they are closer; by this method, half the quantity of Beans will be sufficient for an acre of land; and by the sun and air being admitted between the rows, the Beans will ripen much earlier and more equally than in the common way.

What has been mentioned must be understood as relating to the old husbandry; but where Beans are planted according to the new, the ground should be four times ploughed before the Beans are set, which will break the clods, and render it much better for planting; then with a drill plough, to which a hopper is fixed for setting of the Beans, the drills should be made at three feet asunder, and the spring of the hopper set so as to scatter the Beans at three inches distance in the drills. By this method less than one bushel of seed will plant an acre of land. When the Beans are up, if the ground is stirred between the rows with a horse plough, it will destroy all the young weeds; and when the Beans are advanced about three or four inches high, the ground should be again ploughed between the rows, and the earth laid up to the Beans; and if a third ploughing, at about five or six weeks after is given, the ground will be kept clean from weeds; and the Beans will stalk out, and produce a much greater crop than in the common way.

When the Beans are ripe, they are reaped with a hook, as is usually practised for Peas; and after having lain a few days on the ground they are turned, and this must be repeated several times, until they are dry enough to stack; but the best method is to tie them in small bundles, and set them upright; for then they will not be in so much danger to suffer by wet, as when they lie on the ground; and they will be more handy to carry and stack, than if they are loose. The common produce is from twenty to twenty-five bushels on an acre of land; but I have known thirty-six on an acre.

The Beans should lie in the mow to sweat, before they are threshed out; for as the haulm is very large and succulent, so it is very apt to give and grow moist; but there is no danger of the Beans receiving damage, if they are stacked tolerably dry, because the pods will preserve the Beans from injury; and they will be much easier to thresh after they have sweat in the mow than before ; and after they have once fweated and are dry again, they never after give.

By the new hufbandry, the produce has exceeded the old by more than ten bufhels on an acre ; and if the Beans which are cultivated in the common method are obferved, it will be found that more than half their ftems have no Beans on them ; for by ftanding clofe, they are drawn up very tall ; fo the tops of the ftalks only produce, and all the lower part is naked ; whereas in the new method, they bear almoft to the ground; and as the joints of the ftems are fhorter, fo the Beans grow clofer together on the ftalks.

In the year 1745 I made the following experiment, in planting a piece of eleven acres of Beans in Berkfhire, viz. the gentleman's bailiff, who was wedded to the old practice of hufbandry, was very unwilling to depart from it ; and having been an old fervant in the family, his mafter was inclinable to hear all he could fay in favour of his opinion : however, at laft I prevailed on the gentleman to let his bailiff plant one half of the land in his way, giving him the choice which half he would have : accordingly the land was divided and planted; but the fummer proving wet, the Beans on that part of the field he had chofen grew fo tall and rank, that they produced no pods but on the upper part of the ftalks ; and when they were threfhed out, there was no more than twenty-two bufhels on an acre, whereas the other half produced near forty.

FABA ÆGYPTIACA, is the Arum Ægyptiacum.

FABA CRASSA, is Anacampferos.

FABAGO. See ZYGOPHYLLUM.

FAGARA. Brown. Hift. Jam. tab. 5. f. 1. Ironwood.

The CHARACTERS are,

It hath male and hermephrodite flowers upon different plants ; the male flowers have a fmall empalement, flightly cut into four fegments, but have no petals, and fix ftamina, terminated by roundifh fummits : thefe are barren. The female flowers have a larger concave permanent empalement with four fpreading petals, and four ftamina, crowned with oval germens, and an oval germen, fupporting a flender ftyle, terminated by an obtufe ftigma ; the germen afterward becomes a globular capfule with two lobes, inclofing two feeds.

This genus of plants is ranged in the firft fection of Linnæus's fourth clafs, intitled Tetrandria Monogynia ; whereas it fhould be put into his fixth fection of the twenty-third clafs, as the flowers are male and hermaphrodite on different plants, and the flowers have fix ftamina ; but this miftake he was led into by Jacquin, who had feen and defcribed the hermaphrodite flowers only.

The SPECIES are,

1. FAGARA (*Pterota*) foliolis emarginatis. Amœn. Acad. 5. p. 393. *Fagara, whofe lobes (or fmall leaves) are indented at the top.* Lauro affinis jafmini alato folio, cofta media membranulis utrinque extantibus alata, ligno duritie ferro vix cedens. Sloan. Hift. Jam. 2. p. 25. *Ironwood.*

2. FAGARA (*Tragodes*) articulis pinnarum fubtus aculeatus. Jacq. Amer. 13. *Fagara with fpines under the leaves at the joints.* Schinoides petiolis fubtus aculeatis. Hort. Cliff. 489.

The firft fort grows naturally in the warmeft parts of America. The late Dr. Houftoun found it growing at Campeachy, from whence he fent me dried fpecimens of the plants in flower, by which I am convinced there are male trees which are barren. It rifes with a woody ftem upwards of twenty feet high, fending out branches great part of its length, garnifhed with fmall winged leaves, having three or five lobes to each. The flowers come from the fide of the branches, ftanding four or five together upon fhort foot-ftalks.

The fecond fort I have placed here after Linnæus, but am not fure it fhould be ranged with it ; for although I have pretty ftrong plants of it growing in the Chelfea garden, they have not yet flowered ; but by the external face of the plant, it feems to agree with the firft.

Thefe are both tender plants, fo muft be kept in the bark-ftove conftantly, and are propagated by feeds, and alfo by cuttings, if properly managed.

FAGONIA. Tourn. Inft. R. H. 265. tab. 141. Lin. Gen. Plant. 475. This plant was fo named by Dr. Tournefort, in honour of Dr. Fagon, who was fuperintendant of the royal garden at Paris.

The CHARACTERS are,

The flower hath a fpreading empalement, compofed of five fmall leaves ; it hath five heart-fhaped petals, which fpread open, and are narrow at their bafe, where they are inferted in the empalement. It hath ten ftamina which are erect, terminated by roundifh fummits. In the center is fituated a five-cornered germen, fupporting an awl-fhaped ftyle, crowned by a fingle ftigma. The germen afterward becomes a roundifh capfule having five lobes, ending in a point, and five cells, each having a fingle roundifh feed.

Linnæus ranges this plant in the firft fection of his tenth clafs, intitled Decandria Monogynia, from the flower having ten ftamina and one ftyle.

The SPECIES are,

1. FAGONIA (*Erecta*) fpinofa, foliolis lanceolatis planis lævibus. Hort. Upfal. 103. *Prickly Fagonia, whofe leaves are fpear-fhaped, plain, and fmooth.* Fagonia Cretica fpinofa. Tourn. *Thorny Trefoil of Candia.*

2. FAGONIA (*Hifpanica*) inermis. Lin. Sp. Plant. 386. *Fagonia without fpines.* Fagonia Hifpanica non fpinofa. Tourn. *Spanifh Fagonia without thorns.*

3. FAGONIA (*Arabica*) fpinofa, foliolis linearibus convexis. Lin. Sp. Plant. 386. *Prickly Fagonia with narrow convex leaves.* Fagonia Arabica, longiffimis aculeis armato. Shaw. Pl. Afr. 229. *Arabian Fagonia, armed with very long fpines.*

The firft fort is a native of the ifland of Candia ; this has been defcribed by fome botanifts under the title of Trifolium fpinofum Creticum, which occafioned my giving it the Englifh name of Thorny Trefoil of Crete ; though there is no other affinity between this and the Trefoil, than that of this having three leaves or lobes on the fame foot-ftalk.

This is a low plant, which fpreads its branches clofe to the ground, which are extended to the length of a foot or more every way, garnifhed with fmall trifoliate oval leaves, placed oppofite ; and at each joint, immediately below the leaves, come out two pair of fpines, one on each fide the ftalk ; and at the fame places come out a fingle blue flower, ftanding upon a fhort foot-ftalk, compofed of five fpear-fhaped petals, which are narrow at their bafe, where they are inferted into the empalement ; after thefe fall away, the germen turns to a roundifh five-lobed capfule, ending in an acute point, having five cells, each containing one roundifh feed. It flowers in July and Auguft, but unlefs the feafon proves warm, the feeds do not ripen in England.

The fecond fort grows naturally in Spain ; this differs from the firft in being fmooth, the branches of this having no thorns ; and the plant will live two years, whereas the firft is annual.

The third fort was difcovered by the late Dr. Shaw in Arabia ; this is a low plant with a fhrubby ftalk, from which come out feveral weak branches armed with long thorns ; the leaves of this are thick, narrow, and convex on their lower fide ; the flowers come out in the fame manner as in the firft fort.

Thefe plants are propagated by feeds, which fhould be fown upon a border of frefh light earth, where the plants are defigned to remain, for they do not bear tranfplanting well ; when the plants come up, they may be thinned out to the diftance of ten inches or a foot ; and if they are kept clean from weeds, they will require no other care.

The firft fort is an annual p ant, which feldom perfects its feeds in England, unlefs the feafons prove very warm ; therefore the beft way is to fow the feeds upon a warm border in the autumn, and in frofty weather fhelter the plants with mats, or fome covering to fecure them ; or if they are fown in

pots

pots and placed under a frame in the winter, and the following spring shaken out of the pots, and planted in a warm border, they will come early to flower, and thereby ripe seeds may be more certainly obtained.

The other two sorts may be treated in the same way; for as these seldom flower the first year from seeds, so the plants should be either kept in pots, and sheltered under a frame in winter, or placed in a warm border, where they may be sheltered with mats, or some other covering, to preserve them from the frost; and the following summer the second sort will flower and produce ripe seeds, but the third has not perfected any seeds as yet in England.

FAGOPYRUM. See Helxine.

FAGUS. Tourn. Inst. R. H. 584. tab. 351. Lin. Gen. Plant. 951. [so called from φάγω, Gr. because supposed to be the food of the first race of mankind.] The Beech-tree; in French, *Hêtre*.

The Characters are,

It hath male and female flowers on the same tree; the male flowers are collected into globular heads; these have no petals, but have several stamina included in an empalement of one leaf, which are terminated by oblong summits. The female flowers have a one-leaved empalement cut into four parts, but have no petals; the germen is fixed to the empalement, supporting three styles, crowned by reflexed stigmas. The germen afterward becomes a roundish capsule, armed with soft spines, opening in three cells, each containing a triangular nut.

This genus of plants is ranged in the eighth section of Linnæus's twenty-first class, which includes those plants that have male and female flowers on the same plant, and the male flowers have many stamina. To this genus he has joined the Chesnut; but as the male flowers of the Chesnut are collected in long katkins, and those of the Beech are globular, and the fruit of the latter being triangular, there is sufficient reason for keeping them separate.

We know but one Species of this genus, viz.

Fagus (*Sylvatica*) foliis ovatis obsolete serratis. Hort. Cliff. 447. Fagus. Dod. Pempt. 832. *The Beech-tree with oval sawed leaves.*

There are some planters, who suppose there are two distinct species of this tree; one they call the Mountain Beech, which they say is a whiter wood than the other, which they distinguish by the title of Wild Beech; but it is certain, that this difference in the colour of the wood arises from the difference of the soils in which they grew, for I have not seen any specific difference in the trees. There have been seeds of a Beech-tree brought from North-America, by the title of Broad-leaved Beech, but the plants which were raised from them proved to be the common sort; so that we know of no other variety, excepting those with striped leaves, which is accidental; and when the trees are in vigour, the leaves become plain again. This tree is propagated by sowing the mast; the season for which is any time from October to February, only observing to secure the seeds from vermin when early sowed; which, if carefully done, the sooner they are sown the better, after they are full ripe: a small spot of ground will be sufficient for raising a great number of these trees from seed, but you must be very careful to keep them clear from weeds; and if the plants come up very thick, you should not fail to draw out the strongest of them the autumn following, that those left may have room to grow; so that if you husband a seed-bed carefully, it will afford a three years draught of young plants, which should be planted in a nursery; and, if designed for timber trees, at three feet distance row from row, and eighteen inches asunder in the rows.

But if they are designed for hedges (to which the tree is very well adapted) the distance need not be so great; two feet row from row, and one foot in the rows will be sufficient. In this nursery they may remain two or three years, observing to clear them from

weeds, as also to dig up the ground between the rows, at least once a year, that their tender roots may the better extend themselves each way: but be careful not to cut or bruise their roots, which is injurious to all young trees; and never dig the ground in summer, when the earth is hot and dry; which, by letting in the rays of the sun to the roots, is often the destruction of young trees.

This tree will grow to a considerable stature, though the soil be stony and barren; as also upon the declivities of hills, and chalky mountains, where they will resist the winds better than most other trees; but then the nurseries for the young plants ought to be upon the same soil; for if they are raised in good soil and a warm exposure, and afterwards transplanted into a bleak barren situation, they seldom thrive, which holds true in most other trees; therefore I would advise the nursery to be made upon the same soil where the plantation is intended, but of this I shall say more under the article of Nursery.

The tree is very proper to form large hedges to surround plantations, or large wilderness quarters; and may be kept in a regular figure, if sheared twice a year, especially if they shoot strong; in which case, if they are neglected but a season or two, it will be difficult to reduce them again. The shade of this tree is very injurious to most sorts of plants which grow near it, but is generally believed to be very salubrious to human bodies.

The timber is of great use to turners for making trenchers, dishes, trays, buckets; and likewise to the joiner for stools, bedsteads, coffins, &c. The mast is very good to fat swine and deer; it also affords a sweet oil, and the nuts have in scarce times supported some families with bread.

This tree delights in a chalky or stony ground, where it generally grows very fast; and the bark of the trees in such land is clear and smooth; and although the timber is not so valuable as that of many other trees, yet as it will thrive on such soils and in such situations where few better trees will scarce grow, the planting of them should be encouraged; especially as the trees afford an agreeable shade, and the leaves make a fine appearance in summer, and continue green as long in autumn as any of the deciduous trees: therefore in parks, and other plantations for pleasure, this tree deserves to be cultivated among those of the first class, especially where the soil is adapted to it.

The two sorts with variegated leaves may be propagated by budding or grafting them upon the common Beech, observing not to plant them in a good earth; which will cause the buds or cyons to shoot vigorously, whereby the leaves will become plain, which often happens to most variegated plants.

FARINA FŒCUNDANS is the impregnating meal or dust on the apices or summits of flowers; which, being conveyed into the uterus or vasculum seminale of plants, fecundates the rudiments of the seeds in the ovary, which otherwise would decay and come to nothing. See Generation of Plants.

FEATHERFEW, or FEAVERFEW. See Matricaria.

FENCES. In hotter climates than England, where they have not occasion for walls to ripen their fruit, their gardens lie open, where they can have water fence and prospects; or else they bound their gardens with groves, in which are fountains, walks, &c. which are much more pleasing to the sight than a dead wall: but in colder countries, and in England, we are obliged to have walls to shelter and ripen our fruit, although they take away much from the pleasant prospect of the garden.

Since therefore we are under a necessity to have walls to secure our gardens from the injury of winds, as well as for the conveniency of partitions or inclosures, and also to ripen our fruit, brick walls are accounted the warmest and best for this purpose: and these walls being built pannel-ways, with pillars at equal distances, will save a great deal of charge, in that

the

the walls may be built thinner, than if they were built plain without thefe pannels, for then it would be neceffary to build them thicker every where: and befides, thefe pannels make the walls look the handfomer.

Stone walls are by fome preferred to thofe of brick, efpecially thofe of fquare hewn ftones; but where they are defigned for fruit, they fhould be faced with brick. Thofe that are made of rough ftones, though they are very dry and warm, yet, by reafon of their unevennefs, are inconvenient to nail up trees to, except pieces of timber be laid in them here and there for to faften a trellis to them.

But in large gardens it is better to have the profpect open to the pleafure-garden, which fhould be furrounded with a foffe, that from the garden the adjacent country may be viewed, but this muft depend on the fituation of the place; for if the profpect from the garden is not good, it had better be fhut out from the fight by a wall, or any other fence, than to be open. As alfo, where a garden lies near a populous town, and the adjoining grounds are open to the inhabitants, if the garden is open, there will be no walking there in good weather, without being expofed to the view of all paffengers, which is very difagreeable.

Where thefe foffes are made round a garden which is fituated in a park, they are extremely proper; becaufe hereby the profpect of the park will be obtained in the garden, which renders thefe gardens much more agreeable than thofe which are confined.

In the making thefe foffes there have been many inventions; but, upon the whole, I have not feen any which are in all refpects preferable to thofe which have an upright wall next the garden; which (where the foil will admit of a deep trench) fhould be fix or feven feet high, fo as to be above the reach of boys; and from the foot of this wall, the ground on the outfide fhould rife with a gradual eafy flope to the diftance of eighteen or twenty feet; and where it can be allowed, if it flopes much farther, it will be eafier and lefs perceptible as a ditch to the eye, when viewed at a diftance. But if the ground is naturally wet, fo as not to admit of a deep foffe, then, in order to make a fence againft cattle, if the wall be four feet high, and flight pofts of three feet and a half high are placed juft behind the wall, with a fmall chain carried on from poft to poft, no cattle or deer will ever attempt to jump againft it, therefore it will be a fecure fence againft them; and if thefe are painted of a dark lead colour, they will not be difcerned at a diftance; and at the fame time the chain will fecure perfons walking in the garden from tumbling over: and if another chain is carried through the pofts at one foot from the ground, it will more effectually prevent cattle from creeping under.

In fuch places where there are no good profpects to be obtained from a garden, it is common to make the inclofure of park-paling; which, if well performed, will laft many years, and has a much better appearance than a wall: and this pale may be hid from the fight within, by plantations of fhrubs and Evergreens; or there may be a quick hedge planted within the pale, which may be trained up, fo as to be an excellent fence by the time the pales begin to decay. There are fome perfons who make ftuckade fences round their gardens to keep out cattle, &c. which, when well made, will anfwer the purpofe of a fence; but this being very expenfive in the making, and not of very long duration, has occafioned their not being more commonly in ufe.

As to fences round parks, they are generally of paling; which, if well made of winter-fallen Oak, will laft many years; but a principal thing to be obferved in making thefe pales, is not to make them too heavy; for when they are fo, their own weight will caufe them to decay; therefore the pale fhould be cleft thin, and the rails fhould be cut triangular, to prevent the wet lodging upon them; and the pofts fhould be good, and not placed too far afunder, burning that part of them as goes into the ground. If thefe things are ob-

ferved, one of thefe pales will laft, with a little care, upward of forty years very well. The common way of making thefe fences is, to have every other pale nine or ten inches above the intermediate ones; fo that the fence may be fix feet and a half high, which is enough for fallow deer; but where there are red deer, the fence fhould be one foot higher, otherwife they will leap over.

Some inclofe their parks with brick walls; and in countries where ftone is cheap, the walls are built with this material; fome with, and others without mortar.

A kitchen-garden, if rightly contrived, will contain walling enough to afford a fupply of fuch fruits as require the affiftance of a wall for any family; and this garden being fituated on one fide, and quite out of fight of the houfe, may be furrounded with walls, which will fcreen the kitchen-garden from the fight of perfons in the pleafure-garden; and being locked up, the fruit will be much better preferved than it can be in the public garden: and the having too great a quantity of walling is often the occafion that fo many fcandalous fences are frequently to be feen in large gardens, where there is not due care obferved in their management.

And befides, the borders of pleafure-gardens are generally too narrow for the roots of fruit-trees, as will be fhewn in its proper place, therefore it is in vain to plant them there.

The height of garden-walls fhould be from ten to twelve feet, which is a moderate proportion; and if the foil be good, it may in time be well furnifhed with bearing wood in every part, efpecially thofe parts planted with Pears, notwithftanding the branches being trained horizontally from the bottom of the walls.

I would recommend the White Thorn, the Holly, the Black Thorn and Crab, for outward fences to a good ground, but I do not approve of the intermixing them.

The White Thorn is the beft quick to plant, becaufe it is the moft common, and may be clipped fo as to render it the clofeft and hardieft fence of any other tree; and being very durable, is preferred to all others for outward fences, or for the divifion of fields, where they are expofed to cattle, &c.

The Black Thorn and Crab make very good fences, and are to be raifed as the White Thorn; but if the kernels of Apples or Crabs be fown, it is beft to fow the pommace with them, and they will come up the fooner, i. e. the firft year, if fown in the autumn, foon after the fruit is ripe.

If Crab-ftocks be planted while young, in the fame manner as quick, they make excellent hedges foon, and fo will fome forts of Plumbs, I mean fuch as have thorns.

The Black Thorn is not accounted fo good for fences as the White Thorn, becaufe it is apt to run more into the ground, and is not certain as to the growing, efpecially if the plants are not fet very young; but then on the other hand, the bufhes are by much the better, and are alfo more lafting than the White Thorn, or any other, for dead hedges, or to mend gaps; nor are they fubject to be cropt by cattle, as the others are. The richer the mould is, the better they will profper, but yet they will grow on the fame fort of foil that the White Thorn does.

The Holly will make an excellent fence, and is preferable to all the reft, but is a flow grower; but when once it does grow, it makes amends by its height, ftrength, and thicknefs.

It is raifed of young feedling plants or berries, as the White Thorn is, and the berries will lie as long in the ground before they come up. It delights moft in ftrong grounds, but will grow upon the drieft gravel, amongft rocks and ftones.

The berries lie till the fecond fpring before they come up, therefore they fhould be prepared before they are fown (for this fee the article AQUIFOLIUM.) It will be beft to fow them in the place where you defign

3

they

they fhould grow, but they fhould be well weeded both before they come up and afterwards.

French Furz will alfo do well upon dry fandy banks, where few other plants will grow; but they muft be kept very clean at the bottom, and cut thin, and never fuffered to grow too high: nor fhould they be cut in dry weather, or late in autumn, nor early in the fpring; the doing either of which is fubject to make it die in patches, which is irrecoverable; nor will it ever break out again from old wood, if cut clofe in, after it has been fuffered long to grow out.

Fences may likewife be made of Elder: if the foil be any thing good, you may put fticks of Elder, or truncheons ten or twelve feet long, flopeways in your banks, fo as to make a chequer-work; and they will make a fence for a garden the quickeft of any thing, and be a good fhelter. But thefe fences are improper for a fine garden, becaufe they fhoot very irregular, and are ungovernable; as likewife the roots of thefe trees fpread very far, and draw away all the heart of the ground, fo as to ftarve whatever plants grow near them: and add to this the fcattering of the berries, which will fill the ground near them with young plants; which, if not timely weeded out, will get the better of whatever grows near them; therefore this fort of fence is feldom planted, where a hedge of White Thorn can be had.

Elder planted on a bank, the fide of which is wafhed with a river or ftream, will make an extraordinary fence, and will preferve the bank from being undermined by the water, becaufe it is continually fending fuckers from the roots and lower branches, which is of great advantage where the ftream wafhes away the bank. For middle fences in a garden, the Yew is the moft tonfile, governable, and durable plant.

For furrounding wildernefs quarters, Elm, Lime, Hornbeam and Beech, are very proper.

FENNEL. See FOENICULUM.

FENNEL-FLOWER. See NIGELLA.

FERRUM EQUINUM. See HIPPOCREPIS.

FERULA. Lin. Gen. Plant. 305. Tourn. Inft. R. H. 321. tab. 170. [takes its name of Ferendo, Lat. becaufe the ftalks of this plant are made ufe of in fupporting the branches of trees; or of Feriendo, becaufe in old time fticks were made of them, with which fchool-mafters ufed to correct their fcholars.] Fennel Giant; in French, Ferule.

The CHARACTERS are,

It hath an umbellated flower; the principal umbel is globular, and is compofed of feveral fmaller called rays, of the fame form; the involucrum is compofed of feveral narrow leaves which fall off; the principal umbel is uniform. The flowers have five oblong erect petals which are equal, and five ftamina of the fame length, terminated by fingle fummits; under the flower is fituated a turbinated germen, fupporting two reflexed ftyles, crowned by obtufe ftigmas. The germen afterward becomes an elliptical, compreffed, plain fruit, dividing in two parts, each having a large elliptical plain feed, marked with three lines on each fide.

This genus of plants is ranged in the fecond fection of Linnæus's fifth clafs, intitled Pentandria Digynia, which contains thofe plants whofe flowers have five ftamina and two ftyles.

The SPECIES are,

1. FERULA (*Communis*) foliolis linearibus longiffimis fimplicibus. Hort. Cliff. 95. *Ferula with the fmaller leaves, very narrow, long, and fingle.* Ferula major, feu famina Plinii. M. Umb. *Pliny's Female Fennel Giant.*

2. FERULA (*Galbanifera*) foliolis multipartitis, laciniis linearibus planis. Hort. Cliff. 95. *Ferula whofe fmaller leaves are divided into many narrow parts which are plain.* Ferula galbanifera. Lob. Obf. *Galbanum-bearing Fennel Giant.*

3. FERULA (*Tingitana*) foliolis laciniatis, lacinulis tridentatis inæqualibus. Hort. Cliff. 95. *Ferula whofe fmaller leaves are cut, and fegments ending in three unequal parts.* Ferula Tingitana, folio latiffimo lucido. H. Edin. *Broad-leaved fhining Fennel Giant from Tangier.*

4. FERULA (*Ferulago*) foliis pinnatifidis, pinnis linearibus planis trifidis. Hort. Cliff. 95. *Ferula with wing-pointed leaves, whofe pinnæ are narrow plain, and trifid.* Ferula latiore folio. Mor. Hift. 3. p. 309. *Fennel Giant with a broader leaf.*

5. FERULA (*Orientalis*) foliorum pinnis bafi nudis, foliolis fetaceis. Hort. Cliff. 95. *Ferula with the wings of the leaves naked at the bafe, and the fmaller leaves briftly.* Ferula Orientalis, Cachyros folio & facie. Tourn. Cor. 22. *Eaftern Fennel Giant with the leaf and appearance of Cachrys.*

6. FERULA (*Meoides*) foliorum pinnis utrinque bafi acutis, foliolis fetaceis. Hort. Cliff. 95. *Ferula with the wings of the leaves pointed at their bafe on every fide.* Laferpitium Orientale mei folio, flore luteo. Tourn. Cor. 23. *Eaftern Laferwort with a Spignel leaf and yellow flower.*

7. FERULA (*Nodiflora*) foliolis appendiculatis, umbellis fubfeffilibus. Lin. Sp. Plant. 247. *Ferula with appendages to the fmaller leaves, and umbels fitting clofe to the ftalks.* Libanotis ferulæ folio & femine. C. B. P. 158. *Libanotis with a Fennel Giant leaf and feed.*

8. FERULA (*Glauca*) foliis fupradecompofitis, foliolis lanceolato-linearibus planis. Hort. Cliff. 95. *Fennel Giant with linear, fpear-fhaped, decompounded leaves.* Ferula folio glauco, femine lato oblongo. J. B. 3. p. 45.

The firft of thefe plants is pretty common in the Englifh gardens: this, if planted in a good foil, will grow to a great height, and divide into many branches: the lower leaves of this fort fpread more than two feet every way, and branch out into many divifions, which are again fubdivided into many fmaller, garnifhed with very long, narrow, fmall leaves that are fingle; they are of a lucid green, and fpread near the ground. From the center of the plant comes out the flower-ftalk, which, when the plants are ftrong, will be near as large as a common broomftick, and will rife ten or twelve feet high, having many joints; if the ftalks are cut, there iffues from the veffels a foetid yellowifh liquor, which will concrete on the furface of the wound. The ftalks are terminated by large umbels of yellow flowers, which come out the latter end of June, or in the beginning of July; thefe are fucceeded by oval compreffed feeds, which have three lines running longitudinally on each fide. Thefe ripen in September, and the ftalks decay foon after. When the ftalks are dry, they are full of a light dry pith, which will foon take fire.

Mr. Ray fays, that the people of Sicily ufe the pith of this plant for tinder to light their fires. And if this was practifed by the ancients, we may eafily guefs why the poets feigned, that Prometheus ftole fire from heaven, and carried it to the earth in a hollow Ferula.

The leaves of thefe plants decay foon after the feeds are formed, fo that before they are ripe, there are feldom any leaves remaining, and the ftalks afterward dry and become very tough; fo it is not unlikely thefe may have been ufed for correction in the fchools, as they are very light, and cannot do much injury. The roots of this fort will continue feveral years, efpecially on a dry foil, and will annually produce flowers and feeds.

The fecond fort doth not grow quite fo large as the firft, but the ftalks of this will rife feven or eight feet high; the lower leaves are large, and greatly divided; the fmall leaves are flat, and not fo long as thofe of the former, and are of a lucid green colour; the umbels of flowers are fmaller, and the feeds are lefs. This flowers and ripens its feeds about the fame time as the former fort.

The third fort hath large fpreading leaves near the root, which are divided and fubdivided into many parts; the fmall leaves of this are much broader than in any of the other forts, and thefe are divided at their end into three unequal fegments; the leaves are of a very lucid green. The ftalks are ftrong, and rife to the height of eight or ten feet, and are terminated by large umbels of yellow flowers, which are

5 N   fucceeded

succeeded by large, oval, compressed seeds, like those of the first sort. This flowers and ripens its seeds about the same time as the former sort; it grows naturally in Spain and Barbary.

The fourth sort grows to much the same height as the second; the leaves of this branch out on every side pretty wide, and the smaller leaves on the divisions of the leaves, are broader than those of the others (excepting the third) but they are longer than those, and are of a darker green colour, ending in three points. The umbels of flowers are large, the flowers are yellow, and are succeeded by oval compressed seeds, like those of the other species. This grows naturally in Sicily.

The fifth sort is of much humbler growth than either of the former; the stalks of this seldom rise much more than three feet high; the lower leaves branch into many divisions, which are closely garnished with very fine bristly leaves; the umbel of flowers is but small, when compared with the others, and the seeds are smaller. It grows naturally in the Levant.

The sixth sort hath very branching leaves, the footstalks are angular and channelled; this sends out at every joint two side branches opposite; those toward the bottom are nine or ten inches long, and the others are diminished gradually to the top; these side branches send out smaller at each joint in the same manner, which are garnished with very fine leaves like those of Spignel, which stand quite round the stalks in shape of whorls; the flower-stalks grow three feet high, having a pretty large umbel of yellow flowers at the top; these are succeeded by oval flat seeds, which ripen in the autumn. It grows naturally in the Levant.

The seventh sort rises about three feet high; the leaves of this sort are much divided, and the small leaves on the divisions are very narrow and entire; the umbels of flowers are small, and are situated close to the stalks between the leaves at the joints; these are like those of the other sorts. It grows naturally in Istria and Carniola.

The eighth sort grows naturally in Italy and Sicily. The leaves of this are composed of many narrow flat segments, of a gray colour, and are divided into many parts: the stalk rises from three to four feet high, and is terminated by an umbel of yellow flowers in July, which are succeeded by oval compressed seeds which ripen in autumn.

All these sorts have perennial roots, which will continue several years; these have thick strong fibres, which run deep in the ground, and divide into many smaller, spreading to a considerable distance every way: the stalks are annual, and decay soon after they have perfected their seeds. As these plants spread very wide, so they should have each four or five feet room; nor should they stand near to other plants, for their roots will rob whatever plants grow near them of their nourishment.

They are all propagated by seeds, which should be sown in the autumn; for if they are kept out of the ground till the spring, they frequently fail, and those which succeed remain a year in the ground, so that much time is lost. The seeds may be sown in drills, by which method the ground may be easier kept clean; they must not be nearer than a foot row from row, and the seeds may be scattered two or three inches asunder in the drills; when the plants come up, they must be kept clean from weeds; and where they are too close together, they should be thinned, to allow them room to grow, for they will not be strong enough to remove till they have had two years growth; then in the autumn so soon as their leaves decay, the roots should be taken up with great care, so as not to cut or injure the tap or downright root, and then planted in the places where they are designed to remain, for after this transplanting they should not be removed. They delight in a soft, gentle, loamy soil, not too wet, and are very rarely injured by the hardest frost.

·FERRARIA. Burman. Lin. Gen. 1018.

The CHARACTERS are,

It hath two keel-shaped spathæ (or sheaths) which alternately inclose the flowers, which have six oblong pointed petals curled at their borders, revolving, and are alternately larger; and three stamina sitting on the style, terminated by twin roundish summits; and a roundish three-cornered germen under the flower, supporting a simple erect stigma, crowned by three bifid, hooded, curled stigma; the germen afterward becomes an oblong three-cornered capsule, having three cells, filled with roundish seeds.

This genus of plants is ranged in the second section of Linnæus's twentieth class, intitled Gynandria triandria, the flower having three stamina which sit upon the style.

The SPECIES are,

1. FERRARIA (Undulata) foliis lanceolatis. Burm. Icon. Ferraria with spear-shaped leaves. Iris stellata, Cyclaminis radice, pullo flore. Barrel. Icon. 1216. Starry Iris with a root like the Sowbread.

2. FERRARIA (Ensiformi) foliis ensiformibus. Burm. Icon. Ferraria with sword-shaped leaves.

These plants grow naturally at the Cape of Good Hope; the roots of the first sort were sent me by Dr. Job Baster, of Zirkzee, who received them from the Cape. The root of this is shaped like that of the Bizantine Cornflag; it has a bright brown skin or cover; on the upper side is a hollow like a navel, from whence the flower-stalk arises. The stalk rises a foot and a half high, and is about the size of a man's middle finger, garnished with leaves the whole length; these are keel-shaped, embracing the stalks with their base. The upper part of the stalk divides into two or three branches, which are garnished with the same shaped leaves, but they are smaller, each of the branches are terminated by a large spathæ or sheath of the same colour with the leaves, but this afterward withers and decays; these sheaths are double, and split at the top, where the flower peeps out its petals; these six petals are three alternately larger than the other, and are curiously fringed on their borders; they are of a pale greenish colour on their outside, but of a tawney purple within, and are of a short duration; in the centre of the flower is situated the style, having the three stamina fixed on the side, and is terminated by twin stigmas; the germen is situated under the flower, which afterward becomes an oblong smooth capsule with three cells, filled with roundish seeds.

The second sort is rare in England; this differs from the former in having smaller roots, and longer sword-shaped leaves, which have deeper veins; the stalk also does not divide so much, and the flowers are smaller, and less fringed on their borders.

They are both propagated by offsets sent out from the roots, in the same way as the Ixia, and should be cultivated in the same manner as is directed for those and the African Gladiolus, being too tender to thrive in the open air in England, nor do they succeed well in a green-house; therefore the best method is, to make a border four feet wide, either in the front of the green-house or stoves, covering it with a proper frame and glasses, so that the plants may enjoy the free air in mild weather, but be protected from frost. In such a frame, most of the African bulbous and tuberous rooted plants may be brought to great perfection.

There is a great singularity in the root of the first species, which is in its vegetating only every other year, and the intermediate years it remains at rest.

FICOIDES. See MESEMBRYANTHEMUM.

FICUS. Lin. Gen. Plant. 1032. Tourn. Inst. R. H. 662. tab. 420. The Fig-tree; in French, Figuier.

It hath male and female flowers, which are included within the covering, or skin of the fruit, so do not appear unless the covering is opened; the male flowers are but few in number, and are situated in the upper part of the fruit; the female flowers are numerous, and situated in the lower part;

part. The male flowers fit each upon a separate foot-stalk, and have an empalement divided into three parts; they have no petals, but three briftly ftamina as long as the empalement, terminated by twin fummits; the female flowers fit upon diftinct foot-ftalks; their empalements are divided into five parts; they have no petals, but a germen as the empalement, fupporting an inflexed ftyle, crowned by two reflexed pointed ftigmas. The germen afterward becomes a large feed, fitting in the empalement.

This genus of plants is ranged in the third fection of Linnæus's twenty-third clafs, intitled Polygamia Polycœcia; the male and hermaphrodite flowers being fituated in the fame common covering, but in the wild Fig they are in diftinct plants.

The SPECIES are,

1. FICUS (*Carica*) foliis palmatis. Hort. Cliff. 471. *Fig-tree with hand-fhaped leaves.* Ficus communis. C. B. P. 457. *The common Fig-tree.*

2. FICUS (*Sycomorous*) foliis cordatis fubrotundis integerrimis. Hort. Cliff. 471. *Fig-tree with roundifh heart-fhaped leaves, which are entire.* Ficus folio mori, fruc-, rum in caudice ferens. C. B. P. 459. *Fig-tree with a Mulberry leaf, bearing fruit on the body or ftem, commonly called Sycamore.*

3. FICUS (*Religiofa*) foliis cordatis oblongis integerrimis acuminatis. Hort. Cliff. 471. *Fig-tree with entire heart-fhaped leaves, ending in acute points.* Ficus Malabarienfis, folio cufpidato, fructu rotundo parvo gemino. Pluk. Alm. 144. *Malabar Fig with a long pointed leaf, and fmall double round fruit.*

4. FICUS (*Benghalenfis*) foliis ovatis integerrimis obtufis, caule inferne radicato. Hort. Cliff. 471. *Fig-tree with oval, obtufe, entire leaves, and the lower part of the ftalk putting out roots.* Ficus Benghalenfis, folio fubrotundo, fructu orbiculato. Hort. Amft. 1. p. 119. *Bengal Fig with a roundifh leaf, and orbicular fruit.*

5. FICUS (*Indica*) foliis lanceolatis petiolatis, pedunculis aggregatis, ramis radicantibus. Lin. Sp. Plant. 1060. *Fig-tree with fpear-fhaped leaves having petals, the foot-ftalks of the fruit growing in clufters, and branches fending out roots.* Ficus Indica Theophrafti. Tabern. Hift. 1370. *Indian Fig of Theophraftus.*

6. FICUS (*Maximus*) foliis lanceolatis integerrimis. Hort. Cliff. 471. *Fig-tree with entire fpear-fhaped leaves.* Ficus Indica maxima, folio oblongo, funiculis è fummis ramis dimiffis radices agentibus fe propagans, fructu minori fphærico fanguineo. Sloan. - Cat. Jam. 189. *The largeft Indian Fig with an oblong leaf, fending out roots from the tops of the branches, and a fmall fpherical blood-coloured fruit.*

7. FICUS (*Racemofa*) foliis ovatis acutis integerrimis, caule arboreo, fructu racemofa. Lin. Sp. Plant. 1060. Amœn. Acad. 1. p. 30. *Fig-tree with oval, entire, acute leaves, tree-like ftalk, and branching fruit.* Alty-alu. Hort. Mal. 1. p. 43.

8. FICUS (*Pumila*) foliis ovatis acutis integerrimis, caule repente. Lin. Sp. Plant. 1060. Amœn. Acad. 1. p. 30. *Fig-tree with oval, acute, entire leaves, and a creeping ftalk.* Ficus fylveftris procumbens, folio fimplici. Koempf. Amœn. 803. *Trailing wild Fig-tree having fingle leaves.*

9. FICUS (*Nymphæefolia*) foliis ovato-cordatis integerrimis glabris. *Fig-tree with oval, heart-fhaped, entire, fmooth leaves,* vulgarly called Ficus nymphææ folio. *Fig-tree with a Water Lily leaf.*

10. FICUS (*Citrifolia*) foliis oblongo-cordatis acuminatis, petiolis longiffimis. *Fig-tree with oblong, heart-fhaped, pointed leaves, and very long foot-ftalks.* Ficus citrii folio, fructu parvo purpureo. Catefb. Hift. Carol. 3. p. 18. *Fig-tree with a Citron-leaf, and fmall purple fruit.*

11. FICUS (*Calyculata*) foliis ovatis integerrimis obtufis, oppofitis, fructu globofo calyculato. *Fig-tree with oval, obtufe, entire leaves placed oppofite, and a globular fruit having a calyx.* Ficus folio lato fubrotundo, fructu globofo, magnitudine nuces mofchatæ. Houft. MSS. *Fig-tree with broad roundifh leaves, and a globular fruit about the bignefs of a nutmeg.*

The firft fort, which is the Fig whofe fruit is va-

luable, is cultivated in moft parts of Europe; of this there are great varieties in the warm countries, which have been obtained from feeds, therefore may be increafed annually, if the inhabitants were careful in propagating the trees from the feeds of their beft forts. In England we had not more than four or five forts till within a few years paft; for as the generality of the Englifh were not lovers of this fruit, fo there were few who troubled themfelves with the culture of it. But fome years paft I had a large collection of thefe trees fent me from Venice, by my honoured friend the Chevalier Rathgeb, which I planted and preferved to tafte of their fruits, feveral of which proved excellent; thefe I have preferved and propagated, and thofe whofe fruit were inferior have been neglected. And as the variety of them is very great, fo I fhall here mention only fuch of them as are the beft worth cultivating, placing them in the order of their ripening.

1. The brown or Chefnut-coloured Ifchia Fig. This is the largeft fruit of any I have yet feen, it is fhort, globular, with a pretty large eye, pinched in near the foot-ftalk, of a brown or Chefnut colour on the outfide, and purple within; the grains are large, and the pulp fweet and high-flavoured; this fort very often burfts open when it ripens. It ripens the latter end of July, or the beginning of Auguft. I have had this fruit ripen well on ftandards, in a warm foil. If this fort is planted againft hot walls, two plentiful crops of fruit may be annually ripened.

2. The black Genoa Fig. This is a long fruit, which fwells pretty large at the top where it is obtufe, but the lower part is very flender toward the ftalk; the fkin is of a dark purple colour, almoft black, and hath a purple farina over it like that on fome Plumbs; the infide is of a bright red, and the flefh is very high flavoured. It ripens early in Auguft.

3. The fmall white early Fig. This hath a roundifh fruit a little flatted at the crown, with a very fhort foot-ftalk; the fkin, when fully ripe, is of a pale yellowifh white colour; the fkin is thin, the infide white, and the flefh fweet, but not high-flavoured. This ripens in Auguft.

4. The large white Genoa Fig. This is a large globular fruit, a little lengthened toward the ftalk; the fkin is thin, of a yellowifh colour when fully ripe, and red within. This is a good fruit, but the trees are not good bearers.

5. The black Ifchia Fig. This is a fhort fruit, of a middling fize, a little flatted at the crown; the fkin is almoft black when ripe, and the infide is of a deep red; the flefh is very high flavoured, and the trees produce a good crop of fruit, but the birds are great devourers of them if they are not protected from them. This ripens in Auguft.

6. The Malta Fig. This is a fmall brown fruit, much compreffed at the top, and greatly pinched toward the foot-ftalk; the fkin is of a pale brown colour, as is alfo the infide; the flefh is very fweet, and well flavoured. If this fort is permitted to hang upon the trees till the fruit is fhrivelled, it becomes a fine fweetmeat.

7. The Murrey, or brown Naples Fig. This is a pretty large globular fruit, of a light brown colour on the outfide, with fome faint marks of a dirty white, the infide is nearly of the fame colour; the grains are pretty large, and the flefh is well flavoured. It ripens the latter end of Auguft.

8. The green Ifchia Fig. This is an oblong fruit, almoft globular at the crown; the fkin is thin, of a green colour, but when it is fully ripe, it is ftained through by the pulp to a brownifh caft; the infide is purple, and will ftain linen, or paper; the flefh is high flavoured, efpecially in warm feafons. It ripens toward the end of Auguft.

9. The Madonna Fig, commonly called here the Brunfwick, or Hanover Fig, is a long pyramidal fruit of a large fize; the fkin is brown; the flefh is of a lighter brown colour, coarfe, and hath little flavour. This ripens the end of Auguft and the beginning of September;

September; the leaves of this fort are much more divided than of moft other.

10. The common blue, or purple Fig is fo well known, as to need no defcription.

11. The long brown Naples Fig. The leaves of this tree are deeply divided. The fruit is long, fomewhat compreffed at the crown. The foot-ftalks are pretty long; the fkin is of a dark brown when fully ripe, the flefh inclining to red; the grains are large, and the flefh well flavoured. It ripens in September.

12. The yellow Ifchia Fig. This is a large fruit, of a pyramidal form; the fkin is yellow when ripe, and the flefh is purple and well flavoured, but the trees do not produce much fruit here; they grow very luxuriant in branches, the leaves are very large, and not much divided. This ripens in September.

13. The fmall Brown Ifchia Fig. This is a fmall pyramidal fruit with a very fhort foot-ftalk; the fkin is of a light brown, the flefh inclining to purple, of a very high flavour; it ripens late in September; the leaves of this tree are lefs divided than any of the other forts. This is not a good bearer.

14. The Gentile Fig. This is a middle fized globular fruit; the fkin, when ripe, is yellow; the flefh alfo inclines to the fame colour; the grains are large, and the flefh is well flavoured, but it ripens very late, and the trees are bad bearers, fo that it is not propagated much in England.

There are feveral other forts which have been lately introduced from Italy, but all thofe which I have yet tafted, are inferior to thofe above-mentioned; fome of them rarely ripen their fruit, and others are very ill bearers, not worth propagating, therefore I have omitted the mentioning of them here; for as thofe which are enumerated, continue in fucceffion during the feafon for thefe fruits, and being preferable to the other, few perfons will care to fill their gardens with a greater variety of thefe trees than are of real ufe, efpecially as they require good walls, and a very large fhare of room.

The firft, fecond, third, ninth, and tenth forts will ripen their fruits on ftandards, where they are in a warm fituation; but the others require the affiftance of walls expofed to good afpects, otherwife their fruit will not ripen in England.

Fig-trees generally thrive in all foils, and in every fituation; but they produce a greater quantity of fruit upon a ftrong loamy foil, than on dry ground; for if the feafon proves dry in May and June, thofe trees which grow upon very warm dry ground, are very fubject to caft their fruit; therefore, whenever this happens, fuch trees fhould be well watered and mulched, which will prevent the fruit from dropping off; and the fruit upon thefe trees are better flavoured, than any of thofe which grow upon cold moift land. I have always obferved thofe Fig-trees to bear the greateft quantity of well-flavoured fruit, which were growing upon chalky land, where there has been a foot or more of a gentle loamy foil on the top. They alfo love a free open air; for although they will fhoot and thrive very will in clofe places, yet they feldom produce any fruit in fuch fituations; and all thofe which are planted in fmall gardens in London, will be well furnifhed with leaves, but I have never feen any fruit upon them which have grown to maturity.

Thefe trees are always planted as ftandards in all warm countries, but in England they are generally planted againft walls, there being but few ftandard Fig-trees at prefent in the Englifh gardens; however, fince fome of the forts are found to ripen their fruit well upon the ftandards, and the crop of Figs is often greater upon them, than upon thofe trees againft walls, it is worthy of our care, to plant them either in ftandards or efpaliers; the latter, I think, will fucceed beft in England; if they were managed as in Germany, where they untie the Fig-trees from the efpalier, and lay them down, covering them in winter with ftraw or litter, which prevents their fhoots being injured by the froft; and this covering is taken away gradually in the fpring, and not wholly removed until all the

danger of froft is over, by which management they generally have a very great crop of Figs; whereas in England, where the trees grow againft warm walls, if the fpring proves warm, the young Figs are pufhed out early, and the cold, which frequently returns in April and May, caufes the greateft part of the fruit to drop off; fo that our crop of Figs is generally more uncertain than moft other forts of fruit: and it frequently happens, that trees which are planted againft north and eaft-afpected walls, produce a greater quantity of fruit in England, than thofe which are planted againft fouth and fouth-eaft afpects; which muft happen from the latter putting out their fruit fo much earlier in the fpring than the former; and if there happen cold frofty nights after the Figs are come out (which is frequently the cafe in this country) the forwardeft of the Figs are generally fo injured as to drop off from the trees foon after. In Italy, and the other warm countries, this firft crop of Figs is little regarded, being few in number; for it is the fecond crop of Figs which are produced from the fhoots of the fame year, which is their principal crop, but thefe rarely ripen in England; nor are there above three or four forts which ever ripen their fecond crop, let the fummer prove ever fo good, therefore it is the firft crop which we muft attend to in England; fo that when thefe trees are growing againft the beft afpected walls, it will be a good method to loofen them from the wall in autumn; and after having divefted the branches of all the latter fruit, to lay the branches down from the wall, faftening them together in fmall bundles, fo that they may be tied to ftakes, to keep them from lying upon the ground; the damp whereof, when covered in frofty weather, might caufe them to grow mouldy, and hereby they will be fecured from being broken by the wind. When they are thus managed in autumn, if the winter fhould prove very fevere, the branches may be eafily covered with Peas-haulm, ftraw, or any other light covering, which will guard the tender fruit-bearing branches from the injury of froft; and when the weather is mild, the covering muft be removed, otherwife the Figs will come out too early; for the intention of this management is, to keep them as backward as poffible: then in the fpring, when the Figs are beginning to pufh out, the trees may be faftened up to the wall again. By this management I have feen very great crops of Figs produced in two or three places.

I have alfo feen great crops of Figs in fome particular gardens, after very fharp winters, when they have, in general, failed in other places, by covering up the trees with Reeds made into pannels, and fixed up againft the walls.

In the pruning of Fig-trees, the branches muft never be fhortened, becaufe the fruit are all produced at the upper part of the fhoots of the former year; if thefe are cut off, there can be no fruit expected, befide the branches are very apt to die after the knife; fo that when the branches are too clofe together, the beft way is to cut out all the naked branches quite to the bottom, leaving thofe which are beft furnifhed with lateral branches at a proper diftance from each other, which fhould not be nearer than a foot; and when they are well furnifhed with lateral branches, if they are laid four or five inches farther afunder, it will be better. The beft feafon for pruning of Fig-trees is in autumn, becaufe at that time the branches are not fo full of fap, and will not bleed fo much, as when they are pruned in the fpring; and at this feafon, the branches fhould be divefted of all the autumnal Figs, and the fooner this is done, when the leaves begin to fall off, the better will the young fhoots refift the cold of the winter. There are fome feafons fo cold and moift, that the young fhoots of the Fig-trees will not harden, but are foft, and full of juice; when this happens, there is little hope of a crop of Figs the fucceeding year, for the firft froft in autumn will kill the upper part of thefe fhoots, for a confiderable length downward; whenever this happens, it is the beft way to cut off all the decayed part of the fhoots, which will

prevent

prevent the infection from destroying all the lower part of the branches; and, by this method, I have seen a moderate crop of Figs put out from the lower part of the shoots; where, if the shoots had not been injured, there would have been no fruit produced, because it is chiefly from the four or five uppermost joints of the shoots that the fruit comes out; and it is for this reason, that as many of the short lateral branches should be preserved as possible, those being the most productive of fruit; for where the long strait shoots are fastened up, there will be no fruit, but at their extremities, so that all the lower part of the trees will be naked, if there is not a particular regard had to supply young shoots in every part of the trees.

Those trees which are laid down from the espaliers, should not be fastened up again till the end of March, for the reasons before given, and those against walls may remain some time longer; and when the large shoots of these are nailed up, if the small lateral branches are thrust behind these, to keep them close to the wall, it will secure the young Figs from being injured by the morning frosts; and when this danger is over, they may be brought forward to their natural position again: during the summer season these trees will require no other pruning, but to stop the shoots in the spring, where lateral branches are wanting; and as the branches are often blown down by wind, therefore, whenever this happens, they should be immediately fastened up again, otherwise they will be in danger of breaking; for the leaves of these trees being very large and stiff, the wind has great power on them; so that where the branches are not well secured, they are frequently torn down.

Those trees which are planted against espaliers may be protected from the injury of frost in the spring, by placing Reeds on each side the espalier, which may be taken down every day, and put up again at night; but this need not be practised in warm weather, but only at such times as there are cold winds and frosty mornings; and although there is some trouble and expence attending this management, yet the plentiful crop of Figs which may this way be obtained, will sufficiently recompense for both: the best way of making this covering is, to fasten the Reeds with rope yarn in such a manner as that it may be rolled up like a mat, that the whole may with great facility be put up or taken down; and if these Reeds are carefully rolled up, after the season for using them is over, and put up in a dry shed, they will last several years.

There are several persons who of late have planted Fig-trees in standards, which have succeeded very well; this practice was revived, by observing some old standard Fig-trees in some gardens, which had been growing many years, and generally produced a much greater plenty of fruit than any of those trees which were growing against warm walls; indeed, these standard Fig-trees are in much greater danger of having their branches killed by severe frost, but in mild winters they generally do better than those against walls; so that where these trees can be covered in very hard winters, there will always be plenty of fruit; and these may be covered by fastening as many of the branches together as can be conveniently brought into a bundle, and winding some Hay-bands, Straw, Peas-haulm, or any such light covering as can be readily procured, which in the spring may be gradually taken off, so as not to expose the shoots all at once to the open air; and if there is some such light covering laid round the stems, and upon the surface of the ground about their roots, it will more effectually secure them from the danger of frost; but when this is practised, great care should be taken that no mice or rats harbour in this covering, for these will eat off the bark from their shoots, and kill them: and I have often observed those trees which were against walls, have suffered greatly by these vermin, by having many of their largest branches disbarked near the ground, which has absolutely killed them; and it is in the winter that these vermin do this mischief to

them, therefore they should be carefully watched at that season.

The common blue and white Figs, which are the sorts which have been the most generally cultivated in England, are not so proper to plant for standards, as some other sorts which have been lately introduced for they are much tenderer, and are often killed almost to the root, when some of the other sorts, which have been growing in the same situation, have received very little injury from the frost; indeed the white sort is generally a great bearer, and the fruit is very sweet but to those palates which are accustomed to Figs, that sort is not much in esteem, from its want of flavour those which have succeeded best with me, are the first and third sorts. Their branches are rarely hurt by frost in winter, and their fruit will always ripen well for in favourable seasons, many of these sorts, which were growing against walls, have ripened their second crop of fruit tolerably well. I have also planted many of these sorts of Fig-trees against north-east and north-west aspects; some of those which were first planted, have produced a good quantity of well tasted fruit, but were ripe much later, which has encouraged me to plant many more of these trees to the same aspects, and also to increase my number of standard trees.

I am aware, that what I have here advanced, in relation to the pruning and dressing of Fig-trees, will be condemned by great numbers of people, who will not give themselves time to consider and examine the reasons upon which I have founded this practice, nor to make one single experiment to try the truth of it, as being vastly different from the general practice of most gardeners, who always imagine, that Fig-trees should never have much pruning; or, at least, that they should always be suffered to grow very rude from the wall, to some distance. That by this management I have often seen great quantities of fruit I cannot deny, but then this has been only after mild winters; for it is very certain, that in sharp frosts few of these outside shoots escape being greatly injured where they are not covered; whereas it rarely happens that those shoots which are closely nailed to the wall in autumn, or laid down and covered, suffer the least damage; and the fruits are always produced a fortnight sooner upon these branches, than they are upon those which grow from the wall: but although the trees which are suffered to grow rude from the walls may produce a good quantity of fruit for a year or two, yet afterward the trees will only bear at the ends of the shoots, which will then be so far from the wall, as to receive little benefit from it; nor can the trees be reduced again to any regularity, without cutting away the greatest number of their branches, by which a year or two will be lost before they will come to bear again.

The season also for pruning, which I have laid down, being vastly different from the common practice and opinion of most gardeners, will also be objected against; but I am sure, if any one will but make trial of it, I doubt not his experience will confirm what I have here advanced; as one great injury to this tree proceeds from the too great effusion of sap at the wounded parts, by this autumn pruning this is prevented; for, at that season, all the parts of European trees which cast their leaves, are less replete with moisture than at any other time of the year; for by the long continuance of the summer's heat, the juices of plants having been exhausted in the nourishment and augmentation of wood, leaves, fruits, &c. and also great quantities being evaporated by perspiration, the root not being able to send up a supply equivalent to this great consumption, the branches must contain a much less quantity of sap than in the spring, when it has had several months supply from the root; which, though but small in proportion to what is sent up when the heat is greater, yet there being little or no waste, either by perspiration or augmentation, there must be a greater quantity contained in the branches; which also is easily to be observed, by breaking or cutting off a vigorous branch of a Fig-tree at both seasons (the sap, being milky, may be readily discerned) when that cut in autumn

tumn fhall be found to ftop its bleeding in one day's time, or lefs; whereas that cut in the fpring will often flow a week or more, and the wound will be proportionably longer before it heals.

Of late years there has been fome of thefe trees planted againft fire-walls, which have fucceeded very well where they have been properly managed; but where they have been kept too clofe, and drawn by glaffes, they have not produced much fruit; therefore whenever this is practifed, the heat fhould not be too great, nor the glaffes, or other covering, kept too clofe, but at all times, when the weather is favourable, a good fhare of free air fhould be admitted; and if the trees are young, that their roots are not-extended beyond the reach of the covering, they muft be frequently watered when they begin to fhew fruit, otherwife it will drop off; but old trees, whofe roots are extended to a great diftance, will only require to have their branches now and then fprinkled over with water. If thefe trees are properly managed, the firft crop of fruit will be greater than upon thofe which are expofed to the open air, and will ripen fix weeks or two months earlier, and a plentiful fecond crop may alfo be obtained, which will ripen early in September, and fometimes in Auguft, which is about the feafon of their ripening in the warmer parts of Europe; but the fires fhould not be ufed to thefe trees till the beginning of February; becaufe when they are forced too early, the weather is frequently too cold to admit a fufficient quantity of frefh air to fet the fruit; but the covers fhould be put over the trees a month before, to prevent the fhoots from being injured by the froft.

It may not be improper in this place to mention the great pains which the inhabitants of the Levant are at in the culture of their Figs; and without which (it is generally faid by all the travellers who have written on this fubject, as alfo by Pliny, and other old naturalifts) their fruit will fall off, and be good for nothing. I fhall here fet it down, as I find it in the travels of Monf. Tournefort, chief botanift to the late king of France.

" Pliny, fays he, obferved, That in Zia they ufed
" to drefs the Fig-trees with much care; they ftill
" continue to do fo. To underftand aright this huf-
" bandry of Figs (called in Latin, Caprificatio) we
" are to obferve, that in moft of the iflands of the
" Archipelago, they have two forts of Fig-trees to
" manage; the firft is called Ornos, from the old
" Greek, Erinos, a wild Fig-tree; or Caprificus,
" in Latin; the fecond is the domeftic, or garden
" Fig-tree; the wild fort bears three kinds of fruit,
" Fornites, Cratitires, and Orni, of abfolute neceffity
" towards ripening thofe of the garden Fig.

" The Fornites appear in Auguft, and continue to
" November, without ripening; in thefe breed fmall
" worms, which turn to a fort of gnats, no where to
" be feen but about thefe trees. In October and No-
" vember thefe gnats of themfelves make a puncture
" into the fecond fruit, which is called Cratitires,
" and do not fhew themfelves till towards the end
" of September; and the Fornites gradually fall away
" after the gnats are gone; the Cratitires, on the
" contrary, remain on the tree till May, and inclofe
" the eggs, depofited by the Fornites, when they
" pricked them. In May the third fort of fruit be-
" gins to put forth from the fame wild Fig-trees
" which produced the other two; this is much
" bigger, and is called Orni; when it grows to a
" certain fize, and its bud begins to open, it is pricked
" in that part by the gnats of the Cratitires, which
" are ftrong enough to go from one fruit to the
" other, to difcharge their eggs.

" It fometimes happens, that the gnats of the Crati-
" tires are flow to come forth in certain parts, while
" the Orni in thofe very parts are difpofed to receive
" them; in which cafe the hufbandman is obliged to
" look for the Cratitires in another part, and fix them
" at the end of the branches of thofe Fig-trees, whofe
" Orni are in fit difpofition to be pricked by the gnats;

" if they mifs the opportunity the Orni fall, and the
" gnats of the Cratitires fly away. None but thofe
" that are well acquainted with this fort of culture,
" know the critical minutes of doing this; and in
" order to it, their eye is perpetually fixed on the
" bud of the Fig; for that part not only indicates
" the time that the prickers are to iffue forth, but
" alfo when the Fig is to be fuccefsfully pricked; if
" the bud be too hard, and too compact, the gnat
" cannot lay its eggs, and the Fig drops when this
" bud is too open.

" Thefe three forts of fruit are not good to eat;
" their office is to help to ripen the fruit of the gar-
" den Fig-trees, in manner following: during the
" months of June and July, the peafants take the Orni
" at a time that their gnats are ready to break out,
" and carry them to the garden Fig-trees; if they do
" not nick the moment, the Orni fall, and the fruit
" of the domeftic or garden Fig-tree not ripening,
" will, in a very little time, fall in like manner. The
" peafants are fo well acquainted with thefe precious
" moments, that every morning, in making their
" infpection, they only transfer to their garden Fig-
" trees fuch Orni as are well conditioned, otherwife
" they lofe their crop. It is true, they have one re-
" medy, though an indifferent one, which is, to
" ftrew over the garden Fig-trees the Afcolimbros,
" a very common plant there, and in whofe fruit
" there is a fort of gnats proper for pricking;
" perhaps they are the gnats of the Orni, which are
" ufed to hover about and plunder the flowers of this
" plant.

" To fum up all in one word, The peafants fo well
" order the Orni, that their gnats caufe the fruit of
" the garden Fig-tree to ripen in the compafs of forty
" days. Thefe Figs are very good green; when they
" would dry them, they lay them in the fun for fome
" time, then put them in an oven to keep them the
" reft of the year. Barley bread and dried figs are
" the principal fubfiftence of the boors and monks of
" the Archipelago; but thefe Figs are very far from
" being fo good as thofe dried in Provence, Italy,
" and Spain; the heat of the oven deftroys all their
" delicacy and good tafte; but then, on the other
" hand, this heat kills the eggs which the prickers
" of the Orni difcharged therein, which eggs would
" infallibly produce fmall worms that would preju-
" dice thefe fruits.

" What an expence of time and pains is here for a
" Fig, and that but an indifferent one at laft! I
" could not fufficiently admire the patience of the
" Greeks, bufied above two months in carrying thefe
" prickers from one tree to another. I was foon told
" the reafon, on one of their Fig-trees ufually produces
" between two and three hundred pounds of Figs,
" and ours in Provence feldom above twenty-five.

" The prickers contribute, perhaps, to the maturity of
" the fruit of the garden Fig-tree, by caufing them to
" extravafate the nutritious juice, whofe veffels they
" tear afunder in depofiting their eggs; perhaps too,
" befides their eggs, they leave behind them fome
" fort of liquor proper to ferment gently with the
" milk of the Fig, and to make their flefh tender.
" Our Figs in Provence, and even at Paris, ripen much
" fooner for having their buds pricked with a Straw
" dipped in olive oil. Plumbs and Pears, pricked by
" fome infects likewife ripen much the fafter for it;
" and the flefh round fuch puncture is better tafted
" than the reft. It is not to be difputed but that con-
" fiderable change happens to the contexture of fruits
" fo pricked, juft the fame as to parts of animals
" pierced with any fharp inftrument.
" It is fcarce poffible well to underftand the antient
" authors who have treated of caprification (or huf-
" banding and dreffing the wild Fig-tree) if one is
" not well apprifed of the circumftances, the particu-
" lars whereof were confirmed to us not only at Zia,
" Tinos, Mycone, and Scio, but in moft of the other
" iflands."

Fig-

Fig-trees are propagated in England, either by the suckers, which are sent out from their roots, and by layers made, by laying down of their branches, which in one year will put out roots sufficient to be removed, or by planting of cuttings, which, if properly managed, will take root ; the first of these is a bad method, because all those trees which are raised from suckers, are very subject to send out great quantities of suckers again from their roots; and the branches of the suckers are not so compact, as those of the layers, but are fuller of sap, so in greater danger of being injured by the frost ; those plants which are propagated by layers, are the best, provided the layers are made from the branches of fruitful trees ; for those which are made from the suckers, or shoots, produced from old stools, are very soft, and full of sap, so are in danger of suffering by the frost, and these will shoot greatly into wood, but will not be very fruitful ; for, when trees have acquired a vicious habit while young, it is seldom they are ever brought to be fruitful afterward ; therefore the shoots which are laid down, should be such as are woody, compact, and well ripened, not young shoots, full of sap, whose vessels are large and open. The best time for laying down of the branches is in autumn ; and if the winter should prove very severe, if they are covered with some old tan, or any other mulch, to keep the frost from penetrating the ground, it will be of great service to them ; by the autumn following, these will be sufficiently rooted for removing, when they should be cut off from the old plants, because at that season the branches are not so full of sap as in the spring, so will not bleed so much as when cut off in the spring. If the place is ready to receive them, the layers should be transplanted in autumn, where they are to remain ; but if it is not, then the layers may remain till the spring, provided they are separated from the old plants in autumn. As these plants do not bear transplanting well when they are large, it is the better way to plant them at first in places where they are to remain ; and after they are planted, the surface of the ground about their roots should be covered with mulch to keep out the frost ; and if the winter should prove very severe, it will be proper to cover the branches with Reeds, Peas-haulm, Straw, or some other light covering, which will prevent their tender ends being killed by the frost, which frequently happens where this care is wanting.

The other method of propagating these trees, is by cuttings, which should be taken from the trees in autumn, for the reason before given : these must be chosen from such branches as are compact, whose joints are near each other ; and they should have a part of the former year's wood at their bottom, and the top of each should be left entire, not shortened as is usually practised with other cuttings ; then they should be planted eight or nine inches deep, in a bed of loamy earth, in a warm situation, covering the surface of the ground, three or four inches thick, with old tanner's bark, to keep out the frost ; and in severe frost their tops should be covered with Straw, Peashaulm, Fern, or other light covering, to protect them from frost, which should be removed in the spring ; but the tan may remain, for that will prevent the drying winds of the spring, and the sun in summer, from penetrating the ground, and will be of great use to secure the cuttings from injury ; these cuttings will be rooted sufficiently by the following autumn, when they should be transplanted, and treated in the same manner as the layers.

If fruitful branches of these trees are cut off, and planted in pots, or tubs, filled with good earth, and these are plunged into a good hot-bed of tanners bark in the stove, they will put out fruit early in the spring, which will ripen in the middle of May.

We shall now return to the other sorts of Figs, which grow naturally in warm countries, but are preserved in the gardens of those who are curious in collecting rare exotic plants, for these do not bear eatable fruit in their native soil ; but their leaves being large and beautiful, the plants make a pleasing variety in the stove.

The second sort grows naturally in the Levant, where it becomes a large tree, dividing into many branches, which are garnished with leaves shaped like those of the Mulberry, and affords a friendly shade in those hot countries. The fruit is produced from the trunk and larger branches of the tree, and not on the smaller shoots, as in most other trees ; the shape is like the common Fig, but is little esteemed. This is called the Sycamore, or Pharaoh's Fig-tree.

The third sort grows naturally in India, where it is sacred, so that none dare destroy them ; it is called by some the Indian God-tree ; this rises with a woody stem to a great height, sending out many slender branches, which are garnished with smooth heart-shaped leaves, ending in a long tail, or point ; they are entire, smooth, and of a light green, having pretty long foot-stalks ; they are between six and seven inches long, and three inches and a half broad toward their base, diminishing gradually to the top, where they run out in a narrow point, an inch and a half long. The fruit comes out on the branches, which are small, round, and of no value.

The fourth sort rises with many stalks, which grow to the height of thirty or forty feet, dividing into a great number of branches, which send out roots from their under branches, many of which reach to the ground ; so that in such places where the trees grow naturally, their roots and branches are so interwoven with each other, as to render the places impassable. In India, the Banyans trail the branches of these trees into regular archades, and set up their pagods under them, these being the places of their devotion. In America, where these trees are equally plenty, they form such thickets, as neither man nor beast can pass through. The leaves of this sort are of a thick substance, smooth, and oval ; they are six inches long, and four inches broad, with obtuse ends. The fruit is the size of a marble, and round, but of no use.

The fifth sort grows naturally in both Indies ; this rises with a woody stalk to the height of thirty feet, sending out many branches, which are garnished with oblong leaves standing upon pretty long foot-stalks ; they are about six or eight inches long, and two inches and a half broad, ending in an obtuse point, of a dark green, and smooth on their upper side, but of a light green, and veined on their under side. The fruit is small, and of no value. The branches of these trees send out roots from their lower side, which sometimes reach the ground.

The sixth sort grows naturally in the West-Indies, where it rises to the height of thirty or forty feet, sending out many slender branches, which put out roots in the same manner as the former. The leaves of this are eight or nine inches long, and two inches broad, ending in points. The fruit is small, round, and of a blood colour when ripe, but is not eatable.

The seventh sort grows naturally in India, where it rises to the height of twenty-five feet, and divides into many branches, which are garnished with oval-pointed leaves, which are smooth, and of a lucid green. The fruit is small, and grows in clusters from the side of the branches ; these are not eatable.

The eighth sort grows naturally in India ; this is a low trailing shrub, whose stalks put out roots at their joints, which strike into the ground, so is propagated plentifully where it naturally grows. The leaves are two inches and a half long, and near two inches broad, ending in points ; they are of a lucid green, and are placed without order on the branches ; the fruit is small, and not eatable.

The ninth sort rises with a strong, upright, woody stalk twenty feet high, sending out several side branches, which are garnished with large, oval, stiff leaves, about fourteen inches long, and near a foot broad, and are rounded at the ends ; they have several transverse veins, which run from the midrib to the sides. The foot-stalks are long, and frequently turned next to the branches ; the upper side of the leaves

leaves are of a lucid green, and the under fide is of a gray, or fea-green colour, they are of a thick fubftance, and very fmooth; this grows naturally in India, from whence it was brought to the gardens in Holland.

The tenth fort grows naturally in the Weſt-Indies, where it riſes twenty feet high, fending out many fide branches, which are covered with a white bark, and garniſhed with oblong .heart-ſhaped leaves, ending in acute points; they are about three inches long, and one inch and a half broad, near the baſe; of a lucid green on their upper fide, but of a pale green on their under, ſtanding upon very long foot-ſtalks. The fruit comes out from the fide of the branches, toward their ends; they are about the fize of large gray Peas, and of a deep purple colour, fitting cloſe to the branches; theſe are not eatable.

The eleventh fort grows naturally at La Vera Cruz, from whence it was ſent me by the late Dr. Houſtoun; this riſes with many ſhrubby ſtalks to the height of twelve or fourteen feet, and divides into many ſmaller branches, which are garniſhed with oval ſtiff leaves, which are obtuſe; they are four inches long, and three broad, of a light green, and ſtand upon very ſhort foot-ſtalks, which are joined to a cup, in which the fruit fits; this is globular, and the fize of a middling nutmeg, of a deep yellow, when ripe, but is not eatable.

The ſecond fort, I believe, is not In England at preſent; I raiſed two or three of theſe plants from ſeeds in the year 1736, which were deſtroyed by the ſevere froſt in 1740, fince which time I have not been able to procure any of the ſeeds. The other ſorts are preſerved in ſeveral curious gardens; they are eaſily propagated by cuttings during the ſummer ſeaſon. When the cuttings are taken from the plants, they ſhould be laid in a dry ſhady place for two or three days, that the wounds may be healed over, otherwiſe they are apt to rot; for all theſe plants abound with a milky juice, which flows out whenever they are wounded; for which reaſon, the cuttings ſhould have their wounded part healed over and hardened before they' are planted; after which they ſhould be placed in pots filled with ſandy light earth, and plunged into a moderate hotbed, where they ſhould be ſhaded from the ſun, and two or three times a week gently refreſhed with water, if the ſeaſon is warm; but they muſt not have too much moiſture, for that will infallibly deſtroy them. When the cuttings have taken root ſufficient to tranſplant, they ſhould be each planted into a ſeparate ſmall pot filled with light undunged earth, and plunged into the hot-bed again, being careful to ſhade them until they have taken freſh root; then they ſhould have a large ſhare of free air admitted to them at all times when the weather is favourable, to prevent their drawing up weak, and to give them ſtrength before the cold comes on. In autumn the pots ſhould be removed into the ſtove, and plunged into the tan-bed, where they ſhould conſtantly remain, and muſt be treated in the ſame manner as other tender plants from the ſame countries; for although two or three of the ſorts may be treated in a hardier manner, yet they will not make much progreſs.

FICUS INDICA. See OPUNTIA.

FILAGO. There are ſeveral ſpecies of this genus, ſome of which grow naturally upon barren land in moſt parts of England. They are called by ſome Cottonweed, by others Cudweed, their leaves being white, and, when broken, have cottony threads. Theſe have been ranged under the genus of Gnaphalium by moſt botaniſts, and one of the ſpecies which is uſed in medicine, ſtands in the liſt of ſimples by that appellation. As theſe plants are not cultivated in gardens, I ſhall not trouble the reader with a farther account of them.

FILBERT. See CORYLUS.

FILIPENDULA. See SPIRÆA.

FILIUS ANTE PATREM [i. e. the ſon before the father] an expreſſion which botaniſts apply to plants, whoſe flower comes out before their leaves;

or thoſe plants which ſend forth fide branches of flowers, which advance above the middle.

FILIX, Fern. There are great varieties of this plant in the different parts of the world, but particularly in America, as may be ſeen in the Natural Hiſtory of Jamaica, publiſhed by Sir Hans Sloane, Bart. and in Plumier's American Ferns: but as they are plants which are ſeldom propagated in gardens, I ſhall paſs them over in this place.

FILM, that woody ſkin which ſeparates the ſeeds in the pods of plants.

FIMBRIATED [of Fimbria, *Lat.* a fringe] a term relating to the leaves of plants when they are jagged on the edges, having, as it were, a fringe about them; theſe are often called furbelowed leaves.

FIRE. However foreign, at the firſt view, this article may ſeem to our preſent purpoſe, yet I am of opinion, that a tolerable acquaintance with its nature, as far as it can be attained, and its effects, will contribute no ſmall aſſiſtance in forwarding the work of vegetation. And though the theory of fire is indeed philoſophical, yet the conſideration of its effects, and how it operates on vegetables, will be of no ſmall uſe in the culture of them.

That which beſt defines and diſtinguiſhes fire from every thing elſe, is its heating; and ſo it may be defined, Whatſoever warms or heats bodies.

Heat is ſomething, the preſence of which is beſt perceived by the dilatation of the air or ſpirit in the thermometer. So then, fire is a body, and a body in motion too. The motion of it is proved by its expanding the air, and that it is a body by experiment. Pure mercury, being incloſed in a phial with a long neck, and kept in a gentle heat for the ſpace of a year, will be reduced into a ſolid, and the weight alſo will be increaſed conſiderably; which increaſe cannot proceed from any thing elſe but the acceſſion of fire.

The nature of fire is ſo obſcure and wonderful, that it was held by many of the ancients as a deity; and ſeveral authors of prime note have taken great pains to diſcover the myſtery of it, without having been able to explain many of the principal effects thereof. The learned Herman Boerhaave has uſed no leſs induſtry in making a new ſet of experiments, in order to come to a clearer knowledge of them; and having laid down a new doctrine of fire, in a courſe of public lectures, I ſhall briefly take notice of ſuch of them as I apprehend may be of uſe.

" Fire (ſays he) in effect, appears to be the general
" inſtrument of all the motion in the univerſe. The
" conſtant tenor of a great number of experiments
" leaves no room to doubt, but that, if there were no
" fire, all things would inſtantly become fixed and
" immoveable. Of this there are inſtances every win-
" ter; for while froſt prevails, the water, which be-
" fore was fluid, by a mere privation of heat, becomes
" ſolid, i. e. hardens into ice, and ſo remains till diſ-
" ſolved again by fire. Thus, were a man entirely
" deſtitute of heat, he would immediately freeze into
" a ſtatue; and thus the air itſelf, which is found in
" continual motion, being always either expanding
" or condenfing, would, upon the abſence of fire, con-
" tract itſelf, and cohere into a firm rigid maſs; ſo
" alſo animals and vegetables, all oils, ſalts, &c.
" would, upon the like occaſion, immediately con-
" geal."

Although this doctrine of fire, here laid down by Boerhaave, ſeems new and extraordinary, at leaſt to thoſe who have been uſed to conſider fire in the light that it has been ſet in by the Lord Bacon, Mr. Boyle, and Sir Iſaac Newton; and though we ought to pay great veneration to thoſe illuſtrious authors, yet, in the judgment of themſelves, we ſhould be in excuſable, if we ſhould abſolutely acquieſce in what they have done, and ſhut the door againſt farther and better information.

It may reaſonably be ſuppoſed, that Dr. Boerhaave has had an opportunity of going beyond them; in that, beſides all the experiments and obſervations that they

have

have had to build upon, he has had the advantage of a new fet, which they were unacquainted with.

As to the nature of fire, the great and fundamental difference is, whether it be originally fuch, formed thus by the great Creator himfelf, at the beginning of things? or, whether it be mechanically producible from other bodies, by inducing fome alteration in the particles of it?

Among the modern writers, Homberg, Boerhaave, the younger Lemery, and Dr. Gravefande, maintain the former, and the Englifh authors chiefly maintain the latter.

Monf. Homberg holds, That the chymical principle or element, fulphur, which is fuppofed one of the fimple, primary, pre-exiftent ingredients of all natural bodies, is real fire; and, of confequence, fire is coeval with all bodies. Effai de Souffre Principe, Mem. de l'Academie, anno 1705.

Dr. Gravefande proceeds much on the fame principle: according to him, fire enters the compofition of all bodies, is contained in all bodies, and may be feparated or procured from all bodies, by rubbing them againft each other, and thus putting their fire in motion: and he adds, That fire is by no means generated by fuch motion. Elem. Phyf. Tom. II. cap. 1.

Mr. Lemery the younger, afferts the abfolute and ingenerable nature of fire, and alfo extends it farther; not contented to confine it, as an element, to bodies, he endeavours to fhew, that it is " Equably diffufed " through all fpace; is prefent in all places; in the " void fpace between bodies, as well as the infenfible " interftices between their parts." Mem. de l'Acad. anno 1713.

This laft fentiment falls in with that of Boerhaave.

Of the contrary opinion is the Lord Bacon, who, in his treatife de Forma Calidi, deduces from a great number of particulars, that heat in bodies is no other than motion, only a motion fo and fo circumftantiated; fo that to produce heat in a body, nothing is required but to excite fuch motion in the parts of it.

His opinion is feconded by Mr. Boyle, in his treatife of the Mechanical Origin of Heat and Cold; where he maintains the fame doctrine, with new obfervations and experiments, of which two are as follow:

He fays, " In the production of heat there appears " nothing on the part either of the agent or patient " but motion, and its natural effects. When a fmith " brifkly hammers a fmall piece of iron, the metal " thereby becomes exceedingly hot; yet there is no- " thing to make it fo, except the forcible motion of " the hammer, impreffing a vehement and varioufly " determined agitation on the fmall parts of the iron; " which, being a cold body before, becomes by that " fuperinduced commotion of its fmall parts hot; " firft, in a more loofe acceptation of the word, with " regard to fome other bodies, compared with which " it was cold before; then fenfibly hot, becaufe this " agitation fenfibly furpaffes that of the parts of our " fingers. And in this inftance oftentimes the ham- " mer and anvil continue cold after the operation; " which fhews, that the heat acquired by the iron " was not communicated by either of thefe imple- " ments, as heat, but produced in it, by a motion " great enough ftrongly to agitate the parts of fo " fmall a body as the piece of iron, without being " able to have the like effect upon fo much greater " maffes of metal as the hammer and anvil; though " if the percuffions were often and brifkly renewed, " and the hammer were fmall, this alfo might be " heated; whence it is not neceffary, that a body it- " felf fhould be hot to give heat.

" If a large nail be driven by a hammer into a " plank of wood, it will receive feveral ftrokes on its " head, ere it grows hot; but when it is once driven " to the head, a few ftrokes fuffice to give it a con- " fiderable heat; for while at every blow with the " hammer the nail enters farther into the wood, the " motion produced is chiefly progreffive, and is of the " whole nail tending one way; but, when the mo- " tion ceafes, the impulfe given by the ftroke being

" unable to drive the nail farther on or break it, muft " be fpent in making a various, vehement, and in- " teftine commotion of the parts among themfelves, " wherein the nature of heat confifts."

That fire is the real caufe of all the changes in nature, will appear from the following confideration.

All bodies are either folid or fluid; the folid of themfelves are either commonly fuppofed to be inactive or motionlefs; the fluid both move and are moved.

And all folids are found to be fo much the more firm and contracted, as they have the lefs fire in them. This is evident in iron, which, when heated, expands itfelf into a much greater fpace than when it was cold; fo that any folid and hard body, by being freed from all fire, would fink into a much lefs bulk, and its parts would cohere more nearly, and with greater force than before.

As to fluids, they all harden, fo as to be vifible to the eye upon the abfence of fire; as water, by the cold of a fevere winter, will form itfelf into a folid globe, and yet even then contains a great deal of fire, as appears evidently upon applying a thermometer to it, which is capable of falling twenty divifions lower before it arrive at the point of the moft intenfe cold: and hence it is, that the fpirit of wine is kept from freezing in the thermometer, which would undergo the common fate of other things, were there not abundantly more fire in it.

The air itfelf expands by a greater quantity of fire, and condenfes by a lefs; but it ftill contains a large quantity of fire, where it is moft of all contracted; this is evident from the ftriking of a flint againft a fteel, which is followed by fparks of fire.

Likewife if this fire could be taken from the air, it would become folid and perfectly at reft, and, by confequence, uncapable of change.

" Fire (fays Dr. Gravefande, in Element. Phyf.) na- " turally unites itfelf with bodies; and hence it is, " that a body brought near to the fire grows hot, " in which cafe it alfo expands or fwells; which ex- " panfion is not only obferved in very folid bodies, " but in thofe whole parts do not cohere; in which " cafe they likewife acquire a great degree of elaf- " ticity, as is obferved in air and vapours."

Fire being thus acknowledged the inftrumental caufe of all motion, it remains that itfelf be moved; nay, to move, muft be more natural and immediate to fire, than to any other body; and hence fome have ventured to make motion effential to fire: but as this is inconfiftent with the notion of matter, which is defined to be inert and paffive, and as fire is capable of being proved material, we ought rather to agree, that the motion of fire itfelf is derived from fome higher and metaphyfical caufe. A property of perpetual mobility may indeed be fuperadded to the other properties of fire, but it has no natural neceffary connexion with them; nor can it be maintained with them otherwife than by fome extrinfic efficacy of a fuperior caufe.

However, that it is by motion that fire produces its effects, is evident; and hence the action of fire cannot make any alteration in the elementary fubftance of bodies; for it is neceffary, that what acts upon an object, be without that object, i. e. the fire muft not penetrate the elementary parts, but only enter the pores and interftices of bodies; fo that it does not feem capable of making thofe tranfmutations, which Sir Ifaac Newton afcribes to it.

In effect, as to all our purpofes, it may perhaps be faid, that fire is always in motion. For inftance, take fix feveral forts of thermometers, and two veffels of water with fal armoniac mixed therein, and apply the thermometers to it; and the confequence will be, that the air being condenfed in them, the fpirit will defcend in all of them: remove the veffels of water, and the air growing warmer, and rarefying, the fpirit will afcend again; fo that the active force in air, which produces fo many effects, does really all arife from the fire contained in it.

Again: As all bodies placed in a very solid air, do, by degrees, grow cold, motionless, rigid, &c. i. e. though there be still some remains of fire, and in proportion as that is diminished, the effect is accelerated; it follows, that cold, a less degree of heat, is the effect of a lesser action of fire: and all action rises apparently from the same source.

Then, as fire can render the most solid bodies, as stone, metals, &c. (as appears very evident in large burning-glasses, in which gold itself immediately calcines, and emits fumes, i. e. becomes fluid) so the want of fire would convert the most fluid bodies, as spirits of wine, &c. into solids.

Fire is distinguished into two kinds, called elementary or pure fire, which is such as exists in itself, and alone is properly called fire; or common or culinary fire, which is raised and kindled from the former, and is that which agitates and affects ignited, combustible, and moveable bodies, the particles of which, joining with those of the pure fire, constitute pure flame.

This latter is improperly called fire, in that not only a small part of it is real or pure fire; and in ignited bodies, that which flames, smokes, &c. is not simply fire; whereas pure fire, such as is collected in a burning-glass, yields no flame, smoke, ashes, or the like.

Fire may be present in the greatest abundance, yet without any heat: this is evident in the tops of the highest mountains, illuminated by the sun, where the cold is always extremely pinching, and this even under the equator, there being mountains there which are perpetually covered with snow, though there can be no want of fire.

So a large burning-glass has no effect: the smallest warmth cannot be felt in its focus in a place where the sun does not shine, or when the sun is covered with a cloud, but a piece of metal may be seen to melt the very moment the sun emerges.

Fire may be in exceeding small quantity, and yet burn with great violence: thus spirit of wine when set on fire, does not burn the hands; and though poured on a piece of red-hot iron, does not take fire; so that the fire that is in, should not appear very great: yet if it meet with some harder body while it is burning, the particles of which body it is capable to agitate by the attrition of its own, it will yield a fierce flame, capable of burning a harder body than the hand.

From this it appears, that the relation of heterogeneous particles, agitated by the fire, has more effect in respect to heat than the action of the fire itself: nor need we be far to seek for the mechanical reason of this, for the particles of fire, being all equal and spherical, must of themselves be harmless; but if they carry certain spicula, or any other bodies along with them, then they become capable of doing much harm.

Hence, though the flame of a piece of wood may give a sense of heat, and burn such things as are applied to it, it does not therefore necessarily follow, that there is any pure fire in it, so that the distinction of pure and common fire is absolutely necessary: though this distinction has been overlooked by most or all the authors before Dr. Boerhaave, who have written on fire; which has led them into egregious mistakes, insomuch that most of them have held, that the flame of a piece of wood is all fire, which appears to be false from what has been already said, and also what follows.

Elementary or pure fire is of itself imperceptible, and only discovers itself by certain effects that it produces in bodies, and these effects are only to be learnt by the changes which arise in bodies. These effects are three; 1st, heat; 2dly, dilatation in all solid bodies, and rarefaction in all fluids; 3dly, motion.

The first effect of elementary fire on bodies is heat: heat arises wholly from fire, and in such a manner, that the measure of heat is always the measure of fire; and that of fire, of heat; so the heat is inseparable from the fire.

The second effect of elementary fire is dilatation in all solid bodies, and rarefaction in all fluids.

Numerous experiments make it evident, that both these are inseparable from heat. If you heat an iron rod, it will increase in all its dimensions; and the more it is heated, the farther it will be increased; and being again exposed to the cold, it will contract, and successively return through all degrees of its dilatation, till it arrive at its first bulk, being never two minutes successively of the same magnitude.

The like may be observed in gold, the heaviest of all bodies, which takes up more space when it is fused than it did before; nay, even mercury, the heaviest of all fluids, has been known to ascend above thirty times its height, being placed over the fire in a tube.

The laws of this expansion are;

1st, That the same degree of fire rarefies fluids sooner, and in a greater degree than it does solids. Without this, the thermometer would be of no use; since, if it were otherwise, the cavity of the tube would be dilated in the same proportion as the fluid is rarefied.

2dly, By how much the liquor is lighter, by so much the more it is dilated by fire: thus air, which is the lightest of all fluids, expands the most, and spirit of wine the next after air.

The third effect of fire on bodies is motion; for fire, in warming and dilating bodies, must necessarily move their parts. And in effect, all the motion of nature arises from fire alone; and if this were taken away, all things would become immoveable. All oils, fats, waters, wines, ales, spirits of wine, vegetables, animals, &c. become hard, rigid, and inert, upon the absence of only a certain degree of fire; and this induration will be both the sooner, and the more violent, the less the degree of fire is.

Hence, if the fire was absolutely taken away, and there were the greatest degree of cold, all nature would grow into one concrete body, solid as gold, and hard as a diamond; but, upon the application of fire, it would recover its former mobility.

And, of consequence, every diminution of fire is attended with a proportionable diminution of motion.

Pure fire is found in two different manners, either as it exists every where, and is diffused equally in all places; or as it exists in certain bodies, in which it makes no great alteration.

That fire should exist in the same quantity in all places, will seem a strange paradox; and yet that it does so, is demonstrable from innumerable experiments.

This elementary fire is present every where, in all bodies, all space, and at all times, and that in equal quantities; for let a person go where he will, to the top of the highest mountains, or descend into the lowest cavern, whether the sun shine or not; either in the most scorching summer, or the sharpest winter; fire may be collected by several methods, as attrition or otherwise. In a word, there is no physical point assignable without fire, no place in nature where the attrition of two sticks will not render it sensible.

The Cartesians, as Marriotte, Perrault, &c. hold, That there is a large stock of fire in a perfect vacuum, i. e. a space out of which all the air has been exhausted, as supposing an absolute vacuum impossible: now, the most perfect vacuum that we can arrive at, is that of Mr. Huygens's contrivance, which is as follows: heat a quantity of the purest mercury to the heat of boiling water, and pour it into a hot tube of about forty inches long; and when the tube is filled, apply a finger upon the orifice of it, and thus invert it into a bason full of mercury: the mercury will now be suspended in the tube to the whole height; but then, if you give it but a little shake, it will sink down to the height of about twenty-nine inches, and thus leave a vacuity of eleven inches.

Yet here the philosophers above-mentioned deny there is any vacuum, and urge, that now so much the more fire is entered into the space as there was of other

matter;

matter; but this is contrary to experience; at least, the fire contained there is no hotter than the mercury itself; for if a drop or two of water be in a frosty season sprinkled both upon the upper part of the tube, supposed to be full of fire, and on the lower that is full of mercury, they will in each place freeze alike; so that there is no more pure fire in a perfect vacuum, than in any other place.

But whereas it has been said, that fire is found in all bodies, to prove this, set gold against the vacuum before-mentioned, and this gold, though the most ponderous of all bodies, will not contain more fire than Huygens's vacuum, as appears from the thermometer.

But the fire in gold, when ready to fuse, is pure fire; for a mass of this being once heated red hot, will retain this fire perfectly for three days; nay, the prince of Mirandola and others, have kept gold ignited for two months, without any diminution of weight.

Mr. Gravesande, Phys. Element, says, That bodies of any kind, being violently moved against one another, will grow hot by such friction; and this to a considerable degree, which shews that all bodies have fire in them; for fire may be put in motion, and separated from a body by such rubbing, but can never be generated that way.

Mr. Boyle, Mech. Prod. of Heat, says, That although quicksilver is allowed to be the coldest of all fluids, insomuch that many deny, that it will produce any heat by its immediate action on any other body, and particularly on gold; yet several trials have assured him, that a particular mercury may by preparation be enabled suddenly to insinuate itself into the body of gold, whether calcined or crude, and become manifestly hot with it in less than two or three minutes.

Mr. Gravesande says, That quicksilver contains fire, is evident hence, that if you shake it about in an exhausted glass, it will appear all luminous.

Elementary fire of itself always lies concealed; nay, it may be perfectly undiscoverable, where it is in the greatest quantity; as is evident in the torrid zone, where the snow never melts, notwithstanding the great abundance of fire.

This fire, in itself thus perfectly latent, may discover itself to be present by five effects; 1st, by rarefying bodies, and particularly air; 2dly, by light; 3dly, by colour; 4thly, by heat; and 5thly, by burning.

That there is a good quantity of fire even in the coldest places, and in the coldest bodies, is confirmed by the following experiment: if you take two large iron plates, and rub them briskly together in Iceland, which is only twelve degrees short of the north pole, in the most frosty season, and at midnight, they will grow warm, glow, shine, and heat to such a pitch as not only to rarefy the spirit in the thermometer, but even to ignite, and at last to fuse.

Now the fire here found is either created de novo, or it was there before, but nobody will assert its creation; and accordingly, unless it be furnished with a proper fuel, it will be soon dissipated again, but not annihilated; and of consequence it pre-existed, and it appears to be true fire by its rarefying the spirit in the thermometer.

From this, and many other experiments, it is evident, that fire is always found in all parts of space, and in all bodies equally spread on the utmost top of the highest mountain, as in the subject valley, or in the deepest cavern under ground, and in every climate, and at every season.

The equable distribution of fire in all places being proved, it should thence follow, that there is the same degree thereof every where; which would really be so, were it not that fire happens by one means or other to be more collected in one place than another.

But, notwithstanding the equable difference, &c. of fire through all the mundane space does not hinder, but that, to our senses, it appears very unequal in different places; and hence we have two vulgarly reputed sources or funds of fire, viz. in the sun, and the center of the earth.

As for the first, we have the concurrent opinions of the philosophers of all ages, but one excepted, who held the sun to be cold.

As to the second, the central fire, it is manifest that there is an ample proportion of fire under ground; and even, that fire appears much more abundant there than on the surface; so that at least, a subterraneous fire must be granted.

Thus they who dig mines, wells, &c. constantly observe, that while they are but a little below the surface, they find it a little cool; and as they proceed lower, it proves much colder, as being beyond the reach of the sun's heat, insomuch that water will freeze almost instantaneously, and hence is the use of houses.

But a little lower, about forty or fifty feet deep, it begins to grow warmer, so that no ice can bear it; and then the deeper they go, still the greater heat; till at length it endangers the stoppage of respiration, and puts out their candles. If they venture yet farther with a lighted candle, the place shall be immediately found full of flame, as once happened in the coal-pits in Scotland, where a hardy digger, descending to an unusual depth, with a light in his hand, the fumes, which were there found very copious, caught fire thereby, and burnt the whole mountain down.

Therefore it seems as if nature had lodged another sun in the center of the earth, to contribute on its part to the giving motion to bodies, and for the promoting of generation, nutrition, vegetation, germination, &c. of animals, vegetables, and fossils.

As to the origin of this subterraneous sun, some doubt whether it were formed there in the beginning, like the sun in the firmament, or gradually produced by a secondary collection of vague fire into this place. What makes in favour of the former opinion, are volcanos or burning mountains, which seem to have existed from the first ages; for the flames of mount Ætna are mentioned as of great antiquity, and there are likewise such mountains found in the coldest regions, viz. Nova Zembla and Iceland, as well as the hottest, as Borneo, &c.

It cannot be reasonably pretended, says Mr. Boyle, that the subterraneous heat proceeds from the rays of the sun, since they heat not the earth above six or seven feet deep, even in the southern countries; and if the lower part of the earth were of its own nature cold, and received the heat it affords only from the sun and stars, the deeper men descend therein, the less degree of heat and steams they would meet with.

The sun contributes much in bringing fire to light, by reason of his rapid motion round his axis; whereby the fiery particles, every where diffused, are directed and determined in parallel lines toward certain places where its effects become apparent.

And from thence it is, that the fire is perceived by us when the sun is above; but that when he disappears, his impulse or pression being then taken away, the fire continues dispersed at large through the ethereal space.

There is not, in effect, less fire in our hemisphere in the night time, than there is in the day time; only it wants the proper determination to cause it to be perceived.

The effects of elemental fire may be increased divers ways, viz. first, by attrition, or a swift rubbing or agitating one body against another. This is very manifest in solids. The attrition of a flint against a steel produces sparks of fire; and likewise in fluids, the violent agitation of cream, by churning, will produce a sensible warmth, and separate it into butter; and this effect is rendered still more discernible by a thermometer.

And the heat of animal bodies is owing to the agitation and attrition of the parts of these juices against each other, and the sides of the vessels.

The second manner of increasing the effect of elementary fire is, by throwing a quantity of moist or green

green vegetables, cut down while full of fap, into a large heap, and preffing them clofe down; by which they grow warm, hot, fmoke, and break out into flame,

A third way is by mixing certain cold bodies: thus water, and fpirit of wine, being firft warmed, grow much hotter by being mixed; alfo oil of cloves, cinnamon, &c. being mixed with fpirit of wine, become exceeding hot, and burft forth like volcanos.

The like effects may be had from feveral hard and dry bodies, as fulphur and fteel filings.

To conclude: on fire and the effects thereof, depend all fluidity of humours, juices, &c. all vegetation, putrefaction, fermentation, animal heat, &c.

As all the four elements, water, air, earth, and fire, are very conducive to the work of vegetation, and no one of them more than this of fire; I conclude, that thefe few hints, which I have collected from the moft approved authors, concerning the nature and properties of it, as they may be ufeful, would not be unacceptable to the ingenious and ftudious practifers of horticulture, which induced me to infert them here.

FIR-TREE. See Abies.

FISTULAR FLOWERS [Flores Fiftulares, of Fiftula, *Lat.* a pipe] fuch as are compounded of many long, hollow, fmall flowers, like pipes.

FLAMMULA JOVIS. See Clematis.

FLESH, among botanifts, is all the fubftance of any fruit that is between the outer rind and the ftone, or that part of any root that is fit to be eaten.

FLORIFEROUS [florifer, *Lat.*] bearing flowers.

FLORIST, one who is converfant with, or fkilled in flowers.

FLORULENT, FLORULOUS [florentulus, florulus, *Lat.*] Flowery, full of flowers; alfo bloffoming.

FLOS AFRICANUS. See Tagetes.

FLOS PASSIONIS. See Passiflora.

FLOS SOLIS. See Helianthus.

FLOS TRINITATIS. See Viola.

FLOWER: a flower is a natural production which precedes the fruit, which includes the grain or feed. Though a flower is a thing fo well known, yet the definition of this part of a plant is as various almoft as the authors who define it. Jungius defines it to be the more tender part of a plant, remarkable for its colour, or form, or both, cohering with the fruit. Yet this author himfelf confeffes, that this definition is too narrow; for fome of thofe bodies which he allows to be flowers are remote from the fruit.

Mr. Ray fays, it coheres, for the moft part, with the rudiments of the fruit. Thus the words, for the moft part are hardly to be admitted into definitions. Tournefort defines it to be a part of a plant very often remarkable for its peculiar colours, for the moft part adhering to the young fruit, to which it feems to afford the firft nourifhment, in order to explicate its moft tender parts. Which definition is ftill more deficient than the former, by this uncertain mode of expreffion.

Pontedera, the profeffor of botany at Padua, defines it to be a part of a plant unlike the reft in form and nature; if the flower has a tube, it always adheres to the embryo, or is very near it, for whofe ufe it is fubfervient; but if it wants a tube, there is no embryo adhering.

This definition is far from being clear, for it is fcarce intelligible, and is liable to this objection, that it may include fome parts of a plant which no perfon ever called by that name; for a root, a ftalk, or a leaf, are parts of a plant unlike the reft in form and nature, having no tube, and fo do not adhere to any embryo, and thus by Pontedera's definition are flowers.

Monf. Juffieu, the Paris profeffor, feems not to have fucceeded much better in this affair: he fays, That is properly called a flower, which is compofed of chives, and a piftillum, and is of ufe in generation. But this is too defective; for there are many plants in which the piftillium or ftyle is found a confiderable diftance from the chives; there are many flowers

that have no piftillum, whether that word be taken to fignify the embryo of the fruit, or its appendix, and many which have no chives.

But the late Monfieur Vaillant feems to be happier, in forming a clearer idea of this part of a plant. We find in the lecture he read in the Royal Garden at Paris, that the flowers, ftrictly fpeaking, ought to be reckoned the organs which conftitute the different fexes in plants; feeing they are fometimes found without any covering, and that the coats or petals, which immediately encompafs them, are defigned only to cover and defend them: but (fays he) as thefe coats are the moft confpicuous and moft beautiful part of the compofition, which is called by the name of flower; to thefe coats therefore I give the name of flower, of whatfoever ftructure or colour they be; whether they encompafs the organs of both fexes together, or contain only one of them, or only fome parts depending on one of them, provided always that they be not of the fame figure of the leaves of the plant.

But, in my opinion, Dr. Martyn has been happier, in his definition of a flower, than all thofe abovementioned: he defines a flower to be the organs of generation of both fexes adhering to a common placenta, together with their common coverings; or of either fex feparately, with its proper coverings, if it have any.

The parts of a flower are, 1. The germen or ovary; which is the rudiment of the fruit, and fo is properly the female organ of generation.

2. The ftyle, which is a body accompanying the ovary, either arifing from the top of it, or ftanding as an axis in the middle, with the embryos of the feeds round it.

3. The fummits, or apices, which are thofe bodies that contain the prolific powder, analogous to the male fperm in animals; and generally hang upon flender threads, which are called the chives or ftamina.

The petals are thofe tender fine coloured leaves, which are generally the moft confpicuous parts of a flower.

The empalement, or calyx, is thofe tender leaves which cover the other parts of a flower.

Flowers, according to the number of their petals, are called monopetalous, dipetalous, tripetalous, tetrapetalous, &c.

The ftructure of flowers is indeed very various; but, according to Dr. Grew, the generality have thefe three parts in common, viz. the empalement, the foliation, and the attire.

Mr. Ray reckons, that every perfect flower has the petals, ftamina, apices, and ftylus or piftil; and fuch as want any of thefe parts, he accounts imperfect flowers.

In moft plants there is a perianthum, calyx, or flowercup; which is of a ftronger confiftence than the flower itfelf, and defigned to ftrengthen or preferve it.

Flowers are diftinguifhed into male, female, or hermaphrodite.

The male flowers are thofe in which are the ftamina, but have no germen or ftyle, the fame which botanifts call ftamineous flowers; thefe have no fruit.

The female flowers are fuch as contain the germen and ftyle, or piftil, which is fucceeded with fruit, and are called fruitful, or knitting flowers.

The hermaphrodite flowers are fuch in which the two fexes are contained, i. e. the male and female parts are found in the fame flower, which are the moft general kind; fuch are the Daffodil, Lily, Tulip, Althæa, Geranium, Rofemary, Sage, Thyme.

The ftructure of parts is much the fame in thofe where the fexes are divided; the difference between them confifting in this, that the ftamina and fummits or apices, i. e. the male parts in thefe are feparate from the ftyles or piftils; being fometimes on the fame plants, and fometimes on different ones.

Among the plants which bear both male and female parts, but at a diftance from each other are reckoned the

the Cucumber, Melon, Gourd, Turky-Wheat, Walnut, Oak, Beech, &c.

FLUIDITY. [Fluiditas, of fluere, Lat. to flow.]
Having occasion to mention fluids and fluidity, in speaking of the properties of the elements air, water, fire, &c. I thought it necessary, in this place, to give the following account of that property, which I have extracted from the most approved authors.

A fluid, or fluid body, is by some defined to be a body, whose particles are but weakly connected, their mutual cohesion being, in a great measure, prevented from some external cause : in which sense, a fluid stands opposed to a solid ; and is, by the excellent Sir Isaac Newton, defined to be one whose parts easily give place, or move out of the way, on any force impelled upon them, and by that means do so easily move one over another. Which definition is much better than that of Descartes, That a fluid is a body whose parts are in continual motion, because it is neither apparent that the parts of all fluids are so, nor that the parts of some solid bodies are not so.

Fluidity is the state or affection of bodies, which denominates or renders them fluid, and stands in direct opposition to firmness and solidity.

It is distinguished from liquidity and humidity, in that the idea of fluidity is absolute, and the property contained within the thing itself ; whereas that of humidity is relative, and implies wetting, or adhering, i. e. something that gives us the sensation of wetness or moisture, and would have no existence, but for our senses.

Thus melted metals, air, æther, and even smoke, and flame itself, are fluid bodies, and not liquid ones ; the parts of them being actually dry, and not leaving any sense of moisture.

Fluidity seems to consist in this, that the parts of any body, being fine and small, are so disposed by motion and figure, as that they can easily slide over one another's surfaces all manner of ways. Mr. Boyle also observes, That it is requisite they should be variously and separately agitated to and fro, and that they should touch one another but in some parts only of their surfaces. And the same gentleman says, in his History of Fluidity, That the conditions requisite to constitute a fluid body, are chiefly the three following.

1st, The minuteness or smallness of its parts : thus we see the fire, by dividing metals into parts very fine and small, will melt them, and make them fluid ; and after the same manner do acid menstruums dissolve them, suspend their liquor, and render them fluid ; and that fire turns the hard body of common salt almost wholly into a liquor by distillation : though it is not improbable, but that the shape and figure of these small parts may conduce much towards producing this quality of fluidity ; for it is found in the distillation of Olive oil (which is a fluid made only by pressure) that most of the oil will, by the action of the parts of the fire (if it be done in a retort) be turned into a kind of consistent substance like butter. Likewise mercury, whose parts are, without doubt, much grosser than those of oil and water, is yet more fluid than either of them.

2dly, It seems requisite to fluidity, that there be store of vacuities, or vacant spaces, interspersed between the corpuscles of the fluid body ; for else there will not be room for each particle to continue its motion and agitation on the surfaces of the neighbouring ones. For,

3dly, The chief condition requisite to constitute a fluid body, is, that particles be agitated variously and apart, either by their own proper motion, or by something of substance, that tumbles them up and down by its passage through them.

That this qualification is chiefly requisite to fluidity, you may gather from that common experiment of putting a little dry powder of alabaster, or plaster of Paris, finely sifted, in a flat-bottomed vessel over the fire ; for in a little time it will boil like water, and imitate all the motions of a boiling liquor ; it will

tumble variously over in great waves like that ; it will bear stirring with a stick or ladle without resisting, as it will do when cold ; nay, if it be stirred strongly near the side of the vessel, its waves will apparently dash up against the sides : yet if any of it be speedily taken out, and laid on a piece of paper, you will see nothing but a dry powder.

So that it is evident from hence, that there is a real difference between a fluid-body and a wetting liquor ; for not only this boiling powder and melted metals, but the air and æther, and even flame itself, are properly fluid bodies, though not moist liquors.

This ingenious gentleman found also, that by blowing the smoke of Rosemary into a glass pipe, and then holding the pipe (when filled) upright, the surface of the smoke would accommodate itself to a level situation ; and which way soever the tube was inclined, the superficies of the smoke would be parallel to the horizon ; and when the glass was much inclined, would run along it like water.

From whence he infers, that, in order to the rendering a body fluid, there is no need that its parts should be closely condensed, as those of water are.

And Dr. Hook, in his Micrograph. p. 12. presents us with a very pretty experiment or two, to prove this account of fluidity, viz. That a dish of sand being set on a drum head, briskly beaten by the sticks, or on the upper stone of a mill, turning swiftly round on the (empty) lower one, it in all respects, emulate the properties of a fluid body ; for a heavy body will immediately sink in it to the bottom, and a light one emerge to the top ; each grain of sand hath a constant vibrating, dancing motion ; and if a hole be made in the side of the dish, the sand will spin out like water.

The corpuscular philosophy, before it was wonderfully improved by Sir Isaac Newton, did not go to the bottom of this matter ; for it gave no account of the cause of the chief condition requisite to constitute a fluid body, viz. the various motions and agitations of its particles : but this may, in a great measure, be accounted for, if it be supposed to be one of the primary laws of nature, That as all particles of matter attract one another when they come within a certain distance, so likewise they fly away from, and avoid one another, at all greater distances from one another.

For then, though their common gravity may keep them together in a mass (it may sometimes be) together with the pressure of other bodies upon them ; yet their continual endeavour to avoid one another singly, and the adventitious impulses of light, heat, or other external causes, may make the particles of fluids continually move round about one another, and so produce this quality.

It is indeed a difficulty not easily got over, to account for the particles of fluids always keeping at such a distance from one another, as not to come within the sphere of one another's attraction.

The fabric and constitution of that fluid body, water, is amazing ; that a body so very rare, and which has a vast over-proportion of pores, or interspersed vacuity, to solid matter, should yet be perfectly incompressible by the greatest force ; and yet this fluid is easily reducible into that firm, transparent, friable body which we call ice, by being only exposed to a certain degree of cold.

One would think, that though the particles of water cannot come near enough to attract each other, yet the intervening frigorific matter doth, by being mingled per minima, strongly attract them, and is itself likewise strongly attracted by them, and wedges or fixes all the mass into a firm body ; which solid body loses its solidity again, when by heat the vinculum is solved, and these frigorific particles are disjoined from those of the water, and are forced to fly out of it ; and, perhaps, just thus may the fumes of lead fix quicksilver.

When a firm solid body, such as a metal, is by heat reduced into a fluid, doth not the fire disjoin and separate

parate its conſtituent particles, which mutual attraction cauſed to cohere before, and keep them at
ſuch a diſtance from each other, as that they are
without the ſphere of one anothers attraction as long
as that violent motion laſts? And do not they, when
that is over, and the heat is flown out, come nearer
to, attract one another, and coaleſce again?

As therefore the cauſe of coheſion of the parts of ſolid
bodies appears to be their mutual attraction, ſo the
chief cauſe of fluidity ſeems to be a contrary motion impreſſed on the particles of fluids, by which
they avoid and fly one another, as ſoon as they come
at, and as long as they keep at, ſuch a diſtance from
each other.

It is obſerved alſo in fluids, that the direction of
their preſſure againſt the veſſels which contain them,
is in lines perpendicular to the ſides of ſuch veſſels;
which property being the neceſſary reſult of the particles of any fluid's being ſpherical, it ſhews that the
parts of all fluids are ſo, or of a figure nearly approaching thereto.

Dr. Clarke ſays, That if the parts of a body do not
touch each other, or eaſily ſlide over one another, and
are of ſuch a magnitude as that they may be eaſily
agitated by heat, and the heat be ſufficiently great to
agitate them, though perhaps it may be leſs than ſuf-
fices to prevent water from freezing; or even though
the parts be not actually moved, yet if they be ſmall,
ſmooth, ſlippery, and of ſuch a figure and magnitude as diſpoſes them to move and give way, that
body is fluid.

And yet the particles of ſuch fluid bodies do, in ſome
meaſure, cohere; as is evident hence, that mercury,
when well purged of air, will be ſuſtained in the barometer to the height of ſixty or ſeventy inches; that
water will aſcend in capillary tubes, even in vacuo;
and that the drops of liquors in vacuo run into a ſpherical form, as adhering by ſome mutual coheſion,
like that between poliſhed marble planes.

To this may be added, that theſe ſaid bodies, if they
conſiſt of particles which are eaſily entangled with
each other, as oil; or if they be capable of being ſtiffened by cold, and joined by the interpoſition of certain
cunei or wedges, as water, they are eaſily rendered
hard; but if their particles are ſuch as can neither be
entangled as air, nor ſtiffened by cold, as quickſilver,
then they never grow hard and fixed.

In ſhort, the Carteſians define a fluid to be a body,
the parts of which are in continual inteſtine motion;
and Dr. Hook, Mr. Boyle, and Dr. Boerhaave, tho'
they differ in opinion widely from Carteſianiſm, ſub-
ſcribe to the definition, and alledge arguments to
prove, that the parts of fluids are in continual motion, and even that it is this motion which conſtitutes
fluidity; and the latter of them aſcribes this, and all
motion, to fire. See FIRE.

Fluids then are either natural, as water and mercury;
or animal, as blood, milk, bile, lympha, urine, &c.
or factitious, as wines, ſpirits, oils, &c.

FŒNICULUM. Tourn. Inſt. R. H. 311. tab.
164. Anethum. Lin. Gen. Plant. 326. *Fennel*; in
French, *Fenouil*.

The CHARACTERS are,

*It hath an umbellated flower; the great umbel is com-
poſed of many ſmaller, which have no involucrum; the
umbel is uniform; the flowers have five incurved petals,
and five ſtamina, terminated by roundiſh ſummits: the
germen is ſituated under the flower, ſupporting two ſmall
ſtyles, crowned by roundiſh ſtigmas. The germen afterward turns to an oblong fruit, deeply channelled, dividing
into two parts, each containing a ſingle ſeed, flat on one
ſide, but convex and channelled on the other.*

This genus of plants is ranged in the ſecond ſection
of Tournefort's ſeventh claſs, which includes the herbs
with umbellated flowers diſpoſed circularly, whoſe empalement turns to two narrow, oblong, thick ſeeds.
Dr. Linnæus has joined this genus to Anethum,
which is placed in the ſecond ſection of his fifth claſs,
with thoſe plants whoſe flowers have five ſtamina and
two ſtyles. But as the ſeeds of Fennel are oblong,

5

thick, and channelled, and thoſe of Dill flat and bordered, it is much better to keep them ſeparate, than
to join them in the ſame genus.

The SPECIES are,

1. FŒNICULUM (*Vulgare*) foliis decompoſitis, foliolis
brevioribus multifidis, ſemine breviore. *Fennel with
decompounded leaves, whoſe ſmell leaves are ſhorter and
end in many points, and a ſhorter ſeed.* Fœniculum
vulgare Germanicum. C. B. P. 147. *Common Fennel.*

2. FŒNICULUM (*Dulce*) foliis decompoſitis, foliolis longioribus, ſemine longiori. *Fennel with decompounded
leaves, whoſe ſmall leaves are very long, and a longer
ſeed.* Fœniculum dulce; majore & albo ſemine. J. B.
3. p. 2, 4. *Sweet Fennel having a larger white ſeed.*

3. FŒNICULUM (*Azoricum*) humilius, radice caule-
ſcente carnoſo, ſeminibus recurvis; radice annuâ.
*Dwarf Fennel with a fleſhy ſtalk, recurved ſeeds, and
an annual root.* Fœniculum dulce Azoricum. Pluk.
Alm. *Sweet Azorian Fennel, called Finochio.*

The firſt ſort is the common Fennel, which is cultivated in the gardens, and has ſown itſelf in many
places, where it has been introduced in ſuch plenty,
as to appear as if it were a native in England; but it
is no where found at a great diſtance from gardens, ſo
has been undoubtedly brought into England. There
are two varieties of this, one with light green leaves,
and the other with very dark leaves; but theſe I believe are only varieties which ariſe from the ſame
ſeeds; but this is very difficult to aſcertain; for unleſs the ſeeds were ſown ſeparately in ſome place where
neither of theſe plants have been growing before, it
cannot be done; for the ſeeds of theſe plants which
have ſcattered, will remain in the ground ſome years,
and when expoſed near the ſurface will grow; ſo that
the plants become troubleſome weeds, wherever
their ſeeds have been ſuffered to ſcatter; and they frequently come up where other ſeeds are ſown, and
thereby the two ſorts may accidentally mix.

The common Fennel is ſo well known, as to need
no deſcription. This hath a ſtrong fleſhy root, which
penetrates deep into the ground, and will continue ſeveral years. It flowers in July, and the ſeeds ripen in
autumn. The beſt time to ſow the ſeeds, is ſoon
after they are ripe; the plants will come up in the autumn or the following ſpring, and require no other
care but to keep them clean from weeds, and thin
the plants where they are too cloſe; it will grow in
any ſoil or ſituation. The leaves, ſeeds, and roots
of this, are uſed in medicine; the root is one of the
five opening roots, and the ſeed one of the greater
carminative ſeeds. There is a ſimple water made
from the leaves, and a diſtilled oil from the ſeed.

The ſweet Fennel has been by many ſuppoſed only a
variety of the common ſort, but I have cultivated it
in the ſame ground with that, where it has always retained its differences. The leaves of this are very
long and ſlender, growing more ſparſedly, and do not
end in ſo many points as thoſe of the common ſort;
the ſtalks do not riſe ſo high, and the ſeeds are longer,
narrower, and of a lighter colour. Theſe ſeeds are
generally imported from Germany or Italy, and are
by ſome preferred to thoſe of the common ſort for
uſe, being much ſweeter.

This may be propagated in the ſame manner as the
former ſort, being very hardy, but the roots are not
of ſo long duration.

The third ſort is ſuppoſed to have been originally
brought from the Azorian Iſlands; it has been long
cultivated in Italy as a ſaliad herb, under the title of
Finochio; and there are ſome few gardens in England,
where it is now cultivated, but in ſmall quantities, for
there are not many Engliſh palates which reliſh it, nor
is it eaſy to be furniſhed with good ſeeds; thoſe which
are annually brought from Italy ſeldom prove good;
and it is difficult to ſave it in England, becauſe the
winter frequently kills thoſe plants which are left for
ſeeds; and when any good plants of the early ſowing
are left for ſeeds, they do not ripen, unleſs the winter proves very favourable.

This

This fort hath very fhort ftalks, which fwell juft above the furface of the ground, to four or five inches in breadth, and almoft two thick, being flefhy and tender: this is the part which is eaten when blanched, with oil, vinegar, and pepper, as a cold fallad. When thefe plants are permitted to run for feeds, the ftalks do not rife more than a foot and a half high, having a large fpreading umbel ftanding on the top. The feeds of this fort are narrow, crooked, and of a bright yellow colour; they have a very ftrong fmell like Anifeed, and are very fweet to the tafte.

The manner of cultivating this plant is as follows: Your firft care muft be to procure good feeds from fome perfon who has been careful in the choice of the plants, otherwife there will be little hope of having it good; for the plants will run up to feeds before they fwell to any fize, fo will not be fit for ufe: then make choice of a good fpot of light rich earth, not dry nor very wet, for in either extreme this plant will not thrive. The firft crop may be fown about a fortnight in March, which, if it fucceeds, will be fit for ufe in July; and by fowing at feveral times, there may be a fupply for the table till the froft puts a ftop to it. After having well dug and levelled the ground fmooth, you muft make a fhallow drill by a line, into which you muft fcatter your feeds pretty thin; for if your plants are fix inches afunder in the rows, it will be full near enough; but however, you muft expect fome of your feeds to fail, and therefore you fhould fcatter them about two inches diftance; then cover the feeds about half an inch thick with earth, laying it fmooth: thefe drills fhould be made eighteen inches afunder, or more, that there may be room to clean the ground, as alfo to earth up the plants when they are full grown. When the plants come up, which will be in about three weeks or a month after fowing, you muft with a fmall hoe cut up all the weeds between them, and where the plants are too clofe, they fhould be thinned to about three inches diftance; and as they advance, and the weeds fpring again, they fhould, from time to time, be hoed; and at the laft time of thinning them, they fhould be left feven or eight inches afunder at leaft. If your kind be good, the ftems of the plants will increafe to a confiderable bulk juft above the furface of the ground; which part fhould be earthed up in the manner of Celery, to blanch, about a fortnight or three weeks before it is ufed, and this will caufe it to be very tender and crifp.

Your fecond crop fhould be fown about three weeks after the firft, and fo continue fowing every three weeks or a month till the end of July, after which time it will be too late for the plants to come to any perfection. But you fhould obferve to fow in April, May, and June, on a moifter foil than that which you fowed the firft on; as alfo what you fow in the latter part of July, fhould be fown on a drier foil, and in a warmer fituation; becaufe this crop will not be fit for ufe till late in autumn, and therefore will be fubject to injuries from too much wet or cold weather, if on a moift foil. But as the ground is often extreme dry in June and July, and the feeds more apt to mifcarry and not come up, you fhould therefore obferve to water and fhade the beds where this feed is fown at that feafon, until the plants come up. And if the feafon fhould prove dry, the plants muft be duly watered, otherwife they will run up to feed before they are of any fize; therefore there fhould be a channel made where every row of plants grow, to detain the water which is poured on them, to prevent its running off. In the autumn, if there fhould happen fharp frofts, it will be very proper to cover the plants with fome Peas-haulm, or other light covering, to prevent their being pinched; by which method they may be continued for ufe till the middle of winter.

A fmall bed of this plant will be fufficient at each fowing for a middling family; and for a large family, a bed of about twenty feet long, and four feet broad, will be full enough at a time.

FŒNUM BURGUNDIACUM. See Me-dica Sativa.

FŒNUM GRÆCUM. See Trigonella.

FOOT-STALKS, are thofe fmall ftalks which immediately fuftain the leaves, flowers, or fruit.

FOUNTAINS are fources or fprings of living water, arifing out of the ground. As to the original of them, fee under the article Springs.

Of artificial fountains there are great variety, the mechanifm of which not being to my purpofe, I will not dwell upon it; though I may affert, that they are not only great ornaments to a fine garden, but alfo of great ufe. But they ought not to be placed too near the houfe by reafon of the vapours that arife from the water, which may be apt to ftrike a damp to the wall, and fpoil the paintings, &c. and the fummer vapours may caufe a malignity in the air, and fo be prejudicial to the health of the family; and likewife the noife may be incommodious in the night.

Fountains in a garden fhould be fo diftributed, that they may be feen almoft all at one time, and that the water-fpouts may range all in a line one with another, which is the beauty of them; for this occafions an agreeable confufion to the eye, making them appear to be more in number than they really are. See Jet d'Eau, Springs, Vapours, Water, &c.

FRAGARIA. Lin. Gen. Plant. 558. Tourn. Inft. R. H. 295. tab. 152. [is fo called for its fragrant aromatic fcent.] Strawberries; in French, *Frafier*.

The Characters are,

The empalement of the flower is of one leaf, which is cut into ten parts at the top. The flower hath five roundifh petals, which are inferted in the empalement, and fpread open. It hath twenty ftamina, which are inferted in the empalement, terminated by moon-fhaped fummits. It hath a great number of germen collected into a head, each having a fingle ftyle, inferted in the fide of the germen, crowned by fingle ftigmas; this head afterward becomes a large, foft, pulpy fruit, which, if left, falls away, leaving many fmall angular feeds in the empalement.

This genus of plants is ranged in the fifth fection of Linnæus's twelfth clafs, which includes thofe plants whofe flowers have at leaft twenty ftamina and many ftyles, which are inferted to the empalement.

The Species are,

1. **Fragaria** (*Vefca*) foliis ovatis ferratis, calycibus brevibus, fructu parvo. *Strawberry with oval fawed leaves, foort empalements, and a fmall fruit.* Fragaria vulgaris. C. B. P. 226. *The common or Wood Strawberry.*

2. **Fragaria** (*Virginiana*) foliis oblongo-ovatis ferratis, inferne incanis, calycibus longioribus, fructu fubrotundo. *Strawberry with oblong, oval, fawed leaves, hoary on their under fide, longer empalements, and a roundifh fruit.* Fragaria Virginiana fructu Coccineo. Hift. Ox. 2. 186. *Virginia Strawberry with a fcarlet fruit, commonly called the Scarlet Strawberry.*

3. **Fragaria** (*Muricata*) foliis ovato-lanceolatis rugofis, fructu ovato. *Strawberry with oval, fpear-fhaped, rough leaves, and an oval fruit.* Fragaria fructu parvi pruni magnitudine. C. B. P. 327. *Strawberry with fruit as large as a fmall Plumb, commonly called Hautboy Strawberry.*

4. **Fragaria** (*Chiloenfis*) foliis ovatis carnofis hirfutis fructu maximo. *Strawberry with oval, flefhy, hairy leaves, and a large fruit.* Fragaria Chiloenfis, fructu maximo foliis carnofis hirfutis. Hort. Elth. 145. tab. 120. *Strawberry of Chili with a large fruit, and hairy flefhy leaves, called Frutilla, in America.*

There are fome other varieties of this fruit, which are now cultivated in England; but I have not feen any other which can be called a diftinct fpecies, than are here enumerated, and thefe, I think, may be allowed to be fo, for they never alter from one to the other, by any cultivation, though the fruit is frequently improved, fo as to be of a larger fize thereby; therefore thofe who have fuppofed them but one fpecies, have greatly erred in fo doing; I fhall therefore mention the feveral varieties of Strawberry, which are

at

at present to be found in the gardens under the species to which they naturally belong.

The first sort is the common Wood Strawberry, which grows naturally in the woods in many parts of England, and is so well known as to need no description ; of this there are three varieties, 1. The common sort with red fruit. 2. The white Wood Strawberry, which ripens a little later in the season, and is by many persons preferred to it for its quick flavour, but as it seldom produces so large crops of fruit as the red sort, it is not very generally cultivated. 3. The green Strawberry, by some called the Pine Apple Strawberry, from its rich flavour. The fruit of this is greenish when ripe ; it is very firm, and hath a very high flavour ; this is a late ripe fruit, but unless it is planted in a moist loamy soil, it is a very bad bearer ; but in such land where it does succeed, it merits cultivation as much as any of the sorts.

The Scarlet Strawberry is the sort which is first ripe, for which reason it merits esteem, but it nothing else to recommend it ; but the fruit is so good, as by many persons of good taste to be preferred to most other sorts. This was brought from Virginia, where it grows naturally in the woods, and is so different from the Wood Strawberry in leaf, flower, and fruit, that there need be no doubt of their being distinct species.

There is a variety of this which hath been of late years introduced from the northern parts of America, which has the appearance of a distinct species. The leaves of this are rounder, and not so deeply veined ; the crenatures on their edges are broader and more obtuse. The leaves which compose the empalement are much longer, and are hairy, and the fruit is larger ; but as in other respects it approaches near to the Scarlet Strawberry, I have chosen to join it to that, rather than make a distinct species of it ; this I have been informed grows naturally in Louisiana.

There has also been another variety of this (if not a distinct species) lately introduced to our gardens, which is commonly known by the title of Alpine Strawberry ; the plants of this greatly resemble those of the Scarlet Strawberry, but the fruit is more pointed ; it is a well flavoured fruit, and continues bearing from the common season of Strawberries, until the frost in autumn puts a stop to it, which renders the sort very valuable : I have frequently gathered the fruit in the beginning of November ; this has occasioned the Dutch gardeners titling it Everlasting Strawberry.

The Hautboy Strawberry, which the French call Capitons, came originally from America, but it has been long cultivated in the English gardens, and is very different from the other sorts in leaf, flower, and fruit, as that no one can doubt of their being different species ; there is an improvement of this sort, which is commonly called the Globe Hautboy. The fruit of this is larger, and of a globular form, but this difference has certainly arisen from culture ; for where these have been neglected a year or two, they have degenerated to the common Hautboy again ; where the ground is proper for this plant, and their culture is well managed, the plants will produce great plenty of fruit, which will be large, and well flavoured, and by some persons are preferred to all the other sorts.

The Chili Strawberry was brought to Europe by Monf. Frazier, an engineer, who was sent to America by the late king of France, and was first planted in the Royal Garden at Paris, from whence it was communicated to several curious persons in Holland, and in the year 1727, I brought a parcel of the plants to England, which were communicated to me by Mr. George Clifford, of Amsterdam, who had large beds of this sort growing in his curious gardens at Hartecamp. The leaves of this sort are hairy, oval, and of a much thicker substance than any sort yet known, and stand upon very strong hairy foot-stalks ; the runners from the plants are very large, hairy, and

extend to a great length, putting out plants at several distances. The foot-stalks which sustain the flowers are very strong ; the leaves of the empalement are long and hairy. The flowers are large, and are often deformed ; and so is the fruit, which is very large, and when cultivated in very strong land, the plants produce plenty of fruit, which is firm, and very well flavoured ; but as it is a bad bearer in most places where it has been cultivated, it has generally been neglected.

The Strawberries in general love a gentle hazelly loam, in which they will thrive and bear greater plenty of fruit than in a light rich soil. The ground should also be moist, for if it is very dry, all the watering which is given to the plants in warm dry seasons, will not be sufficient to procure plenty of fruit ; nor should the ground be much dunged, for that will cause the plants to run into suckers, and grow luxuriant, and render them less fruitful.

The best time to remove these plants is in October, that they may get new roots before the hard frost sets in, which loosens the ground ; so that if the roots of the plants are not pretty well established in the ground, the plants are frequently turned out of the ground by the first thaw ; therefore the sooner they are planted when the autumnal rains begin, the better will their roots be established, so there will be less danger of their miscarrying, and sometimes those which are well rooted, will produce a few fruit the first year ; there are some who transplant their plants in the spring ; but where that is done, they must be duly supplied with water in the dry weather, otherwise they will not succeed.

The ground in which these are planted should be thoroughly cleaned from the roots of Couch, and all other bad weeds ; for as the Strawberry plants are to remain three years before they are taken up, so if any of the roots of those bad weeds are left in the ground, they will have time to multiply so greatly as to fill the ground, and overbear the Strawberry plants. The ground should also be well trenched and made level ; then the usual method is to lay it out into beds of four feet broad, with paths two feet or two feet and a half broad between each ; these paths are necessary for the convenience of gathering the fruit, and for weeding and dressing of the beds, and also far watering the plants ; after the beds are marked out, there should be four lines drawn in each, at a foot distance, which will leave six inches space on each side, between the outside rows and the paths ; then the plants should be planted at about a foot distance from each other in the rows, in a quincunx order, being careful to close the ground to the roots of the plants when they are planted ; and if there should not happen rain soon after, the plants should be well watered to settle the earth to their roots.

The distance here mentioned for the plants to be placed must be understood for the Wood Strawberries only, for as the other sorts grow much larger, their distances must be proportioned to their several growths ; therefore the Scarlets and Hautboys should have but three rows of plants in each bed, which should be at fifteen inches distance, and the plants in the rows should be allowed the same space from each other, and the Chili Strawberry must have but two rows of plants in each bed, which should also be two feet apart in the rows ; for as these grow very strong, if they have not room to spread, they will not be very fruitful.

In chusing proper plants of any of the sorts, depends the whole success ; for if they are promiscuously taken from beds without care, great part of the plants will become barren ; these are generally called blind, which is when there are plenty of flowers, but no fruit produced ; if these flowers are well examined, they will be found to want the female organs of generation, most of them abounding with stamina, but there are few, if any styles ; so that it frequently happens among these barren plants, that some of them will have a part of an imperfect fruit formed, which will

will fometimes ripen ; this barrennefs is not peculiar to Strawberries, but is general to all thofe plants which have creeping roots, or ftalks ; and the more they increafe from either, the fooner they become barren, and this in fome degree runs through the vegetable kingdom ; for trees and fhrubs which are propagated by cuttings, are generally barren of feeds in two generations, that is, when they are propagated by cuttings, which were taken from plants raifed by cuttings ; this I have conftantly found to hold in great numbers of plants, and in fruit-trees it often happens, that thofe forts which have been long propagated by grafts and buds, have no kernels. But to return to the choice of the Strawberry plants ; thefe fhould never be taken from old neglected beds, where the plants have been fuffered to fpread or run into a multitude of fuckers, nor from any plants which are not very fruitful ; and thofe offsets which ftand neareft to the old plants, fhould always be preferred to thofe which are produced from the trailing ftalks at a farther diftance ; and the Wood Strawberry is beft when the plants are taken frefh from the woods, provided they are taken from fruitful plants, becaufe they are not fo liable to ramble and fpread, as thofe which are taken from plants, which have been long cultivated in gardens ; therefore thofe who are curious in cultivating this fruit, fhould be very careful in the choice of their plants.

When the plants have taken new root, the next care is if the winter prove fevere, to lay fome old tanners bark over the furface of the bed between the plants, to keep out the froft : this care is abfolutely neceffary to the Chili Strawberry, which is frequently killed in hard winters, where they are expofed without any covering ; therefore where tanners bark cannot eafily be procured, faw-duft, or fea-coal afhes may be ufed ; or in want of thefe, if decayed leaves of trees, or the branches of Evergreen-trees with their leaves upon them, are laid over the beds, to prevent the froft from penetrating deep into the ground, it will fecure the plants from injury.

The following fummer the plants fhould be conftantly kept clean from weeds, and all the runners fhould be pulled off as faft as they are produced ; if this is conftantly practifed, the plants will become very ftrong by the following autumn ; whereas when this is neglected (as is too frequently feen) and all the runners permitted to ftand during the fummer feafon, and then pulled off in the autumn, the plants will not be half fo ftrong as thofe where that care has been taken ; therefore there will not be near the fame quantity of fruit upon them the following fpring, nor will the fruit be near fo large and fair ; and where proper care is taken of the plants the firft fummer, there is generally a plentiful crop of fruit the fecond fpring ; whereas when this is neglected, the crop will be thin and the fruit fmall.

As this fruit is very common, there are but few perfons who cultivate it with proper care ; therefore I fhall give fome directions for the doing of it, which, if carefully practifed, will be attended with fuccefs. The old plants of Strawberries are thofe which produce the fruit, for the fuckers feldom produce any till they have grown a full year ; therefore it appears how neceffary it is to diveft the old plants of them ; for wherever they are fuffered to remain, they rob the fruitful plants of their nourifhment in proportion to their number ; for each of thefe fuckers fend out a quantity of roots, which interfere, and are fo clofely matted together, as to draw away the greateft part of the nourifhment from the old roots, whereby they are greatly weakened ; and thefe fuckers alfo render each other very weak, fo that from hence the caufe of barrennefs arifes ; for I have known where the old plants have been conftantly kept clear from fuckers, they have continued very fruitful four or five years without being tranfplanted ; however, it is the beft way to have a fucceffion of beds, that after three years ftanding they may be taken up ; becaufe by that time they will have exhaufted the ground of thofe vegetable

falts, neceffary for the nourifhment of that fpecies of plants ; for it is always obferved, that Strawberries planted on frefh land are the moft fruitful.

The next thing to be obferved, is in autumn to diveft the plants of any ftrings, or runners, which may have been produced, and alfo of all the decayed leaves, and the beds cleared from weeds ; then the paths fhould be dug up, and the weeds buried which were taken from the beds, and fome earth laid over the furface of the beds between the plants ; this will ftrengthen the plants, and prepare them for the following fpring ; and if after this, there is fome old tanners bark laid over the furface of the ground between the plants, it will be of great fervice to them. In the fpring, after the danger of hard froft is over, the ground between the plants in the beds fhould be forked with a narrow three-pronged fork, to loofen it, and break the clods ; and in this operation, the tan which was laid over the furface of the ground in autumn will be buried, which will be a good dreffing to the Strawberries, efpecially in ftrong land ; then about the end of March, or the beginning of April, if the furface of the beds is covered with mofs, it will keep the ground moift, and prevent the drying winds from penetrating the ground, and thereby fecure a good crop of fruit ; and the mofs will preferve the fruit clean, that when heavy rains may fall after the fruit is full grown, there will be no dirt wafhed over them, which frequently happens, fo that the fruit muft be wafhed before it is fit for the table, which greatly diminifhes its flavour ; therefore where this method is practifed, the fruit may be had in perfection.

The foil in which the Chili Strawberry is found to fucceed beft, is a very ftrong brick earth, approaching near to clay ; in this foil I have feen them produce a tolerable good crop, and the fruit has been extremely well flavoured ; and if fome care be taken to pull off the runners as they are produced, fo as to leave only the old plants, I make no doubt but thefe plants may be as fruitful as the common Hautboy : this I mention from one or two experiments, which have been made by my direction, and not from theory.

There are fome perfons who are fo fond of Strawberries, as to be at any expence to obtain them early in the year, and to continue them as late in the feafon as poffible ; and fhould I omit to give fome directions for both thefe managements, they would fuppofe the book very defective ; therefore I fhall mention the practice of fome few, who have fucceeded beft in the management of thefe fruits ; I fhall begin with directions for obtaining thefe fruits early in the fpring. Where there are any hot walls erected in gardens for the producing early fruit, it is very common to fee Strawberries planted in the borders, that the fire which is applied for ripening the fruit againft the walls, may alfo ferve the purpofe of bringing forward the Strawberries ; but where this is practifed, the Strawberry plants fhould be annually renewed, taking up the plants as foon as their fruit is over, and all the earth of the borders fhould be taken out, at leaft two feet deep, and frefh earth brought in, which will be equally good for the wall trees ; but, as was before obferved, that the old plants of Strawberries only are thofe which produce the fruit, there fhould be a fufficient number of plants brought up in pots ; to fupply the border annually ; and the fame muft be done if they are to be raifed in a common hot-bed, or in ftoves ; therefore I fhall begin with giving directions for raifing and preparing plants for thofe purpofes. The forts which are the moft proper for forcing early, are the Scarlet, the Alpine, and the Wood Strawberries, for the Hautboy grows too large for this purpofe. In the choice of the plants, there fhould be an efpecial care taken to have them from the moft fruitful plants, and thofe which grow immediately to the old plants ; they fhould be taken off in autumn, and each planted in a feparate fmall pot filled with loamy foil, and placed in a fhady fituation till they have taken root ; after which they may be removed to an open fituation, where they may remain till the middle or

       end

end of November, when the pots should be plunged into the ground up to their rims, to prevent the frost from penetrating through the side of the pots; if these are placed near a wall, pale, or hedge, exposed to an east aspect, or north-east, they will succeed better than in a warm situation, because they will not be forced too forward; the only care they require, is to secure them from being turned out of the pots after frost. The spring following the plants will be so far advanced as to have filled the pots with their roots by the end of April, when they should be turned out of the pots, and their roots pared; then planted into penny pots filled with the like loamy soil, and plunged into the ground in a shady situation, where they should remain the following summer; during which time they must be duly kept clean from weeds, and all the runners must be taken off as fast as they are produced; likewise if there should be any flowers come out, they should also be pinched off, and not suffered to bear fruit, which would weaken the plants, for there cannot be too much care taken to have the plants as strong as possible, that they may produce plenty of fruit, without which they are not worth the trouble of forcing.

About the middle of October, or earlier, if the autumn proves cold, the pots should be removed into a warmer situation, to prepare them for forcing; for they should not be suddenly removed from a very cold situation immediately into the stove or hot-bed, but be gradually prepared for it; but where they are designed for the borders near a hot wall, they may then be turned out of the pots, and planted into the borders, that they may have time to get fresh rooting, before the fires are made to heat the walls; when these are planted, they may be placed very close to each other; for as they are designed to remain there no longer than till they have ripened their fruit, they will not require much room, as their roots will find sufficient nourishment below, and also from the earth which is filled into the spaces between the balls of earth, about their roots; and it is of consequence to get as much fruit as possible in a small space, where there is an expence to force them early. If the fires are lighted about Christmas, the Strawberries in these borders will be ripe the end of March; or if the season should prove very cold, it may be the middle of April before they will be fit for the table.

In the management of the plants there must be care taken to supply them with water when they begin to shew their flowers, otherwise they will fall off without producing any fruit; and, in mild weather, there should be fresh air admitted to them every day; but as fruit-trees against the wall must be so treated, the same management will agree with the Strawberries. If the Strawberries are intended to be forced in a stove, where there are Pine-apples, and no room to plunge them in the tan-bed, then the plants should be transplanted into larger pots in September, that they may be well rooted before they are removed into the stove, which should not be till December; but if they are placed under a frame the beginning of November, where they may be screened from the frost, it will prepare the plants better for forcing; and those who are desirous to have them very early, make a hot-bed under frames, upon which they place their plants the latter end of October, which will bring them forward to flower, and then they remove the plants into the stove; when these plants are removed into the stove, they should be placed as near to the glasses as possible, that they may enjoy the full sun and air; for when they are placed backward, the plants will draw up weak, and the flowers will drop without producing fruit. As the earth in the pots will dry pretty fast when they stand dry upon the pavement of the hot-house, or on shelves, so the plants must be duly watered; but it must be done with discretion, and not too much given to them, which will be equally hurtful to them; if these plants are properly managed, they will produce ripe fruit in February, which is as early as most people will chuse to eat them. When the fruit is all gathered from the plants, they

should be turned out of the stove; for as they will be of no farther service, they should not remain to take up the room; nor should those plants which are planted in the borders near the hot walls be left there after their fruit is gathered, but immediately taken up, that they may rob the fruit-trees of their nourishment as little as possible.

Where there is no conveniency of stoves, or hot-walls for this purpose, the fruit may be ripened upon common hot-beds; and though they may not be quite so early as with the other advantages, yet I have seen great crops of the fruit ripe in April, which were upon common hot-beds under frames, and executed at a small expence in the following manner.

The plants were prepared in pots after the manner before directed, which were placed in a warm situation in the beginning of October, and about Christmas the hot-bed was made in the same manner as for Cucumbers, but not so strong; and as soon as the first violent steam of the dung was over, some old rotten dung laid over the hot-bed to keep down the heat, or where it can be easily procured, neats dung is preferable for this purpose; then the plants should be turned out of the pots, and placed upon the bed as close together as possible, filling up the interstices between the plants with earth; afterward the plants must have air admitted to them every day; and if the heat of the bed is too great, the plants should be raised up, to prevent their roots being scorched; and if the bed is too cold, the sides of it should be lined with some hot dung: this first bed will bring the plants to flower by the latter end of February, or the beginning of March, by which time the heat of the bed will be spent, therefore another hot-bed should be prepared to receive the plants, which need not be so strong as the first; but upon the hot dung should be laid some neats dung about two inches thick, which should be equally spread and smoothed; this will prevent the heat of the bed from injuring the roots of the plants, upon this should be laid two inches of a loamy soil; when this has laid two days to warm, the plants should be taken out of the first hot-bed, and turned carefully out of the pots, preserving all the earth to their roots, and placed close together upon this new hot-bed, filling up the vacuities between the balls with loamy earth: the roots of the plants will soon strike out into this fresh earth, which will strengthen their flowers, and cause their fruit to set in plenty; and if proper care is taken to admit fresh air to the plants, and supply them properly with water, they will have plenty of ripe fruit in April, which will be full two months before their natural season.

The methods practised to retard this fruit, is first by planting them in the coldest part of the garden, where they may be as much in shade as possible, and the soil should be strong and cold; when there are such places in a garden, the fruit will be near a month later than in a warm situation; the next is to cut off all the flowers when they first appear, and if the season proves dry, to water them plentifully, which will cause them to put out a fresh crop of flowers; and if they are supplied with water, there will be a late crop of fruit, but these are not so well flavoured as those which ripen in their natural season.

But since the Alpine Strawberry has been introduced in the English gardens, there is little occasion for practising this method of retarding the fruit; because this sort will supply the table the whole summer, especially if care is taken to pull off the runners; and in dry seasons to water the plants, without which the blossoms will fall off, without producing fruit.

There are some persons so curious as to raise the plants from seeds, by which they have greatly improved some of the sorts; and if this was more practised, I am certain it would be found of singular service, where the fairest of the fruit of each kind are chosen. The seeds should be immediately sown when the fruit is eaten; the best way is to sow the seeds in pots, placing them in the shade.

In the spring of the year 1724, there was scarce any rain from February till about the middle of July, so that most of the Strawberries and Raspberries in the gardens near London, were burnt up, and came to no perfection; but upon plenty of rain falling in July, they recovered and put out plenty of flowers, which were succeeded by fruit, which ripened in September, when the markets of London were supplied with a great plenty of both those fruits at that season of the year.

FRANGULA. Tourn. Inst. R. H. 612. tab. 383. Rhamnus. Lin. Gen. Plant. 235. [is so called of frangendo, breaking, because of the brittleness of its wood.] Berry-bearing Alder.

The CHARACTERS are,
The empalement of the flower is of one leaf, cut at the top into five segments, which are erect. The flower hath one petal, which is cut into five acute segments; these are placed between the segments of the empalement, into which they are inserted, but are shorter, and stand erect. It hath five stamina, which are the length of the petal, terminated by obtuse summits; in the center is situated a globular germen, supporting a slender style, crowned by an obtuse stigma. The germen afterward becomes a round berry, inclosing two plain roundish seeds.
This genus of plants is ranged in the second section of Tournefort's, twenty-first class, which includes the trees and shrubs with a Rose flower, whose pointal turns to a berry. Dr. Linnæus has joined this genus with the Paliurus, Alaternus, and Ziziphus, to the Rhamnus, making them only species of one genus; but according to his own system, they should be separated to a great distance from Rhamnus, and be placed in his twenty-second class, because it hath male and female flowers on different plants; whereas it is placed in the first section of his fifth class, from the flower having five stamina and but one style.

The SPECIES are,
1. FRANGULA (*Alnus*) foliis ovato-lanceolatis glabris. *Frangula with oval, spear-shaped, smooth leaves.* Frangula, sive alnus, nigra baccifera. Park. Theat. Black Berry-bearing Alder.
2. FRANGULA (*Latifolia*) foliis lanceolatis rugosis. *Frangula with rough spear-shaped leaves.* Frangula rugosiore & ampliore folio. Tourn. Berry-bearing Alder with a larger and rougher leaf.
3. FRANGULA (*Rotundifolia*) foliis ovatis nervosis. *Frangula with oval veined leaves.* Frangula montana pumila saxatilis, folio subrotundo. Tourn. Low mountain, rocky, berry-bearing Alder, with a round leaf.
4. FRANGULA (*Americana*) foliis oblongo-ovatis nervosis, glabris. *Frangula with oblong, oval, smooth veined leaves.* Frangula Americana foliis glabris. Dale. *American Berry-bearing Alder with smooth leaves.*

The first sort grows naturally in the woods in many parts of England, so is seldom planted in gardens; this rises with a woody stem to the height of ten or twelve feet, sending out many irregular branches, which are covered with a dark bark, and garnished with oval spear-shaped leaves, about two inches long, and one inch broad, having several transverse veins from the midrib to the sides, and stand upon short foot-stalks. The flowers are produced in clusters at the end of the former year's shoots, and also upon the first and second joints of the same year's shoot, each standing upon a short separate foot-stalk, on every side the branches; these are very small, of an herbaceous colour, and do not expand; they are succeeded by small round berries, which turn first red, but afterward black when ripe. The flowers appear in June, and the berries ripen in September; this stands in the Dispensary as a medicinal plant, but is seldom used.
The second sort hath larger rough leaves than the first. It grows naturally on the Alps and other mountainous parts of Europe, and is preserved in some gardens for the sake of variety.
The third sort is of humble growth, seldom rising above two feet high; this grows on the Pyrenean Mountains, and is seldom preserved unless in botanic

gardens for variety; it may be increased by laying down the branches, but must have a strong soil.
The fourth sort grows naturally in North America, from whence I received the seeds; this is pretty like the first sort, but the leaves are longer and broader; they are smooth, of a lucid green, and have many veins. The flowers are very like those of the first sort. These shrubs are easily propagated by seeds, which should be sown as soon as they are ripe, and then the plants will come up the spring following; but if they are kept out of the ground till spring, the plants will not come up till the year after. When the plants come up, they must be kept clean from weeds till autumn, then they may be taken up and planted in a nursery in rows, two feet asunder, and at one foot distance in the rows; in this nursery they may remain two years, and may then be planted where they are to remain; they may also be propagated by layers and cuttings, but the seedling plants are best.
The fruit of the first sort is often brought into the markets of London, and sold for Buckthorn berries; of which cheat, all such as make syrup of Buckthorn should be particularly careful; they may be easily distinguished by breaking the berries, and observing how many seeds are contained in each, the berries of this tree having but two, and those of Buckthorn generally four seeds in each berry, and the juice of the latter dies paper of a green colour.

FRAXINELLA. See DICTAMNUS.

FRAXINUS. Lin. Gen. Plant. 1026. Tourn. Inst. R. H. 577. tab. 343. The Ash-tree; in French, *Frêne.*

The CHARACTERS are,
It hath hermaphrodite and female flowers on the same tree, and sometimes on different trees. The hermaphrodite flowers have no petals, but a small four-pointed empalement, including two erect stamina, which are terminated by oblong summits, having four furrows. In the center is situated an oval compressed germen, supporting a cylindrical style, crowned by a bifid stigma. The germen afterward becomes a compressed bordered fruit, shaped like a bird's tongue, having one cell, inclosing a seed of the same form. The female flowers are the same, but have no stamina.
This genus of plants is ranged in the second section of Linnæus's twenty-third class, which includes the plants which have flowers of different sexes on the same or different plants, which are fruitful.

The SPECIES are,
1. FRAXINUS (*Excelsior*) foliolis serratis, floribus apetalis. Lin. Sp. Plant. 1057. *Ash-tree whose smaller leaves are serrated, and flowers having no petals.* Fraxinus excelsior. C. B. P. 416. *The common Ash.*
2. FRAXINUS (*Rotundifolia*) foliolis ovato-lanceolatis serratis, floribus coloratis. *Ash-tree whose smaller leaves are oval, spear-shaped, and sawed, and the flowers coloured.* Fraxinus rotundiore folio. C. B. P. 416. *Ash-tree with a rounder leaf, commonly called Manna Ash.*
3. FRAXINUS (*Ornus*) foliolis serratis, floribus coloratis. Lin. Sp. Plant. 1057. *Ash-tree whose smaller leaves are sawed, and flowers having petals.* Fraxinus humilior sive altera Theophrasti, minore & tenuiore folio. C. B. P. 416. *Dwarf Ash of Theophrastus with smaller and narrower leaves.*
4. FRAXINUS (*Paniculata*) foliolis lanceolatis glabris, floribus paniculatis terminatricibus. *Ash-tree with smooth spear-shaped leaves, and flowers growing in panicles at the ends of the branches.* Fraxinus florifera botryoides. Mor. Præl. 265. *The flowering Ash.*
5. FRAXINUS (*Nova Anglia*) foliolis integerrimis, petiolis teretibus. Flor. Virg. 122. *Ash-tree with the small leaves entire, and taper foot-stalks.* Fraxinus ex Novâ Angliâ, pinnis foliorum in mucronem productioribus. Rand. Cat. Hort. Chelf. *New England Ash with long acute points to the wings of the leaves.*
6. FRAXINUS (*Caroliniana*) integerrimis petiolis teretibus fructu latiore. Prod. Leyd. 533. *Ash-tree with entire leaves and taper foot-stalks.* Fraxinus Caroliniana, latiore fructu. Rand. Cat. H. Chelf. *Carolina Ash with a broad fruit.*

The

The firſt ſort is the common Aſh-tree, which grows naturally in moſt parts of England, and is ſo well known as to need no deſcription. The leaves of this ſort have generally five pair of lobes, and are terminated by an odd one; they are of a very dark green, and their edges are ſlightly ſawed. The flowers are produced in looſe ſpikes from the ſide of the branches, which are ſucceeded by flat ſeeds, which ripen in autumn; there is a variety of this with variegated leaves, which is preſerved in ſome gardens.

The ſecond ſort grows naturally in Calabria, and is generally ſuppoſed to be the tree from whence the manna is collected, which is an exſudation from the leaves of the tree. The ſhoots of this tree are much ſhorter, and the joints cloſer together than thoſe of the firſt ſort; the ſmall leaves are ſhorter, and deeper ſawed on their edges, and are of a lighter green. The flowers come out from the ſide of the branches, which are of a purple colour, and appear in the ſpring before the leaves come out. This tree is of humble growth, ſeldom riſing more than fifteen or ſixteen feet high in England.

The third ſort is a low tree, which riſes about the ſame height as the ſecond; the leaves of this ſort are much ſmaller and narrower than thoſe of the firſt, but are ſawed on their edges, and are of the ſame dark colour. The flowers of this ſort have petals, which are wanting in the common Aſh.

The fourth ſort was raiſed by the late Dr. Uvedale at Enfield, from ſeeds which were brought from Italy by Dr. William Sherard, where the trees grow naturally; but it was ſuppoſed to be a different ſort from that mentioned by Dr. Morriſon, in his Præludia Botanica, but by comparing them together they appear to be the ſame.

The leaves of this ſort have but three or four pair of lobes (or ſmall leaves) which are ſhort, broad, and ſmooth, of a lucid green, and irregularly ſawed on the edges; the midrib of the great leaf is jointed, and ſwelling where the leaves come out. The flowers grow in looſe panicles at the end of the branches; theſe are moſt of them male, having two ſtamina in each, but no germen or ſtyle; they are of a white herbaceous colour, and appear in May. As this ſort very rarely produces ſeeds in England, it is propagated by grafting or budding it upon the common Aſh.

The fifth ſort was raiſed from ſeeds, which were ſent from New England in the year 1724, by Mr. Moore. The leaves of this tree have but three, or at moſt but four pair of lobes (or ſmall leaves) which are placed far diſtant from each other, and are terminated by an odd lobe, which runs out into a very long point; they are of a light green and entire, having no ſerratures on their edges: this tree ſhoots into ſtrong irregular branches, but doth not grow to a large ſize in the trunk. It is propagated by grafting it upon the common Aſh.

The ſixth ſort was raiſed from ſeeds which were ſent from Carolina in the year 1724, by Mr. Cateſby. The leaves of this ſort hath ſeldom more than three pair of lobes, the lower being the leaſt, and the upper the largeſt; theſe are about five inches long and two broad, of a light green colour, and ſlightly ſawed on their edges; the foot-ſtalk, or rather the midrib, of the leaves is taper, and has ſhort downy hairs; the ſeeds are broader than thoſe of the common Aſh, and are of a very light colour. As this ſort hath not yet produced ſeeds in England, it is propagated by grafting it upon the common Aſh.

Theſe trees are now propagated in plenty in the nurſeries for ſale, as there has been of late years a great demand for all the hardy ſorts of trees and ſhrubs, which will live in the open air; but all thoſe trees which are grafted upon the common Aſh, are not ſo valuable as thoſe which are raiſed from ſeeds, becauſe the ſtock grows much faſter than the grafts; ſo that the lower part of the trunk, ſo far as the ſtock riſes, will often be twice the ſize of the upper; and if the trees ſtand much expoſed to the wind, the grafts are frequently broken off to the ſtock, after they are

grown to a large ſize, which is a great diſappointment to a perſon after having waited ſeveral years, to ſee their trees ſuddenly deſtroyed. Beſide, if the wood of either of the ſorts is valuable, it can be of little uſe when the trees are ſo raiſed.

The fourth ſort is generally planted for ornament, the flowers making a fine appearance when they are in beauty, for almoſt every branch is terminated by a large looſe panicle; ſo that when the trees are large, and covered with flowers, they are diſtinguiſhable at a great diſtance.

All the other ſorts ſerve to make a variety in plantations, but have little beauty to recommend them; and as their wood ſeems to be greatly inferior to that of the common Aſh, ſo there ſhould be few of theſe planted, becauſe they will only fill up the ſpace where better trees might grow.

The common Aſh propagates itſelf in plenty by the ſeeds which ſcatter in the autumn, ſo that where the ſeeds happen to fall in places where cattle do not come, there will be plenty of the plants come up in the ſpring; but where any perſon is deſirous to raiſe a quantity of the trees, the ſeeds ſhould be ſown as ſoon as they are ripe, and then the plants will come up the following ſpring; but if the ſeeds are kept out of the ground till the ſpring, the plants will not come up till the year after, which is the ſame with all the ſorts of Aſh; that when any of their ſeeds are brought from abroad, as they ſeldom arrive here before the ſpring, the plants muſt not be expected to appear till the next year; therefore the ground ſhould be kept clean all the ſummer where they are ſown, and not diſturbed, left the ſeeds ſhould be turned out of the ground, or buried too deep to grow; for many perſons are too impatient to wait a year for the growth of ſeeds, ſo that if they do not come up the firſt year, they dig up the ground, and thereby deſtroy the ſeeds.

When the plants come up, they muſt be kept clean from weeds during the ſummer; and if they make good progreſs in the ſeed-bed, they will be fit to tranſplant by the autumn; therefore there ſhould be ſome ground prepared to receive them, and as ſoon as their leaves begin to fall, they may be tranſplanted. In taking them up, there ſhould be care taken not to break or tear off their roots; to prevent which, they ſhould be taken up with a ſpade, and not drawn up, as is frequently practiſed; for as many of the plants which riſe from ſeeds will out-ſtrip the others in their growth, ſo it is frequently practiſed, to draw up the largeſt plants, and leave the ſmaller to grow a year longer before they are tranſplanted; and to avoid hurting thoſe which are left, the others are drawn out by hand, and thereby many of their roots are torn off or broken; therefore it is much the better way to take all up, little or big together, and tranſplant them out, placing the larger ones together in rows, and the ſmaller by themſelves. The rows ſhould be three feet aſunder, and the plants a foot and a half diſtance in the rows; in this nurſery they may remain two years, by which time they will be ſtrong enough to plant where they are to remain; for the younger they are planted out, the larger they will grow; ſo that where they are deſigned to grow large, they ſhould be planted very young; and the ground where the plants are raiſed, ſhould not be better than that where they are deſigned to grow; for when the plants are raiſed in good land, and afterward tranſplanted into worſe, they very rarely thrive; ſo that it is much the beſt method to make the nurſery upon a part of the ſame land, where the trees are deſigned to be planted, and then a ſufficient number of trees may be left ſtanding upon the ground, and theſe will out-ſtrip thoſe which are removed, and will grow to a larger ſize.

Where people live in the neighbourhood of Aſh-trees, they may ſupply themſelves with plenty of ſelf-ſown plants, provided cattle are not ſuffered to graze on the land, for they will eat off the young plants, and not ſuffer them to grow; but where the ſeeds fall in hedges, or where they are protected by buſhes, the

plants

plants will come up and thrive; and in thefe hedges the trees frequently are permitted to grow till they have deftroyed the hedge, for there is fcarce any tree fo hurtful to all kinds of vegetables as the Afh, which robs every plant of its nourifhment within the reach of its roots, therefore fhould never be fuffered to grow in hedge rows; for they not only kill the hedge, but impoverifh Corn, or whatfoever is fown near them. Nor fhould Afh-trees be permitted to grow near pafture grounds, for if any of the cows eat of the leaves or fhoots of the Afh, all the butter which is made of their milk will be rank and of no value; which is always the quality of the butter which is made about Guildford, Godalmin, and fome other parts of Surry, where there are Afh-trees growing about all their paftures, fo that it is very rare to meet with any butter in thofe places which is fit to eat; but in all the good dairy countries, they never fuffer an Afh-tree to grow.

If a wood of thefe trees is rightly managed, it will turn greatly to the advantage of its owner; for by the under-wood, which will be fit to cut every feven or eight years, for poles or hoops, there will be a continual income more than fufficient to pay the rent of the ground, and all other charges; and ftill there will be a ftock preferved for timber, which in a few years will be worth forty or fifty fhillings per tree. This timber is of excellent ufe to the wheelwright and cartwright, for ploughs, axle-trees, wheel-rings, harrows, bulls, oars, blocks for pullies, and many other purpofes.

The beft feafon for felling of thefe trees is from November to February; for if it be done either too early in autumn, or too late in the fpring, the timber will be fubject to be infefted with worms, and other infects; but for lopping pollards, the fpring is preferable for all foft woods.

FREEZING is the fixing of a fluid, or the depriving it of its natural mobility by the action of cold; or it is the act of converting a fluid fubftance into a firm, coherent, rigid one, called ice.

The principal phænomena of freezing are,

1ft, That Water being dilated or rarefied, and all fluids, oil excepted, i. e. in freezing, take up more fpace, and are fpecifically lighter than they were before. That the bulk and dimenfions of water are increafed by freezing, is found by many experiments, and it may not be improper here to take notice of the procefs of nature.

A glafs veffel then, I A, full of water to A, being immerged in a veffel of water mixed with falt G H K L, the water prefently rifes from D to C; which feems owing to the fudden conftriction of the veffel, haftily plunged into fo cold a medium: foon after, from the point C, it continually defcends condenfing, till it arrives at the point F; where, for fome time, it feems to remain at reft: but it foon recovers itfelf, and begins to expand, rifing from F to E, and from thence foon after, by one violent leap, mounts to B; and here the water in I is immediately feen all thick and cloudy, and, in the very inftant of this leap, is converted into ice. Add, that while the ice is growing harder, and fome of the water near the neck of the veffel I is freezing, the flux of the water is continued above B towards A, and at length runs out at the veffel.

2dly, That they lofe not only of the fpecific, but alfo of their abfolute gravity, by freezing; fo that when they are thawed again, they are found confiderably lighter than before.

3dly, That frozen water is not quite fo tranfparent as when it was liquid, and that bodies do not perfpire fo freely through it.

4thly, That water, when frozen, evaporates almoft as much as when fluid.

5thly, That water does not freeze in vacuo, but requires the prefence and contiguity of air.

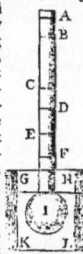

6thly, That water which has been boiled, does not freeze fo readily as that which has not.

7thly, That water, being covered over with a furface of oil of Olives, does not freeze fo readily as it does without it; and that not oil abfolutely preferves it under a ftrong froft, when Olive oil will not.

8thly, That fpirit of wine, nut oil, and oil of turpentine, do not freeze at all.

9thly, That the furface of the water, in freezing, appears all wrinkled; the wrinkles being fometimes in parallel lines, and fometimes like rays proceeding from a center to the circumference.

The theories of freezing, or the method of accounting for thefe phænomena, are very many.

The chief principles that different authors have gone upon, are, either that fome foreign matter is introduced within the pores of the fluid, by means of which it is fixed, its bulk increafed, &c.

Or that fome matter which was naturally contained in the fluid is now expelled, by reafon of the abfence of which, the body becomes fixed.

Or that there is fome alteration produced in the texture or form, either of the particles of the fluid itfelf, or of fomething that is contained within it.

To fome one of thefe principles all the fyftems of freezing are reducible.

The Cartefians explicate freezing by the recefs or going out of the ethereal matter from the pores of the water, or other liquor; which being once done, the finer parts are too fmall and flexible to keep the long, flender, and eel-like particles of water fluent, or in the form of a liquor.

But the Corpufcularians, or Gaffendifts, afcribe the freezing of water, with more probability, to the ingrefs of multitudes of cold or frigorific particles, as they call them; which, entering the liquor in fwarms, and difperfing themfelves every way through it, croud into the pores of the water, and hinder the wonted agitation of its parts, and wedge it up, as it were, into the hard or confiftent body of ice; and from hence proceeds its increafe of dimenfions, coldnefs, &c.

That ice is fpecifically lighter than the water out of which it is by freezing made, is certain by its fwimming in it; and that this lightnefs of ice proceeds from thofe numerous bubbles which are produced in it by its congelation, is equally plain; but how thofe bubbles come to be generated in freezing, and what fubftance they contain in them, if they are not quite empty, is an inquiry of great importance; and, perhaps, if difcovered, may contribute much to the underftanding the nature of cold.

Mr. Hobbes will have it common air, which, intruding into the water in congelation, entangles itfelf with the particles of the fluid, prevents their motion, and produces thofe numerous bubbles, thus expanding its bulk, and rendering it fpecifically lighter.

But, in anfwer to this, no fuch ingrefs of air into water appears in its coagulation; and that it does not get into frozen oil is plain, becaufe that body is condenfed by being frozen.

And Mr. Boyle has alfo fhewn, by undoubted experiments, that water will freeze in veffels hermetically fealed; and in brafs bodies or veffels. clofely ftopped, and into which the air can have no ingrefs, hath yet been turned into ice, abounding with thefe bubbles as numerous as thofe frozen in the open air. He alfo has proved by experiment, that water kept a while in the exhaufted receiver, till all its bubbles were emerged and gone, being afterwards turned into ice by a freezing mixture, the ice had fcarce any bubbles in it; whence it is plain, that thefe bubbles are filled with fome matter which is within the water, if they are filled with any thing. But he proves alfo, by plain experiments, that they have none, or exceedingly little, true elaftic air contained in them.

Others, and thofe of the greateft number, are of opinion, that the freezing matter is a falt; and they argue that an excefs of cold will render water torpid, but never congeal it without falt: they fay that thofe

particles

particles that are the chief caufe of freezing are faline, mixed in a due proportion, congelation bearing a near relation to cryftallization.

This falt is fuppofed to be of the nitrous kind, and to be furnifhed by the air, which is generally found to abound in nitre.

It is indeed no difficult matter, to account for the particles of nitre preventing the fluidity of water. Thefe particles are fuppofed to be fo many rigid pointed fpicula, which are eafily impelled or driven into the ftamina or globules of water; which, by this means, becoming varioufly mingled and entangled with it, do, by degrees, weaken and deftroy the motion of it.

The reafon that this effect arifes only in fevere winter weather, is, that it is then only that the retracting action of the nitrous fpicula is more than equal to the power or principle by which the fluid is otherwife kept in motion, or difpofed for motion.

Several experiments of artificial freezing fupport this opinion.

For if you mix a quantity of common faltpetre with fnow, or ice pulverized, and diffolve the mixture in the fire, and then immerge a tube full of water in the folution; the water, that part of it next the mixture, will freeze prefently, even in a warm air.

Whence they argue, that the fpicula of the falt are driven through the pores of the glafs, and mixed with the water, by the gravity of the mixture, and of the incumbent air; for that it is evident, that the falt has this effect, inafmuch as it is certainly known, that the particles of water cannot find their way through the pores of the glafs.

In thefe artificial freezings, in whatever part the mixture is applied, there is prefently a fkin or lamina of ice produced, whether at the top, bottom, or fides, by reafon that there is always a ftock of faline corpufcles, fufficient to overpower the particles of fire; but natural congelations are confined to the top of the water, where the laft moft abounds.

But this fyftem is oppofed by the author of the Nouvelle Conjecture pour expliquer la Nature de la Glace, who objects, that it does not appear, that the nitre always enters the compofition of ice; but if it did, it would fall fhort of accounting for fome of the principal effects; as,

How fhould the particles of nitre, by entering the pores of the water, and fixing the parts, caufe the water to dilate, and render it fpecifically lighter? They fhould naturally augment its weight.

This and fome other difficulties, fhew the neceffity of a new theory; and therefore the ingenious author advances this which follows, which feems to folve the phænomena in a manner that is more eafy and fimple, as not depending upon the admiffion or extrufion of any heterogeneous matter.

The water freezes in the winter only, becaufe its parts, then being more clofely joined together, mutually embarrafs one another, and lofe all the motion they had; and that the air, or rather an alteration in the fpring and force of the air, is the caufe of this clofer union of water.

It is evident from experiment, that there are an infinite number of particles of grofs air interfperfed among the globules of water; and it is allowed, that each particle of air has the virtue of a fpring; and hence this author argues, that the fmall fprings of grofs air, mixed with water, have more force in cold winter weather, and do then unbend themfelves more, than at other times. Hence thofe fprings thus unbending themfelves on one fide, and the external air continuing to prefs the furface of the water on the other, the particles of the water, being thus conftringed and locked up together, much lofe their motion and fluidity, and form a hard, confiftent body, till a relaxation of the fpring of the air, from an increafe of heat, reduce the particles to their old dimenfions, and leave room for the globules to flow again.

But this fyftem feems to be built upon a falfe prin-

ciple, for the fpring or elafticity of the air is not increafed by cold, but diminifhed; air condenfes by cold, and expands itfelf by heat; and it is demonftrable in pneumatics, that the elaftic force of expanded air is to that of the fame air condenfed, as the bulk when rarefied is to its bulk when condenfed.

Indeed, fome authors, in order to account for the increafe of the bulk and dimenfion of the fpecific gravity of frozen water, have advanced as follows, viz. That the aqueous particles, in their natural ftate, were nearly cubes, and fo filled their fpace without the interpofition of many pores; but that they are changed from cubes to fpheres, by congelation; from whence it will neceffarily follow, that there muft be a great deal of empty fpace between them.

But, in oppofition to this hypothefis, the nature of fluidity and firmnefs eafily fuggefts, that fpherical particles are much properer to conftitute a fluid than cubical ones, and lefs difpofed to form a fixed than cubic one.

But after all, in order to come to a confiftent theory of freezing, we muft either have recourfe to the frigorific matter of the Corpufcularians, confidered under the new light and advantages of the Newtonian philofophy, or to the ethereal matter of the Cartefians, under the improvements of Monf. Gauteron.

The true caufe of freezing, or the congelation of water into ice, fay the former, feems plainly to be the introduction of the frigorific particles into the pores or interftices between the particles of the water, and by that means getting fo near them, as to be juft within the fpheres of one another's attracting force, and then they muft cohere into one folid or firm body; but heat afterwards feparating them, and putting them into various motions, breaks this union, and feparates the particles fo far from one another, that they get out of the diftance of the attracting force, and into the verge of the repelling force, and then the water re-affumes its fluid form.

Now, that cold and freezing proceed from fome fubftance of a faline nature floating in the air, feems probable from hence:

That all falts, and more eminently fome particular ones, do prodigioufly increafe the force and effects of cold, when mixed with fnow or ice. It is alfo evident, that all faline bodies produce a ftiffnefs and rigidity in the parts of thofe bodies into which they enter.

It appears, by microfcopical obfervations upon falts, that the figure of fome falts, before they fhoot into maffes, are thin, double wedged, like particles which have abundance of furface, in refpect to their folidity; and is the reafon why they fwim in water, when once raifed in it, though fpecifically heavier.

Thefe fmall points, getting into the pores of the water, whereby they are alfo, in fome meafure, fufpended in the winter time, when the heat of the fun is not ordinarily ftrong enough to diffolve the falts into a fluid, to break their points, and to keep them in perpetual motion, being lefs difturbed, are at more liberty to approach one another; and, by fhooting into cryftals of the form above-mentioned, do, by both their extremities, infinuate themfelves into the pores of the water, and by that means freeze it into a folid form. And it is apparent, that the dimenfions of water are increafed by freezing, the particles of it being kept at fome diftance from one another, by the intervention of the frigorific matter.

But befides this, there are many little volumes, or fmall particles of air, included at feveral diftances, both in the pores of the watery particles, and in the interftices formed by their fpherical figure: Now, by the infinuation of the cryftals, the volumes of air are driven out of the watery particles, and many of them uniting, form larger volumes, which thereby have a greater force to expand themfelves than when they are difperfed; and fo both enlarge the dimenfions, and leffen the fpecific gravity of water thus congealed into ice.

And hence (fays Dr. Cheyne, from whom this laft account is taken) we may guefs at the manner how water,

ter, impregnated with falts, fulphurs, or earths, which are not eafily diffolvable, may form itfelf into metals, minerals, gums, and other foffils; the parts of thefe mixtures becoming a cement to the particles of water, or getting into their pores, change them into thefe different fubstances.

For the fecond: as an ethereal matter or medium is generally allowed to be the caufe of the motion of fluids, and as the air itfelf has all its motion from the fame principle, it follows, that all fluids muft remain in a ftate of reft or fixity, when that matter lofes of its neceffary force. And confequently, the air being lefs warmed in the winter time, by reafon of the obliquity of the fun's rays, is more denfe and fixed in winter than any other feafon of the year.

But farther: it is evident, from divers experiments, that the air does contain a falt which is fuppofed to be of the nature of nitre. If this be granted, and the denfity of the air allowed, it will follow, that the particles of this nitre muft likewife be brought nearer together, and thickened by the condenfation of the air; as on the contrary, a rarefaction of the air, and an augmentation of its fluidity, muft divide and feparate them.

And if the fame happens to all liquors that have imbibed or diffolved any falt, if the warmth of the liquid keep the falt exactly divided, and if the coolnefs of a cellar, or of ice, caufe the particles of the diffolved falt to approach, run into each other, and fhoot into cryftals; why fhould the air, which is allowed to be a fluid, be exempt from the general law of fluids?

It is true, that the nitre of the air, being groffer in cold weather than in hot, muft have a lefs velocity; but ftill the product of its augmented mafs into the velocity that remains, will give it a greater momentum, or quantity of motion. Nor is there any thing farther required to make this falt act with greater force againft the parts of fluids, and this may probably be the caufe of the great evaporation in frofty weather.

This aereal nitre muft neceffarily promote the concretion of liquids; for it is not the air, nor yet the nitre that it contains, which gives the motion to fluids; it is the ethereal medium, therefore a diminution of the motion of reft arifes from the diminution of that force.

Now the ethereal matter, which in the winter time is weak enough, muft ftill lofe more of its force by its action againft air condenfed, and loaded with large particles of falt. It muft therefore lofe of its force in cold weather, and become lefs difpofed to maintain the motion of the fluids.

In fine, the air, during froft, may be efteemed like the ice impregnated with falt wherewith liquors are iced in fummer time. It is very probable that thefe liquors freeze by reafon of a diminution of the motion of the ethereal medium, by its acting againft the ice and falt together, and the air is not able to prevent its concretion by all its fcorching heat.

The air (fays Mr. Boyle) being a fluid as well as water, and impregnated with falts of different kinds, it is not improbable, that what happens in water impregnated with fuch falts, may alfo happen in the air. Two proper quantities of different falts being diffolved in hot water, they floated undiftinguifhably in it, and retained a capacity to act in conjunction upon feveral occafions; yet when the liquor becomes cold, the faline particles of one kind being no longer agitated by a due degree of heat, fhot into cryftals; and, lofing their fluidity and motion, vifibly feparated themfelves from the other, which ftill continued fluid in the liquor, and capable of acting feparately. We have divers accounts in the Philofophical Tranfactions, of a freezing rain which fell in the weft of England in December 1672. This rain, as foon as it touched any thing above the ground, as a bough, or the like, immediately fettled into ice; and, by multiplying and enlarging the icicles broke all down with its weight; the rain that fell on the fnow im-

mediately froze into ice, without finking into the fnow at all.

It made an incredible deftruction of trees beyond any thing in all hiftory. A certain gentleman weighed a fprig of an Afh-tree of juft three quarters of a pound, the ice which was on it weighed 16 pounds; that fome perfons were frighted with the noife in the air, till they underftood that it was the clatter of icy boughs dafhed againft each other.

Dr. Beale remarks, that there was no confiderable froft obferved on the ground during the whole time; whence he concludes, that a froft may be very fierce and dangerous on the tops of fome hills and plains, while in other places it keeps at two, three, or four feet diftance above the ground, rivers, lakes, &c. and may wander about very furious in fome places, and remifs in others not far off. The froft was followed by glowing heats, and a wonderful forwardnefs of flowers and fruits. The effects of freezing vegetables, is farther explained under the article of Frost.

FRITILLARIA. Lin. Gen. Plant. 372. Tourn. Inft. R. H. 376. tab. 201. Corona Imperialis. Tourn. Inft. R. H. 372. tab. 197, 198. Fritillary, or Chequered Tulip and Crown Imperial.

The Characters are,

The flower hath no empalement; it hath fix oblong petals, is bell-fhaped, and fpreading at the bafe; in the hollow, at the bafe of each petal, is fituated a nectarium; the flower hath fix ftamina ftanding near the ftyle, which are terminated by oblong four-cornered fummits. In the center is fituated an oblong three-cornered germen, fupporting a fingle ftyle which is longer than the ftamina, crowned by a fpreading obtufe ftigma. The germen afterward becomes an oblong capfule with three lobes having three cells, which are filled with flat feeds, ranged in a double order.

The capfule of Fritillaria is oblong and fmooth, but that of Corona Imperialis hath acute borders, or membranaceous wings.

This genus of plants is ranged in the firft fection of Linnæus's fixth clafs, which includes the plants which have fix ftamina in their flowers, and but one ftyle. Thefe two genera of Fritillary and Crown Imperial, have been always feparated, till Dr. Linnæus joined them together; indeed by their flowers they may be properly enough placed in the fame genus; but, if their fruit may be allowed as a characteriftic note, they fhould be feparate; however, as this new fyftem is generally received, I fhall, in compliance with the prefent tafte, join them together.

The Species are,

1. Fritillaria (*Melagris*) foliis linearibus alternis, floribus terminalibus. *Fritillary with narrow leaves placed alternate, and flowers terminating the ftalk.* Fritillaria præcox, purpurea, variegata. C. B. P. 64. *Early, purple, variegated, chequered Tulip.*

2. Fritillaria (*Aquitanica*) foliis infimis oppofitis. Hort. Cliff. 81. *Fritillary whofe lower leaves are oppofite.* Fritillaria Aquitanica, flore luteo obfcuro. Swert. Floril. *Aquitain chequered Tulip, with an obfcure yellow flower.*

3. Fritillaria (*Nigra*) floribus adfcendentibus. *Fritillary with flowers growing above each other.* Fritillaria nigra. Lob. Adver. 2. 496. *Black chequered Tulip.*

4. Fritillaria (*Lutea*) foliis lanceolatis, caule unifloro maximo. *Fritillary with fpear-fhaped leaves, and one large flower on each ftalk.* Fritillaria lutea maxima Italica. Park. Parad. 43. *Largeft yellow Italien Fritillary.*

5. Fritillaria (*Umbellata*) floribus umbellatis. *Fritillary with flowers growing in umbels.* Fritillaria umbellifera. C. B. P. 64. *Umbellated chequered Tulip.*

6. Fritillaria (*Perfica*) racemo nudiufculo, foliis obliquis. Hort. Upfal. 82. *Fritillary with a naked fpike of flowers and oblique leaves.* Lilium Perficum. Dod. Pempt. 220. *The Perfian Lily.*

7. Fritillaria (*Racemofa*) floribus racemofis. *Fritillary with flowers growing in bunches.* Fritillaria ramofa, feu lilium Perficum minus. Mor. Hort. Reg. Blef. *Branching Fritillary, or fmaller Perfian Lily.*

8. Fri,

8.
FRITILLARIA (*Imperialis*) racemo comofo infernè nudo, foliis integerrimis. Lin. Hort. Upfal. 82. *Fritillary with a tufted bunch of leaves over the flowers, which is naked below, and entire leaves.* Corona Imperialis. Dod. Pempt. 202. *Crown Imperial.*

9. FRITILLARIA (*Regia*) racemo comofo infernè nudo, foliis crenatis. Lin. Sp. Plant. 303. *Fritillary with a tufted bunch of leaves over the flowers, which is naked below, and crenated leaves.* Corona regalis lilii folio crenato. Hort. Elth. 110. *Royal Crown with a crenated Lily leaf.*

10. FRITILLARIA (*Autumnalis*) racemo infernè nudo, foliis oblongis mucronatis. *Fritillary with a naked ftalk, and oblong pointed leaves.*

The firft fort grows naturally in Italy, and other warm parts of Europe; and from the feeds of this there have been great varieties raifed in the gardens of the florifts, which differ in the fize and colour of their flowers; and as there are frequently new varieties produced, fo it would be to little purpofe to enumerate thofe which are at prefent in the Englifh and Dutch gardens, which amount to a great number in the catalogues of the Dutch florifts, who are very fond of any little diftinction, either in the colour or fhape, to enlarge their lifts.

The forts which are here enumerated, I think may be allowed as diftinct fpecies, notwithftanding Dr. Linnæus has reduced them to five; for I have raifed many of all the forts from feed, which have conftantly produced the fame as the feeds were taken from, and have only differed in the colour or fize of the flowers; for the fort with broad leaves produced the fame fort again, and the umbellated and fpiked forts produced the fame, though there are feveral varieties in the colours of their flowers.

The firft hath a round compreffed root, in fhape like that of Cornflag, but is of a yellowifh white colour; the ftalk rifes about fifteen inches high, having three or four narrow long leaves placed alternately, and the top is divided into two flender foot-ftalks which turn downward, each fuftaining one bell-fhaped inverted flower, compofed of fix petals, which are chequered with purple and white like a chefs-board; and in the center is fituated a germen fupporting one ftyle, crowned by a trifid ftigma; the fix ftamina ftand about the ftyle, but are fhorter. At the bottom of each petal there is a cavity, in which is fituated a nectarium, filled with a fweet liquor; after the flower is fallen, the germen fwells to a pretty large three-cornered blunt capfule, and then the foot-ftalk is turned and ftands erect; when the feeds are ripe, the capfule opens in three parts and lets out the flat feeds, which were ranged in a double order. The flowers of this appear the latter end of March or beginning of April, and the feeds are ripe in July. There is a variety of this with a double flower.

The fecond fort grows naturally in France; the leaves of this are broader, and of a deeper green than the former; the lower leaves are placed oppofite, but thofe above are alternate; the ftalk rifes a foot and a half high, and is terminated by two flowers of an obfcure yellow colour, which fpread more at the brim than thofe of the firft fort, but are turned downward in the fame manner. This flowers three weeks after the firft. There is a variety of this with greenifh flowers, which grows naturally in fome parts of England.

The third fort feldom rifes more than a foot high, the leaves are narrow like thofe of the firft fort, but are fhorter; each ftalk is terminated by three or four flowers, which arife above each other; they are of a very dark purple, chequered with yellowifh fpots. This flowers in April, about the fame time with the fecond.

The fourth fort rifes about a foot high, the ftalk is garnifhed with fpear-fhaped leaves four inches long and one broad, of a grafs-green colour; thefe are fometimes placed oppofite, but are generally alternate; the ftalk is terminated by one large bell-fhaped flower of a yellowifh colour, chequered with light

purple. This fort flowers about the fame time as the firft. There are two or three varieties of this, which differ in the fize and colour of their flowers and the breadth of their leaves, but retain their fpecific difference, fo as to be eafily diftinguifhed from the other forts.

The fifth fort rifes a foot and a half high; the ftalk is garnifhed with fhorter and broader leaves than the firft fort, which are of a yellow colour; the flowers are produced round the ftalks like thofe of the Crown Imperial; they are of a dark purple colour, chequered with a yellowifh green. This flowers about the fame time with the fecond fort.

The fixth fort is commonly called the Perfian Lily, and is fuppofed to grow naturally in Perfia, but has been long cultivated in the Englifh gardens; the root of this fort is round and large, the ftalk rifes three feet high; the lower part of it is clofely garnifhed with leaves which are three inches long, and half an inch broad, of a gray colour, ftanding on every fide of the ftalks, but are twifted obliquely; the flowers grow in a loofe fpike at the top of the ftalk, forming a pyramid; they are fhaped like thofe of the other fpecies, but are much fhorter, and fpread wider at their brims, and are not bent downward like thofe. They are of a dark purple colour, and appear in May, but are feldom fucceeded by feeds in England, fo are only propagated by offsets.

The feventh fort hath a much fhorter ftalk than the laft, but is garnifhed with leaves like thofe, only they are fmaller; the ftalks branch out at the top into feveral fmall foot-ftalks, each fuftaining one dark coloured flower. This is commonly called the fmall Perfian Lily, from its refemblance to the former fort. Thefe plants are propagated either by feeds, or offsets from the old roots; by the firft of which methods new varieties will be obtained, as alfo a larger ftock of roots in three years, than can be obtained in twenty or thirty years in the latter method: I fhall therefore firft treat of their propagation by feeds.

Having provided yourfelf with fome good feeds, faved from the faireft flowers, you muft procure fome fhallow pans or boxes, which muft have fome holes in their bottoms to let out the moifture; thefe you fhould fill with light frefh earth, laying a few potfheards over the holes, to prevent the earth from ftopping them; then, having laid the earth very level in the boxes, &c. you muft fow the feeds thereon pretty thick, covering it with fine fifted earth a quarter of an inch thick. The time for fowing the feed is about the beginning of Auguft, for if it be kept much longer out of the ground it will not grow; then place the boxes or pans where they may have the morning fun until eleven o'clock, obferving, if the feafon proves dry, to water them gently, as alfo to pull up all weeds as foon as they appear; for if they are fuffered to remain until they have taken deep root into the earth, they would draw the feeds out of the ground whenever they are pulled up. Toward the latter end of September you fhould remove the boxes, &c. into a warmer fituation, placing them clofe to a hedge or wall expofed to the fouth; if they are fown in pots, thefe fhould be plunged into the ground, but they are beft in tubs; thefe fhould be covered in fevere froft. In this fituation they may remain until the middle of March, by which time the plants will be come up an inch high; you muft therefore remove the boxes, as the weather increafes hot, into a more fhady fituation; for while the plants are young, they are liable to fuffer by being too much expofed to the fun: and in this fhady fituation they may remain during the heat of the fummer, obferving to keep them clear from weeds, and to refrefh them now and then with a little moifture; but be careful not to give them much water after their leaves are decayed, which would rot their roots. About the beginning of Auguft, if the roots are very thick in the boxes, you fhould prepare a bed of good light frefh earth, which muft be levelled very even, upon which you fhould fpread the earth in the boxes in

which

which the small roots are contained, equally covering it about one fourth of an inch thick with the same fresh earth: this bed should be situated in a warm position, but not too close to hedges, walls, or pales, which would cause their leaves to be long and slender, and make the roots weaker than if placed in a more open exposure.

In this bed they may remain until they flower, which is generally the third year from sowing; at which time you should put down a mark to the roots of all such as produce fair flowers, that at the time of taking them out of the ground (which ought to be soon after their green leaves are decayed) they may be selected into a bed amongst your old roots of this flower, which, for their beauty, are preserved in the best gardens; but the other less valuable flowers may be planted in the borders of the parterre-garden for their variety, where, being intermixed with other flowers of different seasons, they will make a good appearance,

The fine sorts of this flower should remain undisturbed three years, by which time they will have produced many offsets; and should be taken up when their leaves are decayed, and planted into a fresh bed, taking such of their offsets as are large enough to produce flowers to plant in the flower-garden; but the smaller roots may be planted into a nursery-bed, until they have obtained strength enough to flower; but you must never suffer these roots to lie out of the ground when you remove them, but plant them again immediately, otherwise they will perish.

During these three years which I have advised the roots to remain in the beds, the surface of the earth should be stirred every autumn with a trowel, observing not to go so deep as to bruise the root, and at the same time lay a thin cover of very rotten dung or tanners bark upon the surface of the beds; which, being washed into the ground, will cause the flowers to be larger, as also the roots to make a greater increase: you must also observe to keep them constantly clear from weeds, and those roots which you would preserve with care, should not be suffered to seed.

When a stock of good flowers are obtained, they may be preserved and increased in the same manner as other bulbous rooted flowers, which is by offsets sent out from their roots, which should be taken off every other year from the finest sorts; but the ordinary flowers may remain three years undisturbed, in which time they will have multiplied so much, as that each root will have formed a cluster; so that if they are left longer together, the roots will be small, and the flowers very weak; therefore, if these are taken up every other year, the roots will be the stronger. These roots may be treated in the same manner as Tulips, and other bulbous rooted flowers, with this difference only, that the roots will not bear to be kept out of the ground so long; therefore, if there should be a necessity for keeping them out of the ground any time, it will be best to put the roots into sand to prevent their shrinking,

As these flowers come out early in the spring, they make a pretty appearance in the borders of the pleasure-garden, where they are planted in small clumps; for when they stand single in the borders, they make but a poor figure.

The eighth sort is the Crown Imperial, which is now very common in the English gardens. This grows naturally in Persia, from whence it was first brought to Constantinople, and about the year 1570, was introduced to these parts of Europe; of this flower there are a great variety now preserved in the gardens of florists, but as they have been produced accidentally from seeds, they are but one species; however, for the satisfaction of the curious, I shall here mention all the varieties which have come to my knowledge.

1. The common Crown Imperial; this is of a dirty red colour.

2. The yellow Crown Imperial; this is of a bright yellow.

3. The bright red Crown Imperial, called Fusai.

4. The pale yellow Crown Imperial.

5. The yellow striped Crown Imperial.

6. The large flowering Crown Imperial.

7. The broad leaved late red Crown Imperial.

8. The double and triple crowned Imperial Crown.

9. The double red Crown Imperial.

10. The double yellow Crown Imperial.

11. The silver striped leaved Crown Imperial.

12. The yellow striped leaved Crown Imperial.

There are some few other varieties which are mentioned in the catalogues of the Dutch florists, but their distinctions are so minute, that they are not distinguishable, so I shall pass them over; as those here inserted are all that I have seen growing either in England or Holland, which deserved any distinction.

The Crown Imperial hath a large round scaly root of a yellow colour, and a strong odour of a fox; the stalk rises to the height of four feet or upward; it is strong, succulent, and garnished two-thirds of the length on every side, with long narrow leaves ending in points, which are smooth and entire; the upper part of the stalk is naked, a foot in length; then the flowers come out all round the stalk upon short footstalks, which turn downward, each sustaining one large, spreading, bell-shaped flower, composed of six spear-shaped petals; at the base of each petal is a pretty large cavity, in which is situated a large white nectarium, filled with a mellous liquor. In the center of the flower is fixed a three-cornered oblong germen, upon which rests the single style, which is the length of the petals, and is crowned by a spreading obtuse stigma; round the style there are six awl-shaped stamina which are shorter than the style, and are terminated by oblong four-cornered summits. These flowers hang downward, and above them rises a spreading tuft of green leaves, which are erect; and from between these come out the foot-stalks of the flowers: when the flowers decay, the germen swells to a large hexagonal capsule, shaped like a watermill, having six cells, which are filled with flat seeds. This plant flowers the beginning of April, and the seeds are ripe in July.

The sort with yellow flowers, that with large flowers, and those with double flowers, are the most valuable; but that which hath two or three whorls of flowers above each other, makes the finest appearance; though this seldom produces its flowers after this manner the first year after removing, but the second and third year after planting, the stalks will be taller, and frequently have three tier of flowers, one above another, which is called the Triple Crown. The stalks of this sort frequently run flat and broad, when they produce a greater number of flowers than usual; but this is only a luxuriancy of nature, not constant, though many of the writers have mentioned it as a particular variety.

As this is one of the earliest tall flowers of the spring, it makes a fine appearance in the middle of large borders, at a season when such flowers are much wanted to decorate the pleasure-garden: but the rank fox-like odour which they emit, is too strong for most people, so hath rendered the flowers less valuable than they would have been; for there is something very pleasing in the sight of them at a distance, so that were it not for the offensive smell of the leaves and flowers, it would be more frequently seen in all gardens for pleasure.

This may be propagated by seeds, or offsets from the root; the first is too tedious for most of the English florists, because the plants so raised, are six or seven years before they flower; but the Dutch and Flemish gardeners, who have more patience, frequently raise them from seeds, so get some new varieties, which rewards their labour. The method of propagating these flowers from seeds, being nearly the same as for the Tulip, the reader is desired to turn to that article, where there are full directions for performing it.

The common method of propagating them here, is by offsets sent out from the old roots, which will

     flower

flower ftrong the fecond year after they are taken from the roots; but in order to have plenty of thefe, the roots fhould not be tranfplanted oftener than every third year, by which time each root will have put out feveral offsets, fome of which will be large enough to flower the following year, fo may be planted in the borders of the flower-garden, where they are to remain; and the fmaller roots may be planted in a nurfery-bed; to grow a year or two according to their fize; therefore they fhould be forted, and the fmalleft roots planted in a bed together, which fhould remain there two years, and the larger by themfelves to ftand one year, by which time they will have acquired ftrength enough to flower, fo may then be removed into the pleafure-garden.

The time for taking up thefe roots is in the beginning of July, when their ftalks will be decayed; and they may be kept out of the ground two months, but they fhould be laid fingle in a dry fhady room, but not in heaps, or in a moift place, which will caufe them to grow mouldy and rot. The offsets fhould be firft planted, for as thefe are fmall, they will be apt to fhrink if they are kept long out of the ground.

As the roots are large, they muft not be planted too near other flowers; and when they are planted in beds by themfelves, they fhould not be nearer than a foot and a half in the rows, and two feet row from row; they fhould be planted fix inches deep at leaft, efpecially the ftrong roots: they delight in a light foil, hot too wet, nor very full of dung; therefore, if any dung is laid upon the borders where they are planted, it fhould be buried pretty deep, fo as to be two or three inches below the roots.

The ninth and tenth forts grow naturally at the Cape of Good Hope, from whence they were brought into the European gardens. The ninth has been many years an inhabitant, where it has been ufually titled Corona Regalis. This has a tuberofe root, from which arife in the autumn fix or eight obtufe leaves, near five inches long and two broad toward the top, growing narrower at their bafe, and are crenated on their borders, lying flat on the ground; thefe continue all the winter: in the fpring arifes the flower-ftalk in the center of the leaves, about fix inches high, naked at the bottom; but the upper part is furrounded by bell-fhaped flowers, compofed of fix greenifh petals, with an oval germen fituate at the bottom, furrounded by fix ftamina, fupporting a triangular ftyle, crowned by a trifid ftigma; the germen afterwards becomes a roundifh capfule, but rarely perfects feeds in England. This flowers in April, and the leaves decay in June. The fecond fort I raifed from feeds, which were fent me from the Cape of Good Hope: the root of this is like that of the ninth fort, but the leaves are more than a foot long, broad at their bafe, but are narrowed to the top, where they end in acute points; the flowerftalk rifes rather higher than that of the ninth, but the flowers are of the fame fhape and colour: this feldom flowers till Auguft. The roots of this fort were ftolen out of the Chelfea garden the following fpring after it had flowered, and were fold to fome perfons whofe love for rare plants exceeded their honefty.

FRITILLARIA CRASSA. See ASCLEPIAS.

FRONDOSE [frondofus, Lat.] full of leaves, or fhoots.

FROST may be defined to be an exceffive cold ftate of the weather, whereby the motion and fluidity of the liquors are fufpended; or, it is that ftate of the air, &c. whereby fluids are converted into ice.

By froft metals contract, or are fhortened. Monf. Auzout found by an experiment, that an iron tube twelve feet long, upon being expofed to the air in a frofty night, loft two lines of its length; but this may be fuppofed to be wholly the effect of cold.

On the contrary, froft does not contract fluids, but, on the other hand, fwells or dilates them near one tenth of their bulk.

Mr. Boyle gives us feveral experiments of veffels made of metals exceeding thick and ftrong, which being filled with water, clofe ftopped, and expofed to the cold, the water, being expanded by freezing, and not finding either room or vent, burft the veffels.

A ftrong barrel of a gun, with water in it, being ftopped clofe, and frozen, was rent the whole length; and a fmall brafs veffel, five inches deep, and two in diameter, filled with water, &c. and frozen, lifted up its lid, which was preffed with a weight of fifty-fix pounds.

There are alfo related many remarkable effects of froft on vegetables. Morery, Hift. de France, fays, That trees are frequently fcorched and burnt up with froft, as with the moft exceffive heat, and that even in fo warm a climate as Provence.

Mr. Bobart relates, That in the great froft anno 1683, Oaks, Afhes, Walnut-trees, &c. were miferably fplit and cleft, fo as they might be feen through; and this too with terrible noifes like the explofion of fire arms; that the clifts were not only in the bodies, but continued to the larger boughs, roots, &c. Philof. Tranfact. Nº 105.

Dr. Derham fays, That the froft in 1708, was remarkable through the greateft part of Europe; and the greateft in degree, if not the moft univerfal, in the memory of man; that it extended throughout England, France, Germany, Denmark, Italy, &c. but was fcarce felt in Scotland and Ireland. All the Orange-trees and Olives in Italy, Provence, &c. and all the Walnut-trees throughout France, with an infinity of other trees, perifhed by the froft.

Monf. Gouteron fays, They had a gangrene on them, which he takes to be the effect of a corrofive falt, which corrupted and deftroyed their texture. He adds, That there is fo much refemblance between the gangrene befalling plants through froft, and that which the parts of animals are liable to, that they muft have fome analogous caufe. Corrofive humours burn the parts of animals, and the aëreal nitre, condenfed, has the fame effects on the parts of plants. Memoires de l' Academie Royale de Sciences, an. 1709.

Dr. Derham fays, That the greateft fufferers in the animal kingdom were birds and infects, but vegetables were much the greateft fufferers; that few of the tender forts of vegetables efcaped the feverity of the froft; Bays, Laurels, Rofemary, Cyprefs, Alaternufes, Phillyreas, Arbutufes, Laruftinufes, and even Furz, with moft fort of the frutefcent herbs, as Lavenders, Abrotanums, Rue, Thyme, &c. were generally deftroyed. He adds, that the fap of the finer wallfruit was fo congealed and deftroyed, that it ftagnated in the limbs and branches, and produced diforders like to chilblains in human bodies, which would turn to mortifications in many parts of the trees; that the very buds of the finer trees, both in the leaf, buds, and bloffom buds, were quite killed, and dried into a farinacious matter.

Dr. Derham relates it as a common obfervation, That vegetables fuffered more from the fun than from the froft, in that the fun-fhine, melting the fnow, and opening the ground, left it more expofed to the rigour of the enfuing night. It was likewife obferved, at a meeting of the Royal Society, That the calamities which befel trees, arofe not purely from their being frozen, but principally from the winds fhaking and rocking them when they are frozen, which rent and parted their fibres. Philof. Tranfact. Nº 324.

Hoar froft, or white froft, is the dew frozen, or congealed early in cold mornings, chiefly in autumn. This (as Mr. Regis obferves) is an affemblage of little parcels of ice or cryftals, which are of various figures, according to the difpofition of the vapours which meet and are condenfed by cold.

Dew is, to all appearance, the matter of hoar froft, though many of the Cartefians fuppofe it to be formed of a cloud, and either congealed in the cloud, and fo let fall, or ready to be congealed as foon as it arrives at the earth.

In the year 1728-9, there was a remakable froft, which continued for fome months, and deftroyed a great number of trees and plants in feveral parts of Europe,

a brief

a brief account of which may not be improper to be here inserted.

The autumn began with cold north and east winds, and early in November the nights were generally frosty, though the frost did not enter the ground deeper than the sun thawed the following day; but toward the end of November the winds blew extremely cold from the north, which was succeeded by a great snow, which fell in such quantities in one night, as to break off large arms, as also the tops of many Evergreen-trees, on which it lodged. After the snow had fallen, it began to freeze again, the wind continuing to blow from the north; the days were dark and cloudy for some time, but afterwards it cleared up; and the sun appeared almost every day, which melted the snow where exposed to it, whereby the frost penetrated deeper into the ground. It was observable, that, during these clear days, a great mist or vapour, appeared in the evenings, floating near the surface of the ground until the cold of the night came on, when it was suddenly condensed, and disappeared. About the 8th of December, the nights were extremely cold; the spirits in the thermometer fell 18 degrees below the freezing point, and on the 10th of the same month the frost was as severe as had been known in the memory of man; the spirits of the thermometer fell to 20 degrees below the freezing point. At this time vast numbers of Laurustinuses, Phillyreas, Alaternuses, Rosemary, Arbutus, and other Evergreen-trees and shrubs began to suffer; especially such as had been trimmed up to heads with naked stems, or had been clipped late in autumn. At this time also there were great numbers of large deciduous trees disbarked by the frost, as Pear-trees, Plane-trees, Walnut-trees, with many other sorts, and it was chiefly on the west and south-west side of the trees, that the bark came off.

About the middle of December the frost abated of its intenseness, and seemed to be at a stand till the 23d of the same month, when the wind blew extremely sharp and cold from the east, and the frost increased again, continuing very sharp till the 28th day, when it began to abate again, and seemed to be going off, the wind changing to the south; but it did not continue long in this point, before it changed to the east again, and the frost returned, though it was not so violent as before.

Thus the weather continued for the most part frosty, till the middle of March, with a few intervals of mild weather, which brought forward some of the early flowers; but the cold returning, soon destroyed them: so that those plants which usually flower in January and February, did not this year appear till March, and before they were fully blown, were cut off by the frost; of this number were all the Spring Crocuses, Hepaticas, Persian Irises, Black Hellebores, Mezereons, with some others.

The Cauliflower plants, which were planted out of the beds in the open ground, during the intervals between the frost, were most of them destroyed, or so much cut, that they lost most of their leaves; the early Beans and Peas were most of them killed, and many fruit and forest trees, which had been lately removed, were quite destroyed. The loss was very great to some curious persons, who had been many years endeavouring to naturalize great numbers of exotic trees and shrubs, abundance of which were either totally killed, or destroyed to the surface of the ground; amongst this number there were many sorts destroyed, which had endured the open air many years, without receiving the least injury from the cold, such as Passion Flowers, Cork-trees, Cistuses, Rosemary, Stœchas, Sage, Mastich, and some others. In some places the young Ash and Walnut-trees were killed; but when the frost went off, there appeared to have been much more damage done in the gardens, than there really was, which occasioned many people to dig up and destroy large quantities of trees and shrubs, which they supposed were killed; whereas those who had more patience, and suffered them to remain, fared better;

for great numbers of them shot out again, some from their stems and branches, and others from their roots, the following summer.

Nor was the frost more severe in England, than in other parts of Europe; but, on the contrary, in comparison, favourable; for in the southern parts of France, the Olives, Myrtles, Cistuses, Alaternuses, and several other trees and shrubs, which grow there almost spontaneously, were either destroyed, or at least were killed to their roots; and about Paris, and the northern parts of France, the buds of their fruit-trees were destroyed, although they remained closed; so that there were very few blossoms which opened that spring. The Fig-trees were in several parts of France quite killed, and in England their tender branches were destroyed, so that there was very little fruit on those trees the following summer, except where they were protected from the frost.

In Holland the Pines and Firs, with several other trees, which are natives of cold countries, were greatly injured by the cold; and most of the trees and shrubs; which were brought from Italy, Spain, or the south parts of France, which had been planted in the full ground, in that country, were entirely killed, though many other sorts, which had been brought from Virginia and Carolina, escaped very well in the same gardens; but the person who suffered most in that country, was the learned Dr. Boerhaave, who had been several years endeavouring to naturalize as many exotic trees and shrubs as he could possibly obtain from the several parts of the world, great numbers of which were entirely destroyed by the frost this winter.

In some parts of Scotland they not only lost many of their curious flowers, plants, and trees; but great numbers of sheep, and other cattle, were buried under the snow, where they perished; and many poor people, who went to look after their cattle, were equal sufferers with them, being buried in the snow, which in some places fell eight or nine feet deep in one night.

It has been observed by thermometers, when that kind of hovering lambent fog arises (either mornings or evenings) which frequently betokens fair weather; that the air, which in the preceding day was much warmer, has, upon the absence of the sun become many degrees cooler than the surface of the earth; which being near 1500 times denser than the air, cannot be so soon affected with the alteration of heat and cold; whence it is probable, that those vapours which are raised by the warmth of the earth, are by the cooler air soon condensed into a visible form. The same difference has been observed between the coolness of the air, and the warmth of water in a pond, by putting a thermometer, which hung all night in the open air in summer time, into the water, just before the rising of the sun, when the like reek, or fog, was rising on the surface of the water.

In the year 1739-40, we had another severe winter, which did great mischief to the gardens, fields, and woods, the effects of which are yet, and will be many years, felt in Europe. Some particulars of these depredations, may not, perhaps, be unacceptable to the reader, if they are here mentioned.

The wind set in blowing from the north and north-east, about the autumnal equinox, and continued to blow from the same quarter, with little variation, upward of six months. Early in November, there was a continued sharp frost for nine days, in which time the ice upon large ponds, and other standing waters, was frozen so hard as to bear persons who skated thereon; but toward the end of November the frost abated, and there was little more than slight morning frosts until Christmas day, when it froze pretty hard that morning, and continued every morning so to do; but on the 28th day of December, the wind blew with great strength from the north-east, and brought on severe cold; that night the frost penetrated very deep into the ground, and the next day, viz. the 29th, the wind changed to the southward of the east, and blew with great fury; the thermometer fell this day to twenty

twenty five degrees below frost; in the morning some little snow fell, but the violence of the wind carried it off; but cold still increasing, the waters were all frozen over, and that day it was so intense, as to freeze the water of the river, which was raised by the force of the wind into ice, before it fell down again. The wind continued to blow with the same force, and from the same quarter, all the 30th day, the cold still increasing, so that at this time the frost penetrated into most of the green-houses in England, but especially into all those whose fronts had the least inclination to the east; and such of them as fronted the south-west escaped best, where the back walls were of a sufficient thickness to keep out the frost; the spirits in the thermometer fell in the night of the 30th day to thirty-two degrees below the freezing point, which was lower than it had been known in England before; the violence of the wind made it very troublesome for persons of the most robust constitutions to be abroad, and this also caused the frost to penetrate through thick walls, and in the space of two days, the Evergreen-trees and shrubs appeared as if they had been scorched by fire, so that they seemed to have no life; the only trees of all the sorts of Evergreens which retained their verdure at this time, were the Portugal Laurel, Savin, and shrubby Hartwood; these in the midst of this severe frost remained unhurt, when all the others were as brown as if they had been dead a year; and it was very late in the spring, before any of them resumed their usual verdure: during these severe days there had but little snow fallen, so that the frost penetrated deep in the ground, and destroyed the roots of great part of the vegetables, where they were not well secured; the Artichoke roots were most of them killed in all the kitchen-gardens, some few only escaped, these were such as were not intended to be preserved. A single row of these roots, which were growing in a place where a great quantity of dung had been wheeled over them, whereby the ground was rendered as hard as that of a common foot-way, though there was no covering upon these roots, yet they survived the frost and did well; another parcel which was growing near a tan-yard, where, by accident, some tan had been thrown, were preserved, so that from some of these accidents we were so lucky as to retrieve the good kind of Artichoke, which the English gardens were so famous for being stocked with.

By the sharp piercing winds the Grass was almost totally burned up, so that there was not the least verdure to be seen in the fields, and in many places the sweetest and best kinds of the herbage were entirely killed, so that there remained only the strong rough kinds of grass, whereby the pastures were in general much damaged; but on the 31st day in the evening, the wind being much abated, the severity of the frost was not so great, and there seemed an appearance of a thaw on the first and second of January, but on the third in the evening the frost set in again with great violence; and on the fourth of January in the morning, the thermometer was fallen one degree lower than it had been before. The same morning there was the greatest hoary frost which had been seen, the woods, trees, and hedges, appeared as if they had been covered with snow; and although there was no wind stirring, yet the air was so sharp and penetrating, as to render it difficult to endure the cold, even with great exercise.

The timber-trees suffered greatly that morning, especially the Oaks, which were split with great violence; and the noise in the woods that morning, resembled that of great branches breaking down in every part of the woods, and when heard at a distance, like the firing of guns. This was little attended to at the time, but the timber which has been since fallen, sufficiently proves the great damage which the woods then sustained; nor was it here the calamity stopped, for the Oaks in general had received so much injury from the frost, as to occasion such a weakness and distemper among them, that the

following spring they were infested with insects to such a degree, as that their leaves were eaten and entirely destroyed by them; so that at Midsummer the trees were as naked as if it had been the beginning of April; and this distemper continued for two years after, almost as bad as at first, and has lessened by degrees, as the trees have recovered their strength; and where the trees were old and weak, they have not yet gotten the better of this distemper.

The herbage was also so much weakened by the severity of the frost, as not to be able to resist the attack made upon it by insects, so that innumerable quantities of them were discovered in the pastures in many parts of Europe, beginning first in the northern countries, and afterward spreading to the south; and these insects in many places were so numerous, as to destroy the sward of Grass, and it is to be feared the distemper which so long raged among the cattle may have been owing to this cause; for wherever the distemper spread, it has been observed, that numbers of these insects have harboured about the roots of the Grass: and as a farther proof of this, it has constantly been remarked, that, when these grubs are changed into a sort of beetle, and take their flight (which is commonly about the beginning of May,) the distemper ceases; and when these beetles have deposited their eggs in autumn, the distemper has raged again. Another remark has been made, that these beetles always chuse to deposit their eggs not at a great distance from rivers, or large pieces of water, and in such places the cattle have been most attacked. There might be many other circumstances mentioned in favour of this opinion, as also the several experiments which have been made by some of the members of the Academy of Sciences at Paris, which are sufficient to prove, that the distemper was not infectious, nor can be communicated by the cattle, notwithstanding it has been treated as such in many countries, where has been an immense loss to the public of such numbers of cattle and their hides; but this may require a particular treatise, therefore I shall not enlarge farther on this head at present.

The frost still continued very hard till toward the end of January, but not so violent as at the beginning; for had the wind continued to blow with so much force as it had done the three first days of the frost, for any considerable time longer, there would have been few vegetables able to have resisted the cold, nor would the animal kingdom have fared much better; for the cold was so intense during those few days, as to kill several of the weaker sort of cattle, where they were much exposed to the wind.

The Walnut-trees, Ash, and several other trees, had most of their shoots of the former year destroyed, which caused them to be very late before they put out their new shoots the following spring, and these shoots were produced from the two and three years branches. The Fig-trees in many places were killed almost to the ground, especially those which were growing against the best aspected walls, for those on the north and north-west aspects, as also the old standard Fig-trees escaped better; but all those stools and layers of these trees, which were growing in the nursery-gardens, were so much injured by the frost, as not to be recovered under three years, during which time there were scarce any of these plants to be sold. The layers of Vines, as also of the Oriental Plane-tree, in the nurseries, were likewise killed to the ground, and the old stools so much injured, that they had better have been dug up and thrown away, than to have continued them; for in ten years after they did not recover their former vigour, making their shoots so late in the summer, that their wood had not time to harden, and the first frost in autumn frequently killed them half way to the ground.

Many other deciduous trees were equal sufferers by this severe frost, and the Evergreens were more generally injured, and abundance of them killed. The Pine and Pinaster were so much hurt, as to lose all their verdure, and in some places the young plants of the

FRU

the former sort were entirely killed. The Rosemary, Lavender, Stœchas, Sage, and many other aromatic plants, were in many places quite destroyed, so that it was two or three years before the markets could be supplied with these; and in general the esculent plants in the kitchen-gardens were killed, so that for some months the markets were not supplied with any quantity of garden stuff. The flower-gardens also were great sufferers by this winter; for as the seasons for some years before had been very temperate, few persons had made any provision for a hard winter; and the cold setting in so very intense at the beginning, the mischief was done before people could be provided with covering.

The Wheat in many parts of England, but especially in the open common fields, was very much hurt, particularly on the top of the ridges, where, in several places there were broad naked spaces on the middle of the ridges, which in the spring appeared like so many foot-paths. And as the spring following was very dry, and the wind continuing to blow from the north and east; these piercing winds entered the ground, which had been loosened by the frost, and dried up the tender roots of the Corn, to the great prejudice of it; but some of the more expert farmers, who rolled their Wheat after the frost was over, were well repaid by the great crops which their land produced them.

Were I to enter into all the particulars of the damages sustained by this severe frost in the gardens and fields, it would swell this work beyond the limits intended; so I hope, on the other hand, I shall not be condemned for having inserted thus much, since, by the mention of these things, persons may be instructed how to save many of their valuable plants in future winters, as also what sorts are more liable to danger from frosts than others.

FRUCTIFEROUS [fructifer, *Lat.*] fruit-bearing, fruitful.

FRUCTUS. See FRUIT.

FRUIT is the production of a tree or plant, for the propagation or multiplication of its kind; in which sense fruit includes all kinds of seeds, with their furniture, &c. botanists use it to signify properly, that part of a plant wherein the seed is contained, which the Latins call Fructus, and the Greeks Καρπός.

The fruit of some plants are produced singly, as are their flowers, and sometimes they are produced in clusters, as in most fruit-trees, which are also fleshy, but in many plants they are dry.

The word fruit is also used to signify an assemblage of seeds in a plant; as in a Pea, Bean, Ranunculus, &c. and in its general signification, for all kinds of grain, whether naked, or inclosed in cover, capsula, or pod, whether bony, fleshy, skinny, membranous, or the like.

Fruit is the product or result of the flower, or that for whose production, nutrition, &c. the flower is intended.

The structure and parts of different fruits are different in some things, but in all the species the essential parts of the fruit appear to be only continuations or expansions of those which are seen in the other parts of the tree.

Dr. Beale suggests some very good reasons for a direct communication between the remotest parts of the tree and the fruit; so that the same fibres which constitute the root, trunk, and boughs, are extended into the very fruit.

Thus, if you cut open an Apple transversly, you will find it to consist chiefly of four parts, viz. 1st, a skin, or cortex, which is only a production of the skin or outer bark of the tree. 2dly, A parenchyma or pulp, which is an expansion and intumescence of the inner bark of the tree. 3dly, The fibres, or ramifications of the woody part of the tree. 4thly, The core, which is the produce of the pith, or medulla of the plant, indurated or strengthened by twigs of the wood and fibres inosculated therewith. This serves to furnish a cell, or lodge, for the kernels, filtrates

the juice of the parenchyma, and conveys it thus prepared to the kernel.

Of the fibres, authors generally reckon fifteen branches, of which ten penetrate the parenchyma, and incline to the basis of the flower; the other five ascend more particularly from the pedicle or stalk, and meet with the former at the base of the flower, to which branches the capsulæ, or coats of the kernels are fastened.

These branches being first extended through the parenchyma to the flower, furnish the necessary matter for the vegetation of it; but as the fruit increases, it intercepts the aliment, and thus the flower is starved, and falls off.

In a Pear there are five parts to be distinguished, viz. the skin, parenchyma, ramification, kernel, and acetarium.

The three first parts are common to the Apple. The kernel, observed chiefly in Choke Pears, or Breaking Pears, is a congeries of strong corpuscles, that are dispersed throughout the whole parenchyma, but in the greatest plenty, and closest together about the center, or acetarium; it is formed of the stony or calculous part of the nutritious juice.

The acetarium is a substance of a tart acid taste, of a globular figure, inclosed in an assemblage of several of the stony parts before-mentioned.

In a Plumb, Cherry, &c. there are four parts, viz. a coat, parenchyma, ramification, and nucleus, or stone. The stone consists of two very different parts; the external or harder part, called the stone, or shell, is a concretion of the stony, or calculous parts of the nutritious juice, like the kernel in Pears, within it. The inner, called the kernel, is soft, tender, and light, being derived from the pith, or medulla of the tree by seminal branches, which penetrate the base of the kernel.

The nut, or acorn, consists of a shell, cortex, and medulla; the shell consists of a coat and parenchyma, derived from the bark and wood of a tree.

The cortex consists of an inner and outer part, the first is a duplicature of the inner tunic of the shell; the second is a mossy substance, derived from the same source as the parenchyma of the shell. But authors are not agreed, whether the medulla, or pulp of the kernel does arise from the pith of the tree, or the cortical part thereof.

Berries, as the Grape, &c. contain (besides three general parts, viz. coat, parenchyma, and ramification) grains of a stony nature, to do the offices of seeds.

Fruits in general are serviceable in guarding, preserving, and feeding the inclosed seed, in filtrating the coarser more earthy, and strong parts of the nutritious juice of the plant, and retaining it to themselves, sending none but the most pure, elaborated, and spirituous parts to the seed, for the support and growth of the tender delicate embryo or plantule, which is therein contained.

FRUMENTACEOUS [Frumentaceous, *Lat.*] a term applied by botanists to all such plants as have a conformity with Wheat (called in *Latin* Frumentum,) in respect either of their fruits, leaves, ears, or the like.

FRUMENTUM INDICUM. See ZEA.

FRUTEX, a shrub; a vegetable of a genus between a tree and an herb, but of a woody substance. It is pretty difficult to determine wherein most of the writers on gardening and agriculture have made the distinction between trees and shrubs, or where to fix the difference or boundary, between the trees and shrubs, to say where one ends, and the other begins, for that cannot be determined by their growth; therefore the best definition which can be made of a shrub, to distinguish it from a tree, is its sending forth many stems from the roots, whereas the trees have a single trunk or body.

FRUTEX PAVONIUS. See POINCIANA.

FRUTICOSE [Fruticosus, *Lat.* shrubby.] are those plants which are of a hard woody substance, and do not rise to the height of trees.

5 U   FUCHSIA.

FUCHSIA. Plum. Nov. Gen. 14. Lin. Gen. Plant. 1097. This plant was fo named by Father Plumier, who difcovered it in America, in honour of the memory of Leonard Fuchfius, a learned botanift.

The CHARACTERS are,

The flower hath no empalement ; it hath one petal, with a clofed tube, which is flightly cut into eight parts at the brim, ending in acute points ; it hath four flamina the length of the tube, which are terminated by obtufe fummits. The oval germen is fituated under the flower, fupporting a fingle flyle, crowned by an obtufe fligma. The germen afterward becomes a fucculent berry with four furrows, having four cells, containing feveral fmall oval feeds.

This genus of plants is ranged in the firft feคtion of Linnæus's fourth clafs, intitled Tetrandria Monogynia, the flower having four flamina and one flyle.

We know but one SPECIES of this genus at prefent, viz.

FUCHSIA (*Triphylla*.) Lin. Sp. Plant. 1191. *Three-leaved Fuchfia.* Fuchfia triphylla, flore coccineo. Plum. Nov. Gen. *Three-leaved Fuchfia with a fcarlet flower.*

This plant is a native in the warmeft parts of America ; it was difcovered by Father Plumier, in fome of the French Iflands in America, and was fince found by the late Dr. William Houftoun, at Carthagena in New Spain, from whence he fent the feeds into England.

This is propagated by feeds, which muft be fown in pots filled with rich light earth, and plunged into a hot-bed of tanners bark, and treated in the fame way as other feeds from warm countries. In about a month or fix weeks after the feeds are fown, the plants will begin to appear, when they fhould be carefully cleared from weeds, and frequently refrefhed with water to promote their growth ; and when they are about two inches high, they fhould be fhaken out of the pot, and feparated carefully ; then plant each into a fmall pot filled with light rich earth, and plunge them again into a hot-bed of tanners bark, being careful to fcreen them from the fun until they have taken new root ; after which time they muft have frefh air admitted to them every day in proportion to the warmth of the feafon, and fhould be frequently watered. As the feafon advances and becomes warm, the glafies of the hot-bed fhould be raifed higher, to admit a greater fhare of air to the plants, to prevent their drawing up weak ; and when the plants are grown fo tall as to reach the glafies, they fhould be removed into the barkftove, and plunged into the tan-bed. In winter thefe plants require to be kept very warm, and at that feafon they muft not have much water, but in fummer it muft be often repeated.

Thefe plants are too tender to thrive in the open air in this country, even in the, hotteft part of the year ; therefore they fhould conftantly remain in the ftove, obferving to let in a large fhare of frefh air in fummer, but in winter they muft be kept warm ; with this management the plants will produce their flowers, and make a beautiful appearance in the ftove, amongft other tender exotic plants.

FUMARIA. Lin. Gen. Plant. 760. Tourn. Inft. R. H. 421. tab. 237. Fumatory ; in French, *Fumeterre.*

The CHARACTERS are,

The empalment of the flower is compofed of two equal leaves placed oppofite. The flower is of the ringent kind, approaching near to the butterfly flowers. The upper lip is plain, obtufe, indented at the top, and reflexed ; the neคtarium at the bafe of this is obtufe, and a little prominent. The under lip is like the upper in all its parts, but the bafe is keel-fhaped ; the neคtarium at the bafe is lefs prominent. The chaps of the flower is four-cornered, obtufe, and perfeคtly bifid ; there are fix equal broad flamina in each flower, divided in two bodies, included in the two lips, each being terminated by three fummits. In the center is fituated an oblong germen, fupporting a fhort flyle, crowned by an orbicular compreffed fligma. The germen afterward becomes a fhort pod with one cell, including roundifh feeds.

This genus of plants is ranged in the firft feคtion

of Linnæus's feventeenth clafs, intitled Diadelphia Hexandria, which includes the plants whofe flowers have their flamina in two bodies, and have fix flamina. To this genus Dr. Linnæus has joined the Capnoides of Tournefort, the Cyfticapnos of Boerhaave, the Corydalis of Dillenius, and the Cucularia of Juffieu, making them only fpecies of the fame genus.

The SPECIES are,

1. FUMARIA (*Officinalis*) pericarpis monofpermis racemofis, caule diffufo. Lin. Sp. Plant. 700. *Fumatory with feed-veffels growing in a racemus, with a fingle feed and a diffufed flalk.* Fumaria officinarum & Diofcoridis, flore purpureo. C. B. 143. *The common Fumatory with a purple flower.*

2. FUMARIA (*Spicata*) pericarpiis monofpermiis fpicatis, caule ereคto, folioliis filiformibus. Sauv. Monfp. 263. *Fumatory with feed-veffels growing in a fpike, with one feed, an upright flalk, and thread-like leaves.* Fumaria minor tenuifolia. C. B. 143. *Leffer narrow-leaved Fumatory.*

3. FUMARIA (*Alba*) filiquis linearibus tetragonis, caulibus diffufis acutangulis. Lin. Sp. Plant. 700. *Fumatory with narrow four-cornered pods, and diffufed flalks, having acute angles.* Fumaria fempervirens & floreas, flore albo. Flor. Bat. *Evergreen Fumatory with a white flower.*

4. FUMARIA (*Capnoides*) filiquis teretibus, caulibus diffufis, angulis obtufis. *Fumatory with taper pods and diffufed flalks, having obtufe angles.* Fumaria lutea. C. B. 143. *Yellow Fumatory.*

5. FUMARIA (*Claviculata*) filiquis linearibus, foliis cirrhiferis. Lin. Sp. Plant. 701. *Fumatory with narrow pods, and leaves having clafpers.* Fumaria claviculis donata. C. B. P. 143. *Fumatory with tendrils.*

6. FUMARIA (*Capreolata*) pericarpiis monofpermis racemofis, foliis fcandentibus fubcirrhofis. Lin. Sp. Plant. 701. *Fumatory with feed-veffels growing in a racemus, with one feed, and climbing leaves having fhort tendrils.* Fumaria major fcandens, flore pallidiore. Raii Hift. 405. *Greater climbing Fumatory with a paler flower.*

7. FUMARIA (*Cava*) caule fimplici, braคteis longitudine florum. Lin. Sp. Plant. 699. *Fumatory with a fingle flalk, and braคteæ as long as the flowers.* Fumaria bulbofa, radice cavâ, major. C. B. P. 143. *Greater bulbous Fumatory with a hollow root.*

8. FUMARIA (*Bulbofa*) caule fimplici, braคteis brevioribus multifidis, radice folida. *Fumatory with a fingle flalk, fhorter many pointed braคteæ, and a folid root.* Fumaria bulbofa, radice non cavâ, major. C. B. P. 144. *Greater bulbous Fumatory with a folid root.*

9. FUMARIA (*Cucularia*) fcapo nudo. Hort. Cliff. 351. *Fumatory with a naked flalk.* Capnorchis Americana. Boerh. Ind. alt. 1. 309. and the Fumaria tuberofa infipida. Cornut. 129. *Tuberous infipid Fumatory.*

10. FUMARIA (*Veficaria*) filiquis globofis inflatis. Hort. Upfal. 207. *Fumatory with globular inflated pods.* Cyfticapnos africana fcandens. Boerh. Ind. alt. 1. 310. *Climbing African Cyfticapnos.*

11. FUMARIA (*Eneaphylla*) foliis triternatis, foliolis cordatis. Lin. Sp. Plant. 700. *Fumatory with leaves compofed of three trifoliate fmall leaves, which are heart-fhaped.* Fumaria enneaphyllos Hifpanica faxatilis. Bocc. Muf. 2. p. 83. *Five-leaved Rock Fumatory of Spain.*

12. FUMARIA (*Sempervirens*) filiquis line* linearibus paniculatis, caule ereคto. Hort. Upfal. 207. *Fumatory with narrow pods growing in panicles, and an upright flalk.* Capnoides. Tourn. Inft. R. H. 423. *Baftard Fumatory.*

The firft fort is the common Fumatory which is ufed in medicine. This grows naturally on arable land in moft parts of England ; it is a low annual plant, and flowers in April, May, and June ; and very often from plants which rife late in the fummer, there will be a fecond crop in autumn. The juice of this plant is greatly commended for bilious cholics. It is never cultivated in gardens.

The fecond fort grows naturally in the fouth of France, Spain, and Portugal, but is preferred in botanic gardens for the fake of variety. It is an annual plant,

2

plant, which rifes from the fcattered feeds better than when it is fown with care ; the ftalks of this grow more erect, the leaves are very finely divided, and the flowers grow in a clofe fpike ; they are of a deep red colour, and flower about the fame time as the common fort.

The third fort grows naturally on the borders of the Mediterranean Sea ; it was firft brought to England from Tangier. This is a perennial plant, which fends out from the root many branching ftalks, which rife about fix or eight inches high, growing in tufts or bunches ; the leaves are very much divided, the ftalks are angular, and the flowers grow in loofe panicles upon naked foot-ftalks, which come out from the divifions of the branches ; they are of a whitifh yellow colour, and there is a fucceffion of them moft part of the year.

The fourth fort hath an appearance very like the third, and by fome it is fuppofed to be only a variety of that, but is undoubtedly a diftinct fpecies ; for I have cultivated both more than forty years, and never yet found either of them to vary. The ftalks of this fort have blunt angles, whereas thofe of the third are acute ; they are of a purplifh colour, and the flowers grow in loofer panicles, each having a longer foot-ftalk than thofe of the other ; they are of a bright yellow colour, and there is a fucceffion of them great part of the year.

Thefe two forts continue green all the year, and except in very fevere froft, are always in flower, which make a pretty appearance ; they grow beft on walls or rocks, and are very proper for the joints of grottos, or any rock-work ; where, if a few plants are planted, or the feeds fcattered, they will multiply faft enough from their fcattering feeds, which are caft out of the pods by the elaftic fpring of the valves when ripe, to a confiderable diftance ; and as the plants will require no care to cultivate them, they fhould not be wanting in gardens.

The fifth fort grows in ftony and fandy places in fome parts of England ; it is an annual plant with trailing ftalks, fending out clafpers from the leaves, which faften to any of the neighbouring plants. It flowers in May and June, but is never cultivated in gardens.

The fixth fort is an annual plant with many trailing ftalks, which grow about a foot long, fending out a few fhort tendrils, whereby they faften to any neighbouring fupport ; the flowers come out from the fide of the ftalks in loofe bunches ; they are of a whitifh herbaceous colour, with a purple fpot on the upper lip. This flowers in May and June. It grows in France and Italy, on ftony places in the fhade.

The feventh fort grows naturally in the fouth of France and Italy, and was fome years paft preferved in the Englifh gardens by way of ornament, but is now rarely to be found here ; it was titled Radix cava, or hollow root, from its having a pretty large tuberous root hollowed in the middle. The ftalk of this fort rifes about fix inches high, and does not divide, but is garnifhed toward the bottom with one ramous leaf, fomewhat like the common Fumatory, but the lobes are broader ; the flowers grow in a fpike at the top of the ftalk ; they are of a pale herbaceous colour, and appear in April. This plant delights in the fhade, and is multiplied by offsets, for it rarely ripens feeds in England.

The eighth fort is pretty common in many of the old gardens in England ; it grows naturally in the fouth of France, in Germany and Italy. This hath a pretty large round folid root of a yellowifh colour, from which come out branching leaves like thofe of the laft fort, but the lobes are longer ; the flowers grow in fpikes on the top of the ftalks ; they are of a purple colour, and come out early in April. The ftalks of this fort are fingle, and rife about four or five inches high.

There is a variety of this with green flowers, which is mentioned in moft of the books ; but all the plants of this fort which I have yet feen, are only abortive,

having no real flower, only a green bractea, which has been generally taken for the flowers : there is alfo mentioned a larger fort ; but if there is one which is really different from the common fort, I have not feen it in the Englifh gardens, nor the yellow and white flowering forts, which are alfo mentioned in many of the books.

The ninth fort grows naturally in North America ; this hath a fcaly root about the fize of a large Hazel Nut, from which come out three or four leaves upon flender foot-ftalks ; thefe are divided into three parts, each of thefe parts is compofed of many fmaller divifions, which have narrow lobes, divided into three parts almoft to the bottom ; the flower-ftalk is naked, and eight or nine inches long ; this is terminated by four or five flowers, growing in a loofe fpike ; thefe have two petals, which are reflexed backward, and form a fort of fork toward the foot-ftalk, and at their bafe are two horned nectariums, which ftand horizantal. The flowers are of a dirty white colour and appear in May, but rarely produce feeds here.

This is propagated by offsets from the root ; it loves a fhady fituation and a light foil ; the beft time to tranfplant the roots is in autumn, when the leaves are decayed, for it fhoots pretty early in the fpring, therefore it would not be fafe to remove them at that feafon.

The tenth fort grows naturally at the Cape of Good Hope ; this is an annual plant, with trailing ftalks which are two or three feet long, dividing into many fmaller, which are garnifhed with fmall branching leaves fhaped like thofe of the common Fumatory, but end with tendrils, which clafp to any neighbouring plants, and thereby the ftalks are fupported ; the flowers are produced in loofe panicles, which proceed from the fide of the ftalks ; they are of a whitifh yellow colour, and are fucceeded by globular fwollen pods, in which are contained a row of fmall fhining feeds.

This is propagated by feeds, which fhould be fown upon a moderate hot-bed in the fpring ; and when the plants are fit to remove, they muft be each planted in a fmall pot filled with light earth, and plunged again into the hot-bed, where they muft be fhaded from the fun till they have taken new root ; after which they fhould have a large fhare of air admitted to them at all times in mild weather, to prevent their drawing up weak ; and as foon as the feafon is favourable, they fhould be inured to bear the open air, to which they may be removed the beginning of June, when they may be fhaken out of the pots, preferving all the earth to their roots, and planted in a warm border, where their ftalks fhould be fupported with fticks to prevent their trailing on the ground ; and in July the plants will flower, and continue a fucceffion of flowers till the froft deftroys the plants ; the feeds ripen in autumn.

The eleventh fort grows naturally upon old walls, or rocky places in Spain and Italy ; this hath weak trailing ftalks which are much divided, and are garnifhed with fmall leaves divided into three parts, each of which hath three heart-fhaped lobes ; the flowers are produced in fmall loofe panicles from the fide of the ftalks, they are of a greenifh white, and appear moft of the fummer months. It is an abiding plant, which propagates itself by the feeds that fcatter, and thrives beft in a fhady fituation, and on old walls or buildings.

The twelfth fort is an annual plant with an upright ftalk, which grows a foot and a half high, round and very fmooth, fending out feveral branches upward ; thefe are garnifhed with fmooth branching leaves, of a pale colour, which are divided like the common fort, but the fmall leaves are larger and more obtufe ; the flowers are produced in loofe panicles from the fides of the ftalks, and at the extremity of the branches ; they are of a pale purple colour, with yellow chaps (or lips) ; thefe are fucceeded by taper narrow pods an inch and a half long, which contain many fmall fhining black feeds. This flowers during moft of the fummer months, and the feeds ripen in July, Auguft, guſt, and September. If the ſeeds of this plant are permitted to ſcatter, the plants will come up without any trouble, and require no other care but to thin them where they are too cloſe, and keep them clean from weeds.

Theſe plants may be ſuffered to grow on walls, and in ſome abject part of the garden ; for if they are admitted into the borders of the pleaſure-garden, they will ſcatter their ſeeds, and become troubleſome weeds ; but they are very proper plants to grow on ruins, or on the ſides of grottos or rock-work, where, by their long continuance in flower, they will have a good effect.

The fifth, ſixth, ſeventh, and eighth ſorts are propa-

gated by offſets, as other bulbous-rooted flowers ; theſe produce their flowers in the beginning of April, and are very pretty ornaments to borders in a ſmall flower-garden. They are extreme hardy, but do not increaſe very faſt, ſeldom producing ſeeds with us ; and their bulbs do not multiply very much, eſpecially if they are often tranſplanted. They love a light ſandy ſoil, and ſhould be ſuffered to remain three years undiſturbed, in which time they will produce ſeveral offſets. The beſt ſeaſon for tranſplanting them is from May to Auguſt, when the leaves begin to die off ; for if they are taken up when their leaves are freſh, it will greatly weaken their roots.

FURZ. See GENISTA.

G.

GALANTHUS. Lin. Gen. Plant. 362. Narciſſo-leucoium. Tourn. Inſt. R. H. 387. tab. 208. The Snow-drop ; in French, Perce-neige.

The CHARACTERS are,

The ſpatha or ſheath of the flower is oblong, blunt, and compreſſed. This opens ſideways, and becomes a dry ſkin ; the flower has three oblong concave petals, which ſpread open, and are equal ; in the bottom is ſituated the three-leaved nectarium, which is cylindrical, obtuſe, and indented at the top ; under the flower is ſituated the oval germen, ſupporting a ſlender ſtyle, which is longer than the ſtamina, crowned by ſingle ſtigma ; this is attended by ſix ſhort hairy ſtamina, terminated by oblong pointed ſummits, which are gathered together. The germen afterward becomes an oval capſule which is obtuſe and three-cornered, opening in three cells, which are filled with roundiſh ſeeds.

This genus of plants is ranged in the firſt ſection of Linnæus's ſixth claſs, intitled Hexandria Monogynia, which includes the plants whoſe flowers have ſix ſtamina and one ſtyle.

This plant, as alſo the great Snow-drop, was by Dr. Tournefort ranged together under the title of Narciſſo-leucoium ; which being a compound name, Dr. Linnæus has altered it to this of Galanthus ; and has ſeparated the great Snow-drop from this, and given the ſimple name of Leucoium to that genus.

We know but one SPECIES of this genus, viz.

GALANTHUS (*Nivalis.*) Lin. Hort. Cliff. 134. The common Snow-drop. *Leucoium bulboſum trifolium minus.* C. B. P. The leaſt bulbous Snow-drop with three leaves.

There is a variety of this with double flowers.

Theſe flowers are valued for their early appearance in the ſpring, for they uſually flower in February when the ground is often covered with ſnow. The ſingle ſort comes out the firſt, and though the flowers are but ſmall, yet when they are in bunches, they make a very pretty appearance ; therefore theſe roots ſhould not be planted ſingle, as is ſometimes practiſed by way of edging to borders ; for when they are ſo diſpoſed, they make very little appearance. But when there are twenty or more roots growing in a cloſe bunch, the flowers have a very good effect ; and as theſe flowers thrive well under trees or hedges, they are very proper to plant on the ſides of the wood-walks, and in wilderneſs-quarters ; where, if they are

ſuffered to remain undiſturbed, the roots will multiply exceedingly. The roots may be taken up the latter end of June, when their leaves decay, and may be kept out of the ground till the end of Auguſt, but they muſt not be removed oftener than every third year.

GALE. See MYRICA.

GALEGA. Lin. Gen. Plant. 770. Tourn. Inſt. R. H. 398. tab. 222. Goat's-rue.

The CHARACTERS are,

The empalement of the flower is ſhort, tubulous, and of one leaf, indented in five parts. The flower is of the butterfly kind ; the ſtandard is oval, large, and reflexed ; the wings are near the length of the ſtandard ; the keel is erect, oblong, and compreſſed ; the under ſide toward the point is rounded, but the upper is acute ; there are ten ſtamina, which join above their middle, and are terminated by ſmall ſummits. In the center is ſituated a narrow, cylindrical, oblong germen, ſupporting a ſlender ſtyle, crowned by a ſtigma terminated by a puncture. The germen afterward becomes a long pointed pod, incloſing ſeveral oblong kidney-ſhaped ſeeds.

This genus of plants is ranged in the third ſection of Linnæus's ſeventeenth claſs, intitled Diadelphia Decandria, which includes thoſe plants whoſe flowers have ten ſtamina joined in two bodies.

The SPECIES are,

1. GALEGA (*Officinalis*) leguminibus ſtrictis erectis, foliolis lanceolatis ſtrictis nudis. Lin. Sp. Plant. 1062. *Goat's-rue with erect cloſe pods, and ſpear-ſhaped naked leaves.* Galega vulgaris, floribus cæruleis. C. B. P. 352. *Common Goat's-rue with blue flowers.*

2. GALEGA (*Africana*) foliolis lanceolatis obtuſis, floribus ſpicatis longioribus, ſiliquis craſſioribus. Galega Africana, floribus majoribus ſiliquis craſſioribus. Tourn. Inſt. R. H. 399. *African Goat's-rue, with larger flowers and thicker pods.*

3. GALEGA (*Fruteſcens*) foliis ovatis, floribus paniculatis alaribus, caule fruticoſo. *Goat's-rue with oval leaves, and flowers growing in panicles from the ſides of the ſtalks, which are ſhrubby.* Galega Americana, foliis ſubrotundis, floribus coccineis. Houſt. MSS. *American Goat's-rue with roundiſh leaves and ſcarlet flowers.*

4. GALEGA (*Virginiana*) leguminibus retrofalcatis compreſſis villoſis ſpicatis, calycibus lanatis, foliolis ovali-oblongis acuminatis. Amœn. Acad. 3. p. 18. *Goat's-rue with hairy, compreſſed, ſickle-ſhaped pods, oblong oval-*

oval-pointed leaves, and woolly empalements. Orobus Virginianus, foliis fulva lanugine incanis, foliorum nervo in spinam aberunte. Pluk. Mant. 142.

5. GALEGA (*Purpurea*) leguminibus strictis adscendentibus glabris racemosis terminalibus; stipulis subulatis, foliis oblongis glabris. Flor. Zeyl. 301. *Goatsrue with close, smooth, ascending pods, terminating the stalks in an oblong bunch, awl-shaped stipulæ, and oblong smooth leaves.* Coronilla Zelanica herbacea, flore purpurascente. Burm. Zeyl. 77.

The first sort grows naturally in Italy and Spain, but is propagated in the English gardens for medicinal use. This hath a perennial root, composed of many strong fibres, which are frequently jointed, from which arise many channelled hollow stalks, from two to three feet high, which are garnished with winged leaves, composed of six or seven pair of narrow spear-shaped lobes, terminated by an odd one, which are smooth and entire; the flowers terminate the stalks growing in spikes, they are of the Pea-blossom shape, and of a pale blue colour, and are disposed in loose spikes. They appear in June, and are succeeded by taper pods about one inch and a half in length, having one row of kidney-shaped seeds, which ripen toward the end of August.

There is a variety of this with white flowers, and another with variegated flowers, which have accidentally been produced from seeds, so are not constant, therefore are only mentioned here.

The second sort grows naturally in Africa; this differs from the former, in having larger leaves, which are composed of eight or ten pair of lobes, broader and blunter at their ends than those of the common sort; the flowers are larger, and the spikes are longer; the seed-pods are also much thicker than those of the common sort, but in other respects are very like it.

These plants are propagated by seeds, which may be sown either in the spring or autumn, upon a bed of ground in an open situation; and when the plants come up, they must be kept clean from weeds till they are strong enough to remove; then a spot of ground should be prepared, in size proportionable to the quantity of plants designed; this should be well dug, and cleared from the roots of all noxious weeds; then the plants should be carefully taken up, and planted in rows at a foot and a half distance, and in the rows one foot asunder, observing to water them till they have taken new root; after which they will require no farther care to keep them clean from weeds, which may be easily done by hoeing of the ground frequently between the plants, and in the spring the ground between the rows should be dug, which will encourage their roots, and cause them to shoot out vigorous stalks; and if their stalks are cut down before the seeds are formed every year, the roots will continue the longer, especially if they grow on a light dry soil. The seeds of these will grow whereever they are permitted to scatter, so that plenty of the plants will come up without any care, and these may be transplanted and managed in the same manner as is before directed.

The first sort is used in medicine; it is accounted cordial, sudorific, and alexipharmic, so very good against pestilential distempers, expelling the venom through the pores of the skin, and is of use in all kinds of fevers. Mr. Boyle, in his treatise of the Wholsomeness and Unwholsomeness of the Air, bestows three or four pages, in celebrating the virtues of Goats-rue in pestilential and malignant diseases, from his own observation and experience.

The third sort was discovered by the late curious botanist Dr. William Houstoun, at Campeachy, from whence he sent the seeds into Europe. This plant is propagated by seeds, which must be sown on a hot-bed early in the spring; and when the plants come up, and are fit to transplant, they must be transplanted each into a separate small pot, and plunged into a hot-bed of tanners bark, shading them from the sun till they have taken new root; then they must be treated as hath been directed for other

tender plants, which are kept in the bark-stove. With this management they will flower in July, and in September they will perfect their seeds, but the plants may be preserved through the winter in the bark-stove.

The fourth sort grows naturally in Virginia and Carolina; this hath a perennial root, and an annual stalk which rises three feet high; the lobes of the leaves are oblong and oval, generally seven or nine to each leaf: the whole plant is covered with a silvery down. The flowers are of a red colour, and are produced in spikes at the end of the branches: these are succeeded by sickle-shaped compressed pods of a silvery colour, containing one row of kidney-shaped seeds.

This plant, although it is tolerable hardy, yet it is with difficulty preserved in gardens; for the seeds rarely ripen in England, and the plants are often destroyed by frost in winter. The only method in which I have been able to keep the plant, has been by potting them, and placing them in a common frame in winter, where they enjoyed the free air in mild weather, but were protected from frost, in this way I have kept the plant three years, but it has not ripened seeds here.

The fifth sort grows naturally in Ceylon, and in many parts of India, from whence I have received the seeds. This sort was annual here, and decayed before the seeds were ripe. It hath an herbaceous stalk, which rises two feet high, garnished with winged leaves, composed of eight or nine pair of oval lobes, terminated by an odd one; the foot-stalks of the flowers come out opposite to the leaves; these sustain a long loose spike or thyrse of small purple flowers, which are succeeded by slender erect pods.

This may be cultivated in the same way as the third sort; and if the plants are brought forward early in the spring, if the summer proves warm, the seeds may ripen.

GALENIA. Lin. Gen. Plant. 443. Sherardia. Ponted. Epist. 14.

The title of this genus was given to it by Dr. Linnæus, from the famous physician Galen.

The CHARACTERS are,

The flower hath a small quadrifid empalement of one leaf; it hath no petals, but hath eight hairy stamina the length of the empalement, terminated by double summits. In the center is situated a roundish germen, supporting two reflexed stylei, crowned by simple stigmas. The empalement afterward becomes a roundish capsule with two cells, containing two oblong angular seeds.

This genus of plants is ranged in the second section of Linnæus's eighth class, intitled Octandria Digynia, which includes those plants whose flowers have eight stamina and two styles.

We know but one SPECIES of this genus, viz.

GALENIA (*Africana.*) Hort. Cliff. 150. *Shrubby Galenia.* Sherardia. Ponted. Epist. 14. and the Atriplex Africana, lignosa frutescens, rosmarini foliis. Hort. Pis. 20. *Shrubby African woody Atriplex, with Rosemary leaves.*

This shrub grows naturally at the Cape of Good Hope, and in other parts of Africa; it rises with a shrubby stalk about four or five feet high, sending out many weak branches, garnished with narrow leaves, which are placed irregularly on every side the branches; they are of a light green, with a furrow running longitudinally through the middle; the flowers are produced in loose panicles from the side and at the end of the branches; they are very small, and have no petals, so make little appearance. The flowers come out in July and August, but are not succeeded by seeds in England.

This plant will not live through the winter in the open air in England, so must be placed in the greenhouse, or under a frame, with other hardy exotic plants, where it may have a large share of air in mild weather, for it only requires to be protected from frost. In the summer it may be exposed in the open air, with other plants of the same country, and in dry weather it must be frequently watered. This may be

     propagated

propagated by cuttings, which, if planted during any of the fummer months, and watered frequently, will take root in about five or fix weeks, and may then be treated as is directed for the old plants.

GALEOPSIS. Lin. Gen. Plant. 637. Tourn. Inft. R. H. 185. tab. 86. Stinking Dead Nettle.

The CHARACTERS are,

The empalement of the flower is tubulous, of one leaf; cut into five fegments, which end in acute points. The flower is of the lip kind, having a fhort tube; the chaps are a little broader, but the length of the empalement; from the bafe to the under lip, it is on both fides fharply indented; the upper lip is concave, roundifh, and fawed at the top; the under lip is trifid, the middle fegment being the largeft, which is crenated. It hath four ftamina inclofed in the upper lip, two being fhorter than the other; terminated by roundifh bifid fummits. In the center is fituated a quadrifid germen, fupporting a flender ftyle, crowned by a bifid acute ftigma. The germen afterward become four naked feeds, fitting in the rigid empalement.

This genus of plants is ranged in the firft fection of Linnæus's fourteenth clafs, intitled Didynamia Gymnofpermia, which includes thofe plants whofe flowers have two long and two fhort ftamina, and the feeds are naked.

The SPECIES are,

1. GALEOPSIS (*Ladanum*) internodiis caulinis æqualibus, verticillis omnibus remotis. Lin. Sp. Plant. 579. *Stinking Hedge Nettle, with equal diftances between the joints, and whorls growing at a diftance.* Sideritis arvenfis anguftifolia rubra. C. B. P. 233. *Red narrow-leaved Field Ironwort.*

2. GALEOPSIS (*Tetrabit*) internodiis fupernè incraffatis, verticillis fummis fubcontiguis. Lin. Sp. Plant. 579. *Stinking Hedge Nettle, whofe joints are thicker above, and the whorls at the top growing near each other.* Lamium cannabino folio vulgare. Raii Syn. Ed. 3. p. 240. *Common Dead Nettle with a hemp leaf.*

3. GALEOPSIS (*Speciofa*) corollâ flavâ, labio inferiore maculato. Flor Lapp. 193. *Stinking Hedge Nettle with a yellow flower, whofe under lip is fpotted.* Lamium cannabinum aculeatum flore luteo fpeciofo, labiis purpureis. Pluk. Alm. 204. *Prickly Hemp Dead Nettle, with a beautiful yellow flower and purple lips.*

4. GALEOPSIS (*Galeobdolon*) verticillis fexfloris, involucro tetraphyllo. Lin. Sp. Plant. 780. *Stinking Hedge Nettle with fix flowers in each whorl, and a four-leaved involucrum.* Galeopfis five urtica iners flore luteo. J. B. 3. 323. *Stinking or Dead Nettle with a yellow flower.*

5. GALEOPSIS (*Orientale*) verticillis bifloris, foliis oblongo-cordatis. *Stinking Hedge Nettle with two flowers in each whorl, and oblong heart-fhaped leaves.* Galeopfis Orientalis ocimaftri folio, flore majore flavefcente. H. R. Par. *Eaftern ftinking Hedge Nettle, with an Ocimaftrum leaf, and a larger yellowifh flower.*

6. GALEOPSIS (*Hifpanica*) caule pilofo, calycibus labio corollæ fuperiore longioribus. Lin. Sp. Plant. 580. *Stinking Hedge Nettle with a hairy ftalk, and the empalement longer than the upper lip of the petal.* Galeopfis annua Hifpanica, rotundiore folio. Inft. R. H. 186. *Annual Spanifh ftinking Hedge Nettle, with a rounder leaf.*

Thefe are all of them annual plants, except the fourth fort; the three firft grow naturally in England. The firft is found upon arable land in many places; the fecond grows upon dunghills, and by the fide of paths, in many parts of England. The third fort grows chiefly in the northern counties, but I have found it growing wild in Effex, within ten miles of London. Thefe plants are feldom cultivated in gardens, for if their feeds are permitted to fcatter, the plants will come up as weeds wherever they are allowed a place.

The fourth is a perennial plant with a creeping root; this grows in the woods and under hedges in moft parts of England. The fifth grows in the Levant; this is a biennial plant, which perifhes foon after the feeds are ripe. It is preferred in botanic gardens for the fake of variety, but hath no great beauty.

GALEOPSIS FRUTESCENS. See PRASIUM.

GALIUM. Lin. Gen. Plant. 117. Tourn. Inft. R. H. 114. tab. 39. Ladies Bedftraw, or Cheefe-rennet; in French, *Caillelait.*

The CHARACTERS are,

The flower hath a fmall empalement indented in four parts, fitting upon the germen. It hath one petal, divided into four fegments almoft to the bottom; and four awl-fhaped ftamina which are fhorter than the petal; terminated by fingle fummits. It hath a twin germen fituated under the flower, fupporting a flender half bifid ftyle, crowned by a globular ftigma. The germen afterward become two dry berries, which are joined together, each inclofing a large kidney-fhaped feed.

This genus of plants is ranged in the firft fection of Linnæus's fourth clafs, intitled Tetrandria Monogynia; which includes thofe plants whofe flowers have four ftamina and one ftyle.

The SPECIES are,

1. GALIUM (*Verum*) foliis octonis linearibus fulcatis, ramis floriferis brevibus. Hort. Cliff. 34. *Ladies Bedftraw with eight narrow furrowed leaves, and fhort flowering branches.* Galium luteum. C. B. P. 335. *Yellow Ladies Bedftraw.*

2. GALIUM (*Mollugo*) foliis octonis ovato-linearibus fubferratis patentiffimis mucronatis, caule flaccido, ramis patentibus. Lin. Sp. Plant. 107. *Ladies Bedftraw with eight oval narrow leaves, which are fpread open, fawed, and pointed, a weak ftalk, and fpreading branches.* Mollugo montana latifolia ramofa. C. B. P. 333. *Branching broad-leaved Mountain Mollugo.*

3. GALIUM (*Purpureum*) foliis verticillaris lineari-fetaceis, pedunculis folio longioribus. Hort. Cliff. 34. *Ladies Bedftraw with narrow briftly leaves growing in whorls, and foot-ftalks of the flowers longer than the leaves.* Galium nigro-purpureum montanum tenuifolium. Col. Ecphr. 1. p. 298. C. B. P. 335. *Narrow-leaved Mountain Ladies Bedftraw, with a black purple flower.*

4. GALIUM (*Glaucum*) foliis verticillatis linearibus pedunculis dichotomis, fummo caule floriferis. Prod. Leyd. 256. *Ladies Bedftraw with narrow leaves growing in whorls, foot-ftalks divided by pairs, and flowers growing at the top of the ftalk.* Galium faxatile glauco folio. Bocc. Muf. 2. p. 172. *Rock Ladies Bedftraw with a gray leaf.*

5. GALIUM (*Rubrum*) foliis verticillatis linearibus patulis, pedunculis breviffimis. Hort. Cliff. 34. *Ladies Bedftraw with narrow leaves growing in whorls, and fhort foot-ftalks.* Galium rubrum. C. B. P. 335. *Red Ladies Bedftraw.*

6. GALIUM (*Boreale*) foliis quaternis lanceolatis trinerviis glabris, caule erecto, feminibus hifpidis. Fler. Lappon. 60. *Ladies Bedftraw with four fmooth fpear-fhaped leaves having three veins, an upright ftalk, and rough feeds.* Rubia pratenfis lævis acuto folio. C. B. P. 333. *Smooth Meadow Madder with an acute leaf.*

7. GALIUM (*Album*) foliis verticillatis, lineari-lanceolatis, ramis floriferis longioribus. *Ladies Bedftraw with narrow fpear-fhaped leaves growing in whorls, and longer branches of flowers.* Galium album vulgare. Tourn. Inft. R. H. 113. *Common white Ladies Bedftraw.*

8. GALIUM (*Linifolium*) foliis lineari-lanceolatis glabris, caule erecto ramofiffimo. *Ladies Bedftraw with feven narrow, fmooth, fpear-fhaped leaves, and an upright branching ftalk.* Galium album linifolium. Barrel. Obfer. 99. *White Ladies Bedftraw with a Flax leaf.*

9. GALIUM (*Paluftre*) foliis quaternis obovatis inæqualibus, caulibus diffufis. Flor. Suec. 119. *Ladies Bedftraw with four unequal oval leaves, and a diffufed ftalk.* Galium paluftre album. C. B. P. 335. *White Marfh Ladies Bedftraw.*

The firft of thefe plants (which is the fort commonly ufed in medicine) is very common in moift meadows, and in pafture grounds, in feveral parts of England. The other varieties are preferved in curious botanic gardens, but as they are plants of very little beauty, and are fubject to fpread very far, and over-run whatever plants grow near them, they are feldom cultivated in other gardens.

Thefe forts may any of them be propagated by parting their roots, which fpread and increafe very faft, either

in

in the spring or autumn, and will grow almost in any soil or situation, especially the first sort; the other sorts require a drier soil, but will all grow in any situation.

GALLERIES, are ornaments made with trees of various kinds, which are very common in all the French gardens, but are seldom introduced into the English gardens, especially since the taste for clipped trees has been exploded; but as there may be some who yet fancy these obsolete ornaments, I shall just mention the way of constructing them.

In order to make a gallery in a garden with porticoes and arches, a line must first be drawn of the length you design the gallery to be; which being done, it is to be planted with Hornbeam, as directed under the article HORNBEAM; which Hornbeam thus planted, is to be the foundation of the gallery.

The management of them is not very difficult; they require only to be digged about, and sheared a little when there is occasion.

The chief curiosity required is in the ordering the fore-part of the gallery, and in forming the arches.

Each pillar of the porticoes or arches ought to be four feet distant one from the other; the gallery twelve feet high, and ten feet wide, that there may be room for two or three persons to walk a-breast.

When the Hornbeams are grown to the height of three feet, the distance of the pillars well regulated, and the ground-work of the gallery finished, the next thing to be done is to form the frontispiece: to perform which you must stop the Hornbeam between two pillars at the height, and run up a trellis made for that purpose, which forms the arch.

As it grows up you must with your shears even those boughs that outshoot the others; in time they will grow strong, and may be kept in form by the shears. Portico galleries may be covered with Lime-trees.

GARCINIA. Lin. Gen. Plant. 526. The Mangosteen.

The CHARACTERS are,

The flower hath a one-leaved empalement, which is permanent. It hath four roundish concave petals, which spread open, and are larger than the empalement. It hath sixteen stamina which are erect, and form a cylinder, terminated by roundish summits. In the center is situated an oval germen, with scarce any style, but is crowned by a buckler-shaped plain stigma divided into eight parts, and is permanent. The germen afterward becomes a thick globular berry with one cell, including eight hairy fleshy seeds, which are convex and angular.

This genus of plants is ranged in the first section of Linnæus's eleventh class, intitled Dodecandria Monogynia, which includes those plants whose flowers have twelve stamina and one style.

We have but one SPECIES of this genus, viz.

GARCINIA (*Mangostana*). Hort. Cliff. 182. *The Mangostan, or Mangosteen.* Arbor peregrina aurantio simili fructu. Cluf. Exot. 12. *Foreign Tree with a fruit like the Orange.*

This tree grows naturally in the Molucca Islands, and also in the inland parts of New Spain, from whence I received perfect specimens, which were sent me by Mr. Robert Millar, who gathered them near Tolu, but did not know the tree. It rises with an upright stem near twenty feet high, sending out many branches on every side, which are placed opposite, and stand oblique to each other, and not at right angles; the bark of the branches is smooth, of a gray colour, but on the tender shoots it is green, and that of the trunk is of a darker colour and full of cracks: the leaves are of the spear-shape, and entire; they are seven or eight inches long, and about half so much in breadth in the middle, gradually diminishing to both ends, of a lucid green on their upper side, and of an Olive colour on their under, having a prominent midrib through the middle, with several small veins running from that to both sides of the leaf. The flower is like that of a single Rose, composed of four roundish petals, which are thick at their base, but are thinner toward their ends; they are of a dark

red colour. The fruit which succeeds the flower is round, the size of a middling Orange; the top is covered by a cap, which was the stigma on the top of the style, and remains to the top of the fruit, and is indented in rays to the number of six or seven, which are obtuse. The shell of the fruit is like that of the Pomegranate, but softer, thicker, and fuller of juice; it is green at first, but changes to a dark brown with some yellowish spots; the inside of the fruit is of a Rose colour, and divided into several parts by thin partitions, as in Oranges, in which the seeds are lodged, surrounded by a soft juicy pulp of a delicious flavour, partaking of the Strawberry and the Grape, and is esteemed one of the richest fruits in the world; the trees naturally growing in the form of Pyrabolas, whose branches are well garnished with large shining green leaves: they have an elegant appearance, and afford a kindly shade in hot countries, therefore are worthy of cultivation, in all those countries where there is warmth enough to ripen the fruit. As there are but few of the seeds in these fruit which come to perfection (for the greatest part of them are abortive) so most of those which have been brought to Europe have failed; therefore the surest way to obtain the plants, is to sow their seeds in tubs of earth in the country, and when the plants have obtained strength, they may be brought to Europe; but there should be great care taken in their passage, to screen them from salt water and the spray of the sea, as also not to give them much water, especially when they are in a cool or temperate climate, for these plants are very impatient of wet. When the plants arrive in Europe, they should be carefully transplanted, each into a separate pot, filled with light kitchen-garden earth, and plunged into the tan-bed, observing to shade them from the sun till they have taken new root; then they must be treated in the same manner as other tender plants from hot countries.

GARDENS are distinguished into flower-gardens, fruit-gardens, and kitchen-gardens: the first, being designed for pleasure and ornament, are to be placed in the most conspicuous parts, i. e. next to, or just against the back front of the house; the two latter being principally intended for use and service, are placed less in sight.

Though the fruit and kitchen-gardens are here mentioned as two distinct gardens, and have by the French gardeners, as also by some of our own countrymen been contrived as such, yet they are now usually in one; and with good reason, since they both require a good soil and exposure, and will equally require to be placed out of the view of the house. And as it will be proper to inclose the kitchen-garden with walls, and to secure the gates, that no persons may have access to it, who have no business in it, for the sake of preserving the product, so these walls will answer the purposes of both. Moreover, in the disposition of the kitchen-garden, when it is properly divided into quarters, the planting of espaliers of fruit-trees round each of the quarters, will be of use in screening from the view the kitchen-herbs growing in the quarters; and, by that means, give an elegancy to both parts, and save besides a great expence. The only objection which has been made to this of any consequence is, that the gardeners are too apt to crowd the borders near the walls with kitchen-herbs, whereby the trees are deprived of their nourishment; but this is in every gentleman's power to redress, by not suffering the borders to be thus crowded. But I shall treat more fully of this under the article of KITCHEN-GARDEN.

In the choice of a place to plan a garden in, the situation and exposure of the ground are the most essential points to be regarded; since, if a failure be made in that point, all the care and expence will in a manner be lost.

In a garden for pleasure, the principal things to be considered, are, 1st, the situation; 2dly, the soil, aspect, or exposure; 3dly, water; 4thly, prospect.

1st, Siift, Situation: this ought to be fuch an one as is wholfome, in a place that is neither too high nor too low; for if a garden be too high, it will be expofed to the winds, which are very prejudicial to trees; if it be too low, the dampnefs of the ground, the vermin, and venomous creatures that breed in ponds and marfhy places, add much to their infalubrity.

A fituation on a rifing ground, or on the fide of a hill, is moft happy, efpecially if the ground be not too fteep; if the flope be eafy, and in a manner imperceptible; if a good deal of level may be had near the houfe; and if it abounds with fprings of water; for, being fheltered from the fury of the winds, and the violent heat of the fun, a temperate air will be there enjoyed; and the water that defcends from the top of the hills, either from fprings or rain, will not only fupply fountains, canals, and cafcades, for ornament, but when it has performed its office, will water the adjacent valleys, and render them fertile and wholfome, if it be not fuffered to ftagnate in them.

Indeed, if the declivity of the hill be too fteep, and if the water be too abundant, a garden on the fide of it may often fuffer, by having the trees torn up by the torrents and floods; and the earth above tumbling down, the walls may be demolifhed, and the walks fpoiled.

It cannot however be denied, that the fituation on a plain or flat, has feveral advantages that the higher fituation has not: floods and rains make no fpoil; there is a continued profpect of champaigns, interfected by rivers, ponds, brooks, meadows and hills, covered with buildings or woods; and the level furface is lefs tirefome to walk on, and lefs chargeable, than that on the fide of a hill; the terrace-walks and fteps are not neceffary; but the greateft difadvantage of flat gardens is the want of an extenfive profpect, which rifing grounds afford.

2dly, The fecond thing to be confidered in chufing a plat for a garden, is a good earth or foil.

It is fcarce poffible to make a fine garden in a bad foil; there are indeed ways to meliorate ground, but they are very expenfive; and fometimes, when the expence has beftowed of laying good earth two feet deep over the whole furface, which for a large garden is an expence too great for moft perfons; and after this a whole garden has been ruined, notwithftanding the expofure has been foutherly and healthful, when the roots of the trees have come to reach the natural bottom.

To judge of the quality of the foil, obferve whether there be any Heath, Thiftles, or fuch like weeds, growing fpontaneoufly in it, for they are certain figns that the ground is poor. Likewife if there be large trees growing thereabouts, obferve whether they grow crooked, ill-fhaped, of a faded green, and full of mofs, or infefted with vermin; if fo, the place is to be rejected: but on the contrary, if it be covered with good Grafs fit for pafture, then you may be encouraged to try the depth of the foil.

To know this dig holes in feveral places, fix feet wide and four feet deep; if you find three feet of good earth it will do well, but lefs than two will not be fufficient.

The quality of good ground is neither to be ftony, nor too hard to work; neither too dry, nor too moift; nor too fandy and light, nor too ftrong and clayey, which is the worft of all for gardens.

3dly, The third requifite is water. The want of this is one of the greateft inconveniencies that can attend a garden, and will bring a certain mortality upon whatever is planted in it, efpecially in the greater droughts that often happen in a hot and dry fituation in fummer; befides the ufefulnefs of it in fine gardens, for making jets d'eau, canals, cafcades, &c. which are the greateft ornaments of a garden.

4thly, The fourth thing required in a good fituation is, the view and profpect of a fine country; and though this is not fo abfolutely neceffary as water, yet it is one of the moft agreeable beauties of a fine garden: befides, if a garden be planted in a low place that is buried, as I may fay, and has no kind of profpect, it will be not only difagreeable but unwholfome, by being too much fhaded and obfcured; as the trees will rather retain infalubrious damps, than communicate the refrefhing air, that is fo purifying to vegetable nature.

In fhort, a garden neceffarily requires (befides the care of the gardener) the fun, a good foil, a full, or at leaft an open profpect, and water, the laft above all; and it would be egregious folly to plant a garden where any of thefe are wanting.

Of the Defigning or Manner of Laying out a Pleafure Garden.

The area of a handfome garden may take up thirty or forty acres, not more.

And as for the difpofition and diftribution of this garden, the following directions may be obferved.

1ft, There ought always to be a defcent from the houfe to the garden not fewer than three fteps, but if there are fix or feven it will be better. This elevation of the building will make it more dry and wholfome, alfo from the head of thefe fteps there will be a farther profpect or view of the garden.

In a fine garden, the firft thing that fhould prefent itfelf to the fight, fhould be an open lawn of Grafs, which, in fize, fhould be proportionable to the garden; in a large garden it fhould not be lefs than fix or eight acres; but in middling or fmall gardens, the width of it fhould be confiderably more than the front of the houfe; and if the depth be one half more than the width, it will have a better effect. The figure of this lawn need not be regular, and if on the fides there are trees planted irregularly, by way of open grove, fome of which may be planted forwarder upon the lawn than the others, whereby the regularity of the lawn will be broken, it will render it more like nature, the beauties of which fhould always be ftudied in the laying out and planting of gardens; for the nearer thefe gardens approach to nature, the longer they will pleafe; for what is a garden, but a natural fpot of ground dreffed and properly ornamented? there are thofe who have erred in copying of what they call nature, as much as thofe who have drawn a whole garden into ftrait lines, great alleys, ftars, &c. by bringing the rougheft and moft deformed part of nature into their compofitions of gardens: as for inftance, where the ground has been naturally level, they have at great expence, made hollows and raifed mole-hills; fo that the turf has been rendered not only more unpleafant to walk upon, but much worfe to keep: and after all the pains that have been taken to ape nature, the whole is as eafily difcovered to be the work of art, as the ftiffeft flopes and the moft finifhed parterres.

The great art in laying out of gardens, is to adapt the feveral parts to the natural pofition of the ground, fo as to have as little earth to remove as poffible; for this is often one of the greateft expences in making of gardens; and it may with truth be affirmed, that wherever this has been practifed, nine times in ten it has proved for the worfe; fo that if inftead of levelling hills to form large terraces, ftiff flopes, and even parterres, as have been too often practifed; or the finking of hollows, and raifing of hills, as hath by others been done; if the furface of the ground had only been fmoothed and well turfed, it would have had a much better effect, and been more generally approved than the greateft number of thefe gardens, which have been made with an infinite expence both of time and money.

The next thing to be obferved is, to contrive a dry walk, which fhould lead quite round the whole garden; for as gardens are defigned to promote the exercife of walking, the greater the extent of this dry walk, the better it will anfwer the intent; fince in bad weather, or in dewy mornings and evenings, when

when the fields are unpleasant or unsafe to walk over, these dry walks in gardens become useful and pleasant; and such walks, if laid either with gravel or sand, may lead through the different plantations, gently winding about in an easy natural way, which will be more agreeable than those long strait walks, which are too frequently seen in gardens.

But as the taste of designing gardens has of late altered from the former method, there are many persons who have gone into the opposite extreme; and in the forming of what they term serpentine walks, have twisted them about in so many short turns, as to render it very disagreeable to walk on them; and at the same time they strike the sight with as much stiffness and appearance of art, as any of the methods formerly practised. In short, the fewer turns there are in these walks, and the more they are concealed, the better they will please; and yet the turns being easy, and at great distances, will take off all the appearance of straitness. And here let me observe, that there can be no better, or more easy or natural method of laying out these walks, than by tracing the easy turns made on a road, where it bends by the track of the coach wheels.

These walks should be so contrived, as to lead into shade as soon as possible; as also into some plantations of shrubs, where persons may walk in private, and be sheltered from the wind; for no garden can be pleasing where there is want of shade and shelter.

Another thing absolutely necessary is, where the boundaries of the garden are fenced with walls or pales, they should be hid by plantations of flowering shrubs, intermixed with Laurels, and some other Evergreens, which will have a good effect, and at the same time conceal the fences, which are disagreeable, when left naked and exposed to the sight.

In situations where there is a good supply of water, the designer has room for adding one of the greatest beauties to the garden, especially if it will admit of a constant stream; for in such places, if the water is properly conducted through the garden, it will afford infinite pleasure; for although these streams may not be sufficient to supply a large surface, yet if these narrow rivulets are judiciously led about the garden, they will have a better effect than many of the large stagnating ponds or canals, so frequently made in large gardens; for where these pieces of water are large, if all the boundaries can be seen from one point of view, they cannot be esteemed by persons of judgment; and frequently these standing waters are brought so near the house, as to render the air damp and unhealthy; and many times they are so situated, as to occasion this inconvenience, and at the same time are not seen to any advantage from the house.

Where wildernesses are intended, these should not be cut into stars, and other ridiculous figures, nor formed into mazes or labyrinths, which in a great design is trifling, but the walks should be noble, and shaded by tall trees; and the spaces of the quarters planted with flowering shrubs and Evergreens, whereby they will be rendered pleasant at all seasons of the year; and if there are hardy sorts of flowers (which will thrive with little care) scattered about near the sides of the walks, they will have a very good effect, in making a variety of natural beauties almost through the year.

The situation of these wildernesses should not be too near the house, lest they should occasion damps; therefore it is much better to contrive some open groves, through which there may be a communication under shade, from the house to these wildernesses; which are much the best when they are planted at the farthest part of the garden, provided they do not obstruct the view of fine objects.

Buildings are also very great ornaments to a garden, if they are well designed and properly placed; but the modern taste of crowding gardens with large useless buildings, I presume to think is censurable, with regard as well to propriety as expence.

Statues and vases are also very beautiful objects, but

these should by no means be placed too near each other; for when several of them appear at once, they fill and confound the eye, and lose the beautiful effect which they would have, if now and then one properly situated engages the sight.

What an expence might be spared, and applied to nobler purposes, if nature only were to be imitated, if simplicity were studied in this delightful art, rather than ostentation! for any thing may be said to be more of nature, than what we miscall grandeur.

Fountains are also very ornamental to a garden, if they are magnificently built, and where a constant supply of water can be obtained; but if they are meanly erected, or have not water to keep them constantly running, they should never be introduced into gardens, for nothing can be more ridiculous than to see a dry fountain; which, perhaps, at a great expence, may have water forced up, to supply it for an hour or two, and no more; and this perhaps not in dry seasons, when there is a general scarcity of water.

The same may also be observed of cascades, and other falls of water, which ought never to be contrived in gardens, where there cannot be a constant run of water; but where the situation of a garden is so happy, as to be naturally supplied with water, these falls and jet's d'eau, may be rendered very great beauties, especially if they are well designed, and not made in the low mean taste, in which too many of those now in being appear, and where the water is made to fall over a parcel of regular steps of stone; but the fall should be in one sheet from top to bottom, where should be placed many large rough stones to break and disperse the water, and to increase the noise of the fall.

Where the ground is naturally uneven, and has gentle rises and falls, there may be so humoured in the laying out of the ground, as to be rendered very great beauties; but these inequalities of the ground must by no means be cut into regular stiff slopes, nor amphitheatres, as has been too much the practice: but if the knolls are properly planted with clumps of trees or shrubs, and the sloping sides smoothed and left in their natural position, they will have a much better effect, than can be given them by all the regular angles, lines, and flat slopes, which have been till of late, introduced by all the designers of gardens. The taste in laying out of gardens has greatly altered, and has been as greatly improved in England, in the compass of a few years; for, with the revolution, the Dutch taste of laying out gardens was introduced, which consisted of little more than flower-borders laid out in several scrolls of Box-work, clipped Evergreens, and such low expensive things; as also the walling round, and dividing the several parts of gardens by cross walls; so that a garden consisting of eight or ten acres, was generally divided by brick walls, into three or four separate gardens; and these were reduced to exact levels, having many gravelwalks, and the borders on each side crowded with clipped trees and Evergreen hedges, dividing these small inclosures again; so that the first making and planting of these small gardens was attended with a greater expence, as was the keeping of them afterward, than gardens of six times the extent, when designed after nature.

Whether this taste so universally prevailed in England, in complaisance to his late Majesty King William, or was owing to the low groveling taste of those persons, who had the designing of most of the English gardens, it is difficult to determine; but it is very certain, that the gentlemen, at that time, attended very little themselves, to the disposition of their gardens, but were contented to leave the whole direction of them to persons of the meanest talents that ever professed the art; so that soon after, when another taste prevailed, these gardens were almost totally demolished, and it would have been well, if a good, that is to say, a natural taste had succeeded the other; but this was not the case; for though a more open and extensive way of laying out gardens was introduced, yet this was lit-

tle

tle more than copying after the French, whose taste was in making long avenues, strait walks, stiff regular slopes, cabinets, fret-work, tall hedges cut into various shapes, jets d'eau, fountains, &c. so that there was little of nature studied; but, on the contrary, all the geometrical figures introduced in wilderness-work, as also in the parterres, and other compartments of the garden: nor is it so much to be wondered at, that this taste prevailed in France, when the designs of all the principal gardens were there formed by architects, who were as studious to have the symmetry of the opposite, or corresponding part of the garden, as exact as the apartments of a habitation; nor has length of time, nor the improvements already made in other countries, amended their taste, or convinced them of its absurdity.

As the gardens of Versailles, Marli, and others, were extolled for their magnificence, so the plans of them were almost universally copied; the designers, or imitators rather, only varying the parts according to the situation or figure of the ground; and this was practised for several years, at a time, when great sums of money were expended in gardens, which might have rendered this country the most beautiful of any in Europe, had a natural taste then prevailed in the designing of gardens; which is the more to be lamented, as the plantations then made, have been many of them rooted out, to make way for the alterations and improvements which have been since introduced. Many persons, I am sensible, will have it, that in the designs of gardens, the taste should alter from time to time, as much as the fashion of apparel; but these cannot be persons of judgment; for wherever there are natural beauties in a country, they will always please persons of real knowledge; and frequently it is observed, that persons of but little skill in the art of gardening, are struck with these beauties without knowing the cause; therefore where the beautiful parts of nature are justly imitated in gardens, they will always be approved by judicious persons, let the taste of gardening alter as it will.

When trees have been long growing in a garden, nothing can be more disagreeable than to have them destroyed, to alter the garden according to the fashion of the time, because it requires much time to bring up trees to such a height as to afford shade and shelter; and, as time is precious, so, where the disposition of the garden is altered, there should be great attention given to the preservation of all the good trees, wherever they can be either useful or ornamental.

There is another essential part of gardening, which cannot be too much considered by persons who design gardens, which is that of adapting the several sorts of trees and shrubs, to the situation and soil of the garden, as also to allow the trees a proper share of room; but, however necessary this will appear, yet very few persons have made this their study, insomuch that when one views many modern gardens, and sees the great number of trees and shrubs, which are crowded into them, one would be induced to believe, that private interest has had a greater influence than any other motive, with the designers. Indeed this fault may often be ascribed to the master, who, perhaps, is too much in haste for shade and shelter, so will have three or four times the number of trees and shrubs planted as should have been, or that can remain long without injury, where the plantations succeed; and to this over-haste are owing the miserable plantations of large trees, so often seen in gardens and parks, where trees of all sorts, and of any age are taken out of woods, hedge-rows, &c. and removed at a great expence to stand and decay annually, till they become so many dead sticks, than which nothing can be a more disagreeable sight to the owner; who, after an expectation for several years, attended with an expence of watering, digging, and cleaning, finds himself under a necessity either of replanting, or giving up the thoughts of having any. Numbers of persons have indeed amused themselves with the hopes of success, by seeing these

new planted trees put out branches for a year or two, which they generally do; but in three or four years after, instead of making a progress, they begin to decay at the top, and continue to do so gradually, until they quite perish, which, perhaps, may not happen in eight or ten years, especially if no severe winter, or very dry summer, intervenes, either of which generally proves fatal to these plantations; so that persons may be led on with hopes, for so many years, in the best part of their lives, when there is a certainty of their failing, or at least of their never increasing in size; but of this I shall treat more fully in the article of PLANTING, and shall proceed.

In the business of designs, a mean and pitiful manner should be studiously avoided, and the aim should be always at that which is noble and great, not to bring too many little things into a garden, nor to make small pieces of water, narrow walks, &c. especially in large gardens; for it is much better to have a few great things, than four times the number of small ones, which are trifling. In small gardens there is more excuse for this, nor indeed would it be right, to have either large lawns, broad walks, or large pieces of water in such; but yet even in these there ought to be a medium, and persons should never attempt to crowd too many things in these, whereby the whole will appear only as a mean and trifling model of a large garden. Before the design of a garden is entered upon, it ought to be considered, what it will be in twenty or thirty years time, when the trees and shrubs are grown up, and spread; for it often happens, that a design, which looks handsome when it is first planted, and in good proportion, in process of time becomes so small and ridiculous, that there is a necessity either of altering or totally destroying it.

The general distribution of a garden, and of its parts, ought to be accommodated to the different situations of the ground, for a design may be very proper for a garden on a perfect level, which will by no means do for one where there are great inequalities in the ground; so that, as I have before intimated, the great art of designing is, in properly adapting the design to the situation, and contriving to save the expence of removing earth, to humour the inequalities of the ground, to proportion the number and sorts of trees and shrubs to each part of the garden, and to shut out, from the view of the garden, no objects that may become ornamental.

There are, besides these, many other rules relating to the proportions, conformity, and disposition of the different parts and ornaments of gardens, of which more may be seen under their several articles.

GARDENIA. See JASMINUM.

GARIDELLA. Tourn. Inst. R. H. 655. tab. 430. Lin. Gen. Plant. 507. [This plant was so named by Dr. Tournefort, in honour of Dr. Garidel, who was professor of physic, at Aix, in Provence.]

The CHARACTERS are,

The flower hath a small, oblong, erect empalement of five leaves; it hath no petals, but five oblong equal nectariums occupy their place; these are bilabiate. The outer part of the under lip is bifid and plain; the interior part of the upper lip is short and single. The flower hath eight or ten awl-shaped stamina, which are shorter than the empalement, and are terminated by obtuse erect summits. In the center is situated three germina, which are oblong, compressed, and sharp-pointed, having no styles, but crowned by simple stigmas; these become three oblong compressed capsules with two valves, inclosing several small seeds.

This genus of plants is ranged in the third section of Linnæus's tenth class, which includes those plants whose flowers have ten stamina and three germen.

We know but one SPECIES of this genus, viz.

GARIDELLA (Nigellastrum.) Hort. Cliff. 170. Garidella foliis tenuissime divisis. Tourn. Garidella with very narrow divided leaves; and the Nigella Cretica folio Fœniculi. C. B. P. 146. Fennel-flower of Crete with a Fennel leaf.

This plant is very near akin to the Nigella, or Fennel-flower, to which genus it was placed by the writers on botany before Dr. Tournefort, and was by

him

him feparated from it, as differing in the form of the flower.

It grows wild in Candia, and on mount Baldus, in Italy, as alfo in Provence, where it was difcovered by Dr. Garidel, who fent the feeds to Dr. Tournefort, for the Royal Garden at Paris.

This is an annual plant, which rifes with an upright ftalk a foot high, dividing into feveral flender branches, garnifhed at their joints with very flender leaves like thofe of Fennel. The ftalks are terminated by one fmall flower, of a pale herbaceous colour, which is fucceeded by three capfules, each containing two or three fmall feeds. It flowers in June and July, and the feeds ripen in September. It is propagated by feeds, which fhould be fown in autumn, on a bed or border of light frefh earth, where the plants are defigned to remain (for they feldom thrive if they are tranfplanted;) when the plants are come up, they muft be carefully cleared from weeds, and where they are too clofe, they muft be thinned, leaving them about four or five inches apart; this is all the culture the plants require, and if the feeds are permitted to fcatter, the plants will come up without any farther care.

GAULTHERIA.

The CHARACTERS are,

It hath a double permanent empalement; the outer has two oval, concave, fhort leaves; the inner has one bell-fhaped leaf cut into five fegments; the flower has one oval petal, cut half-way into five fegments, which are reflexed; it has ten awl-fhaped nectarii, which are fhort, furrounding the germen and ftamina, and ten awl-fhaped incurved ftamina inferted to the receptacle, terminated by bifid horned fummits, and a roundifh depreffed germen, fupporting a cylindrical ftyle, crowned by an obtufe ftigma; the germen afterward becomes an obtufe five-cornered capfule, having five cells, faftened to the interior empalement, which turns to a berry open at the top, filled with hard angular feeds.

This genus of plants is ranged in the firft fection of Linnæus's tenth clafs, intitled Decandria Monogynia, the flower having ten ftamina and one ftyle.

We know but one SPECIES of this genus, viz.

GAULTHERIA (*Procumbens.*) Amœn. Acad. 3. p. 14. *Trailing Gaultheria.* Vitis Idæa Canadenfis, pyrolæ folio. Tourn. Inft. 608. *Canada Wortle-berry with a winter green leaf.*

This plant grows naturally in feveral parts of North America upon fwampy ground, fo is with difficulty preferved in the Englifh gardens. The branches of this trail upon the ground, and become ligneous, but never rife upward; they are garnifhed with oval entire leaves, placed alternate; the flowers are produced on the fide of the branches; they are of an herbaceous colour, fo make little appearance, and very rarely are fucceeded by fruit in England.

The only method in which I have fucceeded to keep this plant, was by planting of it in a pot, filled with loofe undunged earth, placing it in the fhade, and frequently watering it; with this management I have kept the plant alive three years, and have had flowers but no fruit.

GAURA.

The CHARACTERS are,

It hath an empalement of one leaf, which falls off, with a long cylindrical tube, having four oblong glands faftened to it; the upper part is cut into four oblong fegments, which are reflexed. The flower hath four oblong rifing petals, which are broad at the top but narrow at their bafe, fitting upon the tube of the empalement; and eight upright flender ftamina which are fhorter than the petals, and a nectarious gland between the bofe of each, with oblong moveable fummits. The oblong germen is fituated under the flower, fupporting a flender ftyle the length of the ftamina, crowned by four oval fpreading ftigmas; the flower is fucceeded by an oval four-cornered compreffed capfule, containing one oblong angular feed.

This genus of plants is ranged in the firft fection of Linnæus's eighth clafs, intitled Octandria Monogynia, the flower having eight ftamina and one ftyle.

We know but one SPECIES of this genus, viz.

GAURA (*Biennis.*) Amœn. Acad. 3. p. 26. *Gaura.* Lyfimachia chamænerio fimilis floridana, foliis nigris punctis capfulis carinatis in ramulorum cymis. Pluk: Amalth. 139. tab. 428. f. 1.

This is a biennial plant, which grows naturally in Virginia and Penfylvania: the ftalk rifes four or five feet high, fending out feveral branches, which are garnifhed with oblong, fmooth, pale, green leaves, fitting pretty clofe. The flowers are produced in clofe tufts at the end of the branches; they are compofed of four oblong petals, of a pale Rofe colour, irregularly placed, having eight ftamina furrounding the ftyle. The flowers appear in September, and when the autumn proves favourable, the feeds will ripen toward the end of October.

If the feeds of this plant are fown on open borders foon after they are ripe, they will more certainly fucceed than when they are fown in the fpring. When the plants come up, they muft be kept clean from weeds; and if they are too clofe, fome of them fhould be drawn out, and planted in a bed to allow room for the other to grow; in the autumn they fhould be all tranfplanted to the place where they are defigned to ftand for flowering and perfecting their feeds, and will require no other culture but to fupport their branches to prevent the autumnal winds from breaking them down.

GENERATION is, by naturalifts, defined to be the act of procreating and producing a thing which before was not; or, according to the fchoolmen, it is the total change or converfion of a body into a new one, which retains no fenfible part or mark of its former ftate.

Thus we fay, fire is generated, when we perceive it to be where before there was only wood, and other fuel, or when the wood is fo changed, as to retain no fenfible character of wood; in the like manner a chick is faid to be generated, when we perceive a chick, where before was only an egg, or the egg is changed into the form of a chick.

In generation there is not properly any production of new parts, but only a new modification or manner of exiftence of the old ones, and thus generation is diftinguifhed from creation.

Generation alfo differs from alteration, in that in alteration the fubject remains apparently the fame, and is only changed in its accidents or affections, as iron, which before was fquare, is now made round; or when the fame body which is well to-day, is fick to-morrow.

Again: generation is the oppofite to corruption, which is the utter extinction of a former thing; as, when that which before was an egg, or wood, is no longer either the one or the other; whence it appears, that the generation of one thing is the corruption of another.

The Peripateticks explain generation by a change of paffage from a privation, or want of a fubftantial form, to the having fuch a form.

The moderns allow of no other change in generation, than what is local; and, according to their notion, it is only a tranfpofition, or new arrangement of parts; and, in this fenfe, the fame matter is capable of undergoing an infinite number of generations.

As for example: A grain of Wheat, being committed to the ground, imbibes the humidity of the foil, becomes turgid, and dilates to fuch a degree, that it becomes a plant; and, by a continual acceffion of matter, by degrees, ripens into an ear, and at length into a feed; this feed, when ground in a mill, appears in the form of a flour, which, being mixed up with water, makes a pafte, of which bread is generated by the addition of yeaft, and undergoing the operation of fire, i. e. by baking; and this bread being cominuted by the teeth, digefted in the ftomach, and conveyed through the canals of the body, becomes flefh, or, in other words, flefh is generated.

Now the only thing effected in all this feries of generation, is a local motion of the parts of the matter, and their fettling again in a different order; fo that where-

wherever there is a new arrangement, or compofition of the elements, there is, in reality, a new generation, and thus generation is reduced to motion.

Generation is more immediately underftood of animal and vegetable bodies from feed, or the coition of others of different fexes, but of the fame genus or kind.

Monf. Perrault, and fome of the modern naturalifts after him, maintained, That there is not properly any new generation, that God created all things at firft, and that what is by us called generation, is no more than an augmentation and expanfion of the minute parts of the body of the feed ; fo that the whole fpecies, which are afterwards produced, were, in reality, all formed at the firft, and inclofed therein, to be brought forth and expofed to view in time, and according to a certain order and œconomy.

And accordingly Dr. Garden fays, It is moft probable, that the ftamina of all the plants and animals that have been formed, ab origine mundi, by the Almighty Creator, within the firft of each refpective kind ; and he who confiders the nature of vifion, that it does not give us the true magnitude, but only the proportion of things ; and that which feems to our naked eye but a point, may truly be made up by as many parts as feem to be in the whole univerfe, will not think this an abfurd or impoffible thing.

Dr. Blair, treating of the generation of plants, fays, That when Almighty God created the world, he fo ordered and difpofed of the materies mundi, that every thing produced from it fhould continue fo long as the world fhould ftand. Not that the fame individual fpecies fhould always remain ; for they were, in procefs of time, to perifh, decay, and return to the earth, from whence they came ; but that every like fhould produce its like, every fpecies fhould produce its own kind, to prevent a final deftruction of the fpecies, or the neceffity of a new creation, in order to continue the fame fpecies upon earth, or in the world.

For which end he laid down certain regulations, by which each fpecies was to be propagated, preferved, and fupported, till, in order, or courfe of time, they were to be removed hence ; for, without that, thofe very beings, which were created at firft, muft have continued till the final diffolution of all things, which Almighty God of his infinite wifdom did not think fit.

But, that he might ftill the more manifeft his omnipotence, he fet all the engines of his providence to work, by which one effect was to produce another by the means of certain laws, or rules laid down for the propagation, maintenance, and fupport of all created beings ; this his divine providence is called nature, and thefe regulations are called the laws, or rules of nature, by which it ever operates in its ordinary courfe, and whatever exceeds from that is faid to be preternatural, miraculous, or monftrous.

Mofes, in his account of the creation, tells us, that plants have their feeds in themfelves, in thefe words : And God faid, Let the earth bring forth grafs, the herb yielding feed, and the fruit-tree yielding fruit, after his kind, whofe feed is in itfelf upon the earth.

The antients, indeed, diftinguifhed the generation of animals into two kinds, i. e. into regular, called univocal ; and anamolous, called alfo equivocal, or fpontaneous.

The firft was effected by parent animals of the fame kind, as that of men, birds, beafts, &c. The fecond they fuppofed to be effected by corruption, the fun, &c. as that of infects, frogs, &c. but this latter is now generally exploded.

Many, indeed, have effayed to treat of the generation of animals, but few have been able to give that fatisfactory account of it that were to be wifhed for, and far fewer yet have been able to treat of the generation of plants as it ought to be ; for that which ftill kept them in the dark, was,

Firft, That though there were two different fexes in animals, by whofe mutual affiftance the fpecies was

propagated, yet there was no fuch thing then known in plants.

Secondly, That though it can now be made appear, that every animal is produced by univocal generation, i. e. from an egg, and not by corruption, &c. as moft of the antients imagined the infects were ; yet there are ftill thofe who maintain, that thofe which they call imperfect plants, are the product of a certain rottennefs in the earth.

The generation of plants bears a clofe analogy to that of fome animals, efpecially fuch as want local motion, as mufcles, and other immoveable fhell-fifh, which are hermaphrodite, and contain both the male and female organs of generation.

The flower of a plant is found to be the pudendum, or principal organ of generation ; but the ufe of fo much mechanifm, and fo many parts, has been but little known till of late years.

The flower of a Lily confifts of fix petala, or flower-leaves, from the bottom of which, in the middle, arifes a kind of tube, called by Tournefort, the piftillum, and by Dr. Linnæus the ftyle ; this refts upon the germen, which is the female organ of generation ; round this are placed pretty fine threads, called the ftamina, or filaments ; thefe ftamina arife likewife from the bottom of the flower, and terminate at the top in little fummits, called by fome apices, which are replete with a fine duft, called farina ; thefe are the male organs of plants.

This is the general ftructure of the flowers of plants, although they are infinite ways diverfified, and to fuch a degree, that fome have no fenfible piftil, and others want the ftamina ; others again have the ftamina, but want the apices, and fome plants exceed all others in this, that they have no vifible flowers ; but if it be allowed, that this before-mentioned is the moft common ftructure of flowers, it will follow, that thefe parts that feem wanting are ufually only lefs apparent, or are fituated in different plants, or in different parts of the fame plant.

The fruit is ufually at the bafe of the piftillum, fo that when the piftillum falls with the reft of the flower, the fruit appears in the ftead of it ; but oftentimes the piftillum is the fruit itfelf, but ftill they have both the fame fituation in the center of the flower, and the petala, or flower-leaves, which are difpofed around the little embryo, feem to be defigned only to prepare a fine juice in the little veffels, for the fupport of it during the little time that they laft, and it requires ; but fome fuppofe the chief ufe of them to be to defend the piftillum, &c.

The apices of the ftamina are fmall capfulæ, or bags, full of a farina, or duft, which falls out when the capfula grows ripe, and burfts.

Monf. Tournefort fuppofed this duft to be only an excrement of the food of the fruit, and the ftamina to be nothing but excretory ducts, which filtrated this ufelefs matter, and thus difcharged the embryo ; but Mr. Morland, Mr. Geoffroy, and others, find nobler ufes for this duft ; on their principle the ftamina, with the apices and farina, make the male part of the plant, and the piftil, the female.

Mr. Morland fays, It hath been long ago obferved, that there is in every particular feed a feminal plant conveniently lodged between the two lobes, which conftitute the bulk of the feed, and are defigned for the firft nourifhment of the tender plant.

But the admirable Dr. Grew, to whofe generous induftry, and happy fagacity, we are indebted for the beft improvements of this part of knowledge, is the only author I can find, who hath obferved that the farina, or fine powder, which is, at its proper feafon, fhed out of thofe thecæ, or apices feminiformes [i. e. feed-forming cafes] which grow at the top of the ftamina, doth fome way perform the office of male fperm. But herein, I think, he falls fhort, in that he fuppofes them only to drop upon the outfide the uterus, or vafculum feminale, and to impregnate the included feed by fome fpirituous emanations, or energetical impref.

                                     That

That which is now subjected to the disquisitions and censure of such whose exquisite skill constitutes them judges of such performances, is, Whether it may not be more proper to suppose, that the seeds which are lodged in the proper involucra, are at the first unimpregnated ova (or eggs) as of animals; that this farina is a congeries of seminal plants, one of which must be conveyed into every ovum before it can become prolific; that the stylus, in Mr. Ray's language, or the upper part of the pistillum, in Mr. Tournefort's, is a tube designed to convey these seminal plants into their nests in the ova; that there is so vast a provision made, because of the odds there are, whether one, of so many, shall ever find its way into, and through so narrow a conveyance.

To make this supposition the more credible, I shall lay down the observations I have made upon the situation of these stamina, and the stylus, in some few species of plants.

First, In the Corona Imperialis, where the uterus, or vasculum seminale of the plant stands upon the center of the flower; and from the top of this ariseth the stylus, the vasculum seminale and stylus together representing a pistillum.

Round this are placed six stamina; upon the ends of each of these are apices, so artfully fixed, that they turn every way with the least wind, being in height almost equal to the styles about which they play, and which in this plant is manifestly open at the top, as it is hollow all the way; to which we must add, that upon the top of the stylus there is a sort of tuft, consisting of pinguid villi, which I imagined to be placed there to catch and detain the farina, as it flies out of the thecæ; from hence, I suppose, the wind shakes it down the tube, till it reach the vasculum seminale.

In the Caprifolium, or Honeysuckle, there rises a stylus from the rudiments of a berry, into which it is inserted to the top of the monopetalous flower; from the middle of which flower are sent forth several stamina, that shed their farina out of the cases upon the orifice of the stylus, which, in this plant, is villous or tufted, upon the same account as in the former.

In Allium, or common Garlic, there arises a tricoccous uterus, or seed-vessel; in the center of which is inserted a short stylus, not so high as the apices, which thus over-topping it, have the opportunity of shedding their globules into an orifice more easily; for which reason, I can discern no tuft upon this (as in the former) to insure their entrance, that being provided for by its situation just under them.

The reader, I hope, will excuse me, if I present him now with some such reasonings or reflections as the foregoing account doth suggest, and will support; and I cannot but hope to persuade those that are candid, that I have assigned to the several parts of the flowers I have mentioned, their true and real use.

For nothing can be more natural than to conclude, that where a fine powder is curiously prepared, carefully reposited, and shed abroad at a peculiar season, where there is a tube so placed as to be fit to receive it, and such care in disposing this tube, where it doth not lie directly under the cases that shed the powder, it hath a particular apparatus at the end, to insure its entrance.

Nothing can be more genuinely deduced from any premises, than it may from this, that this powder, or some of it, was designed to enter this tube. If these stamina had been only excretory ducts, as has been hitherto supposed, to separate the grosser parts, and leave the juice designed for the nourishment of the seed more reserved, what need was there to lodge these excrements in such curious repositories? They would have been conveyed any where, rather than where there was so much danger of their dropping into the seed-vessel again, as there is here.

Again: the tube, over the mouth of which they are shed, and into which they enter, leads always directly into the seed-vessel.

To which we must add, that the tube always begins to die when these thecæ are emptied of their contents; if they last any longer, it is only whilst the globules, which enter at their orifice, may be supposed to have finished their passage. Now, can we well expect a more convincing proof of these tubes being designed to convey these globules, than that they wither when there are not more globules to convey.

If I could now shew, that the ova, or unimpregnated seeds, are ever to be observed without this seminal plant, the proof would arise to a demonstration; but having not been so happy as to observe this, I shall content myself at present with suggesting, that hence one would conclude, that the petala of the flower were rather designed to sever superfluous juices from what was left to ascend in the stamina, than the stamina to perform this office, either for them, or the unimpregnated femina, and observe the analogy between animal and vegetable generation, as far as was necessary there should be an agreement between them. I shall recommend the enquiry to those gentlemen who are masters of the best microscopes, and address in using them; though, in the mean time, I have made some steps toward a proof of this sort, and have met with some such hints, as make me not despair of being able, in a short time, to give the world even this satisfaction. For, not to insist upon this, that the seminal plant always lies in that part of the seed which is always nearest to the insertion of this stylus, or some propagation of it into the seed-vessels, I have discovered in Beans, Peas, and Kidney-beans, just under one end of that we call the eye, a manifest perforation, (discernible by the grosser sort of magnifying glasses) which leads directly to the seminal plant, and at which I suppose the seminal plant did enter; and, I am apt to think, the Beans or Peas that do not thrive well, may be found destitute of it.

But I must now proceed to describe some other plants, whereby it will appear, that there is a particular care always exercised to convey this powder, so often mentioned, into a tube, which may convey it to the ova.

Now, in leguminous plants, if we carefully take off the petala of the flower, we shall discover the pod, or siliqua, closely covered with an involving membrane, which, about the top, separates into nine stamina, each fraught with its quantity of farina; and these stamina closely adhere to the style, which is observable at the end of that tube, which here also leads directly to the pod; it stands not upright, indeed, but so bent, as to make near a right angle with it.

In Roses there stands a column, consisting of many tubes closely clung together, though easily separable, each leading to their particular cell, the stamina in a great number placed all round about.

In Tithymalus, or Spurge, there rises a tricoccous vessel, that, whilst it is small, and not easily discernible, lies at the bottom till it is impregnated, but afterwards grows up, and stands so high upon a tall pedicle of its own, as would tempt one to think, that there were to be no communication betwixt this and the apices.

In the Strawberries and Raspberries, the hairs which grow upon the ripe fruit (which, I suppose, may be surprising to some) are so many tubes leading each to their particular seed; and therefore we may observe, that in the first opening of the flower there stands a ring of stamina, within the petala, and the whole inward area appears like a little wood of these hairs or pulp, which, when they have received and conveyed their globules, the seeds swell, and rise in a carneous pulp. Thus far Mr. Morland.

We may observe a vessel at the bottom of the pistil of the Lily, which vessel we may call the uterus, or womb, in which are three ovaries filled with little eggs, or rudiments of seed found in the ovaria, which always decay, and come to nothing, unless impregnated with the farina of the same plant, or some other of the same kind; the stamina also serve for the conveyance of the male seed of the plant to be per-

fected

Fected in the apices, which, when ripe, burst forth in little particles like dust; some of them fall into the orifice of the pistil, and are either conveyed thence into the utricle, to fecundify the female ova, or lodged in the pistil, where, by their magnetic virtue, they draw the nourishment from the other parts of the plant into the embryos of the fruit, making them swell, grow, &c.

In flowers that turn down, as the Cyclamen, and the Imperial Crown, the pistil is much longer than the stamina, that their dust may fall from their apices in sufficient quantities on the pistil, for the business of impregnation.

Mr. Geoffroy assures us, That in all the observations he had made, the cutting off the pistil before it could be impregnated by the farina, actually rendered the plant barren for the season, and the fruit abortive.

In many kinds of plants, as the Oak, Pine, Willow, &c. the flowers, Mr. Geoffroy observes, have their stamina and apices, whose farina may easily impregnate the rudiments of the fruit, which are not far off.

Indeed there is some difficulty in reconciling this system with a certain species of plants, which bear flowers without fruit; and another species of the same kind and denomination, which bear fruit without flowers; such are the Palm, Hemp, Hop, Poplar, &c. which are hence distinguished into male and female; for how should the farina of the male here, come to impregnate the ova of the female?

This difficulty Mr. Geoffroy solves, by supposing the wind to be the vehicle that conveys the male dust to the female uterus, which is confirmed by an instance of Jovianus Potanus, of a single female Palm-tree growing in a forest, which never bore fruit, till, having risen above the other trees of the forest, and being then in a condition to receive the farina of the male by the wind, it began to bear fruit in abundance.

As to the manner wherein the farina fecundifies, Mr. Geoffroy advances two opinions:

First, That the farina being always found of a sulphureous composition, and full of subtil and penetrating parts (as appears from its sprightly odour) which, falling on the pistils of the flowers, there resolves, and the subtilest parts of it, penetrating the substance of the pistil, excite a fermentation, which putting the latent juices of the young fruit in motion, occasions the parts to unfold the young plant that is inclosed in the embryo of the seed.

In this hypothesis, the plant in miniature is supposed to be contained in the seed, and to want only a proper juice to unfold its parts, and to make them grow.

The second opinion is, That the farina of the male plant is the first germ or semen of the new plant, and stands in need of nothing to enable it to grow or unfold, but a suitable nidus with the juice it finds prepared in the embryo of the seed or ovary.

It may be observed, that these two theories of vegetable generation bear a strict analogy to those two of animal generation, viz. either that the young animal is in the semen masculinum, and only stands in need of the juice of the matrix to cherish and bring it forth; or that the female ovum contains the animal, and requires only the male seed to excite a fermentation.

Mr. Geoffroy rather makes the proper seed to be in the farina, inasmuch as the best microscopes do not discover the least appearance of any bud in the little embryos of the grains, when they are examined, before the apices have shed their dust.

In leguminous plants, if the petala and stamina be removed, and the pistil, or that part which becomes the pod, be viewed with the microscope before the flower be open, those little green transparent vesiculæ, which are to become grains, will appear in their natural order, yet still shewing nothing else but the mere coat, or skin of the grain.

If you continue to observe the flowers as they advance for several days successively, you will find them to swell, and, by degrees, to become replete with a limpid liquor; in which, when the farina comes to be shed, and the leaves of the flower to fall, there may be observed a little greenish speck, or globule, floating about at large.

There is not at first any appearance of an organization in this little body; but in time, as it grows, you may begin to distinguish two little leaves like two small horns; as the little body grows, the liquor diminishes insensibly, till at length the grain becomes quite opake; and upon opening it, the cavity will be found filled with a young plant in miniature, consisting of a little germ, or plantula, a little root, and the lobes of the Bean, or Pea.

The manner wherein this germ of the apex enters the vesicula of the grain, is not very difficult to determine: for, besides that the cavity of the pistil reaches from the top to the embryos of the grains, or those vesiculæ, have a little aperture corresponding to the extremity of the cavity of the pistil, so that the small dust, or farina, may easily fall, or find an easy passage in the aperture in the mouth of the vessels, which is the embryo of the grain.

The aperture, or cicatricula, is much the same in both grains; and it is easily observed in Peas, Beans, &c. without a microscope.

Dr. Patrick Blair, treating of the generation of plants, says, That a vegetative life is common to them, as well as animals; and that the propagation or production of the species is the effect of the vegetative, not the sensitive life in animals, as well as in plants; and that if there be a necessity of the concurrence of two different sexes in animals, at the beginning or generating of the species, the same necessity must be in plants too; for as a cow, a mare, a hen, a she-reptile, an insect, &c. cannot produce an animal without the male, no more can it be supposed, that a plant can produce fertile seed without the concurrence of the male plant, or the male parts of the plant.

Mr. Ray says, That he will not deny, that both trees and herbs may produce fruit, and even come to maturity, without the male seed being sprinkled upon them. For though most birds do not lay eggs without congress of the male, yet the hen often does it without copulating with the cock, but then these eggs are barren and wind eggs; just so, though a female plant may produce seed of itself, yet that seed is never fertile. For,

First, As the work of generation in animals does not proceed from their animal or sensitive life but from their vegetative, which being the same as in plants, that operation must be performed after the same manner in both; therefore, as there is a necessity of two different sexes in animals, it must be so too in plants.

Secondly, As passive seminal matter in female animals cannot be productive or fertile of itself, without being impregnated, animated, or its particles set in motion and dilated by the active principles of the male seminal matter; neither can the female seed in plants be rendered fertile, until it be impregnated by the farina foecundans from the male parts of the plants.

As to the flowers of plants, if they were not assisting to, or if there were not some extraordinary use from them in the perfection of the seed, they would not be so often observed upon plants as they are. But since there is no fruit or seed without a previous flower; and since where the one is obvious the other is conspicuous, and since one is scarce to be observed with the naked eye, neither is the other; this implies a relation between them, that the one of them is not to be expected without the other.

It is true, there may be flowers upon a plant, where the fruit is seldom seen, especially in these northern climates; such as the Pervinca, the Nymphæa alba minima, and several others; where the plant exhausts
the

the nutritious juice, in pushing forth tendrils or creeping roots, which so weaken the plants, as not to be able to bring the fruit to perfection; but there is no fruit or seed to be seen, unless a flower has been sent as a messenger before it, to give notice of its approach; though it is not always upon the same plant, yet it is still upon some other plant of the same species; for the flowers are to be seen upon distinct plants, different branches, or different parts of the branch from the fruit, in the Abies, Corylus, Nux Juglans, &c. the Mercurialis, Spinachia, &c.

But the fruit never appears, or never begins to increase upon these plants, till the flower is spent and gone; therefore they must serve for another use, than to be merely ornamental; for if that were their principal use, they would be always conspicuous, which they are not for the most part in apetalous flowers; and they would always be to be seen, and never be hid; which is not so in the Asarum, Hydrocotyle, &c. where, though the flower is large enough in proportion to the fruit, yet it is not to be seen, unless the leaf be turned up, and both flower and fruit be narrowly searched for.

The Frumenta and Gramina have their stamineous flowers; yet in some of them the flower is seldom to be seen, unless the spike be shaken; and then the apices will appear.

The Polypodium, and other capillary plants, have regular flowers, which precede the minute capsulæ or seed-vessels, but neither of them are conspicuous without a microscope.

From these instances it appears, that the flowers are not constantly a guard to preserve the tender embryos from the injuries of the air, for then the flowers must always have been upon the same pedicle with the fruit.

Therefore, since the appearance of the flower is the first step towards the production of the seed, whether both be upon the same pedicle or not, it necessarily follows, that the one must contribute towards the bringing of the other to perfection.

The antients taking notice, that several plants did produce flowers and had no seeds, and that other plants of the same species, and sown from the same seed, did produce the seed without a previous flower, they were ready to call the one male, and the other female, without any notion that the one was assisting to the other; for they looked upon such flowers to be only barren; and therefore they called those which had flowers female, and those that produced the fruits, male plants. Thus Mercurialis is called Spicata Fœmina, and Testiculata Mas. That which produces the fruit must needs be the female, as the female animal brings forth the fœtus; therefore the testiculata must needs be the female, and the spicata the male.

Wherever the plants are annual, these with the flowers, and such as have the seed, are always near to each other; but where the root is perennial, and where the plant is more frequently propagated by the root than the seed, the case alters; for there being no need of the seed to propagate the plant, there is the less need of the flower to be nearer to the plant which produces the seed.

So the Spinachia and the Lupulus are frequently seen to grow, to produce the seed, and the other the squamous fruit; when the plants which produce the male flowers of the one or the other, are at some distance. And this is so far from being an objection against the necessity of two sexes in plants as well as in animals, that it is an argument to confirm it; for it shews the wonderful contrivances in order to preserve the species, when the ordinary means of propagating it by the seed cannot be so conveniently attained.

These, and more that might be produced, being evident proofs of two sexes in plants, as well as in animals, we shall in the next place, give some experiments to confirm this in a negative way, as have been already done in a positive.

When plants have been deprived of their male flowers,

or male parts in the flower, they either produced no seed at all, or if they did, they became abortive, dried up, or dwindled away; or though the seeds did come to perfection, they were barren; or did not produce.

Experiment 1. Mr. Geoffroy having cut off all the stamineous tufts of male flowers from the top of the stalk in the Maiz or Turky-wheat, as soon as they appeared, and before the spike loaded with the embryos of the semen had put forth from the alæ of the leaves, several of these embryos decayed and dried up after they were pretty big; but some grains upon their pedicles all along the spike swelled considerably, and seemed to be full of the bud, and were consequently fertile, while all the others miscarried, and there was not one spike where the whole seeds did not ripen to the full.

This experiment is a sufficient proof of the use of the male flowers of this plant; for whatsoever that is which flows from the racemi of these flowers, it seems it must be conducive not only for the impregnation of the seed, but also for the growth and impregnation of the fruit.

At present we shall shew, that what nourishment is usually furnished by the pedicle to the embryos, does not appear to be capable to dilate or expand itself, or contribute to the continual supply of nutritious particles, unless the embryos were animated or enlivened by the spirit which should have flowed from the male flowers; so that they were so debilitated and weakened, in ascending from the body of the plant towards the embryos, before they could arrive at them, that they which otherwise might have served for the augmentation and increase of all the embryos upon the spike, could not now do any thing more than contribute to the ripening of a few. And although Mr. Geoffroy might have imagined, that these few seeds which came to perfection were fertile also, because they were full of germs, yet he could not be sure of that, unless he had sown the same seeds next season, and tried whether they would chit or not.

Gardeners who buy Onion and Leek-seed brought from Strasburgh, commonly try the following experiment: they put a few of the seeds into a pot of water mixed with earth, and if they find they begin to spring, or send forth the seminal leaf or fibre of the root, after a few days, they judge of the produce of it; and notwithstanding all the seeds without this trial may seem to be productive, being equally firm, hard, and solid, perhaps not more than one third of them will prove fertile.

And this barrenness may proceed, either because they had never been impregnated by the male parts of the flower, or that they had been too much exposed to the air; being some time or other too much moistened, and not afterwards been carefully dried, or have been kept too long, by which neglect they lose their spirit or life.

Now, if the fulness, solidity and firmness of a seed is not a sure sign of its fertility, then Mr. Geoffroy might have been mistaken in his opinion of the fertility of these seeds in the Maiz, since he did not make any trial of it, by committing it to the ground.

In like manner, as to his second experiment of the Mercurialis Dioscoridis, where he raised some plants which had the fruit, and others which had the stamineous flowers, and removed the floriferous plants before the flowers were blown, every one of the seeds upon the fructiferous plants, except five or six, miscarried; which seeds were so full, that he was persuaded they were capable of producing new plants, and the like was found by Camerarius in the Cannabis. Yet inasmuch as neither of them tried the experiment, by sowing the same seed the second year, they could not be sure but that they might have failed in their expectation.

Mr. Bobart, overseer of the physic-garden at Oxford, many years since, which was before the doctrine of the different sexes of plants was well understood, being herbarizing, found a plant of the Lychnis sylvestris simplex,

ſimplex, no apices; and taking notice that this was not only in one, but in all the flowers upon the ſame plant, he imagined it might be a new ſpecies; and therefore marked the plant, and took care to have it preſerved till the ſeeds were ripe; and then, they being full, hard, and firm, and to outward appearance full of germ, he ſowed them in a proper place in the garden the next ſeaſon, but not a plant ſprung up from them.

Theſe and other inſtances, ſet the opinion of the different ſexes of plants upon another footing than has been received by moſt of our modern authors; for it imports, that it is not the nouriſhment of the groſs ſubſtance of the ſeed itſelf which is hereby meant, nor the increaſe of the ſeed-veſſel, which is thereby deſigned; for (as is already obſerved) a hen can lay an egg, without having before had congreſs with a cock; and this, when newly laid, ſhall be of the ſame bigneſs, colour, taſte, and ſmell, with another egg which has been cocked (as they call it;) i. e. which has been fecundated by the maſculine ſeminal materies: but the difference will appear, when both are put under the hen, in order to be hatched; for the one ſhall pullulate or chit, and the other ſhall become fetid and rot.

The caſe is juſt the ſame with the ſeed of a plant, it may be augmented and increaſed in its bulk; it may become firm, hard, and ſolid, and have all the tokens of a perfect ripeneſs; the ſeed-veſſels may be enlarged, and the pulp or parenchyma of the fruit may be augmented; and yet the particles of the ſeed may remain crude, indigeſted, and incapable to be explicated and dilated, or ſet in a ſuitable motion, whereby to protrude the fibrilla of the root at one end, and the ſeminal leaves at the other; except it has before received ſome extraneous matter, or ſome active particles from the male parts of the flower, or from the male flower itſelf.

In order to confirm the neceſſity of two ſexes of plants, as well as in animals, this familiar conſideration may be added: that the fertility or barrenneſs of any tree, in the more or leſs fruitful ſeaſons, may be known to ignorant or leſs curious perſons, by the quantity of the flowers which appear in the ſpring time; and that not only in trees alone, where the flower and fruit are upon one and the ſame foot-ſtalk, but alſo in ſuch trees, where the flowers are upon diſtinct trees, or ſeparate places upon the ſame tree; for it is eaſy to determine by the catkins or iuli upon the Walnut, Filbert, or Hazle-trees, whether ſuch or ſuch trees will be fertile or barren for the enſuing ſeaſon, before any of the embryos begin to break, be puſhed forth, or appear.

Having already treated of the male and female parts of flowers, we ſhall next conſider their uſe.

Flowers, in this reſpect, may aptly be divided into that of male flowers, which (as has been before obſerved) were formerly reputed barren; and the plants which produce them were alſo called female plants, becauſe thoſe perſons not having any notion of different ſexes in plants, they were called female, upon account of their weakneſs; or if they had any thought of ſexes in them, it was only illuſive.

The ancients were ignorant of thoſe which are now-a-days called hermaphrodite flowers; and they, not having a true notion of ſexes of plants, could not imagine that the parts of both ſexes ſhould be in one flower, upon one and the ſame foot-ſtalk.

And although hermaphrodite animals bear the leaſt proportion in the animal kingdom, yet hermaphrodites have the greateſt ſhare in the vegetable, though they are not ſo numerous as they have been ſuppoſed to be; for upon a ſtrict examination it will be found, that a great many more plants have diſtinct male and female ſexes, than was formerly believed.

The neceſſity of different ſexes in plants having been demonſtrated, and that the female ſeed, though it ſhould ripen to the full, cannot be fertile, except it be impregnated by what it receives from the male parts of flowers, we ſhall next explain the organs of generation in both ſexes.

In the animal œconomy, there are, beſides thoſe veſſels that are deſtinated for nutrition, and the ſecretion of the ſeveral juices in the body, ſpermatic veſſels, which conſiſt of præparantia, deferentia, and continentia ſemen. The præparantia in males, are the blood-veſſels and the teſtes; the one conveys the blood, and the other ſeparates the ſemen from blood, and elaborates it.

So likewiſe in plants there are veſſels that receive the nutritious particles from the earth, and convey it to the extremity of the plant; ſome of which tend directly to the leaf, and others to the flowers.

Thoſe which go to the foot-ſtalk of the flower may not improperly be called ſpermatic-veſſels, for it is from them that the ſeminal particles in male, female, and hermaphrodite flowers are ſeparated; therefore the foot-ſtalks of the hermaphrodite flowers are proportionably larger than thoſe either of the male or female; they have a double office, and contribute ſucceſſively to both.

In thoſe where the calyx becomes the fruit, the greateſt ſupply is furniſhed to it firſt, and diſtributed in its cortical parts, as is viſible in the Roſe; in which the foot-ſtalk is ſo far enlarged at firſt, as to be of an equal bigneſs with the bud.

After the calyx is thus formed, the next diſtribution is to the inner or centrical part of the flower, which Dr. Grew calls attire, and where the piſtillum becomes the fruit; the piſtillum and ſtylus are formed at the ſame time with the ſtamina and apices.

The ſtylus at the very firſt acquire both its due length and bigneſs; for the nutritious particles aſcending in the center never ſtop till the ſtylus is ſtretched out to its full length; and in ſuch as are furniſhed with a peculiar apex, that is formed firſt; the neck of the ſtylus, or that part next to it, is the biggeſt; from thence it gradually decreaſes in its groſſneſs, till it comes to the piſtillum. This is eaſily perceived by thoſe who will take the pains to open the bud of a Lily, Tulip, &c. before they are half blown.

The ſtamen is furniſhed next with an extraordinary ſupply of the nutritious particles before the flower is blown; theſe, whether fewer or more, are at firſt brought to their proportional largeneſs, being round and juicy.

The apex is the third which receives this extraordinary ſupply of the nouriſhment, for after that the ſtylus is formed, that it may lean to it after the veſſels of the ſtamen and ſummit are extended to their full length, and ſo formed, that they can convey ſuch an extraordinary quantity of particles as may fill up the capacity of the apex, it is then more enlarged than ever after; for if the flower of a Lily be opened before it be blown, the apex will be found to be full as long as the ſtamen; for as the one half of the apex covers the ſtamen, fixed to its center, ſo the other half of it is ſo far extended above the ſtamen, as the ſtamen remained uncovered below it, towards the pedicle or foot-ſtalk.

The fourth part of a flower is the petala, which receives this extraordinary ſupply of nouriſhment before the blowing; theſe upon the reverſe, are firſt enlarged towards the pedicle, and are afterwards extended and ſtretched forth in proportion to the enlargement of the attire; at firſt they are all groſſer, and more ſucculent towards the origin, and gradually become thinner and broader. The ſtamina of monopetalous flowers do, for the moſt part, ariſe partly from the petalon itſelf, and partly from the calyx; eſpecially if the ſtamina correſpond in number to the petala, as in the Hexapetalæ, or Polypetalæ Liliaceæ of Tournefort, where every ſtamen ariſes oppoſite to the middle of the petalon.

This obſervation (how and when this more than ordinary ſupply of nouriſhment is carried to the flowers) eaſily demonſtrates wherein the analogy of the organs of generation in plants and animals conſiſts.

In animals, the ſeminal matter is received by proper veſſels from the ſame blood from whence the other ſecretions, fit for the preſervation of the animal œconomy

nomy

nomy proceed; fo that the blood in animals being the fame with the fap in plants, and both being conveyed after the fame manner throughout the feveral bodies, it neceffarily follows, that the one as well as the other, muft have proper veffels for fecretion of the feminal matter.

Let it then be confidered, that the fap or nutritious juice afcends in common to the pedicle of the flower, as the blood flows by the aorta defcendens; and that at the calyx or bottom of the flower, fome fhare goes to one part of it, and fome to another; as the aorta fends one branch to the fpermatic veffels, and the remainder of it goes to perform the other functions; and as a part of the fap is feparated by the pedicle of the flower, when the remainder is diftributed throughout the remaining parts of the plant, fo the arteria præparans goes directly to the teftes in the males, and ovarium in the female: and in flowers fome veffels tend directly to the calyx (if it becomes the fruit) or to the perianthium (if there be any,) fome to the petala, fome to the ftamina, fome to the piftillum or uterus, as it is called by Malpighius.

Thefe things being ferioufly reflected on, we muft of neceffity conclude,

1. That the fame due care is taken to elaborate and prepare the more fubtile and impenetrable particles of the nutritious juice in plants, as of the blood in animals.

2. This fubftance fo prepared, as it muft be defigned for fome extraordinary ufe, fo this ufe can be no other than that of being the means of fecundating the female feed in plants, as the other is of the feminine oval in animals.

If any one fhall take a flower full blown, and pull one of the ftamina from the pedicle, he will find a rough vifcid liquor, like to the fperma, which remains here till its moft fubtle parts have afcended the ftamen, or perhaps the more grofs particles might have remained there, after the moft fubtile had afcended, before the flower was blown; this is as plain and demonftrable as can be in the Lilies, particularly in the Orange Lily, and moft of the Martagon Lilies, there is a contrivance more obvious.

This vifcid liquor afcending by parallel ducts to the apex, there this fubtile matter is retained till it is farther elaborated by the evaporations of the more humid and aqueous particles, by the heat of the fun; and then it becomes a moft fubtile, fine, impalpable duft, which is then faid to be ripe, and is called the farina.

Dr. Blair, after having given the fentiments of feven different authors upon the fubject, proceeds to give his own, without fubfcribing to the fentiment of either the one or the other; and endeavours by a ftrict examination of the flowers themfelves, to find out which of thefe two opinions, fo diametrically oppofite to each other, are moft agreeable to fact.

But before he begins, he lays down this general maxim, which he takes for granted, that nature is uniform in all her operations, and never recedes from thofe rules laid down by the wife Difpofer of all things at the creation, by performing the fame thing after two different and contrary methods; and thence concludes, that if the farina be a congeries of feminal plants in one fpecies, it muft be fo in all.

If there be an open and direct paffage, or though it be not fo direct, yet if by any direct paffage, by which it can be demonftrated, that one fingle grain of the farina can enter every individual feed in one plant, it muft be fo in all; but if neither of thefe hold good, and if it can be proved by ocular infpection, without the affiftance of a microfcope, in thofe very plants exemplified by Mr. Morland, Mr. Geoffroy, and Mr. Bradley, that the farina in fubftance cannot enter the feminal veffel; or if it does, that there is no direct paffage for it to enter each particular feed, after it has fo got into the capfula or filiqua; then he hopes, both their queries, fuppofitions, and affertions, muft fall.

As for the Corona Imperialis, the firft example given by Mr. Morland, the flower of which hangs downwards, though he does not deny but its ftylus may be hollow all the way, and that it may be open at the extremity, yet by its fituation, and feveral other circumftances, it does not feem to him to favour this opinion.

For firft, as there is a continual conflux of particles through the fkin in animal bodies, it is alfo fo in vegetables: this appears by the immediate fading of flowers, or any other part of the plant, after it has been plucked off; which proceeds from the evaporation of the particles in the little tubes, without any more fucceeding in their place.

He thinks it as reafonable to fuppofe, that thefe particles flow out by the hollow ftylus, as by any other part, and alfo more fenfibly there than elfewhere, becaufe of their being concentrated within fuch narrow bounds; and that if thefe particles defcend by the ftylus hanging downwards, the particles, or rather grains of the farina, can never afcend the fame way.

2dly, That if it fhould be granted, that thefe grains did afcend by the ftylus, how do they get into the feminal veffel; that being clofely fhut up, as will appear to any one who fhall obferve it.

3dly, Whereas Mr. Morland fuppofes, that the rain either wafhes it, or the wind fhakes it down the tube, till it reaches the feminal veffel; Dr. Blair obferves, that the extremity which is the upper part of the ftylus in an erect flower, muft be the lower in a dependent one; fo that if either the rain or wind have accefs to it, it muft neceffarily either wafh or drive it away from the feminal veffel, which is now the ftylus.

But here the Doctor takes notice of another contrivance, for anfwering that purpofe, i. e. a fort of a pelvis or ciftern, called by Linnæus nectarium, fituated at the origin or root of each petalon, filled with a vifcous liquor which continues there, and never exceeds its bounds fo long as the petalon is in health: for fince the apices are here fo artfully fixed, that they turn every way with the leaft wind, as Mr. Morland rightly obferves, when they burft, and the farina is driven to and fro, though it cannot fo eafily enter the tube, yet it may conveniently be blown up towards the orifice of the petala furrounding the ftylus, where it is ftopped or faid by this vifcofity, till it has performed its office.

To confirm this, he inftances Mr. Fairchild, who, he fays, being perfuaded that this vifcous liquor did fome way or other contribute towards the fructifying of this plant, but not underftanding how it did fo, he tried the experiment, by wiping this liquor off as foon as it was depofited in the pelvis, and the flower which he fo ferved did not bear any fruit.

And the way the doctor accounts for this is, that the humidity being removed, the farina is no fooner blown upwards, than it immediately falls down, without producing any effect; and that which he takes to be a confirmation of this is, that both Tulips and Fritillarias have this pelvis or bafon, yet it is for the moft part dry and empty; becaufe the flowers of the former being erect, they have no fuch need of this liquor to retain the duft; for that the rain, having immediate accefs to them, may wafh the duft towards the origin of the petala, where it can remain till it has performed its office; whereas the rain having no accefs to the inner furface of the flower of the Corona Imperialis, it is naturally endowed with this humidity, depofited there by feveral excretory ducts, in order to render it fit for the purpofe: and Malpighius himfelf takes notice of this fingularity in this flower, though he afcribes no ufe to it.

The next example propofed by Mr. Morland, is the Yellow Lily, which, according to his figure, is reprefented as having the apices equally high with the top of the ftylus, and the petala over-topping each other; whereas he fays, that by the narroweft infpection he ever could make, the top of the apices (they being then perpendicularly fituated) reaches no higher than the neck of the button upon the top of the ftylus, and that this is before the apices begin to burft and

fhed

thed the duſt; but as ſoon as the flower begins to open, they depart from the ſtylus, and force the petala outwards, by a certain elaſticity, and expand themſelves; this being done, they immediately change their poſture from a perpendicular to an oblique or horizontal one; nor do they ever pour out their duſt or farina, till they can conveniently drop it upon the bottom of the flower, and towards the root of the piſtillum.

But taking it for granted that it was ſo, the top of the ſtylus (which the Doctor calls the button, in oppoſition to the apices ſtaminum,) he ſays, is ſo compact, and of ſo firm a ſubſtance, that it is next to impoſſible, that the farina in ſubſtance, or in integral parts, can paſs through it.

If the integral parts, the complete grain, the minute globuli, in which the whole ſeminal plant is contained, cannot then enter, the whole compound muſt be diſſolved, and the minute ſeminal particles in this ſmall grain of duſt muſt be diſunited; and if ſo, how ſhall theſe again come to cement, ſo as to make up one continued body? or how ſhall this little body, ſo united, penetrate a ſecond time the partition-wall betwixt the ſtylus and piſtillum? and again, how ſhall it find out its way to its neſt, in the proper embryo of the ſeed? The Doctor takes notice of the White Lily, the Orange Lily, the Martagon Lily, &c. as objections to the opinions of Mr. Morland, Bradley, &c. and alſo mentions the Iris, as a moſt pregnant inſtance, that the farina cannot ſo much as come at the piſtillum; for having ſix petals, the three ſtamina with long apices lie hid between the three petala which hang downwards, and three large expanſions of the bifid ſtylus, and the upper part of the down-hanging petalon: the farina can never reach the center of the ſtylus, though it were hollow, which it is not, but muſt deſcend along its outſide, to the top and outſide of the rudiment of the fruit, there to emit its effluvia. Theſe inſtances he concludes, are ſufficient proof, that the farina cannot enter the ſtylus, penetrate into the piſtillum, or inner part of the ſeminal veſſel, nor have the leaſt acceſs to the embryo of the ſeed. As to the objection, that there is not paſſage ſufficient to admit the male ſeed into the uterus, or even into the ovaries, it is thus anſwered:

If it be conſidered how every flower, when it is prepared for the act of receiving the male ſeed, is ſo much under the influence of the ſun, that the petals open at its approach, and ſhut up again at its departure, it very well explains how the pi:tillum, or female parts of generation, are relaxed at one time more than another, i. e. that the female parts are more relaxed at the opening of the flower, than when the flower is ſhut up; for the flower-leaves adhering to the bottom of the piſtillum, muſt conſequently, when they bend back, put every part of the piſtillum into a different poſture to that in which it was when the petals were ſhut.

And it is certain, that it is the preſence of the ſun that ripens the male duſt in the apices, and opens the little caſes in which it is contained, giving them a ſpringineſs that flings forth that duſt as ſoon as it is ripe, ſo as to ſcatter it to a conſiderable diſtance. The female parts are at this time dilated by the opening of the flower-leaves, and the apices and chives, concurring at the ſame time in flinging forth their male duſt, anſwer the ſame end in the generation of plants, that the act of copulation does among animals.

Having thus given ſeveral reaſonings and arguments uſed by various authors, who have made it their ſtudy to inveſtigate the mode of generation of vegetables, whether the impregnation of them proceeds from the farina fœcundans, or male duſt, entering the uterus of plants in ſubſtances, or by effluvia, I ſhall not take upon me to determine the diſpute; eſpecially ſince Mr. Boyle has proved, that all effluvia are ſubtile particles of matter; ſo that it matters not how ſmall or minute theſe particles are, ſince a body in its firſt ſtate may be ſo minute as to be ſcarcely perceptible.

I ſhall therefore conclude with mentioning a few experiments of my own, which I communicated to Dr. Patrick Blair, which he improved as a proof of his opinion of effluvia; and Mr. Bradley alſo, as a proof of the farina entering the uterus in ſubſtance, and leave the curious enquirer to determine on that ſide of the queſtion, to which reaſoning and experiment ſhall influence him.

I ſeparated the male plants of a bed of Spinach from the female; and the conſequence was, that the ſeed did ſwell to the uſual bigneſs, but when ſown it did not grow afterwards; and ſearching into the ſeed, I found it wanted the punctum vitæ, or what Geoffroy calls the germen.

I ſet twelve Tulips by themſelves, about ſix or ſeven yards from any other, and as ſoon as they blew, I took out the ſtamina with their ſummits ſo very carefully, that I ſcattered none of the male duſt; and about two days afterwards I ſaw bees working on a bed of Tulips, where I did not take out the ſtamina; and when they came out, they were loaded with the farina or male duſt on their bodies and legs; and I ſaw them fly into the Tulips; where I had taken out the ſtamina, and when they came out, I found they had left behind them ſufficient to impregnate theſe flowers, for they bore good ripe ſeeds which afterward grew.

In a parcel of Savoys, which were planted for ſeed near white and red Cabbages, the ſeeds, when ſown, produced half red, and ſome white Cabbages, and ſome Savoys with red ribs, and ſome neither one ſort nor the other, but a mixture of all ſorts together in one plant, which I ſuppoſe might happen by the effluvia of the different ſorts impregnating the uterus of each other.

In a letter communicated by Paul Dudley, Eſq; to the Royal Society, written from New England, he mentions the interchanging of the colours of the Indian Wheat, if the various colours are planted in rows near each other; but if they are planted ſeparately, they conſtantly keep to their own colour; and this interchanging of colours has been obſerved, when the diſtance between the rows of Corn has been ſeveral yards, though he ſays, if there happens to be a high board fence between the different coloured Corns, the alteration of colours is entirely prevented.

It is from different flowers impregnating each other, that the ſeveral varieties have been produced; and this gives new light to the floriſts, for raiſing a much greater variety of flowers; for by planting the different coloured flowers near each other, ſo that the flowers when fully blown may be intermixed, their farina will impregnate each other, ſo that the ſeeds will produce variegated flowers partaking of both colours. But it muſt be obſerved, that flowers of different genera will not impregnate each other, therefore the plants muſt be of the ſame genus which are placed together.

Cucumbers and Melons always produce male and female flowers upon different parts of the ſame plant; the male flower (which appears upon a ſlender footſtalk, and has a large ſtyle in the middle, covered with an Orange-coloured farina) is by the gardeners commonly called falſe bloſſoms, and are ſometimes by unſkilful perſons pulled off ſoon after they appear, ſuppoſing that they weaken the plants, if ſuffered to remain, which is a very great miſtake; for, in order to try this experiment, I planted four holes of Melons in a place pretty far diſtant from any other; and when the flowers began to appear, I conſtantly pulled off all the male flowers from time to time before they opened; the conſequence was, that all the young fruit dropt off ſoon after they appeared, and not one ſingle fruit remained to grow to any ſize, though the vines were equally ſtrong with thoſe which I had planted in another place, where I ſuffered all the flowers to remain upon them, from which I had a great quantity of fruit. But this doctrine is now ſo well eſtabliſhed among the gardeners, being confirmed by experience, that they now carry the male flowers of the Cucumbers and Melons to the female, if there are none
ſituated

fituated very near them, and gently ftrike the farina o the male, into the bofom of the female flowers, and thereby fet the young fruit, which would otherwife drop off.

There are fome perfons, who ftill object to this theory of the generation of plants, from having obferved fome plants, which were termed female, growing fingly, and at a very great diftance from any male plants of the fame kind, which had for fome years produced feeds which were perfect, and grew when fown; and indeed I was myfelf a little ftaggered in my opinion, on having obferved a female plant of the white Briony, which grew fingly in a garden, where there were no other plants of the fame kind; which for feveral years produced berries, which grew and flourifhed perfectly well. This put me upon examining the plant more carefully than I had before done, when I found there were great numbers of male flowers intermixed with the female, on the fame plant; and fince then I have frequently found the fame in many other plants, which are fometimes male and female in different plants, yet have fometimes both fexes on the fame plant; fo that the objections which have been made to this doctrine, may not have proper evidence for their fupport.

It is certain, that the female plants may produce fruit, without the impregnation of the male; but it is not certain, that this fruit or feed will, if fown, produce another plant. What has been fo often related by travellers and hiftorians, of the neceffity of the male Palm-tree being near the female, in order to render it fruitful, hath been fully confirmed by Father Labat, in his account of Africa, where he has treated of the feveral forts of Palms: he fays, that he obferved in Martinico a large Palm-tree, which grew by the fide of a convent, which produced plenty of fruit, though there was no other Palm-tree growing within two leagues of this; but he alfo obferved, that none of thefe fruit would grow, though they had made many trials of them; fo that they were obliged to procure fome fruit from Barbary, in order to propagate thefe trees. He likewife adds, that the fruit which grew on this female tree, never ripened fo perfectly, nor was fo well tafted, as thofe which came from trees which had ftood near fome of the male: therefore we may conclude, that the fruit or feed may be produced by the female plants of moft kinds, without the affiftance of the male fperm, which may appear to fight perfect, and fit to produce others; but if we examine the feeds, we fhall find that moft of them have not the germ or little plant inclofed, nor will grow if they are fown.

From thefe and many other experiments, it is very plain, that there is a neceffity that the embryo of the female flower fhould be impregnated by the farina or male duft, in order to render the fruit perfect; but how, or in what manner it is performed, is what we can only guefs at, fince in the generation of animals, our greateft naturalifts differ very much in their opinions; nor can any of them afcertain any particular method how it is performed. I fhall therefore conclude with quoting the words of the Rev. Dr. Hales, which are a moft ingenious fummary of the whole doctrine of the generation of plants.

" If I (fays he) may be allowed to indulge conjecture
" in a cafe in which the moft diligent enquirers are,
" as yet, after all their laudable refearches, advanced
" but little farther than mere conjecture, I would
" propofe it to their confideration, whether from the
" manifeft proof we have, that fulphur ftrongly at-
" tracts air, a hint may not be taken, to confider
" whether this may not be the primary ufe of the fa-
" rina fœcundans, to attract or unite with elaftic or
" other refined active particles. That this farina
" abounds with fulphur, and that a very refined fort,
" is probable from the fubtile oil which chymifts ob-
" tain from the chives of Saffron; and if this be the
" ufe of it, was it poffible that it could be more aptly
" placed for the purpofe on very moveable apices

" fixed on the flender points of the ftamina, whereby
" it might eafily, with the leaft breath of wind, be
" difperfed in the air, thereby furrounding the plant,
" as it were, with an atmofphere of fublimed fulphu-
" reous pounce? for many trees and plants abound
" with it, which uniting with the air particles, may,
" perhaps, be infpired at feveral parts of the plant,
" and efpecially at the piftillum, and be thence con-
" veyed to the capfula feminalis, efpecially towards
" evening, and in the night, when the beautiful pe-
" tala of the flowers are clofed up, and they, with all
" the other parts of the vegetable, are in a ftrongly
" imbibing ftate. And if to thefe united, fulphureous
" and aereal particles, we fuppofe fome particles of
" light to be joined (for Sir Ifaac Newton has found,
" that fulphur attracts light ftrongly;) then the re-
" fult of thefe three by far the moft active principles
" in nature, will be a punctum faliens to invigorate
" the feminal plant; and thus we are at laft con-
" ducted, by the regular analyfis of vegetable nature,
" to the firft enlivening principle of their minuteft
" origin."

GENISTA. Lin. Gen. Plant. 766. Tourn. Inft. R. H. 643. tab. 412. Broom; in French, *Genêt.*

The CHARACTERS are,

The empalement of the flower is of one leaf, tubulous, and divided into two lips; the upper lip is deeply cut into two, and the under into three equal parts. The flower is of the butterfly kind; the ftandard is oval, acute, and remote from the keel, being wholly reflexed; the wings are a little fhorter than the ftandard, and are loofe: the keel is erect, and longer than the ftandard, and is indented at the top. It hath ten ftamina joined in two bodies, which are fituated in the keel, terminated by fingle fummits. In the center is an oblong germen, fupporting an afcending ftyle, crowned by an acute twifted ftigma. The germen afterward becomes a roundifh turgid pod with one cell, opening with two valves, inclofing kidney-fhaped feeds.

This genus of plants is ranged in the third fection of Linnæus's feventeenth clafs, which includes the plants with flowers having ten ftamina, joined in two bodies; and to this he adds fome of Tournefort's fpecies of Spartium, and the Geniftella of Tournefort.

The SPECIES are,

1. GENISTA (*Sagittalis*) ramis ancipitibus articulatis; foliis ovato-lanceolatis. Hort. Cliff. 355. *Jointed Broom, with two-edged branches, and jointed, oval, fpear-fhaped leaves.* Chamæ Genifta fagittalis. C. B. P. 395. *Dwarf arrow-fhaped Broom.*

2. GENISTA (*Florida*) foliis lanceolatis, ramis ftriatis teretibus racemis fecundis. Hort. Cliff. 355. *Broom with fpear-fhaped leaves, and erect taper branches abounding with flowers.* Genifta tinctoria Hifpanica. C. B. P. 395. *Spanifh Dyers Broom.*

3. GENISTA (*Tinctoria*) foliis lanceolatis glabris ramis ftriatis teretibus erectis. Hort. Cliff. 355. *Broom with fpear-fhaped leaves which are acute, and taper channelled branches proceeding from the fide of the ftalk.* Genifta tinctoria Germanica. C. B. P. 395. *Common Dyers Broom, or Wood-waxen.*

4. GENISTA (*Purgans*) fpinis terminalibus, ramis teretibus ftriatis, foliis lanceolatis fimplicibus pubefcentibus. Lin. Sp. 999. *Broom with taper-ftreaked branches terminated by fpines, and fimple, fpear-fhaped, hairy leaves.* Genifta five fpartium purgans. J. B. 1. p. 404.

5. GENISTA (*Candicans*) foliis ternatis fubtus villofis, pedunculis lateralibus fubquinqueflofis foliatis, leguminibus hirfutis. Amœn. Acad. 4. p. 284. *Trifoliate Broom with hairy leaves, foot-ftalks from the fide of the branches having five flowers, and hairy pods.* Cytifus Monfpef-fulanus, medicæ folio, filiquis denfe congeftis & villofis. Tourn Inft. 648.

6. GENISTA (*Tridentata*) ramis triquetris fubarticulatis, foliis tricufpidatis. Lin. Sp. Plant. 710. *Broom with three-cornered jointed branches, and leaves ending in three points.* Geniftella fruticofa Lufitanica. Tourn. Inft. 646. *Shrubby Portugal Dyers Broom.*

7. GENISTA (*Pilofa*) foliis lanceolatis obtufis, caule tuberculato decumbente. Hort. Cliff. 355. *Broom with obtufe*

obtuse spear-shaped leaves, and a declining stalk having tubercles. This is the Genista ramosa, foliis Hyperici. C. B. P. 395. Branching Broom with leaves like St. Johnswort.

8. GENISTA (Anglica) spinis simplicibus, ramis floriferis inermibus, foliis lanceolatis. Hort. Cliff. 355. Broom with single spines, flower-branches without spines, and spear-shaped leaves. Genista spartium minus Anglicum. Tourn. Inst. R. H. 645. Small English Broom, called Petty Whin.

9. GENISTA (Hispanica) spinis decompositis, ramis floriferis, inermibus, foliis lanceolatis. Lin. Sp. Plant. 711. Broom with decompounded spines, flower-branches without spines, and narrow hairy leaves. Genista spinosa minor Hispanica villosissima. C. B. P. 395. Most hairy, small, Spanish, prickly Broom.

The first sort grows naturally in France, Italy, and Germany. This plant sends out several stalks from the root, which spread flat on the ground, and divide into many flat branches which are jointed, and their two sides are ridged like a broad sword; these are green and herbaceous, but are perennial. At each of the joints is placed one small spear-shaped leaf, without any foot-stalk. The flowers are produced in close spikes at the ends of the branches; they are yellow, and of the Pea-bloom kind, and are succeeded by short hairy pods, which contain three or four kidney-shaped seeds. The plants flower in June, and the seeds ripen in September.

This sort is propagated by seeds, which, if sown in the autumn, the plants will come up the following spring; but when they are sown in the spring, the plants rarely come up the same year: when the plants come up, they will require no other culture but to keep them clean from weeds, and thin them where they are too close; at Michaelmas they may be transplanted where they are designed to remain, and after that they will only require to be kept clean, for they are very hardy, and will live several years.

The second sort rises with ligneous stalks about two or three feet high, sending out many taper channelled branches which grow erect, garnished with small spear-shaped leaves placed alternate, and are terminated by several spikes of yellow flowers, which are of the Pea-bloom kind; these are succeeded by short pods, which turn black when ripe, and contain four or five kidney-shaped seeds. It flowers in June and July, and the seeds ripen in autumn.

The third sort grows naturally in England. This hath shrubby stalks, which rise about three feet high, garnished with spear-shaped leaves, which are broader, and end in sharper points than those of the former; the branches come out from the side of the stalks, almost their whole length, and do not grow so upright as those of the second; these are terminated by loose spikes of yellow flowers, which are succeeded by pods like those of the second sort. It flowers, and the seeds are ripe about the same time as the former. The branches of the plant are used by the dyers, to give a yellow colour, from whence it is called Dyers Broom, Green-wood, Wood-waxen, or Dyers-weed.

The fourth sort grows naturally about Montpelier. This rises with shrubby, striated, taper stalks four feet high, sending out several branches which are terminated by spines; the leaves are spear-shaped, single, and hairy; the flowers are produced in spikes at the end of the branches, they are larger than those of the other sorts, and are of a paler yellow colour. They appear in June and July, and are succeeded by pods like the former sorts.

This sort is tender, and in severe frosts is often killed in England, where the plants are not protected.

The fifth sort grows naturally about Montpelier. This rises with a woody stalk to the height of seven or eight feet, sending out many slender branches, garnished with trifoliate leaves, hairy on their under side; the upper part of these branches, for more than a foot in length, send out small flowering branches on their side, supporting five yellow flowers. These

appear in June and July, and the seeds ripen in autumn.

The sixth sort hath a low shrubby stalk, which seldom is more than a foot high, sending out several weak branches which are jointed, garnished with small leaves ending in three acute parts. The flowers are produced in loose spikes at the top of the branches, they are of a pale yellow colour, and appear the latter end of June and in July, and the seeds ripen in September. This plant grows naturally in Portugal.

The seventh sort hath a shrubby stalk which declines toward the ground, and is set over with tubercles; it divides into a few small branches, which are garnished with small obtuse leaves. The flowers are disposed in small loose spikes at the end of the branches; they are small, of a pale yellow colour, and are succeeded by short pods filled with kidney-shaped seeds. It flowers in June, and the seeds ripen in autumn. This grows naturally in Germany and France.

The eighth sort grows naturally upon open heaths in many parts of England. It hath a shrubby stalk which rises about two feet high, sending out many slender branches, which are armed with long single spines, and garnished with very small spear-shaped leaves, placed alternate on every side the branches: the flower-branches have no spines; these are short, and have five or six yellow flowers growing in a cluster at the end. They come out in April and May, and are succeeded by short turgid pods, which contain four or five small kidney-shaped seeds. These ripen in July.

The ninth sort grows naturally in Spain. This hath a low shrubby stalk, which sends out many ligneous branches, armed with branching thorns, composed of several sharp thorns, which come out from each other, but the short branches which produce the flowers have no spines; these are garnished with small hairy leaves of different forms, some of them being as narrow as hairs, and others are of the spear-shape; the branches are terminated by clusters of yellow flowers, which are succeeded by short, compressed, hairy pods, filled with kidney-shaped seeds. The whole plant has much the appearance of the common Furz or Gorse, but is very hairy, and the flower-branches being without thorns, are the most obvious distinctions.

All these sorts of Brooms are propagated by seeds, which, if sown in the autumn, will succeed much better than if sown in the spring, and a year will be thereby saved; as these plants send out long, stringy, tough roots, which run deep into the ground, they do not bear transplanting well, especially if they are not removed young; therefore the best way is to sow a few seeds in those places where the plants are designed to remain, and to pull up all except the most promising plants as soon as they are past danger; after this the plants will require no other culture, but to keep them clean from weeds: but where this cannot be practised, the seeds may be sown thin upon a bed of light earth, and when the plants come up, they must be kept clean from weeds till the following autumn, when the plants should be carefully taken up and transplanted where they are designed to remain. They are all very hardy plants except the fourth, fifth, and ninth sorts, which must have a warm sheltered situation and dry soil, otherwise they will not live through the winter, but the others will grow in almost any soil or situation.

GENISTA SPINOSA, the Furz, Whins, or Gorse. See ULEX.

GENTIANA. Lin. Gen. Plant. 285. Tourn. Inst. R. H. 80. tab. 40. [takes its name from Gentius, a king of Illyrium, who first discovered the virtues of this plant.] Gentian, or Fellwort; in French, Gentiane.

The CHARACTERS are,

It hath a permanent empalement, which is cut into five acute segments. The flower hath one petal, which is tubulous, cut into five parts at the top, which are flat. It hath

hath five awl-shaped stamina, which are shorter than the petal, terminated by single summits. In the center is situated an oblong cylindrical germen, having no style, but is crowned by two oval stigmas. The germen afterward becomes an oblong taper-pointed capsule, with one cell, containing many small seeds fastened to the valves of the capsule.

This genus of plants is ranged in the second section of Linnæus's fifth class, intitled Pentandria Digynia, which includes the plants whose flowers have five stamina and two stigmas.

The SPECIES are,

1. GENTIANA (*Lutea*) corollis quinquefidis rotatis verticillatis, calycibus spathaceis. Hall. Helv. 479. *Gentian with quinquefid wheel-shaped petals growing in whorls, and hood-like empalements.* Gentiana major lutea. C. B. P. 187. *Greater yellow Gentian.*

2. GENTIANA (*Pneumonnthe*) corollis quinquefidis campanulatis oppositis peduncularis, foliis linearibus. Lin. Sp. Plant. 228. *Gentian with bell-shaped quinquefid petals placed opposite upon foot-stalks, and very narrow leaves.* Gentiana augustifolia autumnalis major. C. B. P. 188. *Greater narrow-leaved autumnal Gentian.*

3. GENTIANA (*Asclepiades*) corollis quinquefidis campanulatis oppositis sessilibus, foliis amplexicaulibus. Lin. Sp. Plant. 227. *Gentian with bell-shaped quinquefid petals sitting close to the stalk opposite, and leaves embracing the stalk.* Gentian Asclepiades folio. C. B. P. 187. *Gentian with a Swallow-wort leaf.*

4. GENTIANA (*Acaulis*) corollâ quinquefidâ campanulatâ, caulem excedente. Lin. Sp. Plant. 228. *Gentian with a bell-shaped quinquefid petal exceeding the stalk.* Gentiana Alpina latifolia, magno flore. C. B. P. 187. *Broad-leaved Alpine Gentian with a large flower, commonly called Gentianella.*

5. GENTIANA (*Nivalis*) corollis quinquefidis infundibuliformibus, ramis unifloris alternis. Lin. Sp. Plant. 229. *Gentian with funnel-shaped quinquefid petals, and alternate branches having one flower.* Gentiana annua, foliis Centaurii minoris. Tourn. Inst. 81. *Annual Gentian with lesser Centaury leaves.*

6. GENTIANA (*Cruciata*) corollis quadrifidis imberbibus verticillatis sessilibus. Lin. Sp. Plant. 231. *Gentian with quadrifid petals without beards, growing in whorls close to the stalks.* Gentiana cruciata. C. B. P. 188. *Crosswort Gentian.*

7. GENTIANA (*Cilliata*) corollis quadrifidis margine ciliatis. Lin. Sp. Plant. 231. *Gentian with a four-pointed petal, whose border is hairy.* Gentianella cærulea oris pilosis. C. B. P. 188. *Blue Gentian with hairy brims.*

8. GENTIANA (*Utriculosa*) corollis quinquefidis hypocrateriformibus, calycibus plicatis alatis. Lin. Sp. Plant. 229. *Gentian with salver-shaped quinquefid petals, and winged plaited empalements.* Gentiana utriculis ventricosis. C. B. P. 188. *Gentian with a ventricose tube.*

9. GENTIANA (*Centaureum*) corollis quinquefidis infundibuliformibus caule dichotomo. Lin. Sp. Plant. 229. *Gentian with a funnel-shaped, five-pointed petal, and a forked stalk.* Centaurium minus. C. B. P. 278. *Lesser Centaury.*

10. GENTIANA (*Perfoliatum*) corollis octifidis, foliis perfoliatis. Lin. Sp. Plant. 232. *Gentian with an eight-pointed petal, and Thorough-wax leaves.* Centaurium luteum perfoliatum. C. B. P. 278. *Yellow perfoliate Centaury.*

11. GENTIANA (*Spicata*) corollis quinquefidis floribus alternis sessilibus. Lin. Sp. Plant. 230. *Gentian with funnel-shaped five-pointed petals, flowers growing alternate, and sitting close to the stalks.* Centaurium minus spicatum album. C. B. P. 278. *Lesser Centaury with a white spiked flower.*

12. GENTIANA (*Exaltata*) corollis quinquefidis coronatis crenatis, pedunculo terminali longissimo dichotomo. Lin. Sp. 331. *Gentian with a five-pointed petal, a very long foot-stalk, and forked branches.* Centaurium minus maritimum amplo flore cæruleo. Plum. Cat. 3. *Lesser maritime Centaury with a large blue flower.*

The first sort is the common Gentian of the shops,

whose root is one of the principal ingredients in bitters.

This plant has a large thick root of a yellowish brown colour, and a very bitter taste; the lower leaves are of an oblong oval shape, a little pointed at the end, stiff, of a yellowish green, and have five large veins on the back of each, and are plaited. The stalk rises to the height of three or four feet, which is garnished with leaves, growing by pairs at each joint, almost embracing the stalk at their base; these are of the same form with the lower, but diminish gradually in their size to the top. The flowers come out in whorls at the joints, toward the upper part of the stalks, standing on short foot-stalks, whose origin is from the wings of the leaves; these are of a pale yellow, and have one petal, which is divided almost to the bottom, having an oblong cylindrical germen, which afterward swells to an oblong taper capsule, which is bifid at the point, and opens in two cells, filled with small seeds.

It grows naturally in the pastures in Switzerland, and in the mountainous parts of Germany, from whence the roots are brought to England for medicinal use; there is a compound water, and an extract made of them. The root of the Gentian is also one of the principal ingredients in bitters, and is frequently used in many disorders.

But a few years ago, there was a mixture of Henbane roots brought over with Gentian, which was unhappily used, and occasioned great disorders in the persons to whom it was administered; upon which great enquiry was then made to find out what that root could be, some suspecting it to be the root of Deadly Nightshade, and others believing it to be some of the poisonous umbelliferous roots, but on comparing it with some dried roots of the Henbane, I found they were the same. We have likewise an account of the noxious quality of these roots, printed in the Synopsis Stirpium Hibernicarum, which was communicated to the author by Dr. Thomas Molyneux, physician to the state; it was as follows:

The Dean of Clonfert was making some alterations in his garden, and, looking over his workmen, he observed them to dig up many roots, which he took for Skirrets, and therefore ordered some of them to be carried in and dressed for dinner, which was accordingly done; but all those who eat of them were in a short time seized with dizziness in their head, sickness at the stomach, attended with an unusual heat and driness in their throats; and two, who had eaten a larger share than the rest, lost the use of their reason, and became delirious, which continued for some days; and as it appeared evident these disorders were occasioned by the roots, the Dean caused some of them to be planted, that he might be assured what the plant was whose roots had this bad quality; and in the spring, when they put out their leaves, they proved to be the Henbane, which has been noticed by old writers to be possessed of these qualities. And as the disorders which were occasioned by these supposed Gentian roots, were nearly the same, as is above related; I thought it might be of use to insert it here, to caution others against eating of roots which they are unacquainted with.

This plant delights in a light loamy soil and a shady situation, where it will thrive much better than in a light dry soil, or in an open exposure. It is propagated by seeds, which should be sown in pots soon after it is ripe, for if it is kept till the spring, it will not succeed; these pots should be placed in a shady situation, and kept clean from weeds. In the spring the plants will appear, when they must be duly watered in dry weather, and kept clean from weeds till the following autumn; then they should be carefully shaken out of the pots, so as not to break or injure their roots, and a shady border of loamy earth should be well dug and prepared to receive them, into which the plants should be planted at about six inches distance each way, observing to let the top of the roots be a little below the surface of the

ground,

ground, then prefs the earth clofe to the roots; after this they will require no farther care, but to keep them conftantly clean from weeds; and if the following fpring fhould prove dry, they fhould be duly watered, which will greatly forward their growth. In this border the plants may ftand two years, by which time they will be fit to tranfplant where they are defigned to remain; therefore in autumn, fo foon as their leaves decay, they may be removed; but as the roots of thefe plants run deep into the ground, like Carrots, there muft be great care taken in digging them up, not to cut or break their roots, for that will greatly weaken, if it does not kill them. After the plants are well fixed in their places, they require no other culture, but to dig the ground about them early in the fpring before they begin to fhoot, and in the fummer to keep them clean from weeds. The roots of thefe plants will continue many years, but the ftalks decay every autumn; the fame roots do not flower two years together, nor feldom oftener than every third year; but when they flower ftrong, they make a fine appearance; and as thefe delight in fhady moift ground, where but few ornamental plants will thrive, fo they fhould not be wanting in good gardens.

The fecond fort grows naturally in moift paftures in many parts of England, but particularly in the north; this rifes with an upright ftalk about a foot high, garnifhed with fmooth leaves an inch and a half long, and lefs than a quarter of an inch broad; they are placed oppofite, and have no foot-ftalks. The flowers are produced on the top of the ftalk, three or four in number, ftanding upon foot-ftalks alternately above each other; they are large, bell-fhaped, and divided into five points at their brim, and are of a deep blue colour, fo make a fine appearance; thefe come out the latter end of July in the warm parts of England, but in the north they are full a month later.

It may be propagated by feeds in the fame manner as the firft fort, and the plants may be treated in the fame way; but as this fort does not fhoot its roots deep into the ground, it may be tranfplanted with lefs hazard; however, if thefe are removed with a ball of earth to their roots, they will not feel their removal fo much as when the earth is all taken from them. This fort fhould be planted in a ftrong, moift, loamy foil, in which the plants will thrive and flower annually, but in a warm dry foil they will not thrive or flower.

The third fort grows naturally upon the Helvetian mountains; this rifes with an upright ftalk near a foot high, garnifhed with fmooth leaves about two inches long, and three quarters of an inch broad at their bafe, where they embrace the ftalk, but they end in acute points; they are placed oppofite, and are of a fine green, and diminifh in their fize as they are nearer the top; they have five longitudinal veins, which join at both ends, but diverge from each other in the middle. The flowers come out by pairs oppofite, from the bottoms of the leaves, ftanding on fhort foot-ftalks, are pretty large, bell-fhaped, and of a fine blue colour, fo make a fine appearance when they are open. This fort flowers in June and July.

It may be propagated by feeds in the fame manner as the firft fort, and the plants may be treated in the fame way, but they muft have a moift loamy foil, otherwife they will not thrive. It may alfo be propagated by offsets, which may be divided from the roots; thefe fhould be taken off in autumn, which is the beft feafon for removing all thefe forts of plants; but thefe fhould not be removed, or parted oftener than every third year, where they are expected to produce ftrong flowers.

The fourth fort grows naturally on the Alps and Helvetian mountains, but may be propagated with a ball of earth to their roots, has been long cultivated in moft of the curious gardens in Europe; this is commonly known by the title of Gentianella. It is a low plant, the ftalks feldom growing more than three or

four inches high; they are garnifhed with fmooth leaves placed oppofite, which are two inches long, and half an inch broad, fitting clofe to the ftalk. The flowers grow erect on the top of the ftalk, fo ftand quite above them; thefe are often fingle, but fometimes, when the plants are ftrong, there will be four or five at the end of each ftalk; they are large, bell-fhaped, and of a deep azure blue, fo is the fineft of that colour of any flower yet known. It ufually flowers in May, but fometimes the plants flower again in autumn.

This is commonly propagated by parting of the roots, in the fame manner as is before directed for the third fort, but thefe muft not be often tranfplanted, or parted, if they are wanted to flower ftrong; this fort fhould have a foft loamy foil and a fhady fituation, where the plants will thrive and flower well every year.

It may alfo be propagated by feeds, which, in a good foil, the plants will produce in plenty; thefe fhould be fown in autumn, in the fame manner as is before directed for the firft fort; and if the plants are planted in a good foil, they will be ftrong enough to flower the fecond year after they come up, and thefe feedling plants will flower much ftronger than thofe which are propagated by offsets.

The fifth and eighth forts are low annual plants, which grow naturally upon the Alps and other mountainous places in Europe, and are very rarely cultivated in gardens. The fifth feldom rifes more than two inches high, branching out from the root into feveral flender ftalks, garnifhed with very fmall leaves placed by pairs, and each ftalk is terminated by one fmaller blue flower ftanding erect. The eighth fort grows about four inches high, with a fingle upright ftalk of a purple colour. The leaves at the root are oval, but thofe upon the ftalk are narrow, and ftand oppofite. The ftalk is terminated by one blue flower, with a large bellied empalement, which is plaited, and the petal of the flower rifes but a little above the empalement, fo does not make much appearance. After the top flower decays, there are frequently two fmaller flowers which come out from the fide of the ftalk, at the two upper joints; thefe flower after each other, the upper one coming firft, fo that there is a fucceffion of flowers till autumn.

As thefe plants ufually grow upon moift fpongy ground, it is very difficult to cultivate them in gardens; for unlefs they have a foil approaching near to that in which they naturally grow, they will not thrive; the only method to obtain them is, either to fow their feeds in pots, or upon a moift boggy ground in autumn, but it muft be in the fhade; and when the plants come up, they may be thinned, and the furface of the ground about them covered with mofs, which fhould be conftantly kept moift; with this management I have feen the plants thrive and flower very well.

The fixth fort is a perennial plant, which grows naturally upon the Appenines and the Helvetian mountains; this rifes with an upright ftalk about fix inches high, garnifhed with fmooth fpear-fhaped leaves about two inches long, and one broad in the middle, fitting clofe to the ftalk; they are placed oppofite, and each pair of leaves crofs one another, from whence it is called Croffwort Gentian. The flowers are produced in whorls round the ftalks at the upper joints, fitting very clofe to the ftalks, and at the top there is a large clufter growing in the fame form; thefe are of a light blue colour, and appear in May. This may be propagated by feeds, or offsets, in the fame manner as the third and fourth forts, and the plants muft be treated in the fame way.

The feventh fort grows naturally upon the Alps, and other mountainous parts of Europe; this is a low perennial plant, whofe ftalks are very flender, and rarely rife more than three or four inches high, garnifhed with fmall, narrow, acute-pointed leaves, placed in pairs; each ftalk is terminated by one large blue flower, which is hairy on the infide at the brim. This

flowers

flowers in July and Auguſt, and may be propagated and treated in the ſame manner as the third and fourth ſorts.

The ninth ſort is the Leſſer Centaury of the ſhops; this grows naturally upon dry paſtures in moſt parts of England, where it riſes in height proportionable to the goodneſs of the ſoil; for in good land it is frequently a foot high, but in poor ſoils not more than three or four inches. It is an annual plant, with upright branching ſtalks, garniſhed with ſmall leaves placed by pairs. The flowers grow in form of an umbel at the top, and are of a bright purple colour; they come out in July, and the ſeeds ripen in autumn. This plant cannot be cultivated in the gardens.

The tenth ſort grows naturally upon chalky grounds in many parts of England. It is an annual plant, riſing with an upright ſtalk a foot high, garniſhed with oval-pointed leaves, whoſe baſe ſurrounds the ſtalk; they grow by pairs, and are of a gray colour; the ſtalks and leaves are very ſmooth. The flowers grow in form of an umbel on the top of the ſtalk; they are of a bright yellow colour, and are cut into eight parts at the top. Theſe appear in July, and the ſeeds ripen in autumn.

The eleventh ſort is an annual plant, which grows naturally in the ſouth of France and in Italy; this riſes with an upright ſtalk about a foot high, ſending out ſeveral branches toward the top, which are garniſhed by ſmall leaves placed oppoſite. The flowers are produced from the ſide and at the top of the ſtalk, in form of looſe irregular umbels; they are white, and about the ſize of thoſe of the common Centaury.

The twelfth ſort grows naturally in the Weſt-Indies, where it was diſcovered by Father Plumier, and the late Dr. Houſtoun found it growing in plenty at La Vera Cruz, in low moiſt places where the water ſtagnates, but at a remoter diſtance from the ſea. The ſeeds of this plant he ſent to England, which ſucceeded in the Chelſea garden; this riſes with an upright branching ſtalk near two feet high, garniſhed with oblong, ſmooth, acute-pointed leaves, placed oppoſite; the upper part of the ſtalk divides into ſeveral forks, between which are ſix or ſeven long naked foot-ſtalks, each ſuſtaining one large blue flower, divided into five ſegments at the brim. The flowers are ſucceeded by oblong capſules with one cell, filled with ſmall ſeeds.

This is propagated by ſeeds, which muſt be ſown on a hot-bed ſoon after they are ripe, and the plants afterward treated in the ſame manner as other tender annual plants from warm countries, being too tender to thrive in the open air in England. If the ſeeds of this plant are ſown in autumn, in pots placed in the tan-bed of the ſtove, they will ſucceed better than when they are ſown in the ſpring, and the plants will flower early, ſo good ſeeds may be obtained.

GENTIANELLA. See GENTIANA.

GERANIUM. Lin. Gen. Plant. 346. Tourn. Inſt. R. H. 266. tab. 142. [takes its name from Γέϱανϐ, Gr. a crane, or ſtork, becauſe its fruit reſembles the bill of a Crane.] Crane's-bill; in French, Bec de Gruë.

The CHARACTERS are,

The flower hath a permanent empalement, compoſed of five ſmall oval leaves. The flower hath five petals, which are oval, or heart-ſhaped, ſpreading open; theſe are in ſome ſpecies equal, and in others, the upper two are much larger than the three lower. It hath ten ſtamina, which are alternately longer, but are ſhorter than the petals, and are terminated by oblong ſummits. In the bottom of the flower is ſituated a five-cornered germen, ſupporting an awl-ſhaped ſtyle longer than the ſtamina, which is permanent, crowned by five reflexed ſtigmas. The flower is ſucceeded by five ſeeds, each being wrapped up in the buſk of the beak, which is extended the length of the ſtyle, where they are twiſted together at the point, ſo as to form the reſemblance of a ſtork's beak.

This genus of plants is ranged in the ſecond ſection of Linnæus's ſixteenth claſs, which includes thoſe plants whoſe flowers have ten ſtamina, and the male and female organs are joined in one body. Tournefort

places it in the ſixth ſection of his ſixth claſs, in which he ranges the herbs with a Roſe flower, whoſe pointal becomes a fruit with ſeveral capſules.

The SPECIES are,

1. GERANIUM (*Pratenſe*) pedunculis bifloris, foliis ſubpeltatis multipartitis pinnato laciniatis rugoſis acutis, petalis integris. Hort. Cliff. 344. *Crane's-bill with two flowers on each foot-ſtalk, target-ſhaped leaves cut into many acute ſegments, and entire petals.* Geranium batrachiodes, Gratia Dei Germanorum. C. B. P. *Crane's-bill with a Crow-foot leaf, and large blue flowers.*

2. GERANIUM (*Macrorrhizum*) pedunculis bifloris, calycibus inflatis, piſtillo longiſſimo. Hort. Cliff. 343. *Crane's-bill with two flowers on each foot-ſtalk, inflated empalements, and a very long pointal to the flower.* Geranium batrachioides, longius radicatum, odoratum. J. B. *Long-rooted ſweet-ſmelling Crane's-bill, with a Crow-foot leaf.*

3. GERANIUM (*Sanguineum*) pedunculis unifloris, foliis quinquepartitis trifidis orbiculatis. Lin. Sp. Plant. 685. *Crane's-bill with one flower on each foot-ſtalk, and orbicular leaves, which are trifid and divided into five parts.* Geranium ſanguineum, maximo flore. H. Ox. *Bloody Crane's-bill with a larger flower.*

4. GERANIUM (*Lancaſtrenſe*) pedunculis unifloris, foliis quinquepartitis laciniis obtuſis brevibus, caulibus decumbentibus. *Crane's-bill with one flower upon each foot-ſtalk, leaves divided into five parts, whoſe ſegments are ſhort, blunt, and declining ſtalks.* Geranium hæmatodes Lancaſtrenſe, flore eleganter ſtriato. Raii Hiſt. *Bloody Crane's-bill with a variegated flower.*

5. GERANIUM (*Nodoſum*) pedunculis bifloris, foliis caulinis trilobis integris ſerratis, ſummis ſubſeſſilibus. Hort. Cliff. 343. *Crane's-bill with two flowers on each foot-ſtalk, the leaves upon the ſtalks having three entire ſawed lobes, the upper leaves ſitting cloſe to the ſtalk.* Geranium 5. nodoſum. Plateau. Cluſ. Hiſt. *Knotty Crane's-bill.*

6. GERANIUM (*Phæum*) pedunculis bifloris, foliiſque alternis, calycibus ſubariſtatis, caule erecto, petalis undulatis. Lin. Sp. Plant. 681. *Crane's-bill with two flowers on each foot-ſtalk, alternate leaves, bearded empalements, an erect ſtalk, and waved petals to the flower.* Geranium phæum ſive fuſcum, petalis reflexis, folio non maculoſo. H. L. *Brown Crane's-bill with reflexed petals, and leaves not ſpotted.*

7. GERANIUM (*Fuſcum*) pedunculis bifloris, foliis quinquelobatis inciſis, petalis reflexis. *Crane's-bill with two flowers upon each foot-ſtalk, leaves divided into five lobes, which are cut, and the petals of the flowers reflexed.* Geranium phæum ſive fuſcum, petalis rectis ſeu planis, folio maculato. H. L. *Brown Crane's-bill with plain petals, and ſpotted leaves.*

8. GERANIUM (*Striatum*) pedunculis bifloris, altero breviore, foliis quinquelobis medio dilatatis, petalis bilobis venoſo reticulatis. Burm. Ger. *Crane's-bill with two flowers upon each foot-ſtalk, one bigger than the other, leaves having five lobes, and flowers with two lobes.* Geranium Romanum, verſicolor five ſtriatum. Park. Par. *Roman Crane's-bill with ſtriped flowers.*

9. GERANIUM (*Sylvaticum*) pedunculis bifloris, foliis ſubpeltatis quinquelobis inciſo-ſerratis, caule erecto, petalis emarginatis. Flor. Lapp. 266. *Crane's-bill with two flowers on each foot-ſtalk, target-ſhaped leaves with five lobes deeply ſawed, an erect ſtalk, and indented petals to the flower.* Geranium batrachioides montanum noſtras. Ger. *Mountain Crane's-bill with a Crow-foot leaf.*

10. GERANIUM (*Orientale*) pedunculis bifloris, foliiſque oppoſitis, petalis integris, calycibus brevioribus. *Eaſtern Dove's-foot Crane's-bill, with oppoſite leaves, two flowers on each foot-ſtalk, and a ſhort empalement.* Geranium Orientale columbinum, flore maximo, aſphodeli radice. T. Cor. *Oriental Dove's-foot Crane's-bill, with an Aſphodel root and large flowers.*

11. GERANIUM (*Perenne*) pedunculis bifloris, foliis inferioribus quinque-partito-multifidis rotundis, ſuperioribus trilobis, caule erecto. Hudſ. Flor. Ang. 265. *Crane's-bill with two flowers on each foot-ſtalk, the lower leaves having five many-pointed lobes, the upper three,*

three, and an erect stalk. Geranium Columbinum perenne Pyrenaicum maximum. Tourn. Inst. R. H. 268. *Greatest perennial Dove's-foot Crane's-bill of the Pyrennes.*

12. GERANIUM (*Alpinum*) pedunculis longissimis multifloris, calycibus aristatis, foliis bipinnatis. *Crane's-bill with very long foot-stalks sustaining many flowers, bearded empalements, and double wing-pointed leaves.* Geranium Alpinum Coriandri folio, longius radicatum, flore majore purpureo. Michel. *Alpine Crane's-bill with a Coriander leaf, a long root, and a larger purple flower.*

13. GERANIUM (*Argenteum*) pedunculis bifloris, foliis subpeltatis septempartitis trifidis tomentoso-sericeis, petalis emarginatis. Amœn. Acad. 4. p. 324. *Crane's-bill with two flowers on each foot-stalk, target-shaped leaves divided into seven parts, which are silvery, and the petals of the flower indented.* Geranium argenteum Alpinum. C. B. P. 318. *Silvery Alpine Crane's-bill.*

14. GERANIUM (*Maculatum*) pedunculis bifloris, caule dichotomo erecto, foliis quinquepartitis incisis summis sessilibus. Flor. Virg. 78. *Crane's-bill with two flowers on each foot-stalk, upright stalks divided by pairs, and cut leaves divided into five parts, the upper sitting close to the stalk.* Geranium batrachioides Americanum maculatum, floribus obsolete cæruleis. Hort. Elth. 158. *American spotted Crane's-bill with obsolete blue flowers.*

15. GERANIUM (*Bohemicum*) pedunculis bifloris petalis emarginatis arillis hirtis cotyledonibus trifidis medio truncatis. Burm. Ger. 4. *Crane's-bill with two flowers on each foot-stalk, indented petals to the flower, hairy beards, and a trifid leaf.* Geranium annuum minus batrachiodes Bohemicum, purpuro-violaceum. Mor. Hist. 2. 511. *Lesser annual Crane's-bill of Bohemia, with a purple Violet flower.*

16. GERANIUM (*Sibiricum*) pedunculis subunifloris, foliis quinquepartitis acutis foliolis pinnatifidis. Lin. Sp. Plant. 683. *Crane's-bill with one flower on a foot-stalk, leaves divided into five acute parts, and the smaller leaves wing-pointed.*

17. GERANIUM (*Moschatum*) pedunculis multifloris, floribus pentandris foliis pinnatis incisis cotyledonibus pinnatifidis. Burm. Ger. 22. *Crane's-bill with many flowers on each foot-stalk, having five stamina to the flowers, and cut winged leaves.* Geranium cicutæ folio, moschatum. C. B. P. *Musked Crane's-bill, frequently called Muscovy.*

18. GERANIUM (*Gruinum*) pedunculis sub multifloris, floribus pentandris, foliis ternatis lobatis. Burm. Ger. 32. *Crane's-bill with many flowers on a foot-stalk, five stamina to the flower, and ternate lobed leaves.* Geranium latifolium annuum, cæruleo flore, acu longissimâ. H. Ox. *Broad-leaved annual Crane's-bill with a blue flower, and a very long beak.*

19. GERANIUM (*Ciconium*) pedunculis multifloris, calycibus pentaphyllis, floribus pentandris, foliis pinnatis acutis sinuatis. Lin. Sp. Plant. 680. *Crane's-bill with many flowers on each foot-stalk, having five-leaved empalements, five stamina to the flowers, and acute, sinuated, winged leaves.* Geranium Cicutæ folio, acu longissimâ. C. B. P. 319. *Crane's-bill with a Hemlock leaf, and very long beaks to the seed.*

20. GERANIUM (*Viscosum*) pedunculis multifloris, calycibus pentaphyllis, floribus pentandris, foliis bipinnatis multifidis caule erecto. *Crane's-bill with many flowers on each foot-stalk, having five-leaved empalements, flowers with five stamina, and many-pointed winged leaves.* Geranium cicutæ folio viscosum erectum, acu longissimâ. Jussieu. *Erect viscous Crane's-bill with a Hemlock leaf, and very long beaks to the seed.*

21. GERANIUM (*Cucullatum*) calycibus monophyllis, foliis cucullatis dentatis. Hort. Cliff. 345. *Crane's-bill with an empalement of one leaf, and indented hooded leaves.* Geranium Africanum arborescens, ibisci folio rotundo, carlinæ odore. H. L. *African-tree Crane's-bill with a round Marshmallow leaf, and smell of the Carline Thistle.*

22. GERANIUM (*Angulosum*) calycibus monophyllis, foliis cucullatis angulosis, acute dentatis. *Crane's-bill*

with a one-leaved empalement, and angular hooded leaves sharply indented. Geranium Africanum arborescens, ibisci folio anguloso, floribus amplis purpureis. Phil. Trans. 388. *African-tree Crane's-bill with an angular Marshmallow leaf, and large purple flowers.*

23. GERANIUM (*Zonale*) calycibus monophyllis, foliis cordato-orbiculatis incisis zona notatis. Hort. Upsal. 196. *Crane's-bill with a one-leaved empalement, and round heart-shaped leaves, which are cut, and marked with a circle.* Geranium Africanum arborescens, alchimillæ hirsuto folio, floribus rubicundis. Com. Præl. *African-tree Crane's-bill with an hairy Ladies Mantle leaf, and red flowers.*

24. GERANIUM (*Inquinans*) calycibus monophyllis, foliis orbiculato-reniformibus tomentosis crenatis integriusculis, caule fruticoso. Hort. Upsal. 195. *Crane's-bill with a one-leaved empalement, and round kidney-shaped leaves which are woolly, crenated, entire, and a shrubby stalk.* Geranium Africanum arborescens, malvæ folio plano lucido, flore elegantissimè kermesino. Di van Leur. Boerh. Ind. *African-tree Crane's-bill, with a plain, shining, Mallow leaf, and an elegant scarlet flower.*

25. GERANIUM (*Capitatum*) calycibus monophyllis, foliis lobatis undatis villosis, caule fruticoso. Hort. Upsal. 196. *Crane's-bill with empalements of one leaf, leaves divided into lobes, which are waved and hairy, and a shrubby stalk.* Geranium Africanum frutescens, malvæ folio odorato laciniato. H. L. *African shrubby Crane's-bill with a jagged, sweet-smelling, Mallow leaf.*

26. GERANIUM (*Vitifolium*) calycibus monophyllis, foliis adscendentibus lobatis pubescentibus, caule fruticoso. Hort. Upsal. 196. *Crane's-bill with one-leaved empalements, ascending leaves which have lobes, are covered with soft hairs, and a shrubby stalk.* Geranium Africanum frutescens, malvæ folio laciniato, odorato instar melissæ, flore purpurascente. Boerh. Ind. *African shrubby Crane's-bill, with a jagged Mallow leaf smelling like Balm, and a purplish coloured flower.*

27. GERANIUM (*Papilionaceum*) calycibus monophyllis, corollis papilionaceis, alis carinaque minutis, foliis angulatis, caule fruticoso. Hort. Cliff. 345. *Crane's-bill with an empalement of one leaf, a butterfly flower, whose wings and keel are very small, and a shrubby stalk.* Geranium Africanum arborescens, malvæ folio mucronato, petalis florum inferioribus vix conspicuis. Phil. Trans. *African-tree Crane's-bill with a pointed Mallow leaf, and the under petals of the flower scarce discernible.*

28. GERANIUM (*Acetosum*) calycibus monophyllis, foliis glabris obovatis carnosis crenatis, caule fruticoso. Hort. Cliff. 345. *Crane's-bill with empalements of one leaf, smooth, oval, fleshy leaves, which are crenated, and a shrubby stalk.* Geranium Africanum frutescens, folio crasso & glauco, acetosæ sapore. Com. Præl. *African shrubby Crane's-bill with a thick glaucous leaf, and an acid taste like Sorrel.*

29. GERANIUM (*Carnosum*) calycibus monophyllis, caule fruticoso, articulis carnoso gibbosis, foliis pinnatifidis laciniatis, petalis linearibus. Lin. Sp. Plant. 67. *Crane's-bill with an empalement of one leaf, a shrubby stalk with fleshy knees, wing-pointed leaves, and very narrow petals to the flower.* Geranium Africanum frutescens, chelidonii folio, petalis florum angustis albidis, carnoso caudice. Phil. Trans. Geranium Africanum, folio alceæ, flore albo. Boerh. Ind. alt. *African shrubby Crane's-bill with a leaf like the Alcea, the petals of the flower white and narrow, and a fleshy stalk.*

30. GERANIUM (*Gibbosum*) calycibus monophyllis, caule fruticoso, geniculis carnosis gibbosis, foliis subpinnatis appositis. Lin. Sp. Plant. 677. *Crane's-bill with a one-leaved empalement, shrubby stalk with fleshy knees, and winged leaves placed opposite.* Geranium Africanum noctu olens, tuberosum & nodosum, aquilegiæ foliis. H. L. *African Crane's-bill smelling sweet in the night, with knotty tuberous stalks, and leaves like Columbine.*

31. GERANIUM (*Fulgidum*) calycibus monophyllis, foliis tripartitis incisis, intermedia majore umbellis, geminis, caule fruticoso carnosa. Lin. Vir. 67. *Crane's-bill*

GER

bill with one-leaved empalements, leaves cut into three segments, the middle one being the largest, double foot-stalks with flowers growing in umbels, and a shrubby fleshy stalk. Geranium Africanum, folio alceæ, flore coccineo fulgidissimo. Boerh. Ind. alt. 1. p. 264. African Crane's-bill with a Vervain Mallow leaf, and a deep scarlet flower.

32. GERANIUM (Peltatum) calycibus monophyllis, foliis, quinquelobis integerrimis glabris peltatis, caule fruticoso. Hort. Cliff. 345. Crane's-bill with empalements of one leaf, and smooth target-shaped leaves, having five lobes, which are entire. Geranium Africanum foliis inferioribus asari, superioribus staphidisagriæ, maculatis, splendentibus, & acetosæ sapore. Com. Præl. African Crane's-bill with the under leaves like Asarabacca, and the upper leaves like Stavesacre, shining, spotted, and tasting like Sorrel.

33. GERANIUM (Alchimilloides) calycibus monophyllis, foliis orbiculatis palmatis incisis pilosis, caule herbaceo. Lin. Vir. 67. Crane's-bill with empalements of one leaf, roundish hand-shaped leaves, which are divided, hairy, and an herbaceous stalk. Geranium Africanum, alchimillæ hirsuto folio, floribus albidis. H. L. African Crane's-bill with a hairy Ladies Mantle leaf, and whitish flowers.

34. GERANIUM (Odoratissimum) calycibus monophyllis, caule carnoso brevissimo, ramis herbaceis longis foliis cordatis. Hort. Cliff. 345. Crane's-bill with empalements of one leaf, a very short fleshy stalk, long herbaceous branches, and heart-shaped leaves. Geranium Africanum, folio malvæ crasso molli odoratissimo, flosculo pentapetalo albo. Boerh. Ind. alt. African Crane's-bill with a thick, soft, sweet-smelling Mallow leaf, and a small white flower composed of five leaves.

35. GERANIUM (Triste) calycibus monophyllis, sessilibus scapis bifidis monophyllis. Lin. Sp. 950. Crane's-bill with sessile empalements of one leaf, a bifid stalk, and a roundish root. Geranium Americanum, noctu olens, radice tuberosâ, triste. Corn. H. Ox. American tuberous-rooted Crane's-bill, smelling sweet in the night.

36. GERANIUM (Myrrhifolium) calycibus monophyllis, foliis bipinnatis, inferioribus cordatis lobatis, caule herbaceo, calycibus strigosis. Burm. Ger. 59. Crane's-bill with empalements of one leaf, doubly wing-pointed leaves, the lower heart-shaped with lobes, and an herbaceous stalk. Geranium Africanum tuberosum, anemones folio, incarnato flore. Par. Bat. Tuberous-rooted African Crane's-bill with an Anemony leaf, and a pale, flesh-coloured flower.

37. GERANIUM (Pastinacæfolium) calycibus monophyllis, foliis decompositis pinnatifidis, acutis pedunculis longissimis. Crane's-bill with empalements of one leaf, decompounded leaves ending in acute winged points, and very long foot-stalks to the flower. Geranium Africanum noctu olens, radice tuberosâ, foliis pastinacæ incanis lanuginosis latioribus, flore pallide flavescente. H. L. B. Night-smelling Crane's-bill with a tuberous root, broad, woolly, hoary, Parsnep leaves, and a pale yellowish flower.

38. GERANIUM (Villosum) calycibus monophyllis, foliis pinnatifidis villosis, laciniis linearibus. Crane's-bill with empalements of one leaf, hairy wing-pointed leaves, having very narrow segments. Geranium Æthiopicum, noctu olens, radice tuberosâ, foliis myrrhidus angustioribus. Breyn. Cent. Night sweet-smelling Ethiopian Crane's-bill with a tuberous root, and narrow Cicely leaves.

39. GERANIUM (Lobatum) calycibus monophyllis, caule truncato, scapis subradicalibus, umbella composita. Lin. Sp. 950. Crane's-bill with empalements of one leaf, a truncated stalk, foot-stalks arising from the root, and a compound umbel of flowers. Geranium Africanum noctu olens, folio vitis hirfuto, tuberosum. H. L. Night sweet-smelling African Crane's-bill with a hairy Vine leaf, and a tuberous root.

40. GERANIUM (Coriandrifolium) calycibus monophyllis, foliis bipinnatis linearibus squarrosis, caule herbaceo lævisculo. Lin. Sp. 949. Crane's-bill with a one-leaved empalement, doubly winged rough leaves, and a very smooth stalk. Geranium Africanum, folio

coriandri, floribus incarnatis, minus. H. L. Lesser African Crane's-bill with a Coriander leaf, and a flesh-coloured flower.

41. GERANIUM (Romanum) pedunculis multifloris, floribus pentandris, foliis pinnatis incisis, scapis radicalibus. Burm. Ger. 30. Crane's-bill with many flowers on each foot-stalk, cut winged leaves, and foot-stalks rising from the root. Geranium myrrhinum tenuifolium, amplo flore purpureo. Barrel. rar. 563.

42. GERANIUM (Grossularoides) calycibus monophyllis, foliis cordatis subrotundis lobatis crenatis, caule herbaceo lævi. Burm. Ger. 53. Crane's-bill with empalements of one leaf, roundish heart-shaped leaves which are crenated, and herbaceous smooth stalks. Geranium Africanum, uvæ crispæ folio, floribus exiguis rubellis. H. L. African Crane's-bill with a Gooseberry leaf, and small reddish flowers.

43. GERANIUM (Betulinum) calycibus monophyllis, foliis ovatis inæqualiter serratis planis, caule fruticoso. Lin. Sp. Plant. 679. Crane's-bill with one-leaved empalements, and oval plain leaves unequally sawed, and a shrubby stalk. Geranium frutescens, folio lato dentato, flore magno rubente. Burm. Afr. 92. tab. 33. Shrubby Crane's-bill with a broad indented leaf, and large reddish flower.

44. GERANIUM (Chium) pedunculis multifloris, floribus pentandris, foliis cordatis incisis, superioribus lyratopinnatifidis. Burm. Ger. 35. Crane's-bill with many flowers on each foot-stalk, heart-shaped cut leaves at bottom, the upper lyre-shaped and winged. Geranium chium vernum Caryphyllatæ folio. Tourn. Cor. 20.

45. GERANIUM (Malacoides) pedunculis multifloris, floribus pentandris foliis cordatis sublobatis. Hort. Cliff. 344. Crane's-bill with many flowers on each stalk, and heart-shaped lobed leaves. Geranium folio Altheæ. C. B. P. 318.

46. GERANIUM (Glaucophyllum) pedunculis multifloris, floribus pentandris, foliis ovatis serratis incanis linearis. Lin. Sp. 952. Crane's-bill with many flowers on each stalk, and oval sawed leaves. Geranium Ægyptiacum glaucophyllon, rostris longissimis plumosis.

47. GERANIUM (Carolinianum) pedunculis bifloris, calycibus aristatis, foliis multifidis, arillis hirsutis. Prod. Leyd. 351. Crane's-bill with two flowers on each stalk, bearded empalements, many pointed leaves, and hairy beaks. Geranium columbinum Carolinum, capsulis nigris hirsutis. Hort. Elth. 162.

48. GERANIUM (Althæoides) calycibus monophyllis, foliis cordato-ovatis plicatis sinuatis crenatis, caule herbaceo prostrato. Hort. Cliff. 354. Crane's-bill with a one-leaved empalement, oval heart-shaped plaited leaves, which are indented, and a prostrate herbaceous stalk. Geranium folio Althææ. Africanum odore melisfæ. Boerh. Ind. 1. p. 263.

The first sort grows naturally in moist meadows in many parts of England, but is frequently planted in gardens for the beauty of its large blue flowers ; of this there is a variety with white flowers, and another with variegated flowers ; but these are apt to degenerate to the common sort, if they are raised from seeds, but by parting of their roots they may be continued. It hath a perennial root, which sends up many stalks, which rise near three feet high, garnished with target-shaped leaves, divided into six or seven lobes ; these are cut into several acute segments, after the manner of winged leaves, ending in many points. The flowers are produced at the top of the stalks, each foot-stalk sustaining two flowers, whose petals are large and equal ; they are of a fine blue colour, and appear in May and June.

The varieties of this may be preserved by parting of their roots in autumn ; they may be planted in almost any soil or situation, and require no other culture but to keep them clean from weeds. They may also be propagated by seeds, but by this method they are very apt to vary in the colour of their flowers. If the seeds of these plants are permitted to scatter, the plants will come up without any farther care.

The second sort grows naturally in Germany and Switzerland ; this hath a thick, fleshy, perennial root.

6 C   from

from which arife feveral branching ftalks, which grow about one foot high, garnifhed with leaves at each joint, which are divided into five lobes; and are divided at the top into many fhort fegments, which are crenated on their edges; they are of a light green, and fmooth. The flowers are produced at the end of the branches, many growing together in a bunch, but each fhort foot-ftalk fuftains two flowers. The flowers have fwollen empalements, refembling inflated bladders. The petals are pretty large, equal, and of a fine bright purple colour, and the ftamina and ftyle are much longer than the petals; the whole plant, when rubbed, emits an agreeable odour. This flowers about the fame time with the firft fort, and may be propagated and treated in the fame manner, the plant being equally hardy.

The third fort grows naturally in many parts of England, but is often admitted into gardens; this hath pretty thick, flefhy, fibrous roots, which grow to a large head, from which arife many ftalks, garnifhed with leaves, divided into five lobes, which are again divided almoft to the midrib. The flowers ftand upon long hairy foot-ftalks, which come out from the fide of the ftalk, each fuftaining one flower, compofed of five broad regular petals, which are of a deep purple colour. This fort flowers in June and July; there are two varieties mentioned of this fort as diftinct fpecies, one whofe ftalks grow more erect, and the other hath leaves more deeply divided; but the plants which I have raifed from feeds of thefe do not come up the fame as the parent plants, fo they are only feminal varieties.

This hath a perennial root, which may be parted in autumn, and thereby propagated; or it may be propagated by feeds, and the plants treated in the fame manner as the firft.

The fourth fort hath been fuppofed by fome to be only a variety of the third, but it is undoubtedly a diftinct fpecies; for I have frequently raifed the plants from feeds, which have always proved to be the fame. The ftalks of this plant are fhorter than thofe of the third, and fpread flat on the ground; the leaves are much lefs, and not fo deeply divided, and the flowers much fmaller and of a pale colour, marked with purple; it grows naturally in Lancafhire and Weftmoreland, where I faw it in plenty. This may be propagated and treated in the fame manner as the others.

The fifth fort is a perennial plant, of fmaller growth than either of the former. It rifes with branching ftalks about fix inches high, garnifhed with leaves, having three pretty broad lobes, which are undivided, and crenated on their edges: thofe on the lower part of the ftalks are placed oppofite, upon pretty long foot-ftalks, but the upper leaves fit clofe to the ftalks and are fingle. The flowers are produced at the end of the ftalks, ftanding together upon two fhort foot-ftalks; they are of a dirty purple colour, and appear in June. It grows naturally in France. This fort may be propagated and treated in the fame manner as the firft.

The fixth fort grows naturally on the Alps and Helvetian mountains, and is found in fome places in the North of England: this hath a perennial root, from which arife feveral ftalks near a foot high, with leaves which are divided into five or fix lobes, which are laciniated on their edges; thofe which grow near the root have long foot-ftalks, but thofe on the upper part of the ftalk fit clofe; the ftalk branches out at the top into three or four divifions, each being terminated by two or three foot-ftalks, fuftaining two flowers of a dark purple colour, with erect petals. This flowers in June, and may be propagated by feeds or parting of the roots, in the fame manner as the firft fort.

The feventh fort is very like the fixth, but the leaves are larger, the lobes fhorter, broader, and not fo much cut; they are ftriped with black; the ftalks rife higher, the flowers are larger, and the petals are reflexed. Thefe differences are permanent, fo are

fufficient to conftitute a fpecific difference between them. This may be propagated and treated in the fame manner as the firft fort. It grows naturally on the Alps.

The eighth fort hath a perennial root, which fends up many branching ftalks a foot and a half high, garnifhed with light green leaves; thofe on the lower part of the ftalk hath five lobes, and ftand upon long foot-ftalks; but thofe on the upper part have but three lobes, fit clofer to the ftalks, and are fharply indented on the edges; the flowers ftand upon long flender foot-ftalks, each fuftaining two flowers, compofed of five obtufe petals, which are deeply indented at the top; they are of a dull white, with many purple ftripes running longitudnally thro' them. Thefe appear in June, and in cool feafons there will be a fucceffion of flowers a great part of July. This fort is very hardy, fo may be propagated by dividing of the roots, or from feeds, in the fame manner as the firft fort.

The ninth fort grows plentifully in the meadows in Lancafhire and Weftmoreland; this hath a perennial root, which fends out three or four upright ftalks about nine inches high, garnifhed with leaves, having five lobes, which are fawed on their edges; they are placed oppofite on the ftalks; thofe on the lower part have pretty long foot-ftalks, but thofe on the upper part fit clofer. The flowers are fituated on the top of the ftalks, ftanding upon fhort foot-ftalks, each fuftaining two pretty large blue flowers, with entire petals. This flowers in May and June, and may be propagated and treated in the fame way as the firft fort.

The tenth fort was difcovered by Dr. Tournefort in the Levant, from whence he fent the feeds to the Royal Garden at Paris; this hath a perennial root, from which arife a few weak ftalks about nine inches long, garnifhed with leaves which are round, and divided into five lobes, which are indented at the top, and placed oppofite on the ftalks. The flowers ftand upon pretty long foot-ftalks, which come fingle from the joints of the ftalks, each fuftaining two purplifh flowers with entire petals, having very fhort empalements. It flowers in June, and may be propagated either from feeds, or by parting of the roots in the fame manner as the firft fort, but the plants require a drier foil and a warmer fituation; for although in common winters it will live in the open air, yet in fevere froft thefe plants are fometimes killed, efpecially when they are planted in moift cold land.

The eleventh fort grows naturally on the Pyrenean mountains; this hath a perennial root, from which arife many branching ftalks a foot and a half high, garnifhed with round lobes, divided into many obtufe fegments at the top, placed oppofite. The flowers are produced upon fhort foot-ftalks, which come out at the divifions on the fides, and at the top of the ftalks; they are in fome of a pale purple colour, and in others white. The petals of the flowers are bifid, like thofe of the common Dove's-foot Crane's-bill, to which the whole plant bears fome refemblance; but the ftalks are erect, the leaves and flowers much larger, and the root is perennial; this will propagate itfelf faft enough by its fcattered feeds where it has once got poffeffion, and will thrive in any foil or fituation.

The twelfth fort grows naturally upon the Alps. The feeds of this were fent me by Sig. Micheli, of Florence; this hath a perennial root, which runs very deep into the ground. The lower leaves of the plant have very long foot-ftalks, they are doubly winged and fmooth. The ftalks rife a foot and a half high, which are garnifhed with leaves of the fame form as the lower, but fmaller, and ftand oppofite. The flowers grow many together upon very long foot-ftalks; they are purple. This flowers in June, but has never ripened any feeds in England. The plant is hardy, and lives in the open air, but as the root puts out no offsets, nor perfects feeds here, we have not been able to propagate it.

The

The thirteenth fort grows naturally on the Alps; this hath a very thick perennial root, from which come out roundish leaves, divided into many parts, standing upon pretty long foot-stalks; they are very filvery, and shining like silk. The flower-stalks rise about four or five inches high, garnished with one or two small leaves like those below, which fit close to the stalk. The stalks are terminated by two pretty large pale flowers, whose petals are entire, and spread open flat. It flowers in June, but rarely ripens feeds here; it may be propagated by parting of the roots in the same manner as the first, and must have a shady situation.

The fourteenth fort grows naturally in North America, from whence the feeds were sent to England; this hath a perennial root, from which arise several stalks about one foot high, which divide by pairs, and from the middle of the divisions come out the foot-stalks of the flowers, which are pretty long and naked, each sustaining two pale purple flowers with entire petals. The leaves are divided into five parts, which are cut on their edges, and are placed opposite, the lower having pretty long foot-stalks, but the upper fit close to the stalks. It flowers in June, and frequently ripens feeds, from which the plant may be propagated; it thrives very well in the open air, and requires no other culture but to keep it clean from weeds.

The fifteenth fort grows naturally in Bohemia; this is an annual plant, which sends out many stalks, dividing into several smaller, which are garnished with leaves divided into five lobes, crenated on their edges; they stand upon long foot-stalks, and are for the most part opposite. The flowers stand by pairs upon pretty long slender foot-stalks, which come out from the side of the stalk; they are of a fine blue colour, and are succeeded by feeds, whose capsules and beaks are black. It flowers most part of summer, and the feeds ripen soon after, which, if permitted to scatter, there will be a supply of plants, which want no other care but to keep them clean from weeds.

The sixteenth fort grows naturally in Siberia. The feeds of this plant were sent me by Sir Charles Linnæus, professor of botany at Upsal; this fort hath a perennial root. The leaves are divided into five acute lobes, which are cut into many sharp wing-like segments on their edges; they are placed opposite, and have long slender foot-stalks. The foot-stalks of the flower come out from the wings of the stalk; they are pretty long, slender, and each sustain one pale purplish flower. This fort flowers in June, and perfects its feeds very well, so may be easily propagated; it will grow on any soil, or in any situation.

The seventeenth fort is an annual plant, which is sometimes found growing naturally in England, but is frequently preserved in gardens for the musky odour of the leaves, which in dry weather is very strong. The leaves of this are irregularly winged, the lobes grow alternate, and are cut into many obtuse segments on their edges. The stalks branch into many divisions, and frequently decline to the ground. The flowers are produced in umbels upon long foot-stalks, which arise from the wings of the stalks; they are small, blue, and have but five stamina in each, their empalements are composed of five leaves. It flowers in May, June, and July, and the feeds ripen soon after; which, if permitted to scatter, there will be a supply of plants without care, which will require no other culture but to keep them clean from weeds, and thin them where they are too close; it will thrive on any soil, or in any situation.

The eighteenth fort grows naturally in Crete; this is an annual plant with very broad leaves, which are cut on their sides regularly, in form of winged leaves, and are crenated on their borders. The flowers are produced on pretty long foot-stalks, which come out from the wings of the stalk; they have five-leaved empalements, and are composed of nine entire blue petals; these are succeeded by the largest and longest beaks of any species of this genus yet known. It

flowers in June and July; this ripens feeds very well, and if they are permitted to scatter, the plants will come up without care; or they may be sown in the spring where they are designed to remain, and will require no other culture but to thin them where they are too close, and keep them clean from weeds.

The nineteenth fort grows naturally in Germany and Italy; this is an annual plant, which hath several prostrate stalks near a foot long, garnished with winged leaves, cut into several acute parts, placed opposite. The flowers come out from the wings of the stalk, upon foot-stalks about three inches long; some of these sustain many flowers, but others have no more than two; they are of a pale blue colour, and are succeeded by very long beaks, but not so long or large as those of the former fort; but the feeds of this are frequently used for hygrometers, to shew the moisture of the air: if the feeds of this are permitted to scatter, the plants will come up and thrive without any other care than to keep them clear from weeds, and the plants which come up in autumn will flower early in May, but those which are sown in the spring seldom flower till July. Dr. Linnæus supposes this and the former fort to be the same, but whoever has seen the two plants, cannot doubt of their being distinct species.

The feeds of the twentieth fort were sent to the Chelsea garden by Dr. Jussieu, professor of botany at Paris; this is an annual plant, which hath upright stalks near two feet high, which are garnished with double winged leaves, ending in many points; these are very viscous, and stand opposite. The flowers are produced on long naked foot-stalks, standing many together upon each; they are of a pale blue colour, and have but five stamina; their empalements are composed of five leaves, which end with awns. It flowers in May, June, and July, according to the times when the feeds are sown, and the feeds ripen a month after; this requires no other culture than the two former forts.

There are several other forts of annual Geraniums, some of which grow naturally in England, and are troublesome weeds in a garden, others grow naturally in France, Spain, Italy, and Germany, and are preserved in botanic gardens for the sake of variety; but as they are plants of little beauty, they are rarely admitted into other gardens, therefore I shall not trouble the reader with an enumeration of the species, which would swell this article too much; so I shall next treat of the African Crane's-bills, which are preserved in most of the curious gardens, where there is conveniency to screen them from the frost in winter.

The twenty-first fort grows naturally near the Cape of Good Hope; this rises with a shrubby stalk eight or ten feet high, sending out several irregular branches, garnished with roundish leaves, whose sides are erect, so form a fort of hood by the hollow cavity made in the leaf. The base of the leaves are cut in form of a heart-shaped leaf, and from the foot-stalk run many nerves arising from a point, but diverge toward the sides; the borders of the leaves are sharply indented, those on the lower part of the branches have long foot-stalks, and are placed without order on every side, but those on the upper part have shorter foot-stalks, and stand opposite. The flowers are produced in large panicles on the top of the branches; their empalements are of one leaf, deeply cut into five segments, and closely covered with soft hairs. The petals are large, entire, and of a purple blue colour. It flowers in June, July, August, and September, and the flowers are succeeded by feeds, having short hairy beaks.

The twenty-second fort has some appearance of the twenty-first, but the leaves are of a thicker substance, divided into many acute angles, having purple edges, which are acutely indented. The stalks and leaves are very hairy. The branches are not so irregular as those of the former, nor are the bunches of flowers near so large; these differences are permanent in the plants which are raised from feeds, so it is undoubtedly

a distinct

a diſtinct ſpecies, though Dr. Linnæus ſuppoſes them to be the ſame.

The twenty-third ſort comes from the Cape of Good Hope, but is one of the oldeſt, and the moſt common ſort in the Engliſh gardens; this riſes with a ſhrubby ſtalk four or five feet high, and divides into a great number of irregular branches, ſo as to form a large head, which is often eight or ten feet high. The branches are garniſhed with roundiſh heart-ſhaped leaves, indented on their edges in ſeveral obtuſe ſegments, which are cut into ſhort teeth at their brims; theſe have a purpliſh circle, or mark, like a horſe-ſhoe, through the leaf, going from one ſide of the baſe to the other, correſponding with the border of the leaf; theſe leaves when gently rubbed, have a ſcent like ſcalded Apples. The flowers are produced in pretty cloſe bunches, ſtanding upon foot-ſtalks about five or ſix inches in length, which come out from the wings of the ſtalk, toward the end of the branches; they are of a reddiſh purple colour, and continue in ſucceſſion great part of ſummer; there is a variety of this with fine variegated leaves, which is preferred in moſt of the Engliſh gardens for the beauty of its leaves; but as this accidentally came from the other, it is not a diſtinct ſpecies, therefore I have not enumerated it.

The twenty-fourth ſort grows naturally at the Cape of Good Hope; this riſes with a ſoft ſhrubby ſtem to the height of eight or ten feet, ſending out ſeveral branches, which are generally erect; theſe are garniſhed with roundiſh kidney-ſhaped leaves, which are of a thick ſubſtance, and of a lucid green, ſtanding on pretty long foot-ſtalks; they are covered with ſoft hairs on their under ſide, and are placed without any order. The flowers grow in looſe bunches upon long ſtiff foot-ſtalks, which come out from the wings of the ſtalk; they are of a bright ſcarlet colour, ſo make a fine appearance, and there is a ſucceſſion of theſe flowers during all the ſummer months.

The twenty-fifth ſort grows naturally at the Cape of Good Hope, but has been many years an inhabitant of the Engliſh gardens; this riſes with a ſhrubby ſtalk four or five feet high, dividing into ſeveral weak irregular branches, garniſhed with leaves divided into three unequal lobes, which are hairy and waved on their edges; they are placed alternate on the branches, and ſtand upon hairy foot-ſtalks. The flowers grow in cloſe roundiſh heads on the top of the foot-ſtalks, forming a ſort of corymbus; they are of a purpliſh blue colour, and continue in ſucceſſion great part of the ſummer. The leaves of this ſort, when rubbed, have an odour like dried Roſes, from whence many have given it the title of Roſe Geranium.

The twenty-ſixth ſort is a native of the Cape of Good Hope; this riſes with an upright ſhrubby ſtalk to the height of ſeven or eight feet, ſending out many pretty ſtrong branches, garniſhed with leaves ſhaped ſomewhat like thoſe of the Vine; thoſe on the lower part ſtand upon long foot-ſtalks, but the upper have ſhort ones; when the leaves of this are rubbed, they have a ſcent of Balm. The flowers grow in compact cluſters on the top of long naked foot-ſtalks, which come out from the wings of the ſtalk, but riſe much higher than the branches; they are ſmall, and of a pale blue colour, ſo make no great figure, but there is a ſucceſſion of them moſt part of the ſummer.

The twenty-ſeventh ſort riſes with an upright ſhrubby ſtalk ſeven or eight feet high, ſending out ſeveral ſide branches, garniſhed with large, angular, rough leaves, ſtanding upon long foot-ſtalks. The flowers are produced in large panicles at the end of the branches; theſe are ſhaped ſomewhat like a Butterfly-flower, the two upper petals, which are pretty large, turn upward like a ſtandard in the leguminous flowers; theſe are finely variegated, but the three under petals are ſo ſmall, as not to appear at a ſmall diſtance; theſe are reflexed downward, ſo are ſcreened from ſight, unleſs the flowers are viewed near. This ſort flowers in May, at which time the plants make a fine appearance, but they are not ſucceeded by any

more afterward, as moſt of the other ſorts are; this grows naturally at the Cape of Good Hope.

The twenty-eighth ſort is from the ſame country; this riſes with a ſhrubby ſtalk ſix or ſeven feet high, ſending out ſeveral ſide branches, garniſhed with oblong, oval, fleſhy, ſmooth leaves, of a gray colour, which are crenated on their edges, and have an acid taſte like Sorrel. The flowers ſtand upon pretty long foot-ſtalks, which ariſe from the wings of the ſtalks, each ſuſtaining three or four flowers, whoſe petals are narrow and unequal in ſize; they are of a pale bluſh colour, with ſome ſtripes of a light red; theſe continue in ſucceſſion moſt part of the ſummer. There is a variety of this with ſcarlet flowers, which is ſaid to have been raiſed from the ſeeds of this ſort. The leaves of it are larger, and ſeem to be an intermediate ſpecies between this and the twenty-fourth ſort, for the flowers are larger than thoſe of the twenty-eighth ſort, and are of a pale ſcarlet colour.

The twenty-ninth ſort hath a thick, fleſhy, knotted ſtalk, which riſes about two feet high, ſending out a few ſlender fleſhy branches, garniſhed thinly with double winged leaves, which, on the lower part of the ſtalk, ſtand upon foot-ſtalks, but thoſe above ſit cloſe to the branches. The flowers are produced in ſmall cluſters at the end of the branches; theſe have five narrow white petals, which make no appearance, and continue in ſucceſſion moſt part of the ſummer. It grows naturally at the Cape of Good Hope.

The thirtieth ſort hath a round fleſhy ſtalk with ſwelling knots at the joints, which riſe about three feet high, and ſend out ſeveral irregular branches, which are ſmooth; they are thinly garniſhed with ſmooth, fleſhy, winged leaves, ending in obtuſe points; they are of a gray colour, and ſtand upon ſhort foot-ſtalks. The flowers ſtand four or five upon each foot-ſtalk, which ariſes from the wings of the ſtalk, and are of a dark purple colour. The petals are broader than thoſe of the former ſort, and have a very agreeable ſcent in the evening, after the ſun has left them ſome time; this and the former ſort are ſuppoſed to be one ſpecies by Dr. Linnæus, but they are very different in many particulars, which are permanent in the plants which come up from ſeeds.

The thirty-firſt ſort hath a fleſhy ſtalk which ſeldom riſes a foot high, and puts out very few branches; theſe are garniſhed with ſmooth, light, green leaves, divided into three lobes, the middle ſegment being much larger than the others. The flowers ſtand upon ſhort foot-ſtalks, each ſuſtaining two or three flowers on the top, which are of a very deep ſcarlet colour, and have unequal petals; this ſort is not regular in its ſeaſon of flowering, ſometimes it is in ſpring, at other times in ſummer, and frequently in autumn. The leaves of this ſort fall off, ſo that the ſtalks are frequently deſtitute of them for three or four months in ſummer, and appear as if they were dead, but in autumn they put out freſh leaves again.

The thirty-ſecond ſort hath many weak ſhrubby ſtalks, which require ſupport to prevent their falling on the ground; theſe extend to the length of two or three feet, and are garniſhed with fleſhy leaves, divided into five obtuſe lobes, which are entire; theſe have ſlender foot-ſtalks, which are faſtened to the middle of the leaf like the handle of a target. The leaves are ſmooth, of a lucid green, and have a circular purple mark in their middle; they have an acid flavour, and are placed alternate on their branches. The flowers are produced upon pretty long foot-ſtalks, which come out from the wings of the ſtalk, each foot-ſtalk ſuſtaining four or five purple flowers, compoſed of five unequal petals. This ſort continues a ſucceſſion of flowers moſt of the ſummer months, and frequently ripen ſeeds here.

The thirty-third ſort ſends out ſeveral herbaceous ſtalks about a foot and a half in length, which trail upon the ground if they are not ſupported; theſe are garniſhed with roundiſh hand-ſhaped leaves, which are cut into many parts, and are very hairy. The flowers are of a pale bluſh colour, and ſtand ſeveral together

together upon very long foot-ftalks; there is a fuc-ceffion of thefe during all the fummer months, and the feeds ripen accordingly about a month after the flowers are fallen: there is a variety of this fort which has a dark circle in the middle of the leaves, which is mentioned as a diftinct fpecies, but I find it is apt to vary from feeds.

The thirty-fourth fort hath a very fhort flefhy ftalk, which divides near the ground into feveral heads, each having many leaves, which arife on feparate foot-ftalks from the heads; thefe are heart-fhaped, foft, and downy, and have a ftrong fcent like Anifeed; from thefe heads come out feveral flender ftalks near a foot in length, which lie proftrate on the ground, and are garnifhed with rounder leaves than thofe near the root, but are of the fame texture, and have the like odour. The flowers are produced from the fide of thefe ftalks, three, four, or five ftanding together upon flender foot-ftalks; they are very fmall and white, fo make little appearance, but the plant is pre-ferved in gardens for the fcent of its leaves.

The thirty-fifth fort hath a thick, roundifh, tuberous root, from which arife feveral hairy leaves, which are finely divided, almoft like thofe of the Garden Carrot; thefe fpread near the ground, and between thefe come out the ftalks, which rife about a foot high, which are garnifhed with two or three leaves of the fame fort with thofe below, but are fmaller, and fit clofer to the ftalks; from thefe come two or three naked foot-ftalks, which are terminated by a bunch of yellowifh flowers, marked with dark purple fpots, which fmell very fweet after the fun hath left them; thefe are frequently fuc-ceeded by feeds, which ripen in autumn. This is the fort which has been long cultivated in the gardens, and is known by the title of Geranium noctu olens, or *Night-fcented Crane's-bill.*

The thirty-fixth fort hath a knobbed tuberous root like the laft, from which come out feveral pretty large leaves, compofed of many lobes, fet along the mid-rib in the form of a winged leaf; thefe are narrow at their bafe, but are very much enlarged at their ends, which are rounded, and cut all along their fide and top into many acute points; the ftalks which fuftain the flowers arife immediately from the root, and fometimes have one or two fmall leaves toward the bottom, where they often divide into two naked foot-ftalks, each being terminated by a bunch of pale reddifh flowers, which fmell fweet at night.

The thirty-feventh fort hath oblong tuberous roots, from which come out feveral decompounded winged leaves, ending in many acute points; the fegments of thefe leaves are broader than thofe of the thirty-fifth fort, and the leaves are very hairy. The ftalks rife a foot and a half high, which are garnifhed with a fingle leaf at the two lower joints; thefe are fingly winged, and the lobes are narrow, ftanding at a wider diftance, and the fegments are more acute than thofe of the lower leaves; at the two lower knots or joints, arife two long naked foot-ftalks, each being termi-nated by a bunch of yellowifh flowers, which have long tubes, and fmell fweet in the evening when the fun has left them. This grows naturally at the Cape of Good Hope.

The thirty-eighth fort hath a tuberous root like the former, from which fpring out many hairy leaves, which are finely divided like thofe of the Pulfatilla, which have a hoary appearance, and rife immediately from the root, fpreading on every fide near the ground. The foot-ftalk of the flower is naked, and rifes from the root; this grows about nine inches high, and is terminated by a loofe bunch of flowers, which are of a very dark purple colour, and fmell fweet in the evening.

The thirty-ninth fort hath flefhy tuberous roots like thofe of the former forts, from which come out three or four broad leaves, divided on their borders into feveral lobes, in form of a Vine leaf; thefe fpread flat on the ground; they are hairy, and crenated on their edges, ftanding upon fhort foot-ftalks. The foot-ftalks of the flowers arife immediately from the root,

and grow about a foot high; they are naked, and are terminated by a bunch of dark purple flowers, with long tubes, fitting clofe to the foot-ftalks, which have a very agreeable odour in the evening.

The four firft forts of tuberous-rooted Crane's-bill, are by Linnæus fuppofed to be but one fpecies, but I have propagated them from feeds feveral times, and have never found either of them vary from their parent plants, fo I make no doubt of their being diftinct fpe-cies, for their difference of leaves is as great as in any of the other fpecies.

The fortieth fort is an annual plant, which grows na-turally at the Cape of Good Hope; this rifes with herbaceous branching ftalks near a foot high, which are garnifhed with doubly-winged leaves at each joint; the lower leaves ftand upon long foot-ftalks, but thofe on the upper part fit clofe to the ftalks. The flowers ftand upon naked foot-ftalks, which proceed from the fide of the ftalks, on the oppofite fide to the leaves; they grow three or four together upon fhort feparate foot-ftalks; thefe are fhaped fomewhat like a papili-onaceous flower; the two upper petals, which are large, form a kind of ftandard, the other three petals are narrow, and reflexed downward; they are of a pale flefh colour, appearing in July, and the feeds ripen in September, foon after which the plants decay.

The forty-firft fort hath a pretty thick tuberous root, from which is fent out feveral irregular ftalks, which divide into branches, and grow diffufed; thefe have fwelling joints, and are fomewhat ligneous; they are garnifhed with one double winged leaf at each of the joints, and oppofite to the leaves come out the foot-ftalks of the flowers; thofe which are fituated on the lower part of the ftalk, are very long and naked, but thofe which terminate the branches are fhorter, and have one or two fmall leaves fet at their bafe; thefe foot-ftalks are terminated by a fmall bunch of flowers, fhaped like thofe of the former fort, but larger, and of a paler colour; thefe continue in fucceffion moft part of the fummer: this and the former fort are fup-pofed to be the fame by Dr. Linnæus, but the former is an annual plant in every country, perifhing foon after the feeds are perfected, and the latter is an abiding plant with ligneous ftalks.

The forty-fecond fort is a biennial plant, which grows naturally at the Cape of Good Hope; this fends out a great number of very flender trailing ftalks, which are proftrate on the ground, and extend a foot and a half in length, garnifhed with fmall, roundifh, hand-fhaped leaves, which are crenated on their edges. The flowers fit upon fhort flender foot-ftalks, which come out at every joint from the fide of the ftalks; they are very fmall, and of a reddifh colour; fome-times they are fingle, and at other times there are two or three flowers upon a foot-ftalk. They con-tinue in fucceffion all the fummer, and the feeds ripen in about five weeks after the flowers decay.

The forty-third fort hath a fhrubby ftalk, which rifes to the height of four or five feet, fending out feveral branches, which are garnifhed with oblong leaves, indented, and unequally fawed on their edges; the flowers ftand upon long foot-ftalks, which come out from the fide of their branches; they are large, of a red colour, and the two upper petals are larger than the other; this fort flowers in June and July.

The forty-fourth fort grows naturally in the ifle of Chio in the Levant. This is an annual plant, which fends out feveral branches a foot long; the lower leaves are almoft heart-fhaped, but thofe on the branches are formed in the fhape of an ancient lyre. Thefe are placed alternate on the branches; the foot-ftalks of flowers are produced on the fide of the branches, thefe are fix inches long, fuftaining many bright purple flowers at the top, which are fucceeded each by five feeds, having long flender beaks; thefe ripen in five or fix weeks after the flowers fall away, and if they are permitted to fcatter, the young plants will come up in the autumn; and if the winter is favourable, they will live in the open air, fo will flower early the

following

following spring: but if these should be killed in the winter, some seeds should be sown in the spring, on a border of light ground, and when the plants come up they should be thinned, and kept clear from weeds; these will flower in July, and their seeds will ripen in August.

The forty-fifth sort grows naturally in Portugal and Spain; this is an annual plant, whose lower leaves are heart-shaped, and divided into three lobes; the foot-stalks of the flowers are placed on the side of the branches, which extend a foot and a half each way; these incline to the ground. The foot-stalks sustain many bright red flowers, which are succeeded each by five seeds, having pretty long beaks. This flowers and seeds about the same time as the former sort, and requires the same culture.

The forty-sixth sort grows naturally in Egypt. This is an annual plant, having oval sawed leaves of a gray colour; the branches extend a foot in length, adorned with small leaves placed alternate, and toward the end have three or four foot-stalks produced from their sides, sustaining several pale blue flowers, which are each succeeded by five seeds, having long feathery beaks.

This sort is much tenderer than the two former, therefore if the seeds are sown on a moderate hot-bed in the spring, and when the weather becomes warm, the plants are carefully transplanted on a sheltered border, there will be greater certainty of their perfecting seeds.

The forty-seventh sort grows naturally in Carolina, and is an annual plant, greatly resembling our common Dove's-foot Crane's-bill, but is smaller, and the branches are shorter; the flowers are very small, of a pale blue colour; these are succeeded by five seeds, having short erect beaks, which are black. If the seeds of this sort are permitted to scatter, the plants will arise without farther care; and if thinned and kept clean from weeds, will produce flowers and seeds.

The forty-eighth sort has some resemblance of the forty-fifth, but the leaves are more of an oval heart-shape; the flowers are also of a bright red colour. This grows naturally at the Cape of Good Hope; the plant is tender, therefore will require the same treatment as the forty-seventh sort, with which they will produce flowers and seeds, after which the plants decay.

All the sorts of African Crane's-bill may be propagated by seeds; these may be sown upon a bed of light earth toward the end of March, where the plants will appear in a month or five weeks after, and by the beginning of June the plants will be fit to remove; when they should be carefully taken up, and each planted into a separate pot, filled with light kitchen-garden earth, and placed in a shady situation till the plants have taken new root; then they may be removed into a sheltered situation, and placed among other of the hardier green-house plants, where they may remain till autumn, when they must be removed into the green-house, and treated in the same manner as other hardy kinds of green-house plants.

But those who are desirous to have their plants large, and flower soon, sow the seeds upon a moderate hot-bed in the spring, on which the plants will come up much sooner, and will be fit to remove long before those which are sown in the open air; but when these plants come up, there must be great care taken not to draw them up weak; and when these are transplanted, the pots should be plunged into another moderate hot-bed, observing to shade them from the sun till they have taken new root; then they must be gradually inured to bear the open air, into which they should be removed the beginning of June, and placed in a sheltered situation with other exotic plants. If these plants are brought forward in the spring, most of the sorts will flower the same summer, and the plants will be very strong before the winter, so will make a better appearance in the green-house.

The shrubby African Geraniums, from the twenty-first to the thirty-second inclusive, and also the for-

ty-first and forty-third sorts, are commonly propagated by cuttings, which, if planted in a shady border in June or July, will take good root in five or six weeks, and may then be taken up and planted into separate pots, placing them in the shade till they have taken new root; after which they may be removed into a sheltered situation, and treated in the same manner as the seedling plants. The twenty-ninth, thirtieth, thirty-first, and thirty-second sorts, have more succulent stalks than either of the other, so the cuttings of these sorts should be planted into pots filled with light kitchen-garden earth, and plunged into a very moderate hot-bed, where they should be shaded from the sun in the heat of the day, and should have but little water; for these are very apt to rot with much moisture, so they must only be gently refreshed now and then with water. When these are well rooted, they may be separated and planted in pots filled with the same sort of earth, and placed in the shade till they have taken new root; then they may be removed into a sheltered situation, where they may remain till autumn. These four sorts should be sparingly watered at all times, but especially in the winter, for they are apt to take a mouldiness with moisture, or in a damp air: they will thrive much better in an airy glass-case than in a green-house, because in the former they will have more sun and air than in the latter, so will not be so liable to have a mouldiness or rot. But all the other shrubby sorts are proper furniture for the green-house, where they will only require protection from frost, but should have a large share of free air when the weather is mild; they will require water every week, in mild weather once or twice, but it should not be given them in too great plenty, especially in frosty weather. These plants should be hardened in the spring gradually, and toward the middle or latter end of May, they may be taken out of the green-house, and at first placed under the shelter of trees, where they may remain a fortnight or three weeks to harden; then should be removed into a situation where they may be defended from strong winds, and enjoy the morning sun till eleven o'clock, where they will thrive better than in a warmer situation.

As these shrubby sorts grow pretty fast, so they soon fill the pots with their roots; and if they stand long unremoved in summer, they frequently put out their roots through the holes at the bottom of the pots into the ground, and then the plants will grow vigorously; but when they are suffered to grow long in this manner, it will be difficult to remove them, for if their roots are torn off, all the younger branches will decay, and many times the plants are killed. Therefore the pots should be moved once in a fortnight or three weeks, in the summer months, and the roots which may be then pushing through the holes in the pots cut off, to prevent their striking into the ground. These plants will also require to be new potted at least twice in the summer; the first time should be after they have been three weeks or a month out of the green-house; the second should be towards the end of August, or the beginning of September, that the plants may have time to establish their new roots before they are removed into the green-house.

When these are new potted, all the roots on the outside of the balls of earth should be carefully pared off, and as much of the old earth drawn away from the roots, as can be done with safety to the plants; then if they require it, they should be put into pots a size larger than those out of which they were taken, putting a quantity of fresh earth into the bottom of the pot; then place the plants upon that, being careful the ball about the roots of the plant is not so high as the rim of the pot, that some room may be left to contain the water which may be given to the plants. Then the cavity all round the ball should be filled up with fresh earth, which should be gently pressed down, and the bottom of the pot beaten upon the ground, to settle down the earth; then the plant should be well watered, and the stem fastened to a rail, to prevent

5   the

the wind from difplacing of the root before they are fixed in the new earth.

The compoſt in which I have always found theſe plants thrive beſt (where there has not been a conveniency of getting ſome good kitchen-garden earth) was freſh hazel loam from a paſture, mixed with a fourth or fifth part of rotten dung; if the earth is inclinable to bind, then a mixture of rotten tan is preferable to dung; but if it is light and warm, then a mixture of neat's-dung is beſt: this compoſt ſhould be mixed three or four months before it is uſed, and ſhould be turned over three or four times, that the parts may be well mixed and incorporated; but where a quantity of good kitchen-garden earth can be had, which has been well worked, and is clean from the roots of bad weeds, there will need no compoſition, for in that they will thrive full as well as in any mixture which can be made for them, eſpecially if the earth has lain in a heap ſome time, and has been two or three times turned over to break the clods, and make it fine: theſe plants ſhould not be planted in very rich earth, for that will cauſe them to grow very luxuriant, but they will not flower ſo well as in a poorer ſoil.

The thirty-third ſort hath herbaceous ſtalks, ſo is beſt propagated by ſeeds, which the plants produce in great plenty; but the cuttings of this will take root as freely as either of the other, but the ſeedling plants are preferable to thoſe propagated by cuttings; and where the ſeeds of this and many other of the African ſorts are permitted to ſcatter, there will be a ſupply of young plants come up the ſpring following, provided the ſeeds are not buried too deep in the ground.

The thirty-fourth ſort may be propagated by ſeeds, or from heads ſlipped off from the ſhort fleſhy ſtalk; theſe heads ſhould have their lower leaves ſtripped off, that the ſtalk which is to be planted may be clear of leaves; then they may be planted ſingle into a ſmall pot, or if the heads are ſmall, there may be two or three put into one ſmall pot; then they may be plunged into a very moderate hot-bed, which will forward their putting out roots, and if they are ſhaded from the ſun and gently refreſhed with water, they will take root in a month or five weeks, when they muſt be hardened gradually, and removed into the open air, where they may remain till autumn, when they muſt be removed into ſhelter for the winter ſeaſon.

The thirty-fifth, thirty-ſixth, thirty-ſeventh, thirty-eighth and thirty-ninth ſorts are generally propagated by parting of their roots; the beſt time for doing this is in Auguſt, that the young roots may be eſtabliſhed before the cold comes on. Every tuber of theſe roots will grow, provided they have a bud or eye to them; they may be planted in the ſame ſort of earth as was before directed, and if the pots are plunged into an old tan-bed, under a good frame in winter, the plants will thrive better than in a greenhouſe; the glaſſes of the frame may be drawn off every day in mild weather, whereby the plants will enjoy the free air; and if in hard froſt the glaſſes are well covered to prevent the cold penetrating to the plants, it is all the ſhelter they will require; but in this ſituation they ſhould have but little wet in winter, therefore the glaſſes ſhould be kept over them in heavy rains to keep them dry; but in mild weather the glaſſes may be raiſed on the upper ſide to admit the freſh air to the plants, which will give them greater ſlope to carry off the wet. With this management the roots will thrive and flower very ſtrong every year. Theſe ſorts may alſo be propagated by ſeeds.

The fortieth ſort is an annual plant, and is only propagated by ſeeds, which ſhould be ſown upon a gentle hot-bed in the ſpring, to bring the plants forward; otherwiſe if the ſeaſon ſhould not prove very warm, the plants will not perfect their ſeeds in this country. When the plants are come up, and grown ſtrong enough to remove, they ſhould be each planted into a ſeparate ſmall pot, and plunged into a moderate hot-bed again, obſerving to ſhade them till they have

taken new root; then they muſt be gradually hardened to bear the open air, into which they ſhould be removed in June; and when the plants have filled the ſmall pots with their roots, they ſhould be ſhaken out, and the ball of earth preſerved to their roots, and put into pots a ſize larger, in which they will flower and ripen ſeeds, and ſoon after the plants will decay.

The forty-ſecond ſort is alſo propagated by ſeeds, which may be either ſown upon a moderate hot-bed in the ſpring, or upon a bed of light earth in the open air, where the plants will come up very well, though they will not be ſo forward as thoſe on the hot-bed. Thoſe which are ſown in the open air will require no other care but to keep them clean from weeds, and thin the plants where they are too cloſe. Theſe plants will flower in July and Auguſt, and if the autumn proves favourable, the ſeeds will ripen in September; but if theſe ſhould fail, thoſe which were raiſed on the hot-bed will come earlier to flower, ſo there will be no danger of their perfecting ſeeds; and theſe plants, if they are in pots, may be preſerved through the winter, if they are plunged into an old tan-bed under a frame, and treated in the ſame manner as the tuberous-rooted ſorts before mentioned.

The ſhrubby ſorts muſt be looked over frequently during the winter, while they are in the green-houſe, to pick off all decayed leaves from them, which, if left on, will not only render the plants unſightly, but by their falling off, they will occaſion litter among the other plants; and if they are ſuffered to rot in the houſe, they will occaſion a foul, naſty, damp air, which will be very prejudicial to all the plants; therefore to avoid this, they ſhould be conſtantly picked off every week; and during the ſummer ſeaſon, they will require to be picked every fortnight or three weeks to keep them clean from dead leaves; for as the branches advance, and new leaves are produced on their top, the under ones as conſtantly decay; and if left on till they drop off, will render the plants very unſightly.

GERMANDER. See Teucrium.

GEROPOGON. Goat's-beard.

The Characters are,

The empalement is ſingle, compoſed of many keel-ſhaped leaves which are longer than the corolla; the flower is compoſed of ſeveral hermaphrodite florets, which are imbricated and ſhorter than the empalement, and are of one petal, divided into five ſegments at the top. Theſe have each five ſhort ſtamina, terminated by cylindrical ſummits, and an oblong germen with a ſlender ſtyle, ſupporting two thread-like ſtigma which are recurved; the ſeeds are included in the empalement, and are crowned by five bearded ſpreading rays.

This genus of plants is ranged in the firſt ſection of Linnæus's nineteenth claſs, intitled Syngeneſia Polygamia Æqualis, the florets having five connected ſtamina, and are fruitful.

The Species are,

1. Geropogon (*Glabrum*) foliis glabris. Lin. Sp. 1109. *Goat's-beard with ſmooth leaves.* Tragopogon gramineo folio glabrum, flore dilute incarnato. Raii Sup. 149.

2. Geropogon (*Hirſutum*) foliis piloſis. Lin. Sp. 1109. *Goat's-beard with hairy leaves.* Tragopogon gramineo folio, ſuave rubente flore. Col. Ecphr. 1. p. 232.

The firſt ſort grows naturally in Italy; this hath an erect ſtalk more than a foot high, garniſhed with ſmooth, Graſs-like, long leaves; the ſtalk branches upward into two or five diviſions, each being terminated by one fleſh-coloured flower, compoſed of ſeveral florets.

The ſecond ſort grows naturally in Italy and Sicily. This riſes with an erect ſtalk a foot high, garniſhed with hairy narrow leaves, and ſeldom divides into branches, but is terminated by one flower compoſed of four or five hermaphrodite florets, which are ſucceeded by ſo many bearded ſeeds.

Theſe plants require the ſame treatment as the Tragopogon, to which article the reader is deſired to turn for their culture.

GESNERA.

GESNERA. Plumier Nov. Gen. 27. tab. 9. Lin. Gen. Plant. 667. This plant was so named by father Plumier, who discovered it in America, in honour of Conrad Gesner, a very learned botanist, and natural historian.

The CHARACTERS are,

The empalement of the flower is of one leaf, cut into five acute parts at the top, and is permanent, in which is situated the germen; the flower hath one petal which is tubulous, and first bent inward, and afterward out again like a bugle-horn; the brim is divided into five obtuse segments which are equal; it hath four stamina which are shorter than the petal, terminated by single summits; the germen which sits under the petal supports a single crooked style, crowned by a headed stigma. The germen afterward becomes a roundish capsule with two cells, filled with small seeds, which are fixed on each side the partition.

This genus of plants is ranged in the second section of Linnæus's fourteenth class, intitled Didynamia Angiospermia, which includes those plants whose flowers have two long and two shorter stamina, and the seeds are included in a capsule.

The SPECIES are,

1. GESNERA (*Tomentosa*) foliis ovato-lanceolatis crenatis hirsutis, pedunculis lateralibus longissimis corymbiferis. Hort. Cliff. 318. *Gesnera with oval, hairy, crenated leaves, and long foot-stalks proceeding from the sides of the stalks, supporting flowers in a corymbus.* Gesnera amplo digitalis folio tomentoso. Plum. Gen. 27.

2. GESNERA (*Humilis*) foliis lanceolatis serratis sessilibus, pedunculis ramosis multifloris. Lin. Sp. Plant. 612. *Gesnera with spear-shaped sawed leaves fitting close to the stalks, and branching foot-stalks having many flowers.* Gesnera humilis flore flavescente. Plum. Nov. Gen. 27. *Low Gesnera with a yellowish flower.*

The first sort grows naturally in the West-Indies; the seeds of this were sent me from Jamaica, which succeeded in the Chelsea garden; this rises with a shrubby stalk to the height of six or seven feet, which divides into two or three irregular branches, covered with a russet wool, and garnished with hairy leaves which are seven or eight inches long, and two and a half broad in the middle, having a russet woolly midrib, and the edges are crenated; these are placed on every side the branches without order, and have short foot-stalks; towards the end of the branches come out the foot-stalks of the flowers at every joint, arising from the wings of the stalk; they are naked, and nine inches in length, branching at the top into many smaller foot-stalks, each sustaining a single flower, having a short crooked tube, indented at the top in five obtuse parts, and of an obsolete purple colour. These are succeeded by roundish capsules sitting close in the empalement, the divisions of which arise above the capsule; which Dr. Linnæus, from Plumier's figure, has taken for the empalement sitting upon the capsule, whereas the capsule is distinct from the empalement and is inclosed by it. The capsule is divided into two cells which are filled with small seeds. It flowers here in July and August, but hath not ripened seeds.

The second sort is a plant of humbler growth; this seldom rises more than three feet high; the leaves are much smaller, and sawed on their edges, and fit close to the stalk; the flowers stand upon branching foot-stalks, each sustaining many yellowish flowers, which are deeper cut at their brims than those of the first sort. This was found growing naturally by the late Dr. Houstoun at Carthagena in New Spain.

There is a third species of this genus mentioned by Plumier, which grows to to a tree, and hath spotted and fringed flowers; but this I have not seen in any of the English gardens. These plants are propagated by seeds, which must be procured from the countries where they grow naturally; these should be brought over in their capsules, which is the best way to preserve the seeds good; for as they are very small and light, so when they are separated from the partition to which they adhere, they soon lose their vegetable quality; for I have received the seeds se-

veral times from America, which were taken out of the vessels, but not one of them grew, till I procured some to be sent in their vessels, which succeeded very well.

The seeds should be sown in pots filled with light earth, and plunged into a hot-bed of tanners bark as soon as they arrive, for they sometimes lie long in the ground; those which I have sown in autumn, came up the following spring; therefore when they happen to arrive here at that season, the pots in which the seeds are sown should be plunged into the tan-bed in the stove, and during the winter the earth should be now and then gently watered to prevent its drying too much, but it must not be too moist. In the spring the pots should be removed out of the stove, and plunged into a fresh hot-bed, which will bring up the plants soon after. When these are fit to remove, they should be each planted into a separate pot, and plunged into a good hot-bed of tan, observing to shade them till they have taken new root; then they must be treated in the same way as other tender plants from the same countries.

In autumn they must be plunged into the tan-bed in the stove, where, during the winter, they should have but little water given to them; for if they receive much wet, it will destroy them. In this stove the plants must constantly remain, for they will not thrive if they are kept out of the tan. In the summer, they should have free air admitted to them at all times when the weather is warm; and they must be frequently refreshed with water during that season, but it must not be given to them in too great plenty. As the plants advance in growth they will require larger pots, but there must be care taken not to over-pot them, for they will not thrive in large pots. With this management the plants will flower the second year, and may be continued three or four years, but they are not of long duration in their native country.

GEUM. Lin. Gen. Plant. 561. Caryophyllata. Tourn. Inst. R. H. 294. tab. 151. Avens, or Herb Bennet; in French, *Benoite.*

The CHARACTERS are,

The flower hath a one-leaved empalement, cut at the top into ten segments, which are alternately smaller than the other. The flower has five roundish petals, which are narrow at their base, where they are inserted in the empalement; it hath a great number of awl-shaped stamina, which are the length of the empalement, into which they are inserted, and are terminated by broad obtuse summits. In the center of the flower is situated a great number of germen collected into a head; these have styles inserted in their sides, which are long, hairy, and crowned by single stigmas. The germen afterward become so many flat rough seeds, which are hairy, and have the style which is bent like a knee adhering to them; these fit in the common empalement.

This genus of plants is ranged in the fifth section of Linnæus's twelfth class, intitled Icosandria Polygynia, in which he places those plants whose flowers have more than twenty stamina, and have many styles inserted into the empalement.

The SPECIES are,

1. GEUM (*Urbanum*) floribus erectis, fructu globoso, aristis uncinatis nudis, foliis lyratis. Hort. Cliff. 195. *Geum with erect flowers, a globular fruit, naked hooked beards, and harp-shaped leaves.* Caryophyllata vulgaris. C. B. P. 321. *Common Avens, or Herb Bennet.*

2. GEUM (*Rivale*) floribus nutantibus, fructu oblongo, aristis plumosis. Hort. Cliff. 195. *Geum with nodding flowers, and an oblong fruit with feathery beards.* Caryophyllata aquatica, nutante flore. C. B. P. 321. *Aquatic Herb Bennet with a nodding flower.*

3. GEUM (*Pyrenaicum*) floribus nutantibus, fructu globoso, aristis nudis, foliis lyratis, foliolis rotundioribus. *Geum with nodding flowers, a globular fruit with naked beards, and harp-shaped leaves with rounder lobes.* Caryophyllata Pyrenaica, amplissimo & rotundiori folio, nutante flore. Tourn. Inst. R. H. 295. *Avens*

Avens with a very large and rounder leaf, and a nodding flower.

4. GEUM (*Montanum*) flore erecto folitario fructu oblongo, ariftis plumofis. Lin. Sp. Plant. 501. *Geum with a fingle upright flower, and an oblong fruit with feathery beards.* Caryophyllata montana flore luteo magno. J. B. 2. p. 398. *Mountain Avens with a large yellow flower.*

5. GEUM (*Alpinum*) flore folitario erecto, fructu globofo, ariftis tenuioribus nudis. *Geum with a fingle erect flower, and a globular fruit with narrower naked beards.* Caryophyllata alpina minor. C. B. P. 322. *Smaller Alpine Avens.*

6. GEUM (*Virginianum*) floribus erectis, fructu globofo, ariftis uncinatis nudis, foliis ternatis. Hort. Cliff. 195. *Geum with upright flowers, a globular fruit with naked beards and trifoliate leaves.* Caryophyllata Virginiana, albo flore minore, radice inodora, H. L. 111. *Virginia Avens with a fmaller white flower, and a root without fcent.*

The first fort grows plentifully by the fide of hedges, and in woods, in moft parts of England, fo is rarely admitted into gardens. This ftands in the lift of medicinal plants; the root is the only part ufed, which is efteemed cephalic and alexipharmic, and is manifeftly of a binding nature, fo is ufeful in all fluxes, &c.

The fecond fort grows naturally in moift meadows in the northern parts of England. This is of an humbler growth than the firft, the lower leaves have two pair of fmall lobes at bottom, and three large ones at the top, that which terminates being the largeft. The leaves upon the ftalks are compofed of three acute lobes which fit clofe to the ftalk; the flowers are of a purplifh colour, and nod on one fide; they appear in May, and the feeds ripen in July.

The third fort grows upon the Alps, and alfo on the mountains in the north; this hath fome refemblance to the fecond, but the leaves are much larger and rounder, and are indented on their edges; the flowers are larger and of a gold colour. This flowers about the fame time as the fecond.

The fourth fort grows naturally upon the Alps; this hath leaves much larger than either of the other fpecies; the lower leaves are compofed of three or four pair of fmall irregular pinnæ fet along the midrib, which is terminated by one very broad roundifh lobe, which is crenated on the edge. The flowers are large, of a bright yellow colour, ftanding fingle on the top of the ftalk, which feldom rifes more than five or fix inches high. It flowers in May and June.

The fifth fort grows naturally on the Alps; it is a very low plant, the flower-ftalks are about three inches long, and bend on one fide; they are each terminated by one bright yellow flower, about the fize of thofe of the common fort. This flowers about the fame time as the former.

The fixth fort grows naturally in North America; the ftalks of this fort rife a foot and a half or two feet high, and branch out at the top into fmall footftalks, each being terminated by a fmall white flower; the leaves of this fort are trifoliate, and the root has no fcent. Thefe are all very hardy plants which require a fhady fituation, but will thrive in any foil; they may be eafily propagated by feeds, which fhould be fown in autumn; for when they are fown in the fpring, they do not grow the fame year.

GILLIFLOWER, or JULY-FLOWER. See DIANTHUS.

GILLIFLOWER, or STOCK-GILLIFLOWER. See CHEIRANTHUS.

GILLIFLOWER, the Queen's or Dame's Violet. See HESPERIS.

GINGER. See AMOMUM.

GINGIDIUM. See ARTEDIA.

GLADE is an open and light paffage made through a wood, by lopping off the branches of trees along that way.

GLADIOLUS. Lin. Gen. Plant. 55. Tourn. Inft. R. H. 365. tab. 190. [takes its name of Gladius, *Lat.*

fword; q. d. little fword; becaufe the leaves of this plant refemble a fword.] Cornflag; in French, Glaieul.

The CHARACTERS are,

The flowers are included in fheaths, which ftand at a diftance from each other; the petal of the flower is cut into fix parts, three of the upper are near together, the three under fpread open, but they all form a fhort incurved tube with their bafe; they have three awl-fhaped ftamina, which are inferted into every other petal, and all of them afcend to the upper petals, and are terminated by oblong fummits. The germen is fituated below the flower, fupporting a fingle ftyle the length of the ftamina, crowned by a concave trifid ftigma. The germen afterward becomes an oblong, fwelling, three-cornered capfule, with three cells, opening with three valves, filled with roundifh feeds.

This genus of plants is ranged in the firft fection of Linnæus's third clafs, intitled Triandria Monogynia, which includes thofe plants whofe flowers have three ftamina and one ftyle.

The SPECIES are,

1. GLADIOLUS (*Communis*) foliis enfiformibus, floribus diftantibus, Lin. Sp. Plant. 36. *Cornflag with Sword-fhaped leaves and flowers ftanding at a diftance.* Gladiolus floribus uno verfu difpofitis. C. B. P. 41. *Cornflag with flowers difpofed on one fide the ftalk.*

2. GLADIOLUS (*Italicus*) foliis enfiformibus, floribus ancipitibus. *Cornflag with fword-fhaped leaves, and flowers ftanding on both fides the ftalk.* Gladiolus utrinque floribus. C. B. P. 41. *Cornflag with flowers on each fide the ftalk.*

3. GLADIOLUS (*Byzantinus*) foliis enfiformibus, fpathis longioribus. *Cornflag with fword-fhaped leaves and longer fheaths to the flowers.* Gladiolus major Byzantinus. C. B. P. 41. *Greater Cornflag of Byzantium.*

4. GLADIOLUS (*Indicus*) foliis enfiformibus, floribus maximis incarnatis. *Cornflag with fword-fhaped leaves, and very large incarnate flowers.* Gladiolus maximus Indicus. C. B. P. 41. *Greateft Indian Cornflag.*

5. GLADIOLUS (*Anguftis*) foliis linearibus floribus diftantibus, corollarum tubo limbis longiore. Lin. Sp. Plant. 37. *Cornflag with very narrow leaves, flowers ftanding at a diftance from each other, and the tube longer than the margins of the petal.* Gladiolus Africanus, folio gramineo, floribus carneis, maculam rhomboideam infcriptis uno verfu pofitis. Boerh. Ind. alt. 2. 127. *African Cornflag, with a graffy leaf, and flefh-coloured flowers, marked with a purple rhomboid fpot ranged all on one fide the ftalk.*

6. GLADIOLUS (*Triftis*) foliis lineari cancellatis corollis campanulatis. *Cornflag with very narrow channelled leaves, and a ftalk bearing bell-fhaped flowers.* Lilio-Gladiolus bifolius & biflorus, foliis quadrangulis. Trew. tab. 39. *Lily Cornflag with two leaves and flowers, and four-cornered leaves.*

The firft fort grows naturally in arable land in moft of the warm countries in Europe, and was formerly cultivated in the Englifh gardens, where the roots have multiplied fo greatly as to become a moft troublefome weed, and are very difficult to eradicate; this hath a round, compreffed, tuberous root, which is of a yellowifh colour, covered with a brown furrowed fkin, like thofe of the large yellow vernal Crocus; from the root arife two flat fword-fhaped leaves, which embrace each other at their bafe, and between thefe arife the flower-ftalk, which grows near two feet high, having one or two narrow leaves embracing it like a fheath; the ftalks are terminated by five or fix purple flowers, ftanding above each other at fome diftance, and ranged on one fide of the ftalk; each of thefe has a fpatha (or fheath) which covers the flower-bud before it expands, but fplits open lengthways when the flowers blow, and fhrivel up to a dry fkin, remaining about the feed-veffel till the feeds are ripe. The flower hath one petal, which is cut almoft to the bottom in fix parts, fo as to appear like a flower of fix petals, the three upper fegments ftand near together, and rife like a labiated flower; the under one turns downward, and the two fide fegments form the chaps of the flower, and fpread open at the top, but are curved downward at the bottom. They are ranged along one side of the stalk, and are of a purplish red colour. This flowers the latter end of May, and in June, and the seeds ripen the beginning of August; it requires no care, for when it is once planted in a garden, it will multiply too fast, so as to become a troublesome weed.

There is a variety of this with white flowers, and another with flesh-coloured flowers, which have accidentally risen from seeds, so are not different species.

The second sort differs from the first, in having the flowers ranged on both sides the stalk, but in other respects it is very like to that; and of this there is a variety with white flowers, but these are not so common in the English gardens as the former.

The third sort hath larger roots than either of the former, but are of the same form; the leaves are also much broader and longer, the veins or channels of the leaves are deeper; the flower-stalks rise higher; the flowers are much larger, and of a deeper red colour than those of the former sorts, and the sheaths are longer. This plant makes a fine appearance in flower, so is worthy of a place in every good garden; and the rather, because the roots do not increase so fast as to become troublesome in the borders. This is propagated by offsets, which are sent off from the roots in the same manner as Tulips. The roots may be taken out of the ground the end of July, when their stalks decay, and may be kept out of the ground till the latter end of September, or the beginning of October; at which time they should be planted in the borders of the flower-garden, where they will thrive in any situation, and being intermixed with other flowers of the same growth, they will add to the variety.

The fourth sort grows naturally at the Cape of Good Hope, from whence I have several times received the seeds. This has been many years cultivated in the English gardens, but very rarely flowers here; for in near thirty years that I have cultivated this sort, I have never seen it but once in flower, though I have kept it in all situations, and placed it in various soils. The roots increase very fast, but will not live in the open air through the winter in this country. The roots of this sort are broader and flatter than those of any of the other sorts, and are covered with a netted skin; the scales come out in the same manner, embracing each other like the former sorts; they are longer, smoother, and of a brighter green, than any of the others; these begin to appear in September, and continue growing in size till after Christmas; they begin to decay in March, and the latter end of June are quite withered, when the roots may be taken up, and kept out of the ground till August; the time of its flowering is in January. The flowers of this sort are placed on each side of the stalk, and sit close to it, like the grains of the flat Barley; the sheaths between the flowers are not so long as those of the other sorts, and form a kind of scaly covering to them. The flowers are of a pale red colour without, but the three lower segments are yellow within toward their base, with a few red stripes. The flowers do not all open at the same time, but the lower ones decay before those on the upper part of the spike are in beauty; however, they make a good appearance at a season when all flowers are valuable.

This sort propagates by offsets very fast; these should be planted in a warm border of kitchen-garden earth, and in winter they should be covered with glasses or mats to guard them from frost; for I have with a flight shelter preserved those which were in pots under a common frame, and some which were planted in the full ground, when the frost has not been severe; and I have always found that those plants which were hardily treated, grew much stronger than those which were placed in a moderate degree of warmth; so that where there is a conveniency of covering a warm border with glasses in the winter, if

these roots are planted in the full ground, where they may be protected from the frost, there will be a greater probability of their flowering, than in any other method of culture.

The fifth sort grows naturally at the Cape of Good Hope, from whence I received the seeds, which succeeded in the Chelsea garden, where the plants annually produce their beautiful flowers.

This hath a round, smooth, bulbous root, which is covered with a thin dark-coloured skin, from which come out in autumn two or three very narrow grassy leaves, folded over each other at their base, but open flat above, and rise near two feet high. In the spring of the year arises a single stalk from between the leaves about two feet long, which always bend on one side; toward the upper part of this come out two or three flowers, ranged on one side of the stalk, standing upright, each having a narrow spatha, or hood, and long slender tubes, which swell large upward, and are divided into six parts, which are nearly equal. The flower is of a dusky flesh colour, and each segment of the petal has a rhomboidal mark of a dark red, or purple colour; afterward the tube of the flower opens, and the deep division of the petals is seen, and the three stamina with their summits appear, attended by the style with its trifid stigma, arising from the germen. This plant flowers in May and the beginning of June; as this plant is a native of a warm country, it requires protection from the frost in winter; therefore the bulbs should be planted in pots filled with light earth, and placed in the green-house in winter; or, where there is not such conveniency, they may be put under a hot-bed frame during that season, where they may have air in mild weather, and be screened from the frost; in such situations I have had them thrive and flower very well.

This is propagated by offsets from the root in the same manner as the last, and also by seeds, which are frequently perfected in England; these should be sown the latter end of August, in pots filled with light earth, and placed in a shady situation till the middle of September; then the pots should be removed where they may have the sun great part of the day, and in October they must be placed under a hot-bed frame, where they may be protected from frost and great rains, but enjoy the free air in mild weather. In the spring the young plants will appear, when they will require a little water once in eight or ten days, but it should be given them sparingly, for too much wet will rot these tender bulbs. In May, when the danger of frost is over, the pots should be removed to a sheltered situation, where they may have the morning sun till noon; and, if the season proves dry, they must be now and then refreshed with water. Toward the latter end of June, the leaves of these plants will decay; then the roots should be taken up, and may be mixed with sand, and kept in a dry room till the end of August, when they should be planted again; and as the roots are small, four or five may be planted in each halfpenny pot, filled with light earth; these should be placed where they may have only the forenoon sun, till the middle of September, when they should have a warmer situation; and in October they must be placed under a hot-bed frame as before, and treated in the same way during the winter season; and in the spring they must be placed in the open air till their leaves decay, when they may be again taken out of the ground, and treated in the same manner as before; but as the roots will have grown to a larger size, so when they are planted again, they should each have a separate half-penny pot, because now they will be large enough to flower, so may be treated as the old roots.

The sixth sort is also a native of the Cape of Good Hope, from whence I have several times received the seeds; the root of this sort is oval, not compressed as those of the common sorts. The leaves are very long and narrow, having two deep furrows running the whole length, the midrib rising very prominent, so as

to

to have the appearance of a four-cornered leaf. The leaves are fingle, and wrapped clofe about the flower-ftalk at their bafe to a confiderable length ; there are feldom more than two of thefe leaves from one root ; the ftalk is flender and round, and rifes about two feet high ; and the top is garnifhed with two flowers, which are placed two inches and a half afunder on the fame fide of the ftalk, each having a fhort fpatha, or fheath, embracing the germen and the bafe of the tube, which is long, narrow, and recurved, but enlarges greatly before it is divided. The upper part of the flower is cut into fix equal fegments, which end in acute points of a purplifh colour, which form a ftripe through the middle of each fegment. The petal is of a cream colour, and fades to a fulphur colour before it decays. This flowers in June, and fometimes the feeds ripen well in England. This may be propagated by offsets from the root, or by feeds in the fame manner as the fifth fort, and the plants require the fame treatment.

GLANDIFEROUS trees, are fuch trees as bear maft, as Acorns, &c.

GLANDULOUS roots, are fuch roots as grow kernel-wife.

GLANS is that fort of fruit which is contained within a fmooth, but hard bark, having but one feed ; its hinder parts covered with a kind of cup, the forepart being bare, as Acorns ; but it is properly the fruit without the cup.

GLASTENBURY THORN. See Mespilus.

GLAUCIUM. See Chelidonium.

GLAUX, Sea Chickweed, or Milkwort, and black Saltwort, is a low trailing perennial plant, with leaves fomewhat like Chickweed, but of a thickerconfiftence, which fit clofe to the ftalks. The flowers come out from the bofom of the leaves ; they are white, and like thofe of Chickweed. This is feldom cultivated in gardens, fo I fhall not trouble the reader with a further account of it. This grows upon the fea-fhores in moft parts of England.

GLECHOMA. Ground Ivy, Gill go by the Ground, Ale-hoof, or Turn-hoof.

This plant grows naturally under hedges, and upon the fides of banks in moft parts of England, fo is rarely cultivated in gardens, for which reafon I fhall pafs over it, with barely mentioning it here.

GLEDITSIA. Lin. Gen. Plant. 1025. Acacia. Raii Meth. 161. Honey Locuft, or three-thorned Acacia.

The Characters are,
It hath male and hermaphrodite flowers in the fame katkin, and female flowers in different plants. The male katkins are long, compact, and cylindrical, and have each a three-leaved fmall empalement ; they have three rounddifh petals, which fpread open in form of a cup ; thefe have a turbinated nectarium, whofe mouth afterward grows to the parts of fructification ; they have fix flender flamina, which are longer than the petals, terminated by oblong compreffed fummits. The hermaphrodite flowers in the fame katkin, are fituated at the end ; thefe have empalements, petals, and flamina like the male, and have a germen, flyle, and feeds like the female, which are fituated on different trees, and are difpofed in a loofe katkin ; thefe have a five-leaved empalement, and have five oblong petals, with two fhort thread-like nectariums, and a broad germen longer than the petals, fupporting a fhort reflexed flyle, crowned by a thick ftigma. The germen afterward becomes a large flat pod, with feveral tranfverfe partitions, having a pulp in each divifion, furrounding one hard roundifh feed.

This genus of plants is ranged in the fecond fection of Linnæus's twenty-third clafs, intitled Polygamia Diœcecia, which includes thofe plants which have male and hermaphrodite flowers in the fame plant, and female flowers in different plants.

The Species are,
1. Gleditsia (*Triacanthus*) fpinis triplicibus axillaribus. Lin. Sp. 1509. *Gleditfia with three thorns on the fide of the branches.* Acacia Americana Abruæ folio triacanthos, five ad axillas foliorum, fpinâ triplici donatâ. Pluk. Mant. 1. *Three-thorned American Acacia.*

2. Gleditsia (*Inermis*) fpinis paucioribus, folis bipinnatis, filiquis ovalibus. *Gleditfia with fewer fpines, winged leaves, and oval pods.* Acacia Abruæ folio triacanthos, capfulâ ovali unicum femen claudente. Catefb. Car. 1. p. 43. *Three-thorned Acacia with an Abrus leaf, and an oval pod containing one feed.*

Thefe trees grow naturally in America ; the firft fort is very common in moft parts of North America; where it is known by the title of Honey Locuft ; this has been many years cultivated in the Englifh gardens, and is known among the gardeners by the title of three-thorned Acacia. It rifes with an erect trunk to the height of thirty or forty feet, and is armed with long fpines, which have two or three fmaller coming out from the fide, and are frequently produced in clufters at the knots on the ftems of the trees ; they are fometimes three or four inches long. The branches of this tree are alfo armed with the fame fort of fpines, and are garnifhed with winged leaves, compofed of ten pair of fmall leaves which fit clofe to the midrib, and are of a lucid green. The flowers come out from the fide of the young branches in katkins ; they are of an herbaceous colour, fo make no figure. The hermaphrodite flowers are fucceeded by pods near a foot and a half long, and two inches broad, divided into many cells by tranfverfe partitions, each containing one fmooth, hard, oblong feed, furrounded by a fweet pulp.

The leaves of this tree feldom come out till June in this country, and the flowers appear the latter end of July, but they do not flower till they are of a large fize : there was one tree in the Chelfea garden which produced flowers feveral years, and there is one now growing in the Bifhop of London's garden at Fulham, which produced pods in the year 1728, and came to their full fize, but the feeds did not ripen. The fecond fort hath much the appearance of the firft, but it hath fewer fpines. The leaves are fmaller, and the pods are oval, containing but one feed ; this was difcovered by the late Mr. Catefby, in Carolina, from whence he fent the feeds to England, by the title of Water Acacia, by which it is known in the gardens.

Thefe trees are propagated by feeds, which muft be procured from America, where the trees grow naturally ; thofe of the firft fort are annually fent to England in plenty, by the title of Locuft, or Honey Locuft, to diftinguifh it from the falfe Acacia, which is frequently called Locuft-tree in America; thefe feeds may be fown upon a bed of light earth in the fpring, burying them half an inch deep ; and if the fpring fhould prove dry, they muft be frequently watered, otherwife the plants will not come up the firft year, for I have fometimes had the feeds remain two years in the ground before they have come up ; therefore thofe who are defirous to fave time, fhould fow the feeds as foon as they arrive, and plunge the pots into a moderate hot-bed, obferving to water them frequently ; by this method moft of the plants will come up the fame feafon, but thefe fhould be gradually inured to bear the open air, for if they are continued in the hot-bed, they will draw up weak ; during the fummer feafon, thofe plants in pots will require frequent waterings, but thofe in the full ground will not dry fo faft, therefore need no water, unlefs the feafon fhould prove very dry. In autumn, thofe in the pots fhould be placed under a hot-bed frame to protect them from froft, for thefe young plants generally keep growing late in the fummer, fo the upper part of their fhoots is tender, and the early frofts of the autumn often kill the ends of them, if they are not protected, and this frequently occafions great part of the fhoots decaying in winter ; for which reafon thofe plants in the full ground fhould be covered with mats in autumn, on the firft appearance of froft ; for a fmall froft in autumn will do more mifchief to thefe young fhoots which are full of fap, than fevere froft when the fhoots are hardened.

The following fpring the plants may be tranfplanted into nurfery-beds, at a foot diftance row from row,
and

and fix inches afunder in the rows; but this fhould not be performed till April, after the danger of hard froft is over; for as the plants do not put out their leaves till very late, fo there will be no hazard in removing them any time before May. If the feafon fhould prove dry, they muft be watered; and if the furface of the beds is covered with mofs, or mulch, to prevent the earth from drying, it will be of great fervice to the plants. In thefe beds the plants may remain two years, during which time they muft be conftantly kept clean from weeds; and in the winter there fhould be fome rotten tan, or other mulch, fpread over the furface of the ground to keep out the froft. If the plants thrive well, they will be fit to tranfplant to the places where they are to remain after two years growth, for they do not bear removing when large; the beft feafon for tranfplanting of thefe trees, is late in the fpring; they thrive beft in a light deep foil, for in ftrong fhallow ground they become moffy, and never grow large; they fhould alfo have a fheltered fituation, for when they are much expofed to winds, their branches are frequently broken in the fummer feafon, when they are fully clothed with leaves.

GLOBULARIA. Lin. Gen. Plant. 106. Tourn. Inft. R. H. 466. tab. 265. *Blue Daify.*

The CHARACTERS are,

It hath a flower compofed of many florets, which are included in one common fcaly empalement; each floret has an empalement of one leaf, which is tubulous, and cut into five fegments at the top. The florets have one petal, whofe bafe is tubulous, but the brim is cut into four parts; the upper fegment, which is the leaft, is reflexed; they have four ftamina the length of the petal, terminated by diftinct fummits; in the bottom of the tube is fituated an oval germen fupporting a fingle ftyle, crowned by an obtufe ftigma. The germen afterward becomes an oval feed, fitting in the common empalement.

This genus of plants is ranged in the firft fection of Linnæus's fourth clafs, intitled Tetandria Monogynia, which includes thofe plants whofe flowers have four ftamina and one ftyle.

The SPECIES are,

1. GLOBULARIA (*Vulgaris*) caule herbaceo, foliis radicalibus tridentatis, caulinis lanceolatis. Flor. Suec. 109. *Globularia with an herbaceous ftalk, the lower leaves divided into three points, and thofe on the ftalks fpear-fhaped.* Globularia vulgaris. Tourn. 467. *Common Globularia.*

2. GLOBULARIA (*Nudicaulis*) caule nudo, foliis integerrimis lanceolatis. Lin. Sp. Plant. 97. *Globularia with a naked ftalk, and fpear-fhaped entire leaves.* Globularia Pyrenaica, folio oblongo, caule nudo. Tourn. 467. *Pyrenean Globularia, with an oblong leaf and naked ftalk.*

3. GLOBULARIA (*Alypum*) caule fruticofo, foliis lancelatis tridentatis integrifque. Prod. Leyd. 190. *Globularia with a fhrubby ftalk, fpear-fhaped leaves, fome ending in three points, and others are entire.* Globularia fruticofa, myrti folio tridentato. Tourn. 467. *Shrubby Globularia with a trifid Myrtle leaf.*

4. GLOBULARIA (*Spinofa*) foliis radicalibus crenato-aculeatis, caulinis integerrimis mucronatis. Lin. Sp. Plant. 96. *Globularia with lower leaves crenated and prickly, thofe on the ftalks entire, ending in a point.* Globularia fpinofa. Tourn. 467. *Prickly Globularia.*

5. GLOBULARIA (*Cordifolia*) caule fubnudo, folis cuneiformibus tricufpidatis, intermedio minimo. Lin. Sp. Plant. 96. *Globularia with a naked ftalk, and wedge-fhaped leaves ending in three points, whofe middle fegment is the leaft.* Globularia Alpina minima, origani folio. Tourn. 467. *Smalleft Alpine Globularia with a wild Marjoram leaf.*

6. GLOBULARIA (*Orientalis*) caule fubnudo, capitulis alternis feffilibus, foliis lanceolato-ovatis integris. Lin. Sp. Plant. 97. *Globularia with a naked ftalk, alternate heads fitting clofe to the ftalks, and oval, fpear-fhaped, entire leaves.* Globularia Orientalis, floribus per caulem fparfis. Tourn. Cor. 35. *Eaftern Globularia with flowers fcattered along the ftalks.*

The firft of thefe plants grows plentifully about Montpelier, as alfo at the foot of the mountains Jura and Saleva, and in many other parts of Italy, and in Germany; this plant hath leaves very like thofe of the Daify, but are thicker and fmoother. The flower-ftalks rife about fix inches high, fupporting a globular head of flowers, compofed of feveral florets, which are included in one common fcaly empalement; they are of a fine blue colour, and appear in June; thefe are fucceeded by feeds, which fit in the empalement, and ripen in autumn.

The fecond fort grows plentifully in the woods, near the convent of the Carthufians, and on the Pyrenean mountains; this is much larger than the former, and hath a fhrubby ftalk a foot and a half high; the foot-ftalk is quite naked. The leaves are narrower, and much longer.

The firft fort may be propagated by parting of the roots after the manner of Daifies. The beft feafon for parting and tranfplanting of the plants is in September, that they may take new root before the frofty weather comes on. They fhould be planted in a fhady fituation, and require a moift loamy foil, in which they will thrive much better than in a light ground and an open fituation; but the plants fhould not be removed oftener than every other year, if they are required to flower ftrong.

The third fort grows about Montpelier in France, and in Valentia, and feveral other parts of Spain. This has a hard woody ftem, which rifes about two feet high, having many woody branches, befet with leaves like thofe of the Myrtle-tree. On the top of the branches the flowers are produced, which are of a blue colour, and globe-fhaped; this plant may be propagated by cuttings, which fhould be cut off in April, juft before they begin to make new fhoots; the cuttings fhould be planted into pots filled with light frefh earth, and then placed into a very moderate hot-bed, obferving to water and fhade them until they have taken root, when they may be taken out of the bed, and inured to bear the open air by degrees. In fummer thefe plants may be expofed with other hardy exotic plants, and in winter they fhould be placed under a hot-bed frame, where they may enjoy the free air in mild weather, but fhould be fcreened from hard froft, which will deftroy them, if they are expofed thereto, but in mild winters they will live in the open air. This plant never produces good feeds in this country.

The fourth fort was found in the mountains of Granada, by Dr. Albinus; this plant is of low growth, and may be propagated as the firft; as may alfo the fifth fort, which is the leaft of all the forts, and the moft hardy; therefore fhould have a fhady fituation, and a cool moift foil.

The fixth fort was found by Dr. Tournefort in the Levant; this is fomewhat tender, and fhould be fheltered from the froft in winter, under a frame, but in fummer it fhould be expofed with other hardy exotic plants, and will require to be frequently watered in dry weather. This may be propagated by feeds, or by parting of their roots, as was directed for the firft fort.

GLORIOSA. Lin. Gen. Plant. 374. Methonica. Tourn. Acad. R. Scien. 1706. *The Superb Lily.*

The CHARACTERS are,

The flower hath no empalement; it hath fix long fpear-fhaped petals, which are waved, and reflexed to the foot-ftalk. It hath fix ftamina, which fpread open each way, and are terminated by proftrate fummits. In the center is fituated a globular germen, fupporting a flender inclining ftyle, crowned by an obtufe triple ftigma. The germen afterward becomes an oval thin capfule having three cells, filled with globular feeds, difpofed in a double range.

This genus of plants is ranged in the firft fection of Linnæus's fixth clafs, intitled Hexandria Monogynia, which includes the plants whofe flowers have fix ftamina and one ftyle.

1. GLORIOSA (*Superba*) foliis longioribus capreolis terminalibus. *Superb Lily with longer leaves ending with clafpers.*

claspers. Methonica Malabarorum. Hort. Lugd. 688. *Methonica of Malabar,* and the Lilium Zeylanicum superbum. Hort. Amst. 1. p. 69. *Superb Lily of Ceylon.*

2. GLORIOSA (*Cærulea*) foliis ovato-lanceolatis acutis. *Superb Lily with oval, spear-shaped, acute leaves.*

The first sort grows naturally on the coast of Malabar, and also in Ceylon, from whence it was first brought to the gardens in Holland, where it has been many years cultivated; this hath a long fleshy root of a whitish colour, and a nauseous bitter taste, from the middle of which arises a round weak stalk, which requires support to prevent its trailing on the ground. The stalks grow to the height of eight or ten feet, garnished with leaves placed alternate on every side, which are smooth, about eight inches long, and one inch and a half broad at the base, growing narrower till within two inches of the end, which runs out in a narrow point, ending with a tendril, or clasper, by which it fastens to the neighbouring plants for support. At the upper part of the stalk the flower is produced from the side, standing upon a slender foot-stalk; it is composed of six oblong petals, ending with acute points, which, on their first opening, are of an herbaceous colour, and spread wide open; the flower hanging downward as the Crown Imperial and Fritillary, but afterward the petals turn quite back, and change to a beautiful red flame colour, their acute points meeting at the top; these petals are finely waved on their edges. The six stamina spread out every way almost horizontal, and are terminated by prostrate summits. In the center of the flower is situated a roundish germen, supporting an inclining style, crowned by a triple stigma. This plant flowers in June and July, but seldom perfects seeds in this country. The stalks decay in autumn, and the roots remain inactive all the winter, and the new stalks come out in March. The roots and every part of this plant is very poisonous, so should not be put in the way of children.

The seeds of the second sort were sent me by Monf. Richard, gardener to the French king at Trianon; these were brought from Senegal by Monf. Adanson, who discovered this plant growing there naturally; this is said to have a blue flower, but the plants which are in the Chelsea garden have not yet flowered. This hath a climbing stalk, which is garnished with smooth leaves about three inches long, and two broad, ending in acute points, but have no tendril or clasper. The stalks as yet have not grown more than two feet high here, but have the appearance of climbing like the other sort. The leaves have a strong disagreeable scent on being handled, so as to be troublesome to the head if too near, or long smelt to.

As these plants rarely produce seeds in this country, they are generally propagated by their roots; those of the first sort creep and multiply pretty fast, but the second hath not as yet put out any offsets; but as the plants are young, we cannot as yet say how they may increase when they are of a proper age. These roots may be taken out of the ground when their stalks are decayed, and preserved in sand during the winter season, but they must be kept in the stove, or a warm room, where they can receive no injury from the cold; and in the spring they must be planted in pots filled with light earth, and plunged into the tan-bed in the stove; but others chuse to let the roots continue in the ground all the winter, keeping the pots always in the tan-bed: where this is practised, the roots should have very little water in the winter; for as they are then in an inactive state, so moisture at that time frequently rots the roots.

Toward the latter end of March, or the beginning of April, their stalks will appear, when there should be some tall sticks put down by them to support them, otherwise they will trail over the neighbouring plants, and the first sort will fasten to the plants by the tendrils, which are at the end of the leaves. The stalks of this sort will rise ten or twelve feet high, if the

roots are strong, and some of the stalks will produce two or three flowers, which come out from the wings of the stalk near the top; these flowers make a fine appearance in the stove, during their continuance, which is seldom more than ten days or a fortnight. In summer, when the plants are growing, they will require frequently to be watered, but they must not have it in too large quantities, for they are very subject to rot with much wet at any season. Those roots which are not taken out of the pots in winter, should be transplanted and parted the beginning of March, before they put out new fibres, or stalks, for they must not be removed when they are in a growing state; the pots in which these roots are planted should not be too large; for unless they are confined, they will not put out strong stalks; the largest roots may be planted in twopenny pots, but the small ones will require only pots of about five or six inches over at the top.

GLYCINE. Lin. Gen. Plant. 797. Apios. Boer. Ind. alt. *Knobbed-rooted Liquorice Vetch.*

The CHARACTERS are,

The empalement of the flower is of one leaf, divided into two lips at the top, the upper lip being obtuse and indented; the lower lip is longer, trifid, and acute, the middle indenture being extended beyond the other. The flower is of the butterfly kind. The standard is heart-shaped, deflexed on the sides, gibbous on the back, and indented at the point. The wings are small, oblong, and oval toward their end, and bend backward. The keel is narrow, sickle-shaped, turning upward with its point to the standard, where it is broadest. It hath ten stamina, nine of which are joined in one body, and the other stands single, terminated by single summits. In the center is situated an oblong germen supporting a spiral cylindrical style, crowned by an obtuse stigma. The germen afterward becomes an oblong pod with two cells, inclosing kidney-shaped seeds.

This genus of plants is ranged in the third section of Linnæus's seventeenth class, which includes the plants whose flowers have ten stamina joined in two bodies. Tournefort places the first sort under this genus of Astragalus, which is ranged in the fifth section of his tenth class, which includes the herbs with a butterfly flower, whose pointal turns to a pod with two cells.

The SPECIES are,

1. GLYCINE (*Apios*) foliis impari-pinnatis ovato-lanceolatis. Hort. Upsal. 227. *Glycine with oval, spear-shaped, winged leaves.* Astragalus tuberosus scandens, Fraxini folio. Tourn. Inst. 415. *Climbing tuberous Milk Vetch with an Ash leaf;* and the Apios Americana. Cornut. 200.

2. GLYCINE (*Frutescens*) foliis impari-pinnatis caule perenni. Hort. Cliff. 361. *Glycine with winged leaves and a perennial stalk.* Phaseoloides frutescens, Caroliniana, foliis pinnatis, floribus cæruleis conglomeratis. Hort. Angl. tab. 15. *Carolina Kidney-bean-tree; with winged leaves, and blue flowers growing in whorls.*

3. GLYCINE (*Abrus*) foliis abrupto-pinnatis pinnis numerosis obtusis. Lin. Sp. 1025. *Glycine with abrupt, winged leaves, whose lobes are obtuse.* Orobus Americanus, fructu coccineo nigrâ maculâ notato. Tourn. Inst. 393. *American Bitter Vetch with a scarlet fruit, marked with a black spot, commonly called wild Liquorice in the West-Indies.*

4. GLYCINE (*Comosa*) foliis ternatis hirsutis, racemis lateralibus. Lin. Sp. Plant. 754. *Glycine with hairy trifoliate leaves, and several flowers growing in long bunches from the sides of the stalks.* Phaseolus Marianus scandens, floribus commosis. Pet. Muf. 453. *Climbing Kidney-bean of Maryland with spiked flowers.*

5. GLYCINE (*Tomentosa*) foliis ternatis tomentosis, racemis axillaribus brevissimis, leguminibus dispermis. Lin. Sp. Plant. 754. *Glycine with woolly trifoliate leaves, and very short spikes of flowers proceeding from the sides of the stalks, with pods containing two seeds.* Anonis phaseoloides scandens, floribus flavis sessilibus. Hort. Elth. 30. tab. 26. *Climbing Rest-Harrow like Kidney-bean, with yellow flowers sitting close to the stalks.*

The

The firſt ſort grows naturally in Virginia ; this hath roots compoſed of ſeveral knobs, or tubers, which hang to each other by ſmall ſtrings ; from theſe come out in the ſpring ſlender twining ſtalks, which riſe to the height of eight or ten feet, garniſhed with winged leaves, compoſed of three pair of oval ſpear-ſhaped lobes, terminated by an odd one. The flowers come out in ſhort ſpikes from the ſide of the ſtalks ; they are of a Pea-bloſſom kind, of a dirty fleſh-colour, having little ſcent. Theſe appear in Auguſt, but do not produce ſeeds in England. The ſtalks decay in autumn, but the roots continue ; this is propagated by parting of the roots, each of the tubers being ſeparated from the principal root, will grow ; the beſt time for this is about the end of March, or the beginning of April, before they put out ſhoots. The roots ſhould be planted in a warm ſituation, and in hard froſt covered with tan or mulch to protect them, otherwiſe they will not live abroad in this country : where they have been planted againſt a ſouth wall, they have thriven and flowered extremely well, which they ſeldom do in any ot'er ſituation ; and thoſe roots which are planted in pots rarely flower, nor do their ſtalks riſe near ſo high as thoſe which are planted in the full ground ; ſome ignorant perſons call this the Twickenham Climber.

The ſecond ſort was brought from Carolina, but has been ſince obſerved in Virginia, and ſome other places in North America ; this ſort has woody ſtalks, which twiſt themſelves together, and alſo twine round any trees that grow near, and will riſe to the height of fifteen feet, or more. The leaves are winged, and in ſhape ſomewhat like the Aſh-tree, but have a greater number of pinnæ. The flowers are produced in cluſters from the wings of the leaves, which are of a purple colour ; theſe are ſucceeded by long cylindrical pods, ſhaped like thoſe of the ſcarlet Kidney-bean, containing ſeveral kidney-ſhaped ſeeds, but theſe are never perfected in England.

This climbing ſhrub is propagated in ſeveral nurſeries near London, where it is known by the name of Carolina Kidney-bean-tree. It is increaſed by laying down the young branches in October, which will be rooted well by that time twelvemonth (eſpecially if they are duly watered in dry weather) and may then be tranſplanted, either in a nurſery for a year to get ſtrength, or to the place where they are to remain for good, which ſhould be in a warm light ſoil and a ſheltered ſituation, where they will endure the cold of our ordinary winters very well ; and if their roots are covered with ſtraw, Fern, Peas-haulm, or any other light covering, there will be no danger of their being deſtroyed by the froſt.

The third ſort grows naturally in both Indies, and alſo in Egypt. This is a perennial plant, with ſlender twining ſtalks, which twiſt about any neighbouring ſupport, and riſe to the height of eight or ten feet, garniſhed with winged leaves, compoſed of ſixteen pair of ſmall, oblong, blunt lobes, ſet cloſe together ; theſe have the taſte of Liquorice, from whence the inhabitants of the Weſt-Indies have given it the name of Wild Liquorice, and uſe the herb for the ſame purpoſe as the Liquorice in Europe. The flowers are produced from the ſide of the ſtalks in ſhort ſpikes or bunches ; they are of a pale purple colour, and ſhaped like thoſe of the Kidney-bean ; theſe are ſucceeded by ſhort pods, each containing three or four hard round ſeeds of a ſcarlet colour, with a black ſpot or eye on that ſide which is faſtened to the pod. The ſeeds of this plant are frequently ſtrung, and are worn as ornaments by the natives of thoſe countries, where the plants grow naturally : they are frequently brought to England from the Weſt-Indies, and are wrought into various forms, with ſhells and other hard ſeeds. This plant is propagated by ſeeds, which muſt be ſown upon a good hot-bed in the ſpring ; but as the ſeeds are very hard, ſo unleſs they are ſoaked in water twelve or fourteen hours before they are ſown, they frequently lie in the ground a whole year before they vegetate ; but when ſoaked, the plants will appear in a fortnight after the ſeeds are ſown, if they are good, and the bed in a proper temperature of heat. When the plants are two inches high, they ſhould be each tranſplanted into a ſeparate pot, filled with light earth, and plunged into a hot-bed of tanners bark, where they ſhould be ſhaded from the ſun till they have taken new root ; after which they muſt be treated in the ſame manner as other tender plants from the ſame countries, always keeping them in the bark-ſtove, for they are too tender to thrive in any other ſituation in England. This ſort will flower the ſecond year from ſeeds, and ſometimes ripens ſeeds here.

There are two other varieties of this plant, one with a white, and the other a yellow ſeed, but the plants do not differ from the other in leaf or ſtalk ; but as theſe have not as yet flowered in England, I do not know how their flowers may differ.

The fourth ſort hath a perennial root and an annual ſtalk, which decays in the autumn. This riſes from two to three feet high, with ſlender herbaceous ſtalks, which are garniſhed with trifoliate hairy leaves, ſitting cloſe to the ſtalks ; the ſmall leaves or lobes, are of the oval ſpear-ſhape, ending in acute points. The flowers come out from the ſide of the ſtalks, at the foot-ſtalk of the leaves ; the naked part of the foot-ſtalk is about two inches long, and the ſpike of flowers is about the ſame length, and is recurved ; the flowers are of a Pea-bloſſom kind, ſitting cloſe together. They are ſmall, and of a fine blue colour, coming out the beginning of June, and are ſometimes ſucceeded by ſeeds in England, which ripen in Auguſt.

This ſort grows naturally in North America, and is hardy enough to live in the open air in England. It may be propagated by ſeeds, or parting of the roots ; the former is the beſt method, where good ſeeds can be obtained : theſe may be ſown on a bed of light earth in the ſpring, and if the ſeaſon ſhould prove dry, they muſt be frequently refreſhed with water, otherwiſe they will remain a long time in the ground before they vegetate : when the plants come up, they muſt be kept clean from weeds in the ſummer, and in the autumn when their ſtalks are decayed, if ſome rotten tanners bark is ſpread over the ſurface of the ground, it will protect the roots from being injured by the froſt. In the ſpring, the roots ſhould be tranſplanted to the places where they are deſiged to remain, which muſt be in a warm ſheltered ſituation, but not too much expoſed to the ſun, and in a light ſoil, where they will thrive and produce flowers annually. If this is propagated by parting of the roots, it ſhould be done in the ſpring, before the roots begin to ſhoot, which is the beſt ſeaſon for tranſplanting the plants : but theſe roots ſhould not be parted oftener than every third year, for if they are often removed they will not flower ſo ſtrong.

The fifth ſort hath a perennial root and a climbing ſtalk, which riſes near four feet high, garniſhed with woolly trifoliate leaves : the flowers come out in ſhort bunches from the ſide of the ſtalks ; they are ſmall, of a yellow colour, and are ſucceeded by ſhort pods, which contain two roundiſh ſeeds in each. This flowers in June, and the ſeeds ripen in autumn. It grows naturally in America, but is too tender to live in the open air in England. This is propagated in the ſame manner, and requires the ſame treatment as the third ſort.

GLYCYRRHIZA. Lin. Gen. Plant. 788. Tourn. Inſt. R. H. 389. tab. 210. [ſo called of γλυκὺς, ſweet, and ῥίζα, Gr. a root, q. d. ſweet root : the ancients called it Scythian Root, becauſe the Scythians firſt brought it into uſe.] Liquorice ; in French, Regliſſe.

The CHARACTERS are,

The flower hath a permanent tubulous empalement of one leaf, divided into two lips ; the upper lip is cut into three parts, the middle one being broad and bifid, the under lip is ſingle. The flower hath four petals, is of the butterfly kind, having a long erect ſtandard, with oblong

oblong wings, and a two-leaved keel which is acute. It hath ten stamina, nine joined and one standing single; they are longer than the keel, and terminated by roundish summits. In the bottom is situated a short germen, supporting an awl-shaped style the length of the stamina, crowned by a rising obtuse stigma. The germen afterward becomes an oblong, or oval compressed pod with one cell, including two or three kidney-shaped seeds.

This genus of plants is ranged in the third section of Linnæus's seventeenth class, intitled Diadelphia Decandria, which includes those plants which have ten stamina joined in two bodies.

The Species are,

1. GLYCYRRHIZA (*Glabra*) leguminibus glabris. Hort. Cliff. 490. *Liquorice with smooth pods.* Glycyrrhiza siliquosa, vel Germanica. C. B. P. *Common Liquorice.*
2. GLYCYRRHIZA (*Echinata*) leguminibus echinatis. Prod. Leyd. 386. *Liquorice with prickly pods.* Glycyrrhiza capite echinato. C. B. P. *Rough-podded Liquorice.*
3. GLYCYRRHIZA (*Hirsuta*) leguminibus hirsutis. Prod. Leyd. 386. *Liquorice with hairy pods.* Glycyrrhiza Orientalis, siliquis hirsutissimis. Tourn. Cor. *Eastern Liquorice with hairy pods.*

The first sort is that which is commonly cultivated in England for medicine; the other two kinds are preserved in curious botanic gardens for variety, but their roots are not so full of juice as the first, nor is the juice so sweet; though the second sort seems to be that which Dioscorides has described and recommended; but I suppose the goodness of the first has occasioned its being so generally cultivated in Europe. The roots of this run very deep into the ground, and creep to a considerable distance, especially where they are permitted to stand long unremoved; from these arise strong herbaceous stalks, four or five feet high, garnished with winged leaves, composed of four or five pair of oval lobes, terminated by an odd one; the leaves and stalks are clammy, and of a dark green; the flowers come out in spikes from the wings of the stalks, standing erect; they are of a pale blue colour, and are succeeded by short compressed pods, each containing two or three kidney-shaped seeds. It flowers the latter end of July, but the seeds do not ripen in England.

This plant delights in a light sandy soil, which should be three feet deep at least, for the goodness of Liquorice consists in the length of the roots: the greatest quantity of Liquorice which is propagated in England, is about Pontefract in Yorkshire, and Godalmin in Surry; though of late years there hath been a great deal cultivated in the gardens near London: the ground in which you intend to plant Liquorice, should be well dug and dunged the year before you plant it, that the dung may be perfectly rotted, and mixed with the earth, otherwise it will be apt to stop the roots from running down; and before you plant it, the ground should be dug three spades deep, and laid very light; when your ground is thus well prepared, you should furnish yourself with fresh plants taken from the sides or heads of the old roots, observing that they have a good bud or eye, otherwise they are subject to miscarry; these plants should be about ten inches long, and perfectly sound.

The best season for planting them is in the beginning or middle of March, which must be done in the following manner, viz. First strain a line cross the ground in which you would plant them, then with a long dibble made on purpose, put in the shoot, so that the whole plant may be set strait into the ground, with the head about an inch under the surface in a strait line, about a foot asunder, or more, in the rows, and two feet distance row from row; and after having finished the whole spot of ground, you may sow a thin crop of Onions, which being plants that do not root deep into the ground, nor spread much above, will do the Liquorice no damage the first year; for the Liquorice will not shoot very high the first season, and the hoeing of the Onions will also keep the ground clear from weeds; but in doing of this you must be careful not to cut off the top shoots

the Liquorice plants when they appear above ground, which would greatly injure them; and also observe to cut up all the Onions which grow near the heads of the Liquorice; and after your Onions are pulled up, you should carefully hoe and clean the ground from weeds; and in October, when the shoots of the Liquorice are decayed, you should spread a little very rotten dung upon the surface of the ground, which will prevent the weeds from growing during the winter, and the rain will wash the virtue of the dung into the ground, which will greatly improve the plants.

In the beginning of March following you should slightly dig the ground between the rows of Liquorice, burying the remaining part of the dung; but in doing of this, you should be very careful not to cut the roots. This stirring of the ground will not only preserve it clean from weeds a long time, but also greatly strengthen the plants.

The distance which I have allowed for planting these plants, will, I doubt not, by some, be thought too great; but in answer to that, I would only observe, that as the largeness of the roots is the chief advantage to the planter, so the only method to obtain this, is by giving them room; and besides, this will give a greater liberty to stir and dress the ground, which is of great service to Liquorice; and if the plantation designed were to be of an extraordinary bigness, I would advise the rows to be made at least three feet distant, whereby it will be easy to stir the ground with a breast plough, which will greatly lessen the expence of labour.

These plants should remain three years from the time of planting, when they will be fit to take up for use; which should not be done until the stalks are perfectly decayed; for when it is taken up too soon, it is subject to shrink greatly, and lose of its weight.

The ground near London being rich, increases the bulk of the root very fast; but when it is taken up, it appears of a very dark colour, and not near so sightly as that which grows upon a sandy soil in an open country.

The second sort grows naturally in some parts of Italy; and in the Levant; the stalks and leaves of this are very like those of the first, but the flowers are produced in shorter spikes, and the pods which succeed them are very short, broad at their base, ending in acute points, and are armed with sharp prickles. This flowers about the same time as the first, and in warm seasons will perfect seeds in England.

The third sort grows naturally in the Levant, from whence the seeds were sent to the royal garden at Paris, by Dr. Tournefort. This hath much the appearance of the other two species, but the pods of it are hairy, and longer than those of the other. Both these sorts may be propagated in the same manner as the first, or from seeds, which may be sown in the spring on a bed of light earth; but as neither of these are used, they are seldom propagated unless for the sake of variety.

GNAPHALIUM. Lin. Gen. Plant. 850. Elichrysum. Tourn. Inst. R. H. 452. tab. 259. Goldylocks, or Eternal Flower; in French, *Immortelle.*

The Characters are,

It hath a compound flower, made up of hermaphrodite florets and female half florets, included in one scaly empalement; the hermaphrodite florets are tubulous, funnel-shaped, and cut into five parts at the brim, which are reflexed; these have five short hairy stamina, terminated by cylindrical summits. In the center is situated a germen, supporting a slender style the length of the stamina, crowned by a bifid stigma; the germen afterward becomes a single seed, which in some species is crowned with a hairy down, and in others a feathery down. The female flowers which are intermixed with these have no stamina, but a germen supporting a slender style, crowned by a bifid reflexed stigma. These are in some species fruitful, and in others they are barren. The empalement of the flower is permanent and shining.

This

This genus of plants is ranged in the first section of Linnæus's nineteenth class, which includes those plants which have hermaphrodite and female flowers inclosed in one common empalement, and are fruitful.

The SPECIES are,

1. GNAPHALIUM (*Stœchas*) fruticosum foliis linearibus, ramis virgatis, corymbo composito. Hort. Cliff. 401. *Goldylocks with a shrubby stalk garnished with very narrow leaves, and a compound corymbus of flowers.* Elichryfum feu stœchas citrina angustifolia. C. B. P. 264. *Cassidony, or narrow-leaved Goldylocks.*

2. GNAPHALIUM (*Angustissimum*) foliis linearibus, caule fruticoso ramoso, corymbo composito. Hort. Cliff. 401. *Goldylocks with a branching shrubby stalk, and very narrow leaves, with a compound corymbus of flowers.* Elichryfum Hort. R. H. 452. *Goldylocks with very narrow leaves.*

3. GNAPHALIUM (*Uniflorum*) foliis alternis, acutè dentatis, subtus villosis, pedunculis longissimis unifloris. *Goldylocks with alternate leaves sharply indented, woolly on their under sides, with a very long foot-stalks sustaining one flower.* Elichryfum sylvestre latifolium, flore parvo singulari. Tourn. Inst. R. H. 452. *Broad-leaved wild Goldylocks, with a single small flower.*

4. GNAPHALIUM (*Luteo-album*) foliis semiamplexicaulibus ensiformibus, repandis obtusis, utrinque pubescentibus, floribus conglomeratis. Prod. Leyd. 149. *Goldylocks with sword-shaped leaves half embracing the stalks, which are obtuse, reflexed, woolly on both sides, and flowers growing in clusters.* Elichryfum sylvestre latifolium capitulis conglobatis. C. B. P. 264. *Broad-leaved wild Goldylocks, with heads growing in clusters.*

5. GNAPHALIUM (*Aquaticum*) caule ramoso diffuso, floribus confertis. Flor. Lapp. 300. *Goldylocks with a diffused branching stalk, and flowers in clusters at the top.* Elichryfum aquaticum, ramosum, minus, capitulis, foliaceis. Tourn. Inst. 452. *Lesser branching aquatic Goldylocks, with leafy heads.*

6. GNAPHALIUM (*Sylvaticum*) caule simplicissimo, floribus sparsis. Flor. Lapp. 298. *Goldylocks with a single stalk, and flowers growing scatteringly.* Elichryfum spicatum. Tourn. Inst. R. H. 453. *Spiked Goldylocks.*

7. GNAPHALIUM (*Dioicum*) caule simplicissimo corymbo simplici terminali, sarmentis procumbentibus. Hort. Cliff. 400. *Goldylocks with a single stalk terminated by a single corymbus, and trailing branches.* Elichryfum montanum flore rotundiori candido. Tourn. Inst. R. H. 453. *Mountain Goldylocks with a rounder white flower.*

8. GNAPHALIUM (*Montanum*) foliis radicalibus cuneiformibus, caulinis acutis sessilibus, caule simplicissimo, capitulo terminali aphyllo, floribus oblongis. *Goldylocks with the lower leaves wedge-shaped, those on the stalks acute, and sitting close, a single stalk without leaves, terminated by oblong flowers.* Elichryfum montanum longiore folio & flore albo. Tourn. Inst. 453. *Mountain Goldylocks, with a longer leaf and white flower.*

9. GNAPHALIUM (*Chrysocomum*) humile, caule suffruticoso, foliis linearibus subtus argenteis, squamis calycinis longioribus acuminatis. *Low Goldylocks with a shrubby stalk, very narrow leaves, silvery on their under side, and longer acute-pointed scales to the empalement.* Chamæchrysocoma prælongis purpurascentibusque Jaceæ capitulis. Barrel. Icon. 406. *Dwarf Goldylocks with longer and purplish heads like Knapweed.*

10. GNAPHALIUM (*Orientale*) subherbaceum, foliis lineari-lanceolatis sessilibus, corymbo composito, pedunculis elongatis. Lin. Sp. 195. *Herbaceous Goldylocks with narrow spear-shaped leaves, and a compound cluster of flowers.* Elichryfum Orientale. C. B. P. 264. *Eastern Goldylocks, called Immortal Flower.*

11. GNAPHALIUM (*Ignescens*) fruticosum, foliis sublanceolatis tomentosis sessilibus, corymbis alternis conglobatis, floribus globosis. Prod. Leyd. 149. *Shrubby Goldylocks, with spear-shaped woolly leaves sitting close to the stalks, and alternate clusters of globular flowers.* Elichryfum Germanicum, calyce ex aureo rutilante. Tourn. Inst. R. H. 452. *German Goldylocks having a reddish gold-coloured empalement.*

12. GNAPHALIUM (*Margaritaceum*) herbaceum foliis lineari-lanceolatis acuminatis, alternis, caule supernè

ramoso corymbis fastigiatis. Hort. Cliff. 401. *Herbaceous Goldylocks with narrow, spear-shaped, pointed leaves placed alternate, and the upper part of the stalk branching, with a compact corymbus of flowers.* Elichryfum Americanum latifolium. Tourn. Inst. R. H. 453. *Broad-leaved American Goldylocks.*

13. GNAPHALIUM (*Fœtidum*) herbaceum foliis amplexicaulibus, integerrimis acutis subtus tomentosis, caule ramoso. Hort. Cliff. 402. Lin. Sp. Plant. 850. *Herbaceous Goldylocks with entire leaves embracing the stalks, woolly on their under side, and a branching stalk.* Elichryfum Africanum fœtidissimum, amplissimo folio. Tourn. Inst. R. H. 454. *Most stinking African Goldylocks with a large leaf.*

14. GNAPHALIUM (*Argenteum*) foliis amplexicaulibus integerrimis ovatis nervosis utrinque tomentosis, caule ramoso. Hort. Cliff. 402. *Goldylocks with entire acute leaves embracing the stalks, woolly on both sides, and a branching stalk.* Elichryfum Africanum fœtidissimum amplissimo folio calyce argenteo. Tourn. Inst. 454. *Most stinking African Goldylocks, with a very large leaf, and a silvery empalement to the flower.*

15. GNAPHALIUM (*Undulatum*) herbaceum foliis decurrentibus lanceolatis acutis, undatis, subtus tomentosis, caule ramoso. Hort. Cliff. 402. *Goldylocks with acute running leaves which are waved, and woolly on their under side, and a branching stalk.* Elichryfum graveolens acutifolium, caule alato. Hort. Elth. 130. *Stinking Goldylocks, with an acute leaf and winged stalk.*

16. GNAPHALIUM (*Cymosum*) herbaceum foliis lanceolatis trinerviis supra glabris caule infernè ramoso terminali. Hort. Cliff. 401. *Goldylocks with spear-shaped leaves, having three veins, smooth on their upper side, and the under branches terminated with flowers.* Elichryfum Africanum folio oblongo, subtus incano, supra viridi, flore luteo. Boerh. Ind. alt. 1. 121. *African Goldylocks with an oblong leaf, hoary on the under side, and green above, with a yellow flower.*

17. GNAPHALIUM (*Americanum*) caule herbaceo simplicissimo, foliis lanceolatis obtusis tomentosis, floribus spicatis lateralibusque. *Goldylocks with a single herbaceous stalk, obtuse, spear-shaped, woolly leaves, and flowers growing in spikes from the sides of the stalks.* Gnaphalium ad stœchadem citrinam accedens. Sloan. Cat. Jam. 125. *Cudweed like golden Cassidony.*

18. GNAPHALIUM (*Rutilans*) herbaceum foliis lineari-lanceolatis, caule infernè ramoso, corymbo composito terminali. Hort. Cliff. 401. *Herbaceous Goldylocks with narrow spear-shaped leaves, the under part of the stalk branching, and a compound corymbus terminating the branches.* Elichryfum Africanum, folio oblongo angusto, flore rubello postea aureo. Boerh. Ind. alt. 121. *African Goldylocks with an oblong narrow leaf and a reddish flower, which is afterwards yellow.*

19. GNAPHALIUM (*Sanguineum*) herbaceum, foliis decurrentibus lanceolatis tomentosis planis apiculo nudo terminali. Amœn. Acad. 4. p. 78. *Herbaceous Goldylocks, with spear-shaped, woolly, running leaves, terminated by a naked point.* Chrysocoma Syriaca, flore atro rubente. Breyn. Cent. 146.

20. GNAPHALIUM (*Fruticosum*) frutescens foliis infernè lanceolatis caulinis lineari-lanceolatis, utrinque tomentosis, corymbo composito terminali. *Shrubby Goldylocks with the under leaves spear-shaped, those on the stalks narrow, spear-shaped, woolly on both sides, and the stalks terminated by a corymbus of flowers.* Elichryfum Africanum frutescens, angustis & longioribus foliis incanis. Hort. Amst. 2. p. 109. *Shrubby African Goldylocks, with longer and narrower leaves which are hoary.*

21. GNAPHALIUM (*Odoratissimum*) foliis decurrentibus obtusis infernè villosis, corymbis conglobatis terminalibus. *Goldylocks with obtuse running leaves, hoary on their under side, and a clustered corymbus of flowers terminating the stalk.* Elichryfum foliis linearibus decurrentibus, subtus incanis, floribus corymbosis. Fig. Plant. tab. 131. fol. 2. *Goldylocks with narrow running leaves, hoary on their under side, and flowers growing in a corymbus.*

22. GNAPHALIUM (*Plantaginifolium*) sarmentis procumbentibus caule simplicissimo, foliis radicalibus ovatis maximis,

maximis, farmentis procumbentibus. Lin. Sp. Plant.
850. *Goldylocks with a fimple ftalk, large oval leaves at bottom, and trailing runners.* Gnaphalium plantaginis folio, Virginianum. Pluk. Alm. 171. *Virginia Goldylocks with a Plantain leaf.*

23. GNAPHALIUM (*Obtufifolium*) herbaceum foliis lanceolatis, caule tomentofo paniculato terminalibus glomeratis conicis. Lin. Sp. Plant. 851. *Goldylocks with fpear-fhaped leaves, a woolly ftalk, terminated by a conical clufter of flowers.* Elichryfum obtufifolium, capitulis argenteis conglobatis. Hort. Elth. 130. *Blunt-leaved Goldylocks, with filvery heads growing in clufters.*

24. GNAPHALIUM (*Spicatum*) foliis lanceolatis decurrentibus tomentofis, floribus fpicatis terminalibus lateralibufque. *Goldylocks with fpear-fhaped, woolly, running leaves, and flowers growing in fpikes at the ends and fides of the ftalks.* Elichryfum caule alato, floribus fpicatis. Sloan. Cat. Jam. 125. *Goldylocks with a winged ftalk and fpiked flowers.*

The firft fort hath a fhrubby ftalk, which rifes about three feet high, branching out into long flender ftalks irregularly; the lower branches are garnifhed with obtufe leaves, two inches and a half long, and an eighth of an inch broad at the point, but thofe upon the flower-ftalks are very narrow, ending in acute points; the whole plant is very woolly: the flowers terminate the ftalks in a compound corymbus; their empalements are of a filvery colour at firft, and very neat, but afterward turn of a yellowifh fulphur colour. If thefe are gathered before the flowers are much opened, the heads will continue in beauty many years, efpecially if they are kept from the air and duft. The plants begin to flower in June, and there is a fucceffion of flowers all the fummer, fome of which will continue in beauty moft part of the winter. This is generally fuppofed to be the true golden Caffidony of the fhops, but the fecond fort is ufually fubftituted for it in England.

It is propagated by flips or cuttings, which may be planted in June or July, in a bed of light earth, and covered with glaffes, or fhaded with mats, obferving to refrefh them frequently with water, but it muft not be given in large quantities; thefe cuttings will put out roots in fix or eight weeks, then they fhould be taken up and planted in pots filled with light earth, and placed in a fhady fituation till they have taken new root, when they may be removed to an open fituation, and placed among other hardy exotics, till about the middle or end of October; at which time they fhould be placed under a common frame, where they may be protected from froft, but in mild weather they fhould be expofed to the open air. With this management in winter, the plants will be much ftronger than thofe which are kept in the green-houfe, where they generally draw too weak; for this fort only wants to be fheltered from hard froft, being fo hardy as in very mild winters to live abroad in warm borders near walls, with little fhelter.

The fecond fort hath a fhrubby ftalk, which divides into many flender branches, covered with a white bark; thefe form a thick bufhy under fhrub, and rife near three feet, garnifhed with very narrow leaves, hoary on their under fide, but green on their upper, placed without order on every fide the ftalks; the flowers are produced in a compound corymbus at the end of the branches; their heads are fmall, and are of a yellow colour when fully blown; thefe are continued in fucceffion moft part of fummer. This grows naturally in France and Germany, and is hardy enough to live in the open air in England. It is propagated by flips or cuttings, which may be planted in a fhady border during any of the fummer months, and in the autumn they may be tranfplanted into the places where they are defigned to remain. This fhould have a dry undunged foil, in which it is rarely injured unlefs in the moft fevere froft.

The third fort is an annual plant, which grows naturally in Italy and Sicily; this hath an herbaceous ftalk, which rifes little more than a foot high, garnifhed with acute indented leaves, which are hoary on

their under fide; the flowers ftand upon long footftalks, which rife far above the branches, each fuftaining one fmall whitifh flower. Thefe appear in July, and the feeds ripen in September. It is propagated by feeds, which fhould be fown in autumn upon a bed of light earth, where the plants are defigned to remain; and when the plants come up in the fpring, they fhould be thinned where they are too clofe, and kept clean from weeds, which is all the culture they require.

The fourth fort is an annual plant with woolly leaves, which rife with woolly ftalks about eight inches high, garnifhed with oblong leaves which embrace the ftalks with their bafe; the flowers grow in clofe clufters at the top, and from the fide of their ftalks, which are included in dry filvery empalements.

There is another fpecies of this with narrower leaves, not quite fo woolly; the ftalks rife higher, and are more branched; the flowers grow in clofe bunches on the top of the ftalks, and are of a pale yellow colour. Both thefe forts will come up better from the fcattered feeds, than when they are fown by art; but if the feeds are fown, it muft be foon after they are ripe, otherwife they will not fucceed. The plants require no other care but to keep them clean from weeds, and thinned where they are too clofe. They flower in July, and the feeds ripen in autumn.

The fifth fort is an annual plant, which grows naturally in many parts of England, on places which are covered with water in the winter; this is a low branching plant, with filvery leaves and dark heads of flowers, but being of no ufe is not cultivated in gardens.

The fixth fort is alfo an annual plant with narrow leaves, which are hoary on their under fide; the ftalks grow erect about a foot high, and at every joint is produced a fhort fpike of white flowers, with darkcoloured empalements. This is found growing naturally in fome parts of England, fo is not often admitted into gardens. If the feeds of this fort are permitted to fcatter, the plants will come up in the fpring with greater certainty than if fown, and they will require little culture. Thefe flower in July, and the plants decay foon after they have ripened their feeds. The feventh fort grows naturally in the northern parts of England, upon the tops of hills and mountains, where the fhoots which are fent out from every fide of the plant put out roots, whereby it is propagated in great plenty: the leaves of this grow clofe to the ground, they are narrow at their bafe, but rounded at the end where they are broad; they are near an inch long, and hoary on their under fide; the ftalks are fingle, and rife about four inches high, terminated by a corymbus of flowers which is fingle. This flowers in May and June.

There are two varieties of this, one with a purple and the other a variegated flower, which have rifen accidentally from feeds, but continue their difference in the gardens. They are eafily propagated by offsets, which fhould be planted in the autumn, in a fhady fituation, where they will require no other care but to keep them clean from weeds. This plant is called Pes Cati, or Catsfoot.

The eighth fort grows naturally on the Alps. This is a low plant, with under leaves like the laft mentioned; the ftalks are fingle, and rife about fix inches high, garnifhed with very fmall acute leaves, and terminated by four or five oblong flowers, which in fome plants are white, and in others of a purplifh colour. They appear about the fame time as the former fort, and the plants may be propagated and treated in the fame manner.

The ninth fort grows naturally in Spain and Italy. This is a low plant with a ligneous ftalk, which feldom rifes more than fix inches high, garnifhed with very narrow leaves, white on their under fide; the flowers are produced from the fide of the ftalks, each ftanding upon a feparate foot-ftalk; their empalements are fcaly and long, ending in acute ftiff points, and are of a purplifh colour. This fort flowers in July, but feldom perfects feeds in this country.

6 G

The tenth fort is fuppofed to have been brought firſt from India to Portugal, where it has been long propagated for the beauty of its golden heads of flowers, which, if gathered before they are too open, will continue in beauty feveral years; fo that in the winter feafon they ornament their churches with thefe flowers, and many of them are annually brought to England, and fold for ornaments to the ladies. Thefe plants have a fhort fhrubby ftalk, feldom rifing more than three or four inches high, putting out many heads; the leaves are narrow and woolly on both fides, and come out without order; the flower-ftalks arife from thefe heads; they grow eight or ten inches high, are garnifhed all the way with narrow hoary leaves, and terminated by a compound corymbus of bright yellow flowers with large heads. Thefe begin to flower in May, and there is a fucceffion of them moſt part of fummer. This is propagated by flipping off the heads during any of the fummer months, and after ftripping off the lower leaves, they fhould be planted in a bed of light earth, covering them with hand-glaffes, which muſt be fhaded every day when the fun is warm; and the cuttings muſt be fupplied with water, which fhould be often repeated, but not in too great quantities; when thefe are rooted they fhould be planted in pots, and treated in the fame manner as hath been directed for the firſt fort. Thefe plants in mild winters will live abroad in a very warm border with little fhelter, and the hardier they are treated, the greater number of flowers they will produce; for when they are drawn weak in a green-houfe, they never flower fo ftrong.

The eleventh fort hath very woolly ftalks and leaves, which are much longer than thofe of the tenth; the ftalks rife a foot high, fending out a few fide branches; thefe are terminated by a compound corymbus of flowers, whofe heads are fmall, and of a gold colour, changing a little red as they fade. This is propagated by flips in the fame manner as the laſt mentioned, but the plants will live in the open air, if they are planted on a dry foil.

The twelfth fort grows naturally in North America, but has been long in the Englifh gardens. This hath a creeping root, which fpreads far in the ground, fo as to become a troublefome weed very often, unlefs it is kept within bounds; the ftalks of this are woolly, rifing a foot and a half high, garnifhed with long leaves ending in acute points, which are placed alternate, and are woolly on their under fide; the upper part of the ſtalk branches into two or three divifions, each being terminated by a clofe corymbus of flowers, with pretty large filvery empalements, which, if gathered and properly dried, will retain their beauty feveral years. This fort will thrive in almoſt any foil or fituation, and is eafily propagated by its creeping roots. It flowers in June and July, and the ftalks decay in autumn.

The thirteenth fort grows naturally at the Cape of Good Hope. This is an annual plant, which fends out many oblong blunt leaves near the root; the ftalks rife a foot and a half high, garnifhed with leaves placed alternate, which are broad at their bafe where they embrace the ftalks, but end in acute points; they are woolly, and when handled, emit a very rank odour; the ftalks are terminated by a corymbus of flowers, in large filvery empalements, which will retain their beauty feveral years.

The fourteenth fort grows naturally at the Cape of Good Hope, and is an annual plant, very like the former fort, but the leaves are of a yellowifh green on their upper fide, and woolly on their under; the ftalks branch, and the heads of flowers are of a bright yellow colour, and thefe differences are permanent. Both thefe plants are propagated by feeds, which, if fown in the autumn on a warm border, will more certainly fucceed, than when they are fown in the fpring; or if the feeds are permitted to fcatter, the plants will come up without care, and may be tranfplanted while they are young, to the places where they are defigned to remain: when the plants have taken root, they will require no other care but to keep them clean from

weeds. They flower in July, and the feeds ripen in autumn.

The fifteenth fort grows in Africa, and alfo in North America, from both thefe countries I have received the feeds. It is an annual plant, with oblong leaves at the bottom, which are a little waved, and hoary on their under fide. The ſtalks rife about a foot high, and are garnifhed with acute-pointed leaves; from their bafe runs a border or wing along the ftalk; the whole plant has a difagreeable odour. The flowers grow in a corymbus on the top of the ftalks, they are white, and appear in July. The feeds ripen in the autumn, which, if permitted to fcatter, the plants will come up without care, as the two former forts.

The fixteenth fort rifes with a fhrubby ftalk three or four feet high, fending out many branches from the lower part, garnifhed with narrow fpear-fhaped leaves, which half embrace the ftalks with their bafe; they are of a dark green on their upper fide, but are hoary on their under; the ftalks are terminated by a compound corymbus of yellow flowers, whofe heads are fmall: thefe continue in fucceffion great part of the fummer, but are rarely fucceeded by feeds in England. It is eafily propagated by cuttings in any of the fummer months, which may be planted in a fhady border, and duly watered. Thefe will take root in a month or five weeks, and may then be taken up and planted in pots, placing them in a fhady fituation till they have taken frefh root; then they may be removed to a fheltered fituation, and placed with other hardy green-houfe plants till autumn, when they muſt be carried into the green-houfe, where, during the winter feafon, they fhould have as much free air as poffible in mild weather, for they only require protection from froft, fo they fhould be treated in the fame manner as other hardy green-houfe plants.

The feventeenth fort is an annual plant, which grows naturally in France, Italy, and Spain. This hath a woolly herbaceous ftalk, which rifes fix or eight inches high, garnifhed with obtufe, fpear-fhaped, woolly leaves. The flowers are produced in fhort fpikes from the fide, and at the top of the ftalks; they are of a filvery colour, and appear in June and July. The feeds ripen in autumn, which, if permitted to fcatter, the plants will come up without care, and require no other culture, but to keep them clean from weeds.

The eighteenth fort grows naturally at the Cape of Good Hope; this rifes with a flender fhrubby ftalk, which fends out many lateral branches below; thefe are garnifhed with very narrow leaves, which are hoary on their under fide. The flowers are produced in a compound corymbus at the end of the branches; they are at their firſt appearance of a pale red colour, but afterward change to a gold colour; the empalements of this fort are fmall, and dry like the other fpecies of this genus. This fort is propagated by cuttings, in the fame manner as the fixteenth, and the plants require the fame treatment.

The nineteenth fort grows naturally in Egypt and Paleftine. This is a perennial plant, whofe under leaves fpread near the ground; they are woolly on their under fide; the ftalks rife about fix inches high; the leaves upon thefe are fpear-fhaped, ending in acute points; the ftalks and leaves are woolly, and the ftalk is terminated by a large corymbus of flowers fitting very clofe; thefe are of a fine foft red colour, fo make a pretty appearance in the month of June, when they are in beauty.

This fort is propagated by offsets in the fame manner as the feventh and eighth forts, but this doth not produce them in plenty, fo is very uncommon in the Englifh gardens at prefent: it requires a drier foil than the feventh, and a warmer fituation, but not too much expofed to the mid-day fun, fo fhould be planted to a fouth-eaſt afpect.

The twentieth fort grows naturally at the Cape of Good Hope, but has been long preferved in many curious gardens in Europe; the ftalk rifes three or four feet high, fending out feveral long irregular branches, which are terminated by a compound corymbus

rymbus of flowers. The heads of this fort are composed of leaves, which are much longer than those of any other fort; the heads of the flowers are of a bright filver colour. This is propagated by cuttings, which fhould be planted in the fame manner as hath been directed for the tenth fort, and the plants fhould alfo be treated in the fame way.

The twenty-firft fort was raifed from feeds in the Chelfea garden, which came from the Cape of Good Hope; the lower leaves of this are oblong and blunt. The ftalks are fhrubby, and divide into many irregular branches, which rife about three feet high; thefe are garnifhed with oblong blunt-pointed leaves, hoary on their under fide, but of a dark green above; from the bafe of the leaves runs a border along the ftalk, like a wing, of the fame confiftence with the leaves, fo is what the former botanifts termed a winged ftalk, but Dr. Linnæus calls it a running leaf. The ftalks are terminated by a compound corymbus of flowers, which are very clofely joined together, and are of a bright gold colour, but the flowers are fmall, and change to a darker colour as they fade; there is a fucceffion of thefe flowers moft part of the fummer, and the early flowers are frequently fucceeded by feeds in England. This fort may be propagated by flips, or cuttings, in the fame manner as the tenth, and the plants may be treated in the fame manner as is directed for that. It is engraven in the 131ft plate of the figures of plants. The twenty-fecond fort grows naturally in North America, from whence the feeds have been brought to England; this is a perennial plant, whofe lower leaves are large and oval; from the main ftalk there come out runners, which take root in the ground, and have young plants at their extremity. The ftalks are fingle, and garnifhed with narrower woolly leaves, placed alternate. The flowers are produced at the top of the ftalks in a corymbus, they are of a white colour and fmall. They appear in June and July, and fometimes are fucceeded by feeds, but the plants propagate fo faft by offsets, that the feeds are little regarded; this will thrive in the open air, if planted in a dry foil and a warm fituation.

The twenty-third fort grows naturally in North America; it is an annual plant, with woolly obtufe leaves. The ftalks are fingle, and rife about nine inches high. The flowers grow in fpikes from the fide of the ftalks; they are of a dirty white colour, fo make no great appearance. If the feeds of this are permitted to fcatter, the plants will rife without trouble, and only require to be kept clean from weeds.

The twenty-fourth fort grows naturally in Jamaica, and other of the hot parts of America; this rifes with a fhrubby ftalk about two feet high, garnifhed with leaves about the fize and fhape of thofe of Sage, but woolly on their under fide, and much veined; from the bafe of each leaf runs a border along the ftalk. The flowers are produced in fpikes from the fide, and at the end of the ftalk; thefe are long, and clofely joined in the fpike. It flowers in July and Auguft, but never perfects feeds in England.

It is propagated by feeds, which fhould be fown on a hot-bed in pots, becaufe the plants do not often rife the fame year; therefore when it fo happens, the pots fhould be placed in the ftove in winter, and the following fpring put upon a frefh hot-bed to bring up the plants; when thefe appear they muft be planted into pots, and kept conftantly in the hot-bed, otherwife they will not thrive in England.

GNAPHALODES. See MICROPUS.

GNIDIA.

The CHARACTERS are,

It hath a funnel-fhaped empalement of one coloured leaf, with a long tube divided into four fegments; the flower hath four plain petals fhorter than the empalement inferted to it, and eight briftly erect ftamina, terminated by fimple fummits, and an oval germen fupporting a flender ftyle on the fide inferted with the ftamina, crowned by a ftinging ftigma; the germen afterward becomes one oval oblique-pointed feed, inclofed in the empalement.

This genus of plants is ranged in the firft order of Linnæus's eighth clafs, intitled Octandria Monogynia, the flower having eight ftamina and one ftyle.

We have but one SPECIES of this genus, viz.

1. GNIDIA (*Pinifolia*) foliis fparfis lineari-fubulatis, floribus verticillatis, aggregatis terminalibus. Lin. Sp. 512. *Gnidia with linear awl-fhaped leaves, and flowers placed clofely in whorls terminating the branches.* Rapunculus foliis nervofis linearibus, floribus argenteis non galeatis. Burm. Afr. 112.

This plant grows naturally in Æthiopia. It hath a low fhrubby ftalk, which rifes three or four feet high, fending out a few fidebranches, garnifhed with narrow, oblong, acute-pointed leaves, which are green on their upper fide, but pale on their under, with a ftrong longitudinal nerve, refembling the leaves of Rofemary: the flowers come out almoft in whorls from between the leaves on the extremity of the branches, ftanding on fhort foot-ftalks; they have long flender tubes, and are divided at the top into four fegments which fpread horizontally, having eight very fhort ftamina in the bottom of the tube, and an oval germen with a flender ftyle faftened to the fide of the ftamina; the germen is afterward fucceeded by one oval-pointed feed. There are two varieties of this, one with a white, and the other hath a blue flower.

This is ufually propagated here by cuttings, which if carefully planted during the fummer months, in pots filled with light earth, plunged into a very moderate hot-bed, covering the pots clofely with either bell or hand-glaffes to exclude the air, being careful to fhade the glaffes daily, the cuttings will put out roots in fix weeks, when they fhould be gradually inured to the open air. In winter the plants fhould be placed in a dry airy glafs-cafe, where they may enjoy free air in mild weather, but protected from froft and damp air.

GOMPHRENA. Lin. Gen. Plant. 279. Amaranthoides. Tourn. Inft. R. H. 654. tab. 420.

The CHARACTERS are,

The flower hath a large three-leaved empalement, which is coloured and permanent. The petal is erect, and cut into five parts at the top; it hath a cylindrical tubulous empalement the length of the petal, cut into five fmall parts at the brim, which fpread open; it hath five ftamina fcarcely difcernible, fituated in the brim of the nectarium, terminated by fummits, fhut up in the mouth of the nectarium. In the center is fituated an oval-pointed germen, with two fmall ftyles, crowned with fingle ftigma the length of the ftamina. The germen afterward becomes one large roundifh feed, inclofed in a thin crufted capfule with one cell.

This genus of plants is ranged in the fecond fection of Linnæus's fifth clafs, intitled Pentandria Digynia, which includes the plants whofe flowers have five ftamina and two ftyles.

The SPECIES are,

1. GOMPHRENA (*Globofa*) caule erecto, foliis ovato-lanceolatis, capitulis folitaris, pedunculis diphyllis. Hort. Cliff. 86. *Gomphrena with an erect ftalk, oval fpearfhaped leaves, fingle heads, and foot-ftalks having two leaves.* Amaranthoides Lychnidis folio, capitulis purpureis. Tourn. Inft. R. H. 654. *Globe Amaranthus with purple heads.*

2. GOMPHRENA (*Serrata*) caule erecto, fpicâ interruptâ. Prod. Leyd. 419. *Gomphrena with an erect ftalk, and an interrupted fpike of flowers.*

3. GOMPHRENA (*Perennis*) foliis lanceolatis, capitulis diphyllis, flofculis perianthio proprio diftinctis. Lin. Sp. Plant. 224. *Gomphrena with fpear-fhaped leaves, two leaves to the heads, and each floret having its proper empalement.* Amaranthoides perenne, floribus ftramineis radiatis. Hort. Elth. 24. tab. 20. *Perennial Globe Amaranthus with radiated ftraw-coloured flowers.*

The firft fort grows naturally in India, from whence the feeds were brought to Europe, and the plants have been many years cultivated in all the curious gardens: it is an annual plant, which rifes with an upright branching ftalk about two feet high, garnifhed with fpear-fhaped leaves placed oppofite. The branches alfo come out oppofite, and the foot-ftalks of the flowers, which are long and naked, having two fhort leaves,

leaves, clofe under each head of flowers arifes from the forks of the branches. The heads at their firft appearance are globular, but as they increafe in fize become oval; thefe are compofed of dry fcaly leaves or petals, placed imbricatim like the fcales of fifh; under each of thefe is fituated a tubulous flower, which juft peeps out of the covering, but thefe are not much regarded by the generality of people; for the fcaly empalement which covers them is fo beautiful, and thefe if gathered before they are too much faded, will retain their beauty feveral years. After the flowers are paft, the germen, which is fituated in the bottom of each, becomes a large oval feed, inclofed in a chaffy covering, which ripens late in autumn, and the plants decay foon after.

There are two varieties of this fort, one with fine bright purple heads, the other hath white or filvery heads, and thefe never alter from feeds, fo that they are permanent varieties, though in other refpects they do not differ: there is alfo one with mixed colours, but whether this arofe accidentally from the feeds of either of the former, I cannot determine, for this variety continues from feeds, and the other two I have cultivated more than thirty years, and have never found either of them vary.

There are alfo two varieties of thefe which grow naturally in the Weft-Indies, one with purple, and the other with white heads, which are much fmaller and rounder than thofe before-mentioned. The plants grow much larger, and fpread more into branches, and they are later before they flower, fo that in cold feafons the feeds rarely ripen in England; thefe are called Bachelors Buttons by the inhabitants of America, but whether they are fpecifically different from the others, I cannot with certainty determine.

The fecond fort hath much flenderer ftalks than the firft, which grow taller, and are irregular. The leaves are fmaller, but of the fame fhape. The flowers grow in fpikes at the end of the branches, which are broken, or divided into three or four parts with fpaces between them. The fpikes are fmall, and of a pale purple colour. The feeds of this fort were fent me by the late Dr. Houftoun from Campeachy.

The third fort hath flender upright ftalks, which are garnifhed with fpear-fhaped leaves placed oppofite; they are hairy, and fit clofe to the ftalks, which alfo are hairy, and terminated by fmall heads of flowers, which fpread open from each other, fo as that the empalement appear diftinct; thefe are of a pale ftraw colour, and appear in July. The feeds fometimes will ripen in England, but the plants will live two or three years, if they are preferved in a ftove.

The two forts with large heads of flowers which are firft mentioned, one with purple, and the other which is filver-coloured, are very ornamental plants in gardens, and are now very commonly cultivated in the Englifh gardens. In Portugal, and other warm countries, they are cultivated to adorn their churches in the winter; for if thefe are gathered when they are fully grown, and dried in the fhade, they will retain their beauty a long time, efpecially if they are not expofed to the air; thefe plants are annual, fo are only propagated by feeds, which fhould be fown on a good hot-bed the beginning of March; but if the feeds are not taken out of their chaffy covering, it will be proper to foak them in water for twelve hours before they are fown, which will greatly facilitate their growing. When the plants are come up half an inch high, they fhould be tranfplanted on a frefh hot-bed, at about four inches diftance, obferving to fhade them till they have taken root; then they fhould have frefh air admitted to them every day, in proportion to the warmth of the feafon; they will alfo require to be frequently refrefhed with water. In about a month's time, if the hot-bed is of a proper warmth, the plants will have grown fo large, as to nearly meet, therefore they will require more room, otherwife they will draw up weak; then a frefh hot-bed fhould be prepared, into which there fhould be a fufficient number of three farthing pots plunged, filled with light

rich earth, and when the bed is in a proper temperature of warmth, the plants fhould be carefully taken up with balls of earth to their roots, and each planted into a feparate pot, obferving to fhade them till they have taken new root, afterward they muft be treated in the fame manner as other tender exotic plants. When the plants have filled thefe pots with their roots, they fhould be fhaken out of the pots, and their roots on the outfide of the ball of earth muft be carefully pared off; then they fhould be put into pots a fize larger, and when there is conveniency of a deep frame, to plunge the pots into another gentle hot-bed, it will bring the plants early to flower, and caufe them to grow much larger than thofe which are placed abroad. In July the plants fhould be inured gradually to bear the open air, into which they may be removed about the middle of that month, and intermixed with other annual plants to adorn the pleafure-garden; but it will be proper to keep a plant or two of each fort in fhelter for feeds, becaufe when the autumn proves cold or wet, thofe plants which are expofed abroad, feldom produce good feeds.

GOOSEBERRY. See GROSSULARIA.

GORTERIA.

The CHARACTERS are,

The empalement of the flower is ftiff, fcaly, ending in briftly fpines; the flower is compofed of hermaphrodite florets in the difk, and female in the rays or border; the hermaphrodite florets are funnel-fhaped, five-pointed, having five fhort ftamina terminated by cylindrical fummits, with a hairy germen fupporting a fiender ftyle, crowned by a bifid ftigma; the germen afterward becomes one roundifh feed, furrounded by fine hairs. The female florets are tongue-fhaped, have no ftyle or ftigma, and are barren.

This genus of plants is ranged in the third fection of Linnæus's nineteenth clafs, intitled Syngenefia Polygamia fruftranea, the flowers being compofed of hermaphrodite florets in the difk which are fruitful, and female florets in the border, having neither ftyle or ftigma, for are barren.

The SPECIES are,

1. GORTERIA (*Ringens*) fcapis unifloris, foliis lanceolatis pinnatifidis, caule depreffo. Amœn. Acad. 6. p. 86. *Gorteria with one flower on each foot-ftalk, fpear-fhaped, wing-pointed leaves, and a depreffed ftalk.* Arctotis ramis decumbentibus, foliis lineari-lanceolatis rigidis fubtus argenteis. Ed. prior.

2. GORTERIA (*Fruticofa*) foliis lanceolatis integris dentato-fpinofis fubtus tomentofis, caule fruticofo. Lin. Sp. 1284. *Gorteria with entire fpear-fhaped leaves, whofe indentures end in fpines, woolly on their under fide, and a fhrubby ftalk.* Carthamus Africanus fruteicens, folio ilicis, flore aureo. Walth. Hort. 13. tab. 7.

The firft fort grows naturally at the Cape of Good Hope; it is a low fpreading plant, with ligneous ftalks fix or eight inches long trailing on the ground, having two or three fide branches, each terminating in a clofe head of leaves, which are narrow, green on their upper fide, but filvery on their under, cut into three or five fegments at their ends. The foot-ftalks of the flowers arife from the heads, and are fix inches long, naked, fupporting one large Orange-coloured flower at the top, compofed of feveral hermaphrodite florets in the difk, which are fruitful; but the female half florets on the border are tongue-fhaped, fpreading open, each having a dark mark toward their bafe, with a white fpot intermixed. The flowers appear in May and June, but are feldom fucceeded by feeds in England.

This plant is eafily propagated by cuttings planted in a fhady border during any of the fummer months, and the plants muft be afterward treated as is directed for ARCTOTIS.

The fecond fort grows naturally at the Cape of Good Hope. This rifes with a fhrubby flender ftalk three feet high, fending out a few weak branches, garnifhed with oblong leaves fitting clofe to the branches; they are fmooth on their upper fide, woolly underneath, and indented on their edges, each indenture ending with a weak fpine. The flowers terminate the ftalks, having

having leafy empalements ending with fpines; the flowers are yellow, and appear in the fummer months, but are not fucceeded by feeds in England.
It is propagated by planting of the fmall heads at the end of the branches, in June or July, which muft be clofely covered with either bell or hand-glaffes, or they will not fucceed, and fhould be carefully fcreened from the fun. When thefe are well rooted, they fhould be put each into a fmall pot, and in winter fhould be placed in an airy glafs-cafe fecure from damps.

GORZ. See ULEX.

GOSSYPIUM. Lin. Gen. Plant. 755. Xylon. Tourn. Inft. R. H. 101. tab. 27. Cotton.

The CHARACTERS are,

The flower has a double empalement; the outer is large, of one leaf, and cut half way into three fegments; the inner is cup-fhaped, of one leaf, cut into five obtufe fegments at the top. It hath five plain heart-fhaped petals, which join at their bafe, and fpread open. It hath a great number of ftamina, which are joined at bottom in a column, but are loofe above, and inferted into the petals; thefe are terminated by kidney-fhaped fummits. It hath a round germen, fupporting four ftyles, joined in the column, and are the fame length of the ftamina, crowned by four thick ftigmas. The germen afterward becomes a roundifh capfule, ending in a point, having four cells, which are filled with oval feeds, wrapped up in down.

This genus of plants is ranged in the third fection of Linnæus's fixteenth clafs, intitled Monodelphia Polyandria, which includes the plants whofe flowers have many ftamina, which are joined together with the ftyles in one column or body.

The SPECIES are,

1. GOSSYPIUM (*Herbaceum*) foliis quinquelobis, caule herbaceo lævi. Hort. Upfal. 203. *Cotton with leaves having five lobes, and a fmooth herbaceous ftalk.* Goffypium. Camer. Epit. 203. *The common herbaceous Cotton.*

2. GOSSYPIUM (*Barbadenfe*) foliis trilobis integerrimis fubtus biglandulofis. Hort. Upfal. 205. *Cotton-tree with entire leaves, having three lobes with three glands under their fide.* Goffypium frutefcens annuum, folio trilobo Barbadenfe. Pluk. Alm. 172. tab. 188. *Shrubby annual Barbadoes Cotton, with leaves having three lobes.*

3. GOSSYPIUM (*Arboreum*) foliis palmatis, lobis lanceolatis, caule fruticofo. Lin. Sp. Plant. 693. *Cotton with hand-fhaped leaves, having five fpear-fhaped lobes, and a fhrubby ftalk.* Xylon arboreum, flore flavo. Tourn. Inft. R. 101. *Tree Cotton with a yellow flower.*

4. GOSSYPIUM (*Hirfutum*) foliis trilobis & quinquelobifque acutis, caule ramofo hirfuto. *Cotton with leaves having three and five lobes, ending in acute points, and a hairy branching ftalk.* Xylon Americanum præftantiffimum, femine virefcente. Lign. Tourn. Inft. R. H. 101. *Fineft American Cotton with a green feed.*

The firft fort is the common Levant Cotton, which is cultivated in feveral Iflands of the Archipelago, is alfo in Malta, Sicily, and the kingdom of Naples; it is fown in tilled ground in the fpring of the year, and is ripe in about four months after, when it is cut down in harveft as Corn is in England; the plants always perifh foon after the feeds are ripe: this plant grows about two feet high, with an herbaceous ftalk, garnifhed with fmooth leaves divided into five lobes. The ftalks fend out a few weak branches upward, which are garnifhed with leaves of the fame form but fmaller. The flowers are produced near the extremity of the branches, at the foot-ftalks of the leaves; thefe have two large empalements, the outer is cut into three parts, and the inner into five. The petals of the flower are of a pale yellow colour, inclining to white; thefe are fucceeded by oval capfules, which open in four parts, having four cells, which are filled with feeds wrapped up in down, which is the Cotton.
The fecond fort grows naturally in feveral iflands of the Weft-Indies; this rifes with a fhrubby fmooth ftalk four or five feet high, fending out a few fide branches, which are garnifhed with fmooth leaves, divided into three lobes. The flowers are produced toward the end of the branches, which are fhaped like thofe of

the former fort, but are larger, and of a deeper yellow colour. The pods are larger, and the feeds are black.
The third fort hath a perennial fhrubby ftalk, which rifes fix or eight feet high, and divides into many fmooth branches, garnifhed with hand-fhaped leaves, having four or five lobes. The flowers are produced toward the end of the branches; thefe are larger than thofe of the two former forts, and are of a deep yellow colour. The pods of this fort are larger than thofe of the former.
The fourth fort is a native of the Eaft and Weft-Indies, from whence the feeds have been brought to Europe; this is alfo an annual plant, which perifhes foon after the feeds are ripe. It rifes to the height of three feet or more, and fends out many lateral branches, which extend to a great diftance, where they are allowed room to grow; thefe are hairy, and garnifhed with leaves, having in fome three, and others five acute-pointed lobes, with fhort hairy down on their furface. The flowers are produced from the fide, and at the end of the branches; thefe are large, of a dirty fulphur colour, each petal having a large purple fpot at the bafe, and are fucceeded by oval pods, which open into four cells, which are filled with oblong green feeds wrapped up in a foft down. Where the plants have room to fpread, their branches will produce four or five pods of Cotton upon each, fo that from a fingle plant, thirty or more pods may be produced; and each of thefe are as large as middling Apples, fo there will be a much greater produce from this than from any other fort, and the ftaple is much finer; therefore it is well worth the attention of the inhabitants of the Britifh colonies in America to cultivate and improve this fort, fince it will fucceed in Carolina, where it It has been cultivated for fome years; and might be a commodity worthy of encouragement by the public, could they contrive a proper gin to feparate the Cotton from the feeds, to which this fort admires much clofer than any of the other forts, the Cotton from this fhrub being preferable to any other yet known. All thefe forts are very tender plants, therefore will not thrive in the open air in England, but they are frequently fown in curious gardens for variety: the firft and fourth forts will produce ripe feeds in England, if their feeds are fown early in the fpring, upon a good hot-bed; and when the plants are come up, planted each into feparate pots, and plunged into a hot-bed of tanners bark to bring them forward; and when they are grown too tall to remain under the frames, removed into the tan-bed in the ftove, and fhifted into larger pots, when their roots have filled the other; with this management I have had their flowers appear in July, and toward the end of September the feeds have been perfectly ripe, and the pods as large as thofe produced in the Eaft and Weft-Indies; but if the plants are not brought forward early in the fpring, it will be late in the fummer before the flowers will appear, and there will be no hopes of the pods coming to perfection.
The Shrub-cotton will rife from the feeds very eafily, if they are fown upon a good hot-bed; and when they are fown early in the fpring, and brought forward in the fame manner as hath been directed for the former forts, the plants will grow to be five or fix feet high the fame fummer; but it is difficult to preferve the plants through the winter, unlefs they are hardened gradually in Auguft during the continuance of the warm weather; for when they are forced on at that time, they will be fo tender, as to render them incapable of refifting the leaft injury. The plants of this fort muft be placed in the bark-ftove in autumn, and kept in the firft clafs of heat, otherwife they will not live through the winter in England.

GRAFTING is the taking a fhoot from one tree, and inferting it into another, in fuch a manner, as that both may unite clofely, and become one tree; this is called by the ancient writers in hufbandry and gardening, incifion, to diftinguifh it from inoculating, or budding, which they call inferere oculos.

The ufe of grafting is to propagate any curious forts of fruits, fo as to be certain of the kinds, which cannot be done by any other method; for as all the good fruits have been accidentally obtained from feeds, fo the feeds of thefe, when fown, will many of them degenerate, and produce fuch fruit as are not worth cultivating; but when fhoots are taken from fuch trees as produce good fruit, thefe will never alter from their kind, whatever be the ftock, or tree, on which they are grafted; for though the grafts receive their nourifhment from the ftocks, yet their varieties are never altered by them, but continue to produce the fame kind of fruit as the tree from which they were taken; the only alteration is, that when the ftocks on which they are grafted do not grow fo faft, and afford a fufficient fupply of nourifhment to the grafts, they will not make near fo great progrefs as they otherwife would do, nor will the fruit they produce be fo fair, and fometimes not fo well flavoured.

Thefe fhoots are termed cions, or graffs; in the choice of thefe the following directions fhould be carefully obferved. 1ft, That they are fhoots of the former year, for when they are older, they never fucceed well. 2dly, Always to take them from healthy fruitful trees, for if the trees are fickly from whence they are taken, the grafts very often partake fo much of the diftemper as rarely to get the better of it, at leaft for fome years; and when they are taken from young luxuriant trees, whofe veffels are generally large, they will continue to produce luxuriant fhoots, and are feldom fo fruitful as thofe which are taken from fruitful trees, whofe fhoots are more compact, and the joints clofer together; at leaft it will be a great number of years before the luxuriant grafts begin to produce fruit, if they are managed with the greateft fkill. 3dly, You fhould prefer thofe grafts which are taken from the lateral, or horizontal branches, to thofe from the ftrong perpendicular fhoots, for the reafons before given.

Thefe grafts, or cions, fhould be cut off from the trees before their buds begin to fwell, which is generally three weeks or a month before the feafon for grafting; therefore, when they are cut off, they fhould be laid in the ground with the cut downwards, burying them half their length, and covering their tops with dry litter, to prevent their drying; if a fmall joint of the former year's wood is cut off with the cion, it will preferve it the better, and when they are grafted, this may be cut off; for at the fame time the cions muft be cut to a proper length before they are inferted in the ftocks; but, till then, the fhoots fhould remain their full length, as they were taken from the tree, which will preferve them better from fhrinking; if thefe cions are to be carried to a confiderable diftance, it will be proper to put their ends into a lump of clay, and to wrap them up in mofs, which will preferve them frefh for a month, or longer; but thefe fhould be cut off earlier from the trees than thofe which are to be grafted near the place where the trees are growing.

Having given directions for the cions and grafts, we next come to that of the ftock, which is a term applied to the trees intended for grafting; thefe are either fuch old trees as are already growing in the places where they are to remain, whofe fruit is intended to be changed, or young trees, which have been raifed in a nurfery for a fupply to the garden; in the former cafe there is no other choice, but that of the branches, which fhould be fuch as are young, healthy, well fituated, and have a fmooth bark; if thefe trees are growing againft walls, or efpaliers, it will be proper to graft fix, eight, or ten branches, according to the fize of the trees, by which they will be much fooner furnifhed with branches again, than when a lefs number of cions are put in; but in ftandard-trees, four, or at moft fix cions will be fufficient.

In the choice of young ftocks for grafting, you fhould always prefer fuch as have been raifed from the

5

feed, and that have been once or twice tranfplanted. Next to thefe, are thofe ftocks which have been raifed from cuttings, or layers, but thofe which are fuckers from the roots of other trees fhould always be rejected, for thefe are never fo well rooted as the others, and conftantly put out a great number of fuckers from their roots, whereby the borders and walks of the garden will be always peftered with them during the fummer feafon, which is not only unfightly, but they alfo take off part of the nourifhment from the trees.

If thefe ftocks have been allowed a proper diftance in the nurfery where they have grown, the wood will be better ripened, and more compact than thofe which have grown clofe and have been there drawn up to a greater height; the wood of thefe will be foft, and their veffels large, fo that the cions grafted into them will fhoot very ftrong, but they will be lefs difpofed to produce fruit than the other; and when trees acquire an ill habit at firft, it will be very difficult to reclaim them afterward.

Having directed the choice of cions and ftocks, we come next to the operation, in order to which you muft be provided with the following tools.

1. A neat fmall hand-faw to cut off the heads of large ftocks.
2. A good ftrong knife with a thick back, to make clefts in the ftocks.
3. A fharp penknife to cut the grafts.
4. A grafting chiffel and a fmall mallet.
5. Bafs ftrings, or woollen yarn, to tie the grafts with, and fuch other inftruments and materials as you fhould find neceffary, according to the manner of grafting you are to perform.
6. A quantity of clay, which fhould be prepared a month before it is ufed, and kept turned and mixed, like mortar every other day, which is to be made after the following manner:

Get a quantity of ftrong fat loam (in proportion to the quantity of trees intended to be grafted, then take fome new ftone-horfe dung, and break it in amongft the loam, and if you cut a little ftraw, or hay, very fmall, and mix amongft it, the loam will hold together the better; and if there be a quantity of falt added, it will prevent the clay from dividing in dry weather; thefe muft be well ftirred together, putting water to them after the manner of making mortar; it fhould be hollowed like a difh, and filled with water, and kept every other day ftirred; but it ought to be remembered, that it fhould not be expofed to the froft, or drying winds, and the oftener it is ftirred and wrought the better.

Of late years fome perfons have made ufe of another compofition for grafting, which they have found to anfwer the intention of keeping out the air, better than the clay before defcribed. This is compofed of turpentine, bees-wax, and rofin, melted together, which, when of a proper confiftence, may be put on the ftock round the graft, in the fame manner as the clay is ufually applied; and though it be not above a quarter of an inch thick, yet it will keep out the air more effectually than the clay; and as cold will harden this, there is no danger of its being hurt by froft, which is very apt to caufe the clay to cleave, and fometimes fall off; and when the heat of fummer comes on, this mixture will melt, and fall off without any trouble. In ufing of this, there fhould be a tin, or copper-pot, with conveniency under it to keep a very gentle fire with fmall-coal, otherwife the cold will foon condenfe the mixture; but you muft be careful not to apply it too hot, left you injure the graft. A perfon who is a little accuftomed to this compofition, will apply it very faft, and it is much eafier for him than clay, efpecially if the feafon fhould prove cold. There are feveral ways of grafting, the principal of which are four:

1. Grafting in the rind, called alfo fhoulder-grafting, which is only proper for large trees; this is called crown-grafting, becaufe the grafts are fet in form of a circle, or crown, and is generally performed

formed about the latter end of March, or the beginning of April.

2. Cleft-grafting, which is alſo called ſtock, or ſlit-grafting; this is proper for trees or ſtocks of a leſſer ſize, from an inch, to two inches or more diameter; this grafting is to be performed in the months of February and March, and ſupplies the failure of the eſcutcheon-way, which is practiſed in June, July, and Auguſt.

3. Whip-grafting; which is alſo called tongue-grafting; this is proper for ſmall ſtocks of an inch, half an inch, or leſs, diameter; this is the moſt effectual way of any, and which is moſt in uſe.

4. Grafting by approach, or ablactation; this is to be performed when the ſtock you would graft on, and the tree from which you take your graft, ſtand ſo near together, that they may be joined; this is to be performed in the month of April, and is alſo called inarching, and is chiefly uſed for Jaſmines, Oranges, and other tender exotic trees.

We come next to the manner of performing the ſeveral ways of grafting.

The firſt method, which is termed rind, or ſhoulder-grafting, is ſeldom practiſed but on large trees, where either the head, or the large branches, are cut off horizontally, and two or four cions put in, according to the ſize of the branch, or item; in doing of this, the cions are cut flat on one ſide, with a ſhoulder to reſt upon the crown of the ſtock; then the rind of the ſtock muſt be raiſed up, to admit the cion between the wood and the bark of the ſtock, which muſt be inſerted about two inches, ſo as the ſhoulder of the cion may reſt, and cloſely join the crown of the ſtock; and after the number of cions are inſerted, the whole crown of the ſtock ſhould be well clayed over, leaving two eyes of the cions uncovered therewith, which will be ſufficient for ſhooting; this method of grafting, was much more in practice formerly than at preſent; the diſcontinuance of it was occaſioned by the ill ſucceſs it was attended with; for as theſe cions were placed between the rind of the ſtock and the wood, ſo they are frequently blown out by ſtrong winds, after they had made large ſhoots, which has ſometimes happened after five or ſix years growth; ſo that whenever this method is practiſed, there ſhould be ſome ſtakes faſtened to ſupport the cions, until they have almoſt covered the ſtock.

The next method is termed cleft, or ſtock-grafting; this is practiſed upon ſtocks, or trees, of a ſmaller ſize, and may be uſed with ſucceſs, where the rind of the ſtock is not too thick, whereby the inner bark of the cion will be prevented joining to that of the ſtock; this may be performed on ſtocks, or branches, which are more than one inch diameter; in the doing of this, the head of the ſtock, or branch, muſt be cut off with a ſlope, and a ſlit made the contrary way, in the top of the ſlope, deep enough to receive the cion, which ſhould be cut ſloping like a wedge, ſo as to fit the ſlit made in the ſtock, being careful to leave that ſide of the wedge, which is to be placed outward, much thicker than the other; and in putting the cion into the ſlit of the ſtock, there muſt be great care taken to join the rind of the cion to that of the ſtock; for if theſe do not unite, the grafts will not ſucceed: when this method of grafting is uſed to ſtocks which are not ſtrong, it will be proper to make a ligature of baſs, to prevent the ſlit of the ſtock from opening; then the whole ſhould be clayed over, to prevent the air from penetrating the ſlit, ſo as to deſtroy the grafts, only leaving two eyes of the cions above the clay for ſhooting.

The third method is termed whip, or tongue-grafting, which is the moſt commonly practiſed of any by the nurſerymen near London, eſpecially for ſmall ſtocks, becauſe the cions much ſooner cover the ſtocks in this method than in any other.

This is performed by cutting off the head of the ſtocks ſloping; then there muſt be a notch made in the ſlope toward the upper part downward, a little more than half an inch deep, to receive the cion, which muſt be cut with a ſlope upward, and a ſlit made in this ſlope like a tongue, which tongue muſt be in-

ſerted into the ſlit made in the ſlope of the ſtock; and the cion muſt be placed on one ſide of the ſtock, ſo as that the two rinds of both cion and ſtock may be equal, and join together exactly; then there ſhould be a ligature of baſs to faſten the cion, ſo as that it may not be eaſily diſplaced; and afterward clay it over; as in the former methods.

The fourth ſort of grafting is termed inarching-grafting by approach, or ablactation. This is only to be performed when the ſtocks; which are deſigned to be grafted, and the tree from which the graft is to be taken, ſtand ſo near together, or may be brought ſo near together, as that their branches may be united; this method of grafting is commonly practiſed on tender exotic plants, and ſome other ſorts which do not ſucceed in any of the other methods.

In performing this operation, a part of the ſtock, or branch, muſt be ſlit off about two inches in length, obſerving always to make choice of a ſmooth part of the ſtock; then a ſmall notch ſhould be made in this ſlit of the ſtock downward, in the ſame manner as hath been directed for whip-grafting; then the branch of the tree deſigned to be inarched, ſhould have a part ſlit off in like manner as the ſtock, and a ſlit made upward in this, ſo as to leave a tongue; which tongue ſhould be inſerted into the ſlit of the ſtock, obſerving to join their rinds equally, that they may unite well together; then make a ligature of baſs, to keep them exactly in their ſituation, and afterward clay this part of the ſtock over well, to keep out the air; in this method of grafting, the cion is not ſeparated from the tree, until it is firmly united with the ſtock, nor is the head of the ſtock, or branch, which is grafted, cut off till this time, and only half the wood pared off with a ſlope, about three inches in length, and the ſame of the cion, or graft.

This method of grafting is not performed ſo early in the ſeaſon as thoſe of the other, it being done in the month of April, when the ſap is flowing, at which time the cion and ſtock will join together, and unite much ſooner than at any other ſeaſon.

The Walnut, Fig, and Mulberry, will take by this method of grafting, but neither of theſe will ſucceed in any of the other methods; there are alſo ſeveral ſorts of Evergreens, which may be propagated by this method of grafting; but all the trees which are grafted in this way are weaker, and never grow to the ſize of thoſe which are grafted in the other methods; therefore this is rarely practiſed, but on ſuch ſorts of trees as will not take by the other methods.

The next thing which is neceſſary to be known, by thoſe who would practiſe this art, is, what trees will take and thrive by being grafted upon each other; and here there have been no ſure directions given by any of the writers on this ſubject, for there will be found great miſtakes in all their books, in relation to this matter; but as it would ſwell this article too great, if all the ſorts of trees were to be here enumerated, which will take upon each other by grafting, I ſhall only mention ſuch general directions, as, if attended to, will be ſufficient to inſtruct perſons, ſo as they may ſucceed.

All ſuch trees as are of the ſame genus, i. e. which will agree in their flower and fruit, will take upon each other: for inſtance, all the Nut-bearing trees may be ſafely grafted on each other, as may all the Plumb-bearing trees, under which head I reckon not only the ſeveral ſorts of Plumbs, but alſo the Almond, Peach, Nectarine, Apricot, &c. which agree exactly in their general characters, by which they are diſtinguiſhed from all other trees; but as many of theſe are very ſubject to emit large quantities of gum from the parts of the trees as are deeply cut and wounded, ſo the tender trees of this kind, viz. Peaches and Nectarines, which are moſt ſubject to this, it is found to be the ſureſt method to bud or inoculate theſe ſorts of fruits, for which ſee INOCULATION.

Then all ſuch trees as bear cones will do well upon each other, though they may differ in one being evergreen, and the other ſhedding its leaves in winter; as is obſervbale in the Cedar of Libanus, and the Larch-tree, which are found to ſucceed upon each other very well;

well, but thefe muft be grafted by approach, for they abound with a great quantity of refin which is apt to evaporate from the graft, if feparated from the tree before it is joined with the ftock, whereby they are often deftroyed; as alfo the Laurel on the Cherry, or the Cherry on the Laurel. All the maft-bearing trees will alfo take upon each other, and thofe which have a tender foft wood will do well if grafted in the common way; but thofe that are of a more firm contexture, and are flow growers, fhould be grafted by approach.

By ftrictly obferving this rule, we fhall feldom mifcarry, provided the operation be rightly performed, and at a proper feafon, unlefs the weather fhould prove very bad, as it fometimes happens, whereby whole quarters of fruit-trees mifcarry; and it is by this method that many kinds of exotic trees are not only propagated, but alfo rendered hardy enough to endure the cold of our climate in the open air; for, being grafted upon ftocks of the fame fort which are hardy, the grafts are rendered more capable to endure the cold, as hath been experienced by moft of our valuable fruits now in England, which were formerly tranfplanted here from more foutherly climates, and were at firft too impatient of our cold to fucceed well abroad; but have been, by budding or grafting upon more hardy trees, rendered capable of refifting our fevereft cold.

And thefe different graftings feem to have been greatly in ufe among the ancients, though they were certainly miftaken in the feveral forts of fruits which they mention to have fucceeded upon each other; as the Fig upon the Mulberry, the Plumb upon the Cheftnut, with many others of the like kind; moft of which I have already tried, and find they will not fucceed; therefore what has been advanced on this head by the ancients, is not founded on experience; or at leaft they did not mean the fame plants, which at prefent are called by thofe names; though I cannot help thinking we are apt to pay too much deference to the writings of the ancients, in fuppofing them feldom to be miftaken, or to affert a falfhood; whereas, if their works are carefully examined, it will be found, that they have often copied from each other's writings, without making experiments to prove the truth of their affertions: and it is well known, that the ranging of plants before Cæfalpinus's time (which is about 170 years fince) was, by their outward appearance, or from the fuppofed virtues of them, which method is now juftly exploded; and it hath been obferved, from many repeated trials, that however plants may refemble each other in the fhape and make of their leaves, manner of fhooting, &c. unlefs they agree in their fruit, and their other diftinctive characters, they will not grow upon each other, though performed with ever fo much art.

GRAMEN. Tourn. Inft. R. H. 516. tab. 297. Raii Meth. Plant. 171. Grafs; in French, *Chien-dent.*

To enumerate all the fpecies of Grafs which are found growing naturally in England, would fwell this article greatly beyond the defign of the work; therefore I fhall only take notice of a few fpecies, which are either ufed in medicine, or cultivated for fodder; for there is fcarce a pafture in this country, where at leaft twenty different fpecies are not to be found intermixed, and in moft of them more than twice that number. Thefe were, by the former writers on botany, all included under the common denomination of Gramen, but were divided into different fections. Mr. Ray has ranged them in the following order, Gramen Triticum, i. e. Wheat-grafs. Gramen Secalinum, i. e. Rye-grafs. Gramen Loliaceum, i. e. Darnel-grafs. Gramen Paniceum, i. e. Panic-grafs. Gramen Phalaroides, i. e. Canary-grafs. Gramen Alopecuroides, i. e. Fox-tail-grafs. Gramen Typhinum, i. e. Cat's-tail-grafs. Gramen Echinatum, i. e. Hedgehog-grafs. Gramen Criftatum, i. e. Crefted-grafs. Gramen Avenacium, i. e. Oat-grafs. Gramen Dactylon, i. e. Cock's-foot-grafs. Gramen Arundinaceum, i. e. Reed-grafs. Gramen Milleacem, i. e.

Millet-grafs. And under each of thefe fections there are many fpecies. And there are many others, which, by older writers, were included under this general title, fome of which have no relation to this clafs; but there are others which are near nearly allied to it, as the Cyperus and Cyprefs Graffes, &c. Thefe Dr. Linnæus has divided into genera; but by this method of claffing them, he has feparated them to a great diftance from each other; for all thofe whofe flowers have three ftamina, are ranged in his third clafs; and others which have male and female flowers, are removed to his twenty-firft clafs. However, it would have been much better to have kept them together, as Dr. Van Royen has done in the Prodromus of the Leyden garden, under one general title to the clafs of Gramina.

As the feveral genera under which the different fpecies of Grafs are ranged, have different characters by which they are diftinguifhed, fo it would be to little purpofe to give them all in this work; and as there are no general characteriftics by which the whole clafs can be known, fo I fhall not trouble the reader with any of them here, but proceed to enumerate a few of the fpecies.

1. GRAMEN fpicâ triticeâ repens vulgare, caninum dictum. Raii Syn. 2. p. 247. *Common creeping Grafs with a fpike like Wheat, called Dog-grafs.* Triticum calycibus fublatis trifloris acuminatis. Lin. Sp. Plant. *Wheat with an awl-fhaped pointed empalement: including three flowers, commonly called Couch, Couch-grafs, or Quick-grafs.*

2. GRAMEN loliaceum, anguftiore folio & fpicâ. C. B. P. *Darnel-grafs, with a narrower leaf and fpike.* Lolium fpicâ muticâ. Lin. Sp. Plant. 83. *Darnel with a chaffy fpike, commonly called Ray, or Rye-grafs.*

3. GRAMEN pratenfe, paniculatum majus anguftiore folio. C. B. P. 2. *Meadow-grafs with larger panicles and a narrower leaf.* Poa paniculâ diffufâ, fpiculis quadrifloris pubefcentibus, culmo erecto tereti. Flor. Suec. 77. *Poa with a diffufed panicle, the fmaller fpikes having four hairy flowers, and a taper erect ftraw.*

4. GRAMEN pratenfe, paniculatum majus, latiore folio. C. B. P. 2. *Meadow-grafs with a larger panicle and broader leaf.* Poa paniculâ diffufâ fpiculis trifloris glabris, culmo erecto tereti. Flor. Suec. 76. *Poa with a diffufed panicle, fmall fpikes with three flowers, and an upright ftraw.*

5. GRAMEN avenacium pratenfe elatius paniculâ flavefcente, locuftis parvis. Raii Syn. 407. *Taller Meadow Oat-grafs, with a yellowifh panicle and fmall bufhes.* Avena paniculâ laxâ, calycibus trifloris brevibus, flofculis omnibus ariftatis. Prod. Leyd. 66. *Oat-grafs with a loofe panicle, three flowers in each empalement, which is fhort, and all the flowers having awns.*

6. GRAMEN fecalinum. Ger. Emac. lib. 1. cap. 22. n. 4. *Tall Meadow Rye grafs.*

7. GRAMEN tremulum maximum. C. B. P. 2. *Greateft Quaking-grafs, or Cowquakes.* Briza fpiculis cordatis, flofculis feptendecim. Hort. Cliff. 23. *Briza with heart-fhaped little fpikes, and feventeen flowers in each.*

The firft fort of Grafs is that which is directed to be ufed in medicine; the roots of this are chiefly ufed, and are accounted aperitive and diuretic, opening obftructions of the reins and bladder, provoking urine, and are of fervice againft the gravel and ftone. The juice of the leaves and ftalks was greatly efteemed by Dr. Boerhaave, who generally prefcribed this in all cafes where he fuppofed there were any obftructions in the bile conduit.

This hath a creeping root, which fpreads far in the ground, and is a very troublefome weed in gardens and arable land; for every fmall piece of the root will grow and multiply exceedingly, fo it is very difficult to extirpate where it once gets poffeffion: in gardens, the common method of deftroying it is, to fork out the roots as often as the blades appear above ground; where this is two or three times carefully repeated, it may be totally rooted out; but when the furface of the ground is very full of the roots of this Grafs, the fhorteft way of deftroying it, is to trench the

the ground two fpits and a fhovelling deep, turning all the couch into the bottom, where it will rot, and never fhoot up ; but this can only be practifed, where there is a fufficient depth of foil ; for in fhallow ground the roots cannot be buried fo deep, as to lie below the depth to which they naturally fhoot.

Where the roots of this Grafs get poffeffion in arable fields, it is very difficult to root out again ; the ufual method is by laying the land fallow in fummer, and frequently harrowing it well over to draw out the roots : where this is carefully practifed, the ground may be fo well cleaned in one fummer, as that the roots cannot much injure the crop which may be fown upon it ; but fuch land fhould be cropped with Beans, Peas, or fuch things as require the horfe-hoeing culture ; for where the land can be frequently ftirred and harrowed afterward, it will be of great fervice in cleaning it from the roots of this Grafs and other bad weeds. The blade of this Grafs is fo rough, that cattle will not feed upon it.

The fecond fort is frequently cultivated, efpecially in ftrong cold land, upon which this Grafs will fucceed better than any other fpecies, and is an earlier feed in the fpring ; but this is a very coarfe Grafs, and unlefs it is cut very early for hay, it becomes hard and wiery in the ftalks, fo that few cattle care to eat it ; for this fpecies has but few leaves, running all to ftalk, fo is ufually called Bents, and in fome counties Bennet ; when this grafs is fed, it will be proper to mow off the Bents in the beginning of June, otherwife they will dry upon the ground, and have the appearance of a ftubble field all the latter part of fummer ; fo that it will not only be very difagreeable to the fight, but alfo be troublefome to the cattle that feed on it, by tickling their noftrils ; fo that the want of better pafture only, will force them to eat of the young Grafs which fprings up between thefe Bents, for thofe they will not touch ; therefore thofe who fuppofe that thefe are eaten in fcarcity of feed by the cattle, are greatly miftaken ; for I have many years clofely attended to this, and have always found thefe Bents remaining on the ground untouched, till the froft, rain, and winds, deftroy it in winter ; and, by permitting thefe to ftand, the after-growth of the Grafs is greatly retarded, and the beautiful verdure is loft for three or four months ; fo that it is good hufbandry to mow them before they grow too dry, and rake them off the ground : if thefe are then made into the hay, it will ferve for cart-horfes or cows feed in winter, and will pay the expence of mowing it.

There is another fpecies of this Grafs called Red Darnel, which is of a worfe nature than the firft, the ftalks growing hard much fooner, and having narrower leaves. This is very common in moft pafture grounds, for as it comes early to flower, fo the feeds are generally ripe before the hay is cut, and from the falling feeds the ground is fupplied with plenty of this fort ; therefore thofe who are defirous to keep their paftures as clear from this Grafs as poffible, fhould always mow it before the feeds are ripe.

This Grafs is ufually fown with Clover, upon fuch lands as are defigned to be ploughed again in a few years, and the common method is to fow it with Spring Corn ; but from many repeated trials, I have always found, that by fowing thefe feeds in Auguft, when there has happened a few fhowers to bring up the Grafs, that the crop has anfwered much better than any which has been fown in the common way ; for the Grafs has often been fo rank, as to afford a good feed the fame autumn ; and the following fpring there has been a ton and a half of hay per acre mowed very early in the feafon, and this has been upon cold four land ; fo that I am convinced of that being the beft feafon for fowing thefe Grafies, though it will be very difficult to perfuade thofe perfons to alter their practice, who have been long wedded to old cuftoms. The quantity of feeds which I allow to an acre is about two bufhels, and eight pounds of the common Clover, which, together, will make as good plants upon the

ground as can be defired ; but this is not to be practifed upon fuch lands where the beauty of the verdure is principally regarded, therefore is fit for thofe who have only profit in view.

The third and fourth forts are the two beft fpecies of Grafs for paftures, fo that if the feeds of thefe were carefully collected and fown feparately without any other mixture of Grafs-feeds, they would not only afford a greater quantity of feed on the fame fpace of land, but the Grafs would alfo be better, the hay fweeter, and the verdure more lafting than of any other forts ; but there requires fome attention to the faving of thefe feeds pure without mixture. I have tried to fave the feeds of feveral fpecies of Grafs feparately, in order to determine their qualities, but have found it very difficult to keep them diftinct in gardens where the feeds of other forts of Grafs have been fcattered : the only method in which I could fucceed, was by fowing each fpecies in a diftinct pot, and when the plants came up, to weed out all the other kinds of Grafs which came up in the pots ; by this means I preferved a great variety of the grafly tribe feveral years, but not having ground enough to propagate the moft ufeful fpecies in any quantity, I was obliged to abandon the purfuit : but I muft recommend this to perfons of leifure and fkill who have a fufficient quantity of land for the purpofe, to carry this project into execution, which may be of fingular benefit to the public ; for we have an inftance of the advantage which the inhabitants of the Netherlands have made, by faving the feeds of the White Clover, or Honeyfuckle Trefoil, which is a plant common to moft of the Englifh paitures ; yet few perfons in this country ever gave themfelves the trouble to collect the feeds from the fields for fowing, but have purchafed vaft quantities of this feed annually, at a confiderable price from Flanders, where the peafants have been fo induftrious, as to collect the feeds and fow great quantities of land with it, with a view of fale to this country only. This is not an inconfiderable article in hufbandry, but deferves the attention of all thofe, who, by choice or otherwife, are engaged in the bufinefs of agriculture ; for one acre of land will produce as much feeds of this fpecies of Trefoil, as will fell for 12 l. where it is well planted and faved from the fpring crop ; and if the Grafs-feeds beforementioned were feparately fown, and carefully weeded from all other fpecies, and permitted to ftand till their feeds were ripe, it might be of equal advantage with the other, efpecially now, when every gentleman is endeavouring to improve the verdure near their habitations.

The fifth and fixth forts are alfo very good Grafies for paftures, and have perennial roots, fo are the next beft forts for fowing to thofe before-mentioned, which, in my opinion, deferve the preference to all the other ; but as it will be difficult to fave a fufficient quantity of feeds of thofe alone, to fupply the demand which may be for their feeds ; fo thefe two fpecies may be admitted in aid of the other, as they are very leafy kinds of Grafs, and their ftalks do not become ftiff and harfh like many other fpecies, but with proper care may be made very fine ; and, if duly rolled, their roots will mat and form a very clofe fward, therefore thefe fhould be included in the number of fown Grafies.

The feventh fort is mentioned for the fake of variety, and not for ufe ; this hath an annual root, which fends up many broad hairy leaves, between which arife flender ftiff ftalks from a foot to near two two feet high, dividing upward into a large loofe panicle, garnifhed with heart-fhaped fmall fpikes, each having about feventeen fmall flofcules or florets ; thefe, after the flowers are paft, have a fingle feed fucceeding them ; the heads hang by flender long foot-ftalks, which are moved by every wind, fo that they generally appear fhaking, from whence it had the title of Quaking Grafs. There are four fpecies of this Grafs, two of them grow naturally in England ; and thefe Grafies coming to head in May, occafioned the following

English proverb, *May come shoe early come shoe late, means the cow quake.* The large sort here mentioned, grows naturally in the south of France and Italy, and is only preserved in some English gardens for the sake of variety.

If the seeds of this sort are sown in the autumn, or permitted to scatter when ripe, the plants will come up stronger, and flower much earlier, than when they are sown in the spring, so good seeds may always be expected from them, which can seldom be attained from the spring plants in England ; and as two or three plants of this sort will be full enough in a garden for variety, so these should be allowed to spread ; for where they grow at a distance from each other, the roots will send out a great number of stalks, which will be stronger, and produce much larger panicles than those which are too near together.

The Cock's-foot Grass, Capon's-tail Grass, and Millet Grasses are too coarse to deserve attention in England, though some of their species are very useful in the warm parts of America, where there is a great scarcity of finer Grass ; and some of these are much better adapted to those warm countries, than any of our European Grasses, for many of them lie flat on the ground, and emit roots from their joints, so are well prepared for heat ; their stalks are large and juicy, so will live in heat where few of the European Grasses can be made to thrive.

The land on which Grass-seed is intended to be sown, should be well ploughed, and cleared from the roots of noxious weeds, such as Couch-grass, Fern, Rushes, Heath, Gorse, Broom, Rest-harrow, &c. which, if left in the ground, will soon get the better of the Grass, and over-run the land. Therefore in such places where either of these weeds abound, it will be a good method to plough up the surface in April, and let it lie some time to dry ; then harrow the roots into small heaps, and burn them. The ashes so produced, when spread on the land, will be a good manure for it. The method of burning the roots is particularly directed under the article LAND, which see : but where Couch-grass, Fern, or Rest-harrow is in plenty, whose roots run far under ground, the land must be ploughed two or three times pretty deep in dry weather, and the roots carefully harrowed off after each ploughing, which is the most-sure method to destroy them. Where the land is very low, and of a stiff clayey nature, which holds water in winter, it will be of singular service to make some drains under-ground drains to carry off the wet ; which, if detained too long on the ground, will render the Grass sour. The method of making these drains is prescribed under the article LAND, which see.

Before the seed is sown, the surface of the ground should be made level and fine, otherwise the seed will be buried unequal. When the seed is sown, it must be gently harrowed in, and the ground rolled with a wooden roller, which will make the surface even, and prevent the seeds being blown in patches. When the Grass comes up, if there should be any bare spots, where the seed has not grown, they may be sown again, and the ground rolled, which will fix the seeds ; and the first kindly showers will bring up the Grass, and make it very thick.

Where the land is designed to continue in pasture, it should be sown with the best sorts of Grass-seeds, and white Dutch Clover, or what is commonly called Honeysuckle Grass in many parts of England, but there is a great difficulty of procuring hay-seeds which are good ; for in all the good pastures near London, which abound with the best sorts of Grass, the hay is commonly cut before the seeds of the Grass are ripe ; so that those seeds are procured from the stables where the horses are fed with the best sort of hay, are little more than chaff, or at best are only such as are of the early kinds of Grass, with a great quantity of Plantain and other weeds : which has discouraged many gentlemen from sowing them, nor has any one attempted to save these seeds properly ; and as it requires longer time, and more attention, to save a quantity of

seeds of the purer sort of Grass than the generality of people care to bestow, so I would recommend the setting some of those upland pastures, which are cleanest from weeds, and have the sweetest herbage aside, to stand for seeds ; and although by so doing the hay will be less valuable, yet from the sale of the seeds, it may answer better to the possessor, than to mow it merely for the hay ; for any gentleman who has regard to the beauty of his land, had better give six times the price for such seeds, as is usually paid for the ordinary seeds, since the first expence of seeds is not to be put in competion with the beauty and advantage of having such as are good ; for when the land is brought to a good sward (which may be done in one year, where it is properly prepared and sown with good seeds) it may be kept in good order, and by good management improved annually, and will continue so, as long as proper care is taken of it. I know some land which was sown in the method hereafter directed above forty years ago, which are now as good pastures as any I have seen, and may be always continued so.

These grounds abounded with many bad weeds, so they had a winter and summer's fallow, in which time they were five times ploughed and ten times harrowed in order to destroy the weeds, and make the surface of the ground fine ; in August they were sown with the best Grass-seeds as could be procured, three bushels of this, and nine pounds of the white Dutch Clover-seeds were allowed to each acre ; as there happened rains soon after the seeds were sown, so the Grass came up well ; but among it were a great number of weeds, which were drawn up and carried off the ground, and in the beginning of October the fields were rolled with a Barley roller ; in the spring the fields were again weeded, and afterward rolled, and that summer there was more than two tons of hay per acre mowed off the land ; and by constant weeding twice a year, sweeping it with a bush-harrow, rolling and dressing of the land, the Grass has been greatly improved since, and is now as good pasture as any in England : and since I have laid down great quantities of land in the same manner, and with equal success ; therefore from many years experience can recommend it, as the surest method of having good pastures.

But I know the generality of farmers will object to the first loss of their crop, and also to the after expence of weeding, rolling, &c. as too great for common practice : however, I am well satisfied from experience, that whoever will be at the expence, will find their account in it ; for the crops of hay will be so much better, and the after pasture also, that it will more than pay the expence, as from many exact accounts, which have been kept of the whole, is sufficiently demonstrated, and the verdure of these pastures is charming to all those who have any taste of natural beauties.

The proper management of pasture land is the least understood of any part of agriculture ; the farmers never have attended to this, being more inclined to the plough, though the profits attending that have not of late years been so great as to encourage them in that part of husbandry ; but these people never think of laying down land for pasture, to continue longer than three years, at the end of which time they plough it up again, to sow it with grain.

There is a sort of striped Grass which is preserved in many gardens for the beauty of its variegated leaves, which continue fresh the greatest part of the summer. This sort is easily propagated by parting the roots, either in spring or autumn, for every offset will increase to be a large root in one year's time. It will grow on any soil or in any situation, therefore may be planted in any abject part of the garden, where it will thrive, and afford an agreeable variety. This sort is by many persons called Ribband-grass, from the stripes of white and green, which run the whole length of the blade, like the stripes in some ribbands.

For the further management of Grafs in fields, fee PASTURE and MEADOW; and for that in gardens, fee GRASS.

Clover-grafs. See TRIFOLIUM.
Saint-foin. See ONOBRYCHIS, or HEDYSARUM.
La Lucerne. See MEDICA.
Nonefuch, See MELILOTUS, or TRIFOLIUM.
Trefoil. See TRIFOLIUM.
Spurry. See SPERGULA.

GRANADILLA. See PASSIFLORA.

GRAPES. See VITIS.

GRASS. The Englifh Grafs is of fo good a quality for walks or Grafs-plats, that if they be kept in good order, they have that exquifite beauty that they cannot come up to in France, and feveral other countries. But green walks and green plats are, for the moft part, not made by fowing the Grafs-feed, but by laying turfs; and, indeed, the turfs from a fine common or down, are much preferable to fown Grafs.

In fowing a fine green plat, there is a difficulty in getting good feed; it ought not to be fuch as is taken out of the hay-loft without diftinction; for that feed fhooting too high and making large ftalks, the lower part will be naked and bare; and although it be mowed ever fo often, it will never make handfome Grafs; but, on the contrary, will come to nothing but tufts of weeds and Quick-grafs, very little better than that of the common fields.

If walks or plats be made by fowing, the beft way is to procure the feed from thofe paftures where the Grafs is naturally fine and clear, or elfe the trouble of keeping it from fpiry and benty Grafs will be very great, and it will fcarce ever look handfome.

In order to fow Grafs-feed, the ground muft be firft dug or broken up with a fpade; and when it has been dreffed and laid even, it muft be very finely raked over, and all the clods and ftones taken off, and covered over an inch thick with good mould, to facilitate the growth of the feed; this being done, the feed is to be fown pretty thick, that it may come up clofe and fhort; and it muft be raked over again to bury and cover the feed, that if the weather fhould happen to be windy, it may not be blown away.

As to the feafon of fowing Grafs, the middle or latter end of Auguft is a good time, becaufe the feed naturally requires nothing but moifture to make it grow: if be not fown till the latter end of February, or the beginning of March, if the weather proves dry, it will not fo foon make the walks or quarters green. It is alfo beft to fow it in a mild day, and inclining to rain; for that, by finking down the feed in the earth, will caufe it to fhoot the fooner. But where Grafs is fown in gardens, either for lawns or walks, there fhould always be a good quantity of the White Trefoil or Dutch Clover fown with it, for this will make a fine turf much fooner than any other fown Grafs, and will continue a better verdure than any of the Grafs tribe.

After the feed is well come up, and the Grafs is very thick and of a beautiful green, it will require a conftant care to keep it in order: this confifts in mowing the Grafs often, for the oftener it is mowed, the thicker and handfomer it grows; it muft alfo be rolled with a cylinder or roller of wood, to level it as much as poffible.

If Grafs be neglected, it will run into Quick-grafs and weeds; and if it does fo, there is no way to recover it, but either by fowing it, or laying it over again, and that once in every two years; but if the ground be well cleared from the roots of ftrong weeds, and the turf be taken from a fine level common, it will continue handfome for feveral years, provided it be well kept.

In order to keep Grafs-plats or walks handfome and in good order, in autumn you may fow fome frefh feed over any places that are not well filled, or where the Grafs is dead, to renew and furnifh them again; but there is nothing which improves Grafs fo much as conftant rolling and polling it, to deftroy wormcafts, and thereby the turf is rendered fine.

It is a general practice when turf is laid in gardens, to cover the furface of the ground under the turf, either with fand or very poor earth; the defign of this is to keep the Grafs fine, by preventing its growing too rank. This is proper enough for very rich ground, but is not fo for fuch land as is but middling or poor; for when this is practifed in fuch places, the Grafs will foon wear out, and decay in patches.

When turf is taken from a common or down, there fhould be regard had to the cleannefs of it, and not to take fuch as is full of weeds: for it will be a very tedious piece of work, to weed them out after the turf is laid; and unlefs this is done, the Grafs will never appear handfome.

Where turf is defigned to remain for years without renewing, there fhould be dreffing laid upon it every other year, either of very rotten dung, afhes, or, where it can be eafily procured, very rotten tan, is a good dreffing for Grafs; but thefe dreffings fhould be laid on early in winter, that the rain may wafh them into the ground, before the drought of the fpring comes on, otherwife they will occafion the Grafs to burn when the warmth of fummer begins. Where Grafs is fo dreffed, and kept well rolled and mowed, it may be kept very beautiful for many years; but where it is not dreffed or fed with fheep, it will rarely continue handfome more than eight or ten years.

GRATIOLA. Lin. Gen. Plant. 27. Raii Meth. Plant. 90. Digitalis. Tourn. Inft. R. H. 165. Hedge Hyffop.

The CHARACTERS are,

The flower hath a permanent empalement, which is cut into five parts; it hath one petal of the grinning kind, with a tube longer than the empalement, cut at the top into four fmall fegments, the upper being broader and indented at the end where it is reflexed; the other three are erect and equal. It hath five awl-fhaped ftamina, three of which are fhorter than the petal, and fteril; the other two are longer, and adhere to the tube of the petal; thefe are fruitful in male duft; they are terminated by roundifh fummits. In the center is fituated a cenical germen, fupporting an erect ftyle, crowned by a ftigma with two lips, which clofe after being facundated. The germen afterward becomes an oval capfule ending in a point, having two cells which are filled with fmall feeds.

This genus of plants is ranged in the firft fection of Linnæus's fecond clafs, intitled Diandria Monogynia, which includes thofe plants whofe flowers have but two ftamina and one ftyle, for he does not efteem the three barren ftamina as worthy notice.

The SPECIES are,

1. GRATIOLA (*Officinalis*) floribus pedunculatis, foliis lanceolatis ferratis. Lin. Mat. Med. 18. *Hedge Hyffop with flowers ftanding on foot-ftalks, and fpear-fhaped leaves.* Digitalis minima Gratiolata dicta. Mor. Hift. 2. 479. *Leaft Foxglove, called Gratiola.*

2. GRATIOLA (*Virginiana*) foliis lanceolatis obtufis fub dentatis. Flor. Virg. 6. *Hedge Hyffop with obtufe indented leaves.*

3. GRATIOLA (*Peruviana*) floribus fubfeffilibus. Lin. Sp. Plant. 17. *Hedge Hyffop with flowers fitting clofe to the branches.* Gratiola latiore folio flore albo. Feuill. Peruv.

The firft fort grows naturally on the Alps, and other mountainous parts of Europe. This hath a thick, flefhy, fibrous, creeping root, which propagates very much when planted in a proper foil and fituation, from which arife feveral upright fquare ftalks, near a foot high, garnifhed with narrow fpear-fhaped leaves placed oppofite; the flowers are produced on the fide of the ftalks at each joint, they are fhaped like thofe of the Foxglove, but are fmall, and of a pale yellowifh colour. Thefe appear in July, but are feldom fucceeded by feeds in England.

It is eafily propagated by parting of the roots; the beft time to do this is in the autumn, when the ftalks decay; the plants fhould have a moift foil and a fhady fituation, in which they will thrive exceedingly; but in dry ground they often decay in fummer, unlefs they are plentifully watered.

This

This ftands in the lift of medicinal plants, but is very rarely ufed in England, though it is recommended by fome good writers as a purger of ferous and choleric humours.

The fecond fort grows naturally in North America, from whence I received the feeds. This grows naturally in moift places, where it rifes more than a foot high, but in England I have not feen it more than eight inches; the leaves are blunt, and indented at their extremities; the flowers are white, and come out from the fide of the ftalks, like thofe of the other, but are not fucceeded by feeds here. It may be propagated in the fame manner as the firft fort, and requires the fame treatment.

The feeds of the third fort were fent me from Carthagena, where it was found growing naturally in places where there had been ftanding waters, which were then dried up; this plant grew about nine inches high, with a weak ftalk, and the leaves placed oppofite; they were about three quarters of an inch long, and half an inch broad, fawed on their edges; the flowers came out fingle on each fide the ftalk; they were white, and much fmaller than thofe of the firft fort, but were not fucceeded by feeds, fo the plant was loft here.

GRAVEL and Grafs are naturally ornaments to a country-feat, and the glory of the Englifh gardens, and things in which we excel all other nations, as France, Holland, Flanders, &c.

There are different forts of Gravel, but for thofe who can conveniently have it, I approve of that Gravel on Blackheath, as preferable to moft that we have in England; it confifting of fmooth even pebbles, which, when mixed with a due quantity of loam, will bind exceeding clofe, and look very beautiful, and continue handfome longer than any other fort of Gravel which I have yet feen.

Some recommend a fort of iron-mould Gravel, or Gravel with a little binding loam amongft it, than which nothing, they fay, binds better when it is dry; but in wet weather it is apt to ftick to the heels of one's fhoes, and will never appear handfome.

Sometimes loam is mixed with Gravel that is over fandy or fharp, which muft be very well blended together, and let lie in heaps, after which it will bind like a rock.

There are many kinds of Gravel which do not bind, and thereby caufe a continual trouble of rolling, to little or no purpofe; as for fuch,

If the Gravel be loofe or fandy, you fhould take one load of ftrong loam, to two or three of Gravel, and fo caft them well together, and turn this mixture over three or four times, that they may be well blended together; if this is done in proper porportion, it will bind well, and not ftick to the feet in wet weather.

There are many different opinions about the choice of Gravel; fome are for having the Gravel as white as poffible, and in order to make the walks more fo, they roll them well with ftone rollers, which are often hewn by the mafons, that they may add a whitenefs to the walks; but this renders it very troublefome to the eyes, by reflecting the rays of light fo ftrongly, therefore this fhould ever be avoided; and fuch Gravel as will lie fmooth, and reflect the leaft, fhould be preferred.

Some fcreen the Gravel too fine, which is an error; for if it be caft into a round heap, and the great ftones only raked off, it will be the better.

Some are apt to lay Gravel-walks too round, but this is likewife an error, becaufe they are not fo good to walk upon, and befides, it makes them look narrow; one inch rife is enough in a crown for a walk of five feet; and it will be fufficient, if a walk be ten feet wide, that it lies two inches higher in the middle than it does on each fide; if fifteen feet, three inches; twenty feet, four; and fo in proportion.

For the depth of Gravel-walks, fix or eight inches may do well enough, but a foot thicknefs will be fufficient for any; but then there fhould always be a depth of rubbifh laid under the Gravel, efpecially if the ground is wet; in which cafe there cannot be too much care to fill the bottom of the walks with large ftones; flints, brick rubbifh, chalk, or any other materials which can be beft procured, which will drain off the moifture from the Gravel, and prevent its being poachy in wet weather; but as it may be difficult in fome places to procure a fufficient quantity of thefe materials to lay in the bottom of the walks, fo there may be a bed of Heath, or Furze, which ever can be procured at the leaft expence, laid under the Gravel to keep it dry: and if either of thefe are ufed green, they will lie a long time, as they will be covered from air, and thefe will prevent the Gravel from getting down into the clay, and will always keep the Gravel dry; and where there is not this precaution in the firft laying of the Gravel upon clay, the water being detained by the clay, will caufe the Gravel to be poachy whenever there is much rain.

In making of Gravel-walks, there muft be great regard had to the level of the ground, fo as to lay the walks with eafy defcents toward the low parts of the ground, that the wet may be drained off eafily; for when this is omitted, the water will lie upon the walks a confiderable time after hard rains, which will render them unfit for ufe, efpecially when the ground is naturally wet or ftrong; but where the ground is level, and there are no declivities to carry off the wet, it will be proper to have fink-ftones laid by the fides of the walks, at convenient diftances, to let off the wet; and where the ground is naturally dry, that the water will foon foak away, the drains of the fink-ftones may be contrived fo as to convey the water in feffpools, from which the water will foak away in a fhort time; but in wet land there fhould be under-ground drains, to convey the wet off, either into ponds, ditches, or the neareft place to receive it; for where this is not well provided for, the walks will never be fo handfome or fo ufeful.

The month of March is the propereft time for laying Gravel; it is not prudent to do it fooner, or to lay walks in any of the winter months before that time. Some indeed turn up Gravel-walks in ridges in December, in order to kill the weeds; but this is very wrong, for befides that it deprives them of the benefit of them all the winter, it does not anfwer the end for which it is done, but rather the contrary; for though it does kill the weeds for the prefent, yet it adds a fertility to them, as to the great future increafe of both them and Grafs.

If conftant rolling them after the rains and froft will not effectually kill the weeds and mofs, you fhould turn the walks in March, and lay them down at the fame time.

In order to deftroy worms that fpoil the beauty of Gravel, or Grafs-walks, fome recommended the watering them well with water, in which Walnut-tree leaves have been fteeped, and made very bitter, efpecially thofe places moft annoyed with them; and this they fay, as foon as it reaches them, will make them come out haftily, fo that they may be gathered; but if, in the firft laying of the walks, there is a good bed of lime rubbifh laid in the bottom, it is the moft effectual method to keep out the worms, for they do not care to harbour near lime.

GREEN-HOUSE, or Confervatory.

As of late years there have been great quantities of curious exotic plants introduced into the Englifh gardens, fo the number of Green-houfes, or Confervatories, have increafed; and not only a greater fkill in the management and ordering of thefe plants has increafed therewith, but alfo a greater knowledge of the ftructure and contrivance of thefe places, fo as to render them both ufeful and ornamental, hath been acquired; and fince there are many particulars to be obferved in the conftruction of thefe houfes, whereby they will be greatly improved, I thought it neceffary not only to give the beft inftructions for this I was capable of, but alfo to give a defign of one in the manner I would chufe to erect it, upon the annexed copper-plate.

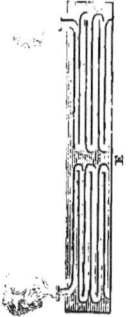

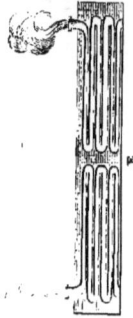

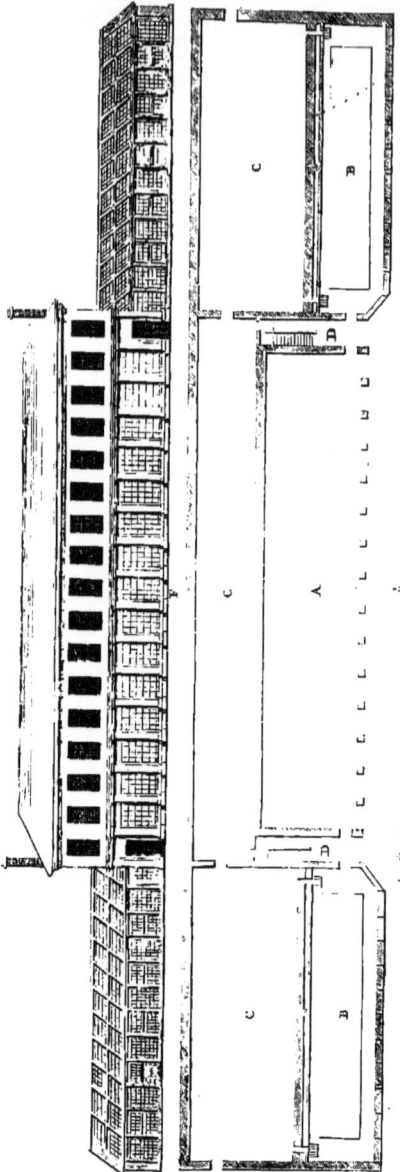

Plan of the Green-house.

A. the Ground-Plan of the Green-house.

B.B. The Ground-Plans of the two Stoves.

C.C.C. The Sheds behind the Green-house and Stoves.

D.D. The passage of communication between the Green-house and Stoves, where the Stairs are placed which lead to the Rooms over the Green-house.

E.E. The Section of the Flues in the back of the Stoves.

F. The upright of the Green-house and Stoves.

J. Hogmer Sculp.

As to the length of these houses, that muſt be proportioned to the number of plants they are to contain, or the fancy of the owner; but their depth ſhould never be greater than their height in the clear, which in ſmall, or middling houſes, may be ſixteen or eighteen feet, but for large ones, from twenty to twenty-four feet, is a good proportion; for if the Green-houſe is long, and too narrow, it will have a bad appearance both within and without, nor will it contain ſo many plants, if proper room be allowed for paſſing in front, and on the backſide of the ſtands on which the plants are placed; and on the other hand, if the depth of the Green-houſe is more than twenty-four feet, there muſt be more rows of plants placed to fill the houſe, than can with conveniency be reached in watering and cleaning; nor are houſes of too great depth ſo proper for keeping of plants, as thoſe of moderate ſize.

The windows in front ſhould extend from about one foot and a half above the pavement, to within the ſame diſtance of the cieling, which will admit of a cornice round the building, over the heads of the windows. As it is neceſſary to have theſe windows ſo long, it will be impoſſible to make them in proportion as to their breadth; for if in the largeſt buildings the ſaſhes are more than ſeven, or ſeven feet and a half broad, they will be ſo heavy and troubleſome to move up and down, as to render it very difficult for one perſon to perform; beſides, their weight will occaſion their ſoon decaying. There is alſo another inconvenience in having the windows too broad, which is that of fixing proper ſhutters to them, in ſuch a manner as that they may fall back cloſe to the piers, ſo as not to be incommodious, or when open to obſtruct any part of the rays of light from reaching the plants. The piers between theſe windows ſhould be as narrow as poſſible to ſupport the building, for which reaſon I ſhould chuſe to have them of ſtone, or of hard well-burnt bricks; for if they are built with fine rubbed bricks, thoſe are generally ſo ſoft, that the piers will require to be made thicker, and the building will be leſs ſtrong, eſpecially if there are any rooms over the Green-houſe; which is what I would always adviſe, as being of great uſe to keep the froſt out in very hard winters. If theſe piers are made of ſtone, I would adviſe them to be two feet and a half in diameter, worked as columns cylindrical, whereby the rays of the ſun will not be taken off, or obſtructed by the corners of the piers, which it would be if they were ſquare; but if they are built with bricks, it will be proper to make them three feet in front, otherwiſe they will be too weak to ſupport the building; theſe I would alſo adviſe to be ſloped off toward the inſide to admit the ſun.

At the back of the Green-houſe there may be erected a houſe for tools, and for many other purpoſes, which will be extremely uſeful, and will alſo prevent the froſt from entering the houſe on the backſide, ſo that the wall between theſe need not be more than two bricks and a half in thickneſs; whereas were it quite expoſed behind, it ſhould be at leaſt three bricks, or three and a half in thickneſs; and by this contrivance, if you are willing to make a handſome building, and to have a noble room over the Green-houſe, you may make the room over the tool-houſe, and carry up the ſtaircaſe in the back, ſo as not to be ſeen in the Green-houſe, and hereby you may have a room twenty-five or thirty feet in width, and of a proportionable length; and under this ſtair-caſe there ſhould be a private door into the green-houſe, at which the gardener may enter in hard froſty weather, when it will not be ſafe to open any of the glaſſes in the front. The floor of the Green-houſe, which ſhould be laid either with Bremen ſquares, Purbeck ſtone, or broad tiles, according to the fancy of the owner, muſt be raiſed two feet above the ſurface of the ground whereon the houſe is placed, which in dry ground will be ſufficient; but if the ſituation is moiſt and ſpringy, and thereby ſubject to damps, it ſhould be raiſed at leaſt three feet above the ſurface; and if the whole is arched with low brick

arches under the floor, it will be of great ſervice in preventing the damps riſing in winter, which are often very hurtful to the plants, eſpecially in great thaws, when the air is often too cold to be admitted into the houſe, to take off the damps. Under the floor, about one foot from the front, I would adviſe a flue of one foot in width, and two feet deep, to be carried the whole length of the houſe, which may be returned againſt the back wall, and carried up in proper funnels adjoining to the tool-houſe, three times over each other, by which the ſmoke may paſs off. The fire-place may be contrived at one end of the houſe, and the door at which the fuel is put in, as alſo the aſhgrate, may be contrived to open into the tool-houſe, ſo that it may be quite hid from the ſight, and be in the dry, and the fuel may be laid in the ſame ſhed, whereby it will always be ready for uſe.

I ſuppoſe many people will be ſurpriſed to ſee me direct the making of flues under a Green-houſe, which has been diſuſed ſo long, and by moſt people thought of ill conſequence, as indeed they have often proved, when under the direction of unſkilful managers, who have thought it neceſſary, whenever the weather was cold to make fires therein; but however injurious flues may have been under ſuch management, yet when ſkilfully looked after they will be found of very great ſervice; for though perhaps it may happen, that there will be no neceſſity to make any fires in them for two or three years together, as when the winters prove mild there will not, yet in very hard winters they will be extremely uſeful to keep out the froſt, which cannot be effected any other way, but with great trouble and difficulty.

Withinſide of the windows, in front of the Green-houſe, you ſhould have good ſtrong ſhutters, which ſhould be made with hinges to fold back, that they may fall back quite cloſe to the piers, that the rays of the ſun may not be obſtructed thereby. Theſe ſhutters need not be above an inch and a half thick, or little more when wrought, which if made to join cloſe, will be ſufficient to keep out our common froſt; and when the weather is ſo cold as to endanger the freezing in the houſe, it is but making a fire in the oven, which will effectually prevent it; and without this conveniency it will be very troubleſome, as I have often ſeen, where perſons have been obliged to nail mats before their windows, or to ſtuff the hollow ſpace between the ſhutters, and the glaſs with Straw, which when done, is commonly ſuffered to remain till the froſt goes away; which if it ſhould continue very long, the keeping the Green-houſe cloſely ſhut up, will prove very injurious to the plants; and as it frequently happens, that we have an hour or two of the ſun-ſhine in the middle of the day, in continued froſts, which is of great ſervice to plants, when they can enjoy the rays thereof through the glaſſes, ſo when there is nothing more to do than to open the ſhutters, which may be performed in a very ſhort time, and as ſoon ſhut again when the ſun is clouded, the plants may have the benefit thereof whenever it appears; whereas, where there is ſo much trouble to uncover, and as much to cover again, it would take up the whole time in uncovering and ſhutting them up, and thereby the advantage of the ſun's influence would be loſt. Beſides, where there is ſo much trouble required to keep out the froſt, it will be a great chance if it be not neglected by the gardener; for if he be not as fond of preſerving his plants, and as much in love with them as his maſter, this labour will be thought too great by him; and if he takes the pains to cover the glaſſes up with mats, &c. he will not care to take them away again until the weather alters, ſo that the plants will be ſhut up cloſe during the whole continuance of the froſt.

There are ſome people who commonly make uſe of pots filled with charcoal to ſet in their Green-houſe in very ſevere froſts, but this is very dangerous to the perſons who attend theſe fires, and I have ſometimes known they have been almoſt ſuffocated therewith, and at the ſame time they are very injurious to the

　　　　　　　　plants;

plants; nor is the trouble of tending upon thefe fmall, and the many hazards to which the ufe of thefe fires is liable, have juftly brought them into difufe with all fkilful perfons; and as the contrivances of flues, and of the fires, are but fmall charges in their firft erecting, they are much to be preferred to any other method for warming the air of the houfe.

The wall on the back part of the houfe fhould be either laid over with ftucco, or plaftered with mortar, and white-wafhed, for otherwife the air in fevere froft will penetrate through the walls, efpecially when the froft is attended with a ftrong wind, which is often the cafe in moft fevere winters. There are fome perfons who are at the 'expence of wainfcotting their Green-houfes, but when this is done, it is proper to plafter the walls with lime and hair behind the wainfcot, to keep out the cold; and when they are lined with wainfcot, they fhould be painted white, as fhould the cieling, and every part withinfide of the houfe; for this reflects the rays of light in a much greater quantity than any other colour, and is of fignal fervice to plants, efpecially in the winter, when the houfe is pretty much clofed, and but a fmall fhare of light is admitted through the windows; for at fuch times I have obferved, that in fome Green-houfes which have been painted black, or of a dark colour, the plants have caft moft of their leaves.

Where green-houfes are built in fuch places as will not admit of rooms over them, or the perfon is unwilling to be at the expence of fuch buildings, there muft be care taken to keep out the froft from entering through the roof. To prevent which it will be very proper to have a thicknefs of Reeds, Heath, or Furz, laid between the cieling and the tiles; in the doing of which there muft be care taken in framing the joifts, fo as to fupport thefe, that their weight may not lie upon the ceiling, which might endanger it; for thefe fhould be laid a foot thick at leaft, and as fmooth as poffible, and faftened down well with laths to prevent their rifing, and then covered over with a coat of lime and hair, which will keep out the air, and alfo prevent mice and other vermin from harbouring in them, which, if left uncovered, they would certainly do. For want of this precaution there are many Green-houfes built, which will not keep out the froft in hard winters, and this is many times attributed to the glaffes in front admitting the cold, when the fault is in the roof; for where there is only the covering, either of tiles or flates, over the cieling, every fevere froft will penetrate through them.

In this Green-houfe you fhould have truffels, which may be moved in and into the houfe, upon which you fhould fix rows of planks, fo as to place the pots or tubs of plants in regular rows one above another, whereby the heads of the plants may be fo fituated, as not to interfere with each other. The loweft row of plants, which fhould be the forwardeft towards the windows, fhould be placed about four feet therefrom, that there may be a convenient breadth left next the glaffes to walk in front; and the rows of plants fhould rife gradually from the firft, in fuch a manner that the heads of the fecond row fhould be entirely advanced above the firft, the ftems only being hid thereby; and at the back fide of the houfe there fhould be allowed a fpace of at leaft five feet, for the conveniency of watering the plants, as alfo to admit of a current of air round them, that the damps occafioned by the perfpiration of the plants, may be the better diffipated, which, by being pent in too clofely, often occafions a mouldinefs upon the tender fhoots and leaves, and when the houfe is clofe fhut up, this ftagnating rancid vapour is often very deftructive to the plants; for which reafon alfo you fhould never croud them too clofe to each other, nor fhould you ever place Sedums, Euphorbiums, Torch Thiftles, and other tender fucculent plants, amongft Oranges, Myrtles, and other Evergreen trees; for, by an experiment which I made, anno 1729, I found that a Sedum placed in a Greenhoufe among fuch trees, almoft daily increafed its weight, although there was no water given to it the

whole time; which increafe of weight was owing to the moifture imbibed from the air, which, being replete with the rancid vapours perfpired from the other plants, occafioned the leaves to grow pale, and in a fhort time they decayed and dropped off; which I have often obferved has been the cafe with many other fucculent plants, when placed in thofe houfes which were filled with many forts of Evergreen trees, that required to be frequently watered.

Therefore, to avoid the inconvenience which attends the placing of plants of very different natures in the fame houfe, it will be very proper to have two wings added to the main Green-houfe, which, if placed in the manner expreffed in the annexed plan, will greatly add to the beauty of the building, and alfo collect a greater fhare of heat. In this plan the Green-houfe is placed exactly fronting the fouth, and one of the wings faces the fouth-eaft, and the other the fouth-weft; fo that from the time of the fun's firft appearance upon any part of the building, until it goes off at night, it is conftantly reflected from one part to the other, and the cold winds are alfo kept off from the front of the main Green-houfe hereby; and in the area of this place you may contrive to place many of the moft tender exotic plants, which will bear to be expofed in the fummer feafon; and in the fpring, before the weather will permit you to fet out the plants, the beds and borders of this area may be full of Anemonies, Ranunculufes, early Tulips, &c. which will be paft flowering, and the roots fit to take out of the ground by the time you carry out the plants, which will render this place very agreeable during the fpring feafon, when the flowers are blown: and here you may walk and divert yourfelf in a fine day, when perhaps the air in moft other parts of the garden will be too cold for perfons not much ufed thereto, to take pleafure in being out of the houfe.

In the center of this area may be contrived a fmall bafon for water, which will be very convenient for watering of plants, and add much to the beauty of the place; befides the water being thus fituated, will be foftened by the heat which will be reflected from the glaffes upon it, whereby it will be rendered much better than raw cold water for thefe tender plants.

The two wings of the building fhould be contrived fo as to maintain plants of differing degrees of hardinefs, which muft be effected by the fituation and extent of the fire-place, and the manner of conducting the flues, a particular account of which will be exhibited under the article of Stoves. But I would here obferve, that the wing facing the fouth-eaft fhould always be preferred for the warmeft ftove, its fituation being fuch, as that the fun, upon its firft appearance in the morning, fhines directly upon the glaffes, which is of great fervice in warming the air of the houfe, and adding life to the plants, after having been fhut up during the long nights in the winter feafon. Thefe wings being in the draught annexed, allowed fixty feet in length, may be divided in the middle by partitions of glafs, with glafs-doors to pafs from one to the other. To each of thefe there fhould be a fire-place, with flues carried up againft the back wall, through which the fmoke fhould be made to pafs, as many times the length of the houfe, as the height will admit of the number of flues; for the longer the fmoke is in paffing, the more heat will be given to the houfe, with a lefs quantity of fuel, which is an article worth confideration, efpecially where fuel is dear. By this contrivance you may keep fuch plants as require the fame degree of heat in one part of the houfe, and thofe which will thrive in a much lefs warmth in the other part, but this will be more fully explained under the article of Stoves.

The other wing of the houfe, facing the fouth-weft, may alfo be divided in the fame manner, and flues carried through both parts, which may be ufed according to the feafons, or the particular forts of plants which are placed therein; fo that here will be four divifions in the wings, each of which may be kept up

to

to a different degree of warmth, which, together with the Green-houfe, will be fufficient to maintain plants from all the feveral countries of the world ; and without having thefe feveral degrees of warmth, it will be impoffible to preferve the various kinds of plants from the feveral parts of Africa and America, which are annually introduced into the Englifh gardens ; for when plants from different countries are placed in the fame houfe, fome are deftroyed for want of heat, while others are forced and fpoiled by too much of it ; and this is often the cafe in many places, where there are large collections of plants.

In the building thefe wings, if there are not fheds running behind them their whole length, the walls fhould not be lefs than three bricks thick ; and if they are more, it will be better, becaufe where the walls are thin, and expofed to the open air, the cold will penetrate them, and when the fires are made, the heat will come out through the walls, fo that it will require a larger quantity of fuel, to maintain a proper temperature of warmth in the houfe. The back part of thefe houfes having floping roofs, which are covered either with tiles or flates, fhould alfo be lined with Reeds, &c. under the covering, as is before directed for the Green-houfe, which will keep out the cold air, and fave a great expence of fuel ; for the clofer and better thefe houfes are built, and the glaffes of the flope, as alfo in front, well guarded by fhutters, or Reeds in hard froft, the lefs fuel will be required to warm the houfes ; fo that the firft expence in building thefe houfes properly, will be the cheapeft, when the after-expence of fires is taken into confideration.

The floping glaffes of thefe houfes fhould be made to flide and take off, fo that they may be drawn down more or lefs in warm weather, to admit air to the plants ; and the upright glaffes in front may be fo contrived, as that every other may open as doors upon hinges, and the alternate glaffes may be divided into two ; the upper part of each fhould be contrived fo as to be drawn down like fafhes, fo that either of thefe may be ufed to admit air, in a greater or lefs proportion, according as there may be occafion.

But befides the Confervatories here mentioned, it will be proper to have a deep hot-bed frame, fuch as is commonly ufed to raife large annuals in the fpring, into which may be fet pots of fuch plants as come from Carolina, Virginia, &c. while the plants are too fmall to plant in the open air, as alfo many other forts from Spain, &c. which require only to be fcreened from the violence of frofts, and fhould have as much free air as poffible in mild weather ; which can be no better effected than in one of thefe frames, where the glaffes may be taken off every day when the weather will permit, and put on every night ; and in hard frofts the glaffes may be covered with mats, Straw, Peas-haulm, or the like, fo as to prevent the froft from entering to the pots to freeze the roots of the plants, which is what will many times utterly deftroy them, though a flight froft pinching the leaves or fhoots, very feldom does them much harm ; if thefe pits are funk a foot or more, below the furface of the ground, they will be the better, provided the ground is dry, otherwife they muft be wholly above ground ; the fides of this frame fhould be built with brick, with a curb of wood laid round on the top of the wall, into which the gutters, on which the glaffes flide may be laid ; the back wall of this frame may be four feet high, and two bricks and a half thick, the front one foot and a half ; the width of the infide of the frame about fix feet, and the length in proportion to the number of plants to be contained therein.

G R E W I A. Lin. Gen. Plant. 914. This genus of plants was conftituted by Dr. Linnæus, who gave it this name in honour of Dr. Grew, F. R. S. who publifhed a curious book of the anatomy of plants.

The CHARACTERS are,

The flower hath a thick leathery empalement, compofed of five fpear-fhaped leaves, which are coloured, and fpread open. The flower hath five petals of the fame form, but fmaller, and are indented at their bafe, where is fituated

a fcaly nectarium to each petal, which is thick and incurved, inclining to the border, to which the ftyle is fixed ; it hath many ftamina, which are briftly, the length of the petals, terminated by roundifh fummits. In the center is fituated the roundifh germen, which is lengthened to a column, fupporting a flender ftyle, crowned by a four-cornered obtufe ftigma. The germen afterward becomes a four-cornered berry with four cells, each inclofing one globular feed.

This genus of plants is ranged in the feventh fection of Linnæus's twentieth clafs, which includes thofe plants whofe flowers have many ftamina joined to the ftyle, forming a column of one body.

The SPECIES are,

1. GREWIA (*Occidentalis*) foliis fubovatis crenatis. *Grewia with oval crenated leaves.* Ulmi facie arbufcula Æthiopica, ramulis alatis, floribus purpurafcentibus. Hort. Amft. 1. p. 165. tab. 85. *Ethiopian Shrub with the appearance of Elm, winged branches, and purplifh flowers.*

2. GREWIA (*Africanus*) foliis ovato-lanceolatis ferratis. *Grewia with oval fpear-fhaped leaves which are fawed.*

The firft fort has been long preferved in many curious gardens, both in England and Holland, and is figured by Dr. Plukenet, by the title of Ulmifolia arbor Africana baccifera, floribus purpureis ; but by Dr. Boerhaave it was fuppofed to be one of Father Plumier's American plants, intitled Guidonia Ulmi foliis, flore rofeo ; but the characters of this do not at all agree with thofe of the Guidonia, that particular fpecies of this genus being in the royal garden at Paris, which is extremely different from this. It grows naturally at the Cape of Good Hope, from whence I have received the feeds, which have fucceeded in the Chelfea garden.

This will grow to the height of ten or twelve feet, and has a ftem and branches very like thofe of the fmall-leaved Elm, the bark being fmooth, and of the fame colour as that of Elm when young ; the leaves are alfo very like thofe of the Elm, and fall off in winter ; the flowers are produced fingly along the young branches from the wings of the leaves, which are of a bright purple colour ; thefe appear toward the end of July, and continue in Auguft, and the beginning of September, but are never fucceeded by fruit in this country.

This may be propagated from cuttings or layers ; the cuttings fhould be taken off, and planted in April, before the buds fwell, for they do not fucceed well after ; thefe cuttings fhould be planted in fmall pots filled with loamy earth, and the pots fhould be plunged into a moderate hot-bed of tanners bark, where, if they are duly watered, and in the heat of the day fhaded from the fun, they will take good root in about two months, and may then be gradually inured to bear the open air, into which they fhould be removed in June, and placed in a fheltered fituation, where they may remain till autumn, when they muft be removed into the green-houfe ; the beft time to lay down the layers of this plant is in the fpring, before the buds come out, and thefe will be rooted by the fame time the following year, when they may be cut off from the old plants, and planted each into a feparate pot filled with a foft loamy foil.

The beft time to remove or tranfplant this plant is, either in the fpring, juft before the buds begin to fwell, or in autumn, when the leaves begin to drop ; for in fummer, when the plants are in full leaf, it will be very improper to difturb them.

In winter thefe plants fhould be placed in the green-houfe, for they are too tehder to live abroad in England ; but they fhould have as much free air as poffible in mild weather, for they only require to be protected from froft, and after their leaves are fallen, they will require very moderate watering ; but in fummer they fhould be conftantly watered three or four times a week in dry weather, and placed in a fheltered fituation, with other hardy green-houfe plants, where they will add to the variety.

The feeds of the fecond fort were fent me by Monf. Richard, gardener to the King of France at Marfeilles,

feilles, which were brought from Senegal in Africa, by Monf. Adanfon; this rifes in this country with a fhrubby ftalk five or fix feet high, fending out many lateral branches, which are covered with a brown hairy bark, and garnifhed with oval fpear-fhaped leaves, about two inches long, and one inch and a quarter broad in the middle, having feveral tranfverfe veins from the midrib to the fides, where they are fawed; thefe are placed alternately on the branches, having very fhort foot-ftalks, and continue in verdure through the year; the plants are young, fo have not as yet flowered in England, therefore I can give no further account of them.

This fort is tender, fo will not live through the winter in England, unlefs it is placed in a warm ftove; nor do thofe plants thrive well, which are placed on fhelves in the dry ftove; therefore the only method to have them fucceed, is to place them in the bark-bed in the tan-ftove, where the plants have grown very well for fome years. In fummer thefe plants require a good fhare of free air to be admitted to them, and fhould have water three or four times a week in warm weather; but in winter they muft be fparingly watered, and require to be kept warm.

GRIAS. Lin. Gen. 659. Anchovy Pear.

The CHARACTERS are,

The empalement is cup-fhaped, of one leaf, cut into four equal fegments; the flower has four leathery concave petals, and many brifly ftamina which are inferted to the receptacle, terminated by roundifh fummits, and a depreffed germen immerfed in the empalement, having no ftyle, crowned by a four-cornered crofs-fhaped ftigma, which afterward becomes a flefhy berry, with a large nut having eight furrows, and one cell containing a large pointed feed.

This genus of plants is ranged in the firft order of Linnæus's thirteenth clafs, intitled Polyandria Monogynia, the flower having many ftamina and one ftyle.

We know but one SPECIES of this genus, viz.

1. GRIAS (*Cauliflora*). Lin. Sp. 732. *Anchovy Pear.* Palmis affinis malus Perfica maxima, caudice non ramofa, foliis longiffimis, flore tetrapetalo pallide luteo, fructu ex arboris trunco prodeunte. Sloan. Hift. Jam. 2. p. 122.

This plant grows naturally in Jamaica, and in many other warm parts of America, where it rifes with a ftrait undivided ftem about twenty feet high, having a gray bark, marked with the veftigia of the fallen leaves; the top of the ftem is garnifhed with leaves near two feet long and fix inches broad, fitting clofe without foot-ftalks; thefe have one longitudinal midrib with feveral tranfverfe veins, and are of a lucid green; the flowers come out from the ftem below the leaves, having no foot-ftalk, in fome places one, and in others they are in clufters, each having four thick yellow petals, and a great number of ftamina which are fixed to the empalement of the flower; the germen is included in the empalement, which afterward becomes a large oval Plumb, including a large pointed nut.

The fruit of this tree is by the Spaniards in the Weft-Indies pickled and fent to old Spain as prefents, who eat them as Mango's, and fome fay the ripe fruit is eaten as a defart.

The plant is propagated by planting of the ftones, which fhould be put into the ground foon after the fruit is gathered, and the plants muft be conftantly kept in the bark-bed in the ftove, otherwife it will not thrive in this country.

GRONOVIA. Martyn. Cent. 4. Lin. Gen. Plant. 284. The name of this genus was given by the late Dr. Houfton, in honour of Dr. Gronovius, a learned botanift at Leyden.

The CHARACTERS are,

The flower hath a permanent empalement of one leaf, which is coloured, and cut to the middle into five fegments. It hath five fmall petals which are fixed to the cuts of the empalement, and five hairy ftamina the length of the petals, which are inferted into the empalement, and are placed alternate with the petals, terminated by twin fummits which are erect. The germen is fituated under the flower, fup-

porting a flender ftyle which is longer than the ftamina, crowned by an obtufe ftigma. The germen afterward becomes a roundifh-coloured fruit with one cell, inclofing one large roundifh feed.

This genus of plants is ranged in the firft fection of Linnæus's fifth clafs, intitled Pentandria Monogynia, which includes thofe plants whofe flowers have five ftamina and one ftyle.

We know but one SPECIES of this genus, viz.

GRONOVIA (*Scandens*). Hort. Cliff. 74. Gronovia fcandens lappacea, pampinea fronde. Houft. *Climbing burry Gronovia.*

This plant was difcovered by the late Dr. Houftoun at La Vera Cruz, from whence he fent the feeds to Europe, which have fucceeded in many gardens. It is an annual plant, which fends forth many trailing branches like thofe of the Cucumber, which are clofely fet with broad green leaves, in fhape like thofe of the Vine; but they are covered with fmall fpines on both fides, which fting like the Nettle: the branches have many tendrils or clafpers, by which they faften themfelves to whatever plants they grow near, and will rife to the height of fix or eight feet; the flowers are fmall, and of a greenifh yellow colour, fo make no great appearance.

This being a very tender plant, muft be raifed on a hot-bed early in the fpring, and afterward placed in the bark-ftove, and treated in the fame way as the Momordica, with which management it will produce ripe feeds; but this having neither ufe or beauty, is rarely cultivated but in botanic gardens for the fake of variety.

GROSSULARIA. Raii Meth. Plant. 145. Tourn. Inft. R. H. 639. tab. 409. Ribes. Lin. Gen. Plant. 247. Goofeberry; in French, *Grofelier.*

This and the Currant are by Tournefort placed in the fame genus, under the title of Groffularia; they are alfo joined together by Dr. Linnæus, under the title of Ribes, for in their principal characters they agree; fo according to the fyftems of botany, they fhould be included in the fame genus; but this may not be quite fo proper in a body of gardening, for as thefe fruits have always paffed under different denominations, fo if they are here joined together, it may occafion fome confufion among thofe who do not enter into the ftudy of botany. Mr. Ray has feparated thefe into different genera, and makes the difference of Goofeberry from the Currant, to confift in the firft having thorns on the branches, and the fruit growing fingle; whereas the latter hath fmooth branches, and the fruit growing in long bunches; and although thefe differences may not be ftrictly fcientific, yet it may be allowed fufficient to diftinguifh them among gardeners.

The CHARACTERS are,

The flower has a permanent empalement of one leaf, cut into five fegments at the top, which is fwollen, concave, and coloured. It hath five fmall, obtufe, erect petals, which rife from the border of the empalement; and five awl-fhaped ftamina, which are inferted into the empalement, terminated by compreffed proftrate fummits. The germen is fituated below the flower, having a bifid ftyle crowned by an obtufe ftigma, and afterward becomes a globular berry having a navel, with one cell, which is filled with roundifh compreffed feeds included in a pulp.

This genus of plants is ranged by Dr. Linnæus in the firft fection of his fifth clafs, intitled Pentandria Monogynia, which contains thofe plants whofe flowers have five ftamina and one ftyle.

The SPECIES are,

1. GROSSULARIA (*Reclinatum*) ramis reclinatis aculeatis, pedunculis triphyllis. *Goofeberry with reclining branches armed with fpines, and a three-leaved foot-ftalk.* Groffularia fpinofa, fructu obfcure purpurafcente. J. B. 1. 48. *Prickly Goofeberry with a dark purplifh fruit.*

2. GROSSULARIA (*Hirfuta*) ramis aculeatis, baccis hirfutis. *Goofeberry with prickly branches and hairy berries.* Groffularia fructu maximo hifpido margaritarum ferè colore. Raii Hift. 1484. *Goofeberry with a very large rough fruit, almoft of a pearl colour.*

3. GROSSULARIA (*Uva Crispa*) ramis aculeatis, erectis, baccis glabris. *Goofeberry with erect prickly branches, and fmooth berries.* Groffularia fimplici acino, vel fpinofa fylveftris. C. B. P. 455. *Goofeberry with a fingle fruit, or wild prickly Goofeberry.*

4. GROSSULARIA (*Oxyacanthoides*) ramis undique aculeatis. *Goofeberry whofe branches are armed on all fides with fpines.* Groffularia oxyacanthæ foliis amplioribus è finu Hudfonis. Pluk. Amalth. 212. *Goofeberry with larger Hawthorn leaves from Hudfon's Bay.*

5. GROSSULARIA (*Cynofbati*) aculeis fubaxillaribus, baccis aculeatis racemofis. *Goofeberry with fpines on the lower part of the branches, and prickly berries growing in clufters.* Ribes aculeis fubaxillaribus, baccis aculeatis racemofis. Lin. Sp. Plant. 202. *Currant with fpines on the lower part of the branches, and prickly berries growing in bunches.*

The forts which are here enumerated, are fuppofed to be diftinct fpecies; but there are feveral other varieties which have been obtained from feeds, and are propagated for fale in the nurferies; moft of thefe are titled from the perfons who raifed them, as Lamb's Goofeberry, Hunt's Goofeberry, Edwards's Goofeberry, &c. and as there are frequently new varieties obtained, it is needlefs to enumerate them here, therefore I fhall proceed to their culture.

Thefe are propagated either by fuckers taken from the old plants, or by cuttings; the latter of which I prefer to the former, becaufe thofe plants which are produced from fuckers are always more difpofed to fhoot out a greater number of fuckers from their roots, than fuch as are raifed from cuttings, which generally form much better roots.

The beft feafon for planting thefe cuttings is in autumn, juft before their leaves begin to fall; obferving always to take the handfomeft fhoots, and from fuch branches as generally produce the greateft quantity of fruit; for if you take thofe which are produced from the ftem of the old plants (which are commonly very luxuriant) they will not be near fo fruitful as thofe taken from bearing branches: thefe cuttings fhould be about fix or eight inches long, and muft be planted in a border of light earth, expofed to the morning fun, about three inches deep, obferving to water them gently when the weather proves dry, to facilitate their taking root; and in the fummer, when they have put out branches, you fhould rub off all the under fhoots, leaving only the uppermoft or ftrongeft, which fhould be trained upright, to form a regular ftem. In October following thefe plants may be removed; at which time you fhould prepare an open fpot of frefh earth, which fhould be well dug, and cleanfed from all noxious weeds, roots, &c. and being levelled, you fhould proceed to take up your plants, trimming their roots, and cutting off all lateral fide branches; then plant them at three feet diftance row from row, and one foot afunder in the rows, obferving to place fome fhort fticks to the plants, in order to train their ftems upright and regular. In this place they may remain one or two years, being careful to keep them clear from weeds, as alfo to trim off all lateral fhoots which are produced below the head of the plant, fo that the ftem may be clear about a foot in height above the furface of the earth, which will be full enough; and as the branches are produced commonly very irregular in the head, you muft cut out fuch of them as crofs each other, or thin them where they are too clofe, whereby the head of the plant will be open, and capable of admitting the air freely into the middle, which is of great ufe to all kinds of fruits.

After thefe plants have remained in this nurfery one or two years at moft, they will be fit to tranfplant to the places where they are defigned to remain; for it is not fo well to let them grow in the nurferies too large which will occafion their roots to be woody, whereby the removing of them will not only hazard the growth of the plants, but fuch of them as may take very well will remain ftinted for two or three years, before they will be able to recover their check. The foil in which thefe plants thrive to the greateft advantage, is a rich light earth; though they will do very well upon middling foils, which are not too ftrong or moift, and in all fituations; but where the fruit is cultivated, in order to procure it in the greateft perfection, they fhould never be planted in the fhade of other trees, but muft have a free open expofure. The diftance they ought to be planted is eight feet row from row, and fix feet afunder in the rows. The beft feafon for tranfplanting them is in October, when their leaves begin to decay; obferving, as was before directed, to prune their roots, and trim off all lateral fhoots, or fuch as crofs each other, fhortening all long branches, fo as to make the head regular.

In the pruning of thefe fhrubs moft people make ufe of garden-fhears, obferving only to cut the head round, as is practifed for Evergreens, &c. whereby the branches become fo much crowded, that what fruit is produced, never grows to half the fize as it would do were the branches thinned, and pruned according to art; which fhould always be done with a pruning-knife, fhortening the ftrong fhoots to about ten inches, and cutting out all thofe which grow irregular, thinning the fruit-bearing branches where they are too thick, obferving always to cut behind a leaf bud. With this management your fruit will be near twice as large as thofe which are produced upon fuch bufhes as are not thus pruned, and the fhrubs will continue in vigour much longer; but you muft obferve to keep the ground clear from weeds, and dig it at leaft once a year; and every other year you fhould beftow a little rotten dung upon it, which will greatly improve the fruit.

It is a common practice with the gardeners near London, who have great quantities of thefe bufhes in order to fupply the markets, to prune them foon after Michaelmas, and then to dig up the ground between the rows, and plant it with Coleworts for fpring ufe, whereby their ground is employed all the winter, without prejudicing the Goofeberries; and in hard winters thefe Coleworts often efcape, when thofe which are planted in an open expofure are all deftroyed; and thefe are generally pulled up for ufe in February or March, fo that the ground is clear before the Goofeberries come out in the fpring; which is a piece of hufbandry well worth practifing where ground is dear, or where perfons are confined for room.

GROVES are the greateft ornaments to a garden, nor can a garden be complete which has not one or more of thefe. In fmall gardens there is fcarce room to admit of Groves of any extent, yet in thefe there fhould be at leaft one contrived, which fhould be as large as the ground will allow it; and where thefe are fmall, there is more fkill required in the difpofition, to give them the appearance of being larger than they really are.

Groves have been in all ages held in great veneration: the ancient Romans had a fort of Groves near feveral of their temples, which were confecrated to fome God, and were called luci by antiphrafis, à non lucendo, as being fhady and dark; and thefe were dedicated to holy ufes, being places of folitude and retirement, and were never to be violated with the ax.

Thefe Groves are not only great ornaments to gardens, but are alfo the greateft relief againft the violent heats of the fun, affording fhade to walk under in the hotteft part of the day, when the other parts of the garden are ufelefs; fo that every garden is defective which has not fhade.

Groves are of two forts, viz. open and clofe Groves: open Groves are fuch as have large fhady trees, which ftand at fuch diftances, as that their branches may approach fo near each other, as to prevent the rays of the fun from penetrating through them; but as fuch trees are a long time in growing to a proper fize for affording a fhade, fo where new Groves are planted, the trees muft be placed clofer together, in order to have fhade as foon as poffible; but in planting of thefe Groves, it is much the beft way to difpofe all the trees irregularly, which will give them a greater magnificence, and alfo form a fhade fooner, than when the trees

trees are planted in lines; for when the fun fhines between the rows of trees, as it muft do fome part of the day in fummer, the walks between them will be expofed to the heat at fuch times, until the branches of thefe trees meet; whereas in the irregular plantations, the trees intervene, and obftruct the direct rays of the fun.

When a perfon who is to lay out a garden, is fo happy as to meet with large full grown trees upon the fpot, they fhould remain inviolate, if poffible; for it will be better to put up with many inconveniencies, than to deftroy thefe, which will require an age to retrieve; fo that nothing but that of offending the habiation, by being fo near as to occafion great damps or obftructing fine views, fhould tempt the cutting of them down.

Moft of the Groves which have been planted either in England, or in thofe celebrated gardens of France, are only a few regular lines of trees; many of which are avenues to the habitation, or lead to fome building, or object; but thefe do not appear fo grand, as thofe which have been made in woods where the trees have grown accidentally, and at irregular diftances; and where the trees have large fpreading heads, and are left at fuch a diftance, as to permit the Grafs to grow under them, then they afford the greateft pleafure: for nothing is more noble than fine fpreading trees with large ftems, growing through Grafs, efpecially if the Grafs is well kept, and has a good verdure; befides, moft of thefe planted Groves have generally a gravel-walk, made in a ftrait line between them, which greatly offends the fight of perfons who have true tafte; therefore whenever a gravelwalk is abfolutely neceffary to be carried through thefe Groves, it will be much better to twift it about, according as the trees naturally ftand, than to attempt regularity; but dry walks under large trees are not fo ufeful as in open places, becaufe the dropping of the trees will render thefe walks ufelefs after rain, for a confiderable time.

Clofe Groves have frequently large trees ftanding in them, but the ground is filled under thefe with fhrubs, or under-wood; fo that the walks which are made in them are private, and fcreened from winds, whereby they are rendered agreeable for walking, at fuch times when the air is too violent or cold for walking in the more expofed parts of the garden.

Thefe are often contrived fo as to bound the open Groves, and frequently to hide the walls, or other inclofures of the garden; and when they are properly laid out, with dry walks winding through them, and on the fides of thefe fweet-fmelling fhrubs and flowers irregularly planted, they have a charming effect; for here a perfon may walk in private, fheltered from the inclemency of cold or violent winds, and enjoy the greater fweets of the vegetable kingdom: therefore where it can be admitted, if they are continued round the whole inclofure of the garden, there will be a much greater extent of walk; and thefe fhrubs will appear the beft boundary, when there are not fine profpects to be gained.

Thefe clofe Groves are by the French termed bofquets, from the Italian word bofquetto, which fignifies a little wood, and in moft of the French gardens there are many of them planted; but thefe are reduced to regular figures, as ovals, triangles, fquares, and ftars; which have neither the beauty or ufe which thofe have that are made irregularly, and whofe walks are not fhut up on each fide by hedges, which prevents the eye from feeing the quarters; and thefe want the fragancy of the fhrubs and flowers, which are the great delight of thefe private walks: add to this, the keeping of the hedges in good order is attended with a great expence, which is a capital thing to be confidered in the making of gardens.

GUAIABARA. See Coccolobos.

GUAJACANA. See Diospyros.

GUAJACUM. Plum. Nov. Gen. 39. tab. 17. Lin. Gen. Plant. 465. Lignum Vitæ, or Pockwood.

The Characters are,

The flower hath a concave empalement of one leaf, which is quinquefid. It hath five oblong, oval, concave petals, which are inferted in the empalement and fpread open, and ten erect ftamina inferted in the empalement, terminated by fmall fummits. The ftyle is long and flender, the germen is oval and pointed, and the ftigma is fingle and flender. The germen afterward becomes a berry which is roundifh, with an oblique point, and deeply furrowed, inclofing an oval hard feed.

This genus of plants is ranged in the firft fection of Linnæus's tenth clafs, intitled Decandria Monogynia, which includes thofe plants whofe flowers have ten ftamina and one ftyle.

The Species are,

1. Guajacum (*Officinale*) foliolis bijugatis obtufis. Lin. Sp. Plant. 381. *Guajacum with obtufe lobes placed by pairs.* Guajacum flore cæruleo, fructu fubrotundo. Plum. Nov. Gen. 391. *Guajacum with a blue flower and a roundifh fruit.*

2. Guajacum (*Sanctum*) foliolis multijugatis obtufis. Lin. Sp. Plant. 382. *Guajacum with many pair of obtufe lobes.* Guajacum flore cæruleo fimbriato, fructu tetragono. Plum. Nov. Gen. 391. *Guajacum with a blue fringed flower, and a four-cornered fruit.*

3. Guajacum (*Afrum*) foliolis multijugatis obtufis. Lin. Sp. Plant. 382. *Guajacum with many pair of acutepointed lobes.* Guilandinoides. Hort. Cliff. 489. and the Afra arbor acaciæ fimilis, foliis myrti aculeatis fplendentibus. Boerh. Ind. alt. 2. p. 57. *African-tree like the Acacia, with fhining, acute-pointed, Myrtle leaves.*

The firft fort is the common Lignum Vitæ, or Guajacum, which is ufed in medicine, and grows naturally in moft of the iflands in the Weft-Indies, where it rifes to be a very large tree, having a hard, brittle, brownifh bark, not very thick; the wood is firm, folid, and ponderous, appearing very refinous, of a blackifh yellow colour within, and of a hot aromatic tafte; the fmaller branches have an Afh-coloured bark, garnifhed with leaves, which are divided by pairs, each pair having two pair of fmall, oval, blunt leaves (or pinnæ) of a ftiff confiftence, and a lucid green; the flowers are produced in clufters at the end of the branches, compofed of five oval concave petals, of a fine blue colour; in the center of thefe is fixed a ftyle with an oval germen, crowned by a flender ftigma; and round this is fituated from ten to twenty ftamina, which are as long as the ftyle, terminated by fickle-fhaped fummits. Dr. Linnæus fuppofes the flowers to have but ten ftamina, whereas they certainly have near twenty.

The bark and wood of this tree are much of the fame nature, only the wood is accounted hotter; they are ufed in diet-drinks to purify and cleanfe the blood, and to caufe fweating; they are efteemed good for the gout and dropfy, the king's-evil, and particularly for the French pox. The gum or refin, which is black, fhining, and brittle, and when powdered, of a greenifh white colour, of an aromatic fmell, and poignant tafte, is fomewhat cathartic, and a good purge in rheumatic cafes, to the quantity of two fcruples mixed with the yolk of an egg, and given in a convenient vehicle.

The wood of this tree is fo hard as to break the tools in felling them, fo they are feldom cut down for fire-wood, being difficult to burn; but the wood is of great ufe to the fugar-planters, for making of wheels and cogs for the fugar-mills, &c. It is alfo frequently brought to Europe, and wrought into bowls, and other utenfils are made of the wood.

This tree can only be propagated by feeds, which muft be procured from the countries where it naturally grows; thefe muft be frefh, otherwife they will not grow; when they arrive, they fhould be fown in pots filled with light earth, and plunged into a good hotbed: if the feeds are good, and the bed in which they are plunged is of a proper temperature of heat, the plants will appear in fix weeks or two months after; and in fix weeks will grow to be of ftrength enough more

for

for tranfplanting ; then they fhould be carefully taken out of the feed-pots, fo as to preferve their roots as entire as poffible, and each planted in feparate fmall pots filled with light earth, and plunged into a new hot-bed of tanners bark, where they muft be fhaded from the fun till they have taken frefh root ; then they muft be treated in the fame manner as other tender exotic plants from warm countries, admitting a large fhare of free air to them when the weather is warm : they will require to be frequently refrefhed with water in warm weather, but it muft be given them with caution, for too much wet will infallibly deftroy them. While the plants are young, they may be kept during the fummer feafon in a hot-bed of tanners bark under a frame ; but in the ' autumn they muft be removed into the bark-ftove, and plunged into the hot-bed of tan, where they fhould conftantly remain, and muft be treated in the fame manner as other tender plants, being careful not to give them too much water in the winter, when it is very prejudicial to them, and in fummer they fhould have a large fhare of free air admitted to them every day. With this treatment the plants will thrive very well, but they are plants of flow growth in their own country, fo cannot be expected to make great progrefs in Europe.

The fecond fort has many fmall leaves placed along the midrib by pairs, which are rounded and obtufe at their ends, but narrow at their bafe : they are of the fame confiftence with thofe of the former fort, but of a darker green colour ; the flowers are produced in loofe bunches toward the end of the branches, which are of a fine blue colour, and their petals are fringed on their edges. This is called in fome of the iflands Baftard Lignum Vitæ ; I received it from Antigua by that title. It requires the fame treatment as the firft fort, and is propagated by feeds in the fame way.

I have alfo received fpecimens from the ifland of Barbuda of one, which feems different from either of thofe before-mentioned : the branches have the fame appearance with thofe of the firft fort, but the leaves are larger and indented at their extremities, and are placed all round the branches, on very fhort footftalks ; the flowers were broken off, fo I cannot determine the difference between them, but by all appearance they feem to be of the fame genus.

The third fort has been long an inhabitant in fome of the curious gardens in England and Holland, but feldom produces flowers in Europe. This grows naturally at the Cape of Good Hope, from whence the feeds were brought firft to Holland, where it paffed for a fpecies of Acacia, until it produced its flowers ; which, by the account given of them by the late Dr. Boerhaave, were of the butterfly kind ; but whether Dr. Linnæus has feen the flowers or not, I cannot fay ; however, he has removed it from that clafs of plants, and has added it to this genus ; and as I have not yet feen the flowers, fo I do not know if it is rightly placed. The plants retain their leaves all the year, and will live in a good green-houfe in winter, but in fummer muft be placed abroad with other green-houfe plants. It is of flow growth, and is with difficulty propagated by layers.

GUAJAVA. See Psidium.

GUANABANUS. See Annona.

GUAZUMA. See Theobroma.

GUIDONIA. See Samyda.

GUILANDINA. Lin. Gen. Plant. 464. Bonduc. Plum. Nov. Gen. 25. rab. 39. The Nickar-tree.

The Characters are,

The empalement of the flower is of one leaf, is bell-fhaped, and cut at the top into five equal fegments : the flower has five concave fpear-fhaped petals which are equal, and fit clofe to the empalement, into which they are inferted. It hath ten awl-fhaped ftamina which are erect, and inferted in the empalement, being alternately fhorter than each other, and terminated by obtufe fummits. In the center is fituated an oblong germen, fupporting a flender ftyle the length of the ftamina, crowned by a fingle ftigma. The germen afterward becomes a rhomboid pod, with

a convex future on the upper fide ; it is fwelling and comprefled, having one cell, including oval hard feeds, which are feparated by partitions.

This genus of plants is ranged in the firft fection of Linnæus's tenth clafs, in which he includes the plants whofe flowers have ten ftamina and one ftyle.

The Species are,

1. Guilandina (Bonduc) aculeata pinnis ovatis foliolis aculeis folitariis. Lin. Sp. 545. Prickly Guilandina with oval-winged leaves, whofe fmall leaves are armed with fingle fpines. Bonduc vulgare majus polyphyllum. Plum. Nov. Gen. 25. Common greater Bonduc, having many leaves, called yellow Nickar.

2. Guilandina (Bonducella) aculeata, pinnis oblongo-ovatis foliolis aculeis geminis. Lin. Sp. 545. Prickly Guilandina with oblong oval leaves, having fpines by pairs. Bonduc vulgare minus polyphyllum. Plum. Nov. Gen. 25. Smaller common Bonduc, or Nickar-tree having many leaves, called gray Nickar.

3. Guilandina (Glabra) inermis foliis bipinnatis, foliolis ovatis acutis alternis. Smooth Guilandina with double winged leaves, whofe fmall leaves are oval-pointed and alternate.

4. Guilandina (Moringa) inermis, foliis fubpinnatis, foliolis inferioribus ternatis. Flor. Zeyl. 155. Smooth Guilandina with winged leaves, whofe under fmall leaves are trifoliate. Moringa Zeylanica, foliorum pinnis pinnatis, flore majore, fructu angulofo. Burm. Zeyl. 162. tab. 75. Morunga of Ceylon, with double-winged leaves, a larger flower, and an angular fruit.

5. Guilandina (Dioica) inermis foliis bipinnatis bafi apiceque fimpliciter pinnatis. Lin. Sp. 546. Guilandina with fmooth branches, doubly winged leaves, whofe bafe and tops are fingle winged. Bonduc Canadenfe polyphyllum, non fpinofum, mas & fœmina. Du Hamel. Canada Nickar-tree having many leaves, which have no fpines, and are male and female in different plants.

The firft and fecond forts grow naturally in moft of the iflands in the Weft-Indies, where they twine their ftalks about any neighbouring fupport, and rife to the height of twelve or fourteen feet. The leaves of the firft fort are near a foot and a half long, and are compofed of fix or feven pair of pinnæ, or wings, each of which has as many pair of lobes, or fmall leaves fet along the midrib ; thefe are oval and entire ; the foot-ftalk or principal midrib of the leaf, is armed with fhort, crooked, fingle thorns, which are placed irregularly ; the ftalks are clofely armed with the like thorns, which are larger. The ftalks at firft grow erect, but afterward they twine about the neighbouring trees or fhrubs, being too weak to ftand without fupport : the flowers come out in long fpikes from the wings of the ftalk ; they are compofed of five concave yellow petals, which are equal ; in the center is fituated the oblong germen, furrounded by ten ftamina. After the flower is paft, the germen becomes a broad thick pod, about three inches long and two broad, clofely armed with flender fpines, opening with two valves, each inclofing two hard feeds about the fize of children's marbles, of a yellowifh colour.

The fecond fort differs from the firft, in having much fmaller leaves, which are fet clofe together ; and below each pair of lobes are fituated two fhort ftiff crooked fpines, which are placed oppofite ; the flowers are of a deeper yellow colour than thofe of the firft fort, and the feeds are of an Afh-colour.

The third fort was difcovered by the late Dr. Houftoun at Campeachy, from whence he fent the dried famples to England, but there was no fruit on the trees at the time when he was there ; but he mentions that this fort had an upright ftem, which was of a large fize, dividing into many branches ; thefe are garnifhed with double winged leaves, which are fmooth ; the wings come out altenrnate, each leaf being compofed of four pair, but the lobes are placed oppofite upon the middle rib ; they are oval, but end in a point, and are of a light green colour.

The fourth fort grows naturally in the ifland of Ceylon, and in feveral places on the Malabar coaft, from

from whence the feeds were brought to England. This in its native country rifes to the height of twenty-five or thirty feet, with a ftrong ftem, covered with a fmooth bark, which in the young branches is green, but on the older it is of an Afh-colour; the root grows knobbed, and very thick. This, when young, is fcraped and ufed by the inhabitants as Horfe-radifh is in Europe, having much the fame fharp tafte; the branches are garnifhed with decompounded winged leaves; thofe which are fituated at the bafe have but three leaves, but above, the leaves are branched out into feveral divifions, which are again divided into fmaller, having each five or fix pair of oval lobes, terminated by an odd one; they are of a light green, and a little hoary on their under fide. The flowers are produced in loofe bunches from the fide of the branches; they are compofed of an unequal number of petals, from five to ten; they have ten fhort ftamina furrounding the germen, which afterward turns to a long taper pod, including feveral angular feeds, covered with a thin membrane. Thefe have a flavour like the root.

Thefe four forts are natives of warm countries, fo will not live through the winter in England, unlefs they are placed in a warm ftove, and the pots plunged into the tan-bed. They are propagated by feeds, but thofe of the two firft forts are fo hard, that unlefs they are foaked two or three days in water before they are put into the ground, or placed under the pots in the tan-bed to foften their covers, they will remain years in the ground without vegetating: when the plants come up, they will be fit to tranfplant in a fhort time; then they fhould be each tranfplanted into a fmall pot filled with light frefh earth, and plunged into a moderate hot-bed of tanners bark, fhading them till they have taken frefh root; then they muft be treated in the fame manner as other tender exotic plants, giving them a large fhare of air in warm weather, and but little water; and when the plants have advanced to be too tall to remain in the frames, they muft be removed into the bark-ftove and plunged into the hot-bed, where they will make great progrefs, provided they have not too much water, efpecially during the winter feafon, for thefe plants are very impatient of moifture in cold weather.

The fourth fort requires the fame treatment as thofe before-mentioned, but the feeds will grow without being fteeped in water; and the plants are with difficulty fhifted from one pot to another, for their roots are large, flefhy, and have but few fibres; fo that unlefs great care is taken, all the earth will fall away from them, which often caufes their ftalks to decay almoft to the root, and fometimes occafions the lofs of the plants. This plant muft be fparingly watered at all times, but particularly in cold weather, when moifture will caufe them to rot in a fhort time.

The fifth fort grows naturally in Canada, from whence the plants were brought to Paris, where it has been fome years cultivated; but about fourteen years paft, it was firft brought to England. This, in the country where it naturally grows, rifes with an erect ftem to the height of thirty feet or more, dividing into many branches, which are covered with a bluifh Afh-colour-ed bark very fmooth, and garnifhed with large decompounded winged leaves which are of the oval fhape, very fmooth and entire, but are ranged alternate on the midrib; thefe fall off in the autumn, and new ones come out late in the fpring.

There are male and female of this fort in different plants; as thefe have not as yet flowered in any of the Englifh gardens, fo I can give no farther account of them nor of the fruit, having never feen any of them. This fort lives abroad in the open air, and is never hurt by froft. It is propagated by cutting off fome of the horizontal roots, which will caufe them to fhoot upward, fo it may be taken from the old root, and planted in pots, whereby the plant may be multiplied, or by fuckers from the root. It requires a light foil, not too moift.

GUNDELIA. Tourn. Cor. 51. tab. 586. Lin. Gen. Plant. 848. Hacub. Vaill. Ac. Reg. Scien. 1718.

This plant was fo named by Dr. Tournefort, in honour of Dr. Gundelfcheimer, who found it in his travels in company with Dr. Tournefort in the Levant.

The CHARACTERS are,

It hath an uniform tubulous flower, compofed of many hermaphrodite florets, which are incircled by leaves. They have but one petal which is clofed at the bottom, but fwells at the top, where it is flightly cut into five fegments: they have five fhort hairy ftamina, terminated by long cylindrical fummits. The oval germen is fituated at the bottom of the flower, crowned by fmall fcales, fupporting a flender ftyle which is longer than the petal, terminated by two revolving ftigmas. The germen afterward becomes a roundifh fingle feed inclofed in the common receptacle, which is conical, and the feeds are feparated by a chaffy down.

This genus of plants is by Tournefort referred to his twelfth clafs, which contains the herbs with flofculous flowers. Dr. Linnæus ranges it in the fifth fection of his nineteenth clafs, intitled Syngenefia Polygamia fegregata, which includes thofe plants whofe flowers have a common empalement, and each of the florets are included in another.

We have but one diftinct SPECIES of this genus at prefent in England, viz.

GUNDELIA. Lin. Sp. Plant. 814. There is no Englifh title to this plant, but there are two varieties of it mentioned by Tournefort, which are fuppofed to arife from the fame feeds, as they were found growing promifcuoufly together. Thefe are,

1. GUNDELIA (*Tournefortii*) Orientalis acanthi aculeati foliis, floribus intenfè purpureis, capite araneofà lanugine obfito. Tourn. Cor. 51. *Eaftern Gundelia with prickly Bear's-breech leaves, deep purple flowers, and a head covered with a down like a cobweb.*

2. GUNDELIA (*Glabro*) Orientalis, acanthi aculeati folio, capite glabro. Tourn. Cor. 51. *Eaftern Gundelia with a prickly Bear's-breech leaf, and a fmooth head.*

This plant was difcovered by Dr. Gundelfcheimer, in company with Tournefort, near Baibout in Armenia, but has fince been foundgrowing naturally in feveral places in the Levant, where it is generally found in dry ftrong land. The ftalks of this plant feldom rife more than a foot and a half high; the under leaves are long, narrow, and fawed on their edges, their teeth ending in a fpine; the other leaves are broader, which are irregularly flafhed to the midrib, and armed at the points with fharp prickles; the ftalks divide upward into feveral branches, which are armed with leaves of the fame form, but are narrower; and each is terminated by a conical head of flowers, refembling thofe of Fuller's Thiftle, being furrounded at the bafe by a circle of long, narrow, prickly leaves: thefe heads are compofed of many hermaphrodite florets, which are fhut up in the fcales, each having an empalement, and a germen with five ftamina furrounding it; but there are few of the feeds which ripen perfectly in each head, in the natural places of its growth. If rain happens at the time when the plants are in flower, the germen perifhes, which is the cafe with feveral other of thofe plants whofe flowers are collected into heads.

Thefe plants are propagated by feed, which fhould be fown the beginning of March, in a warm dry border of frefh, but lean earth, in the place where the plants are defigned to remain. When the plants come up, they muft be carefully cleared from weeds; as they grow large, they fhould be thinned, leaving the plants which are defigned to remain, about two feet afunder, that they may have room to fpread. After this there is no other culture required, but to keep them clear from weeds; and if the froft fhould prove fevere in winter, the plants fhould be covered with ftraw or Peas-haulm to protect them, but this covering muft be taken off in mild weather; in two years they will produce their flowers, when they will make a fine appearance amongft other hardy plants in the pleafure-garden. They flower in May, and the plants lofe their ftalks and leaves in autumn, but their roots will abide many years.

GYPSOPHYLA. Lin. Gen. Plant. 498. We have no Englifh title for this genus.

The CHARACTERS are,

The flower hath a permanent, angular, bell-fhaped empalement, cut into five parts at the top. It hath five oval blunt petals, which fpread open, and ten awl-fhaped ftamina, terminated by roundifh fummits. In the center is fituated a globular germen, fupporting two flender ftyles, crowned by fingle ftigmas. The germen afterward becomes a globular capfule with one cell, opening with five valves, filled with fmall roundifh feeds.

This genus of plants is ranged in the fecond fection of Linnæus's tenth clafs, which includes thofe plants whofe flowers have ten ftamina and two ftyles.

The SPECIES are,

1. GYPSOPHYLA (*Aggregata*) foliis mucronatis recurvatis, floribus aggregatis. Lin. Sp. Plant. 406. *Gypfophyla with pointed recurved leaves, and flowers gathered in a head.* Lychnis Hifpanica kali folio multiflora. Tourn. Inft. R. H. 338. *Spanifh Lychnis with a Glaffwort leaf and many flowers.*

2. GYPSOPHYLA (*Faftigiata*) foliis lanceolato-linearibus, obfoletè triquetris lævibus obtufis fecundis. Lin. Sp. Plant. 407. *Gypfophyla with narrow fpearfhaped leaves, having three blunt angles, and fmooth obtufe leaves in clufters.* Saponaria caule fimplici, foliis linearibus ex alis foliorum confertis teretibus. Hort. Cliff. 166. *Sopewort with a fingle ftalk, very narrow leaves, coming out in clufters from the wings of the ftalks.*

3. GYPSOPHYLA (*Proftrata*) foliis lanceolatis lævibus, caulibus diffufis, piftillis corollâ campanulatâ longioribus. Lin. Sp. Plant. App. 1195. *Gypfophyla with fmooth fpear-fhaped leaves, diffufed ftalks, and the pointal longer than the petal, which is bell-fhaped.*

4. GYPSOPHYLA (*Perfoliata*) foliis ovato-lanceolatis, femiamplexicaulibus. Lin. Sp. Plant. 408. *Gypfophyla with oval fpear-fhaped leaves, half embracing the ftalks.* Lychnis Orientalis, faponariæ folio & facie, flore parvo & multiplici. Tourn. Cor. 24. *Eaftern Lychnis with the leaf and appearance of Sopewort, having many fmall flowers.*

5. GYPSOPHYLA (*Paniculata*) foliis lanceolatis fcabris, floribus dioicis corollis revolutis. Lin. Sp. Plant. 407. *Gypfophyla with rough, fpear-fhaped leaves, male and female in different plants, and the petals of the flowers recurved.* Alfine frutefcens caryophylli folio, flore parvo albo. Gerb. *Shrubby Chickweed with a Clove Gilliflower leaf, and a fmall white flower.*

The firft fort grows naturally in the fouth of France, Spain, and Italy, upon the mountains. This hath a perennial root, from which arife many narrow leaves ending in acute points, which are recurved; the ftalks rife about a foot high, garnifhed with narrower leaves placed oppofite, and at fome of the joints there are fmaller leaves growing from the ftalks in clufters; the upper part of the ftalk divides into fmaller branches, each being terminated by a clofe bunch of fmall white flowers. Thefe appear in July, and are fucceeded by fmall oval capfules, filled with fmall feeds.

The fecond fort is fomewhat like the firft, but the leaves are much narrower, and almoft three-cornered; they are placed in clufters, which come out from the fide of the ftalk; the bunches of the flowers are fmaller, and not fo clofely joined. This hath a perennial root, and grows naturally upon the Helvetian mountains.

The third fort hath a perennial root, from which arife fmooth fpear-fhaped leaves in clufters; the ftalks are near a foot long, but are proftrate on the ground; the flowers have a purplifh caft, and the ftamina are much longer than the petals of the flowers. This flowers in June and July, and the feeds ripen in autumn.

The fourth fort grows naturally in the Levant, and alfo in Spain. It hath a ftrong, flefhy, fibrous root, which ftrikes deep in the ground, fending up feveral thick, flefhy ftalks, which rife near two feet high, garnifhed with oval fpear-fhaped leaves, which half embrace the ftalks with their bafe; the upper part of the ftalk divides into many fmaller branches, which are terminated with loofe bunches of fmall white flowers. Thefe open in July, and the feeds ripen in autumn.

The fifth fort grows naturally in Siberia and Tartary, the feeds of it were fent me from Peterfburgh. This hath a perennial root, from which arife many branching ftalks a foot and a half high, garnifhed with narrow fmooth-pointed leaves, fhaped like thofe of Gilliflowers; at the top of the ftalks are produced loofe clufters of very fmall white flowers, which appear at the fame time with the former forts, and the feeds ripen in the autumn.

Thefe plants have no great-beauty, fo are rarely cultivated but in botanic gardens for the fake of variety.

They are propagated by feeds, which fhould be fown in a bed of light earth, and when the plants are fit to remove, they may be tranfplanted into the places where they are defigned to remain, and will require no other culture but to keep them clean from weeds; for the roots will continue feveral years, and annually produce flowers and feeds.

H.

HÆMANTHUS. Tourn. Inft. R. H. 657. tab. 433. Lin. Gen. Plant. 394. Dracunculoides. Boerh. Ind. alt. 2. 226. [Αἱμανθὸς, of Αἷμα, blood, and Ἄνθος, flos, a flower, i. e. Blood-flower.]

The CHARACTERS are,

The flower has a permanent empalement of fix leaves, which is large, and fhaped like an umbel. It hath one erect petal, which is cut into fix parts, having a fhort angular tube, and fix awl-fhaped ftamina, which are inferted in the petal, but are longer, terminated by oblong proftrate fummits. The germen is fituated under the flower, fupporting a fingle ftyle the length of the ftamina, crowned by a fingle ftigma. The germen afterward becomes a roundifh berry with three cells, each containing one triangular feed.

This genus of plants is ranged in the firft fection of Linnæus's fixth clafs, intitled Hexandria Monogynia, which includes the plants whofe flowers have fix ftamina and one ftyle.

The SPECIES are,

1. HÆMANTHUS (*Coccineus*) foliis linguiformibus planis lævibus. Prod. Leyd. 42. *Blood-flower with plain, tongue-shaped, smooth leaves.* Hæmanthus Africanus. H. L. Bat. *African Blood-flower, or Cape Tulip.*

2. HÆMANTHUS (*Carinatus*) foliis longioribus carinatis. *Blood-flower with longer keel-shaped leaves.*

3. HÆMANTHUS (*Puniceus*) foliis lanceolato ovatis undulatis erectis. Hort. Cliff. 127. *Blood-flower with spear-shaped, waved, erect leaves.* Hæmanthus colchici foliis perianthio herbaceo. Hort. Elth. 167. *Blood-flower with Meadow Saffron leaves, and an herbaceous involucrum.* Dracunculoides. Boerh. Ind. alt. 2. 226. *Bastard Dragon.*

The first sort has been many years in several curious gardens in Europe, where it hath seldom flowered. This hath a large bulbous root, from which in the autumn comes out two broad flat leaves, of a fleshy consistence, shaped like a tongue, which turn backward on each side, and spread flat on the ground, so have a singular appearance all the winter; and in the spring these leaves decay, so that from the end of May to the beginning of August, they are destitute of leaves: when these produce their flowers, it is always in the autumn, just before the new leaves come out. In the books where this plant is figured, the flowers are represented growing upon a strong upright foot-stalk; but all those which I have seen in flower, never have risen more than two or three inches from the bulb, with a large cluster of bright red flowers, inclosed in a common leafy-coloured empalement; these were tubulous, with one petal cut into six parts, each having six long stamina, standing out beyond the petal, and in the center appears the germen sitting under the flower, supporting a single style, crowned with a stigma. The germen never ripens to a seed in England, but decays with the flower, and then the green leaves grow and spread on the ground.

The second sort hath a large bulbous root like the first, which sends out three or four leaves, that grow a foot long or more; these are not flat like those of the other, but are hollowed like the keel of a boat, and stand more erect than those of the former sort, but are not quite so broad; the flowers of this are like those of the first, but are of a pale red; this is certainly different from the other. I received the roots of this from Dr. Van Royen, professor of botany at Leyden.

The third sort hath roots composed of many thick fleshy tubers, which join at the top, where they form a head, out of which arises a fleshy spotted stalk, like that of the dragon, which spreads out at the top into several spear-shaped leaves, which are waved on their edges. The stalks grow about a foot high, and the leaves are six or eight inches long, and two broad in the middle; from the side of this stalk near the ground, breaks out a strong fleshy foot-stalk, about six or eight inches long, sustaining at the top a large cluster of flowers, included in one common empalement or covering, which is permanent; the flowers are shaped like those of the other sorts, but are of a yellowish red colour. These appear in May, June, or July, and are succeeded by berries which are of a beautiful red colour when ripe.

The two first sorts are with difficulty propagated in Europe, for their roots put out offsets but sparingly, so the gardens in Holland are supplied with them from the Cape of Good Hope, where they naturally grow, and produce seeds; the plants are too tender to thrive in this country in winter in the open air, therefore the roots must be planted in pots filled with light loamy earth, and, in the winter, placed in a dry glass-case, where, during that season, the leaves will be in full vigour, so will make a pretty appearance, when intermixed with other plants in the stove; and though they seldom flower here, yet are they worthy of a place in every garden where there is conveniency of keeping them. The roots may be taken up when their leaves are decayed, and kept out of the ground till August, when they should be new pot-

ted, and may remain abroad till the end of September, at which time they may be removed into the glass-case; and during the time they are growing, will require to have frequent waterings, but it must not be given to them in large quantities.

If a border is made either against the front of the green-house or stoves, which may be contrived so as to be covered with glasses in winter, in which these roots, with the African Gladiolus's, Ixia's, Persian Cyclamens, &c. are planted in the full ground, they will flower more constantly, and the foot-stalks will rise much higher than those kept in pots.

The third sort is also a native of the Cape of Good Hope, from whence it was first brought to Holland, where it has been propagated and dispersed over Europe; this may be propagated by parting of the roots; the best time for this is in the spring, before the plants put out new stalks, which is also a right time to shift and new-pot them; but as the roots do not multiply very fast in offsets, the best way is to propagate them from seeds, which they ripen plentifully in England; these should be sown soon after they are ripe, in pots filled with light earth, and kept in the stove all the winter; if these pots are plunged into the tan-bed in the bark-stove, in the vacancies between the plants, the earth will be kept warm, and will not dry so fast, as when they are placed in a dry stove, so the seeds will be sooner prepared to vegetate; in the spring the pots may be taken out of the stove, and plunged into a hot-bed, which will bring up the plants; these must have air admitted to them every day in mild weather, to prevent their drawing up weak; and when they are fit to remove, they may be each planted in a separate small pot filled with light earth, and plunged into the hot-bed again, to promote their taking new root; then they must be gradually hardened, and afterward may be removed into the dry stove, where they should constantly remain, otherwise the plants will not thrive and flower in this country. In the winter season they must not have too much wet, for as their roots are fleshy and succulent, so they are apt to rot with moisture. In the summer they must have a large share of air in warm weather, and require to be frequently watered, especially during the time of their flowering.

HÆMATOXYLUM. Lin. Gen. Plant. 417. Bloodwood, Logwood, or Campeachy Wood.

The CHARACTERS are,

The flower hath a permanent empalement, which is cut into five oval segments. It hath five oval petals which are equal, and larger than the empalement, and ten awl-shaped stamina, which are longer than the petals, terminated by small summits. In the center is situated an oblong oval germen, supporting a single style, crowned by a thick indented stigma. The germen afterward becomes a compressed obtuse capsule, with one cell opening with two valves, containing two or three oblong kidney-shaped seeds.

This genus of plants is ranged in the first section of Linnæus's tenth class, intitled Decandria Monogynia, which includes those plants whose flowers have ten stamina and one style.

We have but one SPECIES of this genus, viz.

HÆMATOXYLUM (*Campechianum*). Hort. Cliff. 161. *Logwood,* Lignum Campechianum, species quædam. Sloan. Cat. Jam 213. *Campeachy Wood.*

This tree grows naturally in the Bay of Campeachy, at Honduras, and other parts of the Spanish West-Indies, where it rises from sixteen to twenty-four feet high. The stems are generally crooked, and very deformed, and are seldom thicker than a man's thigh. The branches come out on every side; they are crooked, irregular, and armed with strong thorns, garnished with winged leaves, composed of three or four pair of lobes, which are obtuse, and indented at the top. The flowers come out in a racemus from the wings of the leaves, standing erect; they are of a pale yellowish colour, with a purple empalement, and are succeeded by flat oblong pods, each containing two or three kidney-shaped seeds.

The

The wood of this tree is brought to Europe, where it is used for dyeing purples, and for the finest blacks, so is a valuable commodity; but the Spaniards, who claim a right to the possession of those places where it naturally grows, are for excluding all other countries from cuting of the wood, which has occasioned many disputes with their neighbours, but particularly with the English; this it is to be hoped will soon be over, as there are some of the planters in Jamaica, and the other islands in America, belonging to the crown of Great-Britain, who have propagated this tree in so great plenty, as to have hopes of supplying the demand for this wood in Britain in a very few years; for the trees grow so fast there, as to be fit for use in ten or twelve years years from seed; and as they produce great plenty of seeds in the British colonies, so those seeds scattering about, the plants come up in all the neighbouring lands, therefore will soon be like an indigenous plant of the country.

Some of the planters in Jamaica have inclosed their estates with hedges formed of these trees, which are very strong and durable; but where the hedges are cut, it will greatly retard the growth of the trees, so that those who propose to make an advantage by the propagation of the wood, should sow the seeds upon swampy lands, which may be unfit for growing of sugar, and permit all their branches to remain, which will be of great use in augmenting the bulk of their stems; and if, while the plants are young, they are kept clean from weeds, &c. it will be of great advantage in promoting of their growth. I have been credibly informed by some of the planters in Jamaica, that they have had some plants of this sort upward of ten feet high in three years, so that it requires but few years to raise a supply of this wood, sufficient to answer all the demands for it.

This plant is preserved in some curious gardens in England, for the sake of variety. The seeds are frequently brought from America, which, if fresh, readily grow when sown upon a good hot-bed; and if the plants are kept in a moderate hot-bed, they will grow to be upward of a foot high the same year, and, while the plants are young, they are generally well furnished with leaves; but afterward they make but little progress, and are frequently but thinly clothed with leaves. These plants are very tender, so should be constantly kept in the bark-stove, where, if they are duly watered, and the stove kept in a good degree of heat, the plants may be preserved very well. There are some of these plants now in England, which are upward of six feet high, and as thriving as those in their native soil.

HALESIA. Lin. Gen. Plant. 596.

The CHARACTERS are,

The flower hath a small permanent empalement of one leaf, indented in four parts; it hath a bell-shaped swelling flower of one petal, divided at the brim into four lobes, and from twelve to sixteen stamina, shorter than the petal, terminated by oblong erect summits; the germen is situated below, is oblong, supporting a slender style longer than the petal, crowned by a simple stigma; the germen afterward becomes an oblong nut, narrowed at both ends, having four angles, with two cells, inclosing a single seed in each. This genus of plants is ranged in the first section of Linnæus's eleventh class, intitled Dodecandria Monogynia, the flower having twelve stamina and one style.

The SPECIES are,

1. HALESIA (*Tetraptera*) foliis lanceolato-ovatis, petiolis glandulosis. Lin. Sp. 636. *Halesia with oval spear-shaped leaves, whose foot-stalks are glandulous.* Frutex padi foliis serratis, floribus monopetalus albis campaniformibus, fructu crasso tetragono. Catesb. Hist. Carol. 1. p. 64.

2. HALESIA (*Diptera*) foliis ovatis, petiolis lævibus. Lin. Sp. 636. *Halesia with oval leaves having smooth foot-stalks.*

This genus of plants received its title from the late learned and reverend Doctor Hales, minister of Teddington, near Hampton-Court.

Both the sorts grow naturally in South-Carolina; the first on the banks of Santee river, where it frequently comes up with two or three stems from the same root, which rise from fifteen to twenty feet high, sending out branches toward their tops, garnished with oval spear-shaped leaves, sawed on their edges: the flowers are produced on the side of the branches in clusters, from two or three to six or seven in each; they are bell-shaped, hanging downward, of one petal, white, which is indented in four parts at the brim; these are succeeded by oblong nuts, having four wings and four cells, each containing one oblong seed.

The second sort hath much resemblance to the first, the leaves are oval, and the foot-stalks are smooth; the fruit has but two angles.

These plants are propagated by seeds, when they can be procured fresh from the places of their natural growth. These should be sown in pots as soon as the seeds arrive, plunging the pots into the ground, in a situation where they may have only the morning sun. The seeds often remain a year in the ground, therefore the earth in the pots should not be disturbed, until there is no probability of the seed growing. When the plants appear, they should be screened from the sun, and frequently, but not too plentifully watered; for while the plants are young, much moisture will rot their shanks. The following autumn, the pots should be placed in a common frame, where the plants may enjoy the free air in mild weather, and be screened from frost. The spring following, before the plants begin to shoot, they should be each put into a separate small pot, plunging them in a frame, where they should be shaded from sun; and in the summer placed in a shady situation, screening them in winter; and the spring following they may be turned out of the pots, and planted in the full ground where they are designed to remain.

HALICACABUM. See PHYSALIS.

HALICACABUS PEREGRINA. See CARDIOSPERMUM.

HALIMUS. See ATRIPLEX.

HALLERIA. Lin. Gent. Plant. 679. Caprifolium. Boerh. Ind. alt 2. p. 226. *African Fly Honeysuckle.*

The CHARACTERS are,

The flower hath a permanent empalement of one leaf, which is cut into three parts at the top, the upper segment being much broader than the other. It hath one petal of the grining kind. The bottom of the tube is roundish. The chaps are swollen and inflexed, the brim is erect and oblique, cut into four segments, the upper being longer than the others, and is blunt, with an indenture at the top; the two side ones are shorter, and pointed, the lower is very short and acute. It hath four stamina, which are bristly, two being longer than the other, terminated by twin summits. In the bottom of the tube is situated an oval germen, with a style longer than the stamina, crowned by a single stigma. The germen afterward becomes a roundish berry with two cells, each containing one hard seed. This genus of plants is ranged in the second section of Linnæus's fourteenth class, intitled Didynamia Angiospermia, which includes the plants with a ringent flower, which have two long and two shorter stamina, and the seeds are included in a capsule.

We have but one SPECIES of this genus, viz.

HALLERIA (*Lucida*). Hort. Cliff. 323. This plant has its title from Dr. Haller, who was professor of botany at Gottingen, in Germany. Caprifolium Africanum folio pruni leviter serrato, flore ruberrimo, baccâ nigrâ. Boerh. Ind. alt. 2. 226. *African Fly Honeysuckle, with a Plumb leaf lightly sawed, a very red flower, and a black berry.*

The English name which I have here added, has been given to this plant by some gardeners, who observed that the shape of the flower had some resemblance to that of the Upright, or Fly Honeysuckle, and for want of an English name gave this to it; or they might take it from the Latin name, by which it was called by Dr. Boerhaave, who made it a species of Honeysuckle.

This

This plant grows to the height of six or eight feet, having a woody stem, which is well furnished with branches; these have oval sawed leaves, which are placed opposite, and continue green through the year; the flowers come out singly, and are of a red colour, but, being intermixed with the leaves, are not seen unless they are looked after, for they grow scatteringly on the branches; these come out in June, and the seeds ripen in September; the leaves are green in winter, so the plants make a variety in the green-house during that season.

It may be propagated by cuttings, which, if planted in pots filled with light earth in June, and plunged into a gentle hot-bed, will soon take root; these plants may be exposed in summer, and will require plenty of water in that season; in winter they must be housed with Myrtles, and other hardy exotic plants, which require a large share of air in mild weather.

HAMAMELIS. Lin. Gen. Plant. 155. Trilopus. Mitch. Gen. 22. *The Witch Hazel.*

The CHARACTERS are,

It is male and female in different plants; the male flowers have a four-leaved empalement, and four narrow petals, which are reflexed; they have four narrow stamina, which are shorter than the petals, terminated by horned reflexed summits. The female flowers have a four-leaved involucrum, in which are four flowers; these have a four-leaved empalement, which is coloured; they have four narrow petals, which are reflexed, and four nectariums adhering to the petals. In the center is situated an oval hairy germen, supporting two styles, crowned by headed stigmas. The germen afterward becomes an oval capsule sitting in the involucrum, having two cells, each containing one hard, oblong, smooth seed.

This genus of plants is ranged in the second section of Linnæus's fourth class, but properly belongs to the second section of his twenty-second class, which includes those plants which have male and female flowers in different plants, whose female flowers have two styles.

We have but one SPECIES of this genus in the English gardens at present, viz.

HAMAMELIS (*Virginiana*). Flor. Virg. 139. *The Witch Hazel.* Pistachia Virginiana nigra, coryli foliis. Pluk. Alm. 296. *Black Virginia Pistachia with Hazel leaves.*

This plant grows naturally in North America, from whence the seeds have been brought to Europe, and many of the plants have been raised in the English gardens, where they are propagated for sale by the nursery gardeners. It hath a woody stem, from two to three feet high, sending out many slender branches, garnished with oval leaves, indented on their edges, having great resemblance to those of the Hazel Nut, placed alternately on the branches; these fall away in autumn, and when the plants are destitute of leaves, the flowers come out in clusters from the joints of the branches; these sometimes appear the latter end of October, and often not till December, but are not succeeded by seeds in this country.

As the flowers of this shrub make very little appearance, so it is only preserved in the gardens of the curious, more for the sake of variety than its beauty.

This is propagated by laying down the young branches in autumn, which will take root in one year, provided they are duly watered in dry weather; but many of the plants which are in the gardens, have been produced from seeds which came from America; these seeds always remain a whole year in the ground, so they should be sown in pots, which may be plunged into the ground in a shady part of the garden, where they may remain all the summer, and require no other care but to keep the pots clean from weeds, and in very dry weather to water them now and then; in autumn the pots may be removed to a warmer situation, and plunged into the ground under a warm hedge; and if the winter should prove very severe, they should have some light covering thrown over the pots, which will secure the seeds from being destroyed.

In the spring the plants will come up, therefore as the season grows warm, the pots may be removed where they may have the morning sun till eleven o'clock; and if they are duly watered in dry weather, the plants will have made good progress by autumn, when they should be transplanted, either into small pots, or in a nursery-bed, where in one, or at most two years time, they will be strong enough to plant where they are designed to remain; they love a moist soil, and a shady situation.

HAMELLIA. Lin. Gen. 232.

The CHARACTERS are,

The empalement of the flower is small, permanent, and cut into five acute segments; the flower is of one petal, having a long tube, whose brim is cut into five acute points; it hath five awl-shaped stamina inserted to the middle of the petal, terminated by linear summits the length of the petal; and an oval germen, whose lower point is conical, supporting a slender style the length of the corolla, crowned by an obtuse linear stigma: the germen afterward becomes an oval furrowed berry, with five cells, filled with small compressed seeds.

This genus of plants is ranged in the first order of Linnæus's fifth class, intitled Pentandria Monogynia, the flower having five stamina and one style: it is named in honour of Monsieur du Hamel des Monceaux, member of the Academy of Sciences at Paris, and fellow of the Royal Society of London; a gentleman well known to the learned, by the many useful books he has published.

We know but one SPECIES of this genus, viz.

1. HAMELLIA (*Patens*) racemis erectos. Jacq. Amer. 71. *Hamellia with erect spikes of flowers.*

This plant grows naturally in Africa, and also in the warm parts of America: I received the seeds from Paris, which were brought from Senegal by Mr. Adanson, with the title of Mortura on the paper; and before that, received a drawing of the plant in flower, from the late Dr. Houstoun, who found it growing naturally in America, where it has since been found growing by Mr. Jacquin, who has figured it. It rises with a ligneous stalk five or six feet high, sending out several erect branches toward the top, garnished with oval woolly leaves, placed by threes round the branches, having red foot-stalks; the flowers terminate the branches in slender spikes; they are tubulous, and cut at their brims into five sharp segments, standing erect, of a bright red colour: these are not succeeded by seeds in England.

This plant is propagated by seeds, when they can be procured fresh from the countries where it grows naturally: these should be sown in small pots, and plunged into a moderate hot-bed: the plants generally appear in about five or six weeks after, and should then be treated in the same way as other plants from the same countries; giving them proper air in warm weather, and gently refreshing them with water; and when they are fit to transplant, they should be each planted in a small pot, plunging them into the hot-bed again, where they should be shaded from the sun until they have taken new root, when they should have air and moisture according to the warmth of the season. In the autumn the plants must be removed into the tan-stove, plunging the pots into the bed, where they should be always continued: this flowers in July and August, when it makes a pretty appearance.

As the seeds of this plant are seldom brought to England, so the plant may be propagated by cuttings, which if planted in small pots, plunged into a moderate hot-bed, and closely covered with either bell or hand-glasses, will put out roots in about six weeks, and may then be treated in the same way as the seedling plants.

HARMALA. See PEGANUM.

HASSELQUISTIA. Lin. Gen. 341.

The CHARACTERS are,

It is an umbelliferous plant, whose universal umbel is composed of six spreading rays; these are for the most part double; the greater involucrum has many short bristly leaves; the proper empalement is very small, and hath five indentures; the general umbel is half radiated; the outer flowers are fruitful, but those in the disk are barren; they have five petals, and five slender stamina longer than the petals, terminated by roundish summits: the turbinated germen is situated under the flower, supporting two slender recurved styles, crowned by obtuse stigmas; the germen afterward becomes an orbicular fruit, composed of two seeds having borders.

This genus of plants is ranged in the second order of Linnæus's fifth class, intitled Pentandria Digynia, the flowers having five stamina and two styles.

It it named after Mr. Hasselquist, who was a pupil of Dr. Linnæus.

1. HASSELQUISTIA (Ægyptiaca). Amœn. Acad. 4. p. 370. Egyptian Hasselquistia. Pastinaca Orientalis, foliis eleganter incisis. Buxb. Cent. 3. p. 16.

This plant is bennial, and being a native of warm countries, is with difficulty preserved in England; for when the plants come up early in the spring, they do not perfect their seeds the same year: and those plants which arise in the autumn, seldom live through the winter; therefore the surest method to procure good seeds in this country, is to sow the seeds in pots about the middle of August, placing the pots where they may have the morning sun only, being careful to water them duly; and as weeds will come up in the pots to take them out, and where the plants are too close, thin them; in October remove the pots into a common frame, where they may enjoy the free air in mild weather, but be screened from frost: in the spring following, if the plants are carefully turned out of the pots, and planted in the full ground, they will flower in June, and the seeds will ripen in August.

HAWTHORN. See MESPILUS.

HAZEL. See CORYLUS.

HEDERA. Lin. Gen. Plant. 249. Tourn. Inst. R. H. 612. tab. 384. The Ivy-tree.

The CHARACTERS are,

The flowers are disposed in form of an umbel, having a small involucrum indented in many parts. The empalement is cut into five parts, and sits upon a germen. The flower hath five oblong petals, which spread open, whose points are incurved; they have five oval-shaped stamina, terminated by prostrate summits, which are cut into two at their base. The germen, which is situated below the flower, supports a short style, crowned by a single stigma. The germen afterward becomes a globular berry with one cell, inclosing four or five large seeds, convex on one side, and angular on the other.

This genus of plants is ranged in the first section of Linnæus's fifth class, which includes those plants whose flowers have five stamina and but one style.

The SPECIES are,

1. HEDERA (Helix) foliis ovatis lobatisque. Flor. Lapp. 91. Ivy with oval lobed leaves. Hedera arborea. C. B. P. 305. Tree Ivy; and the Hedera communis major. J. B. 2. 111. Great common Ivy.

2. HEDERA (Quinquefolia) foliis quinatis, ovatis, serratis. Hort. Cliff. 74. Ivy with leaves composed of five lobes, which are sawed. Vitis quinquefolia Canadensis scandens. Tourn. Inst. 613. Climbing Canada Vine with five leaves, commonly called Virginia Creeper.

The first sort grows naturally in most parts of England, where it meets with any neighbouring support. The stalks will fasten to it, and rise to a very great height, sending out roots on every side, which get into the joints of walls, or the bark of trees, and thereby are supported; or if there is no support near, the stalks trail upon the ground, and take root all their length, so that they closely cover the surface, and are difficult to eradicate; for where any small parts of the stalks are left, they will soon spread and multiply. While these are fixed to any support, or trail upon the ground, their stalks are slender and flexible; but when they have reached to the top of their support, they shorten and become woody, forming themselves

into large bushy heads, and their leaves are larger, more of an oval shape, and not divided into lobes like the lower leaves, that it hath a different appearance, which has occasioned some to take them for distinct species.

In the latter part of the last century, when it was the fashion to fill gardens with all sorts of sheered Evergreens, there were many of these plants trained into round heads, which were clipped into balls, or in form of a cone; and as these were so hardy as not to be injured by weather, and would grow in any soil, so they were then much esteemed; but since that unnatural taste has been exploded, these plants are seldom admitted into gardens, unless to cover walls, or run over grottos, &c. for which purpose there is no plant so well adapted:

There are two varieties of this, one with silver-striped leaves, and the other with yellowish leaves on the top of the branches; these are preferred in some gardens for the sake of variety.

These plants are easily propagated by their trailing branches, which send forth roots their whole length; which branches being cut off, and planted, will grow in almost any soil or situation, and may be trained up to stems, or suffered to remain as climbers, to cover walls, pales, &c.

They may also be propagated by seeds, which should be sown soon after they are ripe, which is in the beginning of April: if these are kept moist and shaded, they will grow the same spring, otherwise they will remain a year in the ground; therefore few persons trouble themselves to propagate the plants in this way, the other being much more expeditious.

While the stalks of this plant trail, either on the ground or upon walls, or other support, they do not produce any flowers, which has occasioned its being called sterile, or barren Ivy; but when the branches get above their support, they produce flowers at the end of every shoot; these appear in September, and are succeeded by berries, which turn black before they are ripe, and are formed into round bunches, which are called corymbi, and from these the epithet of corymbus, so frequently used by botanists, is taken.

The leaves of this plant are frequently applied to issues to keep them cool, and free from inflammations; they are also used for curing of scabs, sores, and scald heads. Mr. Boyle, in his Usefulness of Experimental Philosophy, commends a large dose of the full ripe berries, as a remedy against the plague; but Schroder says, they purge upward and downward. The gum of Ivy is caustic, but is recommended by some to take spots and freckles out of the face.

There is mention made of another species of Ivy, which is titled Hedera Poetica, by Caspar Bauhin; this grows in many of the islands of the Archipelago, and produces yellow berries; but as I have not seen this plant, I cannot determine if it is a distinct species. Dr. Linnæus supposes it to be only a variety, though he has not seen the plant; but Tournefort, who gathered it in the Levant, puts it down as a different sort.

The second sort grows naturally in all the northern parts of America; it was first brought to Europe from Canada, and has been long cultivated in the English gardens, chiefly to plant against walls, or high buildings to cover them, which these plants will do in a short time, for they will shoot almost twenty feet high in one year, and will mount up to the top of the highest building; but as the leaves fall off in autumn, the plants make but an indifferent appearance in winter; and as it is late before they come out in the spring, they are not much esteemed, unless it is for such situations, where better things will not thrive; for this plant will thrive in the midst of London, and is not injured by smoke, or the closeness of the air, so are very proper for such situations. The stalks of these plants put out roots, which fasten themselves in-

into the joints of the walls, whereby they are supported.

This may be propagated by cuttings, which if planted in autumn on a shady border, will take root, and by the following autumn will be fit to plant where they are defigned to remain.

HEDERA TERRESTRIS. See GLECHOMA.

HEDGES. Hedges are either planted to make fences round inclofures, or to part off and divide the feveral parts of a garden: when they are defigned as outward fences, they are planted either with Hawthorn, Crabs, or Black Thorn, which is the Sloe; but thofe Hedges which are planted in gardens, either to furround wilderneffs quarters, or to fcreen the other parts of a garden from fight, are planted with various forts of plants, according to the fancy of the owner; fome preferring ever-green Hedges, in which cafe the Holly is beft, next the Yew, then Laurel, Lauruftinus, Phillyrea, &c. others, who make choice of the deciduous plants, prefer the Beach and Hornbeam, Englifh Elm, or the Alder, to any other; I fhall firft treat of thofe Hedges which are planted for outfide fences, and afterward briefly touch on the other.

Thefe Hedges are moft commonly made of Quick, yet it will be proper, before planting, to confider the nature of the land, and what forts of plants will thrive beft in that foil, whether it be clay, gravel, fand, &c. likewife what the foil is from whence the plants are to be taken; for if the land they are taken from is much better than that in which they are to be planted, it will be more difficult to get them to grow. As for the fize, the fets ought to be about the bignefs of a goofe quill, and cut within about four or five inches of the ground; they fhould be frefh taken up, ftrait, fmooth, and well rooted. Thofe plants which are raifed in the nurfery, are to be preferred to all others, and if raifed on a fpot near the place, it will be beft.

Secondly, If the Hedge has a ditch, it fhould be made fix feet wide at top, and one foot and a half at bottom, and three feet deep, that each fide may have a proper flope; for when the banks are made too upright, they are very fubjeft to fall down after every froft or hard rain; befides, if the ditches are made narrower, they are foon choked up in autumn by the falling leaves, and the growth of weeds, nor are they a fufficient fence to the Hedge againft cattle, where they are narrower.

Thirdly, If the bank be without a ditch, the fets fhould be fet in two rows, almoft perpendicular, at the diftance of a foot from each other, in the quincunx order, fo that in effeft they will be but fix inches afunder.

Fourthly, The turf is to be laid with the Grafs fide downwards, on that fide of the ditch the bank is defigned to be made, and fome of the beft mould fhould be laid upon it, to bed the Quick; then the Quick is to be planted upon it a foot afunder, fo that the ends of the Quick may ftand upright.

Fifthly, When the firft row of Quick is planted, it muft be covered with mould, and the turf laid upon it as before; fo that when the bank is a foot high, you may plant another row of fets againft the fpaces of the lower Quick, and cover them as the former was done; and the bank is to be topped with the bottom of the ditch, and a dry, or dead Hedge laid on the other fide, to defend the under plantation from the cattle.

In making of thefe dead Hedges, there fhould be ftakes driven into the loofe earth, at about two feet and a half diftance, fo low as to reach the firm ground.

Oak ftakes are accounted the beft, and Black Thorn and Sallow the next; then let the fmall bufhes be laid at bottom, but not too thick, for that will caufe the bufhes to rot; but the upper part of the Hedge fhould be laid with long bufhes to bind the ftakes in with, by interweaving them.

And, in order to render the Hedge yet ftronger, you may edder it (as it is called,) i. e. bind the top of the ftakes in with fome fmall long poles, or fticks on each fide; and when the eddering is finifhed, drive the ftakes anew, becaufe the waving of the Hedge and eddering is apt to loofen the ftakes.

The Quick muft be conftantly kept weeded, and fecured from being cropped by the cattle, and in February it will be proper to cut it within an inch of the ground, if it was not done before; which will caufe it to fhoot ftrong, and help it much in the growth.

When a Hedge is of about eight or nine years growth, it will be proper to plafh it; the beft time for this work is either in Oftober or February.

When a Hedge is grown old, i. e. of about twenty or thirty years growth, and there are in it old ftubs as well as new fhoots, the old ftubs fhould be cut floping off within two or three inches of the ground, and the beft and longeft of the middle fize fhould be left to fhoot up, and fome of the ftrongeft, at the height of five or fix feet, according as you defign the height of the Hedge to be, may be left to ferve inftead of ftakes, and frefh ftakes fhould be put in thofe places where they are wanting; the Hedge fhould be then thinned, fo as to leave on the ftubs only fuch fhoots as are defigned to be of ufe, that there may be room left to put a fpade in between them; the ditch alfo fhould be cleanfed, and each fide of the flopes kept as in a new ditch; and where the earth is wafhed from the roots of the Quick, or is hollow, face it anew with fo much of the firft fpit of earth that is dug out of the ditch, as there is occafion for, and lay what is dug out at the fecond fpit, on the top of the bank; for if it be laid on the fide, or face of the bank, it will flip into the ditch again when wet comes, and alfo take a great deal of the bank along with it.

In plafhing Quicks, there are two extremes to be avoided; the firft is, laying it too low and too thick; becaufe it makes the fap run all into the fhoots, and leaves the plafhes without nourifhment, which, with the thicknefs of the Hedge, kills them.

Secondly, It muft not be laid too high, becaufe this draws all the fap into the plafhes, and fo caufes but fmall fhoots at the bottom, and makes the Hedge fo thin, that it will neither hinder the cattle from going through, nor from cropping of it.

When the fhoot that is defigned to be plafhed is bent, give it a fmall cut with a bill, half through, floping a little downwards, and then weave it about the ftakes; and when the whole is finifhed, trim off the fmall fuperfluous branches that ftraggle too far out on both fides of the Hedge.

If the ftubs are very old, cut them quite down, and fecure them with good dead Hedges on both fides, till the young fhoots are got up tall enough to plafh, and plant new fets in the void fpaces.

In making a Hedge, if it be fet with Crab Stocks, it will be proper to leave one ftanding uncut up at every thirty or forty feet, if the ground on both fides of the Hedge be your own; which being done, they may be fo ordered, by pruning or ftaking, that one may lean into one ground, and the other into another, &c.

Thefe ftocks fhould be pruned up every year, till they are brought out of the reach of the cattle, and then they may be grafted with the Red Streak, Gennetmoil, or what other kind of cyder Apple you pleafe.

If the ftocks be of Apple kernels, they may ftand ungrafted, for many of them will yield very good cyder fruit; but then fuch ftocks as are not grafted, will be longer before they bear; and alfo when you do graft, you may be certain of your kind; but if you find a very natural ftock, which by leaf, fhoot, and bud, appears likely, you may try it, and fo you may have a new fine fruit; and if you do not like it, you may graft it when you pleafe.

As for the reft of the Hedge, when it has fhot four or five years, you may lay it to make a fence for the doing of which, take the following directions:

3   Firft,

First, At every laying to lay down some old plashes; or, if the Hedge be thin, young ones; but they must be so laid, as to point with their ends to the ditch side of the bank, the ends being kept low on the bank ; by being so ordered, they will the better thicken the bottom of the Hedge, and keep up the earth of the bank.

Secondly, To heighten the bank every time you lay earth on it, so as to cover the layers, and but the ends, this earth will very much help the Quick ; and by heightening the banks, and deepening the ditch, you will render the fence the better.

Thirdly, Not to cut the plashes too much, but just so as they may bend down well ; nor to lay them too upright, as some do, but to lay them near to a level ; for by so doing, the sap will the better break out at several places, and not run so much to the ends, as it will when they lie too much upon the slope.

If you have much wood to spare, you may cut up great part of those that grow near the ditch, but then you ought to hang the bank with bushes, to prevent cattle from cropping them the first year; these will shoot strong, secure the Hedge, keep up the bank, and thicken the bottom of the Hedge.

Fourthly, Take care to lay the Hedge pretty thick, and turn the beard on the ditch side ; but you must not let the beard hang uncut (though it makes a good shew at the first making), but you must cut off all the straggling boughs within half a foot of the Hedge on both sides, which will cause it to shoot strong at these places, and make the Hedge much the thicker.

Fifthly, If the bank be high, make the Hedge so low, that it may just serve for a fence the first year, for it will soon grow higher; and the lower the Hedge is made, the faster the Quick will grow, and also will be the thicker at the bottom ; but care must be taken to preserve it from cattle on the field side for the two first years that it is made.

Sixthly, If you would have a good Hedge, or fence, you should new lay it once in fourteen or fifteen years, and constantly root out Elder, Travellers Joy (which some call Bull-bine), Briony, &c. and do not leave too many high standards, or pollards in it, though the Elm is one of the best; also no dead wood is to be left in the bottom of the Hedges, for that will choke the Quick ; but if there be a gap, the dead Hedge should be made at a distance.

The Crab is also frequently planted for Hedges, and if the plants are raised from the kernels of the small wild Crab, they are much to be preferred to those which are raised from kernels of all sorts of Apples without distinction ; because the plants of the true small Crab never shoot so strong as those of the Apples, so may be better kept within the proper compass of a Hedge ; and as they have generally more thorns upon them, they are better guarded against cattle, &c. than the other ; besides, the plants of the Crab will grow more equal than those which are raised from the kernels of various kinds of Apples, for these always produce a variety of plants, which differ from each other in their manner of growth, as much as in the size and flavour of their fruits ; so that Hedges made of these will not appear so well, nor can be so well managed as the other.

Some persons intermix Crab with the White Thorn in their Hedges, but this is not a good method ; for the plants of the Crab will grow much stronger than those of the White Thorn, so that the Hedge will not be of equal growth ; which is not near so beautiful or useful, as when the plants of a Hedge keep pace in their growth.

The Black Thorn, or Sloe, is also frequently planted for Hedges, and is a strong durable plant for that purpose, especially as it is so strongly armed with thorns, that cattle seldom care to brouze upon it ; but where this is planted, the best way is to raise the plants from the stones of the fruit ; for all those which are taken from the roots of old trees, spawn, and put out suckers in such plenty from their roots, as to spread over, and fill the neighbouring ground to a consider-

able distance on each side of the Hedge ; and this plenty of suckers drawing away the nourishment from the old plants of the Hedge, they never grow so well as where there are few or no suckers produced, which those plants which are propagated from the stones send not forth, or at least but sparingly, therefore may with little trouble be kept clear of them. The best method of raising these Hedges is, to sow the stones in the place where the Hedge is intended (where it can be conveniently done), for then the plants will make a much greater progress than those which are transplanted ; but the objection to this method will arise from the difficulty of securing the young plants from the cattle ; but this can have little force, when it must be considered, that if the Hedge is planted, it must be fenced for some years, to prevent the cattle from destroying it ; therefore the same fence will do for it when sown, nor will this require a fence much longer than the other. For the plants which stand unremoved, will make a better fence in seven years, than that which is planted, though the plants should be of three or four years growth when planted ; which is what I have seen two or three times, where the experiment has been tried. The stones of this fruit should be sown early in January, if the weather will permit ; but when they are kept out of the ground longer, it will be proper to mix them with sand, and keep them in a cool place. The bushes of the Black Thorn are by much the best of any for making of dead Hedges, being of longer duration, and having many thorns, neither the cattle nor the Hedge-breakers, will care to meddle with them ; these bushes are also the best to be used for under ground drains, for the draining of land, for they will remain found a long time when the air is excluded from them.

The Holly is sometimes planted for Hedges, and is a very durable strong fence; but where it is exposed, there will be great difficulty to prevent its being destroyed, otherwise it is by far the most beautiful plant, and being an Evergreen, will afford much better shelter to cattle in winter, than any other sort of Hedge; and the leaves being armed with thorns, the cattle will not care to brouze upon it. Another objection to this plant is the slow growth, so that Hedges planted with this plant, require to be fenced a much longer time than most others. This is a reason which must be admitted, to prevent this being generally practised ; but in such grounds as lie contiguous to, or in sight of gentlemen's houses, these sorts of Hedges will have an exceeding good effect, especially when they are well kept, as they will appear beautiful at all seasons of the year ; and in the spring of the year, when the sharp winds render it unpleasant to walk abroad in exposed places, these Hedges will afford good shelter, as they will effectually keep off the cold winds, if they are kept close and thick. The surest method of raising these Hedges is, by sowing the berries in the place where they are to stand ; but these berries should be buried in the ground one year before they are sown, by which method they will be prepared to grow the following spring. The way of doing this is, to gather the berries about Christmas (which is the time they are usually ripe,) and put them into large flower-pots, mixing some sand with them ; then dig holes in the ground, into which the pots must be sunk, covering them over with earth about ten inches thick ; in this place they may remain till the following October, when they should be taken up, and sown in the place where the Hedge is intended. The ground for this Hedge should be well trenched, and cleared from the roots of all bad weeds, bushes, trees, &c. Then two drills should be made at about a foot distance from each other, and about two inches deep, into which the seeds should be scattered pretty close, left some should fail ; for it is better to have too many plants come up, than to want. The reason of my advising this is, that the Hedge may be thick to the bottom, which in a single row rarely happens, especially if there is not great care taken of them in the beginning. When the plants come up, they must be carefully weeded ; for if the

weeds

weeds are permitted to grow among them, they will soon deftroy them, or weaken them fo much, that they will not recover their ftrength in a long time. This fhould be conftantly obferved, by every perfon who is defirous to have good Hedges of either fort ; for when the weeds are fuffered to grow near the plants, they will not only rob them of a great part of their nourifhment, but alfo prevent their putting out fhoots near the ground, which will occafion the bottom of the Hedge to be thin and naked.

When thefe Holly Hedges are defigned to be kept very neat, they fhould be fheered twice a year, in May and Auguft ; but if they are only defigned as fences, they need not be fheered oftener than once a year, which fhould be about the latter end of June, or the beginning of July ; and if this is well performed, the Hedges may be kept very beautiful.

The fences which are made to fecure thefe Hedges from cattle while they are young, fhould be contrived fo as to admit as much free air as poffible, which is abfolutely neceffary for the growth of the plants ; for when they are crowded on each fide with dead Hedges, the plants feldom thrive well. The beft fort of fences for this purpofe, are thofe which are made with pofts and rails ; or inftead of rails, three ropes drawn from poft to poft, and holes made in the pofts to draw the ropes through ; this is the cheapeft fence of this kind, and will appear very handfome ; but if fheep are not admitted into the fields, there will be occafion for two ropes only, which will be enough to keep off larger cattle ; and if the ropes are painted over with a compofition of melted pitch, brown Spanifh colour, and oil, mixed well together, they will laft found feveral years ; and thefe fort of fences never obftruct the air, and the place, at the fame time being open to view, the weeds will be better difcovered than when the fences are clofe. In the latter cafe, the Hedges are fometimes fuffered to be over-run with weeds, by their being excluded from the fight, fo are frequently forgotten, efpecially in moift weather, when the weeds grow more luxuriant.

There are fome perfons who intermix Holly with the White Thorn in making their Hedges, which if rightly managed, will have a good effect, efpecially when young ; but when this is practifed, the Holly fhould be planted fo near, as that the Hedge may be entirely formed of it as it grows up, when the White Thorn fhould be quite rooted out ; for as thefe advance, they will not keep pace in their growth, fo will not appear beautiful when intermixed.

When a Hedge of Holly is intended to be made by plants, the ground fhould be well trenched, as was before advifed for the feeds ; and (unlefs the ground be very wet) the plants fhould be fet in October, but, in wet ground, March is preferable. The plants fhould not be taken from a better foil than that in which they are to be planted ; for when it fo happens, the plants are much longer before they recover this change, than thofe are which are taken from a leaner foil. If the plants have been before removed two or three times, they will have better roots, and will be in lefs danger of mifcarrying ; befides, they may be removed with balls of earth to their roots. When the froft comes on, if mulch be laid upon the ground near the roots of the plants, it will prevent the tender fibres, which may then have been put out, from being deftroyed by the cold. I would never advife the planting of Hedges with Holly plants, of above five or fix years growth from the berries ; for when the plants are older, if they take to grow, they are longer before they form a good Hedge, than plants which are much younger ; and if the plants have been twice before tranfplanted, they will more certainly grow.

I fhall next treat of Hedges for ornaments in gardens : thefe are fometimes planted with Evergreens, efpecially if they are not intended to grow very high ; in which cafe, they are planted with deciduous trees. Evergreen Hedges are planted with Holly, Yew,

Laurel, Lauruftinus, Phillyrea, Alaternus, evergreen Oak, and fome others of lefs note. The Holly is preferable to any other, for the reafons before given. Next to this, moft people prefer the Yew, on account of its growing very clofe ; for when thefe Hedges are well kept, they will be fo thick as that a bird cannot get through them ; but the dead colour of the Yew, renders thefe Hedges lefs agreeable. The Laurel is one of the moft beautiful greens of any of the evergreen trees, but then it fhoots fo luxuriant, as to render it difficult to keep the Hedges which are planted with it, in tolerable fhape ; befides, the leaves being very large, if the Hedge is clipped with fheers, the leaves will be cut through, which gives them a bad appearance ; therefore where there are Hedges of this kind, it will be the beft way to prune them with a knife, cutting the fhoots juft down to a leaf. And although by this method the Hedge cannot be rendered fo even as when cut with fheers, yet it will have a much better appearance than that of moft of the leaves being cut through and ftubbed, in the manner they muft be when fheered.

The Lauruftinus is alfo a very fine plant for this purpofe, but the fame objection is to be made to this as hath been to the Laurel ; and as one of the great beauties of this plant is in its flowers, which are produced in the winter and fpring, fo when thefe are fheered, the flowers are generally cut off, by which their beauty is loft. Nor can this be avoided, where the Hedge is to be kept in clofe order, therefore this plant is not fo proper for the purpofe ; but in fuch places where walls or other fences are defigned to be hid, there is not any plant better adapted than this, provided it is rightly managed ; for the branches of this plant are flender and pliable, fo may be trained up clofe to the fence, whereby it may be entirely covered ; and if, inftead of clipping thefe with fheers, they are pruned with a knife, they may be fo managed, as to have them full of flowers from the ground upward. This may be effected by pruning them in April, when the flowers are going off, cutting out thofe fhoots that have flowered, or project too far from the fence ; always cutting clofe to the leaf, that no ftubs may be left : but thofe new fhoots of the fame fpring muft by no means be fhortened, becaufe the flowers are always produced at the extremity of the fhoots of the fame year ; therefore when thefe are topped, as they muft be by fheering, there can be few or no flowers upon thefe plants, except toward the top, where the fheers have not paffed. By this method of knife pruning, the leaves will alfo be preferved entire, and the Hedge may always be kept enough within compafs ; and fo thick, as fully to anfwer the purpofe of covering the fence ; and by the fhoots growing a little irregular, it will make a much better appearance than any fhorn Hedge whatever.

The fmall leaved and the rough leaved Lauruftinus are the beft forts for this purpofe, becaufe their branches grow clofer together than thofe of the fhining leaved ; they are alfo more hardy, and flower much better than the other, when growing in the open air.

The True Phillyrea is the next beft plant for Hedges; it is by the gardeners called the True Phillyrea, to diftinguifh it from the Alaternus, which they fimply call the Phillyrea. The branches of this are ftrong, the leaves pretty large, and of a ftrong green colour. And as this is a plant of middling growth, the Hedges planted with this may be led up to the height of ten or twelve feet ; and if thefe Hedges are kept narrow at the top, that there may not be too much width for the fnow to lodge upon them, they may be rendered very clofe and thick, and being a very good green, will make a fine appearance.

The Alaternus was formerly much more cultivated in the Englifh gardens than at prefent. This was often planted to form Hedges, but the branches of this plant are too pliant for this purpofe, being frequently difplaced by ftrong winds, which render thefe Hedges unfightly ; they alfo fhoot very irregular and thin, fo that

that the middle of the Hedge is frequently open and wide, and only the sides of them can be kept tolerably close, and that muft be by often clipping them. If we add to this, their being frequently laid or broken down by fnow in the winter, it muft be deemed an improper plant for this purpofe.

The Ilex, or evergreen Oak, is alfo planted for Hedges, and where thefe are defigned to grow pretty tall, it is a fit plant for the purpofe ; becaufe it is a plant of large growth, efpecially the fort which is moft common in England ; for there are two forts of them which grow in the fouth of France and Italy, that are of much humbler growth, fo are better adopted to this purpofe, efpecially where the Hedge is not intended to be high, but thefe are not at prefent common here. When thefe Hedges are planted very young, and kept clofe trained from the beginning, they may be very clofe from the ground to the height of twenty feet or more ; but thefe muft always be kept narrower at the top than below, that there may not too much fnow lodge upon them in the winter, which is apt to break and difplace the branches, whereby the Hedges will be rendered unfightly.

There are alfo fome perfons who have planted the Pyracantha, or evergreen Thorn, Juniper, Box, Cedar of Virginia, Bay, &c. as alfo the Halimus, or Sea Purflane, and the Furz, Rofemary, and feveral other plants for Hedges ; but the five forts firft mentioned having very pliant branches, which will require to be fupported, and the three laft being often deftroyed by fevere froft, renders them unfit for this purpofe ; nor are there other forts of evergreen plants in the Englifh gardens, which are fo well adapted for Hedges, as thofe before-mentioned,

The deciduous trees, which are ufually planted to form Hedges in gardens, are the following forts.

The Hornbeam is much efteemed for this purpofe, efpecially in fuch places where they are not required to be very high, or not wanted to grow very faft ; for this plant, while young, doth not make fo great progrefs as many others ; but as it is of flower growth, the Hedges may be kept neat with lefs trouble than moft other plants will require ; and the branches naturally growing very clofe, they will make one of the clofeft Hedges of all the deciduous trees ; but as the leaves of this tree continue upon the branches all the winter, and until the buds in the fpring force them off, they have a bad appearance during the winter feafon.

The Beech is alfo a very proper tree for this purpofe, having the fame good qualities as the Hornbeam ; but the leaves of this continue late in winter upon the branches, when they will have a bad appearance ; befides, the litter which is occafioned by their leaves gradually falling moft part of the winter, prevents the garden from being made clean a great while longer than if there are none of thefe trees planted.

The fmall-leaved Englifh Elm, is alfo a proper tree for tall Hedges ; if thefe are planted young, and kept clofely clipped from their firft fetting out, the Hedges may be trained up to the height of thirty or forty feet, and be very clofe and thick the whole height. But when thefe trees are planted for this purpofe, they fhould not be crowded fo clofe together as they ufually are by moft people ; by which method, when the trees have ftood fome years, if they have thriven well, their ftems will approach fo near each other, as that few branches can be maintained below, whereby the bottom of the Hedge will be naked ; therefore they fhould not be planted clofer together than feven or eight feet, or if they are ten feet it will be ftill better. And although at this diftance they will not form a clofe Hedge fo foon as when the trees are planted clofer together, yet they will in a few years recompenfe for that, by their growing much clofer and better from the ground upward.

The Dutch Elm was formerly in great efteem for Hedges, being quick of growth, and thriving in fuch foils as the Englifh Elm would not grow ; but the wretched appearance which thefe Hedges made, after

they had been growing a few years, very juftly occafioned their being almoft univerfally rooted out of gardens, for a more abominable plant was never introduced into gardens than this.

The Lime-tree hath alfo been recommended for Hedges, and in fome of the old gardens there were many planted with this tree, which, for a few years after planting, made a tolerable appearance, efpecially when they grow upon a moift foil ; but after they had ftood fome years, they grew very thin at bottom, and by being fheered at the top, they were rendered very ftubby and unfightly, their leaves growing very thinly upon the branches, and thefe frequently turning of a black difagreeable colour, and falling off very foon in the autumn, and fometimes in the fummer in dry feafons, has brought thefe trees fo much into difrepute, as that few perfons make ufe of them at prefent for this purpofe : nor fhould any of the very ftrong fhooting trees be applied to this ufe ; for the more they are cut, the ftronger they will fhoot, and of courfe will appear very unfightly ; befides, the often cutting of thefe Hedges occafions great trouble and expence, and frequent litters in gardens.

The Alder is frequently planted for Hedges, and where the foil is moift, there is not any of the deciduous trees equal to it for this purpofe ; for the leaves are of a lively green, continuing frefh till late in the autumn ; and when they decay, their litter is foon over, for they all drop in a fhort time.

There are, befides the trees before-mentioned, many of the flowering fhrubs which have been planted to form Hedges ; fuch as Rofes, Honeyfuckles, Sweetbriar, &c. but thefe make a bad appearance, being more difficult to train ; and if they are cut to keep them within compafs, their flowers, which are their greateft beauty, will be entirely deftroyed. But as thefe are but of low growth, they are not proper to plant where the Hedges are to be of any height.

Although I have given thefe full directions for planting and ordering of thefe Hedges for the pleafure-garden, yet I am far from recommending them as ornamental or ufeful. But as there are numbers of perfons who may differ from me in their opinion, and therefore might think it a deficiency in my book, had I not given thefe inftructions ; to avoid their reproach, I have inferted as much as I think will be neceffary for the obtaining thefe Hedges wherever they are defired, and at a lefs expence than the late method of planting them hath been generally attended with ; where it is not uncommon to fee four times the number of trees planted in thefe Hedges as would have been neceffary, or that can remain long clofe together with any beauty. But moft people who plant, are in too great a hurry to have their garden filled ; and therefore frequently plant fo clofe, as that in three or four years (if their trees thrive) three-fourths of them will require to be taken away again, to make room for thofe which are left to grow ; and there are not wanting perfons, who are ready enough to encourage this practice, fince their own intereft is thereby promoted.

The tafte in gardening having been greatly altered of late years for the better, thefe clipped Hedges have been almoft excluded ; and it is to be hoped, that a little time will entirely banifh them out of the Englifh gardens, as it has already been done by the fhorn Evergreens, which, a few years fince, were efteemed the greateft beauties of gardens. The latter was introduced by the Dutch gardeners, and that of tall Hedges with treillage-work, was in imitation of the French gardens ; in fome of which, the expence of the iron treillage, to fupport the trees which compofe their cabinets, pavillions, bowers, porticoes, and other pieces of rural architecture, amounted to a very great fum. I have been informed in this work, in one garden, has coft above twenty thoufand crowns ; and this only to train up trees in the diftorted fhape of pilafters, niches, cornices, pediments, &c. when at the fame time, thefe can no longer retain the forms intended,

tended, than they are kept clofely fhorn into them; for no fooner do the trees begin to make frefh fhoots, but the whole frame is altered; and inftead of carrying the fine finifhed appearance of a regular piece of architecture, it is grown into a rude unpolifhed form. This expenfive fort of work never has made much progrefs in England, but that part of the French tafte, in furrounding all the feveral divifions of gardens with tall clipped Hedges, making great alleys, forming the walks into ftars, and the like ftiff performances, have too much obtained for fome years paft in England: and the taller thefe clipped Hedges were, the more they were admired; though many times they fhut out from the view the fight of fome of the nobleft Oaks, and other timber trees, growing in the quarters, which are infinitely more pleafing to a perfon of true tafte, than all the ridiculous forms it is poffible for trees to be framed in by art. Befides, when the expence of keeping thefe Hedges, together with the great litter they occafion when clipped, is confidered, thefe, added to many other reafons which might be given, are fufficient to exclude them out of gardens; where they can never be efteemed neceffary, but to fhut out from the view the fight of worfe objects.

HEDYPNOIS. See Hyoseris.

HEDYSARUM. Lin. Gen. Plant. 793. Tourn. Inft. R. H. 401. tab. 225. French *Honeyfuckle*.

The Characters are,

The flower hath a permanent empalement of one leaf, cut into five fegments at the top. It is of the butterfly kind, having an oblong compreffed ftandard, which is indented at the point and reflexed; the wings are oblong and narrow; the keel is compreffed, broader at the end, but convex at the bafe. It hath nine ftamina joined, and one ftanding feparate, which are terminated by roundifh compreffed fummits; the ftamina are reflexed, having an angle or knee. In the center is fituated a long narrow germen, fupporting an awl-fhaped inflexed ftyle, crowned by a fingle ftigma. The germen afterward becomes a jointed pod which is compreffed, each joint being roundifh, and inclofes a fingle kidney-fhaped feed.

This genus of plants is ranged in the third fection of Linnæus's feventeenth clafs, intitled Diadelphia Decandria, which includes thofe plants whofe flowers have ten ftamina joined in two bodies.

The Species are,

1. Hedysarum (*Coronarium*) foliis pinnatis, leguminibus articulatis aculeatis, nudis, rectis, caule diffufo. Hort. Cliff. 365. *French Honeyfuckle with winged leaves, naked, prickly, jointed pods, and a diffufed ftalk.* Hedyfarum clypeatum, flore fuaviter rubente. H. Eyft. *French Honeyfuckle, with a delicate red flower.*

2. Hedysarum (*Spinofiffimum*) foliis pinnatis, leguminibus articulatis, aculeatis tomentofis, caule diffufo. Hort. Upfal. 231. *French Honeyfuckle with winged leaves, jointed, prickly, woolly pods, and a diffufed ftalk.* Hedyfarum clypeatum minus, flore purpureo. Raii Hift. *Smaller French Honeyfuckle with a purple flower.*

3. Hedysarum (*Canadenfe*) foliis fimplicibus ternatifque, floribus racemofis. Hort. Cliff. 232. *French Honeyfuckle with fingle and trifoliate leaves, and flowers in bunches.* Hedyfarum triphyllum Canadenfe. Cornut. *Three-leaved French Honeyfuckle of Canada.*

4. Hedysarum (*flexuofum*) foliis pinnatis, leguminibus articulatis, aculeatis, flexuofis, caule diffufo. Lin. Sp. Plant. 750. *French Honeyfuckle with winged leaves, jointed prickly pods which are waved, and a diffufed ftalk.* Hedyfarum annuum, filiquâ afperâ undulatâ intortâ. Tourn. *Annual French Honeyfuckle, with a rough, waved, writhed pod.*

5. Hedysarum (*Diphyllum*) foliis binatis petiolatis, floralibus feffilibus. Flor. Zeyl. 291. *French Honeyfuckle with two leaves upon a foot-ftalk, fitting clofe to the ftalks.* Hedyfarum minus diphyllum, flore luteo. Sloan. Cat. 73. *Smaller two-leaved French Honeyfuckle, with a yellow flower.*

6. Hedysarum (*Purpureum*) foliis ternatis, foliolis obovatis floribus paniculatis terminalibus, leguminibus intortis. *French Honeyfuckle with trifoliate oval leaves, flowers growing in panicles at the ends of the ftalks, and*

intorted pods. Hedyfarum triphyllum fruticofum, flore purpureo, filiquâ varie diftortâ. Sloan. Cat. 73. *Three-leaved fhrubby French Honeyfuckle, with a purple flower and a varioufly diftorted pod.*

7. Hedysarum (*Canefcens*) foliis ternatis fubtus nervofis, caule glabro fruticofo floribus fpicatis terminalibus. *Three-leaved fhrubby dwarf Honeyfuckle, with veins on the under fide, a fmooth fhrubby ftalk, with flowers growing in fpikes at the ends.* Hedyfarum triphyllum fruticofum fupinum, flore purpureo. Sloan. Cat. *Three-leaved fhrubby dwarf French Honeyfuckle, with a purple flower.*

8. Hedysarum (*Sericeum*) foliis ternatis, foliolis ovatis fubtus fericeis, floribus fpicatis alaribus terminalibufque. *Three-leaved French Honeyfuckle, with oval leaves fitting on their under fide, and flowers in fpikes from the fide and the end of the ftalks.* Hedyfarum triphyllum frutefcens, foliis fubrotundis & fubtus fericeis, flore purpureo. Houft. *Three-leaved fhrubby French Honeyfuckle with roundifh leaves, which are filky underneath, and a purple flower.*

9. Hedysarum (*Villofum*) foliis ternatis, caulibus diffufis villofis, floribus fpicatis terminalibus, calycibus, villofiffimis. *Three-leaved French Honeyfuckle, with diffufed ftalks which are hairy, flowers growing in fpikes at the ends of the branches, and very hairy empalements.* Hedyfarum triphyllum humile, flore conglomerato calyce villofo. Houft. *Dwarf three-leaved French Honeyfuckle, with flowers growing in clufters, and a hairy cup.*

10. Hedysarum (*Procumbens*) foliis ternatis caulibus procumbentibus racemofis, floribus laxè fpicatis terminalibus, leguminibus contortis articulis quadrangularibus. *Three-leaved French Honeyfuckle, with branching trailing ftalks, flowers growing in loofe fpikes at the ends of the branches, and twifted pods with fquare joints.* Hedyfarum triphyllum procumbens, foliis rotundioribus & minoribus, filiquis tenuibus & intortis. Houft. *Trailing three-leaved French Honeyfuckle, with fmaller and rounder leaves, and narrow contorted pods.*

11. Hedysarum (*Intortum*) foliis ternatis, foliolis obcordatis, caule erecto triangulo villofo, racemis terminalibus, leguminibus articulatis incurvis. *French Honeyfuckle, with trifoliate leaves whofe lobes are heart-fhaped, a triangular upright hairy ftalk, flowers growing in long bunches at the ends of the branches, and and jointed incurved pods.* Hedyfarum triphyllum, caule triangulari, foliis mucronatis, filiquis tenuibus intortis. Houft. *Three-leaved French Honeyfuckle, with a triangular ftalk, pointed leaves, and a narrow contorted pod.*

12. Hedysarum (*Glabrum*) foliis ternatis obcordatis, caule paniculato, leguminibus monofpermis glabris. *French Honeyfuckle with trifoliate heart-fhaped leaves, a paniculated ftalk, and fmooth pods containing one feed.* Hedyfarum triphyllum, annuum, erectum, filiquis intortis, & ad extremitatem amplioribus. Houft. *Three-leaved, annual, upright French Honeyfuckle, with contorted pods, which are broad at their extremity.*

13. Hedysarum (*Scandens*) foliis ternatis, foliolis obversè-ovatis, caule volubili, fpicâ longiffimâ reflexâ. *Three-leaved French Honeyfuckle, with obverfe oval lobes, a twining ftalk, and a very long reflexed fpike of flowers.* Hedyfarum triphyllum Americanum fcandens, flore purpureo. *Three-leaved, climbing, American French Honeyfuckle, with a purple flower.*

14. Hedysarum (*Repens*) foliis ternatis obcordatis, caulibus procumbentibus racemis lateralibus. Lin. Sp. 1056. *Three-leaved French Honeyfuckle, with oval heart-fhaped leaves, trailing hairy ftalks, and flowers on the fide of the ftalks.* Hedyfarum procumbens, trifolii fragiferi folio. Hort. Elth. 172. *Trailing French Honeyfuckle, with leaves like the Strawberry Trefoil.*

15. Hedysarum (*Maculatum*) foliis fimplicibus ovatis obtufis. Hort. Cliff. 449. *French Honeyfuckle, with oval, obtufe, fingle leaves.* Hedyfarum humile, capparidis folio maculato. Hort. Elth. 170. *Low French Honeyfuckle, with a fpotted Caper leaf.*

16. Hedysarum (*Frutefcens*) foliis ternatis ovato-lanceolatis, fubtus villofis, caule frutefcente villofo.

3   *Trifoliate*

Trifoliate French Honeyſuckle, with oval ſpear-ſhaped leaves, hairy on their under ſide, and a ſhrubby hairy ſtalk. Quere, Whether this be not the Hedyſarum foliis ternatis ſub-ovatis ſubtus villoſis caule frutef-cente. Flor. Virg. 174. *Three-leaved French Honey-ſuckle, with oval leaves and a ſhrubby ſtalk.*

17. HEDYSARUM (*Pedunculatum*) foliis ternatis, foliolo intermedio pediculo longiore, racemis alaribus erectis longiſſimis. *French Honeyſuckle with trifoliate leaves, the middle lobe ſtanding on a longer foot-ſtalk, and very long bunches of flowers coming from the ſides of the ſtalks.*

18. HEDYSARUM (*Albagi*) foliis ſimplicibus lanceo-latis obtuſis, caule fruticoſo ſpinoſo. Lin. Sp. Plant. 745. *French Honeyſuckle with ſingle, ſpear-ſhaped, ob-tuſe leaves, and a prickly ſhrubby ſtalk.* Alhagi Mau-rorum. Rauwolf. 94. *The Albagi of the Moors.*

19. HEDYSARUM (*Triquetrum*) foliis ſimplicibus cordato-oblongis integerrimis glabris. *French Honeyſuckle with ſingle, oblong, heart-ſhaped leaves, which are ſmooth and entire.* Onobrychis Zeylanica aurantii folio. Pet. Hort. Scic. 247. *Cockſhead of Ceylon with an Orange-leaf.*

20. HEDYSARUM (*Echaſtaphyllum*) foliis ſimplicibus ova-tis ſubtus ſericeis, petiolis muticis. Amœn. Acad. 5. p. 403. *French Honeyſuckle with oval ſingle leaves, ſilky on their under ſide, and a ſpiked foot-ſtalk.* Spar-tium ſcandens, citri foliis, floribus albis ad nodos con-fertim naſcentibus. Plum. Sp. 19.

21. HEDYSARUM (*Gangeticum*) foliis ſimplicibus ova-tis acuminatis, ſpicis longiſſimis nudis terminalibus. *French Honeyſuckle with oval-pointed ſingle leaves, and very long naked ſpikes of flowers terminating the ſtalks.* An Hedyſarum foliis ſimplicibus ovatis acutis baſi ſtipulatis. Lin. Sp. 1052.

The firſt ſort has been long cultivated in the Engliſh gardens for ornament. This grows naturally in Italy ; there are two varieties of this, one with a bright red, and the other a white flower, which very rarely vary from one to the other ; but as there is no other dif-ference but in the colour of their flowers, ſo they are ſuppoſed to be the ſame ſpecies.

It is a biennial plant, which flowers the ſecond year, and ſoon after the ſeeds are ripe, the roots ge-nerally periſh : this ſends up ſeveral hollow ſmooth ſtalks two or three foot long, which branch out on each ſide, garniſhed with winged leaves, compoſed of five ˙or ſix pair of oval lobes, terminated by an odd one ; the leaves are placed alternate, and from their baſe comes out foot-ſtalks which are five or ſix inches long, ſuſtaining ſpikes of beautiful red flowers ; theſe are ſucceeded by compreſſed jointed pods, which are very rough, ſtanding erect ; in each of the joints is lodged one kidney-ſhaped ſeed. This ſort flowers in June and July, and the ſeeds ripen in September. The white is only a variety of this, and as ſuch, is ſometimes preſerved in gardens.

They are propagated by ſowing their ſeeds in April, in a bed of light freſh earth ; and when the plants come up, they ſhould be tranſplanted into other beds of the like earth, and in an open ſituation, at about ſix or eight inches diſtance from each other, leaving a path between every four rows, to go between them to hoe, and clear them from weeds. In theſe beds they may remain until Michaelmas, then may be tranſplanted into the large borders of a parterre or pleaſure-garden, allowing them at leaſt three feet diſtance from other plants, amongſt which they ſhould be interſperſed, to continue the ſucceſſion of flowers ; where they will make a fine appearance when blown, eſpecially the red ſort, which produces very beautiful flowers.

As theſe plants decay after they have perfected their ſeeds, ſo there ſhould annually be a freſh ſupply of plants raiſed, where they are deſired, for the old roots ſeldom continue longer. They are very proper or-naments for large borders, or to fill up vacancies among ſhrubs, but they grow too large for ſmall bor-ders, unleſs their ſtalks are pruned off, leaving only two or three on each plant ; which, if kept upright

with ſticks, will prevent their hainging over other flowers. They are propagated for ſupplying the markets with plants to adorn the London gardens and balconies, by the gardeners in the neighbour-hood of London.

The ſecond ſort is an annual plant, which grows na-turally in Spain and Portugal ; the leaves of this are narrow and oblong, four or five pair being placed along the midrib, with an odd one at the end ; the ſtalks are terminated by ſmall ſpikes of purple flowers, which are ſucceeded by ſmall rough pods, ſhaped like thoſe of the former ſort. This plant is preſerved in botanic gardens for the ſake of variety ; it is propa-gated by ſeeds, which ſhould be ſown the beginning of April, in the place where the plants are to remain, and will require no other culture but to thin them where they are too near, and keep them clean from weeds. This flowers in July, and the ſeeds ripen in autumn.

The third ſort hath a perennial root, which will abide many years if planted in a dry ſoil. This is propagated by ſowing the ſeeds in the manner directed for the former ; but when the plants are come up two inches high, they ſhould be tranſplanted where they are to remain for good ; but if they are not too thick in the ſeed-bed, they may be ſuffered to remain there until the following autumn ; at which time they ſhould be carefully taken up, and tranſplanted into the borders where they are deſigned to ſtand ; for their roots generally run down very deep, ſo that it is not ſafe to remove them often. This plant produces its flowers about the ſame time of the year as the for-mer, and if the ſeaſon proves favourable, perfects its ſeeds in autumn ; and the roots will abide in the open air very well, reſiſting the ſevereſt cold, pro-vided they are planted in a dry ſoil.

The fourth ſort is an annual plant, which grows na-turally in the Levant. This hath ſome reſemblance of the firſt, but is much ſmaller ; the ſtalks ariſe near a foot high, and are garniſhed with winged leaves, compoſed of two or three pair of oval lobes, terminated by an odd one ; the flowers come out in ſpikes at the top of the ſtalks, which are of a pale red intermixed, with a little blue. Theſe appear in July, and are ſucceeded by jointed pods which are waved on both ſides, forming an obtuſe angle at each joint ; the ſeeds ripen in the autumn. This is propagated in the ſame way as the ſecond ſort, and is equally hardy.

The fifth ſort grows naturally in both Indies ; the ſeeds of this were ſent me from La Vera Cruz, by the late Dr. Houſtoun. This is an annual plant, with a long tap root which runs deep in the ground, ſend-ing out one or two ſtalks, which riſe about nine inches high, the lower part being garniſhed with oval leaves by pairs on each foot-ſtalks; but the upper part of the ſtalk where the flowers come out, is garniſhed with ſmall leaves, ending in acute points, ſitting cloſe to the ſtalks, and at each of theſe is ſituated a ſingle, ſmall, yellow flower, incloſed by the two leaves. Theſe make but little appearance, and are ſucceeded by oblong pods, containing one kidney-ſhaped ſeed. The ſixth ſort was ſent me by the the late Dr. Houſ-toun from La Vera Cruz, where he found it growing naturally, as it alſo does in Jamaica. This is an annual plant, which riſes with a ſhrubby ſtalk upward of four feet high, dividing into ſeveral branches, which are garniſhed with oblong oval leaves that are trifo-liate, ſtanding upon pretty long foot-ſtalks, the mid-dle lobe ſtanding an inch beyond the other two ; the branches are terminated by long looſe panicles of purple flowers, which are ſucceeded by narrow jointed pods which are twiſted. Theſe plants flower in July, and their ſeeds ripen in autumn.

The two laſt mentioned are tender plants, ſo their ſeeds muſt be ſown in the ſpring upon a hot-bed ; and when the plants-are fit to remove, they ſhould be each planted in a ſeparate ſmall pot, filled with light earth, and plunged into a hot-bed, keeping them ſhaded from the ſun till they have taken new root ;
then

then they muſt be treated in the ſame way as other tender plants from hot countries, always keeping them in the ſtove or glaſs-caſe, otherwiſe they will not flower or produce ſeeds in England.

The ſeventh ſort grows naturally in Jamaica, from whence the ſeeds were ſent me by the late Dr. Houſtoun. This is a ſhrubby plant, which riſes about five feet high, and divides into ſeveral branches, which are garniſhed with trifoliate leaves which are oval, the middle lobe being much larger than the other two; the ſtalks are terminated by long ſpikes of ſmall purple flowers, which are ſucceeded by narrow pods, ſtrait on one ſide, but jointed on the other.

The eighth ſort was ſent me from La Vera Cruz by the late Dr. Houſtoun, who found it growing there naturally. This riſes with a ſhrubby ſtalk ſix or ſeven feet high, dividing into ſeveral branches, which are garniſhed with trifoliate oval leaves, ſilky and white on their under ſide, but of a pale green on their upper ſide; the flowers come out in long narrow ſpikes from the wings, and at the end of the branches, ſitting cloſe to the ſtalks; they are ſmall, of a bright purple colour, and are ſucceeded by flat, ſmooth, jointed pods, about one inch long, each joint having one kidney-ſhaped ſeed.

The two laſt ſorts will continue two or three years, if the plants are placed in the bark-ſtove. They are propagated by ſeeds, which muſt be ſown upon a hot-bed, and the plants treated in the ſame manner as thoſe juſt before-mentioned; and when they have obtained height, they ſhould be removed into the bark-ſtove, where they ſhould conſtantly remain, allowing them a large ſhare of air in warm weather. Theſe plants ſeldom flower till the ſecond year, when they will produce ſeeds which ripen in the autumn.

The ninth ſort is an annual plant, which grows naturally at La Vera Cruz, from whence it was ſent me by the late Dr. Houſtoun. This ſeldom riſes more than eight or nine inches high, ſending out ſeveral branches from the root, which are diffuſed and hairy; they are cloſely garniſhed with ſmall, oval, trifoliate leaves, a little hoary. The flowers grow in cloſe ſhort ſpikes; they are purple, and have very hairy empalements.

The tenth ſort grows naturally in Jamaica. This hath ligneous trailing ſtalks a foot and a half long, ſending out ſeveral branches on each ſide, which are garniſhed with ſmall, round, trifoliate leaves, of a pale green colour; the flowers are produced in very looſe ſpikes at the ends of the branches; they are ſmall, and of a pale purpliſh colour, ſucceeded by narrow twiſted pods which are jointed, each joint being four cornered, containing a ſingle, ſmall, compreſſed ſeed.

The two laſt ſorts being annual, require the ſame treatment as the fifth and ſixth ſorts before-mentioned, with which management they will flower and ripen their ſeeds in this country.

The eleventh ſort is a ſhrubby plant, which riſes with triangular ſtalks five or ſix feet high, dividing into ſeveral branches, garniſhed with heart-ſhaped trifoliate leaves, ending in acute points; the flowers are produced in very long ſpikes at the end of the branches, which are of a pale purple colour, and are ſucceeded by narrow jointed pods which are variouſly twiſted; the ſeeds are ſmall and compreſſed.

This plant grows naturally in Jamaica, from whence the ſeeds were ſent me by the late Dr. Houſtoun. It will continue three or four years, if the plants are treated in the ſame manner directed for the ſeventh and eighth ſorts, and will perfect ſeeds in this country.

The twelfth ſort is annual, the ſeeds of it were ſent me by the late Dr. Houſtoun from Campeachy. This hath a paniculated ſtalk, which riſes about two feet high, garniſhed with heart-ſhaped trifoliate leaves; the upper part of the ſtalk branches out into panicles of flowers, which are of a pale purple colour; theſe are ſucceeded by lunulated compreſſed pods, which ſtand oblique to the ſtalk, each containing one com-

preſſed kidney-ſhaped ſeed. This ſort is propagated by ſeeds, and requires the ſame treatment as the fifth and ſixth ſorts.

The thirteenth ſort was ſent me from La Vera Cruz, by the late Dr. Houſtoun. This hath a twining ſtalk, which gets round the trees and ſhrubs which grow near it, and climbs to the height of ten or twelve feet, garniſhed with obverſe, oval, trifoliate leaves, ſtanding upon pretty long foot-ſtalks; the flowers are produced in very long ſpikes, which are reflexed; they are of a dark purple colour, and ſit cloſe to the ſtalk. This is an abiding plant, which requires a ſtove to preſerve it in this country, ſo the plants ſhould be treated in the ſame manner as the ſeventh and eighth ſorts.

The fourteenth ſort is an annual plant, which grows naturally in both Indies. The ſeeds of this were ſent me from the Havannah by the late Dr. Houſtoun; it hath trailing branches near a foot long, which are garniſhed with round trifoliate leaves, a little indented at the top, very like in ſhape to thoſe of the Strawberry Trefoil; the ſtalks and under ſide of the leaves are hairy; the flowers are produced toward the end of the branches, ſometimes ſingle, and at other times two at a joint; they are of a purple colour and ſmall; theſe are ſucceeded by pods about an inch long, which are ſtrait on one ſide, and jointed on the other. This flowers the end of July, and ſometimes perfects ſeeds here.

The fifteenth ſort is a low annual plant, having ſlender ſtalks near a foot long, their lower part being garniſhed with ſingle oval leaves, ſtanding upon ſlender foot-ſtalks; their upper part is adorned with flowers, which come out by pairs above each other, to the end of the ſtalk; they are but ſmall, and of a reddiſh yellow colour; theſe are ſucceeded by jointed narrow pods, which ſit cloſe to the ſtalk, and are ſickle-ſhaped. The two laſt mentioned are annual plants, which require the ſame culture as the fifth and ſixth ſorts.

The ſixteenth ſort was ſent me by the late Dr. Dale, from South Carolina: This hath a perennial root, from which ariſe two or three ſhrubby hairy ſtalks near two feet high, branching out on every ſide near the top, garniſhed with oval, ſpear-ſhaped, trifoliate leaves, which are hairy on their under ſide, and ſtand upon ſhort foot-ſtalks; the flowers are produced at the end of the branches in ſhort ſpikes; they are of a purpliſh yellow colour, and ſmall; the ſtalks of this ſort decay every autumn, and new ones ariſe in the ſpring. It is propagated by ſeeds, which ſhould be ſown upon a hot-bed in the ſpring, and when the plants are fit to remove, they ſhould be planted in ſeparate ſmall pots filled with light earth, and plunged into a moderate hot-bed, obſerving to ſhade them until they have taken new root; then they ſhould have a large ſhare of air admitted to them in warm weather, and in ſummer they may be expoſed to the open air, but in the autumn they muſt be placed under a frame to ſcreen them from froſt; the following ſpring ſome of theſe plants muſt be ſhaken out of the pots and planted in a warm border, where, if the ſummer proves warm, they will flower, but theſe ſeldom perfect their ſeeds; therefore two or three plants ſhould be put into larger pots, and plunged into a moderate hot-bed, which will bring them early into flower; ſo that if the glaſſes are kept over them in bad weather, theſe will ripen their ſeeds in autumn, and the roots will continue ſome years, if they are ſcreened from froſt in winter.

The ſeventeenth ſort was ſent me with the laſt, by the ſame gentleman, from South Carolina. This hath a perennial root and an annual ſtalk, which grows erect about two feet high, garniſhed with long trifoliate leaves, which are rounded at their baſe where they are broadeſt, and narrowed all the way to a point; they are near three inches and a half long, and half an inch broad at their baſe, of a light green colour, and ſmooth; the two ſide lobes ſit pretty cloſe to the ſtalk, but the _middle_

middle one fits upon a foot-ftalk an inch long ; the flowers are produced in long fpikes from the wings of the ftalk, growing erect, the lower part of the fpike is but thinly fet with flowers, but on the upper part they are difpofed very clofe ; thefe are fmall, and of a bright yellow colour, fitting very clofe to the ftalks, and are fucceeded by jointed pods ftrait on one fide. This plant is propagated by feeds, and requires the fame treatment as the laft mentioned, with which it will flower and produce ripe feeds.

The eighteenth fort grows naturally in Syria, where it is one of the beauties of the country. It rifes with fhrubby ftalks about three feet high, which branch out on every fide, and are garnifhed with fingle leaves, fhaped like thofe of the broad-leaved Knot-grafs; they are very fmooth, of a pale green colour, and ftand on fhort foot-ftalks ; under thefe leaves come out thorns, which are near an inch long, of a reddifh brown co- lour ; the flowers come out from the fide of the branches in fmall clufters ; they are of a purple colour in the middle, and reddifh about the rims ; thefe are fucceeded by pods; which are ftrait-on one fide, and jointed on the other, bending a little in fhape of a fickle. This plant is at prefent pretty rare in the Englifh gardens ; it is propagated by feeds, which will frequently lie a year in the ground before they vege- tate, therefore fhould be fown in pots filled with light earth, and plunged into a moderate hot-bed; and if the plants do not appear by the beginning of June, the pots fhould be taken out of the bed, and placed where they may have only the morning fun, keeping them clean from weeds; and in the autumn, they fhould be plunged into an old bed of tanners bark un- der a frame, where they may be fcreened from the froft and hard rains in the winter, and in fpring plunged into a frefh hot-bed, which will bring up the plants : when thefe are fit to remove, they fhould be each planted into a feparate fmall pot, filled with light earth, and plunged into a very moderate hot-bed, fhading them from the fun till they have taken new root ; then they fhould be gradually hardened to bear the open air, in- to which they fhould be removed in June, placing them in a fheltered fituation, where they may remain till the autumn ; when, if they are plunged into an old tan-bed under a frame, where, in mild weather they may enjoy the free air, and be protected from froft, they will fucceed better than if placed in a green- houfe, or more tenderly treated. I have feen this plant growing in the full ground, in a very warm border, where, by covering it in frofty weather, it had endured two winters, but a fevere froft happening the third winter entirely killed it.

From this fhrub the Perfian Manna is collected, which is an exfudation of the nutritious juice of the plant. This drug is chiefly gathered about Tauris, a town in Perfia, where the fhrub grows plentifully. Sir George Wheeler found it growing in Tinos, and fuppofed it was an undefcribed plant. Tournefort found it in plenty in many of the plains in Armenia and Georgia, and made a particular genus of it under the title of Alhagi.

The nineteenth fort grows naturally in India, from whence the feeds have been lately brought to Europe, and feveral plants have been raifed in the Englifh gar- dens ; thefe have leaves fo like thofe of the Orange- tree, as fcarcely to be diftinguifhed while young ; but as there are not any plants here of a large fize, fo I can give no further account of this fort at prefent.

The twentieth fort was fent me from Carthagena in New Spain, by the late Dr. Houftoun : this is a peren- nial plant with a twining ftalk, which twifts round any neighbouring fupport, rifing to the height of ten or twelve feet, fending out a few fmall branches from the fide, garnifhed with oval leaves four or five inches long, and an inch and a half broad in the middle ; the under fide of the leaves are like fattin ; the flowers are white, coming out from the fide of the ftalk in clofe bunches ; they are of the fame form with the other fpecies of this genus, and are fucceeded by fhort pods, containing one or two kidney-fhaped feeds.

The feeds of the twenty-firft fort I received from the

Eaft-Indies ; this is an annual plant, which rifes about three feet high, having a flender ftalk inclining to be fhrubby, garnifhed with oval leaves placed fingle on very fhort foot-ftalks; fome of the plants fend out one or two flender branches from the main ftalk, the lower part of which are garnifhed with leaves of the fame form with thofe on the principal ftalk, but are fmaller : the upper part of the principal ftalk and the branches are garnifhed with flowers near a foot in length, which are of a worn-out purple colour, ftanding fingle at each joint : thefe are fucceeded by jointed pods an inch and a half long, containing three or four kidney-fhaped feeds in each.

Thefe two forts are too tender to thrive in the open air in England ; they are both propagated by feeds, which muft be fown on a hot-bed early in the fpring ; and when the plants are come up, and fit to remove, they fhould be parted, and each planted in a fe- parate fmall pot, plunging them into a frefh hot-bed, where they fhould be fcreened from the fun till they have taken new root ; after which, they fhould be treated in the fame manner as other tender plants. The twenty-firft fort muft be placed in the bark-ftove in autumn, but the other will ripen feeds the fame year the beginning of October.

HEDYSARUM Zeylanicum majus & minus. See Æfchynomene.

HEDYSARUM mimofæ foliis. See Æfchyno- mene.

HELENIUM. Lin. Gen. Plant. 863. Heleniaf- trum. Vaill. Act. R. Par. 1720. Baftard Sun-flower.

The Characters are,

It hath a flower compofed of feveral hermaphrodite florets, which form the difk, and female half florets which com- pofe the rays. The hermaphrodite florets are tubulous, and cut into five parts at the brim ; thefe have each five fhort hairy ftamina, terminated by cylindrical fummits, with an oblong germen fupporting a flender ftyle, crowned by a bifid ftigma. The germen afterward becomes an an- gular fingle feed, crowned by a fmall five-pointed empale- ment. The female florets in the border have fhort tubes, and are ftretched out on one fide like a tongue to form the ray ; thefe are cut into five fegments at their points, where they are broad. The female flowers have no ftamina, but have an oblong germen, which turns to a fingle feed like thofe of the hermaphrodite flowers ; thefe are all in- cluded in one common fingle empalement, which fpreads open, and is cut into feveral fegments.

This genus of plants is ranged in the fecond fection of Linnæus's nineteenth clafs, which includes thofe plants which have compound flowers, the hermaphrodite florets in the center, and the female half florets in the border, being both fruitful.

The Species are,

1. Helenium (*Autumnale*) foliis lanceolatis-linearibus integerrimis glabris, pedunculis nudis unifloris. He- lenium with fpear-fhaped narrow leaves, which are fmooth, entire, and naked foot-ftalks with fingle flowers. Heleniaftrum folio longiore & anguftiore. Vaill. Act. R. Par. 1720. Baftard Sun-flower with a longer and narrower leaf.

2. Helenium (*Latifolium*) foliis lanceolatis acutis fer- ratis, pedunculis brevioribus, calycibus multifidis. Helenium with pointed, fpear-fhaped, fawed leaves, fhorter foot-ftalks, and a many-pointed empalement. Heleniaf- trum folio breviore & latiore. Vaill. Act. R. S. 1720. Baftard Sun-flower with a broader and fhorter leaf.

Thefe plants rife to the height of fix or feven feet in good ground ; the roots, when large, fend up a great number of ftalks, which branch toward the top ; thofe of the firft fort are garnifhed with fmooth leaves, which are three inches and a half long, and half an inch broad in the middle, with entire edges fitting clofe to the ftalks, and from their bafe is extended a leafy border along the ftalk, fo as to form what was generally termed a winged ftalk, but Linnæus calls it a running leaf ; the upper part of the ftalk divides, and from each divifion arifes a naked foot-ftalk about three inches long, fuftaining one yellow flower at the top, fhaped like a Sun-flower, but much fmaller, having long rays, which are jagged pretty

deep into four or five fegments ; thefe appear in Auguft, and there is a fucceffion of flowers on the plants
till the froft puts a ftop to them.

The fecond fort hath the appearance of the firft, but
the leaves are not three inches long, and are more
than an inch broad in the middle, ending in acute
points, and are fharply fawed on their edges. The
flowers ftand upoh fhorter foot-ftalks, growing clofer
together, but the ftalks of this do not branch near fo
much as thofe of the other ; they both flower at the
fame feafon.

There is alfo another fort with leaves as narrow as the
firft, which are acutely indented on the edges. The
ftalks branch at the top fomewhat like thofe of the
firft, but the middle flowers have much fhorter foot-
ftalks than thofe which branch on the fide, and
are garnifhed with fmall leaves, almoft to the top ;
but I am not certain if this is a diftinct fpecies,
or only a variety which has accidentally rifen from
the feeds of the other.

Thefe plants are both of them natives of America ;
the feeds of both forts I have received from Virginia
and New England, where they grow wild in great
plenty in the woods, and other fhady places where
the ground is moift. They may be propagated by
feeds, or by parting their roots ; but the latter is generally practifed in this country, becaufe they feldom
perfect their feeds here ; but if the feeds are procured
from abroad, they fhould be fown the beginning of
March on a border of light earth ; and if the feeds
fhould not come up the firft year, the ground fhould
not be difturbed, becaufe they often remain a whole
year in the ground before the plants come up ; in which
cafe there is nothing more to be done, but to keep
the ground clear from weeds, and wait until the plants
rife. When they appear, if the feafon proves
dry, they muft be often watered, which will greatly
forward their growth ; and where the plants come up
too clofe to each other, they fhould be thinned, and
tranfplanted out into beds a foot afunder every way,
being careful to fhade them until they have taken
root, as alfo to water them in dry weather. In autumn they may be tranfplanted where they are to
remain, and the following fummer they will produce their flowers, which will continue till the froft
prevents them; and their roots will abide many years,
and afford many offsets, by which they may be increafed.

The beft feafon to tranfplant the old roots, and to
part them for increafe, is in the end of October, when
their flowers are paft, or the beginning of March, juft
before they begin to fhoot ; but if the fpring fhould
prove dry, they muft be duly watered, otherwife they
will not produce many flowers the fame year ; thefe
plants fhould not be removed oftener than every other
year, if they are expected to flower ftrong; they delight in a foil rather moift than dry, provided it be
not too ftrong, or holds the wet in winter ; but if
they are planted in a dry foil, they muft be often and
plentifully watered in dry weather, to make them
produce plenty of flowers.

HELENIUM, Elecampane. See INULA.

HELIANTHEMUM. Tourn. Inft. R. H. 248.
tab. 128. Ciftus. Lin. Gen. Plant. 598. Dwarf Ciftus,
or Sun-flower.

The CHARACTERS are,
The flower has a three-leaved empalement, which is permanent, which afterward covers the feed-veffel. It hath
five roundifh petals which fpread open, with a great
number of erect ftamina, which are terminated by fmall
roundifh fummits. In the center is fituated an oval germen, fupporting a fingle ftyle the length of the ftamina,
crowned by an obtufe ftigma. The germen afterward
becomes a roundifh, or oval capfule, with three cells,
opening in three parts, filled with fmall roundifh feeds.
This genus of plants is joined by Dr. Linnæus to
that of Ciftus, and is ranged in the firft fection of his
thirteenth clafs, which includes thofe plants whofe
flowers have many ftamina and one ftyle. As the
empalement of the flower has but three leaves, and

thofe of Ciftus five, and the capfule of the Helianthemum has but three cells, and that of Ciftus five,
fo thefe characters are fufficient to admit of their being feparated into different genera ; and as there are
a great number of fpecies of both forts, fo by this
feparation they may be better afcertained.

The SPECIES are,
1. HELIANTHEMUM (Chamæciftus) caulibus procumbentibus fuffruticofis, foliis oblongis fubpilofis, ftipulis
lanceolatis. Dwarf Ciftus with trailing fhrubby ftalks,
oblong hairy leaves, and fpear-fhaped ftipule. Helianthemum vulgare flore luteo. J. B. 2. 15. Common
Dwarf Ciftus with a yellow flower.
2. HELIANTHEMUM (Germanicum) caulibus procumbentibus fuffruticofis, ramofiffimis, fpicis florum longioribus. Dwarf Ciftus with trailing fhrubby ftalks
full of branches, and longer fpikes to the flowers. Helianthemum album Germanicum. Tab. Icon. 1062.
White German Dwarf Ciftus.
3. HELIANTHEMUM (Pilofus) caulibus fuffruticofis pilofis foliis lanceolatis obtufis, fpicis reflexis. Dwarf
Ciftus with hairy fhrubby ftalks, blunt fpear-fhaped leaves,
and reflexed fpikes of flowers. Helianthemum foliis
majoribus, flore albo. J. B. 2. 16. Dwarf Ciftus with
larger leaves and a white flower.
4. HELIANTHEMUM (Apenninum) incanum, caulibus
fuffruticofis erectis, foliis lanceolatis hirfutis. Hoary
Dwarf Ciftus with erect fhrubby ftalks, and hairy fpear-
fhaped leaves. Helianthemum faxatile, foliis & caulibus incanis, floribus albis, Appenini montis.
Mentz. Pug. tab. 8. Rock Dwarf Ciftus of the Apennines, with hoary ftalks and leaves, and white flowers.
5. HELIANTHEMUM (Umbellatum) caule procumbente
non ramofo, foliis linearibus incanis oppofitis. Dwarf
Ciftus with an unbranched trailing ftalk, and narrow
hoary leaves placed oppofite. Helianthemum folio thymi incano. J. B. 2. 19. Dwarf Ciftus with a hairy
Thyme leaf.
6. HELIANTHEMUM (Fumana) caule fuffruticofo procumbente, foliis linearibus alternis, floribus auriculatis. Dwarf Ciftus with a fhrubby trailing ftalk, very
narrow leaves placed alternate, and auriculated flowers.
Helianthemum tenuifolium glabrum luteo flore, per
humum fparfum. J. B. 2. 18. Smooth narrow-leaved
Dwarf Ciftus, with a yellow flower and trailing ftalks.
7. HELIANTHEMUM (Sampfuchifolium) caule fuffruticofo
procumbente, foliis lanceolatis oppofitis, pedunculis
longioribus, calycibus hirfutis. Dwarf Ciftus with a
fhrubby trailing ftalk, fpear-fhaped leaves placed oppofite,
longer foot-ftalks to the flowers, and hairy empalements.
Helianthemum five Ciftus humilis, folio fampfuchi,
capitulis valde hirfutis. J. B. 2. 20. Dwarf Ciftus
with a Marjoram leaf, and very hairy heads.
8. HELIANTHEMUM (Serpillifolium) caule fuffruticofo
procumbente, foliis linearibus oppofitis, floribus umbellatis. Dwarf Ciftus with a fhrubby trailing ftalk,
very narrow leaves placed oppofite, and flowers growing
in an umbel. Helianthemum folio thymi floribus umbellatis. Tourn. Inft. 250. Dwarf Ciftus with a Thyme
leaf and umbellated flowers.
9. HELIANTHEMUM (Ciftifolium) caulibus procumbentibus fuffruticofis glabris, foliis ovato lanceolatis oppofitis, pedunculis longioribus. Dwarf Ciftus with
fhrubby trailing ftalks which are fmooth, oval fpear-
fhaped leaves placed oppofite, and longer foot-ftalks to the
flowers. Helianthemum Germanicum luteum Cifti
folio. Boerh. Yellow German Dwarf Ciftus with a Rock
Rofe leaf.
10. HELIANTHEMUM (Tuberaria) caule lignofo perenne,
foliis radicalibus ovatis trinerviis tomentofis caulinis
glabris lanceolatis alternis. Perennial Dwarf Ciftus
with a woody ftalk, whofe lower leaves are oval, woolly,
with three veins, thofe on the ftalks fmooth, fpear-fhaped,
and placed alternate. Helianthemum plantaginis folio
perenne. Tourn. Inft. 250. Perennial Dwarf Ciftus
with a Plantain leaf.
11. HELIANTHEMUM (Polifolium) caulibus feffilibus fuffruticofis, foliis lanceolatis oppofitis tomentofis caule
florali racemofo. Dwarf Ciftus with very fhort fhrubby
ftalks, woolly fpear-fhaped leaves placed oppofite, and a
branching

branching flower-ftalk. Helianthemum foliis polii montani. Tourn. Inſt. 249. *Dwarf Ciſtus with leaves like Poley Mountain.*

12. HELIANTHEMUM (*Nummularium*) caule ſuffruticoſo procumbente, foliis ovatis nervoſis, ſubtus incanis. *Dwarf Ciſtus with a ſhrubby trailing ſtalk, and oval veined leaves, white on their under ſide.* Helianthemum ad nummulariam accedens. J. B. 2. 20. *Dwarf Ciſtus reſembling Moneywort.*

13. HELIANTHEMUM (*Lavendulæfolium*) caule ſuffruticoſo, foliis lineari-lanceolatis oppoſitis ſubtus tomentoſis. *Dwarf Ciſtus with a ſhrubby ſtalk, and narrow ſpear-ſhaped leaves placed oppoſite, which are woolly on their under ſide.* Helianthemum lavendulæ folio. Tourn. Inſt. 249. *Dwarf Ciſtus with a Lavender leaf.*

14. HELIANTHEMUM (*Hirtum*) caule ſuffruticoſo erecto, foliis linearibus margines revolutis ſubtus incanis. *Dwarf Ciſtus with a ſhrubby erect ſtalk, and narrow leaves reflexed on their edges, with their under ſide hoary.* Helianthemum foliis Roriſmarini ſplendentibus, ſubtus incanis. Tourn. Inſt. 250. *Dwarf Ciſtus with ſhining Roſemary leaves, which are hoary on their under ſide.*

15. HELIANTHEMUM (*Surrejanum*) caulibus ſuffruticoſis procumbentibus, foliis oblongo-ovatis ſubhirſutis, petalis acuminatis reflexis. *Dwarf Ciſtus with trailing ſhrubby ſtalks, oblong oval hairy leaves, and acute-pointed reflexed petals to the flowers.* Helianthemum vulgare petalis florum peranguſtis. Hort. Elth. 177. tab. 145. *Common Dwarf Ciſtus with narrow petals to the flowers.*

16. HELIANTHEMUM (*Luſitanicum*) caule ſuffruticoſo erecto, foliis lanceolatis incanis glabris caule florali ramoſo. *Dwarf Ciſtus with a ſhrubby upright ſtalk, hoary ſpear-ſhaped leaves, which are ſmooth, and branching flower-ſtalks.* Helianthemum Luſitanicum, mari folio incano, flore luteo. Tourn. Inſt. 250. *Portugal Dwarf Ciſtus with a hoary Marum leaf, and a yellow flower.*

17. HELIANTHEMUM (*Roſeum*) caule ſuffruticoſo, foliis oblongo-ovatis oppoſitis, ſummis linearibus alternis. *Dwarf Ciſtus with a ſhrubby ſtalk, oblong oval leaves placed oppoſite, thoſe toward the top being narrow and alternate.* Helianthemum ampliore folio, flore roſeo. Sherard. Act. Phil. N°. 383. *Dwarf Ciſtus with a larger leaf, and Roſe-coloured flower.*

18. HELIANTHEMUM (*Guttatum*) caule herbaceo hirſuto, foliis lanceolato-linearibus piloſis, pedunculis longioribus. *Dwarf Ciſtus with an herbaceous ſtalk which is hairy, narrow ſpear-ſhaped hairy leaves, and longer foot-ſtalks to the flowers.* Helianthemum flore maculoſo. Col. Cephr. 2. p. 78. *Dwarf Ciſtus with a ſpotted flower.*

19. HELIANTHEMUM (*Fugacium*) caule herbaceo, foliis ſubovatis piloſis, flore fugaci. *Dwarf Ciſtus with an herbaceous ſtalk, hairy oval leaves, and a fugacious flower.* Helianthemum annuum humile, foliis ſubovatis, flore fugaci. Allion. *Annual Dwarf Ciſtus with oval leaves, and a fugacious flower.*

20. HELIANTHEMUM (*Ledifolium*) caule herbaceo erecto, foliis lanceolatis oppoſitis, floribus ſolitariis, capſulis maximis. *Dwarf Ciſtus with an erect herbaceous ſtalk, ſpear-ſhaped leaves placed oppoſite, flowers growing ſingly, and very large capſules.* Helianthemum Ledi folio. Tourn. Inſt. 249. *Dwarf Ciſtus with a Ledon leaf.*

21. HELIANTHEMUM (*Salicifolium*) caule herbaceo ramoſo, foliis oblongo-ovatis oppoſitis, ſummis alternis, floribus ſolitariis. *Dwarf Ciſtus with a branching herbaceous ſtalk, oblong oval leaves placed oppoſite, thoſe toward the top growing alternate, and ſolitary flowers.* Helianthemum ſalicis folio. Tourn. Inſt. 249. *Dwarf Ciſtus with a Willow leaf.*

22. HELIANTHEMUM (*Faſciculatum*) foliis faſciculatis. Royen. *Dwarf Ciſtus with leaves growing in bunches.*

23. HELIANTHEMUM (*Ægyptiacum*) herbaceum erectum, foliis lineari-lanceolatis petiolatis, calycibus inflatis corolla majoribus. *Dwarf Ciſtus with erect herbaceous ſtalks, linear ſpear-ſhaped leaves, and ſwelling empalements larger than the petals.*

24. HELIANTHEMUM (*Mariſolium*) caule herbaceo procumbente, foliis ovatis tomentoſis ſeſſilibus. *Dwarf Ciſtus with an herbaceous trailing ſtalk, and oval woolly leaves ſitting cloſe to the branches.* Helianthemum Alpinum, folio piloſellæ minoris Fuchſii. J. B. 2. 18. *Hoary Dwarf Ciſtus of the Alps, with leſſer Cat's-foot leaves.*

The firſt ſort grows naturally on the chalky hills and banks in many parts of England; the ſtalks of this plant are ligneous and ſlender, trailing upon the ground, extending themſelves near a foot each way; theſe are garniſhed with ſmall oblong leaves, of a dark green on their upper ſide, but of a grayiſh colour on their under. The flowers are produced at the end of the ſtalks in looſe ſpikes; they are compoſed of five deep yellow petals, which ſpread open in the day, but ſhut cloſe in the evening; theſe appear in June and July, and are ſucceeded by roundiſh capſules, incloſing many angular ſeeds, which ripen in Auguſt and September, and the roots laſt ſeveral years.

The ſecond ſort grows naturally in Germany; the ſtalks of this are much larger, and extend farther than thoſe of the firſt; the leaves are longer, and are hoary; there are three accuminated ſtipula at each of the lower joints, which are erect. The ſpikes of flowers are much longer than thoſe of the former, and the flowers are white and larger. The empalement of the flowers are hairy and whitiſh; theſe differences are laſting from ſeeds.

The third ſort grows naturally in the ſouth of France, in Italy, and Germany. The ſtalks of this grow more erect than either of the former, and are more ligneous. The joints are farther aſunder; the leaves are longer and hairy; the ſpikes of flowers are generally reflexed; they are white, and the ſize of thoſe of the ſecond; the ſtipula of this are very narrow.

The fourth ſort grows naturally on the Apennine mountains; the ſtalks of this are more erect than thoſe of the third. The leaves are not ſo long, the ſtipula are very ſmall, and the whole plant is very hoary. The flowers are white, and the ſpikes are ſhorter and more compact than either of the former.

The fifth ſort grows naturally in the ſouth of France, in Spain, and Iſtria, from the laſt country I have received the ſeeds; this hath low trailing ſtalks, which are ligneous, but ſeldom branch, and are not more than four or five inches long. The leaves are narrow and hoary, and have no ſtipula at their baſe. The flowers are white, and are in ſmall cluſters at the end of the ſtalks; this ſort ſeldom continues longer than two years.

The ſixth ſort hath trailing ſhrubby ſtalks, which extend a foot in length, and are garniſhed with very narrow ſmooth leaves placed alternate; but thoſe ſhort ſtalks near the root, which do not flower, have ſhorter and finer leaves growing in cluſters; theſe have no ſtipula at their baſe. The flowers are placed thinly toward the end of the branches, they are yellow and auriculated; this ſort grows in the ſouth of France and Italy.

The ſeventh ſort hath very long, trailing, ligneous ſtalks, which are garniſhed with ſpear-ſhaped leaves placed oppoſite, which are very hairy, and gray on their under ſide, having at their baſe three long narrow ſtipula. The ſpikes of flowers are near a foot in length, but grow thinly; they are large, and of a deep yellow colour, with very hairy empalements; this grows naturally in the ſouth of France and Spain.

The eighth ſort hath very ſhrubby crooked ſtalks, covered with a purpliſh brown bark like the common heath. The branches are ſlender, and garniſhed with narrow ſtiff leaves like thoſe of Thyme, which ſtand oppoſite, having no ſtipula at their baſe. The flowers are produced on naked foot-ſtalks, which terminate the branches in a ſort of umbel; they are of a pale yellow colour, and a little ſmaller than thoſe of the common ſort; this grows naturally on the ſands near Fontainbleau, in France.

The

The ninth fort grows naturally in Germany, from whence the feeds were fent to the late Dr. Boerhaave, in whofe curious garden near Leyden I gathered the feeds; this fends out from a ligneous root a great number of trailing ftalks, which are fmooth, and extend more than a foot each way, garnifhed with oval, fpear-fhaped, fmooth leaves, placed oppofite, having at their bafe three fpear-fhaped ftipula. The flowers are large, yellow, and grow in fhort clufters at the end of the branches; this always continues the fame from feeds.

The tenth fort grows naturally in Spain, from whence I received it; this hath a fhort, thick, woody ftalk, from which come out feveral fhort fide-branches, which are garnifhed with oval woolly leaves, having three longitudinal veins. The flower-ftalk which arifes from the main ftem grows about nine inches high, having two or three narrow leaves placed alternate. The flowers are produced in pretty long pedicles toward the top of the ftalk, and have very fmooth empalements.

The eleventh fort was fent me from Verona, where it grows naturally; this hath a low fhrubby ftalk, from which come out a few fhort branches, garnifhed with fmall woolly fpear-fhaped leaves, placed oppofite. The flower-ftalk rifes about fix inches high, and branches toward the top, where the flowers are produced on pretty long foot-ftalks; they are white, and fmaller than thofe of the common fort.

The twelfth fort hath long fhrubby ftalks which trail on the ground, and divide into many branches, which are garnifhed with oval veined leaves of a light green on theirupper fide,but of a grayifh colour below, with three narrow erect ftipula at their bafe. The flowers are pretty large, white, and grow in clufters at the end of the branches.

The thirteenth fort hath fhrubby ftalks which grow pretty upright, garnifhed with narrow fpear-fhaped leaves, placed oppofite, woolly on their under fide, with three very narrow ftipula growing at their bafe. The flowers are white, growing in long fpikes at the end of the branches; this grows naturally in the fouth of France.

The fourteenth fort hath an erect fhrubby ftalk, which fends out many fide branches, whofe joints are pretty clofe, and are garnifhed with very narrow leaves, placed oppofite, whofe borders are reflexed; their upper fide is of a lucid green, and their under fide hoary. The flowers are pretty large, white, and grow in fmall clufters at the end of the branches; this grows naturally in Spain, from whence the roots were fent me.

The fifteenth fort was found by Mr. Edmund Du Bois, near Croydon, in Surry, and was at firft fuppofed to be only an accidental variety of the common fort, but the feeds of this always produce the fame. I have cultivated this above thirty years, and never have found it vary from feeds; this is very like the common fort, but the leaves are hairy. The petals of the flowers are ftar-pointed, and fmaller than thofe of the common fort.

The fixteenth fort hath upright fhrubby ftalks, which rife a foot and a half high, fending out branches the whole length; thefe are garnifhed with fmall fpear-fhaped filvery leaves, placed oppofite, which are fmooth. The flower-ftalks branch, and the flowers, which are white, are produced in fhort fpikes at the end of the branches.

The feventeenth fort was found growing naturally by the late Dr. William Sherrard, near Smyrna, who fent the feeds to England; this hath fhrubby ftalks which do not trail on the ground, garnifhed with oblong oval leaves placed oppofite, but thofe toward the top are narrow and placed alternate. The flowers are produced at the end of the branches in long loofe fpikes; they are of a Rofe colour, and the fize of thofe of the common fort.

The eighteenth fort is annual; this grows naturally in France, Spain, Italy, and in Jerfey, where the late Dr. William Sherrard found it, and fent the feeds to

England; this hath a branching herbaceous ftalk, which rifes four or five inches high, garnifhed with narrow fpear-fhaped leaves, placed oppofite, which are covered with hairs; thofe on the upper part of the ftalks are placed alternate, and are narrower. The flowers are produced in loofe fpikes at the end of the branches, ftanding upon long foot-ftalks; they are fmall, and compofed of five yellow petals, with a dark purple fpot at the bafe of each; thefe flowers are very fugacious, for they open early in the morning, and their petals drop off in a few hours after, fo that by ten of the clock the flowers are all fallen.

The nineteenth fort grows naturally upon Mount Baldus, from whence the feeds were fent me; this is an annual plant, which fends out many herbaceous ftalks from the root, garnifhed with oval leaves, which are hairy. The flowers are produced in loofe fpikes at the end of the branches; they are of a pale yellow colour, and very fugacious, feldom lafting two hours before the petals fall off: there is another variety of this which grows about Verona, with upright ftalks.

The twentieth fort grows naturally in the fouth of France and Italy, and was found by the late Dr. William Sherrard, growing near Smyrna, who fent the feeds to England and Holland by a new title, fuppofing it to be a different plant; but when it was cultivated here, it proved to be the fame with that growing in the fouth of France; for this plant puts on different appearances, according to the foil and fituation where it grows; for, in a good foil, where the plants ftand fingle, and are not injured by weeds, they will rife near a foot and a half high, the leaves will be two inches and a half long, and near half an inch broad in the middle; but in a poor foil, or where the plants ftand too clofe, or are injured by weeds or neighbouring plants, they do not rife more than half that height. The leaves are much narrower, and the feed-veffels not half fo large; fo that any perfon finding thefe plants in two different fituations may be deceived, and take them for different fpecies; but when they are cultivated in a garden in the fame foil and fituation, they do not differ in any particular. This is an annual plant, which perifhes foon after the feeds are ripe.

The twenty-firft fort is an annual plant, which grows naturally in Spain and Portugal; this hath branching ftalks, which rife a foot high, garnifhed with oval oblong leaves placed oppofite on the lower part of the ftalk; but on the upper part they are alternate and narrow, a fingle leaf being placed between each flower, which occafions the title of Solitary Flowers, for they grow in loofe fpikes at the end of the branches, in the fame manner as the other fpecies.

The twenty-fecond fort was fent me by Dr. Adrian Van Royen, who received the feeds from the Cape of Good Hope. This rifes with a fhrubby ftalk about nine inches high, garnifhed with very narrow fine leaves, growing in clufters; the flowers come out from the fide and at the end of the branches, ftanding upon flender foot-ftalks; they are of a pale Straw colour, and very fugacious, feldom continuing longer than two hours before the petals fall off. This feldom continues longer than two years.

The twenty-third fort grows naturally in Egypt; this is an annual plant having fhrubby erect ftalks, garnifhed with narrow fpear-fhaped leaves, ftanding on foot-ftalks; the upper part of the ftalks are adorned with white flowers, whofe petals are not fo large as the empalement, and being very fugacious they make but little appearance: it flowers in July, and the feeds ripen in September, foon after which the plants decay.

The twenty-fourth fort grows naturally about Kendal in Weftmorland, and in fome parts of Lancafhire, upon rocky fituations. This hath trailing herbaceous ftalks, which feldom extend more than three or four inches, garnifhed with oval leaves, which are very woolly, and fit clofe to the branches; the flowers are produced at the upper part of the branches; they are white and fmall, fo make no great appearance.

All

Moſt of the perennial ſorts of Dwarf Ciſtus are hardy, ſo will thrive in the open air in England; they are propagated by ſeeds, which may be ſown in places where the plants are to remain, and will require no other care but to keep them clean from weeds, and thin them where they are too cloſe, always obſerving to leave thoſe ſorts at a farther diſtance, whoſe ſtalks trail on the ground, and grow to the greateſt length. Theſe plants will continue ſeveral years, eſpecially in a poor dry ſoil; but in rich ground or moiſt ſituations, they ſeldom laſt long: but as they ripen ſeeds in plenty, ſo they may be eaſily repaired. They all flower about the ſame time as the common ſort, and their ſeeds ripen in the autumn.

The annual ſorts may be propagated with as great facility; for if their ſeeds are ſown upon a bed of common earth in April, the plants will come up in May, and require no other culture, but to thin them where they are too cloſe, and keep them clear from weeds. Theſe will flower in July, and the ſeeds ripen in the autumn. The twenty-ſecond ſort will thrive in the full ground in the ſame manner as the other; but unleſs the ſummer proves favourable, the ſeeds will not ripen: the roots have ſtood through the winter when the ſeaſon has proved mild, without any ſhelter, and have flowered the following ſummer.

The twenty-fourth ſort requires a ſhady ſituation, otherwiſe it will not thrive here.

HELIANTHUS. Lin. Gen. Plant. 877. Corona ſolis. Tourn. Inſt. R. H. 489. tab. 279. [of 'Ηλιۈ, the ſun, and 'Ανθۈ, a flower,] i. e. Sun-flower; in French, *Soliel.*

This genus of plants was titled Corona ſolis, by moſt of the botanic writers; but this being a compound name, Dr. Linnæus has altered it to this of Helianthus: it has alſo by ſome been titled Heliotropium, which name is now applied to another genus of plants, very different from this.

The CHARACTERS are,

It hath a compound radiated flower, the border or rays being compoſed of female half-florets, which are barren, and the diſk of hermaphrodite florets, which are fruitful: theſe are contained in one common ſcaly empalement, whoſe ſcales are broad at their baſe, pointed at their ends, and expand. The hermaphrodite florets are cylindrical, ſwelling at their baſe, cut at the brim into five acute ſegments, which ſpread open; theſe have five ſtamina which are curved at bottom, as long as the tube, and terminated by tubulous ſummits. The germen, which is ſituated at the bottom of the tube, ſupports a ſlender ſtyle the length of the tube, crowned by a reflexed ſtigma, divided in two parts; the germen afterward becomes an oblong, blunt, four-cornered ſeed. The female half florets, which compoſe the border, are ſtretched out on one ſide like a tongue, which is long and entire; theſe have a germen in the bottom, but no ſtyle or ſtamina, and are not fruitful.

This genus of plants is ranged in the third ſection of Linnæus's nineteenth claſs, in which he includes thoſe plants whoſe flowers are compoſed of hermaphrodite fruitful flowers in the center, and female barren flowers in the circumference.

The SPECIES are,

1. HELIANTHUS (*Annuus*) foliis omnibus cordatis trinervatis, floribus cernuis. Lin. Sp. 1276. *Sun-flower, whoſe leaves are all heart-ſhaped, with three veins and a nodding flower.* Corona ſolis. Tabern. Icon. 763. and the Helenium Indicum maximum. C. B. P. 276. *Greateſt Indian Sun-flower, commonly called annual Sun-flower.*

2. HELIANTHUS (*Multifloris*) foliis inferioribus cordatis trinervatis, ſuperioribus ovatis. Lin. Sp. Plant. 1277. *Sun-flower whoſe under leaves are heart-ſhaped, with three veins, and the upper leaves oval.* Corona ſolis minor fœmina. Tabern. Icon. 764. *Leſſer female Sun-flower, commonly called perennial Sun-flower.*

3. HELIANTHUS (*Tuberoſus*) foliis ovato-cordatis triplinerviis. Lin. Sp. Plant. 1277. *Sun-flower with oval heart-ſhaped leaves with three nerves.* Corona ſolis parvo flore tuberoſâ radice. Tourn. Inſt. 489. Sun-

flower *with a ſmall flower and a tuberous root, commonly called Jeruſalem Artichoke*; in French, *Taupinambours.*

4. HELIANTHUS. (*Strumoſis*) radice fuſſi formi. Hort. Cliff. 420. *Sun-flower with a ſpindle-ſhaped root.* Corona ſolis latifolia altiſſima. Tourn. Inſt. 489. *Talleſt broad-leaved Sun-flower.*

5. HELIANTHUS (*Giganteus*) foliis alternis lanceolatis ſcabris, baſi ciliatis, caule ſtricto ſcabro. Lin. Sp. Plant. 1278. *Sun-flower with ſpear-ſhaped leaves, and a ſlender rough ſtalk.* Chryſanthemum Virginianum altiſſimum anguſtifolium puniceis caulibus. Mor. Hiſt. 3. p. 24. *Talleſt Virginia Chryſanthemum, with a narrow leaf and purple ſtalks.*

6. HELIANTHUS (*Divaricatus*) foliis oppoſitis ſeſſilibus ovato oblongis trinerviis, paniculâ dichotomâ. Lin. Sp. Plant. 1279. *Sun-flower with oblong, oppoſite, oval leaves, having three veins ſitting cloſe to the ſtalk, and a forked panicle.* Chryſanthemum, Virginianum repens, foliis aſperis binatim ſeſſilibus acuminatis. Mor. Hiſt. 3. p. 24. *Creeping Virginia Chryſanthemum, with rough-pointed leaves, ſitting cloſe by pairs.*

7. HELIANTHUS (*Tracheliſolius*) foliis lanceolatis oppoſitis, ſupernè ſcabris, infernè trinerviis, caule dichotomo ramoſo. *Sun-flower with ſpear-ſhaped leaves placed oppoſite, whoſe upper ſurface is rough, the under having three veins and a divided ſtalk.* Corona ſolis trachelii folio, radice repente. Tourn. Inſt. 490. *Sun-flower with a Throatwort leaf, and a creeping root.*

8. HELIANTHUS (*Ramoſiſſimus*) caule ramoſiſſimo, foliis lanceolatis ſcabris, inferioribus oppoſitis, ſummis alternis petiolatis, calycibus folioſis. *Sun-flower with a very branching ſtalk, rough ſpear-ſhaped leaves placed oppoſite at bottom, but alternate toward the top, having foot-ſtalks, and leafy empalements.* Corona ſolis trachelii folio tenuiore, calyce floris ſolinato. Act. Phil. N° 412. *Sun-flower with a narrow Throatwort leaf, and a leafy flower-cup.*

9. HELIANTHUS (*Atrorubens*) foliis ovatis crenatis trinerviis ſcabris, ſquamis calycinis erectis longitudine diſci Flor. Virg. 103. *Sun-flower with oval, rough, crenated leaves, having three nerves, the ſcales of the empalement being erect, and as long as the diſk of the flower.* Corona ſolis Caroliniana, parvis floribus, folio trinervi amplo aſpero, pediculo alato. Martyn. Cent. 1. 20. *Carolina Sun-flower with ſmall flowers, large rough leaves having three veins, and a winged foot-ſtalk.*

10. HELIANTHUS (*Decapetalus*) caule infernè lævi, foliis lanceolato-cordatis, radiis decapetalis. Lin. Sp. Plant. 905. *Sun-flower with a ſmooth ſtalk, heart ſpear-ſhaped leaves, ſmooth on their upper ſide, and ten petals in the rays.* All theſe ſpecies of Sun-flowers are natives of America, from whence we are often ſupplied with new kinds, and it is very remarkable, that there is not a ſingle ſpecies of this genus that is European; ſo that before America was diſcovered, we were wholly unacquainted with theſe plants. But although they are not originally of our own growth, yet they are become ſo familiar to our climate, as to thrive and increaſe full as well as if they were in their native country, (ſome of the very late flowering kinds excepted, which require a longer ſummer than we generally enjoy, to bring them to perfection;) and many of them are now ſo plentiful in England, that perſons unacquainted with the hiſtory of theſe plants, would imagine them at leaſt to have been inhabitants of this iſland many hundred years; particularly the Jeruſalem Artichoke, which, though it doth not produce ſeeds in our climate, yet doth ſo multiply by its knobbed roots, that, when once well fixed in a garden, it is not eaſily to be rooted out.

The firſt ſort is annual, and ſo well known as to require no deſcription. There are ſingle and double flowers of two different colours, one of a deep yellow, and the other of a ſulphur colour; but theſe vary, ſo are not worthy to be mentioned as different. They are eaſily propagated by ſeeds, which ſhould be ſown in March, upon a bed of common earth; and when the plants come up, they muſt be thinned where they are too cloſe, and kept clean from weeds; when

the

the plants are grown fix inches high, they may be taken up with balls of earth to their roots, and planted into the large borders of the pleasure-garden, observing to water them till they have taken new root; after which they will require no other care, but to keep them clear from weeds.

In July the great flowers upon the tops of the stems will appear, amongst which, the best and most double flowers of each kind should be preserved for seeds; for those which flower later upon the side branches are neither so fair, nor do they perfect their seeds so well, as those which are first in flower: when the flowers are quite faded and the seeds are formed, you should carefully guard the heads from the sparrows, which will otherwise devour most of the good seeds; and about the beginning of October, when the seeds are ripe, you should cut off the heads with a small part of the stem, and hang them up in a dry airy place for about a month, by which time the seeds will be perfectly dry and hard; when you may easily rub them out, and put them into bags or papers, preserving them from vermin until the season for sowing them.

The seeds of this sort of Sun-flower are excellent food for domestic poultry; therefore where a quantity of it can be saved, it will be of great use, where there are quantities of these fowls.

The other perennial sorts rarely produce seeds in England, but most of them increase very fast at their roots, especially the creeping rooted kinds, which spread too far for small gardens. The second sort, which is the most common in the English gardens, is the largest and most valuable flower, and is a very proper furniture for large borders in great gardens, as also for bosquets of large growing plants, or to intermix in small quarters with shrubs, or in walks under trees, where few other plants will thrive; it is also a great ornament to gardens within the city, where it grows in defiance of the smoke, better than most other plants; and for its long continuance in flower, deserves a place in most gardens, for the sake of its flowers for basons, &c. to adorn halls and chimneys, in a season when we are at a loss for other flowers. It begins flowering in July, and continues until October; there is a variety of this with very double flowers, which is now become so common in the English gardens, as to have almost banished the single sort from hence.

The third, fourth, fifth, sixth, and seventh sorts may also have a place in some large borders of the garden, for the variety of their flowers; which, though not so fair as those of the common sort, yet will add to the diversity; and as many of them are late flowerers, so we may continue the succession of flowers longer in the season.

These sorts are all of them very hardy, and will grow in almost any soil or situation; they are propagated by parting their roots into small heads, which in one year's time will spread and increase greatly. The best season for this work is in the middle of October, soon after the flowers are past, or very early in the spring, that they may be well rooted before the droughts come on; otherwise their flowers will be few in number, and not near so fair, and by this means their roots will be weak; but if they are planted in October, you will save the trouble of watering them; their roots being surely fixed before the dry weather, they will need no other trouble than to clear them from weeds.

The Jerusalem Artichoke is propagated in many gardens for the roots, which are by some people as much esteemed as Potatoes; but they are more watery and flashy, and are very subject to trouble the belly by their windy quality, which hath brought them almost into disuse.

These are propagated by planting the smaller roots, or the larger ones cut in pieces, observing to preserve a bud to each separate piece, either in the spring or autumn, allowing them a good distance, for their roots will greatly multiply; the autumn following,

when their stems decay, the roots may be taken up for use. These should be planted in some remote corner of the garden, for they are very unsightly while growing, and their roots are apt to over-run whatever grows near them, nor can they be easily destroyed when they are once well fixed in a garden.

The other species which have been ranged under this genus by Tournefort and others, are now removed to the following genera, under which titles they may be found.

Corona Solis. See { COREOPSIS. HELENIUM. RUDBECKIA. SILPHIUM.

HELICTERES. Lin. Gen. Plant. 913. Isora. Plum. Nov. Gen. 34. tab. 27. Screw-tree.

The CHARACTERS are,

The flower has a coriaceous empalement of one leaf, which is narrow at bottom, but spreads open at the top, where it is indented in five parts. The flower hath five oblong equal petals, which are longer than the empalement to which they are fixed. It hath ten short stamina at the base of the germen, terminated by oblong summits, and five nectariums surrounding the germen, which have the appearance of petals. The style is very long, slender, and supports the germen at the top, which is roundish, and crowned by an acute stigma. The germen afterward turns to a twisted spiral fruit with one cell, inclosing many kidney-shaped seeds.

This genus of plants is ranged in the sixth section of Linnæus's twentieth class, which includes those plants whose flowers have ten stamina which are connected to the style.

The SPECIES are,

1. HELICTERES (*Isora*) foliis cordato-ovatis serratis, subtus tomentosis, fructu tereti contorto. *Helicteres with oval heart-shaped leaves which are sawed, and woolly on their under side, and a taper twisted fruit.* Isora althææ foliis, fructu longiore & angustiore. Plum. Nov. Gen. 24. *Screw-tree with Marshmallow leaves, and a longer narrower fruit.*

2. HELICTERES (*Breviore*) foliis cordatis acuminatis serratis, subtus tomentosis, fructu brevi contorto. *Helicteres with heart-shaped, pointed, sawed leaves, woolly on their under side, and a short twisted fruit.* Isora althææ foliis, fructu breviore & crassiore. Plum. Nov. 34. *Screw-tree with a Marshmallow leaf, and a shorter thicker fruit.*

3. HELICTERES (*Arborescens*) caule arboreo villoso, foliis cordatis crenatis nervosis subtus tomentosis fructu ovato contorto villosissimo. *Helicteres with a tree-like hairy stalk, heart-shaped, nervous, crenated leaves, woolly on their under side, and an oval, twisted, very hairy fruit.* Isora althææ folio amplissimo, fructu crassissimo & villoso. Edit. prior. *Screw-tree with a very large Marshmallow leaf, and a very thick hairy fruit.*

The first sort grows naturally in the Bahama Islands, from whence I received the seeds. This rises with a shrubby stalk five or six feet high, sending out several lateral branches, which are covered with a soft yellowish down, garnished with heart-shaped leaves four inches long, and two and a half broad, sawed on their edges, woolly on their under side, standing on long foot-stalks; at the upper part of the branches the flowers come out opposite to the leaves, upon slender foot-stalks which are jointed; these are composed of five oblong white petals, and in the center arises the style, which is curved, three inches long, upon the top of which is situated the germen, crowned by an acute stigma. The germen afterward turns to a taper fruit two inches and a half long, composed of five capsules, which are closely twisted over each other like a screw; these are hairy, and have each one cell, containing several kidney-shaped seeds.

The second sort grows naturally in Jamaica, from whence the late Dr. Houstoun sent me the seeds. This rises with a shrubby stalk nine or ten feet high, sending out many lateral branches, covered with a smooth brown bark, garnished with heart-shaped leaves,

2

leaves, which end in acute points, fawed on their edges, a little woolly on their under fide; the flowers are produced on the fide of the branches, on fhorter foot-ftalks than the former; they are compofed of five petals, and the ftyle in the center, which is ftrait, upright, and not half fo long as the other; the fruit is thicker,· not an inch long, but twifted in the fame manner,

The third fort rifes with a ftrong woody ftalk twelve or fourteen feet high, fending out many ligneous branches, which are clofely covered with hairy down, garnifhed with large heart-fhaped leaves, which are crenated on their edges, having large veins running from the midrib ·to the fides; they are of a light yellowifh green, and woolly on their under fide:, the flowers are produced from the fide of the branches, they are of a yellowifh white colour, and larger than thofe of the other forts. The ftyle is near four inches long, curved like that of the firft fort; the fruit is oval, about one inch long, very thick at the bottom, and clofely covered with hairy down. This fort was fent me by Mr. Robert Millar, from Carthagena.

Thefe plants are propagated by feeds, which muft be fown upon a hot-bed in the fpring, and when the plants are come up ftrong enough to remove, they fhould be each planted in a feparate fmall pot, filled with light earth, and plunged into a moderate hot-bed of tan, obferving to fhade them from the fun till they have taken new root; then they fhould be treated in the fame way as other tender plants from hot countries, raifing the glaffes every day in proportion to the weather, that the plants may enjoy frefh air, which will ftrengthen them, and prevent their drawing up weak. In the fummer the plants may remain under the frames, if there is fufficient height for them to grow; but in autumn they muft be plunged into the tan-bed in the ftove, where they fhould always remain, being careful to fhift them into larger pots when they require it, and not give them too much wet in the winter; but in fummer they fhould have a large fhare of air in warm weather, and require to be often refrefhed with water: the fecond year from the feeds thefe plants have often flowered in the Chelfea garden, and the feeds have fome years ripened there, but the plants will live feveral years with proper management.

HELIOCARPOS. Lin. Gen. Plant. 533. Montia. Houft. Gen. We have no· title in Englifh for this plant.

The CHARACTERS are,

The flower hath one petal which is tubulous at the bottom, and cut into five fegments which expand. It hath an empalement of one leaf, which is cut into five parts fpreading open. In the center is fituated a roundifh germen, fupporting two erect ftyles, crowned by acute ftigmas which ftand apart; thefe are attended by twelve ftamina, which are of the fame length with the ftyles, terminated by narrow twin fummits which are proftrate. The germen afterward becomes an oval compreffed capfule, about three lines long and two broad, with a tranfverfe partition dividing it in two cells, each containing a fingle roundifh feed ending in a point; the borders of the capfule are fet with hairs, refembling rays.

This genus of plants is ranged in the fecond fection of Linnæus's eleventh clafs, intitled Dodecandria Digynia, which includes the plants whofe flowers have twelve ftamina and two ftyles.

We have but one SPECIES of this plant, viz.

HELIOCARPOS (*Americana.*) Hort. Cliff. 211. tab. 16. Montia arborefcens mori folio fructu racemofo. Houft. MSS. *Tree Montia with a Mulberry leaf and branching fruit.*

This plant was difcovered by the late Dr. Houftoun, growing naturally about Old La Vera Cruz in New Spain, from whence he fent the feeds to England, which fucceeded in the Chelfea garden, where the plants have produced flowers, and ripened feeds feveral years. It rifes with a thick, foft, woody ftalk, from fifteen to eighteen feet high, fending out feve-

ral lateral branches toward the top, garnifhed with heart-fhaped leaves full of veins, fawed on their edges, and ending in acute points; they have foot-ftalks three inches long, which ftand oblique to the leaves, and are placed alternate; the flowers are produced at the end of the fhoots, in branching clufters; they are of a yellowifh green, and are fucceeded by flat compreffed feed-veffels of an oval fhape, whofe borders are clofely fet with threads reprefenting rays, of a brownifh colour when ripe; thefe capfules are divided into two cells by an intermediate partition, in each of thefe is lodged a fingle roundifh feed ending in a point.

This plant is propagated by feeds, which muft be fown upon a hot-bed in the fpring; and when the plants are fit to remove, they fhould be each planted in a feparate fmall pot filled with light kitchen-garden earth, andd plunged into a hot-bed, treating them in the fame way as other tender plants, which will not bear the open air in this country at any feafon of the year; and while the plants are young, they require to be plunged in the tan-bed, but after they have acquired ftrength, they will thrive in the dry ftove. In winter they fhould have but little water, and muft be kept warm; but in fummer they fhould have plenty of frefh air in mild weather, and muft be frequently refrefhed with water. With this management the plants will flower the third year, and produce good feeds, but may be preferved feveral years with proper care.

I have fowed the feeds of this plant which had been kept ten years, and came up as well as if it had been faved the former year; though from the appearance of the feeds, it feems as unlike to grow after the firft year as any which I know.

HELIOPHILA. Lin. Gen. 816.

The CHARACTERS are,

It hath a four-leaved empalement, whofe borders have membranes; the two outer have fmall bladders at their bafe. The flower has four roundifh plain petals, placed in form of a crofs, and two nectariums, which are recurved toward the bladders of the empalement. It hath fix ftamina, four of which are longer than the other, terminated by oblong erect fummits; and a cylindrical germen fupporting a fhort ftyle, crowned by an obtufe ftigma; the germen afterward becomes a taper pod, with two cells filled with feeds.

This genus of plants is ranged in the fecond fection of Linnæus's fifteenth clafs, intitled Tetradynamia Siliquofa, the flower having four long and two fhort ftamina, and the feeds being included in long pods.

The SPECIES are,

1. HELIOPHILA (*Integrifolia*) foliis lanceolatis indivifis. N. Burman. *Heliophila with fpear-fhaped undivided leaves.* Leucoium Africanum, cœruleo flore, latifolium. H. L. 364. *African Gilliflower with a broad leaf and a blue flower.*

2. HELIOPHILA (*Coronopi folia*) foliis linearibus pinnatifidis. Lin. Sp. Plant. 927. *Heliophila with linear wing-pointed leaves.* Leucoium Africanum, cœruleo flore, angufto coronopi folio majus. H. L. 364. *African Gilliflower, with narrow Hartfhorn leaves and blue flowers.*

Thefe are both annual plants, which grow naturally at the Cape of Good Hope; the firft rifes with an erect ftalk about four or five inches high, fending out two or three fide branches, garnifhed with long, narrow, entire green leaves, and terminated by a loofe bunch of blue flowers without fcent, which are fucceeded by taper pods near three inches long, having a double row of flat feeds.

The fecond fort grows about the fame height, but branches more; the leaves are cut into many wing-pointed divifions, and the flowers are like thofe of the other fort.

The feeds of both forts may be fown in the fpring on a fouth border, and when the plants come up, if they are thinned and kept clean from weeds, it is all the culture they require.

HELIO-

HELIOTROPIUM. Lin. Gen. Plant. 164. Tourn. Inſt. R. H. 138. tab. 57. [Ἡλιοτρόπιον, of Ἥλιος, the ſun, and τρέπω, to tuin.] Turnſole.

The CHARACTERS are,

The empalement of the flower is of one leaf, tubulous at bottom, but cut into five ſegments at the brim. The flower hath one petal, with a tube the length of the empalement, ſpreading flat above, where it is cut into five ſegments, which are alternately larger than the other ; the chaps of the tube is cloſed, and hath five prominent ſcales, joined in form of a ſtar. It hath five ſhort ſtamina within the tube, terminated by ſmall ſummits, and four germen at the bottom of the tube, with one ſlender ſtyle the length of the ſtamina, crowned by an indented ſtigma. The germen. afterward becomes ſo many ſeeds, ſitting in the empalement.

This genus of plants is ranged in the firſt ſection of Linnæus's fifth claſs, intitled Pentandria Monogynia, which includes thoſe plants whoſe flowers have five ſtamina and one ſtyle.

The SPECIES are,

1. HELIOTROPIUM (*Europæum*) foliis ovatis integerrimis tomentoſis rugoſis ſpicis conjugatis. Hort. Upſal. 33. *Heliotrope with oval, entire, woolly, rough leaves, and conjugated ſpikes.* Heliotropium majus Dioſcoridis. C. B. P. 253. The greater Turnſole of Dioſcorides.

2. HELIOTRIPIUM (*Indicum*) foliis cordato-ovatis acutis ſcabriuſculis, ſpicis ſolitariis, fructibus bifidis. Flor. Zeyl. 70. *Heliotrope with heart-ſhaped oval leaves, which are pointed and rough, ſingle ſpikes of flowers and bifid ſeeds.* Heliotropium Americanum cœruleum, foliis hormini. Acad. Reg. Sc. *Blue American Turnſole with Clary leaves.*

3. HELIOTROPIUM (*Horminifolium*) foliis lanceolato-ovatis acuminatis rugoſis, ſpicis ſolitariis gracilioribus alaribus & terminalibus. *Heliotrope with ſpear-ſhaped oval leaves, which are rough, and end in acute points, having ſlender ſingle ſpikes of flowers proceeding from the ſides and tops of the ſtalks.* Heliotropium Americanum cœruleum, foliis hormini anguſtioribus. H. L. *Blue American Turnſole with narrower Clary leaves.*

4. HELIOTROPIUM (*Capitatum*) foliis oblongo-ovatis integerrimis glabris ſubtus incanis, floribus capitatis alaribus, caule arboreſcente. *Heliotrope with oblong, oval, entire, ſmooth leaves, which are hoary on their under ſide, flowers growing in heads from the wings of the ſtalks, and a tree-like ſtalk.* Heliotropium arboreſcens, folio teucrii, flore albo in capitula denſa congeſto. Boerh. Ind. *Tree-like Turnſole, with a Germander leaf, and white flowers growing in thick ſhort heads.*

5. HELIOTROPIUM (*Canarienſe*) foliis ovatis crenatis oppoſitis, floribus capitatis alaribus dichotomis, caule arboreſcente. *Heliotrope with oval crenated leaves placed oppoſite, flowers growing in heads from the wings of the ſtalks, which diverge, and a tree-like ſtalk.* Heliotropium Canarienſe arboreſcens, folio ſcorodonæ. Hort. Amſt. *Canary tree-like Turnſole, with a Wood Sage leaf.*

6. HELIOTROPIUM (*Peruvianum*) foliis lanceolato-ovatis, caule fruticoſo, ſpicis numeroſis aggregato-corymboſis. Lin. Sp. 187. *Peruvian Heliotrope with oval ſpear-ſhaped leaves, a ſhrubby ſtalk, and many ſpikes of flowers joined in a corymbus.*

7. HELIOTROPIUM (*Curaſſavicum*) foliis lanceolato-linearibus glabris aveniis, ſpicis conjugatis. Hort. Cliff. 45. *Heliotrope with narrow, ſpear-ſhaped, ſmooth leaves without veins, and conjugated ſpikes of flowers.* Heliotropium Curaſſavicum, foliis lini umbilicati. Par. Bat. Prod. *Heliotrope of Curaſſao, with a Venus Navelwort leaf.*

8. HELIOTROPIUM (*Gnaphalodes*) foliis linearibus obtuſis tomentoſis, pedunculis dichotomis, ſpicarum floribus quaternis, caule fruteſcente. Lin. Sp. 188. *Heliotrope with linear, obtuſe, woolly leaves, forked foot-ſtalks, with four ſpikes of flowers and a ſhrubby ſtalk.* Heliotropium arboreum maritimum, tomentoſum, gnaphalii Americani foliis. Sloan. Cat. 93. *Tree maritime woolly Heliotrope, with a Sea Cudweed leaf.*

9. HELIOTROPIUM (*Fruticoſum*) foliis lineari-lanceolatis piloſis, ſpicis ſolitariis ſeſſilibus. Lin. Sp. 187. *Heliotrope with linear, ſpear-ſhaped, hairy leaves, and ſingle ſpikes of flowers ſitting cloſe to the ſtalk.* Heliotropium

minus lithoſpermi foliis. *Smaller Heliotrope with leaves like Gromwell.*

10. HELIOTROPIUM (*Procumbens*) caule procumbente, foliis ovatis tomentoſis integerrimis, ſpicis ſolitariis terminalibus. *Heliotrope with a trailing ſtalk, oval, woolly, entire leaves, and ſingle ſpikes of flowers terminating the branches.* Heliotropium Americanum ſupinum & tomentoſum, foliis ſubrotundis. Houſt. MSS. *Low American woolly Heliotrope with roundiſh leaves.*

11. HELIOTROPIUM (*Americanum*) foliis oblongo-ovatis tomentoſis, ſpicis conjugatis terminalibus, caule fruticoſo. *Heliotrope with oblong, oval, woolly leaves, and double ſpikes of flowers terminating the ſtalk, which is ſhrubby.* Heliotropium Americanum fruteſcens & tomentoſum, foliis oblongis, floribus albis. Houſt. MSS. *Shrubby and woolly American Heliotrope, with oblong leaves and white flowers.*

The firſt ſort grows naturally in the ſouth of France, in Spain, Italy, and moſt of the warmer countries in Europe. It is an annual plant, which ſucceds better from ſeeds which ſcatter in the autumn, or ſown at that ſeaſon, than in the ſpring ; for when they are ſown in the ſpring, they ſeldom come up the ſame year ; but if the plant is once obtained, and the ſeeds ſuffered to ſhed, it will maintain itſelf without any trouble, requiring no other culture but to keep it clean from weeds, and thin the plants where they are too cloſe.

This riſes about ſeven or eight inches high, dividing into two or three branches, garniſhed with oval rough leaves, two inches long and one broad in the middle, of a light green, ſtanding upon pretty long foot-ſtalks alternately ; the flowers are produced at the end of the branches in double ſpikes, joined at the bottom, which are about an inch and a half long, turning backward like a ſcorpion's tail. The flowers are white, and appear in June and July ; the ſeeds ripen in autumn, ſoon after which the plant decays.

The ſecond ſort grows naturally in the Weſt-Indies. This is annual ; the ſtalk riſes a foot and a half, or two feet high, branching out toward the top : the leaves are rough and hairy, ſtanding upon pretty long foot-ſtalks ; they are two inches and a half long, and one and a half broad in the middle, ending in acute points ; the flowers are produced toward the end of the branches in ſingle ſpikes, which are ſix inches long, turning backward at the top like the other ſpecies. The flowers are blue, and appear in July and Auguſt, the ſeeds ripen in September and October.

The third ſort grows naturally in the Weſt-Indies. This is a ſmaller plant than the former, ſeldom growing above two feet high ; the leaves are one inch and a half long, and about half an inch broad ; the ſpikes of flowers are very ſlender, and not more than two inches long ; the flowers are ſmall, and of a light blue colour. They appear at the ſame time with the former, and the ſeeds ripen in autumn.

The ſeeds of theſe two ſorts muſt be ſown on a hot-bed in the ſpring, and when the plants are fit to remove, they muſt be tranſplanted on another hot-bed to bring them forward, treating them in the ſame way as the Balſamine, and other tender annual plants ; and in June they may be taken up with balls of earth, and planted in the borders of the flower-garden, where they will flower, and in warm ſeaſons produce ripe ſeeds.

The fourth ſort riſes with a ſhrubby ſtalk ſix. or ſeven feet high ; the young branches are cloſely covered with a white down, and the leaves on thoſe are very hoary and entire, but thoſe on the older branches are greener, and ſome of them are notched on their edges ; at each joint of the ſtalks come out two ſhort branches oppoſite, which are garniſhed with ſmall hoary leaves placed oppoſite : theſe, when bruiſed, emit a ſtrong odour, which to ſome perſons is very diſagreeable, but others are pleaſed with it. The plants rarely flower in England, for in near forty years which I have cultivated them, I have but once ſeen them in flower. The flowers are white, collected in roundiſh heads, which turn backward, and ſit cloſe to the branches ;

the

the leaves continue all the year, for which the plants are preferved in green-houfes, to add to the variety in winter.

The fifth fort grows naturally in the Canary Iflands. This rifes with a woody ftalk three or four feet high, dividing into many branches, which are garnifhed with oval leaves notched on their edges, growing oppofite upon long foot-ftalks ; they are hairy, and of an Afh colour on their under fide ; the flowers are produced from the fide of the branches on pretty long foot-ftalks, each fuftaining four fhort roundifh fpikes or heads, which divide by pairs, and fpread from each other. The flowers are white, and appear in June and July, but are not fucceeded by feeds in England. The leaves of this plant, when bruifed, emit an agreeable odour, for which it is by fome perfons much efteemed ; the gardeners have given it the title of Madam Maintenon, but for what reafon I know not.

The two laft forts are too tender to live through the winter in the open air in this country, fo muft be kept in a green-houfe during that feafon ; but they only require to be fcreened from froft, fo may be placed with Myrtles and the other hardy greenhoufe plants, where they may have a large fhare of air in mild weather, and be treated in the fame way ; they are eafily propagated by cuttings during any of the fummer months, which, if planted in a fhady border and duly fupplied with water, will take root in five or fix weeks ; then they may be potted, and placed in a fhady fituation till they have taken new root, after which they may be treated as the old plants.

The fixth fort grows naturally in Peru, from whence the feeds were fent by the younger Juffieu to the Royal Garden at Paris, where the plants produced flowers and feeds ; and from the curious garden of the Duke D'Ayen, at St. Germains, I was fupplied with fome of the feeds, which have fucceeded in the Chelfea garden, where the plants have flowered and perfected their feeds for fome years.

This rifes with a fhrubby ftalk two or three feet high, dividing into many fmall branches, garnifhed with oval, fpear-fhaped, rough leaves, fet on without order ; they are three inches long, and one inch and a half broad in the middle, ftanding on fhort foot-ftalks ; they are hairy, and greatly veined on their under fide, which is of an Afh colour. The flowers are produced at the end of the branches in fhort reflexed fpikes, growing in clufters. The footftalks divide into two or three, and thefe divide again into lefs, each fuftaining a fpike of pale blue flowers, which have a ftrong fweet odour. The plants continue in flower great part of the year, and thofe flowers which come out in fummer, are fucceeded by ripe feeds in autumn.

It may be propagated either by feeds or cuttings. The feeds fhould be fown upon a moderate hot-bed in the fpring, and when the plants are fit to remove, they fhould be tranfplanted into fmall pots filled with light earth, and plunged into a hot-bed, where they fhould be fhaded till they have taken new root ; then they fhould be inured to the open air by degrees, into which they fhould be removed in fummer, placing them in a fheltered fituation ; and in autumn they muft be houfed with other exotic plants in a good green-houfe, where they will flower great part of winter, fo will make a good appearance among the Orange-trees, and other green-houfe plants, with whofe culture this plant will thrive. If the cuttings of this plant are put into pots filled with light earth, during any of the fummer months, and plunged into a moderate hot-bed, they will take root very freely, but thefe do not make fo good plants as thofe raifed from feeds.

The feventh fort grows naturally on the fea-fhore in the Weft-Indies ; this is an annual plant, whofe branches trail upon the ground, and grow a foot long ; they are garnifhed with narrow grayifh leaves, which are fmooth. The flowers are produced in double fpikes

from the fide of their branches ; they are white and fmall, fo make no great appearance. It is propagated by feeds, and requires the fame treatment as the fecond and third forts.

The eighth fort rifes with an upright woody ftalk fix or feven feet high, with a hoary bark, full of marks where the leaves have grown ; the upper part of the ftalk divides into two or three ftrong woody branches, which grow erect, and are very clofely garnifhed with long, narrow, woolly leaves, which ftand on every fide the branches without order. The flowers come out from the fide of the ftalks, to which they fit clofe ; they are fhort and reflexed, like thofe of the other fpecies. The flowers are purple, fitting in very woolly empalements, which are divided into five fegments, which fpread open ; the whole plant is very white and woolly, like the Sea Cudweed, fo makes an odd appearance when intermixed with other exotic plants : this is propagated by feeds, which muft be procured from the places where it naturally grows, for it never produces any in Europe ; thefe feeds fhould be fown in a tub of earth in the country, for when the dried feeds come over they feldom grow ; and if they do, it is not before the fecond year : and from feveral parcels of the feeds which I have received from the Weft-Indies, I have not raifed more than two plants, and thefe came up from the feeds which had been fown more than a year ; fo that if the feeds are fown as foon as they are ripe in a tub of earth, when they arrive in England, the tub fhould be plunged into a hot-bed of tanners bark, which will bring up the plants ; and when thefe are fit to remove, they fhould be each planted in a feparate fmall pot filled with earth, compofed of fand and light undunged earth, with a little lime rubbifh well mixed together, then plunged into a hot-bed of tanners bark, and fhaded until they have taken new root ; after which, they muft be treated as other tender exotic plants, always keeping them in the tan-bed in the ftove, giving them but little water, efpecially during the winter feafon.

The ninth fort is a native of the Weft-Indies, where it grows plentifully on the fea-fhore ; it rifes with an upright fhrubby ftalk a foot and a half high, garnifhed with fmall fpear-fhaped leaves, fcarce one inch long, and one-third of an inch broad in the middle, ending in acute points, fitting clofe to the ftalk ; they are hoary on their under fide, but fmooth above. The flowers are produced in fingle flender fpikes, which come out from the fide, and at the top of the ftalks ; they are but little recurved, efpecially thofe on the fide, but thofe at the top are more bent ; they are white, fo make but little appearance.

The tenth fort was fent me from Carthagena in New Spain, where it grows naturally on the fandy fhores. This is an annual plant, with trailing ftalks which grow fix or feven inches long, garnifhed with fmall oval leaves, which are woolly and entire. The flowers are produced at the end of the branches, in fingle fhort fpikes, which are reflexed ; they are fmall and white, fo make little appearance.

The eleventh fort was fent me by the late Dr. Houftoun from La Vera Cruz, where he found it growing in plenty ; this rifes with a fhrubby ftalk three feet high, dividing into flender branches, which are clofely garnifhed with oblong, oval, woolly leaves, placed without order. The flowers are produced at the end of the branches in double fpikes, which are flender, fhort, and ftrait, not recurved as the other fpecies. The flowers are fmall and white, and the plant is perennial.

Thefe three laft mentioned are propagated by feeds, but the difficulty of getting them frefh from America, and the uncertainty of their growing, unlefs they are fown abroad, and brought over in earth, has rendered them rare in Europe ; and as they are plants of little beauty, fo few perfons have taken the trouble to procure them : befides, as they require a ftove to preferve them in this country, and muft have a peculiar foil and management like the eighth fort, fo, unlefs for the fake of variety in botanic gardens, they are not worth cultivating here.

HELLEBORE. See HELLEBORUS.

HELLEBORINE. See SERAPIAS and LIMADORUM.

HELLEBOROIDES HYEMALIS. See HELLEBORUS.

HELLEBORO RANUNCULUS. See TROLLIUS.

HELLEBORUS. Lin. Gen. Plant. 622. Tourn. Inft. R. H. 271. tab. 144. ['Ελλέβορ@.] Black Hellebore, or Chriftmas flower; in French, Ellebore-Noire.

The CHARACTERS are,

The flowers hath no empalement; it hath five large roundish petals, which are permanent, and many small nectarii placed circularly, each being of one piece, with a narrow tube at the bottom, divided at the brim into two lips, the under being short and indented; it hath a great number of stamina, terminated by compressed erect summits, and several germen, which are compressed, supporting awl-shaped styles, crowned by thick stigmas. The germen afterward turn to compressed capsules with two keels, the lower being short, and the upper convex, which are filled with round seeds adhering to the seam.

This genus of plants is ranged in the feventh fection of Linnæus's thirteenth clafs, intitled Polyandria Polygynia, which includes thofe plants whofe flowers have many ftamina and ftyles.

The SPECIES are,

1. HELLEBORUS (*Fœtidus*) caule multifloro foliofo, foliis pedatis. Lin. Sp. Plant. 784. *Hellebore with many flowers on a ftalk, which are intermixed with leaves, and ramofe leaves fitting on the foot-ftalk.* Helleborus niger fœtidus. C. B. P. *Stinking Black Hellebore, Bears-foot, or Setterwort.*

2. HELLEBORUS (*Viridis*) caule multifloro foliofo, foliis digitatis. Lin. Sp. Plant. 558. *Hellebore with many flowers on a ftalk, which are intermixed with leaves, and hand-fhaped leaves.* Helleborus niger hortenfis, flore viridi. C. B. P. *Green flowered Black Hellebore, or Bears-foot.*

3. HELLEBORUS (*Niger*) fcapo fub-unifloro fub-nudo, foliis pedatis. Hort. Upfal. 157. *Hellebore with one flower on a ftalk, which is naked, and hand-fhaped leaves fitting on the foot-ftalk.* Helleborus niger, flore albo, etiam interdum valde rubente. J. B. *True Black Hellebore, or Chriftmas Rofe.*

4. HELLEBORUS (*Trifolius*) caule multifloro, foliis ternatis integerrimis. *Hellebore with many flowers on a ftalk, and leaves compofed of three entire lobes.* Helleborus niger trifoliatus. Hort. Farn. *Trifoliate Black Hellebore.*

5. HELLEBORUS (*Hyemalis*) flore folio infidente. Hort. Cliff. 227. *Hellebore with the flower fitting on the leaf.* Aconitum Hyemale, or *Winter Aconite.*

6. HELLEBORUS (*Latifolius*) caule multifloro foliofo, foliis digitatis ferratis amplioribus. *Hellebore with many flowers upon a ftalk, intermixed with leaves, and large fingered leaves which are fawed.* Helleborus niger amplioribus foliis. Tourn. Inft. R. H. 272. *Black Hellebore with larger leaves.*

The firft fort grows naturally in woods in feveral parts of England, but particularly in Suffex, where I have feen it in great plenty; this hath a jointed herbaceous ftalk, which rifes two feet high, dividing into two or three heads, garnifhed with leaves compofed of eight or nine long narrow lobes, which join at their bafe; four of thefe on each fide are joined together at their tails, and the middle one ftands on the center of the foot-ftalk; thefe are fawed on their edges, and end in acute points; thofe on the lower part of the ftalk are much larger than the upper, which are fmall and narrow. The flower-ftalk arifes from the center of the plant, dividing into many branches, each fuftaining feveral fmaller foot-ftalks, with one entire fpear-fhaped leaf upon each, and one large greenifh flower at the top with purplifh rims;

thefe appear in winter, and the feeds ripen in the fpring; which, if permitted to fcatter, the plants will rife without care, and may be tranfplanted into woods, or in wildernefs quarters, where they will grow in great fhade, and make a good appearance at a feafon when there are but few plants in beauty.

The fecond fort grows naturally at Ditton, near Cambridge, and in the woods near Stoken Church, in Oxfordfhire. The ftalks of this fort grow more upright than thofe of the firft, and do not branch fo much. The leaves are compofed of nine long lobes, which unite to the foot-ftalk at their bafe, and are fharply fawed on their edges; they are of a lighter green than thofe of the firft fort. The flowers are produced at the top of the ftalk, having one or two leaves fet on the foot-ftalk; they are compofed of five oval green petals, with a great number of ftamina furrounding the germen in the middle; thefe appear the beginning of February, and the feeds ripen the end of May, which if fown foon after they are ripe, the plants will come up early the following fpring; and, when they have obtained ftrength, may be planted in fhady places under trees, where they will thrive and flower very well. The leaves of this fort decay in autumn, and new ones arife from the roots in the fpring, but the firft fort is always green.

The third fort is fuppofed to be the Hellebore of the antients; this grows naturally on the Alps and Apennine mountains. The root of this fort is compofed of many thick flefhy fibres, which fpread far into the ground, from which arife the flowers upon naked foot-ftalks, immediately from the root, each fupporting one large white flower, compofed of five roundifh petals, with a great number of ftamina in the middle. The leaves of this are compofed of feven or eight thick, flefhy, obtufe lobes, which are flightly fawed on their edges, and unite with the foot-ftalk at their bafe; this plant flowers in winter, from whence the title of Chriftmas Rofe was applied to it: it is propagated by parting of the roots in autumn, for the feeds feldom ripen well in England; it fhould have a more fheltered fituation than either of the former, otherwife it will not flower well.

The fourth fort is like the fecond, but differs from it in having trifoliate leaves, which are broader and entire, their furface is fmoother; this flowers early in winter, and the ftalks rife higher than either of the former forts, but is at at prefent rare in England.

The fifth fort is the common Winter Aconite, which is fo well known as to need no defcription. It flowers very early in the fpring, which renders it worthy of a place in all curious gardens, efpecially as it requires but little room; this is propagated by offsets, which the roots fend out in plenty; thefe roots may be taken up and tranfplanted, any time after their leaves decay, which is generally by the beginning of June till October, when they will begin to put out new fibres; but as the roots are fmall, and nearly of the colour of the ground, fo, if care is not taken to fearch them, many of the roots will be left in the ground; thefe roots fhould be planted in fmall clufters, otherwife they will not make a good appearance; for fingle flowers fcattered about the borders of thefe fmall kinds, are fcarce feen at a diftance; but when thefe and the Snowdrops are alternately planted in bunches, they will have a good effect, as they flower at the fame time, and are much of a fize.

The fixth fort is like the firft, but the lobes of the leaves are broader, and the ftalks grow taller; this grows naturally in Iftria and Dalmatia, from whence I received fome of the feeds; it has been fuppofed to be only a feminal variety of the firft, and as fuch I fowed the feeds; but the plants had a very great difference, and the firft winter proving fevere, they were all deftroyed; fo that it is not fo hardy as our common fort, and depending on their being fo, occafioned the lofs of the plants.

HEL-

HELLEBORUS florè globofo. See TROLLIUS.

HELLEBORUS ALBUS. See VERATRUM.

HELMET FLOWER, or MONK's HOOD. See ACONITUM.

HEMEROCALLIS. Lin. Gen. Plant. 391. Lilio-Afphodelus. Tourn. Inft. R. H. 344. tab. 179. Liliaſtrum. Tourn. Inft. R. H. 369. tab. 194. *Lily Afphodel, or Day Lily*; in French, *Lis de Saint Bruno*.

The CHARACTERS are,

The flower has no empalement; in fome fpecies the flower is of one petal, cut into fix parts, in others it hath fix petals, with a fhort tube, fpreading open at the top, which is reflexed. There are fix awl-fhaped declining ſtamina furrounding the ſtyle, terminated by oblong proſtrate fummits. The roundiſh furrowed germen is ſituated in the middle, fupporting a ſlender ſtyle, crowned by an obtuſe three-cornered ſtigma. The germen afterward becomes an oval three-cornered capfule with three lobes, opening with two valves, filled with roundiſh feeds.

This genus of plants is ranged in the firſt fection of Linnæus's fixth clafs, which includes the plants whoſe flowers have fix ſtamina and one ſtyle. Tournefort places the firſt in the firſt fection of his ninth clafs, which includes the plants with a Lily-flower of one leaf, cut into fix parts, whofe pointal becomes the fruit; the fecond he places in his fourth fection of the fame clafs, with the flowers of the fame form which have fix petals.

The SPECIES are,

1. HEMEROCALLIS (*Flava*) corollis flavis. Lin. Sp. 462. Hort. Upſal. 88. *Day Lily with a yellow flower.* Lilio-Afphodelus luteus. Park. Par. 148. *Yellow Afphodel Lily.*

2. HEMEROCALLIS (*Minor*) fcapo compreffo corollis monopetalis campanulatis. *Day Lily with a compreffed ſtalk, and a bell-ſhaped flower of one petal.* Lilio-Afphodelus luteus, minor. Tourn. Inft. R. H. 344. *Smaller yellow Afphodel Lily.*

3. HEMEROCALLIS (*Fulva*) corollis fulvis. *Day Lily with a copper-coloured flower.* Lilio-Afphodelus phœnicius. Park. Par. 148. *Afphodel Lily with a reddiſh flower.*

4. HEMEROCALLIS. (*Liliaſtrum*) fcapo fimplici, corollis hexapetalis campanulatis. Hort. Cliff. 128. *Day Lily with an unbranched fingle ſtalk, and bell-ſhaped flowers with fix petals.* Liliaſtrum Alpinum majus. Tourn. Inft. R. H. 369. *Greater Alpine Baſtard Lily, called Savoy Spiderwort;* and in French, *Lis de Saint Bruno, i. e. St. Bruno's Lily.*

The firſt fort grows naturally in Hungary, Dalmatia, and Iſtria, but has long been an inhabitant in the Engliſh gardens; this hath ſtrong fibrous roots, to which hang knobs, or tubers, like thofe of the Afphodel, from which come out keel-ſhaped leaves, which are two feet long, with a rigid midrib, the two fides drawing inward, fo as to form a fort of gutter on the upper fide. The ſower-ſtalks rife two feet and a half high, having two or three longitudinal furrows; thefe are naked, and at the top divide into three or four ſhort root-ſtalks, each fuſtaining one pretty large yellow flower fhaped like a Lily, having but one petal, with a ſhort tube, fpreading open at the brim, where it is divided into fix parts, thefe have an agreeable fcent, from which fome have given it the title of yellow Tuberofe. It flowers in June, and the feeds ripen in Auguſt; this plant is eafily propagated by offsets, which the roots fend out in plenty; thefe may be taken off in autumn, that being the beſt feafon for tranfplanting the roots, and planted in any ſituation, for they are extremely hardy, and will require no other culture but to keep them clean from weeds, and to allow them room that their roots may fpread; they may alfo be propagated by feeds, which, if fown in autumn, the plants will come up the following fpring, and thefe will flower in two years; but if the feeds are not fown till fpring, the plants will not come up till the year after.

The fecond fort grows naturally in Siberia; this hath roots like thofe of the former fort, but are fmaller. The leaves are not near fo long, nor more than half the breadth of the former, and of a dark green co-

lour. The flower-ſtalk rifes a foot and a half high, is naked and compreffed, but has no furrows; at the top is produced two or three yellow flowers, which are nearer the bell-fhape than thofe of the other fpecies, and ſtand on ſhorter foot-ſtalks; thefe flower the beginning of June, and the feeds ripen early in Auguſt. It is propagated by offsets from the root, or by feeds, in the fame manner as the former, but the roots do not increafe fo faſt; it fhould have a moiſt foil and a fhady ſituation, where it will thrive much better than in dry ground.

The third fort is a much larger plant than either of the former, and the roots fpread and increafe much more, therefore is not proper furniture for fmall gardens; the roots of this hath very ſtrong fleſhy fibres, to which hang large oblong tubers. The leaves are near three feet long, hollowed like thofe of the other, turning back toward the top. The flower-ſtalks are as thick a man's finger, and rife near four feet high; they are naked, without joints, and branching at the top, where are feveral large copper-coloured flowers, fhaped like thofe of the Red Lily, and as large. The ſtamina of this fort are longer than thofe of the other, and their fummits are charged with a copper-coloured farina, which ſheds on being touched; or if a perfon fmells to the flowers, it will fly off and fpread over the face, dyeing it all over of a copper colour, which is a trick often played by fome unlucky people to the ignorant: thefe flowers never continue longer than one day, but there is a fucceſſion of flowers on the fame plants for a fortnight or three weeks; this fort flowers about the fame time as the former, and the roots propagate too faſt for thofe gardens where there is but little room. It will grow on any foil or in any ſituation, the beſt time to tranfplant the roots is in autumn.

The Savoy Spiderwort, or, as the French call it, St. Bruno's Lily, is a plant of humbler growth than either of the former: there are two varieties of this, one is titled Liliaſtrum Alpinum majus, and the other Liliaſtrum Alpinum minus by Tournefort; the firſt of thefe rifes with a flower-ſtalk more than a foot and a half high; the flowers are much larger, and there is a greater number upon each ſtalk than the fecond; but as there is no other eſſential difference between them, I have not put them down as different fpecies; but the firſt is by much the finer plant, though not common in England, for the fecond fort is what I have always obferved in the gardens here. I received fome roots of the fecond fort from Monſ. Richard, gardener to the King of France, which continue their difference in the fame foil and ſituation with the firſt, which flowers earlier in the year; the leaves of this fort are fomewhat like thofe of the Spiderwort, are pretty firm, and grow upright; the flower-ſtalks grow about a foot and a half high, and have feveral white flowers at the top, fhaped like thofe of the Lily, which hang on one fide, and have an agreeable fcent; thefe are but of ſhort duration, feldom continuing in beauty above three or four days; but when the plants are ſtrong, they will produce eight or ten flowers upon each ſtalk, fo they make a good appearance while they laſt.

This fort is uſually propagated by parting the roots; autumn is the beſt feafon for doing this work, as it alfo is for tranfplanting the roots; for when they are removed in the fpring, they feldom flower the fame year, or if they do, it is but weakly: thefe plants ſhould not be tranfplanted oftener than every third year, when the roots may be parted to make an increafe of the plants, but they ſhould not be divided too fmall; for if they are, it will be two years before they flower: thefe plants delight in a light loamy foil and in an open expofure, fo muſt not be planted under the drip of trees; but if they are planted to an eaſt aſpect, where they may be protected from the fun in the heat of the day, they will continue in beauty longer than when they are more expofed.

HEMIONITIS ['Ημιωνῖτις, of 'Ημίονος, a Mule, q. d. Mulewort, becaufe this plant was believed to be as barren as a mule.] Moonfern.

This

This is a plant which is feldom propagated in gardens, therefore I fhall not trouble the reader with any account of it more than this. That whoever hath a mind to cultivate any of the forts, muft procure the plants from the countries where they naturally grow ; there are two forts which are natives of the warmer parts of Europe, but in America there is a great number of very different kinds ; thefe muft be planted in pots filled with loamy undunged earth, and fuch of them as are natives of hot countries, muft be placed in the ftove ; the others may be fheltered under a common frame in winter, and during the ſummer they muft be frequently watered, but in winter they will require but little. In ſummer they fhould alſo have plenty of free air admitted to them ; with this management the plants will thrive.

HEPATICA. Boerh. Ind. Plant. Ranunculus. Tourn. Inft. R. H. 286. Anemone. Lin. Gen. Plant. 614. ['Ηπατιτης, of 'Ηπαρ, the liver, fo called, becauſe the leaves of this plant are divided into lobes, like the liver (but it does not at all take its name from its uſe, for it is of no virtue againft the difeafes of the liver, as many have erroneoufly imagined ;) and trifolia, from its fimilitude thereto.] Hepatica, or Noble Liverwort.

The CHARACTERS are,
The flower hath a three-leaved empalement. It hath fix petals, which are oval, and expand to the bottom, with a great number of flender ftamina fhorter than the petals, terminated by obtufe ſummits ; and feveral germen collected into a head, fupporting acuminated ſtyles, crowned by obtuſe ſtigmas. The germen afterward turns to acuminated ſeeds ſitting round the ſtyles.

This genus of plants is by Tournefort ranged among the Crowfoots, and by Linnæus it is placed under Anemone ; but as the flowers of Anemone have no empalement, and the Hepatica hath a three-leaved one, it may be feparated from that genus ; and as it is well known in the gardens by this title, fo fhould we range it with the Anemone, it might occafion confufion. This is ranged in the feventh fection of Linnæus's thirteenth claſs, which includes the herbs with flowers having many ftamina and ſtyles.

The VARIETIES of this plant are,
1. HEPATICA (*Nobilis*) trifolio, cœruleo flore. Cluf. *The fingle blue Hepatica, or Noble Liverwort.*
2. HEPATICA (*Plena*) trifolia cœruleo pleno. Cluf. *The double blue Hepatica, or Noble Liverwort.*
3. HEPATICA (*Alba*) trifolia, flore alba fimplici. Boerh. Ind. *The fingle white Hepatica, or Noble Liverwort.*
4. HEPATICA (*Vulgaris*) trifolia, rubro flore. Cluf. *Single red Hepatica, or Noble Liverwort.*
5. HEPATICA (*Rubra*) trifolia, flore rubro pleno. Boerh. Ind. *Double red, or Peach-coloured Hepatica.*

Theſe plants are fome of the greateft beauties of the fpring ; the flowers are produced in February and March in great plenty, before the green leaves appear, and make a very beautiful figure in the borders of the pleaſure-garden, efpecially the double forts, which commonly continue a fortnight long in flower than the fingle kinds, and the flowers are much fairer. I have feen the double white kind often mentioned in books, but could never fee it growing, though I do not know but fuch a flower might be obtained from feeds of the fingle white, or blue kinds. I have fometimes known the double blue fort produce fome flowers in autumn, which were inclining to white, and thereby fome people have been deceived, who have procured the roots at that feafon, and planted them in their gardens ; but the fpring following their flowers were blue, as before ; and this is what frequently happens, when the autumn is fo mild as to cauſe them to flower; but whether the double white fort, mentioned in the books, was only this accidental alteration in the colour of the flower, I cannot fay, though it feems very probable it was, fince I never could hear of any perfon who ever faw the double white fort flower in the fpring.

The fingle forts produce feeds every year, whereby

they are eafily propagated, and alfo new flowers may be that way obtained. The beft feafon for fowing of the feeds is in the beginning of Auguft, either in pots or boxes of light earth, which fhould be placed fo as to have only the morning fun until October, when they fhould be removed into the full fun, to remain during the winter feafon ; but in March, when the young plants will begin to appear, they muft be removed again to a fhady fituation, and in dry weather fhould be frequently watered, and about the beginning of Auguft they will be fit to be tranfplanted ; at which time you fhould prepare a border facing the eaft, of good, frefh, loamy earth, into which you fhould remove the plants, placing them about fix inches diftance each way, clofing the earth pretty faft to their roots, to prevent the worms from drawing them out of the ground, which they are very apt to do at that feafon ; and, in the fpring following, they will begin to fhew their flowers ; but it will be three years before they flower ftrong, and till then you cannot judge of their goodnefs ; when, if you find any double flowers, or any of a different colour from the common forts, they fhould .be taken up, and tranfplanted into the borders of the flower-garden, where they fhould continue at leaft two years before they are taken up or parted ; for it is remarkable in this plant, that where they are often removed and parted, they are very fubject to die ; whereas, when they are permitted to remain undifturbed for many years, they will thrive exceedingly, and become very large roots.

The double flowers, which never produce feeds, are propagated by parting their roots, which fhould be done in March, at the time when they are in flower ; but you fhould be careful not to feparate them into very fmall heads, nor fhould they be parted oftener than every third or fourth year, if you intend to have them thrive, for the reafon before given. They delight in a ftrong loamy foil, and in an eaftern pofition, where they may have only the morning fun, though they will grow in almoft any afpect, not too warm, and are never injured by cold.

HEPATORIUM. See EUPATORIUM.

HEPTAPHYLLUM. See POTENTILLA.

HERACLEUM. Lin. Gen. 345. Sphondylium. Tourn. Inft. 1. Cow Parfnep.

The CHARACTERS are,
The calyx of the greater umbel is large, compoſed of many ſmaller, which are plain ; the general involucrum is compoſed of many leaves which fall off ; the partial umbels have involucrums of three to ſeven leaves, the outer being the longeft. The general umbel is deformed, the florets are moſtly fruitful ; thoſe of the difk have five equal petals, which are inflexed ; thoſe of the rays have the ſame number of unequal petals, the outer being the largeſt ; they have each five ſtamina longer than the petals, terminated by ſmall ſummits. The germen is ſituated under the flower, and is almoſt oval, ſupporting two ſtyles, crowned by ſimple ſtigmas. The germen afterward becomes an elliptical fruit, compoſed of two oval compreſſed ſeeds.

This genus of plants is ranged in the fecond order of Linnæus's fifth claſs, intitled Pentandria Digynia, the flowers having five ftamina and two ftyles.

The SPECIES are,
1. HERACLEUM (*Sphondylium*) foliolis pinnatifidis. Hort. Cliff. 103. *Cow Parfnep with wing-pointed leaves.* Sphondylium vulgare hirſutum. C. B. P. 157. *Common Cow Parfnep.*
2. HERACLEUM (*Panaces*) foliis pinnatis, foliolis quinis, intermediis feſſilibus, floribus radiatis. Hort. Upſal. 65. *Cow Parfnep with winged leaves having five lobes, and radiated flowers.* Panax Sphondylii folio, fc. Heracleum, C. B. P. 157.
3. HERACLEUM (*Alpinum*) foliis fimplicibus, floribus radiatis. Lin. Sp. 359. *Cow Parfnep with fimple leaves and radiated flowers.* Sphondylium Alpinum glabrum. C. B. P. 157. *Smooth Alpine Cow Parfnep.*
4. HERACLEUM (*Sibricum*) foliis pinnatis, foliolis quinis, intermediis feſſilibus, corollulis uniformibus. Hort. Upſal. 65. *Cow Parfnep with winged leaves, having five lobes*

lobes, and a uniform corolla. Paftinaca foliis fimpliciter pinnatis, foliolis pinnafidis. Flor. Siber. 1. p. 218.

The firft fort grows naturally in moft parts of England, fo is rarely admitted into gardens; there is a variety (if not a diftinct fpecies of this) with narrower leaves, which are more divided than thofe of the firft; however, as they are feldom cultivated, I fhall not trouble the reader with their defcription.

The fecond fort is placed in moft of the Pharmacopœias as a medicinal plant, but is rarelyufed as fuch, efpecially in England. This rifes with a tall ftalk near fix feet high, which is embraced by the bafe of the leaves; thefe are winged, having generally five roundifh lobes, whofe furface is rough, of a dark green colour: the flowers are produced at the top of the ftalks, being clofely inclofed by the empalement when they firft appear; but this afterward burfting, the umbel expands, having large petals on their exteriorrow, which are almoft heart-fhaped, and are fucceeded by flat compreffed feeds like thofe of Parfnep, but larger, having black ftreaks on their outfide. This grows naturally on the Appenines.

The third fort grows naturally on the Alps, as alfo in Siberia: the ftalks of this rife as high as thofe of the former, but the leaves are fmooth. This is feldom cultivated.

The fourth fort grows naturally in Siberia and Tranfylvania; in the former country, the inhabitants eat the ftalks and leaves of the plant for want of better food.

As thefe plants are rarely cultivated, unlefs in botanic gardens, fo I fhall recommend to thofe who are defirous to propagate either of the fpecies, to fow their weeds in the autumn; and in the fpring, when the plants are up, to hough the ground, cutting up the feeds, and thinning of the plants, in the fame manner as is directed for Parfneps, with which culture the plants will thrive.

HERBA GERARDI. See ANGELICA SYLVESTRIS MINOR.

HERBALIST, HERBARIST, a perfon who is fkilled in diftinguifhing the kinds, natures, or virtues of herbs or plants.

HERBA PARIS. See PARIS.

To **HERBARIZE,** to go abroad in the fields in queft of different or new herbs or plants.

HERBIFEROUS fignifies bearing or bringing forth herbs.

HERBIVOROUS, i. e. devouring or feeding on herbs or Grafs.

HERBOSE, graffy, or full of Grafs or herbs.

HERBOSITY, graffinefs, or abundance of Grafs or herbs.

HERBULENT, graffy, full of Grafs or herbs.

HERMANNIA. Tourn. Inft. R. H. 656. tab. 432. Lin. Gen. Plant. 742. The title of this genus was given by Dr. Tournefort in honour of that great botanift, Paul Herman, M. D. Profeffor of Botany at Leyden.

The CHARACTERS are,

The flower hath a pitcher-fhaped permanent empalement, divided into five parts at the brim. It hath five petals, which are narrow at their bafe, and twift againft the fun within the tubulous empalement, but fpread open above, where they are broad and obtufe. It hath five broad ftamina, which are joined in one body, terminated by pointed fummits, which are joined. In the center is fituated a roundifh five-cornered germen, fupporting an awl-fhaped ftyle which is longer than the ftamina, crowned by a fingle ftigma. The germen afterward becomes a five-cornered roundifh capfule, with five cells opening at the top, inclofing many feeds.

This genus of plants is ranged in the firft fection of Linnæus's fixteenth clafs, which includes the plants whofe flowers have five ftamina joined in one body to the ftyle.

The SPECIES are,

1. HERMANNIA (*Alnifolia*) foliis cuneiformibus plicacatis, crenato-emarginatis. Hort. Cliff. 342. *Herman-*

nia with wedge-fhaped folded leaves, which are crenated and indented. Hermannia frutefcens, folio oblongo ferrato latiori. Boerh. Ind. *Shrubby Hermannia with a broader, oblong, ferrated leaf.*

2. HERMANNIA (*Groffulariæfolia*) foliis obovatis acutè incifis, pedunculis bifloris. Prod. Leyd. 347. *Hermannia with oval leaves acutely cut, end foot-ftalks having two flowers.* Hermannia frutefcens folio groffulariæ parvo hirfuto. Boerh. Ind. *Shrubby Hermannia with a fmall, hairy, Goofeberry leaf.*

3. HERMANNIA (*Althæafolia*) foliis obovatis plicatis crenatis tomentofis. Hort. Cliff. 343. *Hermannia with oval, folded, woolly leaves, which are crenated.* Hermannia frutefcens, folio ibifei hirfuto molli, caule pilofo. Boerh. Ind. *Shrubby Hermannia with a foft, hairy, Marfhmallow leaf, and woolly ftalk.*

4. HERMANNIA (*Hyffopifolia*) foliis lanceolatis obtufis ferratis. Hort. Cliff. 342. *Hermannia with obtufe fpear-fhaped leaves, which are fawed.* Hermannia frutefcens, folio oblongo ferrato. Tourn. *Shrubby Hermannia with an oblong ferrated leaf.*

5. HERMANNIA (*Trifoliata*) foliis oblongo-ovatis crenatis tomentofis flore mutabili. *Hermannia with oblong, oval, crenated woolly leaves, and a changeable flower.* Hermannia frutefcens, folio oblongo molli cordato hirfuto. Boerh. Ind. *Shrubby Hermannia with a foft, oblong, hairy, heart-fhaped leaf.*

6. HERMANNIA (*Pinnata*) foliis tripartitis, media pinnatifida. Hort. Cliff. *Hermannia with tripartite leaves ending in many points.* Hermannia frutefcens, folio multifido tenui, caule rubro. Boerh. Ind. alt. *Shrubby Hermannia with a narrow multifid leaf, and a red ftalk.*

7. HERMANNIA (*Lavendulifolia*) foliis lanceolatis obtufis integerrimis. Hort. Cliff. 342. *Hermannia with obtufe fpear-fhaped leaves, which are entire.* Hermannia frutefcens, folio lavendulæ latiori & obtufo, flore parvo aureo. Boerh. Ind. alt. *Shrubby Hermannia with a broad, blunt, Lavender leaf, and a fmall golden flower.*

8. HERMANNIA (*Hirfuta*) foliis fimplicibus ternatifque hirfutis feffilibus. *Hermannia with fingle and trifoliate leaves which are hairy, and fit clofe to the ftalk.*

The firft fort rifes with a fhrubby ftalk fix or eight feet high, dividing into many erect irregular branches, covered with a brown bark, garnifhed with wedge-fhaped leaves, which are narrow at their bafe, but broad and round at the top; they are about an inch long, and three quarters broad at the point, where they are indented and crenated. The flowers are produced in fhort fpikes on the upper part of the branches; they are of a pale yellow colour, but fmall; thefe appear in April and May, and are often fucceeded by feeds, which ripen in Auguft.

The fecond fort is a fhrub of lower ftature than the firft, but fends out a great number of branches, which fpread wide on every fide, garnifhed with fmaller leaves than thofe of the former, which are rough, and fit clofe to the branches. The flowers are produced in fhort clofe fpikes at the end of every fhoot, fo that the whole fhrub feems covered with flowers; they are of a bright yellow, and appear toward the end of April, but are not fucceeded by feeds in England.

The third fort is a plant of humbler growth than either of the former, feldom rifing more than two feet and a half high; the ftem is not fo woody, and the branches are foft and flender, garnifhed with oval woolly leaves, which are plaited and crenated on the edges; the flowers are produced in loofe panicles at the end of the branches; they are larger than thofe of the other fpecies, and have very hairy empalements. This fort flowers in June and July, and frequently puts out more in the autumn.

The fourth fort has been longer in the European gardens than either of the other. This rifes with a fhrubby upright ftalk to the height of feven or eight feet, fending out many ligneous branches from the fide, which alfo grow more erect than any of the other; thefe are cloathed with obtufe fpear-fhaped leaves,

about

about an inch and a half long, and half an inch broad, fawed on the edges toward the end: the flowers come out in fmall bunches from the fide of the ftalk; they are of a pale Straw colour, and appear in May and June; thefe are frequently fucceeded by feeds, which ripen the latter part of Auguft.

The fifth fort feldom rifes more than two feet high, with a foft ligneous ftalk, fending out flender irregular branches, garnifhed with oblong, oval, woolly leaves, ftanding upon pretty long footftalks; the flowers are produced in loofe fpikes at the end of the branches; thefe are, at their firft appearance, of a gold colour, but after they have been fome days open, they change to yellow. This flowers in June and July.

The fixth fort rifes with a fhrubby ftalk near three feet high, fending out many flender branches, covered with a reddifh bark, garnifhed with narrow wing-pointed leaves; the flowers come out from the fide of the branches in fmall clufters; they are fmall, and of a deep yellow colour. This flowers in June and July.

The feventh fort hath fhrubby branching ftalks, which are very bufhy, but feldom rife more than a foot and a half high; the branches are very flender, and garnifhed with hairy, pale, green leaves of different fizes; fome of them are two inches long, and one broad at their ends; but their common fize is feldom more than one inch long, and half an inch broad at their points; they are entire, and fit pretty clofe to the branches; the flowers come out from the fide of the ftalk fingly, they are fmall, and of a yellow colour. This fort flowers moft part of fummer.

The eighth fort I raifed from feeds which came from the Cape of Good Hope. This rifes with a fhrubby hairy ftalk about two feet high, fending out many fide branches, which grow more erect than thofe of the former, garnifhed with oblong, veined, hairy leaves, which are fometimes fingle, and at other times come out by threes, the middle one being the largeft; the flowers are produced toward the end of the branches; they are large, and of a deep yellow colour, with large, fwollen, hairy empalements. This fort continues flowering moft part of fummer.

All the fpecies of this genus yet known, are natives of the country about the Cape of Good Hope, from whence moft of them were brought to the gardens in Holland, where they have been propagated and fpread through moft parts of Europe.

The plants are all propagated by planting cuttings of them during any of the fummer months, in a bed of frefh earth, obferving to water and fhade them until they are well rooted, which will be in about fix weeks after planting; then you fhould take them up, preferving a ball of earth to their roots, and plant them into pots filled with light frefh earth, placing them in a fhady fituation until they have taken frefh root; after which they may be expofed to the open air, with Myrtles, Geraniums, &c. until the middle or latter end of October, when they muft be removed into the green-houfe, obferving to place them in the cooleft part of the houfe, where they may have as much free air as poffible; for if they are too much drawn in the houfe, they will appear very faint and fickly, and feldom produce many flowers; whereas, when they are only preferved from the froft, and have a great fhare of free air, they will appear ftrong and healthy, and produce large quantities of flowers in April and May, during which feafon they make a very handfome appearance in the green-houfe: they muft alfo be frequently watered, and will require to be new potted at leaft twice every year, i. e. in May and September; otherwife their roots will be fo matted, as to prevent their growth.

Thefe plants rarely produce good feeds with us, except the fourth and eighth forts, which ripen their feeds every year in England; the other rarely producing any, I fuppofe this may be accounted for by their having been long propagated from cuttings; for thofe plants which I have raifed from feeds, have been fruitful two or three years after, but I have always found thofe plants which have been propagated ·by cuttings taken from thefe, have foon become barren: the fame thing I have obferved in many other plants, therefore thofe who are defirous to continue their plants fruitful, fhould conftantly raife them from feeds. Thefe, as alfo thofe which are obtained from abroad, muft be fown upon a moderate hot-bed; and when the plants come up, they muft be tranfplanted into fmall pots, and plunged into another very moderate hot-bed, in order to promote their rooting; after which they muft be hardened by degrees, to endure the open air in fummer, and may then be treated as the old plants.

HERMODACTYLUS, the Hermodactyl, commonly called Snake's-head Iris.

This genus is by Dr. Linnæus joined to Iris, the characters of the flower agreeing pretty well with thofe of that genus; from which Tournefort has feparated it from the difference of the root, which is not according to his own fyftem, where he makes the fhape of the petals with their number and pofition, the principal characteriftics in diftinguifhing the claffes and genera; but as this plant requires a particular treatment, fo I have continued it under Tournefort's title.

The Characters are,

It hath a Lily-fhaped flower, confifting of one leaf, and fhaped exactly like an Iris, but has a tuberous root, divided into two or three digs, like oblong bulbs.

We have but one Species of this plant, viz.

Hermodactylus (*Tuberofa*) folio quadrangulo. C. B. P. *Snake's-head Iris*, vulgo. This is alfo called Iris tuberofa Belgarum, i. e. *Tuberous Iris of the Dutch.*

This plant is eafily propagated by its tubers, which fhould be taken off foon after the green leaves decay, which is the proper feafon for tranfplanting the root; but they fhould not be kept long out of the ground, left they fhrink, which will caufe them to rot when they are planted. They fhould have a loamy foil, not too ftrong nor deep, and muft be planted to an eaft afpect, where they will flower very well. The roots fhould not be removed oftener than once in three years, if you defign to increafe them; but then they fhould be planted at a farther diftance from each other, than if they were to remain but one year; and the beds fhould be kept clear from weeds, and at Michaelmas there fhould be fome fine earth laid over the beds, which will greatly ftrengthen their roots. The diftance which thefe plants fhould be allowed is fix inches fquare, and they fhould be placed three inches deep in the ground. Thefe produce their flowers in May, and their feeds are ripe in Auguft; but as they multiply pretty faft by their roots, few people are at the trouble of raifing them from feeds; but thofe who have an inclination fo to do, muft treat them in the manner directed for the bulbous Irifes.

The roots of this plant are very apt to run deep into the ground, and then they feldom produce flowers; and many times they fhoot fo deep as to be loft, efpecially where the foil is very light; therefore to prevent this, it will be proper to lay a thicknefs of rubbifh under the border where thefe are planted, to hinder them from getting down. This fhould always be practifed in light ground, but in ftrong land there will be no occafion to make ufe of this precaution, becaufe they do not fhoot downward fo freely in that.

This plant has by fome botanic writers been fuppofed the true Hermodactyl, but what has been long ufed in Europe for that is the root of a Colchicum.

HERNANDIA. Plum. Nov. Gen. 8. tab. 40. Lin. Gen. Plant. 931. Jack-in-a-Box, vulgo.

The Characters are,

It hath male and female flowers on the fame plant; the male flowers have a partial involucrum, compofed of four oval fmall leaves, which inclofe three flowers; each of thefe has a proper bell-fhaped empalement of one leaf; the petal is funnel-fhaped, cut into fix fegments at the brim; it hath three fhort ftamina inferted in the empalement, terminated by erect fummits. The female flowers are

are ſhaped like the male, but want ſtamina; they have a roundiſh germen, ſupporting three ſlender ſtyles, crowned by acute ſtigmas. The empalement afterward becomes a large, ſwollen, oblong fruit, perforated at each end, incloſing one hard globular nut.

This genus of plants is ranged in the third ſection of Linnæus's twenty-fiſt claſs, intitled Monœcia Triandria, which includes thoſe plants which have male and female flowers in the ſame plant, whoſe male flowers have three ſtamina.

We have but one SPECIES of this genus in England, viz.

HERNANDIA (*Senera*) foliis peltatis. Hort. Cliff. 485. tab. 13. Hernandia amplo umbilicato.

Plum. *Hernandia with a large umbilicated Ivy leaf, commonly called in the Weſt-Indies, Jack-in-a-box.*

This plant is very common in Jamaica, Barbadoes, St. Chriſtopher's, and many other iſlands in the Weſt-Indies, where it is known by the name of Jack-in-a-box. The fruit of this plant when ripe, is perforated, and the nut in the inſide becomes hard; ſo that when the wind blows through the fruit, it makes a whiſtling noiſe, which may be heard at a diſtance; fom whence, I ſuppoſe, the inhabitants gave this name to the plant. It grows in the gullies, where there are rills of water.

In Europe this plant is preſerved in curious gardens, with other tender exotic plants. It is propagated by ſowing the ſeeds in a hot-bed in the ſpring; and when the plants have ariſen two inches high, they ſhould be tranſplanted each into a ſeparate pot, filled with freſh rich earth, and plunged into the hot-bed again, obſerving to water and ſhade them until they have taken root; after which time they muſt have air admitted to them, (by raiſing the glaſſes) in proportion to the warmth of the air, or the heat of the bed in which they are placed; and ſhould be frequently watered, otherwiſe they will not thrive. As the plants advance, they ſhould be removed into larger pots, which ſhould be filled with rich earth; but in doing this, you ſhould be very careful not to break the roots, as alſo to preſerve a good ball of earth to them; and if their leaves ſhould hang after being removed, the plants muſt be ſcreened from the ſun until they have taken new root. The beſt time to ſhift theſe plants is in July, that they may be well rooted before the cold approaches; the plants muſt be conſtantly kept in the bark-ſtove: in winter they ſhould have a moderate ſhare of heat, and in the ſummer they muſt have plenty of air in hot weather. With this management, the plants will grow to the height of ſixteen feet or more, and the leaves being very large, will make a beautiful appearance in the ſtove. It hath not as yet flowered in England, though we may expect ſome of the large plants to flower in a ſhort time.

HERNIARIA. Tourn. Inſt. R. H. 507. tab. 228. Lin. Gen. Plant. 272. [of *Hernia*, Lat. a rupture.] Rupturewort.

The CHARACTERS are,

The flower hath no petals, but a coloured empalement of one leaf, cut into five parts which ſpread open. It hath five ſmall awl-ſhaped ſtamina, ſituated in the diviſions of the empalement, terminated by ſingle ſummits, and five others which are barren, placed alternately between them. In the center is an oval germen which have acute points; the germen afterward turns to a ſmall capſule incloſed in the empalement, having one oval-pointed ſeed.

This genus of plants is ranged in the ſecond ſection of Linnæus's fifth claſs, intitled Pentandria Digynia, which includes the plants whoſe flowers have five ſtamina and two ſtyles.

The SPECIES are,

1. HERNIARIA (*Glabra*) glabra herbacea. J. B. 3. 378. *Smooth Rupturewort.*

2. HERNIARIA (*Hirſuta*) hirſuta herbacea. J. B. 3. 379. *Rough or hairy Rupturewort.*

3. HERNIARIA (*Alſines folia*) alſines folio. Tourn. Inſt. 507. *Rupturewort with a Chickweed leaf.*

4. HERNIARIA (*Fruticoſa*) caulibus fruticoſis, floribus quadrifidis. Amœn. Acad. 4. p. 369. *Rupturewort with ligneous ſtalks and quadrifid flowers.* Herniaria fruticoſa, viticulis lignoſis. C. B. P. 382.

The two firſt ſorts grow naturally in England, but not very common; they are low trailing plants, their branches lying on the ground, and extend ſeven or eight inches each way; they have leaves like the ſmaller Chickweed, the firſt is ſmooth, and thoſe of the ſecond are hairy; the flowers come out in cluſters from the ſide of the ſtalks at the joints; they are ſmall, and of a yellowiſh green, ſo make no appearance.

The fourth ſort hath ſhrubby ſtalks which trail upon the ground, garniſhed with ſmall hairy leaves like the ſecond ſort; the flowers are alſo very like that.

The third ſort is an annual plant, which grows naturally in France and Italy. This doth not ſpread ſo much as either of the other ſorts, but the flowers and leaves are ſomewhat like the firſt, but larger.

Theſe plants are ſeldom cultivated, but in botanic gardens for the ſake of variety. The three firſt are annual plants, ſeldom continuing longer than one year; and muſt be permitted to ſhed their ſeeds, whereby they are better preſerved than if ſown with art. The fourth ſort is an abiding plant, which may be propagated by cuttings; but as they are plants of no beauty, they are rarely preſerved in gardens. The firſt ſort is what ſhould be uſed in the ſhops, but is rarely ſeen in London, the herb-women commonly bringing the Parſley Breakſtone to the markets, which is ſold inſtead of this plant.

HESPERIS. Tourn. Inſt. R. H. 222. tab. 108. Lin. Gen. Plant. 731. [ſome derive the name of this plant from Heſperia, Italy, from whence the people were anciently called Heſperides; but it is pretty plain, that the name was taken from Ἕσπερος, becauſe the flower commonly ſmells moſt in an evening; either of theſe may be admitted. It is called Viola Matronalis, becauſe it reſembles the Violet, and was at firſt cultivated by women.] Dame's Violet, Rocket, or Queen's Gilliflower; in French, *Juliane*, or *Juliene.*

The CHARACTERS are,

The flower is compoſed of four oblong petals in form of a croſs, whoſe baſe or tails are narrow, and are ſituated in a four-leaved empalement, which falls away. It hath ſix awl-ſhaped ſtamina, four of them as long as the tube of the flower, and two much ſhorter, terminated by narrow erect ſummits, reflexed at their points. It hath a honey-gland ſituated between the two ſhort ſtamina, and a four-cornered germen the length of the ſtamina, but no ſtyle, the oblong erect ſtigma ſitting on the germen; the ſtigma is divided into two parts, which join at their points. The germen afterward becomes a plain, long, compreſſed pod with two cells, divided by an intermediate partition, incloſing many oval compreſſed ſeeds.

This genus of plants is ranged in the ſecond ſection of Linnæus's fifteenth claſs, intitled Tetradynamia Siliquoſa, the flowers having four long and two ſhort ſtamina, and are ſucceeded by long pods.

The SPECIES are,

1. HESPERIS (*Matronalis*) caule ſimplici erecto, foliis ovato-lanceolatis denticulatis, petalis mucrone emarginatis. Lin. Sp. 927. *Dame's Violet with a ſingle erect ſtalk, oval, ſpear-ſhaped, indented leaves, and the petals of the flowers indented at the top.* Heſperis hortenſis, flore purpureo. C. B. P. 202. *Garden Rocket with a purple flower.*

2. HESPERIS (*Alba*) caule ſimplici erecto, foliis lanceolatis ſerratis, petalis integris. *Dame's Violet with a ſingle upright ſtalk, ſpear-ſhaped ſawed leaves, and the petals of the flower entire.* Heſperis hortenſis flore candido. C. B. P. 202. *Garden Rocket with a white flower.*

3. HESPERIS (*Inodora*) caule ſimplici erecto, foliis ſubhaſtatis dentatis petalis obtuſis. Lin. Sp. 727. *Dame's Violet with a ſingle upright ſtalk, halbert-ſhaped, indented, obtuſe leaves and petals.* Heſperis ſylveſtris inodora. C. B. P. 202. *Unſavoury wild Rocket.*

4. HES-

4. Hesperis (*Triſtis*) caule hiſpido ramoſo patente. Hort. Upſal. 187. *Dame's Violet with a prickly, branching, ſpreading ſtalk.* Heſperis montana, pallidia, odoratiſſima. C. B. P. 202. *Sweeteſt pale Mountain Rocket.*

5. Hesperis (*Siberica*) caule ſimplici, foliis lanceolatis dentato-ferratis, petalis obtuſiſſimis integris. Lin. Sp. 927. *Dame's Violet with a ſingle ſtalk, ſpear-ſhaped ſawed leaves, and blunt entire petals to the flower.*

6. Hesperis (*Exigua*) caule ramoſiſſimo diffuſo, foliis lineari-lanceolatis dentatis, ſiliquis apice truncatis. *Dame's Violet with a very branching diffuſed ſtalk, narrow, ſpear-ſhaped, indented leaves, and the points of the pods ſhaped like a truncheon.* Heſperis exigua lutea, folio dentato anguſto. Boerh. Ind. 146. *Rocket with a very ſmall yellow flower, and a narrow indented leaf.*

7. Hesperis (*Dentata*) foliis dentato-pinnatifidis, caule lævi. Lin. Sp. Plant. 664. *Dame's Violet with wing-pointed indented leaves, and a ſmooth ſtalk.* Heſperis flore albo minimo, ſiliquâ longâ, folio profundè dentato. Boerh. Ind. alt. 2. 20. *Rocket with a ſmall white flower, a long pod, and leaves deeply indented.*

8. Hesperis (*Africana*) caule ramoſiſſimo diffuſo, fo liis petiolatis lanceolatis acute dentatis ſcabris ſiliquis ſeſſilibus. Lin. Sp. Plant. 928. *Dame's Violet with very branching diffuſed ſtalks, ſpear-ſhaped, rough, ſawed leaves, and pods fitting cloſe to the ſtalks.* Heſperis Africana, hieracii folio hirſuto, flore minimo purpuraſcente. Niſſol. Act. *African Rocket with a hairy Hawkweed leaf, and a very ſmall purpliſh flower.*

9. Hesperis (*Verna*) caule erecto ramoſo, foliis cordatis amplexicaulibus ſerratis villoſis. Lin. Sp. Plant. 664. *Dame's Violet with an erect branching ſtalk, and hairy, ſawed, heart-ſhaped leaves embracing the ſtalk.* Turritis annua verna, purpuraſcente flore. Tourn. Inſt. 224. *Annual vernal Tower Muſtard, with a purpliſh flower.*

The firſt ſort grows naturally in Italy ; this was formerly in greater plenty in the Engliſh gardens than at preſent, having been long neglected becauſe the flowers were ſingle, and made but little appearance ; however, as the flowers have a very grateful ſcent, ſo the plant is worthy of a place in every good garden. This riſes with an upright ſtalk a foot and a half high, garniſhed with ſpear-ſhaped leaves which fit cloſe to the ſtalk, and are ſlightly indented on their edges, ending in acute points : the flowers are produced in a looſe thyrſe on the top of the ſtalks ; they are compoſed of four petals, which are roundiſh and indented at their points, of a deep purple colour, and ſmell very ſweet, eſpecially in the evening or in cloudy weather. It flowers in June, and the ſeeds ripen the latter end of Auguſt. It is a biennial plant, ſo that young plants ſhould be raiſed every year, to ſupply the place of thoſe which decay : if the ſeeds are permitted to ſcatter, the plants will come up without trouble in the ſpring ; and if the ſeeds are ſown, the beſt ſeaſon for it is in the autumn ; becauſe thoſe which are ſown in the ſpring often fail if the ſeaſon proves dry, or will remain a long time in the ground before they vegetate. This plant ſhould have a loamy undunged ſoil, in which it will thrive better than in rich land.

There is a variety of this with double flowers, in ſome of the gardens in France ; but that which we have in England, is a variety of the third ſort with unſavoury flowers.

The ſecond ſort has been generally ſuppoſed only a variety of the firſt, differing in the colour of the flower, but is certainly a diſtinct ſpecies ; the leaves of this are not ſo long, but much broader than thoſe of the firſt, and their borders are entire ; the flowers are not quite ſo large, nor do they form ſo good ſpikes ; they are white, and have not ſo fine a ſcent as the firſt. This is alſo a biennial plant, requiring the ſame treatment as the firſt.

The third ſort grows naturally in Hungary and Auſtria. This riſes with an upright ſtalk near two feet high, garniſhed with ſpear-ſhaped leaves, ending in acute points, and ſharply indented on their edges ; they are of a dark green, and fit cloſe to the ſtalks ;

4

the flowers grow in looſe ſpikes on the top of the ſtalks ; in ſome they are white, in others purple, and ſometimes both colours ſtriped in the ſame flower ; theſe have no odour, ſo are not deſerving of a place in gardens, but may be propagated in the ſame manner as the two former.

From this ſort, the double white and purple Rockets have been accidentally obtained, which are much eſteemed for the beauty of their flowers ; and if they had the agreeable odour of the Garden Rocket, they would be ſome of the beſt furniture for the borders of the flower-garden, but they are without ſcent ; however, for the beauty of their flowers, they are by ſome greatly eſteemed, therefore I ſhall here inſert the beſt method of propagating them yet known.

Theſe plants are naturally biennial, ſo the plants with ſingle flowers rarely ſurvive the ſecond year ; nor will thoſe with double flowers continue much longer ; ſo that unleſs young plants are annually raiſed to ſupply the place of the old ones, there will ſoon be a want of them, which is what few perſons are careful enough to obſerve ; but thinking the roots to be perennial, truſt to their putting out offsets, or the plants remaining after they have flowered ; and finding them decay, are apt to think their ſoil very improper for them, and are at a loſs to account for their decaying ; whereas, when the plants have flowered, they have finiſhed their period, and ſeldom continue to flower a ſecond time from the ſame root ; though in poor land, they will often put out a few weak offsets, which may flower again, but ſeldom ſo ſtrong as the principal roots ; therefore thoſe who are deſirous to propagate theſe plants, ſhould do it in the following manner :

There ſhould be ſome ſtrong roots of each ſort kept apart for this purpoſe, which are not intended to flower ; when theſe have ſhot up their flower-ſtalks about ſix inches high, they ſhould be cut cloſe to the bottom ; each of theſe may be divided in the middle to make two cuttings, which ſhould be planted in a ſoft, gentle, loamy ſoil, to an eaſt expoſure, where they may have only the morning ſun ; and theſe may be planted pretty near together, ſo as to be covered with hand or bell-glaſſes, which ſhould be put over them after the cuttings have been well watered, and cloſely ſhut down, drawing the earth round the rim of the glaſſes to exclude the air ; then the glaſſes ſhould be ſhaded with mats every day when the ſun is hot ; and if the cuttings are gently refreſhed with water once in ſeven or eight days, it will be ſufficient, for too much moiſture will cauſe them to rot : when theſe are watered, the glaſſes ſhould be cloſely ſhut down again as before ; with this management the cuttings will put out roots in five or ſix weeks, and will begin to ſhoot above ; then the glaſſes ſhould be gently raiſed on one ſide to admit the air to them, and ſo gradually harden them to the open air, to prevent their drawing up weak. When theſe have made good roots, they ſhould be carefully removed, and planted in an eaſt border at about eight or nine inches aſunder, obſerving to ſhade and water them till they have taken new root ; after which they will require no other care, but to keep them clean from weeds till the autumn, when they may be tranſplanted into the borders of the pleaſure-garden, where they are deſigned to flower.

The roots which are thus cut down, will ſend up more ſtalks than before ; and when theſe are of a proper height, they may be cut off and treated in the ſame way ; ſo that if the roots are ſound, there may be two or three crops of theſe cuttings taken from them, and by ſo doing, the old roots may be continued much longer than if they are permitted to flower ; and by this management, there may be always a ſupply of good plants for the flower-garden.

Theſe plants are very ſubject to canker and rot when they are planted in a light rich ſoil, but in poor ſtrong ground, I have ſeen them thrive and flower in the utmoſt perfection, where the ſtems of flowers have been as large, and the flowers as fair as the fineſt double

Stock-

Stock-gilliflowers. Their season of flowering is in the beginning of June, and I have frequently raised young plants from the stalks after the flowers have decayed, by cutting them in lengths, and planting them in the manner before directed; but these seldom make so good plants as the young cuttings, nor are they so certain to grow, therefore the other are to be preferred.

The fourth sort grows naturally in Hungary. This is much cultivated in the gardens abroad, for the great fragrancy of its flowers, which in the evening is so strong, as to perfume the air at a great distance, especially where there are any number of the plants. The ladies in Germany are very fond of this plant, and during the season of their flowering, have the pots placed in their apartments every evening, that they may enjoy the fragrancy of their flowers; for they have but little beauty, being smaller than those of the Garden Rocket, and of a pale colour, but the scent of their flowers is much preferable to them; though in the day-time, if the weather is clear, they have very little odour; but when the sun leaves them, their fragrancy is expanded to a great distance. To this species it is supposed, that the title of Dame's Violet was first applied.

This sort is very rarely seen in the English gardens: I suppose it has been neglected, because the flowers make no appearance. It is a biennial plant like the Garden Rocket, which is propagated by seeds in the same manner; but the plants are not quite so hardy, and are very subject to rot in winter, especially on a moist soil, or in rich land, where they are apt to grow very rank, so are soon injured by wet and cold in the winter; therefore the plants of this sort should be planted in a dry poor soil, and a warm situation; and if some of them are planted in pots to be placed under a common frame in winter, where they may be sheltered from hard rains and frost, but enjoy the free air at all times when the weather is mild, it will be a sure way to preserve them.

The leaves of this sort are much larger than those of the Garden Rocket, and of a paler green; the stalks are closely set with bristly hairs; the flowers grow in loose panicles at the top of the stalk, and appear about the same time with the Garden Rocket.

The seeds of the fifth sort were sent me from Germany without any title, nor any account of the country from whence it came; but as it was sent with the seeds of some Siberian plants, I suppose this came from the same country. This is a biennial plant, which rises with a strong branching stalk between two and three feet high, which is very hairy, garnished with oblong heart-shaped leaves, ending in acute points, sitting close to the stalk; they are four inches long, and one and a half broad at their base, gradually diminishing to the point, and are slightly sawed on their edges; the upper part of the stalk divides into two or three branches, which are garnished with small leaves of the same shape with those below, and are terminated with loose panicles of single, large, purple flowers of great fragrancy. This sort flowered the end of June 1757, but the great rains which fell in August, rotted the plants before the seeds were ripe.

The sixth sort grows naturally in the warm parts of Europe; this is annual; the stalks rise about eight or nine inches high, branching out greatly on every side in a confused order; they are garnished with small, narrow, indented leaves, and are terminated by clusters of small yellow flowers, which make no appearance.

The seventh sort grows naturally in Sicily. This is an annual plant, which seldom rises more than six inches high; the stalk branches toward the top into three or four smaller, which are terminated by small white flowers; the leaves are two inches long and one broad, cut almost to the midrib on each side, so as to resemble a winged leaf.

The eighth sort grows naturally in Africa. This is an annual plant with a very branching stalk, which rises about nine inches high, garnished with rough

spear-shaped leaves sawed on their edges, and terminated by loose panicles of small purple flowers, which appear in June and July; these are succeeded by long pods fitting close to the stalks, and are filled with small seeds which ripen in September.

These three sorts are rarely cultivated, except in botanic gardens for the sake of variety. If the seeds of these are permitted to scatter, the plants will come up without care, and only require to be kept clean from weeds; or they may be sown either in the spring or the autumn where they are to stand, for they do not bear transplanting well.

The ninth sort is an annual plant, which grows naturally in the south of France. This sends out several heart-shaped leaves from the root, which spread on the ground; they are sawed and hairy: the stalk rises nine inches high, branching toward the top, garnished with leaves of the same shape, which embrace the stalks with their base; the flowers are produced in loose panicles at the end of the branches; they are of a lively purple colour, and those plants which rise in the autumn, flower early in the spring. If these seeds are sown in the autumn, they succeed much better than in the spring.

HEUCHERA. Lin. Gen. Plant. 283. Sanicle.

The CHARACTERS are,

The flower is composed of five narrow petals, which are inserted in the border of the one-leaved empalement. It hath five erect awl-shaped stamina, which are much longer than the empalement, terminated by roundish summits. It hath a roundish bifid germen, with two erect styles the length of the stamina, crowned by obtuse stigmas. The germen afterward turns to an oval-pointed capsule with two horns, which are reflexed, having two cells filled with very small seeds.

This genus of plants is ranged in the second section of Linnæus's fifth class, which includes those plants whose flowers have five stamina and two styles.

We have but one SPECIES of this genus, viz.

HEUCHERA,(*Americana.*) Hort. Cliff. 82. Mitella Americana, flore squallidè purpureo villoso. Boerh. Ind. alt. *Mitella of America, with hairy flowers of a dirty purple colour.*

This plant grows naturally in Virginia, but is hardy enough to thrive in the open air in England. It hath a perennial root, which sends out many heart-shaped oval leaves, which are indented into four or five lobes, and are crenated on their edges, of a lucid green, and smooth; from between these come out the foot-stalks of the flower, which are naked, and rise a foot high, dividing at the top into a loose panicle, sustaining many small hairy flowers, of an obsolete purple colour. This flowers in May, and the seeds ripen in August.

It is propagated by parting the roots in autumn, and should be planted in a shady situation; there is little beauty in this plant, but it is preserved in some gardens for the sake of variety.

HIBISCUS. Lin. Gen. Plant. 756. Ketmia. Tourn. Inst. R. H. 99. tab. 26. *Syrian Mallow.*

The CHARACTERS are,

The flower has a double empalement, which is permanent; the outer is composed of eight or ten narrow leaves, the inner is shaped like a cup, and is of one leaf, cut at the brim into five acute points. It hath five heart-shaped petals, which join at their base into one. It hath many stamina, which are joined to the style, in form of a column, within the tube of the flower, but expand toward the top, and are terminated by kidney-shaped summits. It has a round germen, with slender styles longer than the stamina, crowned by roundish stigmas. The germen afterward turns to a capsule with five cells, opening in five parts, inclosing kidney-shaped seeds.

This genus of plants is ranged in the third section of Linnæus's sixteenth class, which includes those plants whose flowers have many stamina joined to the styles in one body, forming a column.

The SPECIES are,

1. HIBISCUS (*Syriacus*) foliis cuneiformi-ovatis, supernè inciso-dentatis, caule arboreo. Hort. Cliff. 350. *Hibiscus*

cus with wedge-shaped oval leaves, whose upper parts are cut, indented, and a tree-like stalk. Ketmia Syrorum quibusdam. C. B. P. 316. *The Syrian Ketmia, commonly called Althæa frutex.*

2. HIBISCUS (*Sinensis*) foliis cordato-quinquangularis obsoletè serratis, caule arboreo. Hort. Upsal. 205. *Hibiscus with heart-shaped leaves, having five angles which are slightly sawed, and a tree-like stalk.* Ketmia sinensis, fructu subrotundo. Tourn. Inst. R. H. 100. *China Ketmia with a roundish fruit, commonly called China Rose.*

3. HIBISCUS (*Abelmoschus*) foliis subpeltato-cordatis septemangularibus, serratis hispidis. Hort. Cliff. 349. *Hibiscus with heart-shaped target leaves, having seven angles which are sawed, and set with prickly hairs.* Ketmia Americana hirsuta, flore flavo, & semine moschato. Tourn. Inst. R. H. 100. *Hairy American Ketmia with a yellow flower and musky seed, commonly called Musk.*

4. HIBISCUS (*Manihot*) foliis palmato-digitatis septempartitis. Hort. Cliff. 350. *Hibiscus with fingered leaves, which are divided into seven parts.* Ketmia Americana, folio Papayæ, flore magno flavescente, fundo purpureo, fructu erecto pyramidali hexagono, semine rotundulo sapore fatuo. Boerh. Ind. alt. 1. 272. *American Ketmia with a Papaw leaf, and a large yellow flower, having a purple bottom, a pyramidal, six-cornered, erect fruit, and round seeds of a flat taste.*

5. HIBISCUS (*Tomentosus*) foliis cordatis angulatis serratis tomentosis, caule arboreo. *Hibiscus with angular, heart-shaped, sawed, woolly leaves, and a tree-like stalk.* Malva arboreo, folio oblongo acuminato veluto dentato & leviter sinuato, flore ex rubro flavescente. Sloan. Cat. 95. *Tree Mallow with oblong, acute-pointed, indented leaves, slightly sinuated, and a reddish yellow flower.*

6. HIBISCUS (*Tiliaceus*) foliis cordatis subrotundis indivisis acuminatis crenatis, caule arboreo. Prod. Leyd. 532. *Hibiscus with entire heart-shaped leaves, and a tree-like stalk.* Ketmia Indica tiliæ folio. Tourn. Inst. R. H. 100. *Indian Ketmia with a Lime-tree leaf.*

7. HIBISCUS (*Javanica*) foliis ovatis acuminatis serratis glabris, caule arboreo. Flor. Zeyl. 260. *Hibiscus with oval-pointed, sawed, smooth leaves, and a tree-like stalk.* Alcea Javanica arborescens, flore pleno rubicundo. Bryen. Cent. 121. tab. 56. *Tree Vervain Mallow of Java, with a double red flower, called in India Shoe-flower.*

8. HIBISCUS (*Vitifolis*) foliis serratis inferioribus ovatis indivisis, superioribus quinquepartitis, caule aculeato. Prod. Leyd. 358. *Hibiscus with sawed leaves, the lower oval and undivided, the upper divided into five parts, and a prickly stalk.* Ketmia Indica vitis folio, magno flore. Tourn. Inst. R. H. 100. *Indian Ketmia with a Vine leaf and large flower.*

9. HIBISCUS (*Sabdariffa*) foliis serratis, inferioribus cordatis, mediis tripartitis, summis quinquepartitis, caule aculeato. *Hibiscus with sawed leaves, the lower ones being heart-shaped, the middle divided into three parts, the upper into five, and a prickly stalk.* Ketmia Ægyptiaca vitis folio, parvo flore. Tourn. Inst. R. H. 100. *Egyptian Ketmia with a Vine leaf and a small flower.*

10. HIBISCUS (*Gossypifolius*) foliis quinquelobatis serratis, caule glabro. *Hibiscus with sawed leaves divided into five lobes, and a smooth stalk.* Ketmia Indica, Gossyppii folio, acetosæ sapore. Tourn. Inst. R. H. 100. *Indian Ketmia with a Cotton leaf, and the taste of Sorrel.*

11. HIBISCUS (*Ficulneus*) foliis quinquefido-palmatis, caule aculeato. Hort. Cliff. 498. *Hibiscus with hand-shaped five-pointed leaves, and a prickly stalk.* Ketmia Zeylanica, fici folio, perianthio oblongo integro. Hort. Elth. 190. tab. 157. *Ketmia of Ceylon with a Fig leaf, and an oblong entire perianthium.*

12. HIBISCUS (*Surattensis*) foliis quinquepartitis, lobis ovato-lanceolatis hirsutis crenatis, caule spinosissimo. *Hibiscus with leaves divided into five lobes, which are oval, spear-shaped, hairy, and crenated, and a very prickly stalk.* Ketmia Indica aculeata, foliis digitatis. Tourn. Inst. 101. *Prickly Indian Ketmia with hand-shaped leaves.*

13. HIBISCUS (*Cordifolius*) foliis cordatis hirsutis crenatis, floribus lateralibus, caule arboreo ramoso. *Hibiscus with heart-shaped, hairy, crenated leaves, flowers growing from the sides of the branches, and a tree-like branching stalk.* Ketmia Americana frutescens foliis subrotundis crenatis hirsutis, flore luteo. Houst. *Shrubby American Ketmia with roundish, hairy, crenated leaves, and a yellow flower.*

14. HIBISCUS (*Babamensis*) foliis oblongo-cordatis glabris, denticulatis, subtus incanis, floribus amplissimis. *Hibiscus with oblong, heart-shaped, smooth, indented leaves, hoary on their under side, and very large flowers.*

15. HIBISCUS (*Ficifolius*) foliis quinquepartito pedatis, calycibus inferioribus latere rumpentibus. Lin. Sp. Plant. 696. *Hibiscus with leaves like a hand, divided into five parts, and the lower empalement torn sideways.* Ketmia Brasiliensis, folio ficus, fructu pyramidato sulcato. Tourn. Inst. R. H. 100. *Ketmia of the Brasils with a Fig leaf, and a pyramidal furrowed fruit.*

16. HIBISCUS (*Pentacarpos*) foliis inferioribus cordatis angulatis, superioribus subhastatis, floribus subnutantibus, pistillo cernuo. Lin. Sp. Plant. 697. *Hibiscus with lower leaves heart-shaped and angular, the upper ones somewhat spear-shaped, nodding flowers, and a recurved pistil.* Ketmia palustris minor, folio angusto, flore parvo purpurascente, fructu depresso pentagona. Zannich. Venet. 155. tab. 91. *Smaller Marsh Ketmia with a narrow leaf, a small purplish flower, and a five-cornered depressed fruit.*

17. HIBISCUS (*Populneus*) foliis ovatis acuminatis serratis, caule simplicissimo, petiolis floriferis. Hort. Upsal. 205. *Hibiscus with oval-pointed sawed leaves, a single stalk, and foot-stalks having flowers.* Ketmia Africana Populi folio. Tourn. Inst. 100. *African Ketmia with a Poplar leaf.*

18. HIBISCUS (*Palustris*) caule herbaceo simplicissimo, foliis ovatis subtrilobis, subtus tomentosis, floribus axillaribus. Lin. Sp. Plant. 693. *Hibiscus with a single herbaceous stalk, oval leaves having three lobes, woolly on their under side.* Ketmia palustris flore purpureo. Tourn. Inst. 100. *Marsh Ketmia with a purple flower.*

19. HIBISCUS (*Trionum*) foliis tripartitis incisis, calycibus inflatis. Hort. Upsal. 206. *Hibiscus with tripartite cut leaves, and a swollen empalement.* Ketmia vesicaria vulgaris. Tourn. Inst. *Common Bladder Ketmia, called Venice Mallow, or Flower of an hour.*

20. HIBISCUS (*Africana*) foliis tripartitis dentatis, lobis angustioribus caule hirsuto calycibus inflatis. *Hibiscus with tripartite indented leaves having narrower lobes, a hairy stalk, and swollen empalements.* Ketmia vesicaria Africana. Tourn. Inst. 101. *African Bladder Ketmia.*

21. HIBISCUS (*Hispidus*) foliis inferioribus trilobis, summis quinque partitis obtusis crenatis calycibus inflatis, caule hispido. *Hibiscus with under leaves having three lobes, the upper being cut into five obtuse segments, which are crenated, swollen empalements, and a prickly stalk.*

22. HIBISCUS (*Malvaviscus*) foliis cordatis-crenatis, angulis lateralibus extimis parvis, caule arboreo. Hort. Cliff. 349. *Hibiscus with heart-shaped crenated leaves, whose outward lateral angles are small, and a tree-like stalk.* Malvaviscus arborescens, flore miniato clauso. Hort. Elth. 210. tab. 170. *Tree-like, viscous, seeded Mallow, with a closed scarlet flower.*

The first sort is commonly called Althæa frutex by the nursery gardeners, who propagate the shrubs for sale ; of this there are four or five varieties, which differ in the colour of their flowers ; the most common hath pale purple flowers with dark bottoms ; another hath bright purple flowers with black bottoms, a third hath white flowers with purple bottoms ; a fourth variegated flowers with dark bottoms ; and a fifth pale yellow flowers with dark bottoms ; but the last is very rare at present in the English gardens ; there are also two with variegated leaves, which are by some much esteemed.

This grows naturally in Syria, from whence it has been introduced to the gardens, and is one of the great ornaments of the autumn season : it rises with a shrubby

stalk

ftalk to the height of fix or feven feet, fending out many ligneous branches, covered with a fmooth gray bark, garnifhed with oval fpear-fhaped leaves, whofe upper parts are frequently divided into three lobes, which are fawed; thefe are placed alternately on the branches, ftanding on fhort foot-ftalks. The flowers come out from the wings of the ftalks at every joint of the fame year's fhoot; they are large, and fhaped like thofe of the Mallow, having five large roundifh petals, which join at their bafe, fpreading open at the top in fhape of an open bell: thefe appear in Auguft, and if the feafon is not too warm, there will be a fucceffion of flowers part of September; the early flowers are fucceeded by fhort capfules with five cells, filled with kidney-fhaped feeds; but unlefs the feafon proves warm, they will not ripen in this country.

It is propagated by feeds, which fhould be fown in pots filled with light earth the latter end of March; and if they are plunged into a gentle heat, it will greatly forward the growth of the feeds. When the plants are come up, they muft be inured to the open air, and in May the pots may be plunged into the ground, in a border expofed to the eaft, where they may have the morning fun: the reafon of my advifing the pots to be plunged into the ground, is to prevent the earth from drying fo faft as it would do when the pots ftand on the furface, fo that the plants will not require fo much water in fummer; thefe plants will require no other culture, but to keep them clean from weeds, and in very dry weather to refrefh them with water during the firft fummer, but in autumn it will be proper to remove the pots under a common frame to fcreen them from the froft; or where there is not fuch conveniency, they may be plunged clofe to a hedge, pale, or wall, to a good afpect; and in fevere froft, they fhould be covered with mats, Straw, or other light covering; for although thefe plants, when they have obtained ftrength, will refift the cold of our winters, yet the young plants, whofe fhoots are tender, are very often injured by the firft froft of autumn: fo that if they are not fcreened the firft year, they are often killed to the ground. Toward the latter end of March will be a good time to tranfplant thefe plants, at which time a fpot of light ground muft be prepared to receive them, which fhould be divided into beds four feet broad, with paths of two feet broad between; then the plants fhould be fhaken out of the pots with the earth about them, and feparated with care, for their roots are very tender, and apt to break with little force; thefe fhould be planted at about nine inches afunder in the beds; fo that if four rows are planted in each bed, there will be fix inches allowed between the outfide rows and the paths. The ground fhould be gently clofed about the roots to prevent the air penetrating to them; and if a little old tanners bark, or mulch, is laid over the furface of the beds, it will prevent the earth from drying, and be of great ufe to the plants; during the following fummer they muft be kept clean from weeds, and if the following winter prove fevere, it will be prudent to cover the plants again in autumn, efpecially if they fhoot late in the feafon, or the autumn proves cold and moift, for then the plants will be in great danger of having their tops killed: in thefe beds the plants may remain two years, by which time they will be fit to tranfplant where they are defigned to remain; for if they are kept longer in the nurfery, they will not remove fo well. The beft time for tranfplanting thefe plants is the end of March, or the beginning of April, for they feldom begin to fhoot till the end of April, or the beginning of May; they fhould have a light foil, not too wet, for in ftrong land their ftems grow mofly, and they never thrive after.

Thefe plants may alfo be propagated by cuttings, which, if planted the latter end of March, in pots filled with light earth, and plunged into a gentle heat, will take root; but the plants fo raifed, are not fo good as the feedlings. The feveral varieties may be

propagated by grafting upon each other, which is the common method of propagating the forts with ftriped leaves.

The fecond fort grows naturally in India, from whence the French firft carried the feeds to their fettlements in the Weft-Indies; and the inhabitants of the Britifh colonies there have been fupplied with the feeds from them, fo have given it the title of Martinico Rofe: of this there are the double and fingle flowering, which from the feeds of the double the fingle is frequently produced, but the feeds of the fingle feldom vary to the double. The flowers of thefe plants alter in their colour, for at their firft opening they are white, then they change to a blufh Rofe colour, and as they decay they turn to a purple. In the Weft-Indies, all thefe alterations happen the fame day, as I fuppofe the flowers in thofe hot countries are not of longer duration: but in England, where the flowers laft near a week in beauty, the changes are not fo fudden.

This plant has a foft fpongy ftem, which, by age, becomes ligneous and pithy. It rifes to the height of twelve or fourteen feet, fending out branches on every fide toward the top, which are hairy, garnifhed with heart-fhaped leaves, cut into five acute angles on their borders, and are flightly fawed on their edges, of a lucid green on their upper fide, but pale below, ftanding alternately upon pretty long footftalks. The flowers are produced from the wings of the ftalk, like thofe of the firft fort; the fingle one is compofed of five large petals, which fpread open, and are firft white, but afterward change in the manner before-mentioned; thefe are fucceeded by fhort, thick, blunt capfules, which are very hairy, having five cells, which contain many fmall kidney-fhaped feeds, having a fine plume of fibrous down adhering to them.

This fort is propagated by feeds, which muft be fown upon a hot-bed in the fpring, and when the plants are fit to remove, they fhould be each planted in a feparate fmall pot filled with kitchen-garden earth, and plunged into a moderate hot-bed, where they muft be fhaded till they have taken new root; then they muft be treated as other plants from warm countries, but not too tenderly, for thefe require a large fhare of air in warm weather, otherwife they will draw up very weak: thefe plants fhould not be quite expofed to the open air the firft feafon, and the firft winter will require the warmth of a moderate ftove; but as they get more ftrength, they may be treated with lefs care, for they will bear the open air in fummer, in a warm fheltered fituation, and will live through the winter in a very good green-houfe, provided they have not too much wet; but the plants thus hardily treated, will not make fo great progrefs, nor flower fo well as with a little additional warmth; and if they are too tenderly managed, they will draw up weak, fo will be lefs likely to flower. This fort ufually flowers in England in November, fo that it keeps to the ufual time of flowering in its native country.

The third fort grows naturally in the Weft-Indies, where it is commonly known by the title of Mufk; the French cultivate great quantities of thefe plants in their American Iflands, the feeds of which are annually fent to France in great quantities, fo that they certainly have fome way of rendering it ufeful, as it feems to be a confiderable branch of trade. This rifes with an herbaceous ftalk about three or four feet high, fending out two or three fide branches, garnifhed with large leaves cut into fix or feven angles, which are acute, and fawed on their edges; thefe ftand on long foot-ftalks, and are placed alternately. The ftalks and leaves of this are very hairy. The flowers come out from the wings of the ftalk upon pretty long footftalks, which ftand erect; they are large, of a fulphur colour, with dark purple bottoms, and are fucceeded by pyramidal five-cornered capfules, which open in five cells, filled with large kidney-fhaped feeds of a very mufky odour.

This

This fort feldom lives more than one year in England, but in its native country will laft two years. It is propagated by feeds, which, if fown on a good hot-bed in the fpring, and the plants afterward planted in pots filled with light earth, and plunged into a frefh hot-bed, treating them afterward in the fame way as the Amaranthus, they will flower in July, and their feeds will ripen in autumn.

The fourth fort grows naturally in both the Indies; this rifes with an herbaceous fmooth ftalk three or four feet high, garnifhed with leaves which are divided into feven fegments almoft to the bottom; the middle fegment being four inches long and half an inch broad, the upper lateral fegments about three inches long and the fame breadth; thefe are indented at their extremities, but the lower fegments are not much more than an inch long, and have foot-ftalks, four inches long. The flowers are produced from the wings of the ftalks toward the top, ftanding on fhort foot-ftalks; they are compofed of five large fulphur-coloured petals, which, when open, fpread five inches wide; they have a dark purple bottom, with a column of ftamina and ftyles rifing in the center, and are fucceeded by large, pyramidal, five-cornered, erect feed-veffels, opening in five cells, which are filled with pretty large kidney-fhaped feeds, which have little fmell or tafte.

It is propagated by feeds in the fame manner as the former fort, and if fo managed, will produce flowers and perfect feeds the fame feafon; but the plants may be continued through the winter in a moderate warmth, though few perfons are at the trouble of preferving the plants after they have ripened their feeds, becaufe the young plants make a better appearance.

The fifth fort grows naturally in the Weft-Indies, where it rifes with a woody ftalk feven or eight feet high, fending out many fide branches toward the top, which are covered with a whitifh bark, and garnifhed with angular heart-fhaped leaves, which are woolly; they are about four inches long, and three broad toward their bafe, ending in acute points, and have feveral longitudinal veins. The flowers are produced from the wings of the ftalk upon long foot-ftalks; they are compofed of five roundifh petals, which are joined at their bafe, but fpread open above, and are of a yellow colour, turning to a red as they decay; thefe are fucceeded by large, obtufe, five-cornered, hairy feed-veffels, which open in five cells, filled with large kidney-fhaped feeds.

This is propagated by feeds, which muft be fown upon a hot-bed in the fpring, and the plants afterward treated in the fame way as the two laft mentioned, during the firft fummer, but in the autumn they muft be plunged into the tan-bed in the ftove, where they fhould conftantly remain, and be treated in the fame way as other tender plants from the fame country, giving them but little water in winter; the fecond year the plants will flower, but they have not as yet perfected feeds in England.

The fixth fort grows naturally in both Indies; this rifes with a woody pithy ftem eight or ten feet high, dividing into feveral branches toward the top, which are covered with a woolly down, and garnifhed with round heart-fhaped leaves, ending in acute points; they are of a lucid green on their upper fide, and hoary on their under, full of large veins, and are placed alternately on the ftalks. The flowers are produced at the end of the branches in loofe fpikes; they are of a whitifh yellow colour, and are fucceeded by fhort acuminated capfules, opening in five cells, filled with large kidney-fhaped feeds.

This fort is propagated in the fame way, and the plants require the fame treatment as the fifth, and flower the fecond year, provided they are brought forward, otherwife they will not flower before the third or fourth feafon; but they will bear the open air in fummer, in a warm fituation, though they will not make great progrefs there.

The feventh fort grows naturally on the coaft of

Malabar, from whence I received the plants; this rifes with a woody ftalk twelve or fourteen feet high, dividing into many fmall branches toward the top, which are garnifhed with oval fawed leaves, ending in acute points; they are of a lucid green above, but are pale on their under fide, and are placed without order. The flowers come out from the fide of the branches, at the wings of the leaves, on pretty long foot-ftalks; they are compofed of many oblong roundifh petals of a red colour, which expand like the Rofe, the flowers being as large when fully blown, as the common red Rofe, and as double. This is a perennial plant, which is propagated by cuttings, and the plants muft conftantly be kept in the ftove, giving them a large fhare of air in warm weather, and but little water in winter. There is a variety of this with white flowers, but I have not feen any of the plants in the Englifh gardens; nor have I feen the fingle flowering kind, for the inhabitants of India propagate that with double flowers by cuttings, which put out roots freely; this they do for the fake of flowers, which the women of that country make ufe of to colour their hair and eye-brows black, which will not wafh off: the Englifh there ufe it for blacking of their fhoes, and from thence have titled it Shoe-flower.

The eighth fort is an annual plant, which rifes with an upright ftalk feven or eight feet high; the lower leaves are oval, ferrated, and entire, but the upper leaves are divided almoft to the foot-ftalk, into five fpear-fhaped fegments, like the fingers of a hand, ftanding on very long foot-ftalks, which have thorns at their bafe, and are fharply fawed on their edges. The flowers come out from the wings of the ftalk, they are large, of a pale fulphur colour, with a dark purple bottom, and are fucceeded by oval acuminated, prickly capfules, which open in five cells, filled with large kidney-fhaped feeds.

This fort is propagated by feeds, which muft be fown upon a hot-bed, and the plants treated in the fame way as the third fort; and when they are grown too tall to ftand under the frames, they muft be placed in the ftove, where they will flower in Auguft, and the feeds will ripen in autumn.

The ninth fort is near of kin to the eighth, but the ftalks do not grow fo tall; the lower leaves are heart-fhaped and entire, the middle leaves are divided into three, and the upper into five fegments, almoft to the foot-ftalks; they are fawed on their edges, and the ftalk is prickly. The flowers come out from the wings of the ftalks; they are of a very pale fulphur colour, with dark bottoms, but not fo large as thofe of the laft.

This is propagated by feeds in the fame way as the eighth, and the plants require the fame treatment. It flowers in July and Auguft, and the feeds ripen in autumn.

The bark of both thefe plants is full of ftrong fibres, which I have been informed the inhabitants of the Malabar coaft prepare and make into a ftrong cordage; and by what I have obferved, it may be wrought into fine ftrong thread of any fize, if properly manufactured.

The tenth fort grows naturally in the Weft-Indies, where the inhabitants ufe the green pods to add an acid tafte to their viands: there are two varieties of this, one with a light green, and the other a deep red pod, which always maintain their difference; but as there is no other difference but that of the colour of their pods, they do not deferve feparate titles. This rifes with an herbaceous ftem about three feet high, fending out feveral lateral branches, which are garnifhed with fmooth leaves divided into five lobes. The flowers come out from the fide of the branches; they are of a dirty white, with dark purple bottoms, and are fucceeded by obtufe feed-veffels, divided into five cells, which are filled with kidney-fhaped feeds.

This fort is propagated in the fame way as the third, and will flower and perfect feeds the fame year, fo is feldom preferved longer in England.

The

The eleventh fort is a native of Ceylon; this rises with an herbaceous ftalk, which is prickly, from two to three feet high, dividing upward into fmall branches, which are garnifhed with hand-fhaped leaves, divided into five fegments. The flowers come out from the wings of the leaves; they are fmall and white, with purple bottoms, and are fucceeded by fhort obtufe capfules with five cells, filled with kidney-fhaped feeds. The feeds of this fort were fent me by Dr. Breynius of Dantzick.

This plant is annual, fo muft be treated in the fame way as the third.

The twelfth fort is alfo annual with us; this rises with an herbaceous ftalk three feet high, clofely fet with prickly hairs, and divides into branches upward, garnifhed with hand-fhaped leaves, divided into five lobes, which are fpear-fhaped, ending in acute points; they are hairy, and crenated on their edges, ftanding upon very long foot-ftalks; the flowers come out from the wings of the ftalk, and are very like thofe of the third; this plant requires the fame culture as the third fort. The feeds of this were fent me by Dr. Juffieu, from Paris.

The thirteenth fort was difcovered by the late Dr. Houftoun in the ifland of Cuba, from whence he fent me the feeds. This rises with a woody ftalk twelve or fourteen feet high, fending out many lateral branches, garnifhed with hairy heart-fhaped leaves, crenated on their edges; the flowers come out fingle from the wings of the leaves; they are of a very bright yellow colour, but not fo large as either of the former forts, and are fucceeded by fhort capfules ending in acute points, divided into five cells, which are filled with kidney-fhaped feeds. This plant is tender, fo requires the fame treatment as the fifth, and other tender kinds, with which management it flowers and produces good feeds here.

The fourteenth fort has a perennial root but an annual ftalk. The feeds of this were fent me from the Bahama Iflands, which fucceeded in the Chelfea garden, where the plants produced plenty of flowers, but did not ripen their feeds. This rises with feveral ftalks from the root, which grow four feet high, garnifhed with oblong, heart-fhaped, fmooth leaves, ending in acute points, of a light green on their upper fide, but hoary on their under, and are flightly indented on their edges, ftanding upon long foot-ftalks; the flowers are produced at the top of the ftalks; they are very large, and of a light purple colour with dark bottoms, and are fucceeded by fhort capfules divided into five cells, filled with kidney-fhaped feeds.

This is propagated by feeds, which muft be fown on a moderate hot-bed in the fpring, and when the plants are fit to remove, they fhould be each planted in a feparate fmall pot, and plunged into a hot-bed, treating them in the fame way as the other tender forts, but allowing them a greater fhare of air in warm weather; for thefe may be brought to ftand in the open air in fummer, but unlefs the feafon is very warm they will not flower there; for thofe which flowered in the Chelfea garden, were plunged into a tan-bed whofe heat was declining, under a deep frame, where they produced plenty of flowers, but they came too late to ripen feeds. The ftalks decay in the autumn, but if the pots are fheltered under a hot-bed frame and fecured from froft, they will continue feveral years, and put out new ftalks in the fpring.

The fifteenth fort is very common in the Weft-Indies, where the inhabitants cultivate it for the pods or feed-veffels, which they gather green to put into their foups; thefe, having a foft vifcous juice, add a thicknefs to their foups, and renders them very palatable. It rises with a foft herbaceous ftalk, from three to five feet high, dividing upward into many branches, garnifhed with hand-fhaped leaves, divided into five lobes; the flowers are produced from the wings of the ftalk; they are of a pale fulphur colour with dark purple bottoms, but are fmaller than either of the other forts, and of very fhort duration, opening in the morning with the

rifing fun, but are faded long before noon in warm weather. Thefe are fucceeded by capfules of very different forms, in the different varieties; in fome the capfules are not thicker than a man's finger, and five or fix inches long; in others they are very thick, and not more than two or three inches long; in fome plants they grow erect, in others they are rather inclined; and thefe varieties are conftant, for I have many years cultivated thefe plants, and have not found them vary.

This fort is propagated by feeds in the fame way as the third, and the plants require the fame treatment, for they are too tender to thrive in the open air in this country; I have often tranfplanted the plants into warm borders, after they have acquired proper ftrength, and have fometimes in very warm feafons had them thrive for a fhort time, but the firft cold or bad weather their leaves have all dropped off; and then they have decayed gradually, fo that they have but rarely flowered, and have never in the beft feafons perfected their feeds; therefore thofe who are inclinable to cultivate thefe plants, muft conftantly fhelter them in bad weather.

The fixteenth fort grows naturally near Venice, in moift land; this hath a perennial root and an annual ftalk, which rises from three to four feet high; the lower leaves are angular and heart-fhaped, but the upper are fpear-fhaped, and flightly indented on their edges; the flowers are produced from the wings of the leaves, upon long foot-ftalks; they are fmall, and of a purple colour with a dark bottom, and are fucceeded by five-cornered compreffed capfules, filled with kidney-fhaped feeds.

This fort is propagated by feeds, which muft be fown on a hot-bed, and the plants fhould be treated in the fame way as the fourteenth fort, otherwife they will not flower; for although the roots will live in the full ground here, yet the fummers are not warm enough to bring them to flower. I have fome of the roots which have remained feven years, putting up many ftalks, which rife upward of three feet, and have the flower-buds formed on their tops; but thefe appear fo late in the feafon, that they feldom have opened.

The feventeenth fort grows naturally in North America; this hath a perennial root and an annual ftalk; the roots of this fort will live in the full ground, but unlefs the fummer is warm, the flowers feldom open. It rises with fingle ftalks from the root, two feet high or more; the leaves are oval and fawed, the flowers are large and purple.

The eighteenth fort grows naturally in North America, in moift ground. This hath a perennial root, and an annual ftalk like the former, which is herbaceous and never branches; the leaves are oval, with three lobes which are not deeply divided; they are of a bright green on their upper fide, but woolly on their under; the flowers are produced from the wings of the ftalk; they are large, and of a bright purple colour. This fort, like the former, feldom flowers in the open air here, unlefs the fummer proves very warm, but the roots will live in the full ground, if they are planted in a fheltered fituation. The only way to have thefe plants flower in this country, is to keep the roots in pots, and fhelter them under a frame in winter, and in the fpring plunge them into a gentle hot-bed, which will caufe them to put out their ftalks early; and when the ftalks are fo high as to reach the glaffes, the pots may be removed into a glafs-cafe; where, if they are duly fupplied with water, and have plenty of air in hot weather, they will flower very well in July, and in warm feafons will ripen their feeds.

The nineteenth fort is an annual plant, which grows naturally in fome parts of Italy, and has been long cultivated in the Englifh gardens, by the title of Venice Malva. Gerard and Parkinfon title it Alcea Veneta, and Flos Hora, or Flower of an hour, from the fhort duration of its flowers, which in hot weather continue but few hours open: however, there is a fucceffion of flowers which open daily for a confiderable time, fo that a few of thefe plants may be allowed a place in every curious garden.

It rifes with a branching ftalk a foot and a half high, having many fhort fpines which are foft, and do not appear unlefs clofely viewed: the leaves are divided into three lobes, which are deeply jagged almoft to the midrib; thefe jags are oppofite, and the fegments are obtufe; the flowers come out at the joints of the ftalks upon pretty long foot-ftalks, having a double empalement, the outer being compofed of ten long narrow leaves, which join at their bafe; the inner is of one thin leaf, fwollen like a bladder, cut into five acute fegments at the top, having many longitudinal purple ribs, and is hairy; both thefe are permanent, and inclofe the capfule after the flower is paft. The flower is compofed of five obtufe petals, which fpread open at the top, the lower part forming an open bell-fhaped flower; thefe have dark purple bottoms, but are of a pale fulphur colour above, having the ftamina and apices joined in a column in the center; after the flower is paft, the germen turns to a blunt capfule opening in five cells, which are filled with fmall kidney-fhaped feeds. It flowers in June, July, and Auguft, and the feeds ripen about a month after. This fort is propagated by feeds, which fhould be fown where the plants are defigned to remain, for they do not bear tranfplanting well; if the feeds are fown in autumn, the plants will come up early in the fpring, fo will flower in the fummer, and thofe which are fown early in the fpring will fucceed them; fo that by fowing them at three different feafons, they may be continued in fucceffion till the froft ftops them. Thefe require no other culture but to keep them clean from weeds, and thin them where they are too clofe; and if the feeds are permitted to fcatter, the plants will come up full as well as when fown, fo that it will maintain its fituation unlefs it is weeded out.

The twentieth fort grows naturally at the Cape of Good Hope; this is alfo an annual plant which refembles the former, but the ftalks grow more erect, are of a purplifh colour, and very hairy; the leaves are compofed of three lobes, which are divided almoft to the foot-ftalk; thefe are narrow, the middle lobe ftretching out more than twice the length of the two fide lobes, and they are but flightly indented on their edges, whereas thofe of the former are cut almoft to the midrib; the flowers are larger, and their colour deeper, than thofe of the other.

The feeds of the twenty-fecond fort were fent me from the Cape of Good Hope, a few years paft. This is alfo an annual plant, having at firft fight fome refemblance of the other forts before-mentioned; but it rifes with ftrong hairy branching ftalks, garnifhed with much broader leaves than either of the former, the lower being divided into three, and the upper into five obtufe lobes, which are crenated on their edges; the flowers are large, but of a paler colour than thofe of the other. This has maintained the difference ten years, fo that there is no doubt of its being a diftinct fpecies.

All thefe are as hardy as the nineteenth fort, fo may be treated in the fame way.

The twenty-third fort grows naturally at Campeachy, from whence the late Dr. Houftoun fent me the feeds. This differs fo effentially from the other fpecies in its fructification, as to deferve another title; for all the other have dry capfules with five cells, including many kidney-fhaped feeds, but this hath a foft vilcous berry, with a hard fhell inclofed, containing five roundifh feeds: it rifes with a fhrubby ftalk ten or twelve feet high, dividing into many branches, which are garnifhed with fmooth, heart-fhaped, angular leaves, which are crenated on their edges; the flowers come out from the wings of the ftalks fingly, ftanding on fhort foot-ftalks; they are compofed of five oblong petals, which are twifted together and never expand; they are of a fine fcarlet, and are fucceeded by roundifh berries of a fcarlet colour when ripe, in-

clofing a hard fhell which opens in five cells, each containing a fingle roundifh feed.

This fort is generally propagated here by cuttings, becaufe the feeds do not often ripen here; if the cuttings are planted in pots filled with light earth, and plunged into a gentle hot-bed, keeping the air from them, they will foon take root, and fhould be gradually inured to bear the open air. Thefe plants require a moderate ftove to preferve them through the winter; and if they are kept in warmth in fummer, they will flower, and fometimes ripen fruit, though they may be placed abroad in a fheltered fituation for two or three months in fummer, but the plants fo treated feldom flower fo well.

HIERACIUM. Lin. Gen. Plant. 818. Tourn. Inft. R. H. 469. tab. 267. [of Ἱέραξ, Gr. a hawk; fo called, becaufe hawks as well as eagles, have a ftrong and quick fight; and it is reported, that if by reafon of the heat of the air, a film grows over the eyes of this bird, then the parent let falls a drop of the juice of it in its eye, which takes it off; and that, in like manner, it is good to clear the human fight.] Hawkweed.

The CHARACTERS are,

It hath a flower compofed of many hermaphrodite florets, which are included in one common fcaly empalement, whofe fcales are narrow, and very unequal in their length and pofition; the florets are equal and uniform; they have one petal which is fhaped like a tongue, indented in five fegments at the point, placed imbricatim over each other; thefe have each five fhort hairy ftamina, terminated by cylindrical fummits. At the bottom of the petal is fituated the germen, fupporting a flender ftyle, crowned by two recurved ftigmas; the germen afterward becomes a fhort four-cornered feed crowned with down, fitting in the empalement.

This genus of plants is ranged in the firft fection of Linnæus's nineteenth clafs, which includes the plants with a compound flower, compofed only of fruitful florets.

There are a great number of fpecies of this genus, many of which grow naturally as weeds in England, and the others are fo in different countries, therefore I fhall only felect thofe which are the moft beautiful, and beft worth cultivating from the number, which to enumerate, would fwell this work greatly beyond its bounds.

1. HIERACIUM (*Aurantiacum*) foliis integris caule fubnudo fimpliciffimo pilofo corymbifero. Hort. Cliff. 388. *Hawkweed with entire leaves, and a fingle, hairy, naked ftalk, terminated by a corymbus of flowers.* Hieracium hortenfe, floribus atro purpurafcentibus. C. B. P. 128. *Garden Hawkweed with dark purple flowers.*

2. HIERACIUM (*Cerinthoides*) foliis radicalibus obovatis denticulatis, caulinis oblongis femiamplexicaulibus. Prod. Leyd. 124. *Hawkweed with oval indented leaves at the root, thofe on the ftalks oblong, and half embracing them.* Hieracium Pyrenaicum folio cerinthes. Schol. Bot. *Pyrenian Hawkweed with a Honeywort leaf.*

3. HIERACIUM (*Blattaroides*) foliis lanceolatis amplexicaulibus dentatis, floribus folitariis, calycibus laxis. Hort. Cliff. 387. *Hawkweed with fpear-fhaped indented leaves embracing the ftalks, flowers growing fingly, and loofe empalements.* Hieracium Pyrenaicum, blattariæ folio minus hirfutum. Tourn. Inft. 472. *Pyrenean Hawkweed with a Moth Mullein leaf, lefs hairy.*

4. HIERACIUM (*Amplexicaule*) foliis amplexicaulibus cordatis fubdentatis, pedunculis unifloris hirfutis, caule ramofo. Hort. Cliff. 387. *Hawkweed with heart-fhaped, indented, hairy foot-ftalks, leaves embracing the ftalks bearing one flower, and a branching ftalk.* Hieracium Pyrenaicum rotundifolium amplexicaule. Schol. Bot. *Pyrenean Hawkweed, with round leaves embracing the ftalks.*

5. HIERACIUM (*Sabaudum*) caule erecto multifloro, foliis ovato-lanceolatis dentatis femiamplexicaulibus. Prod. Leyd. 124. *Hawkweed with an erect ftalk bearing many flowers, and oval fpear-fhaped leaves half embracing the ftalk.* Hieracium fabaudum altiffimum, foliis latis brevibus, crebrius nafcentibus. Mor. Hift. 3. p. 71.

6. HIE-

6. HIERACIUM (*Umbellatum*) foliis linearibus fubdentatis fparfis, floribus fubumbellatis. Flor. Lapp. 287. Hawkweed with linear indented leaves placed thinly, and flowers almoft in an umbel. Hieracium fruticofum, anguftiffimo incano folio. H. L. 316.

The firft fort grows naturally in Syria; this fends out from the root many oblong oval leaves, which are entire and hairy; from between the leaves arife a fingle ftalk, little more than a foot high, covered with hairs; the flowers are produced in a corymbus at the top; they are of a dark red colour, compofed of many florets, which are fucceeded by oblong black feeds, crowned with a white down, which, when ripe, by the elafticity of the down, is drawn out of the empalement, and by the firft ftrong gale of wind, are wafted to a confiderable diftance. The flowers appear the beginning of June, and the feeds ripen in about five or fix weeks after, but there is frequently a fucceffion of flowers till the autumn.

It is propagated by feeds, which fhould be fown on an eaft afpected border in March; and when the plants come up, they muft be kept clean from weeds, till they are ftrong enough to remove, which will be by the beginning of June; then they fhould be tranfplanted to a fhady border of undunged ground, at fix inches diftance, obferving to water them if the weather fhould prove dry, till they have taken new root; after which, if they are kept clean from weeds, they will require no other culture: in the autumn they fhould be tranfplanted where they are defigned to remain; the following fummer they will flower and produce ripe feeds, and the roots will continue fome years, if they are not planted in a rich moift foil, which frequently occafions their rotting in winter.

The fecond fort grows naturally on the Pyrenean mountains. It is a perennial plant, whofe lower leaves are oval, indented, and of a grayifh colour; thofe on the ftalks are fmaller, but of the fame fhape and colour, and half embrace the ftalks with their bafe; the ftalks rife a foot high, branching out in feveral divifions, each being terminated by one yellow flower. This is propagated by feeds as the firft fort.

The third fort grows on the Pyrenees; this hath a perennial root, which fends up feveral erect ftalks, garnifhed with fpear-fhaped leaves which are indented; the flowers are produced from the wings of the ftalks, upon fhort foot-ftalks, each fuftaining one large yellow flower, having a loofe empalement; this flowers in June; it is propagated by parting of the roots in autumn, and will thrive in any fituation.

The fourth fort rifes with a branching ftalk a foot and a half high, garnifhed with heart-fhaped leaves which are indented at their bafe, where they embrace the ftalks; each divifion of the branches terminate in a hairy foot-ftalk, fuftaining one large yellow flower, which appears in June, and the feeds ripen in the end of July. This is a perennial plant, which is propagated by feeds as the firft fort, and requires the fame treatment.

The fifth fort grows naturally in Savoy; the root of this is perennial, fending up feveral erect ftalks near two feet high, garnifhed with fhort, fpear-fhaped, indented leaves, half embracing the ftalk with their bafe; the flowers are pretty large, of a deep yellow colour, terminating the ftalks; it flowers in July.

The fixth fort grows naturally in Holland; it is a perennial plant, rifing with three or four flender ftalks, garnifhed with hoary linear leaves, and terminated by yellow flowers. This rarely produces feeds in England, fo is propagated by parting of the roots in autumn: but the fifth may be propagated either in the fame manner, or from feeds as the firft fort, as it produces plenty of feeds here.

HILLS have many ufes, of which I fhall only mention three or four.

1ft, They ferve as fcreens, to keep off the cold and nipping blafts of the northern and eaftern winds.

2dly, The long ridges and chains of lofty mountains,

being generally found to run from eaft to weft, ferve to ftop the evagation of thofe vapours toward the poles, without which they would all run from the hot countries, and leave them deftitute of rain.

3dly, They condenfe thofe vapours, like alembic heads into clouds; and fo by a kind of external diftillation, give origin to fprings and rivers; and by amaffing, cooling, and conftipating them, turn them into rain, and by that means render the fervid regions of the torrid zone habitable.

4thly, They ferve for the production of a great number of vegetables and minerals, which are not found in other places.

It hath been found by experience and calculation, that Hills, though they meafure twice as much as the plain ground they ftand upon, yet the produce of the one can be no more than the other; and therefore, in purchafing land, the Hills ought not to be bought for more than their fuperficial meafure, i. e. to pay no more for two acres upon the fide of a Hill, than for one upon the plain, if the foil be equally rich.

It is true, that thefe lands that are hilly and mountainous, are very different as to their valuable contents, from what are found in flat and plain ground, whether they be planted, fown, or built upon, as for example:

Suppofe a Hill contains four equal fides, which meet in a point at top; yet the contents of thefe four fides can produce no more grain, or bear no more trees, than the plain ground on which the Hill ftands, or than the bafe of it; and yet by the meafure of the fides, there may be double the number of acres, rods, and poles, which they meafure on the bafe or groundplot.

For as long as all plants preferve their upright method of growing, hilly ground can bear no more place in number than the plain or the bafe.

Again, as to buildings on a Hill, the two fides of a Hill will bear no more than the fame number of houfes that can ftand in the line at the bafe.

And as to rails, or pailing over a Hill, though the meafure be near double over the Hill to the line at the bottom, yet both may be inclofed by the fame number of pales of the fame breadth.

HIPPOCASTANUM. See Æsculus.

HIPPOCRATEA. Lin. Gen. Plant. 54. Coa. Plum. Nov. Gen. 8. tab. 35.

The CHARACTERS are,

It hath a large fpreading empalement of one leaf, cut at the top into five fegments; the flower hath five oval petals, which are indented at the points. It hath three awl-fhaped ftamina, terminated by broad fummits, and an oval germen fituated below the petal, with a ftyle the length of the ftamina, crowned by an obtufe ftigma. The germen afterward becomes a heart-fhaped capfule winged at the top, inclofing five feeds.

This genus of plants is ranged in the firft fection of Linnæus's third clafs, intitled Triandria Monogynia, the flowers having three ftamina and one ftyle.

We have but one SPECIES of this genus, viz.

HIPPOCRATEA (*Volubilis.*) Lin. Sp. 50. Plum. Gen. 8. *Hippocratea with a triple roundifh fruit and a twining ftalk.* Coa fcandens, fructu trigemino fubrotundo. Plum. Nov. Gen. 8. *Climbing Coa with a triple roundifh fruit.*

The feeds of this plant were fent me from Campeachy by Mr. Robert Millar, and feveral of the plants were raifed in England, which continued two years in feveral gardens, but not one of them lived to flower; they grew to the height of eight or ten feet, twining round ftakes, but their ftalks were very flender, and decayed at the bottom, probably from their having too much wet.

It is a very tender plant, fo muft be conftantly kept in the bark-bed in the ftove, and fhould have but little wet in winter.

HIPPOCREPIS. Lin. Gen. Plant. 791. Ferrum equinum. Tourn. Inft. 400. tab. 225. Horfefhoe Vetch; in French, *Fer de Cheval.*

The

The CHARACTERS are,

The empalement of the flower is permanent, of one leaf, divided into five parts, the two upper being joined. The flower is of the butterfly kind; the standard hath a narrow base the length of the empalement, but is heart-shaped above; the wings are oval, oblong, and blunt; the keel is moon-shaped and compressed. It hath ten stamina, nine joined and one separate, which stand erect, terminated by single summits. It hath an oblong narrow germen, sitting on an awl-shaped style, crowned by a single stigma. The germen afterward becomes a long, plain, compressed pod, which is cut into many parts from the under seam to the upper, each part forming a roundish sinus, with obtuse three-cornered joints connected to the upper seam, each joint being shaped like a horse-shoe, inclosing a single seed.

This genus of plants is ranged in the third section of Linnæus's seventeenth class, intitled Diadelphia Decandria, which includes the plants with a leguminous flower, having ten stamina joined in two bodies.

The SPECIES are,

1. HIPPOCREPIS (Unisiliquosa) leguminibus sessilibus solitariis. Hort. Cliff. 364. *Horse-shoe Vetch with single pods sitting close to the stalk.* Ferrum equinum, siliquâ singulari. C. B. P. 349. *Horse-shoe Vetch with a single pod.*

2. HIPPOCREPIS (Comosa) leguminibus pedunculatis confertis, margine exteriore repandis. Prod. Leyd. 384. *Horse-shoe Vetch, with pods growing in clusters upon foot-stalks, whose outer border is turned inward.* Ferrum equinum Germanicum, siliquis in summitate. C. B. P. 346. *German Horse-shoe Vetch having pods on the tops of the stalks.*

3. HIPPOCREPIS (Multisiliquosa) leguminibus pedunculatis confertis, margine altero lobatis. Hort. Cliff. 364. *Horse-shoe Vetch with pods growing in clusters upon foot-stalks, one border of which has lobes.* Ferrum equinum siliquâ multiplici. C. B. P. 346. *Horse-shoe Vetch with many pods.*

The first sort grows naturally in Italy and Spain. This is an annual plant, which sends from the root several trailing stalks a foot long, that divide upward into smaller branches, garnished with winged leaves, composed of four or five pair of narrow small lobes, terminated by an odd one, which are obtuse, and indented at their ends; from the wings of the stalk come out single flowers of the butterfly kind, which are yellow, and succeeded by single pods sitting close to the stalks, which are about two inches long, and a third of an inch broad, bending inward like a sickle, and divided into many joints shaped like a horse shoe. This flowers in June and July, and the seeds ripen in the autumn, soon after which the plants decay.

The second sort is found growing naturally in some parts of England, upon chalky hills, particularly at Hogmagog hills near Cambridge; this is a smaller plant than the former, and hath a perennial root, sending out slender trailing stalks about six inches long, which are garnished with narrow winged leaves; the flowers grow in clusters on the top of long foot-stalks; these are succeeded by pods which are shorter, and twisted inward in roundish curves, but have joints shaped like those of the former sort.

The third sort grows naturally in the south of France, Germany, and Italy. This is an annual plant, with trailing stalks greatly resembling the first, but the flowers are produced in clusters on the top of pretty long foot-stalks; they are shaped like those of the other sorts, and the pods are jointed in like manner, but the joints are fixed to the opposite border. These plants flower in June and July, and the seeds ripen in August and September.

These plants are propagated by seeds, which should be sown in the autumn, where the plants are designed to remain; and when the plants come up, they must be kept clean from weeds, and thinned where they are too close, which is all the culture they require. The two annual sorts will decay in the autumn after they have perfected their seeds, but the roots of the

other will continue two or three years, provided they are not in too good ground.

HIPPOLAPATHUM. See RUMEX.

HIPPOMANE. Lin. Gen. Plant. 1099. Mançanilla. Plum. Nov. Gen. 50. tab. 30. The Manchineel.

The CHARACTERS are,

It hath male and female flowers in the same spike; the male flowers come out in small clusters, from a small cup-shaped empalement; these have no petals; from the center of each empalement arises a single style, terminated by two bifid summits. The female flowers have no petal, but an oval germen wrapped up in a three-leaved empalement; they have no style, but are crowned by a triparite bifid stigma. The germen afterward becomes a roundish fruit with a fleshy cover, inclosing a rough hard shell with several cells, each inclosing one oblong seed.

This genus of plants is ranged in the ninth section of Linnæus's twenty-first class, which includes the plants with male and female flowers, which have but one stamina.

The SPECIES are,

1. HIPPOMANE (Mançinella) foliis ovatis serratis. Hort. Cliff. 484. *Hippomane with oval sawed leaves.* Mançanella pyrie facie. Plum. Nov. Gen. 50. *Manchineel with the appearance of the Pear-tree.*

2. HIPPOMANE (Biglandulosa) foliis ovato-oblongis, basi glandulosis. Lin. Sp. Plant. 1431. *Hippomane with oval oblong leaves, which have glands at their base.* Mançanilla lauri foliis oblongis. Plum. Nov. Gen. 50. *Manchineel with oblong Bay leaves.*

3. HIPPOMANE (Spinosa) foliis subovatis dentato spinosis. Lin. Sp. Plant. 1191. *Hippomane with oval leaves which have prickly indentures.* Mançanilla aqui-folii foliis. Plum. Nov. Gen. 50. *Manchineel with Holly leaves.*

The first sort grows naturally in all the islands of the West-Indies. This is a very large tree in its native soil, almost equalling the Oak in size; the wood is much esteemed for making of cabinets, book-cases, &c. being very durable, and taking a fine polish; it is also said, that the worms will not eat it: but as the trees abound with a milky caustic juice, so before they are felled. they make fires round their trunks to burn out their juice, otherwise they who fell them, would be in danger of losing their sight, by the juice flying in their eyes; and wherever this falls on the skin, it will raise blisters; and if it comes upon linen, it will immediately turn it black, and on being washed will come into holes: it is also dangerous working of the wood after it is sawn out, for if any of the saw-dust happens to get into the workmens eyes, it causes inflammations, and the loss of sight for some time; to prevent which, they generally cover their faces with fine lawn, during the time they are working the wood.

This tree hath a smooth brownish bark; the trunk divides upward into many branches, which are garnished with oblong leaves about three inches long, and one inch and a half broad, ending in acute points; they are slightly sawed on their edges, and are of a lucid green, standing on short foot-stalks. The flowers come out in short spikes at the end of the branches, being of both sexes in the same spike, but having no petals they make but little appearance; these are succeeded by fruit, about the size and of the same shape as the Golden Pippin, turning of a yellow colour when ripe, which has often tempted strangers to eat of them to their cost, for they inflame the mouth and throat to a great degree, causing violent pains in the throat and stomach, which is dangerous, unless remedies are timely applied.

The inhabitants of America believe it is dangerous to sit or lie under these trees, and affirm, that the rain, or dew, which falls from the leaves, will raise blisters; but it is very certain, that unless the leaves are broken, and the juice of them mix with the rain, it will do no injury.

The second sort grows naturally at Carthagena in New Spain, and the third at Campeachy, from which

places

places the late Dr. Houstoun sent me their seeds. The second sort grows to as large a size as the first. The leaves of this are much longer than those of the first, and have two small glandules growing at their base; they are sawed on their edges, and are of a lucid green.

The third sort is of humbler growth, seldom rising more than twenty feet high; the leaves of this greatly resemble those of the common Holly, and are set with sharp prickles at the end of each indenture; they are of a lucid green, and continue all the year. These plants are preserved in some of the curious gardens in Europe, where they can never be expected to rise to any great height, for they are too tender to live in these northern countries, but in stoves; they rise easily from seeds, provided they are good. The seeds must be sown upon a good hot-bed, and when the plants come up, they should be each planted in a small separate pot filled with light sandy earth, and plunged into a good bed of tanners bark, treating them in the same way as other tender plants; but they must not have much wet, for these plants abound with an acrid milky juice, and it is certain that most plants which do, are soon killed by much moisture: these plants must be removed into the stove, and plunged into the tan-bed in autumn, where they should constantly remain, giving them very little water in winter; and in summer when the weather is warm, they should have a good share of air admitted to them, and once or twice a week refreshed with water; by this management I have raised many of these plants to the height of five or six feet, which have, by their shining green leaves, made a pretty variety during the winter season in the stove.

HIPPOPHAE. Lin. Gen. Plant. 980. Rhamnoides. Tourn. Cor. 52. tab. 481. Bastard Rhamnus, or Sea Buckthorn.

The CHARACTERS are,

It is male and female in different plants; the male flowers have an empalement of one leaf, cut into two segments, which close at their points; they have no petals, but have four short stamina, terminated by oblong angular summits, which are equal to the empalement. The female flowers have no petals, but have a one-leaved empalement, which is oval, oblong, tubulous, and bifid at the brim; these have no stamina, but in the center is situated a small roundish germen, with a short style, crowned by an oblong thick stigma, twice the length of the empalement. The germen afterward turns to a globular berry with one cell, inclosing one roundish seed.

This genus of plants is ranged in the fourth section of Linnæus's twenty-first class, intitled Diœcia Tetrandria, in which are included those plants which are male and female in distinct plants, and the male flowers have four stamina.

The SPECIES are,

1. HIPPOPHAE (*Rhamnoides*) foliis lanceolatis. Lin. Sp. Plant. 1023. *Hippophae with spear-shaped leaves.* Rhamnoides salicis folio. Tourn. Cor. 53. *Sea Buckthorn with a Willow leaf.*

2. HIPPOPHAE (*Canadensis*) foliis ovatis. Lin. Sp. Plant. 1024. *Hippophae with oval leaves, called Canada Sea Buckthorn.*

The first sort grows naturally on the sea-banks in Lincolnshire, and also on the sand-banks between Sandwich and Deal, in Kent; there are two varieties of this, one with yellow, and the other with red fruit, but it is the first only which I have observed growing naturally in England; the other I saw growing on the sand-banks in Holland.

These rise with shrubby stalks eight or ten feet high, sending out many irregular branches, which have a brown bark silvered over, garnished with very narrow spear-shaped leaves, about two inches long, and a quarter of an inch broad in the middle, lessening gradually to both ends, of a dark green on their upper side, but hoary on their under, having a prominent midrib; the two borders of the leaves are reflexed like the Rosemary; these are placed alternate on every side the branches, sitting very close. The flowers

come out from the side of the younger branches, to which they sit very close; the male flowers growing in small clusters, but the female come out singly; these make but little appearance. They appear in July, and the berries on the female plants are ripe in autumn.

This fort is easily propagated by suckers from the root, for the roots spread wide, and send up a great number of shoots, so as to form a thicket: if these are taken off in autumn, and transplanted into a nursery, they will be fit to transplant after one year's growth, to the places where they are to remain: as there is little beauty in this plant, so one or two of them may be allowed a place in a plantation of shrubs for the sake of variety.

The second sort grows naturally in North America; this hath much the appearance of the former sort, but the leaves differ in their shape, these being much shorter and broader, and are not so white on their under side. This hath not as yet flowered in this country, but the plants seem equally hardy with the former, and may be easily propagated by suckers or layers.

HIPPOSELINUM. See SMYRNIUM.

HIRUNDINARIA. See ASCLEPIAS.

HOEING is necessary and beneficial to plants, for two things: 1st, For destroying of weeds; 2dly, Because it disposes the ground better to imbibe the night dews, keeps it in a constant freshness, and adds a vigour to the plants and trees, whose fruit by that means, becomes better conditioned than otherwise it would be.

This operation is performed by the hand, with an instrument called a Hoe, which is well known to every gardener. There are several sizes of these; the smallest, which is called an Onion Hoe, is not more than three inches broad; and is used for Hoeing of Onions; not only to cut up the young weeds, but also to thin the Onions, by cutting up all those which are too close. The next size is near four inches and a half broad, and is called a Carrot Hoe; this is used for Hoeing of Carrots, or any other crop which requires the same room as those. The largest size is about seven inches broad, and is frequently called a Turnep Hoe, being used for Hoeing of Turneps; but this is generally used by the kitchen-gardeners, for Hoeing between all their crops which are planted out, or stand so far asunder as to admit an instrument of this breadth to pass between the plants. Beside, these sort of Hoes, which are contrived to draw toward the person who uses them, there is another sort of a different form, which is called a Dutch Hoe; this is made for the person who uses it to push from him, so that he does not tread over the ground which is hoed. This is a very proper instrument for scuffling over the ground to destroy weeds, in such places where the plants will admit of its being used, and a person will go over a much greater space of ground in the same time with one of these instruments, than with the common Hoe; but this instrument is not so proper for Hoeing out crops, so as to leave the plants at a proper distance, nor will it penetrate the ground so far; therefore the other sort of hoe is to be preferred to this, because it stirs the ground and loosens the surface, whereby the dews penetrate the ground, and thereby promote the growth of the plants. Of late years there has also been another instrument introduced in the field culture, called the Horse Hoe, which is a sort of plough with the shear set more inclining to a horizontal position than the common plough; but as most of the farmers are at a loss how to use this instrument, so it has been but little practised in this country as yet; nor is it likely to be brought into use, unless the garden farmers near London, who are undoubtedly the best husbandmen in Europe, introduce it; for the common farmers can never be supposed to alter their old established methods, till by necessity they are drove to it: a strong instance we have of this kind, in the culture of Turneps, which for many years were sown in most of the counties in England, but till within about sixty years past, they were never hoed,

         hoed,

hoed, except within twenty or thirty miles of London, where the gardeners who had been bred in the kitchengardens near London, every feafon went out in particular gangs to the different parts of the neighbouring country, and each party engaged to hoe the Turneps in fuch a particular diftrict, at a certain price per acre; and from the fuccefs of the farmers who firft employed them, their neighbours were at length tempted to follow their example, fo that it became neceffary for fome of their labourers to underftand this work; and from that time it has prevailed fo much, as that many of the diftant counties have now engaged in this practice: and if the Horfe-hoeing hufbandry was but well eftablifhed among the farmers near London, there would be little doubt of its fpreading into the diftant counties; but there are great prejudices againft it at prefent, moft of them arifing from the ignorance of the farmers in general, and others from the over-fondnefs of the author to his own fchemes, which has in many particulars carried him into many known abfurdities; and thefe being well known to every practical farmer and gardener, are fufficient arguments with them againft making trial of the ufeful part of his fcheme.

The utility of this method of hufbandry, is firft, in proportioning the number of plants to the pafture, which the ground is fuppofed capable of nourifhing properly. The fecond is, by frequent ftirring of the furface of the land, all weeds which rob the crop of its nourifhment is deftroyed, and the clods of earth are hereby divided and pulverized, fo that the roots of the plants can more eafily penetrate them, and fearch their proper food; befides, the dews and moifture are eafily imbibed in the loofe ground, whereby the plants receive a greater fhare of nourifhment.

There are few perfons who properly confider of what confequence the ftirring and breaking of the furface of the ground is to all crops growing therein. I have frequently made trial of this, when the crop has been fo bad as to be thought not worth ftanding, which has been occafioned by the great quantity of rain which has fallen, whereby the furface of the ground has been fo clofely bound, as that the plants could find no nourifhment, but have changed their ufual verdure to a purple colour, and have made no progrefs; but upon Hoeing the ground and breaking the clods, the plants have put out new roots, and have flourifhed exceedingly. From many repeated trials of this kind I can affirm, that if the Wheat in general was fowed in rows, fo as that the plough may be brought between them in the fpring, to loofen the ground, which by the winter's rains may have been too clofely bound, the crop would more than double what is the common produce.

But the author of this fcheme was too fanguine in his propofals, firft, by afferting, that in this method of hufbandry, the land would conftantly produce the fame fort of crops without diminution; and fecondly, it might be done without dreffing or manuring the ground; and his fondnefs for his own fcheme carried him fo far in the profecution of it, as at laft to have much worfe crops than any of his neighbours; however, this fhould not difcourage others from the practice of it, though upon different principles: for although the land thus cultivated, will not nourifh the fame plant without manuring feveral years, yet by this method of hufbandry I can affirm, that all crops will be fo much improved, as to doubly anfwer the difference of expence, and lefs than a fixth part of the feed will be enough for the fame fpace of ground. The common fwing plough will anfwer all intents of Horfehoeing.

HOLCUS. Lin. Gen. Plant. 1015. Milium. Tourn. Inft. R. H. 514. tab. 298. Sorgum. Mich. Indian Millet, or Corn.

The CHARACTERS are,

It hath male and hermaphrodite flowers fometimes on the fame plant, at others on different plants. The male flowers are fmall, and have a bivalve chaff; thefe velves are oval, fpear-fhaped, and twifted, ending with

an acute beard; they have a fmall hairy corolla with three hairy ftamina, terminated by oblong fummits. The hermaphrodite flowers are fingle, in a ftiff bivalve chaff; the inner of thefe is flender, hairy, and lefs than the empalement; the outer valve terminates in a rigid beard, and is larger than the empalement; they have three hairy ftamina, terminated by oblong fummits, with a roundifh germen, fupporting two hairy ftyles, crowned with plumofe fummits. The germen afterward becomes an oval fingle feed wrapped up in the chaff.

This genus of plants is ranged in the firft fection of Linnæus's twenty third clafs, intitled Polygamia Monœcia which includes thofe plants which have male and hermaphrodite flowers in different parts of the fame plant, whofe flowers have feveral ftamina.

The SPECIES are,

1. HOLCUS (*Sorgum*) glumis villofis, feminibus ariftatis. Hort. Upfal. 301. *Holcus with hairy chaff and bearded feeds.* Milium arundinaceum, fubrotundo femine, Sorgo nominatum. C. B. P. 26. *Reed-like Millet, with a roundifh feed, called Sorgum.*

2. HOLCUS (*Saccharatus*) glumis glabris, feminibus muticis. Lin. Sp. Plant. 1047. *Holcus with fmooth hufks, and feeds without awns.* Milium Indicum, arundinaceo caule, granis flavefcentibus. H. L. 425. *Indian Millet with a reedy ftalk, and yellowifh grains.*

There are feveral other of the graffy tribe which belong to this genus, but as they are not cultivated for ufe, fo I fhall not enumerate them here.

The two forts here mentioned, grow naturally in India, where their grain is often ufed to feed poultry, and the feeds of thefe are frequently fent to Europe for the fame purpofe; but the fummers are feldom warm enough to ripen the feeds in the open air in England, but in Italy they are both cultivated. The ftalks of thefe plants rife five or fix feet high, which are ftrong reedy, and like thofe of the Maiz, or Turkey Wheat, but fmaller. The leaves are long and broad, having a deep furrow through the center, where the midrib is depreffed on the upper furface, and is very prominent below. The leaves are two feet and a half long, and two inches broad in the middle, embracing the ftalks with their bafe. The flowers come out in large panicles at the top of the ftalks, refembling, at firft appearance, the male fpikes of the Turkey Wheat; thefe are fucceeded by large roundifh feeds, which are wrapped round with the chaff. Thefe plants are propagated in a few gardens for the fake of variety, but as they are late in ripening their grain here, fo they are not worth cultivating for ufe. The feeds fhould be fown on a warm border, or upon a gentle hot-bed in March; and when the plants come up, they fhould be thinned and planted at the diftance of a foot afunder in the rows, and the rows fhould be three feet diftance; the culture after this, is to keep the ground clean from weeds, and draw the earth up with a hoe to the ftems of the plants; if the feafon proves warm, their panicles will appear in July, and the grain will ripen in September, but in bad feafons their grain will not ripen here.

HOLLOW ROOT. See FUMARIA.

HOLLY. See ILEX.

HOLLYHOCKS. See ALCEA.

HOMOGENEAL or HOMOGENEOUS plants, are fuch plants as are of the fame kind, or nature, with others.

HONEYSUCKLE. See PERICLYMENUM.

HOPS. See LUPULUS.

HORDEUM. Lin. Gen. Plant. 94. Tourn. Inft. R. H. 513. tab. 293. Barley; in French, Orge.

The CHARACTERS are,

It hath a partial involucrum of fix narrow-pointed leaves, which contain three flowers. The petal of the flower opens with two valves; the under valve is angular, fwelling, oval, and pointed, being longer than the empalement, ending in a long beard; the inner is fmall and fpear-fhaped. The flower hath three hairy ftamina fhorter than the petal, terminated by oblong fummits. It hath an oval turned germen, fupporting two hairy reflexed ftyles, crowned by the like ftigmas. The germen afterward becomes an oblong bellied feed,

3

feed, pointed at both ends, having a longitudinal furrow, surrounded by the petal of the flower, which does not fall off. This genus of plants is ranged in the second section of Linnæus's third class, which includes the plants whose flowers have three stamina and two styles.

The SPECIES are,

1. HORDEUM (*Vulgare*) flosculis omnibus hermaphroditis aristatis ordinibus duobus erectioribus. Lin. Sp. Plant. 84. *Barley with all the flowers hermaphrodite, and two orders of beards, which are erect.* Hordeum polysticum vernum. C. B. P. 22. *Spring Barley with many rows of grain.*

2. HORDEUM (*Zeocriton*) flosculis lateralibus masculis muticis, seminibus angularibus imbricatis. Hort. Upsal. 23. *Barley with male flowers on the side, without awns, and angular seeds placed over each other.* Hordeum distichon. C. B. P. 22. *Common long-eared Barley.*

3. HORDEUM (*Distichon*) flosculis lateralibus masculis muticis, seminibus angularibus imbricatis. Hort: Upsal. 23. *Barley with male flowers on the side, without awns, and angular imbricated seeds.* Hordeum distichum, spicâ breviore & latiore, granis confertis. Raii Syn. 246. *Barley with shorter and broader spikes, commonly called Sprat, or Battledore Barley.*

4. HORDEUM (*Hexastichon*) flosculis omnibus hermaphroditis aristatis, seminibus sexfariàm æqualiter positis. Hort. Upsal. 23. *Barley with all the flowers hermaphrodite, bearded, and six rows of seeds equally ranged.* Hordeum hexasticum pulchrum. J. B. 2. 429. *Winter, or Square Barley, Bear Barley, or Big.*

The first sort is the common Spring Barley, which is principally cultivated in England; of this the farmers make two sorts, viz. the common and rath-ripe Barley, which are the same: for the rath-ripe has only been an alteration, occasioned by being long cultivated upon warm gravelly lands. The seeds of this, when sown in cold or strong land; will the first year ripen near a fortnight earlier than the seeds taken from strong land; therefore the farmers in the vales, generally purchase their seed Barley from the warm land; for if saved in the vales two or three years, it will become full as late in ripening as the common Barley of their own product; and the farmers on the warm land are also obliged to procure their seed Barley from the strong land, otherwise their grain would degenerate in bulk and fineness, which by thus changing is prevented. This sort of Barley is easily distinguished by the two orders of beards, or awns, which stand erect; the chaff is also thinner than that of the two last species, so is esteemed better for malting. The second sort is the long-eared Barley, which is cultivated in many parts of England; and is an exceeding good sort; but some farmers object to this sort, because they say the ears being long and heavy, it is more apt to lodge; this hath the grains regularly ranged in a double row, lying over each other like tiles on a house, or the scales of fishes. The husk, or chaff of this Barley is also very thin, so is much esteemed for malting.

The third sort is usually called Sprat Barley; this hath shorter and broader ears than either of the other sorts; the awns, or beards, are longer, and the grains are placed closer together, and the awns being long, the birds cannot so easily get out the grains; this seldom grows so tall as the other species, the straw is shorter and coarser, so not very good fodder for cattle. The fourth sort is rarely cultivated in the southern parts of England, but in the northern counties, and in Scotland, is generally sown, being much hardier than the other species, so will bear the cold; this hath its grains disposed in six rows: the grain is large and plump, but it is not so good for malting, which is the reason for its not being cultivated in the southern parts of England, where the other sorts, which are much better for that purpose, do thrive well.

All these sorts of Barley are sown in the spring of the year, in a dry time; in some very dry light land, the Barley is sown early in March; but, in strong clayey soils, it is not sown till April,' and sometimes not until the beginning of May; but when it is sown late, if the season doth not prove very favour-

able, it is very late in autumn before it is fit to mow, unless it be the rath-ripe sort, which is often ripe in nine weeks from the time of sowing. Some people sow Barley upon land where Wheat grew the former year; but when this is practised, the ground should be ploughed the beginning of October in a dry time, laying it in small ridges, that the frost may mellow it the better, and this will improve the land greatly; and if this can be ploughed again in January, or the beginning of February, it will break and prepare the ground better; then in March the ground is ploughed again, and laid even where it is not very wet; but in strong wet lands the ground should be laid round, and the furrows made deep to receive the wet. When this is finished, the common method is to sow the Barley-seed with a broad cast at two sowings; the first being harrowed in once, the second is harrowed until the seed is buried; the common allowance of seed is four bushels to an acre. This is the quantity of grain usually sown by the farmers; but if they could be prevailed on to alter this practice, they would soon find their account in it; for if less than half that quantity is sown, there will be a much greater produce, and the corn will be less liable to lodge, as I have many years experienced; for when corn or any other vegetable stands very close, the stalks are drawn up weak, so are incapable to resist the force of winds, or bear up under heavy rains; but when they are at a proper distance, their stalks will be more than twice the size of the other, so are seldom laid. I have frequently observed in fields where there has been a foot-path through the middle, that the corn which has stood thin on each side the path hath stood upright, when all the rest on both sides has been laid flat on the ground: and whoever will observe these roots of corn near the paths, will find them tiller out (i. e. have a greater number of stalks) to more than four times the quantity of the other parts of the field. I have seen experiments made by sowing Barley in rows across divers parts of the same field, and the grains sowed thin in the rows, so that the roots were three or four inches asunder in the rows, and the rows at a foot distance; the intermediate spaces of the same field were at the same time sown broad cast in the usual way; the success was this, the roots which stood thin in the rows tillered out from ten or twelve, to upward of thirty stalks on each root, the stalks were stronger, the ears longer, and the grains larger than any of those sown in the common way; and when those parts of the field where the corn was sown in the usual way has been lodged, these parts sown thin have supported their upright position against wind and rain, though the rows have been made not only lengthways, but cross the lands, in several positions, so that there could be no alteration in regard to the goodness of the land, or the situation of the corn; therefore where such experiments have been frequently made, and always attended with equal success, there can be no room to doubt which of the two methods is more eligible; since if the crops were only supposed to be equal in both, the saving more than half the corn sown is a very great advantage, and deserves a national consideration, as such a saving, in scarce times, might be a very great benefit to the public. I know the farmers in general are very apt to complain if their corn does not come up so thick as to cover the ground green in a short time, like Grass fields; but I have often observed, that from the badness of the season it has come up thin, or by accident has been in part killed, their corn has been stronger, the ears longer, and the grain plumper, so that the produce has been much greater than in those years when it has come up thick; for the natural growth of corn is to send out many stalks from a root, and not rise so much in height; therefore it is entirely owing to the roots standing too near each other, when the stalks are drawn up tall and weak. I have had eighty-six stalks upon one root of Barley, which were strong, produced longer ears, and the grain was better filled than any which I ever saw grow in the common method of husbandry, and the land upon which this

grew

grew was not very rich: but I have frequently obferved on the fides of hot-beds in the kitchen-gardens, where Barley-ftraw has been ufed for covering the beds, that fome of the grains left in the ears has dropped out and grown, the roots have produced from thirty to.fixty ftalks each, and thofe been three or four times larger than the ftalks ever arrive at in the common way: but to this I know it will be objected, that although upon rich land in a garden, thefe roots of corn may probably have fo many ftalks, yet in poor land they will not have fuch produce; therefore unlefs there is a greater quantity of feeds fown, their crop will not be worth ftanding, which is one of the greateft fallacies that can be imagined; for to fuppofe that poor land can nourifh more than twice the number of roots in the fame fpace as rich land, is fuch an abfurdity, as one could hardly fuppofe any perfon of common underftanding guilty of; and yet fo it is, for the general practice is to allow a greater quantity of feed to poor land, than for richer ground, not confidering that where the roots ftand fo clofe, they will deprive each other of the nourifhment, fo ftarve themfelves, which is the cafe where the roots ftand clofe; which any perfon may at-firft fight obferve, in any part of the fields where the corn happens to fcatter when they are fowing it; or in places where, by harrowing, the feed is drawn in heaps, thofe patches will ftarve, and never grow to a third part of the fize as the other parts of the fame field; and yet common as this is, it is little noticed by farmers, otherwife they furely would not continue their old cuftom of fowing. I have made many experiments for feveral years in the pooreft land, and have always found that all crops which are fown or planted at a greater diftance than ufual, have fucceeded beft; and I am convinced, if the farmers could be prevailed on to quit their prejudices, and make trial of this method of fowing their corn thin, they would foon fee the advantage of this hufbandry.

The noblemen and gentlemen in France are very bufy in letting examples of this hufbandry in moft of their provinces, being convinced by many trials of its great utility; and it were to be wifhed, the fame was done in England.

When the Barley is fown, the ground fhould be rolled after the firft fhower of rain, to break the clods and lay the earth fmooth, which will render it better to mow, and alfo caufe the earth to lie clofer to the roots of the corn, which will be of great fervice to it in dry weather.

Where Barley is fown upon new broken up land, the ufual method is, to plough up the land in March, and let it lie fallow until June, at which time it is ploughed again, and fown with Turneps, which are eaten by fheep in winter, by whofe dung the land is greatly improved; and then in March following the ground is ploughed up again, and fown with Barley as before. There are many people who fow Clover with their Barley, and fome have fown the Lucern with Barley; but neither of thefe methods is to be commended, for where there is a good crop of Barley, the Clover or Lucern muft be fo weak as not to pay for ftanding; fo that the better way is to fow the Barley alone without any other crop among it, and then the land will be at liberty for any other crop, when the Barley is taken off the ground; but this practice of fowing Clover, Rye-grafs, and other Grafs-feeds, with corn, has been fo long and univerfally eftablifhed among farmers, that there is little hope of prevailing.with thofe people to alter a cuftom which has been handed down to them from their predeceffors, although there fhould be many examples produced, to fhew the abfurdity of this practice.

When the Barley has been up three weeks or a month, it will be a very good method to roll it.over with a weighty roller, which will prefs the earth clofe to the roots of the corn, and thereby prevent the fun and air from penetrating the ground, which will be of fingular fervice in dry feafons; and this rolling of it before it ftalks,.will caufe it to till out into agreater number of ftalks; fo that if the plants fhould be thin,

this will caufe them to fpread fo as to fill the ground, and likewife to ftrengthen the ftalks.

The time for cutting of Barley is, when the red colour of the ears is off, and the ftraw turns yellow, and the ears begin to hang down: in the north of England they always reap their Barley, and make it up in fheaves, as practifed here for Wheat, by which method they do not lofe near fo much corn, and it is alfo more handy to ftack; but this method cannot fo well be practifed where there are many weeds amongft the corn, which is too frequently the cafe in the rich lands near London, efpecially in moift feafons; therefore when this is the cafe, the Barley muft lie on the fwarth till all the weeds are dead; but as it is apt to fprout in wet weather, it muft be fhook up, and turned every fair day after rain to prevent it. When it is carried in, it fhould be thoroughly dry, otherwife if it be ftacked wet, it will turn mufty; or if too green, it is fubject to burn in the mow. The common produce of Barley, is two and a half, or three quarters on an acre, but I have fometimes known fix or feven quarters on an acre.

HORIZONTAL SHELTERS have, by fome perfons, been greatly recommended to preferve fruit-trees from blights; but with how little reafon, or upon what flight experiments, every one who has ever made ufe of them will eafily judge; efpecially thofe which are contrived by placing tiles in the wall at certain diftances, nothing being more obvious, than that vegetables, when prevented from receiving the advantage of dews, rains, &c. thofe kindly benefits of heaven, grow weak, languid, and at laft entirely decay: and fince, from vaft numbers of experiments which have been lately made, we find that trees imbibe great quantities of nourifhment through the pores of their leaves and branches, whereby they are rendered vigorous and healthy, even in fuch feafons, and upon fuch foils, where one would think it impoffible they fhould receive much nourifhment from the earth; to deprive them of this advantage, is no lefs than deftroying them; though perhaps, if the trees are vigorous, it may not be effected fuddenly; but there will be very vifible figns of decay on them daily, and a few years will put a period to their lives, as I have more than once obferved, where fuch walls were built.

The only fort of thefe fhelters which I have ever obferved ufeful for fruit-trees, was made with two leaves of flit deal, joined over each other, and painted; this being fixed upon the top of the wall with pullies, to draw up and down at pleafure, formed a fort of penthoufe; which being let down in great rains, or cold nights, during the time that the trees were in flower, or the fruit was fetting, proved ferviceable; but then thefe fhelters were removed away foon after the fruit was fet, fo that the trees might enjoy all the advantages of rain, dew, &c. in the fummer, which is abfolutely neceffary, if we would have healthy trees or good fruit.

HORMINUM. Tourn. Inft. 178. tab. 82. Salvia. Lin. Gen. Plant. 36. Clary; in French, Ormin.

The Characters are,

The empalement of the flower is permanent, of one leaf, tubulous, and channelled, having two lips; the upper is broad, ending in three acute points; the under is fhorter, ending in two points. The flower has one petal, divided into two lips; the upper is concave, compreffed on the two fides, and incurved with a flight indenture at the point, the lower is broader and more indented. It hath two fhort ftamina, fituated in the tube of the flower, terminated by fhort proftrate fummits, and two other which decay foon after the flowers open. In the bottom of the tube are four roundifh germen, fupporting a fingle ftyle crowned by a bifid ftigma, fituated in the upper lip of the petal. The germen afterward becomes four feeds, lodged in the empalement.

This genus of plants is ranged in the firft fection of Tournefort's fourth clafs, which includes the herbs with a lip flower of one leaf, whofe upper lip is forked, or fhaped like a helmet. Dr. Linnæus has joined this genus, and alfo the Sclarea of Tournefort to the Salvia, including them all in that genus; but

but as there are many species of each genus, so it is better to keep them asunder, whereby their old titles, by which they have always been known in the shops and market will be retained, though there is no very essential difference in their characters.

  The SPECIES are,

1. HORMINUM (*Verbenacea*) foliis sinuatis serratis, corollis calyce angustioribus acutis. *Clary with sinuated sawed leaves, and the petal of the flower narrower than the cup.* Horminum sylvestre lavendulæ flore. C. B. P. 239. *Wild Clary with a Lavender flower.*

2. HORMINUM (*Lyrata*) foliis pinnato-sinuatis rugosis, calycibus corollâ longioribus. *Clary with wing-shaped sinuated leaves, which are rough, and the empalements longer than the petal of the flower.* Horminum folio querno. Volk. *Oak-leaved Clary.*

3. HORMINUM (*Verticillatum*) verticillis subnudis, stylo corollarum labio inferiore incumbente. *Clary with heart-shaped, crenated, indented leaves, naked whorls, and the style lying under the lip of the petal.* Horminum sylvestre latifolium verticillatum. C. B. P. 283. *Broad-leaved wild Clary, with flowers growing in whorls.*

4. HORMINUM (*Napifolium*) foliis radicalibus pinnato-incisis, caulinis cordatis crenatis, summis semiamplexicaulibus. *Clary, whose lower leaves are cut and winged, those on the stalks heart-shaped and crenated, and those on the top half embracing the stalks.* Horminum napi folio. Mor. Hort. R. Blæff. *Clary with a Navew leaf.*

5. HORMINUM (*Sativum*) foliis obtusis crenatis, bracteis summis sterilibus majoribus coloratis. *Clary with obtuse crenated leaves, the bractæ on the top of the stalks large, coloured, and barren.* Horminum comâ purpuro-violaceâ. J. B. 3. 309. *Clary with a purple Violet top.*

The first sort grows naturally on sandy and gravelly grounds, in many parts of England. This a perennial plant; the lower leaves grow upon pretty long foot-stalks, and are near four inches long and two broad; they are sinuated on their borders, and bluntly crenated; their surface is rugged and wrinkled; the stalks are a foot long, square, and inclining toward the ground; the leaves upon these are smaller, and crenated on their edges; the flowers grow in a whorled spike at the top of the stalk, generally with two shorter spikes, one on each side; the flowers are small and blue; these are scarce so long as their empalements; they have but one petal, which is divided into two lips, the upper being a little longer than the under, and almost shuts over it; there are but two perfect stamina in each flower, and four germen at the bottom, supporting a single style; the germen afterward become so many naked seeds, sitting in the empalement. It flowers in June and July, and the seeds ripen in August and September. This sort propagates itself in plenty, if the seeds are permitted to scatter, and requires no other culture but to keep the plants clean from weeds.

This is sometimes called Oculus Christi, from the supposed virtues of its seeds in clearing of the sight, which it does by its viscous covering; for when any thing happens to fall into the eye, if one of the seeds is put in at one corner, and the eye-lid kept close over it, moving the seed gently along the eye, whatever happens to be there will stick to the seed, and so be brought out. The virtues of this are supposed to be the same as the Garden Clary, but not quite so powerful.

The second sort grows naturally in the south of France and Italy; the lower leaves are upward of four inches long, and not more than one broad, regularly sinuated on both sides, in form of a winged leaf; the stalks rise about the same height with the former, but all the leaves upon the stalks are sinuated in the same manner as the lower; the flowers are smaller than those of the first, but grow in whorled spikes like them. This is a perennial plant, which is very hardy, and will propagate itself in plenty by the scattered seeds. It is seldom kept in gardens but for the sake of variety.

The third sort is a perennial plant, which grows na-

turally in Austria and Bohemia. This sends out from the root a great number of heart-shaped leaves, which are sawed on their edges and deeply veined, standing upon pretty long foot-stalks which are hairy; the stalks arise from between these, which are square, and grow two feet and a half high, which are garnished with two heart-shaped leaves at each joint, whose base sits close to the stalks, half embracing them; the stalks at the two or three upper joints, put out on each side a long foot-stalk; these, and also the principal stalk, are garnished with whorls of small blue flowers, not much unlike those of the common sort, but larger; the spikes are more than a foot long, and toward the top the whorls are nearer together. It flowers in June, and the seeds ripen in August.

The fourth sort grows naturally in the south of France, and in Italy. This is also a perennial plant, which has some resemblance of the third, but the lower leaves of this are cut at their base to the mid-rib, into one or two pair of ears or lobes, which are but small, and are often at a distance from each other; the leaves are not sawed, but are bluntly indented; the stalks of this are slenderer, and do not grow so tall as those of the third, nor are the spikes of flowers so long. This flowers and seeds at the same time with the third.

Both sorts may be easily propagated by seeds, which, if sown in the spring on an open spot of ground, the plants will come up, and require no other care but to keep them clean from weeds, and allow them room to grow; for the plants should not be nearer than two feet apart, for they grow very large, and will last several years.

The fifth sort is an annual plant, which grows naturally in Spain; of this there are three varieties which are constant, one with purple tops, another with red tops, and a third with green tops. As they differ in nothing but the colour of their bractæ on the top of the stalks, so I have not put them down as different species, though from more than thirty years cultivating them, I have not known them alter.

These plants have obtuse crenated leaves, shaped like those of the common red Sage; the stalks are square and grow erect, about a foot and a half high; their lower parts are garnished at each joint with two opposite leaves of the same shape, but gradually diminishing in size toward the top: the stalks are garnished upward with whorls of small flowers, and are terminated by clusters of small leaves, which in one are red, in another blue, and a third green, which make a pretty appearance, and are preserved in gardens for ornament. They flower in June and July, and their seeds ripen in the autumn.

The seeds of these are sown in the spring, in the places where they are designed to remain, and require no other care but to keep them clean from weeds, and thin them where they come up too close.

Garden Clary. See SCLAREA.

HORNBEAM. See CARPINUS.

HORSE CHESTNUT. See ESCULUS.

HORSE DUNG is of great use to make hot-beds for the raising all sorts of early garden crops, as Cucumbers, Melons, Asparagus, Sallading, &c. for which purpose no other sort of Dung will do so well, this fermenting the strongest; and, if mixed with long litter, and sea-coal ashes in a due proportion, will continue its heat much longer than any other sort of Dung whatsoever; and afterwards when rotted, becomes an excellent manure for most sorts of lands, more especially for such as are of a cold nature; and for stiff clayey lands, when mixed with sea-coal ashes, and the cleansing of London streets, it will cause the parts to separate much sooner than any other compost will do; so that where it can be obtained in plenty, I would always recommend the use of it for such lands.

HOSE IN HOSE, a term used in gardening, to signify one tube or petal within another, as in the

Polyanthus, where there are in some varieties two petals.

HOT-BEDS are of general use in these northern parts of Europe, without which we could not enjoy so many of the products of warmer climes as we do now; nor could we have the tables furnished with the several products of the garden, during the winter and spring months, as they are at present in most parts of England, better than perhaps in any other country in Europe: for although we cannot boast of the clemency of our climate, yet England is better furnished with all sorts of esculent plants for the table, much earlier in the season, and in greater quantities, than in the gardens of our neighbours, which is owing to our skill in Hot-beds.

The ordinary Hot-beds which are commonly used in the kitchen-gardens, are made with new horse dung, in the following manner:

1st, There is a quantity of new horse dung from the stable (in which there should be part of the litter or straw which is commonly used in the stable, but not in too great proportion to the dung,) the quantity of this mixture must be according to the length of the bed intended; which, if early in the year, should not be less than one good load for each light; this dung should be thrown up in a heap, mixing therewith a few sea-coal ashes, some leaves of trees, and tan, which will be of service to continue the heat of the dung; it should remain five or seven days in this heap; then it should be turned over, and the parts well mixed together, and cast into a heap again, where it may continue five or six days longer, by which time it will have acquired a due heat; then in some well sheltered part of the garden, you must dig a trench in length and width, proportionable to the frames you intend it for; and if the ground be dry, about a foot deep; but if wet, not above six inches; then wheel the dung into the opening, observing to stir every part of it with a fork, and lay it exactly even and smooth thro' every part of the bed; as also to lay the bottom part of the heap (which is commonly free from litter) upon the surface of the bed; this will prevent the steam from rising so plentifully as it would otherwise do. To prevent this, and the heat from rising so violently as to burn the roots of whatever plants are put into the ground, it will be a very good way to spread a layer of neats dung all over the surface of the horse dung, which will prevent the mould from burning: if the bed is intended for Cucumbers or Melons, the earth should not be laid all over the bed at first, only a hill of earth should be first laid in the middle of each light on which the plants should be planted, and the remaining space should be filled up from time to time as the roots of the plants spread; but this is fully explained under those two articles. But if the hot-bed is intended for other plants, then after the bed is well prepared, it should be left two or three days for the steam to pass off, before the earth is laid upon the dung.

In the making of these hot-beds, it must be carefully observed to settle the dung close with a fork; and if it be full of litter, it should be equally trod down close in every part, otherwise it will be subject to heat too violently, and consequently the heat will be much sooner spent, which is one of the greatest dangers these sort of beds may be liable to. During the first week or ten days after the bed is made, you should cover the glasses but slightly in the night, and in the day time carefully raise them to let out the steam, which is subject to rise very copiously while the dung is fresh; but as the heat abates, so the covering should be increased; otherwise the plants in the beds will be stinted in their growth, if not entirely destroyed. But to remedy this evil, if the bed be very cold, you must put a pretty good quantity of new hot dung round the sides of it, which will add a fresh heat thereto, and cause it to continue a considerable time after; and as the spring advances, the sun will supply the loss of the dung's heat; but then it will be advisable to lay some mowings of Grass round

the sides of the bed, especially if the nights should prove cold, as it often happens in May, which is many times, even at that season, very hurtful to tender plants on Hot-beds.

But although the Hot-bed I have described is what the kitchen-gardeners commonly use, yet those made with tanners bark are much preferable, especially for all tender exotic plants or fruits, which require an even degree of warmth to be continued for several months, which is what cannot be effected by horse dung only. The manner of making these beds is as follows:

There must be a trench dug in the earth about three feet deep, if the ground be dry; but if wet, it must not be above a foot or six inches deep at most, and must be raised in proportion above ground, so as to admit of the tan being laid three feet thick. The length must be proportioned to the frames intended to cover it, but should never be less than eleven or twelve feet; but if it is twice that length it will be better, and the width not less than six, which is the least size of these beds for to continue the heat. This trench should be bricked up round the sides to the above-mentioned height of three feet, paving the bottom with bricks to prevent the earth mixing with the tan, and should be filled in the spring with fresh tanners bark (i. e. such as the tanners have lately drawn out of their vats, after they have used it for tanning leather) which should be laid in a round heap for a week or ten days before it is put into the trench, that the moisture may the better drain out of it, which, if detained in too great a quantity, will prevent its fermentation; then put it into the trench, and gently beat it down equally with a dung-fork; but it must not be trodden, which would also prevent its heating, by settling it too close; then you must put on the frame over the bed, covering it with the glasses, and in about ten days or a fortnight it will begin to heat; at which time you may plunge your pots of plants or seeds into it, observing not to tread down the bark in doing it.

A Bed thus prepared (if the bark be new and not ground too small) will continue in a good temper of warmth for two or three months; and when you find the heat decline, if you stir up the bark again pretty deep, and mix a load or two of fresh bark amongst the old, it will cause it to heat again, and preserve its warmth two or three months longer. There are many people who lay some hot horse dung in the bottom of the trench, under the bark, to cause it to heat; but this is what I would never practise, unless I wanted the bed sooner than the bark would heat of itself, and then I would put but a small quantity of dung at bottom, for that is subject to make it heat too violently, and will occasion its losing the heat sooner than ordinary; and there will never be any danger of the bark's heating if it be new, and not put into the trench too wet, though it may sometimes be a fortnight or more before it acquires a sufficient warmth, but then the heat will be more equal and lasting.

The frames which cover these Beds should be proportioned to the several plants they are designed to contain: for example, if they are to cover the Ananas or Pine-apple, the back part of the frame should be three feet and a half high, and the lower part fifteen inches, which will be a sufficient declivity to carry off the wet; and the back side will be high enough to contain the large fruiting plants, and the lower side will be sufficient for the shortest plants; so that by placing them regularly according to their height, they will not only have an equal distance from the glasses, but also appear much handsomer to the sight. And although many people make their frames deeper than what I have allotted, yet I am fully persuaded, that where there is but height enough to contain the plants, without bruising their leaves, it is much better than to allow a larger space; for the deeper the frame is made, the less will be the heat of the air inclosed therein, there being no artificial warmth but what the bark affords, which will not heat a large space of air; and

a3

as the Pine-apple requires to be constantly kept very warm, in order to ripen the fruit well, so it will be found upon trial, that the depth I have allowed will answer that purpose better than a greater.

But if the Bed be intended for taller plants, then the frame must be made in depth proportionable thereto; but if it be for sowing of seeds, the frame need not be above fourteen or sixteen inches high at the back, and seven inches deep in the front, by which means the heat will be much greater; and this is commonly the proportion allowed to the frames usually made use of in the kitchen-gardens. As to their length, that is generally according to the fancy of the owner; but they commonly contain three lights each, which is in the whole about eleven feet in length, though sometimes they are made to contain four lights; but this is too great a length for the boxes, for the frames thus made are not so handy to remove, as when they are shorter, and are more subject to decay at their corners. Some indeed have them to contain but two lights, which is very handy for raising Cucumber and Melon plants while young; but this is too short for a Bark-bed, as not allowing room for a proper quantity of bark to continue a warmth for any considerable time, as was before-mentioned; but for the other purposes, one or two such frames are very convenient for common Dung-beds.

As to those frames which are made very deep, it is much the better way to have them made to take asunder at the four corners, so that they may be removed with ease; otherwise it will be very difficult to take the frame off, when there is occasion to put in new bark, or take out the old. The manner of making these frames is generally known, or may be much better conceived by seeing them than can be expressed in writing, therefore I shall forbear saying any thing more on this head.

HOTTONIA. Boerh. Ind. alt. 1. p. 207. Lin. Gen. Plant. 203. Stratoites. Vaill. Act. Par. 1719. Water Violet.

The CHARACTERS are,

The flower is funnel-shaped; it has one petal, with a tube the length of the one-leaved empalement, but is cut above into five oblong oval segments, which spread open, and are indented at their extremity. It hath five short awl-shaped stamina standing on the tube of the petal, opposite to the cuts, terminated by oblong summits. In the center is situated a globular germen ending in a point, supporting a short slender style crowned by a globular stigma, which afterward becomes a capsule of the same form, with one cell, filled with globular seeds, sitting upon the empalement.

This genus of plants is ranged in the first section of Linnæus's fifth class, intitled Pentandria Monogynia, which includes the plants whose flowers have five stamina and one style.

We know but one SPECIES of this genus, viz.

HOTTONIA (*Palustris.*) Boerh. Ind. alt. 1. p. 207. Water Violet. Millifolium aquaticum five viola aquatica caule nudo. C. B. P. 141. *Water Milfoil, or Water Violet, with a naked stalk.*

This plant grows naturally in standing waters in many parts of England; the leaves which are for the most part immersed in the winter, are finely winged and flat, like most of the sea plants; these extend pretty wide, and at the bottom have long fibrous roots, which strike into the mud; the flower-stalks rise five or six inches above the water; they are naked, and toward the top have two or three whorls of purple flowers, terminated by a small cluster of the same. These flowers have the appearance of those of the Stock-gilliflower, so make a pretty appearance on the surface of the water. The flowers appear in June.

It may be propagated in deep standing waters, by procuring its seeds, when they are ripe, from the places of their natural growth, which should be immediately dropped into the water where they are designed to grow, and the spring following they will appear; and

if they are not disturbed, they will soon propagate themselves in great plenty.

HUMIDITY is the quality commonly called moisture, or the power of wetting others, which quality some liquors and fluids are endowed with; and it differs very much from fluidity, in that it depends altogether on the congruity of the component particles of any liquor to the pores or surfaces of such particular bodies, as it is capable of adhering to.

Thus, quicksilver is not a moist liquor, in respect to our hands or clothes, and many other things it will not stick to; but it may be called a moist liquor, in respect to gold, lead, or tin, to the surfaces of which it will presently adhere.

Nay, water itself, that wets almost every thing, and is the great standard of Humidity, or moisture, is not capable of wetting every thing; for it stands, and runs easily off in globular drops, on the leaves of Cabbages, and many other plants; and will not wet the feathers of ducks, swans, and other water fowl.

And it is very plain, that it is only the texture that may cause the fluid to be humid; because neither quicksilver alone, nor bismuth, will stick upon glass; yet being mixed together, they will form a mass that will stick on it; as it is very well known in the foliating of looking-glasses, in which such a composition is used.

HUMULUS. See LUPULUS.

HURA. Lin. Gen. Plant. 965. Hura, or Sand-box-tree.

The CHARACTERS are,

It hath male and female flowers on the same plant. The male flowers have no petal, or scarce any empalement, but a column of stamina, which are joined at bottom to the style, forming a cylinder; these spread out at the top, and are terminated by single summits lying over each other. The female flowers have a swelling empalement of one leaf, with one tubulous petal; the roundish germen is situated in the bottom of the empalement, supporting a long cylindrical style, crowned by a large funnel-shaped stigma, which is a plain convex, divided into twelve equal obtuse parts. The germen afterward becomes an orbicular ligneous fruit, depressed at top and bottom, having twelve deep furrows, with so many cells, which open at the top with an elasticity, each containing one round flat seed. This genus of plants is ranged in the ninth section of Linnæus's twenty-first class, intitled Monœcia Monodelphia, which includes those plants which have male and female flowers at separate distances in the same plant, whose stamina are joined to the style, forming one body.

We know but one SPECIES of this genus, viz.

HURA (*Crepitans.*) Hort. Cliff. 486. *Sand-box-tree.* Hura Americana, Abutili Indici folio. Hort. Amst. 2. 131. tab. 66. *American Hura with the leaf of the Indian Abutilon, commonly called in the West-Indies Sandbox-tree.*

This grows naturally in the Spanish West-Indies, from whence it has been introduced into the British colonies of America, where some of the plants are preserved by way of curiosity. It rises with a soft ligneous stem to the height of twenty-four feet, dividing into many branches, which abound with a milky juice, and have scars on their bark, where the leaves have fallen off. The branches are garnished with heart-shaped leaves; those which are the biggest are eleven inches long, and nine inches broad in the middle, indented on their edges, having a prominent midrib, with several transverse veins from that to the sides, which are alternate; these stand upon long slender foot-stalks. The male flowers come out from between the leaves, upon foot-stalks which are three inches long; they are formed into a close spike, or katkin, forming a column, lying over each other like the scales of fish. The female flowers are situated at a distance from the male; these have a swelling cylindrical empalement, out of which rises the petal of the flower, which hath a long funnel-shaped tube, spreading at the

top,

top, where it is divided into twelve parts, which are reflexed. After the flower is paft, the germen fwells and becomes a round, compreffed, ligneous capfule, having twelve deep furrows, each being a diftinct cell, containing one large round compreffed feed; when the pods are ripe, they burft with an elafticity, and throw out their feeds to a confiderable diftance.

It is propagated by feeds, which fhould be fown early in the fpring, in pots filled with light rich earth, and plunged into a hot-bed of tanners bark. If the feeds are frefh, the plants will appear in about five or fix weeks after the feeds are fown. As the plants will advance very faft, where due care is taken of them, fo they fhould have a large fhare of frefh air admitted to them in warm weather, otherwife they will draw up too weak. When the plants are about two inches high, they fhould be tranfplanted each into a feparate fmall pot filled with light rich earth, and plunged again into the hot-bed of tanners bark, being careful to fhade them from the heat of the fun, until they have taken new root; after which time they muft have free air admitted to them, by raifing of the glaffes in proportion to the warmth of the feafon, and fhould be frequently, but gently, watered. When the plants have filled thefe fmall pots with their roots, they muft be fhaken out of them, and their roots trimmed, and then placed in larger pots, which fhould be filled with the like rich earth, and plunged again into the hot-bed, where they fhould remain till Michaelmas, provided the plants have room, without touching of the glaffes, at which time they muft be removed into the bark-ftove, and plunged in the warmeft part thereof: during the winter feafon they muft be fparingly watered, for as the plants have fucculent ftalks, much moifture will rot them; they muft alfo be kept very warm, otherwife they will not live in this country. In fummer they muft have a large fhare of frefh air in warm weather, but they muft not be removed into the open air, for they are too tender to live abroad in the warmeft part of the year in this country.

This plant is now pretty common in the Englifh gardens, where there are collections of tender plants preferved, fome of which are grown to the height of twelve or fourteen feet, and many of them have produced flowers, but there has not been any of their fruit produced as yet in England.

As thefe plants have ample leaves, which are of a beautiful green colour, they afford an agreeable variety among other tender exotic plants in the ftove; for where they are kept warm, and duly refrefhed with water, they retain their leaves all the year in verdure.

The fruit of this plant is, by the inhabitants of the Weft-Indies, cut open on the fide where the foot-ftalk grew, and the feeds carefully taken out, after which the fhells are ufed to contain fand for writing, which gave rife to the name of Sand-box. When thefe fruit are brought entire into England, it is very difficult to preferve them; for when the heat of the fummer comes on, they ufually burft with an explofion, and fcatter their feeds about; and from the noife made by the ripe fruit, it was by Hernandez titled, Arbor crepitans.

HYACINTHUS. Tourn. Inft. R. H. 344. tab. 180. Lin. Gen. Plant. 427. Hyacinth; in French, Jacinte.

The CHARACTERS are,

The flower has no empalement. It has one bell-fhaped petal, whofe rim is cut into fix parts, which are reflexed; and three nectariums on the point of the germen, with fix fhort awl-fhaped ftamina, terminated by fummits, which clofe together. In the center is fituated a roundifh three-cornered germen, having three furrows fupporting a fingle ftyle, crowned by an obtufe ftigma. The germen afterward becomes a roundifh three-cornered capfule, having three cells, which contain roundifh feeds.

This genus of plants is ranged in the firft fection of Linnæus's fixth clafs, intitled Hexandria Monogy-

nia, which includes thofe plants whofe flowers have fix ftamina and but one ftyle.

The SPECIES are,

1. HYACINTHUS (Nonfcriptus) corollis campanulatis fexpartitis apice revolutis. Hort. Cliff. 125. Hyacinth with a bell-fhaped petal divided into fix parts, which are reflexed at their tops. Hyacinthus oblongo flore cæruleus major. C. B. P. 43. Greater Hyacinth with an oblong blue flower; and the Hyacinthus Anglicus. Ger. 99. Englifh Hyacinth, or Hare Bells.

2. HYACINTHUS (Serotinus) corollarum exterioribus petalis fubdiftinctis, interioribus coadunatis. Lin. Sp. Plant. 453. Hyacinth whofe exterior part of the flower has diftinct petals, but the interior joined. Hyacinthus obfoleto flore. C. B. P. 44. Hyacinth with a worn-out flower.

3. HYACINTHUS (Utrinque Floribus) corollis campanulatis fexpartitis, floribus utrinque difpofitis. Hyacinth with a bell-fhaped petal which is divided into fix parts, and flowers ranged on each fide of the ftalk. Hyacinthus floribus campanulæ utrinque difpofitis. C. B. P. 44. Hyacinth with bell-fhaped flowers difpofed on every fide the ftalk.

4. HYACINTHUS (Cernuus) corollis campanulatis fexpartitis racemo cornuo. Lin. Sp. Plant. 217. Hyacinth with bell-fhaped petals divided into fix parts, and a nodding branch of flowers. Hyacinthus floribus campanulæ, uno verfu difpofitis. C. B. P. 44. Hyacinth with bell-fhaped flowers ranged on one fide the ftalk.

5. HYACINTHUS (Amethyftinum) corollis campanulatis femifexfidis bafi cylindricis. Hort. Upfal. 58. Hyacinth with bell-fhaped petals cut half way into fix parts, and a cylindrical bafe. Hyacinthus oblongo cæruleo flore minor. C. B. P. 44. Leffer, Hyacinth with an oblong blue flower.

6. HYACINTHUS (Orientalis) corollis infundibuliformibus femifexfidis bafi ventricofis. Hort. Upfal. 85. Hyacinth with a funnel-fhaped petal cut half into fix parts, and fwelling at their bafe. Hyacinthus Orientalis albus primus. C. B. P. 44. Early White Eaftern Hyacinth.

The forts here mentioned are all of them diftinct fpecies, of which there are feveral varieties, efpecially of the fixth, which have been cultivated with fo much art, as to render fome of them the moft valuable flowers of the fpring; in Holland the gardens abound with them, where the florifts have raifed fo many varieties as to amount to fome hundreds; and fome of their flowers are fo large, double, and finely coloured, as that their roots are valued at twenty or thirty pounds fterling each root; to enumerate thefe varieties here, would fwell this work to very little purpofe, as every year produces new kinds.

The firft fort grows naturally in woods and near hedges, in lands which have lately been woods, in many parts of England, fo is feldom admitted into gardens; but the poor people, who make it their bufinefs to gather the wild flowers of the fields and woods for nofegays, &c. bring great quantities of thefe in the fpring to London, and fell them about the ftreets.

There is a variety of this with white flowers, which is kept in fome gardens, which only differs in the colour of their flowers from the other.

The fecond fort is preferved in fome few gardens for the fake of variety, but as it hath as little beauty as the firft, fo is feldom allowed a place in the flowergarden. The flowers of this are narrower than thofe of the firft fort, and feem as if their petals were divided to the bottom, three of the outer fegments being feparated from the other, ftanding at a fmall diftance from the three interior, but they are all joined at their bafe; when the flowers firft appear, they are of a light blue colour, but before they decay, they fade to a worn-out purple colour. This flowers early in the fpring, and grows naturally in Spain and Mauritania.

The third fort grows naturally in Spain and Italy; this hath blue flowers of the open fpread bell-fhape, which are divided into fix fegments almoft to the bottom,

tom, and are difpofed on every fide the ftalk. The ftalks rife about nine inches high, and when the roots are ftrong, the thyrfe of flowers is large. This flowers about the fame time with the firft fort, and was formerly preferved in gardens, but fince there have been fo many finer flowers raifed from the feeds of the Eaftern Hyacinths, thefe have been almoft totally neglected, fo that they are feldom feen but in old gardens The fourth fort feems to be a variety of the firft, the flowers being ranged for the moft part upon one fide of the ftalk, and the top of the fpike is always bent on one fide. The flowers are of a blufh Peach colour, and appear about the fame time as the firft fort. The fifth fort grows naturally in Spain; this hath a fmaller flower than either of the former forts, and comes earlier in the feafon. The petal is cut into fix parts half the length, and is reflexed at the brim; the lower part is cylindrical, a little fwelling at the bafe, and is of a deeper blue than either of the former. This was formerly called by the gardeners the Coventry blue Hyacinth.

The fixth fort is the Eaftern Hyacinth, of which we formerly had no other varieties in the Englifh gardens, but the fingle and double white and blue flowering; but from the feeds of thefe there were a few others raifed in England; and alfo by the Flemifh gardeners, who came over annually with their flowerroots to vend in England; but the gardeners in Holland have within the laft fifty years raifed fo many fine varieties, as to render the former forts of little or no value.

But thofe who are defirous to preferve any of the old forts, need not be at much trouble about it, for their roots propagate in great plenty in any foil or fituation, and will require no other care but to take up their roots every other or third year, foon after their leaves decay, and plant them again in autumn; for if they are permitted to remain longer in the ground, their roots will have multiplied fo great a degree, as to render their flowers very fmall and weak, fo of little worth.

All the different forts of Hyacinths are propagated by feeds or offsets from the old bulbs; the former method has been but little practifed in England till very lately, but in Holland and Flanders it hath been followed for many years, whereby they have obtained a very great variety of the moft beautiful flowers of this kind : and it is owing to the induftry of the florifts in thofe countries, that the lovers and delighters in gardening are fo agreeably entertained, not only with the curious variety of this, but of moft other bulbous rooted flowers, few other florifts thinking it worth their trouble to wait four or five years for the flowers of a plant, which when produced, perhaps there might not be one in forty that may deferve to be preferred; but they did not confider that it was only the lofs of the four or five firft years after fowing, for if they continued fowing every year after they began, there would be a fucceffion of flowers annually, which would conftantly produce at leaft fome forts that might be different from what they had before feen; and new flowers being always the moft valuable to fkilful florifts (provided they have good properties to recommend them) it would always be a fufficient recompence for their trouble and lofs of time.

The method of raifing thefe flowers from feed is as follows : having provided yourfelf with fome good feed (which fhould be faved from either femi-double, or fuch fingle flowers as are large, and have good properties) you muft have a parcel of fquare fhallow boxes or pots, with holes in their bottoms to let off moifture, which muft be filled with frefh light fandy foil, laying the furface very level; then fow your feeds thereon as equally as poffible, covering it about half an inch thick with the fame light earth; the time for this work is about the middle or latter end of Auguft. Thefe boxes, or pots, fhould be placed where they may enjoy the morning fun only until the latter end of September, at which time they fhould be removed into a warmer fituation, and towards the end of October they fhould be placed under a common hot-bed frame, where they may remain during the winter and spring

months, that they may be protected from hard frofts; though they fhould be expofed to the open air when the weather is mild, by taking off the glaffes. In the latter end of February or the beginning of March, the young plants will begin to appear above ground; at which time they muft be carefully fcreened from frofts, otherwife they will be foon deftroyed when they are fo young; but you muft never cover them at that feafon but in the night, or in very bad weather; for when the plants are come up, if they are clofe covered, they will draw up very tall and flender, and thereby prevent the growth of their roots. About the middle of April, if the weather proves good, you may remove the boxes out of the frame, placing them in a warm fituation, obferving, if the feafon be dry, to refrefh them now and then gently with a little water, as alfo to keep them very clear from weeds, which would foon overfpread the tender plants, and deftroy them, if permitted to remain.

Towards the beginning of May thefe boxes fhould be removed into a cooler fituation; for the heat of the fun at that feafon would be too great for thefe tender plants, caufing their blades to decay much fooner than they would naturally do, if they were fcreened from its violence. In this fhady fituation they fhould remain during the heat of fummer, obferving to keep them conftantly clear from weeds; but you muft not place them under the dripping of trees, &c. nor fhould you give them any water after their blades are decayed, for that would infallibly rot the roots. About the latter end of Auguft you fhould fift a little light rich earth over the furface of the boxes, and then remove them again into a warmer fituation, and treat them, during the winter, fpring, and fummer months, as was before directed : and about the middle of Auguft following you fhould prepare a bed of light rich fandy foil, in proportion to the quantity of your feedling plants; and having levelled the furface very even, you fhould take the earth from the boxes in which your plants were raifed, into a fieve, in order to get out all the roots, which by this time, (if they have grown well) will be about the thicknefs of a fmall quill; thefe roots fhould be placed upon the bed at about two or three inches afunder, obferving to fet the bottom part of their roots downwards; then cover them over two inches thick with the fame light earth; but as it will be impoffible to get all the fmall roots out of the earth in the boxes, you fhould fpread the earth upon another bed equally, and cover it over with light earth; by which method you will not lofe any of the roots, be they ever fo fmall.

Thefe beds muft be arched over with hoops, and in very hard frofty weather they muft be covered with mats, &c. to protect them from froft; and in the fpring, when the green leaves are above ground, if the weather fhould be very dry, you muft refrefh them with water; but do this fparingly, for nothing is more injurious to thefe bulbs than too great quantities of moifture. During the fummer feafon you muft conftantly keep the beds clear from weeds; but after the blades are decayed, you muft never give them any water; and in autumn you fhould ftir the furface of the bed with a very fhort hand-fork, being exceeding careful not to thruft it fo deep as to touch the roots, which, if hurt, are very fubject to perifh foon after. Then fift a little frefh, light, rich earth over the bed about an inch thick, or fomewhat more, and in winter cover them again (as was before directed.) In this bed the roots may continue two years, obferving to treat them, both in fummer and winter, as before; then the third year the roots fhould be carefully taken up a little before their leaves decay, laying the roots horizontally in the ground to ripen for three weeks, after which they may be kept out of the ground till the end of Auguft, when they fhould be planted into new beds prepared as before, placing them at the diftance of fix inches afunder; in thefe beds the roots may remain till they flower, during which time they fhould be treated as before; with this difference only, that inftead of covering them with mats in the winter, the furface of the ground fhould be covered with tanners bark.

When their flowers begin to shew themselves, you should mark all such as appear to have good properties, by thrusting a small stick down by each root; which roots, at the time for taking them up, should be selected from the rest, and planted by themselves; though I would by no means advise the rejecting any of the other roots, until they have blown two years, before which you cannot be ascertained of their value. When the green leaves of these plants begin to decay, their roots must be taken up, and a bed of light earth, in a shady situation, should be raised into a ridge; the better to shoot off the moisture, the roots should be laid into the earth again in an horizontal position, leaving the green leaves hanging out of the ground from the roots, whereby the great moisture contained in their very succulent leaves and flower-stalks may be exhaled, and prevented from returning to the roots, which, when suffered so to do, is very often the cause of their rotting after they are out of the ground. In this ridge the roots should remain until the leaves are quite dried off, which they must be taken up, and after being cleared of all manner of filth, which would be hurtful to them, they must be laid up in boxes, where they may be preserved dry until September, which is the proper season for planting them again; the method of doing this shall be hereafter mentioned, when we treat of the management of old roots.

I shall now proceed to the culture of such Hyacinths as have either been obtained from Holland, or are of our own product from the seeds of such flowers as were very beautiful, and worthy to be preserved in collections of good flowers: and it hath been the want of skill in the management of these noble flowers, which has ocasioned the ill success most people have had with them in England, whereby they have been neglected, supposing their roots to degenerate after they have flowered in England, which is a great mistake; for were the roots managed with the same art as hath been practised in Holland, I am fully convinced they would thrive near as well in England as there, or elsewhere, as I have experienced; for, from some hundreds of roots which I have received from Holland at two or three different times, I have had a very great increase of their roots, which were as large, and produced as many flowers upon their stems, as the same sorts generally do in Holland.

The soil in which these flowers succeed best, is a light, sandy, fresh, rich earth, which may be composed after the following manner: take half fresh earth from a common, or pasture land, which is chiefly of a sandy loam; this should be off the surface, and not taken above eight or nine inches deep at most; and if you take the turf, or green sward with it, it will still be better, provided you have time to let it rot before it is used; to this you should add a fourth part of seafand, and the other fourth part of rotten cow dung; mix these well together, and cast it into a heap, where it may remain until you use it, observing to turn it over once in three weeks or a month, that it may be well mixed. If this compost is made two years before it is used, it will be much the better; but if you are obliged to use it sooner, then it should be oftener turned, that the parts may the better unite.

This soil should be laid two feet deep on the beds which are designed for Hyacinths, and if you lay a little rotten cow dung, or tanners bark, at the bottom, which may be within reach of the fibres, but should by no means touch the bulb, it will be better. If the soil is very wet where these beds are made, you should raise them ten or twelve inches above the surface of the ground; but if it be dry, they need not be raised above three or four inches.

The manner of preparing the beds is as follows: First, take all the former old earth out of the bed to the depth you intend, which should be near three feet; then spread some rotten neats dung, or tan, in the bottom, about six inches thick, laying it very level; upon this you should lay the above-mentioned earth two feet thick, levelling it very even; then score out the distances for the roots, which should be eight inches square, in strait rows each way; after which, place your roots exactly in the squares, observing to set the bottom part downward; then cover the roots six inches deep with the same prepared earth, being very careful in doing this not to displace any of the roots; and if the tops of these beds are made a little rounding, to shoot off the wet, it will be of service in moist ground, provided the middle of the beds are not made too high, which is a fault the other way.

The best season for planting these roots is the middle or latter end of September, according to the earliness or lateness of the season, or the weather when it happens; but I would advise you never to plant them when the ground is extreme dry, unless there be a prospect of some rain soon after; for if the weather should continue dry for a considerable time after, the roots will receive a mouldiness, which will certainly destroy them. The beds will require no farther care until the frost comes on very severe, at which time they should have some rotten tan spread over them, about four inches thick; and if the alleys on each side of the bed are filled up, either with rotten tan, dung, or sand, it will prevent the frost from penetrating the ground on each side to the roots, and secure them from being destroyed; but when the winters prove very severe, it will also be proper to have some Peashaulm, Straw, or such like covering laid over them, which will keep out the frost better than mats; and lying hollow, will admit the air to the surface of the ground, and also permit the exhalations to pass off, whereby the earth will remain dry, and prevent the roots from rotting, which has often happened when the beds have been too close covered. But you must observe to take off this light covering whenever the weather is mild, and only let it continue on in very hard frosts; for where the beds are covered with tan or sea-coal ashes, no common frost can penetrate through, so the coverings are useless, except in very severe frost; for a small frost cannot injure the roots before the green leaves appear above ground, which is seldom before the beginning of February, at which time the beds must be arched over with hoops, that they may be covered either with mats, canvas, or some other light covering, to prevent the frost from injuring the buds as they arise above ground; but these coverings must be constantly taken off every day when the weather is mild, otherwise the flowerstems will be drawn up to a great height, and become very weak, and the foot-stalks of the flowers will be long and slender, and so rendered incapable of supporting the bells; which is a great disadvantage to the flowers, for one of their greatest beauties consists in the regular disposition of their bells. When these hoops are fixed over the beds, the rotten tan should be most of it taken off them; in doing of which, great care should be taken not to bruise or injure the leaves of the Hyacinths, which by that time will be breaking out of the ground with the flower-stem, therefore the tan should be removed by the hands; or if any instrument is made use of in the doing of it, there must be great caution how it is performed. When the stems of the flowers are advanced to their height before the flowers are expanded, you should place a short stick down by each root, to which, with a wire formed into a hoop, the stem of the flowers should be fastened, to support them from falling; otherwise, when the bells are fully expanded, their weight will incline them to the ground, especially if they are not screened from the wind and rain.

During their season of flowering they should be covered in the heat of the day from the sun, as also from all heavy rains; but they should be permitted to receive all gentle showers, as also the morning and evening sun; but if the nights are frosty, they must be constantly defended therefrom. With this management you may continue your Hyacinths in beauty at least one whole month, and sometimes more, according to their strength, or the favourableness of the season.

When

3

/

When their flowers are quite decayed, and the tops of their leaves begin to change their colour, you must carefully raife the roots out of the ground with a narrow fpade, or fome other handy inftrument; this is what the Dutch gardeners term lifting of them: in the doing of this, the inftrument muft be carefully thruft down by the fide of the root, being careful not to bruife or injure it, as alfo to put it below the bottom of the root; then by the forcing of this inftrument on one fide, the fibres of the root are raifed and feparated from the ground. The defign of this is, to prevent their receiving any more nourifhment from the ground; for by imbibing too much moifture at this feafon, the roots frequently rot after they are taken up: about a fortnight after this operation the roots fhould be entirely taken out of the ground, and then carried to beds fituated where the morning fun only fhines upon them; the earth of the beds fhould be loofe and raifed into a fharp ridge, laying the roots into it in a horizontal pofition, with their leaves hanging out, by which means a great part of the moifture contained in their thick fucculent ftalks and leaves will evaporate; which, if it were permitted to return back to the roots, would caufe them to rot and decay after they are taken up, which has been the general defect of moft of the Hyacinths in England.

In this pofition the roots fhould remain until the green leaves are entirely decayed, which perhaps may be in three weeks time. This is what the Dutch gardeners term the ripening of their roots, becaufe by this method the roots become firm, and the outer cover is fmooth, and of a bright purple colour; whereas thofe roots which are permitted to remain undifturbed, till the leaves and ftalks are quite decayed, will be large, fpongy, and their outer coats will be of a pale colour; for the ftems of many of thefe flowers are very large, and contain a great quantity of moifture, which, if fuffered to return into the roots, will infallibly caufe many of them to perifh. After they are fo ripened, you muft take them out of the ground, and wipe them clean with a foft woollen cloth, taking off all the decayed parts of the leaves and fibres, putting them into open boxes where they may lie fingly, and be expofed to the air, but they muft be preferved carefully from moifture; nor fhould they be fuffered to remain where the fun may fhine upon them; in this manner they may be preferved out of the ground until September, which is the feafon for planting them again, at which time yon muft feparate all the ftrong flowering roots, planting them in beds by themfelves, that they may make an equal appearance in their flowers; but the offsets and fmaller roots fhould be planted in another feparate bed for one year, in which time they will acquire ftrength, and by the fucceeding year will be as ftrong as the older roots.

The fingle and femi-double flowers fhould be planted alfo in a bed by themfelves, where they fhould be carefully fheltered (as was directed before) from the froft, until the flowers are blown; at which time their covering fhould be entirely removed, and they fuffered to receive the open air, but the flower-ftalks fhould be fupported with fticks; which, though the weather may foon deface the beauty of the flowers, yet is abfolutely neceffary to promote their feeding; and when the feeds are quite ripe, you muft cut off the veffels and preferve them, with the feeds therein, until the feafon for fowing it. But you muft obferve, that after thefe flowers have produced feeds, they feldom flower fo well again, at leaft not in two years after; fo that the beft method to obtain good feeds is, to plant new roots every year for that purpofe. Although thefe roots are, by moft perfons, taken up every year, yet if the beds are well prepared for them, they may remain two years in the ground unremoved, and the roots will increafe more the fecond year than the firft, though the flowers are more liable to degenerate; therefore thofe who cultivate thefe for fale, take up their roots annually when

they are large and faleable; but the offsets and fmall roots, they ufually leave two years in the ground.

There are fome perfons who let their Hyacinth roots remain three or four years unremoved, by which they have a much greater increafe of roots, than when they are annually taken up; but the roots by this great increafe are frequently degenerated, fo as to produce fingle flowers; therefore I fhould advife the taking up of the roots every year, efpecially thofe of the moft valuable kinds, which is the moft certain method to preferve them in their greateft perfection, though the increafe may not be fo great; and if thefe roots are planted a fortnight or three weeks earlier in the autumn than is before directed, it will caufe them to produce ftronger flowers; and thofe roots which are annually removed, will be rounder and firmer than fuch as ftand two years unremoved.

For the other forts of Hyacinth, fee MUSCARI and ORNITHOGALUM.

HYACINTHUS TUBEROSUS. See CRINUM and POLYANTHES.

HYDRANGEA. Gron. Flor. Virg. 50. Lin. Gen. Plant. 492. We have no Englifh title for this genus.

The CHARACTERS are,

The flower hath a fmall permanent empalement of one leaf, indented in five parts, and five roundifh petals which are equal, and larger than the empalement. It hath ten ftamina which are alternately longer than the petal, terminated by roundifh fummits. Under the flower is fituated a roundifh germen, fupporting two fhort ftyles ftanding apart, crowned by permanent obtufe ftigmas. The germen afterward turns to a roundifh capfule, crowned by the two horned ftigmas, divided tranfverfly into two cells, filled with fmall angular feeds.

This genus of plants is ranged in the fecond fection of Linnæus's tenth clafs, intitled Decandria Dygynia, which includes the plants whofe flowers have ten ftamina and two ftyles.

We have but one SPECIES of this genus, viz.

HYDRANGEA (*Arborefcens*.) Gron. Flor. Virg. 50. This plant grows naturally in North America, from whence it has been brought within a few years paft to Europe, and is now preferved in gardens for the fake of variety more than its beauty. It hath a fpreading fibrous root, from which is fent up many foft, pithy, ligneous ftalks, which rife about three feet high, garnifhed at each joint with two oblong heart-fhaped leaves placed oppofite, ftanding upon footftalks about one inch long; the leaves are three inches long, and two broad near their bafe, fawed on their edges, and have many veins running from the mid-rib upward to their borders; they are of a light green, and fall away in the autumn; the flowers are produced at the top of the ftalks, in form of a corymbus; they are white, compofed of five petals, with ten ftamina furrounding the ftyle. Thefe appear toward the end of July and in Auguft, but feldom perfect their feeds in England.

This is eafily propagated by parting of the roots; the beft time for this is the latter end of October, which is alfo the beft time to tranfplant them: the plants fhould have a moift foil, for they grow naturally in marfhy places; they require no other culture but to keep them clear from weeds, and dig the ground between them every winter. The roots are perennial, and if in very fevere froft the ftalks are killed, they will put out new ones the following fpring.

HYDRASTIS. See WARNERIA.

HYDROCOTYLE, [of ὕδωρ, water, and κοτύλη, a cavity; becaufe this plant has a cavity in the leaves which contains water, and the plant grows in marfhes.] Water Navelwort.

This plant grows in great plenty in moift places in moft parts of England, and is never cultivated for ufe, fo I fhall pafs it over with only naming it.

HYDROLAPATHUM. See RUMEX.

HYDROPHYLLON. Lin. Gen. Plant. 187. Hydrophyllon. Tourn. Inft. R. H. 81. tab. 16. Water Leaf.

The

The CHARACTERS are,

The flower has a permanent empalement of one leaf, cut into five segments which spread open. It hath one bell-shaped petal, which is divided into five parts, indented at their points; under each of these segments is fixed a nectarium, which is situated about the middle, and shut up lengthways by two lamellæ. It hath five stamina which are longer than the petal, terminated by oblong prostrate summits, and an oval-pointed germen, supporting an awl-shaped style the length of the stamina, crowned by a bifid spreading stigma. The germen afterward becomes a globular capsule with one cell, inclosing one large round seed.

This genus of plants is ranged in the first section of Linnæus's fifth class, intitled Pentandria Monogynia, which includes the plants whose flowers have five stamina and one style.

We know but one SPECIES of this genus, viz.

HYDROPHYLLON (*Virginianum*) foliis pinnatifidis. Lin. Sp. 208. Morini. Joncq. Hort. *Water Leaf with wing-pointed leaves.*

This plant grows naturally in many parts of North America, on moist spongy ground. The root of it is composed of many strong fleshy fibres, which spread wide on every side, from which arise many leaves with foot-stalks-five or six inches long, which are jagged into three, five, or seven lobes, almost to the midrib; these are indented on their edges, and have several veins running from the midrib to the sides; they are of a lucid green, and in the spring have water standing on the cavities, from whence I suppose Morinus gave it the title of Water Leaf, and not from the plant growing in water, as Tournefort conjectures. The flowers rise with foot-stalks from the root, having one or two small leaves of the same shape with the lower; the flowers are produced in loose clusters hanging downward; they are of a dirty white and bell-shaped, so make no great figure. They appear in June, and the seeds sometimes ripen here in August.

This plant is very hardy in respect to cold, but it should be planted in a moist rich soil; for if it is planted in a dry warm soil, it will not live, unless it is constantly watered in dry weather. It may be propagated by parting of the roots, which should be done in autumn, that the plants may be well rooted before spring, for otherwise they will require a great deal of water. It requires a moist soil and shady situation.

HYDROPIPER, the common biting Arse-smart, which grows in great plenty in moist places near ditches sides almost every where.

HYDROSTATICS [ὑδροςατικὴ, of ὕδωρ, water, and ςατικὴ, of ςατὸς, standing, of ἵςημι, I stand or stop; Hydrostatics being conceived as the doctrine of the æquilibrum of liquors,] or the doctrine of the gravitation of fluid; or it is that part of the mechanics which considers the weight or gravity of fluid bodies; particularly of water, and of solid bodies immerged therein.

To Hydrostatics belongs whatever relates to the gravities and æquilibria of liquors, with the art of weighing bodies in water, in order to estimate their specific gravities.

Of the use of this science in horticulture, the Rev. Dr. Hales, in his excellent Treatise of Vegetable Staticks, has given many examples, by experiments, shewing the quantities of moisture imbibed and perspired by plants and trees, necessary to be known, in order to promote the business of vegetation.

Some of the most useful heads of this science are;

1. That the upper parts of all fluids press upon the lower.

2. That a lighter fluid may gravitate or press upon a heavier.

3. That if a body that is contiguous to the water, be altogether, or in part, lower than the upper surface of the water, the lower part of the body will be pressed upwards by the water which touches it beneath.

4. There needs only a competent weight of an external fluid, to account for the rising of water in pumps, &c.

5. If a body be placed under water, so that its uppermost surface lie parallel to the horizon, the direct pressure that it sustains is no more than that of a column of water, whose base is the horizontal superficies of the body, and its heighth the perpendicular depth of the water. And if the water which leans on the body be contained in pipes which are open at both ends, the pressure of the water is to be estimated by the weight of a pillar of water, the base of which is equal to the lower orifice of the pipe, and whose height is equal to a perpendicular, which reaches from thence to the top of the water, although the pipe should be much inclined any way, or though it should be ever so regularly shaped, and much broader in some other place than the bottom.

6. A body which is immersed in a fluid, sustains a natural pressure from the fluid, which also increases as the body is placed deeper beneath the surface of the fluid.

7. The reason why water ascends in siphons, and by which it flows through them, may be explained from the external pressure of some other fluid, without having recourse to the abhorrence of a vacuum.

8. The most solid body, which will sink by its own weight at the surface, yet if it be placed at a depth twenty times greater than that of its own thickness it will not sink, if its descent be not assisted by the incumbent water.

9. If a body which is specifically lighter than a fluid, be immersed in that fluid, it will rise with a force proportionable to the excess of gravity in that fluid.

10. If a body which is heavier than a fluid be immersed, it will sink with a force that is proportionable to the excess of its gravity.

11. If any vessel be filled with water, or any other liquor, the surface of which is capable of being even, it will continue so till disturbed by some other external cause.

12. When the fluids are pressed, they are pressed undiquaque, i. e. on all sides.

How far the knowledge of any of these properties of fluids may conduce to the philosophical improvement of gardening, and the business of vegetation, will be more clearly perceived when well considered by the ingenious artist, than being set forth by words.

HYGROMETER [ὑγρόμετρον, of ὑγρὸς, moist, and μέτρον, measure, of μετρέω, to measure,] is a machine or instrument contrived to shew or measure, the moistness and driness of the air, according as it abounds with moist or dry vapours, and to measure and estimate the quantity of such moistness and driness.

There are divers kinds of Hygrometers; for whatever body either swells or shrinks by driness or moisture, is capable of being formed into an Hygrometer; such are the woods of most kinds, particularly Ash, Deal, Poplar, &c. such also is a cord, cat-gut, &c.

Stretch a hempen cord or fiddle-string along a wall, bringing it over a truckle or pully; and to the other end tie a weight, unto which fit a style or index; on the same wall fit a plate of metal, divided into any number of equal parts, and the Hygrometer is complete.

For it is a matter of undoubted observation, that moisture sensibly shortens the length of cords and strings; and that as the moisture evaporates, they return to their former length, and the like may be said of a fiddle-string.

The weight therefore, in the present case, upon an increase of the moisture of the air, will ascend, and upon a diminution of the same will descend.

Hence, as the index will shew the spaces of ascent and descent, and those spaces are equal to the increments and decrements of the length of the cord or gut, the instrument will discover whether the air be more or less humid now, than it was at another given time.

The

The ordinary contrivance with whip-cord is one of the eafieft, for that will infallibly fhorten and lengthen as the air grows moifter and drier.

Some recommend a cat-gut as the beft, which may be a yard in length fufpended, having a plumbet or piece of lead, with an index or pointer hanging at the lower end, by means of which the cat-gut will twift or untwift as the air dries or moiftens, and fhorten and lengthen fo as to raife and fink the plumbet with the index, and this index will point out the degree fought for.

The weight of this lead or plumbet, fhould be about two ounces.

Some perfons who approve a fine whip-cord inftead of cat-gut, ufe a greater weight of lead; the twifting and untwifting of the cat-gut or whip-cord, will make the lead with the index turn round, as well as rife and fall. The degrees may be made upon an open fcrew of brafs within, with which the plumbet and index has its motion.

When you are provided with a barometer and Hygrometer, compare the motions of the one with the other, in order to judge what proportion the rife or fall of the quickfilver in the barometer bears to the twifting of the cat-gut or whip-cord; the degrees of which motion may be obferved by the index or pointer of the Hygrometer; and at the fame time both thefe muft be compared with the rifing and falling of the fpirit in a thermometer, to know what degree of heat or cold attends every different change of weather.

HYGROSCOPE [of ὑγρὸς, moift, and σκοπέω, to view or confider,] a machine the fame as the hygrometer, and for the fame ufes.

Thefe inftruments are of good ufe in confervatories, for meafuring or fhewing the dampnefs or drinefs of them in the winter feafon.

HYMENÆA. Lin. Gen. Plant. 512. Courbaril. Plum. Nov. Gen. 49. tab. 14. Locuft-tree.

The CHARACTERS are,

The outward involucrum of the flower is divided into two parts, the inward is of one leaf, indented in five parts; the flower hath five petals, which are equal in fize, and fpread open. It hath ten declining ftamina, which are fhort, terminated by oblong fummits. In the center is fituated an oblong germen, fupporting a declining ftyle, crowned by an acute ftigma; the germen afterward becomes a large oblong pod, with a thick ligneous fhell, divided into feveral partitions transverfly, in each of which is lodged one comprefled large feed, furrounded with a farinaceous pulp.

This genus of plants is ranged in the firft fection of Linnæus's tenth clafs, intitled Decandria Monogynia, which includes the plants whofe flowers have ten ftamina and one ftyle.

We know but one SPECIES of this genus, viz.

HYMENÆA (Courbaril.) Hort. Cliff. 484. Locuft-tree. Courbaril bifolia, flore pyramidato. Plum. Nov. Gen. 49. Two-leaved Courbaril with a pyramidal flower, commonly called Locuft-tree in America.

This is a very large fpreading tree in the Weft-Indies, where it grows in great plenty: it hath a large ftem, covered with a ruffet bark, which divides into many fpreading branches, garnifhed with fmooth ftiff leaves, which ftand by pairs, their bafe joining at the foot-ftalk, to which they ftand oblique, one fide being much broader than the other, the two outer fides being rounded, and their infide ftrait, fo that they refemble a pair of fheep-fhears; they are pointed at the top, and ftand alternately on the ftalk. The flowers are produced in loofe fpikes at the end of the branches, fome of the fhort ligneous foot-ftalks fupporting two, and others three flowers, which are compofed of five yellow petals ftriped with purple; the petals are fhort and fpread open; the ftamina are much longer, and of a purplifh colour; thefe flowers are fucceeded by thick, flefhy, brown pods, fhaped like thofe of the Garden Bean; they are fix inches long, and two inches and a half broad, of a purplifh brown colour, and a ligneous confiftence, with a large fu-

ture on both edges; thefe contain three or four roundifh comprefled feeds, divided by tranfverfe partitions.

The wood of this tree is efteemed as good timber in the Weft-Indies, and it yields a fine clear refin which is called gum anime in the fhops, which makes an excellent varnifh.

It is eafily raifed from the feeds if they are frefh; thefe muft be fown in pots, and plunged into a hot-bed of tanners bark: there fhould be but one feed put into each pot, or if there is more, when the plants appear, they fhould be all drawn out to one foon after they come up, before their roots entangle, when it will be hazardous doing it; for if great care is not taken, the plant intended to be left may be drawn out with the other. As the roots of this plant are but flender, fo they are very difficult to tranfplant; for unlefs a ball of earth is preferved to their roots, they feldom furvive their removal, therefore they muft be feldom tranfplanted from one pot to another. The plants muft conftantly remain in the tan-bed in the ftove, and fhould be treated in the fame way with other tender plants of the fame country, giving but little water to them, efpecially in the winter. When thefe plants firft appear, they make confiderable progrefs for two or three months, after which time they are at a ftand perhaps a whole year without fhooting, being in their growth very like the Anacardium, or Cafhew Nut, fo is very difficult to preferve long in this country.

HYOSCYAMUS. Tourn. Inft. R. H. 117. tab. 42. Lin. Gen. Plant. 218. [of ὗς, a fwine, and κύαμος, a Bean, q. d. Hog's-bean,] Henbane; in French, Jufquaime.

The CHARACTERS are,

The flower has a cylindrical empalement of one leaf, which is permanent, fwelling at the bottom, and cut into five acute fegments at the top. It hath one funnel-fhaped petal, with a fhort cylindrical tube, and an erect fpreading rim, cut into five obtufe parts, one being larger than the others; it hath five inclined ftamina, terminated by roundifh fummits. In the center is fituated a roundifh germen, fupporting a flender ftyle, crowned by a round ftigma. The germen afterward becomes an oval obtufe capfule fitting in the empalement, divided in two cells by an intermediate partition, opening with a lid at the top, to let out the many fmall feeds which adhere to the partition.

This genus of plants is ranged in the firft fection of Linnæus's fifth clafs, intitled Pentandria Monogynia, in which he includes thofe plants whofe flowers have five ftamina and one ftyle.

The SPECIES are,

1. HYOSCYAMUS (Niger) foliis amplexicaulibus finuatis, floribus feffilibus. Hort. Cliff. 56. Henbane with finuated leaves embracing the ftalks, and feffile flowers. Hyofcyamus vulgaris, vel niger. C. B. P. Common Black Henbane.

2. HYOSCYAMUS (Major) foliis petiolatis, floribus pedunculatis terminalibus. Henbane with leaves having foot-ftalks, and flowers with foot-ftalks terminating the branches. Hyofcyamus major, albo fimilis, umbilico floris atro-pupureo. T. Cor. Great Henbane like the white, but with a dark purple bottom to the flower.

3. HYOSCYAMUS (Albus) foliis petiolatis, floribus feffilibus. Hort. Upfal. 56. Henbane with leaves having foot-ftalks, and flowers fitting clofe to the branches. Hyofcyamus major, albo fimilis, umbilico floris virenti. Juffieu. Greater Henbane like the white, with a green bottom to the flower.

4. HYOSCYAMUS (Minor) foliis petiolatis, floribus folitariis lateralibus. Henbane with leaves having foot-ftalks, and flowers proceeding fingly from the fides of the branches. Hyofcyamus minor albo fimilis, umbilico floris atro purpureo. Tourn. Cor. 5. Smaller Henbane like the white, with a dark purple bottom to the flower.

5. HYOSCYAMUS (Reticulatis) foliis caulinis petiolatis cordatis finuatis acutis, floribus integerrimis, corollis ventricofis. Lin. Sp. 257. Henbane with heart-fhaped, finuated,

finuated, acute leaves upon foot-ftalks, and entire fwollen flowers. Hyofcyamus rubello flore. C. B. P. *Henbane with a reddifh coloured flower.*

6. HYOSCYAMUS (*Aureus*) foliis petiolatis erofo-dentatis acutis, floribus pedunculatis fructibus pendulis. Lin. Sp. 257. *Henbane with acute indented leaves ftanding on foot-ftalks, the flower having foot-ftalks, and the fruit hanging.* Hyofcyamus Creticus luteus major. C. B. P. *Greater yellow Henbane of Candia.*

7. HYOSCYAMUS (*Pufillus*) foliis lanceolatis dentatis, floralibus inferioribus binis, calycibus fpinofis. Hort. Upfal. 44. *Henbane with fpear-fhaped indented leaves, and a prickly empalement.* Hyofcyamus pufillus aureus Americanus, antirrhini foliis glabris. Pluk. Alm. 188. tab. 37. fol. 5. *Low, golden, American Henbane, with a fmooth Snapdragon leaf.*

The firft of thefe forts is very common in England, growing upon the fides of banks and old dunghills almoft every where. It is a biennial plant with long flefhy roots, which ftrike deep into the ground, fending out feveral large foft leaves, which are deeply flafhed on their edges, and fpread on the ground; the following fpring the ftalks come out, which rife about two feet high, garnifhed with leaves of the fame fhape, but fmaller, which embrace the ftalks with their bafe; the upper part of the ftalk is garnifhed with flowers ftanding on one fide in a double row, fitting clofe to the ftalks alternately; thefe are of a dark purplifh colour with a black bottom, and are fucceeded by roundifh capfules, fitting within the empalement; thefe open with a lid at the top, and have two cells filled with fmall irregular feeds. This is a very poifonous plant, and fhould be rooted out in all places where children are fuffered to come; for in the year 1729, there were three children poifoned with eating the feeds of this plant, near Tottenham-court; two of which flept two days and two nights before they could be awakened, and were with difficulty recovered; but the third being older and ftronger, efcaped better.

The roots of this plant are ufed for anodyne necklaces to hang about children's necks, being cut to pieces and ftrung like beads, to prevent fits and caufe an eafy breeding of their teeth, but they are very dangerous to ufe inwardly. For fome years paft there was a mixture of thefe roots brought over with Gentian, and ufed as fuch, which was attended with very bad effects, as hath been mentioned under the article of Gentian, fo I fhall not repeat it here.

The fecond fort grows naturally in the iflands of the Archipelago. This hath rounder leaves, which are obtufely fituated upon their borders, and ftand upon foot-ftalks; the ftalks branch more than thofe of the firft, and the flowers grow in clufters toward the end of the branches, ftanding upon fhort foot-ftalks; they are of a pale yellow colour, with very dark purple bottoms.

The third fort is much like the fecond, but the flowers are in larger bunches, fitting very clofe on the ends of the branches; they are of a greenifh yellow colour, with green bottoms. It grows naturally in the warm parts of Europe, and is the fort whofe feeds fhould be ufed in medicine, being the white Henbane of the fhops.

The fourth fort was brought from the Levant by Dr. Tournefort. This hath a fmaller ftalk than either of the former, whofe joints are further diftant; the leaves are roundifh, and deeply indented in obtufe fegments, ftanding upon pretty long foot-ftalks; the flowers come out fingly from the fide of the ftalks, at a good diftance from each other; they are of a yellow colour with dark bottoms.

The fifth fort grows naturally in Syria; this rifes with a branching ftalk two feet high, garnifhed with long fpear-fhaped leaves having foot-ftalks; the lower leaves are regularly cut on both fides into acute fegments which are oppofite, fo are fhaped like the winged leaves; but the upper leaves are entire; the flowers grow at the end of the ftalks in bunches; they are of a worn-out red colour, and fhaped like

thofe of the common fort, but their tubes are fwollen.

All thefe are biennial plants, which perifh foon after they have perfected their feeds. They flower in June and July, and their feeds ripen in the autumn, which, if permitted to fcatter, will produce plenty of the plants the following fpring; or if the feeds are fown at that feafon, they will fucceed much better than in the fpring; for when they are fown in fpring, the plants feldom come up the fame year. They are all hardy except the fifth fort, and require no other culture but to keep them clean from weeds, and thin the plants where they are too clofe. The fifth fort fhould have a warm fituation and a dry foil, in which it will live much better through the winter than in rich ground.

The fixth fort grows naturally in Candia; this is a perennial plant with weak ftalks, which require a fupport; the leaves are roundifh, and acutely indented on their edges, ftanding upon pretty long foot-ftalks; the flowers come out at each joint of the ftalk; they are large, of a bright yellow, with a dark purple bottom; the ftyle of this fort is much longer than the petal. It flowers moft part of fummer, and fometimes ripens feeds in the autumn. If thefe feeds are fown in pots as foon as they are ripe, and placed under a hot-bed frame in winter, the plants will come up in the fpring; but if they are kept out of the ground till fpring, they rarely fucceed. This fort will continue feveral years, if they are kept in pots and fheltered in winter, for they will not live in the open air at that feafon, but it only requires to be protected from froft; therefore if thefe plants are placed under a common hot-bed in winter, where they may enjoy as much free air as poffible in mild weather, they will thrive better than when they are more tenderly treated. This fort may be eafily propagated by cuttings, which, if planted in a fhady border during any of the fummer months, will take root in a month or fix weeks, and may be afterward planted in pots, and treated like the old plants.

HYPECOUM. Tourn. Inft. R. H. 230. tab. 115. Hypecoum; Lin. Gen. Plant. 157. We have no Englifh name for this plant.

The CHARACTERS are,

The empalement of the flower is compofed of two fmall oval leaves, which are oppofite and erect. The flower hath four petals; the two outer which are oppofite, are broad, and divided into three obtufe lobes; the two other which are alternate, are cut into three parts at their points. It hath four ftamina fituated between the petals, which are terminated by oblong fummits. In the center is placed an oblong cylindrical germen, fupporting two fhort ftyles, crowned by acute ftigma. The germen afterward becomes a long, compreffed, jointed pod, which is incurved, with one roundifh compreffed feed in each joint.

This genus of plants is ranged in the fecond fection of Linnæus's fourth clafs, which contains the plants whofe flowers have four ftamina and two ftyles.

The SPECIES are,

1. HYPECOUM (*Procumbens*) filiquis arcuatis compreffis articulatis. Hort. Upfal. 31. *Hypecoum with compreffed jointed pods bent inward.* Hypecoum latiore folio. Tourn. *Broad-leaved Hypecoum.*

2. HYPECOUM (*Pendulum*) filiquis cernuis teretibus cylindricis. Hort. Upfal. 31. *Hypecoum with taper, cylindrical, nodding pods.* Hypecoum tenuiore folio. Tourn. *Narrow-leaved Hypecoum.*

3. HYPECOUM (*Erectum*) filiquis erectis teretibus torulofis. Hort. Upfal. 32. *Hypecoum with taper, erect, wreathed pods.* Hypecoum filiquis erectis teretibus. Anim. Ruth. 58. *Hypecoum with erect taper pods.*

The firft fort hath many wing-pointed leaves of a grayifh colour, which fpread near the ground, and flender branching ftalks, which lie proftrate on the furface of the ground; thefe are naked below, and at the top are garnifhed with two or three fmall leaves of the fame fhape and colour with the under ones; from between thefe leaves come out the foot-ftalks of the flower, each fuftaining one yellow flower with four petals,

petals, and a pointal ftretched out beyond the petals, which afterward turns to a jointed compreffed pod about three inches long, which bends inward like a bow, having one roundifh compreffed feed in each joint. This flowers in June and July, and the feeds ripen in Auguft.

The fecond fort hath flender ftalks which ftand more erect, and the fegments of the leaves are longer and much narrower than thofe of the firft; the flowers are fmaller, and come out at the divifion of the branches; thefe are fucceeded by narrow taper pods, which hang downward. It flowers and feeds at the fame time with the firft.

The third fort grows in the eaft; Dr. Amman received the feeds from Dauria, and I received the feeds from Iftria, where it was found growing naturally. This hath much the appearance of the fecond fort in leaf and flower, but the pods grow erect, and are wreathed and twifted about. It flowers and feeds at the fame time with the others.

Thefe plants are all of them annual, fo their feeds fhould be fown foon after they are ripe, otherwife it will be a year before the plants will appear, on a bed of light frefh earth where they are to remain, for they feldom fucceed if they are tranfplanted. When the plants are come up, they fhould be carefully cleared from weeds; and where the plants are too clofe, they muft be thinned, leaving them about fix or eight inches apart; after this they will require no other cul-, ture, but to keep them conftantly clear from weeds. In June thefe plants will flower, and their feeds will be ripe in Auguft.

When the feeds are fown in the fpring, and the feafon proves dry, the feeds will not grow the firft year; but if the ground is kept clear from weeds and not difturbed, the plants will come up the following fpring. I have known the feeds of thefe plants remain in the ground two years, and the plants have come up the third fpring very well; fo that it will be very proper to fow fome of the feeds in autumn, foon after they are ripe, in a warm border, where the plants may come up early the following fpring; and thefe will be ftronger, and more likely to perfect feeds, than thofe fown in the fpring, by which method the kinds may be preferred.

If the feeds of thefe plants are permitted to fcatter, the plants will come up the following fpring without any care; and if they are treated in the fame way as the others, they will thrive equally; but when the feeds are fown in the fpring, they fhould be taken out of the pods, and divefted of their fungous covering, which adheres clofe to them, fo prevents their growing, till that is rotted and decayed.

Thefe plants are feldom propagated but by thofe who are curious in botany, though for the fake of variety they may have a place in large gardens, becaufe they require very little trouble to cultivate them; and as they take up but little room, fo they may be intermixed with other fmall annual plants in large borders, where they will make a pretty appearance.

The juice of thefe plants is of a yellow colour, refembling that of Celandine, and is affirmed by fome eminent phyficians to have the fame effect as opium.

HYPERICUM. Tourn. Inft. R. H. 254. tab. 131. Lin. Gen. Plant. 808. St. Johnfwort; in French, Millepertuis.

The CHARACTERS are,

The flower hath a permanent empalement, divided into five oval concave fegments; it hath five oblong oval petals which fpread open, and a great number of hairy ftamina, which are joined at their bafe in three or five diftinct bodies, terminated by fmall fummits. It hath in the center a roundifh germen, fupporting one, three, or five ftyles, the fame length of the ftamina, crowned by fingle ftigmas. The germen afterward becomes a roundifh capfule, having the fame number of cells as there are ftyles in the flower, which are filled with oblong feeds.

This genus of plants is ranged in the third fection of Linnæus's eighteenth clafs, intitled Polyadelphia

Polygynia, which contains the plants whofe flowers have many ftamina joined in diftinct bodies, and feveral ftyles.

The SPECIES are,

1. HYPERICUM (*Perfoliatum*) floribus trigynis, caule ancipiti, foliis obtufis pellucido-punctatis. Hort. Cliff. 383. *St. Johnfwort with three ftyles to the flower, and obtufe leaves having pellucid punctures.* Hypericum vulgare. C. B. P. 279. *Common St. Johnfwort.*

2. HYPERICUM (*Quadrangulum*) floribus trigynis, caule quadrato herbaceo. Hort. Cliff. 380. *St. Johnfwort with three ftyles to the flowers, and a fquare herbaceous ftalk.* Hypericum Afcyron dictum, caule quadrangulo. J. B. 3. p. 382. *St. Johnfwort with a fquare ftalk, commonly called St. Peterfwort.*

3. HYPERICUM (*Hircinum*) floribus trigynis, ftaminibus corollâ longioribus, caule fruticofo ancipiti. Hort. Cliff. 331. *St. Johnfwort with three ftyles to the flower, ftamina longer than the petals, and a fhrubby ftalk with two fides.* Hypericum foetidum frutefcens. Tourn. 255. *Stinking fhrubby St. Johnfwort.*

4. HYPERICUM floribus trigynis, calycibus obtufis, ftaminibus corollâ longioribus caule fruticofo. Hort. Cliff. 381. *St. Johnfwort with three ftyles to the flower, obtufe empalements, ftamina longer than the petals, and a fhrubby ftalk..* Hypericum frutefcens Canarienfe multiflorum. Hort. Amft. 2. p. 135. *Shrubby St. Johnfwort from the Canaries, having many flowers.*

5. HYPERICUM (*Olympicum*) floribus trigynis, calycibus acutis, ftaminibus corollâ brevioribus, caule fruticofo. Hort. Cliff. 380. *St. Johnfwort with three ftyles to the flower, acute empalements, ftamina fhorter than the petals, and a fhrubby ftalk.* Hypericum Orientale, flore magno. T. Cor. 19. *Eaftern St. Johnfwort, with a large flower.*

6. HYPERICUM (*Inodorum*) floribus trigynis, calycibus obtufis, ftaminibus corollâ longioribus, capfulis coloratis, caule fruticofo. *St. Johnfwort with three ftyles to the flower, obtufe empalements, ftamina longer than the petals, coloured feed-veffels, and a fhrubby ftalk.* Hypericum Orientale, foetido fimile, fed inodorum. Tourn. Cor. 19. *Eaftern St. Johnfwort, like the ftinking kind, but without fmell.*

7. HYPERICUM (*Afcyron*) floribus pentagynis, caule tetragono herbaceo fimplici, foliis lævibus integerrimis. Hort. Upfal. 236. *St. Johnfwort with five ftyles to the flower, a fquare, fingle, herbaceous ftalk, and fmooth entire leaves.* Afcyrum magno flore. C. B. P. 280. *Tutfan with a large flower.*

8. HYPERICUM (*Balearicum*) floribus pentagynis, caule fruticofo, foliis ramifque cicatrifatis. Lin. Sp. Plant. 783. *St. Johnfwort with five ftyles to the flower, a fhrubby ftalk, and fcarifed leaves and branches.* Afcyron Balearicum, frutefcens, maximo flore luteo, foliis minoribus, fubtus verrucofis falvad. Boerh. Ind. alt. 1. 242. *Shrubby Balearick St. Peterfwort with a large yellow flower, and fmaller leaves warted on their under fide.*

9. HYPERICUM (*Androfæmum*) floribus trigynis pericarpiis baccatis, caule fruticofo ancipiti. Hort. Upfal. 237. *St. Johnfwort with three ftyles to the flower, a flefhy feed-veffel, and a fhrubby ftalk with two fides.* Androfæmum maximum frutefcens. C. B. P. 280. *Common Tutfan, or Park-leaves.*

10. HYPERICUM (*Bartramium*) floribus pentagynis calycibus obtufis, ftaminibus corollâ æquantibus, caule erecto herbaceo. *St. Johnfwort with five ftyles to the flower, obtufe empalements, ftamina equalling the petals, and an erect herbaceous ftalk.*

11. HYPERICUM (*Monogynum*) floribus monogynis, ftaminibus corollâ longioribus, calycibus coloratis, caule fruticofo. *St. Johnfwort with one ftyle to the flowers, ftamina longer than the petals, coloured empalements, and a fhrubby ftalk.*

There are fome other fpecies of this genus, which are preferved in botanic gardens for the fake of variety, but as they are feldom admitted into other gardens, I have not enumerated them here, left the work fhould fwell too large.

The

The firſt and ſecond ſorts are both very common plants, growing in the fields in moſt parts of England; the firſt is uſed in medicine, but the ſecond is of no uſe: theſe are rarely propagated in gardens, but I chuſe to mention them, in order to introduce the other ſorts, which deſerve a place in every good garden.

The firſt ſort hath a perennial root, from which ariſe ſeveral round ſtalks a foot and a half high, dividing into many ſmall branches, which are garniſhed at each joint with two ſmall oblong leaves, ſtanding oppoſite, without foot-ſtalks; the branches alſo come out oppoſite. The leaves have many pellucid ſpots in them, which appear like ſo many holes when held up againſt the light. The flowers are numerous on the tops of the branches, ſtanding on ſlender foot-ſtalks; they are compoſed of five oval petals, of a yellow colour, with a great number of ſtamina, not quite ſo long as the petals, terminated by roundiſh ſummits. In the center is ſituated a roundiſh germen, ſupporting three ſtyles, crowned by ſingle ſtigmas. The germen afterward becomes an oblong angular capſule, with three cells, filled with ſmall brown ſeeds. It flowers in June and July, and the ſeeds ripen in autumn. The root is perennial, ſo will continue many years; and if the ſeeds are permitted to ſcatter, the plants will come up in too great plenty, ſo as to be very troubleſome weeds. The leaves and flowers of this are uſed in medicine; it is eſteemed an excellent vulnerary plant, and of great ſervice in wounds, bruiſes, and contuſions: there is a compound oil made from this plant, which is of great uſe in the foregoing accidents. From the ſtamina of the flower is expreſſed a red juice, which is ſometimes uſed in colouring, but fades very ſoon.

The ſecond ſort hath ſquare ſtalks, which riſe about the ſame height with the firſt, but do not branch ſo much. The leaves are ſhorter and broader than thoſe of the firſt, and have no pellucid ſpots. The flowers ſit upon ſhort foot-ſtalks at the end of the branches, which are ſhaped like thoſe of the other. This flowers and ſeeds at the ſame time with the other, and will propagate in as great plenty if the ſeeds are permitted to ſcatter.

The third ſort grows naturally in Sicily, Spain, and Portugal; this riſes with ſhrubby ſtalks about three feet high, ſending out ſmall branches at each joint oppoſite, which are garniſhed with oblong oval leaves, placed by pairs, ſitting cloſe to the ſtalks, which have a rank ſmell like a goat. The flowers are produced in cluſters at the end of the branches; they are compoſed of five oval yellow petals, with a great number of ſtamina which are longer than the petals, and three ſtyles which are longer than the ſtamina. The germen which ſupports theſe, afterward becomes an oval capſule with three cells, filled with ſmall ſeeds. It flowers in June, July, and Auguſt, and the ſeeds ripen in autumn.

The fourth ſort grows naturally in the Canary Iſlands, ſo was formerly preſerved in green-houſes during the winter ſeaſon, but is found to be hardy enough to reſiſt the greateſt cold of this country, ſo is now cultivated in the nurſeries as a flowering ſhrub; this riſes with a ſhrubby ſtalk ſix or ſeven feet high, dividing into branches upward, which are garniſhed with oblong leaves, ſet by pairs cloſe to the branches. The leaves of this have alſo a ſtrong odour, but not quite ſo bad as the former. The flowers are produced at the end of the ſtalks in cluſters, and are very like thoſe of the former ſort, having a great number of ſtamina which are longer than the petals; this flowers at the ſame time with the former, and perfects its ſeeds in autumn. Both theſe plants have a very ſtrong odour like that of a goat; ſo that where the plants grow in large quantities, the ſcent is carried by the wind to a great diſtance; or if the leaves are handled, they emit the ſame odour.

Theſe two ſorts are propagated by ſuckers, which are plentifully ſent forth from the old plants. The beſt ſeaſon for taking off the ſuckers is in March, juſt

before they begin to ſhoot; they ſhould be planted in a light dry ſoil, in which they will endure the ſevereſt cold of our climate very well. They may alſo be propagated by cuttings, which ſhould be planted at the ſame ſeaſon; or by ſeeds, which muſt be ſown in Auguſt or September, which is as ſoon as they are ripe; for if they are kept till ſpring, few of them will grow; but as they multiply ſo faſt by ſuckers, the other methods of propagating them are ſeldom practiſed in England. The fifth ſort grows naturally on Mount Olympus, where it was diſcovered by Sir George Wheeler, who ſent the ſeeds to the Oxford garden; this riſes with many upright ligneous ſtalks about a foot high, garniſhed with ſmall ſpear-ſhaped leaves, ſitting cloſe to the ſtalks oppoſite. The flowers are produced at the the top of the ſtalks, three or four together; they are compoſed of five oblong petals, of a bright yellow colour, with a great number of ſtamina, which are of unequal lengths, ſome being longer, and others ſhorter than the petals, terminated by ſmall roundiſh ſummits. In the center is ſituated an oval germen, ſupporting three ſlender ſtyles, which are longer than the ſtamina. The germen afterward becomes an oval capſule with three cells, filled with ſmall ſeeds. This flowers in July and Auguſt, and in warm ſeaſons ripens its ſeeds in autumn.

This plant is uſually propagated by parting of the roots, becauſe the ſeeds ſeldom ripen in this country; the beſt time for doing of this is in September, that the plants may have time to get root before winter; this will live in the open air, if it is planted in a warm ſituation and a dry ſoil, but it will be proper to keep a plant or two in pots, to be ſheltered under a frame in winter, leſt in very ſevere winters, thoſe in the open air ſhould be deſtroyed. If this is propagated by ſeeds, they ſhould be ſown ſoon after they are ripe, in pots filled with light earth, and placed under a frame in the winter, to ſhelter them from froſt, and in the ſpring the plants will appear; when theſe are fit to remove, ſome of them may be planted in a warm border, and others in pots, and treated in the ſame way as the old plants.

The ſixth ſort riſes with a ſhrubby ſtalk ſeven or eight feet high, with a reddiſh bark, and ſends out many ſmaller branches, garniſhed with oval heart-ſhaped leaves, whoſe baſe ſits cloſe to the ſtalks; they are placed oppoſite. The flowers are produced at the end of the ſtalks in cluſters; they are ſmaller than thoſe of the third ſort, and have obtuſe empalements. The ſtamina are longer than the petals, and are of a deeper colour. The flowers are ſucceeded by conical capſules of a purpliſh red colour, having three cells, filled with ſmall ſeeds. It flowers in May, June, and July, and the ſeeds ripen in autumn. This is now propagated in the nurſeries as a flowering ſhrub, and may be treated in the ſame way as the third and fourth ſorts.

The ſeventh ſort was firſt brought to England from Conſtantinople, but has long been very common in the Engliſh gardens, for the roots ſpread and increaſe very faſt, where it is permitted to ſtand long unremoved. The ſtalks of this are ſlender, and incline downward; they are garniſhed with oval, ſpear-ſhaped, ſmooth leaves, placed by pairs, ſitting cloſe to the ſtalks. The flowers are produced at the end of the ſtalks; theſe are very large, and of a bright yellow colour, with a great number of ſtamina, which ſtand out beyond the petals; there are five ſtyles in each flower, which are of the ſame length with the ſtamina. The flowers are ſucceeded by pyramidal ſeed-veſſels with five cells, containing many ſmall ſeeds. It flowers in June and July.

This plant is eaſily propagated by parting of the root; the beſt time for this is in October, that the plants may be well eſtabliſhed before the drought of ſpring, otherwiſe they will not produce many flowers. As this will grow under trees, ſo it is a very proper plant to place under ſhrubs and trees to cover the ground, where they will make a good appearance during the ſeaſon of their flowering.

The

The eighth fort grows naturally in the ifland of Minorca, from whence the feeds were fent to England, by Mr. Salvador, an apothecary at Barcelona, in the year 1718; this rifes with a flender fhrubby ftalk in this country about two feet high, but in its native foil rifes feven or eight feet high, fending out feveral weak branches of a reddifh colour, which are marked where the leaves have fallen off with a cicatrice. The leaves are fmall, oval, and waved on their edges, having feveral fmall protuberances on their under fide, fitting clofe to the ftalks, half embracing them with their bafe. The flowers are produced at the top of the ftalks; they are large, of a bright yellow colour, with a great number of ftamina, which are a little fhorter than the petals; thefe flowers have five ftyles, and are fucceeded by pyramidal capfules with five cells, which have a ftrong fmell of turpentine, and are filled with fmall brown feeds: this plant has a fucceffion of flowers great part of the year, which renders it valuable; it is too tender to live through the winter in the open air in England, but requires no artificial heat: if the plants are placed in a dry airy glafscafe in winter, where they may be protected from froft, and enjoy a good fhare of frefh air in mild weather, they will thrive better than in a warmer fituation; but they muft by no means be placed in a damp air, for their fhoots foon grow mouldy and decay with damp, nor fhould the plants have much water during the winter; but in fummer they fhould be expofed in the open air, and in warm weather they fhould be gently watered three times a week; they fhould have a loofe fandy foil, not over rich. This is propagated by cuttings, which fhould be planted in June, in pots filled with light earth, and plunged into a very moderate hot-bed, whofe heat is declining, fhading them from the fun in the heat of the day, and now and then refrefhing them with water; thefe cuttings, fo managed, will put out roots in fix or feven weeks, when they fhould be carefully taken up, and each planted into a feparate fmall pot, placing them in the fhade till they have taken new root; then they may be removed to a fheltered fituation, where they may remain till the froft comes, when they fhould be removed into fhelter.

If thefe are propagated by feeds, they fhould be fown in autumn, in the fame way as is before directed for the fifth fort, and the plants treated in the fame manners as thofe raifed from cuttings.

The ninth fort is the common Tutfan, or Park-leaves, which is fometimes ufed in medicine. It grows naturally in woods in feveral parts of England, fo is not often admitted into gardens; this hath a fhrubby ftalk, which rifes two feet high, fending out fome fmall branches toward the top; thefe, and alfo the ftalks, are garnifhed with oval heart-fhaped leaves, fitting clofe to them with their bafe, they are placed by pairs at every joint. The flowers are produced in fmall clufters at the end of the ftalk; thefe are yellow, but fmaller than either of the forts here mentioned; they have many long ftamina, which ftand out beyond the flower, and three ftyles. The germen afterward turns to a roundifh fruit, covered with a moift pulp, which, when ripe, is black. The capfule has three cells, containing fmall feeds. It flowers in June, and the feeds are ripe in autumn. It hath a perennial root, and may be propagated by parting it in autumn; it loves fhade and a ftrong foil.

The tenth fort grows naturally in North America; this rifes with an upright herbaceous ftalk three feet and a half high, fending out feveral fmall branches upward, which come out oppofite, and are garnifhed with oblong leaves placed oppofite, which half embrace the ftalk with their bafe. At the end of each ftalk is produced one pretty large yellow flower, with an obtufe empalement, having many ftamina, which are equal in length with the petals, and five ftyles which are fo clofely joined as to appear but one. The ftigmas are reflexed, which denote their number. This fort feldom ripens feeds here, fo is propagated by

parting the roots. The beft time for this is in autumn; it fhould have a light foil and an open fituation. The flowers appear the latter end of July, and in Auguft.

The eleventh fort grows naturally in China, from whence the feeds were brought to the Right Hon. the Earl of Northumberland, and the plants were raifed in his Lordfhip's curious garden at Stanwick, and by his Lordfhip's generofity the Chelfea garden was furnifhed with this plant.

The root of this plant is compofed of many ligneous fibres, which ftrike deep in the ground; from which arife feveral fhrubby ftalks near two feet high, covered with a purplifh bark, and garnifhed with ftiff fmooth leaves about two inches long, and a quarter of an inch broad, placed by pairs, fitting clofe to the ftalk; they are of a lucid green on their upper fide, and gray on their under, having many tranfverfe veins running from the midrib to the border. The flowers are produced at the top of the ftalks, growing in fmall clufters, each ftanding upon a fhort diftinct foot-ftalk; thefe have an empalement of one leaf, divided into five obtufe fegments almoft to the bottom, which is of a deep purple colour. The flower is compofed of five large obtufe petals, of a bright yellow colour; thefe are concave, and in the center is fituated an oval germen fupporting a fingle ftyle, crowned by five flender ftigmas, which bend on one fide; the ftyle is attended by a great number of ftamina which are longer than the petals, and terminated by roundifh fummits.

This plant continues in flower great part of the year, which renders it the more valuable; and if it is planted in a very warm fituation, it will live in the open air; but thofe plants which ftand abroad will not flower in winter, as thofe do which are removed into fhelter in autumn.

It may be propagated by flips from the root, or by laying down of the branches; if by flips, they fhould be planted in the fpring on a moderate hot-bed, which will forward their putting out new roots; the layers fhould alfo be laid down at the fame time, which will have taken root by autumn, when they may be tranfplanted into pots, and fheltered under a frame in winter; and in the fpring, part of thefe may be planted in a warm border, and the others continued in pots to be fcreened in winter, left thofe in the open air fhould be killed.

HYPERICUM FRUTEX. See SPIRÆA.

HYPOCHÆRIS, a fort of Hawkweed, of which there are two or three fpecies, which grow naturally in England; the others are feldom admitted into gardens, therefore I fhall not enumerate them.

HYPOPHYLLOSPERMOUS PLANTS [of ὑπὸ, under, φύλλον, a leaf, and σπέρμα, feed,] are fuch plants as bear their feeds on the backfides of their leaves.

HYSSOPUS. Tourn. Inft. R. H. 200. tab. 95. Lin. Gen. Plant. 628. [takes its name from the Hebrew word אזוב, in which language Hyffop fignifies a holy herb, or for purging or cleanfing facred places, as it is faid in the Pfalms, Purge me with Hyffop. But what plant the Hyffop of the antients was, is not known, but that it feems to have been a low plant, becaufe Solomon is faid to have defcribed the plants from the Cedar to the Hyffop.] Hyffop; in French, Hifope.

The CHARACTERS are,

The empalement of the flower is oblong, cylindrical, ftreaked, and permanent. It is of one leaf, cut into five acute parts at the top. The flower is of one petal, of the griuning kind, with a narrow cylindrical tube the length of the empalement. The chaps are inclining. The upper lip is fhort, plain, roundifh, erect, and indented at the top. The under lip is trifid, the two fide fegments being fhorter than the middle one, which is crenated. It hath four ftamina, which ftand apart; two of them are longer than the petal, the other two are fhorter, terminated by fingle fummits. It hath four germen, with a fingle ftyle

fituated

fituated under the upper lip, crowned by a bifid ftigma. The germen afterward becomes fo many oval feeds fitting in the empalement.

This genus of plants is ranged in the firft fection of Linnæus's fourteenth clafs, intitled Didynamia Gymnofpermia, which contains thofe plants whofe flowers have two long and two fhort ftamina, and are fucceeded by naked feeds in the empalement.

The Species are,

1. Hyssopus (*Officinalis*) fpicis fecundis. Hort. Cliff. 304. *Hyffop with fruitful fpikes.* Hyffopus officinarum cœrulea feu fpicata. C. B. P. 217. *Hyffop of the fhops with blue fpikes, or the common Hyffop.*
2. Hyssopus (*Rubra*) fpicis brevioribus, verticillis compactis. *Hyffop with fhorter fpikes, and whorls more compact.* Hyffopus rubro flore. C.B.P. 217. *Hyffop with a red flower.*
3. Hyssopus (*Altiffimis*) fpicis longiffimis verticillis diftantibus. *Hyffop with the longeft fpikes, and whorls at a greater diftance.* Hyffopus verticillis florum rarioribus. Houft. *Hyffop with the whorls of flowers thinly ranged.*
4. Hyssopus (*Nepetoides*) caule acuto quadrangulo. Hort. Upfal. 163. *Hyffop with an acute fquare ftalk.* Sideritis Canadenfis altiffima, fcrophulariæ folio, flore flavefcente. Tourn. Inft. 192. *Talleft Canada Ironwort, with a Figwort leaf and a yellowifh flower.*
5. Hyssopus (*Lophanthus*) corollis fubrefupinatis ftaminibus corollâ brevioribus. Hort. Upfal. 162. *Hyffop with tranfverfe petals, and the lower ftamina fhorter than the petal.* Nepeta floribus obliquis. Dill. *Catmint with oblique flowers.*

The firft fort, which is the only one cultivated for ufe, grows a foot and a half high. The ftalks are firft fquare, but afterward become round; their lower parts are garnifhed with fmall fpear-fhaped leaves placed oppofite, without foot-ftalks, and feven or eight very narrow erect leaves (or bractæa) rifing from the fame joint. The upper part of the ftalk is garnifhed with whorls of flowers, the lower ones ftanding half an inch apart, but the upper are almoft joined together. The upper lip of the flower is indented at the top, and the under is cut into three parts, the middle being deeply indented at the point. There are four ftamina in each flower, which fpread at a diftance from each other; the two upper are the fhorteft, which are fituated on each fide the upper lip; the two longer ftand clofe to the two fide fegments, and are terminated by twin fummits. At the bottom of the tube are fituated four naked germen, fupporting a flender ftyle, fitting clofe to the upper lip, crowned by a bifid ftigma; thefe germen afterward become four oblong black feeds, fitting in the empalement. The whole plant has a ftrong aromatic fcent. It flowers in July and Auguft, and the feeds ripen in September, but the roots will abide many years; it grows naturally in the Levant. There is a variety of this with white flowers, but doth not differ from the blue in any other particular.

The fecond fort doth not grow fo tall as the firft; the ftalks branch more, and the fpikes of flowers are much fhorter than that of the firft. The whorls are clofer together, and have long narrow leaves fituated under each. The flowers are of a fine red colour, and appear at the fame time with the former. This fort is not quite fo hardy as the common, for in 1739 the plants were all deftroyed by the cold; this is certainly a diftinct fpecies, for I cultivated it from feeds twenty years, and never obferved it to vary.

The third fort grows much taller than either of the other. The leaves are narrower, the whorls of flowers are farther afunder, the fpikes of flowers are much longer, the flowers are larger, and of a deeper blue than thofe of the common fort, and the plant hath not fo ftrong an odour. It flowers at the fame time as the firft.

Thefe three forts of Hyffop are propagated either by feeds or cuttings; if by the feeds, they muft be fown in March, upon a bed of light fandy foil; and when the plants come up, they fhould be tranfplanted out

to the places where they are to remain, placing them at leaft a foot afunder each way; but if they are defigned to abide in thofe places for a long time, two feet diftance will be fmall enough, for they grow pretty large, efpecially if they are not frequently cut, to keep them within compafs; they thrive beft upon a poor dry foil, in which fituation they will endure the cold of our climate better than when they are planted on a richer foil. If you would propagate them by cuttings, they fhould be planted in April or May, in a border where they may be defended from the violent heat of the fun; and being frequently watered, they will take root in about two months; after which, they may be tranfplanted where they are to continue, managing them as was before directed for the feedling plants.

The firft fort was formerly more cultivated than at prefent in England, that being the fort commonly ufed in medicine. The other fpecies are preferred in curious gardens for their variety, but they are feldom cultivated for ufe.

They are very hardy plants, which will endure the cold of our winters in the open air, provided they are planted in a dry undunged foil; for when they are planted in a rich foil, they grow very luxuriant in fummer, and are lefs able to refift the cold in winter; fo that when any of thefe plants grow out of the joints of old walls, (as they frequently do) they will refift the moft fevere froft, and will be much more aromatic than thofe which grow in a rich foil.

The fourth fort grows naturally in North America; this hath a perennial root and an annual ftalk, which decays in autumn. It rifes with an upright fquare ftalk near four feet high, garnifhed with oblique heart-fhaped leaves, which are fawed on their edges, and end in acute points; they are placed oppofite on fhort foot-ftalks. The flowers grow in clofe thick fpikes four or five inches long, at the top of the ftalks. The upper lip is divided into two roundifh fegments, the lower one is divided into three, the two fide fegments ftanding erect, and the middle one is reflexed, and acutely fawed at the end. The two upper ftamina, which are fituated on each fide the upper lip are the longeft, the other two fhorter join the two fide fegments of the lower lip; they are terminated by fmall fummits. The germen are fituated at the bottom of the tube, having a flender ftyle under the upper lip, crowned by a bifid ftigma. The germen afterward becomes four oblong brown feeds, fitting in the tubulous empalement. This fort flowers in July, and the feeds ripen in September.

There is a variety of this fort with purple ftalks and purplifh flowers. The leaves ftand upon longer foot-ftalks, and the fpikes of flowers are thicker, but I cannot fay if it is a diftinct fpecies or only a variety. It grows naturally in the fame country with the other. It is titled, Betonica maxima, folio fcrophulariæ, floribus incarnatis, by Herman. Par. Bat. 106.

The fifth fort grows naturally in Siberia. The feeds of this were fent me from the Imperial garden at Peterfburgh, by the title of Lophanthus, and afterward I received fome from Holland, which were titled, Nepeta floribus obliquis. Dill. This is a perennial plant with a ftrong fibrous root, fending out many fquare ftalks, which divide into fmaller branches, garnifhed with oblong leaves, crenated on their edges, fet on by pairs. The flowers are produced at each joint in fmall clufters, two foot-ftalks arifing from the bafe of the leaves, about half an inch long, both inclining to one fide of the ftalk; each of thefe foot-ftalks divide again into two fmaller, and thefe do each fupport a clufter of four or five flowers, which have fwelling tubulous empalements, cut into five acute fegments at the top. The tube of the petal is longer than the empalement. The lips of the flower are oblique to it, being fituated horizontally. The two upper ftamina and the ftyle ftand out beyond the petal, but the other are fhorter. The flowers are blue, and appear in June and July, and the feeds ripen in September.

Both
```
```

Both these sorts are very hardy, and may be easily propagated by seeds, which should be sown in autumn; for those sown in the spring, often lie a year in the ground before they vegetate; when the plants come up, they must be kept clean from weeds, and thinned where they are too close. The following autumn they should be transplanted where they are to remain, and the plants will flower in summer, and produce seeds, but the roots will abide some years.

It hath been a great dispute amongst modern writers, whether the Hyssop now commonly known is the same which is mentioned in scripture; about which there is great room to doubt, there being very little grounds to ascertain that plant, though it is most generally thought to be the Winter Savory, which plant is now in great request amongst the inhabitants of the eastern countries, for outward washings or purification.

J.

JAC

JACEA. See CENTAUREA.

JACOBÆA. See SENECIO and OTHONNA.

JACQUINIA. Lin. Gen. 254.

The CHARACTERS are,

The empalement of the flower is composed of five roundish concave leaves, and is permanent. The flower has one bell-shaped petal, which is bellied, cut into ten segments. It hath five awl-shaped stamina arising from the receptacle, terminated by halbert-shaped summits, and an oval germen supporting a style the length of the stamina, crowned by a headed stigma. The germen afterward becomes a roundish berry with one cell, containing one seed. This genus of plants is ranged in the first section of Linnæus's fifth class, intitled Pentandria Monogynia, the flowers having five stamina and one style.

The SPECIES are,

1. JACQUINIA (*Ruscifolia*) foliis lanceolatis acuminatis. Jacq. Amer. 15. Lin. Sp. 271. *Jacquinia with spear-shaped acute-pointed leaves.* Fruticulus foliis rusci stellatis. Hort. Elth.

2. JACQUINIA (*Armillaris*) foliis obtusis cum acumine. Jacq. Amer. 15. Lin. Sp. 272. *Jacquinia with blunt leaves ending in acute points.* Chrysophyllum Barbasco. Lœfl. it. 204.

3. JACQUINIA (*Lineari*) foliis linearibus acuminatis. Jacq. Amer. 15. Lin. Sp. 272. *Jacquinia with linear sharp-pointed leaves.*

The first sort grows naturally in the island of Cuba, and in some other warm parts of America; it rises with a shrubby stalk about a foot high, which is ligneous at the bottom, and about the size of a swan's quill, covered with a dark brown bark, sending out a few slender branches, garnished at intervals with hand-shaped stiff leaves, placed in whorls round them; these are stiff like those of Butcher's Broom, ending with sharp points, of a deep green on their upper side, but pale on their under; the flowers are (according to Plumier's figure) produced from between the leaves on the top of the branches; but having seen no flowers in England, so I can give no farther account of them.

The second sort grows naturally at Carthagena, Martinico, and other parts of South America, where it rises with a shrubby stalk four or five feet high, dividing toward the top into four branches, which are situated in whorls round the principal stalk, garnished with oblong blunt leaves, placed also in whorls, having a short slender apex. The flowers are produced in a racemus on the end of the branches, each containing five or six white flowers of a thick consistence, which

JAS

have a scent like Jasmine flowers, which they retain after they decay, so are worn by the ladies of those countries for ornament.

The third sort grows naturally on the borders of the sea, in the island of Dominica; this is an under-shrub, of a very low growth, rarely rising about two feet high, dividing into several branches, garnished with linear stiff leaves, ending with a thorn; these are placed in whorls round the branches, and from the middle of the whorls come out the foot-stalks of the flowers, each being terminated by one small white flower without scent.

As these plants are natives of hot countries, so they will not live in England, unless they are placed in a warm stove, and treated in the manner directed for other plants from the same countries, giving them little water in winter, and in warm weather plenty of fresh air. They are raised from seeds, when they can be procured from the countries where they naturally grow; which must be sown on a hot-bed, and may afterward be propagated by cuttings, though it is with difficulty they take root.

JALAPA. See MIRABILIS.

JASIONE. Lin. Gen. Plant. 896. This is the Rapunculus scabiosæ capitulo cœruleo. C. B. P. 22. Rampions with Scabious heads. This plant grows naturally on sterile ground in most parts of England, and is rarely admitted into gardens.

JASMINOIDES. See CESTRUM and LYCIUM.

JASMINUM. Tourn. Inst. R. H. 597. tab. 368. Lin. Gen. Plant. 17. [This name is Arabic.] The Jasmine, or Jessamine-tree; in French, *Jasmin.*

The CHARACTERS are,

The flower hath a tubulous empalement of one leaf, which is permanent, and cut into five segments at the brim, which are erect. The flower is of one petal, having a long cylindrical tube, cut into five segments at the top, which spread open. It hath two short stamina, which are terminated by small summits, and are situated within the tube of the petal. In the center is situated a roundish germen, supporting a slender style, crowned by a bifid stigma. The germen afterward turns to an oval berry, with a soft skin inclosing two seeds, which are flat on those sides which join, and convex on the other. This genus of plants is ranged in the first section of Linnæus's second class, intitled Diandria Monogynia, in which he ranges those plants whose flowers have two stamina and one style.

The SPECIES are,

1. JASMINUM (*Officinale*) foliis oppositis pinnatis, foliolis acuminatis. *Jasmine with winged leaves placed opposite,*

posite, whose lobes end in acute points. Jasminum vulgatius, flore albo. C. B. P. 397. *The common white Jasmine.*

2. JASMINUM (*Humile*) foliis alternis ternatis simplicibusque, ramis angulatis. Hort. Upsal. 5. *Jasmine with trifoliate winged leaves placed alternate, and angular branches.* Jasminum humile luteum. C. B. P. 397. *Dwarf yellow Jasmine, commonly called the Italian yellow Jasmine.*

3. JASMINUM (*Fruticans*) foliis alternis ternatis simplicibusque, ramis angulatis. Hort. Cliff. 5. *Jasmine with trifoliate single leaves placed alternate, and angular branches.* Jasminum luteum, vulgò dictum bacciferum. C. B. P. 398. *The common yellow Jasmine.*

4. JASMINUM (*Grandiflorum*) foliis oppositis pinnatis, foliolis brevioribus obtusis. *Jasmine with winged leaves placed opposite, whose lobes are shorter and obtuse.* Jasminum humilis, magno flore. C. B. P. 398. *The Spanish white, or Catalonian Jasmine with a larger flower.*

5. JASMINUM (*Odoratissimum*) foliis alternis ternatis, foliolis ovatis, ramis teretibus. *Jasmine with trifoliate leaves placed alternate, whose lobes are oval, and taper branches.* Jasminum Indicum flavum odoratissimum. Fer. Flor. *The sweet-scented yellow Indian Jasmine.*

6. JASMINUM (*Azoricum*) foliis oppositis ternatis, foliolis cordato-acuminatis. *Jasmine with trifoliate leaves placed opposite, whose lobes are heart-shaped and pointed.* Jasminum Azoricum trifoliatum, flore albo, odoratissimum. Hort. Amst. *The three-leaved Azorian Jasmine, with very sweet white flowers, commonly called the Ivy-leaved Jasmine.*

7. JASMINUM (*Capense*) foliis lanceolatis oppositis integerrimis, floribus triandris. *Jasmine with spear-shaped entire leaves placed opposite, and flowers with three stamina.*

The first sort is the common white Jasmine, which is a plant so generally known as to need no description. This grows naturally at Malabar, and in several parts of India, yet has been long inured to our climate, so as to thrive and flower extremely well, but never produces any fruit in England; this hath weak trailing branches, so requires the assistance of a wall or pale to support them. It is easily propagated by laying down the branches, which will take root in one year, and may then be cut from the old plant, and planted where they are designed to remain : it may also be propagated by cuttings, which should be planted early in the autumn, and if the winter should prove severe, the surface of the ground between them should be covered with tan, sea-coal ashes, or saw-dust, which will prevent the frost from penetrating deep into the ground, and thereby preserve the cuttings; or where these are wanting, some Peas-haulm, or other light covering should be laid over the cuttings in hard frost; but these must be removed when the weather is mild, for they will keep off the air and occasion damps, which often destroy them.

When these plants are removed, they should be planted where they are designed to be continued, which should be either against some wall, pale, or other fence, where the flexible branches may be supported; for although it is sometimes planted as a standard, and formed into a head, yet it will be very difficult to keep it in any handsome order; or if you do, you must cut off all the flowering branches; for the flowers are always produced at the extremity of the same year's shoots, which, if shortened before the flowers are blown, will entirely deprive the trees of flowers. These plants should be permitted to grow rude in the summer, for the reason before given; nor should you prune and nail them until the middle or latter end of March, when the frosty weather is past; for if it should prove sharp frosty weather after their rude branches are pruned off, and the strong ones are exposed thereto, they are very often destroyed; and this plant being very backward in shooting, there will be no danger of hurting them by late pruning.

There are two varieties of this with variegated leaves, one with white, and the other yellow stripes, but the

latter is the most common : these are propagated by budding them on the plain Jasmine, and it often happens, that the buds do not take, but yet they have communicated their gilded miasma to the plants; so that in a short time after, many of the branches both above and below the places where the buds have been inserted have been thoroughly tinctured; and the following year I have often found very distant branches, which had no other communication with those which were budded than by the root, have been as compleatly tinged as any of the nearer branches, so that the juices must have descended into the root. The two striped sorts should be planted in a warm situation, especially the white striped; for they are much more tender than the plain, and are very subject to be destroyed by great frosts, if they are exposed thereto; therefore the white striped should be planted to a south or south-west aspect, and in very severe winters their branches should be covered with mats or straw, to prevent their being killed : the yellow striped is not so tender, so may be planted against walls to east or west aspects; but these plants with variegated leaves, are not so much in esteem as formerly.

The second sort is frequently called Italian yellow Jasmine by the gardeners, the plants being annually brought from thence by those who come over with Orange-trees. These plants are generally grafted upon the common yellow Jasmine stocks, so that if the graft decays, the plants are of no value. This sort is somewhat tenderer than the common, yet it will endure the cold of our ordinary winters, if it is planted in a warm situation. The flowers of this kind are generally larger than those of the common yellow sort, but have very little scent, and are seldom produced so early in the season. It may be propagated by laying down the tender branches, as was directed for the common white sort; or by budding or inarching it upon the common yellow Jasmine, the latter of which is preferable, as making the plants hardier than those which are obtained from layers : they should be planted against a warm wall, and in very severe winters will require to be sheltered with mats, or some other covering, otherwise they are subject to be destroyed. The manner of dressing and pruning being the same as was directed for the white Jasmine, I shall not repeat it.

The third sort was formerly more cultivated in the gardens than at present, for as the flowers have no scent, so few persons regard them. This hath weak angular branches which require support, and will rise to the height of eight or ten feet, if planted against a wall or pale; but the plants do often produce a great number of suckers from their roots, whereby they become troublesome in the borders of the pleasure-garden; and as they cannot be kept in any order as standards, so there are few of the plants at present introduced into gardens. It is easily propagated by suckers or layers.

The fourth sort grows naturally in India, and also in the island of Tobago, where the woods are full of it; the late Mr. Robert Millar sent me over a great quantity of it from thence. This hath much stronger branches than the common white sort; the leaves are winged, and are composed of three pair of short obtuse lobes, terminated by an odd one, ending in an acute point; these lobes are placed closer than those of the common Jasmine, and are of a lighter green; the flowers come out from the wings of the stalks, standing on foot-stalks which are two inches long, each sustaining three or four flowers, which are of a blush red on their outside, but white within; the tube of the flower is longer, the segments are obtuse, twisted at the mouth of the tube, and are of a much thicker texture than those of the common sort, so that there is no doubt of its being a distinct species: the reason for Dr. Linnæus's supposing it to be so, was by mistake; for as these plants are generally grafted upon stocks of the common Jasmine, so there are always shoots coming out from the stocks of that sort, which,

if

if permitted to stand, will produce flowers; and these often starve and kill the grafts, so that there will be only the common sort left; and this has been the case with some plants which he examined, therefore supposed the difference of the other sort was wholly owing to culture; whereas, if he had only observed the difference of their leaves, he would have certainly made two distinct species of them, which he has now done in the last edition of his species.

This plant is propagated by budding or inarching it upon the common white Jasmine, on which it takes very well, and is rendered hardier than those which are upon their own stocks. But the plants of this kind being brought over from Italy every spring in so great plenty, they are seldom raised here: I shall therefore proceed to the management of such plants as are usually brought into England from the place above-mentioned, which are generally tied up in small bunches, containing four plants, and their roots wrapped about with mofs, to preserve them from drying; which, if it happen that the ship has a long passage, will often occasion them to push out strong shoots from their roots, which must always be taken off before they are planted, otherwise they will exhaust the whole nourishment of the plant, and destroy the graft.

In the making choice of these plants, you should carefully observe if their grafts are alive, and in good health: for if they are brown and shrunk, they will not push out, so that there will be only the stock left, which is of the common sort.

When you receive these plants, you must clear the roots of the mofs, and all decayed branches should be taken off; then place their roots into a pot or tub of water, which should be set in the green-house, or some other room; where it may be screened from the cold; in this situation they may continue two days, after which you must prune off all the dry roots, and cut down the branches within four inches of the place where they were grafted, and plant them into pots filled with fresh light earth; then plunge the pots into a moderate hot-bed of tanners bark, observing to water and shade them, as the heat of the season may require. In about a month or six weeks after they will begin to shoot, when you must carefully rub off all such as are produced from the stock below the graft; and you must now let them have a great share of air, by raising the glasses in the heat of the day; and as the shoots extend, they should be topped, to strengthen them, and by degrees should be hardened to endure the open air, into which they should be removed the beginning of June, but must have a warm situation the first summer; for if they are too much exposed to the winds, they will make but indifferent progress, being rendered unhealthy tender by the hot-bed. If the summer proves warm, and the trees have succeeded well, they will produce some flowers in the autumn following, though they will be few in number, and not near so strong as they will be the succeeding years, when the trees are stronger and have better roots.

These plants are commonly preserved in green-houses, with Oranges, Myrtles, &c. and during the winter season, will require to be frequently watered; which should be performed sparingly each time, especially in cold weather, for too much wet at that season will be apt to rot the fibres of their roots; they should also have a great share of fresh air when the weather, will permit, for which purpose they should be placed in the coolest part of the green-house, among plants that are hardy, where the windows may be opened every day, except in frosty weather; nor should they be crowded too close among other plants, which often occasions the tender part of their shoots to grow mouldy and decay. In April the shoots of these plants should be shortened down to four eyes, and all the weak branches should be cut off; and if you have the conveniency of a glass-stove, or a deep frame, to place the pots in at that season, to draw them out again, it will be of great service in forwarding their flowering; yet still you should be careful

not to force them too much; and as soon as they have made shoots three or four inches long, the glasses should be opened in the day time, that the plants may, by degrees, be inured to the open air, into which they should be removed by the latter end of May, or the beginning of June; otherwise their flowers will not be so fair, nor continue so long. If the autumn prove favourable, these plants will continue to produce fresh flowers until November; and sometimes when they are strong, they will continue flowering later; but then they must have a great share of air when the weather is mild and will admit of it, otherwise the flower-buds will grow mouldy and decay. But notwithstanding most people preserve these plants in green-houses, yet they will endure the cold of our ordinary winters in the open air, if planted against a warm wall, and covered with mats in frosty weather; they will also produce ten times as many flowers in one season as those kept in pots, and the flowers will likewise be much larger; but they should not be planted abroad till they have acquired strength, so that it will be necessary to keep them in pots three or four years, whereby they may be sheltered from the frost in winter; and when they are planted against the wall, which should be in May, that they may take good root in the ground before the succeeding winter, you must turn them out of the pots, preserving the earth to their roots; and having made holes in the border where they are to be planted, you should place them therein, with their stems close to the wall; then fill up the holes round their roots with good, fresh, rich earth, and give them some water to settle the ground about them, and nail up their shoots to the wall, shortening such of them as are very long, that they may push out new shoots below to furnish the wall, continuing to nail up all the shoots as they are produced. In the middle, or toward the latter end of July, they will begin to flower, and continue to produce new flowers until the frost prevents them; which, when you observe, you should carefully cut off all the tops of such shoots as have buds formed upon them, as also those which have the remains of faded flowers left; for if these are suffered to remain on, they will soon grow mouldy, especially when the trees are covered, and thereby infect many of the tender branches, which will greatly injure the trees.

Toward the middle of November, if the weather proves cold and the nights frosty, you must begin to cover your trees with mats, which should be nailed over them pretty close; but this should be done when the trees are perfectly dry, otherwise the wet being lodged upon the branches, will often cause a mouldiness upon them, and the air being excluded therefrom, will rot them in a short time: it will also be very necessary to take off the mats as soon as the weather will permit, to prevent this mouldiness, and only keep them close covered in frosty weather, and in the nights; at which time you should also lay some mulch upon the surface of the ground about their roots, and fasten some bands of hay about their stems, to guard them from the frost; and in very severe weather, you should add a double or treble covering of mats over the trees; by which method, carefully performed, you may preserve them through the hardest winters. In the spring, as the weather is warmer, you should by degrees take off the covering; but you should be careful not to expose them too soon to the open air, as also to guard them against the morning frosts and dry easterly winds, which often reign in March, to the no small destruction of tender plants if they are exposed thereto; nor should you quite remove your covering until the middle of April, when the season is settled; at which time you should prune the trees, cutting out all decayed and weak branches, shortening the strong ones to about two feet long, which will cause them to shoot strong, and produce many flowers. There is a variety of this with semi-double flowers, which is at present more rare in England, and only to be found in some curious gardens; though in Italy it is pretty common, from whence it is sometimes

brought

brought over amongst the single; the flowers of this kind have only two rows of leaves, so that it is rather cultivated for itscuriosity, than for any extraordinary beauty in the flowers. This may be propagated by budding it upon the common white Jasmine, as hath been directed for the single, and must be treated in the same manner.

The fifth sort grows naturally in India; this rises with an upright woody stalk eight or ten feet high, covered with a brown bark, sending out several branches which want no support; these are closely garnished with trifoliate leaves of a lucid green, which are placed alternate on the branches; the two side lobes of these leaves which grow opposite, are much less than the end one; they are oval and entire, continuing green all the year: the flowers are produced at the end of the shoots in bunches, which have long slender tubes, and are divided at the top into five obtuse segments which spread open; these flowers are of a bright yellow, and have a most grateful odour. They come out in July, August, September, and October, and sometimes continue to the end of November; they are frequently succeeded by oblong oval berries, which turn black when ripe, and have each two seeds.

This sort of Jasmine is propagated either by seeds, or laying down the tender branches; if you would propagate them by seeds, which they sometimes produce in England, you should make a moderate hot-bed in the spring, into which you should plunge some small pots, filled with fresh light earth; and in a day or two after, when you find the earth in the pots warm, you must put your seeds therein; about four in each pot will be sufficient, covering them about an inch thick with the same light earth, and observe to refresh the pots with water as often as you shall perceive the earth dry; but do not give them too much at each time, which would be apt to rot the seeds.

In about six or eight weeks after sowing, the plants will appear above ground, at which time it will be necessary to remove the pots into another fresh hot-bed, of a moderate temperature, in order to bring the plants forward; you must also be careful to water them as often as is necessary, and in the great heat of the day the glasses should be tilted pretty high, and shaded with mats, to prevent the plants from being scorched with heat. About the middle of May you should begin to harden them to the open air, by taking off the glasses when the weather is warm; but this must be done cautiously, for you should not expose them to the open sun in a very hot day at first, which would greatly injure them; but rather take off the glasses in warm cloudy weather at first, or in gentle showers of rain, and so by degrees inure them to bear the sun; and in June you should take the pots out of the hot-bed, and carry them to some well sheltered situation, where they may remain until the beginning of October; at which time they must be carried into the green-house, observing to place them where they may enjoy as much free air as possible when the windows are opened, as also to be clear from the branches of other plants.

During the winter season they will require to be often watered, but you must be careful not to give them too much at each time; and in March you must remove these plants each into a separate pot, being careful not to take the earth from their roots; and if at this time you plunge them into a fresh moderate hot-bed, it will greatly facilitate their rooting again, and be of great service to the plants; but when they are rooted, you must give them a great deal of air; for if you draw them too much, they will become weak in their stems, and incapable to support their heads, which is a great defect in these trees.

You must also harden them to the open air, into which they should be removed about the middle of May, observing, as was before directed, to place them in a situation that is defended from strong winds, which are injurious to these plants, especially while they are young. In winter house them as before, and

continue the same care, with which they will thrive very fast, and produce annually great quantities of flowers.

These plants are pretty hardy, and will require no other care in winter, than only to defend them from hard frosts; nor do I know whether they would not live in the open air, if planted against a warm wall, which is what should be tried by planting some against a wall for that purpose; and I think we have little reason to doubt of the success, since they are much hardier than the Spanish; but there is this difference between them, viz. these plants have large, thick, Evergreen leaves, so that if they were covered with mats, as was directed for the Spanish Jasmine, the leaves would rot and decay the shoots; but as these will only require to be covered in extreme frost, so if their roots are well mulched, and a mat or two loosely hung over them in ordinary frosts, it will be sufficient; and these mats being either rolled up, or taken quite off in the day, there will be no great danger of their being hurt, which only can proceed from being too long close covered.

In the spring these should be pruned, when you should cut off all decayed branches; but you must not shorten any of the other branches, as was directed for the Spanish sort, for the flowers of this kind are produced only at the extremity of the branches, which, if shortened, they would be cut off; and these growing of a more ligneous substance than the other, will not produce shoots strong enough to flower the same year. If you would propagate this plant from layers, the shoots should be laid down in March; and if you give them a little cut at the joint, as is practised in laying of Carnations, it will promote their rooting: you should always observe to refresh them often with water, when the weather is dry; which, if carefully attended to, the plants will be rooted by the succeeding spring, fit to be transplanted, when they must be planted in pots filled with light earth, and managed as was before directed for the seedling plants.

This sort is frequently propagated, by inarching the young shoots into stocks of the common yellow Jasmine, but the plants so raised do not grow so strong as those which are upon their own stock; besides, the common yellow Jasmine is very apt to send out a great number of suckers from the root, which renders the plants unsightly; and if these suckers are not constantly taken off as they are produced, they will rob the plants of their nourishment.

The sixth sort grows naturally in the Azores; this hath long slender branches which require support, and may be trained twenty feet high; they are garnished with trifoliate leaves, whose lobes are large and heart-shaped, of a lucid green, and are placed opposite on the branches; they continue all the year. The flowers are produced at the end of the branches, in loose bunches; they have long narrow tubes, which at the top are cut into five segments spreading open; they are of a clear white, and have a very agreeable scent. This flowers at the same time with the former; the gardeners call it frequently the Ivy-leaved Jasmine.

The Azorian Jasmine is also pretty hardy, and requires no more shelter than only from hard frosts; and I am apt to think, if this sort was planted against a warm wall, and managed as hath been directed for the yellow Indian Jasmine, it would succeed very well; for I remember to have seen some plants of this kind growing against a wall in the gardens at Hampton Court, where they had endured the winter, and were in a more flourishing state than ever I saw any of the kind in pots, and produced a greater quantity of flowers. These plants are propagated in the same manner as the yellow Indian, and require the same management.

These plants are as deserving of a place in all greenhouses, as any which are there preserved; for their leaves being of a shining green, make a good appearance all the year; and their flowers having a fine scent, and continuing so long in succession, renders them very valuable.

The

The feventh fort, was brought from the Cape of Good Hope, by Captain Hutchinfon of the Godolphin, who difcovered it growing naturally, a few miles up the land from the fea, being drawn to it by the great fragrancy of its flowers, which he fmelt at fome diftance from the plant, which was then in full flower; and after having viewed the plant, and remarked the place of its growth, he returned thither the following day with proper help, and a tub to put it in, and caufed it to be carefully taken up, and planted in the tub with fome of the earth on the fpot, and conveyed on board his fhip, where it continued flowering great part of the voyage to England, where it arrived in good health, and from for fome years continued flowering, in the curious garden of Richard Warner, Efq; at Woodford in Effex, who was fo obliging as to favour me with branches of this curious plant in flower, to embellifh one of the numbers of my figures of plants, where it is reprefented in the 180th plate.

This plant feems not to have been known to any of the botanifts, for I have not met with any figure or defcription of it in any of the books; there is one fort which is figured in the Malabar garden, and alfo in Burman's plants of Ceylon, which approaches near this; it is titled Nandi ervatum major. Hort. Mal. But it differs from this, in having longer and narrower leaves; the tube of the flower is larger, and the fegments do not fpread fo much as this; the flowers alfo of the Cape Jafmine fade to a buff colour before they decay, therefore there is no doubt of its being a different fpecies from that of Dr. Burman; but it is furprizing that this plant fhould be unknown to the people at the Cape of Good Hope, for there was not one plant of it in their curious garden, nor could the captain fee any other plant of it but that which he brought away.

The ftem of this plant is large and woody, fending out many branches, which are firft green, but afterward the bark becomes gray and fmooth; the branches come out by pairs oppofite, and have fhort joints; the leaves are alfo fet oppofite, clofe to the branches; they are five inches long, and two inches and a half broad in the middle, leffening to both ends, terminating in a point; they are of a lucid green, having feveral tranfverfe veins from the midrib to the borders; they are entire, and of a thick confiftence. The flowers are produced at the end of the branches, fitting clofe to the leaves; they have a tubulous empalement, with five corners or angles, cut deep at the brim, into five long narrow fegments, ending in acute points: the flower hath but one petal, for although it is cut into many deep fegments at the top, yet thefe are all joined in one tube below; fome of thefe flowers are much more double than others, having three or four orders of petals; thefe which have fo many, have only a bifid ftigma, but thofe which are lefs double have trifid ftigmas. All thofe flowers which I have examined have but one or two ftamina, which may be occafioned by the fulnefs of the flowers; as is often obferved in many kinds of plants, whofe flowers have a greater number of petals than ufual, many of which want both parts of generation, and fome of them have no male parts. This flower, when fully blown, is as large as a middling Rofe, and fome of them are as double as the Damafk Rofe; they have a very agreeable odour; on the firft approach it is fomething like that of the Orange flower, but when more clofely fmelt to, has the odour of the common double white Narciffus. The feafon of this plant flowering in England, is in July and Auguft, but in its native country it is fuppofed to flower great part of the year; for Captain Hutchinfon, who brought the plant over, faid there was a fucceffion of flowers on it, till the fhip arrived in a cold climate, which put a ftop to its growth.

Dr. Linnæus has been induced from what has been printed in the Tranfactions of the Royal Society, to alter the title of this plant to Gardenia; but as the defcription of the plant with its characters as there

printed, was taken from a double flower by fome hafty people, who fhould have remembred what Linnæus has written to caution perfons againft regarding the double flowers of all kinds, in ranging them in their claffes and genera, which if they had adhered to, they would not have made this miftake; for I have fince raifed feveral of the plants from feeds, fome of which have produced flowers which were fingle, having all the marks of the double, the flowers altering to a buff colour before they faded, and all thefe flowers had each but three ftamina and a trifid ftigma; whereas in the characters fet down by Linnæus, there is no ftamina, but five linear antheræ, by which it is plain from the increafe of the number of petals (or rather their fegments) has occafioned an alteration in the parts of generation; which is alfo very confpicuous in the double flowers of Dianthus, where fome flowers have but two or three ftamina, when the fame fpecies with fingle flowers have ufually ten. Linnæus alfo fuppofes the capfule of the feed to have two cells full of fmall feeds; but the perfons who led him into this miftake, have fince fuppofed the figure given by Dr. Plukenet in his 448th plate, under the title of Um-ky, to be the fruit of this plant; whereas this has three cells filled with angular fweet-fcented feeds, as the fpecimens I have of that demonftrate, by which it is certain they are the fruit of a different plant; for the feeds which I fowed of this Jafmine, were a berry compofed of two feeds like the other Jafmines; therefore I have continued it under the fame genus, with an addition to the title of its having three ftamina.

This plant is eafily propagated by cuttings during the fummer feafon; the cuttings fhould be planted in pots, and plunged into a moderate hot-bed, covering them clofe with either bell or hand-glaffes to exclude the external air, being careful to fcreen them from fun in the day time; when they have taken root they fhould be carefully parted, and put each into a feparate fmall pot, plunging them again into the hot-bed, and fhading them until they have taken new root, after which they fhould be gradually inured to the open air.

Though the cuttings of this plant take root freely, and make ftrong fhoots a year or two after, yet in three or four years they are very apt to ftint in their growth, their leaves turning pale and fickly, and frequently die foon after; this has happened every where within my knowledge, although the plants have been kept in various degrees of heat in winter; and in fummer when they have been differently managed, they have frequently failed. I have alfo been informed by a gentleman who lived fome years in India, where he had the plants in his garden, they frequently went off in the fame manner. This has greatly leffened the value of the plants in England.

JASMINUM ARABICUM. See Coffee.

JASMINUM ILICIS FOLIO. See Lantana.

JASMINE, the Arabian. See Nyctanthes.

JASMINE, the Perfian. See Syringa.

JATROPHA. Lin. Gen. Plant. 961. Manihot. Tourn. Inft. R. H. 958. tab. 438. Caffada, or Caffava; in French Caffave.

The Characters are,

It hath male and female flowers in the fame plant; the male flowers have a fcarce vifible empalement; they are falver-fhaped, of one petal, with a fhort tube, whofe brim is cut into five roundifh fegments which fpread open; they have ten awl-fhaped ftamina, five being alternately fhorter than the other, and are joined clofe together, ftanding erect in the center of the flower, terminated by roundifh loofe fummits. The female flowers which are fituated in the fame umbel have no empalement, but have five petals fpread open like a Rofe. In the center is a roundifh germen with three deep furrows, fupporting three ftyles, crowned by fingle ftigmas. The germen afterward becomes a roundifh capfule with three cells, each containing one feed.

This genus of plants is ranged in the ninth fection of Linnæus's twenty-firft clafs, intitled Monœcia Monodelphia,

nodelphia, which includes thofe plants which have male and female flowers on the fame plant, and the ftamina are collected in one body.

The SPECIES are,

1. JATROPHA (*Manihot*) foliis palmatis, lobis lanceolatis integerrimis lævibus. Lin. Sp. Plant. 1007. *Jatropha with hand-fhaped leaves, whofe lobes are fpear-fhaped, entire, and fmooth.* Manihot Theveti, juca & caffavi. J. B. 2. 794. *The Manihot of Thevet, and the Juca or Caffava of John Bauhin.*

2. JATROPHA (*Quinquelobatus*) foliis quinquelobatis, lobis acuminatis, acutè dentatis lævibus, caule fruticofo. *Jatropha with leaves compofed of five fmooth lobes ending in points, which are fharply indented on their edges, and a fhrubby ftalk.* Juffievia frutefcens, non fpinofa, foliis glabris & minus laciniatis. Houft. MSS. *Shrubby Juffievia without fpines, and fmooth leaves lefs divided.*

3. JATROPHA (*Urens*) aculeata, foliis quinquelobatis acutè incifis, caule herbaceo. *Prickly Jatropha, with leaves having five lobes which are fharply cut on their edges, and an herbaceous ftalk.* Juffievia herbacea, fpinofiffima, urens, foliis digitatis & laciniatis. Houft. MSS. *The moft prickly ftinging and herbaceous Juffievia, with fingered leaves which are jagged.*

4. JATROPHA (*Herbacea*) aculeata, foliis trilobis, caule herbaceo. Lin. Sp. Plant. 1007. *Prickly Jatropha, with leaves having three lobes and an herbaceous ftalk.* Juffievia herbacea fpinofiffima, urens, foliis trilobatis minimè incifis. Houft. MSS. *Prickly ftinging herbaceous Juffievia, with leaves having three lobes, which are very flightly indented.*

5. JATROPHA (*Vitifolius*) foliis palmatis dentatis aculeatis. Hort. Cliff. 445. *Jatropha with hand-fhaped, indented, prickly leaves.* Manihot fpinofiffima, folio vitigineo. Plum. Cat. 20. *The moft prickly Caffava with a Vine leaf.*

6. JATROPHA (*Aconitifolius*) foliis lobatis dentatis acuminatis, urentibus, caule arboreo. *Jatropha with lobated leaves which are indented, acute-pointed, and ftinging, and a tree-like ftalk.* Juffievia arborea, minùs fpinofa, floribus albis umbellatis, foliis aconiti urentibus. Houft. MSS. *Tree Juffievia which is lefs prickly, with white flowers growing in umbels, and ftinging leaves like thofe of Wolfsbane.*

7. JATROPHA (*Multifida*) foliis multipartitis lævibus, ftipulis fetaceis multifidis. Hort. Cliff. 445. *Jatropha with fmooth leaves divided into many parts, and briftly ftipulæ with many points.* Ricinoides arbor Americana, folio multifido. 656. *Tree American Baftard Ricinus with a many pointed leaf, commonly called French Phyfic Nut in America.*

8. JATROPHA (*Curcas*) foliis cordatis angulatis. Hort. Cliff. 445. *Jatropha with angular heart-fhaped leaves.* Ricinoides Americana goffypii folio. Tourn. Inft. 656. *American Baftard Ricinus with a Cotton leaf, commonly called Phyfic Nut in America.*

9. JATROPHA (*Staphyfagrifolia*) foliis quinquepartitis, lobis ovatis integris, fetis glandulofis ramofis. Flor. Leyd. Prod. 202. *Jatropha with leaves divided into five parts, the lobes whereof are oval and entire, and branching briftles arifing from the glands.* Ricinoides Americana ftaphyfagriæ folio. Tourn. Inft. 656. *American Baftard Ricinus, with a Stavefacre leaf, commonly called Belly-ach Weed in America.*

The firft fort here mentioned, is the common Caffada or Caffava, which is cultivated for food in the warm parts of America, where, after the juice is expreffed out of the root (which has a poifonous quality) it is ground into a kind of flour, and made up in cakes or puddings, and is efteemed a wholefome food.

This rifes with a fhrubby ftalk fix or feven feet high, garnifhed with fmooth leaves, ftanding upon long foot-ftalks alternately; they are compofed of feven lobes, which are joined at their bafe in one center, where they are narrow, but increafe in their breadth till within an inch and a half of the top, where they diminifh to an acute point; the three middle lobes are about fix inches long, and two-broad in their broadeft part; the two next are about an inch fhorter, and the two outfide lobes are not more than three

inches long; the middle lobes are finuated on each fide near the top, but the two outer are entire. The flowers are produced in umbels at the top of the ftalks, thefe are fome male and others female in the fame umbel; they are compofed of five roundifh petals which fpread open; the male flowers have their ten ftamina joined together in a column, and the female flowers have a roundifh germen with three furrows in the center, fupporting three ftyles; two are feparated at a diftance, and the third arifes between them, but is not fo long; they are crowned by fingle ftigmas. The germen afterward turns to a roundifh capfule with three lobes, each having a diftinct cell, containing one feed.

The fecond fort was difcovered by the late Dr. Houftoun at the Havanna, from whence he fent the feeds. This rifes with an upright ftalk ten or twelve feet high, which is firft green and herbaceous, but afterward becomes ligneous, fending out a few branches at the top, which are garnifhed with fmooth leaves, compofed of five oval lobes, which end in acute points; the edges are alfo indented in feveral irregular points, which are acute. The flowers are produced in an umbel at the extremity of the ftalks, they are of an herbaceous white colour, and are male and female in the fame umbel, as the other fort; the capfule is fmooth and has three cells, each including a fingle feed.

The third fort was difcovered by the late Dr. Houftoun, growing naturally in the fandy grounds about the town of La Vera Cruz, from whence he fent the feeds, which fucceeded in the Chelfea garden. This hath a very thick flefhy root, in fhape like the white Spanifh Radifh; the ftalk rifes from one to two feet high, it is taper, herbaceous, and branching, and clofely armed on every fide with long white fpines, which are not very ftiff, but are pungent and ftinging; the leaves are divided into five lobes, the middle being the longeft; the others are fhortened, the two next being about an inch fhorter, but the two outer are not more than half the length of the middle; thefe are deeply jagged on both fides, and are waved on their edges; all the veins of the leaves are clofely armed with ftinging fpines, fo that it is dangerous handling them; for all the intermediate parts of the leaves have fmall ftinging fpines like thofe of the Nettle, but they do not appear fo vifible. At the end of the branches the flowers are produced in umbels; they are white, and have empalements clofely armed with the fame fpines as the ftalks and leaves: there are male and female flowers in the fame umbel; the female flowers are fucceeded by tricapfular veffels, containing three feeds.

The fourth fort rifes with an herbaceous ftalk about a foot high, dividing into two or three branches, which are garnifhed with leaves ftanding alternate upon long foot-ftalks; they are compofed of three oblong lobes which are flightly finuated on their edges, ending in acute points; the whole plant is clofely armed with long, briftly, ftinging fpines. The flowers grow in an umbel at the end of the branches; they are fmall, of a dirty white colour, and are male and female in the fame umbel: the female flowers are fucceeded by oval capfules with three lobes, which are covered with the fame fpines as the plant; thefe have three cells, each containing a fingle feed. This plant is annual.

The fifth fort was found growing naturally at Carthagena in New Spain, by the late Mr. Robert Millar, who fent the feeds to England, which fucceeded in feveral curious gardens. This hath a thick, fwelling, flefhy root, from which arifes an herbaceous ftalk as big as a man's thumb, which is four or five feet high, and divides into feveral branches; thefe are very clofely armed with long brown fpines; the foot-ftalks of the leaves are fix or feven inches long, which are alfo armed with fpines, but not fo clofely, nor are the fpines fo long as thofe on the ftalk and branches; the leaves are deeply cut into five lobes, which are jagged deeply on their fides, and the nerves are armed with
ftinging

ftinging fpines; the flowers are produced in umbels at the top of the branches, ftanding upon long naked foot-ftalks; they are of a pure white colour, and are male and female in the fame umbel: the male flowers appear firft, which are compofed of five petals, forming a fhort tube at bottom, and the ftamina arife the length of the tube, joined in a column: the petals fpread open flat above, and the ftamina fills the mouth of the tube, fhutting it up: the female flowers are fmaller, but of the fame fhape, having no ftamina, but an oval three-cornered germen, which afterwards becomes a capfule with three lobes, each having a diftinct cell, with one feed inclofed.

The fixth fort was difcovered by the late Dr. Houftoun at La Vera Cruz, where it is frequently permitted to grow about the town by way of ornament; this rifes with a ftrong, brittle, ligneous ftalk, ten or twelve feet high, covered with a gray bark, and divides into many branches, which are garnifhed with leaves, that are divided into parts like thofe of the common Woolfsbane, but are armed with fmall ftinging fpines like thofe of the Nettle; at the end of the branches come out the flower-ftalks, which are five or fix inches long, fuftaining an umbel of white flowers. The male flowers are of one petal, having a pretty long tube, which is divided at the top into five fegments. The female flowers expand in form of a Rofe, having the germen in the center, which afterward becomes a globular prickly fruit with three lobes, opening in three cells, each containing a fingle feed.

The feventh fort is now very common in moft of the iflands in the Weft-Indies, but was introduced from the continent, firft into the French iflands, and from thence it was brought into the Britifh iflands, where it is titled French Phyfic Nut, to diftinguifh it from the following fort, which is called Phyfic Nut, from its purging quality.

This rifes with a foft thick ftem eight or ten feet high, dividing into feveral branches, covered with a grayifh bark. The leaves come out on every fide the branches on ftrong foot-ftalks, which are feven or eight inches long; they are divided into nine or ten lobes in form of a hand, which are joined at their bafe; thefe are feven inches long, and about two inches broad, with many jagged points on their borders ftanding oppofite. The upper fide of the leaves are of a lucid green, but their under fide gray, and a little cottony. The flowers come out upon long foot-ftalks from the end of the branches, formed into an umbel, in which there are male and female flowers, as in the other fpecies; thefe umbels are large, and the flowers being of a bright fcarlet, they make a fine appearance; and the leaves being very remarkable for their beauty, has occafioned the plant being cultivated for ornament in moft of the iflands of the Weft-Indies.

The eighth fort grows naturally in all the iflands of the Weft-Indies; this rifes with a ftrong ftalk twelve or fourteen feet high, which divides into feveral branches; thefe are garnifhed with angular heart-fhaped leaves, which end in acute points. The flowers come out in umbels at the end of the branches; they are male and female, of an herbaceous colour, fo make but little appearance; the female flowers are fucceeded by oblong oval capfules with three cells, each containing one oblong black feed.

The feeds of the two laft forts have been ufed as a purgative by the inhabitants of the Weft-Indies, but they operate fo violently, that now they are feldom ufed; three or four of thefe nuts have worked upward and downward near forty times, on a perfon who was ignorant of their effects; but it is affirmed that this purgative quality is contained in a thin film, fituated in the center of the nut, which, if taken out, the nuts are harmlefs, and may be eaten with fafety. The leaves of the laft fort are ufed in baths and fomentations.

The ninth fort grows naturally in all the iflands of the Weft-Indies, where it is fometimes called wild Caffada, or Caffava, and at others Belly-ach Weed, the leaves of this plant being accounted a good remedy for the dry belly-ach. This plant rifes with a foft herbaceous ftalk to the height of three or four feet, covered with a purple bark, and at the joints have branching briftly hairs rifing in fmall bunches, not only upon the principal ftalk, but alfo on the branches, and the foot-ftalks of the leaves. The ftalk divides upward into two or three branches; thefe are garnifhed with leaves ftanding on very long foot-ftalks, divided into five lobes which are oval, entire, and end in acute points. The flowers are produced at the end of the branches, upon flender naked foot-ftalks, in fmall umbels; they are fmall, of a dark purple colour, having male and female flowers in the fame umbel; the female flowers are fucceeded by oblong tricapfular veffels, fmooth, and covered with a dark fkin, when ripe; in each of the cells is lodged one oblong brown feed.

All thefe plants are natives of the warm parts of America, fo are too tender to thrive in the open air in England. The firft fort is cultivated in the Weft-Indies for food, where it is propagated by cutting the ftalks into lengths of feven or eight inches, which, when planted, put out roots; the method of doing this having been mentioned in various books, I fhall not repeat it here.

The other forts are eafily propagated by feeds, which fhould be fown on a good hot-bed in the fpring, and when the plants are fit to remove, they fhould be each tranfplanted into a fmall pot filled with light earth, and then plunged into a frefh hot-bed of tanners bark, carefully fhading them till they have taken frefh root; after which they muft be treated in the fame manner as other tender plants from hot countries, admitting frefh air to them daily, in proportion to the warmth of the feafon; but as many of the forts have fucculent ftalks, fome of which have a milky juice, they fhould have but little water given them, for they are foon deftroyed by wet.

The fourth fort is an annual plant, fo if the feeds are fown early in the fpring, and the plants are brought forward, they will perfect their feeds the fame year; but the other forts are perennial, fo do not flower till the fecond or third year; therefore the plants fhould be plunged into the tan-bed in the ftove, where they fhould conftantly remain, giving them a large fhare of air in warm weather; but in winter they muft be tenderly treated, and in that feafon muft have very little water. With this management the plants will continue feveral years, and produce their flowers, and frequently perfect their feeds in England.

I B E R I S. Dillen. Nov. Gen. 6. Lin. Gen. Plant. 721. Thlafpidium. Tourn. Inft. R. H. 214. tab. 101. Sci-atica Crefs.

The CHARACTERS are,

The flower hath an empalement of four oval leaves, which fpread open, are hollowed and fall away. It hath four unequal petals, which are oval, obtufe, and fpread open, having oblong erect tails; the two outer petals are longer than the other. It hath fix awl-fhaped erect ftamina, the two on the fides being fhorter than the reft, terminated by roundifh fummits. In the center of the tube is fituated a round compreffed germen, fupporting a fhort fingle ftyle, crowned by an obtufe ftigma. The germen afterward becomes a roundifh compreffed veffel, having two cells, each containing one oval feed.

This genus of plants is ranged in the firft fection of Linnæus's fifteenth clafs, intitled Tetradynamia Siliculofa, which includes thofe plants whofe flowers have four long and two fhort ftamina, and the feeds grow in fhort pods.

The SPECIES are,

1. IBERIS (*Sempeflorens*) frutefcens, foliis cuneiformibus obtufis integerrimis. Lin. Hort. Cliff. 330. *Shrubby Sciatica Crefs with entire, wedge-fhaped, blunt leaves, commonly called the Tree Candy Tuft.* Thlafpidium fruticofum, leucoii folio, femperflorens. Tourn. Inft. 214. *Shrubby Thlafpidium with a Gilliflower leaf, always flowering.*

 2. IBERIS

2. IBERIS (*Sempervirens*) frutefcens foliis linearibus acutis integerrimis. Lin. Hort. Cliff. 330. *Shrubby Sciatica Crefs with narrow-pointed whole leaves, commonly called Perennial Candy Tuft.* Thlafpi montanum, fempervirens. C. B. P. 106. *Evergreen Mountain Candy Tuft.*

3. IBERIS (*Umbellata*) herbacea foliis lanceolatis acuminatis, inferioribus ferratis, fuperioribus integerrimis. Lin. Hort. Cliff. 330. *Herbaceous Sciatica Crefs with fpear-fhaped pointed leaves, the under ones being fawed, but the upper entire, commonly called Candy Tuft.* Thlafpi Creticum quibufdam, flore rubente & albo. J. B. 2. 924. *True Cretan Treacle Muftard with a red and white flower.*

4. IBERIS (*Odorata*) foliis linearibus fupernè dilatatis ferratis. Flor. Leyd. 330. *Sciatica Crefs with narrow leaves dilated at their top, and fawed.* Thlafpi umbellatum Creticum, flore albo odoro, minus. C. B. P. 106. *Small umbellated Treacle Muftard of Crete with a white fweet flower.*

5. IBERIS (*Nudicaulis*) herbacea foliis finuatis, caule nudo fimplici. Lin. Hort. Cliff. 328. *Sciatica Crefs with finuated leaves, and a fingle naked ftalk.* Nafturtium petræum. Tab. Ic. 451. *Rock Crefs.*

6. IBERIS (*Amara*) herbacea foliis lanceolatis acutis fubdentatis, floribus racemofis. Lin. Hort. Upfal. 184. *Sciatica Crefs with acute, fpear-fhaped, indented leaves, and flowers growing in bunches.* Thlafpi avenfe umbellatum amarum. J. B. 2. 925. *Bitter, umbellated, Field Treacle Muftard.*

7. IBERIS (*Rotundifolia*) foliis fubrotundis crenatis. Royen. Lin. Sp. Plant. 49. *Iberis with roundifh crenated leaves.* Thlafpi Alpinum, folio rotundiore carnofo, flore purpurafcente. Tourn. Inft. 112. *Alpine Treacle Muftard with a rounder flefhy leaf, and a purplifh flower.*

8. IBERIS (*Linifolia*) frutefcens, foliis linearibus acutis, corymbis hemifphæricis. *Shrubby Sciatica Crefs with narrow acute leaves, and hemifpherical bunches of flowers.* Thlafpi Lufitanicum umbellatum, gramineo folio, purpurafcente flore. Tourn. Inft. R. H. 213. *Portugal, umbellated, Treacle Muftard, with a Grafs leaf and a purplifh flower.*

The firft fort here mentioned is a low fhrubby plant, which feldom rifes above a foot and a half high, having many flender branches, which fpread on every fide, and fall toward the ground if they are not fupported. Thefe branches are well furnifhed with leaves toward their extremity, which continue green all the year; and in fummer the flowers are produced at the end of the fhoots, which are white, and grow in an umbel. Thefe flowers continue long in beauty, and are fucceeded by others, fo that the plants are rarely deftitute of flowers for near eight months, from the end of Auguft to the beginning of June, which renders the plant valuable.

This plant is fomewhat tender, therefore is generally preferved in green-houfes in winter, where, being placed among other low plants toward the front of the houfe, it makes an agreeable variety, as it continues flowering all the winter. But although it is commonly fo treated, yet in moderate winters this plant will live in the open air, if it be planted in a warm fituation and on a dry foil; and if, in very hard froft, they are covered either with mats, Reeds, Straw, or Peas-haulm, they may be preferved very well; and thefe plants which grow in the full ground, will thrive better, and produce a greater number of flowers, than thofe which are kept in pots; but the foil in which thefe are planted, fhould not be over rich, nor too wet, for in either of thefe they will grow too vigorous in fummer, fo will be in greater danger of fuffering by the froft in winter; but when they grow on a gravelly foil, or among lime rubbifh, their fhoots will be fhort, ftrong, and not fo replete with moifture, fo will better refift the cold.

This plant very rarely produces feeds in England, therefore is only propagated by cuttings, which, if planted during any of the fummer months, and fhaded from the fun, and duly watered, will be rooted in two months, and may afterward be either planted

in pots, or into the borders where they are defigned to ftand.

There is a variety of this with variegated leaves, which is preferved in fome of the gardens where perfons delight in thefe ftriped-leaved plants. This is not fo hardy as the plain fort, therefore muft be treated more tenderly in winter; this is alfo increafed by cuttings in the fame manner as the other.

The fecond fort is a plant of humbler growth than the firft; this feldom rifes more than fix or eight inches high, nor do the branches grow woody, but are rather herbaceous; the leaves of this plant continue green through the year, and the flowers are of as long duration as thofe of the firft fort, which renders it valuable. This rarely produces feeds in England, but is propagated by flips, which in fummer eafily take root, and the plants may be treated in the fame manner as hath been directed for the firft fort, and will thrive in the open air.

The third fort is a low annual plant, the feeds of which were formerly fown to make edgings for borders in the pleafure-garden, for which purpofe all the low annual flowers are very improper, becaufe they do not anfwer the intent, which is to prevent the earth of the borders falling into the walks, which thefe plants never can do; and though they make a pretty appearance during their continuance in flower, which is feldom more than a fortnight or three weeks, yet after their flowers are paft they become very unfightly; therefore all thefe forts of flowers fhould be fown in fmall patches in the borders of the flower-garden, where, if they are properly mixed with other flowers, they will have a very good effect; and by fowing of them at three or four different feafons, there may be a fucceffion of them continued in flower till autumn.

There are two different varieties of this third fort, one with red, and the other hath white flowers; but the white is not common in the gardens, but the feeds of the fixth fort are generally fold for it, and is feldom diftinguifhed but by thofe who are fkilled in botany; this plant feldom rifes more than five or fix inches high, and if they have room will branch out on every fide, but when they are left too clofe, they draw each other up, and are weak: as thefe do not bear tranfplanting well, fo the feeds fhould be fown thin in patches, and when the plants are grown pretty ftrong, they fhould be thinned, leaving but fix or eight in in each patch to flower; and by thus treating them, they will put out fide branches, and flower much ftronger, and continue longer in beauty than when they are left clofer together; thefe plants will require no other culture but to keep them clean from weeds.

The fourth fort feldom grows fo large as the third, and the flowers are much fmaller, but have an agreeable odour. It grows naturally in Helvetia, and is preferved in botanic gardens for variety. It is annual, and requires the fame treatment as the third.

The fifth fort grows on fandy and rocky places in feveral parts of England, fo is rarely admitted into gardens. The leaves of this are fmall, and cut to the midrib into many jags; thefe are fpread on the ground. and between them arife a naked foot-ftalk two or three inches long, fuftaining fmall umbels of white flowers. This is an annual plant, whofe feeds fhould be fown in autumn where the plants are defigned to remain, and require no other care but to keep them clean from weeds.

The fixth fort is very like the third, but differs in the fhape of the leaves. The flowers of this are white, fo may be fown to make a variety with the red. It requires the fame treatment.

The feventh fort grows naturally on the Alps, from whence it was fent me; this is a perennial plant, which roots pretty deep in the ground. The lower leaves which rife from the root, are round, flefhy, and crenated on their edges. The ftalk rifes four or five inches high, and is garnifhed with fmall oblong leaves which half embrace the ftalks with their bafe. The flowers terminate the ftalk in a round compact

pact umbel ; they are of a purple colour, and appear in June, but are seldom succeeded by seeds in England.

It is propagated by seeds, which should be sown on a shady border in autumn, and when the plants are strong enough to remove, they should be transplanted on a shady border where they are designed to remain, and will require no other care but to keep them clean from weeds.

The eighth sort grows naturally in Spain and Portugal ; this hath a great resemblance of the second, but the stalks do not spread so much ; they grow erect, about seven or eight inches high, are ligneous and perennial. The leaves are very narrow, and seldom more than an inch long, standing thinly upon the stalks, having no foot-stalks. The flowers grow in hemispherical umbels on the top of the stalks, and are of a purple colour. It flowers in May and June, but seldom produces good seeds here.

This sort may be propagated by cuttings, which should be treated in the same way as is before directed for the first sort ; and some of the plants may be planted on a warm border in a dry soil, where they will endure the cold of our ordinary winters very well ; but it will be proper to have two or three plants in pots, which may be sheltered under a frame in winter, to preserve the kind, if, by severe frost, those in the open air should be destroyed.

IBISCUS. See HIBISCUS.

ICACO. See CHRYSOBALANUS.

ICE is a hard transparent body, formed from some liquor congealed, or fixed.

Ice is said to be the natural state of water, which remains firm, and not liquid, when no external cause acts upon it.

The true cause of the congelation of water into Ice, seems to be the introduction of frigorific particles into the pores or interstices between the particles of water, and by that means getting so near them, as to be just within the spheres of one another's attractions, and then they must cohere into one solid or firm body.

It may be wondered why Ice goes to the top of the water, for one would imagine, that being colder than flowing water, it ought to be more condensed, and consequently heavier ; but is to be considered, that there are always some bubbles of air interspersed in Ice. It is certain, by the swimming of Ice upon water, that it is specifically lighter than the water out of which it is made by freezing ; and it is as certain, that this lightness of Ice proceeds from those numerous bubbles that are produced in it by congelation.

Water, when it is frozen into Ice, takes up more space than it did before it was congealed. It is visible, that the dimensions of water are increased by freezing, its particles being kept at some distance the one from the other, by the intervention of the frigorific matter.

And, besides, there are many little volumes of air included at several distances, both in the pores of the watery particles, and in the interstices made by the spherical figures. Now, by the insinuation of these chrystals, the volumes of air are driven out of the watery particles, and many of them uniting, form larger volumes ; these have thereby a greater force to expand themselves than when they are dispersed, and so both enlarge their dimensions, and lessen the specific gravity of water thus congealed into Ice.

It seems very probable, that cold, and freezing, and consequently Ice, are produced by some substance of a saline nature floating in the air ; in that salts, and more eminently some particular ones, when mixed with Ice or snow, do wonderfully increase the force and effects of cold.

It is also visible, that all saline bodies cause a stiffness and frigidity in those bodies into which they enter.

It is manifest, by observing salts by microscopes, that the figures of some salts, before they shoot into

masses, are then double wedge-like particles, which have abundance of surface in respect to their solidity ; and this is the reason why they swim in water, when once they are raised in it, although they are specifically heavier, these small points of salts getting into the pores of the water, whereby they are, in some measure, suspended in the winter, when the heat of the sun is not ordinarily strong enough to dissolve the salts into fluid, to break their points, and to keep them in perpetual motion ; which being less disturbed, are more at liberty to approach one another, and by shooting into chrystals, of the form above-mentioned, do, by their extremities, insinuate themselves into the pores of water, and by that means freeze it into a solid form, called Ice.

Monf. Mariotte, in his Treatise of Hydrostatics, gives the subsequent account of what happens to water in freezing, which he discovered by the following experiment.

Having filled a cylindric vessel, of about seven or eight inches high, and six inches diameter, within two inches of the top, with cold water, he exposed it to the open air in a great frost, and observed exactly the whole progress of the freezing of it.

The first congelation was in the upper surface of the water, in little long water shoots, or laminæ, which were jagged like a saw, the water between them remaining still unfrozen, though the rest of the surface was already frozen to the thickness of more than two lines ; he observed that several bubbles of air were formed in the Ice, that began to fix on the bottom and sides of the vessel, some would rise up, and others remained entangled in the Ice, which made him imagine that these bubbles taking up more space in the water, than when their matter was, as it were, dissolved in it, they pushed up a little water through the hole at the top, after the same manner that new wine works out at the bung-hole of a vessel when it begins to heat, and the little water that oozed out at this little hole in the Ice, spreading itself upon the upper surface of the water, which was already frozen, became Ice also, and there began to form a hill of Ice ; and that hole continuing open, by reason of the water which passed successively through it, being pushed up by the new bubbles which formed themselves in the Ice, which continue to increase about the sides and bottom of the vessel, he observed that the upper surface of the water was frozen above an inch thick towards the edges of the vessel, and above an inch and a half round about the little hole, before the water that was contained in it, as in a pipe, became frozen, but at last it was frozen ; then the middle of the water remaining unfrozen, and the water which was compressed by the new bubbles, which formed themselves for two or three hours, having no vent at the little hole, the Ice broke at once towards the top, by the spring of the included air.

In like manner the frost acts upon vegetables, by these frigorific particles entering the tender shoots of plants, and insinuating between the pores of the sap, thereby increasing its bulk, so that the tender vessels of the plants are torn, and those parts of the plants are soon killed ; and the greater the quantity of moisture is in vegetables, the more they are in danger of being destroyed, for we frequently see many plants which grow on the top, and from the joints of walls, escape the severest frosts, when those of the same kinds are all destroyed which were in the ground ; which is entirely owing to their vessels being stronger and more compact, and not so replete with moisture : so when the autumn proves cold and moist, whereby the vessels of plants are not properly hardened, and are replete with moisture, a small frost will do great mischief to them ; whereas when the autumn is dry and warm, the tender shoots of trees and shrubs are hardened, and drained of their moisture, so are not liable to the like accidents.

ICE-HOUSE is a building contrived to preserve ice for the use of a family in the summer season.

These

These are more generally used in warm countries, than in England, but particularly in Italy, where the meaneſt perſon who rents a houſe, is not without a a vault or cellar for keeping of ice; but as the uſe of ice in England is much greater of late than it was formerly, ſo the number of Ice-houſes has been greatly increaſed; and although the mention of theſe may, at firſt ſight, ſeem foreign to my ſubject, yet if it is conſidered, that theſe buildings are generally erected in gardens, and as often put under the care of gardeners, it may not be amiſs for me to give ſome general directions for the choice of the ſituation and ſtructure of the building, as alſo for the management of the ice.

In the choice of a ſituation for an Ice-houſe, the principal regard ſhould be, that of a dry ſpot of ground, for wherever there is moiſture, the ice will melt; therefore in all ſtrong lands, which detain the wet, there cannot be too much care taken to make drains all round the building to carry off all moiſture; for when this is lodged near the building, it will occaſion a damp there, which will always be prejudicial to the keeping of the ice.

The next conſideration muſt be, to have the place ſo elevated, that there may be deſcent enough to carry off whatever wet may happen near the building, or from the ice melting; alſo, that the place be as much expoſed to the ſun and air as poſſible, and not placed under the drip, or in the ſhade of trees, as hath been too often practiſed, under a falſe notion, that if it ſhould be expoſed to the ſun, the ice will melt away in ſummer, which never can be the caſe where there is ſufficient care taken to exclude the outward air (which muſt always be regarded in the building of theſe houſes) for the heat of the ſun can never penetrate through the double arches of the building, ſo as to add any warmth to the air; but when the building is entirely open to the ſun and wind, all damps and vapours will thereby be removed from about the building, which can never be kept too dry, or free from moiſt vapours. As to the figure of the building, that may be according to the fancy of the owner; but for the well into which the ice is to be put, a circular figure is the moſt convenient; the depth of the well, as alſo the diameter of it, muſt be proportioned to the quantity of ice wanted, but it is always beſt to have enough; for where the ice is well built, it will keep the ice for two or three years; and there will be this advantage in having it large enough to contain ice for two years conſumption, that if a mild winter ſhould happen, when there is not ice to be had, there will be a ſtock to ſupply the want.

If the quantity wanting is not great, a well of ſix feet diameter, and eight feet deep, will be large enough; but for large conſumption, it ſhould not be leſs than nine or ten feet diameter, and as many deep: where the ſituation is either dry chalk, gravel, or ſand, the pit may be entirely below the ſurface of the ground; but in ſtrong loam, clay, or moiſt ground, it will be the beſt way to raiſe it ſo high above the ſurface, as that there may be no danger from the wet.

At the bottom of the well there ſhould be a ſpace left, about two feet deep, to receive any moiſture which may drain from the ice, and a ſmall underground drain ſhould be laid from this, to carry off the wet; over this ſpace of two feet, ſhould be placed a ſtrong grate of wood, to let the moiſture fall down, which may at any time happen, from melting of the ice. The ſides of this well muſt be bricked up with a wall, at leaſt two bricks and a half thick; but if it is yet thicker, it will be better, becauſe the thicker the walls are made, the leſs danger there will be of the well being affected by any external cauſe. When the well is brought within three feet of the ſurface, there muſt be another outer arch or wall begun, which muſt be carried up to the height of the top of the intended arch of the well; and if there is a ſecond arch turned over from this well, it will add to the goodneſs of the houſe; but this muſt be ſubmitted to the

perſon who builds, if he will be at the expence; but if not, then the plate into which the roof is to be framed, muſt be laid on this outer wall, which ſhould be carried high enough above the inner arch, to admit of a door-way in, to get out the ice. If the building is to be covered with ſlates or tiles, there ſhould be a thickneſs of Reeds laid under, to keep out the ſun and external air; if theſe Reeds are laid two feet thick, and plaſtered over with lime and hair, there will be no danger of the heat getting through it.

The external wall need not be built circular, but of any other figure, either ſquare, hexangular, or octangular; and where this ſtands much in ſight may be ſo contrived as to make it a good object. I have ſeen an Ice-houſe built in ſuch a manner as to have a handſome alcove ſeat in the front, and behind this ſeat was contrived a paſſage to get out and put in the ice; and by having the entrance behind, to the north aſpect, a ſmall paſſage being next the ſeat, through which a perſon might enter to take out the ice, and a large door being contrived with a porch, wide enough for a ſmall cart to back in, to ſhoot down the ice upon the floor near the mouth of the well, where it may be well broken, before it is put down. The aperture of this mouth of the well need not be more than two feet and a half diameter, which will be large enough to put down the ice, and if it was greater, it would be inconvenient; there ſhould be a ſtone fitted to ſtop this aperture, which muſt be cloſed up as ſecure as poſſible, after the ice is put in, and all the vacant ſpace above and between this and the outer door, muſt be filled cloſe with Barley Straw, to exclude the air; ſo the door to enter for taking out the ice ſhould be on the oppoſite ſide, immediately behind the alcove ſeat, as was before-mentioned; and this door ſhould be no larger than is abſolutely neceſſary for the coming at the ice, and muſt be ſtrong and cloſe to exclude the air; and at five or ſix feet diſtance from this another door ſhould be contrived, which ſhould be cloſely ſhut before the inner door is opened, whenever the ice is taken out.

The building being finiſhed, ſhould have time to dry before the ice is put into it; for when the walls are green, the damp of them frequently melts the ice. At the bottom of the well, upon the wooden grate, ſhould be laid ſome ſmall faggots; and if upon theſe a layer of Reeds is placed ſmooth for the ice to lie upon, it will be better than Straw, which is commonly uſed; and in the choice of the ice, the thinner it is, the better it may be broken to powder; for the ſmaller it is broken, the better it will unite when put into the well: in putting of it in, there muſt be care taken to ram it cloſe, as alſo to allow a vacancy all round next the wall, of about two inches; this is to give paſſage to any moiſture, which may be occaſioned by the melting of ſome of the ice on the top, which, if pent up, will melt the ice downward; when the ice is put into the well, if there is a little ſalt-petre mixed at every ten inches or a foot thickneſs, it will cauſe the ice to join more cloſely into a ſolid maſs. The inſtructions here given, being carefully obſerved, will be ſufficient to guide perſons wholly ignorant in theſe matters.

JET D'EAU is a French word, which ſignifies a fountain that caſts up water to any conſiderable height in the air.

Monſ. Mariotte, in his Treatiſe of Hydroſtatics, ſays, That a Jet d'Eau will never riſe ſo high as its reſervatory, but always falls ſhort of it by a ſpace which is in a ſubduplicate ratio of that height; and this he proves by ſeveral experiments; that though Jets ought to riſe to the height of the reſervatories, yet the friction of the ſides of the ajutages, and the reſiſtance of the air, are the cauſes that in Jets that have very high reſervatories, the height of the Jets does not come up to that of the reſervatory by a great deal.

He adds, That if a greater branches out in many ſmaller ones, or is diſtributed through ſeveral Jets, the ſquare of the diameter of the main pipe muſt be proportioned

portioned to the fum of all the expences'of its branches; that if the refervatory be fifty-two high, and the ajutages half an inch in diameter, the pipe ought to be three inches in diameter.

He fays, That the beauty of Jets of water confifts in their uniformity and tranfparency at the going out of the ajutage, and fpreading but very little, and that to the higheft part of the Jet.

That the worft fort of ajutages are thofe that are cylindrical, for they retard very much the height of the Jets, the conic retard it lefs; but the beft way is, to bore the horizontal plane, which fhuts the extremity of the pipe, or conduit, with a fmooth and polifhed hole, taking care that the plate be perfectly plain, polifhed, and uniform.

Thefe fpouts of water are fome of the greateft beauties of the Italian gardens, and are certainly better adapted for gardens in thofe warm countries, than they are for our climate, becaufe, in the great heats of fummer, the fight of thefe water-fpouts is cooling and refrefhing to the imagination, and they certainly add a real coolnefs to the air; but in cold countries they cool the air too much, therefore fhould not be erected; or if they are, they fhould be placed at fuch diftances from the habitation, as that the damp may no ways affect it.

Where thefe Jets are contrived, if there is not a conftant fupply for a large column of water, they fhould by no means be made, for nothing can have a meaner appearance, than thofe pitiful piffing fpouts, fo frequently to be feen in England, which perhaps have not a fupply of water to play above an hour or two; therefore where there is not a natural body of water, to fupply thefe Jets, without the expence of raifing it, there fhould never be any of thefe contrived in gardens.

ILEX. Lin. Gen. Plant. 158. Aquifolium. Tourn. Inft. R. H. 600. tab. 371. The Holly-tree; in French, *Houx*.

The CHARACTERS are,

They have male, female, and hermaphrodite flowers on different plants. The male flowers have a fmall permanent empalement of one leaf, which is indented in four parts; they have but one petal, which is cut into four fegments almoft to the bottom; they have four awl-fhaped ftamina, which are fhorter than the petal, and are terminated by fmall fummits. The female flowers have their empalements and petals the fame as the male, but have no ftamina; in their center is placed the roundifh germen, having four obtufe ftigmas fitting on it. The germen afterward becomes a roundifh berry with four cells, each containing a fingle hard feed.

This genus of plants is ranged in the third fection of Linnæus's fourth clafs, intitled Tetrandria Tetragynia, which includes thofe plants whofe flowers have four ftamina and four ftyles; but according to his own fyftem, it fhould be placed in the third fection of his twenty-fecond clafs, with thofe plants which have male and hermaphrodite flowers on different plants.

The SPECIES are,

1. ILEX *(Aquifolium)* foliis oblongo-ovatis, undulatis, fpinis acutis. *Holly-tree with oblong leaves which are waved, and have acute fpines.* Ilex aculeata baccifera. C. B. P. 425. *Prickly berry-bearing Ilex*; and the Aquifolium five agrifolium vulgò. J. B. 1. 114. *The common Holly.*

2. ILEX *(Echinata)* foliis ovatis, undulatis, marginibus aculeatis, paginis fupernè fpinofis. *Holly with oval waved leaves, whofe borders are armed with ftrong thorns, and their upper furface prickly.* Aquifolium echinata folii fuperfice. Cornut. Canad. 180. *Holly-tree whofe upper furface of the leaves are prickly, commonly called Hedge-hog Holly.*

3. ILEX *(Caroliniana)* foliis ovato-lanceolatis ferratis. Hort. Cliff. 40. *Holly with oval, fpear-fhaped, fawed leaves.* Aquifolium Carolinienfe, foliis dentatis, baccis rubris. Catefb. Carol. 1. p. 31. *Carolina Holly with indented leaves and red berries, commonly called Dahoon Holly.*

There are feveral varieties of the common Holly with variegated leaves, which are propagated by the nurfery gardeners for fale, and fome years paft were in very great efteem, but at prefent are but little regarded, the old tafte of filling gardens with fhorn Evergreens being pretty well abolifhed; however, in the difpofition of the clumps or other plantations of Evergreen trees and fhrubs, a few of the moft lively colours may be admitted, which will have a good effect in the winter feafon, if they are properly difpofed. As the different variegations of the leaves of Hollies, are by the nurfery gardeners diftinguifhed by different titles, fo I fhall here mention the moft beautiful of them, by the names they are generally known:

Painted Lady Holly, Britifh Holly, Bradley's beft Holly, Phyllis, or Cream Holly, Milkmaid Holly, Pritchet's beft Holly, Gold-edged Hedge-hog Holly, Cheyney's Holly, Glory of the Weft Holly, Broaderick's Holly, Partridge's Holly, Herefordfhire white Holly, Blind's Cream Holly, Longftaff's Holly, Eales's Holly, Silver-edged Hedge-hog Holly.

All thefe varieties are propagated by budding or grafting them upon ftocks of the common green Holly: there is alfo a variety of the common Holly with fmooth leaves, but this is frequently found intermixed with the prickly-leaved on the fame tree, and often on the fame branch, there are both forts of leaves.

The common Holly grows naturally in woods and forefts in many parts of England, where it rifes from twenty to thirty feet high, and fometimes more, but their ordinary height is not above twenty-five feet. The ftem by age becomes large, and is covered with a grayifh fmooth bark; and thofe trees which are not lopped or browzed by cattle, are commonly furnifhed with branches the greateft part of their length, fo form a fort of cone; the branches are garnifhed with oblong oval leaves about three inches long, and one and a half broad, of a lucid green on their upper furface, but are pale on their under, having a ftrong midrib: the edges are indented and waved, with fharp thorns terminating each of the points, fo that fome of the thorns are raifed upward and others are bent downward, and being very ftiff, renders them troublefome to handle. The leaves are placed alternate on every fide of the branches, and from the bafe of their footftalks come out the flowers in clufters, ftanding on very fhort foot-ftalks; each of thefe fuftain five, fix, or more flowers. In fome plants I have obferved the flowers were wholly male, and produced no berries; in others I have obferved female and hermaphrodite flowers, but upon fome large old trees growing on Windfor foreft, I have obferved all three upon the fame trees. The flowers are of a dirty white, and appear in May; they are fucceeded by roundifh berries, which turn to a beautiful red about Michaelmas, but continue on the trees if they are not deftroyed, till after Chriftmas before they fall away.

The fecond fort grows naturally in Canada, from whence it was brought to Europe. The leaves of this fort are not fo long as thofe of the common Holly, and their edges are armed with ftronger thorns ftanding clofer together; the upper furface of the leaves is fet very clofe with fhort prickles, from whence the gardeners have given it the title of Hedge-hog Holly. This fort is ufually propagated in the nurferies, by budding or grafting it upon the common Holly; but I have raifed it from the berries, and found the plants to be the fame as thofe from whence the feeds were taken, fo make no doubt of its being a diftinct fpecies.

There are two varieties of this with variegated leaves, one of which is yellow, and the other white. There is alfo a variety of the common Holly with yellow berries, which is alfo accidental, and is generally found on thofe plants which have variegated leaves, and but feldom on plain Hollies.

The common Holly is a very beautiful tree in winter, therefore deferves a place in all plantations of

Evergreen

Evergreen trees and shrubs, where its shining leaves and red berries make a fine variety; and if a few of the best variegated kinds are properly intermixed, they will enliven the scene. The Holly was also formerly planted for hedges, and is a very proper plant for that purpose; but then it should not be clipped with shears, because when the leaves are cut through the middle, they are rendered unsightly, so they should be cut with a knife close to the leaf; and although in this method they are not shorn so even as with shears, yet they will have a much better appearance, and may be made as close and secure as by any other method generally practised.

The Holly is propagated by seeds, which never come up the first year, but lie in the ground as the Haws do; therefore the berries should be buried in the ground in a large pot or tub one year, and then taken up and sown in the autumn upon a bed exposed only to the morning sun; the following spring the plants will appear, which must be kept clean from weeds; and if the spring should prove dry, it will be of great service to the plants if they are watered once a week; but they must not have it oftener, nor in too great quantity, for too much moisture is very injurious to these plants when young.

In this seed-bed the plants may remain two years, and then should be transplanted in the autumn, into beds at about six inches distance each way, where they may stand two years longer, during which time they must be constantly kept clean from weeds; and if the plants have thriven well, they will be strong enough to transplant where they are designed to remain; for when they are transplanted at that age, there will be less danger of their failing, and they will grow to a larger size than those which are removed when they are much larger; but if the ground is not ready to receive them at that time, they should be transplanted into a nursery in rows at two feet distance, and one foot asunder in the rows, in which place the plants may remain two years longer; and if they are designed to be grafted or budded with any of the variegated kinds, that should be performed after the plants have grown one year in this nursery; but the plants so budded or grafted should continue two years after in the nursery, that they may make good shoots before they are removed; though the plain ones should not stand longer than two years in the nursery, because when they are older, they do not transplant so well. The best time for removing of Hollies is in the autumn, especially in dry land; but where the soil is cold or moist, they may be transplanted with great safety in the spring; if the plants are not too old, or if they have not stood long unremoved, there is great odds of their dying when removed.

The Dahoon Holly grows naturally in Carolina, from whence the seeds were sent by the late Mr. Mark Catesby, who found the trees growing on a swamp at a distance from Charles-town, but it hath since been discovered in other countries in North America. This rises with an upright branching stem to the height of eighteen or twenty feet; the bark of the old stems is of a brown colour, but that of the branches or younger stalks is green and smooth, garnished with spear-shaped leaves, which are more than four inches long, and one and a quarter broad in the broadest part, of a light green and thick consistence; the upper part of the leaves are sawed on their edges, each serrature ending in a small sharp spine; they stand alternately on every side the branches, upon very short foot-stalks. The flowers come out in thick clusters from the side of the stalks; they are white, and shaped like those of the common Holly, but are smaller; the female and hermaphrodite flowers are succeeded by small roundish berries in its native country, which make a fine appearance in winter, but they have not as yet produced fruit in England, so far as I can learn.

Dr. Linnæus supposes this plant and the evergreen Cassine to be the same, but they are undoubtedly dis-

tinct plants: he may probably have been led into this mistake, by receiving seeds of this sort mixed together with the berries of Cassine from America, which I have more than once done; but whoever sees the two plants growing, cannot doubt of their being different.

This sort is tender while young, so requires protection in the winter till the plants are grown strong and woody, when they may be planted in the full ground in a warm situation, where they will endure the cold of our ordinary winters pretty well; but in severe frost they should be protected, otherwise the cold will destroy them.

This sort is propagated from seeds, in like manner as the common sort; the seeds of it will lie as long in the ground, so the berries should be buried in the ground a year, and then taken up and sown in pots filled with light earth, and placed under a frame in winter; in the spring the pots should be plunged into a hot-bed, which will bring up the plants; these must be preserved in the pots while young, and sheltered in winter under a common frame till they have obtained strength, when in the spring they may be turned out of the pots and planted in the full ground, in a warm situation.

From the bark of the common Holly is made the bird-lime, and the wood is made into hones for setting of razors. The wood is very white, and takes a fine polish, so is very proper for several kinds of furniture. I have seen a floor of a room laid in compartments with Holly and Mahogany, which had a very pretty effect.

ILLECEBRUM. Lin. Gen. 291. Corrigiola. Dill. Gen. p. 169. Paronychia. Tourn. Inst. 281.

The Characters are,

It hath a five-cornered coloured empalement of five leaves, which is permanent, but has no petals; it hath five slender stamina within the empalement, terminated by simple summits, and an oval germen with a short style, crowned by an obtuse stigma. The empalement afterward becomes a roundish capsule with five angles, having one cell, containing one large seed, which is pointed on every side.

This genus of plants is ranged in the first section of Linnæus's fifth class, intitled Pentandria Monogynia, the flowers having five stamina and one style.

The Species are,

1. Illecebrum (*Suffruticosum*) floribus lateralibus solitariis, caulibus suffruticosus. Lin. Sp. 298. *Illecebrum with an under-shrub stalk, having single flowers on the sides.* Paronychia Hispanica fruticosa, myrti folio. Tourn. Inst. 508.

2. Illecebrum (*Paronychia*) floribus bracteis nitidis obvalatis, caulibus procumbentibus. Lin. Sp. 299. *Illecebrum with neat bractea inclosing the flowers, and trailing stalks.* Paronychia Hispanica. Clus. Hist. 2. p. 183.

3. Illecebrum (*Capitatum*) floribus bracteis nitidis occultantibus capitula terminalia, caulibus erectis, foliis ciliatis. Lin. Sp. 299. *Illecebrum with neat bractea terminating the erect stalks, and silvery leaves.* Paronychia Narbonensis erecta. Tourn. Inst. 508.

4. Illecebrum (*Achyrantha*) caulibus repentibus pilosis, foliis ovatis mucronatis oppofito minore, capitulis subglobosis subspinosis. Lin. Sp. 299. *Illecebrum with creeping stalks, small oval-pointed leaves placed opposite, almost globular heads of flowers, having small spines.* Achyrantha repens, foliis bliti pallidi. Hort. Elth. 8. tab. 9.

5. Illecebrum (*Polygonoides*) caulibus repentibus hirtis, foliis lato-lanceolatis petiolatis, capitulis orbiculatis nudis. Lin. Sp. 300. *Illecebrum with heiry creeping stalks, broad spear-shaped leaves on foot-stalks, and orbicular naked heads of flowers.* Amaranthoides humile Curassavicum, foliis polygoni. Herm. Parad. 17.

6. Illecebrum (*Vermiculatum*) caulibus repentibus glabris foliis, subteretibus carnosis, capitulis oblongis glabris terminalibus. Lin. Sp. 300. *Illecebrum with smooth creeping stalks, almost taper fleshy leaves, and oblong smooth heads terminating the branches.* Amaranthoides humile Curassavicum, cepæ foliis lucidis, capitulis. Herm. Parad. 15.

The

The three firſt ſorts grow naturally in Spain, Portugal, and the ſouth of France; the firſt has ligneous ſtalks about a foot high, garniſhed with ſmall leaves like thoſe of Knot-graſs; the flowers come out ſingly on the ſide of the ſtalks, which make little appearance, ſo is ſeldom preſerved in gardens.

The ſecond and third ſorts have trailing ſtalks near two feet long, which ſpread on the ground, garniſhed with leaves like thoſe of the firſt ſort; the heads of flowers come out from the joints of the ſtalk, having neat ſilvery bractea ſurrounding them, which make a pretty appearance. Their flowers appear in june, and there is generally a ſucceſſion of them for at leaſt two months; and when the autumn proves warm, they will ripen their ſeeds the beginning of October.

Theſe three ſorts may be propagated by ſeeds, which ſhould be ſown on a bed of light earth the beginning of April; the plants will come up in May, when they ſhould be kept clean from weeds till the plants are fit to remove; then the plants ſhould be carefully taken up, planting ſome of each ſort in ſmall pots, and the other into a warm dry border, obſerving to water and ſhade them until they have taken new root; after which, thoſe which are planted in the full ground will require no other culture but to keep them clean from weeds; for in the ordinary winters of England, they will live in the open air: but as theſe plants are ſometimes killed in ſevere winters, therefore I adviſe ſome plants to be planted in pots, which may be placed in a common frame in winter, where they may enjoy the open air in mild weather, but be ſcreened from froſt.

As the ſeeds of theſe plants do not conſtantly ripen in England, ſo they may be propagated by cuttings, which, if carefully taken off in May or June, and planted in a ſhady border, will in two months put out roots; then in moiſt weather they may be tranſplanted, and afterward treated as the old plants.

The other three ſorts are natives of the warm parts of America; the fourth ſort grows naturally at Beunos Ayres; the fifth and ſixth, in many of the iſlands in the Weſt-Indies.

Theſe have creeping ſtalks, which ſend out roots from the joints, which faſten to the ground in their native ſoil, whereby they ſpread to a great diſtance; and in this country, when the pots are plunged into a tan-bed, they will multiply as faſt, by taking root in tan, or any of the other pots of plants which are near them.

The flowers of the fourth ſort make little appearance, therefore the plant is rarely propagated, except in botanic gardens for variety; but thoſe of the fifth and ſixth ſort have dry heads of flowers, reſembling thoſe of the Amaranthoides, under which genus they were formerly ranged.

Theſe three ſorts are tender, ſo will not thrive in the open air in England; therefore their ſeeds ſhould be ſown on a hot-bed in the ſpring, at the ſame time as the Amaranthus, Gomphrena, and other tender plants; and afterward, if they are plunged into the tan-bed in the ſtove, their branches will put out roots, whereby they may be propagated in plenty.

IMPATIENS. Rivin. Ord. 4. Lin. Gen. Plant. 899. Balſamina. Tourn. Inſt. R. H. 418. tab. 235. Female Balſamine; in French, Balſamine.

The CHARACTERS are,

The flower has a two-leaved ſmall empalement, which is coloured, and placed on the ſide of the petals. It hath five petals which are unequal, and ſhaped like a lip-flower; the petals are roundiſh, the upper is erect, ſlightly cut at the point into three parts, where it is ſharp-pointed, forming the upper lip; the two lower petals are broad, obtuſe, irregular, and reflexed; theſe conſtitute the lower lip; the intermediate pair are alike, and are placed oppoſite, joining at their baſe. It hath a nectarium in the bottom of the flower, ſhaped like a hood or cowl, which is oblique to the mouth, riſing on the outſide, whoſe baſe ends in a tail or ſpur. It hath five ſhort ſtamina which are narrow toward their baſe, and incurved, terminated by

ſummits, which join at the top round the ſtamina, but are divided at their baſe. In the bottom is ſituated an oval ſharp-pointed germen, having no ſtyle, but a ſingle ſtigma ſhorter than the ſummits. The germen afterward becomes a capſule with one cell, opening with an elaſticity in five valves, which twiſt ſpirally, and contain ſeveral roundiſh ſeeds fixed to a column.

This genus of plants is ranged in the fifth ſection of Linnæus's nineteenth claſs, which includes thoſe plants which have ſingle flowers in the empalement, whoſe ſtamina vary in number and ſituation.

The SPECIES are,

1. IMPATIENS (*Noli tangere*) pedunculis multifloris ſolitariis, foliis ovatis, geniculis caulinus tumentibus. Flor. Suec. 722. *Impatiens with foot-ſtalks ſuſtaining many ſingle flowers, oval leaves, and ſtalks having ſwelling joints.* Balſamina lutea, five, Noli me tangere. C. B. P. 306. *Yellow Balſamine, or Touch me not.*

2. IMPATIENS (*Balſamina*) pedunculis unifloris aggregatis, foliis lanceolatis, nectaris floribus brevioribus. Hort. Upſal. 276. *Impatiens with foot-ſtalks ſuſtaining ſingle flowers, which ariſe in cluſters, ſpear-ſhaped leaves, and nectariums which are ſhorter than the flower.* Balſamina fœmina. C. B. P. 306. *The female Balſamine.*

3. IMPATIENS (*Triflora*) pedunculis trifloris ſolitariis, foliis anguſto-lanceolatis. Flor. Zeyl. 315. *Impatiens with three flowers on a foot-ſtalk, and narrow ſpear-ſhaped leaves.* Balſamina erecta, ſc. fœmina, Perſicæ anguſto folio Zeylanica. Herm. Par. Bat. 105. *Upright, or female Balſamine of Ceylon, with a narrow Peach leaf.*

There are ſeveral other ſpecies of this genus, which grow naturally in India, which are plants of little beauty, ſo have not been introduced into the Engliſh gardens; the ſorts here mentioned, are all I have yet ſeen growing here, except one tall ſort from North America.

The firſt ſort grows naturally in ſeveral parts of Weſtmoreland and Yorkſhire, but is frequently introduced into gardens by way of curioſity. It is an annual plant, which riſes about a foot and a half high, with an upright ſucculent ſtalk, whoſe joints are ſwollen, garniſhed with oval ſmooth leaves, which ſtand alternate on every ſide the ſtalk. The flowers come out from the wings of the ſtalks upon long ſlender foot-ſtalks, which branch into ſeveral other ſmaller, each ſuſtaining one yellow flower, compoſed of five petals, which in front are ſhaped like the lip or grinning flowers, but at their baſe have a nectarium with a long tail like the flowers of Indian Creſs; theſe are ſucceeded by taper pods, which, when ripe, burſt open upon being touched, and twiſt ſpirally like a ſcrew, caſting out the ſeeds with great elaſticity. If the ſeeds of this plant are permitted to ſcatter, they generally ſucceed better than when they are ſown; for unleſs they are ſown in the autumn ſoon after they are ripe, they very rarely grow. The plants require no care but to keep them clean from weeds, and thin them where they are too cloſe. It flowers in June, and the ſeeds ripen about a month or five weeks after; this delights in a ſhady ſituation and a moiſt ſoil.

The ſecond ſort is the female Balſamine, of which there are ſeveral varieties; the common ſort has been long an inhabitant in the Engliſh gardens, of this there is the white, the red, and ſtriped flowered, and likewiſe the ſingle and double flowering, with variegated flowers of two colours. Theſe ſorts are ſo hardy as to riſe in the full ground; and where the ſeeds ſcatter, the plants will come up the following ſpring; but ſuch ſelf-ſown plants do not come to flower ſo early as thoſe which are raiſed upon a hot-bed; however, they generally are ſtronger plants, and continue much longer in the autumn in flower than the others, ſo are an ornament to the garden, when there is a greater ſcarcity of flowers.

This ſort riſes a foot and a half high, dividing into many ſucculent branches, which are garniſhed with long, ſpear-ſhaped, ſawed leaves. The flowers come out from the joints of the ſtalks, upon ſlender foot-
ſtalks

ſtalks about an inch long, each ſuſtaining a ſingle flower; but there are two, three, or four of theſe foot-ſtalks ariſing from the ſame joint. The flowers are compoſed of five large unequal petals, which are ſhaped like thoſe of the former ſort, but are larger, and ſpread open much wider; there are white, purple, and red of this ſort, as alſo ſingle and double flowers. If the ſeeds of theſe are ſown on a moderate hot-bed in the ſpring, the plants will flower in June; but thoſe which are ſown in the full ground, will not flower before the middle of July; and theſe will continue flowering till the froſt puts a ſtop to them in the autumn.

There are two other varieties of this, if not diſtinct ſpecies; one of them grows naturally in the Eaſt, and the other in the Weſt-Indies; that which comes from the Eaſt-Indies, by the title of Immortal Eagle Flower, is a moſt beautiful plant; the flowers are double, much larger than thoſe of the common ſort; they are ſcarlet and white variegated, and purple and white in others; and the plants producing many flowers, render them very valuable; and if the ſeeds of theſe are carefully ſaved, the kinds may always be preſerved; but I have raiſed ſome plants from foreign ſeeds, whoſe flowers were ſo very double as to loſe their male parts, ſo did not produce any ſeeds.

The ſeeds of theſe plants ſhould be ſown on a moderate hot-bed in the ſpring, and when the plants are come up about an inch high, they ſhould be tranſplanted on another moderate hot-bed at about four inches diſtance each way, obſerving to ſhade them from the ſun till they have taken new root; after which they ſhould have a large ſhare of free air admitted to them, at all times when the weather is favourable, to prevent their drawing up tall and weak: they will require to be often refreſhed with water, but it ſhould not be given to them in too great plenty; for as their ſtems are very ſucculent, ſo they are apt to rot with much moiſture. When the plants are grown ſo large as to touch each other, they ſhould be carefully taken up with balls of earth to their roots, and each planted into a ſeparate pot filled with light rich earth, and plunged into a very moderate hod-bed under a deep frame, to admit the plants to grow, ſhading them from the ſun until they have taken freſh root; then they ſhould have a large ſhare of air admitted to them every day, and by degrees hardened, ſo as to bear the open air, into which part of the plants may be removed in July, placing them in a warm ſheltered ſituation; where, if the ſeaſon proves favourable, they will flower and make a fine appearance; but it will be proper to keep part of the plants either in a glaſs-caſe or a deep frame, in order to get good ſeeds, becauſe thoſe in the open air will not ripen their ſeeds unleſs the ſummer proves very warm; and the plants in ſhelter muſt have a good ſhare of free air every day, otherwiſe they will grow pale and ſickly; nor ſhould they have too much of the ſun in the middle of the day, in very hot weather, for that occaſions their leaves hanging and their requiring water, which is often very hurtful; therefore if the glaſſes are ſhaded in the middle of the day for three or four hours, the plants will thrive better, and continue longer in beauty than when they are expoſed to the great heat. Thoſe who are curious to preſerve theſe plants in perfection, pull off all the ſingle and plain coloured flowers from the plants which they preſerve for ſeeds, leaving only thoſe flowers which are double and of good colours; where this is carefully done, they may be continued without the leaſt degeneracy conſtantly.

The ſort which grows in the Weſt-Indies, is there called Cockſpur. This hath ſingle flowers as large as the laſt-mentioned ſort, but I never ſaw any of them more than half double, and only with white and red ſtripes: the plants are very apt to grow to a very large ſize before they produce any flowers, ſo that it is late in the autumn before they begin to flower; and ſometimes in bad ſeaſons they will ſcarce have any flowers,

and but rarely ripen their ſeeds here, ſo that few perſons care to cultivate this ſort, eſpecially if they can have the other.

The third ſort here mentioned grows naturally in Ceylon, and in many parts of India; this hath very narrow ſpear-ſhaped leaves, which are ſawed on their edges; the foot-ſtalks ſuſtain each three flowers, which are ſmaller than thoſe of the common ſort, ſo are not worthy of a place in gardens, except for the ſake of variety. This is a tender plant, and requires the ſame treatment as the Immortal Eagle Flower.

IMPERATORIA. Lin. Gen. Plant. 321. Tourn. Inſt. R. H. 316. tab. 168. Maſterwort; in French, *Imperatoire.*

The CHARACTERS are,

It hath an umbellated flower; the principal umbel is plain, and compoſed of many ſmaller; the greater umbel has no involucrum, but the ſmall ones have, which are compoſed of many narrow leaves, almoſt as long as the umbel; the principal umbel is uniform; the flowers have five heart-ſhaped petals, which are equal and inflexed. They have five hairy ſtamina, terminated by roundiſh ſummits. The germen is ſituated under the petals, ſupporting two reflexed ſtyles, crowned by obtuſe ſtigmas. The germen afterward becomes a roundiſh compreſſed fruit divided in two parts, containing two oval-bordered ſeeds.

This genus of plants is ranged in the ſecond ſection of Linnæus's fifth claſs, intitled Pentandria Digynia, which contains the plants whoſe flowers have five ſtamina and two ſtyles.

We have but one SPECIES of this genus, viz.

IMPERATORIA (*Oſtruthium.*) Hort. Cliff. 103. *Maſterwort.* Imperatoria major. C. B. P. 156. *Greater Maſterwort*; and the Aſtrantia of Dodonæus. Pempt. 320. *Maſterwort, or falſe Pellitory of Spain.*

This plant grows naturally on the Auſtrian and Styrian Alps, and upon other mountainous places in Italy; the root is as thick as a man's thumb, running obliquely in the ground; it is fleſhy, aromatic, and has a ſtrong acrid taſte, biting the tongue and mouth like Pellitory of Spain; the leaves ariſe immediately from the root; they have foot-ſtalks ſeven or eight inches long, dividing into three very ſhort ones at the top, each ſuſtaining a trilobate leaf, indented on the border; the foot-ſtalks are deeply channelled, and when broken emit a rank odour. The flower-ſtalks riſe about two feet high, and divide into two or three branches, each being terminated by a pretty large umbel of white flowers, whoſe petals are ſplit; theſe are ſucceeded by oval compreſſed ſeeds, ſomewhat like thoſe of Dill, but larger. It flowers in June, and the ſeeds ripen in Auguſt.

This plant is cultivated in gardens to ſupply the markets. It may be propagated either by ſeeds, or by parting the roots: if you would propagate it by ſeeds, they ſhould be ſown in autumn ſoon after they are ripe, on a bed or border, in a ſhady ſituation; obſerving not to ſow the ſeeds too thick, nor ſhould they be covered too deep. In the ſpring the plants will appear, when they ſhould be carefully weeded; and if the ſeaſon ſhould prove very dry, they ſhould be now and then refreſhed with water, which will greatly promote their growth. Toward the beginning of May, if you find the plants come up too cloſe together, you ſhould prepare a moiſt ſhady border (and thin the plants carefully, leaving them about ſix inches aſunder;) and plant thoſe which you draw up into the border about the ſame diſtance apart every way, being careful to water them duly, if the ſeaſon ſhould prove dry, until they have taken root; after which time, theſe plants (as alſo thoſe remaining in the ſeed-beds) will require no other culture but to keep them clear from weeds; which may be eaſily effected, by hoeing the ground between the plants now and then in dry weather, which will deſtroy the weeds; and by thus ſtirring the ground, will be of great ſervice to the plants. The following autumn theſe plants ſhould be tranſplanted where they are deſigned to remain, which ſhould be in a rich moiſt ſoil and a ſhady ſituation;

tation; where they will thrive much better than if too much exposed to the sun, or in a dry soil, for they delight in shade and moisture; so that where these are wanting the plants will require a constant supply of water in dry weather, otherwise they will thrive but slowly. The distance which these plants should be placed, must not be less than two feet every way, for where they like their situation, they will spread and increase much. When these plants are rooted, they will require no other culture but to keep them clear from weeds; and in the spring, before they shoot, the ground should be every year gently dug between the plants; in doing of which, great care should be had not to cut or bruise their roots. These plants, with this management, will continue several years, and will produce seeds in plenty.

If you would propagate these plants by offsets, their roots should be parted at Michaelmas, and planted in a shady situation, at the same distance as has been directed for the seedling plants, observing to water them until they have taken root, after which time they must be managed as the seedlings.

The roots of this plant are used in medicine, and are greatly recommended for their virtue in contagious distempers, or the bites of venomous creatures; they are alexipharmic and sudorific; by some they are recommended for cholics and asthmas, for the cramp, and all cold diseases of the nerves.

INARCHING is a method of grafting, which is commonly called grafting by approach. This method of grafting is used when the stock you intend to graft on, and the tree from which you would take the graft stand so near (or can be brought so near) that they may be joined together. The method of performing it is as follows: take the branch you would Inarch, and having fitted it to that part of the stock where you intend to join it, pare away the rind and wood on one side about three inches in length. After the same manner cut the stock or branch in the place where the graft is to be united, so that the rind of both may join equally together, at least on one side, that the sap may meet; then cut a little tongue upwards in the graft, and make a notch or slit in the stock downward to admit it; so that when they are joined, the tongues will prevent their slipping, and the graft will more closely unite with the stock. Having thus placed them exactly together, you must tie them with some bass, or other soft bandage; then cover the place with grafting clay, to prevent the air from entering to dry the wound, or the wet from getting in to rot the stock: you should also fix a stake into the ground to which that part of the stock, as also the graft should be fastened, to prevent the wind from breaking them asunder, which is often the case when this precaution is not observed.

In this manner they are to remain about four months, in which time they will be sufficiently united, and the graft may then be cut from the mother tree, observing to slope it off close to the stock; and if at this time you cover the joined parts with fresh grafting clay, it will be of great service to the graft.

This operation is always performed in April or May, that the graft may unite with the stock before the succeeding winter, and is commonly practised upon Oranges, Myrtles, Jasmines, Walnuts, Firs, Pines, and several other trees, which will not succeed so well by common grafting or budding. But although I have mentioned Orange-trees among the rest, yet I would by no means advise this practice where the trees are designed to grow large, which, in this method, they rarely ever will do; and it is chiefly practised upon those trees only as a curiosity, to have a young plant with fruit upon it, in a year or two from seed, by Inarching a bearing branch into a young stock, whereby it is effected, yet these plants are seldom long lived.

INDIGOFERA. Lin. Gen. 889. Indigo.

The CHARACTERS are,

The empalement is of one leaf, spreading almost flat, and cut into five segments; the flower is of the butterfly kind, having a roundish spreading standard, which is indented at the point and reflexed: the wings are oblong, obtuse, and their under borders spreading; the keel is obtuse, spreading, and acute-pointed. It hath ten stamina digested in a cylinder whose points ascend, terminated by roundish summits, and a cylindrical germen, supporting a short style, crowned by an obtuse stigma. The germen afterward becomes a long taper pod, inclosing kidney-shaped seeds.

This species of plants is ranged in the third section of Linnæus's seventeenth class, intitled Diadelphia Decandria, from the flowers having ten stamina formed in two bodies.

The SPECIES are,

1. INDIGOFERA (Tinctoria) leguminibus arcuatis incanis, racemis folio brevioribus. Flor. Zeyl. 273. Indigo with hoary arched pods, and the bunches of flowers shorter than the leaves. Anil five Indigo Americana, siliquis in falculæ modum contortis. Acad. R. Scien. 1718. Guatimala Indigo.

2. INDIGOFERA (Suffruticosa) leguminibus arcuatis incanis, caule fruticosa. Indigo with a shrubby stalk, and hoary arched pods. Colutea affinis fruticosa argentea, floribus spicatis è viride purpureis, siliquis falcatis. Sloan. Cat. Jam. 142.

3. INDIGOFERA (Caroliniana) leguminibus teretibus, foliolis quinis spicis longissimis sparsis, radice perenne. Indigo with taper pods, leaves with five lobes, long loose spikes of flowers, and a perennial root.

4. INDIGOFERA (Indica) leguminibus pendulis lanatis compressis, foliis pinnatis. Indigo with woolly, compressed, hanging pods, and winged leaves.

5. INDIGOFERA (Glabra) leguminibus glabris teretibus, foliolis trifoliatis. Indigo with smooth taper pods, and trifoliate leaves.

The first and fifth sorts are annual plants with us; the seeds of these must be sown on a hot-bed early in the spring of the year, and when the plants are come up two inches high, they should be transplanted into small pots filled with good fresh earth, and the pots plunged into a hot-bed of tanners bark; when the plants have obtained some strength, they must have a great share of free air, by raising the glasses in the day time; and in June they may be exposed more to the open air, by which time they will begin to produce their flowers, which will be succeeded by pods in a short time after, and in August their seeds will be perfected, if the plants are brought forward in the spring.

The second sort grows to the height of five or six feet, and will abide two or three years, if it is preserved in a very warm stove in winter; this produces spikes of flowers from the wings of the leaves on the sides of the stems of the plant, and sometimes will perfect its seeds in England. This must be raised in a hot-bed, as was directed for the two former, but must not be wholly exposed to the open air, even in the hottest weather.

The fourth sort is supposed to be promiscuously used to make the Indigo, but the first is the common sort which is cultivated in the English plantations in America; but I have been assured by a person of great credit, that he has made as good Indigo from the second sort, as any that was produced in our plantations; and this being a much larger plant, will afford a greater quantity from the same compass of ground, than any one of the other species, especially if cut before the stalks grow ligneous; and this sort will grow on poorer land, so may be cultivated in such places where the first sort will not thrive so well, by which means great improvements may be made with this plant in our American plantations. There are some other sorts of this plant which are natives of India, from which this commodity is made; two of which, viz. the fourth and fifth sorts I have had growing in the garden at Chelsea, both which are very different in their leaves and pods from either of the American sorts which have been cultivated. I have also received seeds from India of the third sort, which is the same species of Indigo which grows naturally in South Carolina, and which was greatly esteemed

7 F   some

fome years ago by the Indigo planters of that country, for the beauty of the commodity which it produced; but the plants being flender and thinly garnifhed with leaves, which were fmall, they did not furnifh a quantity of Indigo in proportion to their bulk, fo of late this fort has not been much cultivated there; though the account which I received with the feeds was, that it was what the beft Indigo of India was made from.

The whole procefs in making the Indigo being exactly defcribed by Pere Labat in his voyages, I thought it would not be unacceptable to the Englifh reader, to tranflate his account in this place, which is as follows:

There was formerly a great deal of Indigo made in the parifh of Macauba: there is not a ftream nor river in it, where one docs not meet with Indigo works, that is, backs or vats of ftone-work well cemented, in which the plant that yields the dye is put to digeft: there are ufually three of thefe vats one above another, in the manner of a cafcade; fo that the fecond, which is lower than the bottom of the firft, may receive the liquor contained in the firft, when the holes which are made in the bottom of the firft are unftopped; and that the third may in its turn receive what was in the fecond.

The firft, largeft, and higheft of thefe vats is called the fteeper or rot; it is ufually made twenty feet long, twelve or fifteen feet wide, and three or four feet deep. The fecond is called the battery, it is almoft half as fmall again as the firft: and the third, which is much lefs than the fecond, is called the devilling. The names of the two firft perfectly agree with their ufes, for the plant is laid to fteep in the firft, where it ferments, is macerated, and becomes like rotten dung: after that the falts and fubftance of the leaf and rind are diffufed in the water by the fermentation, which the heat and ripenefs of the plant has excited in it. It is in the fecond that they agitate and beat this water, impregnated and loaded with the falts of the plant, till having collected, re-united, and, as it were, coagulated them with one another, they form the particles which compofe the dye.

As for the name of the third, I do not fee how it agrees with it, unlefs it be becaufe this vat is deeper coloured than the others; for the Indigo already formed remaining in it, confequently dyes and colours it much deeper than the others.

To which I fhould add, that it is only at St. Domingo that they make ufe of this name. In the Windward Iflands they call this laft vat the fettler, and this name fuits it perfectly well, becaufe it is in this, that the Indigo begun in the fteeper, and perfected in the battery unites, grows into a mafs, feparates itfelf from the particles of water which remained in it, leaves them at top, and fettles at the bottom of the vat; whence it is taken out to be put into little bags, and then into the boxes, as I fhall mention hereafter.

Nothing ought to be omitted in the building and making thefe vats fubftantial; the ftrength of the fermentation is fo great, that unlefs the ftone-work and plafter be very well done, and the mortar carefully chofen and wrought, they crack; and a very moderate crack is fufficient to let out a vat of Indigo, and caufe a confiderable lofs to the owner.

When this misfortune happens, the following is an eafy and infallible remedy, which I can anfwer for, as having experienced it. Take fome fea fhells of any kind whatever, pound them without burning them, powder them, and fift them through a fine fieve. Take an equal quantity of quick lime and fift it; mix thefe together with water enough to make a ftiff mortar, and as quick as you can, ftop the cracks of your vats with it. This mixture incorporates, flicks, and dries in a moment, and immediately prevents the matter's running out of the vat.

Every body does, or fhould know, that Indigo is a dye ufed to dye wool, filk, cloths, and ftuffs, blue: the Spaniards call it Anilo: the fineft they make, i. e. in New Spain, comes from Guatimala, which makes

a great many people call it barely Guatimalo. It is made alfo in the Eaft-Indies, particularly in the dominions of the Great Mogul, the kingdom of Golconda, and other places thereabouts, as Mr. Tavernier relates in his voyages. This fort is in Europe oftener called India than Indigo or Anil, people taking for its proper name the name of the place it was made at. Some authors, and among others, Father du Tertre of our order, having fancied that the Indigo which comes from the Eaft-Indies is more beautiful, finer, and dearer, than that which comes from the Weft-Indies, which they call flat Indigo, while they call that from the Eaft barely India. They would have fpoken more properly, if they had called the latter round India; for, by their leave, all the difference between the two Indias, or Indigos, is, that that made in the Eaft-Indies is fhaped like half eggs, and that of the Weft like cakes: for as for goodnefs and beauty, the one will not be a whit fuperior to the other, if both are wrought with equal care and fidelity.

The fhape of the Oriental Indigo obliges the merchants who would carry it into Europe to pound it, that they may put the more into the chefts, or barrels they put it up in. It is certain, that being thus pounded, its grain having been broken under the peftle, ground, and reduced to powder, makes it finer than the Weft-Indian Indigo, which coming in cakes juft as it was dried, fhews its grain entire, and confequently muft appear coarfer; but what is that to the intrinfic goodnefs of the commodity; I maintain it is the fame in both, though there feems to be a difference.

To be convinced of this truth, take a lump of fugar equally white throughout, break it in two, pound one part of it, and reduce it to powder; this will look finer and whiter than that which is whole, which proceeds only from this, that the grain of the one has been feparated and divided into a greater number of parts, which, though very fmall, and almoft infenfible, yet have a greater number of furfaces, and confequently reflect more light; whereas the other remaining entire, prefenting to the fight only a large grain, which has but little furface, of courfe reflects lefs light, and by a neceffary confequence muft appear lefs white; which is the fame as appearing lefs beautiful, fince the beauty of fugar confifts in its whitenefs. Methinks we may reafon in the fame manner upon Indigo, and fay, that cæteris paribus, the Weft-Indian Indigo is as beautiful as the Eaft-Indian, when they are both wrought alike.

I think I fhould add, that the American Indigo is better for ufe than the other; for who does not fee, that there is no pounding this dye, without the moft fubtle parts being diffipated in the air, as Mr. Tavernier allows? And who can doubt that thefe parts are the beft, and thofe that go fartheft when it is ufed?

I grant that the Indigo which comes from the Eaft-Indies, is dearer than that which is made in the Weft-Indies; the reafon is plain, it comes farther, runs greater rifks; and thofe who bring it would not find their account in felling it, at the fame price with that which comes from a much nearer place; but that does not at all prove it to be more beautiful, or better.

Indigo is compofed of the falt and fubftance of the leaves and rind of a plant of the fame name; fo that one may fay, it is a diffolution or digeftion of the plant, caufed by the fermentation it has excited in the water it was laid to fteep in. I know fome writers pretend, that the fubftance of the leaves does not produce the Indigo, which (as they would have it) is only a vifcous tincture, or colour, which the fermentation of the plant diffufes in the water: but before I take their words for it, I defire they would tell me what becomes of the fubftance of the plant; for when it is taken out of the fteeper, it is certain, that it has no longer the fame weight, confiftence, nor colour, it had before. The leaves, which were very

plump,

plump, and very full of juice, are light, flabby, and withered, and look more like dung than any thing else, which makes them frequently give the name of rot to the steeper. If then we no longer find in the leaves, and the rest of the plant, the same substance that was observable in it before it was laid to steep, is it not most natural to believe, that it is the same substance and salts, which, being freed from their inclosures, and diffused in the water, have thickened it, and by their union or coagulation have formed that blue mass which they call Indigo, so useful in painting and dyeing?

The culture.] This plant requires a good rich level soil, not too dry; it greatly robs and impoverishes the ground where it grows, and must be alone. There cannot be too much care taken to keep it clean, and to hinder herbs of any kind whatever from growing near it. They weed and cleanse the ground where they intend to plant the Indigo seed, five times over. I should think they should call it sowing, but the term of planting is consecrated in our isles, and I do not think I ought for the sake of a word to fall out with our planters, who deserve our esteem upon a thousand accounts, though they have got a habit of murdering the French language. They sometimes carry their neatness to such a pitch, that they sweep the piece of ground as they do a room. After that they make the holes wherein the seeds are to be put for this purpose; the slaves, or others, who are to work at it, range themselves in the same line, at the top of the piece of ground; and going backwards they make little drills the breadth of their hoe, of the depth of two or three inches, at about a foot distance every way, and as much as possible in a strait line. When they are come to the end of the ground, each furnishes himself with a little bag of seeds, and returning that way they came, they put eleven or thirteen seeds into each of the holes they have made. A relick of superstition has taught them that the number must be odd. I by no means approve of this practice, but I shall take care not to endeavour to shew them the uselessness and folly of it, being satisfied I shall only lose my time and labour. This work is the most toilsome of any in the manufacture of Indigo; for those who plant it must be always stooping, without rising up, till the planting of the whole length of the piece is ended; so that when that is large, which almost always happens, they are obliged to remain two hours, and often more, in this posture.

When they come to the top of the piece, they go back again, and cover the holes where they have put the seed in, by thrusting in with their feet the earth they had taken out of them, and so the seed is covered with about two inches of earth.

The culture of this plant may be rendered very easy, provided the inhabitants of our colonies in America could be brought to make use of the drill plough; for with this instrument two persons and a horse or mule will sow more land with Indigo in one day, than twenty persons can perform in the same time, in the method now practised; for the plough makes the drill, and the hopper which is fixed to the plough follows, and scatters the seeds at equal distances in the drills; and another instrument behind the hopper covers in the drills, whereby the whole operation is performed at the same time, and with great ease. Indeed the use of this machine must be understood by the persons who are to perform it, otherwise they will do it in a bad manner, but a little practice will bring any person to the right use of it.

As the Indigo is sown in rows, a hoeing plough may be made of a proper dimension, in order to clean the ground between the rows; with this contrivance it may be performed in much less time than in the method now practised. But in doing of this, I would advise the stirring of the ground, soon after the Indigo plants are come up, before the weeds have got much strength, at which time they are soon destroyed; and by stirring of the ground the plants will be greatly

encouraged; and the strongest and most thriving plants will always make the best Indigo.

What Le Bat says of cutting the plants before they are too old, in order to have the Indigo of a better colour, is certainly right. Therefore as soon as the flowers begin to appear, it should be cut; for if it stands much longer the stems of the plants will grow hard and stringy, and the lower leaves will change to a yellowish colour, which will render the Indigo less valuable; as will also the plants being too close together, which will occasion their bottom leaves to decay for want of free air: the same will happen if weeds are suffered to grow among the plants. Therefore there must be great regard to their being kept always clean.

Though all seasons are good for the planting of Indigo, yet care must be taken not to put it in the ground in a dry time: it is true, the seed may keep a whole month in the ground, without being spoiled; but when it is planted so, one runs the risk of having it eaten up by vermin, or carried away by the wind, or choked by the weeds that spring up with it; so that the prudent planters never run the risk of planting it dry, i. e. at a time when they do not probably expect rain in two or three days after the planting is ended: they chuse therefore, usually, a moist season, which promises rain, and then they are sure of seeing the plant spring up in three or four days after its being planted.

Notwithstanding all the care that has been taken in clearing the ground where the seeds have been planted, the planter must not be careless when the Indigo is got above ground; because the goodness of the soil, joined to the moisture and warmth of the climate, and the plentiful dews that fall every night, makes a prodigious quantity of weeds spring up, which would choke and absolutely spoil the Indigo, if extreme care was not taken to weed them up as soon as they appear, and to keep the plant extraordinary neat; and very often the weeds are partly the cause of the breeding of a kind of caterpillars, which devour all the leaves in a short time.

From the time of the plants rising above ground, to its perfect maturity, is but two months, and then it is fit to cut: if one was to stay longer it would blossom, its leaves would grow drier and harder, and consequently they would yield less substance, and the colour would not be near so beautiful.

After this first cutting, the new branches and leaves which the plant produces may be cut about every six weeks, provided the season be rainy, and that care be taken not to cut it in a time of drought, because then we should infallibly lose the plant, or, as they call it there, the Choupues, and be obliged to plant again; but all things being rightly managed, the plant may last two years; after which it must be plucked up, and new ones planted.

When the plant is ripe, which is known by the leaves, which grow brittle and less supple, they cut it some inches from the ground. They use for the cutting of it great crooked knives made like sickles. Some planters make it into bundles, like double bottles of hay, that a negro may easily carry them to the steeper; but most people put it into large pieces of coarse cloth, which they tie by the four corners; and this is more convenient, the plant is less handled and squeezed, and the small are carried away as safely as the great; and besides the work goes on quicker this way, than in making bottles; and as time is precious every where, and especially in America, there cannot be too much care taken not to lose any.

Eighteen or twenty packets of plants, each about the size of two bottles of hay, are sufficient to fill a steeper of the afore-mentioned size. When it is filled with water, so that it covers the plants, they put pieces of wood on the top, that the plants may not rise above the water (much after the manner as they do upon the Grapes that are put into the press) and let all ferment. According as the heat is greater or less, or the plant more or less ripe, the fermentation is raised sooner or later,

later, fometimes in fix, eight, or ten hours; and fometimes one is obliged to wait eighteen or twenty hours, but very feldom longer. Then the effect of the fermentation vifibly appears, the water heats, and boils up on all fides, as the Grapes do in the vat; and the water which at firft was clear, infenfibly grows thick, and becomes of a blue, inclining to a Violet colour. Then without meddling at all with the plants, they open the cocks, which are at the bottom of the fteeper, and let all this water, loaded with the falts and fubftance of the plant, which were freed by the fermentation, run into the battery; and while they throw away as ufelefs, and almoft rotten, the plants that were in the fteeper, and clean it, that it may be filled with frefh, they beat the water, which they have let out of the fteeper into the battery.

They formerly ufed for this purpofe a battledoor wheel, whofe axle was placed upon the middle of the vat, and which they turned by two handles that were at the end of the fame axle. Since that, in the room of battledoors, they have put little bottomlefs boxes, and afterwards others, whofe bottoms were bored full of holes: at prefent they ufe a kind of pretty large pails, faftened to ftrong poles, placed upon chande- liers, by means of which, the negroes violently and continually raife, beat, and ftir the water, till the falts and other parts of the fubftance of the plant are united, and fufficiently, as it were, coagulated to in- corporate.

The hitting this minute exactly fhews the fkill of him who overfees the making of the Indigo; for if he makes them leave off beating a little too foon, the grain not yet formed, remains difperfed in the water, without finking and gathering together at the bottom of the vat, and is loft with the water, when they are obliged to let it out, which is a great lofs to the owner; or if when it is formed they continue to beat, they diffolve it, and the fame inconvenience follows. This minute then muft be nicked, and when it is found, they muft leave off beating and let the matter reft.

To find this minute, they make ufe of a little filver cup, defigned for this ufe alone; they fill it with this water, while the negroes beat it, and according as they obferve that the fæces fink to the bottom of the cup, or remain difperfed in the water, they ceafe, or continue beating.

The General Dictionary printed at Trevoux, relates very ferioufly, upon the credit of father Plumier a minim, that the Indigo-maker having taking up fome of the water of this battery in his cup, fpits in it; and that if the Indigo be formed, the fæces immediately fink to the bottom of the cup, and that then he makes them leave off beating, if not, he makes them con- tinue it. This is not the only incident in which people have impofed upon father Plumier's credulity and fimplicity. I have been a witnefs of it upon other occafions.

When they have left off beating they let the matter reft, the fæces fink to the bottom of the vat, and gather together like a kind of mud; and the water freed from all the falts it was impregnated with, fwims above it, and grows clear. Then they open the cocks, which are placed in the battery at different diftances from the bottom, and let this water run away; and when they come to the furface of the fæ- ces, they open the cocks of the bottom, that the fæces may all fall into the devilling or fettler. There they let it fettle a little while longer, after which they put it into linen bags, fifteen or eighteen inches long, made with a point, where it perfectly purges itfelf from the reft of the water, which remained among its particles. When that is done, they fpread it in little boxes three or four feet long, two feet broad, and about three inches deep, and expofe it to the air to dry it perfectly. They obferve not to expofe it to the fun, becaufe it would ftarve the colour in drying it; and they take a great deal of care to keep it from the rain, becaufe that would diffolve and utterly fpoil it.

It fometimes happens that the caterpillars get among the Indigo; and if they are let alone ever fo little a while they eat all the leaves, and often the very rind, and ends of the branches, and kill the ftocks; it is but loft time to endeavour to deftroy them, or hinder them from ravaging a whole piece, by ftopping them with a ditch. The fureft way is to cut down the In- digo with all fpeed, let its age be what it will, and to throw both plants and caterpillars together into the fteeper; there they burft, and part with what they had devoured, and the Indigo is not the lefs beau- tiful for it. It is true, when the plant is not come to its perfect maturity, it yields much lefs; but many experiments have taught us, that the colour it yields is much more beautiful; fo that what is loft one way is gained another.

I would not wait for fo perfect a ripenefs before I cut the plant. Perhaps all the fecret of thofe, whofe In- digo is fo much extolled beyond ours, lies only in cutting the plant when it yields the livelieft colour. I have experienced that in leaving fome cochineal flies upon fome Indian Figs, which were too ripe, inftead of being red, they grew of a filemot colour, like the fruit they fed upon. The fame thing might happen in Indigo; and what I here propofe is not a ground- lefs doubt, fince it is backed by the experiment I have juft related; which plainly proves, that the fame plant, cut at different ages, produces colours different in beauty. I would not venture to give this advice to men wedded to their intereft, who value the quan- tity rather than the quality of their commodity; but I believe I have nothing to fear from our iflanders, who are generous and magnificent, fometimes even beyond their abilities: I advife them therefore to make different trials, as to the foil, the feafon, the age of the plant, the water they fteep it in, the point of dif- folution, &c. and I am fure, that with a little time, labour, and patience, they will make Indigo that will equal, and even excel, the moft boafted Indigo of foreign countries. The planters of St. Domingo know that in 1701 their coarfe fugar was very bad, and was not made without infinite trouble; and at prefent every body allows, that by their labour, affiduity, and enquiries, it is grown much more efteemed than that of the Windward Iflands: why may not the fame be hoped for in Indigo?

Mr. Pomet, author of the General Hiftory of Drugs, fays in his firft part, chap. 10. That the Indians of the village of Sarqueffe, near Amadabat, ufe only the leaves of the Indigo, and throw away the plant and branches; and that it is from thence the moft efteemed Indigo comes.

I am pretty much of his opinion; for we fee, that thofe who take the pains to ftrip off the Grapes from the branches, before they put them into the vat, and throw away the ftalks entirely, make much the beft wine; becaufe the ftalks always contain an acid, which mixes with the juice of the Grape in the treading and preffing them both together; and for the fame reafon, the ftalks of the Indigo plant muft contain a liquid much lefs perfect in colour than that of the leaves: but one ought to have the leifure and patience of the Indians to undertake fuch a work, and have work- men as cheap as they are in that country, fuppofing the fact true, as Mr. Pomet delivers it from the re- lation of Mr. Tavernier.

Though I am a great friend to thofe experiments which may carry our manufactures to a greater per- fection, yet I dare not propofe this, becaufe of the expence they muft be at, who would try it; and be- caufe the profit arifing from it would not perhaps quit coft: however, I have here given the method of the Indians of Sarqueffe, that I may have no reafon to re- proach myfelf with having omitted a thing which may be of fome ufe to my country.

Good Indigo ought to be fo light, as to fwim upon water; the more it finks the more it is to be fufpected of being mixed with earth, afhes, or powdered flate. Its colour ought to be a deep blue, inclining to a Violet, brilliant, lively, and bright: it ought to be
more

more beautiful within than without, and look fhining, and as it were filvered.

If it is too heavy in proportion to its bulk, it ought to be fufpected, and its quality examined into ; for as it often bears a confiderable price, it is fit that thofe who buy it, fhould be acquainted with the frauds that may be committed in it.

The firft is the beating the plant too much in the fteeper, that the leaves and rind of it may be entirely confumed. It is certain that the quantity of the matter is very confiderably increafed by this diffolution, but the Indigo is a great deal the lefs beautiful for it ; it is blackifh, thick, heavy, and fitter to be thrown away than ufed.

The fecond is the mixing afhes, earth, or a certain brown fhining fand (which is pretty commonly found in the bays by the fea-fide) and efpecially powdered flate, with the fæces, as they fall into the devilling, and ftirring all well together, that it may incorporate, and the fraud not appear : and this fraud is much more eafily committed in the powdered Indigo, than in that which is in cakes ; becaufe it is very difficult for thofe heterogeneous bodies to unite fo well together, as not to make in many places, as it were, beds of a different matter ; and then, by breaking the piece of Indigo, they are eafily perceived.

The two following expedients may be made ufe of, in order to know the goodnefs or badnefs of Indigo.

The firft is to diffolve a bit of it in a glafs of water. If it is pure and well made, it it will entirely diffolve ; but if it is adulterated, the foreign matter will fink to the bottom of the glafs.

The fecond is to burn it. The good Indigo will burn all away, whereas the afhes, earth, fand, and flate, remain after the true Indigo is confumed.

In 1694, Indigo was fold at the Windward Iflands, from three livres ten fols, to four livres per pound, according to its beauty, and the number of veffels to be freighted with it. I have known it fince at a much lower price ; however, the planter would not fail of making a very confiderable profit of it, though he fhould fell it for no more than forty fols per pound, becaufe this commodity requires fewer utenfils and lefs charges than a fugar-work.

Since the cultivation of Indigo was introduced in South Carolina, great quantities of that ufeful dye has been brought from thence to England ; and it may be hoped that the encouragement granted by parliament to the planters, will enable them to profecute this branch of commerce with fuch fuccefs, as to be a great national benefit, and of equal advantage to that colony : but as yet the planters have not arrived to fo much perfection in the making of it as could be wifhed ; for moft of the Indigo which I have feen of the produce of that country, has been fo hard as to render it difficult to diffolve, occafioned by their pouring a quantity of lime-water into the vat, in order to make the fæces of the plant fubfide. I have alfo been informed by letters from many of the planters, that after the fermentation of the plant in the vat, it comes out again almoft entire, being but in a very fmall proportion leffened, either in bulk or weight. This may probably be owing, in great part, to their culture of the plant, as alfo from their vats not being large enough to contain a fufficient quantity of the herb, to make the fermentation ftrong enough to diffolve it ; or from the vats being built in the open air, whereby the fermentation may be impeded, by the cooler breezes of the evening air : for in the iflands where the beft Indigo is made, their vats are all built under cover, where their heat is much greater than that in Carolina, therefore this requires the attention of the planters of Indigo.

As to the culture of the plant, by all the information I have been able to procure from thence, they commit a great error in fowing their feeds too thick, whereby the plants are drawn up with flender ftems, which are not fufficiently garnifhed with leaves ; nor are the leaves fo large and fucculent as they would naturally grow, were the plants allowed a greater fhare of room, fo that the ftalks confift of little elfe but ftrong veffels which are not diffolvable by the fermentation, and it is only the upper parts of the plant which are furnifhed with leaves, like young trees growing clofe together which are drawn up with flender ftems, having no lateral branches, nor leaves, but at their tops ; therefore it is not to be fuppofed, a great quantity of Indigo can be produced from plants fo managed ; for it is a common obfervation of the cultivators of Woad, that when their plants fpire, and have narrow thin leaves, they produce but little of the dye ; fo that they make choice of rich ftrong land for fowing the feeds of this plant, and are careful to thin them, that they may have room to fpread, and produce large fucculent leaves, from which they always reap the greateft profit. If the planters of Indigo in America would but imitate the cultivators of Woad in this particular, they would certainly find their advantage in fo doing.

Another thing in which they err is, letting the plant ftand too long before they cut it, fuppofing from the height of the plant to procure a great quantity of the dye ; but in this they are greatly miftaken, for the older the plant is before it is cut, the drier and firmer will be the ftalks ; therefore but little of the plant will be diffolved by fermentation, nor will the fæces of the old plants be near fo beautiful as that of the young. Therefore it is to be wifhed, that they would try fome few experiments in the culture and management of the plants, by fowing thin, and keeping the plants perfectly clean from weeds ; as alfo to cut them while young and full of juice, and hereby they will be better informed how to improve it to the greateft advantage. But as labour is dear in that country, fo many perfons probably object to the expence of cultivating the Indigo in this method ; therefore, to avoid this, I have before propofed fowing the feeds with a drill plough, whereby the firft expence will be greatly leffened, and the feeds more equally fown ; and by the ufe of the hoe plough, ten acres may be kept clean from weeds with as fmall expence, as one when managed by the hand hoe ; and by ftirring of the ground often, and earthing up the plants, they would grow much ftronger, be lefs liable of being deftroyed by flies, and have larger and more fucculent ftalks and leaves.

INGA. See MIMOSA.

INOCULATING, or Budding. This is commonly practifed upon all forts of ftone fruit, in particular, fuch as Peaches, Nectarines, Cherries, Plums, &c. as alfo Oranges and Jafmines, and is preferable to any fort of grafting for moft forts of fruit. The method of performing it is as follows : you muft be provided with a fharp penknife, having a flat haft (the ufe of which is to raife the bark of the ftock, to admit the bud) and fome found bafs mat, which fhould be foaked in water to increafe its ftrength, and make it more pliable ; then having taken off the cuttings from the trees you would propagate, you fhould choofe a fmooth part of the ftock about five or fix inches above the furface of the ground, if defigned for dwarfs, and for half ftandards at three feet ; but for ftandards, they fhould be budded fix or more feet above ground ; then with your knife make an horizontal cut crofs the rind of the ftock, and from the middle of that cut make a flit downwards about two inches in length, fo that it may be in the form of a T ; but you muft be careful not to cut too deep, left you wound the ftock : then having cut off the leaf from the bud, leaving the foot-ftalk remaining, you fhould make a crofs cut about half an inch below the eye, and with your knife flit off the bud, with part of the wood to it, in form of an efcutcheon : this done, you muft with your knife pull off that part of the wood which was taken with the bud, obferving whether the eye of the bud be left to it, or not (for all thofe buds which lofe their eyes in ftripping, fhould be thrown away, being good for nothing) then having gently raifed the bark of the ftock where the crofs in-

7 G   cifion

tifion was made, with the flat haft of your penknife clear to the wood, you should thruſt the bud therein, obſerving to place it ſmooth between the rind and the wood of the ſtock, cutting off any part of the rind belonging to the bud, which may be too long for the ſlit made in the ſtock; and ſo having exactly fitted the bud to the ſtock, you muſt tie them cloſely round with baſs mat, beginning at the under part of the ſlit, and ſo proceed to the top, taking care that you do not bind round the eye of the bud, which ſhould be left open.

When your buds have been inoculated three weeks or a month, you will ſee which of them have taken; thoſe of them which appear ſhrivelled and black, being dead, but thoſe which remain freſh and plump, you may depend are joined; and at this time you ſhould looſen the bandage, which, if not done in time, will pinch the ſtock, and greatly injure, if not deſtroy, the bud.

The March following you muſt cut off the ſtock about three inches above the bud, ſloping it that the wet may paſs off, and not enter the ſtock; to this part of the ſtock left above the bud, it is very proper to faſten the ſhoot which proceeds from the bud, and would be in danger of being blown out, if not prevented; but this muſt continue no longer than one year, after which it muſt be cut off cloſe above the bud, that the ſtock may be covered thereby.

The time for Inoculating is, from the middle of June until the middle of Auguſt, according to the forwardneſs of the ſeaſon, and the particular ſorts of trees to be propagated; but the time may be eaſily known, by trying the buds, whether they will come off well from the wood. However, the moſt general rule is, when you obſerve the buds formed at the extremity of the ſame year's ſhoots, which is a ſign of their having finiſhed their ſpring growth. The firſt ſort commonly inoculated is the Apricot, and the laſt the Orange-tree, which ſhould never be done until the middle of Auguſt; and in doing of this work, you ſhould always make choice of cloudy weather; for if it be done in the middle of the day, in very hot weather, the ſhoots will perſpire ſo faſt, as to leave the buds deſtitute of moiſture; nor ſhould you take off the cuttings from the trees long before they are uſed; but if you are obliged to fetch your cuttings from ſome diſtance, as it often happens, you ſhould then be provided with a tin box or caſe, having a ſocket about ten inches long, and a cover to the top, which muſt have five or ſix holes; in this ſocket you ſhould put as much water as will fill it about two or three inches high, and place your cuttings therein in an upright poſition, ſo that that part which was cut from the tree may be ſet in the water, and ſo faſten down the cover to keep out the air; and the holes in the cover will be ſufficient to let the perſpiration of theſe branches paſs off, which, if pent in, would be very hurtful to them; you muſt alſo be careful to carry it upright, that the water may not reach to the buds; for it is a very wrong practice in thoſe who throw their cuttings all over in water, which ſo ſaturates the buds with moiſture, that they have no attractive force left to imbibe the ſap of the ſtock, whereby they very often miſcarry.

But before I leave this head, I beg leave to obſerve, that though it is the ordinary practice to diveſt the bud of that part of the wood which was taken from the ſhoot with it; yet, in many ſorts of tender trees, it is beſt to preſerve a little wood to the bud, without which they often miſcarry. The not obſerving this, has occaſioned ſome people to imagine, that ſome ſorts of trees are not to be propagated by Inoculation; whereas, if they had performed it in this method, they might have ſucceeded, as I have ſeveral times experienced.

INTYBUS. See Cichorium.

INULA. Lin. Gen. Plant. 860. Enula. Cæſalp. Helenium. Raii Meth. 33. After. Tourn. Inſt. R. H. 481. tab. 274. Elecampane.

The Characters are,

It hath a radiated compound flower, with an imbricated empalement, compoſed of looſe, ſpreading, ſmall leaves, the outer being the broadeſt. The diſk, or middle of the flower, is compoſed of hermaphrodite florets, and the border, or ray of the female half florets, ſtretched out like a tongue. The hermaphrodite florets are funnel-ſhaped, erect, and cut into five ſegments at the top; theſe have five ſhort ſlender ſtamina, terminated by cylindrical ſummits, which coaleſce at the top: they have one long germen, crowned with down, ſupporting a ſlender ſtyle the length of the ſtamina, crowned by an upright bifid ſtigma. The female half florets have a narrow entire tongue, no ſtamina, but a long crowned germen with a hairy ſtyle, and an upright ſtigma. The germen in both flowers become a ſingle, narrow, four-cornered ſeed, crowned with a down, ſitting on a naked receptacle.

This genus of plants is ranged in the ſecond ſection of Linnæus's nineteenth claſs, intitled Syngeneſia Polygamia ſuperflua, which includes the plants with a compound flower, made up of hermaphrodite florets in the diſk, and female half florets for the rays, which are fruitful.

The Species are,

1. Inula (Helenium) foliis amplexicaulibus ovatis, rugoſis, ſubtus tomentoſis, calycum ſquamis ovatis. Amœn. Acad. 1. p. 410. Elecampane with oval rough leaves, which embrace the ſtalks, woolly on their under ſide, and the ſcales of the empalement oval. After omnium maximus, Helenium dictus. Tourn. Inſt. 483. The greateſt Starwort, called Elecampane.

2. Inula (Odora) foliis amplexicaulibus dentatis hirſutiſſimis radicalibus ovatis, caulinis lanceolatis caule paucifloro. Lin. Sp. Plant. 1236. Inula with hairy indented leaves embracing the ſtalks, thoſe at the bottom oval, but thoſe on the ſtalks ſpear-ſhaped, which have but few flowers. After luteus radice odorâ. C. B. P. 266. Yellow Starwort with a ſweet root.

3. Inula (Salicina) foliis ſeſſilibus lanceolatis recurvis ſerrato-ſcabris, floribus inferioribus altioribus, ramis ſub-angulatis. Amœn. Acad. 1. p. 410. Inula with ſpear-ſhaped, recurved, rough, ſawed leaves, ſitting cloſe to the ſtalks, and the under flowers growing taller than the upper, and angular branches. After montanus luteus, ſalicis glabro folio. C. B. P. 266. Yellow Mountain Starwort with a ſmooth Willow leaf.

4. Inula (Germanica) foliis ſeſſilibus lanceolatis recurvis, ſcabris, floribus ſubfaſciculatis. Lin. Sp. Plant. 883. Inula with ſpear-ſhaped recurved leaves ſitting cloſe to the ſtalks, which are rough, and flowers growing in cluſters. After Thuringiacus altiſſimus latifolius, montanus, flore luteo parvo. Jen. 181. Talleſt broad-leaved Mountain Starwort of Thuringia, with a ſmall yellow flower.

5. Inula (Crithmoides) foliis linearibus carnoſis tricuſpidatis. Lin. Sp. Plant. 883. Inula with narrow fleſhy leaves ending in three points. After maritimus flavus crithmum chryſanthemum dictus. Raii Syn. Ed. 3. p. 174. Yellow maritime Starwort, called Golden Samphire.

6. Inula (Montana) foliis lanceolatis hirſutis integerrimis, caule unifloro calyce brevi imbricato. Lin. Sp. Plant. 124. Inula with hairy, ſpear-ſhaped, entire leaves, one flower on a ſtalk, having a ſhort ſcaly cup. After montanus luteo magno flore. C. B. P. 267. Mountain Starwort with a large yellow flower.

7. Inula (Oculis Chriſti) foliis amplexicaulibus oblongis, integerrimis hirſutis, caule piloſo, corymboſo. Lin. Sp. Plant. 1237. Inula with oblong, entire, hairy leaves, and flowers growing in a corymbus. Conyza Pannonica lanuginoſa. C. B. P. 265. Hungarian woolly Fleabane.

8. Inula (Britanica) foliis amplexicaulibus lanceolatis, diſtinctis ſerratis, ſubtus villoſis, caule ramoſo villoſo erecto. Flor. Suec. 756. Inula with ſpear-ſhaped ſawed leaves embracing the ſtalk, hairy on their under ſide, and an erect branching ſtalk. After paluſtris luteus, folio longiore lanuginoſo. Tourn. Inſt. 483. Yellow Marſh Starwort with a longer woolly leaf.

9. Inula

9. INULA (*Hirta*) foliis feffilibus lanceolatis, recurvatis, fubferrato-fcabris, floribus inferioribus, altioribus, caule teretiufculo fubpilofo. Lin. Sp. 1239. *Inula with fpear-fhaped, recurved, rough leaves, fitting clofe to the ftalks, and the lower flowers rifing above the other.* Af- ter luteus, falicis folio hirfuto. C. B. P. 266. *Yellow After with a hairy Willow leaf.*

10. INULA (*Bifrons*) foliis oblongis decurrentibus den- ticulatis, floribus congeftis terminalibus fubfeffilibus. Lin. Sp. 1236. *Inula with oblong indented leaves run- ning along the ftalks, and flowers in clufters terminating the ftalks.* Conyza Pyrenaica, foliis primulæ veris. Par. Bat. 127.

11. INULA (*Squarofa*) foliis ovalibus lævibus reticulato- venofis fubcrenatis, calycibus fquarrofis. Lin. Sp. 1240. *Inula with fmooth oval leaves and netted veins, with rough empalements to the flowers.* After Conyzoides odora- tus luteus. Tourn. Inft. 483.

12. INULA (*Canarienfis*) foliis linearibus carnofis tricuf- pidatis, caule fruticofo. *Inula with narrow, flefhy, three-pointed leaves, and a fhrubby ftalk.* After Cana- rienfis frutefcens, folio tridentato craffa. Hort. Chelf. 26. *Shrubby Canary Starwort with a thick leaf, ending in three points.*

13. INULA (*Saturejaoides*) foliis linearibus hirfutis op- pofitis, pedunculatis nudis unifloris. *Inula with narrow hairy ftalks placed oppofite, and naked foot-ftalks, having one flower.* After faturejæ foliis conjugatis & pilofis, flore luteo. Houft. MSS. *Starwort with hairy Savoury leaves growing by pairs, and a yellow flower.*

14. INULA (*Mariana*) caule erecto hifpido, foliis lan- ceolatis afperis, floribus alaribus folitariis feffilibus, terminalibus umbellatis. *Inula with an erect prickly ftalk, fpear-fhaped rough leaves, flowers proceeding fingly from the fides of the ftalks, fitting clofe, and terminating in an umbel.* After luteus Marianus Saligneis brevio- ribus foliis hirfutis pubefcentibus, fummo caule ra- mofus. Pluk. Mant. 30. *Yellow Starwort of Maryland, with fhorter, fallow, hairy leaves, and the top of the ftalk branching.*

15. INULA (*Fruticofa*) foliis lanceolatis acutis, fubtus trinerviis, fquamis calycinis acutis caule fruticofa. *Inula with fpear-fhaped acute leaves, having three veins on their under fide, the fcales of the empalement fharp- pointed, and a fhrubby ftalk.*

The firft fort grows naturally in feveral parts of Eng- land, but it is alfo cultivated in gardens for the fake of the roots, which are ufed in medicine, and are ac- counted carminative, fudorific, and alexipharmic, of great fervice in fhortnefs of breath, coughs, ftuffing of the lungs, and infectious diftempers.

This hath a perennial root, which is thick, branching, and of a ftrong odour. The lower leaves are a foot long, and four inches broad in the middle, rough on their upper fide, but downy on their under. The ftalks rife about three feet high, and divide toward the top into feveral fmaller branches, garnifhed with oblong oval leaves, which are indented on their edges, and end in acute points. The flowers terminate the ftalks, each branch ending with one large, yellow, radiated flower, fitting in a fcaly empalement, whofe fcales are oval, and placed like the fcales on fifh over each other. The flowers are fucceeded by narrow four-cornered feeds crowned with down. It flowers in June and July, and the feeds ripen the latter end of Auguft.

This fort may be propagated by feeds, which fhould be fown in autumn foon after they are ripe; for if they are kept till the fpring, they feldom grow; but where they are permitted to fcatter, the plants will come up the following fpring without any care, and may be either tranfplanted the following autumn; or if they are defigned to remain, they fhould be hoed out to the diftance of ten inches, or a foot each way, and conftantly kept clean from weeds; thefe roots will be fit for ufe the fecond year.

But moft people propagate the plant by offsets, which, if carefully taken from the old roots, with a bud, or eye, to each, will take root very eafily; the beft time for this is the autumn, as foon as the leaves begin to

decay; thefe fhould be planted in rows about a foot afunder, and nine or ten inches diftance in the rows; the fpring following the ground muft be kept clean from weeds, and if in autumn it is flightly dug, it will promote the growth of the roots; thefe will be fit for ufe after two years growth, but the roots will abide many years, if they are permitted to ftand; how- ever, the young roots are preferable to thofe which are old and ftringy. It loves a gentle loamy foil, not too dry.

The fecond fort hath a perennial root, from which arife feveral ftalks, about two feet high. The leaves at bottom are oval, indented, and hairy; thofe above embrace the ftalks with their bafe. The ftalks are divided into feveral branches, garnifhed with a few fcattering yellow flowers. The root has a very fweet odour when broken. It flowers in July, but rarely ripens feeds here.

The third fort hath a perennial root, from which arifes many fpear-fhaped leaves, which are fmooth and recurved. The ftalks rife near two feet high; they are angular, and branch at the top into feveral foot-ftalks, each fuftaining one yellow radiated flower. It flowers in June, July, and Auguft, and the feeds ripen in September.

The fourth fort rifes with an upright ftalk between three and four feet high, with fpear-fhaped leaves, which are turned backward, indented on their edges, and rough on their upper fide. The flowers are col- lected in clofe bunches on the upper part of the ftalks; they are fmall and yellow. It grows on the Alps, and other mountainous parts of Europe. It flowers in June, and the feeds ripen in autumn.

The fifth fort grows naturally on the fea-coafts in ma- ny parts of England. I have feen it growing plenti- fully near Sheernefs, in the ifle of Sheepy, in Kent; this rifes with an upright ftalk a foot and a half high, garnifhed with flefhy fucculent leaves, which come out in clufters, and are about an inch and a quarter long, and one eighth of an inch broad, ending in three points. The flowers come out at the top of the ftalks in fmall umbels; they are yellow, and have a border of rays; this flowers in July, and the feeds ripen in autumn. The younger branches of this plant are frequently fold in the London markets for Samphire; but this is a great abufe, becaufe this plant has none of the warm aromatic tafte of the true Samphire.

The fixth fort grows naturally in Germany; this rifes with upright ftalks a foot and a half high, garnifhed with fpear-fhaped leaves which are covered with foft hairs, and are entire. The ftalks each fupport one large yellow flower, which appears in July, but rarely ripens feeds here.

The feventh fort hath a perennial root and an annual ftalk; this grows naturally in Hungary. The leaves are oblong and hairy; the ftalks branch at the top in form of a corymbus. The flowers are fmall, yellow, and are in clofe clufters; thefe appear in July, but feldom perfect feeds in England.

The eighth fort grows naturally in Auftria, Bohemia, and other parts of Germany; it hath a perennial root, and an annual ftalk which rifes near two feet high, garnifhed with fpear-fhaped woolly leaves, which are fawed, and clofely embrace the ftalks with their bafe. The upper part of the ftalk divides into two or three erect branches, or foot-ftalks, each fuftaining one pretty large deep yellow flower; thefe are in beauty in July, but feldom ripen feeds here.

The ninth fort grows naturally in the fouth of France, Spain, and Italy; this hath a perennial root, from whence arife feveral ftalks about one foot high; the lower leaves are fpear-fhaped and prickly; the upper half embrace the ftalks, which divide into feveral branches, each being terminated by one yellow flower, which appears in July, but feldom perfects feeds here.

The tenth fort rifes about a foot high, dividing into many branches, which are garnifhed by oval hairy leaves, which half embrace the ftalks with their bafe;

each

each of the branches is terminated by one large yellow flower, whofe empalement is compofed of oval fcales. It flowers in July and Auguft, but never perfects feeds in this country.

The eleventh fort grows naturally in Hungary; this rifes with fingle upright ftalks near two feet high, garnifhed with oval fpear-fhaped leaves, which are flightly indented on the edges, and fit clofe to the ftalks, which are hairy, and divide in form of a corymbus at the top. The flowers are pretty large, of a pale yellow colour, and appear in July, but are not fucceeded by feeds in this country.

The twelfth fort grows naturally in the Canary Iflands; this rifes with feveral fhrubby ftalks near four feet high, which divide into fmaller branches, garnifhed with clufters of narrow flefhy leaves, which are divided into three fegments at their points. The flowers come out on the fide of the branches at the top of the ftalks; they are fmall, and of a pale yellow colour, appearing in Auguft.

The fecond, third, fourth, fixth, feventh, eighth, and ninth forts are abiding plants, which will thrive and flower in the open air in England; they may be all propagated by parting of their roots. The beft time for doing of this is in autumn, at which time the plants may be removed; thefe may be intermixed with other flowering plants in the borders of large gardens, where they will make an agreeable variety during their continuance in flower. As thefe roots multiply pretty faft, they fhould be allowed room to fpread, therefore fhould not be planted nearer than two feet from other plants; and if they are removed every third year, it will be often enough, provided the ground between them is dug every winter, and, in fummer, if they are kept clean from weeds, they will require no other care.

As fome of thefe forts produce good feeds in England; they may be propagated by fowing of the feeds in the autumn, on a border of light earth expofed to the eaft, where the morning fun only is admitted; and in the fpring, when the plants appear, they fhould be kept clean from weeds till they are fit to remove, when they fhould be tranfplanted on a fhady border, fix inches afunder, obferving to fhade and water them till they have taken new root; and during the fummer feafon they fhould be kept clean from weeds, and in autumn they may be tranfplanted into the borders where they are to remain.

The tenth fort grows naturally in the fouth of France, and on the Pyrenean mountains. This hath a thick fibrous root, which is perennial, fending out many oblong indented leaves, whofe bafe runs along the ftalks from one joint to another: from the root arife three or four ftalks about two feet high, which divide each into three or four fmall branches, which are terminated by clufters of fmall yellow flowers, fitting clofe between the fmall leaves; thefe appear in June and July, and are fucceeded by narrow feeds, crowned with down, which ripen in the autumn.

It is propagated by feeds, which fhould be fown on a bed of light earth early in the fpring; in May the plants will appear, which fhould be kept clean from weeds till they are fit to tranfplant, when they fhould be planted in an eaft border, at about fix inches diftance each way, watering and fhading them till they have taken new root; after which they will require no other culture but to keep them clean from weeds till the autumn, when they fhould be planted where they are defigned to remain.

The eleventh fort grows naturally near Montpelier, and alfo in Italy; this hath a fibrous root, from which arife two or three erect ftalks about two feet high, garnifhed with fmooth oval leaves placed alternate, fitting clofe to the ftalks; thefe grow clofe to the ftalks, and are flender, and formed like net-work. The ftalks are terminated by one yellow flower inclofed in a rough fcaly empalement, and at the two joints of the ftalk immediately under the flower, come out fmall footftalks, with fmaller flowers than thofe on the top. This plant feldom continues above two or three years,

therefore young plants fhould be raifed from feeds to fucceed them. The feeds may be fown at the fame time, and in the fame manner as is directed for the tenth fort, and the plants afterward treated in the fame way.

The fifth fort grows naturally in the falt marfhes in feveral parts of England, which are flowed by the tides, therefore is feldom admitted into gardens. The roots of this are perennial, but the ftalks decay in autumn; and if any one has curiofity to keep a plant or two of it in their gardens, they may tranfplant it into a fhady border from the place of its natural growth, and, by keeping it moift in dry weather, it will thrive pretty well, but the ftalks will not rife fo high, nor will the leaves be near fo flefhy as in the falt marfhes.

The twelfth fort will not live abroad in the open air in England, during the winter feafon, fo muft be removed into fhelter in autumn, but fhould have as much free air as poffible at all times, when the weather is mild, otherwife it is apt to draw up weak. In cold weather the plants muft have very little water, for their ftalks and leaves being fucculent, they are very apt to rot with too much wet; in fummer they fhould be placed abroad with other hardy exotic plants in a fheltered fituation, where they will add to the variety, though they are plants of no great beauty, and feldom flower in England, unlefs the fummer is very warm. This is eafily propagated by cuttings, any time in fummer, which, if planted in a fhady border, will take root in a fhort time.

The thirteenth fort was difcovered by the late Dr. Houftoun, growing naturally at La Vera Cruz; this rifes with a fhrubby ftalk about two feet high, dividing into many fmaller branches, which are hairy, and garnifhed with narrow ftiff leaves placed oppofite, without foot-ftalks; from the edges of thefe arife long hairs, which are ftiff, and come out by pairs; at the end of the branches arife the naked foot-ftalks, which are four or five inches long, fuftaining one fmall, yellow, radiated flower.

This is propagated by cuttings during the fummer feafon, which muft planted on a bed of light earth, and fhaded till they have taken root; after which the plants muft be treated in the fame manner as other hardy exotics, fheltering them from froft in winter.

The fourteenth fort was fent me from Maryland, where it grows naturally; this rifes with a ftrong ftalk about a foot and a half high, which is pretty clofely fet with prickly hairs, and garnifhed with rough fpear-fhaped leaves, about three inches long, and near one inch broad in the middle: toward the upper part of the ftalk there are fingle flowers coming from the wings at each joint, and the ftalk is terminated by a clufter of fmall yellow flowers, difpofed in form of an umbel. This plant flowers here in Auguft, but has not as yet perfected feeds in England.

The fifteenth fort was difcovered growing naturally at Carthagena, by the late Dr. Houftoun; this rifes with a fhrubby ftalk to the height of ten or twelve feet, divided into feveral ligneous branches, garnifhed with fpear-fhaped leaves five inches long, and one inch and a half broad in the middle, and fmooth on their upper fide, but on their under have three longitudinal veins. The flowers are produced at the end of the branches, having very large fcaly empalements; they are as large as a fmall Sun-flower, of a pale yellow colour. This plant is too tender to live in the open air in England, fo muft be conftantly kept in the bark-ftove. It is propagated by feeds, which muft be procured from the country where it naturally grows, for it does not produce any here; thefe muft be fown upon a hot-bed, and when the plants are fit to remove, they fhould be each planted into a fmall pot filled with light earth, and plunged into a frefh hot-bed, treating them in the fame manner as other tender plants from the fame country.

JOHNSONIA. Dale. Callicarpa. Lin. Gen. Plant. 127. Spondylococus. Mitch. 20. This plant was fo titled by the late Dr. Dale, of South Carolina, in memory of Dr. Johnfon, who publifhed an edition of Gerard's Herbal, corrected and much improved.

The

The CHARACTERS are,

The flower hath an empalement of one leaf, cut at the brim into four short segments, which are erect. It hath one petal, which is tubulous, and divided into four parts at the brim, which spread open. It hath four slender summits, which are longer than the petal, terminated by oblong yellow summits. In the center is situated a roundish germen, supporting a slender style, crowned by a thick obtuse stigma. The germen afterward becomes a smooth globular berry, inclosing four hard oblong seeds.

Dr. Linnæus ranges this genus of plants in the first section of his fourth class, intitled Tetrandria Monogynia, which includes the plants whose flowers have four stamina and one style. As the seeds of this plant were sent me from Carolina by the late Dr. Dale with this title, in the year 1739, and with them the characters of the genus, which was before it was mentioned by Dr. Linnæus, I have continued it under the Doctor's title.

We have but one SPECIES of this genus, viz.

JOHNSONIA (*Americana*) floribus verticillatis sessilibus, foliis ovato lanceolatis oppositis, caule fruticoso. Dale. *Shrubby Johnsonia with oval spear-shaped leaves placed opposite, and flowers growing in whorls sitting close to the stalks.* Callicarpa. Act. Upsal. 1741. Mr. Catesby, in his History of Carolina, has figured it under the following title, Frutex baccifer verticillatus, foliis scabris latis dentatis & conjugatis, baccis purpureis densè congestis, vol. ii. p. 47.

This shrub grows plentifully in the woods near Charles-town, in South Carolina. It rises from four to six feet high, sending out many branches from the root, which are woolly when young, like those of the Wayfaring-tree, garnished with oval spear-shaped leaves placed opposite, standing on short foot-stalks; they are about three inches long, and one inch and a quarter broad in the middle, growing narrow at both ends, and a little indented on their edges, their surface rough, and a little hoary. The flowers come out in whorls round the stalks, sitting very close to the branches at the foot-stalks of the leaves; they are small, tubulous, cut into four obtuse segments at the top, which expand, and are of a deep purple colour; these are succeeded by soft succulent berries, which turn first to a bright red colour, but afterward change to a deep purple when ripe, and inclose four hard oblong seeds.

The seeds of this plant were sent me by Mr. Catesby, from Carolina, in 1724; and many of the plants were then raised in several curious gardens in England; most, if not all of them were afterward planted in the open air, where they flourished very well for some years, and several of the plants produced flowers in the Chelsea garden for four or five years, but these were not succeeded by fruit; and in the severe frost in 1740, they were most of them destroyed, as were also the young plants which were raised from Dr. Dale's seeds that year before, which were only sheltered under a frame; so that until the Doctor sent a fresh supply of seeds in 1744, there were scarce any of the plants living in the English gardens; but since then, there has been quantities of the seeds brought to England. This plant rises easily from seeds, if they are sown in a moderate hot-bed; the best way is to sow the seeds in pots, and plunge them into a tan-bed of a moderate warmth; and when the plants come up, and have obtained some strength, they should be gradually inured to the open air, into which they should be removed in June, and placed in a sheltered situation, where they may remain till autumn; during which time they must be kept clear from weeds, and gently refreshed with water in dry weather; but as these young plants are tender, they should be placed under a frame before the early frost comes on; for a frost in autumn will kill the tender part of their shoots, which often causes their stalks to decay most part of their length before the spring. During the winter season they should be screened from frost, but in mild weather they must enjoy the free air, otherwise their shoots will turn mouldy and decay. The following spring, just before the plants shoot, they should be carefully

turned out of the pots, so as not to break their roots; and part of them may be planted in small pots filled with light earth, and the others into a nursery-bed in a warm situation, at about four or five inches asunder; those in the pots should be plunged into a moderate hot-bed, which will forward their taking root, but afterward must be hardened to bear the open air as before; these plants in the pots should be sheltered under a frame in winter for three or four years, till they have obtained strength; then they may be turned out of the pots, and planted in a warm situation, where they will live in the open air in common winters; but in severe frost they are in danger of being killed, if they are not sheltered; therefore the surface of the ground about their roots should be covered with old tan to keep out the frost, and their tops covered with straw, Peas-haulm, or Fern, which will protect them.

Those plants in the beds should also be covered with mats, or Straw, in frosty weather, and after they have obtained strength, they may be transplanted into a warm situation, and treated every winter in the same manner as the other.

The leaves of this shrub were often used by Dr. Dale, in dropsical cases, with very good success. A particular account of the virtues of this, and many other plants of Carolina, was sent me with dried samples of each, by the Doctor, during the last war; but as the ships were taken in their passage, they were all lost, and the Doctor dying soon after, I could never recover them.

JONTHLASPI. See CLYPEOLA.

JONQUIL. See NARCISSUS.

IPOMOEA. Lin. Gen. Plant. 199. Quamoclit. Tourn. Inst. R. H. 116. tab. 39. *Quamoclit, or Scarlet Convolvulus.*

The CHARACTERS are,

The flower hath a small permanent empalement, cut into five parts at the top. The petal is funnel-shaped, having a long cylindrical tube, whose brim is five-pointed, spreading open flat. It hath five awl-shaped stamina, nearly the length of the petal, terminated by roundish summits. In the bottom of the tube is situated a round germen, supporting a slender style, crowned by a roundish stigma. The germen afterward becomes a roundish capsule with three cells, inclosing three oblong seeds.

This genus of plants is ranged in the first section of Linnæus's fifth class, intitled Pentandria Monogynia, which includes those plants whose flowers have five stamina and one style.

The SPECIES are.

1. IPOMOEA (*Quamoclit*) foliis pinnatifidis linearibus, floribus subsolitariis. Hort. Cliff. 60. *Ipomoea with very narrow many-pointed leaves, and solitary flowers.* Quamoclit foliis tenuiter incisis & pennatis. Tourn. Inst. R. H. 116. *Quamoclit with narrow, cut, winged leaves.*

2. IPOMOEA (*Coccinea*) foliis cordatis acuminatis, basi angulatis, pedunculis multifloris. Hort. Upsal. 39. *Ipomoea with heart-shaped pointed leaves, angular at the base, and many flowers on a stalk.* Quamoclit Americana folio hederæ flore coccineo. Com. Rar. Plant. 21. *American Quamoclit with an Ivy leaf and a scarlet flower, commonly called Scarlet Convolvulus.*

3. IPOMOEA (*Solanifolia*) foliis cordatis acutis integerrimis, floribus solitariis. Prod. Leyd. 430. *Ipomoea with acute, heart-shaped, entire leaves, and solitary flowers.* Quamoclit Americana solani folio, flore roseo. Plum. Cat. 3. *American Quamoclit with a Nightshade leaf, and a Rose-coloured flower.*

4. IPOMOEA (*Violacea*) foliis cordatis integerrimis, floribus confertis corollis indivisis. Sauv. Monsp. 114. *Ipomoea with heart-shaped entire leaves, flowers growing in clusters, and undivided petals.* Quamoclit foliis amplissimis cordiformibus. Plum. Cat. 4. *Quamoclit with large heart-shaped leaves.*

5. IPOMOEA (*Tuberosa*) foliis palmatis, lobis septenis lanceolatis integerrimis pedunculis trifloris. Hort. Upsal. 39. *Ipomoea with hand shaped leaves, composed of seven spear-shaped entire lobes, and foot-stalks having three flowers.* Convolvulus major heptaphyllus, flore luteo purpureo odorato. Sloan. Cat. 55. *Greater seven leaved Bind-*

Bindweed with a yellow sweet flower, called Spanish Arbour Vine.

6. IPOMOEA (*Triloba*) foliis trilobis cordatis, pedunculis trifloris. Lin. Sp. Plant. 161. *Ipomea with heart-shaped leaves having three lobes, and three flowers on a foot-stalk.* Convolvulus pentaphyllos minor, flore purpureo. Sloan. Cat. 55. *Smaller five-leaved Bindweed with a purple flower.*

7. IPOMOEA (*Hepaticaefolia*) foliis palmatis, floribus aggregatis. Flor. Zeyl. 79. *Ipomoea with hand-shaped leaves, and flowers growing in clusters.* Volubilis Zeylanica pes tigrinus dicta. Hort. Elth. 318. *Volubilis of Ceylon, called Tyger's-foot.*

8. IPOMOEA (*Digitata*) foliis digitatis glabris floribus sessilibus, caule laevi. Lin. Sp. Plant. 162. *Ipomoea with smooth hand-shaped leaves, whose lobes fit close, and a smooth stalk.* Convolvulus quinquefolius glaber Americanus. Pluk. Alm. 116. *Smooth five-leaved American Bindweed.*

The first sort grows naturally in both Indies; in the West-Indies it is called Sweet-William, and by some Indian Pink. It rises with a twining stalk seven or eight feet high, sending out many slender twining branches, which twist about any neighbouring plants for support; the leaves are winged, being composed of several pair of very fine narrow lobes, not thicker than fine sowing thread; they are about an inch long, of a deep green, and sometimes are by pairs opposite, and at others they are alternate; the flowers come out singly from the side of the stalks, standing upon slender foot-stalks about one inch long; they are funnel-shaped, having a tube an inch-long, which is narrow at bottom, but gradually widens to the top, which spreads open flat, with five corners or angles: they are of a most beautiful scarlet colour, so make a fine appearance. This is an annual plant in England, but whether it is so in its native place I cannot tell; for as the seeds fall to the ground, so there is a succession of young plants, which continue flowering great part of the year.

This is a tender plant, so will not thrive in the open air in England; it is propagated by seeds, which should be sown on a hot-bed in the spring; and as the plants will soon appear, they should be each transplanted into a small pot filled with light earth, before they twine about each other, for then it will be difficult to disengage them without breaking their tops. When they are potted, they should be plunged into a new hot-bed; and sticks placed down by each plant for their stalks to twine about; after they have taken new root, they should have a good share of air in warm weather to prevent their drawing up weak; and when they are advanced too high to remain under the frame, they should be removed into the tan-bed in the stove, where they should have support, for their branches will extend to a considerable height. They will begin to flower in June, and there will be a succession of flowers till the end of September, and the seeds will ripen well in this situation every autumn.

The second sort grows naturally in Carolina and the Bahama Islands; this is also an annual plant in England, but is not so tender as the former. It hath a twining stalk, which rises six or eight feet high, garnished with heart-shaped leaves ending in acute points, which are divided into angles at their base; the flowers come out from the side of the branches, upon slender foot-stalks, which support three or four flowers of the same form and size as the former, but are not so deep coloured. There is a variety of this with Orange-coloured flowers, but they do not differ in any other respect. If the seeds of this sort are sown on a hot-bed in the spring, and when the plants come up, if they are gradually hardened, and afterward transplanted into a warm border, in favourable seasons they will flower and produce good seeds; but most people raise the plants on a very gentle hot-bed, and transplant them afterward into another; by which method they are brought forward, so will perfect their seeds earlier.

The third sort is like the second, but the leaves have

no angles, and the flowers are of a Rose colour, each foot-stalk sustaining one flower. This may be treated in the same manner as the second sort.

The fourth sort grows naturally in the West-Indies, where it twines about any neighbouring support, and rises ten or twelve feet high, garnished with large heart-shaped entire leaves: the flowers come out from the side of the branches upon slender foot-stalks, in clusters; they are of a blue colour, and their brims are not angular as in the former species, but entire. This sort is propagated by feeds, which should be sown on a hot-bed in the spring, and the plants afterward treated in the same way as is before directed for the first sort, for it is too tender to thrive in the open air here.

The fifth sort is cultivated in most of the islands in the West-Indies, but is supposed to have been introduced there from the Spanish Main. These plants rise to a very great height, and send out many branches, so are planted to cover arbours for shade in the islands, from whence it had the appellation of Spanish Arbour Vine. The stalks of this plant are covered with a purple bark; they twine about any neighbouring support, sending out many side branches, so that one plant will cover an arbour of fifty feet long. The leaves are divided into seven lobes almost to the bottom; the flowers come out from the side of the stalks; they are large, funnel-shaped, of a bright yellow colour, and smell very sweet; these are succeeded by large roundish capsules with three cells, containing one large feed in each, which are of a dark colour.

This is a perennial plant, but too tender to thrive in the open air in England; the feeds of this must be sown upon a hot-bed in the spring, and when the plants come up, they must be transplanted into separate pots, and plunged into a fresh hot-bed; but as they will soon grow too tall to stand under a frame, they should be removed into the bark-stove, where they must be supported, otherwise they will twine about all the neighbouring plants. As these plants extend their shoots to a very great length, they require a tall stove, where they may have room to grow, without which they will never produce any flowers. I have had these plants several years, but have only seen one flower produced from them; for they grow so very large before they begin to have flowers, as that few of the stoves in England have height enough for their growth.

The sixth sort grows naturally in most of the islands in the West-Indies; this hath a twining stalk, which rises ten or twelve feet high, garnished with leaves divided into three lobes, which are heart-shaped; the foot-stalks arise from the side of the stalks, each sustaining three purple flowers. This is also tender, so the plants must be raised on a hot-bed in the spring, and afterward planted in separate pots, plunging them into another hot-bed, where they may remain till they reach the glasses, when they should be removed into a glass-case where they may have room, and be screened from the cold, but should have a large share of free air admitted to them in warm weather; with this treatment the plants will flower and produce ripe seeds.

The seventh sort grows naturally in India; this rises with a twining hairy stalk four or five feet high, garnished with hand-shaped leaves which are hairy, and divided at the bottom into several lobes; the flowers come out in clusters, inclosed in a five-cornered involucrum; they are of a purplish colour, but small, and open only in the evening, so make no figure. This is propagated by feeds, and requires the same treatment as the sixth sort.

The eighth sort grows naturally in the West-Indies; this hath a smooth twining stalk which rises four or five feet high, garnished with hand-shaped leaves having five lobes, which fit close to the stalks; the flowers come out from the side of the stalks upon short foot-stalks, which sustain two or three purple flowers; these are succeeded by round tricapsular feed-vessels; in each cell there is one brown feed.

This

This fort requires the fame treatment as the two former, with which it will produce flowers and perfect its feeds in England.

IRESINE. Lin. Gen. 1113. Amaranthus. Sloan. Cat. Jam. 49.

The CHARACTERS are,

It hath male and female flowers on different plants; the male flowers have an empalement compofed of two neat fmall leaves, and five erect, fmall, fpear-fhaped petals, and five nectarii fituated between the five erect ftamina, which are terminated by roundifh fummits; the female flowers on the other plants; have the flore empalement and corolla as the male, with an oval germen but no ftyle, crowned by two roundifh ftigma, the empalement afterward becomes an oval capfule, inclofing woolly feeds.

This genus is ranged in the fifth order of Linnæus's twenty-fecond clafs of plants, intitled Dicecia Pentandria, from their having male and female flowers on different plants, and the male flowers having five ftamina.

We know but one SPECIES of this genus, viz.

IRESINE (Celofioides.) Lin. Sp. 1456. Amaranthus panicula flavicante gracili holofericea. Sloan. Cat. Jam. 49. Amaranthus with flender yellowifh panicles of filky flowers.

This plant grows naturally in Jamaica, and moft of the other iflands in the Weft-Indies, from whence I have received the feeds. It is perennial; the ftalks are weak, fo require fupport; they rife ten or twelve feet high, having large knots at each joint, garnifhed with oval, fpear-fhaped, fmooth leaves. The ftalks are very diffufed, branching out on every fide; the flowers are produced on the top, in flender loofe panicles, covered with a filky down, of a pale yellow colour; thefe appear in July and Auguft, and in warm feafons the feeds will ripen in the autumn.

It is propagated by feeds, which fhould be fown upon a hot-bed in the fpring, and the plants fhould be afterward treated in the fame manner as hath been directed for the tender forts of Amaranthus, till they are grown too tall to remain in the frame, when they fhould be removed to the bark-ftove, plunging the pots into the tan-bed, and fupporting the branches of the plants with a trellis to prevent their falling on other plants; in this fituation they will produce flowers and feeds the fecond year, but the plants may be continued three or four years longer.

IRIS. Tourn. Inft. R. H. 358. tab. 186, 187, 188. Lin. Gen. Plant. 57. Flower-de-luce; in French, Flambe.

The CHARACTERS are,

The flowers are inclofed in fpatha (or fheaths) which are permanent; the flowers are divided into fix parts; the three outer petals are oblong, obtufe, and reflexed, the three inner are erect, and end in acute points; thefe all join at their bafe: they have three awl-fhaped ftamina, which lie upon the reflexed petals, and are terminated by oblong depreffed fummits. Under the flower is fituated an oblong germen, fupporting a flender ftyle, crowned by a large three-pointed ftigma; the germen afterward becomes an oblong angular capfule with three cells, filled with large feeds.

This genus of plants is ranged in the firft fection of Linnæus's third clafs, intitled Triandria Monogynia, which contains thofe plants whofe flowers have three ftamina and one ftyle.

The SPECIES are,

1. IRIS (Pfeudoacorus) corollis imberbibus, petalis interioribus ftigmate minoribus, foliis enfiformibus. Hort. Cliff. Iris with an unbearded flower, the inner petals fmaller than the ftigma, and fword-fhaped leaves. Iris paluftris lutea. Tabern. Icon. 643. Yellow Marfh Flower-de-luce.

2. IRIS (Squalens) corollis barbatis, caule foliis longiore multifloro. Hort. Cliff. 18. Iris with bearded flowers, and the ftalks longer than the leaves, having many flowers. This is the Iris vulgaris Germanica five fylveftris. C. B. P. 30. Common German, or wild Flower-de-luce.

3. IRIS (Aphylla) corollis barbatis, fcapo nudo longitudine foliorum multifloro. Prod. Leyd. 17. Iris with a bearded flower, and a naked ftalk the length of the leaves, with many flowers. Iris latifolia, caule aphyllo. C. B. P.

32. Broad-leaved Flower-de-luce, whofe ftalks are without leaves.

4. IRIS (Variegata) corollis barbatis, caule fubfoliofo longitudine foliorum multifloro. Prod. Leyd. 17. Iris with a bearded flower, and a leafy ftalk the length of the leaves, with many flowers. Iris latifolia pannonica, colore multiplici. C. B. P. 31. Broad-leaved Hungarian Flower-de-luce of many colours.

5. IRIS (Sufiana) corollis barbatis, caule foliis longiore unifloro. Hort. Cliff. 18. Iris with a bearded flower, and a ftalk longer than the leaves, having one flower. Iris Sufiana, flore maximo ex-albo nigricante. C. B. P. 31. Flower-de-luce with a very large flower of a black and white colour, commonly called Chalcedonian Iris.

6. IRIS (Biflora) corollis barbatis, caule foliis breviore trifloro. Hort. Upfal. 17. Iris with a bearded flower, and a ftalk fhorter than the leaves, with three flowers. Iris humilis major, faturatè purpurea biflora. Tourn. Inft. 361. Greater Dwarf Flower-de-luce of a dark purple colour, and having two flowers on each ftalk.

7. IRIS (Pumila) corollis barbatis, caule foliis breviore unifloro. Hort. Cliff. 38. Iris with a bearded flower, and a ftalk fhorter than the leaves, with one flower. Iris humilis minor, flore purpureo. Tourn. Inft. 361. Smaller Dwarf Flower-de-luce with a purple flower.

8. IRIS (Germanica) corollis barbatis, caule foliis longiore multifloro, floribus inferioribus pedunculatis. Lin. Sp. 55. Iris with a bearded flower, a ftalk longer than the leaves with many flowers, and the lower flowers on foot-ftalks. Iris Afiatica cærulea polyanthos. C. B. P. Blue Afiatic Flower-de-luce with many flowers, called greater Dalmatian Iris.

9. IRIS (Orientalis) corollis barbatis, germinibus trigonis, foliis enfiformibus longiffimis caule foliis longiore bifloro. Pluk. 154. Iris with a bearded flower, a three-cornered germen, very long fword-fhaped leaves, and a ftalk longer than the leaves, with two flowers.

10. IRIS (Graminea) corollis imberbibus, germinibus fexangularibus, caule ancipiti, foliis linearibus. Hort. Cliff. 19. Iris with flowers having no beards, a fix-cornered germen, a ftalk having flowers on both fides, and narrow leaves. Iris anguftifolia prunum redolens minor. C. B. P. 33. Smaller narrow-leaved Flower-de-luce fmelling like Plums.

11. IRIS (Maritima) corollis imberbibus, caule foliis breviore trifloro, foliis lineari-enfiformibus. Iris whofe flowers are not bearded, the ftalk fhorter than the leaves, having three flowers, and narrow fword-fhaped leaves. Iris anguftifolia maritima major. C. B. P. 33. Greater narrow-leaved maritime Flower-de-luce.

12. IRIS (Anguftifolia) corollis imberbibus, caule foliis æqualibus multifloro, fpatha majoribus erectis. Iris whofe flowers have no beards, the ftalks equal in length with the leaves, having many flowers which are larger and more erect than the fpatha. Iris anguftifolia, maritima minor. C. B. P. Smaller narrow-leaved maritime Flower-de-luce.

13. IRIS (Bicolor) corollis imberbibus, caule foliis longiore multifloro, germinibus fexangularibus, foliis linearibus. Iris whofe flowers have no beards, the ftalks longer than the leaves, with many flowers, a fix-cornered germen, and very narrow leaves. Iris anguftifolia, bicolor. C. B. P. 33. Narrow-leaved Flower-de-luce with two colours.

14. IRIS (Spuria) corollis imberbibus, germinibus fexangularibus, caule tereti, foliis fublinearibus. Hort. Cliff. 19. Iris whofe flowers have no beards, with a fix-cornered germen, a taper ftalk, and very narrow leaves. Iris pratenfis anguftifolia, folio fœtido. C. B. P. 32. Narrow-leaved Meadow Flower-de-luce, with a ftinking leaf.

15. IRIS (Sativa) corollis imberbibus, fpathâ bifoliâ, caule foliofo longitudine foliorum, pedunculis longioribus. Iris with flowers having no beards, a fheath containing two leaves, a leafy ftalk the length of the leaves, and longer foot-ftalks to the flowers. Iris fativa lutea. C. B. P. 32. Yellow Garden Flower-de-luce.

16. IRIS (Picta) corollis imberbibus, caule longitudine foliorum multifloro, foliis enfiformibus. Iris with an unbearded flower, a ftalk the length of the leaves, with

3   many

many flowers, and sword-shaped leaves. Iris humilis minor, flore picto. Tourn. Inst. 362. *Lesser Dwarf Flower-de-luce with a painted flower.*

17. IRIS (*Verna*) corollis imberbibus, caule unifloro foliis breviore, radice fibrosâ. Flor. Virg. 10. *Iris with an unbearded flower, a stalk shorter than the leaves, with one flower, and a fibrous root.* Iris Virginiana pumila five chamæiris verna angustifolia, flore purpuro-cæruleo odorato. Pluk. Alm. 196. *Dwarf Spring Virginia Flower-de-luce, with a narrow leaf, and a purple blue sweet smelling flower.*

18. IRIS (*Versicolor*) corollis imberbibus, germinibus subtrigonis, caule tereti, foliis ensiformibus. Lin. Sp. Plant. 39. *Iris with an unbearded flower, a three-cornered germen, a taper stalk, and sword-shaped leaves.* Iris Americana versicolor stylo crenato. Dill. Hort. Elth. 188. *Party-coloured American Flower-de-luce, with a crenated style.*

19. IRIS (*Fœtidissima*) corollis imberbibus petalis interioribus patentissimis, caule uniangulato foliis ensiformibus. Hort. Cliff. 19. *Iris with an unbearded flower, the inner petals spreading, a stalk with one angle, and sword-shaped leaves.* Iris fœtidissima, seu Xyris. Tourn. Inst. 360. *Most stinking Flower-de-luce, or Xyris, called Stinking Gladwyn.*

20. IRIS (*Siberica*) corollis imberbibus, germinibus trigonis, caule tereti, foliis linearibus. Lin. Hort. Cliff. 19. *Iris with an unbearded flower, a three-cornered germen, a taper stalk, and narrow leaves.* Iris pratensis, angustifolia non fœtida altior. C. B. P. 32. *Taller narrow-leaved Meadow Flower-de-luce, not stinking.*

21. IRIS (*Tuberosa*) corollis imberbibus, foliis tetragonis. Vir. Cliff. 6. *Iris with an unbearded flower and four-cornered leaves.* Hermodactylus folio quadrangulo. Tourn. Cor. 50. *Hermodactyle with a four-cornered leaf.*

22. IRIS (*Florentina*) corollis barbatis, caule foliis altiore subbifloro floribus sessilibus. Lin. Sp. 55. *Iris with a bearded corolla, stalks taller than the leaves, having two sessile flowers.* Iris alba Florentina. C. B. P. 31. *White Florentine Iris.*

23. IRIS (*Sambucina*) corollis barbatis, caule foliis altiore multifloro, petalis deflexis planis, erectis emarginatis. Lin. Sp. 55. *Iris with a bearded corolla, stalks taller than the leaves, having many flowers whose petals are deflexed, and the upright are indented.* Iris latifolia Germanica, sambuci odore. C. B. P. 31.

The first sort grows naturally in ditches and standing waters in most parts of England; this is titled in the Pharmacopeia, Acorus adulterinus, or Pseudo acorus. *Bastard Accorus.* The roots of this are pretty thick, fleshy, and spread every way near the surface of the ground; the leaves are sword-shaped, very long, of a deep green colour, and not so stiff as those of the Garden Iris; the stalks rise from two to three feet high, toward the top of which grow three or four flowers one above another, which gradually succeed each other; they are shaped like the ordinary Flower-de-luce, but the three inner petals are less than the stigmas, so they want the three upright petals which are termed standards. These appear in June, and are succeeded by large three-cornered capsules, containing three rows of flat seeds.

This sort is not cultivated in gardens, but being an officinal plant, it is here mentioned to introduce the other.

The second sort grows naturally in Germany, but has been long cultivated in the English gardens for ornament; the roots of this are very thick, fleshy, and divided into joints, spreading just under the surface of the ground; they are of a brownish colour on their outside, but white within; the leaves arise in clusters, embracing each other at their base, but spread asunder upward in form of wings; they are a foot and a half long, and two inches broad, having sharp edges, ending in points like swords; the stalks between these, which are a little longer than the leaves, having at each joint one leaf without a foot-stalk; these diminish in their size upward; the stalks divide into three branches, each of which produce two or three flowers one above another at distances, each inclosed in a sheath; they have three large Violet-coloured petals which turn backward, and are called falls; these have beards near an inch long on their midrib toward their base, and have a short arched petal which cover the beard, with three broad erect petals of the same colour, called standards; the stamina lie upon the reflexed petals. Under each flower is situated an oblong germen, which turns to a large three-cornered capsule with three cells, filled with large compressed seeds. This flowers in June, and the seeds ripen in August.

There is a variety of this with blue standards and purple falls, which is titled Iris hortensis latifolia, by Caspar Bauhin; and one with pale purple standards, another with white, and a third with a smaller flower, but these are accidental varieties which have come from seeds.

The third sort has broader leaves than the last, the stalks have no leaves upon them, and are equal in length with the leaves; they have three or four large bright purple flowers, which stand above each other, having purplish sheaths or hoods; the three bending petals or falls are striped with white, from the base to the end of the beard; the flowers are succeeded by large blunt triangular capsules with three cells, filled with compressed seeds. It flowers the latter end of May, and the seeds ripen the beginning of August.

The fourth sort grows naturally in Hungary; the leaves of this are like those of the second sort, but are of a darker green; the stalks rise as tall as the leaves, and toward the bottom are garnished with one leaf at each joint, whose base embrace the stalks; the upper part is naked, and branches into three, each having two or three flowers above one another; the three upright petals or standards are yellow, and the bending petals or falls are variegated with purple stripes. This flowers in June, but is rarely succeeded by seeds in England.

The fifth sort grows naturally near Constantinople, and in other parts of the east. The leaves of this sort are not so broad as those of the second, and are of a grayish colour; the stalks rise two feet and a half high, supporting one very large flower; the three upright petals are almost as broad as a hand, but very thin, of mixed black and white stripes; the three bending petals or falls are of a darker colour, from whence some gardeners have called it the Mourning Iris. This flowers the latter end of May, or the beginning of June, but never has any seeds in England.

The sixth sort hath broad leaves like those of the second sort, but shorter; the stalks rise nine or ten inches high, branching into two or three at the top, each sustaining two deep purple flowers. This flowers in May, but is not succeeded by seeds in England.

The seventh sort hath narrower and shorter leaves than the former; the stalks are shorter than the leaves, and support one flower on the top, of a light purple colour. This flowers the beginning of May, but rarely produces seeds in this country. There are two or three varieties of this, which differ in the colour of their flowers.

The eighth sort hath the largest leaves of any of the Flower-de-luce, they are of a grayish colour and spread wide, embracing each other at their base, where they are purplish. The stalks rise near four feet high, and divide into several branches, each supporting three or four flowers above each other at distances, covered with a thin sheath; the three bending petals or falls, are of a faint purple inclining to blue, with purple veins running lengthways; the beard is yellow, and the three erect petals or standards are of a bright blue, with some faint purple stripes, the flowers have an agreeable scent. They appear the latter end of June, but are seldom succeeded by seeds in England.

The seeds of the ninth sort were brought from Carniola, by the Right Rev. Dr. Pocock, Bishop of Ossory, who found the plants growing there naturally: these were sown in the Chelsea garden, where they succeeded very well, and the plants have been since communicated to many curious gardens in Europe.

This

This plant hath a thick fleshy root, divided into many knots or tubers, which spread and multiply in the ground; these send out many strong, thick, fleshy fibres, which strike deep in the earth, putting out several smaller fibres from their sides. From these roots arise clusters of flat sword-shaped leaves of a deep green colour, which are more than three feet long, and little more than one inch broad in the broadest part, ending in points; these leaves are connected together at their base into several heads or bundles, wrapping over each other; and between these arise the flower-stalks, which grow four feet high and are jointed, having very long spathæ or sheaths at each of the upper joints, which include the flowers. These stalks generally sustain two flowers, one coming out of each sheath or spatha; these are permanent, and when the flowers are past, closely cover the seed-vessel. The flowers are divided into nine leaves, three of these stand erect, which are white, and six turn down, which are joined together at their base, the lower spreading out into a broad, obtuse, reflexed fall, having a beard which is of a bright yellow colour; the upper segment is arched over the lower, so as to form a sort of lip, which is reflexed backward; under these is situated an oblong three-cornered germen, which afterward becomes an oblong, swollen, three-cornered seed-vessel, ending in a long point, which opens into three longitudinal cells, in which the seeds are ranged; these are angular and compressed. This plant flowers the latter end of June, or the beginning of July, and the seeds ripen in the autumn. It is very hardy, and thrives well in the open air without any protection. The leaves decay to the root in the autumn, and new ones arise in the spring. The roots also propagate very fast, when they are in a light moist soil, so that it may soon be had in plenty, without waiting for plants from seeds.

The tenth sort grows naturally in Austria; this hath narrow, flat, Grass-like leaves, about a foot long, of a light green colour; between these arise the stalks about six inches high, having two narrow green leaves, which are much longer than the stalks; these stalks sustain two or three flowers, which are smaller than any of the former species, the petals have no beards, but have a broad yellow line adorned with purple stripes; the three falls are of a light purple colour striped with blue, and have a convex ridge running longitudinally; the other are of a reddish purple variegated with violet; they have a scent like fresh Plums. It flowers in July, and is succeeded by seed-vessels which are short, having three borders or wings running lengthways, opening in three cells, which are filled with angular seeds, which ripen in September.

The eleventh sort grows naturally near the sea, in the south of France, and in Italy. This hath narrow sword-shaped leaves, little more than a foot long, of a deep green colour; the stalks do not rise so tall as the leaves; they sustain at the top two or three flowers which stand near together; they are of a bright purple colour with very deep falls, and the three standards are blue; the bending petals have no beards, but instead of that white broad stripes through the middle. This flowers in July, and the seeds ripen in September.

The twelfth sort hath narrower leaves than the former, but of the same deep green colour; the stalks do not rise higher than the leaves, and support two or three flowers, which have long permanent empalements standing erect, which cover the seed-vessel till the seeds are ripe; the flowers are smaller, and of a paler colour than those of the eleventh sort.

The thirteenth sort has very narrow, long, Grass-like leaves, of a light green; the stalks rise two feet and a half high, sustaining three or four flowers above each other, which have blue falls, and purple standards striped with pale blue lines. This flowers in July, and the seeds ripen at Michaelmas.

The fourteenth sort grows naturally in Germany; this hath leaves like those of the eleventh sort, which, when broken, have a disagreeable scent; but this is accidental, and not common to all the plants; the stalks of this are taper, and rise a little above the leaves, and sustain three or four flowers one above another, which have light blue standards, and purple variegated falls without beards; instead of which, they have a broad white line in the middle; these are succeeded by short thick capsules, which have scarce any angles, opening in three cells, which are filled with angular seeds. It flowers in July, and the seeds ripen in September.

The fifteenth sort has narrower leaves than those of the second, of a pale green colour, and not so stiff; the stalks are equal in height with the leaves, and branch out on both sides with long foot-stalks, each sustaining one pretty large yellow flower, inclosed in a long two-leaved sheath; at each joint where the foot-stalks come out there is a single leaf, which embraces the stalks with their base. This flowers in June, but rarely produces seeds in this country.

There are two varieties of this sort, one with a sulphur-coloured, and the other with a variegated flower, which are supposed to be only varieties which have been accidentally produced from seeds.

The sixteenth sort hath broad sword-shaped leaves about eight inches long; the stalks rise about the same height with the leaves, and divide into two or three foot-stalks, each sustaining two or three flowers one above another, which have yellow standards, and the falls are variegated with dark stripes. This flowers in June, but does not produce seeds here.

The seventeenth sort grows naturally in North America; this hath tufted fibrous roots, from which arise many Grass-like leaves about nine inches long; from between these come out the stalks, which are shorter than the leaves, supporting one purple flower with blue standards. This sort flowers in May, but seldom produces seeds in England.

The eighteenth sort grows also in North America; this hath narrow sword-shaped leaves about a foot long, of a light green colour; the stalks rise a little above the leaves, they are taper, and support two or three flowers one above another; the standards are of a light blue, and the falls are purple variegated, with a broad white line instead of a beard through the middle. The germen, which is situated under the flower, is three-cornered below, but taper toward the top. This flowers in June, and often produces seeds here.

The nineteenth sort grows naturally in moist places in many parts of England, so is seldom admitted into gardens. This hath thick tufted fibrous roots; the leaves are of a Grass-green, sword-shaped, and when broken emit a strong odour, not much unlike that of hot roast beef at the first scent, but if smelt too close, becomes disagreeable. It is generally called stinking Gladwyn in England; the stalks rise about the same height with the leaves, supporting two small flowers, of a purple colour, variegated. It flowers in June, and the seeds ripen in autumn.

The twentieth sort grows naturally in Austria and Bohemia; this hath narrow sword-shaped leaves near a foot and a half long, of a dark green colour; the flower-stalks rise above the leaves, and support two or three flowers with light blue standards, and deep blue falls, with a broad stripe of white, instead of the beard. This flowers in July, and the seeds ripen in September.

There are several varieties of these flag or sword-leaved Irises, which chiefly differ in the colour of their flowers, so are not to be regarded as distinct species; those which are here enumerated are supposed to be specifically different, great part of them I have cultivated by seeds, and found them constantly produce the same as the parent plants.

All these sorts are generally propagated by parting of their roots, which most of them multiply fast enough. The best time to remove and part the roots is in autumn, that they may get good root before the spring, otherwise they will not flower strong the following summer. All those sorts which spread much;

'at their roots fhould be tranfplanted every other year, to keep them within bounds, otherwife they will fpread fo much as to become troublefome, efpecially if they are planted near other flowers; indeed, the large growing kinds are moft of them too fpreading for the flower-garden, fo are only fit to fill up the fpaces between trees and fhrubs in large plantations, where they will have a good effect during the time of their flowering.

The fifth, fixth, feventh, tenth, eleventh, fixteenth, feventeenth and eighteenth forts, grow in lefs compafs, fo may be admitted into the large borders, or in clumps of flowers in the pleafure-garden, where they will add to the variety. The fifth fort fhould have a warmer fituation, being a little tender, but all the other forts will grow in almoft any foil or fituation; thefe may all be propagated by feeds, which fhould be fown foon after they are ripe, then the plants will come up the following fpring; but if the feeds are fown in the fpring, they will lie a year in the ground before they vegetate: when the plants come up they muft be kept clean from weeds, and the following autumn fhould be tranfplanted into beds at ten inches or a foot diftance, where they may remain till they flower, which will be the fecond fummer after tranfplanting; but as moft of the forts are fo eafily propagated by their roots, few people care to wait for feedling plants, unlefs of thofe forts which are fcarce.

The twenty-firft fort grows naturally in the iflands of the Archipelago; this hath a tuberous knobbed root, from which arife five or fix long, narrow, four-cornered leaves, between which arife the ftalk, which fupports one flower, fhaped like thofe of the Iris, but fmall, and of a dark purple colour. This flowers in April, but does not produce feeds in England. It is propagated by the roots, which fend out offsets; thefe may be taken up and tranfplanted when their leaves decay, but fhould not be kept too long out of the ground. If thefe are planted in a deep loofe foil, the roots will run down, and be loft in a few years where they are not difturbed, fo they fhould be annually tranfplanted, and have a fhallow foil; they are hardy in refpect to cold, and require no farther care but to keep them clean from weeds.

The twenty-fecond fort grows naturally in the warm parts of Europe, but is hardy enough to thrive in the open air in England; the leaves of this fort are broad, of a pale green colour; the flower-ftalks rife taller than the leaves, fupporting one or two white flowers which fit clofe to the ftalks. The roots of this are ufed in medicine, and is ufually called Sweet Iris.

The twenty-third fort hath broad leaves, of a deeper green than thofe of the laft fort. The ftalks rife much above the leaves, each having four or five flowers, which have a yellow ground, variegated with dark brown ftripes, and have a fcent like Elder; the two forts flower the latter end of May, or beginning of June.

They are fo hardy as to thrive as well as the fecond fort in the open air in this country, and may be propagated by parting of their roots, or by feeds, in the fame way as is directed for that fort.

IRIS bulbofa. } See XIPHIUM.
IRIS Perfica. }

ISATIS. Tourn. Inft. R. H. 211. tab. 100. Lin. Gen. Plant. 738. Woad; in French, *Paftel*.

The CHARACTERS are,

The empalement of the flower is compofed of four oval coloured leaves, which fpread open and fall away. The flower hath four oblong petals, placed in form of a crofs, which are narrow at their bafe, but broad and obtufe at their ends. It hath fix ftamina, four of which are as long as the petals, the other two are fhorter; thefe are terminated by oblong lateral fummits. It has an oblong comprefed germen, the length of the two fhorter ftamina, crowned by an obtufe ftigma. The germen becomes an oblong comprefed pod with one cell, opening with two valves, inclofing one oval comprefed feed in the center.

This genus of plants is ranged in the fecond fection of Linnæus's fifteenth clafs, intitled Tetradynamia

Siliquofa, which includes the plants whofe flowers have four long and two fhorter ftamina, and their feeds in pods.

The SPECIES are,

1. ISATIS (*Tinctoria*) foliis radicalibus oblongo-ovatis obtufis integerrimis, caulinis fagittatis filiculis oblongis. *Woad with oblong, oval, blunt, entire leaves at bottom, but thofe on the ftalks arrow-pointed, and oblong pods.* Ifatis fativa vel latifolia. C. B. P. 113. *Broadleaved cultivated Woad.*

2. ISATIS (*Dalmatica*) foliis radicalibus lanceolatis crenatis, caulinis lineari-fagittatis, filiculis brevioribus emarginatis. *Woad with fpear-fhaped lower leaves which are flightly crenated, thofe on the ftalks very narrow and arrow-pointed, and fhorter indented pods.* Ifatis Dalmatica major. Bobart. *Greater Woad of Dalmatia.*

3. ISATIS (*Lufitanica*) foliis radicalibus crenatis, caulinis fagittatis, pedunculis fubtomentofis. Lin. Sp. 936. *Woad with crenated lower leaves, thofe on the ftalks halbert-fhaped, and the foot-ftalks of the flowers woolly.* Ifatis fylveftris, minor Lufitanica. H. L. App. *Smaller wild Portugal Woad.*

4. ISATIS (*Ægyptiaca*) foliis omnibus dentatis. Lin. Sp. 937. *Woad whofe leaves are all indented.*

The firft fort is cultivated in feveral parts of England for the purpofes of dyeing, this being ufed as a foundation for many of the dark colours.

This is a commodity well worth propagating in all places where the land is fuitable for it, which muft be a pretty ftrong foil, but not too moift.

The plant is biennial, in which it differs from the third and fourth fort, which are annual. The lower leaves of this are of an oblong oval figure, and pretty thick confiftence, when growing in a proper foil; they are narrow at their bafe, but broad above, and end in obtufe roundifh points, entire on their edges, and of a lucid green. The ftalks rife near four feet high, dividing into feveral branches, garnifhed with arrow-fhaped leaves, fitting clofe to the ftalks; the ends of the branches are terminated by fmall yellow flowers, in very clofe clufters, which are compofed of four fmall petals, placed in form of a crofs; thefe are fucceeded by pods fhaped like a bird's tongue, half an inch long, and one eighth of an inch broad, which when ripe turn black, and open with two valves, having one cell, in which is fituated a fingle feed. It flowers in July, and the feeds ripen the beginning of September.

The third fort has been fuppofed to be the fame fpecies as the firft, only differing by culture; but I have propagated both forts more than forty years, and have not found either of them alter; there. are alfo very effential differences between the two plants, particularly in the fhape of the under leaves, which in the wild fort are narrow and fpear-fhaped, and thofe on the ftalks are not more than half the breadth of thofe of the cultivated Woad. The ftalks do not branch fo much, and the pods are narrower than thofe of the other fort, nor do the roots abide fo long, for they generally die the fame year.

The fecond fort grows naturally in Dalmatia; this is a biennial plant; the lower leaves are fpear-fhaped, and crenated on their edges, but thofe on the ftalks are very narrow and arrow-pointed. The ftalks branch more than thofe of the firft fort, and rife higher. The flowers are larger, and of a brighter yellow colour. The feed-veffels are fhorter, and broader at their ends, which are indented. Thefe plants all flower in July, and their feeds ripen in September.

The fourth fort grows naturally in Egypt, and is an annual plant, which is too tender to thrive in the open air in England, therefore the feeds fhould be fown on a hot-bed in the fpring; and when the plants are fit to remove they muft be tranfplanted on a frefh hot-bed to bring them forward, but as foon as they have taken new root, they fhould have a large fhare of frefh air admitted to them daily, to prevent their being drawn up weak. In this bed they may remain five or fix weeks, by which time they will be fit to tranfplant into pots, which fhould be carefully performed, not

to

to let the earth fall from their roots; the pots should also be plunged into a moderate hot-bed, giving the plants plenty of air at all times when the weather will permit, and supporting their stalks, which will otherwise trail on the ground; with this management the plants will flower in June, and ripen their seeds in September.

The three last sorts are not cultivated for use, so are only preserved in botanic gardens for the sake of variety; the second and third sorts are propagated by seeds, which should be sown in autumn; and when the plants come up, they must be thinned, leaving them six inches apart; afterward they must be kept clean from weeds: the summer following they will flower and produce ripe seeds, after which these sorts soon decay; the roots of the first sort will live another year. The first sort which is propagated for use, is sown upon fresh land which is in good heart, for which the cultivators of Woad pay a large rent; they generally chuse to have their land situated near great towns, where there is plenty of dressing, but they never stay long on the same spot, for the best ground will not admit of being sown with Woad more than twice; for if it is oftener repeated, the crop seldom pays the charges of culture, &c.

Those who cultivate this commodity, have gangs of people, who have been bred to this employment, so that whole families travel about from place to place, wherever their principal fixes on land for the purpose; but these people go on in one track, just as their predecessors taught them; nor have their principals deviated much from the practice of their ancestors, so that there is a large field for improvement, if any of the cultivators of Woad were persons of genius, and could be prevailed on to introduce the garden culture so far as it may be adapted to this plant; this I know from experience, having made numbers of trials in the culture of this plant, therefore I shall insert them here for the benefit of those who may have ingenuity enough to strike out of the old beaten track.

As the goodness of Woad consists in the size and fatness of the leaves, the only method to obtain this, is by sowing the seed upon ground at a proper season, and allow the plants proper room to grow, as also to keep them clean from weeds; which, if permitted to grow, will rob the plants of their nourishment. The method practised by some of the most skilful kitchen-gardeners in the culture of Spinach, would be a great improvement to this plant, for some of them have improved the round-leaved Spinach so much by culture, as to have the leaves more than six times the size they were formerly; and their fatness has been in the same proportion, upon the same land, which has been effected by thinning of the plants when young, and keeping the ground constantly clean from weeds; but to return to the culture of Woad.

After having made choice of a proper spot of land, which should not be too light and sandy, nor over stiff and moist, but rather a gentle hazel loam, whose parts will easily separate: the next is to plough this up just before winter, laying it in narrow high ridges, that the frost may penetrate through the ridges, to mellow and soften the clods; then in the spring plough it again crossway, laying it again in narrow ridges; after it has lain some time in this manner, and the weeds begin to grow, it should be well harrowed to destroy them; this should be twice repeated while the weeds are young, and if there are any roots of large perennial weeds, they must be harrowed out, and carried off the ground. In June the ground should be a third time ploughed, when the furrows should be narrow, and the ground stirred as deep as the plough will go, that the parts may be as well separated as possible; and when the weeds appear again, the ground should be well harrowed to destroy them. Toward the end of July, or the beginning of August, it should be ploughed the last time, when the land should be laid smooth, and when there is a prospect of showers, the

ground must be harrowed to receive the seeds, which should be sown either in rows with the drill plough, or in broad-cast, after the common method; but it will be proper to steep the seeds one night in water before they are sown, which will prepare them for vegetation: if the seeds are sown in drills with a plough, they will be covered by an instrument fixed to the plough for that purpose; but those which are sown broad-cast in the common way, must be well harrowed in. If the seeds are good and the season favourable, the plants will appear in a fortnight, and in a month or five weeks after will be fit to hoe; for the sooner this is performed when the plants are distinguishable, the better they will thrive, and the weeds being then young, will be soon destroyed. The method of hoeing these plants is the same as for Turneps, with this difference only, that these plants need not be thinned so much; for at the first hoeing, if they are separated to the distance of three or four inches, and at the last to six inches, it will be space enough for the growth of the plants; if this is carefully performed, and in dry weather, most of the weeds will be destroyed: but as some of them may escape in this operation, and young weeds will arise, so the ground should be a second time hoed in October, always chusing a dry time for this work; at this second operation, the plants should be singled out to the distance they are to remain. After this the ground will be clean from weeds till the spring, when young weeds will come up, therefore about a fortnight in April will be a good time to hoe the ground again, when the weeds will be young, so may be performed in less than half the time it would require if the weeds were permitted to grow large, and the sun and wind will much sooner kill them; this hoeing will also stir the surface of the ground, and greatly promote the growth of the plants; if it is performed in dry weather, the ground will be clean till the first crop of Woad is gathered, after which it must be again well cleaned; if this is carefully repeated, after the gathering of each crop, the land will always lie clean, and the plants will thrive the better. The expence of the first hoeing will be about six shillings per acre; and for the after-hoeings half that price will be sufficient, provided they are performed when the weeds are young; for if they are suffered to grow large, it will require more labour, nor can it be so well performed; therefore it is not only the best husbandry to do this work soon, but it will be found the cheapest method; for the least number of men will hoe a field of ten acres three times, when it is performed while the weeds are young, as is required to hoe it twice only, because the weeds have longer time to grow between the operations. If the land in which the seed is sown, should have been in culture before for other crops, so not in good heart, it will require dressing before it is sown, in which case rotten stable dung is preferable to any other; but this should not be laid on till the last ploughing before the seeds are sown, and not spread but as the land is ploughed, that the sun may not exhale the goodness of it, which in summer is soon lost, when spread on the ground. The quantity should not be less than twenty loads to each acre, which will keep the ground in heart till the crop of Woad is spent.

The time for gathering the crop is according to the season, but it should be performed as soon as the leaves are fully grown, while they are perfectly green; for when they begin to change pale, great part of their goodness is over; for the quantity will be less, and the quality greatly diminished. If the land is good, and the crop well husbanded, it will produce three or four gatherings, but the two first are the best; these are commonly mixed together in the manufacturing of it, but the after-crops are always kept separate; for if these are mixed with the other, the whole will be of little value. The two first crops will sell from twenty-five to thirty pounds a ton; but the latter will not bring more than seven or eight pounds, and sometimes not so much.

An acre of land will produce a ton of Woad, and in good feafons near a ton and a half.

When the planters intend to fave the feeds, they cut three crops of the leaves, and then let the plants ftand till the next year for feed; but if only one crop is cut, and that only of the outer leaves, letting all the middle leaves ftand to nourifh the ftalks, the plants will grow ftronger, and produce a much greater quantity of feeds.

Thefe feeds are often kept two years, but it is always beft to fow new feeds when they can be obtained. The feeds ripen in Auguft; when the pods turn to a dark colour, the feeds fhould be gathered; it is beft done by reaping the ftalks in the fame manner as Wheat, fpreading the ftalks in rows upon the ground, and in four or five days the feeds will be fit to threfh out, provided the weather is dry; for if it lies long, the pods will open and let out the feeds.

There are fome of the Woad planters who feed down the leaves in winter with fheep, which is a very bad method; for all plants which are to remain for a future crop, fhould never be eaten by cattle, for that greatly weakens the plants; therefore thofe who eat down their Wheat in winter with fheep are equally blameable.

ISOPYRUM. Lin. Gen. Plant. 621. Helleborus. Amman.

The CHARACTERS are,

The flower has no empalement. It hath five equal oval petals, which fall off, and five fhort tubulous nectarii, fituated within the petals, divided at their brim into three lobes, the middle one being the largeft. It hath a great number of fhort hairy ftamina, terminated by fingle fummits, and feveral oval germen, with fingle ftyles of the fame length, crowned by an obtufe ftigma the length of the ftamina. The germen afterward become fo many recurved capfules with one cell, filled with fmall feeds.

This genus of plants is ranged in the feventh fection of Linnæus's thirteenth clafs, intitled Polyandria Polygynia, which includes thofe plants whofe flowers have many ftamina and ftyles.

The SPECIES are,

1. ISOPYRUM (*Fumaroides*) ftipulis fubulatis, petalis acutis. Hort. Upfal. 157. *Ifopyrum with awl-fhaped ftipulæ, and acute petals.* Helleborus fumariæ foliis. Amman. Ruth. 57. tab. 12. *Hellebore with Fumitory leaves.*

2. ISOPYRUM (*Thalictroides*) ftipulis ovatis, petalis obtufis. Lin. Sp. Plant. 557. *Ifopyrum with oval ftipulæ, and obtufe petals.* Ranunculus nemorofus, thalictri folio. C. B. P. 178. *Wood Crowsfoot with a Meadow Rue leaf.*

3. ISOPYRUM (*Aquilegioides*) ftipulis obfoletis. Lin. Sp. Plant. 557. *Ifopyrum with obfolete ftipulæ.* Aquilegia montana, flore parvo, thalictri folio. C. B. P. 144. *Mountain Columbine with a fmall flower, and Meadow Rue Leaf.*

The firft fort grows naturally in Siberia, from whence the feeds were fent to the Imperial garden at Peterfburgh, and the late Dr. Amman, profeffor of botany there, fent me part of the feeds; this is an annual plant, which feldom rifes more than three or four inches high. The leaves are fhaped like thofe of Fumitory; they are fmall, and of a gray colour. The ftalk is naked to the top, where there is a circle of leaves juft under the flowers. The flowers are fmall, of an herbaceous colour on their outfide, but yellow within, having five acute petals, and as many honey glands, with a great number of ftamina which are fhorter than the petals, and feveral reflexed moon-fhaped germen, having fo many fingle ftyles, crowned by obtufe ftigmas. The flowers are fucceeded by many recurved feed-veffels with one cell, filled with fmall fhining black feeds. It flowers the beginning of April, and the feeds ripen in May, then the plants decay.

The feeds of this plant fhould be fown in a fhady border foon after they are ripe, for when they are kept long out of the ground, they feldom grow the firft year; therefore when the feeds are permitted to

scatter, they fucceed better than thofe which are fown, and the plants will require no other care, but to keep them clean from weeds; as there is no great beauty in this plant, fo a fmall patch or two of them in any fhady part of the garden, by way of variety, will be fufficient.

The fecond and third forts were fent me from Verona, near which place they grow naturally. The fecond fort hath leaves very like thofe of the fmalleft Meadow Rue. The ftalks rife four or five inches high, fupporting a few fmall white flowers, with obtufe petals, containing many fmall feeds. It flowers the latter end of March, and the feeds ripen in May.

The third fort hath leaves like the fecond, but a little larger, and of a greener colour. The ftalks rife about fix inches high, fupporting two or three fmall white flowers, fhaped like thofe of the fecond fort; thefe are fucceeded by recurved feed-veffels, filled with fmall feeds. It flowers in April, and the feeds ripen in June.

Both thefe plants delight in a moift fhady fituation; they are propagated by feeds in the fame way as the firft fort, but thefe will live two or three years.

ISORA. See HELICTERES.

ITEA. Lin. Gen. Plant. 243. Flor. Virg. 143. Diconangia. Mitch. Gen. 5.

The CHARACTERS are,

The empalement of the flower is fmall, permanent, and erect, ending in five acute points. The flower has five petals, which are inferted in the empalement. It hath five awl-fhaped ftamina inferted in the empalement, which are as long as the petals, terminated by roundifh fummits, and an oval germen fupporting a cylindrical ftyle, which is permanent, crowned by an obtufe ftigma. The germen afterward becomes a long oval capfule, with the ftyle at the top, having one cell filled with fmall feeds.

This genus of plants is ranged in the firft fection of Linnæus's fifth clafs, intitled Pentandria Monogynia, which includes thofe plants whofe flowers have five ftamina and one ftyle.

We have but one SPECIES of this genus, viz.

ITEA (*Virginica.*) Flor. Virg. 143. We have no English title for this plant,

This fhrub grows in moift foils in feveral parts of North America, where it rifes to the height of fix or feven feet, fending out many branches from the ground upward, garnifhed with fpear-fhaped leaves placed alternately, flightly fawed on their edges, which are reflexed, veined, and of a light green. At the extremity of the fame year's fhoots, in the month of July, are produced fine fpikes of white flowers, three or four inches long, erect; and when thefe fhrubs are in vigour, they will be entirely covered with thefe fpikes of flowers, fo that they make a fine appearance at their feafon of flowering.

This fhrub is now pretty common in England; but the garden where I have feen it in the greateft vigour, is that of his late Grace the Duke of Argyle, at Whitton, near Hounflow, where the foil agrees fo well with this plant, that it thrives and flowers there as well as in its native country.

This fhrub will live in the open air in England, the cold never injuring it, but it will not thrive upon dry gravelly ground, being very apt to die in fuch places in the fummer feafon. It is propagated by layers, which, if laid down in the autumn, will put out roots fo as to be fit to remove by the following autumn; when they may be tranfplanted into a nurfery, or to the place where they are to remain. This fhrub flowers at a feafon when there are few others in beauty, fo it is the more valuable on that account.

IVA. Lin. Gen. 1059. Tarconanthus. Vail. Act. Par. 1719.

The CHARACTERS are,

It hath male and female flowers in the fame plant; the flowers have a roundifh permanent empalement, including feveral florets, which are convex; the male flowers have one petal, which is funnel-fhaped, and indented in five parts at the brim; thofe are fituated in the difk; they have five briftly ftamina, terminated by erect fummits, approach ing each other; the female half florets have neither petal or stamina; they have an oblong germen supporting two hair-like styles, crowned with acute stigmas. The empalement afterward becomes the capsule, including one naked seed.

This genus of plants is ranged in the fifth section of Linnæus's twenty-first class, intitled Monœcia Pentandria, from the plants having male and female florets, and the male florets having five stamina.

The SPECIES are;

1. IVA (*Annua*) foliis lanceolato-ovatis, caule herbaceo. Hort. Upsal. 285. *Ivy with oval spear-shaped leaves and an herbaceous stalk.* Tarconanthus foliis cordatis serratis trinervis. Prod. Leyd. 538.

2. IVA (*Frutescens*) foliis lanceolatis, caule fruticoso. Amœn. Acad. 3. p. 25. *Iva with spear-shaped leaves and a shrubby stalk.* Agerato affinis, Peruviana frutescens. Pluk. Alm. 12.

The first sort grows naturally in many parts of the West-Indies; it is an annual plant, with an herbaceous stalk, which rises from two to three feet high, sending out several branches from the sides, which are garnished with oval spear-shaped leaves, having three deep longitudinal veins, and are sawed on their edges; the stalks and branches are terminated by small clusters of pale blue flowers, which appear in July, and are succeeded by seeds which ripen in the autumn.

This is propagated by seeds, which should be sown in the spring upon a moderate hot-bed: and when the plants are fit to remove, they should be transplanted on another hot-bed to bring them forward, treating them in the same way as is directed for Impatiens, with which management the plants will flower and perfect their seeds.

The second sort has been long an inhabitant of the English gardens, where it has been known by the title of Jesuits Bark-tree. It hath slender ligneous branches which rise eight or ten feet high, garnished with spear-shaped sawed leaves; the branches (in warm seasons) are terminated by small clusters of flowers, of a pale purple colour, which appear the latter end of August, but are not succeeded by seeds in England.

This shrub was some years past preserved in greenhouses, being supposed too tender to live through the winter in the open air; but late trials have made it appear, that the ordinary winters in England seldom hurt it, provided it is planted in a dry soil and a sheltered situation. It is propagated in the nursery-gardens about London for sale, and if the branches are layed into the ground in the spring, they will put out roots in six months; or if cuttings are planted in a shady border in May, they will take root.

JUDAICA ARBOR. See CERCIS.

JUGLANS. Lin. Gen. Plant. 950. Nux. Tourn. Inst. R. H. 581. tab. 346. Walnut; in French, *Noisetier.*

The CHARACTERS are,

It hath male and female flowers at separate distances on the same tree. The male flowers are disposed in an oblong rope, or katkin; which is cylindrical and imbricated, with spaces between the scales; each scale has one flower, with one petal fixed in the outer center, toward the outside of the scale. The petal is divided into six equal parts; in the center is situated many short stamina, terminated by erect acute summits. The female flowers grow in small clusters, sitting close to the branches; these have a short, erect, four-pointed empalement, sitting on the germen, and an acute erect petal, divided into four parts. Under the empalement sits a large oval germen, supporting two short styles, crowned by large reflexed stigmas. The germen afterward becomes a large oval dry berry, with one cell, inclosing a large oval nut with netted furrows, whose kernel hath four lobes, which are variously furrowed.

This genus of plants is ranged in the eighth section of Linnæus's twenty-first class, intitled Monœcia Polyandria, including those plants which have male and female flowers on the same plant, and the male flowers have many stamina.

1. JUGLANS (*Regia*) foliolis ovalibus glabris subserratis subæqualibus. Hort. Cliff. 449. *Walnut with oval small leaves or lobes, which are smooth, sawed, and equal.* Nux juglans sive Regia vulgaris. C. B. P. 417. *Common Walnut.*

2. JUGLANS (*Nigra*) foliolis quindenis lanceolatis serratis, exterioribus minoribus gemmulis super axillaribus. Lin. Sp. 1415. *Walnut-tree with spear-shaped lobes which are sharply sawed; the middle being the largest.* Nux juglans. Virginiana nigra. H. L. 452. *Black Virginia Walnut.*

3. JUGLANS (*Oblonga*) foliolis cordato-lanceolatis inferne nervosis, pediculis foliorum pubescentibus. *Walnut with heart spear-shaped lobes, having many veins on their under side, and downy foot-stalks to the leaves.* Juglans nigra, fructu oblongo profundissime insculpto. Cat. Hort. Chelf. *Black Virginia Walnut, with an oblong fruit very deeply furrowed.*

4. JUGLANS (*Alba*) foliolis lanceolatis serratis, exterioribus latioribus. Lin. Sp. Plant. 997. *Walnut with spear-shaped sawed lobes, the outer being the broadest.* Nux juglans alba Virginiensis. Park. Theat. 1414. *White Virginia Walnut called Hickery Nut.*

5. JUGLANS (*Glabra*) foliolis cuneiformibus serratis, exterioribus majoribus. *Walnut with wedge-shaped lobes which are sawed, the outer being the largest.* Juglans alba fructu minori cortice glabro. Clayt. Flor. Virg. *White Walnut with a smaller fruit, and a smooth bark.*

6. JUGLANS (*Ovata*) foliolis lanceolatis serratis glabris subæqualibus. *Walnut with smooth, spear-shaped, sawed lobes, which are equal.* Juglans alba fructu ovato compresso, nucleo dulce, cortice squamoso. Clayt. Flor. Virg. *White Walnut with an oval compressed fruit, a sweet kernel, and a scaly bark, commonly called Shagbark in America.*

There are several varieties of the common Walnut, which are distinguished by the following titles: the large Walnut, the thin shelled Walnut, the French Walnut, the late ripe Walnut, and the double Walnut; but these do all of them vary when raised by the seed; so that the nuts from the same tree will produce plants whose fruit will differ; therefore there can be no dependence upon the trees which are raised from nuts, till they have produced fruit; so that those persons who plant the trees for their fruit, should make choice of them in the nurseries when they have their fruit upon them, otherwise they may be deceived, by having such as they would not chuse.

The second sort is commonly called Black Virginia Walnut; this grows to a large size in North America. The leaves of this sort are composed of five or six pair of spear-shaped lobes, which end in acute points, and are sawed on their edges; the lower pair of lobes are the least, the other gradually increase in their size to the top, where the pair at the top, and the single lobe which terminates the leaf, are smaller; these leaves, when bruised, emit a strong aromatic flavour, as do also the outer cover of the nuts, which are rough, and rounder than those of the common Walnut. The shell of the nut is very hard and thick, and the kernel small, but very sweet.

The third sort grows naturally in North America, where the trees grow to a large size. The leaves of this sort are composed of seven or eight pair of long heart-shaped lobes, broad at their base, where they are divided into two round ears, but terminate in acute points; they are rougher, and of a deeper green than those of the second sort, and have nothing of the aromatic scent which they have. The fruit is very long. The shell is deeply furrowed, and is very hard. The kernel is small, but well flavoured.

The fourth sort is very common in most parts of North America, where it is called Hickery Nut. The leaves of this sort are composed of two or three pair of oblong lobes, terminated by an odd one; these are of a light green, and sawed on their edges; the lower pair of lobes are the smallest, and the upper the largest. The fruit is shaped like the common Walnut;

nut;

nut; but the fhell is not furrowed, and is of a light colour.

The fifth fort is not fo large as the fourth. The leaves are compofed of two pair of lobes, terminated by an odd one; thefe are narrow at their bafe, but broad and rounded at their ends; they are fawed on their edges, and are of a light green. The nuts are fmall, have a fmooth fhell, and are very hard and white.

The fixth fort grows naturally in North America, where it rifes to a middling ftature. The leaves of this fort are compofed of three pair of fmooth fpear-fhaped lobes, of a dark green colour, fawed on their edges, and ending in acute points. The fruit is oval, the fhell white, hard, and fmooth; the kernel fmall, but very fweet. The young fhoots of the tree are covered with a very fmooth brownifh bark, but the ftems and older branches have a rough fcaly bark, from whence it had the appellation of Shagbark, in America.

The common Walnut is propagated in many parts of England for the fruit, and formerly the trees were propagated for their wood, which was in very great efteem, till the quantity of Mahogany, and other ufeful woods which have been of late years imported into England, have almoft banifhed the ufe of Walnut.

Thefe trees are propagated by planting their nuts, which, as was before obferved, feldom produce the fame fort of fruit as are fown; fo that the only way to have the defired fort, is to fow the nuts of the beft kinds; and if this is done in a nurfery, the trees fhould be tranfplanted out when they have had three or four years growth, to the place where they are defigned to remain; for thefe trees do not bear tranfplanting when they are of a large fize, therefore there may be a good number of the trees planted, which need not be put at more than fix feet apart, which will be diftance enough for them to grow till they produce fruit; when thofe whofe fruit are of the defired kind may remain, and the others cut up, to allow them room to grow; by this method a fufficient number of the trees may be generally found among them to remain, which will thrive and flourifh greatly when they have room; but as many people do not care to wait fo long for the fruit, fo the next beft method is to make choice of fome young trees in the nurferies, when they have their fruit upon them; but though thefe trees will grow and bear fruit, yet they will never be fo large or fo long lived, as thofe which are planted young.

All the forts of Walnuts which are propagated for timber, fhould be fown in the places where they are to remain; for the roots of thefe trees always incline downward, which being ftopped or broken, prevent their afpiring upward, fo that they afterwards divaricate into branches, and become low fpreading trees; but fuch as are propagated for fruit, are greatly mended by tranfplanting; for hereby they are rendered more fruitful, and their fruit are generally larger and fairer; it being a common obfervation, that downright roots greatly encourage the luxuriant growth of timber in all forts of trees; but fuch trees as have their roots fpreading near the furface of the ground, are always the moft fruitful and beft flavoured.

The nuts fhould be preferved in their outer covers in dry fand until February, when they fhould be planted in lines, at the diftance you intend them to remain; but in the rows they may be placed pretty clofe, for fear the nuts fhould mifcarry; and the young trees, where they are too thick, may be removed, after they have grown two or three years, leaving the remainder at the diftance they are to ftand.

In tranfplanting thefe trees, you fhould observe never to prune either their roots or large branches, both which are very injurious to them; nor fhould you be too bufy in lopping or pruning the branches of thefe trees when grown to a large

fize, for it often caufes them to decay; but when there is a neceffity for cutting any of their branches off, it fhould be done early in September (for at that feafon the trees are not fo fubject to bleed) that the wound may heal over before the cold increafes; the branches fhould always be cut off quite clofe to the trunk, otherwife the ftump which is left will decay, and rot the body of the tree.

The beft feafon for tranfplanting thefe trees is as foon as the leaves begin to decay, at which time if they are carefully taken up, and their branches preferved entire, there will be little danger of their fucceeding, although they are eight or ten years old, as I have feveral times experienced; though, as was before obferved, thefe trees will not grow fo large, or continue fo long, as thofe which are removed young. This tree delights in a firm, rich, loamy foil, or fuch as is inclinable to chalk or marl; and will thrive very well in ftony ground, and on chalky hills, as may be feen by thofe large plantations near Leatherhead, Godftone, and Carfhalton in Surry, where are great numbers of thefe trees planted upon the downs, which annually produce large quantities of fruit, to the great advantage of their owners; one of which I have been told, farms the fruit of his trees, to thofe who fupply the markets, for 30 l. per annum.

The diftance thefe trees fhould be placed, ought not to be lefs than forty feet, efpecially if regard be had to their fruit; though when they are only defigned for timber, if they ftand much nearer, it promotes their upright growth. The black Virginia Walnut is much more inclinable to grow upright than the common fort, and the wood being generally of a more beautiful grain, renders it preferable to that, and better worth cultivating. I have feen fome of this wood which hath been beautifully veined with black and white, which, when polifhed, has appeared at a diftance, like veined marble. This wood is greatly efteemed by the cabinet-makers for inlaying, as alfo for bedfteads, ftools, tables, and cabinets; and is one of the moft durable woods for thofe purpofes of Englifh growth, being lefs liable to be infected with infects than moft other kinds (which may proceed from its extraordinary bitternefs;) but it is not proper for buildings of ftrength, it being of a brittle nature, and exceeding fubject to break very fhort, though it commonly gives notice thereof, by its cracking fome time before it breaks.

The general opinion is, that the beating of this fruit improves the trees, which I do not believe, fince in the doing of this, the younger branches are generally broken and deftroyed; but as it would be exceeding troublefome to gather it by hand, fo in beating it off, great care fhould be taken that it be not done with violence, for the reafon before affigned. In order to preferve the fruit, it fhould remain upon the trees till it is thorough ripe, when it fhould be beaten down, and laid in heaps for two or three days; after which they fhould be fpread abroad, when, in a little time, their hufks will eafily part from the fhells; then you muft dry them well in the fun, and lay them up in a dry place, where mice or other vermin cannot come to them, in which place they will remain good for four or five months; but there are fome perfons who put their Walnuts into an oven gently heated, where they let them remain four or five hours to dry, and then put them up in oil jars, or any other clofe veffel, mixing them with dry fand, by which method they will keep good fix months. The putting of them in the oven is to dry the germ, and prevent their fprouting; but if the oven be too hot it will caufe them to fhrink, therefore great care muft be had to that.

All the other forts are propagated in the fame way, but as few of the forts produce fruit in England, fo their nuts muft be procured from North America; which fhould be gathered when fully ripe, and put up in dry fand, to preferve them in their paffage to England: when they arrive here, the fooner they are planted the greater chance there will be of their fucceeding;

ceeding ; when the plants come up, they fhould be kept clean from weeds; and if they fhoot late in the autumn, and their tops are full of fap, they fhould be covered with mats, or fome other light covering, to prevent the early frofts from pinching their tender fhoots, which often caufes them to die down a confiderable length before the fpring ; but if they are fcreened from thefe early frofts, the fhoots will become firmer and better able to refift the cold. Some of thefe forts are tender while young, fo require a little care for the two firft winters, but afterward will be hardy enough to refift the greateft cold of this country.

The black Virginia Walnut is full as hardy as the common fort: there are fome large trees of this kind in the Chelfea garden, which have produced great quantities of fruit upward of forty years; the nuts have generally ripened fo well there as to grow, but their kernels are fmall, fo are of little value.

The trees all require the fame culture as the common Walnut, but they grow beft in a foft loamy foil not too dry, and where there is a depth of foil for their roots to run down. The Hickery, when young, is very tough and pliable, fo the fticks of it are much efteemed ; but the wood when grown large is very brittle, fo not of any great ufe. The black Virginia Walnut is the moft valuable wood of all the forts ; fome of the trees are beautifully veined, and will take a good polifh, but others have very little beauty, which is the cafe of many other forts of wood.

JUJUBE. See ZIZIPHUS.
JULIANS, or ROCKETS. See HESPERIS.
JULY FLOWER. See DIANTHUS.
JUNCUS. Tourn. Inft. R. H. 246. tab. 127. Lin. Gen. Plant. 396. Rufh; in French, Jonc.

The CHARACTERS are,
It hath a chaff opening with two valves, an empalement with fix oblong pointed little leaves which are permanent ; the flower hath no petals, but the coloured empalement is by fome taken for petals. It hath fix fhort hairy ftamina, terminated by oblong erect fummits, and a three-cornered pointed germen, crowned by three long, hairy, flender ftyle, crowned by three long, hairy, flender ftigmas, which are reflexed. The germen afterward becomes a clofe three-cornered capfule with one cell, opening with three valves, inclofing roundifh feeds.

This genus of plants is ranged in the firft fection of Linnæus's fixth clafs, intitled Hexandria Monogynia, which contains the plants whofe flowers have fix ftamina and one ftyle.

The SPECIES are,
1. JUNCUS (*Acutus*) culmo fubnudo tereti mucronato, paniculâ terminali, involucro diphyllo fpinofo. Lin. Sp. Plant. 325. *Rufh with a naked, taper, pointed ftalk, terminated by a panicle, and a prickly two-leaved involucrum.* Juncus acutus, capitulis forghi. C. B. P. 11. *Prickly large Sea Rufh.*
2. JUNCUS (*Filiformis*) culmo nudo, apice membranaceo incurvo, paniculâ laterali. Lin. Sp. Plant. 326. *Rufh with a naked ftalk, an incurved membranacous apex, and a lateral panicle.* Juncus acutus, panicula fparfa. C. B. P. *Common hard Rufh.*
3. JUNCUS (*Effufus*) culmo nudo ftricto, paniculâ laterali. Flor. Leyd. 44. *Rufh with a naked clofe ftalk, and a lateral panicle.* Juncus lævis, paniculâ fparsâ, major. C. B. P. *Larger common foft Rufh, with a fpreading panicle.*
4. JUNCUS (*Conglomeratis*) culmo nudo ftricto, capitulo laterali. Prod. Leyd. 44. *Rufh with a clofe naked ftalk and lateral heads.* Juncus lævis, paniculâ non fparsâ. C. B. P. *Soft Rufh with a more compact panicle.*

There are many other fpecies of this genus, fome of which grow naturally in England, and are very troublefome weeds in many places, fo are not worthy of being enumerated here ; and thofe which are here mentioned, is only to point out a method of deftroying them.

The firft and fecond forts grow on the fea-fhores, where they are frequently watered by the falt water. Thefe two forts are planted with great care on the

banks of the fea in Holland, in order to prevent the water from wafhing away the earth ; which being very loofe, would be in danger of removing every tide, if it were not for the roots of thefe Rufhes, which faften themfelves very deep in the ground, and mat themfelves near the furface, fo as to hold the earth clofely together. Therefore, whenever the roots of thefe Rufhes are deftroyed, the inhabitants immediately repair them to prevent farther damage. In the fummer time, when the Rufhes are fully grown, the inhabitants cut them, and tie them up into bundles, which are dried, and afterward carried into the larger towns and cities, where they are wrought into bafkets, and feveral other ufeful things, which are frequently fent into England. Thefe forts do not grow fo ftrong in England, as they do on the Maefe, and fome other places in Holland, where I have feen them upward of four feet high.

The third and fourth forts grow on moift, ftrong, uncultivated lands in moft parts of England, and confume the herbage where they are fuffered to remain. The beft method of deftroying thefe Rufhes is, to fork them up clean by the roots in July, and after having let them lie a fortnight or three weeks to dry, to lay them in heaps, and burn them gently ; and the afhes which thefe afford, will be good manure for the land ; but in order to prevent their growing again, and to make the pafture good, the land fhould be drained, otherwife there will be no deftroying thefe Rufhes entirely ; but after it is well drained, if the roots are annually drawn up, and the ground kept duly rolled, they may be fubdued.

JUNIPERUS. Tourn. Inft. R. H. 588. tab. 361. Lin. Gen. Plant. 1005. Juniper; in French, Genévrier.

The CHARACTERS are,
It hath male and female flowers in different plants, and fometimes at feparate diftances on the fame plant. The male flowers grow on a conical katkin ; the flowers are placed by threes, two of them faftened along the common tail oppofite, terminated by a fingle one ; the fcales are broad, fhort, lying over each other, and fixed to the column by a very fhort foot-ftalk. The flower has no petal, but three ftamina in the male flower which are joined in one body below, having three diftinct fummits, adhering to the fcales of the lateral flowers. The female flowers have a fmall three-pointed empalement fitting upon the germen, which is permanent ; they have three ftiff, acute, permanent petals, the germen fitting below the empalement, fupports three fingle ftyles, crowned by ftigmas. The germen afterward becomes a roundifh berry, inclofing three ftony feeds, which are oblong and angular on one fide, but convex on the other.

This genus of plants is ranged in the twelfth fection of Linnæus's twenty-fecond clafs, intitled Diœcia Monodelphia, which includes thofe plants which have male and female flowers in different plants, whofe ftamina are joined in one body.

The SPECIES are,
1. JUNIPERUS (*Communis*) foliis ternis patentibus mucronatis bacca longioribus. Lin. Sp. Plant. 1040. *Juniper with fpreading fharp-pointed leaves placed by threes.* Juniperis vulgaris fruticofa. C. B. P. 488. *The common Englifh Juniper.*
2. JUNIPERUS (*Suecia*) foliis ternis patentibus, acutioribus, ramis erectioribus, bacca longioribus. *Juniper with longer and more acute-pointed leaves placed by threes, erect branches, and longer berries.* Juniperis vulgaris arbor. C. B. P. 488. *The Tree, or Swedifh Juniper.*
3. JUNIPERUS (*Virginiana*) foliis ternis omnibus patentibus. *Juniper with leaves placed by threes, which are all of them fpreading.* Juniperus Virginiana. H. L. Folio ubique juniperino. Boerh. Ind. *Cedar of Virginia, or red Cedar.*
4. JUNIPERUS (*Caroliniana*) foliis ternis bafi adnatis, junioribus imbricatis, fenioribus patulis. Hort. Cliff. 464. *Juniper with leaves placed by threes adhering at their bafe, the young ones lying over each other, and the old ones fpreading.* Juniperus Virginiana, foliis inferioribus juniperinis, fuperioribus fabinam, vel cypreffum referentibus. Boerh. Ind. *Carolina Cedar.*

5. JUNI-

5. JUNIPERUS (*Bermudiana*) foliis inferioribus ternis, fuperioribus quadrifariàm imbricatis. *Juniper with fpreading under leaves placed by threes, and the upper by fours, which lie clofe over each other.* Juniperis Bermudiana. H. L. *Cedar of Bermudas.*

6. JUNIPERIS (*Thurifera*) foliis quadrifariàm imbricatis acutis. Lin. Sp. 1471. *Juniper with awl-fhaped acute leaves placed by fours, lying over each other.* Juniperus major baccâ cæruleâ. C. B. P. *Greater Juniper with blue berries.*

7. JUNIPERUS (*Phœnicia*) foliis ternis obliteratis imbricatis obtufis. Lin. Sp. 1471. *Juniper with leaves placed by threes, which are obliterate, obtufe, and lying over each other.* Cedrus folio cupreffi major, fructu flavefcente. C. B. P. *Greater Cedar with a Cyprefs leaf and yellowifh fruit.*

8. JUNIPERUS (*Lycia*) foliis ternis undique imbricatis ovatis obtufis. Flor. Leyd. 90. *Juniper with oval blunt leaves, which every where lie over each other.* Cedrus folio cupreffi media, majoribus baccis. C. B. P. 488. *Middle Cedar, with a Cyprefs leaf and larger berries.*

9. JUNIPERUS (*Barbadenfis*) foliis ternis quadrifariàm imbricatis junioribus ovatis fenioribus acutis. Prod. Leyd. 90. *Juniper with all the leaves placed by fours, lying over each other, the young being oval, the older acute.* Juniperus maxima cupreffi folio minimo, cortice exteriore in tenues philyras fpiralis ductili. Sloan. Cat. Jam. 128. *Greateft Juniper with the leaft Cyprefs leaf, and the outer bark fplitting off in thin ductile pieces, commonly called Jamaica Berry-bearing Cedar.*

10. JUNIPERUS (*Sabina*) foliis oppofitis erectis decurrentibus, ràmis patulis. *Juniper with oppofite, erect, running leaves, and fpreading branches.* Sabina folio tamarifci. C. B. P. 487. *Savin with a Tamarifk leaf, or common Savin.*

11. JUNIPERUS (*Lufitanica*) foliis oppofitis patulis decurrentibus, ramis erectioribus. *Juniper with oppofite fpreading leaves, which run over each other, and more erect branches.* Sabina folio cupreffi. C. B. P. 487. *Savin with a Cyprefs leaf, commonly called Berry-bearing Savin.*

12. JUNIPERUS (*Oxycedrus*) foliis undique imbricatis obtufis, ramis teretibus. *Juniper with obtufe leaves everywhere lying over each other, and taper branches.* Juniperus major, baccâ rufefcente. C. B. P. 489. *Greater Juniper with a brownifh berry.*

13. JUNIPERUS (*Hifpanica*) foliis quadrifariàm imbricatis acutis. Prod. Leyd. 90. *Juniper with acute leaves lying over each other, placed four ways.* Cedrus Hifpanica procerior, fructu maximo nigro. Tourn. Inft. 588. *Taller Spanifh Cedar, with a very large black fruit.*

The firft fort grows naturally upon chalky lands in many parts of England. This is a low fhrub, feldom rifing more than three feet high, fending out many fpreading branches, which incline on every fide, covered with a brown bark, and garnifhed with narrow awl-fhaped leaves ending in acute points, which are placed by threes round the branches, pointing outward ; thefe are of a grayifh colour, and continue through the year ; the male flowers fometimes are fituated on the fame plant with the female, but at diftances, at other times they are upon diftinct plants : the female flowers are fucceeded by roundifh berries, which are firft green, but when ripe, are of a dark purple colour. The berries ripen in the autumn.

The wood, the berries, and the gum, are ufed in medicine ; the gum is titled Sandaracha.

The fecond fort is known in the gardens by the title of Swedifh Juniper : this is by many fuppofed to be only a variety of the firft, but is undoubtedly a diftinct fpecies, for I have many years raifed both forts from the feeds, and have never found them alter. This fort rifes to the height of ten or twelve feet, the branches grow more erect, the leaves are narrower, and end in more acute points : they are placed farther afunder on the branches, and the berries are longer. It grows naturally in Sweden, Denmark, and Norway.

The third fort grows naturally in moft parts of North America, where it is called red Cedar, to diftinguifh it from a fort of Cyprefs, which is called white Cedar there. Of this there are two, if not three varieties, befides the fpecies here enumerated ; one of which has leaves in every part, like thofe of the Savin, and upon being rubbed, emit a very ftrong ungrateful odour : this is commonly diftinguifhed in America, by the title of Savin-tree. There is another with leaves very like thofe of Cyprefs, but as thefe generally arife from the fame feeds when they are fent from America, fo they may be fuppofed to be only feminal variations.

The fourth fort are like thofe of the Swedifh Juniper, but the upper leaves are like thofe of the Cyprefs ; and this difference is conftant, if the feeds are carefully gathered from the fame tree ; but as moft of thofe people who fend over thefe feeds, are not very careful to diftinguifh the difference, fo it often happens that the feeds of two or three forts are mixed together, which has given occafion to people to imagine them but one fpecies ; but all the leaves of the third are like thofe of the Juniper, fo the gardeners call this the red Virginia Cedar ; and the fourth they call Carolina Cedar, though all the forts grow naturally in Virginia.

The fifth fort is the Bermudas Cedar, whofe wood has a very ftrong odour; and was formerly in great efteem for wainfcotting of rooms, and alfo for furniture ; but the odour being too powerful for many perfons, has rendered it lefs vaiuable, and at prefent there is not much of it imported into England. Thefe plants, while young, have acute-pointed leaves, which fpread open, and are placed by threes round the branches ; but as the trees advance, fo their leaves alter, and the branches are four-cornered ; the leaves are very fhort, and placed by fours round the branches, lying over each other like the fcales of fifh ; the berries are produced toward the end of the branches ; thefe are of a dark red colour; inclining to purple. As there are few of thefe trees of any great fize in England, fo I have not had an opportunity of examining their flowers, therefore do not know if they have male and female flowers on the fame plant, or if they are on different plants ; for although I have received very fine fpecimens from Bermudas, yet they are all with fruit on them almoft fully grown, and not one with male flowers; and as thefe trees are commonly deftroyed in England whenever there happens a fevere winter, where they are not fheltered, fo we have little hopes of feeing them in flower here.

The fixth fort grows naturally in Iftria, from whence I received the berries; which have fucceeded with me in the Chelfea garden. This hath fpreading branches, growing thinly, which are garnifhed with acutepointed leaves, placed by fours round the branches : they are of a deep green, and not very clofe to each other, but grow horizontally, pointing outward ; the berries are much larger than thofe of the common Juniper, and are blue when ripe.

The feventh fort grows naturally in Portugal, from whence I have frequently received the berries. This fort grows with its branches in a pyramidical form; the lower ones are garnifhed with fhort, acute-pointed, grayifh leaves, placed by threes round the branches, pointing outward ; but thofe on the upper branches are of a dark green, lying over each other like the fcales of fifh, but end in acute points. The male flowers are produced at the extremity of the branches ; they are fituated in a loofe, fcaly, conical katkin, ftanding upon a fhort foot-ftalk erect ; the fruit is produced fometimes upon the fame tree, at diftances from the flowers, and at other times they are upon feparate trees ; the berries of this are of a pale yellow when ripe, and about the fize of thofe of the common Juniper.

The eighth fort grows naturally in Spain and Italy, from both which countries I have received it. The branches of this fort grow erect, and are covered with a reddifh brown bark ; the leaves are fmall, obtufe, and

and lie over each other like the scales of fish; the male flowers grow at the extremity of the branches in a conical katkin, and the fruit grows single from the side of the branches below the katkins, on the same branch; the berries are large, oval, and, when ripe, are brown.

The ninth sort grows naturally in Jamaica, and also in the other islands of the West-Indies, where it rises to be one of the largest timber trees in those countries; the wood is frequently fetched from thence by the inhabitants of North America, for building of ships. This sort is generally confounded with the Bermudas Cedar, and taken for the same, but the specimens of it which were sent me by the late Dr. Houstoun, prove them to be different trees; for the branches of this spread very wide, the leaves are extremely small, and are every where lying imbricatim over each other; the bark is rugged, and splits off in strings, and is of a very dark colour; the berries are smaller than those of the Bermudas Cedar, and are of a light brown colour when ripe: this sort is male and female in different trees.

The tenth sort is the common Savin; this grows naturally in Italy, Spain, and the Levant, upon the mountains where it is cold. It sends out its branches horizontally, so seldom rises more than three or four feet high, but spreads to a considerable distance every way; the branches are garnished with very short acute-pointed leaves placed opposite, which run over each other along the branches, whose ends point upward. This sort very rarely produces either flower or seed in the gardens; I have frequently examined old plants which have been standing more than fifty years, and have not more than three times found any male flowers upon them, and but once have seen any berries, which were upon a separate tree from the flowers; these berries were smaller than those of the common Juniper, but of the same colour, and were a little compressed; the whole plant has a very rank strong odour when touched. The leaves of this shrub are much used by the farriers for horses when they have worms; and Mr. Ray commends the juice of it mixed with milk, and sweetened with sugar, as an excellent medicine for children who are troubled with worms. The leaves beaten into a cataplasm with hog's-lard, will cure children's scabby heads.

The eleventh sort has, by many, been supposed to be only an accidental variety of the former, but there is a a manifest difference between them; for the branches of this grow more erect than those of the eleventh sort, the leaves are shorter, and end in acute points which spread outward. This sort will rise to the height of seven or eight feet, and produces great quantities of berries. I have propagated this sort from seeds, but have never found it vary. It has been distinguished by most of the old botanists, by the title of Berry-bearing Savin. It grows naturally on the Alps, from whence I have received the berries.

The twelfth sort grows naturally in Spain, Portugal, and the south of France, where it rises ten or twelve feet high, sending out branches the whole length of the stem, which are garnished with small obtuse leaves, lying over each other like the scales of fish; the branches are small and taper, having no angles or corners, as most of the others have; the male flowers are situated at the end of the branches in conical scaly katkins, and the berries grow below from the side of the same branches. These are larger than those of the common Juniper, and when ripe are brown.

The thirteenth sort grows naturally in Spain and Portugal, where it rises from twenty-five to thirty feet high, sending out many branches which form a sort of pyramid; the branches are garnished with acute-pointed leaves, which lie over each other four ways, so as to make the branches four-cornered; the berries of this sort are very large, and black when ripe.

These plants are all propagated by sowing their seeds, the best season for which is as soon as they are ripe, if they can then be procured; for when they are kept until spring before they are sown, they will not come up until the second year. The ground in which the seeds of the hardy sorts are sown, should be fresh and light, but it should not be dunged: it should be well dug and levelled very even; then sow your seeds thereon pretty thick, and sift some earth over them about half an inch thick; this bed will require no farther care than only to keep it clear from weeds, and toward the middle or latter end of April, you will find some of your plants appear above ground, though, perhaps, the greatest part of them may lie till the spring following before they come up; therefore you should carefully clear the beds from weeds, and in very dry weather refresh them with some water, which will greatly promote the growth of those plants which are up, and also cause the other seeds to vegetate; but if the bed in which these seeds are sown is much exposed to the sun, it should be shaded with mats in the day; for when the plants come first up, they will not bear too much heat. In this bed they should remain till the second autumn, when you must prepare some beds to transplant them into, which should also be of light, fresh, undunged soil; and having well dug and cleansed the ground from all noxious weeds and roots, you should make it level; and then in the beginning of October, which is the proper season for removing these plants, you should raise up the young plants with a trowel, preserving as much earth as possible to their roots, and plant them into beds about five or six inches asunder each way, giving them some water to settle the earth to their roots; and if it should prove very dry weather, you may lay a little mulch upon the surface of the ground round their roots, which will be of great service to the plants. But as many of the seeds will be yet left in the ground where they are sown, so the beds should not be disturbed too much in taking up the plants; for I have known a bed sown with these berries, which has supplied plants for three years drawing, some of the berries having lain so long in the ground before they sprouted; therefore the surface of the beds should be kept level, and constantly clean from weeds.

The plants may remain two years in these beds, observing to keep them clear from weeds; in the spring you should stir the ground gently between them, that their roots may with greater ease strike into it; after which time they should be transplanted, either into a nursery, at the distance of three feet row from row, and eighteen inches asunder in the rows, or into the places where they are to remain for good. The best season to transplant them (as I before observed) is in the beginning of October, when you should take them up carefully, to preserve a ball of earth to their roots; and when planted, their roots should be mulched; all which, if carefully attended to, as also observing to refresh them with water in very dry weather until they have taken new root, will preserve them from the danger of not growing; and they being extreme hardy in respect to cold, will defy the severest of our winters to injure them, provided they are not planted in a moist or rich soil.

In order to have these trees aspire in height, their under branches should be taken off, especially where they are inclined to grow strong, but they must not be kept too closely pruned, which would retard their growth; for all these Evergreen trees do more or less abound with a resinous juice, which in hot weather is very apt to flow out from such places as are wounded; so that it will not be adviseable to take off too many branches at once, which would make so many wounds, from which their sap in hot weather would flow in such plenty, as to render the trees weak and unhealthy.

The two sorts of Virginian Cedars grow to a much greater height than the former, and in their native country afford excellent timber for many uses; but with us there are very few which are above twenty-five

five or thirty feet high, though there is no doubt of their growing larger; for they thrive very fast after the three firft years, and refift the fharpeft froft of our climate exceeding well, and are very apt to grow ftrait and regular, provided they are not fuffered to fhoot out too much at bottom.

Thefe plants are alfo propagated by feeds, which muft be procured from Virginia or Carolina (for they rarely produce ripe feeds in England) and fown as was directed for the other Junipers; but as this feed cannot be procured in England till fpring, fo when fown at that feafon, it remains in the ground until the fucceeding fpring before the plants appear; therefore you muft obferve to keep the beds clear from weeds, and not fuffer the feeds to be difturbed, which is often the fault of fome impatient people, who think, becaufe the plants do not rife the firft year, that they will never come up, and fo dig up the ground again, whereby their feeds are buried; but if they are let remain, they feldom fail to grow, though fometimes it is two years after fowing before they come up. When the plants come up they muft be carefully weeded, and in dry weather fhould be refrefhed with water, which will greatly forward their growth; and the autumn following they fhould have a little rotten tan laid between them, to keep out the froft. In this bed the plants may remain till they have had two years growth, then they fhould be tranfplanted into other beds, as was directed before for the other forts, obferving to preferve a ball of earth to their roots; and after they are planted, if the feafon proves dry, they muft be carefully watered, and the furface of the ground covered with mulch, to prevent the fun and wind from entering the earth to dry their fibres; but they fhould not be too much watered, which often proves injurious to thefe trees, by rotting their tender fibres foon after they are emitted, whereby the plants have been often deftroyed.

In thefe beds they may remain two years, obferving to keep them clear from weeds; and in winter you fhould lay a little frefh mulch upon the furface of the ground round their roots, which will prevent the froft from penetrating to them, and effectually preferve them; for while the plants are fo young, they are liable to be injured by hard frofts, when too much expofed thereto; but when they have attained a greater ftrength, they will refift the fevereft of our cold.

After two years, they fhould either be removed into a nurfery (as was directed for the common Juniper) or tranfplanted where they are defigned to remain, obferving always to take them up carefully, otherwife they are fubject to fail upon tranfplanting; as alfo to mulch the ground, and water them as was before directed, until they have taken root; after which they will require no farther care, than only to keep the ground clear about their roots, and to prune up their fide branches to make them afpire in height. The foil in which you plant thefe trees fhould be frefh and light, but muft not be dunged, efpecially at the time when they are planted; for dung is very hurtful to them, if it be not quite rotted to mould; therefore the mulch which is laid upon the furface of the ground fhould not be dung, but rather fome old tanners bark or fea-coal afhes, which will prevent the froft from penetrating deep in the ground.

Thefe trees being thus managed, will in a few years rife to a confiderable ftature, and by the variety of their evergreen leaves and manner of growth, will greatly add to the beauty of all plantations, if rightly difpofed, which indeed is what we feldom obferve in any of the Englifh gardens or wildernefles; for there are few people who confider the different growths of the feveral trees with which they compofe fuch plantations, fo as to place the . talleft growing trees the backwardeft from fight, and the next degree to fucceed them, and fo gradually diminifhing till we come to the common Juniper, and othersof the fame growth, whereby all the trees will be feen, and the gradual de-

clivity of their tops will appear like a verdant flope, and be much more agreeable to the fight, as alfo more advantageous to the growth of the trees, than to place fhrubs of humble growth near fuch plants as will grow to the firft magnitude, whereby the fhrub is hid from fight, and will be over-fhadowed and deftroyed; nor can the diftance which each tree requires, be fo juftly proportioned any other way; for in this diftribution, the largeft trees being feparated by themfelves, may be placed at a due diftance; and then thofe of a middling growth fucceeding, may be accordingly allowed fufficient room; and the fmaller, which are next the fight, being placed much clofer, will hide the naked ftems of the larger trees, and have an agreeable effect to the fight.

The timber of thefe trees is of excellent ufe in America, for building of veffels, wainfcotting houfes, and for making many forts of utenfils, it abounding with a bitter refin, which prevents its being deftroyed by vermin, but it is very brittle, therefore not fo proper for ftubborn ufes; but however, by increafing the number of our timber trees, we fhall find many advantages, befides the pleafure their variety affords; for we may hereby have trees of very different kinds, which are adapted to grow in various foils and fituations, whereby we fhall never want proper trees for all the different forts of foils in England, if proper care be taken in their choice; which would be a great improvement to many parts of this kingdom, which now lie unplanted, becaufe the owner, perhaps, find that neither Oaks nor Elms will thrive there, and confequently concludes, that no other fort of tree will, which is a great miftake; for if we confider how different the ftructure of trees are (being defigned by the wife Author and contriver of all things, to grow on different foils and fituations) and only obferve what forts are adapted for growing on dry barren mountains, and what are defigned for the lower and richer valleys, we need never be at a lofs for proper trees for all forts of ground.

The Bermudas Cedar being a native of that ifland, and alfo of the Bahama Iflands, is much tenderer than either of the former forts, except that of Jamaica, fo is not likely to thrive well in this country; for although many of thefe plants have lived feveral years in the open air in England, yet whenever a fevere winter happens, it either kills them, or fo much defaces them, that they do not recover their verdure in a year or two after.

Thefe plants are propagated by feeds in the fame manner as the former, with only this difference, that thefe fhould be fown in pots or tubs of earth, that they may be removed into fhelter in the winter time, otherwife the young plants are often hurt by hard frofts; but they will require no more care than only to be placed under a common hot-bed frame, where the glaffes may be conftantly kept off in mild weather, when they cannot have too much free air, and only covered in hard frofts. Thefe feeds conftantly remain in the ground until the fecond year before they come up, therefore the earth in the pots fhould not be difturbed; and in the fummer time they fhould be placed in the fhade, to prevent the earth from drying too faft; and in very dry weather they fhould be often watered, but do not give too much water to them at once, which would rot the feeds.

The fpring following, when the young plants come up, they muft be carefully cleared from weeds, and in dry weather refrefhed with water; but fhould ftand, during the fummer feafon, in a place defended from ftrong winds; and in winter muft be placed under frames, where they may be covered in hard frofty weather, but muft have open air when the weather is mild. In April following you fhould tranfplant them each into a fingle halfpenny pot filled with frefh light earth, being careful to raife them up with a ball of earth to their roots; and when they are planted, you fhould water them, to fettle the earth to their roots; then place the pots in a warm fituation, where they may be defended from fun and wind: but if you will beftow a moderate hot-bed to plunge the pots in, it

will

will greatly promote their taking new root; however, you muſt carefully defend them from the great heat of the ſun, which is injurious to them when freſh removed; but when they have taken root, you may expoſe them by degrees to the open air. If you ſuffer the pots to remain plunged all the ſummer, it will preſerve the earth therein from drying ſo faſt as it would do, if they were ſet upon the ground.

In October you ſhould again remove theſe plants into ſhelter, or elſe plunge their pots into the ground under a warm hedge, where they may be protected from the cold north and eaſt winds; and in the ſpring following you muſt ſhift the plants into pots a ſize larger, taking away ſome of the earth from the outſide of the ball, and adding ſome freſh, which will promote their growth; and ſo continue to manage them as was before directed, until you plant them out in the places where they are deſigned to remain; which ſhould not be done till they are four or five years old, by which time they will be ſtrong enough to bear the cold of our common winters.

The reaſon for my directing theſe plants to be preſerved in pots until they are planted out for good is, becauſe they are difficult to tranſplant, and being tender will require ſome ſhelter while young; and whoever obſerves the method here laid down, will find the plants ſo managed to gain two years growth in ſix, from thoſe raiſed in the open air, and be in leſs danger of being deſtroyed; and as the trouble and expence in raiſing them this way is not great, ſo it is worth practiſing, ſince in a few years the trees will recompenſe the trouble.

The timber of this tree is of a reddiſh colour, and very ſweet, and is commonly known in England by the name of Cedar Wood; though there are divers ſorts of wood called by that name, which come from very different trees, eſpecially in the Weſt-Indies, where there are ſeveral trees of vaſtly different appearances and genera, which have that appellation: it is this wood which is uſed for pencils, as alſo to wainſcot rooms, and make ſtair-caſes, it enduring longer found than moſt other ſorts of timber, which, perhaps, may be owing to ſome extreme bitter taſte in the reſin, with which the tree abounds; for it is very remarkable, that the worms do not eat the bottoms of the veſſels built with this wood, as they do thoſe built with Oak; ſo that the veſſels built with Cedar are much preferable to thoſe built with any other ſort of timber, for the uſe of the Weſt-India ſeas, but they are not fit for ſhips of war, the wood being ſo brittle as to ſplit to pieces with a cannon ball.

The Jamaica Juniper is more impatient of cold than the Bermudas, ſo will not live through the winter in the open air in England, and the plants muſt be preſerved in pots and houſed in the winter; this is propagated by ſeeds, in the ſame way as the Bermudas Cedar; but if the pots are plunged into a moderate hot-bed the ſecond ſpring after the ſeeds are ſown, it will bring up the plants ſooner, and they will have more time to get ſtrength before winter.

All the other ſorts are hardy enough to live in the open air, ſo are very well worth propagating, as they will add to the variety of Evergreen plantations; ſome of the ſorts will riſe to a very conſiderable height, ſo may prove to be uſeful timber, and may be adapted to ſuch ſoils as will not ſuit many other trees.

The common Savin ſhould not be neglected, becauſe it is ſo very hardy as never to be injured by the ſevereſt froſt; and as this ſpreads its branches near the ground, ſo if the plants are placed on the borders of woods, they will have a good effect in winter, by ſcreening the nakedneſs of the ground from ſight.

All theſe ſorts are propagated by their ſeeds, which may be ſown in the ſame way as the common Juniper, and the plants afterward ſo managed; and moſt of the ſorts may be propagated by cuttings, which, if planted in autumn in a ſhady border will take root; but thoſe plants which are raiſed from cuttings will never grow ſo upright, nor to ſo large a ſize as the plants

which are raiſed from ſeeds; ſo that when theſe can be procured, it is much the better method, but the other is frequently practiſed on thoſe ſorts which do not perfect their ſeeds in England.

As ſeveral of theſe ſorts grow to the height of eighteen or twenty feet, the procuring as many of the ſorts as can be gotten from the countries of their growth, will be adding to the variety of our Evergreen plantations, which cannot be too much propagated in England, where, in general, our winters are temperate enough for them to thrive to advantage; and as the ſorts which are a little more tender than the others obtain ſtrength, they will be in leſs danger of ſuffering by ſevere winters, as we find by many other plants, which were ſo tender as not to live in the open air at firſt, but now defy the ſevereſt cold of our climate.

JUSSIÆA. Lin. Gen. Plant. 478.

The CHARACTERS are,

It hath a ſmall permanent empalement, divided into five ſegments at the top, ſitting upon the germen. The flower has five roundiſh ſpreading petals, and ten ſhort ſlender ſtamina, terminated by roundiſh ſummits. The oblong germen ſupports a ſlender ſtyle, crowned by a flat ſtigma, marked with five ſtripes. The germen afterward becomes a thick oblong capſule, crowned by the empalement, which opens lengthways, and is filled with ſmall ſeeds.

This genus of plants is ranged in the firſt ſection of Linnæus's tenth claſs, intitled Decandria Monogynia, which includes the plants whoſe flowers have ten ſtamina and one ſtyle.

The SPECIES are,

1. JUSSIÆA (Suffruticoſa) erecta villoſa, floribus tetrapetalis, decandriis ſeſſilibus. Lin. Sp. Plant. 555. Upright hairy Juſſiæa, with flowers ſitting cloſe to the ſtalk, having four petals and ten ſtamina. Lyſimachia Indica non pappoſa, flore luteo minimo, ſiliquis caryophyllum aromaticum æmulantibus. H. L. 396. Indian Primroſe with a very ſmall yellow flower, and pods reſembling Cloves.

2. JUSSIÆA (Pubeſcens) villoſa, caule erecto ramoſo, floribus pentapetalis, decandriis ſeſſilibus. Hairy Juſſiæa with an erect branching ſtalk, flowers having five petals, and ten ſtamina which ſit cloſe to the ſtalk. Lyſimachia lutea erecta, non pappoſa major, foliis hirſutis, fructu caryophylloide. Sloan. Cat. Jam. 85. Yellow upright larger Tree-Primroſe with hairy leaves, and a fruit like Cloves.

3. JUSSIÆA (Erecta) erecta glabra, floribus tetrapetalis octandris ſeſſilibus. Flor. Zeyl. 170. Smooth upright Juſſiæa with four petals, and eight ſtamina to the flowers, which ſit cloſe to the ſtalk. Lyſimachia lutea non pappoſa, erecta, foliis glabris, fructu caryophylloide. Sloan. Cat. Jam. 85. Yellow upright Tree-Primroſe with ſmooth leaves, and a fruit like Cloves.

4. JUSSIÆA (Onagra) caule erecta ramoſo glabro, floribus tetrapetalis octandris ſeſſilibus, foliis lanceolatis. Juſſiæa with an upright, branching, ſmooth ſtalk, flowers having four petals, and eight ſtamina ſitting cloſe to the ſtalk, and ſpear-ſhaped leaves. Onagra foliis perſicariæ amplioribus, parvo flore luteo. Plum. Cat. 7. Tree-Primroſe with a large Arſeſmart leaf, and a ſmall yellow flower.

5. JUSSIÆA (Hirſuta) caule erecto ſimplici hirſuto, foliis lanceolatis, floribus pentapetalis decandris ſeſſilibus. Juſſiæa with a ſingle, upright, hairy ſtalk, ſpear-ſhaped leaves, and flowers which have five petals, and ten ſtamina ſitting cloſe to the ſtalk. Onagra erecta, caule rubro hirſuto, foliis oblongis, flore magno luteo. Houſt. MSS. Upright Primroſe with a hairy leaf of a reddiſh colour, oblong leaves, and a large yellow flower.

The firſt ſort grows naturally at Campeachy, from whence the ſeeds were ſent me by the late Mr. Robert Millar; this riſes with a ſhrubby ſtalk near three feet high, ſending out ſeveral ſide branches, which are garniſhed with oblong hairy leaves placed alternate. The flowers come out from the ſide of the ſtalks ſingly, having ſhort foot-ſtalks; they have four ſmall yellow petals with eight ſtamina; theſe ſit upon the germen, which afterward becomes an oblong ſeed-veſſel, crowned by the four-leaved empalement, and has a great reſemblance.

femblance to Cloves. This plant flowers in July and Auguſt, and the feeds ripen in October.

The fecond fort grows naturally in Jamaica. The feeds of this were fent me by the late Dr. Houſtoun; this riſes with a hairy branching ſtalk two feet high, and is garniſhed with narrow ſpear-ſhaped leaves, placed alternate. The flowers come out toward the end of the branches ſingly from the wings of the leaves, ſitting cloſe to the ſtalk; they are compoſed of five pretty large yellow petals, and ten ſtamina; theſe ſit upon a long germen, which afterward becomes the feed-veſſel, crowned by the empalement; theſe are filled with ſmall ſeeds. It flowers and feeds about the ſame time with the laſt.

The third fort grows naturally in Jamaica, from whence the feeds were ſent me with thoſe of the former fort; this riſes with a ſmooth erect ſtalk three feet high, garniſhed with long, narrow, ſmooth, ſpearſhaped leaves, ſitting cloſe to the ſtalk; theſe are ſucceeded by long feed-veſſels, ſhaped like thoſe of the other forts. It flowers and feeds at the ſame time with the former.

The fourth fort was ſent me from Carthagena by the late Dr. Houſtoun; this hath a branching ſmooth ſtalk near three feet high, garniſhed with ſpearſhaped leaves, ſtanding upon ſhort foot-ſtalks. The flowers are ſmall, yellow, and are compoſed of four petals and eight ſtamina; theſe ſit very cloſe to the ſtalk, and are ſucceeded by feed-veſſels, ſhaped like thoſe of the former forts.

The fifth fort was ſent me from La Vera Cruz, by the late Dr. Houſtoun; this riſes with ſingle upright red ſtalks three feet high, which are hairy and channelled. The leaves are ſpear-ſhaped, and placed alternate on the ſtalks, ſtanding nearer together than in any of the other forts. The flowers come out from the wings of the leaves, toward the top of the ſtalk; they are compoſed of five large yellow petals, and ten ſtamina ſitting cloſe to the ſtalks, and are ſucceeded by feed-veſſels which are one inch long, and ſhaped like thoſe of the former forts.

The firſt, ſecond, and fourth forts are annual plants, at leaſt they are ſo in England; for if the plants are raiſed early in the ſpring, they will flower in July, and ripen their feed the beginning of October; and thoſe plants which are raiſed later in the ſpring, cannot be preſerved through the winter, though they are placed in a warm ſtove; nor do their ſtalks ever grow ligneous, or ſhew any ſigns of their being perennial in their native country.

The third and fifth forts have continued through the winter in the bark-ſtove, but thoſe have been ſuch plants as did not flower and feed the firſt year; for after they had perfected feeds, the following ſummer the plants decayed.

All theſe forts are propagated by feeds, which ſhould be ſown early in the ſpring, in pots filled with a ſoft loamy ſoil, and plunged into a moderate hot-bed; but as theſe feeds often lie a whole year in the ground before they vegetate, the earth muſt be kept moiſt, and the glaſſes of the hot-bed ſhaded in the heat of the day, by this method the feeds may be brought ſoon to vegetate; when the plants come up, and are fit to remove, they ſhould be each planted into a ſmall ſeparate pot, filled with light loamy earth, and plunged into a hot-bed of tanners bark, where they ſhould be ſhaded from the ſun till they have taken new root; after which they ſhould have free air admitted to them every day, in proportion to the warmth of the ſeaſon; they muſt alſo be frequently refreſhed with water, but it muſt not be given to them in too great plenty: when the roots of the plants have filled theſe ſmall pots, the plants ſhould be removed into others a ſize larger; and if the plants are too tall to ſtand under the ſtraws of the hot-bed, they ſhould be removed into the bark-ſtove, where they may remain to flower and perfect their feeds; for when the plants riſe early in the ſpring, and are brought forward in hot-beds, all the forts will flower and perfect their

feeds the ſame year, which is better than to have them to keep through the winter.

JUSTICIA. Houſt. Nov. Gen. Lin. Gen. Plant. 27. Adhatoda. Tourn. Inſt. R. H. 175. tab. 79. This plant was ſo named by the late Dr. Houſtoun, in honour of James Juſtice, Eſq; a great lover and encourager of gardening and botany.

The CHARACTERS are,

The empalement of the flower is ſmall, and divided into five acute ſegments at the top. The flower hath one petal, which is divided into two lips almoſt to the bottom, which are entire. The upper lip is raiſed archways, and the under is reflexed. It hath two awl-ſhaped ſtamina ſituated under the upper lip, terminated by erect ſummits which are bifid at their baſe. It hath an oblong germen, ſupporting a ſlender ſtyle which is longer than the petal, crowned by a ſingle ſtigma. The germen afterward becomes an oblong capſule with two cells, divided by a partition, which is contrary to the two valves, which open with an elaſticity, and caſt out the roundiſh ſeeds.

This genus of plants is ranged in the firſt ſection of Linnæus's ſecond claſs, intitled Diandria Monogynia, which includes thoſe plants whoſe flowers have two ſtamina and one ſtyle. To this genus of Dr. Houſtoun's is joined the Adhatoda of Tournefort, but there is a diſtinction in their flowers; the two lips of Juſticia are entire, but the upper lip of Adhatoda is indented at the end, and the under is divided into three parts; and in the capſule of Juſticia there are ſeldom more than two feeds, but in Adhatoda ſeveral.

The SPECIES are,

1. JUSTICIA (*Scorpioides*) foliis oblongo-ovatis hirſutis, ſeſſilibus, floribus ſpicatis alaribus, caule fruticoſo. *Juſticia with oblong, oval, hairy leaves ſitting cloſe to the ſtalks, and flowers growing in ſpikes proceeding from the ſide of the ſtalks, which are ſhrubby.* Juſticia fruteſcens, floribus ſpicatis majoribus, uno verſu diſpoſitis. Houſt. MSS. *Shrubby Juſticia with larger flowers growing in ſpikes, which are ranged on one ſide.*

2. JUSTICIA (*Sexangularis*) caule erecto ramoſo hexangulari, foliis ovatis oppoſitis, bracteis cuneiformibus confertis. *Juſticia with an erect branching ſtalk, having ſix angles, oval leaves placed oppoſite, and wedge-ſhaped ſmall leaves (or bractea) growing in cluſters.* Juſticia annua hexangulari caule, foliis Circææ conjugatis, flore miniato. Houſt. MSS. *Annual Juſticia with an hexangular ſtalk, Enchanters Nightſhade leaves ſet by pairs, and a carmine flower.*

3. JUSTICIA (*Fruticoſa*) foliis ovato-lanceolatis, pediculatis, hirſutis, bracteis cordatis acuminatis, caule fruticoſo. *Juſticia with oval ſpear-ſhaped leaves growing on foot-ſtalks, heart-ſhaped acute-pointed bractea, and a ſhrubby ſtalk.* Juſticia fruteſcens & hirſuta, foliis oblongis pediculis longiſſimis, flore rubro. Houſt. MSS. *Shrubby and hairy Juſticia with oblong leaves growing on very long foot-ſtalks, and a red flower.*

4. JUSTICIA (*Adhatoda*) arborea, foliis lanceolato-ovatis, bracteis ovatis perſiſtentibus, corollarum galea concavâ. Flor. Zeyl. 16. *Tree-Juſticia with oval ſpear-ſhaped leaves, oval permanent bractea, and a concave helmet to the flower.* Adhatoda Zeylanenſium. H. L. 642. *Adhatoda of Ceylon, commonly called Malabar Nut.*

5. JUSTICIA (*Hyſſopifolia*) fruticoſa, foliis lanceolatis integerrimis, pedunculis trifloris ancipitibus, bracteis calyce brevioribus. Lin. Sp. Plant. 15. *Shrubby Juſticia with entire ſpear-ſhaped leaves, foot-ſtalks having three flowers placed different ways, and a bractea ſhorter than the empalement.* Adhatoda Indica, folio ſaligno, flore albo. Boerh. Ind. alt. 1. 239. *Indian Adhatoda with a Willow leaf and white flower, commonly called Snaptree.*

6. JUSTICIA (*Spinoſa*) ſpinoſa, foliis oblongo-ovatis emarginatis, caule fruticoſo ramoſo. *Prickly Juſticia with oblong oval leaves indented at their edges, and a ſhrubby branching ſtalk.* Adhatoda Antegoana, Lycii facie, ſpinoſa. Petiv. *Prickly Adhatoda of Antigua, with the appearance of Boxthorn.*

7. JUSTICIA (*Arborea*) arborea, foliis lanceolato-ovatis ſeſſilibus, ſubtus tomentoſis, floribus ſpicatis congeſtis terminalibus. *Tree-Juſticia with ſpear-ſhaped oval leaves, wooly*

4

woolly on their under side, sitting close to the stalks, with spikes of flowers growing in clusters at the ends of the branches. Adhatoda arborea, foliis oblongis, subtus villosis, floribus spicatis albis. Houst. *Tree-Adhatoda with oblong leaves, hairy on their under side, and spikes of white flowers.*

8. Justicia (*Echolium*) arborea, foliis lanceolato ovatis, bracteis ovatis deciduis mucronatis, corollarum galeâ reflexâ. Flor. Zeyl. 17. *Tree-Justicia with spear-shaped oval leaves, oval-pointed bractea which fall off, and a reflexed helmet to the flowers.* Adhatoda spicâ longissimâ, flore reflexo. Burman. Zeyl. 7. tab. 4. f. 1. *Adhatoda with a very long spike, and a reflexed flower.*

The first sort was discovered growing naturally at La Vera Cruz, by the late Dr. Houstoun, who sent the seeds to England ; this rises with a shrubby brittle stalk five or six feet high, sending out many branches, which are garnished with oblong oval leaves, two inches long, and one inch broad, which are hairy and placed opposite ; from the wings of the leaves come out the spikes of flowers, which are reflexed like a scorpion's tail. The flowers are large, of a carmine colour, and ranged on one side of the spike ; these are succeeded by short pods about half an inch long. The second sort was discovered by the same gentleman, in the same country ; this is an annual plant with an upright stalk, having six angles, which rises two or three feet high, dividing into many branches, garnished with oval leaves placed opposite, an inch and a half long, and one inch broad ; they are smooth, as are also the stalks. At each joint come out clusters of small wedge-shaped leaves, which are by Dr. Linnæus termed bracteæ, and long before the stalks decay, most of the larger leaves fall off, so there are only these small leaves remaining. The flowers are produced in small spikes at the side of the branches, sitting very close among the leaves ; they are of a beautiful carmine colour, and have but one petal, which has two lips. The upper lip is arched, bending over the lower, which is also a little reflexed, but both are entire. The flowers are succeeded by short wedge-shaped capsules, opening lengthways, inclosing two small oval seeds.

The third sort was discovered by the same gentleman at Campeachy ; this rises with a hairy shrubby stalk four or five feet high, dividing into several branches, garnished with oval, spear-shaped, hairy leaves, four inches long, and two inches and a half broad, standing upon foot-stalks which are above an inch long, placed opposite. At the base of the foot-stalks come out a cluster of small heart-shaped leaves, ending in acute points, which are termed bracteæ. The flowers come out in loose clusters from the wings of the stalks, toward the end of the branches ; they are of a pale red colour, and shaped like those of the former sort.

These plants are propagated by seeds, which should be sown early in the spring, in small pots filled with fresh light earth, and plunged into a moderate hotbed of tanners bark, observing to water the earth gently as it appears dry. The seeds of these plants frequently lie a year in the ground, so that the pots must not be disturbed, if the plants do not come up the same year ; but in the winter should be kept in the stove, and the spring following plunged into a fresh hot-bed, which will bring up the plants if the seeds were good. When the plants begin to appear, the glasses of the hot-bed should be raised every day, when the weather is warm, to admit fresh air to them. The plants must also be frequently watered in warm weather ; but water should not be given in large quantities while the plants are young, because they are then very tender, and subject to rot at the bottom of their stems, with much moisture.

When the plants are about two inches high, they should be carefully taken up, and each transplanted into a separate small pot filled with fresh light earth, and then plunged into the hot-bed again, being careful to water and shade them until they have taken new root ; after which time they should have air admitted to them every day, in proportion to the warmth of

the season, and should be duly watered every two or three days in hot weather.

As the plants advance in their growth, they should be shifted into larger pots, for if their roots are too much confined, the plants will not make any considerable progress ; but they should not be over potted, for that will be of worse consequence than the other ; because when they are planted in very large pots, they will starve and decay, without producing any flowers. They are too tender to endure the open air in this country, therefore they should always remain in the hot-bed, being careful to let them have a due proportion of air in hot weather ; and the annual sort should be brought forward as fast as possible in the spring, that the plants may flower early, otherwise they will not produce good seeds in England.

The first and third sorts should remain in the hot-bed during the summer season (provided there is room under the glasses, without being scorched ;) but at Michaelmas they should be removed into the stove, and plunged into the bark-bed, where they must remain during the winter season, observing to keep them warm, as also to water them gently once or twice a week, according as they shall require. The following summer these plants will flower, and abide several years, but they rarely produce good seeds in Europe. The fourth sort grows naturally in the island of Ceylon, but has been long in the English gardens, where it is commonly known at present by the title of Malabar Nut ; but was formerly called Beetle Nut, and was by some supposed to be the tree of which the Chinese chew the leaves and nuts : this, though a native of so warm a country, is hardy enough to live in a good green-house in England, without any artificial heat. It rises here with a strong woody stalk to the height of twelve or fourteen feet, sending out many spreading branches, which are garnished with spear-shaped oval leaves more than six inches long, and three inches broad, placed opposite. The flowers are produced on short spikes at the end of the branches, which are white, with some dark spots ; these appear in July, but are not succeeded by any seeds in England.

This sort may be propagated by cuttings, which, if planted in pots in June or July, and plunged into a very moderate hot-bed, will take root ; but they must be every day screened from the sun, and if the external air is excluded from them, they will succeed better than when it is admitted to them. It may also be propagated by laying down their young branches, which will take root in the tubs or pots in one year ; then the young plants should be put each into a separate pot, filled with soft loamy earth, and placed in the shade till they have taken new root, when they may be placed in a sheltered situation during the summer, but in winter they must be housed, and treated in the same way as Orange-trees, with only this difference, that these require more water.

The fifth sort grows naturally in India ; this rises with a shrubby stalk from three to four feet high, sending out branches on every side from the bottom, so as to form a kind of pyramid ; these are covered with a white bark, and garnished with spear-shaped entire leaves, near two inches long, and one third of an inch broad ; they are smooth, stiff, and of a deep green, standing opposite. At the base of the foot-stalks come out clusters of smaller leaves, of the same shape and texture. The flowers come out upon short foot-stalks from the side of the branches, each foot-stalk supporting one or two white flowers, having long empalements ; these are succeeded by oblong seed-vessels, which, when ripe, cast out their seeds with an elasticity, from whence it had the title of Snap-tree.

This is propagated by cuttings during any of the summer months ; they should be planted in pots filled with light loamy earth, and plunged into a moderate hot-bed, and shaded from the sun, and now and then gently refreshed with water, and not too much air admitted to them. In about two months the cuttings will have taken root, then they must be gradually

inured

inured to bear the open air, into which they should be removed, placing them in a sheltered situation, where they may stay till autumn; but if they get root pretty early in the summer, it will be proper to separate them each into a single small pot, setting them in the shade till they have taken new root, after which they may be placed as before directed; but when it is late in the season before they take root, it will be better to let them remain in the same pots till the following spring. In winter these plants must be placed in a warm green-house, or in a moderately warm stove, for they are impatient of cold and damp, nor will they thrive in too much warmth; they will often require water in winter, but during that season it must be given them moderately; in summer they must be removed into the open air, but should have a warm sheltered situation, and in warm weather they must have plenty of water. This plant flowers at different seasons, but never produces fruit here.

The sixth sort grows naturally in Jamaica, from whence the late Dr. Houstoun sent it to England; this rises with many shrubby slender stalks about five feet high, sending out branches on every side from the root upward, which grow erect, and are covered with a whitish bark, garnished with small, oblong, oval leaves, coming out on each side the stalk opposite, and under the leaves are placed at every joint two sharp thorns like those of the Berberry; the flowers come out singly from the wings of the leaves, they are small, and of a pale red colour, shaped like those of the other sorts.

The seventh sort was found by the late Dr. Houstoun, growing naturally at Campeachy. This rises with a strong woody stem twenty feet high, dividing into many crooked irregular branches, covered with a light brown bark, garnished with spear-shaped oval leaves, near four inches long and two broad, which are covered with a soft down on their under side. The flowers grow in spikes from the end of the branches, three, four, or five of these spikes arising from the same point, the middle spike being near three inches long, and the others about half that length. The flowers are small and white, but shaped like those of the other species.

The eighth sort grows naturally at Malabar and in Ceylon; this rises in its native soil with a strong woody stem ten or twelve feet high, dividing into many branches, which are garnished with spear-shaped oval leaves five inches long, and two and a half broad, of a lucid green, placed opposite. The flowers grow in very long spikes from the end of the branches, they are of a greenish colour with a shade of blue; the helmet of the flower is reflexed.

These three sorts are propagated by seeds in the same manner as the three first, and the plants must be treated in the same way, especially while they are young; but afterward the eighth sort may be more hardily treated, when they have gotten strength. This sort may also be propagated by cuttings, in the same manner as the fifth sort; and when the plants are two or three years old, they will thrive in a moderate degree of warmth in winter, and in the summer they may be placed abroad for two months in the warmest season of the year; but they should have a warm sheltered situation, and when the nights begin to grow cold, they must be removed into the stove, but they must have free air admitted to them at all times when the weather is warm. The other two sorts should constantly remain in the bark-stove, and require the same treatment as other tender plants from the warmest countries.

I X I A. Lin. Gen. Plant. 54. Sisyrinchium. Com. Hort. Amst.

The CHARACTERS are,
It hath oblong permanent spathe (or sheaths) which inclose the germen; the flower has six oblong spear-shaped petals which are equal, and three awl-shaped stamina which are shorter than the petals, situated at equal distances, terminated by single summits. It hath an oval three-cornered germen situated below the flower, supporting a single style

which is the length of the stamina, crowned by a thick trifid stigma; the germen afterward becomes an oval three-cornered capsule with three cells, filled with roundish seeds.

This genus of plants is ranged in the first section of Linnæus's third class, intitled Triandria Monogynia, which includes those plants whose flowers have three stamina and one style.

The SPECIES are,

1. IXIA (*Chinensis*) foliis ensiformibus, floribus remotis panicula dichotoma, floribus peduncularis. Hort. Upsal. 16. *Ixia with sword-shaped leaves, and flowers standing remote in forked panicles upon foot-stalks.* Bermudiana iridis folio majori flore croceo, eleganter punctato. Krauf. Hort. 25. tab. 25. *Bermudiana with a larger Iris leaf, and a Saffron-coloured flower, which is beautifully spotted.*

2. IXIA (*Africana*) floribus capitatis, spathis laceris. Lin. Sp. Plant. 36. *Ixia with flowers growing in heads, having ragged sheaths.* Bermudiana Capensis, capitulis lanuginosis. Pet. Hort. Sicc. 242. *Bermudiana from the Cape of Good Hope, with woolly heads.*

3. IXIA (*Scillaris*) foliis gladiolatis, nervosis, hirsutis, floribus spicatis terminalibus. Icon. tab. 155. fig 1. *Ixia with sword-shaped, hairy, veined leaves, and flowers growing in spikes at the ends of the stalks.*

4. IXIA (*Polystacia*) foliis lineari-gladiolatis, floribus alaribus & terminalibus. Icon. tab. 155. fig. 2. *Ixia with narrow sword-shaped leaves, and flowers proceeding from the sides and tops of the stalk.*

5. IXIA (*Crocata*) foliis gladiolatis glabris, floribus corymbosis terminalibus. Icon. tab. 156. *Ixia with smooth spear-shaped leaves, and flowers growing in a corymbus terminating the stalk.* Sisyrinchium Africanum majus, flore luteo maculâ notato. Olden. *Greater African Sisyrinchium with a yellow spotted flower.*

6. IXIA (*Bulbifera*) foliis lineari-gladiolatis, floribus alternis, caule bulbifero. *Ixia with narrow sword-shaped leaves, flowers placed alternate, and stalks bearing bulbs.*

7. IXIA (*Sparsa*) foliis gladiolatis, floribus distantibus. *Ixia with sword-shaped leaves, and flowers growing distant.*

8. IXIA (*Flexuosa*) foliis lineari-gladiolatis, floribus spicatis sessilibus terminalibus. *Ixia with narrow sword-shaped leaves, and sessile flowers growing in spikes at the top of the stalk.*

The first sort grows naturally in India, where the stalks rise to the height of five or six feet, but in England they are seldom more than half that height. It hath a pretty thick fleshy root, divided in knots or joints of a yellowish colour, sending out many fibres; the stalk is pretty thick, smooth, and jointed, garnished with sword-shaped leaves a foot long and one inch broad, with several longitudinal furrows embracing the stalks with their base, ending in acute points; the upper part of the stalk divaricates into two smaller, with a foot-stalk arising between them, which supports one flower; the smaller branches divaricate again in the same manner into foot-stalks, which are two inches long, each sustaining one flower. At each of these joints is a spatha or sheath embracing the stalk, which at the lower joints are three inches long, but the upper are not more than one inch, ending in acute points which are permanent; the flowers are composed of six equal petals, of a yellow colour within, and variegated with dark red spots; the outside is of an Orange colour. These appear in July and August, and in warm seasons are succeeded by seeds.

This sort may be propagated either by seeds or parting of the roots: if by seeds they should be sown in pots, and plunged into a moderate hot-bed, which will bring up the plants much sooner than when they are sown in the full ground; when the plants are fit to remove, they should be each planted in a small separate pot filled with light earth, and if they are placed under a frame till they have taken good root in the pots, it will greatly forward their growth; afterward they may be placed in the open air in a sheltered situation, where they may remain till the autumn, when
they

they muſt be placed under a frame to ſcreen them from froſt; and in the ſpring moſt of the plants may be turned out of the pots and planted in a warm border, where they will abide through the common winters very well, but in ſevere froſts they are often killed, unleſs they are covered with tan, or other covering to keep out the froſt; therefore a few of the plants may be kept in pots, and ſheltered under a frame in winter.

The ſtalks and leaves of this plant decay to the root in autumn, ſo that if the ſurface of the ground about the roots is covered two or three inches thick with tan, it will ſecure them from the danger of froſt; and in the ſpring, before the roots ſhoot, will be the beſt time to remove and part the roots; but this ſhould not be done oftener than every third year, for when they are often parted they will be weak, and will not flower ſo well.

The ſecond ſort grows naturally at the Cape of Good Hope; this is a low plant, which rarely riſes more than three or four inches high; the leaves are narrow and veined, the flowers are ſmall, growing in a downy head on the top of the ſtalk, but they make little appearance, ſo are only kept for the ſake of variety.

The third ſort I raiſed from ſeeds, which were ſent me from the Cape of Good Hope. This hath a round bulbous root a little compreſſed, covered with a red ſkin, from which ariſe five or ſix ſword-ſhaped leaves about three or four inches long, hairy, and with ſeveral longitudinal furrows; theſe embrace each other at their baſe, but ſpread aſunder at the top; between theſe come out the flower-ſtalk, which riſes ſix or eight inches high, is naked to the top, and terminated by a cluſter of flowers, each having a ſpatha or hood, which dries and is permanent; the flowers are of a deep blue colour, and appear in May; theſe are ſucceeded by roundiſh three-cornered ſeed-veſſels with three cells, filled with roundiſh ſeeds which ripen in July, then the leaves and ſtalks decay.

The fourth ſort was raiſed from ſeeds in the Chelſea garden, which came with thoſe of the former ſort. This hath a ſmall round bulbous root, from which ariſe four or five narrow, long, ſword-ſhaped leaves, ſix or ſeven inches long; between theſe come out a very ſlender round ſtalk about ten inches long, from the ſide of which there comes out one or two cluſters of flowers, ſtanding upon ſhort foot-ſtalks, and at the top of the ſtalk the flowers grow in a looſe ſpike; they are of a pure white, and ſhaped like thoſe of the other ſpecies. Theſe appear in May, and the ſeeds ripen in July.

The ſeeds of the fifth ſort were ſent me from the Cape of Good Hope; this has an oval bulbous root which is a little compreſſed, from which come up three or four narrow, thin, ſword-ſhaped leaves, near a foot long; the flower-ſtalk riſes a little above the leaves, it is very ſlender, naked, and terminated by a round cluſter of flowers, each having a ſpatha or hood; they are compoſed of ſix pretty large oblong petals which are concave, and of a deep yellow colour, each having a large black ſpot at the baſe. This flowers early in May, and the ſeeds ripen the latter end of June.

The ſixth ſort hath narrow ſpear-ſhaped leaves about ſix or ſeven inches long; the ſtalk riſes near a foot and a half high, garniſhed with one leaf at each of the lower joints, of the ſame ſhape with the other, but ſmaller; theſe embrace the ſtalk with their baſe, and ſtand erect; the upper part of the ſtalk is adorned with flowers, compoſed of ſix oblong oval petals of a ſulphur colour, which are placed alternate on the ſtalk, which is bent at each joint where the flowers ſtand; the flowers have three ſhort ſtamina which are joined at their baſe, terminated by long, flat, erect ſummits; the germen is ſituated under the flower, ſupporting a long ſlender ſtyle, crowned by a trifid ſtigma; the germen afterward becomes a roundiſh capſule with three cells, filled with roundiſh ſmall ſeeds. The ſtalks at each of the lower joints thruſt out ſmall bulbs, which, if planted, will grow and produce flowers.

The ſeventh ſort hath ſhorter and broader leaves than the former; the ſtalk is ſlender and furrowed, and at each of the lower joints is garniſhed with one leaf of the ſame ſhape, embracing the ſtalk with their baſe; the flowers come out toward the top of the ſtalk, at two or three inches diſtance, each ſtalk ſupporting two or three ſulphur-coloured flowers, which are each compoſed of ſix ſpear ſhaped petals an inch and a half long, equal in their ſize and regular in poſition; they have a ſhort permanent empalement, cut into two long and two ſhorter acute ſegments; theſe are ſucceeded by round capſules with three cells, filled with round ſeeds. This ſort flowers in March, and the ſeeds ripen about two months after.

The eighth ſort hath very ſmall, round, bulbous roots, from which ariſe three or four long, ſlender, Graſs-like leaves, of a dark green colour; between theſe come out the ſtalk, which is very ſlender and round, riſing a foot and a half high; at the top the flowers are collected in a ſpike ſitting cloſe to the ſtalk, each having a thin, dry, permanent ſpatha or ſheath, which covers the capſule after the flower is fallen. The flowers are of a pure white, and ſhaped like thoſe of the other ſpecies, but are ſmaller; they are ſucceeded by ſmall round ſeed-veſſels with three cells, each containing two or three round ſeeds. It flowers the latter end or May, and the ſeeds ripen in July.

There are ſome other varieties of this genus, which have flowered in the Chelſea garden, differing only in the colour of their flowers, ſo are not ſuppoſed to be diſtinct ſpecies; one of which is purple on the outſide, and white within; another has white flowers, with a blue ſtripe on the outſide of each petal, and a third has white flowers with yellow bottoms. Theſe have already flowered in the Chelſea garden, where there are many more, which have been ſince raiſed from ſeeds, whoſe flowers have not as yet appeared; and at the Cape of Good Hope, where theſe plants grow naturally, there are more than thirty varieties mentioned in a catalogue of Dr. Herman's. The roots of moſt, if not all theſe ſorts, are frequently eaten by the inhabitants at the Cape of Good Hope, who greatly eſteem them.

All the ſorts multiply very faſt by offsets, ſo that when once obtained, there will be no occaſion to raiſe them from ſeeds; for the roots put out offsets in great plenty, moſt of which will flower the following ſeaſon, whereas thoſe from ſeeds are three or four years before they flower. Theſe plants will not live through the winter in the full ground in England, ſo ſhould be planted in ſmall pots filled with light earth, and placed under a frame in winter, where they may be protected from froſt, but in mild weather ſhould enjoy the free air; but during the winter they muſt be guarded from mice, who are very fond of theſe roots, and if not prevented will devour them.

IXORA. Lin. Gen. 131. Jaſminum. Burman.

The CHARACTERS are,

It hath a ſmall permanent empalement cut into four ſegments; the flower has one funnel-ſhaped petal, having a ſlender tube, cut into four ſegments at the top. It hath four ſhort ſtamina ſituated in the diviſions of the petal, terminated by oblong ſummits, and a roundiſh germen ſituated at the bottom of the involucrum, ſupporting a ſlender ſtyle the length of the tube, crowned by a bifid ſtigma; the germen afterward becomes a berry with two cells, containing two convex angular ſeeds.

This genus of plants is ranged in the firſt order of Linnæus's fourth claſs, intitled Tetrandria Monogynia, the flowers having four ſtamina and one ſtyle.

The SPECIES are,

1. IXORA (*Coccinea*) foliis ovatis ſemiamplexicaulibus, floribus faſciculatis. Flor. Zeyl. 22. *Ixora with oval leaves half embracing the ſtalks, and flowers growing in bunches.* Jaſminum Indicum lauri folio, inodorum umbellatum, floribus coccineis. Pluk. Phyt. tab. 59. f. 2.

2. IXORA

Ixora (*Alba*) foliis ovato-lanceolatis, floribus fafciculatis. Lin. Sp. 160. *Ixora with oval fpear-fhaped leaves, and flowers growing in bunches.* Jafminum Indicum, lauri folio, inodorum, floribus albicantibus & fchetti album. Pluk. Phyt. 109. f. 2.

3. Ixora (*Americana*) foliis ternis lanceolato-ovatis, floribus thyrfoideis. Amœn. Acad. 5. p. 393. *Ixora with oval fpear-fhaped leaves placed by threes, and flowers in a loofe fpike.* Pavetta foliis oblongo-ovatis oppofitis, ftipulis fetaceis. Brown. Jam. tab. 6. f. 2.

The firft fort grows naturally in India, where it rifes with a woody ftalk five or fix feet high, fending out many flender branches covered with a brown bark, garnifhed with oval leaves, placed fometimes oppofite, and at others there are three or four at each joint. The flowers terminate the branches in clufters; they have very long flender tubes, are cut into four oval fegments at the top, and are of a deep red colour.

The fecond fort grows alfo in India; this hath a woody ftalk rifing fix or feven feet high, fending out weak branches, garnifhed with oval fpear-fhaped leaves placed oppofite, fitting clofe to the branch; the flowers terminate the branches in fmall clufters; they have long flender tubes, divided into four fegments at the top, and are white, without fcent.

The third fort grows naturally in Jamaica, and fome other iflands in the Weft-Indies, where it is called Wild Jafmine. This rifes with a fhrubby ftalk four or five feet high, fending out flender branches oppofite, which are garnifhed with oval fpear-fhaped leaves placed oppofite, which are fix inches long, and

two inches and a half broad, having fhort foot-ftalks; the flowers are produced at the end of the branches in a loofe fpike, they are white, and have a fcent like Jafmine.

Thefe plants are propagated by feeds, when they can be procured from the countries where they grow naturally, for they do not perfect any feeds in England. They fhould be fown in fmall pots as foon as they arrive, and plunged into a hot-bed; if they arrive in autumn or winter, the pots may be plunged in the tan-bed in the ftove, between the other pots of plants, fo will take up little room; but when they arrive in the fpring, it will be beft to plunge them in a tan-bed under frames; the feeds will fometimes come up in about fix weeks, if they are quite frefh; otherwife they will lie in the ground four or five months, and fometimes a whole year, therefore the earth fhould not be thrown out of the pots till there is no hopes of their growing; when the plants come up, and are fit to remove, they fhould be each planted in a feparate fmall pot, filled with light earth, and afterward treated in the manner directed for the Coffee-tree.

They may alfo be increafed by cuttings during the fummer months, and planted in fmall pots plunged into a moderate hot-bed, covering them clofe either with bell or hand-glaffes to exclude the external air, fhading them carefully from the fun during the heat of the day, until they have put out good roots, when they fhould be parted, and each put into a feparate pot, treating them as the feedling plants.

K.

K A L   K A L

KA L I. See Salsola.
    KALMIA. Lin. Gen. Plant. 482. Chamærhododendros. Tourn. Inft. R. H. 604. tab. 373.

The Characters are,

The flower has a fmall permanent empalement cut into five parts, and one petal cut into five fegments, which fpread open and are roundifh. It hath ten ftamina the length of the petal, which decline to the middle, terminated by oval fummits. In the center is fituated a roundifh germen, fupporting a flender ftyle as long as the petal, crowned by an obtufe ftigma. The germen afterward becomes an oval or globular capfule with five cells, filled with very fmall feeds.

This genus of plants is ranged in the firft fection of Linnæus's tenth clafs, intitled Decandria Monogynia, which includes thofe plants whofe flowers have ten ftamina and one ftyle.

The Species are,

1. Kalmia (*Latifolia*) foliis ovatis, corymbis terminalibus. Amœn. Acad. 3. p. 19. *Kalmia with oval leaves, and flowers growing in bunches terminating the branches.* Chamædaphne foliis tini, floribus bullatis umbellatis. Catefb. Carol. 2. p. 98. tab. 98. *Dwarf Laurel with a Tinus leaf, and ftudded flowers growing in umbels, commonly called Ivy-tree in America.*

2. Kalmia (*Anguftifolia*) foliis lanceolatis corymbus lateralibus. Lin. Gen. Nov. 1079. *Kalmia with fpearfoaped leaves, and flowers growing in round bunches on the fides of the ftalk.* Chamædaphne fempervirens, foliis

oblongis anguftis, foliorum fafciculis oppofitis. Catefb. Carol. 3. p. 17. *Evergreen Dwarf Laurel, with oblong narrow leaves growing in bunches, which are placed oppofite.* The firft fort grows naturally upon rocks and in barren foils in Virginia and Penfylvania, where it rifes with a branching ftalk to the height of ten or twelve feet, garnifhed with very ftiff leaves, which are two inches long and one broad, of a lucid green on their upper fide, but of a pale green on their under; they have fhort foot-ftalks, and ftand without order round the branches; between thefe the buds are formed for the next year's flowers, at the extremity of the branches; thefe budsfwell during the autumn and fpring months, till the beginning of June, when the flowers burft out from their empalements, forming a round bunch (or corymbus) fitting very clofe to the branch; they are of a pale blufh colour, the outfide of the petals is of a Peach colour. The flower has but one petal, whofe bafe is tubulous, but is cut into five roundifh fegments, ftudded with purple fpots, which are prominent; after the flowers are paft, the germen in the center becomes an oval capfule, crowned by the permanent ftyle, having five cells, which are full of very fmall feeds. This fhrub in its native foil continues flowering great part of the fummer, and is one of the greateft ornaments to the country; but as yet it is not fo well naturalized to our climate as could be wifhed, though the plants are not injured by the cold, and fome of them have flowered feveral years paft in the Chelfea garden.

In

In the country where this shrub grows naturally, it sends out plenty of suckers from the roots, so that they form thickets which are almost impassable; but here they have not as yet produced any suckers, nor do the seeds come to maturity, so that the plants are not very common in England; for the seeds which are sent from America lie in the ground a whole year before the plants appear, and afterward they make very slow progress, which has discouraged most people from attempting to raise the plants in that method. The only person who has succeeded well in the raising of these, is Mr. James Gordon of Mile End, who has a good number of the plants which have arisen from seeds.

The second sort is a native of the same country with the first, where it rises from three to six feet high, dividing into small ligneous branches which are very close, covered with a dark gray bark, garnished with stiff leaves about two inches long and half an inch broad, of a lucid green, placed without order upon the branches, standing upon slender foot-stalks; the flowers grow in loose bunches on the side of the branches, upon slender foot-stalks; they are of one petal, having a short tube, but spread open at the top, where they are cut into five angles: the flowers are of a bright red colour when they first open, but afterward fade to a blush or Peach bloom colour; these are succeeded by roundish compressed seed-vessels crowned by the permanent style, divided into five cells, which are filled with small roundish seeds. This shrub flowers great part of summer in its native country, but is not yet so well naturalized to this country as to do the like.

The leaves of this elegant plant are supposed to have a noxious quality, destroying sheep and oxen when they feed upon them, yet the deer eat them with impunity.

Both these sorts multiply by their creeping roots in their native soil, and at Whitton, where they have stood unremoved a considerable time, they put out suckers in pretty great plenty; and as these plants which come from suckers, are much more likely to produce others than those which are raised from seeds, and will flower much sooner, so the plants should not be removed, but encouraged to spread their roots and send out suckers.

KARATAS, the Penguin or wild Ananas.

The Characters are,

It hath a tubulous bell-shaped flower, which is divided into three parts at the mouth, from whose empalement where the germen is situated arises the pointal, fixed like a nail in the hinder part of the flower, attended by six short stamina; the germen afterward becomes a fleshy almost conical fruit, which is divided by membranes into three cells, that are full of oblong seeds.

There is but one sort of this plant at present known in England, which is,

Karatas (*Penguin*) foliis ciliato spinosis mucronatis, racemo terminali. *The wild Ananas or Penguin.*

Father Plumier has made a great mistake in the figure and description of the characters of this plant, and the Caraguata; for he has joined the flower of the Caraguata to the fruit of the Karatas, and vice versâ; this has led many persons into mistakes, who have joined the Bromelia and Ananas to this, making them all of the same genus, whereas by their characters they should be separated.

This plant is very common in the West-Indies, where the juice of its fruit is often put into punch, being of a sharp acid flavour. There is also a wine made of the juice of this fruit which is very strong, but it will not keep good very long, so is only for present use. This wine is very intoxicating and heats the blood, therefore should be drank very sparingly.

In England this plant is preserved as a curiosity, for the fruit seldom arrives to any degree of perfection in this country, though it has often produced fruit in the gardens, which sometimes has ripened pretty well; but if it were to ripen as thoroughly here as in its native country, it would be little valued on account

of its great austerity, which will often take the skin off from the mouths and throats of those people who eat it incautiously.

This plant is propagated by seeds, for though there are often suckers sent forth from the old plants, yet they come out from between the leaves, and are so long, slender, and ill-shapen, that if they are planted they seldom make regular plants. These seeds should be sown early in the spring, in small pots filled with light rich earth, and plunged into a hot-bed of tanners bark. When the plants are strong enough to transplant, they should be carefully taken up, and each planted into a separate pot filled with light rich earth, and plunged into the hot-bed again, observing to refresh them frequently with water, until they have taken new root, after which time they should have air and water in proportion to the warmth of the season. In this bed the plants may remain till Michaelmas, at which time they should be removed into the stove, and plunged into the bark-bed, where they should be treated in the same manner as the Ananas.

These plants will not produce their fruit in England until they are three or four years old, so they should be shifted into larger pots, as the plants advance in their growth; for if their roots are too much confined, they will make but little progress. They should also be placed at a pretty great distance from each other, for their leaves will be three or four feet long, which turning downward occupy a large space.

The leaves of this plant are strongly armed with crooked spines, which renders it very troublesome to shift or handle the plants; for the spines catch hold of whatever approaches them by their crooked form, being some bent one way, and others the reverse, so that they catch both ways, and tear the skin or clothes of the persons who handle them, where there is not the greatest care taken of them.

The fruit of this plant is produced in clusters, growing upon a stalk about three feet high, and having generally a tuft of leaves growing on the top, so has, at first sight, the appearance of a Pine Apple; but, when closer viewed, they will be found to be a cluster of oblong fruit, each being about the size of a finger.

A KATKIN is an aggregate of summits, hanging down in form of a rope, or Cat's tail, as in the Sallow, Hazel, Birch, &c. and is called in Latin iulus.

KÆMPFERIA. Lin. Gen. Plant. 7.

The Characters are,

It hath a single spatha (or sheath) of one leaf; the flower hath one petal, with a long slender tube, divided into six parts above; three of them are alternately spear-shaped and equal, the other are oval, and at bottom cut into two segments which are vertically heart-shaped. It hath but one stamen, which is membranaceous, oval, and indented, terminated by a linear summit, fastened to it all the length, scarcely emerging out of the tube of the petal. It hath a round germen supporting a style the length of the tube, crowned by an obtuse stigma; the germen afterward becomes a roundish three-cornered capsule with three cells, filled with seeds.

This genus of plants is ranged in the first section of Linnæus's first class, intitled Monandria Monogynia, which includes those plants whose flowers have one stamen and one style.

The Species are,

1. KÆMPFERIA (*Galanga*) foliis ovatis sessilibus. Flor. Zeyl. 8. *Kæmpferia with oval leaves sitting close to the root.* Katsjuli Kelengu. Hort. Mal. and the Wanhom. Kæmpf. Amœn. 901. *Galangale.*

2. KÆMPFERIA (*Rotunda*) foliis lanceolatis petiolatis. Flor. Zeyl. 9. *Kæmpferia with spear-shaped leaves having foot-stalks.* Zedoaria rotunda. C. B. P. *Round Zedoary.*

These plants are both natives of the East-Indies, where their roots are greatly used in medicine as sudorific and carminative. The first sort hath much the scent of green Ginger, when fresh taken out of the ground; the roots are divided into several fleshy tubers, which are sometimes jointed, and grow about four or five inches long; the leaves are oval, about four inches long and two broad; thefe are without foot-ftalks, growing clofe to the root, and feem as if fet on by pairs, fpreading open each way; and from between thefe leaves the flowers are produced fingly, having no foot-ftalks, but are clofely embraced by the leaves; the flowers are white, having a bright purple bottom. Thefe are not fucceeded by any fruit in England.

The fecond fort hath roots fomewhat like thofe of the firft, but are fhorter, growing in large clufters, covered with an Afh-coloured fkin, but within are white; from the roots arife the leaves, which fold over each other at their bafe; they are fix or eight inches long, and three broad in the middle, gradually ending in acute points; the flowers arife immediately from the roots, each having a fpatha (or fheath) at bottom cut into two fegments, which clofely embrace the foot-ftalk; thefe have fix petals, the three lower which decline downward are long and narrow, the two upper are divided fo deeply as to appear like a flower with four petals, and the fide petal is bifid; they are of mixed colours, blue, purple, white and red, having a fragrant odour: they flower in July and Auguft, but do not produce feeds in England.

Thefe plants being natives of hot countries, will not bear the open air in England, fo requires a warm ftove to preferve them through the winter; but as their leaves decay in the autumn, fo the plants fhould not have too much wet while they are in an inactive ftate. If the plants are placed in the bark-ftove, and treated in the fame manner as is directed for the Ginger, they will thrive, and produce plenty of flowers every fummer. They are both propagated by parting of their roots; the beft time for this is in the fpring, juft before they begin to put out their leaves.

KETMIA. See Hibiscus.

KIGGELARIA. Lin. Gen. Plant. 1001. Laurus. Sterb. We have no Englifh title for this plant.

The Characters are,

It hath male and hermaphrodite flowers fituated on different trees; the male flowers have an empalement of one leaf, cut into five concave fegments, and five concave petals which are longer than the empalement, fhaped like a pitcher; each of the petals have a honey gland fastened to their bafe, which have three obtufe lobes and are coloured, faftened to the tails of the petals; they have ten fmall ftamina, terminated by oblong fummits. The hermaphrodite flowers have empalements and petals like the male, but few of them have ftamina. In the center is fituated a roundifh germen, fupporting five ftyles, crowned by obtufe ftigmas. The germen afterward becomes a rough globular fruit with a thick cover, having one cell, filled with angular feeds.

This genus of plants is ranged in the ninth fection of Linnæus's twenty-fecond clafs, intitled Diœcia Decandria; but it fhould be removed to his twenty-third clafs, as the hermaphrodite flowers are fruitful, tho' they are fituated upon diftinct plants, whofe male flowers have ten ftamina.

We have but one Species of this genus, viz.

Kiggelaria (*Africana*.) Hort. Cliff. 462. fol. 29. Euonymo-affinis Æthiopica fempervirens, fructu globofo fcabro, foliis falicis rigidis ferratis. H. L. 139. *An Ethiopian Evergreen plant refembling the Spindle-tree, with a rough globular fruit, and ftiff fawed Willow leaves.*

This plant grows naturally at the Cape of Good Hope, where it rifes to be a tree of middling ftature; but as it will not live in the open air here, they cannot be expected to grow to a great magnitude in England. There are plants of it in the Chelfea garden upward of ten feet high, with ftrong woody ftems and pretty large heads; the branches have a fmooth bark, which is firft green, but afterward changes to a purplifh colour; the leaves are about three inches long and one broad, of a light green colour, and fawed on their edges, ftanding upon fhort foot-ftalks alternately. The flowers come out in clufters from the fide of the branches, and hang downward; they are of an herba-

ceous white colour, and appear in May, at which time the plants are thinly garnifhed with leaves, for moft of the old leaves drop juft before the new ones appear. The male flowers fall away foon after their farina is fhed, but the hermaphrodite flowers are fucceeded by globular fruit about the fize of common red Cherries; the cover of thefe is very rough, and of a thick confiftence, opening in five valves at the top, having one cell filled with fmall angular feeds. Thefe fruit have grown to their full fize in the Chelfea garden, but the feeds have rarely come to maturity here.

Thefe plants were not very common in Europe fome years paft, being very difficult to propagate, unlefs by feeds, which fome plants both in Holland and England have lately produced, fo that they are now much more plenty than they were in both countries; for when any of the young branches are laid down, they are two years before they put out roots, and fearce one in five will then have any roots; nor do the cuttings fucceed better, for not one in twenty of them will take root, when planted with the utmoft care: the beft time to plant the cuttings is in the fpring, juft before the plants begin to fhoot; thefe fhould be planted in pots filled with a foft loamy earth, and plunged into a very moderate hot-bed, covering them clofe with a glafs, to exclude the air from them, and fhade them every day from the fun; they fhould have very little water after their firft planting. If any of them grow, they fhould be planted into feparate fmall pots, filled with loamy earth, and may be expofed to the air in a fheltered fituation till autumn, when they muft be removed into the green-houfe, and treated in the fame manner as Orange-trees.

KITCHEN-GARDEN. A good Kitchen-garden is almoft as neceffary to a country feat, as a kitchen to the houfe; for without one, there is no way of being fupplied with a great part of neceffary food; the markets in the country being but poorly furnifhed with efculent herbs, and thofe only upon the market days, which are feldom oftener than once a week; fo that unlefs a perfon has a garden of his own, there will be no fuch thing as procuring them frefh, in which their goodnefs confifts; nor can any variety of thefe be had in the country markets; therefore whoever propofes to refide in the country, fhould be careful to make choice of a proper fpot of ground for this purpofe; and the fooner that is made and planted, the produce of it will be earlier in perfection; for fruit-trees and Afparagus require three years to grow, before any produce can be expected from them; fo that the later the garden is made, the longer it will be before a fupply of thefe things can be had for the table. And although the ufefulnefs of this garden is acknowledged by almoft every one, yet there are few who make a proper choice of foil and fituation for fuch a garden; the modern tafte, which is, perhaps, carried to as extravagant lengths, in laying open and throwing every obftruction down, as the former cuftom of inclofing within walls was ridiculous; fo that now one frequently fees the Kitchen-garden removed to a very great diftance from the houfe and offices, which is attended with great inconveniencies; and often fituated on a very bad foil, fometimes too moift, and at others without water, fo that there is a great expence in building walls and making the garden, where there can be little hopes of fuccefs. Nor will a Kitchen-garden be well attended to, when it is fo fituated as to be out of fight of the poffeffor, efpecially if the gardener has not a love and value for it, or if it lies at a great diftance from his habitation, or the other parts of the garden; for when it fo happens, a great part of the labourer's time will be loft in going from one part to the other: therefore, before the general plan of the pleafure-garden is fettled, a proper piece of ground fhould be chofen for this purpofe, and the plan fo adapted, as that the Kitchen-garden may not become offenfive to the fight, which may be effected by proper plantations of fhrubs to fcreen the walls; and through thefe fhrubs may be
contrived

contrived fome winding walks to lead to the Kitchen-garden, which will have as good an effect as thofe which are now commonly made in gardens for pleafure only. In the choice of the fituation, if it does not obftruct the view of better objects, or fhut out any material profpect, there can be no objection to the placing it at a reafonable diftance from the houfe or offices; for as particular things may be wanted for the kitchen, which were not thought of at the time when directions were given to the gardener what to bring in; fo if the garden is fituated at a great diftance from the houfe, it will be found very inconvenient to fend thither as often as things are wanting: therefore it fhould be contrived as near the ftables as poffible, for the conveniency of carrying the dung thither; which, if at a great diftance, will add to the expence of the garden.

As to the figure of the ground, that is of no great moment, fince in the diftribution of the quarters all irregularities may be hid; though if you are at full liberty, an exact fquare or an oblong, is preferable to any other figure.

The great thing to be confidered is, to make choice of a good foil, not too wet, nor over dry, but of a middling quality; nor fhould it be too ftrong or ftubborn, but of a pliable nature, and eafy to work; and if the place where you intend to make the Kitchen-garden fhould not be level, but high in one part and low in another, I would by no means advife the levelling it; for by this fituation you will have an advantage which could not be obtained on a perfect level, which is, the having one part dry ground for early crops, and the low part for late crops, whereby the kitchen may be the better fupplied throughout the feafon with the various forts of herbs, roots, &c. And in very dry feafons, when in the upper part of the garden the crop will greatly fuffer with drought, then the lower part will fucceed, and fo vice verfà; but I would by no means direct the chufing a very low moift fpot of ground for this purpofe; for although in fuch foils garden-herbs are commonly more vigorous and large in the fummer feafon, yet they are feldom fo well tafted or wholefome as thofe which grow upon a moderate foil; and efpecially fince in this garden your choice fruits fhould be planted, it would be wrong to have a very wet foil.

This garden fhould be fully expofed to the fun, and by no means overfhadowed with trees, buildings, &c. which are very injurious to your kitchen plants and fruit-trees; but if it be defended from the north wind by a diftant plantation, it will greatly preferve your early crops in the fpring; as alfo from the ftrong fouth-weft winds, which are very hurtful in autumn to fruit and garden-herbs. But thefe plantations fhould not be too near nor very large; for I have generally found where Kitchen-gardens are placed near woods or large plantations, they have been much more troubled with blights in the fpring, than thofe which have been more expofed.

The quantity of ground neceffary for a Kitchen-garden muft be proportioned to the largenefs of the family, or the quantity of herbs defired: for a fmall family, one acre of ground may be fufficient; but for a large family, there fhould not be lefs than three or four acres; becaufe, when the ground is regularly laid out, and planted with efpaliers of fruit-trees, as will hereafter be directed, this quantity will be found little enough, notwithftanding what fome perfons have faid on this head.

This ground muft be walled round, and if it can be conveniently contrived, fo as to plant both fides of the walls which have good afpects, it will be a great addition to the quantity of wall fruit; and thofe flips of ground which are without fide of the walls, will be very ufeful for planting of Goofeberries, Currants, Strawberries, and fome forts of kitchen plants, fo that they may be rendered equally ufeful with any of the quarters within the walls; but thefe flips fhould not be too narrow, left the hedge, pale, or plantation

of fhrubs, which inclofe them, fhould fhade the borders where the fruit-trees ftand: the leaft width of thefe flips fhould be twenty-five or thirty feet, but if they are double that, it will be yet better, and the flips will be more ufeful, and the fruit-trees will have a larger fcope of good ground for their roots to run. Thefe walls fhould be built about twelve feet high, which will be a fufficient height for any fort of fruit. If the foil where you intend to place your Kitchen-garden be very ftrong, then you fhould plough or dig it three or four times before you plant any thing therein; and if you throw it up in ridges to receive the froft in winter, it will be of great fervice to meliorate and loofen its parts.

The manure which is moft proper for fuch foils, is fea-coal afhes, and the cleanfing of ftreets or ditches, which will render it light much fooner than any other dung or manure; and the greater the quantity of afhes the better, efpecially if the ground be cold; and where thefe afhes are not to be obtained in plenty, fea-fand is a very proper dreffing, where it can be eafily procured, or rotten wood, or the parts of vegetables rotted are very good; all which will greatly loofen the foil, and caufe it to be not only eafier to work, but alfo more advantageous for the growth of plants.

But, on the contrary, if your foil be light and warm, you fhould manure it with rotten neats dung, which is much preferable to any other dreffing for hot foils; but if you ufe horfe dung, it muft be well rotted, otherwife it will burn up the crops upon the firft hot dry weather.

The foil of this garden fhould be at leaft two feet deep, but if deeper it will be ftill better; otherwife there will not be depth enough of foil for many forts of efculent roots, as Carrots, Parfneps, Beets, &c. which run down pretty deep in the ground, and moft other forts of efculent plants delight in a deep foil; and many plants, whofe roots appear fhort, yet if their fibres by which they receive their nourifhment are traced, they will be found to extend to a confiderable depth in the ground; fo that when thefe are ftopped by meeting with gravel, chalk, clay, &c. the plants will foon fhew it by their colour and ftinted growth.

You fhould alfo endeavour to have a fupply of water in the different parts of the garden, which, if poffible, fhould be contained in large bafons or refervoirs, where it may be expofed to the open air and fun, that it may be foftened thereby; for fuch water as is taken out of wells, &c. juft as it is ufed, is by no means proper for any fort of plants.

In the diftribution of this garden, after having built the walls, you fhould lay out banks or borders under them, which fhould be at leaft eight or ten feet broad, whereby the roots of the fruit-trees will have greater liberty than in fuch places where the borders are not above three or four feet wide; and upon thefe banks you may fow many forts of early crops, if expofed to the fouth; and upon thofe expofed to the north, you may have fome late crops; but I would by no means advife the planting any fort of deep rooting plants too near the fruit-trees, efpecially Peas and Beans; tho' for the advantage of the walls, to preferve them in winter, and to bring them forward in the fpring, the gardeners in general are too apt to make ufe of thofe borders, which are near the beft afpected walls, to the great prejudice of their fruit-trees; but for thefe purpofes it is much better to have fome Reed-hedges fixed in fome of the warmeft quarters, under which you fhould fow and plant early Peas, Beans, &c. where they will thrive as well as if planted under a wall, and hereby your fruit-trees will be entirely freed from fuch troublefome plants.

Then you fhould proceed to dividing the ground out into quarters, which muft be proportioned to the largenefs of the garden; but I would advife never to make them too fmall, whereby your ground will be loft in walks; and the quarters being inclofed by efpaliers of fruit-trees the plants therein will draw up flender,

and

and never arrive to half the fize as they would do in a more open expofure.

The walks of this garden fhould be alfo proportioned to the fize of the ground, which in a fmall garden fhould be four feet, but in a large one fix; and on each fide of the walk fhould be allowed a border five for fix feet wide between the efpalier and the walk, whereby the diftance between the efpaliers will be greater, and the borders being kept conftantly worked and manured, will be of great advantage to the roots of the trees; and in thefe borders may be fown fome fmall fallad, or any other herbs, which do not continue long or root deep, fo that the ground will not be loft.

The breadth of thefe middle walks which I have here affigned them, may by many perfons be thought too great; but my reafon for this is to allow proper room between the efpaliers, that they may not fhade each other, or their roots interfere and rob each other of their nourifhment: but where the walks are not required of this breadth, it is only enlarging of the borders on each fide, and fo reducing the walks to the breadth defired.

But the walks of thefe gardens fhould not be gravelled, for as there will conftantly be occafion to wheel manure, water, &c. upon them, they would foon be defaced, and rendered unfightly; nor fhould they be laid with turf; for in green walks, when they are wheeled upon or much trodden, the turf is foon deftroyed, and thofe places where they are much ufed, become very unfightly alfo; therefore the beft walks for a Kitchen-garden are thofe which are laid with a binding fand; but where the foil is ftrong and apt to detain the wet, there fhould be fome narrow under ground drains made by the fide of the walks, to carry off the wet, otherwife there will be no ufing of the walks in bad weather; and where the ground is very wet, and the water is detained by the ftiffnefs of the foil, if fome lime-rubbifh, flints, chalk, or any fuch material as can be procured with the leaft expence, and is laid at the bottom of thefe walks; or if neither of thefe can be had, a bed of Heath or Furze fhould be laid, and the coat of fand laid over it; the fand will be kept drier, and the walks will be found and good in all feafons. Thefe fand-walks when they are well laid, are by much the eafieft kept of any; for when either weeds or Mefs begin to grow, it is but fcuffling them over with a Dutch hoe in dry weather, and raking them over a day or two after, and they will be as clean as when firft laid.

The beft figure for the quarters to be difpofed into, is a fquare or an oblong; where the ground is adapted to fuch a figure; otherwife they may be triangular, or of any other fhape, which will be moft advantageous to the ground.

When the garden is laid out in the fhape intended, if the foil is ftrong, and fubject to detain the moifture, or is naturally wet, there fhould always be underground drains made, to carry off the wet from every quarter of the garden, for otherwife moft forts of kitchen plants will fuffer greatly by moifture in winter; and if the roots of the fruit-trees get into the wet, they will never produce good fruit, fo that there cannot be too much care taken to let off all fuperflous moifture from the Kitchen-garden.

Thefe quarters fhould be conftantly kept clear from weeds, and when any part of the ground is unoccupied, it fhould always be trenched up into ridges, that it may fweeten and imbibe the nitrous particles of the air, which is of great advantage to all forts of land, and the ground will then be ready to lay down whenever it is wanted.

The ground in thefe quarters fhould not be fown or planted with the fame crop two years together, but the crops fhould be annually changed, whereby they will prove much better than when they conftantly grow upon the fame fpot. Indeed the kitchen-gardeners near London, where the land is dear, are often obliged to put the fame crop upon the ground for two or three years together; but then they dig and manure

their land fo well every year, as to render it almoft new; though notwithftanding all this, it is conftantly obferved, that frefh land always produces the beft crops.

In one of thefe quarters, which is fituated neareft to the ftables, and beft defended from the cold winds; or if either of the flips without the garden wall, which is well expofed to the fun, lies convenient, and is of a proper width, that fhould be preferred for a place to make hot-beds for early Cucumbers, Melons, &c. The reafons for my giving the preference to one of thefe flips, is, firft, there will be no dirt or litter carried over the walks of the Kitchen-garden in winter and fpring, when the weather is generally wet, fo that the walks will be rendered unfightly; fecondly, the view of the hot-beds will be excluded from fight; and laftly, the convenience of carrying the dung into thefe flips, for by making of a gate in the hedge, or pale, wide enough for a fmall cart to enter, it may be done with much lefs trouble than that of barrowing it thro' the garden; and where there can be a flip long enough to contain a fufficient number of beds for two or three years, it will be of great ufe; becaufe by the fhifting of the beds annually, they will fucceed much better than when they are continued for a number of years on the fame fpot of ground; and as it will be abfolutely neceffary to fence this Melon-ground round with a Reed-hedge, it may be fo contrived as to move away in pannels; and then that hedge which was on the upper fide the firft year, being carried down to a proper diftance below that which was the lower hedge, and which may remain, there will be no occafion to remove more than one of the crofs hedges in a year; therefore I am perfuaded, whoever will make trial of this method, will find it the moft eligible.

The moft important points of general culture confift in well digging and manuring the foil, and giving a proper diftance to each plant, according to their different growths (which is conftantly exhibited in their feveral articles in this book) as alfo in keeping them clear from weeds; for if weeds are permitted to grow until their feeds are ripe, they will fhed upon the ground, and fill it fo as not to be gotten out again in feveral years. You fhould alfo obferve to keep your dunghills always clear from weeds, for it will be to litte purpofe to keep the garden clean, if this is not obferved; for the feeds falling among the dung, will be brought into the garden, whereby there will be a conftant fupply of weeds yearly introduced, to the no fmall damage of your plants, and a perpetual labour occafioned to extirpate them again. Another thing which is abfolutely neceffary to be obferved, is, to carry off all the refufe leaves of Cabbages, the ftalks of Beans and haulm of Peafe, as foon as they are done with, for the ill fcent which moft people complain of in the Kitchen-gardens, is wholly occafioned by thefe things being fuffered to rot upon the ground; therefore when the Cabbages are cut, all leaves fhould be carried out of the garden while they are frefh, at which time they may be very ufeful for feeding of hogs, or other animals, and this will always keep the garden neat and free from ill fcents. As for all other neceffary directions, they will be found in the articles of the feveral forts of kitchen plants, which renders it needlefs to be repeated in this place.

KLEINIA. See CACALIA.

KNAUTIA. Lin. Gen. Plant. 109. Lychni-Scabiofa. Boerh. Ind. 1. 131.

This name was applied to this plant by Dr. Linnæus, in honour of the memory of Dr. Chriftian Knaut, who publifhed a method of claffing plants.

The CHARACTERS are,

It hath a fingle oblong empalement, containing feveral floscular flowers, which are ranged fo as to appear regular, but each irregular, having tubes the length of the empalement, but are cut at the brim into four irregular fegments, the outer being the biggeft; it hath four ftamina the length of the tube, inferted in the receptacle, terminated by oblong incumbent fummits; and a germen under the petal, fupporting a flender ftyle, crowned by a thick bifid ftigma,
                                                          which

which afterward becomes a four-cornered seed with a hairy apex.

This genus of plants is ranged in the first section of Linnæus's fourth class, intitled Tetrandria Monogynia, the flowers having four stamina and one style.

The Species are,

1. Knautia (*Orientalis*) foliis omnibus pinnatifidis, corollis calyce longioribus. Lin. Sp. App. 1679. *Knautia with all the leaves wing-pointed, and the petal longer than the empalement.* Lychni-scabiosa, flore rubro, annua. Boerh. Ind. alt.

2. Knautia (*Propontica*) foliis superioribus lanceolatis indivisis, corollis calyce æqualibus. Lin. Sp. App. 1666. *Knautia whose upper leaves are spear-shaped and whole, and the petal of the flower equal to the empalement.* Scabiosa Orientalis villosa, flore suaverubente, fructu pulchro oblongo. Tourn. Cor. 35.

These plants are natives of the East, they are both annual; the first has been long cultivated in the English gardens; this rises with an erect branching stalk four feet high, garnished with wing-pointed leaves; the branches are terminated by single foot-stalks, each supporting one flower, having a tubular empalement cut into four segments at the top, and each contain four florets of a bright red colour, cut into four unequal segments, the outer being much larger than the other; these have four stamina the length of the tube of the petal, terminated by oblong summits; and the flowers are succeeded by oblong four-cornered seeds, which, when ripe, soon fall out of the cup if they are not gathered.

The second sort differs from the first in its upper leaves being whole, and the petal of the flower being equal to the cup. The lower leaves of this are sawed on their edges, and terminate in acute points.

These plants propagate easily; if their seeds are permitted to scatter in the autumn, the plants will come up soon after; and if some of these are planted in the borders of the pleasure-garden, or among low shrubs near the walks in October, the plants will live through the winter, and flower in June; so their seeds will ripen the end of July or beginning of August, therefore require no other culture but to keep them clean from weeds.

KNIGHTS CROSS, or SCARLET CROSS, is the Scarlet Lychnis. See Lychnis.

L.

LABIATE FLOWERS are such as have lips, or more properly a labiated flower, is an irregular monopetalous flower, divided into two lips; the upper is called the crest, the under the beard; sometimes the crest is wanting, and then the style and chives supply its place, as in the Ground Pine, Scordium, Bugula, &c. but the greatest part have two lips, which, in some species the upper lip is turned upwards, as the Ground Ivy, &c. but most usually the upper lip is convex above, and turns the hollow part down to the lower lip, and so represents a kind of helmet, or monk's hood, from whence these are called galeate, cucullate, and galericulate flowers, in which form are most of the verticillate plants.

LABLAB. See Phaseolus.

LABRUM VENERIS. See Dipsacus.

LABRUSCA. See Vitis.

LABURNUM. See Cytisus.

1. ABYRINTH [Λαβύρινθος,] a winding, mazy, and intricate turning to and fro, through a wilderness or a wood.

The design of a Labyrinth is, to cause an intricate and difficult labour to find out the center, and the aim is, to make the walks so intricate, that a person may lose himself in them, and meet with as great a number of stops and disappointments as is possible, they being the most valuable that are most intricate.

As to the contrivance of them, it will not be possible to give directions in words, there are several plans and designs in books of gardening; they are rarely met with but in great and noble gardens, as Hamptoncourt, &c.

There are two ways of making them, the first is with single hedges; this method has been practised in England. These, indeed, may be best, where there is but a small spot of ground to be allowed for the making

them, but where there is ground enough, the double are most eligible.

Double ones, or those that are made with double hedges of a considerable thickness of wood between hedge and hedge, are approved as much better than single ones, as is the manner of making them in France, and other places, of all which, that of Versailles is allowed by all to be the noblest of its kind in the world.

It is an error in Labyrinths in making them too narrow, for by that means the hedges must be kept close clipped; whereas, if the walks are made wider, according to the foreign practice, they will not stand in so much need of it.

The walks are made with gravel, and the hedges are usually set with Hornbeams; the pallisades ought to be ten, twelve, or fourteen feet high; the Hornbeam should be kept cut, and the walks rolled.

LACRYMA JOBI [so called, because the seed of it resembles a tear, or drop.] Job's Tears. See Coix.

LACTIFEROUS PLANTS are such as abound with a milky juice, as the Euphorbia, Sonchus, Lactuca, &c.

LACTUCA. Tourn. Inst. R. H. 473. tab. 267. Lin. Gen. Plant. 814. [so called from lac, *Lat.* milk, because the leaves, stalks, flower, and branch, being broken, plentifully emit a milk, or white milky juice, quickly turning yellow and bitterish.] Lettuce; in French, *Laitue.*

The Characters are,

The flowers are composed of several hermaphrodite florets, inclosed in one scaly oblong empalement; these lie over each other like the scales of fish. The florets have one petal, which is stretched out on one side like a tongue, and is slightly indented at the end in three or four parts; these have each five short hairy stamina; the oval germen sup-

ports

ports a slender style, crowned by two reflexed stigmas, and afterward becomes one oblong pointed seed, crowned with a single down, sitting in the scaly empalement.

This genus of plants is ranged in the first-section of Linnæus's nineteenth class, intitled Syngenesia Polygamia æqualis, which includes those plants whose flowers are composed of all hermaphrodite, or fruitful florets, and have their stamina and style connected.

It would be beside my purpose to mention in this place the several sorts of Lettuce that are to be found in botanic writers, many of which are plants of little use, and are never cultivated but in botanic gardens for variety; some of them are found wild in many parts of England. I shall therefore pass over those, and only mention the several varieties which are cultivated in the kitchen-garden for use: 1. Common or Garden Lettuce. 2. Cabbage Lettuce. 3. Cilicia Lettuce. 4. Dutch Brown Lettuce. 5. Aleppo Lettuce. 6. Imperial Lettuce. 7. Green Capuchin Lettuce. 8. Versailles, or Upright White Cos Lettuce. 9. Black Cos. 10. Red Capuchin Lettuce. 11. Roman Lettuce. 12. Prince Lettuce. 13. Royal Lettuce. 14. Egyptian Cos Lettuce.

The first of these forts is commonly sown for cutting very young, to mix with other small sallad herbs, and is only different from the second fort, in being a degeneracy therefrom, or otherwise the second is an improvement by frequent cultivation from the first; for if the seeds are saved from such plants of the second fort as did not cabbage closely, the plants produced from that seed will degenerate to the first fort, which is by the gardeners called Lapped Lettuce, to distinguish it from the other, which they call Cabbage Lettuce. The seeds of the first, which are commonly saved from any of the plants, without having regard to their goodness, are generally sold at a very cheap rate (especially in dry seasons, when these plants always produce the greatest quantity of seeds,) though sometimes this seed is sold in the seed-shops, and by persons who make a trade of selling seeds, for the Cabbage Lettuce, which is often the occasion of peoples being disappointed in their crop; so that this fort should never be cultivated but to be cut up very young, for which purpose this is the only good fort, and may be sown any time of the year, observing only in hot weather to sow it in shady borders; and in the spring and autumn upon warm borders, but in winter it should be sown under glasses, otherwise it is subject to be destroyed by severe frosts.

The Cabbage Lettuce may also be sown at different times of the year, in order to have a continuation of it through the whole season. The first crop is generally sown in February, which should be upon a warm spot of ground, and when the plants are come up, they should be thinned out to the distance of ten inches each way, which may be done by hoeing them out, as is practised for Turneps, Carrots, Onions, &c. provided you have no occasion for the superfluous plants, otherwise they may be drawn up, and transplanted into another spot of good ground at the same distance, which, if done before the plants are too large, they will succeed very well, though they will not be so large as those which are left upon the spot where they were sown, but they will come somewhat later, which will be of service where people do not continue sowing every fortnight or three weeks in summer.

You must also observe in sowing the succeeding crops, as the season advances, to chuse a shady moist situation, but not under the drip of trees, otherwise, in the heat of summer they will run up to seed before they cabbage. In the beginning of August you should sow the last crop, which is to stand over winter; the seeds should be sown thin upon a good light soil, in a warm situation, and when the plants are come up they must be hoed out, so as they may stand singly, and cut down all the weeds to clear them. In the beginning of October they should be transplanted into warm borders, where, if the winter is not very severe, they will stand very well; but in order to be sure of

a crop, it will be adviseable to plant a few upon a bed pretty close together, where they may be arched over with hoops, and in severe frosts they should be covered with mats and straw, or Peas-haulm, to secure them from being destroyed; and in the spring of the year they may be transplanted out into a warm rich soil, at the distance before-mentioned; but still those which grew under the wall, if they escaped the winter, and were suffered to remain, will cabbage sooner than those which are removed again; but you must observe not to place them too close to the wall, which would occasion their growing up tall, and prevent their being large or hard.

In order to save good seeds of this kind, you should look over your Lettuces when they are in perfection, and such of them as are very hard, and grow low, should have sticks thrust into the ground, by the sides of as many of them as you intend for seed, to mark them from the rest; and you should carefully pull up all the rest from amongst them as soon as they begin to run up, if any happen to be left, left when they are run up to flower, they should, by the intermixing their farina with the good ones, degenerate the seeds. It may be some persons may object, that suppose some bad ones should happen to be left among them (for seeds to sow for small sallads,) yet the good ones being marked, the seeds need not be mixed, and so no danger can ensue from thence; but notwithstanding ever so much care be taken to keep the seeds separate, yet, whether from the intermixing of the farina during the time of their being in flower, or what other cause, I cannot say, but it hath been frequently observed, that where good and bad plants have been left for seed upon the same spot, the seeds of the good plants which were carefully saved separately, have very much degenerated, and proved worse than such as have seeded by themselves. The seeds should always be saved either from those which stood through the winter, or those which were sown early in the spring, for the late ones very seldom perfect their seeds.

The Cilicia, Imperial, Royal, Black, White, and Upright Cos Lettuces may be sown at the following times; the first season for sowing these seeds is at the latter end of February, or the beginning of March, upon a moderate hot-bed, or on a warm light soil in a sheltered situation; and when the plants are come up and are fit to transplant, those which were sown on the hot-bed should be planted on another warm bed about four inches asunder, row from row, and two inches distance in the rows, observing to shade them from the sun till they have taken new root; after which they should have a larger share of air admitted to them daily, to prevent their drawing up weak; but if the season proves favourable, they should be transplanted the beginning of April to the place where they are to remain, allowing them sixteen inches room every way, for these large forts must not be planted too near each other; those which were sown in the full ground will be later before they come up, so should be either hoed out, or transplanted into another spot of ground (as was directed for those sown on the hot-bed allowing them as much room) especially if the soil be good; after they have taken new root, you must carefully keep them clear from weeds, which is the only culture they will require, except the Black Cos Lettuce, which should be tied up when they are full grown (in the manner as was directed for blanching of Endive,) to whiten their inner leaves, and render them crisp, otherwise they are seldom good for much, rarely cabbaging without this assistance.

When your Lettuces are in perfection, you should look over them, and mark as many of the best of them as you intend for seed (in the same manner as was before directed for the common Cabbage Lettuce,) being very careful not to suffer any ordinary ones to feed amongst them, as was before observed, which would prove more injurious to these forts than to the common, as being more inclinable to degenerate with us, if they are not carefully saved.

You

You may also continue thefe forts through the whole feafon of Lettuce, by fowing them in April, May, and June, obferving, (as was before directed) to fow the late crops in a fhady fituation, otherwife they will run up to feed before they grow to any fize ; but in the middle of September you may fow of thefe forts, to abide the winter ; which plants fhould be tranfplanted either under glaffes, or into a bed, which fhould be arched over with hoops, in order to be covered in the winter, otherwife in hard winters they are often deftroyed ; but you muft conftanly let thefe plants have as much free air as poffible, when the weather is mild, only covering them in hard rains or frofty weather ; for if they are kept too clofely covered in winter, they will be fubject to a mouldinefs, which foon rots them.

In the fpring thefe plants fhould be planted out into a rich light foil, allowing them at leaft fixteen inches diftance each way ; for if they are planted too clofe, they are very fubject to grow tall, but feldom cabbage well ; and from this crop, if they fucceed well, it will be proper to fave your feeds ; though you fhould alfo fave from that crop fown on the hot-bed in the fpring, becaufe fometimes it happens, that the firft may fail by a wet feafon, when the plants are full in flower, and the fecond crop may fucceed, by having a more favourable feafon afterwards ; and if they fhould both fucceed, there will be no harm in that, fince the feeds will grow very well when two years old, and if well faved, at three, but this will not always happen.

The moft valuable of all the forts of Lettuce in England, are the Egyptian Green Cos, and the Verfailles, or White Cofs, and the Cilicia, though fome people are very fond of the Royal and Imperial Lettuces, but they feldom fell fo well in the London markets as the other, nor are fo generally efteemed. Indeed of late years, fince the White Cos has been commonly cultivated, it has obtained the preference of all the other forts, until the Egyptian Green Cos was introduced, which is fo much fweeter and tenderer than the White Cos, that it is by all good judges efteemed the beft fort of Lettuce yet known. This fort will endure the cold of our ordinary winters full as well as the White Cos ; but at the feafon of its cabbaging, if there happens to be much wet, this being very tender, is very fubject to rot.

The Brown Dutch and Green Capuchin Lettuces are very hardy, and may be fown at the fame feafons as was directed for the common Cabbage Lettuce, and are very proper to plant under a wall, or hedge, to ftand the winter, where many times thefe will abide, when moft of the other forts are deftroyed, and therefore they will prove very acceptable at a time when few other forts are to be had ; they will alfo endure more heat and drought than moft other forts of Lettuce, which renders them very proper for late fowing ; for it very often happens, in very hot weather, that the other forts of Lettuce will run up to feed in a few days after they are cabbaged, whereas thefe will abide near a fortnight in good order, efpecially if care be taken to cut the forwardeft firft, leaving thofe that are not fo hard cabbaged to be laft. If fome plants of thefe two laft forts are planted under frames, on a moderate hot-bed in October, they will be fit for ufe in April, which will prove acceptable to thofe who are lovers of Lettuce, and being covered by glaffes, will render them tender. In faving of thefe feeds, the fame care fhould be taken to preferve only fuch as are very large and well cabbaged, otherwife the feeds will degenerate, and be good for little.

The Red Capuchin, Roman, and Prince Lettuces are pretty varieties, and cabbage very early, for which reafon a few of them may be preferved, as may alfo fome of the Aleppo, for the beauty of its fpotted leaves ; though very few people care for either of thefe forts at table, when the other more valuable ones are to be obtained ; but in a fcarcity, thefe may fupply the place pretty well, and thefe forts are very proper for foups. The feeds of thefe muft alfo be faved from

fuch as cabbage beft, otherwife they will degenerate, and be good for little.

In faving feeds of all thefe forts of Lettuce, you fhould obferve never to let two forts ftand near each other, for by their farina mixing, they will both vary from their original, and partake of each other ; and there fhould be a ftake fixed down by the fide of each, to which the ftem fhould be faftened, to prevent their being broken, or blown out of the ground by wind, to which the Cilicia, Cos, and the other large growing Lettuces, are very fubject when they are in flower. You muft alfo obferve to cut fuch branches of the large growing Lettuce as ripen firft, and not wait to have the feed of the whole plant ripe together, which never happens ; but, on the contrary, fome branches will be ripe a fortnight or three weeks before others ; and when you cut them, they muft be fpread upon a coarfe cloth in a dry place, that the feeds may dry, after which you fhould beat them out, and dry them again, and then preferve them for ufe, being careful to hang them up where mice and other vermin cannot come at them ; for if they do, they will foon eat them up.

LACTUCA AGNINI. See VALERIANELLA.
LADY's SLIPPER. See CYPRIPEDIUM.
LADY's SMOCK. See CARDAMIN.
LAGŒCIA, Baftard Cumin.

The CHARACTERS are,

It hath many flowers collected into a head, which have one common empalement, compofed of eight indented leaves, but the fimple empalement to each flower hath five leaves, which are very narrow and pinnated, ending in many hair-like points. The flower confifts of five horned petals, which are fhorter than the empalement ; at the bottom of each flower is fituated the germen, fupporting a ftyle crowned by a fimple ftigma, attended by five ftamina, which are long and narrow ; the germen afterward changes to an oval feed, crowned with the empalement.

There is but one SPECIES of this plant, viz.

LAGOECIA *(Cuminoides.)* Lin. Hort. Cliff. *Baftard, or Wild Cumin.*

We have no other Englifh name for this plant, nor is this a very proper one, but as it has been titled by fome of the antient botanifts Cuminum fylveftre, i. e. Wild Cumin, and by Dr. Tournefort it is made a diftinct genus, by the title of Cuminoides, it may be ftyled Wild, or Baftard Cumin.

This is an annual plant, which grows about a foot high. The leaves refemble thofe of the Honeywort. The flowers, which are of a greenifh yellow colour, are collected in fpherical heads at the extremity of the ftalks ; but there being little beauty in the plant, it is rarely cultivated, except in botanic gardens. It grows plentifully about Aix, in Provence, as alfo in moft of the iflands of the Archipelago. It is annual, and perifhes foon after the feeds are ripe. The feeds of this plant fhould be fown in autumn on a warm border, foon after they are ripe ; or if they are permitted to fcatter, the plants will come up, and require no other care but to clear them from weeds. When the feeds are fown in the fpring, they commonly remain in the ground a year before they grow, and fometimes I have known them to lie two or three years in the ground, fo that if the plants do not come up the firft year, the ground fhould not be difturbed.

LAGOPUS. See TRIFOLIUM.

LAMINATED fignifies platted. Thofe things are faid to be laminated, whofe contexture difcovers fuch a difpofition as that of plates lying over one another, or the fcales of fifh.

LAMIUM. Tourn. Inft. R. H. 183. tab. 89. Lin. Gen. Plant. 636. Dead Nettle, or Archangel.

The CHARACTERS are,

The flower hath a permanent empalement of one leaf, which is tubulons, and cut into five equal fegments at the top, which end in beards. The flower is of the lip kind ; it hath one petal, with a fhort cylindrical tube, fwollen at the chaps and compreffed ; the upper lip is arched, roundifh, obtufe, and entire ; the under is fhort, heart-fhaped, reflexed, and indented at the end. It hath four awl-fhaped
ftamina

stamina joined to the upper lip, two of which are longer than the other, terminated by oblong hairy summits. It hath a four-cornered germen, supporting a slender style situated with the stamina, and crowned by an acute two-pointed stigma; the germen afterward become four three-cornered seeds, sitting in the open empalement.

This genus of plants is ranged in the first section of Linnæus's fourteenth class, intitled Didynamia Gymnospermia, in which he ranges those plants whose flowers have two long and two shorter stamina, and are succeeded by naked seeds sitting in the empalement.

The Species are,

1. Lamium (*Purpureum*) foliis cordatis obtusis petiolatis. Hort. Cliff. 314. *Dead Nettle with heart-shaped obtuse leaves standing on foot-stalks.* Lamium purpureum fœtidum, folio subrotundo, sive Galeopsis Dioscoridis. C. B. P. *Purple stinking Archangel, or Dead Nettle, or the Galeopsis of Dioscorides with a roundish leaf.*

2. Lamium (*Album*) foliis cordatis acuminatis serratis petiolatis. Hort. Cliff. 314. *Dead Nettle with pointed heart-shaped leaves, which are sawed, and have foot-stalks.* Lamium album, non fœtens, folio oblongo. C. B. P. *White Archangel or Dead Nettle which does not stink, with an oblong leaf.*

3. Lamium (*Garganicum*) foliis cordatis pubescentibus, corollis fauce inflata, tubo recto dente utrinque gemino. Lin. Sp. 808. *Dead Nettle with heart-shaped hairy leaves, and the chaps of the flower inflated, indented with two teeth.* Lamium garganicum subincanum, flore purpurascente, cum labio superiore crenato. Micheli. *Hoary Dead Nettle with a purplish flower, whose upper lip is crenated.*

4. Lamium (*Moschatum*) foliis cordatis obtusis glabris, floralibus sessilibus, calycibus profundè incisis. *Dead Nettle with heart-shaped, obtuse, smooth leaves, the upper sitting close to the stalks, and empalements deeply cut.* Lamium Orientale, nunc moschatum, nunc fœtidum, magno flore. Tourn. Cor. *Eastern Dead Nettle, sometimes sweet-scented and sometimes stinking, with a large flower.*

5. Lamium (*Melissæfolium*) foliis cordatis nervosis serratis, petiolis longioribus, caule erecto. *Dead Nettle with heart-shaped veined leaves which are sawed, and longer foot-stalks with an erect stalk.* Lamium montanum melissæ folio. C. B. P. 231. Icon. Pl. 158. *Mountain Dead Nettle with a Balm leaf.*

There are several other species of this genus, as also some varieties of it, but as most of them are weeds, I have passed them over, for there are few who care to admit them into their gardens.

The first sort grows naturally in most parts of England, under hedges and by the side of highways; it is also a troublesome weed in gardens, but as it stands in most of the dispensaries as a medicinal plant, I have chosen to insert it. This is an annual plant, whose stalks seldom rise more than four or five inches high; the under leaves are heart-shaped, blunt, and stand upon pretty long foot-stalks, but the upper leaves sit nearer to the stalks; the flowers come out in whorls on the upper part of the stalk; they are of a pale purple colour, and are succeeded by four naked seeds sitting in the empalement; after the seeds are ripe the plant decays. It flowers in the middle of March, when the autumnal self-sown plants appear; these are succeeded by others, which continue in succession all the summer.

The second sort is commonly called Archangel; this is also used in medicine, for which reason I have enumerated it here. The roots of this are perennial, and creep much in the ground, so is difficult to extirpate, where it happens to grow under bushes and hedges; for the roots intermix with those of the bushes, and every small piece of them grow and spread. The stalks of this rise much higher than those of the last, the flowers are larger, white, and grow in whorls round the stalks; these continue in succession most part of the summer.

The third sort grows naturally upon the mountains

in Italy; this hath a perennial creeping root, from which arise many thick square stalks a foot high, garnished with heart-shaped leaves which are hairy, placed opposite, standing upon pretty long foot-stalks; the flowers come out in whorls at the upper joints of the stalk, they are large, and of a pale purplish colour; these continue in succession most part of the summer, and the flowers are succeeded by seeds which ripen about six weeks after. This may be propagated by seeds, but as the roots spread greatly in the ground, so when once it is obtained, it will propagate fast enough without culture.

The fourth sort grows naturally in the Archipelago; this is an annual plant, which, if permitted to scatter its seeds, the plants will come up and thrive better than when sown by the hand. The plants come up in the autumn, and during the winter their leaves make a pretty appearance, for they are marked with white somewhat like those of the autumnal Cyclamen; the stalks rise eight or nine inches high, and are garnished with smooth heart-shaped leaves placed opposite; these in dry weather have a musky scent, but in wet weather are fetid; the flowers are white, standing in whorls round the stalks. They appear in April, and the seeds ripen in June, then the plants decay; this requires no culture, but to keep the plants clear from weeds.

The fifth sort grows naturally in Portugal; this hath a perennial root and an annual stalk, which rises a foot and a half high; it is strong, square, and grows erect; the leaves are large, heart-shaped, and much veined; they are deeply sawed on their edges, and are placed opposite. The flowers come out in whorls round the stalks at every joint; they are very large, and of a deep purple colour; those on the lower part of the stalks appear the beginning of May, which are succeeded by others above, so that there is a continuance of flowers almost two months on the same stalks. This plant very rarely produces good seeds in England, nor do the roots propagate very fast, so that it is not common here.

The best time to remove and part these roots is in October, but they must not be transplanted oftener than every third year if they are required to flower strongly; for the great beauty of this plant consists in the number of stalks, which are always proportional to the size of the plants; for small plants will put out one or two stalks only, whereas the larger ones will have eight or ten. The roots are hardy, and will thrive best in a soft loamy soil.

LAMPSANA. See Lapsana.

LAND. Its improvement.

1. By inclosing.

Inclosing of Lands, and dividing the same into several fields, for pasture or tillage, is one of the principal ways of improvement; first, by ascertaining to every man his just property, and thereby preventing an infinity of trespasses and injuries, that Lands in common are subject unto, beside the disadvantage of being obliged to keep the same seasons with the other people who have Land in the same field; so that the sowing, fallowing, and tilling the ground, must be equally performed by all the landholders; and when there happens a slothful negligent person, who has Land intermixed with others, it is one of the greatest nuisances imaginable. Secondly, it being of itself a very great improvement; for where Land is properly inclosed, especially in open countries, and the hedge-rows planted with timber trees, &c. it preserves the Land warm, and defends and shelters it from the violent cold nipping winds, which, in severe winters, destroy much of the corn, pulse, or whatever grows on the open field or champain grounds. And where it is laid down for pasture, it yields much more Grass than the open fields, and the Grass will begin to grow much sooner in the spring. The hedges and trees will afford shelter for the cattle from the cold winds in winter, as also shade for them in the great heats of summer. And these hedges afford the diligent husbandman plenty of fuel, as plough-boot, cart-boot, &c. And where they are carefully planted and preferved, furnifh him with timber and alfo maft for his fwine ; or where the hedge-rows are planted with fruit-trees, there will be a fupply of fruit for cyder, perry, &c. which in moft parts of England are of no fmall advantage to the hufbandman.

By this method of inclofing, there is alfo much more employment for the poor, and is therefore a good remedy againft beggary ; for in thofe open countries, where there are great downs, commons, heaths, and waftes, there is nothing but poverty and idlenefs to be feen amongft the generality of their inhabitants. It is very obfervable of late years, how much advantage the inclofing of the Land in Worcefterfhire, and fome other counties at a diftance from London, has been to the inhabitants : for before this method was introduced amongft them, the Lands for the moft part lay in commons, &c. Upon which the poorer fort of people built themfelves cottages with mud walls, where they contented themfelves with a cow or two, and fome fwine ; and thofe of them who were more induftrious than the reft, travelled to the neighbourhood of London every fpring, where they were employed in the gardens and fields for the fummer feafon ; and in autumn they returned to their native countries, where they lived in winter upon what money they had faved in fummer. But fince they have converted their waftes and commons into inclofures, there are but few of the inhabitants of thofe countries, who come to London for work, in comparifon to the numbers that formerly came ; fo that moft of the labourers, who come to London for employment, are either Welch, or inhabitants of fome more diftant counties, or from Ireland, where this improvement hath not as yet been introduced.

The advantages of inclofing Land are now fo generally known, that there is no occafion for me to enumerate them here ; fince the improvements which have been made of late years in feveral parts of England, and the increafe of rent that is every where made by thofe who inclofe, are fufficient arguments to enforce the practice, and render it general ; more efpecially in the north, where it is moft neglected, becaufe it would greatly fhelter the Lands, and render them much warmer than they now are.

In inclofing of Land, regard fhould be had to the nature of the foil, and what it is intended for, becaufe Corn Land fhould not be divided into fmall parcels ; for befides the lofs of ground in hedges, &c. the Corn doth feldom thrive fo well in fmall inclofures, as in more open fields, efpecially where the trees are large in the hedge-rows. The Grafs alfo in paftures is not fo fweet near hedges, or under the drip of trees, as in an open expofure ; fo that where the inclofures are made too fmall, or the Land overplanted with trees, the herbage will not be near fo good, nor in fo great plenty, as in larger fields ; therefore, before a perfon begins to inclofe, he fhould well confider how he may do it to the greateft advantage ; as for inftance, it is always neceffary to have fome fmaller inclofures near the habitation, for the fhelter of cattle, and the conveniency of fhifting them from one field to another, as the feafon of the year may require ; and hereby the habitation, barns, ftables, and outhoufes, will be better defended from ftrong winds, which often do great damage to thofe that are expofed to their fury. Thefe fmall inclofures may be of feveral dimenfions, fome of them three, four, fix, or eight acres in extent ; but the larger divifions for Corn fhould not contain lefs than twenty or thirty acres or more, according to the fize of the farm, or the fituation of it.

The ufual method of inclofing Land is, with a ditch and bank fet with quick. But in marfh Land, where there is plenty of water, they content themfelves with only a ditch, by the fides of which they ufually plant Sallows or Poplars, which being of quick growth, in a few years afford fhade to the cattle ; and when they are lopped, produce a confiderable profit to their owners. In fome counties the divifion of their Lands is

by dry walls made of flat ftones, laid regularly one upon another, and laying the top courfe of ftones in clay, to keep them together, the weight of which fecures the under ones. But in fome parts of Suffex and Hampfhire, they often lay the foundation of their banks with flat ftones, which is of a confiderable breadth at bottom ; upon which they raife the bank of earth, and plant the hedge on the top, which in a few years makes a ftrong durable fence, efpecially if they are planted with Holly, as fome of thofe in Suffex are.

In marfhes and open paftures, where there are no hedges, the ditches are generally made fix feet wide at the top, efpecially thofe which are on the fide of highways or commons ; but the common ditches about inclofures are feldom more than three feet and a half wide at top, and one foot and a half at bottom, and two feet deep, that the fides may have a good flope, and not be too upright, as they are frequently made about London, fo that they are continually wafhing down with great rains. In thefe narrow bottomed ditches, the cattle cannot ftand to turn themfelves, fo as to crop the quick ; but where the ditches are made wider, they fhould be proportionally deeper : as for inftance, if the ditch is made five feet broad, it muft be three feet deep ; and if fix feet broad, three feet and a half deep, and fo in proportion.

The method of inclofing Lands, by raifing high banks of earth, on the fide of which the quick is planted (as is too much practifed in many places near London) is intolerable, for it is not only unfightly, but very expenfive ; becaufe thefe banks are continually wafhing down, fo that they muft be repaired every year at leaft, if not oftener, otherwife the earth will be in a few years wafhed from the roots of the quick, and for want of proper nourifhment, the hedge will foon decay, which is the cafe with the greateft number of the hedges about London : befides, it is a very uncertain way of planting quick on the fide of a fteep bank, where all the moifture runs off ; fo that if the fpring fhould prove dry after it is planted, there is a great hazard whether half the plants will grow, and thofe that take feldom make much progrefs ; whereas thofe planted on the plain furface, where they enjoy the advantages of fun and moifture, will in four years make a better fence than one of thefe bank hedges will in eight or ten, and will continue good much longer than the other. Therefore I advife, that the banks on which the hedges are to be planted, fhould not be raifed more than one foot above the furface of the ground, where the Land is dry, and in wet Land not more than two feet, which will be enough.

I fhall now mention the moft proper plants for making of fences for the different foils and fituations, fo as to anfwer the expectation of the planter : and firft, the white Thorn is efteemed the beft for fencing, and will grow upon almoft any foil and in any fituation, but it fucceeds beft on a hazle loam. Of this there are three or four varieties, which differ in the breadth of their leaves and the fize of their Haws, but that fort with the fmalleft leaves and Haws will make the clofeft fence. For it is very certain, that the branches of all forts of trees are produced at a diftance, in proportion to the fize of their leaves ; fo that Yews, and other Evergreen trees with fmall leaves, will always make a clofer hedge than other trees whofe leaves are larger. Therefore, for the clofeft hedge, the fmalleft Haws fhould be chofen ; but where the moft vigorous fhooters are required, for the advantage of lopping, there the largeft Haws fhould be preferred. But as thefe hedges are ufually planted from a nurfery, where the Haws are promifcuoufly fown, it is very common to fee two or three forts planted in the fame hedge ; which may be eafily diftinguifhed, when they have obtained ftrength, by the difference of their growth. Indeed, where a perfon is curious in raifing of his own quick, it is worth while to gather the Haws feparately, and fow them apart ; and each fort fhould be planted in a feparate hedge, which will render the

hedges

hedges more equal in their growth. If thefe Haws are fown in the places where they are defigned to remain for a fence, they will make a much greater progrefs in a few years, than thofe which are tranfplanted; but as the feeds remain a whole year in the ground before the plants appear, few people care to practife this method; however, thofe who are defirous to raife their hedges this way, fhould bury the Haws, by putting them in pots foon after they are ripe, and burying the pots two feet deep in the ground, where they may remain one year, then take them up and fow them; by this preparation the plants will come up the following fpring; but before they are fown, the Haws fhould be bruifed with hands, and their outer coverings wafhed off, whereby the feeds may be fown at a more regular diftance; for as moft of the Haws inclofe four or five feeds, fo if they are fown entire there will be as many plants arife in a clufter, which if permitted to ftand, will prevent each other's growth; and in drawing out the fuperfluous plants, there will be great danger of injuring thofe which are to remain.

The next to the white Thorn is the black Thorn, which, though not fo generally efteemed as the white, yet it will make an excellent fence, where proper care is taken in the planting and after management of it; and the loppings of this hedge make much the beft bufhes for draining of Land, and are of longer duration for dead hedges than thofe of any other fort of tree, and are very proper to mend gaps in fences; for their branches being befet with fharp thorns, the cattle are not fo apt to crop them as the white Thorn, and fome other forts. Thefe hedges are alfo better, if the ftones of the Plumbs are fown on the fpot where they are to remain, than where the plants are taken from a nurfery; if thefe are fown in the autumn foon after the fruit is ripe, the plants will come up the fpring following.

The Crab will alfo make a ftrong durable fence; this may be raifed by fowing the kernels in the place where the hedge is defigned; but then there fhould be great care taken of the plants while they are young, to keep them clear from weeds, as alfo to guard them from cattle. When thefe ftocks have obtained ftrength, fome of them may be grafted with Apples for cyder, where the fence is not expofed to a public road; but thefe grafts fhould not be nearer than thirty-five or forty feet, left they fpoil the hedge, by their heads overgrowing and dripping on it.

The Holly is alfo an excellent plant for evergreen hedges, and would claim the preference to either of the former, were it not for the flownefs of its growth while young, and the difficulty of tranfplanting the plants when grown to a moderate fize. This will grow beft in cold ftony Lands, where, if once it takes well, the hedges may be rendered fo clofe and thick, as to keep out all forts of animals, and will grow to a confiderable height, and is of long duration. Thefe hedges may be raifed, by fowing the berries, either in the place where they are defigned to remain, or by planting young plants of three or four years growth; but as the berries continue in the ground an entire year before the plants appear, few perfons care to wait fo long; therefore the ufual method is, to plant the hedges with plants of the before-mentioned age. But where this is practifed, they fhould be tranfplanted, either early in the autumn, or deferred till toward the end of March; then the furface of the ground fhould be covered with mulch near their roots after they are planted, to keep the earth moift; and if the feafon fhould prove dry, the plants fhould be watered at leaft once a week, until they have taken root, otherwife they will be in danger of mifcarrying; for which reafon the autumnal planting is generally preferred to the fpring, efpecially in dry grounds.

The Alder will alfo make a good hedge, when planted on a moift foil, or on the fide of rivers, or large ditches; and will preferve the bank from being wafhed away, where there are running ftreams; for they fpread pretty much at bottom, and fend forth fuckers from their roots in great plenty; but thefe hedges fhould be fheared at leaft once a year, in order to make them thick. Thefe Alder hedges are very ornamental, when they are well kept in large gardens; and as they will thrive beft on wet fwampy Lands, where many other plants will not live, they fhould be felected for fuch fituations.

Of late years the Furz has been much propagated for hedges in feveral parts of England, and indeed will make a good fence on poor, fandy, or gravelly foils, where few other plants will grow. The beft method of raifing thefe hedges is, to fow the feed about the latter end of March, or the beginning of April, in the place where the hedge is defigned; for the plants will not bear to be tranfplanted, unlefs it be done while they are young, and then there is great hazard of their taking. The ground where the feeds are to be fown fhould be well cleanfed of weeds, and the furface made light; then there fhould be two or three drills made (according to the width which the hedge is intended) about half an inch deep, into which the feeds fhould be fcattered pretty thick; and then the drills fhould be filled up with the head of a rake, to cover the feeds. This work fhould be performed in dry weather, for if much wet falls foon after the feeds are fown, it is apt to burft them. When the plants are come up, they fhould be kept clear from weeds, that they may fpread and grow thick at bottom; and if thefe hedges are fecured from cattle broufing on them, and are cut every fpring juft before they begin to fhoot, they will make an exceeding clofe fence; but where they are defigned to be cut for fuel, then the beft way is to let them fpread in width; and when they are two years old, to cut them down in the fpring, juft before they begin to fhoot, within two or three inches of the ground, which will caufe them to fend forth a number of fhoots from each root, and thereby increafe the width of the hedge; and by fo doing, the plants will not run up tall and weak, and be in danger of being weighed down by great falls of fnow. Thefe hedges when they are well grown, may be cut down every third or fourth year for fuel; wherefore if there is a treble row of Furz fown, at about three feet apart, they may be cut down alternately, fo that there will be a fence always remaining. But this is only recommended for fuch fandy Lands as lett for a fmall rent, and where fuel is fcarce. The beft fort of Furz for this purpofe is the greater kind, commonly called the French Furz, which will grow to eight or ten feet high, and is not apt to fpread fo much as the ordinary fmall fort.

Elder is fometimes planted for hedges, being very quick of growth; fo that if fticks or truncheons about four or five feet long be thruft into a bank flopewife each way, fo as to crofs each other, and thereby form a fort of chequer work, it will make a fence for fhelter in one year. But as this is a vigorous growing plant, it will never form a clofe fence; and the young fhoots being very foft and pithy, are foon broken by cattle or boys in their fport. Befides, where they are fuffered to bear berries, and thefe are fcattered over the neighbouring Land, they will come up the following fpring, and become very troublefome. Where thefe hedges are planted, they may be cut down every third year near the ground; and thefe ftakes (when divefted of their bark, fo as to prevent their growing) will laft longer in the ground, to fupport Vines or any other plants, which do not require tall ftakes, than any other fort of tree yet known. And where the trees are fuffered to grow to any confiderable fize, the wood is as hard as Box, and therefore very ufeful for turners and inftrument makers. The beft feafon for planting thefe truncheons is foon after Michaelmas, becaufe the plants fhoot very early in the fpring. Of late years there have been many hedges, and other plantations, made of the white berried Elder, for the fake of their fruit to make wine; which, if rightly made, hath the flavour of Frontiniac wine, and is by fome perfons mixed with white wines, and vended for it.

There

There are some other plants which have been recommended for fences, but those here enumerated are the most useful sorts for such purposes; wherefore I shall pass over the others, as not worthy of the care of the husbandman. And as to the farther directions for planting and preserving of hedges, with instructions for plashing or laying them, the reader is desired to turn to the articles of FENCES and HEDGES, where there are particular directions for these works exhibited, which I shall not here repeat.

The draining of Land is also another great improvement to it; for though meadows and pastures, which are capable of being overflowed, produce a greater quantity of herbage than dry Land, yet where the wet lies too long upon the ground, the Grass will be four and extremely coarse; and where there is not care taken in time to drain this Land, it will produce little Grass, and soon be overun with Rushes and Flags, so as to be of small value. The land which is most liable to this, is cold stiff clays where the water cannot penetrate, but is contained as in a dish; so that the wet which it receives in winter, continues till the heat of the sun exhales the greatest part of it.

The best method for draining of these Lands is, to cut several drains across the Land, in those places where the water is subject to lodge; and from these cross drains to make a convenient number of other drains, to carry off the water to either ponds or rivers in the lower parts of the Land. These drains need not be made very large, unless the ground be very low, and so situated as not to be near any river to which the water may be conveyed; in which case there should be large ditches dug at proper distances, in the lowest part of the ground, to contain the water; and the earth which comes out of the ditches should be equally spread on the Land, to raise the surface. But where the water can be conveniently carried off, the best method is, to make under ground drains at proper distances, which may empty themselves into large ditches, which are designed to carry off the water. These sort of drains are the most convenient, and as they are hid from the sight do not incommode the Land, nor is there any ground lost where these are made.

The usual method of making these drains, is to dig trenches, and fill the bottoms with stones, bricks, Rushes, or bushes, which are covered over with the earth which was dug out of the trenches; but this is not the best method, because the water has not a free passage through these drains, so that whenever there is a flood, these drains are often stopped by the soil which the water frequently brings down with it. The best method I have yet observed to make these drains, is to dig trenches to a proper depth for carrying off the water, which for the principal drains should be three feet wide at their top, and sloped down for two feet and a half depth, where there should be a small ledge or bank left on each side, upon which the cross stakes or bearers should be laid, and below these banks there should be an open drain left, at least one foot deep, and ten or eleven inches wide, that there may be room for the water to pass through. These larger drains should be at convenient distances, and smaller drains of about seven or eight inches wide at top, and the hollow under the bushes eight or nine inches deep, should be cut across the ground, which should discharge the water into these larger drains. The number and situation of them must be in proportion to the wetness of the Land; and the depth of the earth above the bushes, must also be proportioned to the intended use of the Land; for if it is arable Land to be ploughed, it must not be shallower than fourteen inches, that there may be sufficient depth for the plough, without disturbing the bushes; but for pasture Land, one foot deep will be full enough; for when the bushes lie too deep in strong Land, they will have little effect, the ground above will bind so hard as to detain the wet on the surface. When the drains are dug, there should be prepared a quantity of good brush wood, the larger sticks should

be cut out to pieces of about sixteen or eighteen inches in length, which should be laid across upon the two side banks of the drain, at about four inches distance; then cover these sticks with the smaller brush wood, Furz, Broom, Heath, or any other kind of brush, laying it lengthwise pretty close; on the top of these may be laid Rushes, Flags, &c. and then the earth laid on to cover the whole. These sort of drains will continue good for a great number of years, and are never liable to the inconveniencies of the other, for the water will find an easy passage through them; and where there is plenty of brush wood, they are made at an easy expence; but in places where wood is scarce, it would be chargeable to make them: however, in this case, it would be a great advantage to these Lands, to plant a sufficient number of cuttings of Willow, or the black Poplar, on some of the moist places, which would furnish brush wood for these purposes in four or five years; and as the expence of planting these cuttings is trifling, there cannot be a greater advantage to an estate which wants draining, than to practise this method, which is in every person's power, since there is little expence attending it.

In countries where there is plenty of stone, that is the best material for making these under ground drains; for when these are properly made, they will never want repairing.

The best time of the year for making these drains is about Michaelmas, before the heavy rains of autumn fall, because at this season the Land is usually dry, so that the drains may be dug to a proper depth; for when the ground is wet, it will be very difficult to dig to any depth, because the water will drain in wherever there is an opening in the ground.

When these drains are made, and the water carried off the Land, it will be proper to pare off the Rushes, Flags, &c. which may be laid in heaps in proper places to rot, and will afford a good manure for the land. The ground must also be ploughed to destroy the roots of noxious weeds, and if it be laid fallow for one season, and ploughed two or three times, it will greatly mend the Land. The Rushes and Flags which were pared off the ground when rotten, should be spread over the surface, and the Grass-seed sown thereon, which will greatly forward the Grass, so that it may soon be brought to a good turf; which Land thus mended, has been lett for four times the rent it was set at before.

There are some persons, who, after they have pared off the Flags, Rushes, &c. from their Land, lay them in small heaps, and burn them in dry weather, then spread the ashes on the Land to improve it, which is a good method, where a person is in haste to have Grass again; but where the ground can be fallowed one year, it will loosen the soil, and more effectually destroy the roots of all noxious weeds; and the Rushes, &c. when rotted, will afford a much larger quantity of manure for the Land than when it is burnt: besides, this can only be practised in the summer season, when the weather is very dry; for if there should fall much rain, the fires will go out, and it will be impracticable to burn it. But where the method of burning is practised, the heaps should not be too great, and it should burn very slowly; which will render the ashes a much better manure, than when the fire is too violent, or the heaps too large; for in this case, the inner part will be over-burnt before the fire reaches the outside of the heap.

As the draining of cold wet Lands is a great improvement to them, so the floating or watering of dry loose Land is not a less advantage to them. This may be easily effected where there are rivers, or reservoirs of water, which are situated above the level of the ground designed to be floated, by under ground drains (made after the manner of those before directed for draining of Land,) through which the water may be conveyed at proper seasons, and let out on the ground: in order to this, there must be good sluices made at the heads of the drains, so that the water may never get out, but at such times as is required;
for

for if this be not taken care of, the water, inſtead of improving the Land, will greatly damage it.

But where the Land lies ſo high, as that there is no water in the neighbourhood lying above its level, it will be more expenſive; becauſe in ſuch caſe, the water muſt be raiſed by machines, from reſervoirs or ſtreams which lie below it. The moſt common engine uſed for this purpoſe is the Perſian wheel (which, being well deſcribed and figured in Woolridge's Art of Huſbandry, is needleſs for me here to repeat.) Yet notwithſtanding the expence of raiſing the water, it has been found greatly advantageous in many parts of England, to drown the Lands, for the profit has many times more than doubled the charge.

The time for drowning of Land, is uſually from November till the end of April; but though this is the general practice, yet I cannot approve of it for many reaſons. The firſt is, that by the wet lying continually on the ground in winter, the roots of the finer ſort of Graſs are rotted and deſtroyed; and by letting on the water, at the ſeaſon when the ſeeds of Docks, and other bad weeds, which commonly grow by river ſides, are falling, theſe ſeeds are carried upon the Land, where they remain and grow, and fill the ground with bad weeds, which is commonly the caſe with moſt of the water meadows in England, the Graſs in general being deſtroyed; ſo that Ruſhes, Docks, and other trumpery, make up the burden of theſe Lands: but if theſe meadows were judiciouſly managed, and never floated till March or April, the quantity of ſweet good Graſs would be thereby greatly increaſed, and the beautiful verdure of the meadows preſerved: but there is little hope of convincing thoſe perſons by any arguments, who are ſo much wedded to their own prejudices, as to ſhut their eyes and ears againſt experiments or reaſon. Where the Land is very hot and dry, and it lieth convenient to be watered at a ſmall expence, it ſhould be repeated every week in dry hot weather, which will prove a great advantage to the Land. But whenever this is done, there ſhould no cattle be admitted while it is wet, for they will poach, and ſpoil the turf.

Another great improvement of Land, is by burning of it, which, for ſour, heathy, and ruſhy Land, be it either hot or cold, wet or dry, is a very great improvement; ſo that ſuch Lands will, in two or three years after burning, yield more, excluſive of the charges, than the inheritance was worth before; but this is not to be practiſed on rich fertile Land; for as the fire deſtroys the acid juice, which occaſions ſterility in the poor Land, ſo it will in like manner conſume the good juices of the richer Land, and thereby impoveriſh it, ſo that it hath been with great reaſon difuſed in deep rich countries.

The uſual method of burning Land is, to pare off the turf with a breaſt plough, turning it over as it is cut, that it may dry the better. And if it proves hot dry weather when this work is done, then it needs no more turning; but if rain ſhould fall, it muſt be turned, and the turfs ſet a little hollow, that they may dry the better; and when they are thorough dry, they may be laid on ſmall heaps, about half a cart load on a heap, or leſs, for the ſmaller the heaps are, provided there is quantity enough to make a good fire, ſo as to conſume the whole to aſhes, it is the better; if the turf be full of fibrous roots, or hath much Moſs or Fern on it, it will burn without any additional fuel; but if it hath not, the heaps ſhould be raiſed on ſmall bundles of Heath, Fern, Gorze, &c. which will ſet the whole on fire; yet there ſhould be no more of theſe things applied, than what is neceſſary to kindle the fire, becauſe the ſlower the turf conſumes, the better will be the aſhes. When the turf is wholly conſumed, the aſhes ſhould be equally ſcattered over the ground in a calm day, leſt the wind ſhould drive it in heaps. Then the Land ſhould be gently ploughed, and the ſeeds ſown thereon; for if the ground is ploughed too deep, the aſhes will be buried too low for the roots of the Graſs or Corn to reach them for a conſiderable time; nor ſhould the

aſhes lie too near the ſurface, becauſe then the roots will reach them too ſoon, and the ſtrength of the aſhes will be ſpent to nouriſh only the blade, ſo that the Corn will grow too rank in winter; and when the roots in the ſpring ſtrike down lower, they will meet with a poorer ſoil, nor will the ſtalks and ears have ſo much advantage from the improvement, as the uſeleſs blade. But when care is taken in this particular, it is wonderful what ſucceſs it hath; for by this method the pooreſt plains, and ſour heathy Lands, have been rendered as fertile as almoſt any good cultivated ground whatever.

It is alſo a very great improvement, where Land is overgrown with Broom, Furz, &c. to ſtub them up by the roots, and when they are dry, lay them on heaps, and cover them with the parings of the earth, and burn them, and ſpread the aſhes over the ground. By this method vaſt tracts of Land, which at preſent produce little or nothing to their owners, might be made good at a ſmall expence, ſo as to become good eſtates to the proprietors.

There are ſeveral other methods of improving Land beſide thoſe here mentioned, as by planting of wood, or adapting the ſeveral ſorts of plants to the particular ſoils with which they agree; but as moſt of theſe things are treated of under the ſeveral articles where theſe plants are mentioned, I ſhall forbear to repeat them in this place, but ſhall beg leave to offer a few general hints on the preſent ſituation of the Lands in England, which may probably excite ſome abler hand to undertake a fuller and more complete diſquiſition of this ſubject.

For ſome years paſt, the quantity of Corn raiſed in England, has greatly exceeded the conſumption, ſo that great quantities of Corn have been exported, by which great ſums of money have been brought into England; but this was accidental; for had not the crops failed in the neighbouring countries, there would have been no demand for the produce of England, ſo that the quantity here grown muſt have reduced the price ſo low, as to have almoſt ruined the farming intereſt; nor is it poſſible to contrive any ſcheme, in a country circumſtanced as this, whereby the public may not, at times, ſuffer from the extravagant price, which, in a ſcarcity, this commodity may be raiſed to; or, on the other hand, the farmers are ſometimes almoſt undone by the low price which it is often reduced to in times of plenty; and ſurely there can be no one thing more worthy of the ſerious attention of every perſon, who has the leaſt regard for the public welfare, than this, of always making ſuch proviſion of Corn, againſt accidental ſcarcities, as that the inhabitants may never be diſtreſſed for want of the ſtaff of life, or the price be ſo high, as that the common people cannot purchaſe it. If I am not greatly miſtaken, there has been, within the ſpace of three or four years, ſuch a diſproportion in the price of Corn, as can hardly be conceived, and this within the memory of numbers of perſons; the time I mean is between 1705 and 1709, in the compaſs of which time the peck loaf of fine bread was riſen from fourteen pence to four ſhillings and twopence; the low price of this commodity was as detrimental to the farmers, as the extravagant price was afterward to the public, neither of which would have ſo ſeverely felt the effects, had there been public granaries where the Corn might have been depoſited, and this purchaſed from the farmer, at a price by which he might live, at the public expence, and ſold out again at an eaſy rate in times of ſcarcity; but I fear this is not an age for encouraging any ſcheme for public utility, when in every thing of this kind, however beneficial it may be to the country, and though propoſed as ſuch to the public, if it meets with any reception, it is with a view to turn it to private intereſt; the practice of turning all things into private jobs, has ſo much prevailed of late years, as to have almoſt extinguiſhed every ſocial virtue;

4

virtue; but I fear I may have incurred the censure of many for this digression; but, be it as it will, I could not omit it, when it so properly came in my way; and as it is from a sincere love and regard to my country, that I have mentioned this, so it may be hoped, that if any harsh expression has been used, it will be forgiven. But to return to my subject; as the quantity of Land now in tillage is very great in England, from the destruction of woods, the ploughing up of downs, the inclosing of commons, &c. so that, unless there happens a failure in the crops of Corn in great part of England, the markets must be so low, as that the farmer will always find it difficult to support his family, and pay his rent; the first must be done, let the landlord fare as he will, for the farmers know, that when the farms are occupied by the landlords, few of them can make the produce of the Land and pay their expence, so that the whole rent of the farm is often sunk, beside the trouble and fatigue of managing the farms; and it is greatly to be feared, from the present condition of the farmers in general, that many landlords will be obliged to undertake this disagreeable affair, which will be the more so, as their Lands will be left without stock, and the soil exhausted, and overgrown with weeds, which will require some years to put into proper condition, and will be attended with great expence.

The extraordinary price which Corn bore some years since, tempted the farmers to break up the downs in many parts of England; and the landlords were brought to comply with the request of the farmer, for the sake of a little advance of the rent, not considering the future consequence of it; so that hereby great extents of downs have been ruined, and not likely to be recovered again; for the soil in many places was not more than four or five inches deep, upon beds of flint or chalk, which, in ploughing, were turned up on the surface, and the little soil which covered them, was in a few years so much exhausted, as not to produce the quantity of grain which was sown upon them; and as there was no probability of procuring dressing for the Lands, the farmers have been obliged to throw them up, which now lie waste, and appear like quarries of flints, or beds of chalk, without Grass, or almost any other plant growing upon them. By this passion for ploughing, the farmers have lessened their stock of cattle, and, of consequence, their quantity of manure has been lessened in proportion, so that they have either been obliged to purchase dressing at a great expence, or destroy their Lands of their vegetative quality: by the former method, when grain bears a low price, the farmer is ruined, and by the latter, every one must know what will be the consequence to both tenant and landlord; therefore it is a matter of great concern to the proprietors of Lands, to see that no more ground in their farms is kept in tillage, than the tenant can supply with dressing, so as to maintain the Land in heart; and that a proper stock of cattle be kept up, in proportion to the size of the farms, which cannot be done where there is not a proportion of pasture kept to that of the arable Land in each farm. There are many persons, who, by a mistake in the article of inclosing Lands, are likely to fall into a great error, by supposing, that the inclosing of commons will be a great advantage to their estates, and perhaps there may be tenants on their estates, who may encourage the gentlemen so to do, from a present interest of their own; but wherever this has been done, the estates have soon fallen in their rents, much lower than the addition made by inclosing the commons, which must always be the case; for if there is not common pasture, where the farmers can turn out their cattle in summer, it cannot be supposed they can keep up a stock of live cattle upon their inclosed pasture; so that, although the dividing and inclosing the Lands in the common fields would be a very great benefit, yet the destroying of pasture commons would on the other extreme be a national disadvantage and loss. There

are many other particulars, which might be here enumerated, to shew the cause of the low condition of the farmers in general; but these few hints may probably lead some persons of abler heads to the consideration of this affair, so I shall not enlarge upon them here.

LANIGEROUS TREES are such as bear a woolly or downy substance, as is commonly contained in the katkins of Willows, &c.

LANTANA. Lin. Gen. Plant. 683. Camara. Plum. Nov. Gen. 32. tab. 2. American Viburnum, or Camara.

The CHARACTERS are,

The empalement of the flower is cut into four segments. The flower is monopetalous, of an irregular shape, having a cylindrical tube, which extends beyond the empalement, and is spread open at the brim, where it is divided into five segments. In the center of the flower is situated the pointal, supporting a crooked stigma, attended by four stamina, two being longer than the other. The pointal afterward changes to a roundish fruit, opening into two cells, and inclosing a roundish seed.

This genus of plants is ranged in the second section of Linnæus's fourteenth class, intitled Didynamia Angiospermia, which includes those plants whose flowers have two long and two shorter stamina, and the seeds are inclosed in the capsule.

The SPECIES are,

1. LANTANA (Aculeata) foliis oppositis, caule aculeato ramoso, floribus capitato-umbellatis. Lin. Sp. 873. Lantana with leaves growing opposite, a branching prickly stalk, and umbellated flowers growing in heads. Viburnum Americanum odoratum, urticæ foliis latioribus spinosum, floribus miniatis. Pluk. Alm. 285. tab. 223. Sweet prickly American Viburnum, with broad Nettle leaves, and carmine flowers.

2. LANTANA (Inerma) caule inermi, foliis lanceolatis dentatis alternis, floribus corymbosis. Lantana with a smooth stalk, spear-shaped indented leaves placed alternate, and flowers growing in round bunches. Periclymenum rectum, salviæ foliis majoribus oblongis, mucronatis, subtus villosis, alternatim sitis, flore & fructu minoribus. Sloan. Cat. Jam. 164. Upright Honeysuckle with larger, oblong, acute-pointed Sage leaves, which are hairy on their under side, placed alternate, and a smaller flower and fruit.

3. LANTANA (Lanuginosa) caule ramoso lanuginoso, foliis orbiculatis crenatis oppositis, floribus capitatis. Lantana with a hairy branching stalk, round crenated leaves placed opposite, and flowers collected in heads. Periclymenum rectum, salviæ folio rugoso minore, subrotundo. Cat. Jam. 164. Upright Honeysuckle with a smaller rough roundish leaf.

4. LANTANA (Trifolia) foliis ternis, caule inermi spicis oblongis imbricatis. Lin. Sp. Plant. 873. Lantana with leaves placed by threes round the stalk, without spines, and oblong imbricated spikes of flowers. Camara trifolia, purpurascente flore. Plum. Nov. Gen. 32. Three-leaved Camara, with a purplish flower.

5. LANTANA (Urticæfolia) caule aculeato, foliis oblongo-cordatis serratis oppositis, floribus corymbosis. Lantana with a prickly stalk, oblong, heart-shaped sawed leaves, and flowers growing in a corymbus. Periclymenum rectum, urticæ folio hirsuto majore, flore flavo. Sloan. Cat. Jam. 163. Upright Honeysuckle with a larger Nettle leaf, and a yellow flower.

6. LANTANA (Camara) caule inermi, foliis ovato-lanceolatis, serratis, rugosis, floribus capitatis lanuginosis. Lantana with a smooth stalk, oval, spear-shaped, rough, sawed leaves, and flowers growing in woolly heads. Periclymenum rectum, salviæ folio rugoso, majore, subrotundo & bullato. Sloan. Cat. Jam. 163. Upright Honeysuckle with a large, rough, Sage leaf, which is roundish and studded.

7. LANTANA (Bullata) foliis oblongo-ovatis acuminatis serratis rugosis alternis, floribus capitatis. Lantana with oblong, oval-pointed, sawed leaves, which are rough, placed alternate, and flowers growing in heads. Periclymenum rectum, salviæ folio rugoso, minore, bullato, flore

flore albo. Sloan. Cat. 163. *Upright Honeyfuckle with a fmaller rough Sage leaf, which is ftudded, and a white flower.*

8. LANTANA (*Alba*) caule inermi, foliis ovatis ferratis, floribus capitatis alaribus feffilibus. *Lantana with a fmooth ftalk, oval fawed leaves, and flowers growing in heads proceeding from the wings of the leaves, fitting clofe to the ftalks.* Camara foliis urticæ, floribus minoribus albis, ex alis foliorum prodeuntibus. Houft. *Camara with a Nettle leaf, and fmaller white flowers proceeding from the wings of the leaves.*

9. LANTANA (*Annua*) foliis quaternis, caule afpero, fpicis oblongis. *Four-leaved Lantana with a rough ftalk, and oblong fpikes of flowers.* Periclymenum rectum humilius, folio rugofo majore, flore purpureo, fructu oblongo, efculento purpureo. Sloan. Cat Jam. 164. *Lower upright Honeyfuckle with a larger rough leaf, a purple flower, and an oblong, purple, efculent fruit.*

10. LANTANA (*Anguftifolia*) caule inermi, foliis ovatolanceolatis oppofitis, floribus capitatis pedunculis longiffimis. *Lantana with a fmooth ftalk, oval fpear-fhaped leaves placed oppofite, flowers collected in heads, and very long foot-ftalks.* Periclymenum rectum, falviæ folio rugofo, longo & anguftiffimo. Sloan. Cat. 164. *Upright Honeyfuckle with a rough Sage leaf, which is long and narrow.*

11. LANTANA (*Africana*) foliis alternis feffilibus, floribus folitariis. Hort. Cliff. 320. *Lantana with alternate leaves fitting clofe to the ftalks, and flowers growing fingly.* Jafminum Africanum, illicis folio, flore folitario ex foliorum alis proveniente albo. Com. Plant. Rar. 6. tab. 6. *African Jafmine with an Ilex leaf, and a folitary white flower coming from the wing of the leaves.*

12. LANTANA (*Salvifolia*) foliis oppofitis feffilibus, floribus racemofis. Lin. Sp. 875. *Lantana with leaves placed oppofite clofe to the ftalks, and flowers in a racemus.* Frutex Africanus, foliis conjugatis falviæ anguftis, floribus hirfutis. Herm. Afr. 10.

The firft fort is pretty common in thofe Englifh gardens, where there are collections of exotic plants; this grows naturally in Jamaica, and moft of the other iflands in the Weft-Indies, where it is called wild Sage, as are feveral of the other forts which are not diftinguifhed by the inhabitants. It rifes with a woody ftalk five or fix feet high, fending out many branches, which have four angles, armed with fhort crooked fpines. The leaves are placed oppofite; they are oval, fpear-fhaped, about an inch and a half long, and three quarters of an inch broad, hairy, and ftand upon fhort foot-ftalks; toward the end of the branches the flowers come out from the wings of the ftalks, two foot-ftalks arifing from the fame joint, one on each fide; they are near two inches long, and are terminated by roundifh heads of flowers, thofe which are on the outfide and form the border, are firft of a bright red, or fcarlet colour; thefe change to a deep purple before they fall. Thofe flowers which are in the center are of a bright yellow, but after fome time fade to an Orange colour. The flowers are fucceeded by roundifh berries, which, when ripe, turn black, having a pulpy covering over a fingle hard feed. This plant in the Weft-Indies continues to flower moft part of the year; but in England they begin to flower in June, and continue in fucceffion till near Chriftmas, and the early flowers are fucceeded by ripe feeds.

The fecond fort grows naturally in Jamaica; this rifes with a flender, fmooth, fhrubby ftalk, about four feet high, dividing into many fmall quadrangular branches which grow erect, garnifhed with fpear-fhaped leaves about two inches long, and one inch broad, indented on their edges, and hoary on their under fide, ftanding alternate upon fhort foot-ftalks. Toward the end of the branches the foot-ftalks of the flowers arife alternately from the wings of the leaves; thefe are very flender, and fupport fmall heads of pale purple flowers, which are fucceeded by fmall purple berries, each having one feed. This flowers at the fame time with the former fort. The feeds of this fort were firft fent me by the late Dr. Houftoun, from La Vera

Cruz, but I have fince received them from Jamaica.

The third fort was fent me from La Vera Cruz, by the late Dr. Houftoun; this rifes with a fhrubby ftalk about three feet high, dividing into feveral upright branches. The leaves are oblong, and fawed on their edges, ftanding oppofite, on the lower part of the branches, but toward the upper part they are placed by threes round the branches. The foot-ftalks of the flowers come out from the wings of the leaves; they are near three inches long, fuftaining an oblong fpike of purple flowers, which come out from imbricated fcales, which end in acute points. The flowers are fucceeded by pretty large purple berries. This flowers at the fame time with the former forts.

The feeds of the fourth fort were fent me from the Havanna, by the late Dr. Houftoun; this rifes with a fhrubby ftalk about three feet high, covered with a gray bark, which is woolly. It divides into branches by pairs, which are garnifhed with round leaves, indented on their edges, whofe upper furface is corrugated and rough, like thofe of Sage; they are placed oppofite, ftanding upon fhort foot-ftalks. At the end of the branches arife the foot-ftalks of the flowers, which are fhort, and fuftain a globular head of purple flowers; thefe are fucceeded by pretty large purple berries containing one feed. This flowers at the fame time with the former forts.

There is a variety of this with white flowers, whofe leaves are not quite fo round, nor are they crenated on their edges; but I fufpect they both come from the fame feeds, fo I have not enumerated it as a diftinct fpecies.

The fifth fort was fent me from La Vera Cruz, by the late Dr. Houftoun; this rifes with a woody branching ftalk four or five feet high, garnifhed with oblong heart-fhaped leaves, which are fawed on their edges, and end in acute points. At the end of the branches the flowers come out in round bunches, ftanding upon flender upright foot-ftalks, about one inch long. The flowers are yellow, and grow in loofer bunches or heads than thofe of the former forts, but flowers at the fame time.

The fixth fort rifes with a woody branching ftalk five or fix feet high, covered with a dark brown bark. The branches are more divided than thofe of the other forts, and are much more ligneous. The leaves are two inches and a half long, and one inch and a quarter broad, deeply fawed on their edges, and their upper furface very rough, and many of them clofely fet with white prominent fpots as if ftudded; thefe are placed alternately on the branches. The flowers come out from the wings of the ftalk, ftanding upon pretty long foot-ftalks; they are white, and are collected in fmall woolly heads. This flowers about the fame time with the former forts.

The feventh fort rifes with a branching fhrubby ftalk about four feet high, covered with a dark brown bark, and garnifhed with fmall, oblong, oval leaves, ending in acute points; they are an inch long, and half an inch broad, very much veined on their upper fide, ftanding alternately pretty clofe to the branches. The flowers come out at the end of the branches upon fhort foot-ftalks, in clofe fmall heads; thefe are white, and make but little appearance. It flowers at the fame time with the former.

The eighth fort was fent me by the late Dr. Houftoun, from Campeachy; this hath a flender fhrubby ftalk which rifes three or four feet high, dividing into many flender, fmooth, fquare branches, which are garnifhed with fmall, oval, fawed leaves placed oppofite; from the wings of the ftalk, at every joint, come out the flowers; they are fmall, white, and are collected in clofe heads; thefe come out by pairs, and fit clofe to the branches. This flowers at the fame time with the former.

The ninth fort is annual; this was firft fent me by the late Dr. Houftoun from La Vera Cruz, but I have fince received the feeds from the north fide of the ifland of Jamaica; it rifes with a ftrong, upright, rough

rough ſtalk near three feet high, dividing toward the top into two or three erect branches, which are garniſhed with oblong, oval, ſawed leaves, ending in acute points; they are placed by fours at each joint, and are a little woolly on their under ſide. The flower-ſtalks ariſe by pairs, and ſometimes three come out at the ſame joint; they are from two to three inches long, and ſuſtain a thick ſpike of large purple flowers, which are ſucceeded by large purple berries that are very ſucculent, and are frequently eaten by the inhabitants. This ſort flowers in July, provided the plants are raiſed early in the ſpring and brought forward, and the ſeeds will ripen in autumn, ſoon after which the plants decay.

The tenth ſort grows naturally in Jamaica, from whence the late Dr. Houſtoun ſent me the ſeeds; this riſes with a ſlender, ſmooth, branching ſtalk three feet high. The branches are garniſhed with oval ſpearſhaped leaves two inches long, and one inch broad; they are crenated on their edges, and rough on their upper ſide, ſtanding by pairs oppoſite, upon very ſhort foot-ſtalks, having an agreeable odour. The flowers come out from the wings of the ſtalk, upon very long foot-ſtalks; they are placed oppoſite the whole length of the young branches, ſuſtaining ſmall round heads of white flowers; theſe appear at the ſame time with the other ſorts, but rarely produce ſeeds in England.

Theſe plants are all of them eaſily propagated by cuttings except the ninth, which is an annual plant, ſo can only be propagated by ſeeds. They may alſo be propagated by ſeeds, which ſeveral of the ſorts produce in England, and the others may be eaſily procured from the Weſt-Indies, where there are a greater variety of theſe plants growing naturally, than are at preſent known in Europe; they are all of them called Wild Sage, by the inhabitants of the Britiſh Iſlands, but they do not diſtinguiſh the ſorts. Theſe ſeeds ſhould be ſown in pots filled with light earth, and plunged into a hot-bed of tan; the reaſon for my adviſing them to be ſown in pots, is, becauſe the ſeeds frequently remain long in the ground before they vegetate; therefore if the plants ſhould not come up the ſame year, the pots ſhould be placed in the ſtove in winter, and the following ſpring plunged into a new hot-bed, which will bring up the plants. When theſe are fit to remove they ſhould be each planted in a ſmall pot, and plunged into another hot-bed, obſerving to ſhade them till they have taken new root; then they ſhould have air admitted to them every day, in proportion to the warmth of the ſeaſon, to prevent their being drawn up with weak ſtalks; afterward they muſt be treated in the ſame manner as other plants from the ſame country, till they have obtained ſtrength; then they may be removed into an airy glaſs-caſe, or a dry ſtove, where they may have a large ſhare of air in warm weather, but protected from the cold. This is neceſſary for the young plants, which ſhould not the firſt year be expoſed to the open air, but afterward they may be placed abroad in the warmeſt part of ſummer, and in winter placed upon ſtands in the dry ſtove, where they will continue long in flower, and many of the ſorts will ripen their ſeeds; but in winter they ſhould be ſparingly watered, for much moiſture will rot their roots.

If they are propagated by cuttings, the beſt time for planting them is in July, after the plants have been expoſed to the open air for about a month, by which time the ſhoots will be hardened ſo as to be out of danger of rotting with a little moiſture. Theſe cuttings ſhould be planted in ſmall pots filled with light earth, and plunged into a moderate hot-bed; and if they are ſcreened from the violence of the ſun in the middle of the day, they will be rooted in about ſix weeks time, when they muſt be hardened gradually to bear the open air, and afterward treated as the old plants.

The eleventh ſort has been long in the Engliſh gardens, and is commonly called the Ilex-leaved Jaſmine. This ſort riſes with a ſhrubby ſtalk five or ſix feet high,

ſending out many irregular branches, which are cloſely garniſhed with thin oval leaves ending in points, and ſawed on their edges, which embrace the branches with their baſe, and from the boſom of each leaf comes out one ſolitary white flower, which is cut at the top into five parts, and at firſt ſight has the appearance of a Jaſmine flower; but when cloſer viewed, the tube will be found curved in the ſame manner with thoſe which Dr. Linnæus titles ringent flowers. The flowers are not ſucceeded by ſeeds in England, but the plants are eaſily propagated by cuttings, which, if planted upon an old hot-bed any time in July, and covered with a bell or hand-glaſs, and ſhaded from the ſun, will put out roots in a month or five weeks; then they may be planted in pots, and placed in the ſhade till they have taken freſh root; after which they may be removed to a ſheltered ſituation, where they may remain till the froſts come on. This plant was brought from the Cape of Good Hope, ſo is not very tender, therefore may be preſerved in a good greenhouſe in winter; but during that ſeaſon it muſt have a large ſhare of air in mild weather, otherwiſe it is apt to grow mouldy, and this will cauſe the tender branches to decay. In the ſummer ſeaſon it may be expoſed in the open air, with other green-houſe plants, in a ſheltered ſituation, where it will add to the variety; and although the flowers are ſmall, and are produced ſingly from between the leaves, ſo do not make any great appearance; yet as there is a ſucceſſion of theſe flowers moſt part of the year, and the leaves continuing green throughout the year, it is rendered worthy of a place in every collection of plants.

The laſt ſort is a native of Africa; this riſes with a ſhrubby four-cornered ſtalk eight or ten feet high, covered with a pale looſe bark, ſending out many ſide branches, garniſhed with rough leaves five or ſix inches long, whoſe baſe embrace the ſtalks, but they end with ſharp points, and are downy on their under ſide; the branches are terminated by looſe ſpikes of pale purple flowers, covered with a meally down; theſe appear in ſummer, but are rarely ſucceeded by ſeeds in England.

This is propagated by cuttings in the ſame manner as the eleventh ſort, and the plants require the ſame treatment.

LANUGINOUS, ſignifies downy, or to be covered with a ſoft down, as a Quince.

LAPATHUM. See Rumex.

LAPSANA. Lin. Gen. Plant. 823. Lampſana & Rhagadiolus. Tourn. Inſt. R. H. 479. tab. 272. Nipplewort.

The Characters are,

The flower is compoſed of ſeveral hermaphrodite florets, which are included in one common imbricated empalement. The florets have one petal, which is tubulous and ſtretched out at the top, in ſhape of a tongue; theſe have each five ſhort hairy ſtamina, terminated by cylindrical ſummits which coaleſce. The germen is ſituated at the bottom of the floret, ſupporting a ſlender ſtyle, crowned by a reflexed bifid ſtigma; the germen afterward becomes an oblong three-cornered ſeed, ſituated in the ſcale of the empalement.

This genus of plants is ranged in the firſt ſection of Linnæus's nineteenth claſs, intitled Syngeneſia Polygamia Æqualis, in which he ranges thoſe plants with hermaphrodite flowers which are fruitful, whoſe ſtamina and ſtyle are connected together; and to this genus he has joined the Rhagadiolus and Zacintha of Tournefort, making them only ſpecies of the ſame genus.

The Species are,

1. Lapsana (*Communis*) calycibus fructûs angulatis, pedunculis tenuibus ramoſiſſimis. Hort. Cliff. 384. *Nipplewort with angular empalements to the fruit, and very narrow branching foot-ſtalks.* Lampſana. Dod. p. 675. *Common Nipplewort.*

2. Lapsana (*Rhagadiolus*) calycibus fructûs undique patentibus, radiis ſubulatis, foliis lyratis. Hort. Upſal. 245. *Nipplewort with empalements to the fruit ſpreading open every way, awl-ſhaped rays, and ſpear-ſhaped undivided*

vided leaves. Rhagadiolus alter. Cæfalp. 511. *Another Rhagadiolus.*

3. LAPSANA (*Lampfanæfoliis*) calycibus fructûs undique patentibus, radiis fubulatis, foliis lyratis. Hort. Upfal. 245. *Nipplewort with empalements to the fruit fpreading open every way, awl-fhaped rays, and harp-fhaped leaves.* Rhagadiolus Lampfanæ foliis. Tourn. Cor. 36. *Rhagadiolus with a Nipplewort leaf.*

4. LAPSANA (*Zacintha*) calycibus fructûs torulofis deprefiis obtufis feftilibus. Lin. Sp. Plant. 811. *Nipplewort with a depreffed knotted empalement which is obtufe, and fits clofe to the branches.* Zacintha five cichorium verrucarium. Tourn. Inft. 476. *Zacintha, or warted Cichory.*

The firft fort is a common weed, which grows by the fide of foot-paths and hedges in moft parts of England, fo is not permitted to have room in gardens.

The fecond and third forts grow naturally in Portugal, from whence I have received their feeds. Thefe are annual plants, of no beauty or ufe, but are preferved in botanic gardens for the fake of variety. If the feeds of thefe are permitted to fcatter, the plants will come up without trouble, and two or three of them will be enough to leave to keep the forts.

The fourth fort grows naturally in Italy ; this is alfo an annual plant, of neither ufe or beauty, but is like the others kept for variety. ·If the feeds of this fort fcatter in the autumn, the plants will come up better than if fown in the fpring. The plants require no culture, but will thrive like weeds.

LARIX. Tourn. Inft. R. H. 586. tab. 353. Pinus. Lin. Gen. Plant. 956. The Larch-tree ; in French, *Melefe.*

The CHARACTERS are,

It hath male and female flowers growing feparate on the fame tree. The male flowers are difpofed in a fcaly katkin ; thefe have no petal, but a great number of ftamina which are connected in a column below, but are feperated at their points, and are terminated by erect fummits. The female flowers are difpofed in a conical fhape, having no petals ; thefe are placed by pairs under each fcale, having a fmall germen, fupporting an awl-fhaped ftyle, crowned by a fingle ftigma. The germen afterward becomes a nut with a membraneous wing, inclofed in the fcales of the cones.

This genus of plants is ranged in the ninth fection of Linnæus's twenty-firft clafs, intitled Monœcia Monodelphia, the fame tree having male and female flowers in different parts, and the ftamina of the male flowers are united in one clufter. Dr. Linnæus has joined this genus, and the Abies of Tournefort, to the genus of Pinus, which, according to his fyftem, may very well be brought together ; but as Tournefort and all former botanifts have feparated them by the form of their leaves, thofe of the Abies coming·out fingle from the branches, thofe of the Pine coming out by two, three, or five out of each fheath, and thofe of this genus arifing in clufters in the bottom, but are fpread above like a painter's pencil ; fo thefe diftinctions being pretty generally known by gardeners, I have chofen to continue them under their former feparate titles to prevent confufion.

The SPECIES are,

1. LARIX (*Decidua*) foliis deciduis, conis ovatis obtufis. *Larch-tree with deciduous leaves, and oval obtufe cones.* Larix folio deciduo, conifera. J. B. 1. p. 265. *Common Cone-bearing Larch-tree.*

2. LARIX (*Chinenfis*) foliis deciduis, conis mucronatis fquamis acutis. *Larch-tree with deciduous leaves, and pointed cones having acute fcales.*

3. LARIX (*Cedrus*) foliis acutis perennantibus, conis obtufis. *Larch-tree with acute evergreen leaves and obtufe cones.* Cedrus conifera, foliis laricis. C. B. P. 490. *Cone-bearing Cedar with a Larch-tree leaf, or the Cedar of Lebanus.*

The firft fort grows naturally upon the Alps and Apennines, and of late years has been very much propagated in England. This tree is of quick growth, and will rife to the height of fifty feet ; the branches are flender, and their ends generally hang downward. Thefe are garnifhed with long narrow leaves, which

arife in clufters from one point, and fpread open above like the hairs of a painter's brufh ; they are of a light green, and fall away in autumn like other deciduous trees. In the month of April the male flowers appear, which are difpofed in form of fmall cones ; the female flowers are collected into oval obtufe cones, which in fome fpecies have bright purple tops, and in others they are white : thefe differences are accidental, for I have found the feeds taken from either of thefe varieties, will produce plants of both forts ; the cones are about one inch long, obtufe at their points, and the fcales lie over each other, and are fmooth ; under each fcale there is generally lodged two feeds which have wings.

There are two other varieties of this tree, one of which is a native of America, and the other of Siberia ; the latter requires a colder climate than England, for they are very apt to die in fummer here, efpecially if they are planted on a dry foil. The cones of this fort which have been brought to England, feem to be in general larger than thofe of the common kind ; but there is fo little difference between the trees in their characteriftic notes, as not to be diftinguifhed as different fpecies, though by the growth of the trees there is a remarkable difference.

The cones of the fecond fort were fent from China, to the Right Hon. the Earl of Northumberland, who was fo good as to communicate fome of the feeds to me, which were fown in the Chelfea garden, where they fucceeded, as they alfo did in his Lordfhip's garden at Stanwick. The cones of this fort were much larger than thofe of the common fort, and ended in acute points ; the fcales were prominent like thofe of the Scotch Pine, and had fo little refemblance to thofe of the Larch, that at every one who faw them, imagined they were a fort of Pine ; they were titled, Fir good to keep up banks. As thefe plants make but little progrefs the firft year, fo they were weak, and in the autumn cafting off their leaves, they were fuppofed to be dead, and moft of the plants were thereby loft ; but thofe which efcaped, afterward fhot their branches out horizontally, fpreading clofe to the ground, and by their prefent appearance, feem to be a fhrub which never will rife upright. This fort is fo hardy, as to thrive in the open air without any protection.

The common Larch is now very plenty in moft of the nurferies in England, and of late years there has been great numbers of the trees planted ; but thofe which have been planted in the worft foil and in bad fituations, have thriven the beft ; for where trees of equal fize have been planted in good garden earth at the fame time, the others on the cold ftiff land, have in twelve years been twice the height of thofe planted in good ground ; which is an encouragement to plant thefe trees, fince they will thrive in the moft expofed fituations, provided they are planted in clumps near each other, and not fingle trees ; nor fhould the plants which are planted in very open expofed places be taken from warm nurferies, but rather raifed as near to the fpot where they are to remain as poffible ; nor fhould the plants be more than three or four years growth when planted, where they are defigned to grow large ; for though trees of greater fize will remove very well, and grow feveral years as well as if they had not been tranfplanted ; yet after twenty or thirty years growth they will frequently fail, where the young planted trees have continued very vigorous.

Thefe trees are raifed from feeds, which moft years ripen well in England : the cones fhould be gathered about the end of November, and kept in a dry place till the fpring, when they fhould be fpread on a cloth and expofed to the fun, or laid before a fire, which will caufe the fcales of the cones to open and emit their feeds. Thefe feeds fhould be fown on a border expofed to the eaft, where the morning fun only comes on it ; or if they are fown on a bed more expofed to the fun, they fhould be fcreened with mats from the fun in the middle of the day ; for when the plants firft appear above ground, they are very impatient of heat ;

and

and when the bed is much expofed to the fun, the furface of the ground will dry fo faft, as to require to have water very often, which frequently rots the tender ftems of the plants; which will be prevented by properly fhading them while young, and afterward they will be in no danger. Thefe young plants fhould be conftantly kept clean from weeds, and if they have made good progrefs, they may be tranfplanted the following autumn, otherwife they may remain in the feed-bed another year, efpecially if the plants are not too clofe together. When they are tranfplanted, it fhould be performed in the autumn as foon as their leaves decay; they may be planted in beds at about fix inches afunder each way, which will be diftance enough for the growth of the plants the two following years, by which time they will be fit to tranfplant where they are to remain.

When the young trees are planted out for good, they need not be more than eight or ten feet diftant from each other, always planting them clofer on expofed fituations, than where they are more defended; after the trees are planted, they will require no other care but to keep them clean from weeds for three or four years till the trees have obtained ftrength, when they will over-top the weeds and prevent their growth; but the ground between thefe trees fhould not be dug, for that I have found has greatly ftopped their growth.

The Siberian Larch is of flow growth in this country, for when the fpring is mild, the trees will begin to fhoot in February, or early in March; and there are frequently fharp frofts after, whereby thefe fhoots are often killed, and this ftops the growth of the trees. Likewife when they are planted on a warm dry foil, they are frequently killed by drought in the fummer; therefore this is a very improper tree for this country, unlefs for fome cold, moift, peary land, where they may probably thrive, and in fuch fituations few other trees will grow.

The American or black Larch, thrives pretty well upon moift land, but on dry ground will make but little progrefs. A few of thefe trees by way of variety, may be allowed to have place in every collection of trees defigned for pleafure; but for profit, the common Larch is to be preferred to any other fpecies.

In Switzerland, where thefe trees abound, and they have a fcarcity of other wood, they build moft of their houfes with it; and great part of their furniture is alfo made of the wood, fome of which is white, and fome red, but the latter is moft efteemed. The rednefs of the wood is by fome fuppofed to be from the age of the trees, and not from any difference between them, but is rather owing to the quantity of turpentine contained in them. They frequently cut out the boards into fhingles of a foot fquare, with which they cover their houfes, inftead of tiles or other covering; thefe are at firft very white, but after they have been two or three years expofed, become as black as charcoal; and all the joints are ftopped by the refin, which the fun draws out from the pores of the wood, which is hardened by the air, and becomes a fmooth fhining varnifh, which renders the houfes fo covered impenetrable to either wind or rain; but as this is very combuftible, the magiftrates have made an order of police, that the houfes fo covered fhould be built at a diftance from each other to prevent fire, which has often done great damage in villages.

In moft countries where this wood is in plenty, it is preferred to all the kinds of Fir for every purpofe; and in many places there are fhips built of this wood, which they fay are durable; therefore this may be a very proper tree for planting upon fome of the cold barren hills in many parts of England, which at prefent produce nothing to their proprietors, and in one age may be large eftates to their pofterity, and a national advantage; which might be effected without a great expence, where the bufinefs is properly conducted.

The beft method for doing this, would be by making fmall nurferies on or near the place where the plantation is intended to be made, in thofe nurferies the feeds fhould be fown; and if there are any poor cottagers there, thefe may be employed in raifing of the plants, keeping of them clean, and afterward in tranfplanting them. This will leffen the number of indigent poor, and by employing them in this fort of hufbandry, they may be brought to have a love and regard for trees of their own planting, fo will not be tempted to deftroy them themfelves, or fuffer others to do it; and as the feafon for planting happens at a time of year when the farmers have little employment for their labourers, fo the finding them ufeful employment this way, will be of infinitely more advantage than the giving them alms from the parifh; and the children may be taught to weed and keep the young plants clean in fummer, whereby they may be rendered ufeful, and kept from being burdenfome to the parifhes.

From the Larch-tree is extracted the Venice turpentine, which the inhabitants of the valley of St. Martin near Lucern, make a confiderable merchandize of. They collect this by boring holes in the trunk of the trees, at about two or three feet from the ground, into which they fix narrow troughs about twenty inches long; the end of thefe are hollowed like a ladle, and in the middle is a fmall hole bored for the turpentine to run into a receiver, which is placed below it; as the turpentine runs from the trees, it paffes along the floping gutter or trough to the ladle, and from thence runs through the holes into the receiver. The people who gather this vifit the trees morning and evening, from the end of May to September, to collect the turpentine from out of the receivers.

The third fort is the Cedar of Libanus, which is a tree of great antiquity; and what is remarkable, this tree is not found as a native in any other part of the world, fo far as hath come to our knowledge.

The cones of this tree are frequently brought from the Levant, which, if preferved entire, will preferve their feeds good for feveral years. The time of their ripening is commonly in the fpring, and fo confequently are near one year old before we receive them, for which they are not the worfe, but rather the better; the cones having difcharged a great part of their refin by lying, and the feeds are much eafier to get out of them than fuch as are frefh taken from the tree.

The beft way to get the feeds out is to fplit the cones, by driving a fharp piece of iron through the center lengthways, which will fplit the cone; then you may pull the feeds out with your fingers, which you will find are faftened to a thin leafy fubftance called wings, as are thofe of the Fir-tree: but before the feeds are taken out, it will be proper to put the cones in water for twenty-four or thirty hours, which will render them eafier to fplit, fo that the feeds may be taken out with greater fafety; for there will require care in the doing of it, otherwife many of the feeds will be fpoiled, as they are very tender, and will bruife where there is any force employed to get them out.

Thefe feeds fhould be fown in boxes or pots of light frefh earth, and treated as was directed for the Firs (to which I refer the reader) but only fhall obferve, that thefe require more fhade in fummer while young than the Firs, and fhould be frequently refrefhed with water.

When the plants come up they muft be guarded from the birds, otherwife they will pick off their tops, as they do of the young Firs where they are not guarded; they muft alfo be conftantly kept clean from weeds, and not placed under the drip of trees. The plants may remain in thefe boxes or pots in which they were fown till the following fpring, but it will be proper to place them under a frame in winter, or cover them with mats; for while they are young they are in danger of lofing their tops, if they are pinched by froft, for the young plants often fhoot late in the autumn. In the fpring, before the plants begin to fhoot, they fhould be carefully taken up and tranfplanted into beds at about four inches diftance, clofing the earth

gently

gently to their roots; thefe beds fhould be arched over with hoops, and covered with mats in the heat of the day, to fhade the plants from the fun till they have taken new root; and if the nights prove frofty, it will be proper to keep the mats over them in the night, but in cloudy or moift weather they muft be always open. After the plants are well rooted, they will require no other care but to keep them clean from weeds, unlefs the feafon fhould prove very dry, in which cafe it will be proper to give them fome water once or twice a week; but it muft be but in fmall quantities, for too much wet is often very injurious to them; fo that it will be better to fcreen 'them from the fun in hot weather, to prevent the earth from drying too faft, or cover the furface of the ground with mofs to keep it cool, than to water the plants often.

In thefe beds the plants may ftand two years, then they fhould be either tranfplanted to the places where they are defigned to remain, or to a nurfery where they may grow two years more; but the younger thefe plants are when they are planted out for good, the better the trees will thrive, and the longer they will continue.

When thefe plants begin to fhoot ftrong, you will generally find the leading fhoot incline to one fide; therefore, if you intend to have them ftrait, you muft fupport them with ftakes, obferving to keep the leader always clofe tied up, until you have got them to the height you defign them, otherwife their branches will extend on every fide, and prevent their growing tall. Thefe trees are by many people kept in pyramids, and fheared as Yews, &c. in which form they lofe their greateft beauty; for the extenfion of the branches is very fingular in this tree, their fhoots for the moft part are declining, and thereby fhewing their upper furface, which is conftantly clothed with green leaves in fo regular a manner, as to appear at fome diftance like a green carpet; and thefe waving about with the wind, make one of the moft agreeable profpects that can be to terminate a vifta, efpecially if planted on a rifing ground.

It is matter of furprife to me, that this tree hath not been more cultivated in England formerly, for till within a few years paft, there were but few here; fince it would be a great ornament to barren bleak mountains, where few other trees will grow fo well, it being a native of the coldeft parts of Mount Libanus, where the fnow continues great part of the year. And from the obfervations I have made of thofe now growing in England, I find they thrive beft on the pooreft foil; for fuch of them as have been planted in a ftrong, rich, loamy earth, have made but a poor progrefs, in comparifon to fuch as have grown upon a ftony meagre foil. And that thefe trees are of quick growth, is evident from four of them now growing in the phyfic garden at Chelfea, which (as I have been credibly informed) were planted there in the year 1683, and at that time were not above three feet high; two of which trees are at this time (viz. 1766) upwards of twelve feet and a half in girt, at two feet above ground, and their branches extend more than twenty feet on every fide their trunks; which branches (though they are produced twelve or fourteen feet above the furface) do at every termination hang very near the ground, and thereby afford a goodly fhade in the hotteft feafon of the year.

The foil in which thefe trees are planted, is a lean hungry fand mixed with gravel, the furface of which is fcarcely two feet deep before a hard rocky gravel appears. Thefe trees ftand at four corners of a pond, which is bricked up within two feet of their trunks, fo that their roots have no room to fpread on one fide, and confequently are cramped in their growth; but whether their ftanding fo near the water may not have been advantageous to them, I cannot fay, but fure I am, if their roots had had full fcope in the ground, they would have made a greater progrefs. I have alfo obferved, that lopping or cutting of thefe trees is very injurious to them (more, perhaps, than to any other of the refinous trees) in retarding their growth;

for two of the four trees above-mentioned, being un-advifedly planted near a green-houfe, when they began to grow large had their branches lopped, to let the rays of the fun into the houfe, whereby they have been fo much checked, as at prefent they are little more than half the fize of the other two.

Thefe trees have all of them produced, for feveral years, large quantities of katkins (or male flowers,) though there are but three of them which have as yet produced cones; nor is it above thirty-five years that thefe have ripened their cones, fo as to perfect the feed; but now the feeds which fall out of the cones on the ground near them, produce plants in plenty, which come up naturally without care: and fince we find that they are fo far naturalized to our country as to produce ripe feeds, we need not fear being foon fupplied with enough, without depending on thofe cones which are brought from the Levant; as there are many trees of this kind in England, which already do, and abundance more which in a few years muft certainly bear: but I find they are more fubject to produce and ripen their cones in hard winters than in mild ones; which is a plain indication, that they will fucceed, even in the coldeft parts of Scotland, where, as well as in England, they might be propagated to great advantage.

What we find mentioned in fcripture of the lofty Cedars, can be no ways applicable to the ftature of this tree; fince, from the experience we have of thofe now growing in England, as alfo from the teftimony of feveral travellers, who have vifited thofe few remaining trees on Mount Libanus, they are not inclined to grow very lofty, but, on the contrary, extend their branches very far; to which the allufion made by the Pfalmift agrees very well, when he is defcribing the flourifhing ftate of a people, and fays, They fhall fpread their branches like the Cedar-tree.

Rauwolf, in his Travels, fays, there were not at that time (i. e. anno 1574) upon Mount Libanus more than 26 trees remaining, 24 of which ftood in a circle; and the other two, which ftood at a fmall diftance, had their branches almoft confumed with age; nor could he find any younger trees coming up to fucceed them, though he looked about diligently for fome. Thefe trees (he fays) were growing at the foot of a fmall hill, on the top of the mountains, and amongft the fnow. Thefe having very large branches, commonly bend the tree to one fide, but are extended to a great length, and in fo delicate and pleafant order, as if they were trimmed and made even with great diligence, by which they are eafily diftinguifhed at a great diftance from Fir-trees. The leaves (continues he) are very like to thofe of the Larch-tree, growing clofe together in little bunches upon fmall brown fhoots.

Maundrel in his Travels, fays, there were but fixteen large trees remaining when he vifited the mountains, fome of which were of a prodigious bulk, but that there were many more young trees of a fmaller fize; he meafured one of the largeft, and found it to be 12 yards 6 inches in girt, and yet found, and 37 yards in the fpread of its boughs. At about five or fix yards from the ground it was divided into five limbs, each of which was equal to a great tree. What Maundrel hath related, was confirmed to me by a worthy gentleman of my acquaintance, who was there in the year 1720, with this difference only, viz. in the dimenfions of the branches of the largeft tree, which he affured me he meafured, and found to be twenty-two yards diameter. Now, whether Mr. Maundrel meant thirty-feven yards in circumference of the fpreading branches, or the diameter of them, cannot be determined by his expreffions, yet either of them well agrees with my friend's account.

Monfieur Le Brun reckons about 35 or 36 trees remaining upon Mount Libanus when he was there, and would perfuade us it was not eafy to reckon their numbers (as is reported of our Stonehenge on Salifbury Plain.) He alfo fays, their cones do fome of them grow dependent. Which is abundantly confuted by the above-mentioned travellers, as alfo from our own experience,

experience, for all the cones grow upon the upper part of the branches, and stand erect, having a strong, woody, central style, by which it is firmly annexed to the branch, so as with difficulty to be taken off; which central style remains upon the branches after the cone is fallen to pieces, so that they never drop off whole, as the Pines do.

The wood of this famous tree is accounted proof against all putrefaction of animal bodies; the sawdust of it is thought to be one of the secrets used by those mountebanks, who pretend to have the embalming mystery. This wood is also said to yield an oil, which is famous for preserving books and writings; and the wood is thought by my Lord Bacon, to continue above a thousand years found. It is also recorded, that in the temple of Apollo at Utica, there was found timber of near two thousand years old. And the statue of the goddess, in the famous Ephesian temple, was said to be of this material also, as was most of the timber work of that glorious structure.

This sort of timber is very dry and subject to split, nor does it well endure to be fastened with nails, from which it usually shrinks, therefore pins of the same wood are much preferable.

LARKSPUR. See DELPHINIUM.

LASERPITIUM. Tourn. Inst. R. H. 324. tab. 172. Lin. Gen. Plant. 306. Laserwort.

The CHARACTERS are,

It hath an umbellated flower, composed of many small umbels; both the small and principal umbels have a many-leaved involucrum. The general umbel is uniform; the flowers have five equal petals, whose points are heart-shaped and inflexed; they have five stamina which are as long as the petals, terminated by single summits; the roundish germen is situated under the flower, supporting two thick acuminated styles, crowned by obtuse spreading stigmas. The germen afterward becomes an oblong fruit with eight longitudinal wings or membranes, resembling the fliers of a water-mill; the fruit divides into two parts, each containing one seed.

This genus of plants is ranged by Dr. Linnæus's in the second section of his fifth class, intitled Pentandria Digynia, which includes those plants whose flowers have five stamina and two styles.

The SPECIES are,

1. LASERPITIUM (*Commune*) foliolis oblongo-cordatis, inciso-serratis. *Laserwort with oblong heart-shaped lobes, which are cut like a saw.* Laserpitium foliis latioribus lobatis. Mor. Umbel. 29. *Laserwort with broader leaves, having lobes.*

2. LASERPITIUM (*Latifolium*) foliolis-cordatis inciso-serratis. Hort. Cliff. 96. *Laserwort with heart-shaped lobes cut like a saw.* Laserpitium foliis amplioribus, semine crispo. Inst. R. H. 324. *Laserwort with large leaves and curled seeds.*

3. LASERPITIUM (*Paludapifolium*) foliolis ovatis obtusis acutè serratis. *Laserwort with oval obtuse lobes sharply sawed.* Laserpitium humilius, paludapii folio, flore albo. Inst. R. H. *Lower Laserwort, with a Smallage leaf and a white flower.*

4. LASERPITIUM (*Gallicum*) foliolis cuneiformibus furcatis. Lin. Sp. Plant. 248. *Laserwort with wedge-shaped forked lobes.* Laserpitium Gallicum. 156. C. B. P. *French Laserwort.*

5. LASERPITIUM (*Angustifolium*) foliolis lanceolatis integerrimis sessilibus. Hort. Cliff. 96. *Laserwort with spear-shaped entire leaves sitting close to the branches.* Laserpitium angustissimo & oblongo folio. Inst. R. H. 324. *Laserwort with a very narrow oblong leaf.*

6. LASERPITIUM (*Selinoides*) foliolis trifidis acutis. *Laserwort with acute trifid lobes.* Laserpitium selinoides, semine crispo. Inst. R. H. *Laserwort resembling sweet Smallage, with a curled seed.*

7. LASERPITIUM (*Trilobum*) foliolis trilobis incisis. Lin. Sp. 357. *Laserwort with trifid leaves.* Libanotis latifolia aquilegiæ folio. C. B. P. 157.

8. LASERPITIUM (*Prutenicum*) foliolis lanceolatis integerrimis extimis coalitis. *Laserwort with spear-shaped entire lobes, whose outer ones coalesce.* Laserpitium

daucoides prutenicum viscoso semine. Breyn. Cent. 167.

9. LASERPITIUM (*Peucedanoides*) foliolis lineari-lanceolatis venoso-striatis distinctis Amœnit. Acad. 4. p. 310. *Laserwort with linear spear-shaped leaves, which are distinct and veined.* Laserpitium exoticum, lobis angustissimis integris. Pluk. Phyt. tab. 96. f. 2.

10. LASERPITIUM (*Siler*) foliolis ovato-lanceolatis integerrimis petiolatis. Hort. Cliff. 96. *Laserwort with oval, spear-shaped, entire leaves, having foot-stalks.* Siler Montanum. Mor. Hist. 3. p. 276.

11. LASERPITIUM (*Chironium*) foliolis oblique cordatis, petiolis hirsutis. Lin. Sp. 358. *Laserwort with oblique heart-shaped lobes, having hairy foot-stalks.* Panax Heracleum. Mor. Hist. 3. p. 315. *Herculus's All-heal.*

12. LASERPITIUM (*Ferulaceum*) foliolis linearibus. Lin. Sp. 358. *Laserwort with linear leaves.* Cachrys Orientalis, ferulæ folio tenuiore, fructu alato plano. Tourn. Cor. 23.

There are some other varieties, if not distinct species of this plant; some of which have been put down as distinct species, which differ only in the colour of their flowers, therefore should not be regarded as such; but the number of species has been greatly lessened by some late writers, who have erred as much in lessening, as those before them had done in multiplying of the species: which mistake they may have fallen into by sowing of the seeds near old plants of the same genus, or on ground where some of these sorts have grown, so that their seeds have been scattered and buried in the ground, where they will remain two or three years, and afterward grow; so that unless their seeds are sown at a distance from any of the other species, there will commonly some other species come up, whereby people have been often confused in distinguishing these plants; nay, I have frequently observed the feeds of one species fall, and the plants come up on the head of another plant which grew near it; and this young plant, if not timely rooted out, has gotten the better of the old plant, and destroyed it; therefore where there is not great care taken to prevent this, the different sorts cannot be preserved in gardens where the species grow near each other.

These plants grow naturally in the south of France, in Italy, and Germany, and are preserved in botanic gardens for the sake of variety; but as they have no great beauty, so are seldom cultivated in other gardens: they require much room, for their roots extend far every way, and the leaves of many sorts will spread three feet, when the plants are strong; their flower-stalks rise four or five feet high, and their umbels of flowers are very large; they have all of them perennial roots but annual stalks. They flower in June, and the seeds ripen in September.

It is generally supposed, that the Silphium of the antients was procured from one species of this genus, but from which of them we are at present ignorant. All the species, if wounded, drop a very acrid juice, which turns to a resinous gummy substance, very acrimonious. This was externally applied by the antients to take away black and blue spots that came by bruises and blows, as also to take away excrescences; it was also by some of the antients prescribed in internal medicines, but others have cautioned people not to make use of it in this way, from the effects which they mention to have seen produced from the violence of its acrimony.

All these plants are extreme hardy, except the last, which requires a warmer situation, otherwise will be killed in sharp winters; the other sorts will thrive in most soils and situations; they are propagated by seed, which if sown in autumn, the plants will come up the following spring; but when they are sown in the spring, the seeds commonly remain in the ground a whole year. The plants should be transplanted the following autumn where they are designed to remain, for they send out long deep roots, which are frequently broken by transplanting if they are large; when the plants are removed, they should be planted

three

three feet afunder, for they grow very large; they decay to the ground every autumn, and come up again the following fpring, but the roots will continue many years, and require no other culture but to clear them from weeds, and to dig between the roots every fpring.

LATHYRUS. Tourn. Inft. R. H. 394. tab. 216, 217. Lin. Gen. Plant. 781. Chichling Vetch; in French, *Geffe.*

The CHARACTERS are,

The flower has a bell-fhaped empalement of one leaf, cut into five parts at the top, the two upper being fhort, and the under longer. The flower is of the butterfly kind. The flandard is heart-fhaped, large, and reflexed at the point. The wings are oblong and blunt; the keel is half round, the fize of the wings. It hath ten flamina, nine of them joined, and one feparate, crowned by roundifh fummits. It hath an oblong, narrow, compreffed germen, fupporting a rifing flyle, which is flat, and the upper part broad, with an acute point, crowned by a hairy ftigma. The germen afterward becomes a long compreffed pod, ending in a point, having two valves, and filled with roundifh feeds.

This genus of plants is ranged in the third fection of Linnæus's feventeenth clafs, intitled Diadelphia Decandria which includes thofe plants whofe flowers have ten ftamina formed in two bodies.

The SPECIES are,

1. LATHYRUS (*Sativus*) pedunculis unifloris, cirrhis diphyllis, leguminibus ovatis compreffis dorfo bimarginatis. Hort. Cliff. 367. *Chichling Vetch with one flower upon a foot-ftalk, tendrils having two leaves, and oval compreffed pods with two borders on their back part.* Lathyrus annuus, flore cæruleo, Ochri filiquâ. H. L. *Annual Chichling Vetch with a blue flower, and a pod like Ochrus.*

2. LATHYRUS (*Cicera*) pedunculis unifloris, cirrhis diphyllis, leguminibus ovatis compreffis, dorfo canaliculatis. Lin. Sp. Plant. 730. *Chichling Vetch with one flower upon a foot-ftalk, two-leaved tendrils, and an oval compreffed pod a little channelled on the back.* Lathyrus fativus flore purpureo. C. B. P. 344. *Cultivated Chichling Vetch with a purple flower.*

3. LATHYRUS (*Setifolius*) pedunculis unifloris, cirrhis diphyllis, foliolis fetaceo-linearibus. Lin. Sp. 1031. *Chichling Vetch with one flower upon a foot-ftalk, a two-leaved tendril, and linear briftly lobes.* Lathyrus foliis anguftis, floribus fingularibus coccineis. Seg. Pl. Veron. *Chichling Vetch, with narrow leaves and fingle fcarlet flowers.*

4. LATHYRUS (*Parifienfus*) pedunculis unifloris, cirrhis polyphyllis, ftipulis lanceolatis. Hort. Cliff. 368. *Chichling Vetch with one flower upon a foot-ftalk, a many-leaved tendril, and fpear-fhaped ftipule.* Clymenum Parifienfe flore cæruleo. Tourn. Inft. R. H. 396. *Chichling Vetch of Paris with a blue flower.*

5. LATHYRUS (*Hifpanicus*) pedunculis bifloris, cirrhis polyphyllis, foliolis alternis. Hort. Cliff. *Chichling Vetch with two flowers upon a foot-ftalk, a many-leaved tendril, and the lobes placed alternate.* Clymenum Hifpanicum, flore vario filiquâ articulatâ. Tourn. Inft. R. H. 296. *Spanifh Chichling Vetch, with a variable flower and jointed pod.*

6. LATHYRUS (*Odoratus*) pedunculis bifloris, cirrhis diphyllis, foliis ovato-oblongis, leguminibus hirfutis. Hort. Cliff. 368. *Chichling Vetch with two flowers on a foot-ftalk, a two-leaved tendril, oblong oval leaves, and hairy pods.* Lathyrus diftoplatyphyllos hirfutus, mollis, magno & peramæno flore odore. Hort. Cath. *The fweet-fcented Pea.*

7. LATHYRUS (*Hirfuta*) pedunculis bifloris, cirrhis diphyllis, foliolis lineari-lanceolatis, leguminibus hirfutis, feminibus fcabris, Flor. Leyd. Prod. 363. *Chichling Vetch with two flowers on a foot-ftalk, a two-leaved tendril, narrow fpear-fhaped lobes, hairy pods, and rough feeds.* Lathyrus anguftifolius filiquâ hirfutâ. C. B. P. *Narrow-leaved Chichling Vetch with a hairy pod.*

8. LYTHYRUS (*Tingitanus*) pedunculis bifloris, cirrhis diphyllis, foliolis alternis lanceolatis. Flor. Leyd.

Prod. 263. *Chichling Vetch with two flowers on a foot-ftalk, a two-leaved tendril, and fpear-fhaped alternate leaves.* Lathyrus Tingitanus filiquis orobi flore amplo ruberrimo. Mor. Hift. 2. 55. *Chichling Vetch of Tangier, with a bitter Vetch pod, and a large red flower.*

9. LATHYRUS (*Annuus*) pedunculis bifloris, cirrhis diphyllis, foliolis enfiformibus, leguminibus glabris, ftipulis bipartitis. Amœn. Acad. 3. p. 417. *Chichling Vetch with two flowers on a foot-ftalk, a two-leaved tendril, fword-fhaped lobes, fmooth pods, and a bifid ftipula.* Lathyrus luteus latifolius. Bot. Monfp. *Yellow broad-leaved Chichling Vetch.*

10. LATHYRUS (*Tuberofus*) pedunculis multifloris, cirrhis diphyllis, foliolis ovalibus, internodis nudis. Hort. Cliff. 367. *Chichling Vetch with many flowers on a foot-ftalk, a two-leaved tendril, oval leaves, and naked between the joints.* Lathyrus arvenfis repens tuberofus. C. B. P. 344. *Creeping Field Chichling Vetch with a tuberous root.*

11. LATHYRUS (*Pratenfis*) pedunculis multifloris, cirrhis diphyllis, foliolis lanceolatis cirrhis fimpliciffimis. Hort. Cliff. 367. *Chichling Vetch with many flowers on a foot-ftalk, a two-leaved tendril, fpear-fhaped leaves, and fingle tendrils.* Lathyrus luteus fylveftris dumetorum. J. B. 2. p. 304. *Yellow wild Chichling Vetch of the woods.*

12. LATHYRUS (*Heterophyllus*) pedunculis multifloris, cirrhis diphyllis tetraphyllifque, foliolis lanceolatis. It. W. Goth. 75. *Chichling Vetch with many flowers on a foot-ftalk, a two-leaved, and fometimes four-leaved tendril, and fpear-fhaped leaves.* Lathyrus major Narbonenfis anguftifolius. J. B. 2. 304. *Greater Chichling Vetch of Narbonne with narrow leaves.*

13. LATHYRUS (*Latifolius*) pedunculis multifloris, cirrhis diphyllis, foliolis lanceolatis, internodiis membranaceis. Hort. Cliff. 367. *Chichling Vetch with many flowers on a foot-ftalk, a two-leaved tendril, fpear-fhaped leaves, and a membranaceous ftalk between the joints.* Lathyrus latifolius. C. B. P. 344. *Broad-leaved Chichling Vetch, commonly called Everlafting Pea.*

14. LATHYRUS (*Magnoflore*) pedunculis multifloris, cirrhis diphyllis foliolis ovato-lanceolatis, internodiis membranaceis. *Chichling Vetch with many flowers on a foot-ftalk, a two-leaved tendril, oval fpear-foeped leaves, and a membranaceous ftalk between the joints.* Lathyrus latifolius minor flore majore. Boerh. Ind. alt. 2. p. 42. *Smaller bread-leaved Chichling Vetch with a larger flower, or large, red, flowering, Everlafting Pea.*

15. LATHYRUS (*Piftformis*) pedunculis multifloris, cirrhis polyphyllis, ftipulis ovatis, bafi acutis. Hort. Upfal. 217. *Chichling Vetch with many flowers on a foot-ftalk, a many-leaved tendril, and oval ftipulæ acute at the bafe.*

16. LATHYRUS (*Niffolia*) pedunculis unifloris, foliis fimplicibus ftipulis fubulatis. Lin. Sp. Plant. 729. *Chichling Vetch with one flower on a foot-ftalk, fingle leaves, and awl-fhaped ftipule.* Niffolia vulgaris. Tourn. Inft. 656. *Crimfon Grafs Vetch.*

17. LATHYRUS (*Amphicarpos*) pedunculis unifloris calyce longioribus, cirrhis diphyllis fimpliciffimis fubtus venofis. *Chichling Vetch with fingle flowers upon a foot-ftalk, which are longer than the empalement, and a two-leaved fingle tendril.*

18. LATHYRUS (*Aphaca*) pedunculis unifloris, cirrhis aphyllis, ftipulis fagitto-cordatis. Lin. Sp. 1029. *Chichling Vetch with one flower on each foot-ftalk, a tendril without leaves, and a heart arrow-fhaped ftipula.* Aphacha. Lob. Ic. 2. p. 70.

19. LATHYRUS (*Americana*) pedunculis bifloris, foliis reniformibus fimpliciffimis fubtus venofis. *Chichling Vetch with two flowers upon a foot-ftalk, and kidney-fhaped fingle leaves, which are veined on their under fide.* Niffolia Americana procumbens, folio rotundo, flore luteo. Houft. MSS. *Trailing American Niffolia, with a round leaf and a yellow flower.*

The firft fort grows naturally in France, Spain, and Italy; this is an annual plant, with a climbing ftalk about two feet high. The leaves come out at each joint alternate; they are compofed of two long narrow
lobes,

lobes, with a tendril or clasper rising between, which fastens to any support near. The flowers come singly upon foot-stalks at each joint; they are blue, and shaped like those of the Pea; these are succeeded by oval compressed pods, with a double membrane or wing running longitudinally on the back. This flowers in June and July, and the seeds ripen in September. It is seldom cultivated, unless in botanic gardens for the sake of variety.

The second sort is cultivated in some countries for the seeds, which are used for feeding of poultry; this grows wild in Italy and Spain. It does not rise so high as the first sort. The leaves are longer, the pods are near twice the length of those, and are channelled on their back side; this is cultivated in the same manner as Vetches or Tares.

The third sort was sent me from Verona, where it grows naturally; this is an annual plant, which seldom rises more than six or eight inches high. The two lobes of the leaves are small, and end with claspers. The flowers are of a bright scarlet, and are succeeded by taper pods, filled with roundish seeds. This is only kept for variety in some botanic gardens.

The fourth sort grows naturally about Paris; this is an annual plant, with a slender stalk about one foot high, garnished with leaves, composed of several narrow lobes placed alternate along the midrib, which end in claspers. The flowers come out singly upon pretty long foot-stalks; they are blue, and about the size of those of the common Tare. It grows naturally in some parts of England, particularly on Windsor forest, in moist meadows, and has often a variable flower.

The fifth sort grows naturally in Spain and Italy; it is an annual plant, with a climbing stalk which rises near three feet high, garnished with leaves composed of several lobes, which are spear-shaped, placed alternately along the midrib, which is terminated by very long claspers. The foot-stalks of the flowers are five or six inches long, upon which stand two flowers one above the other, shaped like those of the Pea. The standard, which is large, is of a bright red colour, but the keel and wings are white. The flowers are succeeded by pretty long jointed pods, filled with roundish seeds. This flowers in June and July, and the seeds ripen in autumn.

The sixth sort is commonly known by the title of Sweet Pea; this grows naturally in Ceylon, but is hardy enough to thrive in the open air in England. It is an annual plant with a climbing stalk, which rises from three to four feet high, garnished with leaves composed of two large oval lobes, whose midrib is terminated by long claspers. The foot-stalks come out at the joints; they are about six inches long, and sustain two large flowers with dark purple standards; the keel and wings are of a light blue colour. The flowers have a strong sweet odour, and are succeeded by oblong inflated pods, which are hairy, containing four or five roundish seeds in each.

There are two other varieties of this sort, one of which has a Pink-coloured standard with a white keel, and the wings of a pale blush colour; this is commonly called Painted Lady Pea. The flowers of the other are all white, which are the only differences between them.

The seventh sort grows naturally in Essex. I have found it in places which were spread over with Brambles, near Hockerel; this hath a perennial root, sending out three or four weak stalks, which are near two feet long, garnished with leaves composed of two oblong lobes, whose midrib is terminated by claspers. The foot-stalks are about four inches long, and sustain two purple flowers, which are succeeded by rough hairy pods, little more than an inch long, containing three or four roundish seeds. This sort is very rarely preserved in gardens.

The eighth sort was originally brought from Tangier to England; this is an annual plant, whose stalk rises four or five feet high, garnished with leaves composed of two oval veined lobes, whose midrib ends

with claspers. The foot-stalks are short, and sustain two large flowers with purple standards, whose wings and keel are of a bright red; these are succeeded by long jointed pods, containing several roundish seeds. This is sometimes titled by the gardeners Scarlet Lupine.

The ninth sort is an annual plant, which grows naturally about Montpelier. I have also received the seeds from Siberia; this rises with a climbing stalk five or six feet high, which has two membranes, or wings, running along from joint to joint. The leaves are composed of two long narrow lobes, whose midrib ends with claspers. The flowers stand upon long foot-stalks, each sustaining two pale yellow flowers, which are succeeded by long taper pods, containing several roundish seeds.

The tenth sort grows naturally amongst the Corn in the South of France, and in Italy, but is cultivated in the Dutch gardens for the roots, which are there sold in the markets, and are commonly eaten: this hath an irregular tuberous root about as big as those of the Pignut, covered with a brown skin; these shoot up several weak trailing stalks, garnished with leaves composed of two oval lobes, ending with claspers. The foot-stalks of the flowers are weak, about three inches long, each sustaining two deep red flowers, which are seldom succeeded by pods, but the roots increase plentifully in the ground. This sort will grow in most soils, but will thrive best on light ground.

The eleventh sort grows naturally on the banks and under thickets in most parts of England; this hath a perennial creeping root, whereby it propagates so fast as to be a very troublesome weed, so should not be admitted into gardens.

The twelfth sort grows naturally by the side of hedges, and in thickets, in several parts of England; this hath a perennial creeping root, which sends out many climbing stalks which rise five or six feet high, garnished with leaves, which have sometimes two, and at others four long narrow lobes, terminated by claspers. The foot-stalks sustain several small flowers with pale standards, whose wings and keels are blue; these are succeeded by long taper pods, containing several roundish seeds. It flowers in June and July, and the seeds ripen in autumn.

The thirteenth sort has been found growing naturally in several parts of England, but is frequently cultivated in gardens for ornament, therefore it is doubtful if it is a native here; this hath a perennial root, from which arise several thick climbing stalks from six to eight feet high, which have membranaceous wings on each side between the joints. The leaves are composed of two spear-shaped lobes, and the midrib is terminated by claspers. The foot-stalks are eight or nine inches long, and sustain several large red flowers, which are succeeded by long taper pods, containing several roundish seeds. It flowers in June, July, and August, and the seeds ripen in autumn, soon after which the stalks die to the root, and new ones arise in the spring, from whence it is called Everlasting Pea.

The fourteenth sort differs from the last in the stalks, being much shorter and stronger. The leaves are broader, and of a deeper green. The flowers are much larger, and of a brighter red colour, so make a better appearance; these differences are lasting from seeds, for I have raised many plants from seeds within forty years past, and have always found them them to be the same as the parent plant.

The fifteenth sort grows naturally in Siberia; this hath a perennial root and an annual stalk, which is garnished with leaves, composed of six or eight pair of oblong acute lobes. The flowers are blue, and many of them stand upon each foot-stalk; these are succeeded by pods, shaped like those of the Pea. It flowers in June, and the seeds ripen in August.

The sixteenth sort grows naturally in moist meadows in many parts of England; this rises with an upright stalk one foot high, which is garnished with

long, narrow, fingle leaves at each joint. The foot-
ftalks of the flowers come out from the joints toward
the upper part of the ftalk ; they are flender, about
three inches long, fome having but one, and others
have two bright red flowers on their tops. It flowers
in May and June, and the feeds ripen in autumn.
This is rarely kept in gardens.

The feventeenth fort grows naturally in Syria ; this
is an annual plant with a trailing ftalk, garnifhed
with leaves compofed of two lobes, whofe midrib is
terminated by a fingle tendril. The foot-ftalk fupports one flower of a pale purple colour, and when
the flowers decay, the germen is thruft into the ground,
where the pods are formed, and the feeds ripen.

The eighteenth fort was difcovered by the late Dr.
Houftoun, growing naturally at La Vera Cruz in
New Spain ; this is annual plant, with a trailing ftalk
a foot long, garnifhed with a fingle kidney-fhaped
leaf at each joint. The flowers grow two together
upon very fhort foot-ftalks ; they are fmall, and of
a deep yellow colour ; thefe are fucceeded by fhort
taper pods, including three or four fmall roundifh
feeds.

This fort is tender, fo the feeds fhould be fown upon a hot-bed in the fpring, and when the plants are
fit to remove, they fhould be each planted into a
fmall pot filled with light earth, and plunged into
a tan-bed, where they fhould conftantly remain,
treating them in the fame manner as other tender
plants from warm countries ; if they are brought forward in the fpring, they will flower in July, and their
feeds will ripen in autumn.

Several of the other forts are preferved in curious
gardens for the variety of their flowers, fome of which
make a fine appearance, and continue long in flower.
Thefe may all be propagated by fowing their feeds,
either in fpring or autumn ; but thofe which are fowed
in autumn fhould have a light foil and a warm fitua-
ation, where the plants will abide the winter, and
come to flower early the following fpring, and their
feeds will ripen in July ; but thofe which are fown in
the fpring fhould have an open expofure, and be
planted upon almoft any foil, if not too wet, for
they are not tender plants, nor do they require
much culture : thefe forts fhould all of them be fown
where they are defigned to remain, for they feldom
fucceed when they are tranfplanted, unlefs it is done
while the plants are young ; fo that where they are
fown for ornament, there fhould be four or five feeds
fown in a fmall patch, in different parts of the borders of the flower-garden ; and when the plants come
up, they fhould be carefully kept clear from weeds ;
but when they are grown two or three inches high,
there fhould be fome fticks put down by them to
fupport them, otherwife they will trail on the ground,
or on whatever plants ftand near them, and become
unfightly.

The fixth fort, with the two varieties of it, are de-
ferving room in every good garden for the beauty
and odour of their flowers; and the eighth fort is
by fome cultivated for the colour of the flowers ;
but there are few of the other forts worthy of room
in gardens, except the thirteenth and fourteenth forts,
which, if they are planted in a proper fituation, and
are rightly trained, will make a fine appearance.

LATIFOLIOUS trees and plants are fuch as have
broad leaves.

LAVATERA. Tourn. Act. Gal. 1706. tab. 3.
Dill. Gen. 10. Lin. Gen. Plant. 752.

The CHARACTERS are,

*The flower has a double empalement ; the outer is of
one leaf, fhort, obtufe, and trifid ; the inner is of one leaf,
and quinquefid ; they are both permanent. The flower hath
five petals, which are joined at their bafe, plain, and
fpread open above. It has many ftamina, which are joined
in a column below, but above are loofe ; they are inferted
in the petal, and terminated by kidney-fhaped fummits.
It has an orbicular germen, fupporting a fhort cylindrical
ftyle, crowned by many briftly ftigmas. The empalement
afterward becomes a fruit with feveral capfules, covered*

in front by a hollow fhield, each capfule having one kidney-fhaped feed.
This genus of plants is by Dr. Linnæus ranged in the
fifth order of his fixteenth clafs, intitled Monodelphia
Polyandria, which includes thofe plants whofe flowers
have many ftamina joined in a column.

The SPECIES are,
1. LAVATERA (Althæafolia) foliis infimis cordato-orbiculatis, caulinis trilobis acuminatis glabris, pedunculis unifloris, caule herbaceo. Lavatera whofe lower
leaves are orbicularly heart-fhaped, thofe on the ftalks fet
with three acute fmooth lobes, and one flower upon a
foot-ftalk, and an herbaceous ftalk. Lavatera folio &
facie althææ. Act. R. P. 1706. Lavatera with the
leaves and appearance of Marfhmallow.
2. LAVATERA (Africana) foliis infimis cordato-angula-
tis, fupernè fagittatis, pedunculis unifloris, caule herbaceo hirfuto. Lavatera with the lower leaves angularly
heart-fhaped, the upper ones arrow-pointed, a fingle
flower upon each foot-ftalk, and a hairy herbaceous ftalk.
Lavatera Africana, flore pulcherrimo. Boerh. Ind.
alt. African Lavatera with a beautiful flower.
3. LAVATERA (Trimeftris) foliis glabris, caule fcabro
herbaceo, pedunculis unifloris, fructibus orbiculo
tectis. Hort. Upfal. 203. Lavatera with fmooth leaves,
a rough herbaceous ftalk, one flower upon a foot-ftalk,
and an orbicular clofed fruit. Malva folio vario. C. B.
P. Mallow with a variable leaf.
4. LAVATERA (Thuringiaca) caule herbaceo, fructibus
denudatis, calycibus incifis. Hort. Upfal. 203. Lavatera with an herbaceous ftalk, naked fruit, and a cut
empalement. Althæa flore majore. C. B. P. 316.
Marfhmallow with a larger flower.
5. LAVATERA (Hirfuta) foliis quinquelobatis hirfutis,
caule erecto fruticofo. Icon. tab. 161. Lavatera with
hairy leaves having five lobes, and a fhrubby upright
ftalk.
6. LAVATERA (Veneta) caule arboreo, foliis fepteman-
gularibus tomentofis plicatis, pedunculis confertis
unifloris axillaribus. Hort. Upfal. 202. Lavatera with
a tree-like ftalk, woolly plaited leaves having feven angles,
and foot-ftalks with fingle flowers arifing in clufters from
the wings of the leaves. Malva arborea veneta dicta,
parvo flore. C. B. P. 215. Tree Mallow with a fmall
flower.
7. LAVATERA (Triloba) caule fruticofo, foliis fubcordatis fubtrilobis rotundatis crenatis ftipulis cordatis,
pedunculis unifloris. Lin. Sp. Plant. 691. Lavatera
with a fhrubby ftalk, heart-fhaped leaves having three
round indented lobes, which are crenated, heart-fhaped
ftipulæ, and foot-ftalks with fingle flowers. Althæa frutefcens, folio rotundiore incano. C. B. P. 316. Shrubby
Marfhmallow with a rounder hoary leaf.
8. LAVATERA (Olbia) caule fruticofo, foliis quinque-
lobo-haftatis. Hort. Upfal. 202. Lavatera with a
fhrubby ftalk, and leaves having five arrow-pointed lobes.
Althæa frutefcens, folio acuto, parvo flore. C. B. P.
316. Shrubby Marfhmallow with an acute leaf, and a
fmall flower.
9. LAVATERA (Hifpanica) caule fruticofo, foliis orbiculatis crenatis tomentofis, pedunculis confertis unifloris axillaribus. Lavatera with a fhrubby ftalk, round,
crenated, woolly leaves, and foot-ftalks growing in clufters at the wings of the ftalk, each fuftaining a fingle
flower. Althæa frutefcens Hifpanica folio rotundiori.
Tourn. Inft. R. H. 97. Spanifh fhrubby Marfhmallow
with a rounder leaf.
10. LAVATERA (Undulata) caule fruticofo tomentofo,
foliis orbiculato-cordatis undatis incanis, ferrato-cre-
natis, pedunculis fæpius trifloris. Lavatera with a
fhrubby woolly ftalk, round heart-fhaped hoary leaves,
which are waved, fcarply indented, and foot-ftalks which
have frequently three flowers. Althæa frutefcens Lufitanica, folio rotundiori undulato. Tourn. Inft. 97.
Portugal fhrubby Marfhmallow with a rounder waved
leaf.
11. LAVATERA (Bryonifolia) caule fruticofo, foliis
quinquelobatis acutis crenatis tomentofis, racemis terminalibus. Lavatera with a fhrubby ftalk, woolly leaves
having five acute lobes, and long fpikes of flowers terminating

nating the stalks. Althæa frutescens, folio bryoniæ. C. B. P. 316. *Shrubby Althæa with a Briony leaf.*

The first sort grows naturally in Syria; it is an annual plant, with an erect, branching, herbaceous stalk, rising two feet high; the under leaves are orbicularly heart-shaped, smooth, and stand upon long foot-stalks, the upper are divided into three acute lobes; the flowers come out upon long foot-stalks from the wings of the leaves; they are very large, and spread open like those of the Marshmallow, and are of a pale red or Rose colour. These come out in July, the seeds ripen in September, and the plants decay in autumn.

There is a variety of this with white flowers, which has accidentally risen from seeds.

The second sort grows naturally at the Cape of Good Hope, from whence the seeds were brought to Holland, and the plants there cultivated, and the seeds have since been communicated to most parts of Europe. This differs from the first in the shape of the leaves, the lower having angles, and the upper being arrow-pointed; the stalks are hairy, the flowers larger, and of a brighter red colour.

This sort is annual, and flowers at the same time with the former, and the seeds are ripe in the autumn.

The third sort grows naturally in Spain and Sicily; this is an annual plant, which rises with slender herbaceous stalks about two feet high, covered with a brown mark; the lower leaves are roundish, and the upper are angular, and some arrow-pointed. The flowers are not half so large as those of either of the former, and are of a pale red colour; these stand upon short foot-stalks, and appear about the same time with the former. This is certainly a distinct species, for I have cultivated it more than forty years, and I have never found it vary.

The fourth sort hath a perennial root and an annual stalk, which rises five or six feet high, is woolly, garnished with angular heart-shaped leaves, standing upon long foot-stalks. The flowers come out from the wings of the leaves toward the top, sitting close to the stalks at every joint; they are of a purplish colour, and shaped like those of the Marshmallow, but are larger. These appear in July and August, and the seeds ripen in the autumn, then the stalks decay to the root. It grows naturally in Austria and Bohemia.

The fifth sort grows naturally at the Cape of Good Hope, the seeds of it were sent me by the ingenious Mr. Storm, gardener at Amsterdam. This rises with a shrubby branching stalk to the height of eight or ten feet, garnished with large hairy leaves, deeply divided into five roundish lobes, which are indented on their edges, of a bright green, standing alternately upon long foot-stalks; as the plants become more shrubby the leaves decrease in size, so that the upper leaves are not more than a sixth part of the bigness of the first or lower leaves. The flowers come out singly at the wings of the leaves at every joint, so that as the branches extend there is a succession of flowers, whereby the plants are seldom destitute of them the whole year. The flowers are of a bright purple colour, but are not very large; these are succeeded by capsules having many partitions, in each of these is one kidney-shaped seed, which ripen in succession as the flowers are produced.

The sixth sort is commonly called Mallow-tree; this rises with a very strong thick stalk the height of eight or ten feet, dividing into many branches at the top, which are garnished with soft woolly leaves that are plaited, and the edges cut into several angles. The flowers are produced in clusters at the wings of the leaves, each standing upon a separate foot-stalk; they are of a purple colour, and shaped like those of the common Mallow, and are succeeded by seeds of the same form. This sort flowers from June to September, and the seeds are ripe in the autumn.

The seventh sort rises with a shrubby stalk seven or eight feet high, sending out several long branches,

garnished with woolly leaves, differing greatly in size and shape, the lower being partly heart-shaped at their base, but divide into five roundish lobes; the upper, which are small, have three lobes, which are indented on their edges. The flowers come out from the wings of the stalk, three or four at each joint, upon very short foot-stalks; they are of a light purple colour, and shaped like those of Marshmallow. There is a succession of these flowers from June to the autumn.

The eighth sort is a shrub which grows to the same size as the seventh, and differs from it in the shape of the leaves, which are divided into three or five acute-pointed lobes; the flowers are smaller, but of the same shape and colour, it continues in flower at the same time. This grows naturally in the south of France.

The ninth sort rises with a shrubby stalk six or eight feet high, sending out many branches, garnished with roundish, crenated, woolly leaves, standing upon long foot-stalks; the foot-stalks of the flowers come out in clusters from the wings of the leaves, each sustaining one large pale blue flower, of the same shape with those of the other species. This flowers at the same time with them, and the seeds ripen in the autumn.

The tenth sort hath a soft, shrubby, woolly stalk, which rises to the height of four or five feet; these stand more erect than either of the former sorts, and do not branch so much; the leaves are heart-shaped at their base, but round on their edges, very hoary and waved, standing upon long foot-stalks. The flowers come out in clusters from the wings of the leaves, standing upon foot-stalks of different lengths; these generally support but one flower, but sometimes they have two or three; the flowers are large, and of a pale blue colour. They appear at the same time with the former, and their seeds ripen in the autumn. It grows naturally in Portugal.

The eleventh sort rises with a shrubby stalk six or seven feet high, sending out several shrubby branches, which are garnished with woolly leaves, divided into five lobes, which end in acute points, and are crenated on their edges; the lower part of the branches are adorned with a single flower at each joint, sitting close to the stalk, but the branches are terminated by loose spikes of flowers, which are of a pale blue colour, and shaped like those of the former.

The six last mentioned sorts, though they have shrubby stalks, yet are but of short duration here; the fifth, tenth, and eleventh sorts, seldom continue longer than two years, unless when they happen to grow upon dry rubbish, where they make but little progress, and their stalks and branches being firmer, so are better able to resist the cold; for when they are in good ground, they are very vigorous and full of sap, so are killed by the frost in common winters. The other three sorts are not quite so tender, nor of so short duration; these will continue three or four years, and sometimes longer, provided the winters are not very severe; or if the plants stand in a warm situation and on a dry soil, but in moist rich ground they seldom continue long.

All these shrubby sorts are easily propagated by seeds, which should be sown in the spring upon a bed of light earth; and when the plants are about three or four inches high, they should be transplanted to the places where they are designed to remain; for as they shoot out long fleshy roots which have but few fibres, so they do not succeed well if they are transplanted after they are grown large. If the seeds of these plants are permitted to scatter on the ground, the plants will come up the following spring; and when they happen to fall into dry rubbish, and are permitted to grow therein, they will be short, strong, woody, and produce a greater number of flowers than those plants which are more luxuriant. As these plants continue a long time in flower, so a few plants of each sort may be allowed a place in all gardens where there is room.

The

The three first forts are annual plants, which are propagated by feeds : the feafon for fowing them is the end of March or the beginning of April, upon a bed of frefh light earth ; and when the plants are come up, you muft carefully clear them from weeds ; and in very dry weather they muft be now and then refrefhed with water. When they are about two inches high, you muft tranfplant them into the places where they are defigned to remain, which fhould be in the middle of the borders in the flower-garden ; for if the foil is good, they will grow two or three feet high ; in tranfplanting them, you muft take them up very carefully, preferving a ball of earth to their roots, otherwife they are apt to mifcarry ; and alfo water and fhade them until they have taken root, after which they will require no other care but to clear them from weeds, and to faften them to ftakes, to prevent their being injured by ftrong winds. You may alfo fow their feeds in autumn, and when the plants are come up, tranfplant them into fmall pots, which, towards the end of October, fhould be placed in a common hot-bed frame, where the plants being defended from fevere frofts, will abide the winter very well ; and in the fpring, you may fhake them out of the pots, and plant them into larger, or elfe into the full ground, where they may remain to flower. The plants thus managed will be larger, and flower ftronger and earlier than thofe fown in the fpring, and from thefe you will conftantly have good feeds, whereas thofe fown in the fpring fometimes mifcarry. The feeds of the third fort fhould be fown in the fpring in the place where they are to remain, for they do not well bear removing in the fummer.

The two firft forts are very ornamental plants in a fine garden, when placed among other annuals, either in pots or borders.

The fourth fort hath a perennial root which abides feveral years, but the ftalks decay in the autumn, and new ones arife in the fpring. This is propagated by feeds, which fhould be fown upon a bed of light earth in the fpring, and when the plants are fit to remove, they fhould be either tranfplanted to the places where they are to remain, or into pots where they may ftand to get more ftrength, before they are planted in the full ground. After the plants are well rooted, they will require no other care but to keep them clear from weeds. And if the winter fhould prove very fevere, it will be proper to cover the ground about them with old tanners bark to keep out the froft ; but they will endure the cold of our ordinary winters very well, and will produce their flowers and ripen their feeds annually.

The fifth fort will not live through the winter in the open air in England, fo the feeds fhould be fown in the fame manner as thofe of the other forts ; and when the plants are fit to remove, they fhould be each planted into a fmall pot filled with light earth, and placed in the fhade till they have taken new root ; then they may be removed to a fheltered fituation, and mixed with other hardy exotic plants. As the plants advance in their growth, fo they will require larger pots, and muft be treated in the fame way as other exotic plants ; in the autumn they muft be removed into the green-houfe, and placed with Myrtles and the other kinds of plants, which only require protection from hard froft, but muft have as much free air as poffible in mild weather.

LAVENDULA. Tourn. Inft. R. H. 198. tab. 93. Lin. Gen. Plant. 630. Lavender ; in French, Lavende. [It takes its name of Lavando, Lat. wafhing, becaufe it was ufed to be thrown into baths for the fragrancy of the fcent ; or becaufe ufed in lye, to give a fragrancy to linen ; and becaufe it is very good to wafh the face with, and give it both beauty and a grateful fcent.]

The CHARACTERS are,

The flower hath an oval permanent empalement of one leaf, which is obfcurely indented at the brim. The flower is of the lip kind, with one petal, having a cylindrical tube longer than the empalement, but fpreading above ; the upper lip is large, bifid, and open ; the under lip is cut into three equal fegments. *It hath four fhort ftamina fituated within the tube of the petal, two being fhorter than the other, terminated by fmall fummits. It hath a germen divided in four-parts, fupporting a flender ftyle the length of the tube, crowned by an obtufe indented ftigma. The germen afterward turns to four oval feeds, fitting in the empalement.*

This genus of plants is ranged in the firft fection of Linnæus's fourteenth clafs, intitled Didynamia Gymnofpermia, which includes thofe plants whofe flowers have two fhort and two longer ftamina, and have four naked feeds fitting in the empalement.

The SPECIES are,

1. LAVENDULA (*Spica*) foliis lanceolatis integerrimis fpicis nudis. Hort. Cliff. 303. *Lavender with entire fpear-fhaped leaves and naked fpikes.* Lavendula latifolia. C. B. P. 216. *Broad-leaved Lavender.*

2. LAVENDULA (*Anguftifolia*) foliis lanceolato-linearibus, fpicis nudis. *Lavender with fpear-fhaped narrow leaves, and naked fpikes.* Lavendula anguftifolia. C. B. P. 216. *Narrow-leaved Lavender.*

3. LAVENDULA (*Multifida*) foliis duplicato-pinnatifidis. Vir. Cliff. 56. *Lavender with leaves doubly wing-pointed.* Lavendula folio diffecto. C. B. P. 216. *Lavender with a cut leaf.*

4. LAVENDULA (*Canarienfis*) foliis duplicato-pinnatifidis hirfutis, fpicis fafciculatis. *Lavender with doubly wing-pointed hairy leaves, and fpikes of flowers growing in clufters.* Lavendula folio longiore tenuius & elegantius diffecto. Tourn. Inft. R. H. 198. *Lavender with a longer, narrower, and more elegant cut leaf.*

The firft fort is cultivated in feveral of the Englifh gardens, and has been generally known by the title of Spike, or Lavender Spike ; the leaves of this fort are much fhorter and broader than thofe of the common Lavender, and the branches are fhorter, more compact, and fuller of leaves. This fort doth not often produce flowers, but when it does, the flower-ftalks are garnifhed with leaves very different from thofe on the other branches, approaching nearer to thofe of the common fort, but are broader ; the ftalks grow taller, the fpikes of the flowers are larger, the flowers are fmaller, and are in loofer fpikes. It generally flowers a little later in the feafon. This has been frequently confounded with the common Lavender, and has been fuppofed the fame fpecies, but is undoubtedly a different plant. This I believe to be the fame with what Dr. Moriffon calls Lavendula latifolia fterilis, for the plants will continue feveral years without producing flowers ; during which time they have a very different appearance from thofe of the common Lavender, as thofe branches of the fame plant always have which do not flower ; but I have planted flips taken from thofe flowering branches with narrow leaves, and others from thofe with the broad leaves, but have always found the plants fo propagated return to their original fort, the cuttings with the narrow leaves have become broad again.

The fecond fort is the common Lavender, which is fo well known as to require no defcription. Both thefe forts flower in July, at which time the fpikes of the fecond fort are gathered for ufe ; there is a variety of this with white flowers.

Thefe are propagated by cuttings or flips ; the beft feafon for which is in March, when they fhould be fhaded with mats until they have taken root, after which they may be expofed to the fun ; and when they have obtained ftrength, may be removed to the places where they are defigned to remain. Thefe plants will abide much longer in a dry, gravelly, or ftony foil, in which they will endure our fevereft winters ; though they will grow much fafter in the fummer, if they are planted upon a rich, light, moift foil, but then they are generally deftroyed in winter ; nor are the plants half fo ftrong fcented, or fit for medicinal ufes, as thofe which grow upon the moft barren rocky foil.

Thefe

Thefe plants were formerly in ufe to make edgings to borders in gardens, for which purpofe they are by no means proper, for they will grow too large for fuch defigns; and if they are often cut in very dry weather, they are fubjeét to decay; and in hard winters they are very often killed, fo that the edging will not be complete: befides, thefe plants greatly exhauft the goodnefs of the foil, whereby the plants in the borders will be deprived of their nourifhment; fo that they fhould never be planted in a fine garden amongft other choice plants and flowers, but rather be placed in beds in the phyfic-garden, or in any part of the kitchen-garden, if the foil is dry. The third fort grows naturally in Andalufia; this is an annual plant, which rifes with an upright branching ftalk two feet high; the ftalks are woolly, and garnifhed with hoary leaves growing oppofite, which are cut into many divifions to the midrib; thefe fegments are again divided on their borders toward the top, into three obtufe fegments, fo that they end in many points. The foot-ftalk of the flower is continued from the end of the branches, which is naked, and about fix inches long, having four corners or angles, and is terminated by a clofe fpike of flowers about one inch long; the fpike has the rows of flowers twifted fpirally: under this fpike there are commonly two fmall ones proceeding from the fide of the ftalk, at about an inch diftance from the middle fpike. This fort flowers in July, and the feeds ripen in autumn. There are two varieties of this, one with blue, and the other with white flowers.

This fort is fown every fpring on borders or beds of light frefh earth, and when the plants come up, they may be tranfplanted into other borders of the flowergarden, or into pots, to remain for good; where they will require no farther care, but to keep them clean from weeds. Thefe are pretty plants to place in large borders, amongft other plants, for variety, but they are never ufed with us; they may alfo be preferved over the winter, if placed in a green-houfe in autumn; but they never continue longer than two years with us, and many times (if they have produced feeds the firft year) they will not continue longer. Nor do thofe plants which are thus preferved, appear handfome the following fummer, fo that, unlefs in bad feafons, when the feeds do not ripen in the open air, it is not worth while to preferve the plants. If the feeds of this fort are permitted to fcatter, the plants will come up the following fpring without care, and may be treated in the manner before directed.

The fourth fort grows naturally in the Canary Iflands, from whence the feeds were fent to the Bifhop of London, which were fown in his Lordfhip's garden at Fulham, where this plant was firft raifed. This rifes with an upright, branching, fquare ftalk four feet high, garnifhed with leaves which are longer, and cut into narrower fegments than thofe of the third fort. They are of a lighter green and almoft fmooth; the naked flower-ftalk is alfo much longer than thofe of the former, and terminated with a clufter of fpikes of blue flowers; at two or three inches below thefe, are two fmall fpikes of flowers, ftanding one on each fide the ftalk. The flowers are fmaller than thofe of the common Lavender, but are of the fame fhape. This fort is tenderer than either of the former, fo the feeds of this muft be fown on a moderate hot-bed in the fpring; and when the plants come up, they fhould be each planted into a feparate fmall pot filled with light earth, and plunged into another hot-bed, to bring the plants forward; and in the beginning of June, they fhould be inured to the open air, when they fhould be placed in a fheltered fituation toward the end of that month; in July the plants will flower, and if the autumn proves warm, the feeds will ripen in September; but when they do not perfeét feeds, the plants may be preferved through the winter in a good green-houfe, where they will produce flowers moft part of that feafon, whereby good feeds may be obtained.

LAUREOLA. See Thymelæa.
LAUROCERASUS. See Padus.
LAURUS. Tourn. Inft. R. H. 597. tab. 367. Lin. Gen. Plant. 452. The Bay-tree; in French, Laurier.

The Characters are,

It hath male and hermaphrodite flowers on different plants, the male flowers have no empalement: they have one petal, which is cut into fix fegments at the top, and nine ftamina which are fhorter than the petal, ftanding by threes, terminated by flender fummits. The hermaphrodite flowers have noempalement; they have one petal, which is flightly cut into fix fegments at the top. In the bottom is fituated an oval germen, fupporting a fingle ftyle of the fame length with the petal, crowned by an obtufe ftigma, attended by fix or eight ftamina: there are two globular glands, ftanding upon very fhort foot-ftalks, fixed to the bafe of the petal. The germen afterward becomes an oval berry with one cell, inclofing one feed of the fame form.

This genus of plants is ranged in the firft feétion of Linnæus's ninth clafs, intitled Enneandria Monogynia, which includes thofe plants whofe flowers have nine ftamina and one ftyle; but it fhould be ranged in his twenty-fecond clafs, which includes thofe plants whofe male and female flowers are upon different plants.

The Species are,

1. Laurus (Nobilis) foliis lanceolatis venofis perennantibus, floribus quadrifidis diœciis. Hort. Cliff. 105. Bay-tree with evergreen, fpear-fhaped, veined leaves, and flowers cut into four points, which are male and female on different plants. Laurus latifolia Difcoridis. C. B. P. The broad-leaved Bay of Diofcorides.

2. Laurus (Undulatis) foliis lanceolatis venofis perennantibus, marginibus undatis. Bay-tree with evergreen fpear-fhaped leaves, which are veined and waved on their edges. Laurus vulgaris folio undulato. H. R. Par. Common Bay-tree with waved leaves.

3. Laurus (Tenuifolia) foliis lineari-lanceolatis venofis perennantibus, floribus quinquefidis diœciis. Bay-tree with narrow fpear-fhaped leaves which are evergreen and veined, flowers cut into five points, which are male and female on different plants. Laurus tenuifolia. Tab. Icon. 925. Narrow-leaved Bay.

4. Laurus (Indica) foliis venofis lanceolatis perennantibus planis, ramulis tuberculatis cicatricibus, floribus racemofis. Hort. Cliff. 154. Bay-tree with evergreen, veined, fpear-fhaped, plain leaves, branches having tubercles and cicatrices, and flowers growing in bunches. Laurus Indica. Ald. Hort. Farnef. 61. The Indian Bay.

5. Laurus (Borbonia) foliis venofis lanceolatis calycibus fruétus baccatis. Lin. Sp. 529. Bay-tree with veined fpear-fhaped leaves, and the empalement becomes berries. Laurus Carolinienfis, foliis acuminatis, bacciscæruleis, pediculis longis rubris infidentibus. Catefb. Carol. 1. p. 63. Carolina Bay-tree with pointed leaves, and blue berries fitting upon long red foot-ftalks.

6. Laurus (Benzoin) foliis ovato-lanceolatis obtufis integris annuis. Bay-tree with oval, obtufe, fpear-fhaped, entire leaves, which are annual. Arbor Virginiana, citreæ vel limonii folio, Benzoinum fundens. Hort. Amft. 1. p. 168. The Benjamin-tree.

7. Laurus (Saffafras) foliis integris trilobifque. Hort. Cliff. 154. Bay-tree with entire leaves, or having three lobes. Cornus mas odorato, folio trifido, margine plano, faffafras diéta. Pluk. Alm. 120. The Saffafras.

8. Laurus (Enervius) foliis venofis oblongis acuminatis annuis, fubtus rugofis. Bay-tree with oblong, acutepointed, veined, annual leaves, which are rough on their under fide. Laurus foliis lanceolatis enervibus annuis. Flor. Virg. 159. Bay-tree with fpear-fhaped, winged, unveined, annual leaves.

9. Laurus (Camphora) foliis trinerviis lanceolato-ovatis, nervis fupra bafin unitis. Lin. Mat. Med. 192. Bay-tree with oval fpear-fhaped leaves, having three veins which unite above the bafe. Camphora officinarum. C. B. P. 500. The Camphire-tree.

10. Laurus (Americana) foliis ovatis planis integerrimis, pedunculis racemofis, floribus in capitulum colleétis. Bay-tree with plain, oval, entire leaves, branching foot-

foot-ftalks, and flowers collected into heads. Laurus Americana, foliis fubrotundis, floribus in capitulum collectis. Houft. MSS. *American Bay-tree with roundifh leaves, and flowers collected into heads.*

11. LAURUS (*Cinnamomum*) foliis trinerviis ovato-oblongis nervis verfus apicem evanefcentibus. Flor. Zeyl. 145. *Laurel with oblong leaves which diminifh toward their end.* Cinnamomum foliis latis ovatis frugiferum. Burm. Zeyl. 62. *Cinnamon-tree.*

12. LAURUS (*Canella*) foliis triplinerviis lanceolatis. Flor. Zeyl. 146. *Laurel with fpear-fhaped leaves, having three veins.* Cinnamomum, fc. Cancella Malabarica, fc. Javanenfis. C. B. P. 409. *Caffia or Wild Cinnamon.*

13. LAURUS (*Perfea*) foliis venofis ovatis coriaceis perennantibus, floribus corymbofis. Lin. Sp. 529. *Bay-tree with oval, thick, veined leaves, which continue through the year, and flowers growing in a corymbus.* Perfea. Cluf. Hift. 1. p. 2.

The firft fort is the broad-leaved Bay, which grows naturally in Afia, Spain and Italy ; from all thofe places I have received the berries feveral times. This is almoft too tender to thrive in the open air in England, for in fevere winters they are frequently killed, or their branches are fo much injured as to appear fo for a long time ; therefore they are generally planted in tubs, and removed into the green-houfe in winter. The leaves of this fort are much broader than thofe of the common Bay, and are fmoother : there are male and female plants of this, as there are alfo of all the other forts.

The fecond is the common Bay ; of this there are plants with plain leaves, and others which are waved on their edges, but they feem to be the fame fpecies ; for the young plants which I have raifed from the berries of one, have been a mixture of both forts ; but this is undoubtedly a different fpecies from the firft, for this fort thrives well in the open air, and is feldom hurt, except in very fevere winters ; whereas the firft will fcarce live abroad, while young, in common winters, without fhelter.

The third fort hath very long narrow leaves which are not fo thick as thofe of the two former, and are of a light green ; the branches are covered with a purplifh bark, and the male flowers come out in fmall clufters from the wings of the leaves fitting clofe to the branches. This fort is too tender to thrive in the open air in England, fo the plants are generally kept in pots or tubs, and houfed in winter as the firft fort.

The fourth fort grows naturally at Madeira and the Canary Iflands, from whence it was formerly brought to Portugal, where it has been propagated in fo great plenty, as to appear now as if it was a native of that country. In the year 1620, this plant was raifed in the Farnefian garden, from berries which were brought from India, and was fuppofed to be a baftard fort of Cinnamon. This grows to the height of thirty or forty feet in temperate countries, but it is too tender to thrive in the open air in England, fo the plants are kept in pots and tubs, and removed into the green-houfe in winter.

The leaves of this fort are much larger than thofe of the common Laurel ; they are thick, fmooth, and of a light green, the foot-ftalks inclining to red ; the branches are regularly difpofed on every fide, and the male flowers are difpofed in long bunches ; they are of a whitifh green colour ; the berries are much larger than thofe of the other forts. It is called by fome the Royal Bay, and by others the Portugal Bay.

The fifth fort grows naturally in Carolina in great abundance, where it is called the Red Bay ; it alfo is found in fome other parts of America, but not in fo great plenty. In fome fituations near the fea, this rifes with a ftrait trunk to a confiderable height, and their ftems are large, but in the inland parts of the country they are of an humbler ftature. The wood of this tree is much efteemed, being of a fine grain, fo is of excellent ufe for cabinets, &c.

The leaves of this fort are much longer than thofe of

the common Bay, and are a little woolly on their under fide, their edges are a little reflexed ; the veins run tranfverfly from the midrib to the.fides, and the male flowers come out in long bunches from the wings of the leaves. The female trees produce their flowers in loofe bunches, ftanding upon pretty long foot-ftalks, which are red ; thefe are fucceeded by blue berries fitting in red cups.

This fort is alfo too tender to thrive in the open air in England ; for although fome plants have lived abroad in a mild winter, which were planted in a warm fituation, yet the firft fharp winter has deftroyed them, fo that thefe plants muft be kept in pots or tubs, and houfed in winter like the former.

Thefe five forts may be propagated by layers, and the common fort is generally propagated by fuckers ; but thofe plants never keep to one ftem, but generally fend out a great number of fuckers from their roots, and form a thicket, but do not advance in height ; therefore the beft way to have good plants, is to raife them from the berries, when they can be procured, for the plants which come from feeds, always grow larger than the others, and do not put out fuckers from their roots, fo may be trained up with regular ftems. The beft way is to fow the berries in pots, and plunge them into a moderate hot-bed, which will bring up the plants much fooner than if they are fown in the full ground, fo they will have a longer time to get ftrength before winter ; but the plants muft not be forced with heat, therefore they fhould be inured to bear the open air the beginning of June, into which they fhould be removed, where they may remain till autumn ; then the pots fhould be placed under a common frame, that the plants may be protected from hard froft, but in mild weather they may enjoy the free air ; for while the plants are fo young, they are in danger of fuffering in hard froft, even the common fort of Bay. The fpring following, thofe forts which will not live in the open air, fhould be each tranf-planted into feparate pots ; but the common fort may be planted in nurfery-beds fix inches afunder each way, where they may grow two years, by which time they will be fit to plant where they are defigned to grow. The other forts muft be conftantly kept in pots, fo fhould every year be new potted, and as they advance in growth, they muft have larger pots. As thefe plants require fhelter in winter, a few of each fort will be enough for a large green-houfe.

The common Bay will make a variety in all evergreen plantations ; and as it will grow under the fhade of other trees, where they are not too clofe, fo it is very proper to plant in the borders of woods, where it will have a good effect in winter.

The fixth fort grows naturally in North America, where it rifes to the height of ten or twelve feet, dividing into many branches, garnifhed with oval fpear-fhaped leaves near three inches long, and one inch and a half broad, fmooth on their upper furface, but with many tranfverfe veins on their under fide ; thefe leaves fall off in the autumn like other deciduous trees. The flowers I have but once feen, thofe were all male, and of a white herbaceous colour ; but if I remember right, they had but fix ftamina in each.

The Saffafras-tree is alfo very common in moft parts of North America, where it fpreads greatly by its roots, fo as to fill the ground with fuckers wherever they are permitted to grow ; but in England this fhrub is with difficulty propagated. In America it is only a fhrub, feldom rifing more than eight or ten feet high ; the branches are garnifhed with leaves of different fhapes and fizes, fome them are oval and entire, about four inches long and three broad ; others are deeply divided into three lobes ; thefe are fix inches long, and as much in breadth from the extremity of the two outfide lobes ; they are placed alternately upon pretty long foot-ftalks, and are of a lucid green ; thefe fall off in the autumn, and in the fpring, foon after the leaves begin to come out, the flowers appear juft below them, upon flender foot-ftalks, each

fuftaining

suſtaining three or four ſmall yellow flowers, which have five oval concave petals, and eight ſtamina in the male flowers, which are upon different plants from the hermaphrodite flowers, which have an oval germen, that afterward becomes an oval berry, which, when ripe, is blue, but thoſe plants do not produce fruit in England.

The eighth ſort grows naturally in North America, in ſwampy lands; this riſes with a ſhrubby branching ſtalk eight or ten feet high, covered with a purple bark. The leaves are placed oppoſite, and are near two inches long and one broad, ſmooth on their upper ſide, but are veined on their under, where they are rough. This hath not as yet produced flowers here, but the berries which were ſent me from Maryland were red, and nearly the ſize and ſhape of the common Bay-berry.

The Camphire-tree grows naturally in Japan, and in ſeveral parts of India, and alſo at the Cape of Good Hope, where it riſes to a tree of middling ſtature, dividing into many ſmall branches, garniſhed with oval ſpear-ſhaped leaves, ſmooth on their upper ſide, having three longitudinal veins which unite above the baſe; if theſe are bruiſed, they emit a ſtrong odour of Camphire, as alſo the branches when broken. Theſe are male and hermaphrodite on different trees; I have only ſeen thoſe of the male, which has flowered plentifully in England; theſe were ſmall, and compoſed of five concave yellow petals, very like thoſe of the Saſſafras-tree, and were produced three or four upon each foot-ſtalk, in like manner.

The tenth ſort was diſcovered by the late Dr. Houſtoun at La Vera Cruz; this riſes with a woody ſtalk to the height of twenty feet, dividing into many branches, which are covered with a gray rough bark; at the extremity of the branches are produced the foot-ſtalks, which are unequal in length, but divide into ſeveral ſmaller, each ſuſtaining a cluſter of ſmall white flowers, which are collected into a head or ſmall umbel, having one general involucrum; theſe are male and hermaphrodite on different trees. The hermaphrodite flowers are ſucceeded by oval berries, not quite ſo large as thoſe of the common Bay. The leaves of this tree are about two inches long and one broad, rounded at the top and entire, ſtanding upon very ſhort foot-ſtalks.

The Saſſafras-tree is commonly propagated by the berries, which are brought from America; but theſe berries generally lie in the ground a whole year, and ſometimes two or three years before they grow, when they are ſown in the ſpring; therefore the ſureſt method of obtaining the plants will be, to get the berries put into a tub of earth ſoon after they are ripe, and ſent over in the earth; and as ſoon as they arrive, to ſow the berries on a bed of light ground, putting them two inches in the earth; and if the ſpring ſhould prove dry, the bed muſt be frequently watered, and ſhaded from the great heat of the ſun in the middle of the day; with this management many of the plants will come up the firſt ſeaſon, but as a great many of the berries will lie in the ground till the next ſpring, ſo the bed ſhould not be diſturbed, but wait until the ſeaſon after, to ſee what will come up. The firſt winter after the plants come up, they ſhould be protected from the froſt, eſpecially in the autumn; for the firſt early froſt at that ſeaſon is apt to pinch the ſhoots of theſe plants, which, when young, are tender and full of ſap, ſo will do them more injury than the ſevere froſt of the winter; for when the extreme part of the ſhoots are killed, it greatly affects the whole plant.

When the plants have grown a year in the ſeed-bed, they may be tranſplanted into a nurſery, where they may ſtand one or two years to get ſtrength, and may then be tranſplanted into the places where they are to remain for good.

There have been ſome of theſe plants propagated by layers, but theſe are commonly two, and ſometimes three years before they put out roots; and if they are not duly watered in dry weather, they rarely take

root; ſo that it is uncertain, whether one in three of theſe layers do ſucceed, which makes theſe plants very ſcarce in England at preſent.

The wood of this ſhrub is frequently uſed to make tea, which is eſteemed a great antiſcorbutic; and in Carolina they frequently give a decoction of the wood and leaves in intermitting fevers; but the flowers of the ſhrub are gathered, and dried by the moſt curious, and are uſed for tea.

The Benjamin-tree, as it is falſly called, may be propagated in the ſame manner as the Saſſafras, by ſowing of the berries: theſe generally lie long in the ground, ſo that unleſs they are brought over in earth, in the ſame way as before directed, they often fail, or at leaſt remain long in the ground; but this is now frequently propagated by layers in England, which put out roots pretty freely, when the young ſhoots are choſen to make layers.

The eighth ſort is alſo a native of the ſame country with the laſt, and may be propagated by ſeeds in the ſame manner as thoſe, and require the ſame treatment. This may alſo be propagated by layers, which put out roots pretty freely; and as the ſhrubs do not produce ſeeds in England, ſo this is the beſt method to propagate them.

Theſe three ſorts will live in the open air in England, but the Saſſafras is often injured by very ſevere froſts, eſpecially if they are in an expoſed ſituation; therefore theſe plants ſhould have a warm ſituation and a looſe ſoil; and in moiſt ground this, and alſo the eighth ſort, will thrive much better than in a dry ſoil; for when they are planted on a hot gravelly ſoil, they frequently die in ſummer when the ſeaſon proves dry. They are all of them now much cultivated in England, to add to the variety of ſhrubs, but they are not very ornamental plants; though indeed the Saſſafras makes a good appearance in ſummer, when it is fully clothed with its large leaves, which being of different ſhapes, makes an agreeable variety, when intermixed with ſhrubs of the ſame growth.

The Camphire-tree is very near a-kin to the Cinnamon-tree, from which it differs in the leaves, thoſe of the Cinnamon-tree having three ribs running longitudinally from the foot-ſtalk to the point, where they ſoon diminiſh; whereas the ribs of the leaves of this tree are ſmall, and extend toward the ſides, and have a ſmooth ſhining ſurface: they are both male and hermaphrodite in different trees.

In Europe this tree is propagated by layers, which are generally two years, and ſometimes longer, before they take root, ſo that the plants are very ſcarce; and as all thoſe which I have ſeen flower are male trees, ſo there can be no hopes of procuring ſeeds from them here: but if the berries of this, and alſo of the Cinnamon-tree, were procured from the places of their growth, and planted in tubs of earth, as hath been directed for the Saſſafras-tree, there may be a number of theſe plants procured in England: and if they were ſent to the Britiſh colonies in America, they might be there cultivated, ſo as to become a public advantage; eſpecially the Cinnamon-tree, which will grow as well in ſome of our iſlands in the Weſt-Indies, as it does in the native places of its growth, and in a few years the trees might be had in plenty; for they propagate eaſily by the berries, as the French experienced in their American iſlands. The Portugueze brought ſome of the Cinnamon-trees from the Eaſt-Indies, and planted them on the iſland of Princes, on the coaſt of Africa, where they now abound, having ſpread over a great part of the iſland; there is alſo one tree now growing at the Madeiras, which I have been informed is a male, ſo never produces berries.

The Camphire-tree does not require any artificial heat in winter, ſo that if they are placed in a warm dry green-houſe they will thrive very well. During the winter ſeaſon they muſt be ſparingly watered, and in the ſummer they ſhould be placed abroad in a warm ſituation, where they may be defended from ſtrong winds, and not too much expoſed to the direct rays of of the fun ; but during this feafon, they muft be frequently refrefhed with water.

They may be propagated by laying down the young branches in autumn, which fhould be treated in the fame manner as is before directed for the Benjamin. The tenth fort requires a ftove to preferve it through the winter in England ; this is propagated by feeds, which muft be procured from the country where it grows naturally.

This plant requires the fame treatment as the Coffeetree, fo fhould be planted in a ftove, with that and other tender plants of thofe warm countries, and always remain there.

The eleventh and twelfth forts have been generally confounded by moft, if not all the writers who have treated of them ; though their bark, which is the material part of thefe trees in ufe, is pretty eafily diftinguifhed by the dealers in thefe commodities.

Dr. Linnæus is certainly miftaken in referring the latter to the figure of Dr. Burman, which he has given in his Hiftory of Ceylon plants, by the title of Cinnamomum perpetuo florens, &c. which is a true reprefentation of the male Cinnamon-tree, and is not the Caffia Lignea ; but as there are plants of all thefe forts now in the Britifh Iflands of America, fo we may hope foon to have their fpecies better afcertained.

The plants of both thefe kinds are not fo tender as moft people do imagine, and the treating of thofe plants which have been brought to England fo tenderly has deftroyed them ; for fo far as I have made trial of their culture it has appeared, that great heat is very prejudicial to them ; therefore I would advife thofe perfons who may have any of the plants come under their care, to treat them in a different manner, otherwife there will be little hopes of keeping them ; for when the plants have taken new root in the pots, they fhould in fummer be placed in a glafs-cafe, where they may have plenty of air in warm weather, and in winter placed in a ftove kept moderately warm.

LAURUS ALEXANDRINA. See Ruscus.

LAURUS TINUS. See Tinus.

LAWN is a great plain in a park, or a fpacious plain adjoining to a noble feat.

As to the dimenfions of it, it fhould be as large as the ground will permit ; but never lefs, if poffible, than thirty or forty acres ; but this is to be underftood of Lawns in gardens, for in gardens a Lawn of fix or eight acres is a reafonable fize for gardens of a moderate extent, ten or twelve acres for thofe of the largeft fize.

As to the fituation of a Lawn, it will be beft to be in the front of the houfe, and to lie open to the neighbouring country, and not pent up too much with trees.

If the houfe front the eaft, or fouth-eaft, it will be moft convenient, becaufe the rooms will be fhaded in the afternoon, and fo the objects to be viewed from the houfe will be much better feen, by the fun's fhining upon them at that time of the day ; for if the beft room of the houfe front the Lawn, as it always fhould do, the afternoon being the moft ufual time for people of fafhion to folace themfelves in fuch rooms, the fun will not be offenfive to thofe rooms, nor will the profpect be interrupted, but rendered more pleafant ; whereas, were it on the weft fide of the houfe, the fun, by fhining from the object, and directly againft thofe rooms, would, by both, hinder the profpect, for the generality of profpects are moft pleafant when the fun fhines upon the objects.

Befides, there is another inconvenience, if the Lawn be on the weft fide of the houfe, it will give the more way to the weft wind (which is commonly the greateft) to injure the houfe, by its having a free paffage to it.

If the Lawn be on the fouth fide of the houfe, it may do well enough, for the reafons before-mentioned, for the fun's rays being then darted obliquely, will not fo much interrupt the profpect, and the fun fhining moft part of the day on that fide of the houfe, will ftill add to the beauty of that front, which ought to

be the beft front in the houfe, therefore a Lawn on that fide will much help the profpect of the houfe.

But the moft defirable afpect for a Lawn is that of the fouth-eaft, which is generally the moft favourable point in England ; for as the fun rifes upon the front of the houfe facing this point, fo it will add a chearfulnefs to the rooms in the morning, and by noon the rays will be oblique to this front, and in the afternoon will have entirely left thefe apartments.

It will not be at all convenient to have the Lawn on the north fide of the houfe, becaufe it will lay the houfe too open to the cold north winds, &c. therefore it will be more eligible to plant wilderneffes and woods on the weft and north fides of the houfe, by way of fcreen to it, provided thefe do not fhut out agreeable objects.

As to the figure of the Lawn, fome contend for an exact fquare, others an oblong fquare, fome an oval, and others a circular figure ; but neither of thefe are to be regarded, for it will be much better if contrived fo as to fuit the figure of the ground ; and as there fhould be trees planted for fhade on the boundaries of the Lawn, fo the fides may be broken by irregular plantations of trees ; for if there are not fome good profpects beyond the Lawn, it will be proper to have it bounded on every fide by plantations, which may be brought round pretty near to each end of the houfe, fo that perfons may foon get into fhade, which is a very defirable thing in hot weather ; for where that is wanting, few perfons care to ftir abroad when the fun fhines warm.

If in the plantations round the Lawn, the trees are placed irregularly, fome breaking much forwarder on the Lawn than others, and not crowded too clofe together, they will make a much better appearance than any regular plantations can poffibly do ; and if there are varieties of trees properly difpofed, they will have a good effect ; but it fhould be obferved, that no other but thofe which make a fine appearance, and that grow large, ftrait, and handfome, fhould be admitted here, as they are placed in the conftant view from the houfe.

Many perfons have preferred the Lime-tree for this purpofe, on account of their regular growth ; but as the leaves of this tree often change their colour, and begin to fall very foon in autumn, occafioning a great litter in the garden ; and from the end of July the trees make but an indifferent appearance, fo they are not to be efteemed for thefe plantations.

The Elm, Oak, Beech, and Cheftnut, among the deciduous trees, are to be preferred to all others, as they keep their leaves late in autumn ; and thefe are all of them large growing trees, fo are very proper for this purpofe.

If there are fome clumps of Evergreen trees intermixed with the deciduous trees in this plantation, if they are properly difpofed, it will add to the beauty, efpecially in the winter feafon ; the beft forts for this purpofe are Lord Weymouth's Pine, the Silver and Spruce Firs, which will grow faft, and become large trees ; and as the two latter forts always grow pyramidically, fo they will have a good effect to the fight, if they are rightly placed, but they fhould not be intermixed in the fame clumps with the deciduous trees; but as thefe generally feather out their branches near the ground, they fhould be planted where they do not obftruct the view of any diftant objects.

But as moft perfons who take pleafure in beautifying their feats in the country, are in hafte for fhade, they generally plant the trees too clofe together, and often in fuch a manner as to render it difficult when the trees are advanced to reduce their number, without injury to the defign ; therefore thofe trees fhould be firft planted, which are defigned to remain, and then there may be fome few others planted for prefent fhade, which may afterward be taken away. When perfons who are beautifying their feats meet with full grown trees on the fpot, it is a great pleafure, for thefe fhould not be deftroyed, if they can poffibly ftand without prejudice.

LAWSONIA. Lin. Gen. Plant. 433. Henna. Ludw. 143.

The CHARACTERS are,

The flower has a small permanent empalement, divided into four parts at the top. The flower is composed of four oval spear-shaped petals, which spread open, and eight slender stamina the length of the petals, which stand by pairs between them, terminated by roundish summits. It hath a roundish germen, supporting a slender permanent style, crowned by a headed stigma. The germen afterward becomes a globular capsule ending in a point, having four cells, filled with angular seeds.

This genus of plants is ranged in the first section of Linnæus's eighth class, intitled Octandria Monogynia, which includes those plants whose flowers have eight stamina and one style.

The SPECIES are,

1. LAWSONIA (*Inermis*) ramis inermibus. Flor. Zeyl. 134. *Lawsonia whose branches have no spines.* Ligustrum Ægyptiacum latifolium. C. B. P. 476. *Broad-leaved Egyptian Privet, called Alhenna, or Henna, by the Arabians.*

2. LAWSONIA (*Spinosa*) ramis spinosis. Flor. Zeyl. 134. *Lawsonia with prickly branches.* Rhamnus Malabaricus MAIL-ANSKI. Pluk. Alm. 38. tab. 220. *Malabar Buckthorn, called Mail-anski.*

The first sort grows naturally in India, Egypt, and other warm countries, where it rises with a shrubby stalk eight or ten feet high. The branches come out by pairs opposite; these are slender, and covered with a whitish yellow bark, and garnished with oblong small leaves of a pale green, ending in acute points, placed opposite. The flowers are produced in loose bunches at the end of the branches; they are of a gray or dirty white colour, and are composed of four small petals which turn backward at the top. The flowers are succeeded by roundish capsules with four cells, filled with angular seeds.

The leaves of this shrub are much used by the Egyptian women to colour their nails yellow, which they esteem an ornament.

The second sort grows naturally in both Indies, for I have received specimens of it from the Spanish West-Indies, where it was found growing naturally in great plenty.

This rises with a woody trunk eighteen feet high or more. The wood is hard and close, covered with a light gray bark. The branches come out alternate, and are garnished with oblong oval leaves, which stand without order; and at the joints where the leaves are placed, come out single, strong, sharp thorns. The flowers are produced in loose bunches from the side of the branches; they are of a pale yellow colour, and of a disagreeable scent; they have four petals, which spread open; between each of these are situated two pretty strong stamina, terminated by roundish summits. After the flowers are past, the germen becomes a roundish capsule with four cells, including many angular seeds.

These plants are both propagated by seeds, which should be sown on a hot-bed early in the spring, that the plants when they come up may have time to get strength before winter. When the plants are fit to remove, they should be each planted in a small pot filled with light sandy earth, and plunged into a hot-bed of tanners bark, where they must be screened from the sun till they have taken new root; then their treatment should be the same as that of the Coffee-tree, with this difference only, not to let these plants have so much water; but especially in the winter, during which season it should be given to them very sparingly, for by over-watering these plants I have known many of them destroyed; these plants are too tender to thrive in the open air in England, so they must constantly remain in the stove, but in hot weather they should have plenty of free air admitted to them.

LAYERS. Many trees and shrubs may be propagated by Layers, which do not produce seeds here, so are not easily increased by any other method.

This is to be performed by slitting the branches a little way upward, and laying them under the mould about half a foot; the ground should first be well digged and made very light, and after they are laid they should have a little water given them.

If they do not comply well in the laying of them down, they must be pegged down with a forked stick cut in form of a hook to keep them down; if the Layers have taken sufficient root by the next winter, they must be cut off from the main plants, and planted in the nursery, as is directed about seedlings.

Some twist the branch or bare the rind, and if it be out of the reach of the ground, they fasten a tub or basket near the branch, which they fill with good mould, and lay the branch in it.

Laying of Trees.

This operation is thus performed:

1st, Take some of the most flexible boughs and lay them into the ground about half a foot deep in fine fresh mould, fastening them down with forked sticks, leaving them with the end of the Layer about a foot or a foot and a half out of the ground, and keep them moist during the summer season, and they will probably have taken root and be fit to remove in autumn, and if they have not by that time taken root they must lie longer.

2dly, Tie a piece of wire hard round the bark of the bough, at the place you intend to lay in the ground, and twist the ends of the wire, so that they may not untie, and prick the place above the wire through the bark, with an awl in several places, and then lay it in the ground as before directed; this will often succeed when the other fails.

3dly, Cut a slit upwards at a joint, as is practised in laying of Carnations, which by gardeners is called tonguing the Layers.

4thly, Twist the part of the branch designed to lay in the ground like a withy, if it is pliable, and lay it into the ground as directed in the first way of laying.

5thly, Cut a circle almost round about the bough (that is designed to be laid) half an inch, at the place that is most convenient to lay into the ground, and manage it as is directed in the first method of laying. The season for laying hardy trees that shed their leaves is in October, but for such as are tender in the beginning of March; for Evergreens, June or July are good seasons.

Though Layers may be laid at any time in the year, yet the before-mentioned seasons are most proper, for the reasons following, because they have the whole winter and summer to prepare and draw root; for at these times of the year the sun has sufficient power on the sap of the tree to feed the leaf and bud, but has not power sufficient to make a shoot.

And if that small quantity of sap that does arise be hindered, as it will by some of the preceding ways of laying, the leaves and buds will gently crave of the Layer, and by that means will prepare the Layer to take root, or put forth roots a little to maintain itself, finding it cannot have it from the mother plant.

And therefore, because it wants but little nourishment at that time of the year, it is better to lay Layers of trees, or to set cuttings than at other times, either in the autumn, when the sap stirs but little, or in the spring when it begins to rise, because it is then apt to come too suddenly to draw sap from the Layer, before the Layer has drawn or prepared for root; but for some sorts the middle of summer is best.

However, the spring or summer may do well for small plants, because such plants being but short-lived draw root the quicker.

If you would lay young trees from a high standard, the boughs of which cannot be bent down to the ground, then you must make use of Osier baskets, boxes, or pots, filled with fine mould, mixed with a little rotten Willow dust, which will keep moisture to assist the Layer in taking root; this basket, box, &c. must be set upon a post or tressel, &c. and the bough must be laid according to either of the four firſt ways of laying, but too much head muſt not be left on, left that be injured by the wind, or by its own motion rub off the tender root; and the ſmaller the boughs are, the leſs way they ſhould be left out of the ground, and care muſt be taken to keep them clear from weeds.

The harder the wood of the tree is, the young ſhoots will take root beſt; but if the wood be ſoft, the older boughs will take root the beſt.

There are many kinds of trees and plants which will not put out roots from their woody branches, though laid down with the utmoſt care; yet if the young ſhoots of the ſame year are laid in July, they will often put out roots very freely, ſo that when any plants are found difficult to propagate by Layers in the common way, they ſhould be tried at this ſeaſon; but as theſe ſhoots will be ſoft and herbaceous, they muſt not have too much wet, for that will cauſe them to rot; therefore it will be a better method to cover the ſurface of the ground over the Layers with Moſs, which will prevent the ground from drying too faſt, ſo that a little water now and then will be ſufficient.

LEAVES. A Leaf is defined to be a part of a plant extended into length and breadth, in ſuch a manner as to have one ſide diſtinguiſhable from the other; they are properly the moſt extreme part of a branch, and the ornament of the twigs, and conſiſt of a very glutinous matter, being furniſhed every where with veins and nerves; one of their offices is, to ſubtilize and give more ſpirit to the abundance of nouriſhing ſap, and to convey it to the little buds.

We ſhall firſt conſider the diſtinctions which are made by botaniſts in their definitions of the ſhape and form of Leaves in their titles and deſcriptions of plants, and afterward conſider their uſes in vegetation.

The Leaf of a plant or tree is diſtinguiſhed from that of flowers, the firſt is called Folium in Latin, and the other Petalum; therefore what is to be underſtood here of Leaves, are thoſe which are ranged on the branches and ſtalks of plants, and have no connection with the flower.

Theſe Leaves are either ſimple or compound.

Simple Leaves are thoſe of which the foot-ſtalk or petiole ſupports but one, compound are thoſe of which the foot-ſtalk ſuſtains many Leaves or ſmall foliola.

Simple Leaves differ in reſpect to circumſcription, angles, ſinus, apices, margin, ſuperficies and ſubſtance; circumſcription conſiders the form of the circumference of Leaves where there are no angles or ſinuations; in which reſpect Leaves are, Orbiculate, or round Leaves (Orbiculatum) are ſuch whoſe breadth are equal to their length, and every part of their edges equally diſtant from the center, as in fig. 1.

A roundiſh Leaf (Subrotundum) when the Leaf is nearly orbiculate, as in fig. 2.

An oval or egg-ſhaped Leaf (Ovatum) when the length of the Leaf exceeds the breadth, and the baſe or lower part of it forms a ſegment of a circle; but the upper extremity is not in proportion, but ſmaller, as in fig. 3.

An obverſe oval Leaf is one whoſe foot-ſtalk is fixed to its ſmaller end.

An oval or elliptic Leaf (Ovale ſive ellipticum) is one whoſe length exceeds its breadth, and both ends are narrower than the ſegments of circles, as fig. 4.

A parabolical Leaf (Parabolicum) is one whoſe length exceeds its breadth, and is narrowed from the baſe upward, ſo becomes half egg-ſhaped, fig. 5.

A ſpatulated Leaf (Spatulatum) is of a roundiſh figure, but narrow at the baſe, and linearly lengthened, fig. 6.

A wedge-ſhaped Leaf (Cuneiforme) is one whoſe length exceeds the breadth, and is narrowed to the baſe, fig. 7.

An oblong Leaf (Oblongum) is one whoſe length greatly exceeds its breadth, and each extremity is narrower than a ſegment of a circle, fig. 8.

A ſpear-ſhaped or ſpear-pointed Leaf (Lanceolatum) is oblong, and grows narrower toward both ends, and terminates in a point, fig. 9.

A linear Leaf (Lineare) is one whoſe two ſides run almoſt parallel to each other; they are uſually narrow, and ſomewhat broader in the middle than at the two ends, fig. 10.

A chaffy Leaf (Acerofum) is when the linear Leaf ſtays on the tree, and is evergreen, as in the Fir, Yew, &c. fig 11.

An awl-ſhaped Leaf (Subulatum) is one which is linear below, but gradually contracting towards the top, fig. 12.

A triangular Leaf (Triangulare) is when the diſk is ſurrounded by three prominent angles, fig. 13.

A quadrangular and quinquangular Leaf, only differ from the former in the number of their ſides or angles, fig. 14.

A deltoide Leaf is one with four angles, of which thoſe of the extremities are farther diſtant from the center than thoſe of the ſides, fig. 15.

A round Leaf (Rotundum) is one without any angles.

A ſinus (or Hollow) is uſed to expreſs thoſe openings or cavities in Leaves which diſtinguiſh them into parts.

A kidney-ſhaped Leaf (Reniforme) is of a roundiſh figure, and hollowed a little at the baſe, but without any angles, fig. 16.

A heart-ſhaped Leaf (Cordatum) when they are ovate, and hollowed a little at the baſe, but without any angles, fig. 17.

A moon-ſhaped Leaf (Lunulatum) is a roundiſh Leaf hollowed at the baſe, with two curvilinear angles in form of ſickles, fig. 18.

An arrow-ſhaped Leaf (Sagittatum) is one which is triangular, and hollowed at the baſe for the inſertion of the foot-ſtalk, fig. 19.

A heart arrow-ſhaped Leaf (Cordatum-ſagittatum) is like the former, but the ſides of it are convex, fig. 20.

A ſpear-pointed Leaf (Haſtatum) is of a triangular form, the ſides and baſe of which are hollowed, and the angles ſpreading ſo as to reſemble a Leaf compoſed of three parts, fig. 21.

A fiddle-ſhaped Leaf (Pandura forme) is oblong, larger at both ends than in the middle, the two ſides being compreſſed like the body of a violin, fig. 22.

A cleft or divided Leaf (Fiſſum) is divided by linear ſinuations and ſtrait margins; from the number of the diviſions they are termed a two, three, or many pointed leaf, fig. 23.

A lobated Leaf (Lobatum) is one which is divided almoſt to the midrib, into parts which ſtand diſtant from each other, and have convex margins according to the number of theſe parts; it is called bilobed, trilobed, or quadrilobed, &c. fig. 24.

A handed Leaf (Palmatum) is one which is divided into ſeveral longitudinal ſegments down to the baſe, where they are united, and reſemble an open hand, fig. 25.

A wing-pointed Leaf (Pinnatifidum) is one which is tranſverſly divided into oblong horizontal diviſions, fig. 26.

A lyre-ſhaped Leaf (Lyratum) is one which is divided into tranſverſe ſegments, the upper ones being larger than the lower, which are farther aſunder, fig. 27.

A laciniated or jagged Leaf (Laciniatum) is one whoſe ſides are variouſly divided into jags, which are again divided without any order, fig. 28.

A ſinuated Leaf (Sinuatum) is one which has many ſinuations on its ſides, but is not indented or notched on its edges, fig. 29.

An indented ſinuated Leaf (Dentato-ſinuatum) is one like the former, but the ſide lobes are of a linear figure.

A divided Leaf (Partitum) is one which is divided into many parts to the baſe, ſo as to appear like many Leaves till cloſely examined. Theſe are called bipartite, tripartite, &c. according to the number of parts, fig. 30.

An entire Leaf (Integrum) is one that is undivided, and has ſmooth edges.

4

Apex

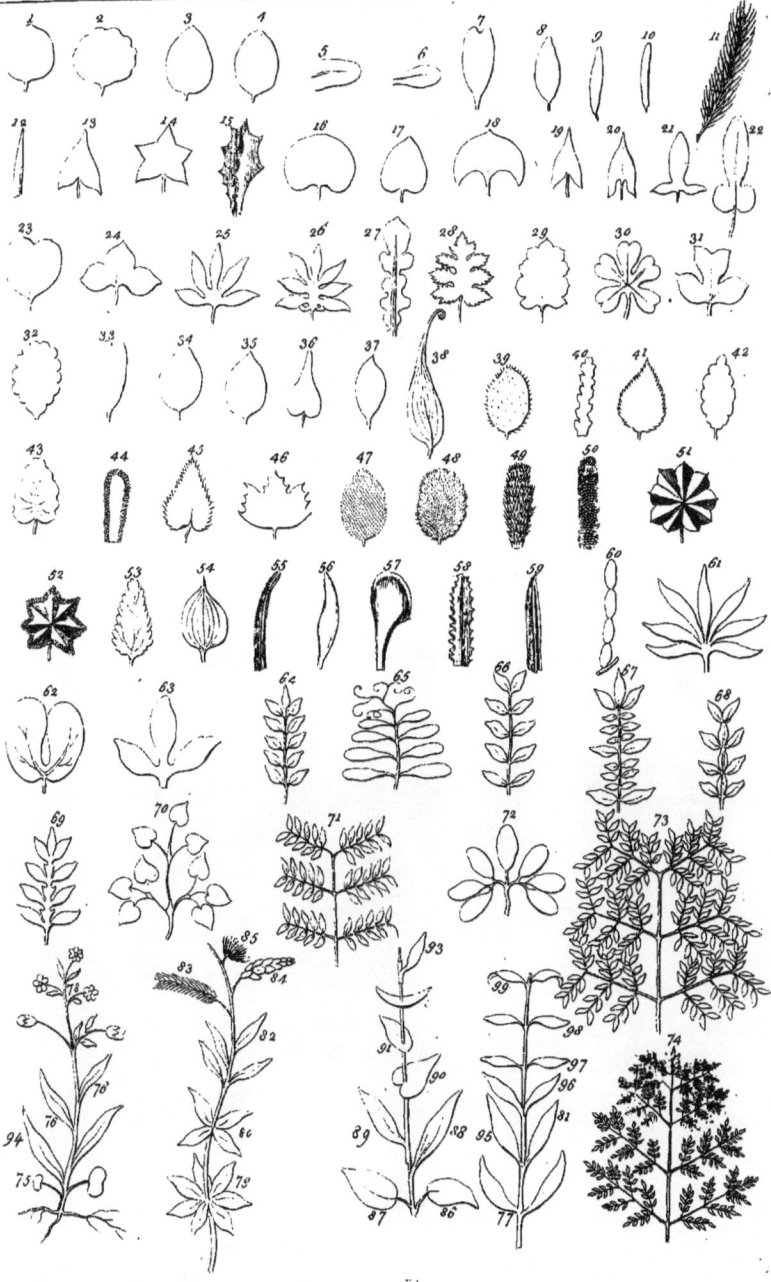

Apex tip, is the extremity in which the Leaf terminates ; Leaves in refpeﬅ to thefe are termed,

A truncated Leaf (*Truncatum*) is one whofe fummit feems as though it were cut off by a ﬅrait line, in a tranfverfe direﬅion.

A bitten Leaf (*Præmorfum*) is one which is terminated by very blunt unequal cuts, ﬁg. 31.

A blunt Leaf (*Retufum*) is one whofe extremity is terminated by an obtufe finus, ﬁg. 32.

A nicked Leaf (*Emarginatum*) is one whofe extremity is a little notched, ﬁg. 33.

An obtufe Leaf (*Obtufum*) is one whofe point is terminated bluntly, or by a fegment of a circle, ﬁg. 34.

A ﬂharp Leaf (*Acutum*) is one whofe point is terminated in an acute angle, ﬁg. 35.

An acuminated Leaf (*Acuminatum*) is one which is terminated by an awl-ﬂhaped point, ﬁg. 36.

A pointed obtufe Leaf (*Obtufum acumine*) is one whofe upper part is rounded, but draws to an acute point, ﬁg. 37.

A clafper Leaf (*Cirrhofum*) is one which terminates with a tendril, ﬁg. 38. as in Gloriofa, Flagellaria, &c. The margin of a Leaf is the outermoﬅ boundary of its difk or middle, fo in refpeﬅ to their margin are,

A fpinous Leaf (*Spinofum*) is one whofe edge or border ends with hard ﬅiff prickles, ﬁg. 39.

An indented Leaf (*Dentatum*) is one whofe edge has horizontal points of the fame confiﬅence with the Leaf, but are feparated from each other, ﬁg. 40.

A fawed Leaf (*Serratum*) is one whofe edges are ﬂharply notched like the teeth of a faw, which make acute angles bending toward the top, ﬁg. 41.

A backward fawed Leaf (*Retrorfo-ferratum*) is one whofe ferratures or teeth, are bent toward the bafe of the Leaf.

A double fawed Leaf (*Duplicato-ferratum*) is one whofe edges are fawed with larger teeth, and the edges of thefe are again fawed in the fame manner.

A notched Leaf (*Crenatum*) is one whofe edges are indented with angles, which neither turn toward the point nor bafe. When thefe indentings terminate obtufely, it is called obtufe crenated ; when acutely, acute crenated ; when the indentures are again indented, it is called double crenated (*Duplicato-crenatum,*) ﬁg. 42.

A bowed or ferpentine Leaf (*Repandum*) is one whofe margin has feveral obtufe finufes which are inferibed with the fegments of circles, ﬁg. 43.

A cartilaginous or grifly Leaf (*Cartilagineum*) is one whofe edge is furniﬂhed with a firm cartilage of a different fubﬅance with the Leaf, ﬁg. 44.

A ciliated Leaf (*Ciliatum*) is one whofe edge is fet with parallel hairs, fo as to refemble the hairs of the eye-lid, ﬁg. 45.

A torn Leaf (*Laceratum*) is one whofe edges are cut into fegments of irregular ﬂhapes.

A gnawed Leaf (*Erofum*) is one which is finuated, and the finufes have their edges again indented with fmall obtufe finuations, ﬁg. 46.

A very entire Leaf (*Integerrimum*) is one whofe margin is entirely free of all notches or indentures.

The furface (*Superficies*) is the outfide, or what covers the difk of the Leaf, and refpeﬅs both the upper and under furface, fo are termed,

A vifcous Leaf (*Vifcidum*) has its fuperfices covered with a clammy moiﬅure which is not fluid, but ﬅicky.

A downy Leaf (*Tomentofum*) is one whofe furface is covered with a nap of interwoven hairs fo ﬂhort and fine, that the eye does not diﬅinguifh them fingly, though the Leaf is evidently downy both to the fight and touch, ﬁg. 47.

A woolly Leaf (*Lanatum*) is one whofe furface is covered with a kind of woolly fubﬅance, like a fpider's web, as in Salvia, Sideritis, &c.

A hairy Leaf (*Pilofum*) has its furface furniﬂhed with long diﬅinﬅ hairs, ﬁg. 48.

A rough or ﬅinging Leaf (*Hifpidum*) is one whofe furface is covered with rigid hairs, which either ﬅing or prick on being touched, ﬁg. 49.

A rough Leaf (*Scabrum*) is one whofe furface has on it feveral little irregular prominences.

A prickly Leaf (*Aculeatum*) is one whofe furface is covered with ﬅrong ﬂharp points or thorns, which adhere lightly to the furface.

A ﬅreaked or channelled Leaf (*Striatum*) is when its furface has a number of parallel longitudinal furrows.

A pimpled Leaf (*Papillofum*) is one whofe furface has many little roundifh protuberances like nipples or bladders, ﬁg. 50.

A punﬅuated Leaf (*Punﬅatum*) is one whofe furface has many hollow points difperfed over it.

A bright or fplendent Leaf (*Nitidum*) is one whofe furface is fmooth and ﬂhining, as if poliﬂhed by art.

A plaited Leaf (*Plicatum*) is one which has feveral angular rifings and hollows towards its borders, as if folded up, as in Alchimilla, ﬁg. 51.

A waved Leaf (*Undulatum*) is one whofe furface toward the edges rifes and falls convexly like the waves of the fea.

A curled Leaf (*Crifpum*) is when the circumference of the Leaf grows larger than the difk will admit, fo that the whole furface is raifed in waves, ﬁg. 52.

A rough leaf (*Rugofum*) is one whofe veins are contraﬅed and funk below the difk, and the intermediate fleﬂhy parts rife in irregular forms, fo as to appear rough, ﬁg. 53.

A hollow or concave Leaf (*Concavum*) is one whofe margin contraﬅs, fo is lefs than the middle, and is funk down or hollowed.

A veined Leaf (*Venofum*) is one whofe veins are branched, and appear to the naked eye.

A convex Leaf (*Convexum*) is one whofe middle rifes into a protuberant form.

A nervous Leaf (*Nervofum*) is when the veins are extended lengthways from the bafe toward the fummit without branching, ﬁg. 54.

A coloured Leaf (*Coloratum*) is one which has other colours than green.

A fmooth Leaf (*Glabrum*) is one whofe furface is fmooth, without any inequalities.

The fubﬅance of a Leaf refpeﬅs the conditions of its fides, in this refpeﬅ Leaves are,

A taper Leaf (*Teres*) is one of a thick fubﬅance, and for the moﬅ part of a cylindrical form.

A half taper Leaf (*Semicylindraceum*) is one which is of a cylindrical form, flatted on one fide.

A hollow Leaf (*Tubulofum*) is one which is hollow like a pipe, as thofe of the Onion.

A fleﬂhy Leaf (*Carnofum*) is one that is fucculent or full of pulp.

A compreffed Leaf (*Compreffum*) is one whofe marginal fides are preffed, fo that the fubﬅance of the Leaf is larger than the difk.

A plane Leaf (*Planum*) is one whofe furfaces are every where parallel.

A gibbous Leaf (*Gibbum*) is one which is convex on both fides, the middle being fuller of pulp.

A depreffed Leaf (*Depreffum*) is one whofe difk is more depreffed than the fides.

A guttered Leaf (*Canaliculatum*) is one which has a longitudinal deep furrow running through the middle of the Leaf, and is almoﬅ cylindrical, ﬁg. 55.

A double-faced Leaf (*Ancipites*) is one whofe difk is convex, and has two prominent longitudinal angles.

A fword-ﬂhaped Leaf (*Enfiforme*) is one with thin edges, with a prominent rib running from the bafe to the point in the middle.

A faulchion or fcymiter-ﬂhaped Leaf (*Acinaciforme*) is one which is fleﬂhy and compreffed, with one of its edges convex and narrow, the other thick and ﬅrait, ﬁg. 56.

An ax-ﬂhaped Leaf (*Dolabriforme*) is one which is roundifh, obtufe, and compreffed, gibbous on the outfide, the infide ﬂharp-edged and taper below, ﬁg. 57.

A tongue-ﬂhaped Leaf (*Linguiforme*) is linear, fleﬂhy, and obtufe, convex on the under fide, and has often cartilaginous edges, ﬁg. 58.

A two-

A two-edged Leaf (*Anceps*) is one which has two prominent angles, running lengthways on a convex difk.
A three-cornered Leaf (*Triquetrum*) has three longitudinal plain fides like an awl-fhaped Leaf.
A three-edged Leaf (*Trigonal*) is much like the former, but in this the ribs are fharp and membranaceous, the furface of the Leaf being channelled. When a Leaf has four or five angles, it is called tetragonal and pentagonal, &c.
A furrowed Leaf (*Sulcatum*) is one that has feveral ridges running lengthways, which have obtufe finufus, fig. 59.
A keel-fhaped Leaf (*Carinatum*) is one that has the under part of the difk prominent the whole length, and the upper concave like the keel of a boat.
A membranaceous Leaf (*Membranaceum*) is one wholly compofed of membranes, without any apparent pulp between.
A compound Leaf (*Compofitum*) in general means one, which is formed of feveral fmall Leaves ftanding upon one foot-ftalk, but thefe Leaves are divifible again to the ftru{ture and pofition of the fmall Leaves. ·
1ft, Into fuch as are properly and diftinctly called compound Leaves; 2dly, the decompound ; 3dly, the fupradecompound, of each of thefe in its place.
In defcribing thefe kinds of Leaves, the whole Leaf which is the refult of the combination, is confidered as one Leaf, called (*Folium*) and the fmall leaves which together compofe it (*Folioli*) or lobes.
A fimple compound Leaf, is one whofe fimple foot-ftalk bears more than one Leaf.
A jointed one (*Articulatum*) is when one Leaf grows out of the point of another, fig. 60.
A fingered Leaf (*Digitatum*) is one which is compofed of feveral fmall Leaves joining to one foot-ftalk at their bafe, fpreading open like the fingers of a hand, fig. 61.
A two-lobed Leaf (*Binatum*) is one with two fmall Leaves on one foot-ftalk, fig. 62.
A three-lobed Leaf (*Ternatum*) is one with three fmall leaves, which is frequently called a trifoliate Leaf, fig. 63.
A cinquefoil Leaf (*Quinatum*) has five fmall Leaves on the fame foot-ftalk.
A winged Leaf (*Pinnatum*) is one which has many fmall Leaves, ranged on each fide a fingle foot-ftalk like wings ; of thefe there are feveral kinds.
An unequal winged Leaf (*Pinnatum cum impare*) is a winged Leaf, terminated by an odd lobe or (*Folioli*) fig. 64.
A clafper-winged Leaf (*Pinnatum cum cirrho*) is a winged Leaf ending with a tendril or clafper, fig. 65.
An abrupt-winged Leaf (*Abruptum*) is a winged Leaf not terminated by an odd lobe or clafper, fig. 66.
An oppofite-winged Leaf (*Oppofite pinnatum*) is when the fmall Leaves or lobes are placed oppofite on the midrib.
An alternate-winged Leaf (*Alternatim pinnatum*) is when the fmall Leaves ftand alternate.
An interrupted-winged Leaf (*Interruptè pinnatum*) is when there are fmaller lobes intermixed with larger upon the fame midrib, fig. 67.
A jointed-winged Leaf (*Articulatè pinnatum*) is when the common foot-ftalk is jointed, fig. 68.
A running-winged Leaf (*Decurfivè pinnatum*) is one whofe fmall Leaves run along the foot-ftalk from one to another, fig. 69.
A conjugated Leaf (*Conjugatum*) is one which has but two fmall Leaves on the fame foot-ftalk.
We next proceed to the decompounded Leaves.
A decompounded Leaf (*Decompofitum*) is one whofe foot-ftalk is once divided, and joins together many fmall Leaves.
A double conjugated Leaf (*Bigeminatum*) is one whofe foot-ftalk divides in forks, and connects four fmall Leaves on the top, or it is compofed of two conjugations.
A double trifolate Leaf (*Biternatum*) is one whofe foot-ftalk is divided, and each divifion fuftains three fmall Leaves, fig. 70.

A double-winged Leaf (*Bipinnatum*) is one whofe foot-ftalk is divided, and thefe divifions have fmall Leaves ranged on their fide like wings, fig. 71.
A foot-fhaped or branched Leaf (*Pedatum*) is one whofe foot-ftalk is divided, and has fome fmall Leaves placed on the inner fide, as in Paffiflora and Arum, fig. 72.
A greater compounded Leaf (*Supra decompofitum*) is one whofe foot-ftalk is many times divided, and each divifion is garnifhed with fmall Leaves.
A triternate Leaf (*Triternatum*) is one whofe foot-ftalk connects three double trifoliate Leaves.
A triple-winged Leaf (*Tripinnatum*) is one compofed of feveral double-winged Leaves ; if thefe are terminated by two fmall Leaves, they are faid to be abrupt, fig. 73. but when they are terminated by an odd one, they are called an irregular, triple, winged Leaf, fig. 74.
We next come to confider the diftinctions of Leaves from their place, pofition, infertion, or their direction, when joined to the other parts of plants.
A feed Leaf (*Seminale*) is the firft Leaf of the plant, and is what former writers called cotyledones ; thefe are different in form and fubftance from the other Leaves, fig. 75.
A bottom Leaf (*Radicale*) is one whofe foot-ftalk rifes immediately from the root.
An upper or ftalk Leaf (*Caulinum*) is one which grows from the ftalk of the plant, fig. 76.
An axillary Leaf (*Axillare*) is one which grows from the infertions of the branches, fig. 77.
A flower Leaf (*Florale*) is one that is inferted near the flower, and never appears but with it, fig. 78.
A ftarry Leaf (*Stellate*) fig. 79. or whorled Leaf (*Verticillata*) is when feveral Leaves are difpofed in whorls round the ftalk, fig. 80.
Oppofite Leaves (*Oppofita*) are when thofe upon the ftalks ftand by pairs on each fide, fig. 81.
Alternate Leaves (*Alterna*) are when they ftand alternate above each other, fig. 82.
Sparfed Leaves (*Sparfa*) are fuch as ftand without order over the whole plant.
Clufter Leaves (*Conferta*) are fuch as come out from the fide of the branches in clufters, and are fo clofe to one another, that it is not eafy to difcover their exact fituation, fig. 83.
Imbricated Leaves (*Imbricata*) are fuch as are placed over each other like tiles on a houfe, or the fcales of fifhes, fig. 84.
Fafciculated Leaves (*Fafciculata*) are fuch as grow in clufters from the fame point, fig. 85.
Difticha is when the Leaves are ranged along only upon two fides of the branches, as in the Fir-tree.
A target or fhield-fhaped Leaf (*Peltatum*) is one whofe foot-ftalk is fixed to the difk, and not to the bafe or edge of the Leaf, fig. 86.
Petiolatum is when the foot-ftalk is inferted to the bafe of the margin, fig. 87.
Seffile is when the Leaf fits clofe to the ftalk or branch, and has no foot-ftalk, fig. 88.
A running Leaf (*Decurrens*) is when the Leaf adheres to the ftalk or branch, and is extended along the ftalk from the bafe, fo as to form a leafy border on each fide the ftalk, fig. 89.
Amplexicaule is when the bafe of the Leaf environs or embraces the fides of the ftalk entirely, fig. 90.
Semiamplexicaule, is when the bafe of the Leaf reach but half round the ftalk.
A perfoliate Leaf (*Perfoliatum*) is one which is perforated by the ftalk or branch, which do not touch the margin, fig. 91.
Connatum, is when the two oppofite Leaves cohere at their bafe, fo as to form one body embracing the ftalk, fig. 92.
Vaginans, is when the bafe of the Leaf forms a kind of cylinder, embracing the ftalk like a fheath, as in Corn, Grafs, fig. 93.
The direction of Leaves.
An adverfe Leaf (*Adverfum*) is one whofe fides refpect the meridian and not the heavens, as the Ginger, &c.

An oblique Leaf (*Obliquum*) is when the base of the Leaf regards the sky, and the summit the horizon.

An inflexed or incurved Leaf (*Inflexum*) is one which grows in form of a bow, turning its point toward the stalk again, fig. 94.

Adpressum, is when the disk of the Leaf approaches near the stalk.

An erect Leaf (*Erectum*) is one so situated as to make a very acute angle with the stalk, fig. 95.

Patens, is when the Leaf does not make so acute an angle with the stalk as the former, and yet does not stand horizontal, fig. 96.

An horizontal Leaf (*Horizontale*) is one which stands perfectly at right angles with the stalk, fig. 97.

A reclined Leaf (*Reclinatum*) is one whose summit is lower than the base, fig. 98.

A rolled Leaf (*Revolutum*) is one whose upper part is rolled downward, fig. 99.

A dependent Leaf (*Dependens*) is one whose summits point to the earth.

A rooting Leaf (*Radicans*) is one which puts out roots.

A floating Leaf (*Natans*) is one which floats on the surface of the water, as the Water Lily, &c.

Demersum, is used to express a Leaf sunk below the surface of the water.

Having explained the several forms of Leaves, by which botanists distinguish them, and also their position, both in regard to the other parts of the tree, or plant, and that of the earth, we shall next proceed to their structure and uses; for these were not designed by the wise Creator only for ornament, but they are of more important use in vegetation, and are as variously constructed in their several parts, as their several uses for which they are designed.

Some plants have very thick fleshy Leaves, whose pulpy substance is always moist; these are such plants as naturally grow upon dry barren rocky places, and for the most part are natives of warm countries; and as they perspire very little in comparison of most other plants, they are adapted to grow in such places where they can receive very little nourishment from the earth. Most of the Leaves of these plants have a thin compact skin over their surface, with very small minute pores, whereby the descending moisture is thrown off, which, if admitted into the substance of the Leaves, or stalks, would in a very short time cause a mortification, and destroy the plant.

The Leaves of all those trees and shrubs which continue their verdure all the year, have also a thin compact skin or cover over their surfaces, as is easily discovered by macerating them in water, in order to separate the parenchyma from the vessels of the leaves, which cannot be effected in any of these Evergreens, till the thin parchment-like cover is taken off; these trees and shrubs are found, by experiment, to imbibe and perspire but little in the same space of time, when compared with the deciduous trees and shrubs; and it is principally owing to this close covering, as also to the small proportion of moisture contained in their vessels, that they retain their verdure, and continue through the winter on the trees. The nutritive juices of these plants always abound more or less with an oily or terebinthinous quality, which secures them from the injury of frost, so that many of these evergreen trees are adapted to grow in the coldest parts of the habitable world.

In all the Leaves of trees and plants which I have examined, there are two orders of veins or nerves, one belonging to each surface; and I have generally observed, that the lower lamina or under side of the Leaf, had the ramifications larger, and were capable of admitting a liquid to pass through them, which those of the upper surface would not; these two orders of veins are inosculated at several places, but not so closely connected, but that they may be easily separated, after they have been macerated in water a proper time, for some Leaves require a much longer time than others, to render the parenchyma soft enough to separate easily from the veins without tearing them.

These two laminæ, or orders of veins, are supposed to be destined for different purposes; the upper lamina is thought to be air-vessels, or trachæ, through which the perspiring matter is protruded, and by which the air is inspired; that these are pores through which that substance passes, which is thrown out of the plants, is pretty evident; for the clammy substance which is commonly called honey-dew, is always found sticking to the upper surface of Leaves, from whence many have supposed that this substance fell from above, and lodged upon the Leaves in the night. This is the Manna which is collected from Ash-trees in Calabria, and from the Alhagi in Persia, &c. and is no other than the nutritive juices, or a substance, separated from that, which issues from the pores of the Leaves, and is concreted on the surface of the Leaves by the cold air; but whenever this is found in quantity upon the Leaves, it is a sure sign of a diseased plant.

The lower lamina of veins are supposed to be destined for another purpose, which is that of receiving, preparing, and conveying the moisture imbibed from the rising vapours of the earth, by which trees and plants are greatly nourished; and for this use we see how differently the two surfaces are formed; the upper one is commonly smooth and lucid, and the under is frequently covered with hairs, or a soft down, the better to stop and detain the rising vapours, and transmit them to the inner vessels; and where the structure of the Leaves are different, it is found by experience, that their functions alter; for those Leaves, whose upper surfaces are garnished with down or hairs, are found to be the receivers and conveyers of the moisture, and not the under ones, as in the other plants.

If the surfaces of these Leaves are altered, by reversing the branches on which they grow, the plants are stopped in their growth, until the foot-stalks are turned, and the Leaves recover their former position. This shews how necessary it is to support all those weak shoots of plants, which are naturally disposed for upright growth, and that either twine about the neighbouring trees for support, or that put out claspers, by which they take hold of whatever trees or plants grow near them, and are thereby supported; and, on the contrary, how absurd is that practice of tying up the shoots of those plants which are naturally disposed to trail upon the ground; for, in both these cases, nature is reversed, and consequently the growth of both sorts of plants is greatly retarded.

This is one of the great functions for which the Leaves of trees and plants are designed; but, besides this, there are others of equal importance to the well-being of plants and fruits; the first is that of the foot-stalks of Leaves nourishing and preparing the buds of the future shoots, which are always formed at the base of these foot-stalks, and during the continuance of the Leaves in perfect health, these buds increase in their magnitude, and, in the deciduous trees, are brought to maturity before the foot-stalks separate from the buds in autumn; but if by accident the Leaves are blighted, or if the entire surface of the Leaves are cut off, and the foot-stalks are left remaining, yet the buds will decay, or not arrive to their proper size, for want of that nourishment which is conveyed to them from the Leaves; so that whenever trees are divested of their Leaves, or those Leaves are cut, or otherwise impaired, though it may in either case happen when the buds may be nearly formed; yet if it is before the foot-stalks separate naturally from the branches, the future shoots will be weakened in proportion to the time when this is done; therefore, as from all the experiments which have been made in order to know how serviceable the Leaves of trees and plants are to their well-being, it has been found, that where the plants have been divested of their Leaves, or their Leaves have been eaten, or cut, during their growth, the plants have been remarkably weakened thereby. This should teach us not to pull, or cut off the Leaves of trees, or plants, on any account, while they retain their verdure or are in health.

health. As also how absurd that common practice is, of feeding down Wheat in the winter and spring with sheep; for by so doing, the stalks are rendered very weak, and the ears are in proportion shorter; nor are the grains of Corn so plump and well nourished, as that which is not fed down upon the same ground: this is a fact which I can assert from many years experience; for when Corn or Grass is fed down close to the root, the succeeding blades will be much finer than if the first Leaves had been left remaining; which is evident from all sheep pastures, where the Grass is much finer and shorter than in other places; as also upon lawns and bowling-greens, where the Grass is often mowed, the blades will be rendered finer in proportion to the frequency of mowing it, yet the species of Grass is the same with that on the richest pastures; so that although this may be a desirable thing for lawns, &c. in gardens, yet where regard is had to the produce, this should be avoided.

Besides these, there are other uses for which Leaves are designed, one of which is that of shading the buds for the future shoots from the sun, which would exhale and dry up all their moisture, as also the shading of the young fruit, which is absolutely necessary during the time of their growth; for I have suspended the Leaves of trees which were growing against walls, so as to expose the fruit to the sun, and not taken any of them off the branches, yet I have always found those fruits so exposed, have been greatly stinted in their growth, and have never arrived to near the size of others above and below them on the same branches, nor were they so well tasted, or replete with juice.

In making this experiment, I was as careful as possible not to reverse the surfaces of the Leaves, having been thoroughly convinced, from many repeated experiments, how prejudicial that is to all plants; but notwithstanding this precaution, the event was as before-mentioned.

Another principal use of the Leaves is to throw off by transpiration, what is unnecessary for the growth of the plants, answering to the discharge made by sweat in animal bodies; and as plants receive and transpire much more, in equal time than large animals, so it appears how necessary the Leaves are to preserve the plants in perfect health; for it has been found by the most exact calculations, made from repeated experiments, that a plant of the Sun-flower receives and perspires, in twenty-four hours, seventeen times more than a man.

As naturalists have generally ascribed a four-fold use to Leaves, I shall beg leave to mention them here, and then shall give an account of the most accurate experiments which have been made to ascertain the truth of their hypotheses.

1. Chiefly, that they do in the spring time receive the crude humours into themselves, divide them very minutely, and move them strongly in the utricles, and perhaps draw in from the air what is necessary, though unknown to us, and carry back great plenty of elaborate juice to the plant.

2. That there may be a transpiration of what is unprofitable, answering to the discharge made by sweat; for sometimes those excretory vessels of the Leaves are so overcharged by the great plenty of distending humour [juice,] that they burst in the middle, and let go the more subtile parts; nor is it seldom, that, in a hot season, great plenty of juices are this way discharged and imbibed. Thus Manna is found to exsude [sweat forth] from the Leaves of certain trees, if a cold night should follow a hot day; and the same thing frequently happens in divers other plants and trees, as we learn from the bees flying to the Lime-tree, that they may gather that gumous substance from their Leaves; and it is from the surfaces of the Leaves, as well as from the flowers, those animals collect their honey; but if the heat should be less, all the superfluous humours, except those which, perhaps, are transmitted by insensible transpiration thro'

the arterial vessels, exhaling naturally, are seen to return into the trunk.

3. That the bibulous vessels, dried by the diurnal heat, and for this reason to be compared to veins, may imbibe, in the night-time especially, those watery parts, which, among others, lie hid in the air under the form of a very thin dew, and so make amends for the loss made by the arteries, by the new moisture received.

4. Lastly, the Leaf serves chiefly for this purpose, that it may keep and nourish the eye, or gem, until the gem, by degrees growing out to a greater bulk, presses together the vessels of the foot-stalk, from whence the humour is by little and little stopped in the Leaf, till it cannot any more return to the foot-stalk; which, by the ceasing of the afflux and reflux of the nutritive juice, grows putrid, whence a consumption being caused, the Leaf dies, and falls off, which is the chief cause of the falling of the Leaves in autumn.

The Rev. Dr. Hales, in his excellent Treatise of Vegetable Statics, speaking of the perspiration of plants, gives an account of the following experiments, viz.

That in July or August he cut off several branches of Apple-trees, Cherry-trees, Pear-trees, and Apricot-trees, two of a sort; they were of several sizes, from three to six feet long; with proportional lateral branches, and the transverse cut of the largest part of the stems was about an inch diameter.

That he stripped off the Leaves of one bough of each sort, and then set their stems in several glasses, pouring in known quantities of water.

The boughs with Leaves on them imbibed some fifteen ounces, some twenty, twenty-five, or thirty, in twelve hours day, more or less, in proportion to the quantity of Leaves they had, and when he weighed them at night, they were lighter than in the morning. While those without Leaves imbibed but one ounce, and were heavier in the evening than in the morning, they having perspired little.

The quantity imbibed by those with Leaves decreased very much every day, the sap-vessels being probably shrunk at the transverse cut, and too much saturate with water, to let any more pass, so that usually in four or five days the Leaves faded and withered much.

He adds, that he repeated the same experiments with Elm branches, Oak, Osier, Willow, Sallow, Aspen, Currant, Gooseberry, and Filbert branches, but none of these imbibed so much as the foregoing, and several sorts of Evergreens very much less.

He adds also another experiment: That on the 15th of August, he cut off a large Pippin with two inches stem, and its twelve adjoining Leaves: that he set the stem in a little phial of water, which imbibed and perspired in three days one third of an ounce:

And that at the same time he cut off from the same tree another bearing twig of the same length, with twelve Leaves, no Apple on it, which imbibed in the same three days near three-fourths of an ounce.

That about the same time, he set in a phial of water a short stem of the same tree, with two large Apples on it, without leaves, and they imbibed near three-fourths of an ounce in two days.

So in this experiment, the Apples and Leaves imbibed four-fifths of an ounce, the Leaves alone near three-fifths, but the two large Apples imbibed and perspired but one third part so much as the twelve Leaves, then the one Apple imbibed the one-sixth part of what was imbibed by the twelve Leaves; therefore two Leaves imbibe and perspire as much as one Apple; whence their perspirations seem to be proportionable to their surfaces, the surface of the Apple being nearly equal to the sum of the upper and under surfaces of the two Leaves.

Whence it is probable that the use of these Leaves (which are placed just where the fruit joins to the tree) is to bring nourishment to the fruit.

And

And accordingly he obferves, that the Leaves next adjoining to the bloffoms are in the fpring very much expanded, when the other Leaves on barren fhoots are but beginning to fhoot, and that all Peach Leaves are very large before the bloffom goes off.

And that, in Apples and Pears, the Leaves are one-third or half grown, before the bloffom opens, fo provident is nature in making timely provifion for the nourifhing the yet embryo fruit.

He alfo adds another experiment: he ftripped the Leaves of an Apple-tree branch, and then fixed the great end of the ftem in the gage, it raifed the mercury $2 + \frac{1}{4}$ inches, but it foon fubfided, for want of the plentiful perfpiration of the Leaves, fo that the air came in almoft as faft as the branch imbibed water.

And as a farther proof of the influence of the Leaves in raifing the fap, he alfo made the following experiment.

On the fixth of Auguft, he cut off a large Ruffet Pippin, with a ftalk $1 + \frac{1}{4}$ inch long, and twelve adjoining Leaves growing to it.

He cemented the ftalk faft in the upper end of a tube, which tube was fix inches long, and one-fourth diameter; as the ftalk imbibed the water, it raifed the mercury four inches high.

That he fixed another Apple of the fame fize in the fame manner, but firft pulled off the Leaves, and it raifed the mercury but one inch; that in the fame manner he fixed a like-bearing twig, with twelve Leaves on it, but no Apple, and it raifed the mercury three inches.

He then took a like-bearing twig, without either Leaves or Apple, and it raifed the mercury one-fourth of an inch.

So a twig, with an Apple and Leaves, raifed the mercury four inches; one with Leaves, only three inches; one with an Apple without Leaves, only one inch.

A Quince, which had two Leaves juft at the twig's infertion, raifed the mercury $2 + \frac{1}{4}$ inches, and held it up a confiderable time.

A fprig of Mint, fixed in the fame manner, raifed the mercury $3 + \frac{1}{4}$ inches, = to 4 feet 5 inches height of water.

Thefe, and many more experiments of the Rev. Dr. Hales, that curious enquirer into the caufes, ftate, and progrefs of vegetation, evidently fhew the great perfpiration of the Leaves of plants, and their great ufe in raifing the fap, and other functions of vegetable nature; to whofe excellent treatife before-mentioned, I refer the curious enquirer.

I fhall add, That nature has directed us as to the true diftance we ought to train the branches of trees againft walls or efpaliers, which fhould always be in proportion to the fize of their Leaves; for if we regard her progrefs in the great varieties of trees, which are within our obfervation, we fhall always find their branches grow diftant from each other in proportion to the breadth of their Leaves; and it was upon this account that the Romans fo much admired the Platanus, becaufe the Leaves, being large, afforded them a kindly fhade in fummer, but in winter, when they are deftitute of Leaves, their branches growing at a great diftance, eafily admitted the beams of the fun.

I fhall next beg leave to mention a few, out of the many experiments which have been made by Monf. Bonnet, of Geneva, to prove that moft Leaves imbibe the moifture of the air on their under furface, and not from their upper: they are as follow:

He gathered the Leaves of fixteen forts of herbaceous plants when fully grown; of each he put feveral Leaves upon the furface of water in glafs vafes, fome were pofited with their upper furface, and others with their under furface upon the water; thefe were adjufted exactly to the furface of the water, with great care not to let any moifture reach their oppofite furfaces, and the fame care was taken to prevent their foot-ftalks from receiving any moifture. The glaffes in which thefe Leaves were thus placed, were kept in a

clofet, where the air was very temperate; and as the water in the glaffes evaporated, there was from time to time a fupply of frefh, which was added with a fyringe, fo that the Leaves were not difturbed. The Leaves were taken from the following plants; the Plantain, the Mullein, the Wake Robin, the great Mallow, the Nettle, the Marvel of Peru, the Kindney-bean, the Sun-flower, the Cabbage, the Balm, the Cock's-comb, the purple-leaved Amaranth, Spinach, and the fmaller Mallow.

Six of thefe forts he found continued green a long time, and thefe were with different furfaces upon the water; they were of the following forts, the Wake Robin, the Kidney-bean, the Sun-flower, the Cabbage, the Spinach, and fmall Mallow; among the others the following forts were found to draw the moifture better with their upper furface than their under, the Plantain, the Mullein, the great Mallow, the Nettle, the Cock's-comb, and the purple Amaranth.

The Leaves of the Nettle whofe under furface was upon the water, were decayed in three weeks, whereas thofe whofe upper furface was next the water continued two months.

The Leaves of Mullein, whofe under furface was next the water, did not continue frefh more than five or fix days, but thofe whofe upper furface was next the water lafted five weeks.

The Leaves of the purple Amaranth, whofe upper furface was next the water, continued frefh three months, whereas thofe whofe under furface was next the water, were decayed in a week.

The Leaves of the Marvel of Peru and the Balm, appeared to have the advantage, whofe under furfaces were next the water.

The Leaves of Wake Robin and of the Cock's-comb, whofe foot-ftalks only were put into the water, continued frefh a longer time than thofe which were placed with either furface next the water.

The Leaves of the Great Mallow, the Nettle, the Sun-flower, the Marvel of Peru, and Spinach, whofe foot-ftalks were plunged into the water, continued frefh a fhorter time than thofe which had either of their furfaces next the water.

The Leaves of the Mullein, of Plantain, and Amaranth. which received the water at their foot-ftalk, continued frefh much longer than thofe, whofe under furface was next the water.

It is not difficult to explain the reafon of this fact, for the orifices of the fap-veffels in the foot-ftalk, are much larger than thofe of either furface, fo that the moifture infinuates in greater quantities, and with more eafe, the firft, than by the fecond way.

After this fame gentleman made experiments on the Leaves of fixteen forts of trees and fhrubs of the following forts, the Lilac, the Pear-tree, the Vine, the Afpen, the Laurel, the Cherry-tree, the Plumb-tree, the Horfe Chefnut, the White Mulberry, the Lime-tree, the Poplar, the Apricot, the Walnut, the Filbert, the Oak, and the Creeper.

Among thefe fpecies, he found that the Lilac and the Afpen imbibed the moifture on their upper furface, equally with the under furface; but in all the other forts, the under furface imbibed it in much greater quantities than the oppofite. The difference was very remarkable in the Leaves of the White Mulberry, for thofe whofe upper furface was laid upon the water, faded in five days, whereas the other whofe under furface was next the water, preferved their verdure near fix months.

The Vine, the Poplar, and Walnut-tree are very remarkable inftances, how little difpofed the upper furfaces of the Leaves of ligneous plants are to imbibe the moifture; for thofe of thefe three forts, whofe upper furfaces were applied to the water, decayed almoft as foon as thofe which had no nourifhment.

In all the experiments made by this curious gentleman upon the various Leaves of trees and herbs, it is remarkable, that all thofe Leaves which imbibed the moifture by their upper furface, were fuch as had
that

that furface covered with either hairs or down; and on the contrary, where the under furface was garnifhed with either hairs or down, the moifture was imbibed by that furface. He likewife mentions many experiments made by himfelf, and alfo by Monf. du Hamel de Monceau, of the Royal Academy of Sciences at Paris, in rubbing the Leaves over with varnifh, oil, wax, and honey, to fee the effect of thefe upon various Leaves, fome of which were rubbed over on both furfaces, others only upon one; fome only a part of the furface, others the edges of the Leaves were rubbed over, and in fome only the foot-ftalks of the Leaves were rubbed with thefe. They likewife anointed the trunks of fome trees and fhrubs, and left the Leaves and branches in their natural ftate.

The refult of thefe experiments was, that where the Leaves were anointed on both furfaces with varnifh, they decayed prefently; and where they were anointed with the other things, in proportion as thofe were moft penetrating, fo the Leaves continued a fhorter time than the others; and where one furface only was anointed, they continued much longer than thofe which were anointed on both; and where the pedicle only was anointed, they continued ftill longer; but the anointing of the trunks, made no fenfible alteration, excepting in very hot weather; when they both imagine, that the anointing them was of fervice, by hindering the too great tranfpiration which might weaken the trees; for they obferved, that thofe trees which were varnifhed, fuffered lefs from the violent heat, than the trees which were left in their natural ftate.

Monf. Bonnet alfo obferved, that thofe Leaves which were varnifhed, the tender parts of the Leaves were deftroyed by it, and the tough fibres only were left remaining.

As it would fwell this work much beyond its intended bulk, were I to mention more of thefe curious experiments, I fhall refer the curious to his book, where they will find a great number of the moft accurate and well conducted experiments related, to afcertain the ufes of the Leaves of plants in vegetation.

The before-mentioned Rev. Dr. Hales, in his Treatife of Vegetation, fays, it is plain from many experiments and obfervations he had before mentioned, that Leaves are very ferviceable in this work of vegetation, by being inftrumental in bringing nourifhment from the lower parts, within the reach of the attraction of the growing fruit, which, like young animals, is furnifhed with proper inftruments to fuck it thence; but the Leaves feem alfo defigned for many other noble and important fervices; for nature admirably adapts her inftruments, fo as to be at the fame time ferviceable to many good purpofes.

Thus the Leaves, in which are many excretory ducts in vegetables, feparate and carry off the redundant watery fluid, which, by being long detained, would turn rancid, and prejudicial to the plant, leaving the more nutritive parts to coalefce; part of which nourifhment, we have good reafon to think, is conveyed into vegetables through the Leaves, which plentifully imbibe the dew which contain falt, fulphur, &c.

For the air is full of acid and fulphureous particles, which, when they abound much, do, by the action and reaction between them and the elaftic air, caufe that fultry heat which ufually ends in lightning and thunder; and thefe new combinations of air, fulphur, and acid fpirit, which are conftantly forming in the air, are doubtlefs very ferviceable in promoting the work of vegetation; when, being imbibed by the Leaves, they may not improbably be the materials, out of which the more fubtile and refined principles of vegetables are formed; for fo fine a fluid as the air feems to be a more proper medium, wherein to prepare and combine the more exalted principles of vegetables, than the groffer watery fluid of the fap;

and for the fame reafon it is likely that the moft refined and active principles of animals are alfo prepared in the air, and thence conveyed through the lungs into the blood; and that there is plenty of thefe fulphureo-aereal particles in the Leaves, is evident from the fulphureous exfudations that are found in the edges of Leaves, of which bees are obferved to make their waxen cells, as well as of the duft of flowers. And that wax abounds with fulphur, is plain from its burning freely, &c.

We may therefore reafonably conclude, that one great ufe of Leaves is what has been long fufpected by many, viz. to perform, in fome meafure, the fame office for the fupport of the vegetable life, as the lungs of animals do for the fupport of animal life; plants, very probably, drawing through their Leaves fome part of their nourifhment from the air.

LEDUM. Raii Syn. 1—142. Lin. Gen. Plant. 483. Marfh Ciftus, or wild Rofemary.

The CHARACTERS are,

The flower has a fmall empalement of one leaf, indented in five parts. It hath five oval, concave, fpreading petals, and ten flender ftamina the length of the petals, which fpread open, terminated by oblong fummits, and a roundifh germen fupporting a flender ftyle, crowned by an obtufe ftigma. The germen afterward becomes a roundifh capfule with five cells, opening at the bafe in five parts, and filled with fmall, narrow, acute-pointed feeds.

This genus of plants is by Dr. Linnæus ranged in the firft fection of his tenth clafs, intitled Decandria Monogynia, which includes thofe plants whofe flowers have ten ftamina and one ftyle.

We have but one SPECIES of this genus, viz.

LEDUM (*Paluftre*) foliis linearibus fubtus hirfutis, floribus corymbofis. Flor. Suec. 341. *Ledum with very narrow leaves, hairy on their under fide, and flowers growing in a corymbus.* Rofmarinum fylveftre minus noftras. Park. Hift. 76. *Our fmall wild Rofemary.*

This plant grows naturally upon moffes and bogs in many parts of Yorkfhire, Chefhire, and Lancafhire, where it rifes with a flender fhrubby ftalk about two feet high, dividing into many flender branches, which are garnifhed with narrow leaves not much unlike thofe of Heath. The flowers are produced in fmall clufters at the end of the branches, which are fhaped like thofe of the Strawberry-tree, but fpread open wider at the top. Thefe are of a reddifh colour, and appear in May, and in the natural places of their growth, are fucceeded by feed-veffels filled with fmall feeds, which ripen in the autumn.

It is with great difficulty this plant is kept in a garden, for as it naturally grows upon bogs, fo unlefs the plants have fome fuch foil and a fhady fituation, they will not thrive. The plants muft be procured from the places of their growth, and taken up with good roots, otherwife they will not live. They cannot be propagated in gardens, but in the moffes their roots fpread and propagate pretty freely.

LEEKS. See PORRUM.

LEGUMES, or LEGUMENS, are a fpecies of plants which are called pulfe, fuch as Peas, Beans, &c. and are fo called, becaufe they may be gathered by the hand without cutting. Mr. Ray reckons all thofe plants which have a papilionaceous flower, among the Legumes; but the French comprehend moft forts of efculent plants, under this general title of Legumes.

LEGUMINOUS, of or belonging to pulfe.

LEMNA. Lin. Gen. 1038. Lens Paluftris, Duck-Meat. This is a very common plant, growing upon ftanding waters in moft parts of England; where, if it is not difturbed, it will foon cover the whole furface.

LEMON-TREE. See LIMON.

LENS. See ERVUM.

LENTISCUS. See PISTACIA.

LEONTICE. Lin. Gen. Plant. 423. Leontopetalon. Tourn. Cor. 49. tab. 484. Lion's Leaf.

The

The CHARACTERS are,

The empalement of the flower is made up of six very narrow leaves, which are alternately smaller and drop off. The flower has six oval acute petals, which are twice the length of the empalement, and six nectariums which are fixed by small foot-stalks to the base of the petals. It has six short slender stamina, terminated by erect summits. In the center is placed an oblong oval germen, supporting a short taper style, inserted obliquely to the germen, crowned by a simple stigma. The germen afterward becomes a globular swollen berry a little succulent, with one cell, inclosing two or three globular seeds.

This genus of plants is ranged in the first section of Linnæus's sixth class, which includes those plants whose flowers have six stamina and one style.

The SPECIES are,

1. LEONTICE (*Chrysogonum*) foliis pinnatis, petiolo communi simplici. Hort. Cliff. 122. *Lion's Leaf, with winged leaves having one common single foot-stalk.* Leontopetalon foliis costæ simplici innascentibus. Tourn. Cor. 49. *Lion's Leaf with a single foot-stalk to the leaves.*

2. LEONTICE (*Leontopetalum*) foliis decompositis, petiolo communi trifido. Hort. Cliff. 122. *Lion's Leaf with decompounded leaves, and a common trifid foot-stalk.* Leontopetalon foliis costæ ramosæ innascentibus. Tourn. Cor. 49. *Lion's Leaf with a branching foot-stalk to the leaves.*

These plants both grow naturally in the islands of the Archipelago, and also in the Corn fields about Aleppo, where they flower soon after Christmas. They have large tuberous roots about the size of those of Cyclamen, covered with a dark brown bark; the leaves arise upon slender foot-stalks immediately from their roots, which grow about six inches high; that of the first sort is single, having many small folioli ranged along the midrib, but the footstalks of the second sort are branched into three smaller; upon each of these are ranged several folioli or small leaves, in the same form as the winged leaves. The flowers sit upon naked foot-stalks, those of the first sort sustain many yellow flowers, but the flowers of the second are smaller and of a paler colour. These in their native country appear soon after Christmas, but in England they do not flower till the beginning of April, and are never succeeded by seeds here. Both these plants are propagated by seeds, which require to be sown soon after they are ripe, otherwise they seldom succeed; but as they are brought from distant countries, they should be preserved in sand to be sent to England. I received a few of the seeds from the Duke D'Ayen, which were sent him from Aleppo, put up in sand, and these came up better than any of those which came over dry; for of several parcels of these seeds which I have sown of both kinds for three years successively, I had not more than two plants arise.

The plants are very difficult to preserve in England, for the roots will not thrive in pots; and when they are planted in the full ground, the frost frequently destroys them in winter, especially where the roots are young. Of late years the winters have proved so very unfavourable, as to kill all the young roots which I had raised in the Chelsea garden: but before the severe winter in 1740, I had some of the roots which were planted in a south-west border that flowered several years, and without any shelter survived the winters; but although I covered many of those roots which I had lately raised, yet I could not preserve them.

The leaves of these plants decay about Midsummer, and the roots remain in an inactive state till the following spring, at which time the flowers and leaves come up nearly at the same time.

When the seeds are procured from abroad, the best way is to sow them as soon as they arrive, and cover them with glasses in the winter to protect them from frost; and in the spring, when the plants begin to appear, they must have the free air admitted to them at all times when the weather is mild, otherwise they are very subject to draw up tall with weak stems, and

their roots do not increase in their bulk. If the plants are not too close, it will be best to let them remain in the place unremoved till the second year; but where they are too close, part of the roots may be taken up in October, and transplanted close to a warm wall, being very careful not to disturb the roots which are left standing; and in November, before the hard frost sets in, it will be a good way to lay some old tanners bark over the surface of the ground, three or four inches thick, to prevent the frost from penetrating to the roots; but this should be most of it taken off in March, before the roots begin to push out their leaves; and if this is removed in part soon after the hard frost is over in February, and another part three weeks or a month after, it will be better than taking it all off at the same time; and if a thin covering of the tan is left at the last over the surface of the ground, it will prevent the drying winds of the spring from drying the ground, which will be of great service to the roots. These roots should have a dry loose soil, and must be seldom removed; but when that is done, October is the best time, for then the roots are inactive.

LEONTODON. Lin. Gen. Plant. 817. Dens leonis. Tourn. Inst. R. H. 468. Dandelion; in French, *Dent de Lion.*

There are four or five species of this genus, which grow naturally in the fields either in England or France, so are seldom cultivated in gardens; but as some people in the spring gather the roots out of the fields, and blanch them in their gardens for a sallad herb, so I have mentioned the genus, but shall forbear saying any thing more of them, than that they are very bad weeds both in gardens and fields; so should be rooted out before their seeds are ripe, otherwise they will spread to a great distance, as they have down adhering to them, by which they are wafted about by the wind.

LEONTOPODIUM. See PLANTAGO.

LEONURUS. Tourn. Inst. R. H. 187. tab. 87. Phlomis. Lin. Gen. Plant. 642. [Λεωνυρ⌀, of Λεων, a lion, and ⌀ρα, a tail, because the crest of this flower seems to resemble the tail of a lion.] Lion's Tail.

The CHARACTERS are,

The flower has a tubulous, five-cornered, permanent empalement of one leaf; the flowers have one petal, of the lip or ringent kind; the upper lip is long, cylindrical, hairy, and entire; the lower is short, reflexed, and cut into three parts. It hath four stamina situated under the lower lip, two of which are shorter than the other; these are terminated by oblong compressed summits. In the bottom of the tube are situated four germen supporting a slender style, situated with the stamina, crowned by a bifid acute stigma. The germen afterward become four oblong angular seeds, sitting in the empalement.

This genus of plants is ranged in the second section of Tournefort's fourth class, which includes the herbs with a lip flower of one leaf, whose upper lip is hollowed like a spoon. Dr. Linnæus has joined the species of this genus to the Phlomis, and has applied this title to the Cardiaca, from which he separates these plants, because they have no punctures on their summits. These he ranges in the first section of his fourteenth class, which includes the plants with a ringent (or grinning) flower, that have two long and two shorter stamina, and naked seeds succeeding, sitting in the empalement.

The CHARACTERS are,

1. LEONURUS (*Africana*) foliis lanceolatis, obtusè serratis. Hort. Cliff. 312. *Lion's Tail with spear-shaped leaves which are bluntly sawed.* Leonurus perennis Africanus, sideritidis folio, flore Phœnicio majore. Breyn. Cent. 1. 171. *Perennial African Lion's Tail with an Ironwort leaf, and a larger scarlet flower.*

2. LEONURUS (*Nepetæfolia*) foliis ovatis, calycibus decagonis, septem dentatis, inæqualibus. Hort. Cliff. 312. *Lion's Tail with oval leaves, an empalement having ten corners, and seven unequal indentures.* Leonurus minor capitis Bonæ Spei, vulgò. Boerh. Ind. alt. 180. *Small Lion's Tail of the Cape of Good Hope.*

The

The firſt ſort is a native of Ethiopia, but has been long cultivated in the Engliſh gardens. This riſes with a ſhrubby ſtalk ſeven or eight feet high, ſending out ſeveral branches from the ſide, which are four-cornered; theſe are garniſhed with oblong narrow leaves, acutely indented on their edges; they are about three inches long, and half an inch broad, hairy on their upper ſide, and veined on their under, ſtanding oppoſite. The flowers are produced in whorls round the branches, each of the branches having two or three of theſe whorls toward their ends, ſitting very cloſe to the branches; they are of the lip kind, ſhaped ſomewhat like thoſe of the Dead Nettle, but their creſts are much longer and covered with ſhort hairs; they are of a golden colour, ſo make a fine appearance. The flowers commonly appear in October and November, and ſometimes continue till the middle of December, but are not ſucceeded by ſeeds here.

There is a variety of this ſort with variegated leaves, which is by ſome admired; but as this ſeldom produces ſo large whorls of flowers as the plain ſort, it is not ſo generally eſteemed.

The ſecond ſort is mentioned by ſeveral authors as an annual plant; they alſo ſuppoſe it to be a native of America, and believe it was brought from Surinam to Holland; but it is undoubtedly a native of the Cape of Good Hope, from whence I have two or three times received the ſeeds; and the late Dr. Boerhaave aſſured me, that he frequently received the ſeeds from that country, as alſo a painting of the plant, ſo that he made no doubt of the plant growing naturally there.

This riſes with a ſquare ſhrubby ſtalk about three feet high, ſending out ſeveral four-cornered branches, which are garniſhed with oval crenated leaves, rough on their upper ſide like the Dead Nettle, but veined on the under, which is of a pale green: theſe are placed oppoſite by pairs, as are alſo their branches. The flowers come out in whorls round the branches, in like manner as the former, but are not ſo long nor ſo deep coloured; they appear at the ſame ſeaſon with the firſt, and continue as long in beauty.

Both theſe ſorts are propagated by cuttings in Europe, for they do not produce any ſeeds here. If the cuttings are planted in July, after the plants have been ſo long expoſed to the open air as to harden the ſhoots, they will take root very freely. They ſhould be planted in a loamy border on an eaſt aſpect, and if they are covered cloſely with a bell or hand-glaſs to exclude the air, and ſhaded from the ſun, it will forward their putting out roots; but when they begin to ſhoot, the glaſſes ſhould be raiſed to admit the free air, to prevent their drawing up weak, and by degrees their muſt be expoſed to the open air. As ſoon as they have taken good root they muſt be taken up, and each planted in a ſeparate pot filled with ſoft loamy earth, and placed in the ſhade till they have taken new root; then they may be removed to a ſheltered ſituation, where they may remain till October, when they muſt be removed into the green-houſe, and afterward treated as the Myrtle, and other hardy green-houſe plants, obſerving to water the firſt ſort plentifully.

LEPIDIUM. Tourn. Inſt. R. H. 215. tab. 103. Lin. Gen. Plant. 718. Dittander, or Pepperwort.

The CHARACTERS are,

The empalement of the flower is compoſed of four oval concave leaves, which fall off. The flower has four oval petals placed in form of a croſs, which are much larger than the empalement, and ſix awl-ſhaped ſtamina the length of the empalement, two of which are ſhorter than the other, terminated by ſingle ſummits. In the center is ſituated a heart-ſhaped germen, ſupporting a ſingle ſtyle, crowned by an obtuſe ſtigma. The germen afterward turns to a ſpear-ſhaped ſeed-veſſel with two cells, divided by an intermediate partition, containing oblong ſeeds.

This genus of plants is ranged in the firſt ſection of Linnæus's fifteenth claſs, intitled Tetradynamia ſiliculoſa, the flower having four long and two ſhorter ſtamina, and the ſeeds being included in ſhort pods.

The SPECIES are,

1. LEPIDIUM (*Latifolium*) foliis ovato-lanceolatis integris ſerratis. Hort. Cliff. 330. *Dittander with entire, oval, ſpear-ſhaped leaves, which are ſawed.* Lepidium latifolium. C. B. P. 97. *Broad-leaved Dittander.*

2. LEPIDIUM (*Arvenſe*) foliis lanceolatis amplexicaulibus dentatis. Hort. Cliff. 331. *Dittander with ſpear-ſhaped indented leaves which embrace the ſtalks.* Lepidium humile, incanum arvenſe. Tourn. Inſt. R. H. 216. *Low hoary Dittander of the fields.*

3. LEPIDIUM (*Chalepenſe*) foliis ſagittatis ſeſſilibus dentatis. Amœn. Acad. 4. p. 321. *Dittander with arrow-ſhaped indented leaves ſitting cloſe to the ſtalks.* Lepidium humile minus incanum, Alepicum. Tourn. Inſt. 216. *Low Dittander of Aleppo with leſs hoary leaves.*

4. LEPIDIUM (*Iberis*) floribus diandris tetrapetalis, foliis inferioribus lanceolatis ſerratis, ſuperioribus linearibus integerrimis. Flor. Leyd. Prod. 334. *Dittander with flowers having four petals and two ſtamina, whoſe under leaves are ſpear-ſhaped and ſawed, and the upper narrow and entire.* Lepidium graminco folio five, Iberis. Tourn. Inſt. 216. *Dittander with a Graſs leaf, or Iberis.*

5. LEPIDIUM (*Perfoliatum*) foliis caulinis pinnato-multifidis, ramiferis cordatis, amplexicaulibus integris. Hort. Cliff. 331. *Dittander with lower leaves wing-pointed, and thoſe on the branches heart-ſhaped, entire, and embracing the ſtalks.* Thlaſpi verum Dioſcoridis. 1 Zan. Hiſt. 193. *The true Mithridate Muſtard of Dioſcorides.*

6. LEPIDIUM (*Virginicum*) floribus ſubtriandris tetrapetalis, foliis linearibus pinnatis. Lin. Gen. Plant. 645. *Dittander with flowers having four petals, chiefly with three ſtamina, and very narrow winged leaves.* Iberis humilior annua Virginiana ramoſior. Mor. Hiſt. 2. p. 311. *Lower, annual, branching Sciatica Creſs of Virginia.*

7. LEPIDIUM (*Lyratum*) foliis lyratis criſpis. Lin. Sp. Plant. 644. *Dittander with curled lyre-ſhaped leaves.* Lepidium Orientale naſturtii criſpi folio. Tourn. Cor. 15. *Eaſtern Dittander with a leaf like curled Creſs.*

8. LEPIDIUM (*Nudicaule*) ſcapo nudo ſimpliciſſimo, floribus tetrandris. Lœfl. It. 155. *Dittander with a ſingle naked ſtalk, and flowers with four ſtamina.* Naſturtium minimum vernum, foliis tantum circa radicem. Magn. Montp. 187.

9. LEPIDIUM (*Petræum*) foliis pinnatis integerrimis, petalis emarginatis calyce minoribus. Flor. Suec. *Dittander with entire winged leaves, and indented petals to the flowers which are ſmaller than the empalement.* Naſturtium pumilum vernum. C. B. P. 105.

10. LEPIDIUM (*Sativum*) floribus tetradynamis, foliis oblongis multifidis. Vir. Cliff. 63. *Dittander with ſix ſtamina in the flowers, and oblong leaves with many points.* Naſturtium hortenſe. *Garden Creſs.*

11. LEPIDIUM (*Subulatum*) foliis ſubulatis indiviſis ſparſis, caule ſuffruticoſo. Lin. Sp. 899. *Dittander with awl-ſhaped undivided leaves, and a ſhrubby ſtalk.* Lepidium capillaceo folio, fruticoſum Hiſpanicum. Tourn. Inſt. 216.

12. LEPIDIUM (*Ruderale*) floribus diandris apetalis, foliis radicalibus dentato-pinnatis, ramiferis linearibus integerrimis. Flor. Suec. 534. *Dittander with two ſtamina in the flowers, ſugacious petals, the bottom leaves indented, and thoſe on the branches linear and entire.* Naſturtium ſylveſtre Oſyridis folio. C. B. P. 105.

13. LEPIDIUM (*Bonarienſe*) floribus diandris tetrapetalis, foliis omnibus pinnato-multifidis. Lin. Sp. 901. *Dittander with two ſtamina and four petals to the flowers, and all the leaves wing-pointed.* Thlaſpi Bonarienſe multiciſſum flore inviſibili. Hort. Elth. 286.

The firſt ſort grows naturally in moiſt places in many parts of England, ſo is now ſeldom cultivated in gardens. It hath ſmall, white, creeping roots, by which it multiplies very faſt, ſo as to render it difficult to eradicate the plant, after it has grown long in any place; the lower leaves are oval, ſpear-ſhaped, about three inches long, and one and a half broad toward the baſe, ſawed upon the edges, having long foot-ſtalks. The ſtalks riſe two feet high, they are ſmooth, and

and fend out many fide branches; the leaves upon the ftalks are longer, narrower, and more acute-pointed than the lower, and are not fawed on their edges. The flowers grow in clofe bunches toward the top of the branches, which come out from the fide; they are fmall, and are compofed of four fmall white petals, which appear in June and July, and the feeds ripen in the autumn. The whole plant has a hot biting tafte like Pepper, and the leaves have been often ufed by the country people to give a relifh to their viands inftead of Pepper, from whence it had the appellation of Poor Man's Pepper.

This plant is eafily propagated, for every piece of the root will grow and multiply wherever it is planted, fo will become troublefome to root out after growing for fome time in a garden. The leaves of this plant bruifed and mixed with hog's lard, and applied as a cataplafm to the hip, help the fciatica; and chewed in the mouth, caufe a great defluxion of rheum, fo is faid to help fcrophulous-tumours in the throat.

The fecond fort grows naturally in Auftria and Italy; this hath a flefhy fibrous root, from whence arife feveral weak ftalks about a foot and a half high, which are garnifhed with fpear-fhaped leaves, three inches long and one and a half broad, deeply cut in upon the edges; thefe are fmooth, a little hoary, and embrace the ftalks with their bafe; the flowers are fmall, white, and grow in loofe bunches at the end of the branches. They flower from June till the beginning of September, and the feeds ripen in the autumn. This is a perennial plant, which propagates very faft by its roots, and is feldom admitted into gardens.

The third fort grows naturally about Aleppo; this hath creeping roots, which extend to a great diftance, fo will foon fpread over a large piece of ground. The leaves of this are longer and narrower than thofe of the former, and are lefs hoary; the flowers grow in loofe bunches at the end of the branches; they are fmall and white like thofe of the firft. This is a hardy perennial plant, which propagates by its creeping roots in as great plenty as either of the former.

The fourth fort grows naturally in the fouth of France, Italy, and Sicily, but is preferved in fome Englifh gardens for variety. This hath a long flefhy root, which runs deep into the ground, and fends out many oblong leaves, which are fawed on their edges, and fpread flat on the ground; the ftalks are flender, ftiff, and branch out horizontally on every fide; they rife about two feet high, and are garnifhed with very narrow entire leaves. The flowers come out in clofe fmall clufters at the ends of the branches; they are white, and appear in June and July, and the feeds ripen in the autumn. If the feeds are permitted to fcatter, the plants will come up early in the fpring, and require no other care but to keep them clean from weeds; the roots will abide feveral years if they are in a dry foil. This plant is alfo commended for its virtues in fciaticas, if bruifed and mixed with hog's lard as the firft, and from its virtues it obtained the title of Sciatica Crefs.

The fifth fort grows naturally in Perfia and Syria; this is fuppofed to be the true Mithridate Muftard of Diofcorides. It is an annual plant, whofe lower leaves are winged, and finely cut into many fegments; the ftalks rife a foot high, dividing into many flender branches, which are garnifhed with heart-fhaped leaves that are entire, and embrace the ftalks with their bafe. The flowers grow in long loofe fpikes from the end of the branches; they are fmall, yellow, and appear in June and July, and the feeds ripen in September, foon after which the plant decays.

The feeds of this plant fhould be fown in the autumn, for thofe which are fown in the fpring feldom flower the fame year, and are often killed by the froft in winter; whereas thofe which are fown in the autumn, or the plants that rife from fcattered feeds, will always flower about Midfummer, and the feeds ripen in Auguft and September following. The plants re-

quire no other care but to thin them, and keep them clean from weeds.

The fixth fort is an annual plant, which grows naturally in Virginia, and alfo in all the iflands of the Weft-Indies, where the inhabitants gather the leaves, and eat them in their fallads, as we do the Garden Crefs.

The lower leaves of this fort are three inches long and one broad, fawed on their edges, and are of a light green, with a biting tafte like Crefs. The ftalk rifes a foot and a half high, fending out a great number of fmall fide branches, which are garnifhed with narrow leaves regularly fawed on their edges, fo as to refemble winged leaves; thefe fit clofe to the branches. The flowers are produced at the end of the branches in loofe fpikes; they are fmall and white, and are fucceeded by roundifh or heart-fhaped compreffed feed-veffels, which have a border round them. It flowers in June and July, and the feeds ripen in the autumn; this fort is eafily propagated by feeds, which may be fown upon an open bed in April, where the plants are defigned to remain; and when they come up, they will require no other care but to thin them where they are too clofe, and keep them conftantly clean from weeds; or if the feeds are permitted to fcatter in the autumn, the plants will come up very well, and may be treated in the fame way as the other.

The feventh fort grows naturally in Afia, and alfo in Spain, from whence I have received the feeds. This is a biennial plant; the lower leaves which fpread on the ground, are near two inches long, and about half an inch broad, indented on both fides in fhape of a lyre, and curled on the edges; the ftalks rife a foot high, and divide into a great number of flender branches, garnifhed with fmall oblong leaves, which are cut on their fides, and a little curled on their edges; the ftalks and leaves are of a gray colour, inclining toward hoarinefs. The flowers are produced in clufters at the end of the branches; they are very fmall and white, appearing in July, and are fucceeded by roundifh bordered feed-veffels, which are compreffed, and have two cells each, containing two fmall oblong feeds, which are ripe in the autumn.

This fort may be propagated by feeds in the fame manner as the former; or if the feeds are permitted to fcatter in the autumn, the plants will come up without care, and fhould be treated in the fame way as the former fort; but this does not flower till the fecond year, fo the plants fhould be left farther afunder.

The eighth fort grows naturally about Montpelier. It is a fmall annual plant, having a few wing-pointed leaves which fpread on the furface of the ground; between which arifes a naked ftalk two or three inches high, fupporting five or fix fmall white flowers, each having four petals placed crofswife, and four ftamina placed near the ftyle; the germen afterward becomes a fhort capfule, including four or five roundifh feeds.

If the feeds of this fort are fown in the autumn, the plants will flower in April and their feeds ripen in May; which, if permitted to fcatter, the plants will come up in autumn, and require no other care but to thin them where they are too clofe, and weed them.

The ninth fort is alfo a low annual plant, which grows naturally on Putney-heath; the leaves of this are winged and entire, thefe are placed near the ground; the flower-ftalks rife two inches high, fupporting a few white flowers, whofe petals are lefs than the empalement, and are indented at their points. This flowers in May and June, and if their feeds are permitted to fcatter, the plants will come up as the former.

The tenth fort is the Garden Crefs, fo much ufed in winter and fpring fallads, and being fo well known requires no defcription. There are three varieties of this, one with broad leaves, another with curled leaves, and the common fort which is ufed; the feeds of of this fhould be fown in drills pretty clofe, in winter, on moderate hot-beds, but in fpring and autumn on borders, and will foon be fit for ufe; therefore fhould be cut while young, otherwife it will be too rank.

The eleventh fort is a low fhrubby plant, garnifhed with entire awl-fhaped leaves, which are very narrow; thefe are placed alternately on the ftalks; the foot-ftalks of the flowers proceed from the wings, and alfo terminate the ftalks; the flowers are white, and fhaped like thofe of the other fpecies.

This fort may be propagated by feeds or cuttings; the feeds fhould be fown in the fpring on a bed of light earth, in the open air; and when the plants are fit to tranfplant, a few of them fhould be planted in pots, which may be fheltered in winter under a common frame; for in fharp winters, thofe plants which are expofed in the open air are frequently killed: the remaining plants fhould be planted in a fheltered fituation in a dry rubbifhing ground, where they will grow flowly, fo will become more fhrubby, and in lefs danger of fuffering by cold.

The twelfth fort is an annual plant, which grows naturally in feveral parts of England, fo is rarely preferved in gardens, being a plant of no great beauty or ufe; yet I have known it eaten in fallads, though the tafte is very rank. The plants, when young, have fome refemblance to the Swine's Crefs. The ftalks rife eight or ten inches high, fupporting a number of fmall white flowers, fhaped like thofe of the other fpecies, which are fucceeded by feeds like thofe of the Garden Crefs, which, if permitted to fcatter, will abundantly fupply the place with young plants.

The thirteenth fort grows naturally in many warm countries, for it has come up in the earth which came from the Brafils, and from feveral parts of America, fo that it may be found in many other parts. The leaves and ftalks are much like thofe of the Garden Crefs, but are more divided, and differ in fmell and tafte from it: the petals of the flowers are fo fmall as to be almoft imperceptible, and there appears but two ftamina in each.

This fort is only cultivated in botanic gardens for variety; the feeds fhould be fown on a moderate hot-bed in the fpring, and when the plants have obtained ftrength, they may be tranfplanted on a warm border, where they will flower and perfect their feeds.

LEPIDOCARPODENDRON. See PROTEA.

LETTUCE. See LACTUCA.

LEUCANTHEMUM. See ANTHEMIS.

LEUCOJUM. Lin. Gen. Plant. 363. Narciffo-leucojum. Tourn. Inft. R. H. 387. tab. 208. [Λευκίον, of Λευκὸν, white, and Ἰον, a Violet; i. e. White Violet,] Snowdrop; in French, *Perce-neige*.

The CHARACTERS are,

It hath an oblong, obtufe, compreffed fpatha or fheath, which opens on the fide. The flower is of the fpreading bell fhape, cut into fix parts, which join at their bafe. It hath fix fhort briftly ftamina, terminated by oblong, obtufe, four-cornered fummits, which are erect. The roundifh germen is fituated under the flower, fupporting a ftyle which is thick and obtufe at the top, crowned by an erect briftly ftigma. The germen afterward becomes a turbinated capfule with three cells, opening with three valves, and filled with roundifh feeds.

This genus of plants is ranged in the firft fection of Linnæus's fixth clafs, which includes the plants whofe flowers have fix ftamina and one ftyle.

The SPECIES are,

1. LEUCOJUM (*Vernum*) fpathâ uniflorâ, ftylo clavato. Lin. Sp. Plant. 289. *Snowdrop with a fheath inclofing one flower, with a key-fhaped ftyle.* Narciffo-leucojum vulgare. Tourn. Inft. R. H. 387. *Common great Snowdrop.*

2. LEUCOJUM (*Æftivum*) fpathâ multiflorâ, ftylo clavato. Loef. Lin. Sp. Plant. 289. *Snowdrop with many flowers in a fheath, and a key-fhaped ftyle.* Narciffoleucojum pratenfe multiflorum. Tourn. Inft. R. H. 387. *Meadow Snowdrop with many flowers, commonly called the tall late Snowdrop.*

The firft fort grows naturally in Switzerland and Germany, as alfo upon the mountains near Turin. This hath an oblong bulbous root, fhaped like that of the Daffodil, but fmaller; the leaves are flat, of a deep green, four or five in number, broader and longer than thofe of the fmall Snowdrop; between thefe arife an angular ftalk near a foot high, which is naked, hollow, and channelled; toward the top comes out a fheath, which is whitifh, opening on the fide, out of which come two or three white flowers, hanging upon flender foot-ftalks; thefe have but one petal, which is cut into fix parts almoft to the bottom, which are much larger than thofe of the fmall Snowdrop, and the ends of the fegments of the petal are tipped with green, where they are of a thicker fubftance than in any other part. Thefe flowers appear in March, foon after thofe of the fmall fort; they have an agreeable fcent, not much unlike that of the flowers of Hawthorn; after the flower is paft, the germen which is fituated below the flower, fwells to a Pearfhaped capfule with three cells, inclofing feveral oblong feeds.

The leaves of this fort decay toward the end of May, after which time the roots may be taken up and tranfplanted, for they fhould not be long kept out of the ground. It is propagated here by offsets, which the roots put out pretty plentifully when they are in a fituation agreeable for them, and when they are not too often removed. They fhould have a foft, gentle, loamy foil, and an expofure to the eaft; the roots fhould be planted fix inches afunder, and four or five inches deep, and muft not be tranfplanted oftener than every third year.

The fecond fort is generally known by the title of late, or tall Snowdrop; this grows naturally in the meadows near Pifa in Italy, in Hungary, and alfo near Montpelier.

The root of this fort is nearly as large as thofe of the common Daffodil, and are very like them in fhape; the leaves alfo are not unlike thofe of the Daffodil, and are more in number than thofe of the other fort; they are of a pale green, and keel fhaped at the bottom, where they fold over each other, and embrace the ftalk, which rifes a foot and a half high; at the top is fituated a fpatha (or fheath) which opens on one fide, and lets out three or four flowers, which hang downward, upon pretty long foot-ftalks; thefe are cut into fix oval concave fegments almoft to the bottom, and are of a clear white, with a large green tip to each fegment, which is of a thicker confiftence than any other part of the petal; within are fituated fix awl-fhaped ftamina, with oblong yellow fummits, ftanding erect round a very flender ftyle, crowned by an obtufe ftigma. Thefe flowers appear the latter end of April or the beginnning of May, and as all flowers in each fheath do not come out together, but following each other, fo there is a fucceffion of them for three weeks or longer, in cool weather. The flowers are fucceeded by large triangular feed-veffels, having three cells, each containing two rows of feeds.

This fort is generally propagated in England by offfets, for the plants raifed by feeds will not come to flower in lefs than four years; and as the roots put out offsets in plenty, fo that is the more expeditious method. Thefe roots may be treated in the fame way as the firft fort, and fhould have a foft loamy foil, and be expofed only to the morning fun, where they will flower ftronger, and continue longer in beauty, than when they are in an open fituation, though they will thrive in almoft any foil or fituation.

LEUCOJUM INCANUM.
LEUCOJUM LUTEUM. } See CHEIRANTHUS.

LEUCOJUM BULBOSUM. See GALANTHUS.

LEVEL, a mathematical inftrument ferving to draw a line parallel to the horizon, not only for various ufes in mafonry, &c. but alfo to meafure the difference of afcent and defcent between feveral places, for the conveying of water, draining of fens, &c.

A Water

A water Level shews the horizontal line, by means of a surface of water, or other liquid, founded on this principle, That water always naturally places itself level.

The most simple instrument for this use is made of a long wooden trough, or canal, whose sides are parallel to its base, so that, being equally filled with water, the surface thereof shews the line of Level.

This Level is also made with two cups fixed to the two ends of a pipe three or four feet long, about an inch in diameter; by means whereof, the water communicates from the one to the other cup, and this pipe being moveable on its stand, by means of a ball and socket, when the two cups become equally full of water, the two surfaces mark the line of Level. Instead of cups, this instrument may be made with two short cylinders of glass three or four inches long, fastened to each end of the pipe with wax or mastich; then the pipe, being filled either with common or coloured water, will shew itself through the cylinder, by means of which the line of Level is determined, the height of the water, with respect to the center of the earth, being always the same in both cylinders. This Level is very commodious in levelling small distances.

If you would level any piece of ground that you can see from side to side, or from the middle to any side, set up your instrument in the middle of it, whether it be a water Level, or a ground Level with sights; place it so high, that you may see over the highest part of the ground half a foot or a foot; then set up a stake in the middle; so that the top may be exactly level with the sights, and another stake on the highest side, the top of which must be level with the middle stake; then either turn the Level, or look-back sight, and set up another stake on the lower ground level with the two first; then you will have three stakes standing in a Level.

Then keeping your Level true to the middle stake, turn it till it makes right angles with the three stakes, and set up two stakes on each side one Level with those three, then you will have five stakes in two lines set true level.

If the ground be large, you may set up two rows more by the Level, but five stakes are enough in a small ground.

When this is done, you may lay your Level aside, and look over the head of one to the head of another, and cause the person who assists you to put down stakes between two and two, till you have set as many stakes level in the ground as you think convenient; or you may use a rule, which being placed level with the head of the stake, you may look over that to the head of the other, and put stakes down between you and the other stake, to what number you please.

The ground being thus staked out with all the stakes heads level, and half a foot higher than the highest ground, in some grounds the middle stake, and the stakes in the cross line, will be the Level line the ground must be brought to; that is, abating the hill, and filling up the low side to the Level of the mid-line. But if the ground be very uneven, then you must measure over all the stakes, and take them middle high for their mean of Level, and, by the rule of three, proportion your ground to that.

As for instance: If a valley be ten poles in length, and two feet in depth from the strait line, and there be a hill five poles long; how many feet deep must a person sink those five poles to fill up the valley? This question may be resolved by the inverse or back rule of three, and will stand thus: As 5 to 2, so is 10 to 4.

$$5 \text{---} 2 \text{---} 10$$
$$2$$
$$5)20(4$$

So that a person must go four feet deep in such a hill to make good such a valley.

If you are to abut the top of the hill four feet deep,

and two poles from the top of that hill, those four feet are to come out.

To perform this, set up a stake on the top of a hill two or three feet above ground, and another of the same height where the depth comes out, set down a stake three rods from that, till the head comes to be in a line with these two, and at that stake you must be one foot deep.

At six poles stake down another as before, and there you must be two feet deep: then stake down another at nine poles, and there you must be three feet deep, and you may set more stakes at equal distances, which will direct you so as that you cannot go amiss.

LEVITY is the privation or want of weight in any body, when compared with another which is heavier, in which sense it is opposed to gravity.

The schoolmen maintain, that there is such a thing as positive and absolute Levity, and impute this to the rise and emergency of bodies lighter in specie than the fluids wherein they rise.

But, besides that the common sense of mankind discovers, that Levity is only a relative term, we find that all bodies tend towards the earth, some slower, and some faster, in all fluids or mediums, whether water, air, &c.

Thus cork is said to be lighter than gold, because under equal dimensions of bulk the gold will sink in, and the cork swim upon the water.

Archimedes has demonstrated, That a solid body will float any where in a fluid of the same specific gravity, and that a lighter body will keep above a heavier.

The reason of this is, because bodies falling towards the earth, those which have a like number of equal parts, have equal gravity, since the gravity of the whole is the sum of the gravity of all its parts.

Now, two bodies having an equal number of equal parts, if under the same dimensions there are no intervals destitute of matter; whence it follows, that as no portion of matter is so small, but that body wherein it is contained may be wholly divided into parts equally small, there can be no reason for the descent of these, which will not hold equally for the descent of that.

Hence it may be concluded, that those bodies which do not equally gravitate under the same dimensions, do not contain the same equal portions of matter, and therefore when we see, that a cube of gold subsides in water, at the same time that an equal bulk of cork swims upon it, it is evident, that the gold must have a greater number of equal parts of matter under the same bulk than the cork, or the cork must have a greater number of vacuities than the gold, and that there are also in the water a greater number of vacuities than in the gold.

Hence we have a clear idea both of density or gravity, and of Levity, and know, that in a strict sense the latter cannot be accounted any thing positive, but a mere negation, or absence of body, which determines that body to be lighter than another which contains more matter.

LICHEN. Liverwort.

There being two sorts of this plant which are used in medicine, and one of those being accounted a sovereign remedy for the bite of mad dogs, I thought it would not be improper to mention them here, though they are plants which cannot be propagated by any method, except by paring up the turf of Grass whereon they grow, and laying it down on some moist shady place, where, if the turf takes root, and thrives, the plants will spread and do well.

The two Sorts are,

1. Lichen (*Petræus*) petræus latifolius, five Hepatica fontana. C. B. P. *Common broad-leaved Liverwort.*

2. Lichen (*Officinarum*) terrestris cinereus. Raii Syn. *Ash-coloured Ground Liverwort.*

The first sort grows on the sides of wells, and in moist shady places, not only on the ground, but on stones, bricks, or wood. Of this there are several varieties,

     which

which are diftinguifhed by the curious in botany; but as they are plants of no ufe, I fhall not enumerate them.

The fecond fort (which is ufed to cure the bite of mad dogs) grows on commons and open heaths, where the Grafs is fhort, and the ground almoft bare, in moft parts of England, efpecially on declivities, and on the fides of pits. This fpreads on the furface of the ground, and, when in perfection, is of an Afh-colour, but as it grows old, it alters, and becomes of a dark colour. This is often carried into gardens with the turf which is laid for walks and flopes; and where the foil is moift and cool, it will fpread, and be difficult to deftroy, fo that it renders the Grafs unfightly; but this is the only method yet known to have it grow in gardens, where it is defired. This is efteemed a fovereign remedy for the bite of mad dogs, and hath been for many years ufed with great fuccefs. It was communicated to the Royal Society by Mr. George Dampier, whofe uncle had long ufed this plant, to cure the bite of mad dogs on men and animals, with infallible fuccefs. The method of taking it he has delivered as followeth : " Take of the " herb, and dry it either in an oven, by the fire, or " in the fun; then powder it, and pafs it through a " fine fieve; mix this with an equal quantity of fine " powdered pepper. The common dofe of this mix- " ture is four fcruples, which may be taken in warm " milk, beer, ale, or broth." He alfo advifes, that the part bitten be well wafhed, as alfo the clothes of the perfon who was bit, left any of the fnivel, or drivel of the mad dog fhould remain. If the perfon bitten be full grown, he advifes, that he be blooded before the medicine is taken, and to ufe the remedy as foon after the bite as poffible, as alfo to repeat the dofe two or three feveral mornings fafting.

LIGHT is ufed in various fenfes: 1. Sometimes it fignifies that fenfation which is occafioned in the mind by the view of luminous bodies.

2. For thofe properties in thofe bodies, whereby they are fitted to excite thofe fenfations in us.

3. A certain action of the luminous body on the medium between that and the eye, by the means of which the one is fuppofed to act on the other, and this is called fecondary Light, or derived Light, in diftinction to that of luminous bodies, which is called primary or innate Light.

As to the phænomenon of light, philofophers have explained it feveral ways; Ariftotle by fuppofing fome bodies to be tranfparent, as air, water, ice, &c. The Cartefians have confiderably refined upon this notion of Light, and own, that Light, as it exifts in the luminous body, is nothing elfe but a power or faculty of exciting in us a very clear and vivid fenfation; and Father Malebranche explains the nature of Light by a fuppofed analogy between it and found, the latter of which is allowed to be produced by the fhaking or vibration of the infenfible parts of the fonorous body.

But the greateft difcoveries into this wonderful phænomenon have been made by Sir Ifaac Newton, that the primary light confifts wholly in a certain motion of the particles of the lucid body, whereby they do not propel any fictitious matter fuppofed to be lodged in the hidden pores of tranfparent bodies, but throw off from the luminous body certain very fmall particles, which are emitted every way with great force. And the fecondary or derived Light, not in a conatus, but in a real motion of thefe particles receding every way from the luminous body in right lines, and with an incredible velocity.

For it has been demonftrated by Mr. Reaumur, from the obfervation on the fatellites of Jupiter, that the progrefs of Light from the fun to our earth is not above ten minutes, and therefore, fince the earth is at leaft 10,000 of its own diameters diftant from the fun, Light muft run 10,000 of thofe diameters in a minute, which is above 100,000 miles in a fecond. And if a bullet, moving with the fame celerity with which it leaves the muzzle of a cannon, requires twenty-five years to pafs from the earth to the fun, as Mr. Huygens has computed; then the velocity of Light will be to that of a cannon ball, as twenty-five years is to ten minutes, which is above 10,000 to 1 : fo that the particles of Light move above a million of times fwifter than a cannon ball, from which rapidity of motion very ftrange effects may be produced; but Sir Ifaac Newton has fhewn, paft contradiction, that the Light of the fun is near feven minutes in its paffage to the earth, which is the fpace of 50,000,000, a velocity 10,000,000 times greater than that wherewith a ball flies out of the mouth of a cannon.

Sir Ifaac Newton alfo obferves, that bodies and Light act mutually on one another: bodies on Light, in emitting, reflexing, refracting, and inflecting it, and Light on bodies, by heating them, and putting their parts into a vibrating motion, wherein heat principally confifts; for he obferves, that all fixed bodies, when heated beyond a certain degree, emit Light and fhine, which fhining, &c. appears to be owing to the vibrating motion of the parts, and all bodies abounding in earthy and fulphureous particles, if they be fufficiently agitated emit Light, which way foever the agitation be effected,

The fame great author obferves, that there are but three affections of Light wherein the rays differ, viz. refrangibility, reflexibility, and colour; and thofe rays which agree in refrangibility, agree alfo in the other two, whence they may be well defined homogeneal. Again, the colours exhibited by homogeneal Light, he calls homogeneal colours, and thofe produced by heterogeneal Light, heterogeneal colours; from which definitions he advances feveral propofitions :

1. That the fun's Light confifts of rays differing by indefinite degrees of refrangibility.

2. That rays, which differ in refrangibility, when parted from one another, do proportionably differ in the colours which they exhibit.

3. That there are as many fimple and homogeneal colours, as there are degrees of refrangibility, for to every degree of refrangibility belongs a different colour.

4. Whitenefs, in all refpects, like that of the fun's immediate Light, and of all the ufual objects of our fenfes, cannot be compounded of fimple colours, without an indefinite variety of them, for to fuch a compofition there are required rays endued with all the indefinite degrees of refrangibility, which infer as many fimple colours.

5. The rays of Light do not act one on another in paffing through the fame medium.

6. The rays of Light do not fuffer any alteration of their qualities from refraction, nor from the adjacent quiefcent medium.

7. There can be no homogeneal colours produced out of Light by refraction, which are not commixed in it before, fince refraction changes not the qualities of the rays, but only feparates thofe that have divers qualities by means of their different refrangibility.

8. The fun's Light is an aggregate of homogeneal colours, whence homogeneal colours may be called primitive or original.

Hence proceeds the whole theory of colours in plants and flowers.

Thofe parts, v. g. which are the moft refrangible, conftitute Violet colour, the dimmeft and moft languid of all colours.

And, on the contrary, thofe particles that are the leaft refrangible, conftitute a ray or a red colour, which is the brighteft and moft vivid of all colours; the other particles being diftinguifhed into little rays, according to their refpective magnitudes and degrees of refrangibility, excite intermediate vibrations, and fo occafion the fenfations of the intermediate colours. See Sir Ifaac Newton's Doctrine of Colours.

Perhaps thefe obfervations of Light may to fome perfons feem foreign to the fubject matter of this book, yet, if thoroughly underftood might probably be found very ufeful. The learned and curious enquirer into the bufinefs of vegetation, the Rev. Dr. Hales,

Hales, in his treatise on that head, does, upon the query put by Sir Isaac Newton [" Are not grofs bo- " dies and Light convertible into one another? And " may not bodies receive much of their activity " from the particles of Light which enter their com- " pofition? The change of bodies into Light, and " of Light into bodies, is very conformable to the " courfe of nature, which feems delighted with tranf- " mutations,"] add this query, " And may not " Light alfo, by freely entering the expanded fur- " faces of leaves and flowers, contribute much to the " ennobling the principles of vegetables?"

That Light has been found to be of infinite fervice to the growth of vegetables, has been fully proved by many experiments: 1. By painting the walls of the infide of a green-houfe black, whereby there will be no reflected rays of Light, when the weather be- comes fo cold, as that the fhutters to the windows have been obliged to be kept fhut a few days, the leaves of thofe plants which have been placed therein have dropped off.

And plants which have been placed in dark rooms, have been found to do the fame. The earthing up plants to blanch them, whereby they become tender, and better for ufe; yet if thefe are not ufed, when properly blanched, will foon decay: the like will happen if plants are covered clofe, fo as no Light can come to them, they will foon grow pale and ficken, and afterward decay.

How much the fine racy flavour of fruits is owing to Light is hard to fay, but from a few experiments it appears, moft of their rich juices are beholden to Light for their excellence; therefore we may truly aver, that Light is as neceffary to promote vegeta- tion as for animal œconomy.

LIGUSTICUM. Tourn. Inft. R. H. 323. tab. 171. Lin. Gen. Plant. 308. [takes its name of Ligu- ria, becaufe this plant, in old time, grew in greateft plenty near a river of Genoa, called Liguria.] Lo- vage; in French, Livéche.

The CHARACTERS are, *It hath an umbellated flower. The general umbel is com- pofed of feveral fmaller, which are alfo compofed of other yet fmaller. The general umbel has an involucrum com- pofed of feven unequal leaves. The perianthium of the flower is indented in five parts, fitting upon the germen. The flower hath five equal petals, which are inflexed at their points, and keel-fhaped within. It hath five hairy ftamina, which are fhorter than the petals, terminated by fimple fummits. The germen, which is fituated under the flower, fupports two fimple ftyles, crowned by fimple ftig- mas. The germen afterward turns to an oblong fruit, di- vided into two parts, which is angular and channelled, containing two oblong fmooth feeds.*

This genus of plants is ranged in the fecond fection of Linnæus's fifth clafs, which contains thofe plants whofe flowers have five ftamina and two ftyles.

The SPECIES are,

1. LIGUSTICUM (*Leviflicum*) foliis multiplicibus, foliolis fuperne incifis. Hort. Cliff. 97. *Lovage with many leaves, whofe lobes are cut outward toward the top.* Le- vifticum vulgare. Mor. Hift. 3. p. 275. *Common Lovage.*

2. LIGUSTICUM (*Scoticum*) foliis biternatis. Lin. Sp. Plant. 250. *Lovage with double trifoliate leaves* Li- gufticum. Scoticum Apii folio. Tourn. Inft. R. H. 324. *Scotch Lovage with a Smallage leaf.*

3. LIGUSTICUM (*Auftriacum*) foliis bipinnatis, foliolis confluentibus incifis integerrimis. Lin. Sp. 360. *Lo- vage with double winged leaves, whofe lobes run together, and have entire fegments.* Ligufticum cicutæ folio glabrum. Tourn. Inft. R. H. 323. *Lovage with a fmooth Hemlock leaf.*

4. LIGUSTICUM (*Lucidum*) foliis pinnatifidis, foliolis li- nearibus planis. *Lovage with wing-pointed leaves, whofe lobes are very narrow and plain.* Ligufticum Pyrenai- cum, fœniculi folio lucidum. Tourn. Inft. 324. *Lo- vage of the Pyrenees, with a fhining Fennel leaf.*

5. LIGUSTICUM (*Peloponnefiacum*) foliis multiplicato- pinnatis, foliolis pinnatim incifis. Lin. Sp. 36. *Lo-*

vage with leaves many times winged, and lobes cut like wings. Cicutaria latifolia fœtida. C. B. P. 161. *Broad- leaved, ftinking, Baftard Hemlock.*

The firft fort is the common Lovage of the fhops; this was formerly cultivated in the kitchen-gardens as an efculent herb, but has been long difufed as fuch in England. It grows naturally upon the Appenines, and alfo near the river Liguria not far from Genoa; this hath a ftrong, flefhy, perennial root, which ftrikes deep into the ground, and is compofed of many ftrong flefhy fibres covered with a brown fkin, and has a ftrong, hot, aromatic fmell and tafte. The leaves are large, winged, and compofed of many large lobes fhaped like thofe of Smallage, but are larger, and of a deeper green. The lobes toward the top are cut into acute fegments. The ftalks rife to the height of fix or feven feet; they are large and channelled, dividing into feveral branches, each being terminated by a large umbel of yellow flowers, which are fuc- ceeded by oblong ftriated feeds. It flowers in June and July, and the feeds ripen in autumn.

This is eafily propagated by feeds, which fhould be fown in autumn foon after they are ripe; for when they are kept out of the ground till fpring, they fel- dom grow the firft year; when the plants come up and are fit to remove, they may be tranfplanted into a moift rich border, at about three feet diftance from each other; and after they have taken new root, they will require no other care but to keep them clean from weeds. The roots will abide many years, and where the feeds are permitted to fcatter, the plants will come up without care.

The roots, leaves, and feeds of Lovage, are heating and drying; they warm and comfort the ftomach, expel wind, and provoke urine.

The fecond fort grows naturally near the fea in many parts of Scotland; this hath a biennial root, but of much lefs fize than the former; the leaves are com- pofed of broader and fhorter lobes, each leaf having two or three trifoliate leaves, whofe lobes are in- dented on their edges. The ftalk rifes about a foot high, fuftaining a fmall umbel of yellow flowers on the top, fhaped like thofe of the former; thefe appear in June, and are fucceeded by oblong chan- nelled feeds, which ripen in autumn. This plant may be cultivated in the fame manner as the former.

The third fort grows naturally on the Alps; this is a perennial plant. The ftalks rife about two feet high, and at every joint are bent alternately, firft to one fide, then to the oppofite; at every joint they are garnifhed with doubly winged leaves, compofed of fmall lobes which run into each other, and juft above each leaf comes out a fide branch; thefe, as alfo the principal ftalks, are terminated by umbels of white flowers, which appear in June, and are fuc- ceeded by oblong channelled feeds, which ripen in autumn.

The fourth fort grows naturally on the Pyrenean Mountains; this hath a biennial root. The leaves are doubly winged. The lobes are very narrow, and finely divided. The ftalks are ftrong, and rife a foot and a half high, garnifhed with fhining winged leaves, and are terminated by pretty large umbels of whitifh flowers, which appear in June, and the feeds ripen in September.

The fifth fort grows naturally on the Peloponefian Mountains; this hath a very thick flefhy root like that of Parfnep, which ftrikes deep in the ground. The leaves are very large, being compofed of many winged leaves, whofe lobes are cut into acute points; thefe are of a deep green, and, when bruifed, emit a fœtid odour. The ftalks rife three or four feet high; they are very large and hollow, like thofe of Hem- lock, and fuftain at their top large umbels of yellowifh flowers, in fhape of a corymbus; thefe appear in June, and are fucceeded by oblong channelled feeds which ripen in autumn.

This has by fome perfons been thought to be the Hemlock of the antients, their conjectures being founded upon the plant anfwering in many particulars

lars to the defcription, and alfo from the poifonous quality of this together with its fœtid fcent ; and as this grows naturally in many parts of Afia, fo they have been induced to believe it might be the fame plant.

All thefe plants are preferved in botanic gardens for the fake of variety, but are feldom cultivated any where elfe ; they rife eafily from feeds, which fhould be fown in autumn, and the plants afterward treated in the fame way as the firft ; they love a moift foil and a fhady fituation.

LIGUSTRUM. Tourn. Inft. R. H. 596. tab. 367. Lin. Gen. Plant. 18. Privet ; in French, Troène.

The CHARACTERS are,

The flower has a fmall tubular empalement, cut at the top into four obtufe fegments. It hath one funnel-fhaped petal, with a cylindrical tube cut into four oval fegments at the top, which fpread open. It hath two ftamina which ftand oppofite, terminated by erect fummits which are the length of the tube of the petal, and one roundifh germen fupporting a fhort ftyle, crowned by an obtufe bifid ftigma. The germen afterward turns to a fmooth round berry with one cell, inclofing two oblong feeds, flat on one fide, but convex on the other.

This genus of plants is ranged in the firft fection of Linnæus's fecond clafs, which includes thofe plants whofe flowers have two ftamina and one ftyle.

The SPECIES are,

1. LIGUSTRUM (*Vulgare*) foliis lanceolato-ovatis obtufls. *Privet with fpear-fhaped, oval, obtufe leaves.* Liguftrum Germanicum. C. B. P. 475. *The common Privet.*

2. LIGUSTRUM (*Italicum*) foliis lanceolatis acutis. *Privet with fpear-fhaped leaves.* Liguftrum foliis majoribus & magis acuminatis toto anno folia retinens. Pluk. Alm. 217. *Privet with larger and more acutepointed leaves, which continue all the year, commonly called the Italian ever-green Privet.*

The firft fort grows common in the hedges in moft parts of England, where it rifes fifteen or fixteen feet high, with a woody ftem, covered with a fmooth gray bark, fending out many lateral branches which are garnifhed with fpear-fhaped, oval, fmooth leaves, ending with obtufe points ; they are placed by pairs oppofite, fitting clofe to the branches, and are of a dark green. The flowers are produced in thick fpikes at the end of the branches ; they are white, with one tubular petal cut at the top into four parts, which fpread open. Thefe come out in June, and are fucceeded by fmall round black berries, which ripen in the autumn ; each of thefe contain two feeds. The leaves of this fort frequently remain green till after Chriftmas, when they alter their colour and fall off. There are two varieties of this fort, one whofe leaves are variegated with white, and the other hath leaves variegated with yellow ; but in order to preferve thefe varieties, they fhould be planted in poor land ; for if they are in a rich foil, they will grow vigorous and foon become plain.

The other fort grows naturally in Italy ; this rifes with a ftronger ftalk than the former, the branches are lefs pliable and grow more erect ; their bark is of a lighter colour ; the leaves are much larger, and end in acute points ; they are alfo of a brighter green, and continue upon the fhrubs in verdure, till they are thruft off by the young leaves in the fpring, as the Phillyrea and moft other Evergreens do ; fo that it is undoubtedly a diftinct fort, though many have fuppofed they were the fame. The flowers of this are rather larger than thofe of the common fort, and are not often fucceeded by berries in this country.

The leaves and flowers of the firft fort are ufed in medicine ; they are reckoned to be cooling, drying, and reftringent, good for ulcers and inflammations of the mouth and throat, bleeding of the gums, and relaxation of the uvula.

This fhrub is frequently cultivated in the nurferies near London, to furnifh the fmall gardens and balconies in the city, it being one of the few plants which will thrive in the fmoke of London ; but although it will live fome years in the clofe part of the town, yet it feldom produces flowers there after the firft year, unlefs it is in fome open places, where there is a free air. In the country, the leaves of this plant will continue green great part of the winter. It flowers in June, and the berries ripen in autumn, which generally hang upon the branches till Chriftmas.

The Italian fort is now generally preferred to the common fort for planting in gardens, the leaves being larger and continuing green all the year, renders it more valuable ; and being fo hardy as to refift the greateft cold in this country, it may be planted in any fituation where the common fort will thrive. I have frequently planted it under the dropping of large trees, where I find it will thrive better than moft other fhrubs.

I cannot but think this fort which is the moft common in Italy, is the Liguftrum mentioned by Virgil in the fecond Eclogue : and my reafon for it is, that as the flowers of this fhrub are of a pure white, but fall off very foon, they are by no means proper to gather for garlands, &c. and the berries being of a fine black colour, and continuing long upon the plants, make a fine appearance. To confirm that thefe berries were gathered for ufe, we find in feveral authors of undoubted credit, that they were ufed in dyeing, as alfo that the beft ink was made of thefe berries. Befides, is it not much more reafonable to fuppofe, that Virgil would rather draw his comparifon from the flowers and fruit of the fame plant, when he is warning the youth not to truft to his beauty, than to mention two different plants, as has been generally fuppofed ? for here are the white flowers of the Privet appearing early in the fpring, which is an allufion to youth ; but thefe are of fhort duration, foon falling away ; whereas the berries, which may be applied to mature age, are of long continuance, and are gathered for ufe.

Thefe plants are eafily propagated by laying down their tender fhoots in autumn, which in one year's time will be rooted enough to tranfplant ; when they may be removed to the places where they are defigned to remain, or planted in a nurfery for two or three years, where they may be trained for the purpofes defigned.

They are alfo propagated by fuckers, which thefe plants fend forth in great plenty ; but thefe are too apt to put out a great number of fuckers from their roots, fo are not eafily kept within bounds ; nor do the plants rife fo high as thofe which are propagated by layers, therefore this method fhould be preferred.

They may alfo be propagated by cuttings, which, if planted in the autumn on a fhady border and in a loamy foil, will take root very freely, and may be afterward treated in the fame way as the layers.

But the ftrongeft and beft plants, are thofe which are raifed from feeds ; indeed, this is a much more tedious method than the other, fo is feldom practifed, for the feeds generally lie a year in the ground before they vegetate ; therefore, whoever would propagate the plants in this method, fhould gather the berries when ripe, and put them into a pot with fand between them, and bury the pot in the ground, as is practifed for Holly berries and Haws ; and after they have laid a year in the ground, take them up in the autumn, and fow them on a border expofed to the eaft, where the plants will come up the following fpring, and thefe will make great progrefs after they have gotten fome ftrength, fo will grow upright, and not fend out fuckers like the other.

Formerly thefe plants were greatly in ufe for hedges, but fince fo many others of great beauty have been introduced, which are much preferable to thefe for fuch purpofes, they have been entirely rejected, the trouble of keeping them in order being very great ; nor are the hedges made with them ever fo thick and handfome, as thofe made with divers other plants. The two variegated kinds are pretty varieties amongft other ftriped fhrubs. Thefe may be propagated by budding, or inarching them upon the plain fort, as alfo

alfo by laying down their branches; but as they feldom shoot so fast, as to produce any branches proper for layers, the other method is chiefly used. The silver striped sort is somewhat tenderer than the plain, but will endure the open air, if planted in a dry soil and in a warm situation. .

LILAC. See SYRINGA.

LILIASTRUM. See HEMEROCALLIS.

LILIO-ASPHODELUS. See HEMEROCALLIS and CRINUM.

LILIO-FRITILLARIA. See FRITILLARIA.

LILIO-HYACINTHUS. See SCILLA.

LILIO-NARCISSUS. See AMARYLLIS.

LILIUM. Tourn. Inst. R. H. 369. tab. 191. Lin. Gen. Plant. 371. [takes its name of λᾶσ, smooth, polished, because its leaves are, as it were, polished; or of λιριὸν, which signifies the same thing,] the Lily; in French, Lis.

The CHARACTERS are,

The flower has no empalement; it hath six petals, which are narrow at their base, but are broad, obtuse, and reflexed at their points. The flower is of the open bell-shape, the petals are thick, obtuse, and keel-shaped; on their back each petal has a narrow longitudinal nectarium at their base. It hath six stamina which are erect and shorter than the petals, terminated by oblong prostrate summits, with a cylindrical oblong germen having six furrows, supporting a cylindrical style the length of the petals, crowned by a thick triangular stigma. The germen afterward becomes an oblong capsule with six rough furrows followed at the top, having three cells which are filled with flat half round seeds, lying above each other in a double order.

This genus of plants is ranged in the first section of Linnaeus's sixth class, which includes those plants whose flowers have six stamina and one style.

The SPECIES are,

1. LILIUM (*Candidum*) foliis sparsis, corollis campanulatis erectis, intus glabris. Hort. Cliff. 120. *Lily with sparsed leaves, and a bell-shaped erect flower which is smooth within.* Lilium album, flore erecto & vulgare. C. B. P. 76. *Common white Lily with an erect flower.*

2. LILIUM (*Peregrinum*) foliis sparsis, corollis campanulatis cernuis, petalis basi angustioribus. *Lily with sparsed leaves, and a bell-shaped nodding flower, whose petals are narrower at their base.* Lilium album, floribus dependentibus, sive peregrinum. C. B. P. 76. *White foreign Lily with pendent flowers.*

3. LILIUM (*Bulbiferum*) foliis sparsis, corollis campanulatis erectis, intus scabris. Hort. Cliff. 120. *Lily with sparsed leaves, and an erect bell-shaped flower, rough within.* Lilium purpureo-croceum majus. C. B. P. 76. *Greater Lily with a purple Saffron-coloured flower, commonly called Orange Lily.*

4. LILIUM (*Humile*) humile, foliis linearibus sparsis, corollis campanulatis erectis, caule bulbifero. *Dwarf Lily with narrow sparsed leaves, erect bell-shaped flowers, and a stalk bearing bulbs.* Lilium bulbiferum minus. C. B. P. 77. *Smaller bulb-bearing Lily, by some called the fiery Lily.*

5. LILIUM (*Pomponium*) foliis sparsis subulatis, floribus reflexis, corollis revolutis. Hort. Cliff. 120. *Lily with awl-shaped sparsed leaves and reflexed flowers, whose petals are turned backward.* Lilium rubrum angustifolium. C. B. P. 78. *Narrow-leaved red Lily or Martagon.*

6. LILIUM (*Angustifolium*) foliis linearibus sparsis, pedunculis longissimis. *Lily with narrow sparsed leaves, and very long foot-stalks to the flowers.* Lilium brevi & gramineo folio. C. B. P. 79. *Lily with a short Grass leaf, commonly called Martagon of Pompony,*

7. LILIUM (*Chalcedonicum*) foliis sparsis lanceolatis, floribus reflexis, corollis revolutis. Hort. Cliff. 120. *Lily with sparsed spear-shaped leaves, and reflexed flowers whose petals turn backward.* Lilium Byzantinum miniatum. C. B. P. 78. *Lily of Byzantium with a carmine flower, commonly called the scarlet Martagon.*

8. LILIUM (*Superbum*) foliis sparsis lanceolatis, floribus pyramidatis reflexis, corollis revolutis. *Lily with sparsed spear-shaped leaves, and pyramidal reflexed flowers,*

whose petals turn backward. Martagon multis & magnis floribus luteis alios superans. Suvert. Icon. Pl. 57. *The great yellow Martagon.*

9. LILIUM (*Martagon*) foliis verticillatis, floribus reflexis, corollis revolutis. Hort. Cliff. 120. *Lily with leaves growing in whorls, and reflexed flowers whose petals turn backward.* Lilium floribus reflexis montanum. C. B. P. 77. *Mountain Lily with reflexed flowers, commonly called purple Martagon.*

10. LILIUM (*Hirsutum*) foliis verticillatis hirsutis, floribus reflexis, corollis revolutis. *Lily with hairy leaves growing in whorls, and reflexed flowers whose petals turn backward.* Lilium floribus reflexis alterum lanugine hirsutum. C. B. P. 718. *Another Lily with reflexed flowers which is hairy and downy, commonly called the red Martagon.*

11. LILIUM (*Canadense*) foliis verticillatis, floribus reflexis corollis revolutis. Lin. Sp. Plant. 303. *Lily with leaves growing in whorls, and reflexed bell-shaped flowers.* Lilium, sc. martagon Canadense maculatum. Mor. Hist. 2. p. 408. *Lily, or Martagon of Canada with spotted flowers.*

12. LILIUM (*Campschatense*) foliis verticillatis, floribus erectis, corollis campanulatis. Amœn. Acad. 2. p. 348. *Lily with leaves growing in whorls, and an erect bell-shaped flower.*

13. LILIUM (*Philadelphicum*) foliis verticillatis brevibus, corollis campanulatis, unguibus petalorum angustioribus, floribus erectis. Icon. tab. 165. *Lily with very short leaves growing in whorls, and bell-shaped flowers whose petals are very narrow at their base.*

There is a greater variety of Martagons than are here mentioned, but as they are supposed to be only accidental arising from culture, so I thought it would be to little purpose to insert them here; therefore I shall only give their common titles hereafter.

The common white Lily is so well known as to need no description; this grows naturally in Palestine and Syria, but has been long cultivated in all the gardens of Europe. It is so hardy that no frost ever injures the roots in England, and it propagates so fast by offsets from the roots, that it is become so common as to be little regarded, though there is great beauty in the flowers, and they emit an agreeable odour. Of this sort there are the following varieties:

The white Lily striped with purple.

The white Lily with variegated leaves.

The white Lily with double flowers.

These are varieties which have accidentally risen from culture; the sort with variegated flowers has not been in England much more than thirty-five years, but is now very common in most of the gardens, and is by some persons esteemed for the variety of its purple stripes; but as the pure white of the flower is stained by the purple, so as to appear of a dull colour, therefore many prefer the common white Lily. The sort with variegated leaves is chiefly valued for its appearance in winter and spring, for as the leaves come up early in the autumn, which spread themselves flat on the ground, and being finely edged with broad yellow stripes, they make a pretty appearance during the winter and spring months. The flowers are the same as those of the common sort, but appear earlier in summer, which may be occasioned by the roots being weaker than those of the plain sort, for all variegated plants are weaker than those which are plain. The white Lily with double flowers is less valuable than either of the other, because their flowers never open well, unless they are covered with glasses to shelter them from the rain and dew, so often rot without expanding. These flowers have none of the agreeable odour which the single sort is valued for, even when they open the fairest; for as by the multiplicity of petals in the flowers, the parts of generation are destroyed, so there is a want of the fecundating powder from whence the odour is sent out.

The roots, leaves, and flowers of the common white Lily are used in medicine; the roots are frequently used to soften, ripen, and digest tumours and hard swellings. Matthiolus says, that the distilled water

8 A   of

of the flowers, is properly and fuccefsfully given to women in hard labour ; and the diftilled water of the leaves is of great ufe in diftempers of the lungs.

The white Lily with dependent flowers, was originally brought from Conftantinople. This is by fome fuppofed to be only a variety of the common fort, but is undoubtedly a diftinct fpecies ; the ftalk is much flenderer than the common, the leaves are narrower and fewer in number ; the flowers are not quite fo large, and the petals are more contracted at their bafe ; thefe always hang downward, whereas thofe of the common fort grow erect. The ftalks of this kind fometimes are very broad and flat, and appear as if two or three were joined together ; when this happens, they fuftain from fixty to a hundred flowers, and fometimes more ; this has occafioned many to think it a different fort, who have mentioned this with broad ftalks and many flowers as a diftinct fpecies, though it is accidental, for the fame root fcarce ever produces the fame two years.

Thefe forts are eafily propagated by offsets, which the roots fend out in fo great plenty, as to make it neceffary to take them off every other, or at moft every third year, to prevent their weakening the principal roots. The time for removing the roots is at the end of Auguft, foon after the ftalks decay ; for if they are left longer in the ground, they will foon put out new fibres and leaves, when it will be improper to remove them, becaufe that will prevent their flowering the following fummer. They will thrive in almoft any foil or fituation, and as they grow tall and fpread, fo they muft be allowed room ; therefore in fmall gardens they take up too much fpace, but in large borders they are very ornamental.

The common Orange or red Lily, is as well known in the Englifh gardens as the white Lily, and has been as long cultivated here. This grows naturally in Auftria and fome parts of Italy. This fort multiplies very faft by offsets from the roots, and is now fo common, as to be almoft rejected ; however, in large gardens thefe fhould not be wanting, for they make a good appearance when in flower, if they are properly difpofed. Of this fort there are the following varieties :

The Orange Lily with double flowers.

The Orange Lily with variegated leaves.

The fmaller Orange Lily.

Thefe varieties have been obtained by culture, and are preferred in the gardens of florifts. They all flower in June and July, and their ftalks decay in September, when the roots may be tranfplanted, and their offsets taken off, which fhould be done once in two or three years, otherwife their bunches will be too large, and the flower-ftalks weak. This doth not put out new leaves till toward fpring, fo that the roots may be tranfplanted at any time after the ftalks decay till near Chriftmas. It will thrive in any foil or fituation, but will be ftrongeft in a foft gentle loam not too moift.

The bulb-bearing fiery Lily feldom rifes much more than half the height of the former ; the leaves are narrower, the flowers are fmaller, and of a brighter flame colour ; they are few in number, and ftand more erect. Thefe come out a month before the common fort, and the ftalks put out bulbs at moft of the joints, which, if taken off, when the ftalks decay, and planted, will produce plants, fo that it may be propagated in plenty. There are feveral varieties of this, which are mentioned as diftinct fpecies, but are fuppofed to have been produced by culture. Thefe are,

The greater broad-leaved bulb-bearing Lily.

The many-flowered bulb-bearing Lily.

The fmall bulb-bearing Lily.

The hoary bulb-bearing Lily.

All thefe forts of Lilies will thrive under the fhade of trees, fo may be introduced in plantations, and on the borders of woods, where they will have a good effect during the time they are in flower.

There is a great variety of the Martagon Lily ;

thefe differ from the common Lilies, in having their petals reflexed backward in form of a Turk's turbant, from whence many give them the title of Turk's Cap. In the gardens of the florifts, particularly thofe in Holland, they make a great variety of thefe flowers, amounting to the number of thirty or upward ; but in the Englifh gardens, I have not obferved more than half that number, and moft of thefe are accidental, for thofe before enumerated, are all that I think may be fuppofed fpecifically different. However, for the fake of fuch as are curious in collecting thefe forts of flowers, I fhall here mention all thofe varieties which are to be found in the Englifh gardens.

The common Martagon with double flowers.

The white Martagon.

The double white Martagon.

The white fpotted Martagon.

The Imperial Martagon.

The early fcarlet Martagon.

The Conftantinople Vermillion Martagon.

The common Martagon with red flowers, which is the fifth fort before enumerated, has very narrow leaves, growing without order. The ftalk rifes near three feet high, fuftaining at the top eight or ten bright red flowers, which ftand at a diftance from each other. Thefe appear in June, and the ftalks decay in Auguft, foon after which time the roots may be tranfplanted.

The fixth fort is called Martagon of Pompony ; the ftalks of this rife higher than thofe of the former, the leaves are fhorter, and fet clofer upon the ftalks ; each of thefe ftalks fuftain from fifteen to thirty flowers of a very bright red, approaching to fcarlet. The foot-ftalks of the flowers are very long, fo that the head of flowers fpreads out very wide ; thefe hang downward, but their petals are reflexed quite back. This flowers foon after the fifth fort.

The feventh fort is commonly known by the title of Scarlet Martagon ; this rifes with a ftalk from three to four feet high ; the leaves are much broader than thofe of the former forts, and appear as if they were edged with white ; they are placed very clofely upon the ftalks, but without any order. The flowers are produced at the top of the ftalk ; they are of a bright fcarlet, and are feldom more than five or fix in number. This flowers late in July, and in cool feafons will continue in beauty great part of Auguft.

The eighth fort rifes with a ftrong ftalk from four to five feet high, garnifhed with leaves as broad as thofe of the laft mentioned, which ftand without order ; the flowers are produced in form of a pyramid, on the upper part of the ftalk. When the roots of this kind are ftrong, they produce forty or fifty flowers upon each ftalk ; they are large, of a yellow colour, fpotted with dark fpots, fo make a fine appearance ; but the flowers have fo difagreeable ftrong fcent, that few perfons can endure to be near them, which has occafioned their being thrown out of moft Englifh gardens. This flowers the latter end of July.

The ninth fort is frequently called the Purple Martagon, though in moft of the old gardens it is known fimply by the title of Turk's Cap. This rifes with a ftrong ftalk from three to four feet high, garnifhed by pretty broad leaves, which ftand in whorls round the ftalk, at certain diftances. The flowers are of a dark purplifh colour, with fome fpots of black ; they are produced in loofe fpikes on the top of the ftalks. This flowers in June ; the flowers of this fort have a very difagreeable odour when near, but it is not fo offenfive as the former fort.

The tenth fort is very like the former, but the leaves are narrower ; the whorls ftand farther afunder, the leaves and ftalks are fomewhat hairy, and the buds of the flowers are covered with a foft down : the flowers are of a brighter colour with few fpots, and come out earlier in the fummer, though the ftalks appear much later above ground. This flowers early in June, and the ftalks decay in Auguft.

The eleventh fort is commonly called the Canada Martagon, as it was firft brought to Europe from thence, but

but it grows naturally in moſt parts of North America. The roots of this are oblong and large, made up of ſcales like the other ſorts; the ſtalks riſe from four to five feet high, garniſhed with oblong pointed leaves placed in whorls round the ſtalk. The flowers are produced toward the top of the ſtalk; they are large, of a yellow colour, ſpotted with black, which are ſhaped like the flowers of the Orange Lily; the petals of them are not turned backward ſo much as thoſe of the other ſorts of Martagon. This flowers the beginning of Auguſt, and when the roots are large, the ſtalks have a good number of flowers, ſo make a fine appearance. There are two varieties of this, one with larger and deeper coloured flowers than the other, but they are ſuppoſed to have accidentally come from ſeeds.

The twelfth ſort grows naturally in North America, and is alſo mentioned to grow at Campſchatſki. This hath erect flowers ſhaped like thoſe of the Canada Martagon, but the petals of this are oval, not narrowed at their baſe as are thoſe, and ſit cloſe to the foot-ſtalk; the flowers are of a deeper colour, and not ſo much ſpotted as the other ſort. It flowers in July, and the ſtalks decay in the autumn. This ſort is at preſent rare in England, being in very few gardens. It was ſent me a few years ago from Maryland, but after it had flowered the root periſhed.

The thirteenth ſort was ſent me from Penſylvania by Mr. John Bartram, who found it growing naturally in that country. The root of this is ſmaller than thoſe of the other ſorts; it is ſcaly and white; in the ſpring it ſends out one upright ſtalk near a foot and a half high; the leaves come out in whorls round the ſtalks, at diſtances; they are ſhort, pretty broad, and have obtuſe points. The ſtalk is terminated by two flowers which ſtand erect, upon ſhort ſeparate foot-ſtalks; they are ſhaped like the flowers of the bulb-bearing fiery Lily, but the petals are narrower at their baſe, ſo that there are ſpaces between each, but upward they enlarge and join, forming a ſort of open bell-ſhaped flower; their petals are ſpear-ſhaped, ſo are contracted at the top, where they terminate in acute points. The flowers are of a bright purple colour, marked with ſeveral dark purple ſpots toward their baſe. In the center of the flower is ſituated a ſix-cornered germen, ſupporting a ſtrong ſtyle, crowned by a three-cornered ſtigma; round this are ſituated ſix awl-ſhaped ſtamina, terminated by oblong proſtrate ſummits; theſe are a little ſhorter than the ſtyle. The germen afterward turns to an oblong capſule with three angles, blunt at the top, divided into three cells, filled with flat ſeeds lying over each other. It flowers in July, and the ſeeds ripen the latter end of September.

This ſort is at preſent very rare in the Engliſh gardens, but as it has ripened ſeeds the laſt ſeaſon here, ſo it may in a few years become very common. As this ſort grows in a ſmall compaſs, and the flowers have no ill ſcent, it is proper furniture for the borders of ſmall gardens. The ſtalks of this decay ſoon after the ſeeds are ripe, when it will be a proper time to remove the roots; theſe do not put out new fibres till after Chriſtmas. The roots of this kind do not put out many offsets, ſo that unleſs it is propagated by ſeeds, it cannot be increaſed in any plenty.

All the ſorts of Martagon may be propagated by offsets from the roots, in the ſame way as the common Lily, which ſome of the ſorts produce in as great plenty; but there are others which ſend out very few offsets, which occaſion their preſent ſcarcity. The roots of all the ſorts of Martagon may be ſafely taken up when their ſtalks decay; and if there is a neceſſity for keeping the roots out of the ground, if they are wrapped in dry Moſs, they will keep perfectly well for two months; ſo that if the roots are to be tranſported to a diſtant place, this precaution of wrapping them up is neceſſary; but where they are to be planted in the ſame garden, there will be no occaſion for this, eſpecially if they are not kept too long out of the

ground; for if the place is ready to receive the roots, they ſhould be planted the beginning of October; ſo if the roots are put in a dry cool place, they will keep very good without any further care; but if the ground is not ready to receive them till later in the year, then it will be proper to cover the roots with dry ſand, or wrap them in Moſs to exclude the air, which, if they are much expoſed to, will cauſe their ſcales to ſhrink, which weakens the roots, often cauſing a mouldineſs, and is ſometimes the occaſion of their rotting.

Theſe roots ſhould be planted five or ſix inches deep in the ground, eſpecially if the ſoil is light and dry; but where the ground is moiſt, it will be proper to raiſe the borders in which theſe are to be planted, five or ſix inches above the level of the ſurface of the ground; for if the water riſes ſo high in winter as to come near the roots, it will cauſe them to rot; and where the ſoil is naturally ſtiff and ſubject to bind, there ſhould be a good quantity of ſea-coal aſhes or rough ſand, well mixed in the border, to ſeparate the parts, and prevent the ground from binding in the ſpring, otherwiſe the roots will not ſend up very ſtrong ſtalks, nor will they make ſo good increaſe.

As the Canada Martagon, the Martagon of Pompony, and the laſt ſort, are ſomewhat tenderer than the others, ſo if in very ſevere winters the ſurface of the ground over them is covered with old tanners bark or ſea-coal aſhes, it will be a good way to ſecure them from being injured by the froſt; and in the ſpring the covering may be removed, before the roots ſhoot up their ſtalks.

The tall growing ſorts of theſe are only proper for large gardens, ſo they may be intermixed with the white and Orange Lilies, the tall growing Iriſes, and other flowers of the ſame growth; where, if they are not too much crowded, and are properly diſpoſed, they will make a good appearance; and as they flower one after another, ſo they may be diſpoſed according to their ſeaſons of flowering. There are ſome of the common Martagons hardy enough to thrive under the ſhade of trees, ſo they may be diſpoſed in wilderneſs quarters, with the common ſort of Lilies, where they will have a good effect.

The roots of all theſe kinds muſt never be tranſplanted after they have made any ſhoots, for that will ſo much weaken them (if it does not entirely kill them) as not to be recovered in leſs than two or three years, as I have experienced to my coſt; for being obliged to remove a fine collection of theſe roots early in the ſpring, I loſt a great part of them, and the others were long recovering their ſtrength.

All the ſorts of Lilies and Martagons may be propagated by ſowing their ſeeds, by which method ſome new varieties may be obtained, provided the ſeeds are ſaved from the beſt ſorts; eſpecially the Martagons, which are more inclinable to vary than the other Lilies. The manner of ſowing them is as follows:

You muſt be provided with ſome ſquare boxes about ſix inches deep, which ſhould have holes bored in their bottoms to let the wet paſs off: theſe boxes ſhould be filled with freſh light ſandy earth, and in the beginning of October, ſoon after the ſeeds are ripe, you muſt ſow them thereon pretty thick, covering them over with light ſifted earth about half an inch; then place the boxes where they may have the morning ſun only, obſerving if the ſeaſon ſhould prove dry, to refreſh them often with water, as alſo to pull out all weeds which may be produced. In this ſituation the boxes ſhould remain until the beginning of November, when you muſt remove them where they may have as much ſun as poſſible, as alſo be ſcreened from the cold north and eaſt winds during the winter ſeaſon; but in the ſpring of the year, about the beginning of April, you muſt remove the boxes into their former poſition; for now the young plants will appear above ground, which are impatient of too much heat; beſides, the earth in the boxes will dry too faſt at this ſeaſon, if expoſed to the full ſun at noon. You muſt alſo obſerve at this ſeaſon to keep them
entirely

entirely clear from weeds, as alſo to refreſh them gently with water, if the ſeaſon ſhould prove dry, but this muſt be done ſparingly and with caution. In this place you ſhould let the boxes remain until the beginning of Auguſt; at which time you ſhould prepare ſome beds of the above mentioned freſh light earth, which muſt be levelled very even; then take the earth out of the boxes, together with the ſmall bulbs, and ſtrew it equally over the beds, covering it over about half an inch thick with fine ſifted earth; and if the ſeaſon ſhould prove very hot and dry, you would do well to ſhade the beds in the middle of the day from the great heat of the ſun, and refreſh them now and then with water.

You muſt alſo obſerve to keep them entirely clear from weeds, and if the following winter ſhould prove very cold, you muſt cover the beds with Peas-haulm, or ſome other light covering, to keep out the froſt, which would prejudice the roots, if ſuffered to enter deep into the ground (eſpecially while they are ſo young:) but you muſt never let the covering remain on in mild weather, which would alſo be very injurious to them.

The end of February, or the beginning of March, when the hard froſts are over, you ſhould gently clear off the earth upon the ſurface of the beds (which, during the winter ſeaſon, will often have contracted a moſſineſs;) and ſift a little freſh earth equally over the beds, which will greatly encourage the root; but in doing this, you muſt be very careful not to ſtir the ground ſo deep as to diſturb or injure the roots; nor ſhould you defer doing it too late, leſt the ſhoots ſhould be coming up, which, by this operation might be broken and greatly hurt; and as the ſeaſon advances, you muſt be careful to clear them from weeds, and in dry weather to water them gently, but they ſhould not have it in great plenty; and in very hot days, if you ſhade them from the ſun, it will be of great ſervice to them; but this need not be done till the latter end of April or the beginning of May, when the ſeaſon is ſometimes very hot and dry. When their leaves are quite decayed, you ſhould ſtir the ſurface of the beds again (but do not go too deep) which will prevent the weeds from growing very faſt, and be of ſervice to the roots; and in September you muſt ſift ſome more freſh earth over the beds about half an inch thick, and in winter and ſpring you muſt manage them as was directed for the preceding year.

In September following theſe roots will require to be tranſplanted to a greater diſtance, when you muſt prepare ſome beds of the ſame freſh light earth as was before directed, making them level; then take up the roots and tranſplant them into the beds, placing them about eight inches aſunder, obſerving to put the roots with their buds uppermoſt, and about four inches below the ſurface.

This work ſhould be done when the weather is moiſt, for if the roots are tranſplanted in a very dry ſeaſon, and there doth not happen rain ſoon after, they will take a mouldineſs which many times rots them.

You muſt alſo obſerve, as was before directed, to keep the beds entirely clear from weeds; and in winter, if the froſt ſhould be very ſevere, you muſt cover them with Peas-haulm or decayed tan, to prevent the roots from being injured thereby; and in the ſpring you ſhould take off the covering, alſo the earth from the ſurface of the beds, as before, laying ſome freſh thereon, and ſo continue the ſummer and winter's work, as before.

The ſecond year after being planted in theſe beds, the ſtrongeſt roots will begin to flower; at which time, if you obſerve any peculiar varieties, you ſhould put down a ſtick by each of theſe roots to mark them; which may be taken up when their leaves are decayed, and removed into the borders of the flower-garden, or tranſplanted into other beds at a greater diſtance, to encourage them to flower ſtrong. But you cannot be ſo good a judge which of thoſe will be

good by their firſt flowers, therefore you ſhould never reject any of them until they have flowered two years; for many times, ſome of theſe flowers will make but a mean appearance the firſt year, and afterwards become fair handſome flowers when they have obtained ſtrength; ſo that you ſhould ſuffer all ſuch, of whoſe worth you are not aſſured, to remain undiſturbed two years, that you may be aſcertained which of them are worth preſerving; theſe ſhould be removed into the flower-garden at a proper ſeaſon, but the ordinary ones may be rejected, or planted in ſhady outer walks, where, though they are mean flowers, they will appear well enough.

LILIUM CONVALLIUM. See CONVALLARIA.
LILIUM PERSICUM. See FRITILLARIA.
LILIUM SUPERBUM. See GLORIOSA.
LIME-TREE. See TILIA.
LIMODORUM. Flor. Virg. 110. Lin. Gen. Plant. 904. Helleborine. Tourn. Inſt. R. H. 436. tab. 249. Baſtard Hellebore.

The CHARACTERS are,

It hath a ſingle naked flower-ſtalk, ariſing immediately from the root. The flowers have no empalement, but a ſpatha (or ſheath) ſituated below them. The flower is compoſed of five oval petals, which are diſſimilar. The ſide petals ſpread open, but the two upper are connected together; the lower one is keel-ſhaped, ſo that it has much the appearance of a butterfly flower. Within the petals is ſituated a concave nectarium of one leaf, which is as long as the petals. It has two ſtamina, which are as long as the petals, terminated by two oval ſummits. It hath a column-ſhaped germen ſituated under the flower, which is as long as the petals, ſupporting a ſlender ſtyle, faſtened to the ſtamina, crowned by a funnel-ſhaped ſtigma. The column-ſhaped germen afterward turns to a capſule of the ſame form, opening with three valves, having one cell, in which are lodged four or five roundiſh ſeeds.

This genus of plants is ranged in the firſt ſection of Linnæus's twentieth claſs, which includes thoſe plants whoſe flowers have but two ſtamina, which are connected with the ſtyle.

We have but one SPECIES of this genus at preſent in England, viz.

LIMODORUM (*Tuberoſum*) foliis longis anguſtis ſulcatis & acuminatis, pedunculis longiſſimis. *Limodorum with long narrow leaves ending in acute points, and a very long foot-ſtalk to the flower.* Helleborine Americana, radice tuberoſâ, foliis longis anguſtis, caule nudo, floribus ex rubro pallide-purpuraſcentibus. Martyn. Cent. 1. Pl. 50. Icon. tab. 165. *American Baſtard Hellebore with a tuberoſe root, long narrow leaves, a naked ſtalk, and flowers of a red and pale purpliſh colour.* This plant grows naturally in Jamaica, eſpecially on the north ſide of that iſland, from whence many of the roots were ſent me by the late Dr. Houſtoun, with the following title, Helleborine purpurea, tuberoſâ radice. Plum. Cat. 9. ſo that it is the ſame plant with Plumier's. It alſo grows naturally in the French Iſlands of America. The roots of this were afterward brought me from the Bahamâ Iſlands, where it was found growing naturally; and it was ſince ſent me from Penſylvania, by Mr. John Bartram, who found it growing naturally in that country.

The root of this plant is ſhaped like that of the true Saffron Crocus, but the outer cover is of a darker brown colour; from this comes out two or three leaves, according to the ſize and ſtrengthof the root; theſe are nine or ten inches long, and near three quarters of an inch broad in the middle, being contracted toward both ends, terminating with long acute points, folding over each other at their baſe; they have five longitudinal furrows, like the firſt leaves of young Palms; theſe leaves come out in the ſpring, and frequently decay the following winter; but when the plants are kept in a warm ſtove, they are not very long deſtitute of leaves. The flower-ſtalk ariſes immediately from the root, on one ſide of the leaves; this is naked, ſmooth, and of a purpliſh colour toward the top. It is near a foot and a half high, and terminated by a looſe ſpike of purpliſh red flowers,

ſtanding

ſtanding upon ſhort foot-ſtalks; they are compoſed of five or ſix petals, the two upper are connected together, forming a ſort of helmet, the two ſide petals expand like the wings of a butterfly flower, and the lower forms a ſort of keel. In the center of the petals is ſituated a column-ſhaped germen, which riſes from the baſe of the petals, ſupporting a ſlender ſtyle, to which adhere two ſtamina, terminated by oval ſummits, as the ſtyle is by a funnel-ſhaped ſtigma; after the flowers are faded, the germen becomes a three-cornered column-ſhaped capſule, with one cell, opening with three valves, containing ſeveral roundiſh ſeeds, but theſe ſeeds are rarely produced in England.

This plant is not conſtant to any particular ſeaſon of flowering; for ſometimes it has flowered in April and May, and in other years it has not flowered till September or October; but the moſt uſual time of its flowering is in June and July, when the flowers appear early in the ſpring; they are ſucceeded by ſeed-veſſels, which ſometimes ripen in this country.

There are ſeveral other ſpecies of this genus mentioned by Father Plumier, but I have only ſeen one more than this here mentioned, which had oval obtuſe leaves, furrowed in the ſame manner as the leaves of this ſort, but were of a thicker conſiſtence; the flowers of this I have not yet ſeen. The root was ſent me from Maryland, where it grew naturally in a thicket.

The ſort here deſcribed is too tender to thrive in the open air in England, and although with care it may be preſerved in a warm green-houſe, yet it ſeldom flowers in ſuch a ſituation; ſo that to have it in perfection, it is neceſſary to keep it in the tan-bed in the ſtove in winter; and if in ſummer the pots are plunged in a tan-bed under a deep frame, the plants will thrive, and flower as ſtrong as in their native ſoil.

It is propagated by offsets from the root, which are ſent out pretty freely when the plants are in vigour; theſe ſhould be taken off, and the roots tranſplanted when they are the moſt deſtitute of leaves. The roots ſhould have a ſoft loamy ſoil, and muſt have but little water, eſpecially in winter.

LIMODORUM. See ORCHIS.

LIMON. Tourn. Inſt. R. H. 621. Citrus. Lin. Gen. Plant. 807. [ſo called of Λειμῶν, a meadow, becauſe the leaves of this tree are of a green colour, as is likewiſe the fruit before it comes to maturity.] The Lemon-tree; in French, Limonier.

The CHARACTERS are,

The flower is compoſed of five oblong thick petals, which are a little concave, ſpreading open; theſe ſit in a ſmall empalement of one leaf, indented at five parts at the top. It hath about ten or twelve ſtamina, which are joined in three or four bodies, which are terminated by oblong ſummits. It hath an oval germen, ſupporting a cylindrical ſtyle the length of the ſtamina, crowned by a globular ſummit. The germen afterward becomes an oval fruit with a fleſhy rind, incloſing a thin pulpy fruit with ſeveral cells, each having two hard ſeeds.

This genus of plants is ranged in the ſixth ſection of Tournefort's twenty-firſt claſs, which includes the trees and ſhrubs with a Roſe-ſhaped flower, whoſe pointal becomes a fleſhy fruit with hard dry ſeeds. Dr. Linnæus has joined the Citron, Orange, and Lemon together, making them only different ſpecies of the ſame genus; but if we admit of the fruit being a characteriſtic note to diſtinguiſh the genus, the Limon cannot be joined with the Orange, for the Orange has a globular fruit, compreſſed at both ends, but the Limon has an oval fruit, prominent at the top, and the latter hath not ſo many cells as the former. It is placed in the ſecond ſection of Linnæus's eighteenth claſs, which includes the plants whoſe flowers have about twenty ſtamina joined in ſeveral bodies.

The SPECIES are,

1. LIMON (*Vulgaris*) foliis ovato-lanceolatis acuminatis, ſubſerratis. *Limon-tree with oval, ſpear-ſhaped, acute-*

pointed leaves, which are little ſawed. Limon vulgaris. Ferr. Heſp. 193. *The common Limon.*

2. LIMON (*Spinoſum*) foliis ovatis integris, ramis ſubſpinoſis. *Limon with oval entire leaves, and branches which are ſomewhat ſpiny.* Limon acris. Ferr. Heſp. 331. *The ſour Limon, commonly called Lime.*

3. LIMON (*Racemoſum*) foliis ovato-lanceolatis ſubſerratis, fructu conglomerato. *Limon with oval ſpear-ſhaped leaves, which are ſomewhat ſawed, and fruit growing in cluſters.* Limon fructu racemoſo. Tourn. Inſt. R. H. 621. *Limon with fruit growing in bunches.* There are great varieties of this fruit, which are preſerved in ſome of the Italian gardens, and in both the Indies there are ſeveral which have not yet been introduced to the European gardens; but theſe, like Apples and Pears, may be multiplied without end from ſeeds, therefore I ſhall only mention the moſt remarkable varieties which are to be found in the Engliſh gardens at preſent, as it would be to little purpoſe to enumerate all thoſe which are mentioned in the foreign catalogues.

The Limon-tree with variegated leaves.
The ſweet Limon.
The Pear-ſhaped Limon.
The imperial Limon.
The Limon called Adam's Apple.
The furrowed Limon.
The childing Limon.
The Limon with double flowers.

The common Limon and the ſweet Limon are brought to England from Spain and Portugal in great plenty, but the fruit of the latter are not much eſteemed. The Lime is not often brought to England, nor is that fruit much cultivated in Europe, but in the Weſt-Indies it is preferred to the Limon, the juice being reckoned wholeſomer, and the acid is more agreeable to the palate; there are ſeveral varieties of this fruit in the Weſt-Indies, ſome of which have a ſweet juice, but thoſe are not greatly eſteemed; and as the inhabitants of thoſe iſlands do not propagate theſe fruits by grafting or budding, being contented with ſowing their ſeeds, ſo there is no doubt but a great variety of them may be found by any perſon who is curious in diſtinguiſhing them.

As I have never known the common Limon ever vary to the Lime, when raiſed from ſeeds, nor the Lime vary to the Limon, I ſuppoſe they are ſpecifically different, for I have frequently raiſed both from ſeeds, and have always found them continue their difference in leaf and branch, for I never waited to ſee their fruit, as they were only deſigned for ſtocks, to bud other ſorts into them.

The Pear-ſhaped Limon is a ſmall fruit with very little juice, ſo is not much propagated any where; the curious, who have room and convenience for keeping many of theſe trees, may preſerve a plant or two of this ſort for the ſake of variety.

The fruit of the Imperial Limon is ſometimes brought to England from Italy, but I do not remember to have ſe n any of this ſort imported from Spain or Portugal, ſo that I ſuppoſe they are not much propagated in either of theſe countries; for the inhabitants of both thoſe fine countries are ſo very incurious, eſpecially in horticulture, as to truſt almoſt entirely to nature, that the products of their gardens are inferior both in numbers and quality, to many other parts of Europe, where the climate is much leſs favourable for theſe productions. And in the article we are now upon, there are many ſtrong inſtances of the ſlothfulneſs, or incurioſity of the Portugueze particularly, for they had many of the moſt curious ſorts of Orange, Limon, and Citron-trees, brought from the Indies to Portugal formerly, which ſeemed to thrive almoſt as well there, as in their native ſoil, and yet they have not been propagated; there are a few trees of theſe ſorts ſtill remaining in ſome neglected gardens near Liſbon, almoſt unnoticed by the inhabitants. As there are alſo ſeveral curious trees and plants, which were formerly introduced from both Indies, ſome of which thrive and produce fruit amidſt the wild

8 B.   buſhes

bushes and weeds, with which those gardens are spread over.

All these sorts are propagated by budding or inarching them either on stocks of Lemons or Citrons, produced from seeds, but they will not so readily unite on Orange stocks, for which reason the Citrons are preferable to either Oranges or Lemons for stocks, as they readily join with either sort, and being of larger growth, cause the buds of the other sorts to shoot much stronger than if they were on stocks of their own kind. The method of raising these stocks, and the manner of budding them, being already exhibited under the article of AURANTIUM, it would be superfluous to repeat it here.

The culture of the Lemon being the same with that of the Orange-tree, it would be needless to repeat it here; therefore I shall only observe, that the common Lemons are somewhat hardier than the Oranges, and will bring their fruit to maturity with us better than they will do, and require to have a greater share of fresh air in winter; for which reason, they should always be placed nearer to the doors or windows of the green-house; and in some curious gardens, these trees have been planted against walls, where, by covering them with glasses in winter, and protecting them from severe frost, they have produced plenty of large fruit: as these trees do generally produce stronger shoots, they require more water to be given them than the Orange; but as to the tender sorts, they must be treated with a little more care, otherwise their fruit will fall in winter, and come to nothing; these things being fully exhibited before, I refer the reader (as I hinted) to the article AURANTIUM, where their culture is fully set forth.

LIMONIUM. Tourn. Init. R. H. 341. tab. 177. Statice. Lin. Gen. Plant. 348. [takes its name of Λιμών, a marsh, as growing in marshes.] Sea Lavender.

The CHARACTERS are,

The flowers have an imbricated perianthium, rising one above another. The flower is funnel-shaped, composed of five petals, which are narrow at their base, but are broad and spreading at the top. It hath five awl-shaped stamina which are shorter than the petals, crowned by prostrate summits. It hath a small germen, supporting five slender styles, crowned by pointed stigmas. The empalement of the flower afterward becomes a capsule, shut close at the neck, but expanded above where the seeds are lodged. This genus of plants is ranged in the second section of Tournefort's eighth class, which includes the herbs with a Clove Gilliflower flower, whose pointal becomes the seed inclosed in the empalement. Dr. Linnæus has joined this genus to the Statice of Tournefort, and places it in the fifth section of his fifth class, which contains the plants whose flowers have five stamina and five styles. As the flowers of this genus are ranged one above another in form of spikes, and those of the Statice are collected in globular heads, they may, without impropriety, be kept separate; and as there are several species of each genus, therefore I have the rather been inclined so to do, than by joining them, to swell the genus.

The SPECIES are,

1. LIMONIUM (*Vulgare*) foliis ovato-lanceolatis, caule tereti nudo paniculato. *Sea Lavender with oval spear-shaped leaves, and a taper paniculated stalk.* Limonium maritimum majus. C. B. P. 192. *Common great Sea Lavender.*

2. LIMONINM (*Narbonense*) foliis oblongo-ovatis, caule paniculato patulo, spicis florum brevioribus. *Sea Lavender with oblong oval leaves, a spreading paniculated stalk, and shorter spikes of flowers.* Limonium maritimum majus alterum serotinum Narbonense. H. R. Par. *Another large late flowering Sea Lavender of Narbonne.*

3. LIMONIUM (*oleæfolium*) foliis ovatis obtusis, petiolis decurrentibus, caule paniculato, spicis florum erectioribus. *Sea Lavender with oval obtuse leaves, running foot-stalks, a paniculated stalk, and more upright spikes of flowers.* Limonium maritimum minus, oleæ folio. C. B. P. 192. *Small Sea Lavender, with an Olive leaf.*

4. LIMONIUM (*Humile*) foliis lanceolatis, caule humile patulo, spicis florum tenuioribus. *Sea Lavender with spear-shaped leaves, a low spreading stalk, and slender spikes of flowers.* Limonium Anglicum minus, caulibus ramosioribus, floribus in spicis rariùs sitis. Rai Hist. 217. *Lesser English Sea Lavender, with more branched stalks, and flowers seldom growing in a spike.*

5. LIMONIUM (*Tartaricum*) foliis lineari-lanceolatis, caule ramoso patulo, floribus distantibus uno versu dispositis. *Sea Lavender with narrow spear-shaped leaves, a branching spreading stalk, and flowers placed asunder on one side the stalk.* Limonium Orientale, plantaginis folio, floribus umbellatis. T. Cor. *Oriental Sea Lavender with Plantain leaves, and flowers growing in an umbel.*

6. LIMONIUM (*Sinuatum*) foliis radicalibus alternatim pinnato-sinuatis, caulinis ternis triquetris subulatis decurrentibus. *Sea Lavender with the lower leaves alternately sinuated like wings, and those upon the stalks three-cornered, awl-shaped, and running along the foot-stalk.* Limonium peregrinum, foliis asplenii. C. B. P. *Foreign Sea Lavender with Spleenwort leaves.*

7. LIMONIUM (*Siculum*) caule fruticoso patulo, foliis lineari lanceolatis crassis, floribus solitariis distantibus. *Sea Lavender with a spreading shrubby stalk, narrow, thick, spear-shaped leaves, and flowers growing singly at a distance from each other.* Limonium Siculum lignosum, gallas ferens, & non ferens. Bocc. Rar. *Woody Sicilian Sea Lavender, sometimes producing galls, at other times not.*

8. LIMONIUM (*Africanum*) foliis inferioribus lanceolatis hirsutis serratis caulinis ternis linearibus acutis decurrentibus. *Sea Lavender with spear-shaped lower leaves which are hairy and sawed, but growing by threes on the stalks, narrow, acute-pointed, and running along the stalk.* Limonium Africanum caule alato, foliis integris hirsutis, petalo pallidè flavo calyce amœnè purpureo. Martyn. Cent. 48. tab. 48. *African Sea Lavender with a winged stalk, entire hairy leaves, pale yellow petals to the flower, and a beautiful purple empalement.*

9. LIMONIUM (*Reticulatum*) foliis cuneiformibus, caule erecto paniculato, ramis inferioribus sterilibus nudis. *Sea Lavender with wedge-shaped leaves, an upright paniculated stalk, and the under branches sterile and naked.* Limonium minus flagellis tortuosis. Bocc. Mus. *Small Sea Lavender with twisted shoots.*

10. LIMONIUM (*Cordatum*) caule nudo paniculato, foliis spathulatis retusis. *Sea Lavender with a paniculated naked stalk, and spatule-shaped blunt leaves.* Limonium maritimum minus, foliolis cordatis. C. B. P. *Small Sea Lavender with little leaves, which are heart-shaped.*

11. LIMONIUM (*Echioideum*) caule nudo paniculato, tereti, foliis tuberculatis. *Sea Lavender with a naked, taper, paniculated stalk, and leaves set with tubercles.* Limonium minus annuum, bullatis foliis vel echioides. Bot. Monsp. *Small annual Sea Lavender with studded leaves.*

12. LIMONIUM (*Fruticosum*) caule erecto fruticoso, foliis lineari-lanceolatis obtusis, floribus alternis. *Sea Lavender with an upright shrubby stalk, narrow spear-shaped leaves, ending in obtuse points, and flowers ranged alternately.* Limonium Egyptiacum fruticosum, foliis lanceolatis obtusis. *Shrubby Egyptian Sea Lavender with blunt spear-shaped leaves.*

The first sort grows naturally in the marshes which are flowed by the sea, in several parts of England. The roots of this plant are thick, of a reddish colour, and an astringent taste, sending out many strong fibres, which strike deep in the ground; and from the upper part of the root comes out several oval spear-shaped leaves, from four to five inches long, and more than two inches broad in the middle; they are smooth, of a pretty thick consistence, and of a dark green. The stalks rise upward of a foot high, is naked of leaves, divided into many branches, which are again divided into smaller toward the top; these are terminated by slender spikes of pale blue flowers, ranged on one side the stalk above each other, coming out of narrow covers like sheaths; these appear in July, and are succeeded by oblong seeds, which are inclosed in the empalement, ripening in autumn.

The

The second fort grows naturally in the fouth of France on the fea-coaft. The leaves of this fort are of an oblong oval form ; they are fix inches long, and three broad, fmooth, entire, and of a deep green. The ftalk rifes fifteen or fixteen inches high, dividing into feveral fpreading branches, which are divided again into fmaller, and are terminated by feveral fhort fpikes of pale blue flowers, ranged on one fide the foot-ftalk. This fort feldom flowers till the end of Auguft, fo never produces any good feeds in England.

The third fort grows naturally in Narbonne and Provence ; this hath fmall, oval, obtufe leaves, about two inches long, and one broad, with pretty long foot-ftalks, which are bordered, or winged with part of the leaves, which runs clofe to, and partly embrace the upper part of the root ; thefe are of a lighter green than either of the former. The ftalk rifes a foot and a half high, fending out branches alternately on each fide ; the lower ones being long, the others gradually diminifhing to the top, fo as to form a loofe kind of pyramid : thefe all point upward, and toward their ends fend out fpikes of pale blue flowers, which are erect. This fort flowers late in Auguft, fo never perfects feeds in England.

The fourth fort grows naturally in England. It was firft difcovered on the fea banks near Walton, in Effex, afterward near Malden, in the fame county, and fince at the mouth of the river that runs from Chichefter, in Suffex. The leaves of this fort are fpear-fhaped, about three inches long, and one broad in the middle, leffening gradually to both ends. The ftalk rifes four or five inches high, dividing into many fpreading branches, which are very thick fet with fhort fpikes of whitifh blue flowers. Thefe appear in Auguft, and the feeds ripen in October.

The fifth fort was difcovered by Dr. Tournefort in the Levant, from whence he fent the feeds to the Royal Garden at Paris, where they grew, and have produced feeds many years, which have been communicated to many of the curious gardens in Europe. The feeds of this fort were fent me from the Dardanelles, where the plants grow in plenty. The leaves of this fort are about four inches long, and three quarters of an inch broad in the middle, diminifhing gradually to both ends. The ftalks rife about five or fix inches high, dividing into feveral fpreading branches, which are again divided into fmaller ; thefe are terminated by fpikes of pale blue flowers, ranged on one fide the foot-ftalk ; the whole, when growing, being fpread wide, has fomewhat the appearance of an umbel of flowers. This fort flowers in Auguft, fo never ripens feeds here.

The fixth fort grows naturally in Sicily and Paleftine ; this is a biennial plant. The lower leaves which fpread on the ground, are indented almoft to the middle rib ; thefe indentures are alternate and blunt. The ftalks rife a foot and a half high, dividing upward into feveral branches, garnifhed at each joint with three narrow leaves fitting clofe to the ftalks, from whofe bafe proceeds a leafy membrane, or wing, which runs along on both fides the ftalk ; thefe are rough, and a little hairy. The ftalks are terminated by panicles of flowers, which fit upon winged foot-ftalks, each fuftaining three or four flowers of a light blue colour, which continue long without fading. This fort flowers in July and Auguft, but unlefs the fummer is very warm and dry, the feeds do not ripen in England.

The feventh fort grows naturally in Sicily ; this hath a fhrubby ftalk, which rifes about two feet high, dividing into feveral ligneous branches, which fpread out on every fide ; the lower part of thefe are clofely garnifhed with gray leaves, like thofe of the Sea Purflain, and are of a thick confiftence. The branches are terminated by panicles of blue flowers, having one funnel-fhaped petal, which come out fingly at a diftance from each other, having long tubes, but divide into five fegments upward, which fpread open. This flowers from June till autumn, but never pro-

duces feeds in England : there is a variety of this, which bears galls like thofe upon the Oak, which grows naturally in Sicily, but I do not know if it is a different fpecies, for thofe plants which are in the Englifh gardens have no appearance of any.

The eighth fort was raifed in the Chelfea garden, from feeds which were brought me from Africa ; this is a biennial plant, which dies foon after it has produced flowers and feeds. The lower leaves are but few in number ; they are fpear-fhaped, hairy, and flightly fawed on their edges, about two inches long, and half an inch broad. The ftalk rifes about fifteen inches high, which at each joint is garnifhed with three narrow leaves, ending in acute points ; from the bafe of thefe leaves is continued a leafy membrane, or wing, running along the ftalk on each fide ; thefe ftalks branch out but little, and are terminated by fhort panicles of flowers, whofe foot-ftalks are not winged as in the former ; each foot-ftalk fuftains two or three flowers of a bright blue colour, out of the middle of which arifes another fmall flower of a pale yellow colour. This fort flowered in July and Auguft, 1757, but did not ripen feeds.

The ninth fort grows naturally in Sicily, and was found growing on the border of the fea in Norfolk, by Mr. Henry Scott, a gardener, and has fince been found in plenty in Lincolnfhire, by —— Banks, Efq; The lower leaves of this fort are narrow at their bafe, but enlarge upward, where they are broad, and rounded at the top, in fhape of a wedge. The ftalks are flender and ftiff, rifing from feven to fourteen inches high, fending out many flender fide branches ; all thofe which proceed from the lower part of the ftalk are barren, having no flowers ; but toward the top they have fhort panicles of whitifh flowers, which are fmall, and fit three or four together upon one foot-ftalk. This fort flowers in July and Auguft.

The tenth fort grows naturally near the fea, about Marfeilles and Leghorn ; this hath many thick flefhy leaves, which are fhaped like a fpatula, growing near the root, and fpread on the ground ; they are fmooth, and of a grayifh colour. The ftalks are naked, and rife about fix inches high, dividing toward the top into many fmaller branches, which are terminated by fhort crooked panicles of fmall flowers, of a pale red colour. This fort flowers in Auguft, but never produces feeds in this country.

The eleventh fort grows naturally about Montpelier and in Italy ; this is an annual plant, with long narrow leaves, which are fet with rough tubercles like the leaves of Viper's Buglofs. The ftalks rife about eight inches high, dividing into two or three fmall branches, which are terminated by reflexed fhort fpikes of pale blue flowers ; thefe come out late in Auguft, and the feeds are feldom perfected in England.

The twelfth fort grows naturally in Egypt, from whence the feeds were fent to the Royal Garden at Paris, part of which were fent me by Dr. Bernard de Juffieu, which grew in the Chelfea garden, where there are feveral plants, which have produced flowers many years. This rifes with an upright fhrubby ftalk to the height of eight or ten feet, divided upward into many branches, garnifhed with narrow fpear-fhaped leaves, placed without order ; they are of a thick confiftence, and of a gray colour, fitting clofe to the branches. The flowers are produced at the end of the branches in loofe panicles, ftanding alternate on each fide the ftalk, one above another, with intervals between them ; they have pretty long tubes, which enlarge upward, where they are cut into five obtufe fegments, which fpread open ; thefe are of a bright fky blue, but fade to a purple before they fall off. The flowers begin to appear in July, and there is a fucceffion of them till winter.

The firft, fecond, third, fourth, fifth, and eighth forts, are abiding plants, which will thrive in the open air in England ; fuch of thefe as grow naturally in England, may be eafily procured from the places where they grow ; thefe plants may be tranfplanted at almoft any time of the year, provided they are

carefully

carefully taken up, preserving some earth to their roots, and in hot weather to shade them till they have taken new root; after which time they will require no other culture but to keep the ground clean from weeds, and in the spring to stir up the ground between them to loosen it. As these plants do not require much culture, nor do they take up much room, so a few of each sort may be allowed to have a place in gardens, where there is room, for the sake of variety. These plants do not propagate very fast in gardens, so the roots need not be removed oftener than every third or fourth year, at which time they may be slipped to increase them; the best time for this is in the autumn, that the plants may be well rooted before the spring, otherwise they will not flower very strong the following summer. They should be planted in a loamy soil, on an east aspected border, where they may enjoy the morning sun, but screened from the great heat in the middle of the day; in such a situation the roots will continue several years, and flower as well as in their native soil.

These plants may also be propagated by seeds, so that such of them as do not grow naturally in England, may be obtained by procuring their seeds from abroad. These should be sown upon a border exposed to the morning sun, and on a soft loamy soil, early in the spring, for the seeds lie a considerable time in the ground before the plant comes up; therefore the ground must be kept entirely clean from weeds, and if the season should prove very dry, the border should be watered two or three times a week, otherwise the seeds will lie a whole year before they vegetate; when the plants come up, they must be kept clean from weeds, and in every dry weather watered, and in the autumn they may be transplanted where they are designed to remain.

The sixth and eighth sorts are biennial plants, which rarely perfect their seeds in England, so that unless fresh seeds can be procured from warm countries, where they ripen well, it will be very difficult to continue the sorts. If the seeds of these can be obtained time enough to sow them in the autumn, the plants will come up the following spring; but when they are sown in the spring, they seldom grow the same year. These seeds should be sown on a border of loamy earth, not stiff or moist, and exposed to the south; but when the sun is warm, the border should be shaded with mats, to prevent the earth from drying too fast. When the plants come up, they must be kept clean from weeds; and if they are too close, some of them should be carefully taken out as soon as they are fit to remove, and planted in small pots, placing them in the shade till they have taken new root; then they may be placed where they may enjoy the morning sun till autumn, when they should be put into a hot-bed frame, where they may be screened from hard frost, but enjoy the free air in mild weather; and those plants which are left in the border where they were sown, must be covered with mats in hard frost; for though they will often live through the winter in mild seasons, yet hard frost will always destroy them. The following summer the plants will flower, and if the season proves warm and dry, they will ripen seeds, and the roots soon after decay.

The seventh and twelfth sorts are shrubby plants, which are too tender to live through the winter in the open air in England, so the plants must be removed into shelter in the autumn, but they only require protection from hard frost: these plants may be placed with Myrtles, Oleanders, and other hardy green-house plants, where they often continue to flower great part of winter, and make a pretty variety. These sorts are easily propagated by cuttings, which, if planted in July on a shady border, and duly watered, will take root in fix or seven weeks, when they should be taken up and planted into pots filled with light loamy earth, placing them in the shade till they have taken root; then they may be exposed till Oc-

tober, at which time they must be removed into shelter.

The eleventh sort is annual, and rarely ripens seeds here, so these must be procured from abroad, and sowed in the same way as the sixth and eighth sorts.

LINARIA. Tourn. Inst. R. H. 168. tab. 76. Antirrhinum. Lin. Gen. Plant. 668. [so called of Linum, *Lat.* flax, because its leaves resemble flax.] Toad-flax; in French, *Linaire*.

The CHARACTERS are,

The flower hath a permanent empalement of one leaf, divided into five parts almost to the bottom. The flower hath one petal, and is of the ringent (or grinning) kind, with an oblong swelling tube, having two lips above, with the chaps shut. The upper lip is bifid and reflexed on the sides, the lower lip is trifid and obtuse. It hath an oblong nectarium, which is awl-shaped and prominent behind, and four stamina, which are included in the upper lip, two of which are shorter than the other, and a roundish germen supporting a single style, crowned by an obtuse stigma. The germen afterward turns to a roundish obtuse capsule with two cells, filled with small seeds.

This genus of plants is ranged in the fourth section of Tournefort's third class, which includes the herbs with a tubulous, anomalous, personated flower, of one petal. Dr. Linnæus joins this genus, and also the Asarina of Tournefort to the Antirrhinum, and places that genus in the second section of his fourteenth class, in which are contained the plants whose flowers have two long and two short stamina, and the seeds are included in a capsule. The plants of this genus agree in their general characters with those of the Antirrhinum, or Calve's Snout, except in one particular, which is in the nectarium of the Linaria, which, from the base of the petal, stretches out like a heel; whereas the flowers of the Antirrhinum, have their nectarium lodged within side the base of the petal: this being so very obvious, and both genera having many species, I thought it might be easier for students in botany to range them under different genera, than to join them under one.

The SPECIES are,

1. LINARIA (*Vulgaris*) foliis lanceolato-linearibus confertis caule erecto, spicis terminalibus sessilibus. *Toad-flax with spear-shaped linear leaves growing in clusters, and an upright stalk terminated by spikes of flowers, sitting close to the stalk.* Linaria vulgaris lutea, flore majore. C. B. P. 212. *Common yellow Toad-flax with a larger flower.*

2. LINARIA (*Triphylla*) foliis ternis ovatis. *Toad-flax with oval leaves placed by threes.* Linaria triphylla minor lutea. C. B. P. 212. *Smaller three-leaved yellow Toad-flax.*

3. LINARIA (*Lusitanica*) foliis quaternis lanceolatis, caule erecto ramoso, floribus pedunculatis. *Toad-flax with spear-shaped leaves placed by fours, an upright branching stalk, and flowers upon foot-stalks.* Linaria latissimo folio Lusitanica. H. R. Par. *Broadest-leaved Portugal Toad-flax.*

4. LINARIA (*Alpina*) foliis subquaternis linearibus caule diffuso, floribus racemosis. *Toad-flax with linear leaves placed by fours on the lower part of the stalk, a diffused stalk and branching flowers.* Linaria quadrifolia supina. C. B. P. 213. *Low four-leaved Toad-flax.*

5. LINARIA (*Purpurea*) foliis lanceolato-linearibus sparsis, caule florifero erecto spicato. *Toad-flax with spear-shaped linear leaves, and the flower-stalks erect and spiked.* Linaria purpurea major odorata. C. B. P. 213. *Greater sweet-scented purple Toad-flax.*

6. LINARIA (*Repens*) foliis linearibus confertis, caule erecto ramoso, floribus spicatis terminalibus. *Toad-flax with linear leaves in clusters, an erect branching stalk, and flowers in spikes terminating the stalks.* Linaria cærulea, foliis brevioribus & angustioribus. Raii Syn. 3. 282. *Blue Toad-flax with shorter and narrower leaves.*

7. LINARIA (*Multicaulis*) foliis inferioribus quinis linearibus. *Toad-flax with linear leaves, placed by fives at the lower part of the stalks.* Linaria Sicula multicaulis, folio molluginis. Bocc. Rar. 38. *Sicilian Toad-flax with many stalks and a Bedstraw leaf.*

8. LI-

8. LINARIA (*Tristis*) foliis lanceolatis sparsis, inferioribus oppositis, nectariis subulatis, floribus subsessilibus. *Toad-flax with spear-shaped sparsed leaves, which on the lower part of the stalk are opposite, awl-shaped nectariums, and flowers sitting almost close.* Linaria Hispanica procumbens, foliis uncialibus glaucis, flore flavescente pulchrè striato, labiis nigro-purpureis. Act. Phil. N° 412. *Trailing Spanish Toad-flax with gray leaves an inch long, yellow flowers beautifully striped, and dark purple lips.*

9. LINARIA (*Monspessulana*) foliis linearibus confertis, caule nitido paniculato, pedunculis spicatis nudis. *Toad-flax with linear leaves in clusters, a paniculated stalk, and flowers in spikes on naked foot-stalks.* Linaria capillaceo folio, odora. C. B. P. 213. *Sweet Toad-flax with hair-like leaves.*

10. LINARIA (*Villosa*) foliis lanceolatis hirtis alternis, floribus spicatis, foliolo calycino supremo maximo. *Toad-flax with alternate, hairy, spear-shaped leaves, flowers in spikes, and the upper leaf of the empalement very large.* Linaria latifolia villosa, laciniis calycinis inæqualibus, flore majore pallido striato rictu aureo. Horteg. Icon. *Broad-leaved hairy Toad-flax, whose empalement is unequally cut, and a large pale striped flower with a golden snout.*

11. LINARIA (*Pelisseriana*) foliis caulinis linearibus sparsis, radicalibus rotundis. *Toad-flax with linear leaves placed sparsedly on the stalks, and on the lower leaves round.* Linaria annua purpurea violacea, calcaribus longis, foliis imis rotundioribus. Vaill. Bot. Par. 118. *Annual purple Violet Toad-flax, with long spurs and rounder leaves at bottom.*

12. LINARIA (*Chalepensis*) foliis lineari-lanceolatis alternis, floribus racemosis, calycibus corollâ longioribus. *Toad-flax with linear spear-shaped leaves placed alternate, branching flowers, and empalements longer than the petals.* Linaria annua angustifolia, flosculis albis, longius caudatis. Triump. 87. *Narrow-leaved annual Toad-flax, with white flowers having long tails.*

13. LINARIA (*Dalmatica*) foliis lanceolatis alternis, caule suffruticoso. *Toad-flax with spear-shaped alternate leaves, and an under shrub stalk.* Linaria latifolia Dalmatica, magno flore. C. B. P. 212. *Broad-leaved Toad-flax of Dalmatia with a large flower.*

14. LINARIA (*Genistifolia*) foliis lanceolatis acuminatis, paniculâ virgatâ. *Toad-flax with spear-shaped acute-pointed leaves, and a rod-like panicle.* Linaria genistæ folio glauco, flore luteo. Par. Bat. App. 9. *Toad-flax with a gray Dyer's Weed leaf and a yellow flower.*

15. LINARIA (*Spuria*) foliis ovatis alternis, caule flaccido procumbente. *Toad-flax with oval leaves placed alternate, and a weak trailing stalk.* Elatine folio subrotundo. C. B. P. 253. *Fluellin with a roundish leaf.*

16. LINARIA (*Elatina*) foliis hastatis alternis, caule flaccido procumbente. *Toad-flax with arrow-pointed leaves placed alternate, and a weak trailing stalk.* Elatine folio acuminato. C. B. P. 253. *Fluellin with an acute-pointed leaf.*

17. LINARIA (*Cymbalaria*) foliis cordatis quinquelobatis alternis glabris. *Toad-flax with heart-shaped leaves having five lobes, which are alternate and smooth.* Linaria hederaceo folio glabro, seu Cymbalaria vulgaris. Tourn. Inst. R. H. 169. *Toad-flax with a smooth Ivy leaf, or common Cymbalaria.*

There are several other species of this genus which are well known and described, which are of less note, so are very rarely admitted into gardens, for which reason I have not enumerated them here.

The first of these plants grows in great plenty upon the sides of dry banks in most parts of England, and is seldom cultivated in gardens; for it is a very troublesome plant to keep within bounds, the roots being very apt to spread under ground, and rise at a great distance from the mother plant, whereby it greatly injures whatever plants stand near it. This is one of the plants mentioned in the catalogue of simples at the end of the College Dispensatory, to be used in medicine.

This hath a great number of slender white roots, which creep far on every side, from which arise se-

veral erect branching stalks a foot and a half high, garnished with narrow gray leaves in clusters, and terminated by spikes of yellow flowers, sitting close to the stalk. The flowers are of one petal, with a long tube, to which is fixed a spur or heel, called a nectarium; the fore parts of the flower has the appearance of the mouth of an animal, the under lip is hairy within; the chaps are of a golden colour, but the other parts of the flower are of a pale yellow; these are succeeded by roundish capsules with two cells, filled with flat black seeds. It flowers in July and August, when it makes a pretty appearance, so that a few plants might be allowed a place in gardens, were it not for their creeping roots, which spread too much, and become troublesome weeds; therefore the roots should be confined in pots to keep them within bounds.

There is an ointment made of this herb and hog's-lard, which is accounted excellent for the piles, being mixed with the yolk of an egg at the time of using it. The plant is reckoned to be aperitive and diuretic, opening obstructions of the liver and spleen, helping the dropsy and jaundice.

The second sort grows naturally about Valencia and in Sicily; this is an annual plant, which rises with an upright branching stalk near a foot and a half high, garnished with oval, smooth, gray leaves, placed often by threes, and sometimes by pairs opposite at the joints; the flowers grow in short spikes at the top of the stalks; they are shaped like those of the common sort, but have not so long tubes; they are yellow, with Saffron-coloured chaps. This sort flowers in July and August, and the seeds ripen in the autumn, and the plants soon after decay.

There is a variety of this whose flowers have a purple standard and spur, which makes a pretty appearance in a garden; but it is generally supposed to be only an accidental variety which has risen from seeds of the former, for which reason I have not enumerated it here; though from many years culture of both sorts, I have never yet perceived either of them alter. The leaves of this are longer than those of the yellow, but in other respects they do not differ.

This sort may be propagated by seeds, or by the roots; the seeds should be sown in the spring, on the borders of the flower-garden where they are designed to remain; and when the plants come up, they should be thinned where they are too close, and kept clean from weeds, which is all the culture they require. If some of the seeds are sown in autumn upon a warm dry border, the plants will live through the winter, unless the frost proves very severe; and these autumnal plants will grow larger, flower earlier, and from these good seeds may always be obtained: the first sort is seldom admitted into gardens.

The third sort rises with upright stalks near two feet high, which are garnished with spear-shaped smooth leaves, placed sometimes by fours round the stalk, and at others by pairs opposite; the stalks are terminated by large purple flowers with long spurs, standing upon foot-stalks. This flowers in July, but seldom ripens seeds in England; it grows naturally in Portugal and Spain.

This sort is tenderer than the last, so should be planted in a dry soil and a warm situation, otherwise the plants are often destroyed in winter. This plant is propagated by seeds in the same manner as the former, as also by parting the roots; but it is adviseable always to keep some of these plants in pots, that they may be removed into shelter in winter, otherwise in hard frosts they will be killed.

The fourth sort grows naturally about Verona, from whence I received the seeds. This is a perennial plant, from whose roots arise several diffused stalks about eight inches long, garnished with narrow, short, gray leaves, placed by fours round the stalk at bottom, but upward they are opposite; the stalks are terminated by short branching tufts of pale yellow flowers with golden chaps. This sort flowers in June, and in warm seasons sometimes the seeds will ripen here in the autumn.

The fifth fort grows naturally in the fouth of France and Italy; this hath a perennial root, fending out many ftalks; thofe of them which fupport the flowers are erect, and near three feet high, but the other ftalks are weaker, and hang loofely on every fide the plants; thefe are garnifhed with long, narrow, fpear-fhaped leaves placed fparfedly; they are fmooth, and of a gray colour. The ftalks are terminated by long loofe fpikes of blue flowers, which appear in June, July, and Auguft, and the feeds ripen in the autumn, which, if permitted to fcatter, will produce plenty of young plants without any further care.

The fixth fort grows naturally about Henley in Oxfordfhire, and alfo in fome parts of Hertfordfhire. This hath a perennial root, from which arife feveral ftalks near two feet high, which branch out on every fide, and are garnifhed with narrow leaves growing in clufters toward the bottom, but upward they are fometimes by pairs, and at others fingle. The flowers are produced in loofe fpikes at the end of the ftalks; they are of a pale blue colour, which appear in June and July, and the feeds ripen in the autumn; which, if permitted to fcatter, will produce plenty of plants. When the feeds happen to fall upon old walls, the plants will grow there and continue longer than thofe planted in the ground.

I received a fpecimen of this fort from abroad, by the title of Linaria arvenfis cærulea. C. B. P.

The feventh fort grows naturally in Sicily; this is an annual plant, from whofe root arifes many ftalks which are very flender and about a foot high, which on their lower part are garnifhed with five very narrow leaves at each joint, but upward they are fometimes by pairs, and at others they are fingle: the ftalks are divided into many fmall branches, which are garnifhed with fmall yellow flowers, coming out fingle at diftances from each other; thefe are fhaped like thofe of the other fpecies. The flowers appear in July, and the feeds ripen in the autumn. There are two varieties of this, one with a deep yellow, and the other a fulphur-coloured flower.

This is propagated by feeds in the fame manner as the fecond fort; if the feeds are permitted to fcatter, the plants will come up without care, and if they are kept clean from weeds, will produce their flowers early in the fummer.

The eighth fort grows naturally on the rocks about Gibraltar, from whence the late Sir Charles Wager brought the feeds, which were fown in his curious garden at Parfon's Green near Fulham, where they fucceeded, and from thence many curious gardens were furnifhed with the plants. This has a perennial root, from which come out many flender fucculent ftalks about eight or nine inches long, which are weak and hang down on every fide the root; they are garnifhed with fhort, narrow, fpear-fhaped leaves, of a gray colour, and fucculent, ftanding without order; they are about one inch long, and a fifth part of an inch broad. The flowers are produced at the end of the ftalks in fmall bunches; they are yellow, marked with purple ftripes, and the chaps of the flower, as alfo the fpur, are of a dark purple colour; the flowers fit clofe upon the top of the ftalk. They appear in June and July, but do not produce feeds in England. This plant is eafily propagated by planting cuttings in any of the fummer months, which, if watered and fhaded, will foon take root, and may be afterwards planted in pots, filled with frefh, light, undunged earth, in which they will fucceed much better than in a richer foil; for if they are planted in a fine rich earth, it, caufes them to grow very faft for a fhort time, but they feldom fail to rot foon after. Thefe muft be removed into fhelter in winter, where they muft have as much free air as poffible in mild weather, and be only protected from fevere cold; fo that if the pots are placed under a hot-bed frame, the plants will fucceed better than in a green-houfe, where they are apt to draw too much, which will caufe them to decay.

The ninth fort grows naturally in Wales, particularly near Penryn. This hath a perennial root, from which arife many branching ftalks near two feet high, garnifhed with very narrow leaves growing in clufters, which are of a grayifh colour. The flowers are produced in loofe fpikes at the end of the branches; they are of a pale blue colour, and fmell fweet. Thefe appear in June, and there is often a fucceffion of flowers on the plants till winter. The feeds ripen in the autumn, which, if permitted to fcatter, will furnifh a fupply of young plants without any further care. If the feeds of this fort get on a wall, the plants will come up, and continue there a much longer time than when they are planted in the ground.

The tenth fort grows naturally in Spain; the feeds of it were fent me by Dr. Hortega from Madrid. This is an annual plant, which rifes with a fingle ftalk about a foot and a half high, garnifhed with hairy fpear-fhaped leaves, fitting clofe to the ftalk, which are placed alternate. The flowers grow on the top of the ftalks in loofe fpikes; they are of a pale yellow colour, with a few dark ftripes, and the chaps are of a gold colour; the upper fegment of the empalement is much larger than the lower. The flowers of this fort are as large as thofe of the common fort; they appear in July, and the feeds will in warm feafons ripen in autumn in England.

The feeds of this fort fhould be fown in the fpring, upon a border of light earth where the plants are defigned to remain; and when the plants come up, they muft be treated in the fame way as thofe of the fecond fort.

The eleventh fort grows naturally in France; this is an annual plant, having round leaves at the root; the ftalks are flender, branching, and rife a foot high, garnifhed with very narrow leaves at each joint. The flowers are produced in loofe fpikes at the end of the branches; they are of a bright blue colour, and appear in July; the feeds ripen in the autumn, at which time they fhould be fown; for thofe which are fown in the fpring frequently lie in the ground till the fpring following, before the plants appear. When the plants come up, they muft be thinned where they are too clofe, and kept clean from weeds, which is all the culture they require.

The twelfth fort grows naturally in Sicily; this is an annual plant, which rifes with a branching ftalk two feet high, garnifhed with very narrow fpear-fhaped leaves placed alternately. The flowers are produced fingly all along the branches the greateft part of their length; they are fmall, white, and have very long tails or fpurs. This flowers in July, and the feeds ripen in the autumn. If the feeds of this fort are permitted to fcatter, the plants will come up and fucceed better than if fown with care, and require no other culture but to keep them clean from weeds.

The thirteenth fort grows naturally in Crete, and alfo in Dalmatia. This rifes with a ftrong ligneous ftalk three feet high, garnifhed with fmooth fpear-fhaped leaves placed alternate, fitting clofe to the ftalk. The flowers are produced at the end of the branches in fhort loofe fpikes; they are of a deep yellow colour, and much larger than thofe of the common fort, ftanding upon fhort foot-ftalks. This fort flowers in July, but the feeds very rarely ripen in England; fo that the plants are feldom feen in any gardens here. It is propagated by feeds, which fhould be fown early in the fpring upon a border of light earth; and when the plants come up and are fit to remove, fome of them fhould be planted in pots filled with light fandy earth, and placed in the fhade till they have taken new root; then they may be expofed with other hardy exotic plants till the end of October, when they fhould be put into a common hot-bed frame, where they may be protected from hard froft; but in mild weather they fhould enjoy the free air, for thefe plants only require to be protected from hard froft, for in mild winters they will live abroad without fhelter, if they are upon a dry foil; therefore a part of the plants may be planted on a warm border of poor fandy foil, where they will live through our common winters

very

very well; and thofe plants which grow in rubbifh and are ftinted, will endure much more cold than the others.

The fourteenth fort grows naturally in Siberia; this is a biennial plant, which rifes with an upright branching ftalk from three to four feet high, garnifhed with fpear-fhaped leaves, ending in acute points, of a grayifh colour; thefe are placed alternate. The flowers are produced at the end of the branches, in loofe panicles; they are of a bright yellow colour, and fhaped like thofe of the other forts. This flowers in June and July, and the feeds ripen in the autumn, which, if permitted to fcatter, the plants will come up the following fpring, and require no other care but to thin them where they are too clofe, and keep them clear from weeds. The plants always decay after they have ripened their feeds, therefore there fhould be a fupply of young ones annually raifed.

The fifteenth fort grows naturally amongft Wheat and Rye, in feveral parts of England. It is an annual plant with weak trailing ftalks, which fpread on the ground, and are a foot and a half long; they are hairy, and garnifhed with oval leaves, placed alternately; from the fetting on of the foot-ftalks of the leaves; at each joint comes out one flower, fhaped like thofe of the other fpecies. The upper lip is yellow, and the under is purple; thefe appear in June and July, and the feeds ripen in autumn, which fhould be then fown, or permitted to fcatter; for if it is fown in the fpring, it feldom grows the fame year, for it is rarely feen among fpring-fown Corn, in thofe lands where it commonly grows.

This plant is ufed in medicine, and is efteemed vulnerary, and good for old cancerous fores and ulcers; it is accounted good for hæmorrhages of all forts.

The fixteenth fort differs from the fifteenth, in nothing but the fhape of the leaves, which in this are fhaped like the point of an arrow, and thofe of the other are oval; this is more commonly found in England than the other.

The feventeenth fort was brought from Italy to England, where it now grows in as great plenty in the neighbourhood of London, as if it was in its native country, growing from the joints of walls, whereever the feeds happen to fcatter. It is a perenial plant, which will thrive in any foil or fituation, fo that where it is once&ftablifhed, it will be difficult to root out, for the feeds will get into any joints of walls, or the decayed parts of pales, as alfo in the hollow of trees, where they grow and propagate plentifully; for the ftalks put out roots at their joints, fo fpread themfelves to a great diftance. It flowers all the fummer, and the feeds ripen in fucceffion. It is never cultivated in gardens, but is fuppofed to be an excellent wound herb.

LINGUA CERVINA. Hart's Tongue.

Thefe plants commonly grow out from the joints of old walls and buildings, where they are moift and fhady, and alfo upon fhady moift banks, but are feldom cultivated in gardens. There is a very great variety of thefe plants, both in the Eaft and Weft-Indies, but there are very few fpecies of them in Europe; all the hardy forts may be propagated by parting their roots, and fhould have a moift foil and fhady fituation.

LINUM. Tourn. Inft. R. H. 339. tab. 170. Lin. Gen. Plant. 349. Flax; in French, *Lin*.

The CHARACTERS are,

The flower hath a permanent empalement, compofed of five fmall, fpear-fhaped, acute leaves. It is compofed of five large oblong petals, which are narrow at their bafe, but broader upward, and fpread open. It hath five awl-fhaped erect ftamina, terminated by arrow-fhaped fummits. In the center is fituated an oval germen, fupporting five flender ftyles, crowned by reflexed ftigmas. The germen afterward turns to a globular capfule with ten cells, opening with five valves; in each cell is lodged one oval, plain, fmooth feed, with an acute point.

This genus of plants is ranged in the fifth fection of Linnæus's fifth clafs, intitled Pentandria Pentagynia,

which contains thofe plants whofe flowers have five ftamina and five ftyles.

The SPECIES are,

1. LINUM (*Ufitatiffimum*) calycibus capfulifque mucronatis petalis crenatis, foliis lanceolatis alternis caule fubfolitario. Lin. Sp. Plant. 277. *Flax with empalements, and capfules ending in acute points, crenated petals to the flower, fpear-fhaped alternate leaves, and the ftalks commonly fingle.* Linum fativum. C. B. P. 214. *Manured Flax.*

2. LINUM (*Humile*) calycibus capfulifque mucronatis, petalis emarginatis, foliis lanceolatis alternis, caule ramofo. *Flax with fharp-pointed empalements and capfules, the petals of the flower indented, fpear-fhaped alternate leaves, and a branching ftalk.* Linum fativum humilius flore majore. Bobart. Boerh. Ind. alt. 1. p. 284. *Low manured Flax with a larger flower.*

3. LINUM (*Narbonenfe*) calycibus acuminatis, foliis lanceolatis fparfis ftrictis fcabris acuminatis, caule tereti bafi ramofo. Lin. Sp. Plant. 278. *Flax with acute-pointed empalements, rough fpear-fhaped leaves placed without order, ending in acute points, and a taper ftalk branching at the bafe.* Linum fylveftre, cæruleum, folio acuto. C. B. P. 107. *Wild blue Flax with an acute leaf.*

4. LINUM (*Tenuifolium*) calycibus acuminatis, foliis fparfis linearibus fetaceis retrorfum fcabris. Lin. Sp. Plant. 278. *Flax with acute-pointed empalements, and narrow briftly leaves placed without order, which are rough on their outfide.* Linum fylveftre anguftifolium, floribus diluté purpurafcentibus vel carneis. C. B. P. 214. *Narrow-leaved wild Flax, with a pale purplifh or flefh-coloured flower.*

5. LINUM (*Anglicum*) calycibus capfulifque acuminatis, caule fubnudo fcabro, foliis acuminatis. *Flax with acute-pointed empalements, an almoft naked rough ftalk, and acute-pointed leaves.* Linum perenne, majus, cæruleum, capitulo majore. Mor. Hift. 2. 573. *Greater blue perennial Flax with larger heads.*

6. LINUM (*Perenne*) calycibus capfulifque obtufis, foliis alternis lanceolatis acutis, caulibus ramofiffimis. Plat. 166. *Flax with obtufe empalements and capfules, alternate, fpear-fhaped, acute leaves, and very branching ftalks, commonly called Siberian perennial Flax.*

7. LINUM (*Hifpanicum*) calycibus acutis, foliis linearilanceolatis fparfis, caule paniculato procumbente. *Flax with acute empalements, linear fpear-fhaped leaves placed without order, and a paniculated ftalk.*

8. LINUM (*Bienne*) calycibus patulis acuminatis, foliis linearibus alternis, caule ramofo. *Flax with fpreading acute-pointed empalements, linear alternate leaves, and a branching ftalk.*

9. LINUM (*Hirfutum*) calycibus hirfutis acuminatis feffilibus alternis, caule corymbofo. Lin. Sp. Plant. 277. *Flax with hairy acute-pointed empalements, placed alternate clofe to the ftalks, whofe flowers are formed in a corymbus.* Linum fylveftre, latifolium, hirfutum cæruleum. C. B. P. 339. *Broad-leaved, hairy, wild Flax, with a blue flower.*

10. LINUM (*Strictum*) calycibus foliifque lanceolatis ftrictis mucronatis, margine fcabris. Lin. Sp. Plant. 279. *Flax with fpear-fhaped leaves, and empalements which end in acute points, and have rough edges.* Pafferina Lobelii. J. B. 3. p. 454.

11. LINUM (*Fruticofum*) calycibus acutis, petalis integris, foliis inferioribus linearibus fafciculatis, fuperioribus alternis, caule fuffruticofo. *Flax with acute empalements, entire petals to the flower, linear under leaves growing in clufters, the upper ones alternate, and a fhrubby ftalk.* Linum fylveftre acutis foliis fruticans. Barrel. Icon. 1008. *Wild Flax with a fhrubby ftalk and acute leaves.*

12. LINUM (*Nodiflorum*) foliis lanceolatis alternis, floribus alternis feffilibus caule fimplici. *Flax with fpear-fhaped leaves placed alternate, flowers growing alternate, and clofe to the ftalks, which are fingle.* Linum luteum ad fingula genicula floridum. C. B. P. 214. *Yellow Flax with fingle flowers growing from the joints.*

13. LI-

13. LINUM (*Catharticum*) foliis oppofitis ovato-lanceolatis, caule dichotomo, corollis acutis. Hort. Cliff. 372. *Flax with fpear-fhaped leaves placed oppofite, a ftalk divided by pairs, and acute petals to the flower.* Linum pratenfe, flofculis exiguis. C. B. P. 214. *Meadow Flax with fmall flowers, commonly called Mountain Flax.*

14. LINUM (*Maritimum*) calycibus ovatis acutis muticis, foliis lanceolatis inferioribus oppofitis. Lin. Sp. Plant. 280. *Flax with oval, acute, chaffy empalements, and fpear-fhaped leaves, the lower of which grow oppofite.* Linum maritimum luteum. C. B. P. 214. *Yellow maritime Flax.*

The firft fort is the Flax which is cultivated in moft parts of Europe, but particularly in the northern parts; this is an annual plant, which ufually rifes with a flender unbranched ftalk a foot and a half high, garnifhed with narrow fpear-fhaped leaves placed alternate, ending in acute points, and are of a gray colour. The flowers are produced on the top of the ftalks, each ftalk fuftaining four or five blue flowers, compofed of five petals, which are narrow at their bafe, but broad at the top, where they are flightly crenated. The empalement of the flower is cut into five parts, which end in acute points. The flowers appear in June, and are fucceeded by roundifh capfules which have ten cells, opening with five valves, which are terminated by acute points; each cell contains one fmooth flattifh feed, ending in a point, of a brownifh colour. The feeds ripen in September, and the plants foon after perifh.

When this plant is cultivated in the fields after the ufual method, it feldom rifes higher than is before mentioned; nor do the ftalks branch out, but when they are allowed more room, they will rife more than two feet high, and put out two or three fide branches toward the top, efpecially if the foil is pretty good where it is fown.

The fecond fort differs from the firft, in having ftronger and fhorter ftalks branching out much more. The leaves are broader, the flowers are larger, and the petals are indented at their extremities. The feedveffels are alfo much larger, and the foot-ftalks are longer; thefe differences are lafting, for I have cultivated this and the common Flax on the fame ground upward of thirty years, and have never found either of them alter.

The third fort grows naturally in the fouth of France, in Italy, and Spain; this rifes from a foot to eighteen inches high, branching out almoft to the bottom into many long flender branches, which are garnifhed with narrow, fpear-fhaped, acute-pointed leaves, placed without order; thefe are rough to the touch. The flowers are produced at the end of the branches, almoft in form of an umbel; they are fmaller than thofe of the manured fort, and are of a pale blue colour. The feed-veffels are much fmaller, and not fo round. It flowers and feeds about the fame time as the former.

The fourth fort grows naturally about Vienna and in Hungary; this fort feldom rifes more than a foot high, with a flender ftalk, which divides into three or four flender naked foot-ftalks at the top, each fuftaining two or three flowers, which are of a pale blue colour. The ftalks are garnifhed with fhort, narrow, briftly leaves, ftanding erect, which are rough on their outfide. This flowers and feeds about the fame time as the former, and the plant foon after decays.

There are two or three varieties of this, which differ in the colour of their flowers, but in other refpects are the fame.

The fifth fort grows naturally in fome parts of England, particularly in Cambridgefhire; this hath a perennial root, from which arife three or four inclining ftalks, garnifhed with fhort narrow leaves toward their bafe, but upward have fcarce any. The flowers are produced at the end of the ftalks, fitting very clofe; they are of a blue colour, and about the fize of thofe of the manured kind, and are fucceeded by pretty large round feed-veffels, ending in acute points. This flowers about the fame time as the common Flax, but the roots will continue four or five years.

The fixth fort grows naturally in Siberia; it hath a perennial root, from which arife feveral ftrong ftalks, in number proportional to the fize of the root, and in height according to the goodnefs of the foil where it grows; for in rich moift ground they will rife near five feet high, but in middling ground about three feet; thefe divide into feveral branches upward, and are garnifhed with narrow fpear-fhaped leaves, placed alternate; they are not much more than an inch long, and an eighth of an inch broad, of a deep green, ending in acute points. The flowers are produced at the end of the branches, forming a kind of umbel, the ftalks rifing nearly of the fame height. The flowers are large, and of a fine blue colour; thefe appear in June, and are fucceeded by obtufe feed-veffels, which ripen in September.

The feventh fort grows naturally in Spain, from whence I received the feeds; this hath a perennial root, from whence come out feveral trailing ftalks, which are clofely garnifhed with leaves; thefe never rife much from the ground, but between thefe come out upright ftalks, which rife upward of two feet high, garnifhed with pretty long, narrow, fpear-fhaped leaves, placed without order. The flowers grow in a fort of panicle toward the upperpart of the branches; they are about the fize of thofe of the common fort, and are of the fame colour. It flowers and ripens its feeds about the fame time, and the roots continue feveral years.

The eighth fort I received from Iftria; this hath a biennial root, from which arife two or three ftalks, which divide into feveral branches, at about fix inches from the root, which divide again into fmaller toward the top; they are garnifhed with fhort, narrow, acute-pointed leaves, placed alternately. The flowers come out from the fide of the branches, ftanding upon long foot-ftalks. The empalement of the flower is compofed of five broadifh leaves ending in acute points, which fpread open; the flowers are of the fame fize and colour as the common Flax, and appear at the fame feafon. The feeds ripen in the autumn, and the roots abide feveral years.

The ninth fort grows naturally in Hungary and Auftria; this hath a perennial root, from which arife feveral ftalks near two feet high, which are thick, firm, and hairy, dividing at the top into feveral branches, and are garnifhed with broader leaves than the other fpecies, which are hairy. The flowers grow along the ftalks alternately; they are large, and of a deep blue colour, appearing at the fame time with the common fort, and the feeds ripen in the autumn.

The tenth fort grows naturally in Germany and the fouth of France, amongft the Corn. This is an annual plant, rifing with an upright ftalk near a foot and a half high, garnifhed with fpear-fhaped acute-pointed leaves, which are rough on their edges; they are about the fame length of thofe of the common Flax, but a little broader, placed alternately. The ftalks divide toward the top into feveral branches, each fuftaining two or three yellow flowers, fitting in fpear-fhaped acute-pointed empalements. Thefe appear in July, but unlefs the autumn proves favourable, the feeds never ripen in England.

The eleventh fort grows naturally in Spain; the feeds of it were fent me from Madrid by Dr. Hortega. This hath a fhrubby ftalk which rifes a foot high, fending out feveral branches which are garnifhed with very narrow leaves coming out in clufters; but the flowering branches are garnifhed with broader and longer leaves, placed alternately at every joint. The flowers are produced at the end of the branches, ftanding erect upon long flender foot-ftalks; they have acute-pointed empalements. The petals of the flower are large, entire, and white, but before the flowers open, they are of a pale yellow colour. Thefe flowers appear in July,

but

but unlefs the autumn proves favourable, the feeds do not ripen in England. The flower-ftalks of this fort decay in the autumn, but the lower fhrubby ftalk continues with the other branches all the year.

The twelfth fort grows naturally upon the Alps ; this hath a perennial root, from whence arife two or three flender ftiff ftalks, which divide at the top into two or three flender branches, garnifhed with fpear-fhaped leaves placed alternately. The flowers come out fingly at the joints, and fit clofe to the ftalks ; their empalements are cut into five flender fegments, which are longer than the petals of the flower. The flowers are yellow, and appear about the fame time with the common fort, and the feeds ripen in the autumn.

The thirteenth fort grows common in many parts of England, upon dry barren hills. It is commonly called Linum cartharticum, purging Flax, and alfo Mountain Flax. This rifes with feveral branching flender ftalks about feven or eight inches high, garnifhed with fmall, oval, fpear-fhaped leaves placed oppofite. The flowers are fmall and white, ftanding upon pretty long foot-ftalks, which come out from the fide of the branches, and alfo where they are divided. They appear in July, and are fucceeded by fmall round cap-fules, containing fmall flat feeds which ripen in the autumn. This is one of thofe plants which refufes culture. I have frequently fown the feeds both in autumn and fpring, but could feldom get up any of the plants, and others who have made the trial have found the fame.

The fourteenth fort grows naturally about Montpelier, and in fome parts of Italy near the fea. This rifes with upright ftalks near two feet high, the lower part of which are garnifhed with fpear-fhaped leaves placed oppofite, but on the upper part they are alternate. The ftalks divide upward into feveral branches, the tops of which are garnifhed with yellow flowers about the fize of thofe of common Flax, which hang downward ; thefe are fucceeded by fmall oval cap-fules, containing fmaller feeds than thofe of the common Flax. The flowers appear in July, and the feeds ripen in the autumn.

There are feveral other fpecies of Flax which grow wild in the different parts of Europe, but thofe here enumerated are all I have feen growing in the Englifh gardens.

The firft fort is that which is cultivated for ufe in divers parts of Europe, and is reckoned an excellent commodity ; the right tilling and ordering of which, is efteemed a good piece of hufbandry.

This fhould be cultivated upon a rich foil, that has not been ploughed for feveral years, upon which Flax always makes the beft improvement ; but as it draws greatly from the foil, it fhould not be fown two years together upon the fame ground, nor in lefs than after five or fix years interval.

This ground fhould be as clean from weeds as pof-fible ; in order to have it fo, it fhould be fallowed two winters and one fummer, obferving to harrow the ground well between each ploughing, particularly in fummer, to deftroy the young weeds foon after they appear, that the fmalleft of them may not ftand to ri-pen their feed ; this will alfo break the clods, and fe-parate their parts fo, that they will fall to pieces on being ftirred. If the land fhould require dung, that fhould not be laid on till the laft ploughing, when it muft be buried in the ground ; but this dung fhould be fuch as is clear from the feeds of weeds, which it always will be where there is care taken to keep the dunghills clean from weeds, and the places near it ; for fuppofing there fhould be any feeds at firft among the dung, yet when it is laid in a heap and well fer-mented, that will deftroy the feeds ; but there are few perfons who are careful to keep their dunghills, and the places near them, clean from weeds ; and the feeds of thefe falling on the dung, are carried upon the land ; from whence fprung that vulgar error, that dung produces weeds, which it can never do, if there is not the feeds mixed with it. Juft before the

feafon for fowing of the Flax feed, the land muft be well ploughed, laid flat and even, upon which the feeds fhould be fown about the latter end of March, or the beginning of April, when the weather is mild and warm.

The common way is to fow the feed in broad-caft, and to allow from two to three bufhels of feeds to one acre of land ; but from many repeated trials, I have found it is a much better method to fow the feeds in drills, at about ten inches diftance from each other, by which half the quantity of feed which is ufually fown, will produce a greater crop ; and when the Flax is thus fown, the ground may be eafily hoed to deftroy the weeds ; which, if twice repeated in dry weather, will keep the ground clean till the Flax is ripe : this may be performed at half the expence which the hand weeding will coft, and will not tread down the plants nor harden the ground, which by the other method is always done ; and it is abfolutely neceffary to keep the Flax clean from weeds, otherwife they will overbear and fpoil the crop.

There are fome people who recommend the feeding of fheep with Flax, when it is a good height ; and fay, they will eat away the weeds and Grafs, and do the Flax good ; and if they fhould lie in it, and beat it down or flatten it, it will rife again the next rain : but this is a very wrong practice, for if the fheep gnaw or eat the Flax, the plants will fhoot up very weak, and never come to half the fize they would have done, if not cropped : and as to the fheep de-ftroying the weeds, they never are fo nice diftin-guifhers, for if they like the crop better than the weeds, they will devour that and leave the weeds untouched.

Toward the latter end of Auguft or the beginning of September, the Flax will begin to ripen, when you muft be careful that it does not ftand to be over ripe ; therefore you muft pull it up as foon as the heads begin to change brown and hang downwards, otherwife the feeds will foon fcatter and be loft ; fo that the pluckers muft be nimble, and tie it up in handfuls, fetting them upright till they be perfectly dry, and then houfe them. If the Flax be pulled when it firft begins to flower, it will be whiter than if it ftand till the feed is ripe, but then the feed will be loft ; but the thread will be ftronger when Flax is left till the feed is ripe, provided it does not ftand too long, but the colour of it will not befo good.

The Siberian perennial Flax has been made trial of, and anfwers very well for making of common ftrong linen, but the thread fpun from this is not fo fine or white as that which is produced from the common fort ; but as the roots of this fort will continue many years, fo there will be a great faving in the culture, as it will require no other care but to keep it con-ftantly clean from weeds ; which cannot be well done, unlefs the feeds are fown in rows, that the ground may be conftantly kept hoed to deftroy the weeds when young ; for if they are fuffered to grow large, it will be difficult to get the ground clean, and they will weaken the roots. This fort muft have the ftalks cut off clofe to the ground when ripe, and tied up in fmall bundles, managing them afterward in the fame way as the common fort ; but this feldom produces more than three crops, which will pay for ftanding.

The eighth fort I received from Iftria, which pro-duced the fineft thread of all the forts which I have tried ; and this grows taller than the common Flax, and having a biennial root, may be wor-thy of trial to fee how it will thrive in the open fields ; for in gardens it lives through the winter with-out receiving the leaft injury from the froft, the roots having furvived through the winter in the Chelfea garden feveral years ; and in order to make trial of its goodnefs, I gave a parcel of the ftalks of this, as alfo of the Spanifh and Siberian perennial forts, to a perfon who is well fkilled in watering, breaking, and dreffing of Flax, who prepared them, and affured me, that the Iftrian Flax was by much the fineft of the three, and was in goodnefs preferable to any he had feen.

        There

There is annually great quantities of the feed. of Flax imported into Scotland and Ireland, from the East Country, particularly from Riga, to the amount of many thousand pounds sterling, per ann. which might be saved to the public, by encouraging the growth of Flax in the northern colonies of America, where the summers are warmer than in England, so that the seeds would ripen perfectly there, and the change of feeds from thence would be greater than that from Riga, but it should be confined to the most northern parts of America; for such feeds as are saved in the warmer parts will not succeed well here, as I have experienced in many other kinds of plants, whose feeds I have sent to Carolina, where they have grown two or three years, after which some of the seeds have been sent me back, which I have always found to be much longer in growing to perfection than before.

The other sorts which are here mentioned, are preserved in gardens for the sake of variety, but none of them are used, except the Mountain Flax, which is esteemed a good purger in dropsical disorders, and has of late years been often prescribed.

They are all of them propagated by seeds, which may be sown in the spring, in the places where they are to remain, and will require no other culture but to keep the plants clean from weeds. The annual forts will flower and perfect their seeds the same year, but the roots of the perennial forts will continue several years, putting out fresh stalks every spring. The shrubby forts will live through the winter in the open air, provided it is in a dry soil and a warm situation; but these rarely produce feeds in England.

The method of watering, piling, braking, &c. being a particular business, and foreign to my design, I shall not pretend to give any directions about it in this place.

The common sort is a plant of the greatest use, in several of the most essential parts of life; from the seeds an expressed oil is drawn, which is of great use in medicine, painting, &c. from the bark of the stalks is made linen, and from the rags of linen is made paper; so that this plant may be esteemed as one of the most valuable, and absolutely necessary in many of the principal conveniencies of life.

LINUM UMBILICATUM. See CYNOGLOSSUM.

LIPPIA. Houst. Gen. Nov. Lin. Gen. Plant. 699.

This plant was so named by the late Dr. William Houstoun, who discovered it at La Vera Cruz, where it grows naturally, in honour of Dr. Augustus Lippi, a famous botanist, who travelled to Egypt, and discovered many new plants.

The CHARACTERS are,

The empalement: of the flower is permanent, roundish, and compressed. The flower hath one petal, which is of the ringent kind; the upper lip is divided into two parts, which are reflexed; the under lip is smaller, and cut into two roundish segments. It hath four short stamina, two of which are a little longer than the other, terminated by single summits, and an oval germen supporting a slender style the length of the stamina, crowned by an indented stigma. The germen afterward turns to a compressed capsule with one cell, opening with two valves, which appear like the scales of the empalement, inclosing two seeds which are joined.

This genus of plants is ranged in the second section of Linnæus's fourteenth class, intitled Didynamia Angiospermia, which includes those plants whose flowers have two long and two shorter stamina, and the seeds are included in capsules.

The SPECIES are,

1. LIPPIA (*Americana*) arborescens foliis conjugatis oblongis, capitulis squamosis & rotundis. Houst. *Tree Lippia with oblong leaves growing by pairs, having round scaly heads.* Lippia capitulis pyramidatis. Lin. Sp. 883. *Lippia with pyramidal heads.*

2. LIPPIA (*Hemisphærica*) capitulis hemisphæricis. Jacq. Amer. 25. *Lippia with hemispherical heads.*

The first sort in the country of its native growth, commonly rises to the height of sixteen or eighteen feet, with a rough bark: the branches come out by pairs opposite, as do also the leaves, which are oblong, pointed, and a little sawed on their edges. From the wings of the leaves come out the foot-stalks, which sustain many pyramidal scaly heads, about the size of a large gray Pea, in which are many small yellow flowers appearing between the scales, which are succeeded by the seed-vessels.

The second sort grows naturally in Carthagena in New Spain, where it rises with shrubby stalks ten or twelve feet high, sending out slender branches toward their top, garnished with oval spear-shaped leaves three inches long, ending in acute points, smooth on their upper surface, which are placed opposite; the foot-stalks of the flowers come out opposite just above the leaves, each supporting a pyramidal head of white flowers, which peep out from the scales of the head; these are succeeded by capsules having two cells, including small seeds.

The seeds of the first sort were sent by Dr. Houstoun to several curious gardens in Europe, where some of the plants have been raised; but as the country from whence they came is very warm, so the plants will not thrive in this climate, unless they are preserved in a warm stove. The feeds should be sown on a hot-bed, and the plants may be treated in the same manner as other shrubby plants which are natives of warm countries: which is, to keep them always in the stove, plunged in the bark-bed, observing to give them a large share of air in warm weather, and frequently refresh them with water; but in winter they must be watered more sparingly, and be kept in a moderate degree of warmth, otherwise they will not live through the winter, especially while they are young; but when they have acquired strength, they may be preserved with a less share of warmth.

As the plants advance in their growth, they should be shifted into larger pots, but this should not be too often repeated; for if they are removed into new pots every spring, it will be as often as they will require; so that when these, and many other exotic plants, are too often removed, they do not thrive so well as when they are permitted to fill the pots with their roots. The best time to shift these plants is in April, at which time the tan of the hot-bed should be stirred, and fresh tan mixed with it, to increase the heat. The earth in which these plants are placed, should be fresh and light, but not too rich.

LIQUIDAMBER. Mitch. Gen. 12. Lin. Gen. Plant. 955. Liquidamber, Sweet Gum, or Storax-tree.

The CHARACTERS are,

It hath male and female flowers sometimes on the same plant, at other times upon different plants; the male flowers are numerous, disposed in long, loose, conical katkins; these have four-leaved empalements, but no petals. They have a great number of short stamina joined in one body, which are convex on one side, but plain on the other, terminated by erect twin summits, with four furrows. The female flowers are often situated at the base of the male spike, collected in a globe; these have a double empalement like that of the male, and each of them has a bell-shaped, angular, distinct empalement, with many protuberances. They have no petals, but an oblong germen fastened to the empalement, supporting two awl-shaped styles, to which is also fixed the recurved stigmas, which are hairy and as long as the styles. The empalement afterward turns to a roundish capsule of one cell, with two valves at the top, which are acute, and collected in a ligneous globe, containing oblong acute-pointed seeds.

This genus of plants is ranged in the eighth section of Linnæus's twenty-first class, which includes those plants with male and female flowers, whose male flowers have many stamina.

The SPECIES are,

1. LIQUIDAMBER (*Styraciflua*) foliis quinquelobatis serratis. *Liquidamber with sawed leaves having five lobes.* Styrax aceris folio. Raii Hist. 1681. *Maple-leaved Storax-tree.*

LIT

LIT

2. LIQUIDAMBER (*Orientalis*) foliis quinquelobatis, finuatis obtufis. *Liquidamber with leaves having five lobes, which are finuated and obtufe.*

The firft fort has by fome writers been ranged with the Maple, but on no other account, except from the fimilitude of the leaves; for in flower and fruit it is very different from the Maple, and moft other genera: nor has it any affinity to the Storax-tree, but the gum which iffues from this tree being tranfparent, and having a great fragrancy, has by fome ignorant perfons been taken for that.

It grows plentifully in Virginia and feveral other parts of North America, where it rifes with a ftrait naked ftem to the height of fifteen or fixteen feet, and afterward branches out regularly to the height of forty feet or upward, forming a pyramidal head. The leaves are angular, and fhaped fomewhat like thofe of the leffer Maple, having five lobes, but are of a dark green colour, and their upper furfaces fhining; a ftrong, fweet, glutinous fubftance exfudes through the pores of the leaves in warm weather, which renders them clammy to the touch.

The flowers are generally produced early in the fpring of the year, before the leaves are expanded, which are of a Saffron colour, and grow in fpikes from the extremity of the branches; after thefe are paft, the fruit fwells to the fize of a Walnut, being perfectly round, having many protuberances, each having a fmall hole and a fhort tail, which extends half an inch.

The planks of this tree being beautifully veined, are often ufed in America for wainfcotting rooms; but it requires a long time to feafon the boards, otherwife they are apt to fhrink.

In Europe this tree is cultivated in the gardens of the curious, for the fake of variety; it is hardy enough to endure the fevereft cold of this country in the open air, and there are fome of them upward of twenty feet high, though I have not heard of any of them which has produced fruit.

This is commonly propagated by layers in England, but thofe plants which are raifed from feeds grow to be much fairer trees.

The feeds of this tree, if fown in the fpring, commonly remain in the ground a whole year before the plants come up; fo that the fureft way to raife them is, to fow the feeds in boxes or pots of light earth; which may be placed in a fhady fituation during the firft fummer, and in autumn they may be removed where they may have more fun; but if the winter fhould prove fevere, it will be proper to cover them with Peas-haulm, or other light covering, which fhould be taken off conftantly in mild weather. In the following fpring, if thefe boxes or pots are placed upon a moderate hot-bed, it will caufe the feeds to come up early, fo that the plants will have time to get ftrength before the winter; but during the firft and fecond winters, it will be proper to fcreen the plants from fevere froft, but afterward they will bear the cold very well.

The feeds of the fecond fort were fent by Mr. Peyfonel from the Levant, to the French king's garden at Marli, a few of which were fent me by Mr. Richard, the king's gardener, which fucceeded in the Chelfea garden. The leaves of this fort differ from thofe of the firft, in having their lobes fhorter, and much more finuated on their borders; they end in blunt points, and are not ferrated; but as I have not feen the fruit of this, fo I do not know how it differs from the other.

LIRIODENDRUM. See TULIPIFERA.

LITHOSPERMUM. Tourn. Inft. R. H. 137. tab. 55. Lin. Gen. Plant. 166. [of Λίθος, a ftone, and Σπέρμα, feed; q. d. Stone-feed; becaufe the feed of this plant is hard, and good againft the ftone.] Gromwell, Gromill, or Graymill; in French, *Gremil.*

The CHARACTERS are,

The flower hath an oblong, erect, acute-pointed, permanent, empalement, which is cut into five parts. It hath one petal with a cylindrical tube the length of the em- palement, *divided into five obtufe points at the brim; which are erect; the chaps are perforated. It hath five fhort ftamina terminated by oblong fummits; which are fhut up in the chaps of the petal. It hath four germen, with a flender ftyle the length of the tube, crowned by a bifid obtufe ftigma. The germen afterward turn to fo many oval, hard, fmooth, acute-pointed feeds, fitting in the fpreading empalement.*

This genus of plants is ranged in the firft fection of Linnæus's fifth clafs, which includes the plants whofe flowers have five ftamina and one ftyle.

The SPECIES are,

1. LITHOSPERMUM (*Officinale*) feminibus lævibus, corollis calycem vix fuperantibus, foliis lanceolatis. Hort. Cliff. 46. *Gromwell with fmooth feeds, the petal of the flower fcarce louger than the empalement, and fpear-fhaped leaves.* Lithofpermum majus erectum. C. B. P. 258. *Greater upright Gromwell.*

2. LITHOSPERMUM (*Arvenfe*) feminibus rugofis, corollis vix calycem fuperantibus. Hort. Cliff. 46. *Gromwell with rough feeds, whofe petals are fcarce longer than the empalement.* Lithofpermum arvenfe, radice rubrå. C. B. P. 258. *Field Gromwell with a red root.*

3. LITHOSPERMUM (*Purpurocæruleum*) feminibus lævibus, corollis calycem multoties fuperantibus. Hort. Cliff. 46. *Gromwell with fmooth feeds, and the petal many times longer than the empalement.* Lithofpermum minus repens latifolium C. B. P. 258. *Smaller, creeping, broad-leaved Gromwell.*

4. LITHOSPERMUM (*Virginianum*) foliis fubovalibus nervofis, corollis acuminatis. Lin. Sp. Plant. 132. *Gromwell with veined leaves which are almoft oval, and acute-pointed petals.* Lithofpermum latifolium Virginianum, flore albido longiore. Mor. Hift. 3. p. 447. *Broad-leaved Gromwell of Virginia with a longer whitifh flower.*

5. LITHOSPERMUM (*Fruticofum*) fruticofum, foliis lineraribus hifpidis, ftaminibus corollam fubæquantibus. Lin. Sp. 190. *Shrubby Gromwell with rough linear leaves, and the ftamina almoft equal to the petal.* Bugloffum famium frutefcens, foliis Rorifmarini obfcure virentibus lucidis & hirfutis. Tourn. Cor. 6.

The firft fort grows naturally upon the banks, and in dry fields in many parts of England, fo is feldom admitted into gardens. This hath a biennial root, from which arife two or three upright ftalks two feet high, which branch out toward the top, garnifhed with fpear-fhaped, rough, hairy leaves, placed alternate, fitting clofe to the ftalks. The flowers come out fingly at every joint of the fmall branches; they are white, of one petal, cut into four parts at the top, and ftand within the empalement; thefe are fucceeded by four hard, white, fhining feeds, which ripen in the empalement. It flowers in May, and the feeds ripen in Auguft.

The feeds of this plant are accounted a powerful diuretic, and a cleanfer of the reins and urethers, being boiled in wine and water, and are of great fervice againft gravel or ftoppage of urine.

The fecond fort is an annual plant, which grows among winter Corn in many parts of England. This rifes with a flender branching ftalk a foot and a half high, garnifhed with narrow, fpear-fhaped, rough leaves placed alternately. The flowers are produced fingly on the upper parts of the ftalks. They are fmall and white; thefe are fucceeded by four rough feeds, which ripen in the empalement. It flowers in June, and the feeds ripen in Auguft, foon after which the plants decay.

The third fort grows naturally in woods in many parts of England; this hath a perennial root, from which come out two or three trailing ftalks fcarce a foot long, garnifhed with long, narrow, fpear-fhaped leaves, placed alternately; thefe are fmoother than thofe of the other forts. The flowers are produced at the end of the ftalks from amongft the leaves; they are white, and the petals are much longer than the empalements. Thefe appear the latter end of May, and each is fucceeded by four fmooth feeds, which ripen in the empalement.

Tha

The fourth fort grows naturally in North America; this hath a perennial root, from which arife feveral very hairy ftalks about a foot and a half high, garnifhed with rough, hairy, veined leaves, which are almoft oval, fitting clofe to the ftalks alternately. The flowers grow in fhort reflexed fpikes at the end of the branches: thefe are white, their petals being longer than the empalement, ending in acute points. It flowers in June, and the feeds ripen in autumn.

The fifth fort grows naturally in the fouth of France, and alfo in the Levant. This hath a perennial root, which runs deep in the ground, from which comes out in the fpring a fhrubby erect ftalk two or three feet high, which is pretty clofely fet with hairs, and garnifhed with narrow leaves placed alternately. The flowers are produced in fhort reflexed fpikes at the end of the ftalk, ftanding in hairy empalements; they are of a reddifh purple colour, but as they decay change to a deep purple; they are tubulous, but cut at the top into four or five fegments; the upper two are reflexed. It flowers in June, but the feeds rarely ripen in England.

Thefe plants may be cultivated by fowing their feeds in rows foon after they are ripe, in a bed of frefh earth, allowing the rows at leaft a foot diftance from each other, obferving to keep them clear from weeds, and they will thrive in almoft any foil or fituation.

LOAM is a common fuperficial earth, that is a mixture of fand and clay, commonly of a yellowifh colour, though there is fome Loam that is blackifh. Some call Loam the moft common fuperficial earth met with in England, without any regard to the proportion it bears to fand or clay; but moft generally the appellation of Loam is applied to a foft fat earth, partaking of clay, but eafy to work.

It is found by experience, that plants of moft forts will grow in it; and wherever it is found, it appears to be a more beneficial foil to plants than any other. A clay ufed in grafting is alfo called Loam.

LOBELIA. Plum. Nov. Gen. 21. tab. 31. Lin. Gen. Plant. 897.

The CHARACTERS are,

The empalement of the flower is fmall, of one leaf, indented in five parts, and grows about the germen. The flower has but one petal, which is tubulous, and a little ringent, cut into five parts at the brim; two of the upper fegments are fmaller than the other, and more reflexed and deeper cut, thefe conftitute the upper lip; the three lower are fpread open, and larger. It hath five awl-fhaped ftamina the length of the tube, terminated by oblong cylindrical fummits, divided at their bafe into five parts. It has a pointed germen under the petal, fupporting a cylindrical ftyle, crowned by an obtufe prickly ftigma. The germen afterward becomes an oval flefhy berry with two cells, each containing a fingle feed.

This genus of plants is ranged in the fifth fection of Linnæus's nineteenth clafs, to which he has joined the Rapuntium of Tournefort; but although the form of theflowers, and the number of their ftamina, agree pretty well, yet as the fruit of this is a pulpy berry, inclofing but two feeds, and the Rapuntii have dry capfules including many fmall feeds, I fhall keep them feparate.

We know but one SPECIES of this genus, viz.

LOBELIA (*Frutefcens*) frutefcens, foliis ovati-oblongis integerrimis. Flor. Zeyl. 313. *Shrubby Lobelia with oblong, oval, entire leaves.* Lobelia frutefcens portulacæ folio. Plum. Nov. Gen. 21. *Shrubby Lobelia with a Purflane leaf.*

This plant rifes with a fucculent ftalk five or fix feet high, garnifhed with oval, oblong, fucculent leaves, which are placed alternately; thefe fit clofe to the ftalk. The flowers are produced upon long foot-ftalks, which come out from the fide of the ftalk, and fuftain two or three white flowers of one petal, cut into five acute fegments at the brim; thefe are fucceeded by two oval berries as large as Bullace, containing a ftone with two cells, in each of which is lodged a fingle feed.

The feeds of this plant were fent to England by Mr. Catefby, in the year 1724, who gathered them in the Bahama Iflands, where the plants grow in plenty, near the fhore of the fea; and fince that time the feeds have been fent to England by Dr. William Houftoun, who gathered them at La Vera Cruz; fo that I believe the plant is common in moft of the warm parts of America.

It is propagated by feeds, which muft be procured from the countries of its natural growth, for the plants will not produce them in Europe; thefe feeds fhould be fown in pots filled with light fandy earth, and plunged into a hot-bed of tanners bark, where the plants will come up in about a month or five weeks, provided the bed is warm, and the earth often watered. When the plants are up, they fhould be kept in a temperate hot-bed, and frequently refrefhed with water, but it muft not be given them in large quantities, for they are very fucculent, and fubject to perifh with much moifture, efpecially while they are young. When the plants are about two inches high, they fhould be carefully taken out of the pots in which they were fown, and each planted in a feparate fmall pot filled with frefh light fandy earth, and then plunged into the hot-bed again, obferving to fhade them in the heat of the day until they have taken new root. In this hot-bed the plants may remain until the middle, or latter end of September, when they muft be removed into the ftove, and plunged into the tan-bed, in the warmeft part of the ftove, for they are very tender plants while young, therefore muft be kept very warm, otherwife they will not live through the firft winter in this country. In the fpring following the plants may be fhifted into fomewhat larger pots, and then plunged into a frefh hot-bed to forward their growth; for if they are not pufhed on while they are young, they feldom grow to any fize, nor will they ever flower; fo that in order to have them in any beauty, they muft be carefully managed. The leaves of this plant are very fubject to contract filth, by being conftantly kept in the ftove, therefore they fhould be wafhed with a fponge frequently, to keep them clean, otherwife they will appear unfightly.

LOBUS ECHINATUS. See GUILANDINA.

LOCULAMENTS are little diftinct cells, or partitions, within the feed-veffels of plants.

LOLIUM. Darnel Grafs.

Of this fort of Grafs we have two or three fpecies, which grow naturally in England; fome in dry Grafs grounds, and one which is an annual Grafs, is frequently found in arable land; but as neither of them are cultivated for ufe, fo I fhall not trouble the reader with any farther account of them.

LONCHITIS [fo called of λόγχη, a lance or fpear, becaufe the leaves are fo fharp-pointed as to refemble the point of a fpear.] Rough Spleenwort.

The CHARACTERS are,

The leaves are like thofe of the Fern, but the pinulæ are eared at their bafe; the fruit alfo is like that of the Fern.

The SPECIES are,

1. LONCHITIS afpera. Ger. *Rough Spleenwort.*
2. LONCHITIS afpera major. Ger. Emach. *Greater rough Spleenwort.*

The firft of thefe plants is very common in fhady woods, by the fides of fmall rivulets, in divers parts of England; but the fecond fort is not quite fo common, and has been brought into feveral curious botanic gardens from the mountains in Wales. There are alfo great variety of thefe plants in America, which at prefent are ftrangers in the European gardens; they are feldom cultivated but in botanic gardens for the fake of variety, where they muft have a moift foil and fhady fituation.

LONGITUDINAL VESSELS, in plants, are fuch as are extended in length through the woody parts of trees and plants, into which the air is fuppofed to enter, and mix with the juices of the plant, and thereby augment its bulk.

LONI.

LONICERA. Lin. Gen. Plant. Chamæcerafus. Tourn. Inft. R. H. 609. tab. 379. *Upright Honeyfuckle.*

The CHARACTERS are,

The flower has a fmall empalement, cut into five parts, upon which the germen fits. It hath one petal, with an oblong tube, cut into five parts at the brim, and five awl-fhaped ftamina, almoft the length of the petal, terminated by oblong fummits. Under the petal is fituated a roundifh germen, fupporting a flender ftyle the length of the petal, crowned by an obtufe ftigma. The germen afterward turns to two berries, which join at their bafe.

This genus of plants is ranged in the firſt ſection of Linnæus's fifth claſs, which includes thoſe plants whoſe flowers have five ftamina and one ftyle; and to this genus he has joined the Caprifolium, Periclymenum, and Xyloſteum of Tournefort, and the Symphoricarpos of Dillenius. Tournefort places this genus in the fixth ſection of his twentieth claſs, in which he ranges the trees and ſhrubs with a flower of one petal, whoſe empalement becomes a berry.

The SPECIES are,

1. LONICERA (*Xyloſteum*) pedunculis bifloris, baccis diſtinctis, foliis integerrimis pubeſcentibus. Prod. Leyd. 238. *Lonicera with two flowers on each foot-ftalk, diftinct berries, and entire woolly leaves.* Chamæceraſus dumetorum fructu gemino rubro. C. B. P. 451. *Dwarf Cherry with twin red fruit, commonly called Fly Honeyfuckle.*

   LONICERA (*Alpigena*) pedunculis bifloris, baccis co-
2. adunatis didymis. Lin. Sp. Plant. 174. *Lonicera with two flowers upon a foot-ftalk, and twin berries which are joined together.* Chamæceraſus Alpina, fructu gemino rubro duobus punctis notato. C. B. P. 451. *Dwarf Alpine Cherry with a red twin fruit, marked with two points, commonly called red-berried upright Honeyfuckle.*

3. LONICERA (*Cærulea*) pedunculis bifloris, baccis coadunatis globofis, ftylis indiviſis. Lin. Sp. Plant. 174. *Lonicera with two flowers on a foot-ftalk, globular berries, which are joined, and undivided ftyles.* Chamæceraſus montana, fructu fingulari-cæruleo. C. B. P. 451. *Mountain Dwarf Cherry with a fingle blue fruit, commonly called fingle, blue-berried, upright Honeyfuckle.*

4. LONICERA (*Nigra*) pedunculis bifloris, baccis diſtinctis, foliis ferratis. Prod. Leyd. 238. *Lonicera with two flowers on a foot-ftalk, diftinct berries, and fawed leaves.* Chamæceraſus Alpina, fructu nigro gemino. C. B. P. 451. *Alpine Dwarf Cherry with a black twin fruit, called black-berried upright Honeyfuckle.*

5. LONICERA (*Tartarica*) pedunculis bifloris, baccis diſtinctis, foliis cordatis obtuſis. Hort. Upfal. 42. *Lonicera with two flowers on a foot-ftalk, diftinct berries, and blunt heart-fhaped leaves.* Chamæceraſus fructu gemino rubro, foliis glabris cordatis. Amm. Ruth. 184. *Dwarf Cherry with a twin red fruit, and fmooth heart-fhaped leaves.*

6. LONICERA (*Pyrenaica*) pedunculis bifloris, baccis diſtinctis, foliis oblongis glabris. Lin. Sp. Plant. 174. *Lonicera with two flowers on a foot-ftalk, diftinct berries, and oblong fmooth leaves.* Xyloſteum Pyrenaicum. Tourn. Inſt. 609. *Pyrenean Dwarf Cherry.*

7. LONICERA (*Symphoricarpos*) capitulis lateralibus pedunculatis, foliis petiolatis. Lin. Sp. Plant. 175. *Lonicera with lateral heads of flowers growing upon foot-ftalks, and leaves having foot-ftalks.* Symphoricarpos foliis alatis. Dill. Hort. Elth. 371. *commonly called ſhrubby St. Peterſwort.*

The firſt ſort has been many years cultivated in the Engliſh gardens under the title of Fly Honeyſuckle. It grows naturally upon the Alps, and in other cold parts of Europe. It riſes with a ſtrong woody ſtalk fix or eight feet high, covered with a whitiſh bark, dividing into many branches, which are garniſhed with oblong oval leaves placed oppoſite; they are entire, and covered with ſhort hairy down. The flowers come out on each ſide of the branches oppoſite, ſtanding upon ſlender foot-ftalks, each ſuſtaining two white flowers ſtanding erect; theſe have one petal, which is cut into five parts; the three lower being narrow, are reflexed, the two broader ſtand upright; theſe appear in June, and are ſucceeded by

two red clammy berries, which are joined at their bafe; and ripen the beginning of September.

The ſecond ſort grows naturally upon the Alps; this has been long cultivated in the Engliſh gardens, by the title of red-berried upright Honeyſuckle; this hath a ſhort, thick, woody ſtem, which divides into many ſtrong woody branches growing erect, garniſhed with ſpear-ſhaped leaves placed oppoſite, ſtanding upon foot-ftalks; they are entire, their under ſide being of a pale green, but their upper of a dark green. The flowers ſtand upon very long ſlender foot-ftalks, which come out oppoſite on each ſide the branches, at the baſe of the leaves; they are red on their outſide, but within, ſhaped like thoſe of the former ſort, but are a little larger, ſtanding erect; theſe appear the latter end of April, and are commonly ſucceeded by two red berries, joined at their baſe, which have two punctures; they ripen the beginning of Auguſt. Sometimes there is but one berry ſucceeding each flower, which is frequently as large as a Kentiſh Cherry; this I believe has led ſome to ſuppoſe it was a diſtinct ſpecies, as I thought myſelf, when I ſaw all the fruit upon the ſhrub were ſingle; but the following years, I found they had twin fruit like the others.

The third ſort grows naturally upon the Appenines; this is a ſhrub of humbler growth than either of the former, ſeldom riſing more than four or five feet high. The branches are ſlender, covered with a ſmooth purpliſh bark. The joints are diſtant, where the leaves come out oppoſite, and ſometimes there are two on each ſide. The foot-ftalks of the flowers are very ſhort, each ſuſtaining two white flowers, ſhaped like thoſe of the former ſorts; theſe are ſucceeded by blue berries, which are ſingle and diſtinct. The flowers appear in May, and the berries ripen in Auguſt.

The fourth ſort grows naturally on the Alps and Helvetian Mountains; this is a ſhrub very like the former, but the branches are ſlenderer. The leaves are a little ſawed on their edges. The flowers have two berries ſucceeding them, in which conſiſts their difference. It flowers at the ſame time with the former.

The fifth ſort grows naturally in Tartary, from whence the ſeeds were ſent to the Imperial Garden at Peterſburgh, where they ſucceeded, and from thence the ſeeds were ſent to me; this is a ſhrub which grows about the ſame height with the two former, to which this has a great reſemblance in its branches; but the leaves of this are heart-ſhaped, and the berries are red, growing ſometimes ſingle, at others double, and frequently there are three joined together, which are about the ſame ſize with the former. It flowers in April, and the fruit is ripe in July.

The ſixth ſort grows naturally on the Pyrenean Mountains, and alſo in Canada, from whence the ſeeds were brought to Duke D'Ayen, which were ſown in his curious garden at St. Germain, where they ſucceeded, and his highneſs was ſo good as to furniſh me with a plant; this ſeldom riſes more than three or four feet high, dividing into ſeveral ſpreading irregular branches, which are garniſhed with oblong ſmooth leaves, placed oppoſite. The flowers come out from the ſide of the branches upon ſlender foot-ftalks, each ſuſtaining two white flowers, which are cut into five ſegments almoſt to the bottom; theſe are ſucceeded by berries as the other ſorts. It flowers in April.

The ſeventh ſort grows naturally in North America, but has been many years propagated in the Engliſh gardens; this hath a ſhrubby ſtalk which riſes about four feet high, ſending out many ſlender plain branches, garniſhed with oval hairy leaves, placed by pairs oppoſite, having very ſhort foot-ftalks. The flowers are produced in whorls round the ftalk; they are of an herbaceous colour, and appear in Auguſt. The fruit, which is hollow, and ſhaped like a pottage pot, ripens in the winter. Dr. Dillenius, in his Hortus Elthamenſis, has titled this plant, Symphoricarpos foliis alatis, ſuppoſing the leaves to be winged;

8 E   but

but as the leaves fall off fingle, and the branches remain upon which they were fixed, they cannot be called winged leaves.

Thefe fhrubs are now propagated in the nurfery-gardens near London, for fale, and are commonly intermixed with other flowering fhrubs for the fake of variety; but as there is little beauty in fome of their flowers, a few of them only fhould be admitted, to fet off thofe which are preferable; they are all of them very hardy plants, fo will thrive in a cold fitu-ation better than in a warm one; they love a moift foil, in which they will thrive, and produce a greater quantity of fruit than in dry ground.

They may be propagated either by feeds or cuttings. The feeds commonly lie in the ground a year before they vegetate, but require no particular culture; if they are fown in autumn, many of them will grow the following fpring. The cuttings fhould be planted in autumn in a fhady border, where they will put out roots the following fpring, and in the following autumn they may be removed into a nurfery, to grow two years to get ftrength, after which they fhould be tranfplanted where they are defigned to remain.

LOPPING. It is very obfervable, that moft old trees are hollow within, which does not proceed from the nature of the trees, but is the fault of thofe who have the management of them, who fuffer the tops to grow large before they lop them, as the Afh, Elm, Hornbeam, &c. and perfuade themfelves, that they may have the more great wood; but, in the mean time, do not confider that the cutting off great tops, or branches, endangers the life of a tree, or, at beft, wounds it fo, that many trees yearly decay more in their bodies, than the yearly tops come to; and at the fame time that they furnifh themfelves with more great wood, they do it at the lofs of the owner. And, indeed, though the Hornbeam and Elm will bear great tops when the body is little more than a fhell, yet the Afh, if it comes to take wet at the head, very rarely bears more top after the body of the tree decays; therefore, if once thefe trees decay much in the middle, they will be worth little but for the fire, fo that if you find a timber tree decay, it fhould be cut down in time, that the timber be not loft.

The Lopping of young trees, that is, at ten or twelve years old at moft, will preferve them much longer, and will occafion the fhoots to grow more into wood in one year, than they do in old tops at two or three. But when great boughs are ill taken off, it often fpoils many a tree, for which reafon they fhould always be fpared, unlefs there is an abfolute neceffity. When they muft be cut off, it fhould be clofe and fmooth, and not parallel to the horizon, and cover the wound with loam and horfe-dung mixed, to prevent the wet from entering the body of the tree.

When trees are at their full growth, there are feve-ral figns of their decay, as, the withering or dying of many of their top branches; or if the wet enters at any knot, or they are any-wife hollow, or difcoloured, if they make but poor fhoots, or if woodpeckers make any holes in them.

This Lopping of trees is only to be underftood for pollard trees, becaufe nothing is more injurious to the growth of timber trees, than that of Lopping or cutting off great branches from them; whoever will be at the trouble of trying the experiment upon two trees of equal age and fize, growing near each other, to lop or cut off the fide branches from one of them, and fuffer all the branches to grow upon the other, will, in a few years, find the latter to exceed the other in growth every way, and this will not decay near fo foon.

All forts of refinous trees, or fuch as abound with a milky juice, fhould be lopped very fparingly, for they are fubject to decay when often cut. The beft feafon for Lopping thefe trees, is foon after Bartholomew tide, at which time they feldom bleed much, and the

wound is commonly healed over before the cold wea-ther comes on.

LORANTHUS. Vaill. Act. R. Sc. 1702. Lin. Gen. Plant. 400. Lonicera. Plum. Nov. Gen. 17. tab. 37.

The CHARACTERS are,

The empalement of the flower is entire, concave, and crowns the germen. The flower is tubulous, and cut into five narrow fegments almoft to the bottom, which are re-flexed. It hath four ftamina which are longer than the tube of the flower, terminated by globular fummits. The germen, which is fituated below the empalement, fupports a fingle ftyle which is longer than the ftamina, crowned by an oval ftigma. The germen afterward becomes an oval pulpy fruit with one cell, including feveral compreffed feeds.

This genus of plants is ranged in the firft fection of Linnæus's fixth clafs, but it fhould be placed in his fourth clafs, for the flower has but four ftamina and one ftyle.

There are feveral fpecies of this genus, which grow naturally upon trees, in feveral parts of America; but as the plants cannot be cultivated in gardens, fo it will be to no purpofe to enumerate them.

LOTUS. Tourn. Inft. R. H. 402. Lin. Gen. Plant. 803. Bird's-foot Trefoil; in French, *Lotier.*

The CHARACTERS are,

The empalement of the flower is of one leaf, permanent, and cut at the top into five parts. The flower is of the butterfly kind. The ftandard is roundifh, and reflexed backward. The wings are broad, roundifh, and fhorter than the ftandard, clofing together at the top. The keel is clofed on the upper fide, and convex on the under, rifing a little. It hath ten ftamina, nine joined and one feparate, terminated by fmall fummits, with an oblong ta-per germen, fupporting a fingle ftyle, crowned by an in-flexed ftigma. The germen afterward becomes a clofe cy-lindrical pod with one cell, opening with two valves, ba-ving many tranfverfe partitions, in each of thefe is lodged one roundifh feed.

This genus of plants is ranged in the third fection of Linnæus's feventeenth clafs, intitled Diadelphia De-candria, which contains the plants whofe flowers have ten ftamina in two houfes.

The SPECIES are,

1. LOTUS (*Corniculatus*) capitulis depreffis, caulibus de-cumbentibus, leguminibus cylindricis patentibus. Lin. Sp. Plant. 775. *Bird's-foot Trefoil with depreffed heads, trailing ftalks, and cylindrical fpreading pods.* Lo-tus corniculata glabra, minor. J. B. 2. 356. *Leffer, fmooth, corniculated Bird's-foot Trefoil.*

2. LOTUS (*Anguftiffimus*) leguminibus fubbinatis lineari-bus ftrictis erectis, caule erecto, pedunculis alternis. Lin. Sp. Plant. 774. *Bird's-foot Trefoil with erect, li-near, ftrait pods, growing in pairs, an erect ftalk, and alternate foot-ftalks.* Lotus pentaphyllos, minor, hir-futus, filiquâ anguftiffimâ. C. B. P. 332. *Smaller, five-leaved, hairy Bird's-foot Trefoil, with very narrow pods.*

3. LOTUS (*Glabrus*) capitulis depreffis, caulibus decum-bentibus, foliis linearibus glabris, leguminibus li-nearibus. *Bird's-foot Trefoil with depreffed heads, trail-ing ftalks, fmooth linear leaves, and very narrow pods.* Lotus pentaphyllos frutefcens, tenuiffimis glabris fo-liis. C. B. P. 332. *Shrubby five-leaved Bird's-foot Tre-foil, with very narrow fmooth leaves.*

4. LOTUS (*Rectus*) capitulis fubglobofis, caule erecto, leguminibus rectis glabris. Hort. Upfal. 221. *Bird's-foot Trefoil with globular heads, an erect ftalk, and ftrait fmooth pods.* Lotus villofus, altiffimus, flore glome-rato. Tourn. Inft. R. H. 403. *Talleft hairy Bird's-foot Trefoil with a glomerated flower.*

5. LOTUS (*Cretica*) leguminibus fubternatis, caule fru-ticofo, foliis fericeis nitidis. Hort. Cliff. 372. *Bird's-foot Trefoil with generally three pods on each foot-ftalk, a fhrubby ftalk, and fhining leaves.* Lotus argentea Cre-tica. Pluk. Alm. 226. *Silvery Bird's-foot Trefoil of Crete.*

6. LOTUS

6. LOTUS (*Hirſutus*) capitulis hirſutis, caule erecto hir-ſuto, leguminibus ovatis. Hort. Upſal. 220. *Bird's-foot Trefoil with hairy heads, an erect hairy ſtalk, and oval pods.* Lotus pentaphyllos ſiliquoſus villoſus. C. B. P. 332. *Five-leaved, hairy, podded Bird's-foot Trefoil.*

7. LOTUS (*Candidus*) capitulis ſubglobofis hirſutis, caule erecto ramoſo, hirſuto, foliis tomentoſis. *Bird's-foot Trefoil with globular heads, which are hairy, an upright branching hairy ſtalk, and woolly leaves.* Lotus hæmorrhoidalis humilior & candidior. Tourn. Inſt. 403. *Lower bird's-foot Trefoil, having whiter leaves.*

8. LOTUS (*Ornithopodioides*) leguminibus ſubquinatis arcuatis compreſſis, caulibus diffuſis. Hort. Cliff. 372. *Bird's-foot Trefoil with five arched compreſſed pods, and diffuſed ſtalks.* Lotus ſiliquis ornithopodii. C. B. P. 332. *Bird's-foot Trefoil with pods like birds feet.*

9. LOTUS (*Peregrinus*) leguminibus ſubbinatis linearibus compreſſis nutantibus. Hort. Cliff. 372. *Bird's-foot Trefoil with two narrow compreſſed nodding pods.* Lotus ſiliquis geminis peregrina. Boerh. Ind. 2. p. 38. *Foreign Bird's-foot Trefoil with twin pods.*

10. LOTUS (*Pratenſis*) leguminibus ſolitariis rectis teretibus terminalibus, caule erecto. Sauv. Monſp. 189. *Bird's-foot Trefoil with an erect ſtalk, terminated by a ſingle, taper, erect pod.* Lotus pratenſis ſiliquoſa lutea. C. B. P. 332. *Yellow, meadow, podded Bird's-foot Trefoil.*

11. LOTUS (*Edulis*) leguminibus ſubſolitariis gibbis incurvis. Hort. Cliff. 370. *Bird's-foot Trefoil with ſingle, convex, incurved pods.* Lotus pentaphyllos, ſiliquâ cornutâ. C. B. P. 332. *Five-leaved Bird's-foot Trefoil with horned pods.*

12. LOTUS (*Maritimus*) leguminibus ſolitariis membranaceo-quadrangulatis, bracteis lanceolatis. It. Oel. 143. Flor. Suec. 610. *Bird's-foot Trefoil with ſingle pods which are quadrangular by a membrane, and a ſpear-ſhaped bractea.* Lotus maritima lutea ſiliquoſa, folio pingui glabro. · Bot. Monſp. *Podded, yellow, maritime Bird's-foot Trefoil with a ſmooth leaf.*

13. LOTUS (*Conjugatus*) leguminibus conjugatis membranaceo quadrangulis, bracteis oblongo-ovatis. Lin. Sp. Plant. 774. *Bird's-foot Trefoil with conjugated pods which are quadrangular by a membrane, and oblong oval bractea.* Lotus lutea, ſiliquâ anguloſâ. Boerh. Ind. alt. 2. p. 37. *Yellow Bird's-foot Trefoil with angular pods.*

14. LOTUS (*Tetragonolobus*) leguminibus ſolitariis membranaceo-quadrangulatis, bracteis ovatis. · Hort. Upſal. 220. *Bird's-foot Trefoil with ſingle pods which are quadrangular, with a membrane, and oval bractea.* Lotus ruber ſiliquâ anguloſâ. C. B. P. 332. *Red Bird's-foot Trefoil with angular pods, commonly called winged Pea.*

15. LOTUS (*Cytiſoides*) capitulis dimidiatis, caule diffuſo ramoſiſſimo, foliis tomentoſis. Prod. Leyd. 387. *Bird's-foot Trefoil with heads divided into two equal parts, a very branching diffuſed ſtalk, and woolly leaves.* Lotus ſiliquoſa maritima lutea, Cytiſi facie. Barrel. Icon. 1031. *Podded, yellow, maritime Bird's-foot Trefoil with the appearance of Cytiſus.*

16. LOTUS (*Jacobæus*) leguminibus ſubternatis, caule herbaceo erecto, foliis linearibus. Hort. Cliff. 372. *Bird's-foot Trefoil with three pods, an erect herbaceous ſtalk and narrow leaves.* Lotus auguſtifolia, flore luteo purpuraſcente, inſulæ St. Jacobi. Hort. Amſt. 2. p. 165. *Narrow-leaved Bird's-foot Trefoil of St. James's iſland, with a yellow purpliſh flower.*

17. LOTUS (*Dorycnium*) capitulis aphyllis, foliis ſeſſilibus quinatis. Lin. Sp. Plant. 776. *Bird's-foot Trefoil with naked heads, and leaves placed by fives ſitting cloſe to the branches.* Dorycnium Monſpelienſium. Lob. Icon. 51. *Dorycnium of Montpelier.*

The firſt, ſecond, and third ſorts grow naturally in many parts of England, ſo are rarely admitted into gardens. When theſe grow in moiſt land and a ſhady ſituation, they ſend out ſtalks near two feet long; but upon dry chalky and gravelly ground, their ſtalks are not more than four or five inches long, and lie flat upon the ground. I have always obſerved

in thoſe paſtures where theſe plants have grown, that the cattle of all ſorts have avoided eating them, but the Graſs all round them has been eaten very bare. I have cut the plants when young, and given it to various kinds of animals, but could never get them to eat it; and yet the ſeeds of theſe have been gathered and ſold by ſome quacks in huſbandry, under the title of Lady's Finger Graſs, to be ſown as an improvement to land for paſture.

The roots of theſe are perennial, ſo are difficult to get out when they have had long poſſeſſion of the land; and they produce great quantities of ſeeds, which is caſt about by the elaſticity of the pods when ripe, to a conſiderable diſtance; they flower in June, and the ſeeds ripen in September.

The fourth ſort grows naturally in the ſouth of France, in Italy, and Sicily; this has by ſome been ſuppoſed the Cytiſus of Virgil, but without foundation, for it does not anſwer the deſcription given of that plant. This hath a ſtrong perennial root, from which ariſe many upright ſtrong ſtalks from three to four feet high, covered with a purpliſh bark, and toward the top ſend out a few ſide branches; theſe are garniſhed at every joint by a trifoliate leaf, whoſe lobes are wedge-ſhaped; at the baſe of the footſtalk are placed two heart-ſhaped lobes ſitting cloſe to the branch; the leaves are hairy on their under ſide; the flowers are produced at the end of the branches almoſt in globular heads, ſitting cloſe to the foot-ſtalk: theſe are of a pale fleſh colour and appear in June, and are ſucceeded by ſmooth ſtrait pods almoſt an inch long, which change to a brown colour when ripe, and contain ſeveral roundiſh ſeeds which ripen in September. It is rarely cultivated but in botanic gardens for variety, but if any perſon has an inclination to cultivate this plant for feeding of cattle, it may be done in the ſame way as the Lucern, for which there is full directions in the article MEDICAGO. It riſes eaſily from ſeeds, is very hardy, and will thrive on any light dry poor ground. Cows and horſes will eat this plant when green, but I have not tried if they will feed on it when made into hay.

The fifth ſort grows naturally in Syria and Crete; this riſes with ſlender ſtalks which require ſupport, from three to four feet high, ſending out a few ſide branches; theſe are garniſhed at each joint with neat ſhining ſilvery leaves which are trifoliate, and have two appendages at the baſe of their foot-ſtalks, as the other ſorts; they are in ſhape like the former, but a little ſmaller, and have an acute point at their top. The foot-ſtalks of the flowers, which are from two to three inches long, ariſe from the ſide of the branches, and ſuſtain heads of yellow flowers, which part in the middle, each head containing four or fix flowers; theſe appear in May, June, and July, and are ſucceeded by long taper pods filled with roundiſh ſeeds which ripen in the autumn.

This ſort has a perennial ſtalk, but is too tender to live through the winter in the open air in England, ſo is kept in pots and removed into the green-houſe in autumn, and treated like other hardy exotic plants which only require protection from froſt, ſo want no artificial heat. It may be propagated by ſeeds, which if ſown on a bed of light earth in April, the plants will come up in about a month after, and in another month will be fit to remove; when they ſhould be each put into a ſeparate ſmall pot filled with freſh light earth, placing them in the ſhade till they have taken new root; then they may be removed to a ſheltered ſituation, where they may remain till autumn.

It may be alſo propagated by cuttings, which may be planted during any of the ſummer months, upon a bed of light earth, covering them cloſe with a bell or hand-glaſs, and ſcreening them from the ſun; in about five or fix weeks they will have taken root, when they muſt be inured to bear the open air, and ſoon after may be planted in pots, and treated in the ſame way as the ſeedling plants.

The

The fixth fort grows naturally in the fouth of France and Italy; this hath a perennial ftalk, which rifes three feet high; when the roots are large, they frequently fend up feveral of thefe ftalks, efpecially if the old ones are cut down; the ftalks are hairy, and divide into feveral branches, which are clofely garnifhed with hoary trifoliate leaves, having two appendages at the bafe of the ftalk; the flowers are collected into heads fitting upon pretty long foot-ftalks, which come out of the fide of the ftalks. They have very hairy em-palements, and are of a dirty white colour with a few marks of pale red. They appear in June and July, and are fucceeded by fhort thick pods of a Cheftnut colour, containing feveral roundifh feeds which ripen in the autumn. This is propagated by feeds in the fame way as the laft fort; the plants will live through the winter in the open air in mode-rate winters, but it will be proper to keep one or two plants in pots to be fheltered in winter, left thofe abroad fhould be deftroyed by fevere froft.

The feventh fort grows naturally in Sicily; this rifes with an upright woody ftalk near three feet high, gar-nifhed with leaves like the fixth, but they are much whiter, covered with a fhort woolly down, as are alfo the ftalks; the flowers grow in clofe heads like the laft, and are fucceeded by fhort pods, which contain many yellow feeds. It flowers in fummer, and the feeds ripen in autumn. This is too tender to live in the open air in England through the winter, fo the plants muft be kept in pots and houfed during that feafon. It is propagated in the fame way as the fifth fort, and requires the fame culture.

The eighth fort grows naturally in Sicily; this is an annual plant, which fends out from the root many ftiff ftalks from one to two feet high, which divide in-to many branches growing diffufed without any or-der, and are garnifhed with trifoliate leaves, having two appendages at their bafe; the foot-ftalks of the flower rife from the wings of the ftalks; they are two or three inches long, terminated by a clufter of yel-low flowers, which are fucceeded by flat pods two inches long, which are bent like an arch, and have many joints, feparating the cells in which the feeds are lodged. It flowers in July, and the feeds ripen in autumn, and the plants decay foon after.

This is propagated by feeds, which fhould be fown early in April upon an open bed or border expofed to the fun, where the plants are to remain: when they come up they muft be thinned, leaving them near two feet afunder, and afterwards they muft be kept clean from weeds, which is all the culture they require.

The ninth fort grows naturally in Spain and Portu-gal: this is an annual plant like the former, but doth not branch fo much; the fmall leaves are rounder at their ends, and they are fmoother; the foot-ftalks are fhorter, and feldom fuftain more than two flowers; thefe are fucceeded by two very narrow pods about two inches long, which hang downward. This re-quires the fame culture as the former.

The tenth fort grows naturally in the fouth of France; this hath a perennial root, from which is fent out fe-veral hairy ftalks near a foot long, garnifhed with tri-foliate hairy leaves, ftanding upon fhort foot-ftalks, with two appendages at the bafe of the foot-ftalk; the flowers ftand upon pretty long foot-ftalks fingly, which rife from the end of the branches; they have long hairy empalements, with two oblong acute-pointed leaves immediately under them. The flowers are yellow, ftanding erect, and are fucceeded by taper erect pods an inch and a half long. It flowers in June and July, and the feeds ripen in the autumn. It is propagated by feeds, which fhould be fown where the plants are to remain, and muft be treated as the two former forts, but the roots of this will continue fe-veral years.

The eleventh fort grows naturally in Sicily and Crete, where the pods are eaten by the poorer inhabitants when they are young. It alfo grows about Nice, from

whence I received the feeds. This is an annual plant, from whofe roots come out feveral trailing ftalks a foot long, garnifhed at each joint with trifoliate round-ifh leaves, having appendages. The flowers ftand fingly upon long foot-ftalks, which arife from the fide of the branches; they are yellow and fmall, and are fucceeded by fingle pods, which are thick, and arched with a deep furrow on the outfide. The flowers appear in June and July, and in warm fea-fons the feeds ripen in the autumn, but in cold fummers they will not ripen here. This muft have the fame culture as the annual forts before mentioned.

The twelfth fort grows near the borders of the fea in France, Spain, and Italy; this hath a perennial root, fending out many flender ftalks about a foot and a half long, which trail upon the ground, and are garnifhed with trifoliate leaves at each joint, which are fmooth, and have two appendages to the bafe of the foot-ftalk. The flowers ftand fingly, upon very long foot-ftalks arifing from the wings of the ftalk; they are yellow, and are fucceeded by fingle pods near two inches long, having four leafy membranes running longitudinally at the four corners. This flowers in June and July, and the feeds ripen in the autumn. It is propagated by feed in the fame way as the tenth fort.

The thirteenth fort grows naturally in the fouth of France and Italy; this is an annual plant, from whofe roots are fent forth feveral branching ftalks a foot long, garnifhed with trifoliate leaves, whofe lobes are acute-pointed, and have two oblong oval appendages at the bafe of their foot-ftalks: the foot-ftalks of the flower arife from the wings of the branches, each fuftaining two yellow flowers, which are fucceeded by taper pods near two inches long, having four leafy membranes running longitudi-nally their length. It flowers in July, and the feeds ripen in autumn. It is propagated by the feeds in the fame way as the annual forts before mentioned.

The fourteenth fort grows naturally in Sicily, but has been long cultivated in the Englifh gardens; it was formerly cultivated as an efculent plant. The green pods of it were dreffed and eaten as Peas, which the inhabitants of fome of the northern counties ftill continue, but they are very coarfe, fo not agreeable to the tafte of thofe who have been accuftomed to better fare.

It is an annual plant which is cultivated in the flower-gardens near London for ornament. This fends out from the root feveral decumbent ftalks about a foot long, garnifhed at each joint with trifoliate oval leaves, having oval appendages at the bafe of their foot-ftalks; from each joint arife alternately the foot-ftalks of the flowers, which are from two to three inches long, each fuftaining one large red flower at the top, with three leaves juft under the flower. Af-ter the flower fades, the germen becomes a fwelling taper pod two inches long, having four leafy mem-branes or wings running longitudinally. It flowers in June and July, and the feeds ripen in autumn.

The feeds of this fort are commonly fown in patches, five or fix feeds being fown near each other, in the borders of the pleafure-garden, where they are de-figned to remain. If the feeds all grow, fome of the plants may be pulled up, leaving only two or three in each patch, and afterward they will require no other care but to keep them clean from weeds.

The fifteenth fort grows near the borders of the fea, in the fouth of France and Spain. This is a perennial plant, fending out from the root many ftalks, which branch out their whole length, and are garnifhed with roundifh trifoliate leaves with two appendages; they are covered with a woolly down: the flowers ftand upon fhort foot-ftalks, four or fix growing in a divided head; they are yellow, and appear in July, and are fucceeded by taper pods filled with roundifh feeds, which ripen in autumn. This is propagated by feeds, which fhould be fown in the fpring in the place where the plants are to remain, and muft be

treated

treated in the fame manner as the hardy perennial forts before mentioned.

The fixteenth fort grows naturally in the Ifland of St. James, from whence the feeds were firft brought to Europe, but I have fince received the feeds from the Cape of Good Hope. This hath a flender ftalk which is woody, rifing from two to three feet high, fending out many flender herbaceous branches, garnifhed with narrow white leaves, which are fometimes trifoliate, and at others there are five narrow lobes to each; thefe fit clofe to the branches, and are hoary. The flowers are produced from the fide of the ftalks towards their upper part, upon very flender footftalks, each fuftaining four or five flowers collected in a head, of a yellowifh deep purple colour, which are fucceeded by taper flender pods little more than an inch long, containing five or fix fmall roundifh feeds. This plant flowers all the fummer and autumn, and many times great part of the winter, efpecially if the plants are placed in a dry airy glafs-cafe, where they may be free from damp, for nothing is more prejudicial to them. It is too tender to live abroad in England, fo the plants muft be kept in pots; and in the winter placed in a warm airy glafs-cafe, but in the fummer they fhould be placed abroad in a fheltered fituation. It may be eafily propagated by cuttings, during the fummer feafon, in the fame way as the fifth fort, and alfo by feeds; but the plants which have been two or three times propagated by cuttings, feldom are fruitful.

The feventeenth fort grows naturally about Montpelier; it rifes with weak fhrubby ftalks three or four feet high, fending out many flender branches, which are thinly garnifhed with fmall hoary leaves, growing with five lobes in form of a hand; they fit clofe to the branches. The flowers are produced at the extremity of the branches in fmall heads; they are very fmall and white, fo make no great appearance; they appear in June, and are fucceeded by fhort pods containing two or three fmall round feeds which ripen in the autumn. This fhrub will live in the open air, if it be planted in a dry foil and a warm fituation. It is propagated by feeds, which will come up in any common border.

LOTUS ARBOR   See CELTIS.

LOVE-APPLE.   See LYCOPERSICON.

LUDVIGIA. Lin. Gen. Plant. 142.

This title was given to this genus of plants by Dr. Linnæus, in honour of M. Chrift. Ludwig, of Leipfic, who publifhed Remarks on Rivinus's Method of claffing Plants, at Leipfic, in 1737.

The CHARACTERS are,

The empalement of the flower is of one leaf, cut into four fegments at the top, and fits upon the germen. The flower confifts of four fpear-fhaped petals, which are equal, and fpread open. In the center of the flower is fituated the four-cornered pointal, attended by four ftamina: the germen afterward becomes a four-cornered fruit, crowned with the empalement, and has four cells which are full of fmall feeds.

This genus of plants is ranged in the firft fection of Linnæus's fourth clafs, which includes thofe plants whofe flowers have four ftamina and one ftyle.

We have but one SPECIES of this genus in the Englifh gardens at prefent, which is

LUDVIGIA (*Alternifolia*) foliis alternis lanceolatis. Lin. Sp. Plant. 118. Ludvigia with alternate fpear-fhaped leaves. Ludvigia capfulis fubrotundis. Hort. Cliff. 491. Ludvigia with roundifh capfules.

We have no Englifh name for this plant, but it is very near akin to the Onagra, or Tree Primrofe, from which it differs in the number of ftamina.

This plant grows naturally in South Carolina, from whence the late Dr. Dale fent me the feeds. It is annual, and rifes with an upright branching ftalk a foot high, garnifhed with fpear-fhaped leaves placed alternate. The flowers come out fingly at the foot-ftalks of the leaves; they are compofed of four fmall yellow petals, which fpread open, ftanding upon fhort footftalks, and have four ftamina; the flowers are fucceeded

by roundifh feed-veffels with four leafy membranes they open in four cells, including many fmall feeds. It flowers in July, and the feeds ripen in the autumn. The plants muft be raifed in a hot-bed in the fpring, and treated in the fame manner as hath been directed for the Amaranthus; for if they are not brought forward in the fpring, they feldom produce good feeds in England.

LUFFA. Tourn. Act. R. S. 1709. Momordica. Lin. Gen. 967. Egyptian Cucumber.

The CHARACTERS are,

It hath a bell-fhaped flower confifting of one leaf, which is divided into five parts to the center; there are male and female flowers on the fame plant. The male flowers are produced on fhort foot-ftalks, having no embryos; but the female flowers reft on the top of the embryos, which afterward become a fruit like a Cucumber to outward appearance, but is not flefhy; the inner part confifting of many fibres, which are elegantly netted; and there are three cells which are filled with feeds, which are almoft of an oval fhape.

We have but one SPECIES of this plant, viz.

LUFFA (*Ægyptiaca*) Arabum. Tourn. Act. R. 170. *The Luffa of the Arabians.*

There are two varieties of this plant, one having white, and the other black feeds; but thefe are not diftinct fpecies.

This plant may be propagated after the fame manner as Cucumbers and Melons, by fowing the feeds on a hot-bed the beginning of March; and when the plants are come up, they muft be pricked into a frefh hot-bed to ftrengthen the plants, obferving to let them have frefh air every day in warm weather, and to refrefh them frequently with water. When the plants have four or five leaves, they fhould be planted out upon a hot-bed where they are defigned to remain, which fhould be under frames, and but one plant put into each light; for as thefe plants fend forth a great number of fide-fhoots, fo where they are planted too clofe, they will entangle one into the other, and become fo thick, as to caufe the fruit to drop. In the management of thefe plants, after they are planted out for good, there muft be the fame care taken as for Melons and Cucumbers, with this difference only, that thefe require a larger fhare of air in warm weather; otherwife the Vines will grow weak, and will not produce fruit.

When the plants have fpread, fo as to fill the frames on every fide, the frames fhould be raifed on bricks, and the ends of the plants drawn out, that they may have room to grow; for when thefe plants are in a vigorous ftate, they will fpread eight or ten feet; fo that if they are confined, they will become fo thick, as to rot the tender branches which are covered from the air, and there will be no fruit produced.

The fruit, when it is young, is by fome people eaten, and made into Mangoes, and preferved in pickle; but it hath a very difagreeable tafte, and is not accounted very wholefome: wherefore thefe plants are feldom cultivated in Europe, except by fuch perfons as are curious in botany, for variety.

LUNARIA. Tourn. Inft. R. H. 218. tab. 105. Gen. Plant. 725. [fo called of Luna, Lat. the moon. becaufe the feed-veffels refemble the form of the moon.] Moonwort, Sattin Flower, or Honefty; in French, *Bulbonac.*

The CHARACTERS are,

The empalement of the flower is compofed of four oblong, oval, fmall leaves, which are obtufe and fall off; the flower has four petals in form of a crofs, which are large, obtufe, and entire: it hath fix awl-fhaped ftamina, four of thefe are the length of the empalement; the other two are fhorter, terminated by erect fummits. It has an oblong oval germen fitting upon a fmall foot-ftalk, fupporting a fhort ftyle, crowned by an entire obtufe ftigma. The germen afterward becomes an erect, plain, comprefled, elliptical pod, fitting upon the fmall foot-ftalk, terminated by the ftyle, having two cells opening with two valves, which are parallel, inclofing feveral comprefled kidney-fhaped feeds, which are bordered, fitting in the middle of the pod.

8 F   This

This genus of plants is ranged in the second section of Linnæus fifteenth class, intitled Tetradynamia siliculosa, which includes those plants whose flowers have four long and two shorter stamina, and the seeds are included in short pods.

The SPECIES are,

1. LUNARIA (*Rediviva*) siliculis oblongis. Lin. Sp. Plant. 653. *Sattin Flower with oblong pods.* Lunaria major, siliquâ longiore. J. B. 2. 881. *Greater Moonwort with longer pods, commonly called Honesty, or White Sattin.*

2. LUNARIA (*Annua*) siliculis subrotundis. Lin. Sp. Plant. 653. *Sattin Flower with roundish pods.* Lunaria major, siliquâ rotundiore. J. B. *Greater Moonwort with a rounder pod.*

3. LUNARIA (*Ægyptiaca*) foliis suprà decompositis, foliolis trifidis, siliculis oblongis pendulis. *Moonwort with leaves decompounded whose lobes are trifid, and oblong hanging pods.* Cardamine foliis suprà decompositis, siliquis unilocularibus pendulis. Lin. Sp. Plant. 656. *Lady's Smock with leaves decompounded above, and hanging pods containing one cell.*

4. LUNARIA (*Perennis*) perennis, siliculis oblongis, foliis lanceolatis incanis. *Perennial Moonwort, with oblong pods and spear-shaped hoary leaves.* Lunaria perennis, lutea, folio leucoii, ramis expansis. Vaill. *Yellow perennial Moonwort, with a Stock Gilliflower leaf and expanded branches.*

The first sort grows naturally in Hungary, Istria, and Austria, but has been long an inhabitant of the English gardens. It is a biennial plant, which perishes soon after the seeds are ripe; it rises with a branching stalk from two to three feet high, covered with a reddish hairy bark, sending out branches on every side from the ground upward; these are garnished with heart-shaped leaves placed alternately, ending in acute points indented on their edges, and are a little hairy; the lower standing upon pretty long foot-stalks, but the upper sit close to the branches. The flowers are produced at the top and from the side of the branches toward their ends, in clusters; they are composed of four purplish heart-shaped petals, placed in form of a cross. These appear in May, and are succeeded by large flat roundish pods with two cells, inclosing two rows of flat kidney-shaped seeds, which have a border round them. These pods, when ripe, turn to a clear white or sattin colour, from whence the title of Sattin Flower has been given to it, and are transparent.

The seed-vessels of this plant, when they are full ripe, become very transparent, and of the appearance of white sattin, at which time the branches are cut off and dried; after which they are preserved to place in the chimneys of halls and large rooms, where they continue a long time in beauty.

This is propagated by seeds, which should be sown in the autumn; for those which are sown in the spring often miscarry, or lie a long time in the ground before they appear. The plants will grow in almost any soil, but love a shady situation; it requires no other culture, but to keep it clean from weeds. If the seeds are permitted to scatter, the plants will rise without any farther care; and if they are left unremoved, they will grow much larger than those which are transplanted; the roots of this sort perish soon after the seeds are ripe.

The second sort grows naturally upon the mountains in Italy; this hath stalks and leaves very like the first, but the flowers are rather larger, and of a lighter purple colour; but the principal difference is in the pods of this being longer and narrower than those of the other. It flowers and seeds at the same time with the first, and requires the same culture.

The third sort is an annual plant, which grows naturally in Egypt. This rises with a smooth branching stalk little more than a foot high, garnished with winged leaves, composed of several pair of lobes ranged along the midrib, terminated by an odd one; these lobes are of unequal sizes, and vary in their form; some of them are almost entire, and others are cut at their extremities into three parts; they are

smooth, and of a lucid green. The flowers stand each upon pretty long slender foot-stalks, which come out from the side, and also at the end of the branches, in loose small clusters; they are of a purple colour, and are succeeded by oblong compressed pods, which hang downward. This sort flowers in June and July, the seeds ripen the beginning of September, and the plants decay soon after.

This is propagated by seeds, which should be sown upon an open border where the plants are to remain; if they are sown soon after they are ripe, the plants will come up in the autumn, and live through the winter in a sheltered situation; these will flower early the following summer, whereby ripe seeds may be obtained; they may also be sown in the spring in like manner. When the plants come up, they will require no other care but to keep them clean from weeds, and thin them where they are too close. If the seeds are permitted to scatter in the autumn, the plants will rise without care, and may be treated in the same way, which is much preferable to the sowing the seeds in the spring.

The fourth sort grows naturally in the Archipelago; this hath a perennial root, from which arise two or three ligneous stalks a foot high, covered with a white hairy bark, dividing upward into several smaller branches, garnished with spear-shaped leaves sitting close to the stalks, which are a little hoary. The branches are terminated by loose spikes of yellow flowers which appear in June, and are succeeded by oblong flat pods, containing flat kidney-shaped seeds, which ripen in the autumn.

This sort is propagated by seeds, which, if sown in the autumn, will succeed better than in the spring; they should be sown on a warm border, and on a dry poor soil, otherwise they will not live through the winter; but in a rubbishing soil the plants will continue two or three years.

LUPINUS. Tourn. Inst. R. H. 392. tab. 213. Lin. Gen. Plant. 774. Lupine; in French, *Lupin.*

The CHARACTERS are,

The empalement is bifid and of one leaf; the flower is of the butterfly kind; the standard is roundish, heart-shaped, indented at the top, and the sides reflexed and compressed. The wings are nearly oval, and almost as long as the standard; they are not fixed to the keel, but close at their base; the keel is as long as the wings, but is narrow, falcated, and ends in a point. It hath ten stamina joined at their base in two bodies, but as they rise are distinct above, terminated by five oblong summits. In the center is situated a hairy, compressed, awl-shaped germen, supporting a rising style, terminated by an obtuse stigma. The germen afterward becomes a large, oblong, thick pod with one cell, ending with an acute point, including several roundish compressed seeds.

This genus of plants is ranged in the third section of Linnæus's seventeenth class, intitled Diadelphia Decandria, which includes those plants whose flowers have ten stamina joined in two bodies.

The SPECIES are,

1. LUPINUS (*Varius*) calycibus semiverticillatis appendiculatis, labio superiore bifido, inferiore subtridentato. Hort. Cliff. 499. *Lupine with empalements half whorled, having appendages, whose upper lip is bifid, and the under one almost trifid.* Lupinus sylvestris, purpureo flore, semine rotundo vario. J. B. 2. 291. *Wild Lupine, with a purple flower and a round variegated seed, commonly called the lesser blue Lupine.*

2. LUPINUS (*Angustifolius*) calycibus verticillatis appendiculatis, labio superiore bipartito, inferiore integro. Lin. Sp. Plant. 721. *Lupine with empalements having alternate appendages, whose upper lip is divided into two, and the under one entire.* Lupinus angustifolius cœruleus elatior. Raii Hist. 908. *Narrow-leaved taller blue Lupine.*

3. LUPINUS (*Luteus*) calycibus verticillatis appendiculatis, labio superiore bipartito, inferiore tridentato. Hort. Cliff. 499. *Lupine with empalements growing in whorls, having appendages to them, whose upper lips are cut into two parts, and the under one into three.* Lupinus sylvestris, flore luteo. C. B. P. 348. *The common yellow Lupine.*

4. Lu-

4. LUPINUS (*Hirſutis*). calycibus verticillatis appendiculatis, labio ſuperiore inferioreque integris. Hort. Cliff. 499. *Lupine with whorl-ſhaped empalements having appendages, and the upper and under lip entire.* Lupinus peregrinus major, vel villoſus, cœruleus, major. C. B. P. *Foreign, greater, hairy Lupine, with a large blue flower, commonly called the great blue Lupine.*

5. LUPINUS (*Albus*) calycibus alternis inappendiculatis, labio ſuperiore integro, inferiore tridentato. Hort. Cliff. 499. *Lupine with alternate empalements having no appendages, and the upper lip entire, but the under cut into three parts.* Lupinus ſativus, flore albo. C. B. P. 347. *Garden or manur'd Lupine, with a white flower.*

6. LUPINUS (*Perennis*) calycibus alternis inappendiculatis, labio ſuperiore emarginato, inferiore integro. Lin. Sp. Plant. 721. *Lupine with alternate empalements having no appendages, the upper lip indented, and the under entire.* Lupinus cœruleus, minor, perennis, Virginianus, repens. Mor. Hiſt. 2. p. 87. *Smaller perennial, creeping, blue Lupine of Virginia.*

The firſt ſort grows naturally among the Corn in the ſouth of France and Italy, and in great abundance in Sicily. This is an annual plant, which riſes with a firm, ſtrait, channelled ſtalk near three feet high, divided toward the top into ſeveral branches, which are garniſhed with hand-ſhaped leaves, compoſed of five, ſix, or ſeven oblong lobes, which join in one center at their baſe, and are hairy. The flowers are produced in ſpikes at the end of the branches, ſtanding half round the ſtalk in ſort of whorls; they are of a light blue colour, ſhaped like thoſe of Peas, and are ſucceeded by ſtrait taper pods with one cell, incloſing a row of roundiſh ſeeds. This ſort flowers in June and July, and the ſeeds ripen in the autumn.

It is propagated in the borders of the pleaſure-garden for ornament, by ſowing the ſeeds in April, in the places where they are to remain; and when the plants come up they ſhould be thinned where they are too cloſe, and kept clean from weeds, which is all the culture they require.

The ſecond ſort has much the appearance of the firſt, but the ſtalks riſe higher; the leaves have more lobes, and ſtand upon longer foot-ſtalks; the lobes are blunt-pointed, and the ſeeds are variegated. This requires the ſame culture as the firſt, and flowers at the ſame time.

The third ſort is the common yellow Lupine, which has been long cultivated in the Engliſh gardens for the ſweetneſs of its flowers. This grows naturally in Sicily; it riſes about a foot high, with a branching ſtalk garniſhed with hand-ſhaped leaves, compoſed of nine narrow hairy lobes, which join at their baſe to the foot-ſtalks; theſe are four or five inches long. The flowers are yellow, and are produced in looſe ſpikes at the end of the branches, ſtanding in whorls round the ſtalks, with ſpaces between them, terminated by three or four flowers, ſitting cloſe at the top; theſe are ſucceeded by flattiſh hairy pods about two inches long, ſtanding erect, incloſing four or five roundiſh ſeeds, a little compreſſed on their ſide, of a yellowiſh white, variegated with dark ſpots. This ſort flowers at the ſame time as the former, but to have a ſucceſſion of the flowers, the ſeeds are ſown at different times, viz. in April, May, and June; but thoſe only, which are firſt ſown, will ripen their ſeeds. It may be cultivated in the ſame manner as the two former, and is equally hardy.

The fourth ſort is ſuppoſed to be a native of India, but has been many years in the Engliſh gardens. It is an annual plant, which riſes with a ſtrong, firm, channelled ſtalk from three to four feet high, covered with a ſoft browniſh down, dividing upward into ſeveral ſtrong branches, garniſhed with hand-ſhaped leaves, compoſed of nine, ten, or eleven wedge-ſhaped hairy lobes, which are narrow at their baſe where they join the foot-ſtalk, but enlarge upward, and are rounded at the top where they are broadeſt; the foot-ſtalks of the leaves are three or four inches long. The flowers are placed in whorls round the ſtalks above each other, forming a looſe ſpike, which

proceeds from the end of the branches; they are large, and of a beautiful blue colour, but have no ſcent. Theſe appear in July, and the ſeeds ripen in the autumn. The pods of this ſort are large, almoſt an inch broad, and three inches long, incloſing three large roundiſh ſeeds compreſſed on their ſides, very rough, and of a purpliſh brown colour. There is a variety of this with fleſh-coloured flowers, which is commonly called the Roſe Lupine; it differs from the blue only in the colour of the flower, but this difference is permanent, for neither of the ſorts vary.

This is generally late in ripening the ſeeds, ſo that unleſs the autumn proves warm and dry, they do not ripen; therefore the beſt way to have good ſeeds, is to ſow them in September cloſe to a warm wall on dry ground, where they will live through our ordinary winters; and theſe plants will flower early the following ſummer, ſo there will be time for the ſeeds to ripen before the rains fall in the autumn, which frequently cauſes the ſeeds to rot which are not ripe. If a few of the ſeeds of both theſe varieties are ſown in ſmall pots the beginning of September, and when the froſts begin, the pots are removed into a common hot-bed frame, where they may be protected from hard froſt, but enjoy the free air in mild weather, the plants may be thus ſecured in winter; and in the ſpring they may be ſhaken out of the pots, preſerving the earth to their roots, and planted in a warm border, where they will flower early, and produce very good ſeeds.

The fifth ſort grows naturally in the Levant, but is cultivated in ſome parts of Italy, as other pulſe, for food. This hath a thick upright ſtalk about two feet high, which divides toward the top into ſeveral ſmaller hairy branches, garniſhed with hand-ſhaped leaves, compoſed of ſeven or eight narrow oblong lobes, which are hairy, and join at their baſe, of a dark grayiſh colour, and have a ſilvery down. The flowers are produced in looſe ſpikes at the end of the branches; they are white, and ſit cloſe to the ſtalk; theſe are ſucceeded by hairy ſtrait pods about three inches long, a little compreſſed on the ſides, containing five or ſix flattiſh ſeeds which are white, having a little cavity like a navel, in that part which is fixed to the pod. This ſort flowers in July, and the ſeeds ripen in the autumn. It is an annual plant, which is cultivated for ornament in the pleaſure-garden. The ſeeds muſt be ſown in the places where the plants are to remain, and may be treated in the ſame way as the firſt ſort.

The ſixth ſort grows naturally in Virginia, and other of the northern parts of America. This hath a perennial creeping root, from which ariſe ſeveral erect channelled ſtalks a foot and a half high, ſending out two or three ſmall ſide branches, garniſhed with hand-ſhaped leaves, compoſed of ten or eleven narrow ſpear-ſhaped lobes, which join at their baſe, ſtanding upon very long foot-ſtalks, having a few hairs on their edges. The flowers grow in long looſe ſpikes, which terminate the ſtalks, and are placed without order on each ſide; they are of a pale blue colour, having ſhort foot-ſtalks. Theſe appear in June, and the ſeeds ripen in Auguſt, which are ſoon ſcattered if they are not gathered when ripe; for after a little moiſture, the ſun cauſes the pods to open with an elaſticity, and caſt out the ſeeds to a diſtance all round. This ſort is propagated by ſeeds as the former, which ſhould be ſown where the plants are to remain; for although the root is perennial, yet it runs ſo deep into the ground as that it cannot be taken up entire; and if the root is cut or broken, the plant ſeldom thrives well after. I have traced ſome of the roots of this plant, which have been three feet deep in the ground in one year from ſeed, and ſpread out as far on every ſide, ſo that they muſt have room, therefore the young plants ſhould not be left nearer than three feet aſunder. If this plant is in a light dry ſoil, the roots will continue ſeveral years, and produce many ſpikes of flowers; and although the uſual ſeaſon of flowering is in June and July,

July, yet when rain happens to fall in Auguſt, there are frequently freſh ſtalks ariſe from the roots, which flower the end of September, or beginning of Octōber.

The ſeeds of the fifth ſort are uſed in medicine; they have a bitter taſte, ſo open, digeſt, diſſolve, and cleanſe; and if they are ſteeped in water for ſome days, till they have loſt their bitterneſs, they may be eaten out of neceſſity, but they are ſuppoſed to breed groſs humours, and are hard of digeſtion. Some women uſe the flower of the ſeed mixed with the juice of Lemons, and a little Alumen ſaccharinum, made into the form of ſoft ointment, to make the face ſmooth, and look more amiable.

The ſmall blue Lupine is frequently ſown in Italy, to dreſs and manure the ground, eſpecially that which is intended for vineyards; where, if they have time, the ground is ſown with Lupines, which grow till they begin to flower; then they cut them down and plough them into the ground, where the ſtalks rot with the winter's rain; but it is doubtful whether this is any real benefit to the ground, for there are few plants which draw and impoveriſh the ground ſo much as Lupines; therefore the dreſſing they yield, is ſcarce an equivalent for what they have drawn from the ground: but when there is not time for this operation, they parboil the ſeeds to prevent their growing, and ſow them upon the ground before it is ploughed, allowing ſixteen buſhels to an acre of land; and this dreſſing is preferable to the former.

All the ſorts of Lupines make a pretty appearance when they are in flower, but the yellow ſort is pre-ferred for its ſweetneſs, though the flowers of this are of ſhort duration, eſpecially in warm weather; therefore the ſeeds of this ſhould be ſown at ſeve-ral times, that there may be a ſucceſſion of flowers through the ſeaſon, for they will continue flowering till they are ſtopped by hard froſt; and thoſe which come in the autumn to flower, will continue in beauty a longer time than the early ones. If ſome of the ſeeds are ſown in the autumn on a warm border, the plants will often live through the winter, and flower early in the ſpring.

LUPULUS. Tourn. Inſt. R. H. 535. tab. 309. Humulus. Lin. Gen. Plant. 989. [This plant takes its name of Lupus, *Lat.* a wolf, becauſe the antients had a notion, that wolves were wont to hide them-ſelves under this plant.] The Hop; in French, *Houblon.*

The CHARACTERS are,

The male and female flowers are upon different plants. The empalement of the male flower is compoſed of five ſmall, concave, obtuſe leaves; it hath no petal, but has five ſhort hairy ſtamina, terminated by oblong ſummits. The female flowers have a general, four-pointed, acute perianthium, and a ſeparate oval one of four leaves, in-cluding eight flowers; each of theſe have an empalement of one leaf, which is cloſed at the baſe. Theſe have nei-ther petal or ſtamina, but a ſmall germen ſituated in the center, ſupporting two awl-ſhaped ſtyles, crowned by acute, reflexed, ſpreading ſtigmas. The germen afterward turns to a roundiſh ſeed covered with a thin ſkin, incloſed in the baſe of the empalement.

This genus of plants is ranged in the fifth ſection of Linnæus's twenty-ſecond claſs, intitled Diœcia Pen-tandria, which includes thoſe plants whoſe male and female flowers are upon different plants, and the male flowers have five ſtamina.

We have but one SPECIES of this genus, viz.

LUPULUS (*Humilus*) mas & femina. C. B. P. 298. *Male and female Hop.*

The male Hop grows wild by the ſide of hedges and upon banks, in many parts of England: the young ſhoots of theſe plants are often gathered in the ſpring by the poor people, and boiled as an eſculent herb; but theſe muſt be taken very young, other-wiſe they are tough and ſtringy; it is eaſily diſtin-guiſhed by the flowers, which are ſmall, and hang in long looſe bunches from the ſide of the ſtalks, abound-

ing with farina on their ſummits; theſe have no Hops ſucceeding to the flowers.

The female Hop is the ſort which is cultivated for uſe; of this ſort, the people who cultivate them reckon three different varieties: as firſt, the long and ſquare Garlick Hop, the long white Hop, and the oval Hop, all which are indifferently cultivated in England, but of the male Hop there is no different varieties.

There being the greateſt plantation of Hops in Kent that are in any county of England, it is very pro-bable, that their method of planting and ordering them ſhould be the beſt.

As for the choice of their Hop-grounds, they eſteem the richeſt and ſtrongeſt grounds as the moſt proper; they chuſe a warm dry ſoil, that has a good depth of hazel mould; and if it be rocky within two or three feet of the ſurface, the Hops will proſper well; but they will by no means thrive on a ſtiff clay, or ſpongy wet land.

If it may be, chuſe a piece of meadow or lay ground to plant Hops on, ſuch as has not been tilled or ſown with other crops for many years, or an old decayed orchard; for land that is worn out by long bearing of Corn, will require abundance of dung to bring it into any tolerable condition to bear a crop of Hops. The Kentiſh planters accounting new land beſt for Hops, they plant their Hop-gardens with Apple-trees at a large diſtance, and with Cherry-trees between; and when the land hath done its beſt for Hops, which they reckon it will in about ten years, the trees may begin to bear. The Cherry-trees laſt about thirty years, and by that time the Apple-trees are large, they cut down the Cherry-trees.

The Eſſex planters account a moory land the pro-pereſt for Hops, though there are ſeveral other ſorts of ſoil that are eſteemed very good.

Some account that land which has a roſſelly top, and a brick earth bottom, the beſt; a true roſſel or light ſand, is what they generally plant in, whether it be white or black.

Moory land is of different ſorts, ſome being ſtrong and heavy, ſo as to crack in ſummer; and ſome ſo light, that in dry ſeaſons it will blow away with the wind; and ſome are of a middle conſiſtence, being compoſed of both.

Theſe moors for goodneſs and value, are according to the nature and goodneſs of the ſoil that is under-neath them; which being flung up upon the ſurface, will make a very good mixture, it being beſt to fling the under ſoil downward for Hops, becauſe they na-turally root downwards, ſometims four or five yards deep, and therefore the deepeſt and richeſt ſoil is beſt for them.

Few are acquainted with the value of moors, becauſe they do not ſearch into the bottom of them, by reaſon of the expenſiveneſs of doing it, and the difficulty of carrying off the water.

If the land be moiſt, it ought to be laid up in high ridges, and to be well drained, and the drains kept clear and open, eſpecially in winter, that the water do not rot or too much chill the roots.

If the land be ſour or cold, it will be very much helped by burning it; and if the haulm and ſtrings of the Hops be burnt every year, and ſome of the pa-ring or ſides of the garden or other earth be laid on them as they burn, and then more haulm be laid over that, and ſo continued layer upon layer, it will make an excellent compoſt to make the hills with.

As to the ſituation of a Hop-ground, one that inclines to the ſouth or weſt is the moſt eligible; but if it be expoſed to the north-eaſt or ſouth-weſt winds, there ſhould be a center of ſome trees at a diſtance; becauſe the north-eaſt are apt to nip the tender ſhoots in the ſpring, and the ſouth-weſt frequently break and blow the poles at the latter end of the ſummer, and very much endanger the Hops.

Hops require to be planted in an open ſituation, that the air may freely paſs round and between them to dry up and diſſipate the moiſture, whereby they will not be be fo fubject to fire blafts, which often deftroy the middles of large plantations, while the outfides remain unhurt.

As for the preparation of the ground for planting, it fhould, the winter before, be ploughed and harrowed even; and then lay upon it in heaps a good quantity of frefh rich earth, or well rotted dung and earth mixed together, fufficient to put half a bufhel in every hole to plant the Hops in, unlefs the natural ground be very frefh and good.

Then lay a line acrofs it from the hedge, in which knots have been tied, at the diftance you defign your Hop-hills to be at, about eight or nine feet diftance the whole length of the ground, and place a fharp pointed ftick at every knot; then lay afide the line, and with two forked fticks of about eight or nine feet long, you may from the firft row fet out the whole ground, by applying the two forks to two of the fticks which were firft fet up, and placing another row at the ends, where the forked fticks meet triangularwife; then you fhould dig a hole at every ftick about a foot and a half wide, and fill it full of the good earth you brought in.

If you plough the ground with horfes between the hills, it will be beft to plant them in fquares chequerwife; but the quincunx form is the moft beautiful, and it will alfo be better for the Hop; but if the ground is intended to be cultivated by the breaftplough, it will be beft to plant them in fquares; but which way foever you make ufe of, a ftake fhould be ftuck down at all the places where the hills are to be made.

Perfons ought to be very curious in the choice of the plants and fets, as to the kind of the Hop; for if the Hop-garden be planted with a mixture of two or three forts of Hops that ripen at different times, it will caufe a great deal of trouble, and be a great detriment to the owner.

The two beft forts are the white and the gray bind; the latter is a large fquare Hop, more hardy, and is the more plentiful bearer, but ripens later than the former.

There is alfo another fort of the white bind, which ripens in a week or ten days before the common; but this is tenderer, and a lefs plentiful bearer, but it has this advantage, it comes firft to market.

But if three grounds, or three diftant parts of one ground, be planted with thefe three forts, there will be this conveniency, that they may be picked fucceffively as they become ripe.

The fets ought to be procured out of grounds that are entirely of the fame fort you would have, they fhould be five or fix inches long, with three or more joints or buds on them, all the old bind and hollow part of the fet being cut off.

If there be a fort of Hop you value, and would increafe plants and fets from, the fuperfluous binds may be laid down when the Hops are tied, cutting off the tops, and burying them in the hill; or when the Hops are dreffed, all the cuttings may be faved, and laid in rows in a bed of good earth; for almoft every part will grow, and become a good fet the next fpring. Some have tried to raife a Hop-ground by fowing feeds, but that turns to no account, becaufe that way is not only tedious, but the Hops fo produced are commonly of different kinds, and many of them wild and barren.

As to the feafons of planting Hops, the Kentifh planters beft approve the months of October and March, both which fucceed very well; but the common fets are not to be had in October, unlefs from fome ground that is to be digged up and deftroyed; and likewife there is fome danger that the fets may be rotted, if the winter prove very wet; but the moft ufual time of procuring them is in March, when the Hops are cut and dreffed.

As to the manner of planting the fets, you fhould put two or three good fets in every hole with a fetting ftick, at about four inches diftance, placing them floping; they muft ftand even with the furface of the

ground; let them be preffed clofe with the hand, and covered with fine earth, and a ftick fhould be placed on each fide the hill to fecure it.

The ground being thus planted, all that is to be done more that funimer, is to keep the hills clear from weeds, and to horfe-hoe the ground about the month of May, gathering up the ftones, if more are turned up by ploughing, and to raife a fmall hill round about the plants; and in June you muft twift the young binds or branches together in a bunch or knot, for if they are tied up to fmall poles the firft year, in order to have a few Hops from them, it will not countervail the weakening the plants.

A mixture of compoft or dung being prepared for your Hop-ground, the beft time for laying it on, if the weather prove dry, is about Michaelmas, that the wheels of the dung-cart may not injure the Hops, nor furrow the ground: if this be not done then, you muft be obliged to wait till the froft has hardened the ground, fo that it will bear the dung-cart; and this is alfo the time to carry on your new poles, to recruit thofe that are decayed, and to be caft out every year.

If you have good ftore of dung, the beft way will be to fpread it in the alleys all over the ground, and to dig or plough it in the winter following. The quantity they will require, will be forty loads to an acre, reckoning about thirty bufhels to the load.

If you have not dung enough to cover all the ground in one year, you may lay it on one part one year, and on the reft in another, or a third; for there is no occafion to dung the ground after this manner, oftener than once in two or three years.

Thofe who have but a fmall quantity of dung, ufually content themfelves with laying on about twenty loads upon an acre every year; this they lay only on the hills, either about November, or in the fpring; which laft fome account the beft time, when the Hops are dreffed, to cover them after they are cut; but if it be done at this time, the compoft or dung ought to be very well rotted and fine.

As to the dreffing of the Hops, when the Hop-ground is dug or ploughed in January or February, the earth about the hills, and very near them, ought to be taken away with a fpade, that you may come the more conveniently at the ftock to cut it.

About the end of February, if the Hops were planted the fpring before, or if the ground be weak, they ought to be dreffed in dry weather; but elfe, if the ground be ftrong and in perfection, the middle of March will be a good time; and the latter end of March, if it be apt to produce over rank binds, or the beginning of April, may be foon enough.

Then having with an iron picker cleared away all the earth out of the hills, fo as to make the ftock bear to the principal roots, with a fharp knife you muft cut off all the fhoots which grew up with the binds the laft year; and alfo all the young fuckers, that none be left to run in the alley and weaken the hill. It will be proper to cut one part of the ftock lower than the other, and alfo to cut that part low, that was left higheft the preceding year. By purfuing this method, you may expect to have ftronger buds, and alfo keep the hill in good order.

In dreffing thofe Hops that have been planted the year before, you ought to cut off both the dead tops, and the young fuckers which have fprung up from the fets, and alfo to cover the ftocks with fine earth a finger's length in thicknefs.

About the middle of April the Hops are to be polled, when the fhoots begin to fprout up; the poles muft be fet to the hills deep into the ground, with a fquare iron pitcher or crow, that they may the better endure the wind; three poles are fufficient for one hill. Thefe fhould be placed as near the hills as may be, with their bending tops turned outwards from the hill, to prevent the binds from entangling; and a fpace between two poles ought to be left open to the fouth, to admit the fun beams.

The poles ought to be in length fixteen or twenty feet, more or lefs, according as the ground is in ftrength ; and great care is to be taken not to over-pole a young or weak ground, for that will draw the ftock too much, and weaken it. If a ground be over-polled, you are not to expect a good crop from it ; for the branches which bear the Hops will grow very little, till the binds have over-reached the poles, which they cannot do when the poles are too long. Two fmall poles are fufficient for a ground that is young. If you wait till the fprouts or young binds are grown to the length of a foot, you will be able to make a better judgement where to place the largeft poles ; but if you ftay till they are fo long as to fall into the alleys, it will be injurious to them, becaufe they will entangle one with another, and will not clafp about the pole fo readily.

Maple or Afpen poles are accounted the beft for Hops, on which they are thought to profper beft, be-caufe of their warmth ; or elfe, becaufe the climbing of the Hop is furthered by means of the roughnefs of the bark. But for laftingnefs, Afhen or Willow poles are preferable ; but Cheftnut poles are the moft dura-ble of all.

If, after the Hops are grown up, you find any of them have been under-polled, taller poles may be placed near thofe that are too fhort, to receive the binds from them.

As to the tying of Hops, the buds that do not clafp of themfelves to the neareft pole when they are grown to three or four feet high, muft be guided to it by the hand, turning them to the fun, whofe courfe they will always follow. They muft be bound with wi-thered Rufhes, but not fo clofe as to hinder them from climbing up the pole.

This you muft continue to do till all the poles are furnifhed with binds, of which two or three are enough for a pole ; and all the fprouts and binds that you have no occafion for, are to be plucked up ; but if the ground be young, then none of thefe ufelefs binds fhould be plucked up, but fhould be wrapt up to-gether in the middle of the hill.

When the binds are grown beyond the reach of your hands, if they forfake the poles, you fhould make ufe of a ftand ladder in tying them up.

Some advife, that if the binds be very ftrong, and overgrow the poles very much, you ftrike off their heads with a long fwitch, to increafe their branching below.

Towards the latter end of May, when you have made an end of tying them, the ground muft have the fum-mer ploughing or digging, which is done by cafting up with the fpade fome fine earth into every hill, and a month after it muft be again repeated, and the hills made up to a convenient bignefs.

It is not at all to be doubted, but that a thorough watering would be of very great advantage to Hops in a hot dry fummer ; but it is fo much charge and trouble to do this, that unlefs you have a ftream at hand to flow the ground, it is fcarce practicable.

When the Hops blow, you fhould obferve if there be any wild barren hills among them, and mark them, by driving a fharpened ftick into every fuch hill, that they may be digged up and replanted.

Hops as well as other vegetables, are liable to dif-tempers and difafters, and among the reft, to the fen. The Rev. Dr. Hales, in his excellent Treatife of Ve-getable Statics, treating of Hops, gives us the follow-ing account of the ftate of Hops in Kent in the year 1725, that he received from Mr. Auften of Canter-bury, which is as follows :

In mid April not half the fhoots appeared above ground, fo that the planters knew not how to pole them to the beft advantage.

This defect of the fhoot, upon opening the hills, was found to be owing to the multitude and variety of vermin that lay preying upon the roots ; the increafe of which, was imputed to the long and almoft uninter-rupted feries of dry weather for three months before. Towards the end of April many of the Hop-vines were infefted with flies.

About the 20th of May there was a very unequal ap-pearance, fome Vines being run feven feet, others not above three or four ; fome juft tied to the poles, and fome not vifible ; and this difproportionate inequa-lity in their fize, continued through the whole time of their growth.

The flies now appeared upon the leaves of the for-wardeft Vines, but not in fuch numbers here, as they did in moft other places. About the middle of June the flies increafed, yet not fo as to endanger the crop ; but in diftant plantations they were exceedingly mul-tiplied, fo as to fwarm towards the end of the month. June the 27th fome fpecks of fen appeared. From this day to the 9th of July was very dry weather. At this time, when it was faid, that the Hops in moft parts of the kingdom looked black and fickly, and feemed paft recovery, ours held it out pretty well, in the opinion of the moft fkilful planters.

The great leaves were indeed difcoloured, and a lit-tle withered, and the fen was fomewhat increafed. From the 9th of July to the 23d, the fen increafed a great deal ; but the flies and lice decreafed, it raining much daily. In a week more the fen, which feemed to be almoft at a ftand, was confiderably increafed, efpecially in thofe grounds where it firft appeared. About the middle of Auguft the Vines had done growing both in ftem and branch, and the forwardeft began to be in the Hop, the reft in bloom ; the fen continued fpreading where it was not before perceived, and not only the leaves, but many of the burs were alfo tainted with it.

About the 20th of Auguft fome of the Hops were in-fected with the fen, and whole branches corrupted by it. Half the plantations had pretty well efcaped hi-therto, and from this time the fen increafed but little ; but feveral days wind and rain the following week fo diftorted them, that many of them began to dwindle, and at laft came to nothing ; and of thofe that then remained in bloom, fome never turned to Hops ; and of the reft which did, many of them were fo fmall, that they very little exceeded the bignefs of a good thriving bur.

We did not begin to pick till the 8th of September, which is eighteen days later than we began the year before ; the crop was little above two hundred on an acre round, and not good. The beft Hops fold this year at Way-hill, for 16 l. the hundred.

The Rev. Dr. Hales, in his aforefaid Treatife, gives us an account of the following experiment that he made on Hop-vines. He tells us, that in July he cut off two thriving Hop-vines near the ground, in a thick fhady part of the garden, the pole ftill ftanding ; he ftripped the leaves off from one of thefe Vines, and fet their ftems in known quantities of water in little bottles ; that with leaves imbibed in a twelve hours day four ounces, and that without leaves three-fourths of an ounce.

He took another Hop-pole with its Vines on it, and carried it out of the Hop-ground into a free and open expofure ; thefe imbibed and perfpired as much more as the former in the Hop-ground, which is, doubtlefs, the reafon why the Hop-vines on the outfides of plantations, where they are moft expofed to the air, are fhort and poor, in comparifon of thofe in the middle of the ground, viz. becaufe being much dried, their fibres harden fooner, and therefore they cannot grow fo kindly as thofe in the middle of the ground, which, by fhade, are always kept moifter, and more ductile.

The fame curious author proceeds as followeth : Now there being 1000 hills in an acre of Hop-ground, and each hill having three poles, and each pole three Vines, the number of Vines will be 9000, each of which perfpiring four ounces, the fum of all the ounces per-fpired by an acre in twelve hours day will be 36000 ounces = 15750000 grains = 62007 cube inches, or 220 gallons, which divided by 6272640, the number of fquare inches in an acre, it will be found, that the quantity of liquor perfpired by all the Hop-vines will be equal to an area of liquor as broad as an acre, and

Ť ť

$\frac{1}{100}$ part of an inch deep, befides what evaporated from the earth.

And this quantity of moifture, in a kindly ftate of the air, if daily carrried off, is a fufficient quantity to keep the Hops in a healthy ftate ; but in a rainy moift ftate of air, without a due mixture of dry weather, too much moifture hovers about the Hops, fo as to hinder, in fome meafure, the kindly perfpiration of the leaves, whereby the ftagnating fap corrupts, and breeds mouldy fen, which often fpoils vaft quantities of flourifhing Hop-grounds.

This was the cafe in the year 1723, when for ten or fourteen days almoft continual rains fell, about the latter half of July, after four months dry weather, upon which the moft flourifhing and promifing Hops were all infected with mould, or fen, in their leaves and fruit, while the then poor and unpromifing Hops efcaped, and produced plenty, becaufe they, being fmall, did not perfpire fo great a quantity as others, nor did they confine the perfpired vapour, fo much as the large thriving Vines did in their fhady thickets. This rain on the then warm earth, made the Grafs fhoot out as faft as if it were in a hot-bed, and the Apples grew fo precipitately, that they were of a flafhy conftitution, fo as to rot more remarkably than had ever been remembered.

The planters obferve, That when a mould, or fen, has once feized any part of the ground, it foon runs over the whole, and that the Grafs, and other herbs under the Hops, are infected with it, probably, becaufe the fmall feeds of this quick-growing mould, which foon come to maturity, are blown over the whole ground ; which fpreading of the feed may be the reafon why fome grounds are infected with fen for feveral years fucceffively, viz. from the feeds of the laft year's fen. Might it not then be advifed to burn the fenny Hop-vines, as foon as the Hops are picked, in hopes thereby to deftroy fome of the feed of the mould? Mr. Auften, of Canterbury, obferves fen to be more fatal to thofe grounds that are low and fheltered, than to the high and open grounds, to thofe that are fhelving to the north, than to thofe fhelving to the fouth ; to the middle of grounds than to the outfides ; to the dry and gentle grounds, than to the moift and ftiff grounds.

This was very apparent throughout the plantations where the land had the fame workmanfhip and help beftowed upon it, and was wrought at the fame time. But if in either of thefe cafes there was a difference, it had a different effect, and the low and gentle grounds, that lay neglected, were then feen lefs diftempered than the open and moift, which were carefully managed and looked after.

The honey dews are obferved to come about the 11th of June, which, by the middle of July, turn the leaves black, and make them ftink.

The faid Dr. Hales relates, That in the month of July (the feafon for fire-blafts, as the planters call them) he has feen the Vines in the middle of the Hop-ground fcorched up almoft from one end of a large ground to the other, when a hot gleam of fun-fhine has come immediately after a fhower of rain, at which time vapours are all feen with the naked eye, but efpecially with reflecting telefcopes, to afcend fo plentifully as to make a clear and diftinct object become immediately very dim and tremulous ; nor was there any dry gravelly vein in the ground along the courfe of this fcorch ; it was therefore, probably, owing to the much greater quantity of fcorching vapours in the middle, than the outfides of the ground, and that being a denfer medium, it was much hotter than a more rare medium.

And, perhaps, the great volume of afcending vapours might make the fun-beams converge a little towards the middle of the ground, that being a denfer medium, and thereby increafe the heat confiderably ; for he obferved, That the courfe of the fcorched Hops was in lines at right angles to the fun-beams about eleven o'clock, at which time the hot gleam was.

The Hop-ground was in a valley which ran from fouth-weft to north-eaft, and to the beft of his remembrance, there was but little wind, and that in the courfe of the fcorch ; but had there been fome other gentle wind, either north or fouth, it is not improbable but that the north wind gently blowing the volume of rifing wreak on the fouth fide of the ground, that fide might have been moft fcorched, and fo vice verfa.

As to particular fire-blafts, which fcorch here and there a few Hop-vines, or one or two branches of a tree, without damaging the next adjoining, what aftronomers obferve, may hint to us no very improbable caufe of it, viz. They frequently obferve (efpecially with reflecting telefcopes) fmall feparate portions of pellucid vapours floating in the air, which, though not vifible to the naked eye, are yet confiderably denfer than the circumambient air ; and vapours of fuch a degree of denfity may very probably either acquire fuch a fcalding heat from the fun as will fcorch what plants they touch, efpecially the more tender.

(An effect which the gardeners about London have too often found to their coft, when they have incautioufly put bell-glaffes over their Cauliflowers early in a frofty morning, before the dew was evaporated off them ; which dew, being raifed by the fun's warmth, and confined within the glafs, did there form a denfe, tranfparent, fcalding vapour, which burned and killed the plants :)

Or, perhaps, the upper or lower furface of thefe tranfparent, feparate, flying volumes of vapours, may, among the many forms they revolve into, fometimes approach fo near to an hemifphere, or hemicylinder, as thereby to make the fun-beams converge, fo as often to fcorch the more tender plants they fhall fall on, and fometimes alfo parts of the more hardy plants and trees, in proportion to the greater or leffer convergency of the fun's rays.

The learned Boerhaave, in his Theory of Chymiftry, p. 245, Shaw's edition, obferves, That thofe white clouds which appear in fummer time, are, as it were, fo many mirrours, and occafion exceffive heat. Thefe cloudy mirrours are fometimes round, fometimes concave, polygonous, &c. When the face of heaven is covered with fuch white clouds, the fun fhining among them, muft, of neceffity, produce a vehement heat, fince many of his rays, which would otherwife, perhaps, never touch our earth, are hereby reflected to us. Thus, if the fun be on one fide, and the clouds on the oppofite one, they will be perfect burning-glaffes, and hence the phænomena of thunder. I have fometimes (continues he) obferved a kind of hollow clouds full of hail and fnow, during the continuance of which the heat was extreme, fince, by fuch condenfation, they were enabled to reflect more ftrongly. After this came a fharp cold, and then the clouds difcharged their hail in great quantity, to which fucceeded a moderate warmth. Frozen concave clouds, therefore, by their great reflexions, produce a vigorous heat, and the fame, when refolved, exceffive cold.

From which the Rev. Dr. Hales obferves as follows : Hence we fee, that blafts may be occafioned by the reflexions of the clouds, as well as by the above-mentioned refraction of denfe tranfparent vapours.

About the middle of July Hops begin to blow, and will be ready to gather about Bartholomew-tide. A judgment may be made of their ripenefs, by their ftrong fcent, their hardnefs, and the brownifh colour of their feed.

When by thefe tokens they appear to be ripe, they muft be picked with all the expedition poffible ; for if at this time a ftorm of wind fhould come, it would do them great damage, by breaking the branches, and bruifing and difcolouring the Hops ; and it is very well known, that Hops, being picked green and bright, will fell for a third part more than thofe which are difcoloured and brown.

The moſt convenient way of picking them is into a long ſquare frame of wood, called a bin, with a cloth hanging on tenter-hooks within it, to receive the Hops as they are picked.

The frame is compoſed of four pieces of wood joined together, ſupported by four legs, with a prop at each end to bear up another long piece of wood, placed at a convenient height over the middle of the bin; this ſerves to lay the poles upon which are to be picked.

This bin is commonly eight feet long, and three feet broad; two poles may be laid on it at a time, and ſix or eight perſons may work at it, three or four on each ſide.

It will be beſt to begin to pick the Hops on the eaſt or north ſide of your ground, if you can do it conveniently; this will prevent the ſouth-weſt wind from breaking into the garden.

Having made choice of a plot of the ground containing eleven hills ſquare, place the bin upon the hill which is in the center, having five hills on each ſide; and when theſe hills are picked, remove the bin into another piece of ground of the ſame extent, and ſo proceed till the whole Hop-ground is finiſhed.

When the poles are drawn up to be picked, you muſt take great care not to cut the binds too near the hills, eſpecially when the Hops are green, becauſe it will make the ſap to flow exceſſively.

And if the poles do not come up without difficulty, they ſhould be raiſed by a piece of wood in the nature of a lever, having a forked piece of iron, with teeth on the inſide, faſtened within two feet of the end.

The Hops muſt be picked very clean, i. e. free from leaves and ſtalks, and, as there ſhall be occaſion, two or three times in a day the bin muſt be emptied into a Hop-bag made of coarſe linen cloth, and carried immediately to the oaſt, or kiln, in order to be dried; for if they ſhould be long in the bin, or bag, they will be apt to heat, and be diſcoloured.

If the weather be hot, there ſhould no more poles be drawn than can be picked in an hour, and they ſhould be gathered in fair weather, if it can be, and when the Hops are dry; this will ſave ſome expence in firing, and preſerve their colour better when they are dried.

The beſt method of drying Hops is with charcoal on an oaſt or kiln, covered with hair-cloth, of the ſame form and faſhion that is uſed for drying malt. There is no need to give any particular directions for the making it, ſince every carpenter, or bricklayer, in thoſe countries where Hops grow, or malt is made, knows how to build them.

The kiln ought to be ſquare, and may be of ten, twelve, fourteen, or ſixteen feet over at the top, where the Hops are laid, as your plantation requires, and your room will allow. There ought to be a due proportion between the height and breadth of the kiln, and the beguels of the ſteddle where the fire is kept, viz. if the kiln be twelve feet ſquare on the top, it ought to be nine feet high from the fire, and the ſteddle ought to be ſix feet and a half ſquare, and ſo proportionable in other dimenſions.

The Hops muſt be ſpread even upon the oaſt a foot thick or more, if the depth of the curb will allow it, but care is to be taken not to overload the oaſt, if the Hops be green or wet.

The oaſt ought to be firſt warmed with a fire before the Hops are laid on, and then an even ſteady fire muſt be kept under them; it muſt not be too fierce at firſt, leſt it ſcorch the Hops; nor muſt it be ſuffered to ſink or ſlacken, but rather be increaſed till the Hops be near dried, leſt the moiſture, or ſweat, which the fire has raiſed, fall back, or diſcolour them. When they have lain about nine hours, they muſt be turned, and in two or three hours more they may be taken off the oaſt. It may be known when they are well dried by the brittleneſs of the ſtalks, and the eaſy falling off of the Hop leaves.

The Dutch and Flemings have another method of drying their Hops: they make a ſquare kiln, or room,

about eight or ten feet wide, built of brick or ſtone, having a door at one ſide, and a fire-place in the middle of the room, on the floor, about thirteen inches wide within, and thirteen inches high in length from the mouth of it, almoſt to the back part of the kiln, a paſſage being left juſt enough for a man to go round the end of it; this they call a horſe, ſuch as is commonly made in malt-kilns, the fire paſſing out at the holes at each ſide, and at the end of it.

The bed, or floor, on which the Hops lie to be dried, is placed about five feet high above; about that is a wall near four feet high, to keep the Hops from falling.

A window is made at one ſide of the upper bed, to ſhove off the dry Hops down into a room prepared to receive them. The beds are made of laths, or rails, ſawn even, lying a quarter of an inch diſtant from one another, with a croſs beam in the middle, to ſupport them; the laths are let in even with the top of the beam, and this keeps them even in the places; this they call an oaſt.

The Hops are laid on this bed by baſkets full, without any oaſt-cloth, beginning at one end, and ſo going on till all is covered, half a yard thick, without treading them; then they even them with a rake, that they may lie of equal thickneſs.

This being done, they kindle the fire below, either of wood or charcoal, but the latter is accounted the better fuel for Hops; this fire is kept as much as may be at an equal or conſtant heat, and only at the mouth of the furnace, for the air will ſufficiently diſperſe it.

They do not ſtir them till they are thoroughly dried, i. e. till the top is as fully dried as the bottom; but if they find any place not to be ſo dry as the reſt, (which may be known by reaching over them with a ſtick or wand, and touching them in ſeveral places,) they obſerve where they do not rattle, and where they do; and where they do not rattle, they abate them there, and diſpoſe of them where the places were firſt dry.

They know when they are thoroughly dry, by the brittleneſs of the inner ſtalk, if it be ſhort when it is rubbed; which when they find, they take out the fire, and ſhove out the Hops at the window that is made for that purpoſe, into the room made to receive them, with a coal-rake made with a board at the end of a pole, and then go in at a door below, and ſweep up the Hops and ſeeds that fall through, and put them to the other Hops; then they lay another bed of green Hops, and renew the fire, and proceed as before.

This method is diſapproved by ſome, becauſe (they ſay) the Hops lying ſo thick, and not being turned, the under part of them muſt needs dry before the upper; and the fire paſſing through the whole bed to dry the uppermoſt, muſt neceſſarily over-dry, and much prejudice the greateſt part of the Hops, both in ſtrength and weight, beſides the unneceſſary expence of firing, which muſt be long continued to dry thoroughly ſo many together.

Therefore ſome have improved on this method, and adviſed to make the kiln much as is before directed as to the Dutch way.

Firſt to make a bed of flat ledges about an inch thick, and two or three inches broad, ſawn, and laid acroſs one another the flat way, chequerwiſe, at about three or four inches diſtance one from the other, the edges being ſo entered one into the other, that the floor may be even and ſmooth; this bed may be made to reſt on two or three joiſts, ſet edgewiſe, to ſupport it from ſinking.

This bed is to be covered with large double tin, foldered together at each joint, and the ledges muſt be ſo ordered, before they are laid, that the joints of the tin may always lie over the middle of the ledge, the bed being wholly covered over with tin: boards muſt be fitted about the edges of the kiln, to keep up the Hops, but one ſide muſt be made to remove, that the Hops may be ſhoved off as before.

On

On this bed, or floor of tin, the Hops may be turned without such hazard or loss, as upon the hair-cloth : and also it will require a less expence of fuel, and, besides, any sort of fuel will serve in this kiln, as well as charcoal, because the smoke does not pass through the Hops as it does the former ways; but then care is to be taken, that there be passages made for it at the several corners and sides of the kiln.

It is found by experience, that the turning of Hops, though it be after the most easy and best manner, is not only an injury and waste to the Hops, but also an expence of fuel and time, because they require as much fuel, and as long a time, to dry a small quantity, by turning them, as a large one.

Now, this may be prevented, by having a cover (to be let down and raised at pleasure) to the upper bed whereon the Hops lie.

This cover may also be tinned, by nailing single tin plates over the face of it, so that when the Hops begin to dry, and are ready to burn, i. e. when the greatest part of their moisture is evaporated, then the cover may be let down within a foot, or less, of the Hops (like a reverbatory) and will reflect the heat upon them, so that the top will soon be as dry as the lowermost, and every Hop be equally dried.

As soon as the Hops are taken off the kiln, lay them in a room for three weeks or a month to cool, give, and toughen ; for if they are bagged immediately, they will powder, but if they lie a while (and the longer they lie the better, provided they be covered close with blankets to secure them from the air,) they may be bagged with more safety, as not being liable to be broken to powder in treading, and this will make them bear treading the better, and the harder they are trodden, the better they will keep.

The common method of bagging is as follows ; they have a hole made in an upper floor, either round or square, large enough to receive a Hop-bag (which consists of four ells and a half of ell-wide cloth, and also contains ordinarily two hundred and a half of Hops) they tie a handful of Hops in each lower corner of the bag, to serve as handles to it, and they fasten the mouth of the hole, so placed that the hoop may rest upon the edges of the hole.

Then he that is to tread the Hops down into the bag, treads the Hops on every side, another person continually putting them in as he treads them, till the bag is full, which being well filled and trodden, they unrip the fastening of the bag to the hoops, and let it down, and close up the mouth of the bag, tying up a handful of Hops in each corner of the mouth, as was done in the lower part.

Hops being thus packed, if they have been well dried, and laid up in a dry place, they will keep good several years ; but care must be taken, that they be neither destroyed nor spoiled by the mice making their nests in them.

The crop of Hops being thus bestowed, you are to provide for another, first by taking care of the poles against another year, which are best to be laid up in a shed. having first stripped off the haulm from them ; but if you have not that conveniency, set up three poles in the form of a triangle, or six poles (as you please) wide at the bottom, and having set them into the ground, with an iron pitcher, and bound them together at top, set the rest of your poles about them ; and being thus disposed, none but those on the outside will be subject to the injuries of the weather, for all the inner poles will be kept dry, unless at the top ; whereas, if they were on the ground, they would receive more damage in a fortnight, than by their standing all the rest of the year.

In the winter time provide your soil and manure for the Hop-ground against the following spring.

If the dung be rotten, mix it with two or three parts of common earth, and let it incorporate together till you have occasion to make use of it in making your Hop-hills ; but if it be new dung, then let it be mixed as before, till the spring come twelvemonths, for new dung is very injurious to Hops.

Dung of all sorts was formerly more commonly made use of than now it is, especially when rotted, and turned to mould, and they who have no other manure must use it; which, if they do, cows or hogs dung, or human ordure mixed with mud, may be a proper compost, because Hops delight most in a manure that is cool and moist.

Some recommend chalk, or lime, as the best manure, except in cold lands, and in such, pigeons dung will do best ; a little of which laid to a hill, and so mixed, that it may not be too hot in a place, is of great advantage.

LUTEOLA. See RESEDA.

LYCHNIDEA. See PHLOX.

LYCHNIS. Tourn. Inst. R. H. 333. tab. 175. Lin. Gen. Plant. 517. [so called of Λύχνος, a candle, or light, because the flowers of this plant imitate the flame or rays of light.] Campion.

The CHARACTERS are,

The flower has a permanent swollen empalement of one leaf, indented in five parts at the top. It hath five petals, whose tails are the length of the empalement, their upper part plain, broad, and frequently cleft in laminæ. It hath ten stamina which are longer than the empalement, alternately ranged, and fastened to the tails of the petals, terminated by prostrate summits. In the center is situated an almost oval germen, supporting five awl-shaped styles, crowned by reflexed hairy stigmas. The empalement afterward becomes an oval capsule with one cell, opening with five valves, filled with roundish seeds.

This genus of plants is ranged in the fifth section of Linnæus's tenth class, intitled Decandria Pentagynia, which includes those plants whose flowers have ten stamina and five styles.

The SPECIES are,

1. LYCHNIS (*Chalcedonica*) floribus fasciculatis fastigiatis. Hort. Cliff. 174. *Campion with flowers gathered into a pyramid.* Lychnis hirsuta, flore coccineo, major. C. B. P. 203. *Greater hairy Campion with a scarlet flower.*

2. LYCHNIS (*Viscaria*) petalis integris. Lin. Sp. Plant. 436. *Campion with entire petals.* Lychnis sylvestris viscosa, rubra, angustifolia. C. B. P. 205. *Wild viscous Lychnis with a red flower and narrow leaves, commonly called the Single Catchfly.*

3. LYCHNIS (*Dioeci*) floribus dioecis. Hort. Cliff. 171. *Campion with male and female flowers on different plants.* Lychnis sylvestris, sive aquatica purpurea, simplex. C. B. P. 204. *Wood or aquatic Lychnis with a single purple flower, frequently called Bachelors Button.*

4. LYCHNIS (*Alba*) floribus dioecis, calycibus inflatis hirsutis. *Campion with male and female flowers growing on different plants, and swollen hairy empalements.* Lychnis sylvestris, alba, simplex. C. B. P. 204. *Wild campion with a single white flower.*

5. LYCHNIS (*Floscuculi*) petalis quadrifidis, fructu subrotundo. Hort. Cliff. 174. *Campion with quadrifid petals, and a roundish fruit.* Lychnis pratensis flore laciniato simplici. Mor. Hist. 2. p. 537. *Meadow Campion with a single jagged flower, commonly called Ragged Robin.*

6. LYCHNIS (*Alpina*) petalis bifidis corymbosis. Lin. Sp. Plant. 436. *Campion with bifid petals, and flowers growing in a corymbus.* Silene floribus in capitulum congestis. Haller. Helv. 376. *Lychnis with flowers collected in a head.*

7. LYCHNIS (*Siberica*) petalis bifidis, caule dichotomo, foliis subhirtis. Lin. Sp. Plant. 437. *Campion with bifid petals, a stalk divided by pairs, and leaves which are somewhat hairy.*

8. LYCHNIS (*Lusitanica*) caule erecto, calycibus striatis acutis, petalis dissectis. Plat. 170. *Campion with an erect stalk, striped acute empalements, and petals cut into many parts.*

9. LYCHNIS (*Apetala*) calyce inflato, corollâ calyce breviore, caule subunifloro. Lin. Sp. Plant. 437. *Campion with a swollen empalement, the petals of the flower shorter than the cup, and stalks having chiefly one flower.* Lychnis sylvestris alba, calyce amplo vesicario

cario. Vaill. *Wild white Campion with a large inflated empalement.*

The firſt ſort is commonly known by the title of Scarlet Lychnis; of which there is one with double flowers, which is moſt eſteemed for the ſize of the flowers and multiplicity of the petals; as alſo for the duration of the flowers, which continue much longer in beauty than the ſingle flowers, ſo that the latter is not much cultivated at preſent, though the flowers of this are very beautiful; and as the plants are ſo eaſily propagated by ſeed, they may ſoon be had in greater plenty than thoſe with double flowers, which do not produce ſeeds. Of the ſingle ſort there are three varieties, the deep ſcarlet, the fleſh-colour, and the white, but the firſt is the moſt beautiful. This is eaſily propagated by ſeeds, which ſhould be ſown on a border expoſed to the eaſt, in the middle of March. The plants will appear in April, when if the ſeaſon is dry, they ſhould be refreſhed with water two or three times a week. By the beginning of June the plants will be fit to remove, when there ſhould be a bed of common earth prepared to receive them; into which they ſhould be planted at about four inches apart, obſerving to water and ſhade them till they have taken root; after which time they will require no other care but to keep them clean from weeds till the following autumn, when they ſhould be tranſplanted into the borders of the pleaſure-garden, where they are to continue. The ſummer following theſe plants will flower and produce ripe ſeeds, but the roots will abide ſeveral years and continue to flower. This ſort flowers in June and July, and the ſeeds ripen in autumn. It may alſo be propagated by off-ſets, but as the ſeeds ripen ſo freely, few perſons trouble themſelves to propagate the plants any other way. The French call this plant Jeruſalem Croſs. The ſort with double flowers is a valuable plant, the flowers are very double, and of a beautiful ſcarlet colour. This hath a perennial root, from which ariſe two, three, or four ſtalks, according to the ſtrength of the roots; theſe in rich moiſt land, grow upwards of four feet high; the ſtalks are ſtrong, erect, and hairy. They are garniſhed the whole length with ſpear-ſhaped leaves ſitting cloſe to the ſtalks, placed oppoſite; and juſt above each pair of leaves, there are four ſmaller leaves ſtanding round the ſtalk. The flowers are produced in cloſe cluſters ſitting upon the top of the ſtalk; when the roots are ſtrong, the cluſters of flowers will be very large, ſo they make a fine appearance, the flowers being very double, and of a bright ſcarlet colour. They appear the latter end of June, and in moderate ſeaſons continue near a month in beauty. The ſtalks decay in autumn, and new ones ariſe in the ſpring. This was originally produced from the ſeeds of the ſingle ſort, and is propagated by ſlips taken from the roots in autumn; but as this is a ſlow method of increaſing the plants, the beſt way to have them in plenty, is to cut off the flower-ſtalks in June before the flowers appear, which may be cut into ſmall lengths, each of which ſhould have three or four joints, which ſhould be planted on an eaſt border of ſoft loamy earth, putting three of the joints into the ground, leaving one eye juſt level with the ſurface; theſe muſt be watered, and then covered cloſe with bell or hand-glaſſes, ſo as to exclude the outward air, and ſhaded with mats when the ſun ſhines hot upon them. The cuttings ſo managed will put out roots in five or ſix weeks, when they muſt be expoſed to the open air, and in very dry weather they ſhould be now and then refreſhed with water, but it muſt not be repeated too often, nor given in large quantities, for too much moiſture will cauſe them to rot. Theſe will make good plants by the following autumn, when they may be tranſplanted into the borders of the pleaſure-garden, where they will flower the following ſummer. Some people who are covetous to have their plants flower, ſuffer the ſtalks to remain till the flowers are decayed, and then cut them off to plant; but by that time the ſtalks are grown hard, ſo but few of them

ſucceed, and thoſe which do, will not be near ſo good plants as thoſe which are planted earlier; therefore it will be better to ſacrifice the flowers of ſome roots for this purpoſe. Theſe plants delight in a ſoft, rich, loamy ſoil, not too moiſt or ſtiff, in which they will thrive and flower very ſtrong, but they do not care for much dung, which very often cauſes the roots to canker and rot, ſo that in the rich dunged lands about London, they do not thrive well. As theſe plants grow tall, they ſhould be planted in the middle of large borders, and not crowded with other plants, for their roots extend to a large diſtance; ſo if they are incommoded by other roots, it will ſtint their growth.

I have not ſeen any double flowers of the two other varieties, but have been informed that there are of both the white and the fleſh-colour with double flowers in ſome of the French gardens. Theſe make a variety, but are not ſo beautiful as the ſcarlet, ſo are not much eſteemed.

The ſecond ſort is commonly called Red German Catchfly. This hath been found growing naturally upon the rocks in Edinburgh Park, and in ſome places in Wales. It was formerly cultivated in flower-gardens for ornament, but ſince this ſort with double flowers hath been produced, the ſingle has been almoſt baniſhed out of the gardens. This hath long, narrow, Graſs-like leaves, which come out from the root without order, ſitting cloſe to the ground; between theſe come up ſtrait ſingle ſtalks, which in good ground riſe a foot and half high; at each joint of the ſtalk come out two leaves oppoſite, of the ſame form as the lower, but decreaſe in their ſize upward; under each pair of leaves, for an inch in length, there ſweats out of the ſtalk a glutinous liquor, which is almoſt as clammy as birdlime, ſo that the flies which happen to light upon theſe places, are faſtened to the ſtalk, where they die, from whence it had the title of Catchfly. The ſtalk is terminated by a cluſter of purple flowers, and from the two upper joints come out on each ſide of the ſtalk a cluſter of the ſame flowers, ſo that the whole form a ſort of looſe ſpike. Theſe appear in the beginning of May, and the ſingle flowers are ſucceeded by roundiſh ſeed-veſſels, which are full of ſmall angular ſeeds ripening in July.

It may be propagated in plenty by parting of the roots in autumn, at which time every ſlip will grow; or if the ſeeds are ſown in the ſame manner as is directed for the firſt ſort, the plants with ſingle flowers may be raiſed in plenty. This delights in a light moiſt ſoil and a ſhady ſituation.

The double flowering of this ſort was accidentally obtained from the ſeeds of the ſingle. This hath not been known forty years in the Engliſh gardens, but it is now ſo common as to have excluded that with ſingle flowers; it differs only from that in the doubleneſs of the flowers. As this never produces ſeeds, ſo it can only be propagated by parting and ſlipping of the roots; the beſt time for this is in autumn, at which time every ſlip will grow. If this is performed in September, the ſlips will have taken good root before the froſt, and will flower well the following ſummer; but if they are expected to flower ſtrong, the roots muſt not be divided into ſmall ſlips, though for multiplying the plants, it matters not how ſmall the ſlips are. Theſe ſhould be planted on a border expoſed to the morning ſun, and ſhaded when the ſun is warm till they have taken root. If the ſlips are planted in the beginning of September, they will be rooted ſtrong enough to plant in the borders of the flower-garden by the middle or latter end of October. The roots of this ſort multiply ſo faſt, as to make it neceſſary to tranſplant and part them every year; for when they are let remain longer, they are very apt to rot. This ſort requires the ſame ſoil and ſituation as the former.

The third ſort grows naturally by the ſide of ditches and in moiſt paſtures in many parts of England, ſo is ſeldom admitted into gardens; it hath a perennial root, from which ariſe many branching diffuſed ſtalks

from

from two to three feet high, garnifhed with oval acute-pointed leaves, placed by pairs at each joint, and are terminated by clufters of purple flowers, which appear in April and May. The male flowers grow upon feparate plants from the female. The latter produces feeds which ripen in July; the ftalks decay in autumn, but the roots continue feveral years.

There is a variety of this with double flowers, which is cultivated in gardens, by the title of Red Bachelor's Button. This is an ornamental plant, and continues long in flower. It is propagated by flips, which fhould be planted the beginning of Auguft in a fhady border of loamy earth, where they will take root in about fix weeks or two months, and may then be tranfplanted into the borders of the flower-garden. Thefe roots fhould be annually tranfplanted, otherwife they frequently rot; and young plants muft be propagated by flips to fupply the decay of the old roots, which are not of very long duration. This fort thrives beft in a foft loamy foil, and in a fhady fituation, where they have only the morning fun.

The fourth fort is very common upon dry banks on the fide of roads in moft parts of England, fo is not admitted into gardens; there is a variety of this with purple flowers, which I find is by fome fuppofed to be the fame as the third, but is very different, for the ftalks of this are branched out much more; the leaves are longer and more veined, and the flowers of this ftand fingly upon pretty long foot-ftalks, fo are not produced in clufters like thofe of the third. This is alfo very hairy, and the empalement of the flowers is fwollen like inflated bladders. This flowers near a month after the other, but the male and female flowers grow upon different plants, as in the former.

There is a variety of this with double flowers, which is propagated in gardens by the title of Double white Bachelor's Button, and is an ornamental plant in the flower-garden; though being white it doth not make fo good an appearance as the other, however it adds to the variety. This is propagated in the fame way as the double fort before-mentioned, but the plants will thrive in a drier foil, and a more open expofure than that.

The fifth fort grows very common in moift meadows, and by the fide of rivers in moft parts of England, where it is intermixed with the Grafs. This rifes with upright unbranched ftalks near a foot and a half high, garnifhed with narrow fpear-fhaped leaves, placed by pairs oppofite at each joint. The ftalks are flender, channelled, and are terminated by fix or feven purple flowers upon pretty long foot-ftalks, which branch out. The empalement of the flower is ftriped with purple, and the petals of the flowers are deeply jagged in four narrow fegments, which appear as if torn; from whence the country people have given it the appellation of Ragged Robin. It flowers in May, and the feeds ripen in July. This fort is never kept in gardens, but there is a variety of it with very double flowers, which is propagated by the gardeners for ornament. It only differs from the fingle in the multiplicity of the petals, and produces no feeds, fo is propagated by flips in the fame manner as the fecond fort. It is commonly known by the title of Double Ragged Robin.

The fixth fort grows naturally on the Alps, in Lapland, and the other cold parts of Europe. This is a perennial plant which delights in a moift foil. The ftalks of this are erect, half a foot high, garnifhed with narrow fpear-fhaped leaves placed by pairs oppofite, like the former fort, but are a little fhorter and broader; the bottom leaves are broader than thofe upon the ftalks, and fit clofe to the ground; they are fmooth, and of a deep green: the flowers are produced in a corymbus on the top of the ftalk, fitting clofe together; they are of a purple colour, and the petals are cut in the middle. This flowers the beginning of June, and the feeds ripen in Auguft. It is propagated by feeds, and alfo by parting of the roots; it muft have a moift foil and a fhady fituation, otherwife the plants will not thrive. The time for tranf-

planting the plants, and parting the roots, is the fame as for the fecond fort, and the feeds may be fown upon a fhady border in March. In dry weather the ground muft be kept moift, otherwife the feeds will not grow. When the plants come up, and are fit to remove, they fhould be tranfplanted into a fhady border, where they may remain to flower.

The feventh fort grows naturally in Siberia: this hath a perennial root, from which arife many narrow leaves fitting clofe to the ground. The ftalks rife a foot high, dividing into branches by pairs. The flowers grow out from the divifion of the branches, as alfo at the top of the ftalks. They are compofed of five white petals, which are divided in the middle; thefe appear in June, and are fucceeded by roundifh capfules filled with fmall angular feeds, which ripen in Auguft. This requires the fame treatment as the former fort.

The eighth fort was brought from Portugal to England, and is probably a variety of one with fingle flowers, which grows naturally in that country, but is different from any we have in England. This approaches neareft to the Double Ragged Robin, but is different from that. It hath a perennial root, from which arife many oblong narrow leaves fitting clofe to the ground. It divides into feparate heads like the fecond fort, and from each of thefe come out an upright ftalk about nine inches high, which divides upwards by pairs, and from the middle of each divifion comes out a flender foot-ftalk two inches long, fuftaining one double purple flower at the top, whofe petals are very much jagged at their points; the empalements of the flowers are marked with deep purple ftripes. From the fide of the ftalks there are alfo foot-ftalks come out at the wings, which for the moft part fuftain but one flower, though fometimes they have two; thefe flowers being very double, are never fucceeded by feeds. The ufual time of this plant flowering is in June, but fometimes it fends out frefh ftalks, which have flowers in the autumn. It is propagated by flips in the fame manner as the third and fourth forts, but coming from a warm country, it is impatient of much cold, and requires a particular treatment, for it does not thrive well in pots; nor will it live through the winter in open borders, fo that the only fituation in which I have feen it thrive, was where it was planted as clofe as poffible to a fouth wall in dry undunged earth; for in rich or moift ground the roots prefently rot, as they alfo do when they are watered. If they are planted in brick rubbifh, they will ftill do better. I was favoured with this plant by John Browning, Efq; of Lincoln's-inn, who received it from Portugal.

The ninth fort grows naturally in the northern parts of Europe. It is like the fourth fort, but the petals of the flowers do not extend beyond the empalement, and the empalements are much larger and more fwollen.

The other SPECIES of LYCHNIS are now ranged under the following genera, viz.

AGROSTEMMA, CUCUBALUS, SAPONARIA, and SILENE, to which articles the reader is defired to turn for thofe which are not here enumerated.

LYCIUM. Lin. Gen. Plant. 232. Jafminoides. Niffol. Act. R. Par. 1711. Rhamnus. C. B. P. 477. Boxthorn.

The CHARACTERS are,

The flower hath a fmall, obtufe, permanent empalement, which is erect, and divided into five parts at the top; the flower is funnel-fhaped, of one petal, with an incurved tube, whofe brim is cut into five obtufe fegments, which fpread open. It has five awl-fhaped ftamina, which are a little inclined and fhorter than the tube, terminated by erect fummits. In the center is fituated a roundifh germen fupporting a fingle ftyle, which is longer than the ftamina, crowned by a thick bifid ftigma; the germen afterwards becomes a roundifh berry with two cells, inclofing kidney-fhaped feeds faftened to the middle partition. This genus of plants is ranged in the firft fection of Linnaeus's fifth clafs, intitled Pentandria Monogynia, which

, which includes thofe plants whofe flowers have five ftamina and one ftyle.

The Species are,

1. Lycium (*Afrum*) foliis lineari-longioribus, tubo florum longiori, fegmentis obtufis. *Boxthorn with longer linear leaves, a longer tube to the flower, and obtufe fegments.* Lycium foliis linearibus. Hort. Cliff. 57. *Boxthorn with linear leaves.*

2. Lycium (*Italicum*) foliis lineari-brevioribus, tubo florum breviori, fegmentis ovalibus patentiffimis. *Boxthorn with fhorter linear leaves, a fhorter tube to the flower, and oval fegments fpreading open.*

3. Lycium (*Salicifolium*) foliis cunciformibus. Vir. Cliff. 14. *Boxthorn with wedge-fhaped leaves.* Jafminoides aculeatum, falicis folio, flore parvo ex albo purpurafcente. Mitchel. Gen. 224. *Prickly Baftard Jafmine with a Willow leaf, and a fmall purplifh white flower.*

4. Lycium (*Barbarum*) foliis lanceolatis craffiufculis, calycibus trifidis. Lin. Sp. Plant. 192. *Boxthorn with fpear-fhaped thick leaves, and trifid empalements.* Jafminoides aculeatum, polygoni folio, floribus parvis albidis. Shaw. Afr. 349. f. 349. *Prickly Baftard Jafmine, with a Knot-grafs leaf, and fmall whitifh flowers.*

5. Lycium (*Chinenfe*) foliis ovato-lanceolatis, ramis diffufis, floribus folitariis patentibus alaribus, ftylo longiori. *Boxthorn with oval fpear-fhaped leaves, diffufed branches, and fingle fpreading flowers proceeding from the fides of the branches, with a longer ftyle.*

6. Lycium (*Halimifolium*) foliis lanceolatis acutis. *Boxthorn with fpear-fhaped acute leaves.* Jafminoides Sinenfe halimi folio longiore & anguftiore. Du Ham. 306. *China Baftard Jafmine with a narrower and longer leef.*

7. Lycium (*Capenfe*) foliis oblongo-ovatis, craffiufculis, confertis, fpinis robuftioribus. *Boxthorn with oblong, oval, thick leaves growing in clufters, and ftronger fpines.*

8. Lycium (*Anguftifolium*) foliis lineari-lanceolatis confertis, calycibus brevibus acutis. *Boxthorn with linear fpear-fhaped leaves growing in clufters, and fhort acute empalements.*

9. Lycium (*Juerme*) inermis, foliis lanceolatis, alternis, perennantibus. *Smooth Boxthorn, with fpear-fhaped evergreen leaves placed alternate.*

10. Lycium (*Cordatum*) foliis cordato-ovatis, feffilibus, oppofitis perennantibus, fpinis craffis bigeminis, floribus confertis. *Lycium with oval heart-fhaped leaves placed oppofite, which are ever-green, and fit clofe to the ftalks, with thick double fpines, and flowers growing in clufters.* Arbor Africana fpinofa, foliis craffis cordatis & conjugatis, fpinis craffis bigeminis. I Term. Cat. 4. *Prickly African-tree with thick heart-fhaped leaves growing by peirs, and thick double fpines.*

The firft fort grows naturally in Spain, Portugal, and at the Cape of Good Hope. This rifes with irregular fhrubby ftalks ten or twelve feet high, fending out feveral crooked knotty branches, covered with a whitifh bark, and armed with long fharp fpines, upon which grow many clufters of narrow leaves; thefe thorns often put out one or two fmaller on their fides, which have fome clufters of fmaller leaves upon them; the branches are garnifhed with very narrow leaves an inch and a half long, and at the bafe of thefe come out clufters of fhorter and narrower leaves. The flowers come out from the fide of the branches, ftanding upon fhort foot-ftalks; they have a fhort permanentempalement of one leaf, which is tubulous, and cut into five fegments at the brim; it is funnel-fhaped, of one petal, with a long incurved tube, cut into five obtufe fegments at the brim; they are of a dull purple colour, and have five ftamina almoft as long as the tube, with erect fummits. In the center is fituated a roundifh germen, fupporting a ftyle which is longer than the ftamina, crowned by a bifid ftigma. The germen afterward turns to a roundifh flefhy berry, of a yellowifh colour when ripe, inclofing feveral hard feeds. This ufually flowers in June and July, and the feeds ripen in the autumn; but there is frequently a few flowers come out in all the fummer months.

It may be propagated either by feeds, cuttings, or

layers. If by feeds, they fhould be fown in the autumn foon after they are ripe; for if they are kept out of the ground till fpring, they feldom come up the firft year. If the feeds are fown in pots, the pots fhould be plunged into fome old tan in the winter, and in very fevere froft covered with Peas-haulm or ftraw, but in mild weather fhould be open to receive the wet; in the fpring the pots fhould be plunged into a moderate hot-bed, which will foon bring up the plants; thefe muft be inured to bear the open air as foon as the danger of froft is over, and when they are three inches high, they may be fhaken out of the pots, and each planted in a fmall feparate pot, filled with loamy earth, and placed in the fhade till they have taken new root, when they may be removed to a fheltered fituation, where they may remain till the autumn; then they fhould be either removed into the green-houfe, or placed under a hot-bed frame to fhelter them from hard froft; for thefe plants are too tender to live in the open air in England, fo they muft be kept in pots and treated in the fame way as Myrtles, and other hardy green-houfe plants; but when the plants are grown ftrong, there may be a few of them planted in the full ground in a warm fituation, where they will live in moderate winters, but in hard frofts they are commonly deftroyed. If the cuttings of thefe plants are planted in a fhady border in July, and duly watered, they will take root, and may then be treated in the fame way as the feedling-plants.

The fecond fort was raifed in the Chelfea garden from feeds which came from the Cape of Good Hope. This hath an irregular fhrubby ftalk like the former, but feldom rife more than four or five feet high; the large leaves are fhorter and a little broader than thofe of the firft, but the tufts of fmall leaves are narrower; the tube of the flower is fhorter, the brim is deeper cut into oval fegments which fpread open; the empalement is fhorter, and cut into acute fegments; the flowers and fruit are alfo fmaller. Thefe differences are permanent, in all the plants which I have two or three times raifed from feeds. It flowers about the fame time as the firft, and may be propagated in the fame way; the plants alfo require the fame culture.

The third fort grows naturally in the hedges in the fouth of France, in Spain and Italy. This hath many irregular fhrubby ftalks, which rife eight or nine feet high, fending out feveral irregular branches, covered with a white bark, and armed with pretty ftrong thorns; the leaves are narrow at bottom, growing broader upward, and are of a pale green colour. The flowers come out from the fide of the branches; they are of a purplifh white colour and fmall, fo make no great appearance. This fort flowers in June and July, but rarely produces any feeds in this country. The leaves of this remain till winter, when they fall off. It may be propagated by cuttings or layers, in the fame manner as the firft fort. The plants will live abroad in a fheltered warm fituation, but in very hard froft they fhould be covered with ftraw or litter, otherwife the branches will be killed, and fometimes the roots are deftroyed where they have not fome cover.

The fourth fort was brought from Africa by the late Dr. Shaw, where it grows naturally. This hath a fhrubby ftalk which rifes feven or eight feet high, fending out feveral irregular branches, which are armed with ftrong fpines, and garnifhed with fhort, thick, fpear-fhaped, oval leaves, which ftand without order. The flowers come out from the fide of the branches; they are fmall and white, fo make little appearance. This flowers in July and Auguft, but does not produce feeds in England. It may be propagated by cuttings in the fame way as the firft fort, but is too tender to live in the open air in winter in this country, fo the plants muft be kept in pots, and removed into the green-houfe in autumn, and treated in the fame way as other hardy kinds of green-houfe plants.

The

The fifth fort grows naturally in China, from whence the feeds were brought to England a few years paft, and the plants were raifed in feveral gardens, and by fome were thought to be the Thea. This rifes with weak, irregular, diffufed branches to a great height, but require fupport, otherwife they will trail upon the ground: I have meafured fome of thefe branches, which in one year has been upward of twelve feet long: the lower leaves are more than four inches long, and three broad in the middle: they are of a light green and a thin confiftence, placed without order on every fide the branches; as the fhoots advance in length, fo the fize of the leaves diminifh, and toward the upper part they are not more than an inch long, and a quarter of an inch broad; they fit clofe to the ftalks on every fide. The flowers come out fingly at every joint toward the upper part of the branches, ftanding upon fhort flender foot-ftalks; they are of a pale colour, with fhort tubes; the brims are fpread open broader than either of the former forts, and the ftyle is confiderably longer than the tube of the flower. This fort flowers in Auguft, September, and October; the plant is very hardy, and retains its leaves till November before they decay. It propagates faft enough by its creeping roots, which fend out fuckers at a great diftance, and the cuttings thruft into the ground will take root as freely as Willows.

The fixth fort grows naturally in China, from whence the feeds were brought to the Royal Garden at Paris, and the feeds were fent me by Dr. Bernard de Juffieu, demonftrator of the plants in that garden. This rifes with a fhrubby ftalk to the height of four or five feet, fending out many irregular branches, covered with a very white bark, and armed with a few fhort fpines; the leaves are about three inches long, and one broad in the middle; they are placed alternately on the branches, and are of a pale green colour. The flowers of this fort appear in June and July, which are fucceeded by fmall round berries that ripen in the autumn, when they are as red as coral. This fort is propagated by cuttings, which fhould be planted in the fpring before they begin to fhoot, in a border expofed to the morning fun, where they will take root very freely; but thefe fhould not be removed till the autumn, when they may be planted to cover walls, for the branches are too weak to fupport themfelves; and as the leaves continue green as long as any of the deciduous plants, fo they are proper plants for fuch purpofes.

The feventh fort was raifed in the Chelfea garden from feeds, which were brought me from the Cape of Good Hope. This rifes with fhrubby branching ftalks feven or eight feet high, which are armed with long ftrong thorns, that have feveral clufters of leaves upon them; the branches are garnifhed with fmall, oblong, oval leaves, which are placed without order; fometimes they come out in fmall clufters from one point, at others they are fingle, ftanding on every fide the ftalk; thefe are of a light green, and a pretty thick confiftence, continuing green all the year. Thefe plants have not as yet flowered here, fo I can give no account of them; but by the fruit which I received entire, I make no doubt of its belonging to this genus.

This fort is pretty hardy, for it has lived abroad four winters, where it was planted againft a fouth-eaft wall. It may be propagated either by layers or cuttings, in the fame manner as the firft; and when the plants have obtained ftrength, they may be planted in a warm fituation, where they will live with very little fhelter in fevere froft. The branches of this fort are ftronger than thofe of the former, fo will not require the fame fupport. It will be proper to keep a plant of this in fhelter to preferve the kind, left thofe in the open air fhould be deftroyed.

The eighth fort has much the appearance of the firft, but the branches are not fo ftrongly armed with thorns; they have alfo a whiter bark, the leaves are

broader and of a lighter green, ftanding in clufters at every joint. The flowers are fmaller, of a deeper purple colour, and have much fhorter empalements, which are cut into acute fegments. It flowers at the fame time with the firft fort, but does not produce any feeds in this country; it is not fo hardy as the former fort, fo requires protection from very hard froft; therefore the plants fhould be kept in pots and houfed in the winter, treating them in the fame way as other hardy green-houfe plants. It may be propagated by cuttings or layers, in the fame way as the firft fort.

The ninth fort has been long an inhabitant of the Chelfea garden; it was raifed from feeds which came from China, and was for many years taken for the Tea-tree, till it produced fome flowers, which difcovered its true genus. This rifes with a ftrong woody ftalk fix or feven feet high, fending out many fmooth branches, which are covered with a brown bark having no thorns; they are garnifhed with fpear-fhaped leaves about three inches long, and near three quarters of inch broad, placed alternately on the branches, ftanding upon fhort foot-ftalks; they are of a deep green, and continue all the year. The flowers are white, and of the fame fhape with the others of this genus, but there has not been any feeds of this fort as yet produced in England.

This plant will live in the open air, if it is planted in a warm fituation and a dry foil; but it is of flow growth, feldom fhooting more than three or four inches in a feafon; it is alfo difficult to propagate, for the branches which are laid down will not take root in lefs than two years, and the cuttings are with difficulty made to grow. The beft time to plant them is in May, in pots filled with light loamy earth, plunging them into an old bed of tanners bark, covering the pots clofe with bell or hand-glaffes, to exclude the external air; thefe fhould be fhaded every day from the fun; thefe cuttings fhould be refrefhed with water once a week, but it muft not be given to them in too great plenty. Thofe cuttings which fucceed, will have put out roots by the beginning of Auguft, when they may be taken up and planted in fmall pots, placing them in the fhade till they have taken new root; and then they may be placed with other hardy exotic plants in a fheltered fituation, till the end of October, when they may be put under a common frame to fhelter them in winter. When the plants have acquired ftrength, they may be fhaken out of the pots, and planted in the full ground in a warm fituation, where, if they are fheltered in fevere frofts, they will thrive better than in pots.

The tenth fort grows naturally at the Cape of Good Hope, from whence the feeds were fent to Holland a few years paft, where the plants were raifed. This is a low fhrubby plant, which fends out branches from the ground upward, which are covered with a dark green bark, and are armed with fhort ftrong thorns, which come out by pairs, and fometimes there are double pairs upon the fame foot-ftalk; thefe are fituated juft below the leaves, and where there are four, two of them point upward, and the other two downward. The leaves are heart-fhaped, not much larger than thofe of the Box-tree, of the fame confiftence and colour, terminating in acute points; they are placed by pairs oppofite, upon very fhort foot-ftalks, ftanding pretty clofe together; thefe continue green all the year. The flowers come out from the fide of the branches upon fhort flender foot-ftalks, each fupporting five or fix fmall white flowers, which grow in a clufter at the top; thefe have very fhort empalements, and pretty long tubes, divided at the brim into five acute fegments. Thefe flowers have an agreeable odour; they appear in July and Auguft, but are feldom fucceeded by feeds in England.

This fort may be propagated by cuttings in the fame manner as the firft fort, which, if planted in July, and fhaded from the fun, will take root very freely; then they fhould be planted into feparate fmall pots, and placed in the fhade till they have

taken

taken new root, after which they may be treated in the same manner as the former fort. This plant has not as yet been planted in the full ground in England, but it lives through the winter under a common frame.

The other species which were included in this genus, are now removed to CELASTRUS.

LYCOPERSICON. Tourn. Inft. R. H. 150. tab. 63. Solanum. Lin. Gen. Plant. 224. [of Λύκ⊙·, a wolf, and Perfica, *Lat.* a Peach.] Love Apples, or Wolf's Peach.

The CHARACTERS are,

The flower has a permanent empalement of one leaf, which is cut into five acute segments at the top, and is permanent. The flower has one petal, which is wheel-shaped, with a very short tube, and a large five-cornered brim, which spreads open and is plaited. It hath five small awl-shaped stamina, terminated by oblong summits which close together. It hath a roundish germen, supporting a slender style the length of the stamina, crowned by an obtuse stigma. The germen afterward becomes a roundish fleshy fruit or berry, divided into several cells, inclosing many flat seeds.

This genus of plants is ranged in the seventh section of Tournefort's second class, which includes the herbs with a wheel-shaped flower of one leaf, whose pointal becomes a soft fruit. Dr. Linnæus has joined this genus, and also the Melongena of Tournefort, to the Solanum, which he places in the first section of his fifth class, which includes those plants whose flowers have five stamina and one style; but as there are numerous species of Solani, so it is much better to keep these separate, and to avoid confusion, which if we allow the fruit as a characteristic note, should be done; for as the fruit of the Solanum has but two cells, and the fruit of this many, so that distinction may be allowed to separate the genera.

The SPECIES are,

1. LYCOPERSICON (*Galeni*) caule inermi herbaceo, foliis pinnatis incisis, fructu rotundo glabro. *Love Apple with an herbaceous unarmed stalk, pinnated cut leaves, and a smooth round fruit.* Lycoperficon Galeni. Ang. 217. *The Wolf Peach of Galen.*

2. LYCOPERSICON (*Esculentum*) caule herbaceo hirsutissimo, foliis pinnatis, incisis, fructu compresso sulcato. *Love Apple with a very hairy herbaceous stalk, winged cut leaves, and a compressed furrowed fruit.* Solanum pomiferum, fructu rotundo striato molli. C. B. P. 167. *Apple-bearing Nightshade, with a soft, round, striated fruit, commonly called Tomatas by the Spaniards.*

3. LYCOPERSICON (*Æthiopicum*) caule inermi herbaceo, erecto, foliis ovatis dentato angulatis, subspinosis fructu subrotundo sulcato. *Love Apple with an herbaceous, erect, unarmed stalk, oval angular leaves indented, having a few spines, with a roundish furrowed fruit.* Lycoperficon fructu striato duro. Tourn. Inft. R. H. 150. *Wolf's Peach with a hard striated fruit.*

4. LYCOPERSICON (*Pimpinellifolium*) caule inermi herbaceo, foliis inæqualiter pinnatis, foliolis obtuse-dentatis, racemis simplicibus. *Love Apple with an herbaceous unarmed stalk, leaves unequally winged, whose lobes are bluntly indented, and simple branches of flowers.* Lycoperficon inodorum. Juff. *Wolf's Peach having no scent.*

5. LYCOPERSICON (*Peruvianum*) caule inermi herbaceo, foliis pinnatis tomentofis incisis, racemis bipartitis foliosis. *Love Apple with an unarmed herbaceous stalk, winged cut leaves, which are downy, and a leafy double spike of flowers.* Lycoperficon pimpinellæ sanguisorbæ foliis. Feuill. Obf. 3. p. 37. *Wolf's Peach with leaves like Burnet.*

6. LYCOPERSICON (*Procumbens*) caule herbaceo, procumbente, foliis pinnatifidis, glabris, floribus folitariis alaribus. *Love Apple with an herbaceous trailing stalk, wing-pointed smooth leaves, and flowers growing singly from the wings of the stalk.*

7. LYCOPERSICON (*Tuberosum*) caule inermo herbaceo, foliis pinnatis integerrimis. *Love Apple with an unarmed herbaceous stalk, and winged leaves which are entire.* Solanum tuberofum efculentum. C. B. P. 167. *Esculent*

tuberous Nightshade, commonly called Potatoe, by the Indians Batatas.

The first fort here mentioned is supposed to be the Lycoperficon of Galen. This is an annual plant, with an herbaceous, branching, hairy stalk, which will rise to the height of six or eight feet, if supported, otherwise the branches will fall to the ground; these are garnished with winged leaves of a very rank disagreeable odour, composed of four or five pair of lobes terminated by an odd one; these are cut on their edges, and end in acute-points. The flowers come out from the side of the branches upon pretty long foot-stalks, each sustaining several yellow flowers, ranged in a single long bunch or thyrfe, and are succeeded by round, smooth, pulpy fruit, about the size of a large Cherry. There are two varieties of this, one with yellow, and the other with red fruit. The plants flower from June till the frost stops them, and the fruit ripens in succeffion from the end of July, till the frost kills the plants; this fort is used in medicine. The second fort is very like the first, excepting the fruit, which differ greatly; for those of the second fort are very large, compressed at both ends, and deeply furrowed all over the sides. This fort never varies to the other, so that it is undoubtedly a distinct species. This is the fort which is commonly cultivated to put into foups; and the Portugueze, Spaniards, and some others, use them in many of their fauces, to which they give an agreeable acid flavour. The third fort is also annual; this rises with an erect herbaceous stalk a foot and a half high, dividing into several branches, garnished with oval angular leaves, from three to four inches long, and almost three inches broad in the middle; they are placed alternately upon pretty long foot-stalks, which have one or two short spines upon them, as there also is upon the midrib of the leaves. The flowers come out singly upon foot-stalks from the side of the branches; they are white, and are succeeded by red striated fruit, which are firmer than those of the other forts, and about the size of Cherries. This fruit ripens in the autumn, and the plants decay soon after. The fourth fort is somewhat like the first, but the leaves are unequally winged, having some smaller lobes placed between the large ones; the lobes of this are shorter, broader, and not cut like those of the first, but have some obtuse indentures toward their base. The leaves of this fort have not that rank disagreeable odour which the two first have; the fruit of it is not so large as those of the first, but they are round and smooth, and are very late before they ripen here; so that unless the plants are raised early in the spring, they will not produce ripe fruit. The fifth fort is also annual; this hath a very branching herbaceous stalk, spreading out into many divisions, and is not so hairy as the two first; the leaves are composed of a greater number of lobes, which are much shorter and more indented on their edges, where they are a little waved, and are downy. The flowers stand upon very long foot-stalks, which branch out and support a large number of flowers at the top; these have a longer style than those of the other species, which is permanent, remaining on the top of the fruit. This fort is late in ripening the fruit, so that unless the plants are raised early in the spring, the fruit will not ripen in England.

The seeds of these two forts were sent from Peru by Mr. Joseph de Juffieu to the Royal Garden at Paris, part of which was sent me by his brother Dr. Bernard de Juffieu, of the Royal Academy of Sciences. The sixth fort was raised by Mr. James Gordon, gardener at Mile-end, who gave me some of the feeds, but from what country it came I could not learn. This hath very weak, trailing, smooth stalks, not more than a foot long, garnished with smooth leaves, standing by pairs opposite; these are regularly cut on the sides almost to the midrib, in form of a winged leaf; and these fegments are also indented on their edges, and at their points. The flowers come out

out on the fide of the ftalks fingly; they are of a whitifh yellow colour, and have a pretty large fpreading empalement, which is deeply cut at the brim into many acute fegments which fpread open. The flowers are fucceeded by fmall roundifh berries a little compreffed at the top, of an herbaceous yellow colour when ripe.

Thefe plants are all propagated by fowing their feeds on a moderate hot-bed in March, and when the plants are come up two inches high, they fhould be tranfplanted into another moderate hot-bed, at about four inches diftance from each other, obferving to fhade them until they have taken root; after which they muft have frequent waterings, and a large fhare of frefh air; for if they are too much drawn while young, they feldom do well afterwards.

In May thefe plants fhould be tranfplanted either into pots filled with rich light earth, or into borders near walls, pales, or Reed-hedges, to which their branches may be faftened to fupport them from trailing on the ground, which they otherwife will do, and then the fruit will not ripen; fo that where thefe plants are cultivated for the fake of their fruit, they fhould be planted to a warm afpect, and the branches regularly faftened as they extend, that the fruit may have the advantage of the fun's warmth to forward them, otherwife it will be late in the feafon before they are ripe, and they are unfit for ufe before; but when the plants are brought forward in the fpring, and thus regularly trained to the fouth fun, the fruit will ripen by the latter end of July, and there will be a fucceffion of it till the froft kills the plants.

Some perfons cultivate thefe plants for ornament, but their leaves emit fo ftrong offenfive an odour on being touched, which renders them very improper for the pleafure-garden, and their branches extend fo wide and irregular, as to render them very unfightly in fuch places; for as their branches cannot be kept within bounds, efpecially when they are planted in good ground, fo they will appear very unfightly in fuch places; therefore the borders in the kitchen-garden, where thefe plants are placed for their fruit, muft not be too rich, for in a moderate foil they will not be fo luxuriant and more fruitful.

The Italians and Spaniards eat thefe Apples, as we do Cucumbers, with pepper, oil, and falt; and fome eat them ftewed in fauces, &c. and in foups they are now much ufed in England, efpecially the fecond fort, which is preferred to all the other. This fruit gives an agreeable acid to the foup, though there are fome perfons who think them not wholefome, from their great moifture and coldnefs, and that the nourifhment they afford muft be bad.

The third fort is never ufed either in the kitchen or for medicine, but the plants are preferved for the fake of variety, efpecially by thofe perfons who are lovers of botany. This fort is propagated by feeds, which fhould be fown upon a hot-bed in the fpring, and the plants afterward treated in the fame manner as hath been directed for the Capficum, with which this plant will thrive and produce plenty of fruit annually.

The feventh fort is the common Potatoe, which is a plant fo well known now, as to need no defcription. Of this there are two varieties, one with a red and the other with a white root; that whofe roots are red, have purplifh flowers, but the white root has white flowers; thefe are fuppofed to be only accidental variations, and not diftinct fpecies.

The common name of Potatoe, feem to be only a corruption of the Indian name Batatas. This plant has been much propagated in England within thirty or forty years paft, for although it was introduced from America about the year 1623, yet it was but little cultivated in England till of late; thefe roots being defpifed by the rich, and deemed only proper food for the meaner fort of perfons; however, they are now generally efteemed by moft people, and the quantity of them which are cultivated near

London, I believe, exceeds that of any other part of Europe.

This plant was always ranged in the genus of Solanum, or Nightfhade, and is now brought under that title again by Dr. Linnæus; but as Lycoperficon has been eftablifhed as a diftinct genus, on account of the fruit being divided into feveral cells, by intermediate partitions; and as the fruit of this plant exactly agrees with the characters of the other fpecies of this genus, I have inferted it here.

This is generally propagated by its roots, which multiply greatly if planted in a proper foil. The common way is, either to plant the fmall roots or offsets entire, or to cut the larger roots into pieces, preferving a bud or eye to each; but neither of thefe methods is what I would recommend, for when the fmaller offsets are planted, they generally produce a greater number of roots, but thefe are always fmall; and the cuttings of the larger roots are apt to rot, efpecially if wet weather happens foon after they are planted; therefore what I would recommend is, to make choice of the faireft roots for this purpofe, and to allow them a larger fpace of ground, both between the rows, as alfo in the rows, plant from plant; by which method I have obferved, the roots have been in general large the following autumn.

The foil in which this plant thrives beft, is a light fandy loam, not too dry or over moift; this ground fhould be well ploughed two or three times, in order to break and divide the parts; and the deeper it is ploughed, the better the roots will thrive. In the fpring, juft before the laft ploughing, there fhould be a good quantity of rotten dung fpread on the ground, which fhould be ploughed into the ground the beginning of March, if the feafon proves mild, otherwife it had better be deferred till the middle or latter end of that month; for if it fhould prove hard froft after the roots are planted, they may be greatly injured, if not deftroyed thereby: but the fooner they are planted in the fpring, after the danger of froft is over, the better it will be, efpecially in dry land. In the laft ploughing, the ground fhould be laid even, and then the furaows fhould be drawn at three feet diftance from each other, about feven or eight inches deep. In the bottom of this furrow the roots, fhould be laid at about one foot and a half afunder; then the furrow fhould be filled with the earth which came out, and the fame continued through the whole field or parcel of land, intended to be planted.

After all is finifhed, the land may remain in the fame ftate till near the time when the fhoots are expected to appear above ground, when the ground fhould be well harrowed over both ways, which will break the clods, and make the furface very fmooth; and by doing of it fo late, it will deftroy the young weeds, which, by this time, will begin to make their appearance; and this will fave the expence of the firft hoeing, and will alfo ftir the upper furface of the ground, which, if much wet has fallen after the planting, is often bound into a hard cruft, and will retard the appearance of the fhoots.

As I have allotted the rows of Potatoes at three feet diftance, it was in order to introduce the hoe-plough between them, which will greatly improve thefe roots, for by twice ftirring and breaking the ground between thefe plants, it will not only deftroy the weeds, but alfo loofen the ground, whereby every fhower of rain will penetrate to the roots, and greatly improve their growth; but thefe operations fhould be performed early in the feafon, before the ftems or branches of the plants begin to fall and trail upon the ground, becaufe after that, it will be impoffible to do it without injuring the fhoots.

If thefe ploughings are carefully performed between the rows, and the ground between the plants in the rows hand-hoed, it will prevent the growth of weeds, till the haulm of the plants cover the ground; fo that afterward there will be little danger of weeds growing fo as to injure the crop; but as the plough can only go between the rows, it will be neceſſary to make uſe of a hoe to ſtir the ground, and deſtroy the weeds in the rows; and if this is carefully performed in dry weather, after the two ploughings, it will be ſufficient to keep the ground clean until the Potatoes are fit to take up.

In places where dung is ſcarce, many perſons ſcatter it only in the furrows, where the roots are planted; but this is a very poor method, becauſe when the Potatoes begin to puſh out their roots, they are ſoon extended beyond the width of theſe furrows, and the new roots are commonly formed at a diſtance from the old, ſo will be out of the reach of this dung, and conſequently will receive little benefit from it. And as moſt of the farmers covet to have a crop of Wheat after the Potatoes are taken off the ground, ſo the land will not be ſo thoroughly dreſſed in every part, nor ſo proper for this crop, as when the dung is equally ſpread, and ploughed in all over the land, nor will the crop of Potatoes be ſo good. I have always obſerved, where this method of planting the Potatoes has been practiſed, the land has produced a fine crop of Wheat afterward, and there has ſcarce one ſhoot of the Potatoe appeared among the Wheat the following ſeaſon, which I attribute to the farmers planting only the largeſt roots; for when they have forked them out of the ground the following autumn, there have been ſix, eight, or ten large roots produced from each, and often many more, and ſcarce any very ſmall roots among them; whereas, in ſuch places where the ſmall roots have been planted, there has been a vaſt number of very ſmall roots produced; many of which were ſo ſmall as not to be diſcovered when the roots were taken up, ſo have grown the following ſeaſon, and have greatly injured whatever crop was on the ground.

The haulm of theſe Potatoes is generally killed by the firſt froſt in the autumn, when the roots ſhould be taken up ſoon after, and may be laid up in ſand in any ſheltered place, where they may be kept dry, and ſecure from froſt. Indeed the people who cultivate theſe roots near London, do not wait for the decaying of the haulm, but begin to take up part of them as ſoon as their roots are grown to a proper ſize for the market, and ſo keep taking up from time to time, as they have vent for them. There are others likewiſe, who do not take them up ſo ſoon as the haulm decays, but let them remain much longer in the ground; in which there is no hurt done, provided they are taken up before hard froſt ſets in, which would deſtroy them, unleſs where the ground is wanted for other crops; in which caſe, the ſooner they are taken up the better, after the haulm is decayed. When theſe roots are laid up, they ſhould have a good quantity of ſand or dry earth laid between them, to prevent their heating; nor ſhould they be laid in too large heaps, for the ſame reaſon. The kitchen-gardeners and farmers who live in the neighbourhood of Mancheſter, cultivate great quantities of this root, as the inhabitants of that populous town conſume abundance of them, and are much fonder of them than of any other eſculent plants; which has occaſioned an emulation among the cultivators, of endeavouring to outvie each other, in getting the roots of a proper ſize for the table early in the ſeaſon: in order to obtain this, they have made choice of thoſe roots which produced the firſt flowers, and have left them to ripen their ſeeds, which they have ſowed with great care; and the plants ſo raiſed, have generally been forwarder than the other; and by frequently repeating of this, they have ſo much improved the forwarding of the roots, as to have them fit for uſe in two months after planting; ſo that great improvements may be made by this practice, of many eſculent plants, by perſons who are curious and careful in trying the experiments.

LYCOPUS [Λυκόπυς, of Λύκος, a wolf, and Πῦς, a foot; q. d. Wolf's-foot; becauſe the ancients fancied, that the leaves of this plant reſembled the foot of a wolf,] it is commonly called Water Horehound.

This plant grows in great plenty on moiſt ſoils by the ſides of ditches and ponds in moſt parts of England, but is never cultivated in gardens, ſo that it would be needleſs to ſay any thing more of it in this place.

LYSIMACHIA. Tourn. Inſt. R. H. 141. tab. 59. Lin. Gen. Plant. 188. [this plant was ſo called of Lyſimachus, the ſon of a king of Sicily, who is ſaid to have firſt found the virtues of it.] Looſtrife; in French, *Corneille.*

The CHARACTERS are,

The empalement of the flower is permanent, and is cut into five acute ſegments, which are erect. The flower is of one petal, cut into five oblong oval ſegments to the bottom, which ſpread open. It hath five awl-ſhaped ſtamina about half the length of the petal, terminated by acute-pointed ſummits. In the center is ſituated a roundiſh germen, ſupporting a ſlender ſtyle the length of the ſtamina, crowned by an obtuſe ſtigma. The germen afterward turns to a globular capſule with one cell, opening with ten valves, and filled with ſmall angular ſeeds.

This genus of plants is ranged in the firſt ſection of Linnæus's fifth claſs, intitled Pentandria Monogynia, which includes the plants whoſe flowers have five ſtamina and one ſtyle.

The SPECIES are,

1. LYSIMACHIA (*Vulgaris*) paniculata, racemis terminalibus. Lin. Sp. Plant. 209. *Paniculated Looſtrife, with bunches of flowers terminating the ſtalks.* Lyſimachia lutea, major, quæ Dioſcoridis. C. B. P. 245. *Greater yellow Looſtrife of Dioſcorides.*

2. LYSIMACHIA (*Thyrſiflora*) racemis lateralibus pedunculatis. Lin. Sp. Plant. 147. *Looſtrife with lateral ſpikes of flowers growing upon foot-ſtalks.* Lyſimachia bifolia flore globoſo, luteo. C. B. P. 242. *Two-leaved Looſtrife with a yellow globular flower.*

3. LYSIMACHIA (*Atropurpurea*) ſpicis terminalibus petalis, lanceolatis, ſtaminibus corolla longioribus. Lin. Sp. Plant. 147. *Looſtrife with ſpear-ſhaped ſpreading ſpikes of flowers terminating the branches, and ſtamina longer than the petals.* Lyſimachia Orientalis anguſtifolia flore purpureo. Tourn. Cor. 7. *Narrow-leaved Eaſtern Looſtrife with a purple flower.*

4. LYSIMACHIA (*Ephemerum*) racemis ſimplicibus terminalibus, petalis obtuſis, ſtaminibus corolla brevioribus. Lin. Sp. Plant. 146. *Looſtrife with ſpikes of flowers terminating the ſtalks, obtuſe petals to the flower, and ſtamina ſhorter than the petal.* Lyſimachia Orientalis minor, foliis glaucis, annuentibus, flore purpureo. Hort. Piſſ. *Smaller Eaſtern Looſtrife, with nodding grayiſh leaves and a purple ſpike of flowers.*

5. LYSIMACHIA (*Ciliata*) petiolis ciliatis, floribus cernuis. Lin. Sp. Plant. 147. *Looſtrife with hairy foot-ſtalks and nodding flowers.* Lyſimachia Canadenſis Jalappæ foliis. Sarr. Canad. *Canada Looſtrife with a Jalap leaf.*

6. LYSIMACHIA (*Salicifolia*) ſpica ſimplici erecto terminali, petalis ovatis, ſtaminibus corolla longioribus. *Looſtrife with a ſingle erect ſpike terminating the ſtalk, oval petals, and ſtamina longer than the flower.* Lyſimachia ſpicata, flore albo, ſalicis folio. Tourn. Inſt. R. H. 141. *Looſtrife with a ſpike of white flowers and a Willow leaf.*

7. LYSIMACHIA (*Nummularia*) foliis ſubcordatis, floribus ſolitariis, caule repente. Vir. Cliff. 13. *Looſtrife with leaves nearly heart-ſhaped, flowers growing ſingly, and a creeping ſtalk.* Nummularia lutea major. C. B. P. 309. *Greater yellow Moneywort.*

8. LYSIMACHIA (*Tenella*) foliis ovatis acutiuſculis, pedunculis folio longioribus, caule repente. Lin. Sp. Plant. 148. *Looſtrife with oval acute-pointed leaves, foot-ſtalks longer than the leaf, and a creeping ſtalk.* Nummularia minor, purpuraſcente flore. C. B. P. 310. *Smaller Moneywort with a purpliſh flower.*

9. LYSIMACHIA (*Nemorum*) foliis ovatis acutis, floribus ſolitariis, caule procumbente. Hort. Cliff. 52. *Looſtrife with oval acute-pointed leaves, flowers growing ſingly, and a trailing ſtalk.* Anagallis lutea nemorum. C. B. P. 252. *Yellow Pimpernel of the woods.*

10. LY-

10. LYSIMACHIA (*Quadrifolia*) foliis fubquaternis, pedunculis verticillatis unifloris. Lin. Sp. Plant. 147.

Loofftrife with leaves generally placed by fours, and foot-ftalks placed in whorls round the ftalks, each fuftaining a fingle flower. Lyfimachia lutea minor, foliis nigris punctatis notatis. C. B. P. 245. *Smaller yellow Loofftrife with leaves marked with black fpots.*

The firft fort grows by the fide of ditches and rivers in many parts of England, fo is not often admitted into gardens, becaufe the roots creep far in the ground, and fend up ftalks at a great diftance, whereby it becomes often a troublefome plant; otherwife for the variety of its flowers, it might deferve a place in large gardens, efpecially in moift places, where better things will not thrive. It rifes with upright ftalks from two to three feet high, garnifhed with fmooth fpear-fhaped leaves placed fometimes by pairs oppofite; at others there are three, and frequently four of thefe leaves placed round the ftalk at each joint. The upper part of the ftalk divides into feveral foot-ftalks, which fuftain yellow flowers growing in a panicle; thefe have one petal which is deeply cut into five fegments, fpreading open. They appear in June and July, and are fucceeded by roundifh feed-veffels, filled with fmall feeds which ripen in the autumn. This is placed in the lift of medicinal plants, but is not often ufed. If the roots of this plant are taken up from the places where it grows naturally in the autumn, and planted in a moift foil, they will thrive faft enough without care.

The fecond fort grows naturally in the northern parts of England; this hath a perennial creeping root, which fends up feveral erect ftalks near a foot and a half high, garnifhed at every joint by two pretty long narrow leaves placed oppofite, whofe bafe fits clofe to the ftalk; they are about three inches long, and more than half an inch broad toward their bafe, leffening gradually to the end, which terminates in acute points; the foot-ftalks of the flowers come out oppofite on each fide of the ftalks; they are an inch long, fuftaining at their top a globular or oval thyrfe of yellow flowers, whofe ftamina are much longer than the petals. This flowers at the fame time with the former fort, but feldom produces feeds, for the roots creep fo much as to render it barren. It is but feldom kept in gardens, for the fame reafon as the former is rejected; but thofe who are defirous to have it, may procure the roots and plant them in a moift foil, where it will foon fpread.

The third fort is a biennial plant, which was difcovered by Dr. Tournefort in the Levant, from whence he fent the feeds to the Royal Garden at Paris, where they fucceeded, and many of the European gardens have from thence been furnifhed with it. This rifes with an upright ftalk about a foot high, garnifhed with fpear-fhaped leaves ending in acute points; thefe are placed by pairs oppofite; they are fmooth, and of a lucid green. The flowers grow in a loofe fpike, terminating the ftalks; the flowers ftand horizontally, fpreading out on each fide the ftalk; they have longer tubes than the other fpecies, and are of a purple colour. Thefe appear in June, and the feeds ripen in September, foon after which the plants decay. It is propagated by feeds, which fhould be fown on a moderate hot-bed in the fpring, often watering the ground to bring up the plants; and if the feafon fhould prove warm, the glaffes of the hot-bed fhould be fhaded in the heat of the day; when the plants are up, they fhould have a large fhare of frefh air admitted to them in warm weather, to prevent their drawing up weak, and fhould be frequently refrefhed with water. When they are fit to remove, they fhould be each planted in a feparate pot, plunging them into a moderate hot-bed to forward their taking new root: after which they fhould be gradually inured to bear the open air, into which they fhould be removed by the beginning of June, where they may remain till October, when they fhould be removed into a common frame, where they may be fheltered from froft in winter, but fhould always enjoy the free air in mild weather. The fpring following fome of the plants fhould be fhaken out of the pots, and planted in borders; but a few of them fhould be put into larger pots, where they may flower and feed: this is called Ephemerum by Linnæus, but is not fo.

When the plants come up, they muft have plenty of air admitted to them in warm weather, to prevent their drawing up weak; then they may be planted into the borders of the pleafure-garden, where they will flower and produce ripe feeds the following fummer.

The fourth fort is an annual plant, which is too tender to rife in the open air in this country, therefore the feeds fhould be fown on a moderate hot-bed in the fpring, and the plants afterward treated in the fame manner as hath been directed for the third fort.

The fifth fort was firft brought from Canada, where it grows naturally; this hath a perennial creeping root, fending up many erect ftalks about two feet high, garnifhed with oblong, oblique, fmooth leaves, placed oppofite; they are veined on their under fide, and end in acute points. The flowers are produced from the wings of the ftalks, each fitting upon a long flender foot-ftalk; there are three or four of thefe arifing from the fhort branches, which come out on each fide the ftalk, at all the upper joints. The flowers are like thofe of the firft fort, but fmaller, and hang downward; thefe appear in June and July, but are feldom fucceeded by any feeds in England.

This fort fpreads and propagates by roots, in as great plenty as the firft, and is equally hardy, fo requires no other culture.

The fixth fort grows naturally in Spain, and was formerly titled by John Bauhin and others, Ephemerum; this hath a perennial root, from which arife feveral upright ftalks upward of three feet high, garnifhed with narrow, fmooth, fpear-fhaped leaves, which ftand oppofite, and at the bafe of thefe come out fhort fide branches, garnifhed with fmaller leaves of the fame fhape. The flowers are produced in a long, clofe, upright fpike, at the top of the ftalk; they are cut into five oval fegments, which are white, fpreading open, and the ftamina ftand out longer than the petal. It flowers in June, and the feeds ripen in autumn.

This is the fineft fpecies of this genus, and as the roots of it do not fpread like thofe of the other, fo deferves a place in the pleafure-garden, where it is a very ornamental plant for fhady borders. It loves a moift foil and a fhady fituation, where it will continue long in beauty. It may be propagated by parting the roots in autumn, but by this method it increafes flowly; fo that the only way to have it in plenty, is by fowing the feeds: thefe fhould be fown upon an eaft-afpected border in autumn, foon after they are ripe, then the plants will come up the following fpring; but thofe which are fown in the fpring will not grow the fame year. When the plants come up they fhould be kept clean from weeds, and if they are too clofe, fome of them may be drawn out and tranfplanted on a fhady border, which will give the remaining plants room to grow till autumn, when they may be tranfplanted into the borders of the flower-garden where they are defigned to flower; after which they will require no other culture but to keep them clean from weeds, and dig the ground between them every fpring.

The feventh fort is commonly called Moneywort, or Herb Two-pence; this is a perennial plant, which grows naturally in moift fhady places in moft parts of England, fo is not cultivated in gardens. The ftalks of this trail upon the ground, and put out roots, by which it foon fpreads to a great diftance. The leaves are almoft heart-fhaped, and placed by pairs. The flowers come out fingly from the fide of the ftalks; they are yellow, appearing in June and July.

The eighth fort is a fmall trailing plant, which grows upon bogs in moffy places in moft parts of England, but cannot be cultivated on dry ground. The ftalks feldom are more than three or four inches long, and are terminated by three or four fmall flowers, of a bright purple colour, growing in a bunch. This flowers in June, but is rarely planted in gardens. The ninth fort is a perennial plant with trailing ftalks, which grow naturally in moift woods in moft parts of England, fo is not cultivated in gardens. The leaves ftand oppofite at each joint ; they are fmooth, oval, and acute-pointed. The flowers come out fingly from the fide of the ftalk, upon long foot-ftalks ; they are yellow, and fpread open like the flowers of Chickweed. This flowers in May and June, and the feeds ripen in autumn.

The tenth fort grows naturally among Rufhes and Reeds, by the rivers fides in Holland; this hath a perennial creeping root like the firft. The ftalks rife a foot high ; they are flender, and are garnifhed by fpear-fhaped leaves an inch and a half long, and a quarter of an inch broad in the middle, placed fometimes by pairs, at others by threes, and often four at each joint, furrounding the ftalk. The flowers alfo come out at each joint, four of them ftanding round the ftalk in whorls, each having a diftinct flender footftalk an inch long. The flowers are fmall and yellow ; they appear in June, and are fometimes fucceeded by seeds which ripen in autumn; it may be treated in the fame manner as the firft fort, and is equally hardy.

LYSIMACHIA GALERICULATA. See SCUTELLARIA.

LYSIMACHIA NON PAPPOSA. See ŒNOTHERA.

LYSIMACHIA SILIQUOSA. See EPILOBIUM.

LYTHRUM. Lin. Gen. Plant. 532. Salicaria. Tourn. Inft. R. H. 253. tab. 129. *Willow Herb, or purple Looftrife.*

The CHARACTERS are,
The flower hath a cylindrical ftriated empalement of one leaf, indented at the brim in twelve parts, which are alternately fmaller. It has fix oblong blunt petals which fpread open, whofe tails are inferted in the indentures of the empalement, and ten flender ftamina the length of the empalement, the upper being fhorter than the lower, terminated by fingle rifing fummits. In the center is fituated an oblong germen, fupporting an awl-fhaped declining ftyle, crowned by a rifing orbicular ftigma. The germen afterward turns to an oblong acute capfule with two cells, filled with fmall feeds.

This genus of plants is ranged in the firft fection of Linnæus's eleventh clafs, intitled Dodecandria Monogynia, which includes thofe plants whofe flowers have twelve ftamina and one ftyle.

The SPECIES are,
1. LYTHRUM (*Salicaria*) foliis oppofitis cordato-lanceolatis, floribus fpicatis dodecandris. Lin. Sp. Plant. 446. *Lythrum with heart fpear-fhaped leaves placed oppofite, and flowers growing in fpikes, having twelve ftamina.* Salicaria vulgaris, purpurea, foliis oblongis. Tourn. Inft. R. H. 253. *Common purple Willow Herb with oblong leaves.*

2. LYTHRUM (*Tomentofum*) foliis cordato-ovatis, floribus verticillato-fpicatis tomentofis. *Lythrum with oval heart-fhaped leaves, and flowers growing in whorly fpikes, which are woolly.* Salicaria purpurea, foliis fubrotundis. Tourn. Inft. R. H. 253. *Purple Willow Herb with roundifh leaves.*

3. LYTHRUM (*Hyffopifolia*) foliis alternis linearibus, floribus hexandris. Hort. Upfal. 118. *Lythrum with linear alternate leaves, and flowers having fix ftamina.* Salicaria hyffopi folio anguftiore. Tourn. Inft. R. H. 253. *Willow Herb with a narrow Hyffop leaf.*

4. LYTHRUM (*Lufitanicum*) foliis lanceolatis ternis glabris, floribus fpicatis decandris. *Lythrum with fmooth fpear-fhaped leaves placed by threes, and flowers growing in fpikes, which have ten ftamina.* Salicaria Lufitanica, anguftiore folio. Tourn. Inft. R. H. 253. *Portugal Willow Herb with a narrower leaf.*

5. LYTHRUM (*Hifpanicum*) foliis oblongo-ovatis infernè oppofitis fupernè alternis floribus hexandris. *Lythrum with oblong oval leaves placed oppofite below, but*

above alternate, and flowers having fix ftamina. Salicaria Hifpanica, hyffopifolia, floribus oblongis faturatè cæruleis. Tourn. Inft. 253. *Spanifh Willow Herb with a Hyffop leaf, and oblong, deep, blue flowers.*

6. LYTHRUM (*Verticillatum*) foliis oppofitis, fubtus tomentofis fubpetiolatis, floribus verticillatis lateralibus. Lin. Sp. Plant. 446. *Willow Herb with oppofite leaves, which are woolly on their under fide, and flowers growing in whorls round the ftalk.*

7. LYTHRUM (*Petiolatum*) foliis oppofitis linearibus petiolatis, floribus dodecandris. Lin. Sp. Plant. 446. *Willow Herb with linear leaves placed oppofite, having foot-ftalks, and flowers with twelve ftamina.*

8. LYTHRUM (*Lineare*) foliis oppofitis linearibus, floribus oppofitis hexandris. Lin. Sp. Plant. 447. *Willow Herb with linear oppofite leaves, and flowers having fix ftamina, which are placed oppofite.*

9. LYTHRUM (*Americanum*) foliis oblongo-ovatis infernè oppofitis fupernè alternis, floribus hexandris, caule erecto. *Willow Herb with oblong leaves placed oppofite below, and above alternate, with flowers having fix ftamina and an erect ftalk.* Salicaria Americana, hyffopi folio latiore, floribus minimis. Houft. MSS. *American Willow Herb with a broader Hyffop leaf, and very fmall flowers.*

The firft fort grows naturally by the fide of rivers and ditches in moft parts of England. It has a perennial root, from which come forth feveral upright angular ftalks, which rife from three to four feet high ; they are of a purple colour, and are garnifhed with oblong leaves, placed fometimes by pairs oppofite, at others there are three leaves at each joint, ftanding round the ftalk. The flowers are produced in a long fpike at the top of the ftalk ; they are of a fine purple colour, and make a fine appearance. This flowers in July, and the feeds ripen in autumn : although this plant is defpifed, becaufe it grows common, yet it merits a place in gardens better than many other which are propagated with care, becaufe they are more rare. It is eafily cultivated by parting the roots in autumn, and fhould be planted in a moift foil, where it will thrive and flower without any other care than the keeping it clean from weeds.

There is a variety of this with an hexangular ftalk, and generally with three leaves at each joint ; but this is only accidental, for the roots of this, when removed into a garden, come to the common fort.

The fecond fort hath perennial roots like the firft, from which come out upright branching ftalks three feet high, garnifhed with oval heart-fhaped leaves about one inch long, and three quarters of an inch broad ; they are downy, and placed by threes round the ftalk. The flowers are produced in long fpikes at the top of the ftalks, but they are difpofed in thick whorls, with fpaces between each ; they are of a fine purple colour, and appear at the fame time with the former. This may be propagated in the fame way as the firft fort, and is equally hardy.

The third fort grows naturally in moift bogs in many parts of England, fo is feldom admitted into gardens ; this hath a perennial root, fending up two or three branching ftalks about a foot high, garnifhed with narrow leaves, placed alternate. The upper part of the ftalk is garnifhed with flowers, which come out from the fide fingly at each joint, ftanding clofe to the bafe of the leaves ; they are fmall, and of a light purple colour, appearing in June, and the feeds ripen in autumn.

The fourth fort grows naturally in Spain and Portugal, in moift places by the fide of waters ; this has a perennial root and ftalks like the firft, which feldom grow more than one foot high, garnifhed with narrower and fhorter leaves than the firft, which are fmooth, and placed by threes round the ftalk. The flowers grow in fpikes at the top of the ftalks ; they are of a light purple colour, and appear in July. The feeds ripen in autumn. This fort is hardy, and may be propagated in the fame way as the firft.

The fifth fort grows naturally in Spain and Portugal, from both which countries I have received the feeds.

The

The root of this is perennial. The ftalks are flender, not more than nine or ten inches long, fpreading out on every fide. The lower part of the ftalks are garnifhed with oblong oval leaves, placed oppofite. On the upper part of the ftalks the leaves are narrower, and placed alternate. The flowers come out fingly from the fide of the ftalks at each joint; they are larger than thofe of the common fort, and of a deeper purple colour, fo make a fine appearance in July, when they are in beauty.

This fort has never produced any feeds in England, and the fevere froft in 1740, killed all the plants here, fince which time I have not feen any of them in the Englifh gardens.

The fixth fort grows naturally in the northern parts of America; this rifes with a ftiff branching ftalk a foot and a half high, garnifhed with oblong leaves, which are downy, and placed oppofite, ftanding upon very fhort foot-ftalks. The flowers are produced in whorls round the ftalks; they are of a pale purple colour, and appear in July; thefe are fucceeded by capfules with two cells, filled with feeds which ripen in autumn.

The feventh fort grows naturally in Virginia, from whence I received the feeds; this rifes with an upright woolly ftalk near two feet high, garnifhed with linear leaves placed oppofite, upon fhort foot-ftalks. The flowers come out from the wings of the ftalks fingly; they are fmall, tubulous, and of a pale purple colour, fo make no great appearance; thefe appear in July, and in warm feafons only will perfect feeds; but the roots of this fort will increafe fo faft, as to render the propagating the plants by feeds unneceffary, when once obtained.

The eighth fort grows naturally in North America. It has a perennial root. The ftalks are flender, about a foot high, garnifhed with linear leaves placed oppofite, which are entire. The flowers come out fingly from the wings of the leaves, on the upper part of the ftalks; they are fmall, white, and have fix petals. The empalement is ftreaked, and cut at the top into fix parts, and the flower has fix ftamina. This flowers in June, and the feeds ripen in autumn.

The ninth fort was difcovered by the late Dr. Houftoun at La Vera Cruz, growing in fwamps, where the water had ftagnated. This hath a ligneous root, from which arife two or three flender ftalks upward of two feet high, garnifhed with oblong, oval, fmooth leaves, which, on the lower part of the ftalks are oppofite, but thofe on the upper part are narrow and alternate. The flowers come out from the wings of the leaves, on the upper part of the ftalk fingly; they are fmall and white, having fix petals and fix ftamina; thefe do not appear till the fecond year from feed, and have not produced any good feeds in England.

This fort is tender, fo will not live in the open air in England. It is propagated by feeds, which fhould be fown in pots, and plunged into an old hot-bed the firft feafon; for the feeds never rife the firft year, unlefs they are fown in autumn; the pots fhould be fheltered in winter, and the fpring following placed on a hotbed to bring up the plants; thefe muft be treated in the fame way as other tender plants from the fame country.

All the other forts, when raifed from feeds, fhould be fown in autumn, otherwife the feeds will remain a year in the ground, fo that thofe feeds which are brought from America, never grow the fame year they are fown; for which reafon the ground fhould not be difturbed in which the feeds are fown, but left till the following fpring, when the plants will come up if the feeds were good.

M.

M A G

M A G

MACALEB. See CERASUS.
MADDER. See RUBIA TINCTORUM.
MAGNOLIA. Plum. Nov. Gen. 38. tab. 7. Lin. Gen. Plant. 610. The Laurel-leaved Tulip-tree, vulgò.

The CHARACTERS are,

The empalement is compofed of three oval concave leaves like petals, which foon fall away. The flower is compofed of nine oblong blunt petals, which foon fall away. It hath a great number of fhort ftamina which are compreffed, and inferted into the germen, terminated by linear fummits, adhering to every fide of the ftamina. It hath many oblong oval germina faftened to the receptacle, fupporting recurved, contorted, fhort ftyles, with longitudinal hairy ftigmas. The germen afterward become oval cones, with roundifh compreffed capfules almoft imbricated, having one cell, opening with two valves, inclofing one kidneyfhaped feed, hanging by a flender thread from the fcale of the cone.

This genus of plants is ranged in the feventh fection of Linnæus's thirteenth clafs, intitled Polyandria Polygynia, which includes thofe plants whofe flowers have many ftamina and ftyles. If Father Plumier's figure of the fection of his fruit is exact, his muft be a different genus from this; for the feeds of his are reprefented within the fruit, lying round a column.

The SPECIES are,

1. MAGNOLIA (*Glauca*) foliis ovato-lanceolatis fubtus glaucis. Lin. Sp. 755. *Magnolia with oval fpear-fhaped leaves, which are gray on their under fide.* Magnolia lauri folio fubtus albicante. Catefb. Hift. Car. 1. p. 39. *Magnolia with a Bay leaf, which is whitifh on the under fide, commonly called Small Magnolia, or Laurel-leaved Tulip-tree.*

2. MAGNOLIA (*Grandiflora*) foliis lanceolatis perfiftentibus, caule erecto arboreo. Fig. Plant. tab. 172. *Magnolia with fpear-fhaped leaves which are evergreen, and an erect tree-like ftalk.* Magnolia altiffima, flore ingenti candido. Catefb. Carol. 2. p. 61. *Talleft Magnolia, with a very large white flower, commonly called Greater Magnolia, or Tulip-tree, with a Laurel leaf.*

3. MAGNOLIA (*Tripetala*) foliis lanceolatis ampliffimis annuis, petalis exterioribus dependentibus. *Magnolia with very large fpear-fhaped leaves which are annual, and the outer petals of the flower declining.* Magnolia ampliffimo flore albo, fructu coccineo. Catefb. Car. 2. p. 80. *Magnolia with a very large white flower and a fcarlet fruit, commonly called Umbrella-tree.*

4. MAGNOLIA (*Acuminata*) foliis ovato-lanceolatis acuminatis annuis, petalis obtufis. *Magnolia with oval, fpear-fhaped, pointed leaves, which are annual, and obtufe petals to the flower.* Magnolia flore albo, folio majore acuminato, haud albicante. Catefb. Car. 3. p. 15. *Magnolia with a white flower, and a larger acute-pointed leaf, not whitifh.*

The firft fort grows pretty common in Virginia, Carolina, and in moft other parts of North America, where it is found in moift places, near brooks; this ufually grows about fifteen or fixteen feet high, with a flender ftem. The wood is white and fpongy, the

the bark is smooth and white, the branches are garnished with thick smooth leaves, resembling those of the Bay, but are of an oval shape, and smooth on their edges, being white underneath. The flowers are produced in May and June at the extremity of the branches, which are white, composed of six petals which are concave, and have an agreeable sweet scent. After these are past, the fruit increases in size to be as large as a Walnut with its cover, but of a conical shape, having many cells round the outside, in each of which is lodged a flat seed, about the size of a Kidney-bean. This fruit is at first green, afterward red, and, when ripe, of a brown colour. The seeds, when ripe, are discharged from their cells, and hang by a slender thread.

In the natural places of its growth, there is a succession of the flowers on the trees for two months or more, during which time the woods are perfumed with them; but all those trees which have produced flowers in England, seldom have more than twelve or fourteen flowers upon each, which are of short duration, and are not succeeded by others; the leaves of this sort fall off in winter.

The young plants of this sort frequently retain their leaves through the greatest part of winter, and often do not fall off till the young shoots thrust them off, which has occasioned some persons to believe the plants were evergreen; but when they are three or four years old, they constantly cast their leaves by the beginning of November.

When these trees are transplanted from the places of their growth into dry ground, they make handsomer trees, and produce a greater number of flowers; this is to be understood of America, for in Europe they do not thrive so well in a dry soil as in a moist loamy land. The greatest number of these trees, which are now growing in England, are at his Grace the Duke of Norfolk's, at Worksop Manor, in Nottinghamshire. The second sort grows in Florida and South Carolina, where it rises to the height of eighty feet or more, with a strait trunk upward of two feet diameter, having a large regular head: the leaves of this tree resemble those of the common Laurel, but are much larger, and of a shining green on their upper side, and, in some trees, they are of a russet, or buff colour, on their under side; these leaves continue all the year, so that this is one of the most beautiful evergreen trees yet known. The flowers are produced at the end of the branches; they are composed of eight or ten petals, which are narrow at their base, but broad at their extremity, where they are rounded, and a little waved; these spread open wide, and are of a pure white colour. In the center is situated a great number of stamina and styles, fastened to one common receptaculum; these flowers are succeeded by oblong scaly cones in the places where it grows naturally, but the summers are not warm enough in England to produce any fruit to perfection, though some old plants do often form cones. These trees in their native places of growth begin to produce their flowers in May, and continue a long time in flower, so that the woods are perfumed with their odour the greatest part of summer; but those which have flowered in England, seldom begin till the middle or latter end of June, and do not continue long in beauty. The largest tree of this kind, which I have met with in England, is in the garden of Sir John Colliton, of Exmouth, in Devonshire, which has produced flowers for several years; there are also many pretty large plants of this sort in the gardens of his Grace the Duke of Richmond, at Goodwood, in Sussex, one of which has produced flowers several years; and in the nursery of Mr. Christopher Gray, near Fulham, there is one very handsome plant, which has also produced many flowers several years.

As this sort is a native of a warm country, it is a little impatient of cold, especially while young, therefore the plants should be kept in pots, and sheltered in winter for some years, until they have acquired strength, when they may be shaken out of the pots,

and planted in the full ground, but they must be planted in a warm situation, where they may be defended from the strong winds, and screened from the north and east, otherwise they will not live abroad.

There were a great number of young plants in England before the year 1739; but a great part of them were destroyed by that severe winter, and since then, there have been few good seeds sent to England, so that there are not many of the plants at present to be sold in the nurseries; and as almost every person who is curious in gardening, is desirous to have some of these beautiful trees in their gardens, the demand for them of late has greatly increased their value. If this tree can be so far naturalized as to endure the cold of our severest winters abroad, it will be one of the greatest ornaments to our gardens; and this we may hope, will, in time, be effected, by diligent observation and care; for the time when these plants suffer most, is in autumn, by the early frosts; for the extremity of the shoots being then tender, as they are then generally growing freely, a small frost will pinch them, and afterward the whole shoot frequently decays; so that the plants should be guarded against these early frosts, by covering their tops with mats until the shoots are hardened, after which time they will not be in so much danger of suffering; for I have constantly observed, that if these plants escape the early frosts of the autumn, they are seldom injured afterward: in the severe winter in the year 1739-40, I had a pretty large plant growing in the open air, which was killed down by the frost, and I supposed was entirely destroyed, as there was not the least appearance of life in the stem; so that after Midsummer I cut it down to the ground, but left the root remaining, which, to my great surprize, shot up again the year after. This I mention, to caution people from being too hasty in destroying plants after hard frost, but to have them wait until there can be no hopes of their recovery.

The third sort grows in Carolina pretty frequent, but in Virginia it is pretty rare; this usually grows from sixteen to twenty feet high, with a slender trunk; the wood is soft and spongy; the leaves of this tree are remarkably large, and are produced in horizontal circles, somewhat resembling an umbrella, from whence the inhabitants of those countries have given it the title of Umbrella-tree. The flowers are composed of ten or eleven white petals, which hang down without any order; the fruit is very like that of the former sort; the leaves of this sort drop off at the beginning of winter.

This tree is as yet very rare in Europe, but as it is propagated from seeds, we may hope to have it in greater plenty soon, if we can obtain good seeds from Carolina, for it is rarely met with in Virginia.

The fourth sort is also very rare in England; there are but few of the plants at present here, nor is it very common in any of the habitable parts of America: some of these trees have been discovered by Mr. John Bartram, growing on the north branch of Susquehannah river. The leaves of this tree are near eight inches long and five broad, ending in a point. The flowers come out early in the spring, which are composed of twelve white petals, shaped like those of the second sort; the fruit of this tree is longer than those of the other species, but in other respects agrees with them. The wood of this tree is of a fine grain, and an Orange colour.

All these sorts are propagated by seeds, which must be procured from the places of their natural growth; these should be put up in sand, and sent over to England as soon as possible; for if they are kept long out of the ground, they very rarely grow, therefore the seeds should be sown as soon as possible, when they arrive here.

Some years past I received a good quantity of these seeds from Carolina, which I sowed in pots as soon as I received them, and plunged the pots into an old hot bed of tanners bark; and with this management

I raised

I raiſed a great number of plants, but from the ſeeds which have been lately brought over, there have been but few plants produced; whether the ſeeds were not perfectly ripe when they were gathered, or from what other cauſe this has happened, I cannot ſay, but it is certain the fault muſt be in the ſeeds, becauſe thoſe before-mentioned were differently ſown and managed by the ſeveral perſons who received them, and the ſucceſs was nearly alike every where.

There have been ſeveral plants of the firſt and ſecond ſort raiſed from layers, and ſome from cuttings; but theſe do not thrive ſo well as thoſe which come from ſeeds, nor will they grow to near the ſize of thoſe, ſo that it is much the beſt way to procure their ſeeds from America, and propagate them that way.

The firſt ſort frequently comes up well from ſeeds, but the young plants are very difficult to keep the two firſt years; for if they are expoſed much to the ſun, their leaves change yellow and the plants decay; ſo the beſt way is to keep the pots plunged in a moderate hot-bed, and ſhade them every day from the ſun with mats, giving them air in plenty when the weather is warm, and frequently refreſh them with water; during the winter ſeaſon they muſt be ſcreened from froſt, and in mild weather they muſt enjoy the free air, to prevent their growing mouldy, and they ſhould have but little wet in winter. With this management the plants may be trained up, and when they have acquired ſtrength, they may be planted in the open air, where they will thrive and flower, if they have a warm ſheltered ſituation.

The ſecond ſort is not ſo difficult to train up as the firſt, but in order to get them forward, it will be proper when they are removed out of the ſeed-pots, to plant them each into a ſeparate ſmall pot, filled with ſoft loamy earth, and plunge them into a gentle hot-bed of tanners bark, obſerving to ſhade them from the ſun, and admit proper air to them; but at Midſummer, if they are well rooted, they ſhould be inured to the open air gradually, and then placed in a ſheltered ſituation, where they may remain till autumn; but on the firſt approach of froſt, they ſhould be removed under ſhelter, otherwiſe the early froſts will pinch their tender ſhoots, which often occaſions their dying downward after. When the plants have got ſtrength, ſome of them may be turned out of the pots, and planted in the full ground in a warm ſheltered ſituation, but part of them ſhould be kept in pots, and ſheltered in the winter, to preſerve them, leſt, by ſevere froſt, the other ſhould be killed. If the plants make good progreſs, they will be ſtrong enough to plant in the full ground in about ſix or ſeven years from ſeeds. The time for removing or ſhifting theſe plants is in March, before they begin to ſhoot, which may ſometimes happen to be too ſoon to turn them out of the pots into the full ground, eſpecially if the ſeaſon proves late; but as there will be no danger in removing them out of the pots, the ball of earth being preſerved to their roots, ſo it is beſt to defer this till the month of April; but it will be neceſſary to harden thoſe plants which are intended to be planted out, by expoſing them to the air as much as poſſible before, which will keep the plants backward, and prevent their ſhooting; for if they make ſhoots in the green-houſe, thoſe will be too tender to bear the ſun, until they are by degrees hardened to it, and the leaſt froſt will greatly pinch them, and ſuch froſts frequently happen very late in the ſpring.

The two or three winters after theſe are planted out, it will be neceſſary to lay ſome mulch on the ſurface of the ground about their roots, as alſo to throw ſome mats over their heads, eſpecially at the beginning of the morning froſts in autumn, for the reaſons before given; but in doing this, the heads of the plant ſhould never be too cloſely covered up, leſt thereby the ſhoots ſhould grow mouldy, for that will certainly kill the leading buds of every ſhoot, and prove to the full as injurious to them as the froſt.

As the plants get ſtrength, they will be better able to endure the cold of our climate, though it will be proper to lay ſome mulch about their roots every winter; and, in very ſevere froſt, to cover their heads and ſtems.

It is the firſt ſort which requires the moſt care, being much tenderer than any of the other, for they will endure the cold very well, without much care, after they have acquired ſtrength; for as theſe loſe their leaves in the winter, the froſt will not have ſo much force upon them as of the firſt ſort, whoſe leaves are frequently tender toward the end of the ſhoots, eſpecially when they grow freely, or ſhoot late in the autumn.

MAHALEB. See Cerasus.

MAJORANA. See Origanum.

MALABAR NUT. See Justicia.

MALA ÆTHIOPICA. See Lycopersicon.

MALA ARMENIACA. See Armeniaca.

MALACOIDES. See Malope.

MALA COTONEA. See Cydonia.

MALA INSANA. See Melongena.

MALLOW. See Malva.

MALLOW-TREE. See Lavatera.

MALOPE. Baſtard Mallow.

The Characters are,

The flower, which is ſhaped like that of the Mallow, hath a double empalement, the outer being compoſed of three heart-ſhaped leaves, and the inner is of one leaf cut into five ſegments; the flower is of one petal, divided into five parts at the bottom, where they are joined, but ſo near the bottom as to have the appearance of five petals. In the center ariſes the pointal, having a great number of ſtamina ſurrounding it, which are joined cloſely, and form a ſort of column. The pointal afterward becomes a fruit compoſed of many cells, which are collected into a head, in each of which is lodged a ſingle ſeed.

We have but one Species of this plant, viz.

Malope (*Malacoides*) foliis ovatis crenatis glabris. Lin. Hort. Cliff. 347. *Baſtard Mallow, with oval ſmooth leaves, which are notched.*

This plant was by Dr. Tournefort ſeparated from the Mallow, and made a diſtinct genus, by the title of Malacoides; but Dr. Linnæus has altered the title of this for Malope, being an enemy to all names which are compounded of oides.

The whole plant has greatly the appearance of the Mallow, but differs from it, in having the cells collected into a button, ſomewhat like a Blackberry; the branches ſpread, and lie almoſt flat upon the ground, extending themſelves a foot or more each way. The flowers are produced ſingly upon long foot-ſtalks, which ariſe from the wings of the leaves, which are in ſhape and colour like thoſe of the Mallow.

This is propagated by ſeeds, which ſhould be ſown in the place where they are deſigned to remain, for they do not bear tranſplanting well. If theſe ſeeds are ſown upon a warm border in Auguſt, the plants will frequently ſtand through the winter, and flower early the following ſeaſon, ſo that good ſeeds may be obtained; for thoſe which are ſown in the ſpring, rarely ripen ſeeds the ſame year in England; and theſe plants being large, are often deſtroyed in winter, unleſs they are ſheltered under a frame; it ſeldom continues longer than two or three years, ſo that young plants ſhould be annually raiſed.

MALPIGHIA. Plum. Nov. Gen. 46. tab. 36. Lin. Gen. Plant. 38. Barbadoes Cherry, vulgò.

The Characters are,

The flower hath a ſmall permanent empalement of five leaves, which are cloſed together. It hath two oval mellous glands, adhering to the ſmall leaves within and without. It has five kidney-ſhaped petals, which are concave, and ſpread open, having long narrow tails, and ten broad awl-ſhaped ſtamina, which are erect, terminated by heart-ſhaped ſummits. In the baſe a ſmall roundiſh germen, ſupporting three ſlender ſtyles, crowned by obtuſe ſtigmas. The germen afterward turns to a large furrowed globular berry with one cell, incloſing three rough ſtony ſeeds, which are angular.

This

This genus of plants is ranged in the third section of Linnæus's tenth class, intitled Decandria Trigynia, which includes the plants whose flowers have ten stamina and three styles.

The SPECIES are,

1. MALPIGHIA (*Glabra*) foliis ovatis integerrimis glabris, pedunculis umbellatis. Hort. Cliff. 169. *Malpighia with smooth, oval, entire leaves, and umbellated foot-stalks.* Cerasus Jamaicensis, fructu tetrapyreno. Hort. Amst. 1. p. 145. *Jamaica Cherry with a fruit having four seeds, commonly called Barbadoes Cherry.*

2. MALPIGHIA (*Punicifolia*) foliis ovato-lanceolatis, acuminatis, glabris, pedunculis umbellatis. *Malpighia with oval, spear-shaped, smooth leaves, ending in acute points, and umbellated foot-stalks.* Malpighia mali punici facie. Plum. Nov. Gen. 46. *Malpighia with the appearance of Pomegranate.*

3. MALPIGHIA (*Incana*) foliis lanceolatis subtus incanis, pedunculis umbellatis alaribus. *Malpighia with spear-shaped leaves, hoary on their under side, and umbellated foot-stalks, proceeding from the wings of the stalk.*

4. MALPIGHIA (*Urens*) foliis cordato-lanceolatis, setis decumbentibus rigidis, racemis lateralibus. *Malpighia with spear heart-shaped leaves, having rigid declining bristles, and bunches of flowers proceeding from the sides of the stalks.* Malpighia latifolia, folio subtus spinoso. Plum. Nov. Gen. 46. *Broad-leaved Malpighia, with spines growing on the under side of the leaf.*

5. MALPIGHIA (*Nitida*) foliis ovatis acutis glabris, pedunculis umbellatis alaribus terminalibusque. *Malpighia with oval, smooth, acute-pointed leaves, and umbellated foot-stalks, proceeding from the sides and at the ends of the branches.*

6. MALPIGHIA (*Paniculata*) foliis oblongo-cordatis acuminatis glabris, pedunculis paniculatis, alaribus terminalibusque. *Malpighia with oblong, heart-shaped, smooth leaves, ending in acute points, and paniculated foot-stalks proceeding from the sides and ends of the branches.* Apocynum fruticosum, folio oblongo acuminato, floribus racemosis. Sloan. Cat. 89. *Shrubby Dogsbane with an oblong acute-pointed leaf, and flowers growing in clusters.*

7. MALPIGHIA (*Angustifolia*) foliis lineari-lanceolatis, setis decumbentibus rigidis, pedunculis umbellatis alaribus. *Malpighia with linear spear-shaped leaves, rigid declining bristles, and foot-stalks having umbels of flowers proceeding from the sides of the branches.* Malpighia angustifolia, folio subtus spinoso. Plum. Nov. Gen. 46. *Narrow-leaved Malpighia with spines under the leaves.*

8. MALPIGHIA (*Ilicifolia*) foliis lanceolatis dentato-spinosis subtus hispidis. Lin. Sp. Plant. 426. *Malpighia with spear-shaped leaves, indented and prickly, whose under sides are set with spiny hairs.* Malpighia angustis & acuminatis aquifolii foliis. Plum. Nov. Gen. 46. *Malpighia with narrow and acute-pointed Holly leaves.*

9. MALPIGHIA (*Lucida*) foliis oblongo-ovatis obtusis glabris, pedunculis racemosis alaribus. *Malpighia with oblong oval leaves, which are obtuse and smooth, and branching foot-stalks of flowers proceeding from the sides of the branches.*

10. MALPIGHIA (*Coccigrya*) foliis subrotundis dentato-spinosis, pedunculis unifloris. *Malpighia with leaves nearly oval, indented, and prickly, and foot-stalks with one flower.* Malpighia humilis, ilicis cocci-glandiferæ foliis. Plum. Nov. Gen. 46. *Low Malpighia with leaves like the Kermes Oak.*

The first sort is commonly cultivated in the West-Indies for the sake of its fruit; this tree usually grows to the height of sixteen or eighteen feet, having a slender stem, covered with a light brown bark. The leaves are produced opposite; they are oval, smooth, ending in acute points, and continue all the year. The flowers are produced in bunches upon pretty long foot-stalks, which come out from the side and at the end of the branches; these are composed of five roundish petals, which are of a Rose colour, joined at their base. The flowers are succeeded by red fruit, shaped like those of the small wild Cherry,

and of the same size, having several furrows, each inclosing four angular furrowed stones, surrounded by a thin pulp, which has an agreeable acid flavour; the fruit of this often ripens in England.

The second sort grows naturally in Jamaica; this rises with a shrubby stalk ten or twelve feet high, dividing into several slender-spreading branches, covered with a light brown bark, garnished with oval, spear-shaped, smooth leaves placed opposite, ending in acute points. The flowers are produced in small umbels at the end of the branches, upon short foot-stalks; they are of a pale Rose colour, and composed of five obtuse concave petals which are indented, having long narrow tails, by which they are joined; these spread open, and in the center is situated the roundish germen, supporting three styles, attended by ten stamina which spread asunder. The germen afterward turns to a roundish pulpy berry with many furrows, red when ripe, inclosing three or four hard angular seeds. The fruit of this sort is eaten by the inhabitants of the isles in America.

The third sort grows naturally at Campeachy, from whence it was sent me by the late Mr. Robert Miliar. This rises with a strong woody stalk eighteen or twenty feet high, dividing into many branches, covered with a brown spotted bark, garnished with spear-shaped leaves placed opposite, which are hoary on their under side. The flowers come out in umbels from the side of the branches; they are of a Rose colour, and are succeeded by oval channelled fruit, like those of the former sort.

The fourth sort grows naturally in Jamaica, from whence the late Dr. Houstoun sent me the seeds. This rises with a woody stalk from fifteen to eighteen feet high, dividing into many pretty strong branches, which are furrowed, and covered with a brown bark. The leaves are from three to four inches long, and one broad at their base, where they are rounded in form of a heart, lessening gradually to the point; they are covered on their under sides with stinging bristly hairs so closely, as to render it very troublesome to handle them, for these hairs fasten themselves into the flesh, and are difficult to get out again. The flowers are produced in umbels from the side of the branches; they are of a light purple colour, and shaped like those of the other species; they are succeeded by oval furrowed fruit like that of the former sort. This is called in the West-Indies, Couhage, or Cowitch Cherry.

The fifth sort grows naturally at Carthagena in New Spain, from whence the late Dr. Houstoun sent me the seeds. This rises with a shrubby stalk about ten feet high, covered with a light brown spotted bark, branching out regularly at the top on every side; the leaves are oval, smooth, and end in acute points, standing opposite, of a light green on the upper side, but paler on the under. The flowers come out from the side of the stalks in small umbels, standing erect; the foot-stalks of the umbels are scarce an inch long. They are of a pale blush colour, shaped like those of the former sorts; these are succeeded by roundish furrowed berries with a red skin, covering three hard angular seeds.

The sixth sort grows naturally in Jamaica, from whence the late Dr. Houstoun sent the seeds to England. This rises with several slender shrubby stalks from five to six feet high, garnished with oblong heart-shaped leaves, four inches long and one inch and a quarter broad at the base, where they are rounded in two heart-shaped lobes, gradually diminishing to the point; they are smooth, and of a pale yellowish green, placed opposite. The flowers are produced in loose panicles from the side and at the end of the branches; they are of a light purple colour, shaped like those of the other species, but smaller; the fruit is more pointed, and not so much furrowed.

The seventh sort was sent me from the island Barbuda: this rises with a shrubby stalk seven or eight feet high, covered with a bright purplish bark which is spotted and furrowed, dividing toward the top into

several

several smaller branches, garnished with narrow spear-shaped leaves, about two inches long and a quarter of an inch broad, of a lucid green on their upper side, but of a russet brown on their under, where they are closely armed with stinging bristles, which fasten themselves into the flesh or clothes of those who touch them; these leaves are placed opposite. The flowers are produced from the side and at the end of the branches in small umbels; they are of a pale purple colour, of the same form of the other species, but smaller; and are succeeded by small, oval, furrowed fruit, of a dark purple colour when ripe.

The eighth sort was sent me from the island Berbuda in the West-Indies, where it grows naturally. This rises with a strong woody stem from fifteen to twenty feet high, dividing into many spreading branches, covered with a gray bark, garnished with oblong oval leaves of a firm consistence; they are about an inch long, and half an inch broad, rounded at their ends, of a lucid green, and placed opposite. The flowers come out from the side, and also at the end of the branches, upon pretty long foot-stalks, which branch in form of a racemus, or long bunch. They are of the same form with those of the other species, but vary in their colour, some of them being of a bright red, and others of an Orange colour in the same bunch; these are succeeded by small oval berries, which are less furrowed than those of the other species, and, when ripe, change to a dark purple colour.

The ninth sort grows naturally in the island of Cuba, where the late Dr. Houstoun found it in plenty. This rises with a shrubby stalk to the height of seven or eight feet, sending out branches the whole length, which are covered with a gray bark, garnished with narrow prickly leaves like those of the Holly, which have many stinging bristles on their under side. The flowers are produced in small clusters from the side of the branches, they are of a pale blush colour, and shaped like those of the other species, but smaller; the fruit is more pointed than those of the common sort, and turns to a dark purple colour when ripe.

The tenth sort grows naturally near the Havanna, from whence the late Dr. Houstoun sent the seeds. This is a very low shrub, seldom rising more than two or three feet high; the stalk is thick and woody, as are also the branches, which come out on every side from the root upward; they are covered with a rough gray bark, garnished with lucid leaves half an inch long, and almost as much broad; they appear as if cut at their ends, where they are hollowed in, and the two corners rise like horns ending in a sharp thorn, as do also the indentures on the sides. The flowers come out from the side of the branches, upon foot-stalks an inch long, each sustaining one small pale blush flower, of the same form with those of the other species; the fruit is small, conical, and furrowed, changing to a purple red colour when ripe.

There are two other species of this genus, which have been lately introduced from America, but as neither of them have yet flowered here, so I have not enumerated them; and if those warm parts of America were searched by persons of skill, there might be many more species discovered; for from a large number of imperfect specimens which were sent me from the Spanish West-Indies, I have selected many which have the appearance of the other species of this genus, but as they are without flowers or fruit, they cannot be ascertained.

The fruit of several of the species here mentioned, are promiscuously gathered and eaten by the inhabitants of the countries where they naturally grow; but the first sort is cultivated in some of the islands for its fruit, though that is but indifferent: the pulp which surrounds the stones is very thin, but has a pleasant acid flavour, which renders it agreeable to the inhabitants of those warm countries, where, to supply the want of those Cherries which are culti-

vated in Europe, they are obliged to eat the fruit of these shrubs.

These plants are preserved in the gardens of those persons who are so curious in botanical studies, as to erect hot-houses for maintaining foreign plants: and where there are such conveniencies, these plants deserve a place; because they retain their leaves all the year, and commonly continue flowering from December to the end of March, when they make a fine appearance at a season, when there is a scarcity of other flowers, and many times they produce ripe fruit here. Those sorts whose leaves are armed with stinging bristles, like the Cowitch, are the least worthy of a place in stoves, because they are so troublesome to handle, nor do their flowers make so good an appearance as many of the other sorts. The tenth sort is the most valuable for its flowers, which are produced in larger bunches than those of any of the other, and there being flowers of different colours in the same bunches, they make a fine variety; and this sort grows more like a tree than the others, the leaves are also of a stronger consistence and of a lucid green.

As these plants are natives of the warmest parts of America, they will not live through the winter in England, unless they are preserved in a warm stove; but when the plants have obtained strength, they may be exposed in the open air in a warm situation, from the middle or latter end of June, till the beginning of October, provided the weather continues so long mild; and the plants so treated, will flower much better than those which are constantly kept in a stove.

They are all propagated by seeds, which must be sown upon a good hot-bed in the spring; and when the plants are fit to transplant, they must be each put into a separate small pot filled with rich earth, and plunged into a hot-bed of tanners bark, and must be treated in the same manner as hath been directed for other tender plants of the same country; and for the two first winters, it will be proper to keep them in the bark-bed in the stove; but afterward they may be placed upon stands in the dry stove in winter, where they may be kept in a temperate warmth, in which they will thrive much better than in a greater heat; these must be watered two or three times a week, when they are placed, in the dry stove, but it must not be given to them in large quantities.

MALT-DUST is accounted a great enricher of barren ground; it contains in it a natural heat and sweetness, which gives the earth whereon it is laid a proper fermentation, as those who live in malting countries have found by experience.

Some are of opinion, that there is not a greater sweetener than Malt-dust, where the grounds are natural clay, and have contracted a sourness and austerity, whether by reason of its having lain long untilled and unexposed to the air, or by reason of water having stood long thereon.

MALVA. Tourn. Inst. R. H. 94. tab. 23. Lin. Gen. Plant. 751. [so called of μαλακίζω, or μαλάσσω, to soften, because it is good to soften the belly.] Mallows; in French, *Mauve*.

The CHARACTERS are,

The flower has a double empalement; the outer is composed of three spear-shaped leaves, and is permanent; the inner is of one leaf, cut into five broad segments at the brim. The flower is, according to Tournefort, Ray, &c. of one petal; but according to Linnæus, it has five; they are joined at the base, and spread open, and fall off joined. It has a great number of stamina which coalesce at bottom in a cylinder, but spread open above, and are inserted in the petal, terminated by kidney-shaped summits. In the center is situated an orbicular germen supporting a short cylindrical style, with many bristly stigmas the length of the style. The empalement afterward turns to several capsules, which are joined in an orbicular depressed head fastened to the column, opening on their inside, each containing one kidney-shaped seed.

4

This

This genus of plants is ranged in the fifth fection of Linnæus's fixteenth clafs, intitled Monodelphia Polyandria, which contains thofe plants whofe flowers have many ftamina joined with the ftyle in one body.

The Species are,

1. MALVA (*Sylveſtris*) caule erecto herbaceo, foliis feptem lobatis acutis pedunculis petiolifque pilofis. Lin. Sp. Plant. 969. *Mallow with an erect herbaceous ſtalk, with ſeven acute lobes to the leaves, and hairy foot-ſtalks both to the leaves and flowers.* Malva fylveftris, folio finuato. C. B. P. 314. *Wild Mallow with a ſinuated leaf.*

2. MALVA (*Rotundifolia*) caule proftrato, foliis cordatoorbiculatis obfolete quinquelobis, pedunculis fructiferis declinatis. Lin. Sp. 969. *Mallow with proſtrate ſtalks, roundiſh heart-ſhaped leaves with five obſolete lobes, and the foot-ſtalks of the fruit declining.* Malva vulgaris, flore minore, folio rotundo. J. B. 2. p. 949. *Common Mallow with a ſmall flower and a round leaf.*

3. MALVA (*Orientalis*) annua, caule erecto herbaceo, foliis lobatis obtufis & crenatis. *Annual Mallow with an erect herbaceous ſtalk, and obtuſe lobed leaves which are crenated.* Malva orientalis, flore magno fuavè rubente. Tourn. Cor. 3. *Eaſtern Mallow with a more upright ſtalk, and a large, ſoft, red flower.*

4. MALVA (*Criſpa*) caule erecto, foliis angulatis crifpis, floribus axillaribus glomeratis. Lin. Sp. 970. *Mallow with an erect ſtalk, angular curled leaves, and flowers in cluſters on the ſide of the ſtalks.* Malva foliis crifpis. C. B. P. 315. *Furbelowed Mallow.*

5. MALVA (*Verticillata*) caule erecto, foliis angulatis, floribus axillaribus glomeratis feffilibus, calycibus fcabris. Vir. Cliff. 356. *Mallow with an erect ſtalk, angular leaves, and flowers growing in whorls at the wings of the ſtalks.*

6. MALVA (*Chinenſis*) annua, caule erecto herbaceo, foliis fuborbiculatis obfoletè quinquelobatis, floribus confertis alaribus feffilibus. *Annual Mallow with an erect, herbaceous, ſingle ſtalk, leaves almoſt round, with five indented lobes, and flowers growing in cluſters, which ſit cloſe to the ſtalks.* Malva Sinenfis erecta, flofculis albis minimis. Boerh. Ind. alt. *Upright annual China Mallow, with very ſmall white flowers.*

7. MALVA (*Cretica*) caule erecto ramofo hirfuto, foliis angulatis, floribus alaribus pedunculis brevioribus. *Mallow with an erect, branching, hairy ſtalk, angular leaves, and flowers proceeding from the wings of the ſtalks, which grow upon ſhorter foot-ſtalks.* Malva Cretica altiffima, flore parvo ad alas umbellato. Tourn. Cor. 2. *Talleſt annual Mallow of Crete, with ſmall flowers growing in umbels on the ſides of the ſtalk.*

8. MALVA (*Peruviana*) caule erecto herbaceo, foliis lobatis, fpicis fecundis axillaribus feminibus denticulatis. Lin. Sp. Plant. 968. *Mallow with an erect herbaceous ſtalk, leaves having lobes, and ſpikes of flowers in fruitful cluſters proceeding from the ſides of the ſtalks, and indented ſeeds.*

9. MALVA (*Alcea*) caule erecto, foliis multipartitis fcabriufculis. Hort. Cliff. 347. *Mallow with an erect ſtalk, and rough leaves divided into many parts.* Alcea tenuifolia crifpa. J. B. 2. 953. *Narrow-leaved curled Vervain Mallow.*

10. MALVA (*Moſchata*) foliis radicalibus reniformibus incifis, caulinis quinque partitis pinnato-multifidis. Hort. Upfal. 202. *Mallow with kidney-ſhaped lower leaves which are cut, and thoſe on the ſtalks divided into five parts, ending in winged points.* Alcea folio rotundo laciniato. C. B. P. 316. *Round cut-leaved Vervain Mallow.*

11. MALVA (*Ægyptia*) foliis palmatis dentatis, corollis calyce minoribus. Lin. Sp. Plant. 690. *Mallow with hand-ſhaped indented leaves, and petals leſs than the empalement.* Alcea Ægyptia, gerani folio. Juff. *Egyptian Vervain Mallow with a Crane's-bill leaf.*

12. MALVA (*Bryonifolia*) foliis palmatis fcabris, caule tomentofo fruticofo, pedunculis multifloris. Prod. Leyd. 356. *Mallow with rough hand-ſhaped leaves, a ſhrubby woolly ſtalk, and foot-ſtalks with many flowers.* Althæa frutefcens bryoniæ folio. C. B. P. 316. *Shrubby Vervain Mallow with a Briony leaf.*

13. MALVA (*Tourneſortia*) foliis radicalibus quinque particis, trilobis linearibus, pedunculis folio caulino longioribus, caule procumbente. Amœn. Acad. 4. p. 283. *Mallow with cut leaves having three lobes, which are linear, and a declining ſtalk.* Alcea maritima Galloprovincialis, geranii folio. Tourn. Inſt. 98. *Maritime Vervain Mallow of Provence, with a Crane's-bill leaf.*

14. MALVA (*Capenſis*) foliis fubcordatis laciniatis hirfutis, caule arborefcente. *Mallow with hairy cut leaves, almoſt heart-ſhaped, and a tree-like ſtalk.* Malva Africana frutefcens, flore rubro. Hort. Amft. 2. p. 171. *African ſhrubby Mallow with a red flower.*

15. MALVA (*Americana*) foliis cordatis crenatis, floribus lateralibus folitariis, terminalibus fpicatis. Prod. Leyd. 359. *Mallow with heart-ſhaped crenated leaves, and flowers growing ſingly from the ſides of the ſtalks, and in ſpikes at the top.* Althæa Americana, pumila, flore luteo fpicato. Breyn. Cent. 124. *Low American Marſhmallow, with a yellow ſpiked flower.*

The two firft forts are found wild in moft parts of England, fo are rarely cultivated in gardens. The firft is the fort commonly ufed in medicine, with which the markets are fupplied by the herbfolks, who gather it in the fields. Thefe are both fo well known, as to need no defcription. There is a variety of the firft with white flowers, which continues the fame from feeds; but as it only differs in the colour of the flower, fo it cannot be reckoned a diftinct fpecies.

The third fort was difcovered by Dr. Tournefort in the Levant, this is an annual plant with an erect ftalk; the flowers are larger than thofe of the common fort, and are of a foft red colour. This is preferved in fome curious gardens for the fake of variety.

The fourth fort is annual; this rifes with an upright ftalk four or five feet high; the leaves are curled on their edges, for which variety it is preferved in gardens.

The fifth fort was difcovered firft by Dr. Tournefort, and afterward by Dr. Sherard, in the Levant, who fent the feeds to feveral gardens, where the plants have produced flowers and feeds; which having fcattered in thofe gardens fo plentifully, as to become as common as our native forts.

The fixth fort was formerly fent from China as a pot-herb, and hath been cultivated in fome curious gardens in England; though it is not likely to obtain here as an efculent plant, fince we have many others which are preferable to it for that purpofe. This is an annual plant, which will propagate itfelf faft enough, provided it be permitted to fcatter its feeds, when they feldom fail to grow, and are often very troublefome when they have gotten poffeffion of the ground.

The feventh fort grows naturally in Crete; this plant is annual, the ftalks rifes rather higher than that of our common Mallow, and the branches extend farther, and are in greater plenty; the leaves are angular, and the flowers ftand on fhort foot-ftalks. This will be very common, provided the feeds are permitted to fcatter.

The eighth fort grows naturally in Peru, from whence the feeds were fent to the Royal Garden at Paris, by Mr. Jofeph de Juffieu. This is an annual plant, rifing with an upright branching ftalk near two feet high, garnifhed with broad hairy leaves, having three lobes. The flowers grow in fpikes from the wings of the ftalks; they are fmall, of a pale blue, and fet very clofely on the fpikes. Thefe appear in June, and are fucceeded by feeds, which, if permitted to fcatter, will come up plentifully the following fpring without care.

The ninth fort is the common Vervain Mallow, which is found growing naturally near London. It is a biennial plant; the ftalks rife higher than thofe of the former, the leaves are cut into obtufe lobes which are indented. The flowers are large, appearing in June and July, and the feeds ripen in autumn.

The tenth fort differs from the ninth, in having taller hairy ftalks, and the leaves being kidney-fhaped,

and

and finely cut into narrow fegments. This grows naturally in the middle counties of England, and about Paris.

The eleventh fort was fent from Egypt to the Royal Garden at Paris, and hath fince been communicated to many other gardens. This is an annual plant, whofe ftalks are about a foot long; they are fmooth, and decline toward the ground. The leaves ftand upon pretty long foot-ftalks, they are fhaped like a hand, having five divifions which join at their bafe to the foot-ftalk, and are indented on their fides. The flowers come out fingle from the wings of the ftalk, and at the top in clufters; they have pretty large acute empalements; the flowers are fmall, and of a pale blue colour. Thefe appear in June, and the feeds ripen in autumn.

The twelfth fort grows naturally in Spain; this rifes with a fhrubby woolly ftalk four or five feet high, fending out branches on every fide, garnifhed with angular woolly rough leaves; the ftalks are longer from the wings of the leaves, each fupporting four or five flowers of a bright purple colour, fhaped like thofe of the common Mallow, which appear in July, and the feeds ripen in autumn. This fort feldom continues more than two or three years; but if the feeds are permitted to fcatter, young plants will come up the following fpring.

The thirteenth fort grows naturally in the fouth of France; this is an annual plant, which has fome refemblance of the former, but the ftalks are longer and more branched; the leaves are cut into five obtufe lobes almoft to the bottom, and thefe are deeply cut on their fide. The flowers ftand upon very long foot-ftalks; the empalement of the flower is large, prickly and acute-pointed; the flowers are blue, and larger than thofe of the other fort. It flowers and ripens its feeds about the fame time.

The fourteenth fort grows naturally at the Cape of Good Hope; this rifes with a woody ftalk ten or twelve feet high, fending out branches from the fide the whole length; the ftalks and branches are clofely covered with hairs, and are garnifhed with hairy leaves, which are indented on the fides, fo as to have the appearance of a trilobate leaf; thefe on the young plants are three inches long and two broad at their bafe, but as the plants grow older, they are fcarce half that fize. The flowers come out from the fide of the branches, upon foot-ftalks an inch long; they are of a deep red colour, and fhaped like thofe of the common Mallow, but are fmaller. This plant continues flowering great part of the year, which renders it valuable.

There are two other varieties of this plant, which have been mentioned by fome authors as diftinct fpecies. The firft is, Alcea Africana frutefcens, groffulariæ folio ampliore, unguibus florum atro-rubentibus. Act. Phil. 1729. Shrubby African Vervain Mallow, with a larger Goofeberry leaf, and the bottoms of the flower of a dark red. The other is, Alcea Africana frutefcens, folio groffulariæ flore parvo rubro. Boerh. Ind. alt. t. 271. Shrubby African Vervain Mallow, with a Goofeberry leaf, and a fmall red flower. The leaves of the laft appear very different from either of the former, being deeply divided into three lobes, which are alfo deeply indented, fo that any perfon upon feeing it would fuppofe it to be a different fpecies; but I have frequently raifed all thefe, with fome other intermediate varieties, from the feeds of one plant.

This plant is eafily propagated by feeds, which, if fown in a common border in the fpring, the plants will come up; but as it is too tender to live abroad in the winter, fo when the plants are three or four inches high, they fhould be each planted into a feparate pot of light frefh earth, placing them in the fhade till they have taken frefh root; then they may be removed to a fheltered fituation, intermixing them with other hardy exotic plants, where they may remain till autumn; when the froft comes on they fhould be removed into the green-houfe, and after-

ward treated in the fame way as the hardy plants from the fame country, always allowing them plenty of free air in mild weather.

The fifteenth fort grows naturally in moft of the iflands in the Weft-Indies. This is an annual plant, which rifes about a foot high, fending out a few fhort branches from the fide, which are woolly, and garnifhed with heart-fhaped woolly leaves which are crenated on their edges, and are placed alternately upon pretty long foot-ftalks. The flowers are produced fingly from the fide of the ftalk, and in a clofe fpike at the top; they are fmall, and of a pale yellow colour. They appear in July, and the feeds ripen in autumn.

This is propagated by feeds, which muft be fown upon a hot-bed in the fpring; and when the plants are fit to remove, they fhould be each planted in a feparate fmall pot filled with light frefh earth, and plunged into a new hot-bed, fhading them until they have taken frefh root; then they muft have free air admitted to them in proportion to the warmth of the feafon, and the latter end of June they may be placed in the open air in a fheltered fituation, where they will flower and produce ripe feeds.

The feeds of the other fpecies fhould be fown the end of March, upon a bed of frefh light earth, and when the plants are up three or four inches high, they fhould be tranfplanted where they are defigned to be continued, allowing them a good diftance; for if they are planted too clofe, they do not appear fo well; but they are beft when intermixed with other flowers of the fame growth, where they afford an agreeable variety.

Thefe feeds may alfo be fown in Auguft, for the plants will endure the greateft cold of our climate, if placed on a dry foil, and will grow larger, and flower fooner than thofe fown in the fpring; or if the feeds are permitted to fcatter, they will come up as the former forts, and thrive equally well.

MALVA ARBOREA. See LAVATERA.

MALVA ROSEA. See ALCEA.

MALUS. The Apple-tree.

The CHARACTERS are,

The empalement of the flower is of one leaf, cut into five fegments. The flower confifts of five leaves, which expand in form of a Rofe, whofe tails are inferted into the empalement. The fruit is hollowed about the foot-ftalk, is for the moft part roundifh, and umbellated at th top; it is flefhy, and divided into five cells or partitions, in each of which is lodged one oblong feed.

Dr. Linnæus has joined the Pear, Apple, and Quince together, making them all of the fame genus, and has reduced all the varieties of each to one fpecies. The Apple he diftinguifhes by the title of Pyrus foliis ferratis, pomis bafi concavis. Hort. Cliff. i. e. *Pear with fawed leaves, and the Apple hollow at the bafe.* But where the fruit is admitted as a diftinguifhing character of the genus, the Apple fhould be feparated from the Pear, this diftinction being founded in nature; for thefe fruits will not take by budding or grafting upon each other, though it be performed with the utmoft care. Indeed I have fometimes fucceeded fo far, as to have the bud or graft of an Apple fhoot when grafted on a Pear, but they foon decayed, notwithftanding all poffible care was taken of them; therefore I fhall beg leave to continue the feparation of the Apple from the Pear, as hath been always practifed by the botanifts before his time.

The SPECIES are,

1. MALUS (*Sylveftris*) foliis ovatis ferratis, caule arboreo. *Apple with oval fawed leaves, and a tree-like ftalk.* Malus fylveftris, fructu valde acerbo. Tourn. Inft. R. H. 635. *Wild Apple with a very four fruit, commonly called Crab.*

2. MALUS (*Coronaria*) foliis ferrato-angulofis. *Apple with angular fawed leaves.* Malus fylveftris Virginiana, floribus odoratis, Cat. Hort. *Wild Crab of Virginia, with a fweet-fcented flower.*

3. MALUS (*Pumila*) foliis ovatis ferratis, caule fruticofo. *Apple with oval fawed leaves and a fhrubby ftalk.* Malus

pumila quæ potiùs frutex quam arbor. C. B. P. 435.

Dwarf Apple, which is rather a ſhrub than a tree, commonly called Paradiſe Apple.

Of the firſt ſort there are two varieties of fruit, one is white, and the other purple toward the ſun, but theſe are accidental variations. There is alſo a variety of this with variegated leaves, which has been propagated in ſome of the nurſeries near London; but when the trees grow vigorous, their leaves ſoon become plain.

The ſecond ſort grows naturally in moſt parts of North America, where the inhabitants plant them for ſtocks to graft other ſorts of Apples upon; the leaves of this are longer and narrower than any of the other ſorts, and are cut into two acute angles on their ſides. The flowers of this have a fragrant odour, which perfumes the American woods at the time they appear. The third ſort is undoubtedly a diſtinct ſpecies from all the others, for it never riſes to any height; the branches are weak, ſcarce able to ſupport themſelves, and this difference is permanent when raiſed from ſeeds.

I have not diſtinguiſhed the Apples from the Crab, as diſtinct ſpecies, though I have never ſeen any Apples produced from the ſeeds of Crabs. I ſhall next mention a few of thoſe ſorts of Apples which have been introduced from France, which were moſt of them grafted on Paradiſe ſtocks, ſo were for ſome time much eſteemed, and ſhall mention thoſe of our own growth afterward.

There is alſo a ſort of Apple, called the Fig Apple, which is common to England and North America, but the fruit is not greatly eſteemed; however, as ſome perſons are fond of variety, ſo I have mentioned it.

Pomme de Rambour. The Rambour is a very large fruit, of a fine red next the ſun, and ſtriped with a pale or yellowiſh green. This ripens very early, commonly about the end of Auguſt, and ſoon grows mealy, therefore is not eſteemed in England.

Pomme de Courpendu, the hanging body. This is a very large Apple, of an oblong figure, having ſome irregular riſing or angles, which run from the baſe to the crown; it is of a red caſt on the ſide toward the ſun, but pale on the other ſide; the foot-ſtalk is long and ſlender, ſo that the fruit is always hanging downward, which occaſioned the French gardeners to give it this name.

The Rennette-blanche, or White Renette, or French Rennette. This is a large fine fruit, of a roundiſh figure, and of a pale green, changing a little yellowiſh when ripe, having ſome ſmall gray ſpots; the juice is ſugary, and it is good for eating or baking; it will keep till after Chriſtmas ſound.

The Rennette-griſe. This is a middle ſized fruit, ſhaped like the Golden Rennette, but is of a deep gray colour on the ſide next the ſun, but on the other ſide intermixed with yellow; it is a very juicy good Apple, of a quick flavour. It ripens in October, and will not keep long.

Pomme d'Api. This is a ſmall hard fruit, of a bright purple colour on the ſide next the ſun, and of a yellowiſh green on the other ſide; it is a very firm fruit, but hath not much flavour, ſo is only preſerved by ſome perſons by way of curioſity. It keeps a long time ſound, and makes a variety in a diſh of fruit.

Le Calville d'Automne, the Autumn Calville. This is a large fruit of an oblong figure, of a fine red colour toward the ſun. The juice is vinous, and much eſteemed by the French.

Fenouillat ou Pomme d'Anis, the Fennel, or Aniſe Apple. This is a middle ſized fruit, a little longer than a Golden Pippin, of a grayiſh colour. The pulp is tender, and has a ſpicy taſte like Aniſe-ſeed; the wood and the leaves are whitiſh.

Pomme Violette, the Violet Apple. This is a pretty large fruit, of a pale green, ſtriped with deep red to the ſun. The juice is ſugary, and has a flavour of Violets, which occaſioned the name.

The Crab, which is the firſt ſort here mentioned, has

been generally eſteemed as the beſt ſtock for grafting Apples upon, being very hardy, and of long duration; but of late years there have been few perſons who have been curious enough to raiſe theſe ſtocks, having commonly ſown the kernels of all ſorts of cyder Apples for ſtocks without diſtinction, as theſe are much eaſier to procure than the other; ſo the gardeners generally call all thoſe Crabs, which are produced from the kernels of any ſort of Apple which has not been grafted; but were the kernels of the Crabs ſown, I ſhould prefer thoſe for ſtocks, becauſe they are never ſo luxuriant in their growth as thoſe from Apple kernels, and they will continue longer ſound; beſide, theſe will preſerve ſome of the beſt ſort of Apples in their true ſize, colour, and flavour; whereas the other free ſtocks produce larger fruit, which are not ſo well taſted, nor will they keep ſo long.

The Paradiſe Apple for ſome years paſt was greatly eſteemed for ſtocks, to graft or bud the other ſorts upon; but theſe are not of long duration, nor will the trees grafted upon them ever grow to any ſize, unleſs they are planted ſo low as that the cion may ſtrike root into the ground, when it will be equal to no ſtock; for as the graft will draw its nouriſhment from the ground, ſo the ſtocks will become uſeleſs after; therefore it is only by way of curioſity, or for very ſmall gardens, that theſe ſtocks are proper, ſince there can never be expected any conſiderable quantity of fruit from ſuch trees.

Theſe trees have been much more eſteemed in France, where they were frequently brought to the table in the pots, growing with their fruit upon them; but this being only a curioſity, it never obtained much in England, ſo that the gardeners do not propagate many of them here at preſent.

There is another Apple, which is called the Dutch Paradiſe Apple, much cultivated in the nurſeries for grafting Apples upon, in order to have them dwarfs; and theſe will not decay or canker as the other, nor do they ſtint the grafts near ſo much, ſo are generally preferred for planting eſpaliers or dwarfs, being eaſily kept within the compaſs uſually allotted to theſe trees.

Some perſons have alſo made uſe of the Codlin ſtocks to graft Apples upon, in order to make them dwarf; but the fruit which are produced on ſuch trees are not ſo firm, nor do they laſt near ſo long as thoſe upon Crab ſtocks; therefore the winter fruits ſhould never be grafted upon them.

The Virginian Crab-tree with ſweet flowers, is often preſerved by ſuch perſons as are curious in collecting great variety of trees; it may be propagated by budding or grafting it upon the common Crab or Apple-tree, but it is ſomewhat tender while young; wherefore it ſhould be planted in a warm ſituation, otherwiſe it will be ſubject to ſuffer by an extreme hard winter. The flowers of this tree are ſaid to be exceeding ſweet in Virginia, where it grows in the woods in great plenty; but I could not obſerve much ſcent in ſome of them which have flowered in England, ſo that I am in doubt whether the ſort at preſent in the gardens is the very ſame with that of Virginia; or perhaps it may have degenerated by ſowing the ſeeds, which is the way it was firſt obtained in England.

The Fig Apple is ſuppoſed by many perſons to be produced without a previous flower. But this opinion is rejected by more curious obſervers, who affirm, there is a ſmall flower precedes the fruit, which is very fugacious, ſeldom continuing above a day or two. Now, which of theſe opinions is the right, I have not, as yet, had an opportunity to determine, not having a tree in my own poſſeſſion which is arrived at maturity to produce fruit; though it might reaſonably be expected, that ſuch who have had trees of this kind ſeveral years, might have determined this point long before this time.

I remember an account of a tree of this kind, mentioned in a letter from New England, written by Paul Dudley, Eſq; to the Royal Society, and publiſhed in the Philoſophical Tranſactions, N° 385. which was
exceeding

exceeding large, and produced great quantities of fruit, without any previous flowers; but it grew at some distance from his habitation, and he having no other opportunity to observe it strictly himself, but by visiting the place two or three times about the season of flowering, and not being apprized of the sudden decay of the flowers, they might easily be supposed to have appeared and dropped off, between the times of his visiting the place.

The other sorts which are above-mentioned, are what have been introduced from France, but there are not above two or three of them, which are much esteemed in England, viz. the French Rennette, the Rennettegrise, and the Violet Apple; the other being early fruit, which do not keep long, and their flesh is generally meally, so they do not deserve to be propagated, as we have many better fruits in England : but as there may be some persons who are willing to have all the sorts, I have mentioned them here for their instruction; but I shall next put down those sorts of Apples which are best esteemed in England, placing them in the order according to their time of ripening.

The first Apple which is brought to the markets, is the Codlin. This fruit is so well known in England, that it is needless to describe it.

The next is the Margaret Apple : this fruit is not so long as the Codlin, of a middling size; the side next the sun changes to a faint red, when ripe; the other side is of a pale green; the fruit is firm, of a quick pleasant taste, but doth not keep long.

The Summer Pearmain is an oblong fruit, striped with red next the sun; the flesh is soft, and in a short time is meally, so that it is not greatly esteemed.

The Kentish Fill Basket is a species of Codlin, of a large size, and somewhat longer shaped than the Codlin; this ripens a little later in the season, and is generally used for baking, &c.

The Transparent Apple : this was brought to England a few years since, and was esteemed a curiosity; it came from Petersburgh, where it is affirmed to be so transparent, as that the kernels may be perfectly seen, when the Apple is held to the light; but, in this country, it is a meally insipid fruit, so not worth propagating.

Loan's Pearmain : this is a beautiful fruit, being of a middling size; the side next the sun is of a beautiful red, and striped with the same colour on the other; the flesh is vinous, but as it soon grows meally, it is not greatly esteemed.

The Quince Apple : this is a small fruit, seldom larger than the Golden Pippin, but is in shape like the Quince, especially toward the stalk; the side next the sun is of a russet colour, on the other side inclining to yellow : this is an excellent Apple for about three weeks in September, but will not keep much longer.

The Golden Renette is a fruit so well known in England, as to need no description; this ripens about Michaelmas, and for about a month is a very good fruit, either for eating raw or baking.

The Aromatic Pippin is also a very good Apple : it is about the size of a Nonpareil, but not so flat, it is a little longer; the side next the sun is of a bright russet colour; the flesh is breaking, and hath an aromatic flavour. It ripens in October.

The Hertfordshire Pearmain, by some called the Winter Pearmain : this is a good sized fruit, rather long than round, of a fine red next the sun, and striped with the same colour on the other side; the flesh is juicy, and stews well, but is not esteemed for eating by any nice palates. This is fit for use in November and December.

The Kentish Pippin is a large handsome fruit, of an oblong figure; the skin is of a pale green colour; the flesh is breaking, and full of juice, which is of a quick acid flavour. This is a very good kitchen fruit, and will keep till February.

The Holland Pippin is larger than the former; the fruit is somewhat longer, the skin of a darker green,

and the flesh firm and juicy. This is a very good kitchen fruit, and will keep late in the season.

The Monstrous Renette is a very large Apple, of an oblong shape, turning red toward the sun; but of a dark green on the other side; the flesh is apt to be meally, so it is not much valued by those who are curious, and only preserved for the magnitude of the fruit.

The Embroidered Apple is a pretty large fruit, somewhat shaped like the Pearmain, but the stripes of red are very broad, from whence the gardeners have given it this title : it is a middling fruit, and is commonly used as a kitchen Apple, though there are many better.

The Royal Russet, by some called the Leather Coat Russet, on account of the deep russet colour of the skin; this is a large fair fruit, of an oblong figure, broad toward the base; the flesh is inclinable to yellow. This is one of the best kitchen Apples we have, and is a very great bearer : the trees grow large and handsome, and the fruit is in use from October till April, and is also a pleasant fruit to eat.

Wheeler's Russet is an Apple of a middling size, flat, and round; the stalk is slender, the side next the sun of a light russet colour, and the other side inclining to a pale yellow, when ripe; the flesh is firm, and the juice has a very quick acid flavour, but is an excellent kitchen fruit, and will keep a long time.

Pile's Russet is not quite so large as the former, but is of an oval figure, of a russet colour to the sun, and of a dark green on the other side; it is a very firm fruit, of a sharp acid flavour, but is much esteemed for baking, and will keep sound till April, or later, if they are well preserved.

The Nonpareil is a fruit pretty generally known in England, though there is another Apple which is frequently sold in the markets for it, which is what the French call Haute-bonne; this is a larger fairer fruit than the Nonpariel, more inclining to the yellow; the russet colour brighter, and it is earlier ripe, and sooner gone; this is not so flat as the true Nonpareil, nor is the juice so sharp, though it is a good Apple in its season; but the Nonpareil is seldom ripe before Christmas, and where they are well preserved they will keep till May perfectly sound; this is justly esteemed one of the best Apples that have been yet known.

The Golden Pippin is a fruit almost peculiar to England; there are few countries abroad where this succeeds well, nor do they produce so good fruit in many parts of England as were to be wished; which, in some measure, is owing to its being grafted on free stocks, which enlarges the fruit, but renders it less valuable, because the flesh is not so firm, nor the flavour so quick, so is apt to be dry and meally; therefore this should always be grafted upon the Crab stock, which will not canker like the others, and though the fruit will not be so fair to the sight, yet it will be better flavoured and keep longer.

There are yet a great variety of Apples, which, being inferior to those here mentioned, I have omitted, as those which are here enumerated will be sufficient to furnish the table and the kitchen, during the whole season of these fruits; so that where these sorts can be had, no person of taste will eat the other. I shall here mention some of the Apples which are chiefly preferred for the making of cyder, tho' there are in every cyder country, new sorts frequently obtained from the kernels; but those hereafter mentioned, have, for some years, been in the greatest esteem.

The Red-streak.
Devonshire Royal Wilding.
The Whitsour.
Herefordshire Under Leaf.
John Apple, or Deux-annes.
Everlasting Hanger.
Gennet Moyle.

All the sorts of Apples are propagated by grafting or budding upon the stocks of the same kind, for they will

will not take upon any other fort of fruit tree. In the nurferies there are three fort of stocks generally ufed to graft Apples upon; the firft are called free stocks; thefe are raifed from the kernels of all forts of Apples indifferently, and fometimes they are alfo termed Crab stocks; for all thofe trees which are produced from the feeds before they are grafted, are termed Crabs without any diftinction; but, as I have before obferved, I fhould always prefer fuch stocks as are raifed from the kernels of Crabs, where they are preffed for verjuice; and I find feveral of the old writers on this fubject of the fame mind. Mr. Auften, who wrote above a hundred years ago, fays, " The " stock which he accounts beft for Apple grafts is " the Crab, which is better than fweeter Apple-trees " to graft on, becaufe they are ufually free from " canker, and will become very large trees; and, I " conceive, will laft longer than stocks of fweeter " Apples, and will make fruits more strong and hardy " to endure froft;" and it is very certain, that by frequently grafting fome forts of Apples upon free stocks, the fruits have been rendered lefs firm and poignant, and of fhorter duration.

The fecond fort of stock is the Dutch Creeper, before-mentioned; thefe are defigned to stint the growth of the trees, and keep them within compafs for dwarfs or efpaliers.

The third fort is the Paradife Apple, which is a very low fhrub, fo only proper for trees which are kept in pots, by way of curiofity, for thefe do not continue long.

Some perfons have made ufe of Codlin stocks for grafting of Apples, in order to stint their growth; but as thefe are commonly propagated by fuckers, I would by no means advife the ufing of them; nor would I chufe to raife the Codlin-trees from fuckers, but rather graft them upon Crab stocks, which will caufe the fruit to be firmer, laft longer, and have a fharper flavour; and thefe trees will laft much longer found, and never put out fuckers, as the Codlins always do, which, if not conftantly taken off, will weaken the trees, and caufe them to canker: and it is not only from the roots, but from the knots of their stems, there are generally a great number of strong fhoots produced, which fill the trees with ufelefs fhoots, and render them unfightly, and the fruit fmall and crumpled.

The method of raifing stocks from the kernels of Crabs, or Apples, is, to procure them where they are preffed for verjuice or cyder, and after they are cleared of the pulp, they may be fown upon a bed of light earth, covering them over about half an inch thick with the fame light earth; thefe may be fown in November or December, where the ground is dry, but in wet ground, it will be better to defer it till February; but then the feeds fhould be preferved in dry fand, and kept out of the reach of vermin, for if mice or rats can get at them, they will devour the feeds; there fhould alfo be care taken of the feeds, when they are fown, to protect them from thefe vermin, by fetting traps to take them, &c. In the fpring, when the plants begin to appear, they muft be carefully weeded, and if the feafon fhould prove dry, it will be of great fervice to water them two or three times a week; and, during the fummer, they muft be kept clean from weeds, which, if fuffered to grow, will foon over-top the plants, and fpoil their growth; if thefe thrive well, they will be fit to tranfplant into the nurfery the October following, at which time the ground fhould be carefully digged, and cleanfed from the roots of all bad weeds; then the stocks fhould be

planted in rows three feet afunder, and the plants one foot diftance in the rows, clofing the earth pretty faft to their roots; when the stocks are tranfplanted out of the feed-bed, the firft autumn after fowing, they need not be headed, but where they are inclined to fhoot downward, the tap root muft be fhortened, in order to force out horizontal roots; if the ground is pretty good in which thefe stocks are planted, and the weeds conftantly cleared away, the stocks will make great progrefs, fo that thofe which are intended for dwarfs, may be grafted the fpring twelve months after they are planted out of the feed-bed; but thofe which are defigned for standards will require two or three years more growth, before they will be fit to graft, by which time they will be upward of fix feet high. The other neceffary work to be obferved in the culture of thefe trees, while they remain in the nurfery, being exhibited under the article of NURSERY, I fhall not repeat in this place.

I fhall next treat of the manner of planting fuch of thefe trees, as are defigned for efpaliers in the kitchen-garden, where, if there is an extent of ground, it will be proper to plant, not only fuch forts as are for the ufe of the table, but alfo a quantity of trees to fupply the kitchen; but where the kitchen-garden is fmall, the latter muft be fupplied from standard-trees, either from the orchard, or wherever they are planted; but as many of thefe kitchen Apples are large, and hang late in the autumn upon the trees, they will be much more expofed to the strong winds on standard trees than in efpaliers, whereby many of the fruit will be blown down before they are ripe, and others bruifed, fo as to prevent their keeping; therefore where it can be done, I fhould always prefer the planting them in efpaliers.

The diftance which I fhould chufe to allow thefe trees, fhould not be lefs than thirty feet, for fuch forts as are of moderate growth (if upon Crab or free stocks:) but the larger growing forts fhould not be allowed lefs room than thirty-five or forty feet, which will be found full near enough, if the ground is good, and the trees properly trained; for as the branches of thefe trees fhould not be fhortened, but trained at their full length, fo in a few years they will be found to meet. Indeed, at the firft planting, the diftance will appear fo great to thofe perfons who have not obferved the vigorous growth of thefe trees, that they will fuppofe they never can extend their branches fo far, as to cover the efpalier; but if thefe perfons will but obferve the growth of standard-trees of the fame kinds, and fee how wide their branches are extended on every fide, they may be foon convinced, that as thefe efpalier-trees are allowed to fpread but on two fides, they will of courfe make make more progrefs, as the whole nourifhment of the root will be employed in thefe fide branches, than where there is a greater number of branches on every fide of the tree, which are to be fupplied with the fame nourifhment.

The next thing to be obferved is the making choice of fuch forts of fruits as grow nearly alike, to plant in the fame efpalier. This is of great confequence, becaufe of the diftance they are to be placed, otherwife thofe forts which make the largeft fhoots, may be allowed lefs room to fpread than thofe of fmaller growth; befide, when all the trees in one efpalier are nearly equal in growth, they will have a better appearance than when fome are tall, and others fhort; but for the better inftruction of thofe perfons who are not converfant in thefe things, I fhall divide the forts of Apples into three claffes according to their different growths.

Largeſt growing tree.	Middle growing tree.	Smalleſt growing tree.
All the ſorts of Pearmains.	Margaret Apple.	Quince Apple.
Kentiſh Pippin.	Golden Renette.	Tranſparent Apple.
Holland Pippin.	Aromatic Pippin.	Golden Pippin.
Monſtrous Renette.	Embroidered Apple.	Pomme d'Api.
Royal Ruſſet.	Renette Griſe.	Fenouillet, or Anis Apple.
Wheeler's Ruſſet.	White Renette.	
Pile's Ruſſet.	Codlin.	
Nonpareil.		
Violet Apple.		

N. B. Theſe are all ſuppoſed to be grafted on the ſame ſort of ſtocks.

If theſe Apples are grafted upon Crab ſtocks, I would willingly place them at the following diſtance from each other, eſpecially where the ſoil is good, viz. the largeſt growing trees at forty feet, the middle growing at thirty feet, and the ſmall growing at twenty-five feet, which, from conſtant experience, I find to be full near enough; for in many places, where I have planted theſe trees at twenty-four feet diſtance, they have ſhot ſo ſtrong, as that in ſeven years their branches have met; and in ſome places where every other tree hath been taken up, the branches have almoſt joined in ſeven years after; therefore it will be much the better way to plant theſe trees at a proper diſtance at firſt, and between theſe to plant ſome Dwarf Cherries, Currants, or other ſorts of fruit, to bear for a few years, which may be cut away when the Apple-trees have extended their branches to them; for when the Apple-trees are planted nearer together, few perſons care to cut down the trees, when they are fruitful, ſo that they are obliged to uſe the knife, ſaw, and chiſel, more than is proper for the future good of the trees; and many times, where perſons are inclinable to take away part of their trees, the diſtances will be ſo irregular (where there was not this conſideration in their firſt planting,) as to render the eſpalier unſightly.

When the trees are upon the Dutch Dwarf ſtock, the diſtance ſhould be for the larger growing trees thirty feet, for thoſe of middle growth twenty-five, and the ſmalleſt twenty feet, which will be found full near where the trees thrive well.

The next is the choice of the trees, which ſhould not be more than two years growth from the graft, but thoſe of one year ſhould be preferred; you ſhould alſo be careful, that their ſtocks are young, ſound, and ſmooth, free from canker, and which have not been cut down once or twice in the nurſery; when they are taken up, all the ſmall fibres ſhould be entirely cut off from their roots, which, if left on, will turn mouldy and decay, ſo will obſtruct the new fibres, which will ſoon puſh out, in their growth; the extreme part of the roots muſt alſo be ſhortened, and all bruiſed roots cut off; and if there are any miſplaced roots which croſs each other, they ſhould alſo be cut away. As to the pruning of the head of theſe trees, there need be nothing more done than to cut off any branches which are ſo ſituated, as that they cannot be trained to the line of the eſpalier: in the planting, there muſt be care taken not to place their roots too deep in the ground, eſpecially if the ſoil is moiſt, but rather raiſe them on a little hill, which will be neceſſary to allow for the raiſing of the borders afterward. The beſt ſeaſon for planting theſe trees (in all ſoils which are not very moiſt) is, from October, to the middle or latter end of November, according as the ſeaſon continues mild; but ſo ſoon as the leaves fall, they may be removed with great ſafety. After the trees are planted, it will be proper to place down a ſtake to each tree, to which the branches ſhould be faſtened, to prevent the winds from ſhaking or looſening their roots, which will deſtroy the young fibres; for when theſe trees are planted pretty early in autumn, they will very ſoon puſh out a great number of new fibres, which, being very tender, are ſoon broken, by the wind ſhaking

of the trees, whereby they are greatly injured. If the winter ſhould prove ſevere, it will be proper to lay ſome rotten dung, tanners bark, or ſome other ſort of mulch about their roots, to prevent the froſt from penetrating of the ground, which might damage theſe tender fibres; but I would not adviſe the laying of this mulch before the froſt begins, for if it is laid over the ſurface of the ground about their roots, ſoon after the trees are planted (as is often practiſed,) it will prevent the moiſture entering the ground, and do much more harm than good to the trees.

The following ſpring, before the trees begin to puſh, there ſhould be two or three ſhort ſtakes put down on each ſide every tree, to which the branches ſhould be faſtened down as horizontally as poſſible, never cutting them down, as is by ſome practiſed, for there will be no danger of their putting out branches enough to furniſh the eſpalier, if the trees are once well eſtabliſhed in their new quarters.

In the pruning of theſe trees, the chief point is, never to ſhorten any of the branches, unleſs there is an abſolute want of ſhoots to fill the ſpaces of the eſpalier; for where the knife is much uſed, it only multiplies uſeleſs ſhoots, and prevents their fruiting; ſo that the beſt method to manage theſe trees is, to go over them three or four times in the growing ſeaſon, and rub off all ſuch ſhoots as are irregularly produced, and train the others down to the ſtakes in the poſition they are to remain: if this is carefully performed in ſummer, there will be little left to be done in the winter, and by bending of their ſhoots from time to time, as they are produced, there will be no occaſion to uſe force to bring them down, nor any danger of breaking the branches. The diſtance which theſe branches ſhould be trained from each other, for the largeſt ſorts of fruits ſhould be about ſeven or eight inches, and for the ſmaller four or five. If theſe plain inſtructions are followed, it will ſave much unneceſſary labour of pruning, and the trees will, at all times, make a handſome appearance; whereas when they are ſuffered to grow rude in ſummer, there will be much greater difficulty to bring down their ſhoots, eſpecially if they are grown ſtubborn, when it may become neceſſary to ſlit the branches to make them pliable. All the ſorts of Apples produce their fruit upon curſons, or ſpurs, ſo that theſe ſhould never be cut off, for they will continue fruitful a great number of years.

The method of making the eſpaliers having been already exhibited under that article, I need not repeat it here, but only obſerve, that it will be beſt to defer making the eſpalier till the trees have had three or four years growth; for before that time, the branches may be ſupported by a few upright ſtakes, ſo that there will be no neceſſity to make the eſpalier, until there are ſufficient branches to furniſh all the lower part.

I ſhall now treat of the method to plant orchards, ſo as to have them produce the greateſt profit. And firſt, in the choice of the ſoil and ſituation for an orchard: the beſt ſituation for an orchard is, on the aſcent of the gentle hills, facing the ſouth, or ſouth-eaſt; but this aſcent muſt not be too ſteep, leſt the earth ſhould be waſhed down by haſty rains. There

       are

are many perfons who prefer low fituations at the foot of hills, but I am thoroughly convinced from experience, that all bottoms where there are hills on each fide, are very improper for this purpofe ; for the air is drawn down into thefe vallies in ftrong currents, which, being pent in renders thefe bottoms much colder than the open fituations ; and during the winter and fpring, thefe bottoms are very damp and unhealthy to all vegetables ; therefore the gentle rife of a hill, fully expofed to the fun and air, is by much the beft fituation. As to the foil, a gentle hazel loam, which is eafy to work, and that doth not detain the wet, is the beft ; if this happens to be three feet deep, it will be better for the growth of the trees, for although thefe trees will grow upon very ftrong land, yet they are feldom fo thriving, nor are their fruit fo well flavoured, as thofe which grow on a gentle foil ; and on the other hand, thefe trees will not do well upon a very dry gravel or fand, therefore thofe foils fhould never be made choice of for orchards.

The ground intended to be planted fhould be well prepared the year before, by ploughing it thoroughly, and if fome dung is laid upon it the year before, it will be of great fervice to the trees ; if in the preceding fpring a crop of Peas or Beans is planted on the ground (provided they are fown or planted in rows, at a proper diftance, fo as that the ground between them is horfe-hoed,) it will deftroy the weeds, and loofen the ground, fo that it will be a good preparation for the trees, for the earth cannot be too much wrought, or pulverifed for this purpofe : thefe crops will be taken off the ground long before the feafon for planting of thefe trees, which fhould be as foon as poffible performed when the trees begin to fhed their leaves.

In chufing of the trees, I would advife the taking fuch as are but of two years growth from the graft, and never to plant old trees, or fuch as are grafted upon old ftocks, for it is lofing of time to plant thefe ; young trees being always more certain to grow, and make a much greater progrefs than thofe which are old. As to pruning of the roots, it muft be done in the fame manner as hath been already directed for the efpalier-trees ; and in pruning their heads, little more is neceffary than to cut out fuch branches as are ill placed, or that crofs each other ; for I do not approve the heading of them down, as is by fome often practifed to the lofs of many of their trees.

The diftance which thefe trees fhould be planted, where the foil is good, muft be fifty or fixty feet ; and where the foil is not fo good, forty feet may be fufficient ; but nothing can be of worfe confequence, than the crowding trees too clofe together in orchards. And although there may be fome who may imagine this diftance too great, yet I am fure, when they have thoroughly confidered the advantages attending this practice, they will agree with me. Nor is it my own opinion in this affair, for in many of the old writers on this fubject, there is often mention made of the neceffity for allowing a proper diftance to the fruit-trees in orchards, particularly Auften, upon planting before quoted, who fays, " He fhould chufe to " prefcribe the planting thefe trees fourteen or fix-" teen yards afunder ; for both trees and fruits have " many great advantages, if planted a good diftance " one from another." One advantage he mentions is, " The fun refrefhes every tree, the roots, body, " and branches, with the bloffoms and fruits ; where-" by trees bring forth more fruit, and thofe fairer and " better." Another advantage he mentions is, " That " when trees are planted at a large diftance, much " profit may be made of the ground under and about " thefe trees, by cultivating garden-ftuff, commo-" dious as well for fale as houfekeeping ; as alfo " Goofeberries, Rafpberries, Currants, and Straw-" berries, may be there planted." Again he fays, " When trees have room to fpread, they will grow " very large and great ; and the confequences of that " will be, not only multitudes of fruits, but alfo

" long lafting, and thefe two are no fmall advan-" tages." For, fays he, " Men are miftaken, when " they fay, the more trees in an orchard, the more " fruits ; for one or two large trees which have room " to fpread, will bear more fruits than fix or ten (it " may be) of thofe that grow near together, and " crowd one another." Again he fays, " Let men but " obferve, and take notice of fome Apple-trees, that " grow a great diftance from other trees, and have " room enough to fpread both their roots and " branches, and they fhall fee, that one of thofe trees " (being come to full growth) hath a larger head, " and more boughs and branches, than (it may be) " four, or fix, or more, of thofe which grow near " together, although of the fame age." And Mr. Lawfon, an ancient planter, advifes to plant Apple-trees twenty yards afunder. As the two authors above quoted have written the beft upon this fubject, and feem to have had more experience than any of the writers I have yet feen, I have made ufe of them as authorities to confirm what I have advanced ; though the fact is fo obvious to every perfon who will make the leaft reflection, that there needs no other proof.

When the trees are planted, they fhould be ftaked, to prevent their being fhaken, or blown out of the ground by ftrong winds ; but in doing of this, there fhould be particular care taken, to put either ftraw, haybands, or woollen cloth, between the trees and the ftakes, to prevent the trees from being rubbed and bruifed, by the fhaking againft the ftakes, for if their bark fhould be rubbed off, it will occafion fuch great wounds, as not to be healed over in feveral years, if they ever recover it.

If the winter fhould prove very fevere, it will be proper to cover the furface of the ground about their roots with fome mulch, to prevent the froft from penetrating the ground, which will deftroy the young fibres ; but this mulch fhould not be laid on too foon, as hath been before mentioned, left the moifture fhould be prevented from foaking down to the roots of the trees, nor fhould it lie on too long in the fpring for the fame reafon ; therefore where perfons will be at the trouble to lay it on in frofty weather, and remove it again after the froft is over, that the wet in February may have free accefs to the roots of the trees ; and if March fhould prove dry, with fharp north or eaft winds, which often happens, it will be proper to cover the ground again with the mulch, to prevent the winds from penetrating and drying the ground, and will be of fingular fervice to the trees. But I am aware, that this will be objected to by many, on account of the trouble, which may appear to be great ; but when it is confidered, how much of this bufinefs may be done by a fingle perfon in a fhort time, it can have little force, and the benefit which the trees will receive by this management, will greatly recompenfe the trouble and expence.

As thefe trees muft be conftantly fenced from cattle, it will be the beft way to keep the land in tillage for fome years, that by conftant ploughing or digging of the ground, the roots of the trees will be more encouraged, and they will make the more progrefs in their growth ; but where this is done, whatever crops are fown or planted, fhould not be too near the trees, left the nourifhment fhould be drawn away from the trees ; and as in the ploughing of the ground where it is fo tilled, there muft be care taken not to go too near the ftem of the trees, whereby their roots would be injured, or the bark of their ftems rubbed off, fo it will be of great fervice to dig the ground about the trees where the plough doth not come, every autumn, for five or fix years after planting, by which time their roots will have extended themfelves to a greater diftance.

It is a common practice in many parts of England, to lay the ground down for pafture, after the trees are grown pretty large in their orchards ; but this is by no means advifeable, for I have frequently feen trees of above twenty years growth, almoft deftroyed by horfes,

horfes, in the compafs of one week; and if fheep are put into orchards, they will conftantly rub their bodies againft the ftems of the trees, and their greafe fticking to the bark, will ftint their growth, and in time will fpoil them; therefore wherever orchards are planted, it will be much the better method to keep the ground ploughed or dug annually, and fuch crops put on the ground as will not draw too much nourifhment from the trees.

In pruning of orchard-trees, nothing more fhould be done, but to cut out all thofe branches which crofs each other, and, if left, would rub and tear off the bark, as alfo decayed branches, but never fhorten any of their fhoots. If fuckers, or fhoots from their ftems, fhould come out, they muft be entirely taken off annually; and when any branches are broken by the wind, they fhould be cut off, either down to the divifion of the branch, or clofe to the ftem from whence it was produced; the beft time for this work is in November, for it fhould not be done in frofty weather, nor in the fpring, when the fap begins to be in motion.

The beft method to keep Apples for winter ufe is, to let them hang upon the trees until there is danger of froft, and to gather them in dry weather, laying them in large heaps to fweat for three weeks or a month; afterward look them over carefully, taking out all fuch as have appearance of decay, wiping all the found fruit dry, and pack them up in large oiljars, which have been thoroughly fcalded and dry, ftopping them down clofe to exclude the external air: if this is duly obferved, the fruit will keep found a long time, and their flefh will be plump; for when they are expofed to the air, their fkins will fhrink, and their pulp will be foft.

MALUS ARMENIACA. See ARMENIACA.
MALUS AURANTIA. See AURANTIA.
MALUS LIMONIA. See LIMONIA.
MALUS MEDICA. See CITREUM.
MALUS PERSICA. See PERSICA.
MALUS PUNICA. See PUNICA.
MAMMEA. Plum. Nov. Gen. 44. tab. 4. Lin. Gen. Plant. 583. The Mammee-tree.

The CHARACTERS are,

The empalement of the flower is compofed of two fmall, oval, concave leaves, which fall off. The flower has four large concave petals, which fpread open. It hath many awl-fhaped ftamina, terminated by roundifh fummits, and in the center a roundifh germen, with a conical ftyle the length of the ftamina, crowned by a fingle permanent ftigma. The germen afterward turns to a large flefhy fruit, of a fpherical figure, inclofing one, two, or three large almoft oval ftones.

This genus of plants is ranged in the firft fection of Linnæus's thirteenth clafs, intitled Polyandria Monogynia, which includes the plants whofe flowers have many ftamina and one ftyle.

There is but one SPECIES of this tree known in the Englifh gardens, viz.

MAMMEA ftaminibus flore brevioribus. *Mammee with the ftamina fhorter than the flower.* Mammea magno fructu, perficæ fapore. Plum. Nov. Gen. 44. *Mammee with a large fruit, having the tafte of a Peach.*

This tree, in the Weft-Indies, grows to the height of fixty or feventy feet; the leaves are large and ftiff, and continue green all the year; the fruit is as large as a man's fift; when ripe, it is of a yellowifh green colour, and is very grateful to the tafte. It grows in great plenty in the Spanifh Weft-Indies, where the fruit is generally fold in their markets, and is efteemed one of the beft fruits in the country. It alfo grows on the hills of Jamaica, and has been tranfplanted into moft of the Caribbee Iflands, where it thrives exceeding well.

In England there are fome few of thefe plants, which are preferved with great care by fuch as are curious in cultivating exotic plants; but there are none of any confiderable fize, fo that we cannot expect to fee either fruit or flowers for fome years. Thefe plants may be propagated by planting the ftones, which are

often brought from the Weft-Indies; (which fhould be very frefh, otherwife they will not grow,) into pots filled with frefh light earth, and plunged into a hotbed of tanners bark, obferving to water the earth. whenever it appears dry. In about a month or fix weeks the plants will appear above ground, after which they muft be frequently refrefhed with water, and in hot weather the glaffes of the hot-bed fhould be raifed to let in frefh air. In two months the roots of the plants will have filled the pots, when you fhould provide fome pots of a little larger fize, into which you fhould tranfplant the plants; being careful to preferve as much earth to their roots as poffible; then you fhould fill up the pots with frefh light earth, and plunge them into the bark-bed again, obferving to water and fhade them until they have taken root, after which they fhould be conftantly refrefhed with water as you fhall find they want it, and muft have air in hot weather. In this bed they may remain till Michaelmas, when they muft be removed into the bark-ftove, where they muft be conftantly kept, obferving to refrefh them with water, but it muft be given to them fparingly at this feafon, as alfo to clean their leaves from the filth they are apt to contract in the ftove; the fpring following they fhould be fhifted into frefh earth, and if they require it, into larger pots, but by no means over-pot them, for they do not produce many roots, therefore if the pots are too large the plants will not thrive; they muft be conftantly kept in the bark-ftove, and may be treated after the manner directed for the Coffee-tree.

If, when the ftones of this fruit are brought over, they are put into the tan-bed, under the bottom of any of the pots, they will fprout fooner than thofe which are planted in the earth.

MANCANILLA. See HIPPOMANE.
MANDRAGORA. Tourn. Inft. R. H. 76. tab. 12. Lin. Sp. Plant. 221. Mandrake; in French, *Mandragore.*

The CHARACTERS are,

The empalement of the flower is large, bell-fhaped, erect, and permanet; it is of one leaf, cut at the top into five acute fegments. The flower hath one erect bell-fhaped petal which fpreads open, and is a little larger than the empalement. It hath five awl-fhaped ftamina, which are arched and hairy at their bafe. In the center is fituated a roundifh germen, fupporting an awl-fhaped ftyle, crowned by a headed ftigma. The germen afterward turns to a large round berry with two cells, having a flefhy receptacle convex on each fide, filled with kidney-fhaped feeds.

This genus of plants is ranged in the firft fection of Linnæus's fifth clafs, intitled Pentandria Monogynia, which contains thofe plants whofe flowers have five ftamina and one ftyle.

We have but one SPECIES of this genus in the Englifh gardens, viz.

MANDRAGORA (*Officinarum.*) Hort. Cliff. 51. *The Mandrake.* Mandragora fructu rotundo. C. B. P. 169. *Mandrake with a round fruit.*

This plant grows naturally in Spain, Portugal, Italy, and the Levant, but is preferved here in the gardens of the curious. It hath a long taper root fhaped like Parfnep, which runs three or four feet deep in the ground; it is fometimes fingle, and at others divided into two or three branches, almoft of the colour of Parfnep, but a little darker; from this arifes a circle of leaves, which at firft ftand erect, but, when grown to their full fize, fpread open, and lie upon the ground; they are more than a foot in length, and four or five inches broad in the middle, growing narrow toward both ends, of a dark green colour, and a fœtid fcent. Thefe rife immediately from the crown of the root, without any foot-ftalk; between them come out the flowers, each ftanding upon a feparate foot-ftalk about three inches long, which alfo arife immediately from the root; they are five-cornered, of an herbaceous white colour, fpreading open at the top like a Primrofe, having five hairy ftamina, with a globular germen in the center, fupporting an awlfhaped ftyle. The germen afterward turns to a globular

bular foft berry lying upon the leaves, which, when fully grown, is as large as a Nutmeg, of a yellowifh green colour when ripe, full of pulp, in which the kidney-fhaped feeds are lodged. It flowers in March, and the feeds are ripe in July.

This plant is propagated by feeds, which, fhould be fown upon a bed of light earth foon after they are ripe, for if they are kept until the fpring, they feldom fucceed well; but thofe 'which are fown in autumn will come up in the fpring, when they fhould be carefully cleared from weeds; and in' very dry weather they muft be refrefhed with water, which will greatly promote their growth. In this bed they fhould remain till the latter end of Auguft, (obferving always to keep them clear from weeds) at which time they fhould be taken up very carefully, and tranfplanted into the places where they are to remain; the foil fhould be light and deep, for their roots always run very deep, fo that if the foil is wet, they are often rotted in winter; and if it be too near the gravel or chalk, they will make but little progrefs; but if the foil be good and they are not difturbed, the plants will grow to a large fize in a few years, and will produce great quantities of flowers and fruit; the roots will abide a great many years.

I have been informed by fome perfons of credit, that one of thefe roots will remain found above fifty years, and be as vigorous as a young plant. I have known fome plants myfelf near that age, which are now in great vigour, and may continue fo many years longer, as there are no figns of their decay; but they fhould never be removed after their roots have arrived to any confiderable fize, which would break their lower fibres, and fo ftint the plants, as that if they live they will not recover their former ftrength in two or three years. Thefe plants fhould have a warm fituation, otherwife in fevere winters they will be deftroyed.

As to the feigned refemblance of a human form, which the roots of this plant are faid to carry, it is all impofture, owing to the cunning of quacks and mountebanks, who deceive the populace and the ignorant with fictitious images, fhaped from the frefh roots of Briony and other plants : and what is reported as to the manner of rooting of this plant, by tying a dog 'thereto, to prevent the certain death of the perfon who fhould care to attempt it, and the groans it emits upon the force offered, &c. is all a ridiculous fable; for I have taken up feveral large roots of this plant, fome of which have been tranfplanted into' other places, but could never obferve any particular difference in this from any other deep rooting plant.

MANGIFERA. Lin. Gen. Plant. 278. The Mango-tree.

The CHARACTERS are,

The empalement of the flower is cut into five fpear-fhaped fegments; the flower hath five fpear-fhaped petals longer than the empalement, and five awol-fhaped ftamina the length of the corolla, crowned with heart-fhaped fummits. It hath a roundifh germen, fupporting a flender ftyle the length of the empalement, terminated by a fingle ftigma; the germen afterward becomes an oblong kidney-fhaped Plumb fomewhat compreffed, inclofing an oblong woolly nut of the fame form.

This genus of plants is ranged in the firft fection of Linnæus's fifth clafs, intitled Pentandria Monogynia, the flower having five ftamina.and one ftyle.

We have but one SPECIES of this genus, viz.

MANGIFERA (*Indica*.) Lin. Sp. 290. *The Mango-tree.* Manga Indica fructu magno reniforma. Raii Hift. 1550.

This tree grows naturally in moft parts of India, as alfo in the Brazils, and fome other parts of the world, where it becomes a large tree ; the wood is brittle, and the bark becomes rough by age ; the leaves are feven or eight inches long, and two or more broad, terminating in points, having feveral tranfverfe veins from the middle rib to the fides, which are oppofite. The flowers are produced in loofe panicles toward the end of the branches, each confifting of 'five fpear-

fhaped petals which fpread open, having five awl-fhaped ftamina the length of the petals, which are fituated between them; the germen at the bottom of the flower afterward becomes a large oblong kidney-fhaped Plumb, inclofing a rough nut of the fame form.

This fruit, when fully ripe, is greatly efteemed by the inhabitants of thofe countries where they grow naturally, or have been tranfplanted; but in Europe we have only the unripe fruit brought over in pickle, which is little better than feveral other fruit when pickled in the fame way : however, from the account given of the ripe fruit, by moft people who have eaten it in the country; it has excited the curiofity of many perfons in Europe to endeavour to procure young plants in their gardens, for which purpofe great quantities of the nuts have been brought to feveral parts of Europe, but without effect; for I have not heard of one plant which has been produced in Europe from the nuts. All thofe which have fallen into my hands have been rotten when received, fo that I am apt to think the vegetative quality of them cannot be long preferved; therefore the only method to obtain the plants in England, is to plant a good quantity of the nuts in a tub of earth in the country where they grow naturally; and when the plants are grown a foot high, to fhip them for England, placing a covering over them to defend them from falt water and the fpray of the fea, being very careful not to let them have much wet in their paffage; as alfo when the fhip arrives in a cold climate, to fcreen the plants from cold, efpecially if it is toward the approach of winter. By carefully obferving thefe rules, the plants may be brought very fafely over, as has been experienced by a plant of this fort, with feveral other forts of plants, which were brought over by Capt. Quick, and are now in good health in the Chelfea garden.

There have been fome plants brought to England before this, which were deftroyed by having too much heat, for this plant will not thrive in a hot-bed of tanners bark; fo that the only way to have them fucceed, is to plant them in pots filled with light kitchen-garden earth, and place them in a dry ftove, where in warm weather they fhould have frefh air daily, and in the winter the air kept up to temperate, as is marked upon the thermometers.

MANIHOT. See JATROPHA.

MANURE.

There are various kinds of Manure, which are now commonly ufed in different parts of England, for enriching of the feveral foils. Some of thefe have been already mentioned under the article of DUNG, fo I fhall not repeat them here, but proceed to take notice of fome other kinds of Manure, which are at prefent neglected by many people, though they might be ufed with equal fuccefs, if not better on many lands, as moft of thofe now commonly in ufe.

Oak bark, after the tanners have ufed it for tanning of leather, when laid in a heap and rotted, is an excellent Manure, efpecially for ftiff cold land; in which one load of this Manure will improve the ground more, and laft longer, than two loads of the richeft dungs; and yet it is very common to fee large heaps of this remaining in the tanners yards for many years, in feveral parts of England, where Manure of other kinds is very fcarce, and often carried to a great diftance. Of late years this tan has been much ufed for hot-beds in feveral parts of England, and is found greatly to exceed horfe dung for that purpofe, the fermentation being moderate and of long continuance; fo that a bed of tan, when rightly made, will continue in a moderate temperature of heat for three or four months; and when the heat begins to decay, if it be ftirred up with a dung fork, and fome frefh tan added to it, the heat will renew again, and laft for fome months, fo that thefe beds are by far the moft kindly for exotic plants; and whatever plants are plunged into thefe beds, if they are permitted to root through the bottom of the pots, they will thrive more in one month after, than they did in four months while

they

they are confined to the pots. I have frequently observed many kinds of plants, which were rooted through the pot into the tan, and have sent forth roots upward of twelve feet each way, in less than three months, and the plants have advanced in proportion; which is a plain indication, that plants are greatly nourished by the rotten tan. After the tan hath been used for a hot-bed, I have spread it on the ground for Manure, and found it has greatly enriched the ground; but it is much better for cold strong land, than for light hot ground, because it is of a warm nature, and will loosen and separate the earth; so that where this Manure hath been used three or four times, it hath made the land very loose which before was strong, and not easy to be wrought. When this Manure is laid upon Grass, it should be done soon after Michaelmas, that the winter rains may wash it into the ground; for if it is laid on in the spring, it will burn the Grass, and instead of improving it, will greatly injure it for that season. Where it is used in Corn land, it should·be spread on the surface before the last ploughing, that it may be turned down for the fibres of the Corn to reach it in the spring; for if it lies too near the surface, it will forward the growth of the Corn in winter: but in the spring, when the nourishment is chiefly wanted to encourage the stems, it will be nearly consumed, and the Corn will receive little advantage from it. Nor will it be proper to have this Manure lie too near the roots of any plants, for when this has happened, I have frequently observed it prejudicial to most plants, but especially to bulbous and tuberose-rooted flowers, which are very subject to rot where it lies near their roots; yet when it is buried just deep enough for the fibres of their roots to reach it in the spring, the flowers have been exceedingly improved by it. And in some places, where this Manure hath been used in kitchen-gardens, it hath greatly improved the vegetables; so that it is to be wondered, that this should not be employed on the land in every country where it can be obtained.

Rotten vegetables of most sorts also will enrich land, so that where other Manure is scarce, these may be used with success. The weeds of ponds, lakes, or ditches, being dragged out before they seed, and laid in heaps to rot, will make good Manure, as will most other sorts of weeds; but wherever any of these are employed, they should be cut down as soon as they begin to flower, for if they are suffered to stand until their seeds are ripe, the land will be stored with weeds, which cannot be easily destroyed; nay, some kinds of weeds, if they are permitted to stand so long as to form their seed, will perfect them after they are cut down, which may be equally prejudicial to the land: therefore the surest method is, to cut them down just as they begin to flower; at which time most sorts of vegetables are in their greatest vigour, being then stronger and fuller of juice, than when their seeds are farther advanced; so that at that time they abound most with salts, and therefore are more proper for the intended purpose. In rotting of these vegetables, it will be proper to mix some earth, mud, or any other such like substance with them, to prevent their taking fire in their fermentation; which they are very subject to, where they are laid in large heaps without any other mixture to prevent it; and it will be also proper to cover the heaps over with earth, mud, or dung, to detain the salts, otherwise many of the finer particles will evaporate in fermenting. When these vegetables are thoroughly rotted, they will form a solid mass, which will cut like butter, and be very full of oil, which will greatly improve land.

In such places where there are neither ponds, lakes, or ditches, to supply these weeds, and the situation being far from the sea (from whence also may be obtained many sorts of weeds for this purpose) there may be many sorts of vegetables sown, in order to plough them into the grounds when they are full grown, to enrich the land; at present those chiefly

used for this purpose are Buck Wheat, Vetches, and Spurry. And in some countries abroad they commonly sow Lupines upon such land as they want to improve, and when they are full grown they mow them down, and plough them into the ground, which they esteem to be good Manure. This is chiefly used in the south of France and in Italy, where some of the sorts of Lupines grow naturally; but these are not proper for this climate, because, if the season should prove cold or wet after the Lupines are sown, they will rot in the ground, so that it is very hazardous to sow them in this country; and there being many other sorts of plants which are hardy, and grow to a much larger size with us than Lupines, they should be preferred to them for this purpose. I have known some land sown pretty thick with Horse-beans which have been mowed down when they were in blossom, and ploughed in for a crop of Wheat, and it hath largely repaid the owner. Almost any of the pulse kind, which grow large, are very proper to be sown for this purpose; and next to these may be sown Mustard, Cole-seed, or any of these large growing plants; which, if cut before they form their seeds, and ploughed in, will greatly enrich the ground.

The refuse of kitchen-gardens, when laid in heaps and rotted, will also afford a good sort of Manure for Corn land; but as this is not to be obtained in any quantity, excepting near great cities, so, in such places, dung being to be had pretty reasonable, the other will not be much sought after.

I have lately been informed of another improvement, which may be of great use in several parts of the kingdom; which is, the mowing down of Fern while it is green and tender, and laying it in heaps to rot, which will make a tolerable Manure for land; and as this is a most troublesome plant in many parts of England, so by frequently mowing, it may be destroyed; and when rotted, a good quantity of this Manure may be obtained, which will more than defray the charges of cutting it down. In some places, where no tan or horse-dung can be obtained, they have cut down Fern and chopped it pretty small, and laid it in a heap to ferment, then have used it for hot-beds, for which purpose it has answered pretty well. The first person who informed me of this, was Mr. Samuel Brewer, a very curious gentleman in gardening, who made several hot-beds of Fern, which, he says, continued their heat for some months; so that he prefers it to dung, where a moderate lasting heat is required.

There are many kinds of weeds which infest the lands in many parts of England, which, if cut down at a proper time and laid to rot, might be used to great advantage for manuring of land; and hereby the weeds may in time be destroyed, and the Manure would more than pay the expence of doing it: but few persons who are employed in husbandry care to go out of their old beaten road to try experiments, even where they are attended with little expence and nothing hazarded; otherwise there is great room to make improvements of this kind, especially in countries where dung, or other common Manure is very scarce; in which places, if some experiments were properly made, of rotting whatever vegetables could be procured in the neighbourhood, it might turn to good account.

The ashes of all kinds of vegetables are an excellent Manure for land, so that where the ground is overrun with bushes, brambles, &c. which are become woody, if they are grubbed up in summer, and spread abroad to dry for a little time, then gently consumed to ashes, and these spread on the land, it will greatly improve it. The method for doing this is already explained under the article of LAND.

Rotten wood, and saw-dust when rotted, is a very good Manure for strong land, because it loosens the parts of the earth and renders it light.

Bones, horns, and other parts of animals, also enrich land greatly, as do decayed fish; so that in some

       places

places where thefe can be eafily obtained, a great improvement may be made of them.

Sea-fand and fhells are in feveral parts of England ufed to great advantage, efpecially in Devonfhire, where they are at the expence of fetching the fand and fhells on horfes backs, twelve or fourteen miles. The land on which they lay this Manure, is a ftrong loam incl'ning to clay; fo that this feparates the parts, and the falts which are contained in the drefling are a very great improvement of their land. Coral, and fuch kinds of ftony plants which grow on the rocks, are filled with falts which are very beneficial to land; but as thefe bodies are hard, the improvement is not the firft or fecond year after they are laid on the ground, becaufe they require time to pulverize them before their falts can mix with the earth to impregnate it. Therefore dreffings of this kind are feldom ufed by tenants, who want to reap the fruit of their labour as foon as poffible. But thefe Manures are much better for cold ftrong land, than for that which is light and fandy. In fome countries, at a great diftance from the fea, have been difcovered great quantities of foffil fhells, which have been dug out of the earth, and ufed as Manure, which have improved the ground a little, efpecially ftrong land: as thefe have little falts, when compared to thofe fhells which are taken from the fhore, therefore where the latter can be obtained, they other are fcarce worth ufing.

Where the land lies near the fea, fo that either fand, fhells, corals, wrecks, or fea-weeds, can be obtained at an eafy expence, they are by far the beft kinds of Manure, becaufe they enrich the land for feveral years; for as their falts are clofely locked up, they are communicated by degrees to the land, as the heat and cold caufes the bodies to pulverize, and fall into fmall parts; fo that where fand and fmaller kinds of fea-weeds are ufed, if they are laid on land in proper quantities it will enrich it for fix or feven years; but fhells, corals, and other hard bodies, will continue many years longer.

In dunging of land, I have frequently obferved in feveral parts of England, but efpecially in Cambridgefhire, a very wrong cuftom continued, by carrying and laying the dung on the land about Midfummer, and fpread abroad perhaps a month or fix weeks before the ground is ploughed; in which time the fun exhales all the goodnefs of the dung, fo that what remains is of little fervice to the land. Therefore when dung or any other Manure is ufed, it fhould not be laid on the ground until the laft time of ploughing, when it fhould be buried as foon as poffible, to prevent the evaporation of the falts. Indeed, where fnells, corals, or any other hard fubftances, are ufed for Manure, if thefe are fpread abroad fome months before the ground is ploughed, the fun, rain, or froft will caufe them to pulverize much fooner than when they are buried and excluded from the air.

The drefling of Grais ground in fummer, foon after the crop of hay is taken off the land, is equally bad; for before Michaelmas the fun will have dried and exhaled moft of the goodnefs, if the drefling is of dung or any other foft Manure, fo that the ground will receive fmall advantage from it; and yet this method is too generally practifed.

MAPLE. See ACER.

MARACOCK. See PASSIFLORA.

MARANTA. Plum. Nov. Gen. 16. tab. 36. Lin. Gen. Plant. 5. Indian Arrow-root.

The CHARACTERS are,

It hath a fmall three-leaved empalement fitting upon the germen; the flower hath one petal, which is of the grinning kind, having an oblong compreffed tube, which is oblique and turned inward; the rim is cut into fix fmall fegments, reprefenting a lip flower, the two fide fegments being the largeft. It has one membranaceous ftamina, appearing like a fegment of the petal, with a linear fummit faftened to the border. It hath a roundifh germen fituated under the flower, fupporting a fimple ftyle the length of the petal, crowned by a three-cornered ftigma.

The germen afterward turns to a roundifh three-cornered capfule with three valves, containing one hard rough feed.

This genus of plants is ranged in the firft fection of Linnæus's firft clafs, intitled Monandria Monogynia, which includes thofe plants whofe flowers have but one ftamina and one ftyle.

The SPECIES are,

1. MARANTA (*Arundinacea*) culmo ramofo. Lin. Sp. 2. *Indian Arrow-root with branching ftalks.* Maranta Arundinacea cannacori folio. Plum. Nov. Gen. 16. *Maranta with a leaf of the Indian flowering Reed.*

2. MARANTA (*Galanga*) culmo fimplici. Lin. Sp. 3. *Indian Arrow-root with a fimple ftalk.* Canna Indica, radice albâ alexipharmica. Sloan. Cat. Jam. 122. *Indian Arrow-root.*

The firft fort was difcovered by Father Plumier in fome of the French fettlements in America, who gave it this name, in honour of one Bartholomew Maranta, an ancient botanift. The feeds of this kind were fent to Europe by the late Dr. William Houftoun, who found the plant growing in plenty near La Vera Cruz in New Spain.

This hath a thick, flefhy, creeping root which is very full of knots, from which arife many fmooth leaves, which are fix or feven inches long, and three broad toward their bafe, leffening toward each end, terminating in points. They are of the confiftence and colour of thofe of the Reed, and ftand upon Reedlike foot-ftalks, which arife immediately from the root; between thefe come out the ftalks, which rife near two feet high; thefe divide upward into two or three fmaller, and are garnifhed at each joint with one leaf of the fame fhape with the lower, but are fmaller. The ends of the ftalks are terminated by a loofe bunch of fmall white flowers, ftanding upon foot-ftalks which are near two inches long. The flowers are cut into fix narrow fegments, which are indented on their edges; thefe fit upon the embryo, which afterward turns to a roundifh three-cornered capfule, inclofing one hard rough feed. It flowers here in June and July.

The other fort was brought from fome of the Spanifh fettlements in America, into the iflands of Barbadoes and Jamaica, where it is cultivated in their gardens as a medicinal plant, it being a fovereign remedy to cure the bite of wafps, and to extract the poifon of the Manchineel-tree. The Indians apply the root to expel the poifon of their arrows, which they ufe with great fuccefs. They take up the roots, and after cleanfing them from dirt, they mafh them, and apply it as a poultice to the wounded part, which draws out the poifon and heals the wound. It will alfo ftop a gangrene, if it is applied before it is gone too far, fo that it is a very valuable plant.

This fort is very like the firft, but has a fingle ftalk; the flowers are fmaller, and the fegments of the petals are entire, in which their principal difference confifts; it flowers alfo at the fame time.

Thefe plants being natives of a warm country, are very tender, and therefore will not live in this climate, unlefs they are preferved in ftoves. They may be propagated by their creeping roots, which fhould be parted in the middle of March, juft before they begin to pufh out new leaves. Thefe roots fhould be planted in pots filled with light rich earth, and plunged into a moderate hot-bed of tanners bark, obferving now and then to refrefh them with water; but it muft not be given to them in large quantities, for too much moifture will foon rot the roots, when they are in an unactive ftate. When the green leaves appear above ground, the plants will require more frequently to be watered, and they fhould have free circulation to them every day, in proportion to the warmth of the feafon, and the heat of the bed in which they are placed. As the plants advance in ftrength, they fhould have a greater fhare of air, but they muft conftantly remain in the ftove plunged in the tan, otherwife they will not thrive; for when the pots are placed on fhelves in the ftove, the moifture paffes too foon from the [...]

which generally spread on the sides and bottoms of the pots, so that the plants do not receive much nourishment from the water. But where they are constantly kept in the tanners bark, and have proper air and moisture, they will thrive, so as from a small root to fill the pot in which it was planted, in one summer. About Michaelmas the first sort will begin to decay, and in a short time after the leaves will die to the ground, but the pots must be continued all the winter in the bark-bed, otherwise the roots will perish; for although they are in an unactive state, yet they will not keep very long from shrinking, when taken out of the ground; and if the pots are taken out of the tan, and placed in any dry part of the stove, the roots often shrivel and decay; but when they are continued in the tan-bed they should have but little water given to them when their leaves are decayed, lest it rot them. The first sort doth flower constantly in July or August, and will often produce ripe seeds in England; but the second sort doth not flower so constant, nor do the flowers appear so conspicuous, being very small and of a short duration. This sort never hath produced any seeds in England, nor could I ever observe any rudiment of a seed-vessel succeeding the flower. The green leaves abide on this sort most part of the winter, seldom decaying till February; and sometimes will continue green until fresh leaves come up, and thrust the old ones off; in which particular there is a more remarkable difference between the two sorts, than can be observed in the face of plants.

MARJORAM. See ORIGANUM.

MARLE is a kind of clay, which is become fatter, and of a more enriching quality, by a better fermentation, and by its having lain so deep in the earth as not to have spent or weakened its fertilizing quality by any product.
Marle is supposed to be much of the nature of chalk, and is believed to be fertile from its salt and oily quality; and that it contracts its salts from the air, and for that reason is the better the longer it is exposed to it.
Marles are of different qualities in different counties of England. There are reckoned to be four sorts of Marles in Sussex, a gray, a blue, a yellow, and a red; of these the blue is accounted the best, the yellow the next, and the gray the next to that; and as for the red, that is the least valuable.
The Marle in Sussex is most like fullers earth, and therefore must certainly be the fattest, whereas that in the north country runs much upon the loam.
In Cheshire they reckon six sorts of Marle:
1. The cowshut Marle, which is of a brownish colour, with blue veins in it, and little lumps of chalk or lime stone; it is commonly found under clay, or low black land, seven or eight feet deep, and is very hard to dig.
2. Stone, slate, or flag Marle, which is a kind of soft stone, or rather slate, of a blue or bluish colour, that will easily dissolve with frost or rain. This is found near rivers and the sides of hills, and is a very lasting sort of Marle.
In Staffordshire they esteem the dice or slate Marle better than the clay Marle, and reckon the blue best for arable land, and the gray for pasture.
3. Peat Marle, or delving Marle, which is close, strong, and very fat, of a brown colour, and is found on the sides of hills, and in wet boggy grounds, which have a light sand in them about two feet or a yard deep. This is accounted the strongest of all Marles, and is very good for sandy land, but the land must have a double quantity laid on.
4. Clay Marle; this resembles clay, and is pretty near akin to it, but is fatter, and sometimes mixed with chalk stones.
5. Steel Marle, which lies commonly in the bottom of pits that are dug, and is of itself apt to break into cubical bits; this is sometimes under sandy land.
6. Paper Marle, which resembles leaves or pieces of brown paper, but something of a lighter colour; this

lies near coals. This sort is less esteemed, it being hard to be got.
The properties of any sorts of Marles, and by which the goodness of them may be best known, are better judged of by their purity and uncompoundedness, than their colour: as if it will break in pieces like dice, or into thin flakes, or is smooth like lead ore, and is without a mixture of gravel or sand; if it will shake like slate stones, and shatter after wet, or will turn to dust when it has been exposed to the sun: or will not hang and stick together when it is thoroughly dry, like rough clay; but is fat and tender, and will open the land it is laid on, and not bind; it may be taken for granted, that it will be beneficial to it.
Some advise to try the goodness of Marle, by putting some of it in a glass of water; and they account it to be good, if it be so tender, that the lumps break, and dissolve as soon as it comes to the bottom; they also reckon it a good sign, if it sparkle in the water, and feel fat between the fingers; but the surest sign of its goodness is, if it dissolve by wet or frost. The strength of Marle may also be known, by putting a lump of it in a glass of good vinegar, where, if the fermentation is great, it is a sure sign of the goodness of the Marle.
Some approve of marling land shallow, because they say, it is apt to work downwards; others of laying it in deep at first, because the sun wastes the fatness of it.
Some recommend Marles for the improving of sandy loose land, but the surest way to know what lands it will best suit with, is to try with a little of it on lands supposed to be of a contrary nature to it.
Marles do not make so good an improvement of lands the first year as afterwards.
Some advise, first to burn the Marle before it is laid on the lands; which if it be done, one load will go as far as five.
The quantity of Marle ought to be in proportion to the depth of the earth, for over-marling has often proved of worse consequence than under-marling, especially where the land is strong; for by laying it in too great quantities, or often repeating the marling, the land has become so strong, and bound so closely, as to detain the wet like a dish, so that the owners have been obliged to drain the ground at a great expence, and have often been obliged to lower their rents; but in sandy land there can be no danger in laying on a great quantity, or repeating it often, for it is one of the best dressings for such land.

MARRUBIASTRUM, Bastard Horehound. See SIDERITIS.

MARRUBIUM. Tourn. Inst. R. H. 192. tab. 91. Lin. Gen. Plant. 640. Pseudodictamnus. Tourn. 188. tab. 89. Lin. Gen. Plant. 640. [some derive the name of מרוב, Heb. Marrob, i. e. bitter juice; others from the Latin word Marcidum, because the leaves of this plant are so wrinkled, that they appear to be withering.] Horehound.

The CHARACTERS are,
The empalement of the flower is funnel-shaped, of one leaf, and equal at the brim, which spreads open. The flower is of the lip or grinning kind, with a cylindrical tube opening at the brim, where it is divided into two lips, the upper being very narrow and acute, the under broad, reflexed, and cut into three segments, the middle one is broad and indented. It has four stamina, which are under the upper lip, two of which are a little longer than the other, terminated by simple summits. It hath a four-pointed germen, supporting a slender style of the same length, and situated with the stamina, crowned by a bifid stigma. The germen afterward turns to four oblong seeds, sitting in the empalement.
This genus of plants is ranged in the first section of Linnæus's fourteenth class, intitled Didynamia Gymnospermia, which includes those plants whose flowers have two long and two short stamina, which are succeeded by naked seeds sitting in the empalement.

The

The Species are,

1. Marrubium (*Vulgare*) dentibus calycinis fetaceis uncinatis. Hort. Cliff. 312. *Horebound with hooked brifly indentures to the empalement.* Marrubium album vulgare. C. B. P. 230. *Common white Horebound.*

2. Marrubium (*Peregrinum*) foliis ovato-lanceolatis ferratis, calycum denticulis fetaceis. Hort. Cliff. 311. *Horebound with oval, fpear-fhaped, fawed leaves, and brifly indentures to the empalement.* Marrubium album latifolium peregrinum. C. B. P. 230. *Broad-leaved, foreign, white Horebound.*

3. Marrubium (*Creticum*) foliis lanceolatis dentatis, verticillis minioribus, dentibus calycinis fetaceis erectis. *Horebound with fpear-fhaped indented leaves, fmaller whorls, and erect brifly indentures to the empalements.* Marrubium album anguftifolium peregrinum. C.B.P. 230. *Narrow-leaved, foreign, white Horebound.*

4. Marrubium (*Abyffon*) foliis cuneiformibus, quinque verticillis involucro deftitutis. Hort. Cliff. 311. *Horebound with wedge-fhaped plaited leaves, with five indentures, and the whorls deftitute of covers.* Marrubium alyffon dictum, foliis profundè incifis. H. L. *Horebound, called Madwort, with leaves which are deeply cut on their fides.*

5. Marrubium (*Supinum*) dentibus calycinis fetaceis rectis villofis. Hort. Cliff. 312. *Horebound with hairy, erect, brifly indentures to the empalement.* Marrubium Hifpanicum fupinum, foliis fericeis argenteis. Tourn. 193. *Low Spanifh Horebound with filken filver-coloured leaves.*

6. Marrubium (*Candidiffimum*) foliis fubovatis lanatis fupernè emarginato-crenatis, denticulis calycinis fubulatis. Hort. Cliff. 312. *Horebound with woolly leaves almoft oval, the upper parts of which are indentd and crenated, with awl-fhaped indentures to the empalements.* Marrubium album candidiffimum & villofum. Tourn. Cor. 1. *Whiteft and villofe Horebound.*

7. Marrubium (*Hifpanicum*) calycum limbis patentibus, denticulis acutis. Hort. Cliff. 312. *Horebound with fpreading borders to the empalement, and acute indentures.* Marrubium album rotundifolium Hifpanicum. Par. Bat. 201. *Round-leaved Spanifh Horebound.*

8. Marrubium (*Crifpum*) calycum limbis planis villofis, foliis orbiculatis rugofis, caule herbaceo. *Horebound with a plain hairy border to the empalement, round rough leaves, and an herbaceous ftalk.* Pfeudodictamnus Hifpanicus, foliis crifpis & rugofis. Tourn. Inft. 188. *Spanifh Baftard Dittany, with rough curled leaves.*

9. Marrubium (*Suffruticofum*) calycum limbis planis villofis, foliis cordatis rugofis incanis, caule fuffruticofo. *Horebound with the border of the empalement plain and hoary, heart-fhaped, rough leaves, and a fhrubby ftalk.* Pfeudodictamnus Hifpanicus, ampliffimo folio candicante & villofo. Tourn. Inft. R. H. 118. *Spanifh Baftard Dittany, with a very large hoary leaf.*

10. Marrubium (*Pfeudodictamnus*) calycum limbis planis villofis, foliis cordatis, caule fruticofo. Hort. Cliff. 312. *Horebound with a plain hairy border to the empalement, heart-fhaped leaves, and a fhrubby ftalk.* Pfeudodictamnus verticillatus inodorus. C. B. P. 232. *Whorled unfavoury Baftard Dittany.*

11. Marrubium (*Acetabulofum*) calycum limbis tubo longioribus membranaceis, angulis majoribus rotundatis. Lin. Sp. Plant. 584. *Horebound with a membranaceous rim to the empalement longer than the tube, and larger rounder angles* Pfeudodictamnus acetabulis Moluccæ. C. B. P. 222. *Baftard Dittany, with a pan or hollow of Molucca Baum.*

The firft fort is the Prafium, or white Horehound of the fhops. This grows naturally in moft parts of England, fo is feldom propagated in gardens. It hath a ligneous fibrous root, from which come out many fquare ftalks a foot or more in length, which branch out upward, and are garnifhed with hoary roundifh leaves, indented on the edges, placed oppofite. The flowers grow in very thick whorls round the ftalks at each joint; they are fmall, white, and of the lip kind, ftanding in ftiff hoary empalements, cut into ten parts at the top, which end in ftiff briftles; thefe are fucceeded by four oblong black feeds fitting

in the empalement. It flowers in June, and the feeds ripen in autumn.

The fecond fort grows naturally in Italy and Sicily; this rifes with fquare ftalks near three feet high, which branch much more than the firft; the leaves are rounder, whiter, and ftand farther afunder; the whorls of flowers are not fo large, but the flowers have longer tubes.

The third fort grows naturally in Spain and Portugal; this rifes with flender hoary ftalks near three feet high; the leaves are very hoary, much longer and narrower than thofe of the fecond; the whorls of flowers are fmaller, and the brifly indentures of the empalement are longer and erect; the whole plant has an agreeable flavour.

The fourth fort grows naturally in Spain and Italy; this is a biennial plant, whofe ftalks are about the fame length as thofe of the firft; the leaves are wedge-fhaped, hoary, and obtufely indented; the whorls of flowers are fmall, and have no covers. The flowers ftand loofer in the whorls, and the cuts of the empalement end in very ftiff prickles, which fpread open; the flowers are purple, and larger than thofe of the firft fort.

The fifth fort grows naturally in the iflands of the Archipelago; the ftalks of this are feldom above eight or nine inches long, covered with a foft hoary down; the leaves are fmall, roundifh, and very foft to the touch; they are hoary, and indented on the edges. The whorls of flowers are fmall, very downy, and white; the flowers are fmall and white.

The fixth fort grows naturally in Spain; this hath ftalks about the fame length as the firft; the leaves are nearly oval, woolly, and crenated toward the top, and the empalement of the flowers are awl-fhaped.

The feventh fort grows naturally in Iftria, from whence I received the feeds. The ftalks of this grow more erect than thofe of the common fort; the leaves are rounder and more fawed on the edges; the empalement of the flowers fpread open, ending in acute fegments. The flowers are like thofe of the common fort; the whole plant is very hoary.

The eighth fort grows naturally in Spain and Sicily; this fends out many ftiff roundifh ftalks, which rife more than two feet high, covered with a white cottony down; the leaves are almoft round, rough on their upper fide, and woolly on their under; the whorls of flowers are large, the borders of the empalement are flat and hairy; the tube of the flower is fcarce fo long as the empalement, fo the two lips are but juft vifible.

The ninth fort grows naturally in Spain; the ftalks of this are fhrubby, and rife near three feet high, dividing into fmall branches; the leaves are heart-fhaped and rough on their upper fide, but hoary on their under; the whorls of flowers are large, the borders of the empalements flat and hairy; the tube of the flower is longer, and the flowers are larger than thofe of the former fort; they are of a pale purple colour, and their upper lips are erect.

The tenth fort grows naturally in Sicily, and the Iflands of the Archipelago. This rifes with a fhrubby ftalk two feet high, which divides into many branches, garnifhed with fmall heart-fhaped leaves, fitting pretty clofe to the ftalks: the whorls of flowers are not fo large as thofe of the two former forts. The rim of the empalements are flat. The flowers are white, and the whole plant is very hoary.

The eleventh fort grows naturally in Crete; this hath very hairy ftalks which rife about two feet high, garnifhed with heart-fhaped leaves, which are rough on their upper fide, but hoary on their under. The whorls of flowers are large, the border of the empalements flat, and cut into many fegments, which are membranaceous, angular, and rounded at the top. The flowers are fmall, of a pale purple colour, but fcarce appear out of their empalements, and their upper lips are erect.

The

The firſt ſort is what the College of Phyſicians has directed to be uſed in medicine. The leaves and tops of the plants are eſteemed hot and dry, pectoral, and good to free the lungs from thick viſcid phlegm, and thereby to help old coughs, eſpecially in cold moiſt conſtitutions, the juice being made into a ſyrup with ſugar or honey; they open obſtructions of the liver and ſpleen, and are very ſerviceable againſt the dropſy, jaundice, green ſickneſs, and obſtructions of the catamenia, and ſuppreſſion of the lochia, and other diſtempers of the female ſex, for which few herbs go beyond this. The officinal preparation is the ſyrupus de Praſſio.

The fourth ſort is ſuppoſed to be Galen's Madwort; this was by the antients greatly recommended for its efficacy in curing of madneſs, and ſome few of the moderns have preſcribed it in the ſame diſorder, but at preſent it is ſeldom uſed; it is a biennial plant, which generally periſhes after it hath perfected ſeeds. All theſe plants are preſerved in botanic gardens for the ſake of variety, but there are not above two of the ſorts which are cultivated in other gardens; theſe are the tenth and eleventh ſorts, whoſe ſtalks are ſhrubby; the plants are very hoary, ſo make a variety when intermixed with other plants; theſe very rarely produce ſeeds in England, ſo are propagated by cuttings, which, if planted in a ſhady border the middle of April, will take root pretty freely.

They are ſomewhat tender, ſo in very ſevere winters are killed, unleſs they are ſcreened from the hard froſts, eſpecially thoſe plants which grow in good ground, where they grow luxuriant in ſummer, ſo their branches are more replete with juice, and very liable to ſuffer by cold; but when they are in a poor dry rubbiſh, the roots will be ſhort, firm, and dry, ſo are ſeldom injured by cold, and will continue much longer than thoſe in better ground.

The other ſorts are eaſily propagated by ſeeds, which ſhould be ſown on a bed of poor earth in the ſpring, and when the plants come up they muſt be kept clean from weeds; and where they are too cloſe they ſhould be thinned, leaving them a foot and a half aſunder, that their branches may have room to ſpread; after this they require no other culture; they may alſo be propagated by cuttings, in the ſame manner as the other two ſorts. If theſe plants are upon a dry poor ſoil, they will live ſeveral years, but in rich land they ſeldom laſt above three or four.

MARRUBIUM NIGRUM. See **BALLOTE.**

MARTAGON. See **LILIUM.**

MARTYNIA. Houſt. Gen. Nov. Martyn. Dec. 1. 42. [This name was given by the late Dr. William Houſtoun to this genus of plants, which he diſcovered in America, in honour of his friend Mr. John Martyn, who was Profeſſor of Botany at Cambridge.]

The CHARACTERS are,

The empalement of the flower is cut into five parts, three of them are erect, and two reflexed. The flower hath one petal, which is bell-ſhaped, with a large ſwelling tube, at the baſe of which is ſituated a gibbous nectarium. The rim of the petal is cut ſlightly into five obtuſe ſegments, two of which are turned upward, the other three downward, repreſenting a lip flower. It hath four ſlender incurved ſtamina, which are inflexed into each other, terminated by ſummits, which are connected together. It hath an oblong germen ſituated under the flower, ſupporting a ſhort ſtyle, crowned by a plain ſtigma. The empalement afterward turns to an oblong gibbous capſule, which divides into two parts, including a hard nut, ſhaped like the body of a ſtag beetle, with two incurved ſtrong horns at the end, having four cells, two of which are generally barren, the other have one oblong ſeed in each.

This genus of plants is ranged in the ſecond ſection of Linnæus's fourteenth claſs, which includes the plants whoſe flowers have two long and two ſhort ſtamina, and the ſeeds are included in a capſule.

The SPECIES are,

1. MARTYNIA (*Annua*) caule ramoſo, foliis angulatis. Lin. Sp. Plant. 618. *Martynia with a branching ſtalk and angular leaves.* Martynia annua villoſa & viſ-

coſa, folio ſubrotundo, flore magno rubro. Houſt. *Annual, hairy, viſcous Martynia, with a roundiſh leaf, and a large red flower.*

2. MARTYNIA (*Perennis*) caule ſimplici, foliis ſerratis. Lin. Sp. Plant. 618. *Martynia with a ſingle ſtalk and ſawed leaves.* Martynia foliis ſerratis. Lin. Hort. Cliff. *Martynia with ſawed leaves.*

3. MARTYNIA (*Louiſiana*) caule decumbente ramoſa, foliis integris fructibus longiſſimis. *Martynia with a decumbent branching ſtalk, entire leaves, and very long fruit.* The firſt of theſe plants was diſcovered by the late Dr. William Houſtoun, near La Vera Cruz, in New Spain, from whence he ſent the ſeeds into England, which ſucceeded very well in the Phyſic Garden at Chelſea; and in the year 1731, ſeveral of the plants were raiſed, which produced their beautiful flowers, and perfected their ſeed, from whence ſeveral plants were raiſed the ſucceeding year.

This riſes with a ſtrong, herbaceous, hairy ſtalk near three feet high, which divides upward into three or four large branches, garniſhed with oblong oval leaves, cut into angles on their ſides; they are five inches long, and three inches and a half broad at their baſe, where they are broadeſt, ending in obtuſe points; they are hairy, and very viſcous, ſticking to the fingers if handled. The flowers are produced in ſhort ſpikes from the forks of the branches, and alſo at their tops; they are ſhaped like thoſe of the Foxglove, but are of a paler purple colour; theſe are ſucceeded by oblong oval capſules, which are thick, tough, and clammy; theſe, when ripe, divide into two parts, leaving a large hard nut hanging on the plant, about the ſize, and much of the ſame form, as the ſtag beetle, with two ſtrong crooked horns at the end. The nut has two deep longitudinal furrows on the ſides, and ſeveral ſmaller croſſing each other in the middle. It is ſo hard, that it is with difficulty cut open without injuring of the ſeeds: within are four oblong cells, two of which have generally a ſingle oblong ſeed in each, but the other two are abortive. If the plants are brought forward in the ſpring, they will begin to ſhew their flowers in July, which are firſt produced at the diviſion of the branches; and afterward at the extremity of each branch, ſo there will be a ſucceſſion of flowers on the ſame plant till the end of October, when the plants decay.

The ſecond ſort was diſcovered by Mr. Robert Millar, growing naturally about Carthagena in New Spain, from whence he ſent the ſeeds to Europe; this hath a perennial root and an annual ſtalk, which decays every autumn, and new ones ariſe in the ſpring. The roots of this plant are thick, fleſhy, and divided into knots, which are ſcaly, ſomewhat like thoſe of Toothwort; theſe ſend up ſeveral ſtalks, which grow about a foot high; they are thick, ſucculent, and of a purpliſh colour, garniſhed with oblong thick leaves, whoſe baſe ſits cloſe to the ſtalk; they are ſawed on their edges, rough on their upper ſide, where they are of a dark green, but their under ſide is purpliſh. The ſtalk is terminated by a ſhort ſpike of blue flowers, which are bell-ſhaped, and do not ſpread open at the rim ſo much as the former ſort; theſe uſually appear in July or Auguſt, but are not ſucceeded by ſeeds in England.

The firſt ſort, being an annual plant, is only propagated by ſeed, which ſhould be ſown in pots filled with light rich earth, and plunged into a hot-bed of tanners bark, where (if the earth is duly watered to promote the vegetation of the ſeed) the plants will appear in about three weeks or a month, and will grow pretty faſt if the bed is warm; they ſhould therefore be tranſplanted in a little time after they come up, each into a ſeparate pot filled with light rich earth, and then plunged into the hot-bed again, obſerving to water them well, as alſo to ſhade them from the ſun until they have taken new root; after which time they ſhould have a large ſhare of freſh air admitted to them in warm weather, by raiſing the glaſſes of the hot-bed every day: with this management the plants will make great progreſs, ſo as to fill the pots with their roots in about a month or six weeks time, when they should be shifted into pots about a foot diameter at the top, which should be filled with light rich earth, and then plunged into the hot-bed in the bark-stove, where they should be allowed room, because they put out many side branches, and will grow three feet high or more, according to the warmth of the bed; and the care which is taken to supply them constantly with water; and should be constantly kept in the tan-bed, giving them plenty of free air at all times when the weather is warm, but they will not bear to be exposed abroad in this country; when these plants thrive well they will send out many side branches, which will all of them produce small spikes of flowers; but it is only from the first spike of flowers that good seeds can be expected in this country, so that particular care should be taken, that none of these are pulled off or destroyed, because it is very difficult to obtain good seeds here; and I believe few of those that are produced on the side branches in the natural country of their growth, are duly ripened; for I have received a great quantity of these seeds from abroad, which have appeared to be very good, and yet few of them have grown.

The seeds of these plants have a strong green covering on them, as thick as the outer covering of an Almond, and when the seeds are ripe, the covering opens, and lets the seeds fall, in the same manner as the covering of Almonds, Walnuts, &c. In each covering there is one hard nut, in shape somewhat like a beetle, having two sharp crooked horns at one end. This nut contains four embryos, but there are seldom more than two seeds which are perfect in any of them. However, when they are sown, the whole nut must be planted, for it is so hard, that it is almost impossible to take out the seeds without spoiling them; so where there are two plants produced from the same nut, they are easily separated, especially if they are transplanted while young. These seeds will continue good for some years, for I saved a pretty large quantity of them in the year 1734, part of which I sowed the following year, but had not one plant produced from them; the remainder of the seeds I divided, and sowed some of them every succeeding year, without any success, until the year 1738, when I sowed all the seeds I had left, from which I had one plant produced; so that if the seeds are good, it is evident they will grow when they are four years old; therefore, whenever we receive good seeds from abroad, or save any in this country which are perfectly ripened, it will be proper to preserve some of them for a year or two, lest a bad season should happen, when the plants may not perfect their seeds; so that if this precaution be not taken, the species may be lost in Europe.

The second sort dies to the root every winter, and rises again the succeeding spring; this must be constantly preserved in the stove, and plunged into the bark-bed, otherwise it will not thrive in this country. During the winter season, when the plants are decayed, they should have but little water given to them, for at that time it will rot the roots. In the middle of March, just before the plants begin to shoot, is the proper season to transplant and part the roots, when they should be planted into pots of a middle size, filled with light rich earth, and then plunged into the bark-bed, which should at this time be renewed with some fresh tan. When the plants come up, they must be frequently refreshed with water, but it must not be given to them in large quantities, lest it rot their tender roots; and as the warmth of the season increases, it will be proper to admit a large share of fresh air, which will greatly strengthen the plants; they must also be placed in the tan-bed, where they are not over-hung, or shaded by other plants; nor should they be shifted or transplanted when they are in leaf, for that will prevent their flowering. As the roots of this plant increase very fast, there is no necessity for using other methods to propagate it; otherwise

the shoots of the young stalks will take root, if they are planted in pots filled with light earth, and plunged into a hot-bed during any of the summer months. The third sort grows naturally in Louisiana, from whence the seeds were brought to France. This is an annual plant, having a succulent viscous stalk, which divides into many branches; these thick succulent stalks become too weighty for the stalk to support them, whereby the stalk generally is brought to the ground, unless it is well supported: the leaves are large, viscous, and hairy; some of them are cut into angles, but for the most part they are entire, five or six inches long, and four broad in the middle. The flowers are produced from the forks of the stalk in short spikes; they are of a pale red colour, and in shape and size like those of the first sort; they are succeeded by fruit four or five inches long, having a thick green cover, which parts and falls off when ripe, leaving a rough beetle-shaped vessel, having two very long horns at the end, opening in two parts, containing several oval seeds, covered with a black skin, which must be taken off before the seeds are sown.

This being an annual plant, should be brought forward in the spring, by sowing the seeds on a hot-bed the latter end of March; and when the plants come up, they should be treated almost in the same manner as the first, with this difference only, that being more hardy than the first, the plants should have more air admitted to them, to prevent their drawing up weak; nor should they have too much water in summer, which is apt to rot their succulent stems before the seeds are perfected.

MARVEL OF PERU. See Mirabilis.

MARUM. See Teucrium.

MARUM VULGARE. See Satureja.

MARYGOLD. See Calendula.

MARYGOLD (AFRICAN.) See Tagetes.

MARYGOLD (FIG.) See Mesembryanthemum.

MARYGOLD (FRENCH.) See Tagetes.

MASTERWORT. See Imperatoria.

MASTICHINA. See Satureja.

MATRICARIA. Tourn. Inst. R. H. 493. tab. 281. Lin. Gen. Plant. 867. [so called from the matrix, because this plant is very good against diseases of the womb; and for the same reason it is called Parthenium, of Παρθένος, a virgin.] Feverfew; in French, *Matricaire*.

The Characters are,

It hath a compound flower. The ray, or border, is composed of many female half florets, and the disk, which is hemispherical, of hermaphrodite florets; these are included in one common hemispherical empalement, composed of linear scales, nearly equal. The female half florets are tongue-shaped, and indented in three parts at the end; these have a naked germen, supporting a slender style, terminated by two twisted stigmas. The hermaphrodite florets are tubulous, funnel-shaped, and cut into five parts at the brim, which spread open; they have each five hairy short stamina, terminated by cylindrical summits, and an oblong naked germen, with a slender style, crowned by a bifid spreading stigma. The germen of both turn to single, oblong, naked seeds.

This genus of plants is ranged in the second section of Linnæus's nineteenth class, which includes the plants with compound flowers, whose stamina and styles are connected, and the florets are all fruitful.

The Species are,

1. Matricaria (*Parthenium*) foliis compositis planis, foliolis ovatis incisis, pedunculis ramosis. Hort. Cliff. 416. *Feverfew with plain compounded leaves, whose lobes are oval and cut, having branching foot-stalks.* Matricaria vulgaris, seu sativa. C. B. P. 133. *Common, or Garden Feverfew.*

2. Matricaria (*Maritima*) receptaculis hemisphæricis, foliis bipinnatis subcarnosis, suprà convexis, subtus carinatis. Lin. Sp. Plant. 891. *Feverfew with hemispherical receptacles, doubly winged leaves, which are fleshy, and convex on their upper side, but keel-shaped below.* Chamæmelum maritimum perenne humilius, foliis brevioribus

brevioribus craffis obfcurè virentibus. Raii Syn. Ed.
3. p. 186. *Dwarf, perennial, maritime Chamomile, with
fhort, thick, dark green leaves.*

3. MATRICARIA (*Indica*) foliis' ovatis finuatis angulis
ferratis acutis. *Feverfew with oval, finuated, angular,
acutely-fawed leaves.* Matricaria latiore folio, flore
pleno. Mor. Hift. 3. p. 33.

4. MATRICARIA (*Argentea*) foliis bipinnatis, pedunculis
folitariis, Hort. Cliff. 415. *Feverfew with winged
leaves, and fingle foot-flalks to the flowers.* Chamæmelum Orientale incanum, Millefolium folio. Tourn.
Cor. 37.

5. MATRICARIA (*Americana*) foliis lineari-lanceolatis integerrimis, pedunculis unifloris. *Feverfew with entire
fpear-fhaped leaves, and foot-flalks with one flower.*

The firft fort is the common Feverfew, which is directed to be ufed in medicine. It grows naturally in
lanes, and upon the fide of banks in many parts of
England, but is frequently cultivated in the phyfic-
gardens to fupply the markets; this is commonly a
biennial plant, which decays foon after it has perfected feeds. The root of this plant is compofed of
a great number of fibres, which fpread wide on every
fide. The ftalks rife upward of two feet high; they
are round, ftiff, and ftriated, branching out on every
fide. The leaves are compofed of feven lobes, which
are cut into many obtufe fegments; they are of a
yellowifh green colour. The ftalks and branches are
terminated by the flowers, which are difpofed almoft
in the form of loofe umbels, each flower ftanding
upon a feparate foot-ftalk, about two inches long.
The flowers are compofed of feveral fhort rays, which
are white, like thofe of the Chamomile, furrounding
a yellow difk, compofed of hermaphrodite florets,
which form a hemifphere; thefe are inclofed in one
common fcaly empalement, and are fucceeded by oblong, angular, naked feeds. It flowers in June, and
the feeds ripen in autumn. The whole plant has a
ftrong unpleafant odour. The leaves and flowers of
this are ufed in medicine, and are particularly appro-
priated to the female fex, being of great fervice in all
cold flatulent diforders of the womb, and hyfteric affections, procuring the catamenia, and expelling the
birth and fecundines.

The following varieties of this plant are preferved in
botanic gardens, many of which are pretty conftant,
if care is taken in faving the feeds; but where the feeds
of thefe plants has been fuffered to fcatter, it will be
almoft impoffible to preferve the varieties without
mixture; but if the feeds are fown upon a frefh fpot
of ground, where there has not grown any of the
plants before, I am inclinable to believe the feeds
will produce the fame plants as thofe they were taken
from; however, as they are fuppofed to be only varieties, fo I fhall only juft infert them here, for the
ufe of thofe who are curious in collecting the varieties.

1. Feverfew with very double flowers.
2. Feverfew with double flowers, whofe borders, or
rays are plain, and the difk fiftular.
3. Feverfew with very fmall rays.
4. Feverfew with very fhort fiftular florets.
5. Feverfew with naked heads, having no rays or border.
6. Feverfew with naked fulphur-coloured heads.
7. Feverfew with elegant curled leaves.

Thefe plants are all propagated by their feeds, which
fhould be fown in March upon a bed of light earth,
and, when they are come up, they fhould be tranfplanted out into nurfery-beds, at about eight inches
afunder, where they may remain till the middle of
May, when they may be taken up, with a ball of
earth to their roots, and planted in the middle of
large borders, where they will flower in July and Auguft; and, if the autumn be favourable, will produce
ripe feeds the fame year. But it is not advifeable to
permit them to feed, which often weakens and decays the roots; therefore, when their flowers are paft,
you fhould cut down their ftems, which will caufe
them to pufh out frefh heads, whereby the roots may
he maintained.

When the different varieties of thefe plants are intermixed with other plants of the fame growth, they
make a handfome appearance during the feafon of
flowering, which commonly continues a full month,
or more, which renders them more valuable. But as
their roots feldom abide more than two, or at moft
three years, frefh plants would be raifed from feeds
to fupply their places; for although they may be
propagated by parting their roots either in fpring or
autumn, yet thefe feldom make fo good plants as
thofe obtained from feeds; but the fecond variety feldom produces any good feeds, therefore that muft be
propagated in this manner, or by planting cuttings
in the fpring or fummer months, which will take
root, and make good plants.

The fecond fort grows naturally near the fea, in feveral parts of England. I have obferved it upon the
Suffex coaft in great plenty, from whence I brought
the plants, which were of no longer duration in the
garden than two years, though in their native foil they
may continue longer. The ftalks of this plant branch
out pretty much, and fpread near the ground; they
are garnifhed with dark green leaves, which are compofed of many double wings, or pinnæ, like thofe of
the common Chamomile, but are much thicker in
fubftance; they have their edges turned backward, fo
are convex on their upper furface, and concave on
their under. The flowers are white, like thofe of
the common Chamomile, and are difpofed almoft in
the form of an umbel; they appear in July, and the
feeds ripen in autumn.

This plant is feldom cultivated but in botanic gardens for variety. It may be propagated by feeds,
which may be fown either in autumn, foon after they
are ripe, or in the fpring, upon a bed of common
earth, in almoft any fituation; and when the plants
come up, they will require no other care but to thin
them where they are too clofe, and keep them clean
from weeds.

The third fort grows naturally in many parts of India, I received it from Nimpu, where it grows plentifully; this plant rifes a foot and a half high, dividing
into many branches, garnifhed with angular oval
leaves, which are acutely fawed on their edges, and
are of a pale colour; the flowers are produced on
foot-ftalks which arife from the wings of the leaves,
and alfo terminate the branches; thefe are, in all I
have yet feen, very double, and full as large as thofe
of the double fort before-mentioned; thefe appear in
July, and in favourable feafons are fucceeded by feeds
which ripen late in the autumn.

This fort is propagated by feeds, which fhould be
fown in the fpring upon a moderate hot-bed, and
when the plants come up, they muft be treated in the
manner already directed for the Chryfanthemum Coronarium, with which culture they will thrive and
flower very well.

The fourth fort grows naturally in the eaft; this fort
rifes a foot high, having winged leaves of a filver
colour, which are for the moft part placed oppofite,
the foot-ftalks of the flowers arife fingle from the fide
of the branches, each fupporting one white flower.
This flowers in July, and in warm feafons will fometimes perfect feeds in autumn.

The feeds of this fort fhould be fown in April, on a
bed of light earth, in a good expofure; and when the
plants are grown of a proper fize to remove, they
fhould be planted in the borders of the flower-garden; where, if they are kept clean from weeds, they
will flower and perfect their feeds.

The fifth fort grows naturally in North America;
this is a perennial plant, whofe ftalks and leaves decay
in the autumn, and new ones come out again in the
fpring; the ftalks rife a foot and a half high, and divide upward into feveral forked branches; at each of
thefe divifions is placed one linear fpear-fhaped leaf
about two inches long, and a quarter of an inch
broad, entire on the edges, and of a deep green.
The branches are terminated by fingle foot-ftalks,
each fupporting one blue flower, very like thofe of
fome kind of Starwort; but the empalement being
fcaly,

scaly, and the seeds having no down, occasions its being here placed. The flowers appear in July and August, and the seeds ripen in the autumn.

This is propagated by seeds, which, if sown in the autumn, soon after they are ripe, will more certainly succeed than when sown in the spring; they should be sown in the full ground, and when the plants are fit to remove, if they are planted in the borders of the flower-garden, they will continue some years without protection, and annually produce flowers and seeds.

MATTED ROOTS are such as are entangled or plaited together.

MAUDLIN. See Achillea.

MAUROCENIA. Lin. Gen. Plant. Edit. 2. 289. Frangula. Hort. Elth. 121. The Hottentot Cherry, vulgo.

The Characters are,

The empalement of the flower is of one leaf, cut into five segments, and is permanent. The flower hath five oval petals, which spread open. It hath five stamina, which are situated between the petals, crowned by obtuse summits. In the center is situated a roundish germen, having no style, crowned by a trifid stigma. The germen afterward turns to an oval berry with one or two cells, each containing a single oval seed.

This genus of plants is ranged in the third section of Linnæus's fifth class, which includes the plants whose flowers have five stamina and three styles or stigmas; and in the last edition of his Genera, he has joined it to the Cassine, making them the same; but as the flower of Cassine has but one petal, and the flower of these have five; and the berries of the former three cells, and those of this but one or two, therefore I have separated them.

The Species are,

1. Maurocenia (Frangula) foliis subovatis integerrimis, floribus confertis lateralibus. Maurocenia with entire leaves which are almost oval, and flowers growing in clusters on the sides of the branches. Frangula sempervirens, folio rigido subrotundo. Hort. Elth. 146. tab. 121. Evergreen berry-bearing Alder with a roundish stiff leaf, commonly called Hottentot Cherry.

2. Maurocenia (Phillyrea) foliis obversè ovatis serratis, floribus corymbosis alaribus & terminalibus. Maurocenia with obverse, oval, sawed leaves, and flowers growing in a corymbus at the sides and ends of the branches. Phillyrea capensis, folio celastri. Hort. Elth. 315. tab. 236. Phillyrea of the Cape with a Staff-tree leaf, by the Dutch called Leplebout.

3. Maurocenia (Cerasus) foliis ovatis nervosis integerrimis. Maurocenia with oval veined leaves, which are entire. Cerasus Hottentotorum. Pluk. Almag. 94. The smaller Hottentot Cherry.

4. Maurocenia (Americana) foliis obversè ovatis emarginatis, floribus solitariis alaribus. Maurocenia with obverse oval leaves which are indented at the edges, and flowers growing singly from the sides of the branches. Frangula folio subrotundo rigido subtus ferrugineo. Houst. MSS. Berry-bearing Alder with a roundish stiff leaf, which is of an iron colour on the under side.

The first sort grows naturally at the Cape of Good Hope, where it rises to a considerable height, but here they are rarely more than five or six feet high. The stalk is strong, woody, and covered with a purplish bark, sending out many stiff branches, garnished with very thick leaves, almost oval, standing for the most part opposite; they are about two inches long, and almost as much in breadth, of a dark green colour, and entire. The flowers come out from the side of the old branches, in clusters, three, four, or five, standing upon one common foot-stalk, which is slender, composed of five plain equal petals, ending in acute points; they are first of a greenish yellow colour, but afterward change to white, spreading wide open. In the center is situated the oval germen, crowned with the trifid stigma, and between each petal is situated a stamina; these spread open in the same manner as the petals, and are terminated by obtuse summits. The germen afterward

turns to an oval pulpy berry, some having but one, and others two cells; in each of these is lodged one oval seed. The berries change to a dark purple when they are ripe. This plant flowers in July and August, and the berries ripen in winter.

The second sort is a native of the Cape of Good Hope; this hath a woody stalk, which in this country seldom rises more than five or six feet high, sending out many branches, covered with a dark purplish bark, and garnished with pretty stiff leaves, which are obversely oval, and sawed on their edges, standing opposite; they are about an inch and a half long, and a little more in breadth, of a light green, having short foot-stalks. The flowers are produced in roundish bunches from the side, and at the end of the branches; they are white, and have five small petals which spread open; between these are situated the stamina, which spread in the same manner; these are terminated by obtuse summits. In the center is situated the roundish germen, which is crowned sometimes by a bifid, and at others by a trifid stigma. The flowers appear in July and August, but are not succeeded by berries in England.

The third sort grows naturally at the Cape of Good Hope; this rises with a woody stalk about the same height as the former, dividing into many branches, which are garnished with stiff oval leaves about two inches long, and nearly as much in breadth, of a lucid green colour, and entire, having three longitudinal veins; these are sometimes placed opposite, and at others they are alternate, having a strong margin, or border, surrounding them. This sort hath produced its flowers in England, and I am fully convinced that the characters of the flowers are the same with the others.

The fourth sort was discovered by the late Dr. Houstoun, growing naturally at the Palisadoes in Jamaica, from whence he sent the seeds to Europe; this rises with a woody stalk from fifteen to twenty feet high, covered with a rough brown bark, and divides into many branches, which are garnished with stiff leaves, placed alternately; they are about an inch and a half long, and a little more in breadth, indented at the top, with a stiff reflexed border, of a gray colour on their upper side, but of a rusty iron colour on their under, standing upon short foot-stalks. The flowers come out singly along the side of the branches; they have five small white petals, which end in acute points, and five slender stamina, which spread open, and are terminated by obtuse summits. In the center is situated a roundish germen, supporting a long bifid stigma, which is permanent. The germen afterward turns to a round berry, with one or two cells, each having one oblong seed.

The first sort is too tender to live abroad in England, but as it requires no artificial heat, so may be preserved through the winter in a good green-house, where it deserves a place for the beauty of its leaves, which are very thick, of a deep green, and differing in appearance from every other plant; this may be propagated by laying down those shoots which are produced near the root, but they are long in putting out roots. The shoots should be twisted in the part which is laid, to facilitate their putting out roots; if these are laid down in the autumn, they will put out roots sufficient to remove by the following autumn; it may also be propagated by cuttings, but this is a tedious method, as they are seldom rooted enough to transplant in less than two years. When this is practised, the young shoots of the former year should be cut off, with a small piece of the old wood at the bottom, in the spring, and planted in pots filled with loamy earth, and plunged into a moderate hot-bed, covering the pots with glasses, which should be close stopped down to exclude the external air; they should be pretty well watered at the time they are planted, but afterward they will require but little wet; the glasses over them should be covered every day with mats, to screen the cuttings from the sun during the heat of the

the day, but in the morning before the fun is too warm, and in the afternoon, when the fun is low, they fhould be uncovered, that the oblique rays of the fun may raife a gentle warmth under the glaffes. With this care the cuttings will take root, but where it is wanting, they feldom fucceed. When the cuttings or layers are rooted, they fhould be each planted in a feparate fmall pot, filled with foft loamy foil, and placed in the fhade till they have taken new root; then they may be removed to a fheltered fituation, where they may remain during the fummer feafon; and, before the frofts of the autumn come on, they muft be removed into the green-houfe, and treated in the fame way as the other plants of that country, giving them but little water in cold weather, and in mild weather admitting the free air. In fummer they muft be removed into the open air, and placed in a fheltered fituation with other exotic plants, and in very warm weather they muft be watered three times a week, but it muft not be given them too freely at any time. When the plants have obtained ftrength, they will produce flowers and fruit, which, in warm feafons, will ripen perfectly; and if the feeds are fown foon after they are ripe, in pots, and plunged into the tan-bed in the ftove, the plants will come up the fpring following, and may then be treated in the fame manner as thofe which are propagated by cuttings and layers.

The fecond fort is not altogether fo hardy as the firft, fo muft have a warmer place in the green-houfe in winter, and fhould not be placed abroad quite fo early in the fpring, nor fuffered to remain abroad fo late in the autumn, but if the green-houfe is warm, the plants will require no additional heat. This may be propagated by layers and cuttings, in the fame manner as the firft, and requires the fame care, for the cuttings are with difficulty made to root; nor will the branches which are laid, put out roots in lefs than a year, and if thefe are not young fhoots, they will not take root.

As this fort does not produce feeds in England, it can be only propagated by layers and cuttings, which being difficult to root, occafions its being fcarce at prefent in Europe.

The third fort is yet more rare than either of the former, and is with greater difficulty propagated, for the layers and cuttings are commonly two years before they get roots fufficient to remove, and as it never produces feeds here, it can be no other way propagated; this is alfo tenderer than either of the other forts, fo requires a moderate degree of heat in winter, for without fome artificial warmth, it will feldom live through the winters in England. In the middle of fummer the plants may be placed abroad in a warm fituation, but they muft be removed into fhelter early in the autumn, before the cold nights come on, otherwife they will receive a check, which will not recover in winter; during the fummer feafon they fhould be gently watered three times a week in dry weather, but in winter they will require to be feldom watered.

The fourth fort is much more impatient of cold than either of the other, being a native of a warmer country. This is propagated by feeds, which muft be procured from the country where it grows naturally, for it does not produce any here. Thefe do not grow the firft year, fo the feeds fhould be fown in pots filled with light earth, and plunged into a moderate hot-bed of tanners bark, where they may remain all the fummer; and in the autumn they fhould be removed into the bark-ftove, and plunged into the tan-bed between the other pots of plants, in any vacant fpaces; there they may remain till fpring, when they fhould be taken out of the ftove, and plunged into a frefh hot-bed, which will bring up the plants. When thefe are fit to remove, they fhould be each tranfplanted into a feparate fmall pot, filled with a foft loamy earth, and plunged into a hot-bed again, being careful to fhade them from the fun till they have taken new root, after which they muft be treated in the

fame manner as other tender plants from the fame country, always keeping them in the tan-bed; and in winter they muft have a temperate warmth, otherwife they will not live here.

All the forts delight in a foft, gentle, loamy foil, not over ftiff, fo as to detain the wet; nor fhould the foil be too light, for in fuch they feldom thrive. They retain their leaves all the year, fo make a good appearance in the winter feafon, their leaves being remarkably ftiff and of a fine green, efpecially the firft fort, whofe fruit ripens in winter, which when it is in plenty on the plants, affords an agreeable variety.

MAYS. See ZEA.

MEADIA. Catefb. Carol. 3. p. 1. Dodecatheon. Lin. Gen. Plant. 183.

The CHARACTERS are,

It hath a fmall involucrum of many leaves, in which are many flowers. The flower hath a permanent empalement of one leaf, cut into five long fegments which are reflexed. The flower hath one petal, cut into five parts, whofe tube is fhorter than the empalement, and the limb is reflexed backward. It hath five fhort obtufe ftamina fitting in the tube, terminated by arrow-pointed ftigmas, which are connected into a head, with a conical germen, fupporting a flender ftyle longer than the ftamina, crowned by an obtufe ftigma. The empalement afterward becomes an oblong oval capfule with one cell, opening at the top, and filled with fmall feeds.

This genus of plants is ranged in the firft fection of Linnæus's fifth clafs, which includes thofe plants whofe flowers have five ftamina and one ftyle. The title of this genus was given to it by Mr. Mark Catefby, F. R. S. in honour of the late Dr. Mead, who was a generous encourager of every ufeful branch of fcience; but being himfelf no great botanift, Dr. Linnæus was unwilling any plant fhould bear his name, fo he has altered it to that of Dodecatheon, which was a title applied by Pliny to a fpecies of Primrofe with a yellow root, and leaves like the Garden Lettuce.

We have but one SPECIES of this genus, viz.

MEADIA (*Dodecatheon.*) Catefb. Hift. Carol. App. 1. tab. 1. *Meadia.* Auricula urfi Virginiana, floribus boraginis, inftar roftratis, cyclaminum more reflexis. Pluk. Alm. 62. tab. 79. fol. 6. *Bear's-ear of Virgina, whofe flower has a beak like that of Borage, and reflexed petals like thofe of Sowbread.*

This plant grows naturally in Virginia, and other parts of North America, from whence it was fent by Mr. Banifter, many years fince, to Dr. Compton, Lord Bifhop of London, in whofe curious garden I firft faw this plant growing in the year 1709; after which the plant was for feveral years loft in England, till within a few years paft, when it was again obtained from America, and has been propagated in pretty great plenty. It hath a yellow perennial root, from which comes out feveral long fmooth leaves in the fpring, which are near fix inches long, and two and a half broad; at firft ftanding erect, but afterward they fpread on the ground, efpecially if the plants are much expofed to the fun; from between thefe leaves arife two, three, or four flower-ftalks, in proportion to the ftrength of the roots, which rife eight or nine inches high, they are fmooth, naked, and are terminated by an umbel of flowers, under which is fituated the many-leaved involucrum. Each flower is fuftained by a pretty long flender foot-ftalk which is recurved, fo that the flower hangs downward. The flower has but one petal, which is deeply cut into five fpear-fhaped fegments, which are reflexed upward like the flowers of Cyclamen or Sowbread; the ftamina, which are five in number, are fhort, and fit in the tube of the flower, having five arrow-pointed fummits, which are connected together round the ftyle, forming a fort of beak. The flowers are purple, inclining to a Peach bloffom colour, and have an oblong germen fituated in the bottom of the tube, which afterward becomes an oval capfule inclofed by the empalement, with the permanent ftyle on its apex, which, when ripe, opens at the top to let out the

the feeds, which are faftened round the ftyle. This plant flowers the beginning of May, and the feeds ripen in July, foon after which the ftalks and leaves decay, fo that the roots remain inactive till the following fpring.

This plant is propagated by offsets, which the roots put out pretty freely when they are ina loofe moift foil and a fhady fituation; the beft time to remove the roots, and take away the offsets, is in Auguft, after the leaves and ftalks are decayed, that they may be fixed well in their new fituation before the froft comes on. It may alfo be propagated by feeds, which the plants generally produce in plenty; thefe fhould be fown in the autumn foon after they are ripe, either in a fhady moift border, or in pots, which fhould be placed in the fhade; in the fpring the plants will come up, and muft then be kept clean from weeds, and if the feafon proves dry, they muft be frequently refrefhed with water; nor fhould they be expofed to the fun, for while the plants are young, they are very impatient of heat, fo that I have known great numbers of them deftroyed in two or three days, which were growing to the full fun. Thefe young plants fhould not be tranfplanted till their leaves are decayed, then they may be carefully taken up and planted in a fhady border, where the foil is loofe and moift, at about eight inches diftance from each other, which will be room enough for them to grow one year, by which time they will be ftrong enough to produce flowers, fo may then be tranfplanted into fome fhady borders in the flower-garden, where they will appear very ornamental during the continuance of their flowers.

At the firft many fuppofed this plant to be tender, fo planted it in warm fituations and nurfed it too much, whereby the plants were often killed; but by experience it is found to be fo hardy, as not to be hurt by the fevereft cold of this country; but it will not thrive in a very dry foil, or where it is greatly expofed to the fun.

MEADOW.

Under the general title of Meadow, is commonly comprehended all pafture land, or at leaft all Grafs land, which is mown for hay; but I chufe rather to diftinguifh fuch land only by this appellation, which is fo low, as to be too moift for cattle to graze upon them in winter, being generally too wet to admit heavy cattle, without poaching and fpoiling the fward; and thofe Grafs lands which are drier, I fhall diftinguifh by the title of pafture.

There are two forts of Meadows in England, one of which is ftiled Water Meadows, and the other are fimply called Meadows.

Water Meadows are thofe which lie contiguous to rivers or brooks, from whence the water can be carried to overflow the Grafs at pleafure. Of thefe there are large tracts in feveral parts of England, which, if fkilfully managed, would become much more profitable to their owners than they are at prefent, as hath been already mentioned in another place; for nothing can be more abfurd than the common practice of flowing thefe low grounds all the winter, whereby the roots of all the fweeteft kinds of Grafs are deftroyed, and only fuch Graffes left as are natives of marfhes, which are coarfe and four: and if people were curious to examine the herbage of thefe Water Meadows, they would find the bulk of them compofed of bad weeds, fuch as grow by the fides of rivers, brooks, and ditches, of which the feveral forts of Docks make no fmall fhare; and although many of thefe Meadows produce a great burden of what the country people call hay, yet this is only fit for cows, cart-horfes, and other animals, which by hard labour and hunger, are driven to eat it; for horfes which have been accuftomed to feed on good hay, will ftarve before they will touch it: and after the Grafs is mown off thefe Meadows, and cattle turned in to graze upon them, how common is it to fee the land almoft covered with thefe rank weeds, which the cattle never will eat! Which muft always be the condition of fuch Meadows,

where the water is let over them in autumn and winter; for, as the fides of rivers and brooks do every where abound with thefe rank weeds, whofe feeds ripen in autumn, and falling into the water, they are carried by the ftream, and depofited on the flowed land, where they grow and fill the ground in every part; but fo incurious are the generality of farmers in this refpect, that if the ground is but well covered, they care not what it is, few of them ever taking any pains to weed or clean their paftures.

The method which I propofe for the management of thefe Meadows is, never to flow them till the middle or latter end of March, excepting once or twice in winter, when there may happen floods, which may bring down a great fhare of foil from the upper lands, at which times it will be of great fervice to let water upon the Meadows, that the foil may fettle there; but the fooner the wet is drained off when this is lodged, the greater advantage the Meadows will receive by it; but from the end of March to the middle of May, in dry feafons, by frequently letting on the water, the growth of the Grafs will be greatly encouraged, and at this feafon there will be no danger of deftroying the roots of the Grafs; and after the hay is carried off the ground, if the feafon fhould prove dry, it will be of great fervice to the Grafs, if the Meadows are flowed again; but when this is practifed, no cattle fhould be turned into the Meadows, till the furface of the ground is become firm enough to bear their weight without poaching the land, for otherwife the Grafs will fuffer more from the treading of the cattle, than it will receive benefit by the flowing; but thefe are things which the country people feldom regard, fo that the Meadows are generally very unfightly, and rendered lefs profitable.

I would alfo recommend the weeding of thefe Meadows twice a year; the firft time in April, and again in October; at which times if the roots of Docks and all bad weeds are cut up with a fpaddle, the Meadows will foon be cleared of this trumpery, and the herbage greatly improved.

Another great improvement of thefe lands might be procured, by rolling them with a heavy roller in fpring and autumn. This will prefs the furface of the ground even, whereby it may be mown much clofer, and it will alfo fweeten the Grafs; and this piece of hufbandry is of more fervice to paftures than moft people are aware of.

As to thofe Meadows which cannot be flowed, there fhould be the fame care taken to weed and roll them, as hath been directed for the Water Meadows; as alfo never to let heavy cattle graze upon them in winter when they are wet; for the cattle will then poach them, and greatly injure the Grafs; therefore thefe fhould be fed down as clofe as poffible in the autumn, before the heavy rains fall to render the ground foft; and thofe paftures which are drier, may be kept to fupply the want of thefe in winter; and where there are not cattle enough to eat down the Grafs in time, it will be much better to cut off what is left, than to fuffer it to rot upon the ground, for that will prevent the Grafs from fhooting early in the fpring; but where people have not cattle enough of their own to eat down the Grafs in time, they had much better take in fome of their neighbours, than fuffer their fog (as it is called) to remain all the winter. When thefe Meadows are fed in the autumn, the greater variety of animals are turned in, the clofer they will eat the Grafs; and I am fully convinced, the clofer it is eaten, the better the Grafs will come up the following fpring; therefore, if during the time while the cattle are feeding, the Meadows are well rolled, the animals will eat the Grafs much clofer than they otherwife would.

Thofe perfons who are beft fkilled in this part of hufbandry, always drefs their Meadows every other, or at leaft every third year, without which it is in vain to expect any good crop of hay; but the generality of the farmers are fo much diftreffed for dreffing to fupply their Corn land, as not to have any to fpare

for

for their Meadows, fo that they are content with what the land will naturally produce, rather than take any part of their manure from their arable ground ; but this is a very imprudent piece of hufbandry ; for if land is to be annually mowed far hay, can it be fuppofed that it will produce a good crop long, unlefs there are proper dreffings allowed it ? And when ground is once beggared for want of manure, it will be fome years before it can be recovered again ; but I fhall referve what is neceffary to be farther enlarged on this fubject, to be fully treated under the article of PASTURE.

MEADOW SAFFRON. See C OLCHICUM.

MEDEOLA. Lin. Gen. Plant. 411.

The CHARACTERS are,

The flower has no empalement ; it hath fix oblong oval petals which are equal, fpread open, and turn backward ; and fix awl-fhaped ftamina the length of the petal, terminated by incumbent fummits, and three corniculated germen terminating the ftyle, crowned by thick recurved ftigmas. The germen afterward turns to a roundifh trifid berry with three cells, each containing one heart-fhaped feed.

This genus of plants is ranged in the third fection of Linnæus's fixth clafs, which includes thofe plants whofe flowers have fix ftamina and three ftyles.

The SPECIES are,

1. MEDEOLA (*Afparagoides*) foliis ovato-lanceolatis alternis, caule fcandente. *Medeola with oval, fpear-fhaped, alternate leaves, and a climbing ftalk.* Afparagus Africanus, fcandens, myrti folio. Hort. Piff. 17. *Climbing African Afparagus, with a Myrtle leaf.*

2. MEDEOLA (*Anguftifolia*) foliis lanceolatis alternis, caule fcandente. *Medeola with fpear-fhaped alternate leaves, and a climbing ftalk.* Alparagus Africanus, fcandens, myrti folio anguftiore. Hort. Piff. 17. *Climbing African Afparagus, with a narrower Myrtle leaf.*

3. MEDEOLA (*Virginiana*) foliis verticillatis, ramis inermibus. Lin. Sp. Plant. 339. *Medeola with leaves growing in whorls and fmooth branches.* Lilium five martagon pufillum, floribus minutiffimè herbaceis. Pluk. Alm. 410. tab. 328. fol. 4. *The Lily or little Martagon, with very fmall herbaceous flowers.*

The firft fort grows naturally at the Cape of Good Hope ; this hath a root compofed of feveral dugs or oblong knobs, which unite together at the top like that of the Ranunculus, from which arife two or three ftiff winding ftalks, which divide into branches rifing four or five feet high, if they meet with any neighbouring fupport to which they can faften, otherwife they will fall to the ground ; thefe are garnifhed with oval fpear-fhaped leaves, ending in acute points, placed alternately, and fitting clofe to the ftalks ; they are of a light green on their under fide, and dark on their upper. The flowers come out from the fide of the ftalks, fometimes fingly, and at others there are two upon a flender fhort foot-ftalk ; they have fix oblong equal petals which fpread open, and are of a dull white colour ; within thefe are ranged fix ftamina, which are as long as the petals, terminated by incumbent fummits. In the center is fituated a germen with three horns, fitting upon a fhort ftyle, crowned by three thick recurved ftigmas ; the germen afterward turns to a roundifh berry with three cells, each containing one heart-fhaped feed. It flowers the beginning of winter, and the feeds are ripe in the fpring.

The fecond fort is alfo a native of the Cape of Good Hope, from whence I received the feeds. This hath a root like the firft, but the ftalks are not fo ftrong ; they climb higher, but do not branch fo much ; the leaves are much longer and narrower, and are of a grayifh colour. The flowers come from the fide of the branches, two or three upon each foot-ftalk ; they are of an herbaceous white colour, fhaped like thofe of the former fort, and appear about the fame time, but this has not produced any fruit here. Thefe are undoubtedly diftinct fpecies, for they never vary when they are propagated by feeds.

Both thefe forts propagate freely by offsets from the roots, fo that when they are once obtained, there will be no neceffity of fowing their feeds, which commonly lie a year in the ground, and the plants will not be ftrong enough to flower in lefs than two years more, whereas the offsets will flower the following feafon. The time for tranfplanting and parting of the roots is in July, when their ftalks are entirely decayed, for they begin to fhoot toward the end of Auguft, and keep growing all the winter, and decay in the fpring. Thefe roots fhould be planted in pots filled with good kitchen-garden earth, and may remain in the open air till there is danger of froft, when they muft be removed into fhelter, for they are too tender to live through the winter in the open air ; but if they are placed in a warm green-houfe, they will thrive and flower very well, but they do not produce fruit unlefs they have fome heat in winter ; therefore where that is defired, the plants fhould be placed in a ftove kept to a moderate degree of warmth. During the winter, when the plants are in vigour, they fhould be frequently, but gently watered ; but when the ftalks begin to decay, they muft have very little wet, for much moifture will rot them while they are in an inactive ftate ; during which time, if the pots are placed where they have only the morning fun, they will require little or no water : but when they begin to fhoot out their ftalks, they fhould be removed to a warmer fituation, and fhould then be frequently but gently watered.

The flowers of thefe plants make no great appearance, fo the plants are not preferved for their beauty ; but as their ftalks are climbing, and their leaves are in full vigour in winter, during that feafon th y add to the variety in the green-houfe.

The third fort is a native of North America ; it is by Dr. Linnæus joined to this genus, in which I have followed him ; though, if I remember rightly, the characters of this fort do not exactly agree with thofe of the other, for the flower is either polypetalous, or is cut into many fegments, and has but five ftamina ; it being fome years fince I faw the flowers, I cannot be very certain if I am right. This hath a fmall fcaly root, from which arifes a fingle ftalk about eight inches high, garnifhed with one whorl of leaves at a fmall diftance from the ground, and at the top there are two leaves ftanding oppofite ; between thefe come out three flender foot-ftalks which turn downward, each fuftaining one pale herbaceous flower with a purple pointal. It flowers in June, but I have not feen any fruit upon it.

This plant is hardy enough to live in the open air, but does not propagate faft here, as it produces no feeds, fo can only be encreafed by offsets.

MEDICA. Tourn. Inft. R. H. 410. tab. 231. Medicago. Tourn. Inft. 412. Lin. Gen. Plant. 805. [This plant takes its name from Media (as Pliny writes) becaufe when Darius Hyftafpis carried his army into Greece, he had with him a great many facks of this feed for provender for his cattle, and fo the feeds came to be fcattered in Greece.] Medick, or La Lucerne.

The CHARACTERS are,

The flower hath a bell-fhaped empalement of one leaf, cut into five equal acute points. The flower is of the butterfly kind ; the ftandard is oval, entire, and the border is reflexed ; the two wings are oblong, oval, and fixed by an appendix to the keel ; the keel is oblong, bifid, obtufe, and reflexed toward the ftandard. It has ten ftamina, nine of which are joined almoft to their tops, the other is fingle ; they are terminated by fmall fummits. It hath an oblong compreffed germen which is incurved, fitting on a fhort ftyle, terminated by a fmall ftigma ; this and the ftamina are involved by the keel and ftandard. The germen afterward turns to a compreffed moon-fhaped pod, inclofing feveral kidney-fhaped feeds.

This genus of plants is ranged in the third fection of Linnæus's feventeenth clafs, which includes the herbs with a butterfly flower, having ten ftamina in two houfes. He alfo has joined the Medica and Medicago

Medicago of Tournefort together, making them one genus under the title Medicago, but Tournefort makes the diftinguifhing character of Medicago to confift in having a falcated compreffed pod. Therefore I fhall here feparate thofe plants whofe pods are of that form, from the others whofe pods are twifted like a fcrew; and as the title of Medica was firftapplied to the Lucern, fo I fhall continue it to thofe fpecies as have fuch pods, and refer the others to the genus of Medicago.

The SPECIES are,

1. MEDICA (*Sativa*) pedunculis racemofis, leguminibus contortis, caule erecto glabro. Lin. Sp. 1096. *Medick with branching foot-ftalks, contorted pods, and an erect fmooth ftalk.* Medica major, erectior, floribus purpurafcentibus. J. B. 2. 382. *Greater upright Medick with purplifh flowers, commonly called La Lucerne, and by the French, Burgundy Hay.*

2. MEDICA (*Falcata*) pedunculis racemofis, leguminibus lunatis, caule proftrato. Flor. Suec. 620. *Medick with branching foot-ftalks, moon-fhaped pods, and trailing ftalks.* Medica fylveftris, floribus croceis. J. B. 2. 383. *Wild Medick with Saffron-coloured flowers.*

3. MEDICA (*Radiata*) leguminibus reniformibus, margine dentatis, foliis ternatis. Hort. Cliff. 377. *Medick with kidney-fhoped pods indented on the borders, and trifoliate leaves.* Medicago annua, trifolii leaves. Tourn. Inft. R. H. 412. *Annual Medicago with the appearance of Trefoil.*

4. MEDICA (*Hifpanica*) caule herbaceo procumbente, foliis pinnatis, leguminibus ciliato-dentatis. *Medick with a trailing herbaceous ftalk, winged leaves, and pods having hairy indentures.* Medicago vulnerariæ facie Hifpanica. Tourn. Inft. R. H. 412. *Spanifh Medicago with the appearance of Ladies Finger.*

5. MEDICA (*Italica*) caule herbaceo proftrato, foliis ternatis, foliolis cuneiformibus fuperne ferratis, leguminibus margine integerrimis. *Medick with a proftrate herbaceous ftalk, trifoliate leaves whofe lobes are wedge-fhoped and fawed at the top, and the borders of the pods entire.* Medicago Italica, annua maritima, trifolia, polycarpos, fructu torofo non fpinofo. Mitchel. Hort. Piff. *Annual, Italian, maritime Medicago with trifoliate leaves, and bearing much fruit, which is thick and without fpines.*

6. MEDICA (*Cretica*) caule herbaceo proftrato, foliis radicalibus integerrimis, caulinis pinnatis leguminibus dentatis. *Medick with a proftrate herbaceous ftalk, the bottom leaves entire, thofe on the ftalks winged, and indented pods.* Medicago vulnerariæ facie Cretica. Tourn. Inft. 412. *Cretan Medicago, with the appearance of Ladies Finger.*

7. MEDICA (*Arborea*) leguminibus lunatis margine integerrimis caule arboreo. Hort. Cliff. 376. *Medick with moon-fhaped pods whofe borders are entire, and a tree-like ftalk.* Medicago trifolia, frutefcens, incana. Tourn. Inft. R. H. 412. *Shrubby, hoary, three-leaved Medica, or the Cytifus Virgilii.*

The firft fort hath a perennial root and annual ftalks, which rifes near three feet high in good land; thefe are garnifhed with trifoliate leaves at each joint, whofe lobes are fpear-fhaped, about an inch and a half long, and half an inch broad, a little fawed toward their top, of a deep green, and placed alternately on the ftalks. The flowers grow in fpikes, which are from two to near three inches in length, ftanding upon naked foot-ftalks which are two inches long, rifing from the wings of the ftalk; they are of a Pea bloom or butterfly kind, of a fine purple colour, and are fucceeded by compreffed moon-fhaped pods, which contain feveral kidney-fhaped feeds. It flowers in June, and the feeds ripen in September.

There are the following varieties of this plant:
One with Violet-coloured flowers.
Another with pale blue flowers.
And a third with variegated flowers.

Thefe variations of their flowers have accidentally rifen from feed, therefore are not to be fuppofed different plants; and thofe with the pale blue and variegated flowers are never fo ftrong as thofe with purple, fo are lefs profitable to the cultivators.

This plant is fuppofed to have been brought originally from Media, and from thence had its name Medica; it is by the Spaniards called Alfafa; by the French, La Lucerne, and Grand Trefle; and by feveral botanic writers it is called Fœnum Burgundiacum, i. e. Burgundian Hay. But there is little room to doubt of this being the Medica of Virgil, Columella, Palladius, and other ancient writers of hufbandry, who have not been wanting to extol the goodnefs of this fodder, and have given direction for the cultivation of it in thofe countries where they lived.

But notwithftanding it was fo much commended by the antients, and hath been cultivated to fo good purpofe by our neighbours in France and Switzerland for many years, it hath not as yet found fo good reception in our country as could be wifhed; nor is it cultivated in confiderable quantities, though it is evident, it will fucceed as well in England as in either of the before-mentioned countries, though will not bear cutting fo often here, yet is extremely hardy, and refifts the fevereft cold of our climate: as a proof of this, I muft beg leave to mention, that the feeds which have have happened to be fcattered upon the ground in autumn, have come up, and the plants have endured the cold of a fevere winter, and made very ftrong plants the following feafon.

About the year 1650, the feeds of this plant were brought over from France, and fown in England; but whether for want of fkill in its culture, whereby it did not fucceed, or that the people were fo fond of going on in their old beaten road, as not to try the experiment whether it would fucceed here or not, was the occafion of its being entirely neglected in England, I cannot fay, but it is very certain that it was neglected many years, fo as to be almoft forgotten. However, I hope, before I quit this article, to give fuch directions for its culture, as will encourage the people of England to make farther trial of this valuable plant, which grows in the greateft heat, and alfo in very cold countries, with this difference only, that in very hot countries, fuch as the Spanifh Weft-Indies, &c. where it is the chief fodder for their cattle at this time, they cut it every week; whereas in cold countries, it is feldom cut oftener than four or five times in a year. And it is very likely that this plant may be of great fervice to the inhabitants of Barbadoes, Jamaica, and the other hot iflands in the Weft-Indies, where one of the greateft things they want is fodder for their cattle; fince by the account given of this plant by Pere Feuillé, it thrives exceedingly in the Spanifh Weft-Indies, particularly about Lima, where they cut it every week; and bring it into the market to fell, and is there the only fodder cultivated.

It is alfo very common in Languedoc, Provence, and Dauphiné, and all over the banks of the Rhone, where it produces abundantly, and may be mowed five or fix times in a year. Horfes, mules, oxen, and other domeftic cattle, love it exceedingly; but above all when it is green, if they are permitted to feed on it, and efpecially the black cattle, which will feed very kindly upon the dried plant; the excefs of which is, by many people, thought to be very dangerous; but it is faid to be exceeding good for milch cattle, to promote their quantity of milk; and is alfo faid to agree with horfes the beft of all, though fheep, goats, and moft other cattle, will feed upon it, efpecially when young.

The directions given by all thofe who have written of this plant are very imperfect, and generally fuch as, if practifed in this country, will be found entirely wrong; for many of them order the mixing of this feed with Oats or Barley, (as is practifed for Clover) but in this way it feldom comes up well, and if it does, it will draw up fo weak by growing amongft the Corn, as not to be recovered under a whole year, if ever it can be brought to its ufual ftrength again. Others have directed it to be fown upon a low, rich, moift foil, which is found to be the worft next to a

clay

clay, of any for this plant; in both which the roots will rot in winter, and in a year or two the whole crop will be deftroyed.

But the foil in which this plant is found to fucceed beft in this country is, a light, dry, loofe, fandy land, which fhould be well ploughed and dreffed, and the roots of all noxious weeds, fuch as Couch Grafs, &c. deftroyed, otherwife they will overgrow the plants while young, and prevent their progrefs.

The beft time to fow the feed is about the middle of April, when the weather is fettled and fair; for if you fow it when the ground is very wet, or in a rainy feafon, the feeds will burft and come to little (as is often the cafe with feveral forts of the leguminous plants;) therefore you fhould always obferve to fow it in a dry feafon, and if there happens rain in about a week or ten days after it is fown, the plants will foon appear above ground.

But the method I would direct for the fowing thefe feeds is as follows: after having well ploughed and harrowed the land very fine, you fhould make a drill quite acrofs the ground, about half an inch deep, into which the feeds fhould be fcattered very thin by a hopper fixed to a drill plough; then cover them over half an inch thick, with the earth that came out of the drill; then proceed to make another drill about two feet and a half from the former, fowing the feeds therein in the fame manner as before, and fo proceed through the whole fpot of ground, allowing the fame diftance between row and row, and fcatter the feeds very thin in the drills. In this manner, an acre of land will require about fix pounds of feeds; for when it is fown thicker, if the feed grows well, the plants will be fo clofe as to fpoil each other in a year or two, the heads of them growing to a confiderable fize, as will alfo the roots, provided they have room. I have meafured the crown of one root, which was in my poffeffion, eighteen inches diameter; from which I cut near four hundred fhoots at one time, which is an extraordinary increafe, and this upon a poor, dry, gravelly foil, which had not been dunged for many years, but the root was at leaft fourteen years old; fo that if this crop be well cultivated, it will continue many years, and be equally good as when it was firft fown; for the roots generally run down very deep in the ground, provided the foil be dry; and although they fhould meet a hard gravel a foot below the furface, yet their roots would penetrate it, and make their way downward, as I have experienced, having taken up fome of them which were above four feet in length, and had run above two feet into a rock of gravel, which was fo hard as not to be loofened without mattocks and crows of iron, and that with much difficulty.

The reafon for directing this feed to be fown in rows is, that the plants may have room to grow; and for the better ftirring the ground between them, to deftroy the weeds, and encourage the growth of the plants, which may be very eafily effected with a Dutch hoe, juft after the cutting the crop each time, which will caufe the plants to fhoot again in a very little time, and be much ftronger than in fuch places where the ground cannot be ftirred; but when the plants firft come up, the ground between them fhould be hoed by hand with a common hoe; and if in doing of this you cut up the plants where they are too clofe in the rows, it will caufe the remaining to be much ftronger. This hoeing fhould be repeated two or three times while the plants are young, according as the weeds are produced, obferving always to do it in dry weather, that the weeds may the better be deftroyed; for if it be done in moift weather, they will take root and grow again.

With this management, the plants will grow to the height of two feet, or more, by the beginning of Auguft, when the flowers will begin to appear, when it fhould be cut for the firft time, obferving to do it in a dry feafon, efpecially if it is to be made into hay, and keep it often turned, that it may foon dry, and be carried off the ground; for if it lie long upon the roots, it will prevent their fhooting again. After the

crop is taken off, you fhould ftir the ground between the rows with a hoe, to kill the weeds, and loofen the furface, which will caufe the plants to fhoot again in a fhort time, fo that by the middle of September there will be fhoots four or five inches high, when you may turn in fheep upon it to feed it down, for it will not be fit to cut again the fame feafon; nor fhould the fhoots be fuffered to remain upon the plants, which would decay when the frofty weather comes on, and fall down upon the roots, and prevent their fhooting early the fucceeding fpring; but thefe fheep fhould not remain fo long upon it as to endanger the crowns of the roots.

So that the beft way is to feed it until November, when it will have done fhooting for that feafon; but it fhould not be fed by large cattle the firft year, becaufe the roots being young, would be in danger of being deftroyed, either by their trampling upon them, or their pulling them out of the ground; but fheep will be of fervice to the roots by dunging the ground, provided they do not eat it too clofe.

The beginning of February, the ground between the roots fhould be again ftirred with the hoe, to encourage them to fhoot again; but in doing of this you fhould be careful not to injure the crown of the roots, upon which the buds are at that time very turgid, and ready to pufh. With this management, if the foil be warm, by the middle of March the fhoots will be five or fix inches high, when, if you are in want of fodder, you may feed it down till a week in April; after which it fhould be fuffered to grow for a crop, which will be fit to cut the beginning of June, when you fhould obferve to get it off the ground as foon as poffible, and ftir the ground again with a Dutch hoe, which will forward the plants fhooting again, fo that by the middle of July, there will be another crop fit to cut, which muft be managed as before: after which it fhould be fed down again in autumn; and as the roots by this time will have taken deep hold in the ground, there will be little danger of hurting them, if you fhould turn in larger cattle; but you muft always obferve not to fuffer them to remain after the roots have done fhooting, left they fhould eat down the crown of the roots below the buds, which would confideraby damage, if not deftroy them. In this manner you may continue conftantly to have two crops to cut, and two feedings upon this plant, and in good fummers there may be three crops cut, and two feedings; which will be a great improvement, efpecially as this plant will grow upon dry barren foils, where Grafs will produce little, efpecially in dry feafons, when it will be of great ufe, the Grafs being often burnt up. And as it is an early plant in the fpring, fo it will be of great fervice when fodder falls fhort at that feafon, when it will be fit to feed at leaft a month before Grafs or Clover; for I have had this plant eight inches high by the tenth of March, old ftyle, at which time the Grafs in the fame place has fcarcely been one inch high.

That the cold will not injure this plant, I am fully fatisfied; for in the very cold winter, anno 1729-30, I had fome roots of this plant which were dug up in October, and laid upon the ground in the open air till the beginning of March, when I planted them again, and they fhot out very vigoroufly foon after; nay, even while they lay upon the ground, they ftruck out fibres from the under fide of the roots, and begun to make fhoots from the crown of the roots. But that wet will deftroy the roots I am fully convinced, for I fowed above an acre upon a moift fpot of ground for a trial, which came up very well, and flourifhed exceedingly during the fummer feafon, but in winter, when the great rains fell, the roots began to rot at bottom, and before the fpring moft of them were deftroyed. There has been lately fome perfons who have advifed the fowing of Lucern in broad-caft, and to make ufe of a ftrong harrow, to tear up and deftroy the weeds which naturally grow up among the plants; but this advice has been given too prematurely, therefore it is to be hoped will not be followed by any difcreet perfons, who are defired to take a furvey of fome of thefe lands which have been fo cultivated three or four years, which I am fully perfuaded will convince them of the bad hufbandry, for no perfon who has any regard to neatnefs and utility, will ever practife this method.

The beft places to procure the feed from, are Switzerland, and the northern parts of France, for the feeds faved in thofe countries fucceed better with us than that which comes from a more fouthern climate; but this feed may be faved full as well in England, and in as great plenty, were people curious enough to let the firft crop ftand for that purpofe; in order to which, a fmall quantity of the plants fhould be fuffered to grow uncut till the feeds are ripe, which is commonly about the beginning of September, when it muft be cut, and laid to dry in an open barn, where the air may freely pafs through, but be defended from the wet; for if it be expofed thereto, it will fhoot while it remains in the pod, whereby it will be fpoiled. When it is quite dry, it muft be threfhed out, and cleanfed from the hufk, and prefeved in a dry place till the feafon for fowing it; and this feed faved in England is much preferable to any brought from abroad, as I have feveral times experienced, the plants produced from it having been much ftronger than thofe produced from French, Helvetian, and Turkey feeds, which were fown at the fame time, and on the fame foil and fituation.

I am inclinable to think, that the reafon of this plant not fucceeding, when it has been fown in England, has either been occafioned by the fowing it with Corn, with which it will by no means thrive (for though the plant be very hardy when grown pretty large, yet at its firft coming up, if it be incommoded by any other plants or weeds, it feldom does well; therefore it fhould always be fown by itfelf, and carefully cleared from weeds until it has ftrength, after which it is not eafily deftroyed;) or, perhaps, people have fown it at a wrong feafon, or in wet weather, whereby the feeds have rotted, and never come up, which hath difcouraged their attempting it again : but however the fuccefs has been, I dare aver, that if the method of fowing and managing of this plant, which is here laid down, be duly followed, it will be found to thrive as well as any other fort of plant now cultivated in England, producing a much greater crop than any other fort of fodder, and will continue much longer; for if the ground be duly ftirred after the cutting each crop, and the laft crop fed as hath been directed, the plants will continue in vigour forty years or more, without renewing, provided they are not permitted to feed, which will weaken the roots more than four times cutting it would do. The hay of this plant fhould be kept in clofe barns, it being too tender to be kept in ricks open to the air as other hay; but it will remain good, if well dried before it be carried in, three years. The people abroad reckon an acre of this fodder fufficient to keep three horfes all the year round.

And I have been affured by perfons of undoubted credit, who have cultivated this plant in England, that three acres of it have fed ten cart-horfes from the end of April to the beginning of October, without any other food, though they have been conftantly worked. Indeed, the beft ufe which can be made of this Grafs is, to cut it, and give it green to the cattle; where this hath been daily practifed, I have obferved that by the time the field has been cut over, that part which was the firft cut hath been ready to cut again; fo that there has been a conftant fupply in the fame field, from the middle of April to the end of October : when the feafon has continued long mild, and when the fummers have proved fhowery, I have known fix crops cut in one feafon, but in the drieft feafons there will be always three or four. When the plant begins to flower, it fhould then be cut; for if it ftands longer, the ftalks will grow hard, and the under leaves will decay, fo that the cattle will not fo greedily devour it. Where there is a quantity of this cultivated, fome of it fhould be cut before the

flowers appear, otherwife there will be too much to cut within a proper time.

When this is made into hay, it will require a great deal of making; for as the ftalks are very fucculent, it muft be often turned, and expofed a fortnight or longer, before it will be fit to houfe; for this requires a longer time to make than Saint Foin; therefore, when it is cut, it fhould be carried to make upon fome Grafs ground, becaufe the earth in the intervals of the rows will wafh up, and mix with the hay in every fhower of rain, and by carrying it off as foon as it is cut, the plants will fhoot up again foon; but it is not fo profitable for hay, as to cut green for all forts of cattle, but efpecially horfes, which are extremely fond of it; and to them it will anfwer in the purpofe both of hay and Corn, and they may be worked at the fame time juft as much as when they are fed with Corn, or dry food.

The fecond fort grows naturally in the fouth of France, in Spain, Italy, and alfo in fome more northern countries, and has been fuppofed only a variety of the firft, but I have frequently cultivated this by feeds, and have never obferved it to alter. The ftalks of this are fmaller, and never rife fo high, generally proftrating on the ground; the leaves are not half fo broad, the flowers are produced in fhort roundifh fpikes, and are of a Saffron colour. This flowers about the fame time as the firft, and the feeds ripen in the latter part of fummer. It may be eafily propagated by feeds, and hath a perennial root which will continue many years, but is feldom cultivated any where. The third fort grows naturally in Italy; this is an annual plant, having feveral flender branching ftalks a foot and a half long, which fpread on the ground, garnifhed with trifoliate leaves, whofe lobes are oval, fpear-fhaped, and entire. The flowers are produced fingly upon flender foot-ftalks, which proceed from the fide of the branches; they are fmall, of a yellow colour, and fhaped like thofe of the former fort; thefe are fucceeded by broad, flat, moon-fhaped pods, whofe borders are indented, and thefe indentures are terminated by fine hairs; in each of thefe pods is lodged four or five kidney-fhaped feeds. It flowers in June and July, and the feeds ripen in the autumn.

The fourth fort grows naturally in Spain; this is alfo an annual plant, whofe ftalks grow a foot and a half long, trailing on the ground, and are garnifhed with winged leaves compofed of two pair of fmall lobes, terminated by one large, oval, fpear-fhaped lobe, which are a little hoary, and placed alternately at the joints. The flowers ftand upon long flender foot-ftalks, each fuftaining four or five gold-coloured flowers at the top, which are fucceeded by compreffed moon-fhaped pods, not half fo large as thofe of the third fort, but have hairy indentures like thofe. This flowers and perfects its feeds about the fame time as the former.

The fifth fort grows naturally on the borders of the fea in feveral parts of Italy; it is alfo an annual plant, with proftrate herbaceous ftalks about a foot long, garnifhed with trifoliate leaves, whofe lobes are wedge-fhaped and fawed toward the top. The flowers are produced upon flender foot-ftalks arifing from the joints of the ftalk; they are about an inch long, each fuftaining five or fix pale yellow flowers, which are fucceeded by fmall, thick, moon-fhaped pods, whofe borders are entire, containing three or four fmall kidney-fhaped feeds in each. It flowers and feeds about the fame time with the two former.

The fixth fort grows naturally in the Archipelago; this is an annual plant, from whofe roots come out feveral oblong leaves about two inches and a half long, narrow at their bafe, but broad toward the top, where they are rounded; thefe fpread on the ground, and between them come out the ftalks which are flender, about a foot long, branching out into fmaller, garnifhed with winged hoary leaves: thofe on the lower part of the ftalk are compofed of two pair of lobes terminated by an odd one; thefe are equal in fize, size, but those on the upper part of the stalks are trifoliate. The flowers are produced at the end of the stalks; they are small, yellow, and shaped like those of the other sorts, and are succeeded by compressed moon-shaped pods, which are acutely indented on their borders, and contain three or four kidney-shaped seeds. This plant flowers and ripens its seeds about the same time as the other.

These annual sorts are preserved in the gardens of those who are curious in botany; the seeds of these should be sown upon an open bed of fresh ground, in the places where the plants are to remain, because they do not bear transplanting well, unless when they are very young. As the plants spread their branches on the ground, so they should not be sown nearer than two feet and a half asunder; when the plants come up, they will require no other care but to keep them clean from weeds. In June they will begin to flower, and as the stalks and branches extend, there will be a succession of flowers produced till the autumn; for the early flowers are such as will have good seeds succeed them; for those which come late in summer, have not time to ripen before the cold weather comes on.

The seventh sort grows naturally in the islands of the Archipelago, in Sicily, and the warmest parts of Italy. This rises with a shrubby stalk to the height of eight or ten feet, covered with a gray bark, and divides into many branches, which, while young, are covered with a hoary down; these are garnished at each joint with trifoliate leaves, standing upon foot-stalks about an inch long; there are two or three of these at each joint, so that the branches are closely covered with them; the lobes are small, spear-shaped, and hoary on their under side; these remain all the year. The flowers are produced on foot-stalks which arise from the side of the branches, they are of a bright yellow, each foot-stalk sustaining four or five flowers; these are succeeded by compressed moon-shaped pods, each containing three or four kidney-shaped seeds.

It flowers great part of the year, and when the winters are favourable all the year; or when the plants are sheltered in winter, they are seldom destitute of flowers; but those in the open air begin to flower in April, and continue in succession till December. Those flowers which appear early in summer will have their seeds ripe in August, or the beginning of September, and the others will ripen in succession till the cold stops them.

This plant may be propagated by sowing the seeds upon a moderate hot-bed, or a warm border of light earth, in the beginning of April; and when the plants come up, they should be carefully cleared from weeds; but they should remain undisturbed, if sown in the common ground, till September following; but if on a hot-bed, they should be transplanted about Mid-summer into pots, placing them in the shade until they have taken root; after which they may be removed into a situation where they may be screened from strong winds, in which they may abide till the latter end of October, when they must be put into a common garden frame, to shelter them from hard frosts; for those plants which have been brought up tenderly, will be liable to suffer by hard weather, especially while they are young. In April following these plants may be shaken out of the pots, and placed in the full ground where they are designed to remain, which should be in a light soil and a warm situation, in which they will endure the cold of our ordinary winters extremely well, and continue to produce flowers most part of the year, and retaining their leaves all the winter renders them the more valuable.

Those also which were sown in an open border may be transplanted in August following, in the same manner; but in doing of this you must be careful to take them up with a ball of earth to their roots, if possible, as also to water and shade them until they have taken root; after which they will require little more care than to keep them clean from weeds, and to prune off the luxuriant branches to keep them with-

in due compass; but you should never prune them early in the spring, nor late in autumn, for if frost should happen soon after they are pruned, it will destroy the tender branches, and many times the whole plant is lost thereby.

These plants have been constantly preserved in the green-house, supposing them too tender to live thro' the winter in the open air; but I have had large plants of this kind, which have remained in a warm situation many years without any cover, and have been much stronger, and flowered better, than those which were housed; though, indeed, it will be proper to keep a plant or two in shelter, left by a very severe winter (which sometimes happens in England) the plants abroad should be destroyed.

They may also be propagated by cuttings, which should be planted in April, and watered and shaded until they have taken root, after which they may be exposed to the open air; but they should remain in the same bed till July or August following, before they are transplanted, by which time they will have made strong roots, and may be removed with safety to the places where they are to remain, observing (as was before directed) to water and shade them until they have taken root; after which you may train them up with strait stems, by fastening them to sticks, otherwise they are apt to grow crooked and irregular; and when you have got their stems to the height you design them, they may then be reduced to regular heads, and with pruning their irregular shoots every year, they may be kept in very good order.

This plant grows in great plenty in the kingdom of Naples, where the goats feed upon it, with whose milk the inhabitants make great quantities of cheese; it also grows in the islands of the Archipelago, where the Turks use the wood of these shrubs to make handles for their sabres, and the Caliogers of Patmos make their beds of this wood.

This is, as hath been before observed, by many people, supposed to be the Cytisus of Virgil, Columella, and the old writers in husbandry, which they mention as an extraordinary plant, and worthy of cultivation for fodder, from whence several persons have recommended it as worthy of our care in England. But however useful this plant may be in Crete, Sicily, Naples, or those warmer countries, yet I am persuaded it will never thrive in England, so as to be of any real advantage for that purpose; for in severe frost it is very subject to be destroyed, or at least so much damaged, as not to recover its former verdure before the middle or latter end of May; and the shoots which are produced will not bear cutting above once in a summer, and then will not be of any considerable length; and the stems growing very woody, will render the cutting of it very troublesome; so that, upon the whole, it can never answer the trouble and expence in cultivating it, nor is it worth the trial, since we have so many other plants preferable to it; though in hot, dry, rocky countries, where few other plants will thrive, this may be cultivated to great advantage, since in such situations this plant will live many years, and thrive very well.

But however unfit this may be for such uses in England, yet for the beauty of its hoary leaves, which will abide all the year, together with its long continuance in flower, it deserves a place in every good garden, where, being intermixed with shrubs of the same growth, it makes a very agreeable variety.

As there are at present so many persons inquisitive to know which is the true Cytisus mentioned by the antients, I have taken the pains of transcribing briefly what they have said as to its description, by which may be judged how uncertain it is to determine in an affair where there is so little to be found in authors to assist us.

Theophrastus says, Cytisus is such an enemy to other plants, that it will kill them, by robbing them of nourishment, and that the medulla of it is so hard and thick, that it comes the nearest of any thing to Ebenum.

The

The fhrub Cytifus, by Ariftomachus, the Athenian, as may be feen in Pliny [who fays much the fame as Varro and Columella, from whom probably he has taken it,] is highly commended for food for fheep, and, being dry, for fwine ; the utility [as to health and fattening, Dal.] the fame as that of Ervum, but the fatiety is quicker, a four-footed animal growing fat with a little of it, fo that cattle fet light by their Barley.

No food makes a greater quantity, nor better milk, and it excels all things as to the difeafes of cattle; moreover, being given dry, or in a decoction of water mixed with wine, to nurfes whofe milk fails, it helps very much,and makes the children ftronger, and take to their feet fooner; green, it is alfo good for them, or dry, if it be made moift.

Democritus and Ariftomachus fay, bees will never want food, if they have Cytifus enough, nor is any thing cheaper.

If, when the feed be fown, fhowers are wanting, Columella directs, That it be watered the fifteen following days.

It is fown [according to the antients] after the equinoxes. It is perfected in three years. It is mown in the vernal equinox [for it flourifhes all the winter, Dal.] with the cheap labour of a boy, or old woman.

The Cytifus is hoary in afpect. If any one would exprefs its likenefs briefly, it is a fhrub of a broader fort of Trefoil.

In winter, being moiftened, ten pounds will fatisfy a horfe, and a lefs quantity other animals. Being dry, it has more virtue, and a lefs quantity fatisfies.

This fhrub was found in the ifle Cythnus, thence it was tranflated into all the Cyclades, and afterwards into the cities of Greece, where it occafioned a great increafe of cheefe.

It fears not the injury of heat nor cold, nor hail nor fnow, and Hyginus adds, nor of enemies, becaufe the wood is of no value.

Alfo Galen, in his book de Antid. writes, " Cytifus " is a fhrub. In Myfia, in that part that is neareft to " our province, there is a tract which they call Brot- " ton, in which there is a place full of Cytifus, from " the flowers of which, all agree, the bees make very " much honey.

" It is a fruticofe plant ; it rifes to the height of a " Myrtle."

He fays, feven fimple leaves have the faculty of digefting, mixed with warm water, as the leaves of Mallows : thus Galen.

Cornarus too fecurely writes, That Cytifus either never came among the Germans, or that it perifhed long ago. From what Pliny fays, That it was very rare in Italy in his time, he cannot perfuade me, that nothing could grow in Germany, that was fcarce in Italy. Jo. Bauh.

Strabo, contrary to Diofcorides, Pliny, and Galen, will have the Cytifus to be a tree, and he likens it to the Balfamum, an odoriferous tree, which probably was the occafion, that Cornarus thought this tree came neareft to a fhrub, becaufe Pliny faid the wood was of no value, therefore he perfuades himfelf, that it produces woody branches, not tender and foft, as in an herb.

But Virgil fhews it is neither a tree nor a fhrub, when he fays :

" —— Non me pafcente, capellæ,
" Florentem Cytifum, & falices capretis amaras."
[Buc. Ecloo. 1.
" Sic Cytifo paftæ diftendunt ubera vaccæ."
Ecloo. 9.
" Nec Cytifo faturantur apes, nec fronde capellæ."
Ecloo. 10.

Virgil, I fay, indicates very plainly in thefe verfes, that it is neither a tree nor a fhrub, for goats do not ufe it ; nor can they, if they were wont to eat flowery trees. Neither will what Cornarus fays avail, when

Pliny fays the wood is of no value, that it muft of neceffity produce woody branches; nay, the contrary is rather true, that there is no value in the wood, that it bears viny pliable branches, with which the goats cannot be fatiated.

Theocritus very plainly exprefies it, That Cytifus is a very grateful food to goats :

Ἡ αἴξ τὸν κύτισον, ὀλλῶ τὴν αἶγα διώκει.

" Capra Cytifum, lupus capellam fequitur."

Which is thus imitated by Virgil :

" Torva leæna lupum fequitur, lupus ipfe capellam :
" Florentem Cytifum fequitur lafciva capella."

Amatus, to avoid this difficulty, concludes Cytifus to be between trees and fhrubs, by the difference of genus, to be diftinguifhed by Pliny, that, as a tree, it may be ufed in the feminine gender, as a fhrub in the mafculine, which is not worth the minding.

Columella ufes Cytifus in the feminine gender, and Theocritus and others in the mafculine; as Cob. Conft. in Lex. who writes that it was called ἀρσένω-λον, and Theocritus calls this fhrub κυτισόν, and others, κύτισος; others again τηλις.

Of Cythnus, or, as others, of Cythifa, the name of an ifland, as Severius has it.

Among thefe words of Diofcorides in fome manufcripts, there are found, falfely written, in fome, Telinen Triphyllon, in others Lotum Grandem.

Diofcorides's defcription of the Cytifus is not fo accurate, that from it the true Cytifus may be afcertained.

Although in the feveral fpecies of Cytifufes it is hard to judge which is the legitimate Cytifus fpecified by the antients ; the moft fkilful take it to be that which Maranthus has defcribed, which is our Medica, which has been ranged under the genus of Cytifus, by moft of the writers before Dr. Tournefort, who eftablifhed the genus of Medicago, on account of the feed-veffel being like that of Medica, or Snail Trefoil.

This plant grows in great plenty at Abruzzo, where the goats feed upon it, and from their milk are made great quantities of cheefe. I have had both feeds and fpecimens of the plant fent me from thence, by perfons of the greateft fkill in botany, who have affured me, that this plant is generally fuppofed, by all the people of learning in that country, to be the plant mentioned by Virgil.

Trifolium fruticans, according to Dodonæus, or Polemonium, according to fome, is improperly called, Cytifus by many.

Trifolium candidum Dodon. by fome is faid to be the Cytifus of Columella, concerning which, fee Lib. Hift. n. 9. 17. of Trifolious herbs.

Tragus writes, That their opinion is to be rejected, who interpret the Trifolium pratenfe to be a Cytifus. Some contend the Trifolium candidum of Dodon. the Rectum Melilotum vulgarem, to be the Cytifus of the antients, as Dodonæus fays, but they have not hit on the truth.

Ruellius writes, That he was afraid that Marcellus took Cytifus for Medica.

MEDICAGO. Lin. Gen. Plant. 805. Medica. Tourn. Inft. R. H. 410. tab. 231. Snail Trefoil.

The CHARACTERS are,

The flower hath a cylindrical erect empalement of one leaf, which is cut at the brim into five equal acute fegments. The flower is of the butterfly kind, having an oval erect ftandard, whofe borders are reflexed. The wings are oblong, oval, and fixed to the keel by an appendix. The keel is oblong, bifid, obtufe, and reflexed. It hath ten ftamina, nine of which are joined, and the other is fingle, terminated by fmall fummits, and an oblong germen, which fits upon a fhort ftyle, is involved with the ftamina by the keel, and crowned by a very fmall ftigma. The germen afterward turns to a long compreffed pod, twifted into the form of a fnail, inclofing many kidney-fhaped feeds.

This

This genus of plants is ranged in the fame fection and clafs, as the former by Tournefort and Linnæus.

The Species are,

1. Medicago (*Marina*) pedunculis racemofis, leguminibus cochleatis, fpinofis, caule procumbente tomentofo. Hort. Cliff. 378. *Medicago with branching footftalks, fnail-fhaped prickly pods, and a trailing woolly ftalk.* Medica Marina. Lob. Icon. 38. *Sea Medick, or Snail Trefoil.*

2. Medicago (*Scutellata*) leguminibus chochleatis, inermibus ftipulis dentatis caule angulofo diffufo, foliolis oblongo ovatis acute dentatis. *Medicago with fmooth fnail-fhaped pods, indented ftipulæ, an angular diffufed ftalk, and oblong, oval, fmall leaves, which are fharply indented.* Medica fcutellata. J. B. 2. 384. *Snail Trefoil, commonly called Snails.*

3. Medicago (*Tornato*) leguminibus tornatis inermibus, ftipulis acutè dentatis foliolis ferratis. *Medicago with a turned fmooth pod, acute indented ftipulæ, and the fmall leaves fawed.* Medica tornata minor lenis. Park. Theat. 1116. *Snail Trefoil with a fmaller, turned, fmooth fruit.*

4. Medicago (*Intortexta*) leguminibus cochleatis fpinofiffimis aculeis utrinque tendentibus. *Medicago with very prickly fnail-fhaped pods, whofe fpines point every way.* Medica magno fructu, aculeis furfum & deorfum tendentibus. Tourn. Inft. R. H. 411. *Snail Trefoil with a large fruit, whofe fpines point upward and downward, commonly called Hedgehog.*

5. Medicago (*Laciniata*) leguminibus chochleatis fpinofis, foliolis acutè dentatis tricufpidifque. *Medicago with prickly fnail-fhaped pods, whofe lobes are acutely indented, and terminate in three points.* Medica cochleata dicarpos capfulâ rotundâ fpinosâ, foliis eleganter diffectis. H. L. B. *Snail-fhaped Trefoil, having a double fruit with a round prickly capfule, and elegant cut leaves.* There are many other fpecies of this genus, which grow naturally in the warm parts of Europe, and are frequently preferved in botanic gardens for the fake of variety; but thefe are rarely cultivated in other gardens, fo it would be befide my purpofe to enumerate them here.

The firft fort grows naturally on the borders of the Mediterranean Sea; this is a perennial plant, with trailing woolly branches about a foot long, which are divided into fmall branches, garnifhed with fmall, trifoliate, downy leaves at each joint, ftanding upon fhort foot-ftalks. The flowers are produced from the fide and at the ends of the branches, in fmall clufters; they are of a bright yellow colour, and are fucceeded by fmall roundifh fnail-fhaped fruit, which are downy, and armed with a few fhort fpines. The flowers appear in June and July, and the feeds ripen in September.

This plant is propagated by feeds, which fhould be fown upon a warm border of dry foil in the fpring, where the plants are defigned to remain; when the plants are come up, two or three of them may be tranfplanted into fmall pots to be fheltered in winter, becaufe in very fevere froft, thofe which are in the open air are frequently deftroyed; though they will endure the cold of our ordinary winters, if they are growing in a dry foil and a fheltered fituation. Thofe plants which are left remaining, will require no other culture but to thin them where they are too clofe, and keep them clean from weeds. This fort may be propagated by cuttings, which may be planted in June or July, in a fhady border, covering them clofe with a glafs to exclude the external air; thefe will take root in about fix weeks time, and may then be either planted in a warm border or in pots, and treated in the fame way as the feedling plants.

The fecond fort is an annual plant, which grows naturally in the warm parts of Europe, but in England it is frequently cultivated in gardens for the oddnefs of its fruit, which is twifted in the form of a fnail; and as it ripens turns to a dark brown colour, fo as to have the appearance of fnails feeding on the plants at a diftant view. This hath trailing branches; the flowers are of a pale yellow, and come out from the

fide of the branches. Thefe appear in June and July, and the feeds ripen in the autumn. It is propagated by feeds, which fhould be fown in the middle of April, where the plants are to remain; and the plants fhould be thinned where they are too clofe, and kept clean from weeds, which is all the culture they require. The third fort is alfo an annual plant, which grows in the fame countries as the former. This hath trailing branches, and yellow flowers like the fecond fort, but the fruit is much longer and clofer twifted, fo as to refemble the figure of a veffel called a pipe, being lefs at each end than in the middle. This is frequently kept in gardens for the fake of variety, and may be propagated and treated in the fame way as the fecond fort.

The fourth fort is an annual plant, which was formerly more cultivated in the Englifh gardens than at prefent. The ftalks, leaves, and flowers, are like thofe of the two former forts, but the fruit is much larger, and clofely armed with long fpines like a hedgehog, from whence it had the title; thefe fpines point every way, fo that it is difficult to handle the fruit without fmarting for it. This is propagated by feeds in the fame way as the fecond fort, and the plants require the fame treatment. It flowers in June, and the feeds ripen in September.

The fifth fort grows naturally in Syria; it is an annual plant, with trailing ftalks like the former; the lobes of the trifoliate leaves are wedge-fhaped, fharply indented on the edges, and at the top have three acute points. The flowers are of a pale yellow, and the fruit is fnail-fhaped, but fmall, armed with many weak fpines. It flowers about the fame time with the former, and may be cultivated in the fame way.

MEDLAR. See Mespilus.

MELAMPYRUM. Tourn. Inft. R. H. 173. tab. 78. Lin. Gen. Plant. 660. Μελάμπυρον, of μίλας, black, and πυρός, Wheat.] Cow Wheat.

The Characters are,

The flower has a permanent empalement of one leaf, which is tubulous, cut into four fegments at the brim. The flower is of the lip kind, having an oblong recurved tube compreffed at the brim; the upper lip is formed like a helmet, and is compreffed and indented at the top; the under lip is plain, erect, and cut into three fegments at the top, which are equal and obtufe. It hath four awl-fhaped ftamina which are curved under the upper lip, two of which are fhorter than the other, terminated by oblong fummits, and in the center is fituated an acute-pointed germen, fupporting a fingle ftyle crowned by an obtufe ftigma. The empalement afterward turns to an oblong acute-pointed capfule with two cells, inclofing two pretty large oval feeds.

This genus of plants is ranged in the fecond fection of Linnæus's fourteenth clafs, which contains thofe plants whofe flowers have two long and two fhorter ftamina, and the feeds are included in a capnfule.

The Species are,

1. Melampyrum (*Pretenfe*) floribus fecundis lateralibus, conjugationibus remotis, corollis claufis. Flor. Suec. 513. *Cow Wheat with fruitful foot-ftalks of flowers ftanding at a diftance, and the petals fhut.* Melampyrum luteum latifolium. C. B. P. 234. *Broad-leeved yellow Cow Wheat.*

2. Melampyrum (*Criftatum*) fpicis quadrangularibus bracteis cordatis compactis denticulis imbricatis. Flor. Suec. 510. *Cow Wheat with quadrangular fpikes, and heart-fhaped bractea, which are imbricated.*Melampyrum luteum anguftifolium. C. B. P. 234. *Yellow narrow-leaved Cow Wheat.*

3. Melampyrum (*Arvenfe*) fpicis conicis laxè bracteis dentato-fetaceis. Flor. Seuc. 511. *Cow Wheat with loofe conical fpikes, and briftly indented bractea.* Melampyrum purpurafcente comâ. C. B. P. 234. *Cow Wheat with purplifh tops.*

4. Melampyrum (*Nemorofum*) floribus fecundis lateralibus bracteis dentato cordato lanceolatis, fummis, coloratis fterilibus, calycibus lanatis. Flor. Suec. 512. *Cow Wheat with fruitful lateral flowers, heart fpear-fhaped bractea, fterile coloured tops, and woolly empalements.*

ments. Melampyrum comâ cæruleâ. C. B. P. 234.
Cow Wheat with blue tops.

These plants are seldom cultivated in gardens. The first sort grows naturally in woods in many parts of England. The second sort grows plentifully in Bedfordshire and Cambridgeshire. The fourth sort grows in the northern parts of Europe. The third sort grows naturally in some of the sandy lands in Norfolk, tho' not in great plenty ; but in West Friezland and Flanders, it grows very plentifully among the Corn ; and Clusius says, it spoils their bread, making it dark ; and that those who eat of it used to be troubled with heaviness of the head, in the same manner as if they had eaten Darnel or Cockle : but Mr. Ray says, He has eaten of this bread very often, but could never perceive that it gave any disagreeable taste, or that it was accounted unwholesome by the country people, who never endeavour to separate it from the Corn : and Tabernæmontanus declares, he has often eaten it without any harm ; and says, it makes a very pleasant bread. It is a delicious food for cattle, particularly for fattening of oxen and cows, for which purpose it may be cultivated.

The seeds of these plants should be sown in the autumn soon after they are ripe, otherwise it seldom grows the first year ; when the plants come up, they must be weeded in the spring while young, and as soon as they begin to shew their flowers, the cattle may be fed upon it ; but they should be confined to a certain space, and not permitted to run over the whole field to trample it down, which would destroy a great part of it.

The third and fourth sorts make a pretty appearance, with their purple and blue tops, during the months of July and August. They are all of them annual plants.

MELANTHIUM, Star-flower.

The CHARACTERS are,

The flower has no empalement (unless the corolla is so called) it hath six oblong, oval, spreading petals, which are permanent, and six slender erect stamina inserted above the tails, with globular summits, with a streaked globular germen, supporting three curved distinct styles, crowned by obtuse stigma ; the germen afterward turns to an oval capsule, having three cells, which are united within, containing several oval compressed seeds.

This genus of plants is ranged in the third section of Linnæus's sixth class, intitled Hexandria Trigynia, the flower having six stamina and three styles.

The SPECIES are,

1. MELANTHIUM (*Virginicum*) petalis unguiculatis. Lin. Sp. Plant. 483. *Star-flower with tender nail-shaped petals.* Asphodelo affinis Floridana, ramoso caule, floribus ornithogali obsoleti. Pluk. tab. 434. f. 8.

2. MELANTHIUM (*Sibericum*) petalis sessilibus. Amœn. Acad. 2. p. 349. *Star-flower with sessile petals.* Ornithogalum spicis florum longissimis ramosis. Flor. Siber. p. 45.

3. MELANTHIUM (*Punctatum*) petalis punctatis, foliis cucullatis. Amœn. Acad. 63. *Star-flower with punctated petals, and hooded leaves.*

The first sort grows naturally in Virginia and in other parts of North America, but being a plant of little beauty, is seldom cultivated except in botanic gardens ; the flower-stalks of this rises from six to eight inches high, branching upward into three or four divisions, garnished below the flower with two or three linear leaves. The flowers are composed of six spreading petals of a dusky worn-out colour, which are rarely succeeded by seeds in England.

If the roots of this plant are planted in a border of light earth, not too dry, they will thrive and produce their flowers here, but seldom increase.

The second sort grows naturally in Siberia, so is at present a stranger in England, but may be propagated here (if once obtained) by planting the bulbous roots in an east border.

The third sort grows at the Cape of Good Hope, so is too tender to thrive in the open air in England. But if the roots are planted in a border, covered in win-

ter with a garden frame, and treated in the same way as is directed for the Ixia, they will thrive and flower annually.

MELASTOMA. Lin. Gen. Plant. 481. Grossularia. Sloan. Hist. Jam. Plum. Sp. 18. The American Gooseberry-tree, vulgò.

The CHARACTERS are,

The flower has a permanent empalement of one leaf, swelling like a bladder, and obtuse. It hath five roundish petals, which are inserted into the border of the empalement, and ten short stamina, terminated by long erect summits a little curved. Under the flower is situated a roundish germen, supporting a slender style, crowned by an incurved indented stigma. The germen afterward turns to a berry with five cells, covered by the empalement which crowns it, and contains many small seeds.

This genus of plants is ranged in the first section of Linnæus's tenth class, intitled Decandria Monogynia, which includes those plants whose flowers have ten stamina and one style.

The SPECIES are,

1. MELASTOMA (*Plantaginis folio*) foliis denticulatis ovatis acutis. Lin. Sp. Plant. 389. *Melastoma with oval, acute-pointed, indented leaves.* Grossularia Americana, plantaginis folio amplissimo. Plum. Sp. 18.

2. MELASTOMA (*Acinodendron*) foliis denticulatis subtrinerviis ovatis acutis. Lin. Sp. Plant. 558. *Melastoma with oval indented leaves ending in acute points, having three veins.* Grossularia alia plantaginis folio, fructu rariore violaceo. Plum. Sp. 18.

3. MELASTOMA (*Hirta*) foliis denticulatis quinquenervibus, ovato-lanceolatis caule hispido. Lin. Sp. 390. *Melastoma with spear-shaped indented leaves, with five veins, and a prickly stalk.* Grossularia plantaginis folio angustiore hirsuto. Plum. Sp. 18.

4. MELASTOMA (*Holosericea*) foliis integerrimis trinerviis oblongo-ovatis tomentosis racemis secundis, spicis bipartitis. Lin. Sp. 559. *Melastoma with very entire oblong oval leaves, which are woolly on their under side, and spikes of flowers dividing in two parts.* Arbor racemosa Brasiliana, folio Malabathri. Breyn. Cent. tab. 2 & 3.

5. MELASTOMA (*Grossularioides*) foliis lanceolatis utrinque glabris nervis tribus ante basin coëuntibus. Hort. Cliff. 162. *Melastoma with spear-shaped leaves smooth on both sides, and three veins which join before they reach the base.* Grossularia fructu non spinoso, Malabathri foliis oblongis, floribus herbaceis racemosis, fructu nigro. Sloan. Cat. 165.

6. MELASTOMA (*Bicolor*) foliis lanceolatis, nervis tribus longitudinalibus, subtus glabris coloratis. Hort. Cliff. 162. *Melastoma with spear-shaped leaves having three longitudinal veins, smooth and coloured on their under side.*

7. MELASTOMA (*Malabathrica*) foliis lanceolato-ovatis quinquenerviis scabris. Flor. Zeyl. 171. *Melastoma with spear-shaped oval leaves which are rough, and have five veins.* Melastoma quinque nervia hirta major, capitulis sericeis villosis. Burm. Zeyl. 155. tab. 73.

8. MELASTOMA (*Lævigata*) foliis oblongo-ovatis minutissimè dentatis infernè sericeis quinquenervibus, floribus racemosis. *Melastoma with oblong oval leaves, having very small indentures on the edges, and silky on their under side, with five veins, and flowers growing in long bunches.* Grossulariæ fructu, arbor maximo non spinosa, Malabathri folio maximo inodora, flore racemoso albo. Sloan. Cat. Jam. 165.

9. MELASTOMA (*Petiolatis*) foliis denticulatis ovatis acuminatis, infernè nitidissimis, petiolis longissimis. *Melastoma with oval acute-pointed leaves, which are indented on their edges, very shining on their under side, and have very long foot-stalks.*

10. MELASTOMA (*Umbellata*) foliis cordatis acuminatis integerrimis, infernè incanis, floribus umbellatis. *Melastoma with heart-shaped, acute-pointed, entire leaves, hoary on their under side, and flowers growing in umbels.* Sambucus Barbadensis dicta, foliis subincanis. Pluk. Phyt. tab. 221. fol. 6.

11. MELASTOMA (*Racemosa*) foliis oblongo-cordatis acuminatis, denticulato-serratis, floribus racemosis sparsis.

fis. *Melastoma with oblong, heart-shaped, acute-pointed leaves, having sawed indentures, and flowers growing thinly in long bunches.*

12. MELASTOMA (*Verticillata*) foliis ovato-lanceolatis, quinquenervibus, subtus aureis, floribus verticillatis, caule tomentoso. *Melastoma with oval spear-shaped leaves having five veins, which are of a gold colour on their under side, and flowers growing in whorls, with a woolly stalk.*

13. MELASTOMA (*Acuta*) foliis lanceolatis acutis denticulatis infernè incanis trinervibus, floribus racemosis. *Melastoma with acute spear-shaped leaves which are indented on their edges, hoary on their under side, have three veins, and flowers growing in bunches.*

14. MELASTOMA (*Glabra*) foliis ovato-lanceolatis acuminatis integerrimis, utrinque glabris trinervibus, floribus racemosis. *Melastoma with entire, oval, spear-shaped leaves ending in acute points, having three veins, and smooth on both sides, with flowers growing in long bunches.* Arbor Syrinamensis, canellæ folio utrinque glabro. Pluk. Phyt. tab. 249. fol. 5.

15. MELASTOMA (*Quinquenervia*) foliis ovatis quinquenervibus scabris, floribus racemosis alaribus. *Melastoma with oval rough leaves having five veins, and flowers growing in bunches from the sides of the branches.*

16. MELASTOMA (*Octandria*) foliis lanceolatis trinervibus glabris, marginibus hispidis. *Melastoma with smooth spear-shaped leaves having three veins, and hairy prickles on the border.*

17. MELASTOMA (*Aspera*) foliis ovatis quinquenervibus glabris, marginibus hispidis. *Melastoma with oval smooth leaves, having five veins, and hairy prickly borders.*

18. MELASTOMA (*Scabrosa*) foliis ovato-lanceolatis scabris acuminatis quinquenervibus, floribus racemosis. *Melastoma with oval, spear-shaped, acute-pointed leaves, having five veins, and flowers growing in long bunches.*

The title of this genus of plants was given to it by Professor Burman, of Amsterdam, in the Thesaurus Zeylanicus; some of these plants have been titled Sambucus, others Christophoriana, and to some of the species Dr. Plukenet gave the title of Acidendron; but Sir Hans Sloane and Father Plumier, gave them the title of Grossularia, from whence I have applied the English name of Goofeberry to them, which is the name by which some of the sorts are known in America.

The first sort rises about four or five feet high, the stem and branches being covered with long ruffet hairs; the leaves are placed on the branches opposite; they are five inches long and two broad, and are also covered with the same ruffet down, having five ribs or veins running through the leaves from end to end, but the three inner join before they reach the base, with small transverse ribs; the fruit is produced at the end of the shoots, which is a pulpy blue berry, as large as a Nutmeg.

The second sort grows to be a large tree, having many crooked branches, covered with a brown bark, the leaves placed opposite on the branches; these are smooth, entire, and above five inches long, and two broad in the middle, with three deep veins running through them; both sides of these leaves are of a light green and smooth, and are sharply indented on their edges, ending in acute points. The fruit grows in loose spikes at the end of the branches; they are thinly placed on the spikes, and are of a Violet colour.

The third sort grows to the height of twenty feet, with a large trunk, covered with a ruffet bark: the leaves of this tree are very large, being above seven inches long, and three and a quarter broad, of a dark ruffet colour on their upper side, but of a yellowish ruffet on their under, soft to the touch, having a soft down over them; the stalks are covered with rough hairs, and the leaves are placed by pairs on the branches, which make a beautiful appearance when the trees are viewed at a distance.

The fourth sort seldom grows more than eight or ten feet high, the leaves are about four inches long,

having three veins, which join before they reach the base; they are entire, and are of a sattin colour on their under side, but of a light green on their upper; these are placed by pairs on the branches.

The fifth sort seldom grows more than seven or eight feet high, spreading out into many branches, which are covered with a smooth purple bark; they are slender, and are garnished with spear-shaped leaves, five inches long and two broad in the middle, where they are broadest; they are smooth on both sides, their edges are entire, and they terminate in acute points. The flowers are produced in pretty long hanging bunches, of an herbaceous colour, with long styles which are stretched out a good length beyond the petals, and are permanent; the fruit is small, and black when ripe.

The sixth sort rises four or five feet high, dividing into many slender branches, which are smooth, and garnished with spear-shaped leaves three inches long, and one and a quarter broad, of a lucid green on the upper side, but white on the under, having three longitudinal veins which join before they reach the base; these are entire, and placed alternately on the branches. The flowers are produced in a loose panicle at the end of the branches; they are small, white, and have pretty long tubes; these are succeeded by small purple fruit.

The seventh sort rises with an angular stalk six or seven feet high, sending out branches opposite, which are garnished with spear-shaped, oval, rough leaves, placed by pairs; they are hairy, of a dark green on their upper side, but of a pale green on their under. The flowers are produced at the end of the branches, two or three standing together; they are large, and of a Rose colour, inclining to purple, sitting in large hairy empalements; these are succeeded by roundish purple fruit crowned by the empalement, which are filled with a purple pulp surrounding the seeds.

The eighth sort grows to the height of twenty feet, with a large strait stem, covered with a gray bark, and at the top divides into many angular branches; these are garnished with oblong oval leaves near a foot long, and six inches broad in the middle, of a dark green on their upper side, but silky on their under, with five strong longitudinal veins; they are indented on their edges, and placed opposite. The flowers are produced in loose long bunches at the end of the branches; these are white, and are succeeded by roundish purple fruit, filled with pulp, in which the seeds are lodged.

The ninth sort rises with a strong erect stalk near thirty feet high, covered with a gray bark, dividing at the top into several angular compressed branches, which are garnished with oval leaves indented on their edges; they are seven inches long and almost five broad, standing by pairs opposite on very long footstalks, of a lucid green on their upper side, but of a pale gold colour and sattiny on their under, with five strong longitudinal veins, and a great number of smaller transverse ones. The flowers are produced in loose panicles at the end of the branches; they are white, and are succeeded by purple fruit, about the same size as those of the former.

The tenth sort rises with a shrubby stalk ten or twelve feet high, covered with a hairy bark, and divides into many branches toward the top, which are garnished with heart-shaped leaves ending in acute points; they are five inches long and three broad toward their base, entire in their borders, of a dark green on their upper side, but hoary on their under, with five longitudinal veins, and many smaller transverse ones; these are placed opposite, and stand upon hairy footstalks, two inches and a half in length. The flowers are produced at the end of the branches, in a sort of umbel; they are of a pale Rose colour and pretty large, sitting on hairy empalements; these are succeeded by small black fruit, a little larger than Elder-berries.

The eleventh sort rises with a shrubby stalk about eight or nine feet high, covered with a dark brown bark,

bark, and divides at the top into many ftraggling branches, which are garnifhed with oblong heart-fhaped leaves fix inches long, and three broad toward their bafe, ending in acute points, indented on their edges with fharp ferratures ; they are fmooth on both fides, and of a light green colour. The flowers are produced in very loofe bunches at the end of the branches; they are fmall, of an herbaceous colour, and are fucceeded by fmall fruit, of a dark colour when ripe.

The twelfth fort rifes with a fhrubby ftalk five or fix feet high, dividing into many fmaller branches, which are covered with a hairy woolly bark, of a rufty iron colour; thefe are garnifhed with oval fpear-fhaped leaves, one inch and a half long, and three quarters of an inch broad in the middle; they are of a dark green on their upper fide, and of a rufty iron colour on their under, having five longitudinal veins; they are placed oppofite, and fit clofe to the branches. The flowers come out in whorls at the joints of the ftalks; they are fmall, of a purplifh colour, and are fucceeded by fmall black fruit.

The thirteenth fort is a low fhrub, feldom rifing more than three feet high, dividing at the bottom into flender branches, which are garnifhed with fpear-fhaped leaves, ending in acute points ; thefe are five inches long, and one and a half broad in the middle, fawed on their edges, of a dark green on their upper fide, but of a hoary white on their under, having three longitudinal veins ; they are placed oppofite, upon fhort foot-ftalks. The flowers are produced in loofe bunches at the end of the branches ; they are white, and fucceeded by fmall purple fruit.

The fourteenth fort hath a fhrubby ftalk eight or nine feet high, divided toward the top into many flender branches which are fmooth, garnifhed with oval fpear-fhaped leaves, which are feven inches long and three broad, ending in acute points; they are entire on their edges, and fmooth on both fides, ftanding oppofite, and have three longitudinal veins. The flowers are produced in loofe panicles at the end of the branches, and are fucceeded by very fmall pur-ple fruit.

The fifteenth fort rifes with feveral fhrubby ftalks five or fix feet high, dividing into feveral crooked branches, garnifhed with oval leaves three inches long, and almoft as much broad, having five longitudinal veins; they are rough, of a dark green on their upper fide, but of a pale green on their under, indented on their edges, ftanding upon very hairy foot-ftalks; they are fometimes oppofite, and at others alternate, on the branches. The flowers are produced in very loofe bunches, which come out from the fide of the ftalks ; they are fmall, of an herbaceous colour, and are fucceeded by fmall purplifh fruit, filled with very fmall feeds.

The fixteenth fort rifes with a fhrubby ftalk feven or eight feet high, and divides into many fmooth branches, which are garnifhed with fpear-fhaped leaves about four inches long, and one inch and a quarter broad in the middle; they are fmooth on both fides, of a dark green colour, and have three longitudinal veins ; the edges of thefe leaves are clofely fet with briftly ftinging hairs. The flowers are produced in loofe bunches at the end of the branches ; they are fmall, of a purplifh colour, and are fucceeded by very fmall black fruit.

The feventeenth fort is in many parts like the former, but the leaves are oval, a little more than two inches long, and one and a quarter broad ; thefe have five lon-gitudinal veins, and are fmooth on both fides, of a dark green colour, and ftand oppofite on fhort foot-ftalks. The flowers grow in loofe bunches at the end of the branches, they are larger than thofe of the former fort, but are of the fame colour. The edges of the leaves of this fort are clofely fet with ftinging hairs, as thofe of the other.

The eighteenth fort rifes with a fhrubby ftalk eight or nine feet high, dividing into branches ftanding oppofite, as do alfo the leaves, which are feven inches

long and three broad, rough on their furface, entire on their edges, ending in acute points ; they are of a light green on both fides, and ftand upon fhort foot-ftalks. The flowers are produced in pretty large loofe panicles at the end of the branches ; they are fmall, white, and are fucceeded by fmall, round, purple fruit.

All the forts are natives of the warm parts of Ame-rica, where there are many more fpecies than are here enumerated. Moft of thefe here mentioned, were found by the late Dr. Houftoun, growing na-turally in Jamaica, from whence he fent many of their feeds to Europe, fome of which fucceeded ; but moft, if not all the plants which were raifed from them, were loft in the fevere winter in 1740, fince which time they have not been recovered in Europe.

There is great beauty in the diverfity of the leaves of thefe plants, many of them being very large, and moft of them are of different colours on the two fur-faces, their under fide being either white, gold co-lour, or ruffet, and their upper of different fhades of green, fo that they make a fine appearance in the hot-houfe all the year ; indeed, their flowers have no great beauty to recommend them, but yet for the fingular beauty of their leaves, thefe plants deferve a place in all curious collections, as much as moft other forts.

There are very few of thefe plants at prefent in any of the European gardens, which may have been oc-cafioned by the difficulty of bringing over growing plants from the Weft-Indies ; and the feeds being fmall when they are taken out of the pulp, foon be-come dry, fo feldom fucceed. The beft way to ob-tain thefe plants is, to have the entire fruits put up in dry fand as foon as they are ripe, and forwarded by the fooneft conveyance to England ; thefe fhould be immediately taken out when they arrive, and the feeds fown in pots of light earth, and plunged into a moderate hot-bed of tanners bark. When the plants come up, and are fit to remove, they muft be each planted into a fmall pot of light earth, and plunged into the tan-bed ; and may afterward be treated in the manner directed for the ANNONA; to which I fhall defire the reader to turn, to avoid repetition.

M E L I A. Lin. Gen. Plant. 473. Azederach. Tourn. Inft. R. H. 616. tab. 387. The Bead-tree.

The CHARACTERS are,

The empalement of the flower is fmall, erect, and of one leaf, cut into five points at the top, which are obtufe. The flower hath five long, narrow, fpear-fhaped petals which fpread open, and a cylindrical nectarium of one leaf, the length of the petals, indented at the brim in ten parts. It has ten fmall ftamina inferted in the top of the necta-rium, terminated by fummits which do not appear above it, with a conical germen fupporting a cylindrical ftyle, crowned by an obtufe indented ftigma. The germen af-terward turns to a foft globular fruit, including a round-ifh nut having five rough furrows, and five cells, each containing one oblong feed.

This genus of plants is ranged in the firft fection of Linnæus's tenth clafs, intitled Decandria Monogy-nia, which includes thofe plants whofe flowers have ten ftamina and one ftyle.

The SPECIES are,

1. MELIA (*Azedarach*) foliis bipinnatis. Flor. Zeyl. 162. *Melia with double winged leaves.* Azederach. Dod. Pempt. 848. *The Bead-tree, or Falfe Sycamore.*
2. MELIA (*Azedirachta*) foliis pinnatis. Hort. Cliff. 161. *Melia with winged leaves.* Olea Malabarica, fraxini folio. Pluk. Alm. 269.

The firft fort grows naturally in Syria, from whence it was brought to Spain and Portugal, where it is now become as common almoft, as if it were a native of thofe countries. This in warm countries grows to a large tree, fpreading out into many branches, which are garnifhed with winged leaves, compofed of three fmaller wings, whofe lobes are notched and indented on their edges ; they are of a deep green on their up-per fide, and paler on their under. The flowers come out from the fide of the branches in long loofe bunches ;

bunches; they are compofed of five long, narrow, fpear-fhaped petals, of a blue colour, and are fucceeded by oblong fruit as large as a fmall Cherry, green at firft, but when ripe changes to a pale yellow, inclofing a nut with five deep furrows, having four or five cells, in each of which is lodged one oblong feed. This produces its flowers in England in July, but are not often fucceeded by feeds here; it drops its leaves in the autumn, and puts out frefh in the fpring. The pulp which furrounds the nut, is faid to have a deadly quality if eaten; and if mixed with greafe, and given to dogs, it will kill them. The nuts are bored through, and ftrung by the Roman Catholics to ferve as beads.

There has been of late years fome of thefe plants introduced to the iflands in the Weft-Indies, where I **am** informed they continue flowering, and produce their fruit moft part of the year. The fruit I have received from thence by the title of Indian Lilac, from which I have raifed many of the plants, and find them to be the fame as that from Syria.

This fort is propagated by feeds (which may be obtained from Italy or Spain, where thefe trees annually produce ripe fruits in the gardens where they are planted:) the feeds or berries fhould be fown in pots filled with good frefh light earth, and plunged into a moderate hot-bed of tanners bark, where (if the feeds are frefh) they will come up in about a month or five weeks time. When the plants are come up they fhould be frequently watered, and fhould have a large fhare of free air, by raifing the glaffes every day; in June they fhould be expofed to the open air, in a well fheltered fituation, that they may be hardened before winter. In October the pots fhould be removed under a hot-bed frame, where they may enjoy free open air when the weather is mild, and be covered in hard froft. During the winter feafon they muft be refrefhed gently with water, but by no means repeat this too often, nor give them too much at a time; for their leaves being off, they will not be in a condition to throw off a fuperfluity of moifture.

In March following, you may fhake out the plants from the feed-pots and divide them, planting each into a feparate fmall pot, filled with light frefh earth, plunging them into a moderate hot-bed, which will greatly promote their rooting, and increafe their growth, but they muft not be drawn too much; and in June you fhould remove them out into the open air as before, and during the three or four winters, while the plants are young, you muft fhelter them, to fecure them from the cold; but when the plants are grown pretty large and woody, they will endure to be planted in the open air againft a fouth wall. The beft feafon for this is in April, at which time you fhould fhake them out of the pots, being careful not to break the earth from the roots, but only pare off with a knife the outfide of the ball of earth; then open your holes and put in the plants, clofing the earth to their roots, obferving if the weather is dry, to give them fome water, which fhould be repeated twice a week until the plants have taken root; but you muft obferve in planting them on a dry foil, otherwife they will be liable to mifcary in fevere frofty weather.

The fecond fort grows naturally in India, where it becomes a large tree; the ftem is thick, the wood of a pale yellow, and the bark of a dark purple colour and very bitter. The branches extend wide on every fide, which are garnifhed with winged leaves, compofed of five or fix pair of oblong acute-pointed lobes, terminated by an odd one; thefe are fawed on their edges, of a light green colour, and a ftrong difagreeable odour; they ftand upon pretty long footftalks, which come out fometimes oppofite, and at others they are alternate. The flowers are produced in long branching panicles which proceed from the fide of the branches; they are fmall, white, and fit in fmall empalements, which are cut in five acute fegments; thefe are fucceeded by oval fruit of the fize of fmall Olives, which are green, afterward yellow, and when ripe, they change to a purple colour;

the pulp which furrounds the nut is oily, acrid, and bitter; the nut is white, and fhaped like that of the former. It grows in fandy land, both in India and the ifland of Ceylon, where it is always green, and produces flowers and fruit twice a year.

This fort is now very rare in England, and alfo in the Dutch gardens, where fome years paft it was more common; it is propagated by feeds in the fame way as the other fort, but being much tenderer, the plants fhould be kept conftantly in the tan-bed while young. In the fummer they may be placed under a frame, but in winter they muft be removed into the bark-ftove, and treated in the fame way with other plants from the fame countries. When the plants have obtained ftrength, they may be treated more hardily, by placing them in winter in a dry ftove, and in the middle of fummer they may be placed abroad for two or three months in a warm fheltered fituation, but they fhould not remain too long abroad; and during the winter feafon they fhould be fparingly watered: with this management the plants will produce flowers annually, and as they retain their leaves all the year, they are ornamental in winter in the ftove. The firft fort is commonly called, Zizyphus alba, in Portugal and Spain, and in Italy, Pfeudocycamorus. It was by moft of the modern botanifts titled, Azederach, but Dr. Linnæus has altered it to this of Melia, which was by Theophraftus applied to a fpecies of Afh.

MELIANTHUS. Tourn. Inft. R. H. 430. tab. 245. Lin. Gen. Plant. 712. [μελίανθ⊙, of μίλι, honey, and ἄνθ⊙, a flower.] Honey Flower.

The CHARACTERS are,

The flower has a large, coloured, unequal empalement, divided into five fegments; the two upper are oblong and erect, the lower is fhort, and fhaped like a bag. The middle are fpear-fhaped and oppofite. It hath four narrow fpear-fhaped petals, reflexed at their points, fpreading open outward, and fhaped like the empalement into two lips, connected on their fides. It has a nectarium of one leaf, fituated in the lower fegment of the empalement, and faftened with it to the receptacle; it is fhort, comprefled on the fides, and cut on the margin. It hath four erect awl-fhaped ftamina, the two under being fomewhat fhorter than the other, terminated by oblong heart-fhaped fummits. In the center is fituated a four-cornered germen, fupporting an erect ftyle, crowned by a quadrifid ftigma. The germen afterward becomes a quadrangular capfule with diftended cells, divided by partitions in the center, each containing one almoft globular feed, fixed to the center of the capfule.

This genus of plants is ranged in the fecond fection of Linnæus's fourteenth clafs, which includes thofe plants whofe flowers have two long and two fhorter ftamina, and their feeds are included in empalemnets.

The SPECIES are,

1. MELIANTHUS (*Major*) ftipulis folitariis petiolo adnatis. Hort. Cliff. 492. *Honey Flower with fingle ftipulæ growing clofe to the foot-ftalk.* Melianthus Africanus. H. L. B. 414. *Greater African Honey Flower.*

2. MELIANTHUS (*Minor*) ftipulis geminis diftinctis. Hort. Cliff. 492. *Smaller Honey Flower with two diftinct ftipulæ.* Melianthus Africanus minor fœtidus. Com. Rar. Pl. 4. tab. 4.

The firft fort grows naturally at the Cape of Good Hope, from whence it was brought to Holland in the year 1672; this hath a ligneous perennial root, which fpreads far on every fide, from which arife many ligneous ftalks which rife four or five feet high, and are herbaceous toward the top, where they are garnifhed with large winged leaves, which embrace the ftalks with their bafe, where they have a large fingle ftipulæ faftened on the upper fide of the foot-ftalk, with two ears at the bafe, which alfo embrace the ftalk. The leaves have four or five pair of very large lobes, terminated by an odd one; thefe are deeply jagged on their edges into acute fegments, and between the lobes runs a double leafy border or wing on the upper fide of the midrib, fo as to connect the bafe of the lobes together; thefe are alfo deeply jagged in the

the fame manner as the lobes; they are of a gray colour. The flowers are produced in pretty long fpikes, which arife from between the leaves toward the top of the ftalks; they are of a brown or chocolate colour, and are formed like the lip flowers, but have four narrow petals, in which it differs from the other plants of this clafs with lip flowers; thefe are fucceeded by oblong four-cornered capfules, divided by a central partition into four cells, each containing one roundifh feed; this plant flowers in June, but unlefs the feafon proves warm, they are not fucceeded by feeds in England.

This plant was formerly preferved in green-houfes as a tender exotic, but if planted in a dry foil and a warm fituation, it will endure the cold of our ordinary winters very well; and if in a fevere froft the tops of them fhould be deftroyed, yet the roots will abide, and put forth again the fucceeding fpring, fo that there is no great danger of lofing it; and the plants which grow in the open air always flower much better than thofe which are preferved in the greenhoufe, as they are lefs drawn, which always is hurtful to the flowering of plants; for it rarely happens that any of the plants of this fort, which are placed in the green-houfe do flower, for they are apt to draw up tall and weak, which prevents their flowering, and thofe branches which produce flowers, generally decay foon after; fo that although the ftems become woody, yet they are not of long duration, but the roots fpread where they have room, and fend out a great number of ftalks annually; and when the plants grow in the full ground, moft of thofe ftalks which are not injured by froft, feldom fail to flower the fpring following, fo that the fureft method to have them flower, is to cover the fhoots of thefe plants in frofty weather with Reeds or mats, to prevent their tops being killed by the cold; therefore it is the beft way to plant them clofe to a good afpected wall, and on a dry rubbifh, in which they will not fhoot fo vigorous as in good ground, fo will be lefs fucculent, and therefore not fo liable to fuffer by cold; but if the winter proves fevere, the ftalks may be faftened up to the wall, and covered to protect them; for want of this care the ftalks are frequently killed to the ground in winter, fo that there is feldom any flowers produced.

This plant may be propagated by taking off its fuckers or fide fhoots, any time from March to September, obferving to chufe fuch as are furnifhed with fibres, and after they are planted and taken root, they will require no farther care but to keep them clear from weeds: they may be alfo propagated by planting cuttings, during any of the fummer months, which, if watered and fhaded, will take root very well, and may afterwards be tranfplanted where they are defigned to remain.

The fecond fort is alfo a native of the country about the Cape of Good Hope, from whence it was brought to Europe; this rifes with round, foft, ligneous ftalks five or fix feet high, which fend out two or three branches from their fide, garnifhed with winged leaves like thofe of the former fort, but not half fo large; thefe have two diftinct ftipulæ adhering to their foot-ftalks; they are of a deep green on their upper fide, and whitifh on their under. The flowers come out from the fide of the ftalks in loofe hanging panicles, each fuftaining fix or eight flowers, which are fhaped like thofe of the firft fort, but fmaller; the lower part of the petals are green, their upper part are of a Saffron colour, and on the outfide, in the fwelling part of the petals, is a blufh of fine red; thefe have two long and two fhorter ftamina, which are terminated by yellow fummits. The flowers are fucceeded by four-cornered feed-veffels, which are fhorter than thofe of the firft fort, in which are lodged four oval feeds in feparate apartments; this flowers at the fame feafon with the former.

This fort does not fpread its roots as the firft, fo is not propagated with fo great facility, but cuttings of this fort planted upon an old hot-bed, whofe heat is over, and covered clofe with bell or hand-glaffes to exclude the air, will take root pretty freely; thefe may be planted in pots, and fheltered in the winter under a common frame for a year or two till they have obtained ftrength, then they may be planted in a warm border, and treated in the fame way as the former fort, with which management I have feen them flower much better than any of thofe which have been treated more tenderly, and thefe plants have perfected their feeds in good feafons.

MELICOCCA. See SAPINDUS.

MELILOTUS. See TRIGONELLA.

MELISSA. Tourn. Inft. R. H. 193. tab. 91. Lin. Gen. Plant. 647. [fo called of μίλι, honey, becaufe the bees procure it from this plant; it is alfo called Meliffophyllon, μίλι, and φύλλον, a leaf, q. d. Honey Leaf.] Baum.

The CHARACTERS are,

The empalement of the flower is of the open, bell-fhape, angular kind, ftreaked with one leaf, whofe brim is formed into two lips; the upper lip is indented in three parts, which are fpread open and reflexed; the under lip is fhort, acute, and indented in two parts. The flower is of the lip kind, having a cylindrical tube; the chaps are gaping, the upper lip is fhort, erect, forked, and roundifh, indented at the end. The under lip is trifid, the middle part being the largeft. It hath four awl-fhaped ftamina, two of which are as long as the petal, but the other are but half fo long; they are terminated by fmall fummits, which join by pairs. It hath a quadrifid germen, fupporting a flender ftyle the length of the petal, which, with the ftamina, are fituated under the upper lip, and is crowned by a flender, bifid, reflexed ftigma. The germen afterward turns to four naked feeds, fitting in the empalement.

This genus of plants is ranged in the firft fection of Linnæus's fourteenth clafs, which includes the plants whofe flowers have two long and two fhort ftamina, whofe feeds are naked.

The SPECIES are,

1. MELISSA (*Officinalis*) racemis axillaribus verticillatis, pedicellis fimplicibus. Lin. Sp. Plant. 592. *Baum with whorled bunches of flowers proceeding from the fides of the ftalks, having fingle foot-ftalks.* Meliffa hortenfis. C. B. P. 229. *Garden Baum, or common Baum.*

2. MELISSA (*Romana*) floribus verticillatis feffilibus, foliis hirfutis. *Baum with whorls of flowers fitting clofe to the ftalks, and hairy leaves.* Meliffa Romana, molliter hirfuta & graveolens. H. R. Par. *Roman Baum with foft hairy leaves, and a ftrong fmell.*

3. MELISSA (*Grandiflora*) pedunculis axillaribus dichotomis longitudine florum. Lin. Sp. Plant. 592. *Baum with foot-ftalks arifing from the wings of the ftalk, which are divided in forks, and are the length of the flowers.* Calamintha magno flore. C. B. P. 229. *Calamintha with a large flower.*

4. MELISSA (*Calamintha*) pedunculis axillaribus dichotomis longitudine foliorum. Lin. Sp. Plant. 592. *Baum with foot-ftalks arifing from the wings of the ftalk, which are forked, and as long as the leaves.* Calamintha vulgaris & officinarum Germaniæ. C. B. P. 228. *Common officinal Calamint of the Germans.*

5. MELISSA (*Nepeta*) pedunculis axillaribus dichotomis folio longioribus, caule decumbente. Lin. Sp. Plant. 593. *Baum with foot-ftalks arifing from the wings of the ftalk, which are forked, and longer than the leaves, with a declining ftalk.* Calamintha pulegii odore five nepeta. C. B. P. 228. *Calamint with the fcent of Penny Royal, or Cat Mint.*

6. MELISSA (*Cretica*) racemis terminalibus, pedunculis folitariis breviffimis. Lin. Sp. Plant. 593. *Baum with fpikes of flowers terminating the ftalks, growing upon very fhort fingle foot-ftalks.* Calamintha incana ocymi foliis. C. B. P. 228. *Hoary Calamint with Bafil leaves.*

7. MELISSA (*Majoranifolia*) foliis ovatis glabris, floribus verticillatis feffilibus, pedunculis folitariis breviffimis. *Baum with oval fmooth leaves, and flowers growing in whorls, fitting clofe to the branches, which have very fhort fingle ftalks.* Calamintha Romana, majoranæ folio,

folio, pulegii odore. Bocc. Muſ. *Roman Calamint with
a Marjoram leaf, and the ſcent of Penny Royal.*

8. MELISSA (*Fruticoſa*) fruticoſa, ramis attenuatis virga-
ris, foliis ſubrus tomentoſis. Lin. Sp. Plant. 593. *Shrubby
Baum with ſlender twig-like branches, and leaves which
are woolly on their under ſide.* Calamintha Hiſpanica
frutefcens, mari folio. Tourn. Inſt. 194. *Shrubby
Spaniſh Calamint with a Marum leaf.*

The firſt ſort grows naturally on the mountains near
Geneva, and in ſome parts of Italy, but is cultivated
here in gardens as a medicinal and culinary herb. It
has a perennial root, and an annual ſtalk, which is
ſquare, branching, and riſes from two to three feet
high, garniſhed with leaves ſet by pairs at each joint,
which are two inches and a half long, and almoſt two
inches broad at their baſe, growing narrower toward
the top, indented about their edges, and the lower
ones ſtanding upon pretty long foot-ſtalks. The
flowers grow in looſe ſmall bunches at the wings of
the ſtalk, in whorls, ſtanding upon ſingle foot-
ſtalks; they are of the lip kind, the upper lip ſtanding erect and is forked; the under lip is divided into
three parts; the middle one is roundiſh, and indented at the top. The flowers are white, and appear in
July. The whole plant has a pleaſant ſcent, ſomewhat like Lemons.

It is reckoned to be cordial, cephalic, and good for
all diſorders of the head and nerves; there is a ſimple water of this herb. It is alſo uſed as Tea, and
is by ſome greatly eſteemed for that purpoſe; there
is a variety of this with ſtriped leaves.

This plant is eaſily propagated by parting of the
root; the beſt time for this is in October, that the
offsets may have time to get root before the froſts
come on. The roots may be divided into ſmall pieces
with three or four buds to each, and planted two feet
apart in beds of common garden earth, in which they
will ſoon ſpread and meet together; the only culture
it requires is to keep it clean from weeds, and cut off
the decayed ſtalks in autumn, ſtirring the ground
between the plants.

The ſecond ſort grows naturally about Rome, and
in ſeveral parts of Italy; this hath a perennial root,
and an annual ſtalk like the former. The ſtalks are
ſlender, the leaves are much ſhorter than thoſe of
the former ſort, and the whole plant is hairy, and
of a ſtrong diſagreeable odour. The flowers grow
in whorls, fitting pretty cloſe to the branches, and
are ſmaller than thoſe of the firſt ſort; it flowers
about the ſame time. It is ſeldom preſerved in
gardens, but may be cultivated in the ſame way as
the former.

The third ſort grows naturally in the mountains of
Tuſcany and Auſtria, but is preſerved in many Engliſh gardens for the ſake of variety. It hath a perennial root, and an annual ſtalk, which riſes about a foot
high, garniſhed at each joint with two leaves ſtanding oppoſite, which are an inch and a half long, and
three quarters of an inch broad, ſawed on their edges,
of a lucid green on their upper ſide, and whitiſh on
their under: from the wings of the ſtalks come out
ſingle foot-ſtalks half an inch long, which divide into two ſmaller, and each of theſe ſuſtain two flowers
upon ſhort ſeparate foot-ſtalks. The flowers are large,
of a purple colour, and ſhaped like thoſe of the other
ſpecies. It flowers in June, and the ſeeds ripen in
Auguſt. This may be propagated in the ſame way
as the firſt ſort, and the plants may be treated in the
ſame manner.

The fourth ſort is the common Calamint of the ſhops,
which grows naturally in many parts of England, ſo is
ſeldom kept in gardens. It hath a perennial root,
from which ariſe ſeveral ſquare ſtalks near a foot long,
which are hairy, and garniſhed with two roundiſh
leaves at each joint, about the ſize of thoſe of Pot
Marjoram, a little indented on their edges, and of a
ſtrong penetrating odour. The flowers come out in
whorls on the ſide of the ſtalks, upon foot-ſtalks,
which divide by pairs, and are as long as the leaves;
theſe ſuſtain ſeveral ſmall bluiſh flowers, which appear

in July, and are ſucceeded each by four ſmall, roundiſh, black ſeeds. The herb is uſed in medicine, and
is hotter, and abounds with more ſubtile and volatile
parts than Mint. It provokes urine, brings down
the menſes, opens the liver, and is good for coughs.
This may be planted in gardens, and treated in the
ſame way as the common Baum.

The fifth ſort is found in greater plenty than the
fourth, growing wild in England. The ſtalks of this
are longer and bend towards the ground. The leaves
are larger, and more indented on their edges, and
have a very ſtrong ſcent like Penny Royal. The
whorls of flowers are ſet cloſer together than thoſe of
the fourth ſort, but in other reſpects they agree.

The ſixth ſort grows naturally in the ſouth of France
and in Italy; this is not of ſo long duration as the
former ſorts, ſeldom continuing more than two or
three years. The ſtalks are ſlender, a little ligneous,
and are garniſhed with ſmall, roundiſh, hoary leaves,
placed oppoſite at each joint. The flowers are produced in whorls toward the upper part of the
ſtalks, which are terminated by a looſe ſpike; they
are ſmall and white, ſhaped like thoſe of the other
ſpecies, and appear in June; theſe are ſucceeded by
ſeeds, which ripen in autumn, and if they are permitted to ſcatter, there will be a ſufficient ſupply of
young plants.

The ſeventh ſort grows naturally in Italy; this is a
biennial plant, whoſe ſtalks are about eight inches
long, declining toward the ground, and are garniſhed
with roundiſh leaves about the ſize of Marjoram, of
a light green colour. The flowers come out in cloſe
whorls on the upper part of the ſtalks, each ſtanding
upon a ſhort ſeparate foot-ſtalk; they are large, and
of a bright purple colour, appearing in July and Auguſt,
and the ſeeds ripen in autumn; this is propagated
by ſeeds, which ſhould be ſown ſoon after they are
ripe, and then the plants will come up in the ſpring;
but when the ſeeds are not ſown till the ſpring,
they ſeldom grow till the next year. The plants may
alſo be propagated by cuttings, which if planted in
the ſummer, and ſhaded from the ſun, will take root
very freely. If theſe plants are on a warm border,
they will live through the winter, but to preſerve the
ſpecies, a plant or two ſhould be kept in pots, and
ſheltered under a frame in winter.

The eighth ſort grows naturally in Spain; this hath
ſlender ſhrubby ſtalks about nine inches long, which
put out ſmall ſide branches oppoſite, and are garniſhed with ſmall, hoary, oval-pointed leaves, placed by
pairs; theſe have much the appearance of thoſe of the
Marum. The flowers grow in whorled ſpikes, at the
end of the ſtalks; they are ſmall and white, appearing in July, and the ſeeds ripen in autumn. The
whole plant has a ſtrong ſcent of Penny Royal; this
plant is of as ſhort a duration as the ſeventh ſort, and
may be propagated either by ſeeds or cuttings in the
ſame way as the ſeventh, and the plants require the
ſame treatment.

MELISSA TURCICA. See DRACOCEPHA-
LON.

MELITTIS. Greater Dead Nettle.

The CHARACTERS are,

*It hath an erect, taper, bell-ſhaped empalement, having
two lips; the upper is tall and indented, the under is ſhort
and bifid; the flower is ringent, the tube is longer than
the empalement, the chaps are thicker; the upper lip is
roundiſh, plain, and erect; the lower is trifid, ſpreading,
and obtuſe. It hath four ſtamina, which are awl-ſhaped,
ſituated under the upper lip, two being a little longer than
the other, terminated by bifid obtuſe ſummits, which are
placed a croſs; it hath an obtuſe, quadrifid, hairy germen
ſupporting a ſlender ſtyle, crowned by a bifid acute ſtigma. The flower is ſucceeded by four ſeeds which ripen in
the empalement.*

This genus of plants is ranged in the firſt ſection of
Linnæus's fourteenth claſs, intitled Didynamia Gym-
noſpermia, the flowers having two long and two ſhort
ſtamina, and are ſucceeded by four naked ſeeds ſitting in the empalement.

We

We know but one Species of this genus, viz.

Melittis (Melyssophyllum.) Hort. Cliff. 309. Greater Dead Nettle. Melissa. Fuchsii.

This plant grows naturally in some woods in the West of England and in Wales, Germany and near Montpelier. It hath a perennial root, which in the spring sends up three, four, or more stalks, according to the age and strength, which rise a foot and a half high; these are square, and garnished with leaves like those of the common Dead Nettle, but are much larger, rougher, and stand on longer foot-stalks, two being placed opposite at each joint. The flowers come out at the joints of the stalks, just above the foot-stalks of the leaves; they are in shape like those of the Dead Nettle, but are much larger, of a redder purple colour, and the upper lip grows erect. These appear in May, when the plants make a handsome appearance, and if the season does not prove hot, the flowers will continue in beauty upward of three weeks. As the plants do rarely produce good seeds in the gardens, so they are usually propagated by parting the roots; but where the plants are intended for ornament, the roots should not be disturbed oftener than every third year; nor should they then be divided into small parts, left thereby they should not flower the first year. The best time to remove and part the roots is the beginning of October, that they may have time to get root before the frost comes on. They should have a loamy soil and an east exposure, where the plants will thrive and produce flowers in plenty.

MELO. Tourn. Inst. R. H. 104. tab. 32. Cucumis. Lin. Gen. Plant. 969. [it takes its name of Μῆλον, an Apple, because the fruit resembles an Apple.] The Melon.

The Characters are,

It hath male and female flowers on the same plant. The male flowers have a bell-shaped empalement of one leaf, whose border is terminated by five awl-shaped bristles. The flower is of one petal, which is bell-shaped, fastened to the empalement, and cut into five segments at the brim; these are veined and rough. It hath three short stamina inserted in the empalement, and are joined together, two of which have bifid points. The summits are linear, and run up and down on the outside of the stamina, to which they adhere. The female flowers have no stamina or summits, but have a large oval germen situated below the flower, supporting a short cylindrical style, crowned by three thick gibbous stigmas. The germen afterward turns to an oval fruit with several cells, filled with oval, acute-pointed, compressed seeds, inclosed in a soft pulp.

This genus of plants is by Dr. Linnæus joined with the Colocynthus and Anguria, to the Cucumis, making them only species of the same genus, which, according to his system, may be allowable; but whoever will admit the fruit as a characteristic note to distinguish the genera, will find marks to separate them; and however properly these may be put together in a system of botany, yet in a work of this nature it cannot be admitted.

There is a great variety of this fruit cultivated in the different parts of the world, and in this country there are too many of them propagated, which are of no value, especially by those who supply the markets, where their size is chiefly regarded; so that by endeavouring to augment their bulk, the fruit is rendered of no value; I shall therefore only mention a very few of the varieties, which are the most deserving of care, excluding the common Melons, as being unworthy of the trouble and expence in cultivating.

The sort of Melon which is in the greatest esteem among all the curious in every part of Europe, is the Cantaleupe; which is so called from a place about fourteen miles from Rome, where the pope has a country seat, in which place this fruit has been long cultivated; but it was brought thither from that part of Armenia which borders on Persia, where this fruit is in so great plenty, that a horse-load is sold for a French crown. The flesh of this Melon, when in perfection, is delicious, and does not offend the most tender stomachs, so may be eaten with safety. The

Dutch are so fond of this fruit, as to cultivate very few other sorts, and by way of pre-eminence, call it only by the appellation of Cantaleupe, and never join the title of Melon to it, which they apply indifferently to all the other sorts. The outer coat of this is very rough, and full of knobs and protuberances like warts; it is of a middling size, rather round than long, and the flesh is for the most part of an Orange colour, though there are some with a greenish flesh, but I have never met with any of that colour so good as those of the other.

The Romana is by some much esteemed, and when the fruit is well conditioned, the plants in perfect health, and the season dry, it is a good Melon, and may be brought forwarder in the season than the Cantaleupe; therefore those who are desirous of early Melons may cultivate this sort.

The Succado is also a good sort, and may also be cultivated for early fruit, but these must give way to the Cantaleupe, when that is in season.

The Zatte is also a very good Melon, but very small. The fruit of this is seldom bigger than a large Orange; it is a little flatted at the two ends, and the outer coat is warted like the Cantaleupe, but there is so little flesh in one of these fruit, that they are scarce worthy the trouble of propagating.

The small Portugal Melon, which is by some called the Dormer Melon, is a pretty good fruit, and the plants generally produce them in plenty, so by many people this is preferred to most other, especially those who love a plenty, and are not so nice in distinguishing the quality: this may also be cultivated for an early crop.

But the best Melon for this purpose is the Black Galloway, which was brought from Portugal by Lord Galloway many years since, but of late years is rarely to be met with in England, it having been degenerated by growing among other sorts. The fruit of this sort will ripen in a shorter time from its first setting, than any other which I have yet seen, and when suffered to ripen naturally, is not a bad fruit.

The few varieties here mentioned, are sufficient to satisfy the curious, who may be fond of variety, for there are scarce any other which deserve the trouble; and indeed those who have a true taste for this fruit, seldom cultivate any but the Cantaleupe; but as I before observed, where this fruit is desired early in the season, the Cantaleupe is not so proper as some of the other, therefore a few plants of one of the other sorts should be raised earlier in the spring, but should be in a different part of the garden from the Cantaleupe Melons; for when two sorts of Melons grow near, they cannot be preserved perfectly right; therefore the Dutch and German gardeners are very careful in this respect, and in order to keep the sort in perfection, do not plant any other sort of Melon, Cucumber or Gourd, near these, left, by the impregnation of the farina of those other, these fruit should be rendered bad; and in this particular, I am convinced, from long experience, they are right; and from the not observing this, many persons who are lovers of this fruit, have gradually diminished their goodness, without knowing the cause, and have imputed it to the long cultivating from the seeds saved in the same garden, believing it absolutely necessary to procure seeds from a distant place frequently to preserve them good: indeed, where a person can securely depend on the care and skill of those he procures the seeds from, it is a very good method to exchange seeds now and then; but there are so few who are exact in making choice of the fruits from which they save the seeds, or careful enough to do it themselves, but often depend on others to clean the seed, that I should advise every one to do it himself, which is the sure way to have it good; for I have frequently been deceived myself, by depending on the fidelity and skill of others; nor could I procure any of these seeds from Cantaleupe which were good, until my much honoured friend, the Chevalier Rathgeb, sent me plentifully of it from thence; though I had often been
supplied

supplied with feeds by perfons who I thought could not be deceived in their choice, and who lived near the place of their growth.

Before I quit this head, I beg leave to caution all perfons againft depending upon feeds which are brought from abroad, either by thofe perfons who import them for fale, or gentlemen who frequently bring or fend over thefe feeds to their friends, for it feldom happens that any of thefe prove tolerable. I have been fo often deceived by thefe myfelf, as to determine never to make trial of any of thefe feeds again, unlefs I receive them from a perfon who is fkilful, and who eat of the fruit himfelf of which he faved the feeds; for in Italy, Spain, Portugal, and many parts of France, the gardeners are very carelefs in the choice of all their feeds, but of the Melons they are remarkably fo; and as for thofe which come from Conftantinople, Aleppo, and other parts of Turkey, I have rarely feen one Melon produced from thofe feeds which was tolerable.

The feeds of Melons fhould not be fown until they are three years old, nor would I chufe to fow them when they are more than fix; for although they will grow at ten or twelve years old, yet the fruit which are produced from thefe old feeds are feldom fo thick flefhed, as thofe which come from feeds which are frefher: and it is the fame of light feeds, which fwim upon water, when they are taken out of the pulp, for I have made fome trials of thefe, and have had them grow at three years old; but not one of the Melons produced on thefe plants was near fo deep flefhed, as thofe which grew upon plants raifed from heavy feeds taken out of the fame fruit, though they grew in the fame bed, and were cultivated exactly in the fame manner; nor was their flefh fo firm, but rather inclining to be mealy; therefore I would not advife the fowing of thefe light feeds, nor thofe which are very old.

Having thus largely treated of the choice of the forts, and of the feeds, I fhall next proceed to the method of cultivating them, in order to obtain plenty of good fruit: the method which I am going to prefcribe being very different from what has been conftantly practifed in England, will, I doubt not, be objected to by many; but it is what has been practifed in all the good gardens in Holland and Germany, where the Cantaleupe Melon is produced in great plenty and perfection; and from feveral years experience, I have found this to be the only method in which thefe Melons can be cultivated with fuccefs; and I am likewife convinced of its being the beft way to obtain plenty of any other fort of Melon.

It is common to hear many perfons valuing themfelves upon having two or three early Melons, which, when brought to the table are not better than a Pumpkin, and thefe are procured at a great expence and with much trouble; and in order to have them ripe a little earlier than they would naturally come, if fuffered to grow to their full fize, the ftem upon which the fruit grows is commonly twifted, to prevent the nourifhment entering the fruit, whereby the growth is checked; then the fruit is clofely covered with the mowings of Grafs-plats, laid of a fufficient depth to caufe a fermentation, by which the fruit becomes coloured: but where this unnatural method is practifed, the fruit has little flefh, and that has neither moifture, firmnefs, or flavour; fo that after four months attendance, with a great expence of dung, &c. there may, perhaps, be three or four brace of Melons produced, which are fitter for the dunghill than the table. Therefore my advice is, never to attempt to have thefe fruit ripe earlier than the middle or latter end of June, which is generally foon enough for this climate; and from that time to the end of September, they may be had in plenty, if they are fkilfully managed; and when the autumn has continued favourable, I have had them very good in the middle of October.

But in order to continue this fruit fo long, the feeds muft be fown at two or three different feafons: the firft

fhould be fown about the middle or end of February, if the feafon proves forward; but if it is otherwife, it will be better to defer it till the end of that month; the future fuccefs greatly depends on the raifing the plants in ftrength, which cannot be fo well effected, if the weather fhould prove fo bad after the plants are come up, as that a fufficient quantity of frefh air cannot be admitted to them, therefore it is not advifeable to be too early in fowing the feeds.

When the feafon is come, thefe feeds may be fown on the upper fide of a Cucumber-bed, where there are any; and if there are none, a proper quantity of new horfe dung muft be provided, which muft be thrown in a heap to ferment, and turned over, that it may acquire an equal heat, in the fame manner as hath been directed for Cucumbers; and the plants muft be raifed and managed in the fame manner as hath been directed for them, until they are planted where they are to remain for good, to which article the reader is defired to turn, to avoid repetition.

The fecond feafon for fowing of thefe feeds is about the middle of March, and both thefe fowings muft be underftood to be planted under frames; for thofe which are defigned for bell or hand-glaffes, or to be covered with oil papers, fhould not be fown till about a week in April; for when thefe are fown earlier, if the plants are properly managed, they will grow fo long, as to extend their fhoots to the fides of the glaffes, before it will be fafe to let them run out; for it often happens in this country, that we have fharp morning frofts in the middle of May; fo that if the ends of the Vines are then without the glaffes, if they are not covered with mats to guard them againft the froft, they will be in danger of fuffering greatly therefrom; and, on the other hand, if the plants have fpread fo much as to fill the glaffes, and not permitted to run out, they will be in equal danger of fuffering by their confinement from the heat of the fun in the day time; therefore it is that I fhould advife the putting of the feed rather a little later into the hot-bed for the glaffes, than thofe which are to be covered with the oil papers. Nor will the times here mentioned be found too late, for I have put the feeds of Cantaleupe Melons into a hot-bed the third of May, which were not tranfplanted, but remained where they were fown, and covered with oiled paper; and from this bed I cut a large crop of good fruit, which ripened about the latter end of Auguft, and continued till the end of October. This I only mention, to fhew what has and may be done, though it muft not be always depended on:

But we next come to the making and preparing of the beds, or, as the gardeners term it, the ridges, into which the plants are to be put out to remain; thefe fhould always be placed in a warm fituation, where they may be defended from all cold and ftrong winds, for the eaft and north winds are generally very troublefome in the fpring of the year; fo that if the place be expofed to thofe afpects, it will be difficult to admit a proper fhare of frefh air to the young plants; and if it is much expofed to the fouth-weft winds, which often are very boifterous in fummer and autumn, thefe will turn up and difplace the Vines, whereby they will fuffer greatly; therefore the beft pofition for thefe beds is where they are open to the fouth, or a little inclined to the eaft, and fheltered at a diftance by trees from the other points: this place fhould be inclofed with a good Reed fence, which is better for this purpofe than any other inclofure, becaufe the winds are deadened by the Reeds, and are not reverberated back again, as they are by walls, pales, and other clofe fences; but in making the inclofure, it fhould be extended to fuch diftance every way from the beds, as not to obftruct the fun's rays during any part of the day; this fhould have a door wide enough to admit of wheelbarrows paffing, to carry in dung, earth, &c. and it fhould be kept looked, that no perfons fhould be allowed to go in but thofe who have bufinefs; for ignorant perfons, having often curiofity to look into the beds, open the glaffes

and

. and let the cold air to the plants, and frequently leave the glasses in part open; or sometimes when they are raised by the gardener to admit the fresh air, the tilts are thrown down, so that the air is excluded; all which are very injurious to the young plants, as is also the handling of the fruit after it is set; therefore none should be admitted, but when the person who is intrusted with the care of them is there.

The next thing is the preparation of the earth for these plants, in which the Dutch and German gardeners are very exact: the mixture which they generally prepare is of the following sorts; of hazel loam, one third part; of the scouring of ditches or ponds a third part, and of very rotten dung a third part; these are mixed up at least one, and often two years, before they make use of it, frequently turning it over, to incorporate their parts and sweeten it; but the compost in which I find these plants succeed best in England, is two thirds of fresh gentle loam, and one third of rotten neats dung; if these are mixed together one year before it is wanted, so as to have the benefit of a winter's frost and summer's heat, observing to turn it over often, and never suffer weeds to grow upon it, this will be found equal to any other compost whatever.

As these plants succeed best when they are planted young, so before the plants appear there should be a quantity of new dung thrown in a heap, proportionable to the number of lights intended, allowing about fifteen good wheelbarrows full to each light; this must be two or three times turned over, to prepare it (as hath been directed for Cucumbers) and in a fortnight it will be fit for use, at which time the trench must be dug to receive the dung, where the bed is intended; this must be made wider than the frames, and in length proportional to the number of frames intended. As to the depth, that must be according as the soil is dry or wet; but in a dry ground it should not be less than a foot, or a foot and a half deep; for the lower these beds are made the better they will succeed, where there is no danger of their suffering by wet. In the well laying and mixing of the dung, the same care must be taken as hath been advised already for Cucumbers, which in every respect must be the same for these beds. When the bed is made, the frames should be placed over it to keep out wet; but there should be no earth laid upon it till after it has been three or four days made, and is found of a proper temperature of heat; for many times these beds will heat so violently when they are first made, as to burn the earth, if covered with it; and when this happens, it is much the best way to take this earth off again, for the plants will never thrive in it. As soon as the bed is found to be of a proper warmth, the earth should be laid upon it, which at first need not be more than two inches thick, except in the middle of each light, where the plants are to be placed, where there must be a hill raised fifteen inches high or more, terminating in a flat cone; in two or three days after the earth is put on the bed, it will be of a proper temper to receive the plants; then in the evening you may transplant the plants, but always do it when there is little wind stirring: in taking up the plants, their roots should be carefully raised with a trowel, so as to preserve all their fibres; for if these are broken off, the plants do not soon recover this; or if they do, they are generally weaker, and seldom make so good Vines as those which are more carefully removed; for these plants are more nice and tender in transplanting than those of Cucumber, especially the Cantaleupe Melon; which, if it is not planted out, soon after the third, (or what the gardeners call the rough) leaf is put out, they are long recovering their vigour; so that when it happens that the beds cannot be ready for them in time, it will be a good method to plant each plant into a small pot while they are young, and these may be plunged into the hot-bed where they were raised, or into the Cucumber-bed where there is room, so that they may be brought for-

ward; and when the bed is ready, these may be turned out of the pots, with the whole ball of earth to their roots, whereby they will receive no check in removing: and this latter method is what I should prefer to any other for the Cantaleupe, because there should never be more than one plant left to grow in each light; therefore in this method there will be no necessity of planting more, as there will be no danger of their succeeding; whereas in the common way, most people plant two or more plants in each light, for fear some should miscarry. When the plants are placed on the top of the hills, they should be gently watered, which should be repeated once or twice after till the plants have taken good root, after which they seldom require more; for when they receive too much wet, they often canker at the root, and when that happens they never produce good fruit. When the plants have established themselves well in the new beds, there should be a greater quantity of earth laid on the bed, beginning round the hills where the plants grow, that their roots may have room to strike out; and as the earth is put in from time to time, it must be trodden or pressed down as close as possible; and it should be raised at least a foot and a half thick upon the dung all over the bed, observing also to raise the frames, that the glasses may not be too near the plants, lest the sun should scorch them.

When the plants have gotten four leaves, the top of the plants should be pinched off with the finger and thumb, but not bruised or cut with a knife, because in either of these cases the wound will not so soon heal over: this pinching is to cause the plants to put out lateral branches, for these are what will produce the fruit; therefore, when there are two or more of these lateral shoots produced, they must also be pinched, to force out more; and this must be practised often, that there may be a supply of what the gardeners call runners, to cover the bed. The management of these beds must be nearly the same as hath been directed for the Cucumbers, therefore I need not repeat it here; but shall only observe, that the Melons require a greater share of air than Cucumbers, and very little water; and when it is given to them, it should be at a distance from their stems.

If the plants have succeeded well, they will spread over the bed, and reach to the frames, in about five or six weeks, at which time the alleys between the beds should be dug out; or where there is but one bed, there should be a trench made on each side, of about four feet wide, as low as the bottom of the bed, and hot dung wheeled in, to raise a lining to the same height as the dung of the bed, which should be trodden down close, and afterward covered with the same earth as was laid upon the bed, to the thickness of a foot and a half or more, treading it down as close as possible; this will add to the width of the bed, so . much as to make it in the whole twelve feet broad, which is absolutely necessary, for the roots of the plants will extend themselves quite through it; and it is for want of this precaution, that it is common to see the Vines of Melons decay, before the fruit is well grown; for where there is no addition made to the width of the bed, the roots will have reached the sides of the beds by the time that the fruit appears, and having no more room to extend themselves, their extremities are dried by the sun and air, which is soon discovered by the plants hanging their leaves in the heat of the day, which is soon attended with a decay of many of those leaves which are near the stem, and the plants from that time gradually languish, so that the fruit cannot be supplied with nourishment; but when ripe, will be found to have little flesh, and that mealy and ill flavoured; whereas those plants which have sufficient breadth for their roots to run, and the earth laid of a proper depth and closely trod down, will remain in vigour until the frost destroys them, so that I have had a second crop of fruit on them, which have sometimes ripened well; but all the first were excellent, and of a larger size

than

than thefe forts ufually grow: the leaves of thefe plants were very large, and of a ftrong green, fo that they were in the utmoft vigour; whereas, in moft places where the Cantaleupe Melons have been raifed in England, the beds have been no wider than they were firft made, and perhaps not more than three inches thicknefs of earth upon them, fo that the plants have decayed many times without producing a fingle fruit; and from thence people have imagined, that this fort of Melon was too tender for this climate, when their ill fuccefs was entirely owing to their not underftanding their culture.

There is alfo another advantage attending this method of widening the beds, as above directed, which is that of adding a frefh warmth to the beds, by the hot dung, which is buried on each fide, which will caufe the dung in the bed to renew its heat; and as the plants will by this time fhew their fruit, this additional heat will be of great fervice in fetting the fruit, efpecially if the feafon fhould prove cold, as it often happens in this country in the month of May. When the beds are made up in the manner here directed, and the Vines have extended fo far as to fill the frames, and want more room, the frames fhould be raifed up with bricks about three inches high, to admit the fhoots of the Vines to run from under them; for if the plants are ftrong, they will run fix or feven feet each way from the ftems; for which reafon, I caution every one to allow them room, and to put but one plant in each light; for when the Vines are crowded, the fruit feldom will fet well, but will drop off when they are as large as an egg; therefore the frames which are defigned for Melons fhould not be made fmall, but rather fix feet wide; for the wider thefe are, the better will the plants thrive, and produce a greater plenty of fruit.

There is no part of gardening, in which the practitioners of this art differ more than in the pruning and managing of thefe plants: nor are there any rules laid down in the feveral books in which the culture of Melons have been treated of, by which any perfon can be inftructed; for there is fuch inconfiftency in all their directions, and what is worfe, the greateft part of them are abfurd, fo that whoever follows them can never hope to fucceed; therefore I fhall, in as few words as poffible, give fuch plain directions, as I hope will be fufficient to inftruct any perfon, who is the leaft converfant in thefe things.

I have before advifed the pinching off the ends of the plants as foon as they have a joint, in order to get lateral fhoots, which are by the gardeners called runners; and when thefe fhoots have two or three joints, to pinch off their tops to force out more runners, becaufe it is from thefe that the fruit is to be produced; but after a fufficient number are put out, they fhould not be ftopped again, but wait for the appearance of the fruit, which will foon come out in plenty; at which time the Vines fhould be carefully looked over three times a week, to obferve the fruit, and make choice of one upon each runner, which is fituated neareft the ftem, having the largeft foot-ftalk, and that appears to be the ftrongeft fruit, and then pinch off all the other fruit which may appear on the fame runner; alfo pinch off the end of the runner at the third joint above the fruit, and if the runner is gently pinched at the next joint above the fruit, it will ftop the fap and fet the fruit. There is alfo another method practifed by fome gardeners to fet this fruit, which is the taking off fome of the male flowers, whofe farina are juft ripe and fit for the purpofe, laying them over the female flowers, which are fituated on the crown of the young fruit, and with their nails gently ftrike the male flowers to fhake the farina into the female flowers, whereby they are impregnated, and the fruit foon after will fwell, and fhew vifible figns of their being perfectly fet; fo that where the plants are under frames, and the wind excluded from them, which is neceffary to convey the farina from the male to the female flowers, this practice may be very neceffary. The taking off all the other fruit

will prevent the nourifhment being drawn away from the fruit intended to grow, which, if they were all left on the plant, could not be fupplied with fufficient nourifhment; fo that when they come to be as large as the end of a man's thumb, they frequently drop off, and fcarce one of them fets; which will be prevented by the method before directed: but there are fome perfons, who are fo covetous of having a number of fruit, as not to fuffer any to be taken off, whereby they generally fail in their expectation. My allowing but one fruit to be left upon each runner is, becaufe if half thefe ftand there will be full as many fruit as the plant can nourifh; for if there are more than eight upon one plant, the fruit will be fmall and not fo well nourifhed: indeed, I have fometimes feen fifteen or twenty Melons upon one plant, but thefe have generally been of the fmaller kinds, which do not require fo much nourifhment as the Cantaleupes, whofe fkins are of a thick fubftance; fo that where a greater number are left of them than the plants can well fupply, their flefh will be remarkably thin.

As I before advifed the ftopping or pinching off the runners three joints above the fruit, fo by this there will be frefh runners produced a little below the places where the others were pinched; therefore it is, that I advife the careful looking over the Vines fo often, to ftop thefe new runners foon after they come out, as alfo to pull off the young fruit which will appear; and this muft be repeated as often as is found neceffary, which will be until thofe intended to ftand are grown fo large as to draw all the nourifhment which the plants can fupply, for then the plants will begin to abate of their vigour. Thefe few directions, if properly made ufe of, is all the pruning which is neceffary to be given them; but at the fame time when this is practifed, it may be neceffary to give fome water to the plants, but at a diftance from their ftems; which will be of fervice to fet the fruit and caufe it to fwell, but this muft be done with great caution.

The glaffes of the hot-bed fhould alfo be raifed high, to admit a large fhare of air to the plants, otherwife the fruit will not fet; and if the feafon fhould prove very warm, the glaffes may be frequently drawn off, efpecially in an evening, to receive the dews, provided there is but little wind ftirring; but the glaffes fhould not remain off the whole night, left the cold fhould prove too great; but in warm weather, the glaffes may be kept off from ten in the morning till evening.

When the plants have extended themfelves from under the frames, if the weather fhould alter to cold, it will be neceffary to cover their extremities every night with mats; for if thefe fhoots are injured, it will retard the growth of the fruit, and often proves very injurious to the plants: and now what water is given to the plants, fhould be in the alleys between the beds; for as the roots of the Vines will by this time have extended themfelves through the alleys, fo when the ground there is well moiftened, the plants will receive the benefit of it; and by this method, the ftems of the plants will be preferved dry, whereby they will continue found; but thefe waterings fhould not be repeated oftener than once a week in very dry warm weather, and be fure to give as much air as poffible to the plants when the feafon is warm.

Having given full inftructions for the management of thofe Melons which are raifed under frames, I fhall next proceed to treat of thofe which are raifed under bell or hand-glaffes. The plants for thefe muft be raifed in the fame manner as hath been already directed, and about the latter end of April, if the feafon proves forward, will be a good time to make the beds; therefore a fufficient quantity of hot dung fhould be provided, in proportion to the intended number of glaffes, allowing fix or eight good wheelbarrows of dung to each glafs. Where there is but one bed, which is propofed to be extended in length, the trench fhould be dug out four feet and a half wide, and the length according to the number of

6

glaffes,

glaffes, which fhould not be placed nearer than four feet to each other; for when the plants are too near each other, the Vines will intermix, and fill the bed fo clofely as to prevent the fruit from fetting: in digging the trench, it fhould be fo fituated, as to allow for the widening of the bed three or four feet on each fide; the depth muft be according as the foil is dry or wet; but, as was before obferved, if the foil is fo dry as that there is no danger of the beds being hurt by the wet, the lower they are made in the ground the better: in the making of the beds, the fame regard muft be had to the well mixing and laying of the dung as was before directed; and after the dung is laid, there fhould be a hill of earth raifed, where each plant is to ftand, one foot and a half high; the other part of the bed need not as yet be covered more than four inches thick, which will be fufficient to keep the warmth of the dung from evaporating; then the glaffes fhould be placed over the hills, and fet down clofe, in order to warm the earth of the hills to receive the plants; and if the beds work kindly, they will be in a proper temperature to receive the plants in two or three days after making; then the plants fhould be removed, in the fame manner as was before directed; and if they are in pots, fo that there will be no danger of their growing, there fhould but one plant be put under each glafs; and if they are not in pots, there fhould be two, one of which may be afterward taken away, if they both grow. Thefe plants muft be watered at firft planting, to fettle the earth to their roots, and fhaded every day until they have taken new root; and if the nights prove cold, it will be proper to cover the glaffes with mats, to preferve the warmth of the bed.

Where there are feveral of the beds intended, they fhould be placed at eight feet diftance from each other, that there may be a proper fpace left between them, to be afterward filled up, for the root of the Vines to have room for extending themfelves, for the reafons before given.

When the plants have taken good root in the beds, their tops muft be pinched off; and their pruning, &c. muft, from time to time, be the fame as for thofe under the frames. In the day time, when the weather is warm, the glaffes fhould be raifed on the oppofite fide to the wind, to admit frefh air to the plants; for where this is not obferved, they will draw up weak and fickly, therefore all poffible care fhould be taken to prevent this; for if the runners are not proper ftrength, they can never fupply the fruit with nourifhment.

When the plants are grown fo long as to reach the fides of the glaffes, if the weather proves favourable, the glaffes muft be fet on three bricks, fo as to raife them about two inches from the furface of the beds, to give room for the Vines to run out from under them; but when this is done, the beds fhould be covered all over with earth to the depth of one foot and a half, and trod down as clofe as poffible; and if the nights fhould prove cold, there fhould be a covering of mats put over the beds, to prevent the cold from injuring the tender fhoots of the Vines; but as the Vines of the Contaleupe Melons are impatient of wet, it will be neceffary to arch the beds over with hoops to fupport the mats, that they may be ready for covering at all times when they require it; which is the only fure method to have thefe Melons fucceed in England, where the weather is fo very uncertain and variable; for I have had fome beds of thefe Melons in as fine order under thefe glaffes as could be defired, which were totally deftroyed by one day's heavy rain in June.

After the thicknefs of earth is laid upon the beds, if the weather fhould prove cold, it will be advifeable to dig trenches on each fide of the beds, into which you fhould lay a fufficient quantity of hot dung, to make it of the fame thicknefs with the bed, after the manner before directed for the frames; or if there is a fufficient quantity of hot dung ready, the whole fpace between the beds may be dug out and filled up with

the dung, laying thereon the earth a foot and a half deep, treading it down clofe; this new dung will add a frefh warmth to the beds, and caufe the plants to fhew fruit foon after.

The watering of thefe plants muft be done with great caution, and not given to their ftems; the pinching off the runners muft alfo be duly attended to, as alfo the pulling off all fuperfluous fruit, to encourage thofe which are defigned to remain: and in fhort, every thing before directed for thofe under frames, muft likewife be obferved for thefe; and the further care is, to cover them in all hard rains and cold nights, with mats, which, if performed with care, there will be little danger of their mifcarrying, and thefe Vines will remain vigorous until the cold in autumn deftroys them.

There have been many perfons, who of late years have raifed their Melons under oiled paper, and in many places they have fucceeded well; but where this is practifed, there muft be great care taken not to keep thefe coverings too clofe over them; for where that is done, the Vines will draw very weak, and rarely fet their fruit in any plenty; therefore where thefe coverings are propofed to be ufed, I fhould advife the bringing up of the plants under hand or bell-glaffes, in the manner before directed, until they are grown far enough to be let out from under the glaffes; and then, inftead of the covering with mats, to put over the oiled paper; and if this covering is prudently managed, it will be the beft that can be ufed. The beft fort of paper for this purpofe is that which is ftrong, and not of too dark a colour; and it fhould be done over with linfeed oil, which will dry foon. There fhould be a proportionable number of fheets of this paper pafted together, as will fpread to the dimenfions of the frame to which it is faftened; and if this is fixed to the frame, before the oil is rubbed over it, fo much the better; but this fhould be done fo long before they are ufed, as that the oil may be thoroughly dry, and the ftench gone off, otherwife it will deftroy the plants.

There are fome perfons who make thefe frames of broad hoops, in imitation of the covers of waggons; but as thefe are cumberfome to move, and there are no conveniencies for admitting air to the plants, but by raifing the whole frame on one fide, I prefer thofe made of pantile laths, framed like the ridge of a houfe; and each flope having hinges, may be raifed at pleafure to admit the air to the plants; but as defcriptions of thefe things are not well comprehended by perfons not fo converfant with them, I fhall exhibit a figure of one of thefe frames, to be added to the article of STOVES.

The further management of the Melons, after their fruit is fet, is to keep pulling off all the fuperfluous fruit, and to pinch off all weak runners, which may draw away part of the nourifhment from the fruit; as alfo to turn the fruit gently twice a week, that each fide may have equal benefit of the fun and air; for when they are fuffered to lie with the fame fide conftantly to the ground, that fide will become of a pale or whitifh colour, as if it were blanched, for want of the advantages of the fun and air. The plants will require a little water in very dry weather, but this fhould be given them in the alleys at a diftance from the ftems of the plants, and not oftener than once in a week or ten days, at which time the ground fhould be well foaked in the alleys. This will encourage the growth of the fruit, and caufe the flefh to be thick; but the great caution which is neceffary to be obferved, is not to over-water the plants, which is certain injury to them: alfo be fure to give as much free air as poffible, at all times, when the weather will permit, for this is abfolutely neceffary to render the fruit good.

When the fruit is fully grown, they muft be duly watched to cut them at a proper time; for if they are left a few hours too long upon the Vines, they will lofe much of their delicacy, therefore they fhould be looked

looked over at leaſt twice every day; and if thoſe fruit which are intended for the table, are cut early in the morning, before the ſun has warmed them, they will be much better flavoured; but if any ſhould require to be cut afterward, they ſhould be put into cold ſpring water, or ice, to cool them, before they are brought to the table: and thoſe cut in the morning, ſhould be kept in the cooleſt place till they are ſerved up to table. The ſign of this fruit's maturity is, that of its beginning to crack near the foot-ſtalk, and its beginning to ſmell, which never fail; for as theſe Cantaleupe Melons ſeldom change their colour until this is too ripe, that ſhould never be waited for. The directions here given for the management of the Cantaleupe Melons, will be found equally good for all the other ſorts, as I have fully experienced; for in the common method of managing them, where the earth is laid but three or four inches thick, the plants are very apt to decay before the fruit is ripe; for their roots ſoon reach the dung, and are extended to the ſides of the bed, where their tender fibres are expoſed to the air and ſun, which cauſe the leaves of the plants to hang down in the heat of the day, ſo it is neceſſary to ſhade them with mats, to prevent their decay; and this alſo occaſions the watering of the plants often to keep them alive, which is alſo prejudicial to their roots; whereas when the beds are made of a proper width, and earthed of a ſufficient thickneſs, the plants will bear the ſtrongeſt heat of the ſun in this climate, without ſhewing the leaſt want of moiſture, or their leaves drooping, and they will continue in health till the autumn cold deſtroys them.

In ſaving of the ſeeds I need not repeat here, that only ſuch ſhould be regarded, which are taken from the firmeſt fruit, and thoſe which have the higheſt flavour; and if theſe are taken out with the pulp entire, without diſplacing the ſeeds, and ſuffered to remain in the pulp two or three days before it is waſhed out, the better; and then to preſerve only the heavy ſeeds, which ſink in the water.

MELOCACTUS.
MELOCARDUUS. } See Cactus.
MELOCHIA, Jews Mallow.

The Characters are,

It hath a permanent empalement of one leaf, cut half way into five ſegments; the flower hath five large ſpreading petals; the ſtamina are involved in the tube of the germen, and have five ſummits. It has a roundiſh germen with five awl-ſhaped erect ſtyles, which are permanent, crowned by ſingle ſtigmas. The flower is ſucceeded by five-cornered roundiſh capſules, having five cells with two horns, in each cell is lodged one angular compreſſed ſeed.

This genus of plants is ranged in the firſt ſection of Linnæus's ſixteenth claſs, intitled Monadelphia Pentandria; the flowers of this claſs have their ſtamina and ſtyles connected in one houſe, and thoſe of this ſection have but five ſtamina.

The Species are,

1. Melochia (*Pyramidata*) floribus umbellatis oppoſitis foliis, capſulis pyramidatis pentagonis, angulis acutis, foliis nudis. Hort. Cliff. 343. *Jews Mallow with umbellated flowers placed oppoſite to the leaves, and five-cornered pyramidal capſules.* Althæa Braſiliana fruteſcens, incarnato flore, fagopyri ſemine. Pluk. Phyt. tab. 131. f. 3.

2. Melochia (*Tomentoſa*) floribus umbellatis axillaribus, capſulis pyramidatis pentagonis, angulis mucronatis, foliis tomentoſis. Lin. Sp. 943. *Jews Mallow with umbellated flowers at the wings of the ſtalk, five-cornered pyramidal capſules, and woolly leaves.* Abutilon herbaceum procumbens, betonicæ folio, flore purpureo. Sloan. Hiſt. Sp. 220.

3. Melochia (*Depreſſa*) floribus ſolitariis capſulis depreſſis pentagonis, anguſtis obtuſis ciliatis. Flor. Leyd. Prod. 348. *Jews Mallow with flowers growing ſingly, and five-cornered depreſſed capſules.* Abutilon Americanum, ribeſii foliis, flore carneo, fructu pentagono aſpero. Houſt. MSS.

4. Melochia (*Coatacenata*) racemis confertis terminalibus, capſulis globoſis ſeſſilibus. Flor. Zeyl. 247. *Jews Mallow with cinſtered ſpikes terminating the ſtalks, and globular capſules ſitting cloſe.*

5. Melochia (*Supina*) floribus capititatis, foliis ovatis ſerratis, caulibus procumbentibus. Lin. Sp. 944. *Jews Mallow with flowers in heads, oval ſawed leaves, and trailing ſtalks.* Alcea ſupina puſilla, gerani exigui maritimi folio & facie, madeiaſpatenſis, fructu in ſummo caule glomerato, pericarpio duro. Pluk. Phyt. tab. 132. f. 4.

The firſt ſort grows naturally in the Brazils as a common weed, having a ſtalk ſomewhat ſhrubby, which riſes four or five feet high; the flowers are produced in umbels from the ſide of the ſtalk, oppoſite to the leaves; they are of a pale fleſh colour, and are ſucceeded by pyramidal capſules with five corners having five cells, each containing one angular ſeed.

The ſecond ſort grows naturally in Jamaica, and other warm parts of America. This has a trailing herbaceous ſtalk, garniſhed with woolly leaves ſhaped like Betony. The flowers are produced in umbels at the wings of the ſtalk; they are of a purple colour, and are ſucceeded by pyramidal capſules, having five corners.

The third ſort was diſcovered growing naturally at the Havannah, by the late Dr. Houſtoun. This riſes with a ſhrubby ſtalk five or ſix feet high, garniſhed with angular leaves reſembling thoſe of the Currant buſh; the flowers are produced ſingly from the ſide of the ſtalk: they are of a fleſh colour, and in ſhape like thoſe of the ſmall flowering Mallow; theſe are ſucceeded by rough five-cornered capſules, incloſing five Mallow-ſhaped ſeeds.

The fourth ſort grows naturally in both Indies; this hath an herbaceous ſtalk, which is terminated by ſeveral oblong bunches of flowers, which are ſucceeded by globular capſules with five cells, in each of which is lodged a ſingle ſeed.

The fifth ſort grows naturally in India; this is an annual plant with trailing ſtalks which ſpread on the ground, garniſhed with ſmall Betony-ſhaped leaves; the flowers and fruit are produced in cluſters at the end of the branches.

Theſe are preſerved in botanic gardens for variety, but having little beauty they are rarely cultivated in other places; they are propagated by ſeeds which muſt be ſown on a hot-bed, and when the plants come up, they ſhould be treated in the ſame way as is directed for Sida, to which the reader is deſired to turn to avoid repetition. The firſt and third ſorts are ſhrubby, ſo may with care be preſerved thro' the winter in a ſtove, whereby good ſeeds may be obtained; for theſe ſeldom ripen their ſeeds well the firſt year, unleſs the plants are brought forward early in the ſpring, and the ſummer proves warm. The other three ſorts generally ripen their ſeeds the ſame year they are ſown.

MELON. See Melo.

MELONGENA. Tourn. Inſt. R. H. 151. tab. 65. Solanum. Lin. Gen. Plant. 224. Mad Apple, by ſome called Egg Plant; in French, *Mayenne.*

The Characters are,

The flower has a permanent empalement of one leaf, which is deeply cut into five acute ſegments, which ſpread open. The flower hath but one petal, which is cut into five parts, which ſpread open and are reflexed. It hath five awl-ſhaped ſtamina, terminated by oblong ſummits which converge together. In the center is ſituated an oblong germen ſupporting a ſlender ſtyle, crowned by an obtuſe ſtigma; the germen afterward becomes an oval or oblong fruit with one cell, which hath a fleſhy pulp, filled with compreſſed roundiſh ſeeds.

This genus of plants is ranged in the ſeventh ſection of Tourneſort's ſecond claſs, which includes the herbs with a wheel-ſhaped flower of one leaf, whoſe pointal changes to a ſoft fruit. Dr. Linnæus has joined this genus, and the Lycoperſicon of Tourneſort, to the Solanum, making them only ſpecies of

8 X   that

that genus ; but as the fruit of this genus has but one cell, so it should be separated from the Solanum, whose fruit have two cells, and of which there are so many species already known, that there need not be any addition of plants which can be separated with propriety added to it ; he places it in the first section of his fifth class.

The Species are,

1. Melongena (*Ovata*) caule inermi herbaceo, foliis oblongo-ovatis tomentosis integris, fructu ovato. *Mad Apple with a smooth herbaceous stalk, oblong, oval, woolly leaves, which are entire, and an oval fruit.* Melongena fructu oblongo violaceo. Tourn. Inst. 151. *Mad Apple with an oblong Violet-coloured fruit.*

2. Melongena (*Tereta*) caule inermi herbaceo, foliis oblongo-ovatis tomentosis, fructu tereti. *Mad Apple with herbaceous, smooth, oblong, oval, woolly leaves, and a taper fruit.* Melongena fructu tereti violaceo. Tourn. Inst. 151. *Mad Apple with a taper Violet-coloured fruit.*

3. Melongena (*Incurva*) caule inermi herbaceo, foliis oblongis sinuatis tomentosis, fructu incurvo. *Mad Apple with a smooth herbaceous stalk, oblong sinuated leaves which are woolly, and an incurved fruit.* Melongena fructu incurvo. Tourn. Inst. R. H. 152. *Mad Apple with an incurved fruit.*

4. Melongena (*Spinosa*) spinosa, foliis sinuatis-laciniatis, fructu tereti, caule herbaceo. *Mad Apple, with a prickly stalk and leaves which are cut into sinuses, a taper fruit, and an herbaceous stalk.* Solanum pomiferum fructu spinoso. J. B. 3. 619. *Apple-bearing Nightshade with a prickly fruit.*

The first sort grows naturally in Asia, Africa, and America, where the fruit is commonly eaten by the inhabitants ; and it is cultivated in the gardens in Spain as an esculent fruit, by the title of Barenkeena ; the Turks who also eat the fruit, call it Badinjan, the Italians Melanzana, and the inhabitants of the British islands in America, Brown John, or Brown Jolly. It is an annual plant with an herbaceous stalk, which becomes a little ligneous, and rises near three feet high, sending out many side branches, garnished with oblong oval leaves seven or eight inches long, and four broad ; they are woolly, and their borders are very slightly sinuated, but not indented, standing without order upon very thick foot-stalks. The flowers come out singly from the side of the branches, having a thick fleshy empalement of one leaf, which is deeply cut into five acute segments, which spread open, and is armed with strong prickles on the outside. The flowers have one petal, which is cut at the brim into five segments, which expand in form of a star, and are a little reflexed ; they are blue, and the summits which are connected together in the bosom of the flower are yellow. The flowers are succeeded by oval fleshy fruit, about the size and shape of a swan's egg, of a dark purple on one side, and white on the other. The flowers come out in June and July, and the fruit ripens in September.

There are the following varieties of these species ; one with white fruit, called by some the Egg Plant ; one with yellow fruit, and another with pale red fruit ; all these varieties are generally constant, the seeds producing the same fruit as those from which they were taken, but as they only differ in colour, so I chuse not to enumerate them as distinct species.

The second sort differs from the first in the shape of the fruit, which is commonly eight or nine inches long, taper and strait ; in other respects they are the same, but as this never varies when propagated in gardens, so there can be no doubt of their being distinct species. There are two varieties of this sort, one with a purplish fruit, and the other white, but the latter is the most common in England.

The third sort differs from the two former in the shape of the leaves, which are deeply sinuated on their borders. The fruit is oblong and incurved, of a yellowish colour, and larger at the end than in any other part.

The seeds of the fourth sort were sent me from India ;

this differs greatly from either of the former. The stalks and leaves are armed with very strong thorns, and the leaves are larger, and deeply jagged on their sides. The flowers are larger, and of a deeper blue colour. The fruit is long, taper, and white.

These fruit are eaten by most of the inhabitants of the warm parts of the globe, and are esteemed a delicacy, but are supposed to have a property of provoking lust.

They are propagated by seeds, which must be sown upon a moderate hot-bed in March, and when the plants come up, they must be transplanted into another hot-bed about four inches asunder, observing to water and shade them until they have taken root ; after which you must give them a great share of air when the weather is warm, otherwise they will draw up very weak. They must be also frequently watered, without which they will make but very indifferent progress ; but when they are grown so strong as to fill the frame (which will be by the middle or end of May,) you must transplant them out into a rich spot of ground, at two feet distance, or in the borders of the pleasure-garden at the same distance from other plants, observing to preserve as much earth to the roots as possible when you take them up, otherwise they are subject to miscarry. You must observe to water them plentifully, and shade them until they have taken root, after which they will require but very little care, more than to keep them clear from weeds, and in very dry weather to give them some water.

About the middle of July the fruit will appear, at which time, if the weather should be very dry, you must often water them, which will cause the fruit to grow very large, and increase their number : toward the latter end of August their fruit will ripen, when you must preserve the seeds of each kind separate ; but those for the table should be gathered before they are quite ripe.

These plants are only preserved as curiosities in the English gardens, the fruit being seldom eaten in this country, except by some Italians or Spaniards, who have been accustomed to eat them in their own countries.

MELOPEPO. See Cucurbita.

MELONRY, or MELON GROUND, is an apartment in the kitchen-garden for the propagation of Melons only.

This spot of ground should be open to the south-east sun, but sheltered from the west, north-west, and north-east winds, by walls, pales, or hedges, the latter of these is the best ; it should also be upon a dry soil, for nothing is more injurious to these plants than much wet ; for in the spring of the year it often proves very wet weather, when, if the soil is very wet, there will be no making the ridges until it is very late. This should also be contrived as near to the dung as possible, which will save a great deal of labour in wheeling the dung ; and, if there should be a pond of water near it, which, in very dry weather, will be very useful to water the Melons when it is necessary, though it is not often that water is wanted for this purpose in England.

As to the size of the ground, that must be proportioned to the quantity of ridges intended, which you may easily calculate, by allowing twelve feet breadth for every ridge, and the holes placed at about four feet asunder ; but it is the best way to allow room enough where you are not streightened to it.

This ground should be inclosed with a Reed fence, and kept constantly locked up during the time that the Melons are growing, for if they are exposed to every person that walks in the garden (most of whom have a curiosity to handle the Vines, and look after the fruit,) it will be of ill consequence, nothing being more injurious to these plants than frequent tumbling or disturbing their leaves.

The common practice in most gentlemens gardens is, to inclose a spot of ground either with walls or pales, which they constantly appropriate to this purpose ; but

but this is by no means a good method, for it rarely happens that thefe fucceed well longer than two years in the fame place, unlefs the foil be removed and frefh brought in, which is very expenfive ; therefore the beft way is, to have a fufficient parcel of Reeds made into pannels, which may be annually moved from place to place, fo that you need not continue your ridges longer than one year in the fame place; and if you have a piece of ground which is large enough to divide into three or four fuch places, the fence may be every year removed till the whole has been occupied, after which you may return to the fpot where you began, which, by that time, will be as good as frefh earth; and hereby, without much trouble, you may remove them every year, for as one of the fides will remain unremoved every time the fence is carried forward, the labour will not be fo great as if it were wholly removed to fome diftance, and thefe Reed fences are much preferable to either walls or pales, for this purpofe.

MELOTHRIA. Lin. Gen. Plant. 48.

The title of this genus was applied to it by Dr. Linnæus in the Hortus Cliffortianus. By fome authors it hath been placed under the genus of Cucumis, and by others under that of Bryonia ; but the Doctor has removed this to a diftance from either of thofe genera, on account of its having but three ftamina; but Dr. Van Royen has brought it next to the genus of Bryonia again, as the plants have male and hermaphrodite flowers.

The CHARACTERS are,

The empalement of the flower is of one leaf, bell-shaped, and cut slightly at the brim into five parts, and in the hermaphrodite flowers, rests upon the embryo. The male flower is of one leaf, wheel-shaped, having a tube the length of the empalement. In the center of the hermaphrodite flower is situated the pointal, supporting a cylindrical style, attended by three conical stamina, which are inserted in the tube of the flower, and are extended to the same length; the male flowers have three stamina, terminated by blunt styles. The pointal afterward becomes an oval small berry, having three divisions, in which are lodged small flat seeds.

We have but one SPECIES of this plant, viz.

MELOTHRIA (*Pendula.*) Lin. Hort. Cliff. 490. *Small creeping Cucumber.* Cucumis minima fructu ovali nigro lævi. Sloan. Hift. 1. p. 227. *Smallest Cucumber with a smooth, black, oval fruit.*

This plant grows wild in the woods in Carolina, Virginia, and alfo in many of the iflands in America ; it creeps upon the ground with flender Vines, having angular leaves, fomewhat refembling thofe of the Melon, but much fmaller. Thefe Vines ftrike out roots at every joint, which faften themfelves into the ground, and thereby a larger fhare of nourifhment is drawn to the plants, by which means their ftalks extend to a great diftance each way, and clofely cover the ground. The flowers are very fmall, in fhape like thofe of the Melon, and of a pale fulphur colour. The fruit, in the Weft-Indies, grow to the fize of a Pea, of an oval figure, and changes black when ripe; thefe are by the inhabitants fometimes pickled when they are green.

In England the fruit are much fmaller, and are fo hidden by the leaves, as to render it difficult to find them. The plants will not grow in the open air here, but the feeds muft be fown upon a hot-bed, and if the plants are permitted, will foon fpread over the furface of a large bed ; and when the fruit is ripe, if they fcatter their feeds, the plants will come up where the earth happens to be ufed on a hot-bed again, and if they are fupplied with water, will require no farther care. This plant is in fome gardens preferved for the fake of variety, but is of no ufe.

MENISPERMUM. Tourn. Act. R. Par. 1705. Lin. Gen. Plant. 1131. Moonfeed.

The CHARACTERS are,

It hath male and female flowers on different plants ; the male flowers have empalements composed of two short linear leaves, and have four oval spreading petals with-

out-fide, *and eight oval concave petals within; which are smaller than those without, ranged in four series, and many cylindrical stamina which are longer than the petals, terminated by short obtuse summits having four lobes. The female flowers have the same empalement and corolla as the male, and have eight stamina with pellucid summits, which are fruitful. These have two oval incurved germina, supporting a solitary recurved style, crowned by a bifid stigma; the germen afterward become two roundish kidney-shaped berries of one cell, inclosing a large kidney-shaped seed.*

This genus of plants is ranged in the tenth fection of Linnæus's twenty-fecond clafs, which includes thofe plants which have male and female flowers on different plants, and the male flowers have twelve ftamina.

The SPECIES are,

1. MENISPERMUM (*Canadense*) foliis peltatis fubrotundis angulatis. Hort. Cliff. 140. *Moonseed with target-shaped, roundish, angular leaves.* Menifpermum Canadenfe fcandens, umbilicatis foliis. Tourn. Act. Par. 1705. *Climbing Moonseed of Canada, with a navel-shaped leaf.*

2. MENISPERMUM (*Virginicum*) foliis cordatis peltatis lobatis. Flor. Virg. 40. *Moonseed with heart and target-shaped leaves, which have lobes.* Menifpermum folio hederaceo. Hort. Elth. 223. tab. 178. *Moonseed with an ivy leaf.*

3. MENISPERMUM (*Carinianum*) foliis cordatis fubtus villofis. Lin. Sp. Plant. 340. *Moonseed with heart-shaped leaves, which are hairy on their under side.*

The firft fort grows naturally in Canada, and moft parts of North America, in the woods; this hath a thick ligneous root, from which are fent out many climbing ftalks, which become ligneous, and rife to the height of twelve or fourteen feet, twifting themfelves about the neighbouring plants for fupport ; thefe are garnifhed with large, fmooth, roundifh leaves, whofe foot-ftalks are placed almoft in the middle of the back of the leaves ; on the upper fide there is a hollow in that part of the leaf refembling a navel. The flowers come out in loofe bunches from the fide of the ftalks; they are of an herbaceous colour, fmall, and compofed of two tiers of oblong oval petals, very fhort ftamina, with ten in the male flowers, terminated by fingle fummits ; the two germen fituated in the center of the female flowers turn to fo many channelled berries, each containing one kidney-fhaped feed. It flowers in July, and the feeds ripen in autumn.

This fort may be eafily propagated by laying down of the branches, which, if performed in autumn, will have made good roots by the following autumn, when they may be feparated from the old plant, and tranfplanted where they are defigned to remain ; thefe plants require fupport, for their branches are flender and weak. In the country where it grows naturally, they climb up the trees to a confiderable height, fo that if thefe are planted near trees in wildernefs quarters, where their ftalks may have fupport, they will thrive better than in an open fituation.

The fecond fort differs from the firft in the fhape of its leaves, which are angular, and fometimes heart-fhaped; their foot-ftalks join to the bafe of the leaves, fo they have no umbilical mark on their furface. The ftalks of this become ligneous, and rife nearly as high as thofe of the firft fort, and the flowers and berries do not differ from them. It is alfo propagated after the fame manner.

The third fort grows naturally in Carolina, from whence the feeds were fent to England ; this has by fome been fuppofed the fame with the fecond fort, from which it differs in its branches, not becoming woody as thofe do. The ftalks are herbaceous ; the leaves are entire and hairy, and are not more than half fo large as thofe of the fecond, nor is the plant fo hardy, for in fevere winters, thofe which are expofed to the open air are fometimes killed, whereas the fecond fort is never injured by cold. This fort does not produce any flowers in England, unlefs the feafon proves very warm.

This

This may be propagated by parting of the roots, which spread out on the side, so that part of them may be cut off every other year; the best time for doing this is in the spring, a little before the plants begin to shoot; these should be planted in a warm situation and; have a light soil, for in strong land, where the wet is detained in winter, the roots are apt to rot; therefore if they are planted close to a wall exposed to the south or west, their stalks may be fastened against the wall, to prevent their trailing upon the ground; and in this situation the plants will frequently flower, and by having a little shelter in severe frost, their stalks may be preserved from injury.

There is little beauty in these plants, but yet they are preserved in many gardens for the sake of variety, for which reason they are here inserted.

MENTHA. Tourn. Inst. R. H. 188. tab. 89. Lin. Gen. Plant. 633. [Μίνθη, according to the ancients, a goddess, as also according to the poets. The ancients also gave it the name of Sweet-smelling, and where this word is found, this plant is understood. Mentha is likewise so called of Mens, Lat. the mind, because this plant is said to strengthen the mind.] Mint; in French, *Menthe*.

The CHARACTERS are,
It hath a lip flower of one petal, sitting on a permanent tubulous empalement of one leaf, which is erect, and cut at the brim into five equal segments. The tube of the petal is a little longer than the empalement. The chaps are cut into four almost equal segments, the upper being a little larger and indented. It hath four awl-shaped stamina, which are erect, standing asunder, the two nearest being longest; they are terminated by roundish summits, and in the bottom of the tube is situated a four-pointed germen, supporting a slender erect style, crowned by a bifid spreading stigma. The germen afterward turns to four naked seeds sitting in the empalement.
This genus of plants is ranged in the first section of Linnæus's fourteenth class, which includes those plants whose flowers have two long and two shorter stamina, and the seeds ripen in the empalement.

The SPECIES are,
1. MENTHA (*Viridis*) floribus spicatis, foliis oblongis serratis. Hort. Upsal. 168. *Mint with spiked flowers, and oblong sawed leaves.* Mentha angustifolia spicata. C. B. P. 227. *Narrow-leaved spiked Mint, commonly called Spear Mint.*
2. MENTHA (*Glabra*) floribus spicatis, foliis oblongis glabris, superne minime serratis. *Mint with spiked flowers, and longer smooth leaves, which are very slightly sawed toward their points.* Mentha angustifolia spicata glabra. Rand. *Narrow-leaved, smooth, spiked Mint.*
3. MENTHA (*Candicans*) foliis lanceolatis serratis, subtus incanis, floribus spicatis hirsutissimis. *Mint with spear-shaped sawed leaves, which are hoary on their under side, and very hairy spiked flowers.* Mentha Sylvestris candicans, odore sativi. Doody. Raii Syn. App. *Wild Mint of a white colour, smelling like that of the garden.*
4. MENTHA (*Sylvestris*) spicis confertis, foliis serratis tomentosis sessilibus. Hort. Cliff. 306. *Mint with spikes of flowers growing in clusters, and woolly sawed leaves sitting close to the stalks.* Mentha sylvestris longiore folio. C. B. P. 227. *Wild Mint with a longer leaf.*
5. MENTHA (*Aquatica*) spicis crassioribus, foliis ovato-lanceolatis serratis subtus tomentosis petiolatis. *Mint with thicker spikes, and oval, spear-shaped, sawed leaves, which are woolly on their under side, and have foot-stalks.* Mentastri aquatici genus hirsutum, spica latiore. J. B. 3. 222. *Hairy Water Mint with a broader spike.*
6. MENTHA (*Piperita*) spicis crassioribus interruptis, foliis lanceolatis acute serratis. *Mint with thicker spikes of flowers, which are interrupted, and spear-shaped leaves which are sharply sawed.* Mentha fervida nigricans, piperis sapore. Rand. Hort. Chel. Cat. *Blackish hot Mint with a taste like Pepper, commonly called Pepper Mint.*

7. MENTHA (*Crispa*) floribus spicatis, foliis cordatis dentatis undulatis sessilibus. Hort. Cliff. 306. *Mint with spiked flowers, and heart-shaped indented leaves, which are waved, and sit close to the stalks.* Mentha crispa Danica sive Germanica speciosa. Mor. Hist. 3. p. 367. *Danish or German curled Mint.*
8. MENTHA (*Rotundifolia*) spicis confertis, foliis ovatis rugosis sessilibus. *Mint with spikes growing together, and oval rough leaves sitting close to the stalk.* Mentastrum folio rugoso rotundiore spontaneum, flore spicato, odore gravi. J. B. 3. 217. *Wild Mint with a rounder rough leaf, and a spiked flower, having a strong scent.*
9. MENTHA (*Rubra*) spicis confertis interruptis, foliis oblongo-ovatis acuminatis dentatis sessilibus. *Mint with interrupted spikes of flowers growing together, and oblong, oval, acute-pointed, indented leaves, sitting close to the stalk.* Mentha rotundifolia rubra, aurantii odore. Mor. Hist. 3. 369. *Round-leaved red Mint, smelling like an Orange, commonly called Orange Mint.*
10. MENTHA (*Chalepensa*) foliis oblongis dentatis, utrinque tomentosis sessilibus, spicis tenuioribus. *Mint with oblong indented leaves, which are woolly on both sides, set close to the stalk, and very narrow spikes of flowers.* Mentastrum chalepense, angustifolium, raro florens. Boerh. Ind. alt. 1. p. 185. *Narrow-leaved wild Mint of Aleppo, which rarely flowers.*
11. MENTHA (*Palustris*) floribus capitatis, foliis ovatis serratis petiolatis, staminibus corolla longioribus. Hort. Cliff. 306. *Mint with flowers growing in heads, oval sawed leaves having foot-stalks, and stamina longer than the petals.* Mentha rotundifolia palustris sive aquatica major. C. B. P. 227. *Greater round-leaved Water Mint.*
12. MENTHA (*Nigricans*) floribus capitatis, foliis lanceolatis serratis subpetiolatis. Lin. Sp. Plant. 576. *Mint with flowers growing in heads, and spear-shaped sawed leaves with very short foot-stalks.* Mentha fervida nigricans latifolia. Rand. *Broad-leaved blackish Pepper Mint.*
13. MENTHA (*Arvensis*) floribus verticillatis, foliis ovatis acutis serratis, staminibus corolla brevioribus. Lin. Sp. Plant. 577. *Mint with flowers growing in whorls, oval, acute, sawed leaves, and stamina shorter than the petals.* Mentha arvensis, verticillata hirsuta. J. B. 3. 2. 217. *Whorled hairy field Mint, or Calamint of the shops.*
14. MENTHA (*Exigua*) floribus verticillatis, foliis ovatis dentatis, staminibus corolla longioribus. *Mint with flowers growing in whorls, oval indented leaves, and stamina longer than the petals.* Mentha aquatica, exigua. Trag. Lib. 1. c. 6. *Smallest Water Mint.*
15. MENTHA (*Gentilis*) floribus verticillatis, foliis ovatis, marginibus ciliatis, staminibus corollam æquantibus. *Mint with whorled flowers, oval leaves whose borders are hairy, and stamina equalling the petals.* Mentha verticillata, rotundiore folio, odore ocymi. Dale. *Whorled Mint with a rounder leaf, smelling like Basil.*
16. MENTHA (*Hirsuta*) floribus verticillatis, foliis ovatis serratis hirsutis, staminibus corolla longioribus. *Mint with whorled flowers, oval, sawed, hairy leaves, and stamina longer than the petals.* Mentha aquatica sive sisymbrium hirsutum. J. B. 3. 2. 224. *Water Mint, or hairy Sisymbrium.*
17. MENTHA (*Verticillata*) floribus verticillatis, foliis lanceolatis acutis serratis, rugosis, staminibus corollam æquantibus. *Mint with whorled flowers, spear-shaped, acute-pointed, sawed, rough leaves, and stamina equalling the petals.* Mentha verticillata, longiori acuminato folio, odore aromatico. Rand. Hort. Chel. Cat. *Whorled Mint with a longer acute-pointed leaf, and an aromatic scent.*
There are several other varieties of this genus, which have been found growing naturally in England, of which I have twelve or more in my own collection; but as I suspect some of them to be only accidental variations, arising from the different soils and situations where they have been found, I have not enumerated them all here; those which are here mentioned, I take to be distinct species, having cultivated them more than thirty

thirty years, in which time I have not obferved them to change from one to another; feveral of thefe I have propagated by feeds, and have found them keep to the kind from which the feeds were faved. The firft fort is what the gardeners cultivate to fupply the markets, and is ufed both as a culinary herb, and for medicine; it is generally called Spear Mint, and by fome Hart Mint; Parkinfon and Gerard title it Roman Mint; this is a plant fo well known, as to need no defcription. There are two varieties of this, one with a curled leaf, and the other has variegated leaves, but both thefe I have had run from the common fort; thefe are by fome preferved in their gardens for the fake of variety, therefore I have mentioned them here.

This herb is greatly efteemed for all diforders of the ftomach, lofs of appetite, and vomiting; there is a fimple water, a fpirit, and compound fyrup, and a diftilled oil of it prepared in the fhops.

The fecond fort hath fmoother leaves than the firft, and they are rather narrower, in other refpects it agrees with that, fo that it is frequently cultivated in the gardens for ufe, without diftinction.

The third fort grows naturally in England; the leaves of this are fhorter, and broader in the middle than either of the former, the ferratures on their edges are more acute, and their under fides are woolly, and very white. The ftalks divide more toward the top, fo are terminated by a greater number of fpikes, the lower part of which are interrupted. The fcent of this fort is very like that of the Garden Mint.

The fourth fort hath longer and broader leaves than either of the former, which are woolly and white. The ferratures on their edges are farther afunder, and are very fharp pointed; they fit clofe to the ftalks, which are hairy. The fpikes of flowers are flender, feveral of them growing together at the top of the ftalk, which are hairy. This is the Mentaftrum, or wild Mint of the fhops, and is an ingredient in the Trochifci de Myrrha.

The fifth fort grows naturally in moift places in feveral parts of England, it is titled Spiked Horfe Mint, or Water Mint. The ftalks of this are fhorter than thofe of either of the former, and are hairy, as are alfo the leaves, which are oval, fpear-fhaped, fawed on their edges, and of a pale colour. The flowers grow in fhort thick fpikes at the top of the ftalks, their ftamina being fhorter than the petal.

The fixth fort is found growing naturally in fome parts of England; I have found it by the fide of the river between Mitcham and Croydon, in Surry; this hath fmooth purple ftalks; the leaves are fmaller than thofe of common Mint; they are fpear-fhaped, fawed on their edges, and of a darker green colour than either of the former; their midrib and veins are purple, and a little hairy on their under fide. The fpikes of flowers are fhorter and thicker than thofe of the common Mint, and are broken or interrupted at the bottom; they are of a dark purple colour, and their ftamina are longer than the petal. The whole plant has a hot biting tafte like Pepper, and a pleafant fcent. There is a diftilled water of this plant kept in the fhops, which is by moft people preferred to that of the common Mint, for all the purpofes which that is ufually prefcribed, and is efteemed an excellent remedy againft the ftone and gravel.

The feventh fort was originally brought from Denmark, where it was thought to grow naturally, but Dr. Linnæus fixes it as a native of Siberia. The ftalks of this fort are hairy, and rife about the fame height with the common. The leaves are heart-fhaped, deeply indented on their edges, waved and curled, and fit clofe to the ftalk, they are of a light green. The flowers are purple, growing in thick interrupted fpikes at the top of the ftalks; their empalements are cut almoft to the bottom, and the ftyle of the flower is bifid, ftanding out beyond the petal.

The eighth fort grows naturally in many parts of England; this rifes with a ftrong, four-cornered, hairy ftalk, about the fame height as the common Mint, branching out toward the top, and garnifhed with oval rough leaves fitting clofe to the ftalks; they are of a dark green, and crenated on their edges. The fpikes of flowers grow in clufters at the top of the ftalks, which are fhort and clofe; the flowers are of an herbaceous white colour, and their ftamina are ftretched out beyond the petal.

The ninth fort is commonly called Orange Mint, from its fcent, which is fomewhat like that of the rind of Orange. This rifes with an upright fmooth ftalk about the fame height with the common Mint, but does not branch out like that; the leaves are much broader than thofe of the common fort; the indentures on their edges are deep, and they end in acute points. The fpikes of flowers grow in clufters on the top of the ftalks, which are interrupted; they are of a pale colour, and their ftamina are fhorter than the petal. It is commonly cultivated in gardens for its pleafant fcent.

The tenth fort grows naturally at Aleppo, but is hardy enough to thrive in the open air in England. This hath flender four-cornered ftalks, which are purple at bottom, but woolly upward, feldom branching; they are garnifhed with oblong indented leaves, which are downy on both fides, fitting clofe to the ftalks. The fpikes of flowers are fingle, and very flender; thefe do not often appear in England, but when they do it is late in the fummer. It creeps much at the root, fo the only way to obtain flowers, is to confine their roots in pots.

The eleventh fort grows naturally in ditches in moft parts of England, and is commonly known by the name of Water Mint. This hath hairy ftalks about a foot high, which branch toward the top, and are garnifhed with oval fawed leaves, ftanding upon pretty long foot-ftalks. The flowers grow in roundifh fpikes at the end of the branches; they are of a purple colour, and their ftamina are longer than the petal. The whole plant has a very ftrong fcent, fomewhat like that of Penny Royal. This fort is fometimes ufed in medicine, and is reckoned hotter than the Garden Mint: it is carminative, expelling wind out of the ftomach, and helping the cholick.

The twelfth fort grows naturally in ditches in feveral parts of England; the ftalks of this are purple, fmooth, and fhort, branching out on every fide; the leaves are broad, fpear-fhaped, of a dark colour; they are but flightly fawed on their edges, and ftand upon fhort foot-ftalks. The flowers grow in roundifh heads on the top of the ftalks, they are purple, and their ftamina are longer than the petal. This fort has a warm biting tafte, but not quite fo hot as the Pepper Mint before defcribed, but is often ufed for it. There is a variety of this which fmells like Penny Royal.

The thirteenth fort grows naturally in arable land in moft parts of England, and is rarely admitted into gardens. This is the Water Calamint of the fhops, but is now feldom ufed in medicine. The ftalks of this fort rife about a foot high and are hairy, garnifhed with oval leaves ending in acute points, and fawed on their edges. The flowers grow in very thick whorls round the ftalks; they are fmall, of a purple colour, and their ftamina are fhorter than the petal. The plant has a ftrong fcent like Penny Royal.

The fourteenth fort grows in watery places in many parts of England; this hath weak trailing ftalks a foot and a half long, garnifhed with fmall oval leaves which are indented on their edges, and ftand upon pretty long foot-ftalks. The flowers grow in thick whorls round the ftalks, they are purple, and their ftamina are longer than the petal.

The fifteenth fort grows plentifully on the fide of the road between Bocking and Gosfield in Effex; the ftalks of this are much fmaller, and not fo long as thofe of the former; the leaves are fhorter and rounder, and are very little indented on their edges, but have their borders fet with hairs. The whorls of flowers are fmaller, and the whole plant has the fcent of Bafil.

The fixteenth fort grows naturally in ditches and on the fides of rivers, in many parts of England. This hath hairy four-cornered ftalks, which are a foot or more in height; the leaves are oval, fawed, and very hairy. The flowers grow in large whorls toward the top of the ftalks; they are purple, and their ftamina are longer than the petals. This hath a pleafanter fcent than the common Water Mint, fo is called Sweet Water Mint by way of diftinction: it ftands in the lift of fimples in moft difpenfaries, but is now feldom ufed in medicine.

The feventeenth grows naturally by the fide of the river Medway, between Rochefter and Chatham. This rifes with fpear-fhaped leaves, ending in acute points, which are fawed on their edges; the ftalks are befet with whorls of flowers almoft their whole length, fo that they have frequently ten or twelve whorls on each. The flowers are purplifh, and their ftamina are equal with the petals; this hath a very pleafant aromatic fcent.

All the forts of Mint are eafily propagated by parting the roots in the fpring, or by planting cuttings during any of the fummer months, but they fhould have a moift foil; and after the cuttings are planted, if the feafon fhould prove dry, they muft be often watered until they have taken root; after which, they will require no farther care but to keep them clear from weeds: they fhould be planted in beds about four feet wide, allowing a path about two feet broad between the beds, to water, weed, and cut the plants. The diftance they fhould be fet is four or five inches, or more, becaufe they fpread very much at their roots; for which reafon, the beds fhould not ftand longer than three years before you plant frefh, for by that time the roots will be matted fo clofely, as to rot and decay each other, if permitted to ftand longer. There are fome people who are very fond of Mint fallad in winter and fpring; in order to obtain which, they take up the roots before Chriftmas, and plant them upon a moderate hot-bed pretty clofe, covering them with fine earth about an inch thick, and cover the bed either with mats or frames of glafs. In thefe beds the Mint will come up in a month's time, and be foon fit to cut for that purpofe.

When the herb is cut for medicinal ufe, it fhould be done in a very dry feafon, juft when it is in flower; for if it ftand longer, it will not be near fo handfome, nor fo well tafted; and if it be cut when it is wet, it will change black and be little worth; this fhould be hung up to dry in a fhady place, where it may remain until it be ufed.

If the foil be good in which thefe plants are fet, they will afford three crops every year, but after July they feldom prove good; therefore what fhoots are produced after that time fhould be permitted to remain till Michaelmas, when they muft be cut down clofe; and after having cleared the beds from weeds, you fhould fpread a little fine rich earth all over them, which will greatly encourage the roots againft the fucceeding fpring.

As the diftilled water of all the forts of Mint is efteemed a very wholefome cordial dram, fo I fhould think it might be fubftituted inftead of thofe vile fpirits with which the common people intoxicate themfelves; for the Pepper Mint water is as warm on the ftomach as any fort of dram, and more-fo than any of thofe noxious fpirits; and if this was mixed with fome other agreeable aromatic herbs, there might certainly be a diftilled liquor much more palatable and wholefome than what is now vended in common; for as the generality of the lower clafs of people are fo debauched, as not to be contented without drams, fo the lefs hurtful thofe are made, the better it will be for the public; and by introducing

the diftilling of herbs, there will be lefs occafion for ufing of Wheat.

MENTHA CATARIA. See Nepeta.

MENTZELIA. Plum. Nov. Gen. Plant. 40. tab. 6. Lin. Gen. Plant. 595.

The name was given to this plant by Father Plumier, who difcovered it in the French fettlements in America, in honour of Dr. Mentzelius, who was phyfician to the Elector of Brandenburgh, and who publifhed an Index of plants in Latin, Greek, and High Dutch.

The CHARACTERS are,

The flower hath a fpreading empalement cut into five parts, which fits upon a long cylindrical germen. It hath five petals which fpread open, and are a little longer than the empalement, and many erect briftly ftamina, terminated by fingle fummits. From the long cylindrical-germen which is fituated under the flower, arifes a briftly ftyle the length of the petals, crowned by a fingle ftigma. The germen afterward turns to a cylindrical long capfule with one cell, containing many fmall feeds.

This genus of plants is ranged in the firft fection of Linnæus's thirteenth clafs, which includes thofe plants whofe flowers have many ftamina and one ftyle.

We know but one SPECIES of this genus, viz.

MENTZELIA (*Afpera*). Hort. Cliff. 492. Plumier titles it Mentzelia foliis & fructibus afperis. Nov. Gen. Plant. 41. *Mentzelia with prickly leaves and fruit.*

This plant grows plentifully at La Vera Cruz, from whence the feeds were fent to England by the late Dr. William Houftoun, which have fucceeded in the phyfic garden at Chelfea.

This plant is annual; it rifes with a flender fmooth ftalk, which is ftiff, and becomes a little woody, rifing more than three feet high, branching out alternately at diftances; the branches are diftorted, and run into one another; thefe are garnifhed with leaves fhaped like the point of an halbert, ftanding alternately on the branches, upon fhort foot-ftalks; they are covered with fhort hooded prickles, which faften themfelves into the clothes of thofe who rub againft them; and thofe parts of the branches eafily feparate from the plants, and adhere to the clothes in like manner as the feeds of Clivers. The flowers come out fingly from the joints of the ftalk, refting upon a cylindrical germen, which is near an inch in length, narrow at the bafe, but widens upward to the top. Upon the top of it comes out the empalement, which is fpread open after the fame manner as thofe of the Onagra; then the petals of the flower fpread open upon the empalement; they are of a pale yellow colour, and longer than the empalement. In the middle arifes a great number of ftamina which are erect, and are terminated by fingle fummits; from the germen arifes a fingle ftyle, which is as long as the petals, crowned by a fingle ftigma. The germen afterward turns to a long cylindrical capfule, armed with the like prickles as the leaves, which alfo faften themfelves to the clothes of thofe who rub againft them; thefe have but one cell, which is filled with fmall feeds.

As this is an annual plant, which perifhes foon after the feeds are ripe, therefore the feeds muft be fown on a hot-bed early in the fpring, that the plants may be brought forward early in the feafon, otherwife they will not produce ripe feed in this country. When the plants are come up about an inch high, they fhould be each tranfplanted into a feparate halfpenny pot filled with light rich earth, and plunged into a hot-bed of tanners bark, being careful to fhade them from the fun until they have taken new root; after which time they muft be conftantly watered every other day in warm weather, and fhould have frefh air every day admitted to them, in proportion to the warmth of the feafon, and the heat of the bed in which they are plunged. In about fix weeks or two months after tranfplanting, if the plants have made a good progrefs, they will have filled the pots with their roots, when they fhould be fhifted into larger pots, which muft be filled with light rich earth, and then plunged into the bark-bed in the ftove, that they may have

room

room to grow in height, obferving, as before, to water them duly, as alfo to admit frefh air to them every day in warm weather: with this management the plants will rife to the height of three feet, and will produce ripe feeds the latter end of Auguft or the beginning of September.

MENYANTHES, is the Trifolium Paluftre, or Bog Bean.

This plant is common upon boggy places in divers parts of England, but is never cultivated in gardens; for which reafon I fhall not trouble the reader with any farther account of it, except the taking notice, that this plant is at prefent in great efteem, being thought an excellent remedy for the rheumatifm, gout, and many other diforders. It is frequently called Bog Bean, or Marfh Trefoil, in the markets, and grows plentifully on bogs in many parts of England, where it is gathered and brought to fupply the markets.

MERCURIALIS. Tourn. Inft. R. H. 534. tab. 308. Lin. Gen. Plant. 998. [This plant takes its name from Mercury, becaufe the ancients had a notion, that the God Mercury brought this plant into ufe.] Mercury; in French, *Mercuriale*.

The CHARACTERS are,

It is male and female in different plants; the male flowers have a fpreading empalement, which is cut into three concave fegments; thefe have no petals, but have nine or twelve erect hairy ftamina, crowned by globular twin fummits. The female flowers have no petals, but have two awl-fhaped acute-pointed nectariums; to each of thefe there is a fingle broad germen, impreffed with a furrow between them; thefe roundifh compreffed germen have a prickly furrow on each fide, and fupport two reflexed prickly ftyles, crowned by acute reflexed ftigmes. The germen afterward turns to a twin capfule fhaped like the fcrotum, having two cells, each containing one roundifh feed.

This genus of plants is ranged in the eighth fection of Linnæus's twenty-fecond clafs, which includes thofe plants whofe male flowers grow on different plants from the fruit, and have nine ftamina in each.

The SPECIES are,

1. MERCURIALIS (*Annua*) caule brachiata, foliis glabris. Hort. Cliff. 461. *Mercury with a branching ftalk and fmooth leaves.* Mercurialis fpicata & tefticulata mas & fœmina. C. B. P. 121. *Mercury with fpiked and tefticulated flowers, which are both male and female, called French Mercury.*

2. MERCURIALIS (*Perennis*) caule fimpliciffimo, foliis fcabris. Hort. Cliff. 461. *Mercury with a fingle ftalk and rough leaves.* Mercurialis montana fpicata & tefticulata. C. B. P. 122. *Mountain Mercury, or Dogs Mercury, with fpiked and tefticulated flowers.*

3. MERCURIALIS (*Tomentofa*) caule fubfruticofo, foliis tomentofis. Hort. Cliff. 461. *Mercury with a ftalk fomewhat fhrubby, and woolly leaves.* Mercurialis fruticofa incana, fpicata & tefticulata. Tourn. Inft. R. H. 534. *Shrubby hoary Mercury, having fpiked and tefticulated flowers.*

The firft fort is commonly called French Mercury, from whence it might have been brought into England; for although it is now become a weed in gardens and upon dunghills, yet it is feldom found growing at a diftance from habitations. This is an annual plant, with a branching ftalk about a foot high, garnifhed with fpear-fhaped leaves about an inch and a half long, indented on their edges, of a pale or yellowifh green colour. The male plants have fpikes of herbaceous flowers growing on the top of the ftalks, thefe fall foon; but the female plants, which have tefticulated flowers proceeding from the fide of the ftalks, are fucceeded by feeds, which, if permitted to fcatter, will produce plenty of plants of both fexes. The leaves and ftalks of this plant are ufed in medicine, and are reckoned aperitive and mollifying.

The fecond fort grows under hedges and in woods in moft parts of England. This hath a perennial root, which creeps in the ground; the ftalks are fingle and

without branches, rifing ten or twelve inches high, garnifhed with rough leaves, placed by pairs at each joint; they are of a dark green colour, and indented on their edges; thefe have their male flowers growing in fpikes upon different plants, from thofe which produce feeds.

This hath a poifonous quality, there have been many late inftances of it, where people in the fpring of the year, when there has been a fcarcity of greens, have boiled the leaves of this, and have fuffered greatly by eating them.

The third fort grows naturally in the fouth of France, in Spain, and Italy. This rifes with a fhrubby branching ftalk a foot and a half high, garnifhed with oval leaves placed by pairs, which are covered with a white down on both fides. The male flowers grow in fhort fpikes from the fide of the ftalks, upon different plants from the fruit, which are tefticulated and hoary. If the feeds of thefe are permitted to fcatter, the plants will come up the following fpring; and if the feeds are fown, it fhould be performed in the autumn, for thofe which are fown in the fpring feldom grow the fame year. This plant fhould have a warm fituation and a dry rubbifhy foil, in which it will live three or four years, but in hard froft thefe plants are frequently killed.

MESEMBRYANTHEMUM. Dill. Gen. 9. Hort. Elth. 179. Ficoides. Tourn. Act. R. Par. 1705. Fig Marygold.

The CHARACTERS are,

The flower hath a permanent fpreading empalement of one leaf, which is cut at the top into five acute parts. It hath one petal, which is cut into many linear fegments almoft to the bottom, and ranged in feveral feries, but are joined together at their bafe; within thefe are ranged a great number of hairy ftamina, terminated by incumbent fummits. Under the flower is fituated an obtufe five-cornered germen, fupporting fometimes five, and often ten or more ftyles, which are reflexed, and crowned by fingle ftigmas. The germen afterward becomes a roundifh flefhy fruit, having as many cells as there are ftyles, filled with fmall feeds.

This genus of plants is ranged in the fourth fection of Linnæus's twelfth clafs, which includes thofe plants whofe flowers have from twenty to thirty ftamina inferted in the empalement, and five ftyles.

The SPECIES are,

1. MESEMBRYANTHEMUM (*Nodiflorum*) foliis alternis teretiufculis obtufis ciliatis. Hort. Upfal. 129. *Mefembryanthemum with taper, obtufe, hairy leaves, placed alternately.* Ficoides Neapolitana, flore candido. H. L. *Fig Marygold of Naples with a white flower, or Egyptian Kali.*

2. MESEMBRYANTHEMUM (*Cryftallinum*) foliis alternis ovatis papulofis undulatis. Hort. Cliff. 216. *Mefembryanthemum with oval, obtufe, waved leaves placed alternately.* Ficoides Africana, folio plantaginis undulato, micis argenteis adfperfo. Tourn. Act. R. Par. 1705. *African Fig Marygold, with a waved Plantain leaf, marked with filvery fpots, commonly called the Diamond Ficoides, or Diamond Plant.*

3. MESEMBRYANTHEMUM (*Geniculiflorum*) foliis femiteretibus papulofis diftinctis floribus feffilibus axillaribus. Lin. Sp. Plant. 481. *Mefembryanthemum with half taper leaves, and flowers fitting clofe to the wings of the ftalks.* Ficoides Capenfe, folio tereti, flore albido. Pet. Gaz. 78. fol. 3. *Fig Marygold of the Cape, with a taper leaf and a whitifh flower.*

4. MESEMBRYANMTHEMUM (*Noctiflorum*) foliis femicylindraceis, impunctatis diftinctis, floribus pedunculatis calycibus quadrifidis. Lin. Sp. Plant. 481. *Mefembryanthemum with almoft cylindrical leaves, and quadrifid foot-ftalks to the flowers.* Ficoides Africana, erecta, arborefcens, lignofa, flore radiato, primo purpureo, dein argenteo, interdiu claufo, noctu aperto. Boerh. Ind. alt. 1. 290. *Upright, ligneous, tree Fig Marygold of Africa, with a radiated flower, which is at firft purple, afterward filvery, fhut in the day, and open at night.*

5. MESEMBRYANTHEMUM (*Splendens*) foliis femiteretibus impunctatis recurvis diftinctis congeftis, calycibus terminalibus

terminalibus digitiformibus. Lin. Sp. 689. *Mesembry-anthemum with taper, unspotted, recurved, distinct leaves in clusters, whose empelement is finger-shaped.*

6. MESEMBRYANTHEMUM (*Umbellatum*) foliis fubulatis, scabrido-punctatis connatis apice patulo, caule erecto, corymbo trichotoma. Lin. Sp. Plant. 481. *Mesembry-anthemum with awl-shaped leaves which join, having rough spots, an erect stalk, and a corymbus of flowers at the triple division of the stalk.* Ficoides africana erecta teretifolia, floribus albis umbellatis. Par. Bat. 166. *Upright African Fig Marygold, with a taper leaf, and white flowers growing in umbels.*

7. MESEMBRYANTHEMUM (*Calamiforme*) acaule foliis subteretibus adscendentibus impunctatis connatis, floribus octagynis. Lin. Sp. Plant. 481. *Mesembryanthe-mum without a stalk, almost taper leaves which join at their base, and flowers having eight styles.* Ficoides Capensis humilis, cepeæ folio, flore stamineo. Brad. Suec. p. 10. fol. 19. *Low Fig Marygold of the Cape, with an Onion leaf, and a stamineous flower.*

8. MESEMBRYANTHEMUM (*Tripolium*) foliis alternis lanceolatis planis impunctatis caulibus laxis simplicibus calycibus pentagonis. Hort. Cliff. 217. *Mesembry-anthemum with plain spear-shaped leaves which are not spotted, a single weak stalk, and a five-cornered empale-ment.* Ficoides Africana, procumbens, tripoli folio, flore argenteo. Hort. Chell. *Trailing African Fig Ma-rygold, with a Tripolium leaf and a silvery flower.*

9. MESEMBRYANTHEMUM (*Bellidiflorum*) acaule, foliis triquetris linearibus impunctatis apice trifariàm dentatis. Hort. Cliff. 218. *Mesembryanthemum without a stalk, having narrow, three-cornered, unspotted leaves, marked with three indentures at their points.* Ficoides Capen-sis humilis, folio triangulari in summitatem dentato, flore minore purpurascente. Brad. Suec. p. 9. tab. 18. *Dwarf Marygold of the Cape, with a triangular leaf in-dented at the top, and a smaller purplish flower.*

10. MESEMBRYANTHEMUM (*Subulatum*) acaule foliis fub-ulatis triquetris dorso supernè serratis. *Mesembryan-themum without a stalk, and awl-shaped three-cornered leaves, whose back part is sawed toward the top.*

11. MESEMBRYANTHEMUM (*Deltoides*) foliis deltoidibus triquetris dentatis impunctatis distinctis. Hort. Cliff. 218. *Mesembryanthemum with three-cornered indented leaves, which are shaped like the Greek delta, without spots, and distinct.* Ficoides Africana, folio triangulari crasso, brevi, glauco, ad tres margines aculeato. Boerh. Ind. alt. 1. 290. *African Fig Marygold, with a short, thick, gray, triangular leaf, with prickles on the three edges.*

12. MESEMBRYANTHEMUM (*Caulescens*) caulescens, fo-liis deltoidibus, lateribus minimè dentatis. *Stalky Me-sembryanthemum, with leaves shaped like the Greek delta, whose sides are a little indented.* Ficoides Africana, fo-lio triangulari glauco, brevissimo, crassissimo, margine non spinoso. Boerh. Ind. alt. 1. 290. *African Fig Ma-rygold, with very thick, short, triangular, gray leaves, having no spines on their edges.*

13. MESEMBRYANTHEMUM (*Barbatum*) foliis subovatis papillosis distinctis apice barbatis. Hort. Cliff. 216. *Mesembryanthemum with almost oval leaves, having dis-tinct bladders bearded at their points.* Ficoides seu ficus aizoides Africana, folio variegato aspero, ad apicem stella spinosa armato. Boerh. Ind. alt. 1. p. 291. *Afri-can Fig Marygold, with a rough variegated leaf, whose point is armed with spines in form of a star.*

14. MESEMBRYANTHEMUM (*Stellatum*) caulibus decum-bentibus, foliis teretibus papulosis apice barbatis. *Mesembryanthemum with decumbent stalks and taper blad-dered leaves, whose points are bearded like a star.* Fi-coides Capensis frutescens, folio tumido, extremitate stellatâ, flore purpureo. Brad. Suec. Dec. 1. tab. 6. *Shrubby Fig Marygold of the Cape, with a star-pointed tumid leaf, and a purple flower.*

15. MESEMBRYANTHEMUM (*Hispidum*) foliis cylindricis papulosis distinctis, caule hispido. Lin. Sp. Plant. 482. *Mesembryanthemum with a prickly stalk, and deflexed cy-lindrical leaves with pulpy bladders.* Ficoides Afra, fru-ticosa, caule lanugine argenteâ ornato, folio tereti, parvo, longo, guttulis argenteis quasi scabro, flore vi-

olaceo. Boerh. Ind. alt. 1. 291. *African shrubby Fig Marygold, having stalks adorned with silvery down, and long, small, taper leaves, spotted as it were with silvery drops, and a Violet-coloured flower.*

16. MESEMBRYANTHEMUM (*Villosum*) caule foliisque pubescentibus. Hort. Cliff. 217. *Mesembryanthemum whose stalks and leaves are garnished with downy hairs.*

17. MESEMBRYANTHEMUM (*Scabrum*) foliis subulatis distinctis subtus undique muricatis, calycibus mu-ticis. Hort. Cliff. 219. *Mesembryanthemum with awl-shaped leaves, which are distinct, every where rough on their under side, and chaffy empalements.* Ficoides Afra, folio triangulari viridi longo aspero, flore violaceo. Boerh. Ind. alt. 290. *African Fig Marygold, with a long, green, rough, triangular leaf, and a Violet-coloured flower.*

18. MESEMBRYANTHEMUM (*Uncinatum*) articulis cauli-nis terminatis in folia connata acuminata subtus den-tata. Hort. Cliff. 218. *Mesembryanthemum whose joints of the stalks are terminated by acute-pointed leaves, which are joined at their base, and indented on their under side.* Ficoides Afra, folio triangulari glauco, perfoliato, brevissimo, apice spinoso. Boerh. Ind. alt. 290. *Afri-can Fig Marygold, with a short, perfoliated, triangular leaf, whose point is prickly, commonly called Buckshorn Ficoides.*

19. MESEMBRYANTHEMUM (*Perfoliatum*) perfoliatum, foliis majoribus, apicibus triacanthis. Hort. Elth. 251. *Perfoliate Mesembryanthemum with larger leaves, whose points have three thorns.* Ficoides Africana frutescens perfoliata, folio triangulari glauco punctato, cortice lignoso candido tenui. Tourn. Act. Par. 1705. *Shrubby, perfoliate, African, Fig Marygold, with a triangular, gray, spotted leaf, and a thin, white, ligneous bark, com-monly called Stag's horn Ficoides.*

20. MESEMBRYANTHEMUM (*Spinosum*) foliis tereti-tri-quetris punctatis distinctis spinis ramosis. Hort. Cliff. 216. *Mesembryanthemum with taper three-cornered leaves, which have distinct spots and branching spines.* Ficoides Africana, aculeis longissimis & foliolis nascentibus ex foliorum alis. Tourn. Act. R. Par. 1705. *African Fig Marygold with long spines, and smaller leaves arising from the wings of the leaves.*

21. MESEMBRYANTHEMUM (*Tuberosum*) foliis subulatis papillosis, distinctis apice patulis radice capitata. Hort. Cliff. 216. *Mesembryanthemum with awl-shaped pimply leaves, and a beaded root.* Ficoides Africana, folio triangulari recurvo, floribus umbellatis obsoleti coloris, extremè purpureis. Tourn. Act. Par. 1705. *African Fig Marygold with a triangular recurved leaf, and umbellated flowers of a dark colour, which are pur-ple on their outside.*

22. MESEMBRYANTHEMUM (*Tenuifolium*) foliis subulatis semiteretibus glabris, distinctis internodio longioribus. Hort. Cliff. 216. *Mesembryanthemum with awl-shaped, half-taper, smooth, distinct leaves, whose joints are far-ther distant.* Ficoides Capensis humilis, teretifolia, flore coccineo. Brad. Suec. p. 13. *Low Fig Marygold of the Cape, with a taper leaf and a scarlet flower.*

23. MESEMBRYANTHEMUM (*Stipulaceum*) foliis subtri-quetris compressis incurvatis punctatis distinctis con-gestis basi marginalis. Lin. Sp. 693. *Mesembryanthe-mum with three-cornered, compressed, incurved leaves, having distinct spots, whose base are bordered and clustered.* Mesembryanthemum frutescens, flore purpureo rari-ore. Hort. Elth. tab. 209.

24. MESEMBRYANTHEMUM (*Crassifolium*) foliis semicy-lindricis impunctatis connatis, apice triquetris caule repente semicylindricis. Hort. Cliff. 217. *Mesembryan-themum with a creeping cylindrical stalk, cylindrical smooth leaves, joining at their base, whose points are three-cor-nered.* Ficoides Africana reptans, folio triangulari, flore saturatè purpureo. Brad. Suec. p. 16. tab. 38. *Creeping African Fig Marygold with a green triangular leaf, and deep purple-coloured flower.*

25. MESEMBRYANTHEMUM (*Falcatum*) foliis sub-acina-ciformibus incurvis punctatis distinctis ramis tereti-bus. Hort. Cliff. 219. *Mesembryanthemum with distinct, smooth, falchion-shaped leaves, and taper branches.* Fi-coides Afra folio triangulari ensiformi brevissimo, flore

flore dilutè purpurafcente filamentofo. Brad. Suec. Dec. 5. tab. 42. *African Fig Marygold with a triangular, cimeter-shaped, short leaf, and a pale purplish flower.*

26. Mesembryanthemum (*Glomeratum*) foliis teretiufculis compreffis punctatis, caule paniculato multifloro. Lin. Sp. 694. *Mefembryanthemum with taper, compreffed, spotted leaves, and a panicled stalk with many flowers.* Mefembryanthemum falcatum minus, flore carneo minore. Hort. Elth. tab. 213.

27. Mesembryanthemum (*Edule*) foliis æquilateri-triquetris acutis strictis impunctatis connatis carina fubferratis, caule ancipiti. Lin. Sp. 695. *Mefembryanthemum with equilateral, acute, unspotted leaves joined at their base, whose keel are sawed.* Ficoides feu ficus aizoides Africana major procumbens, triangulari folio, fructu maximo eduli. H. L. 244. *Greater trailing African Fig Marygold, with a triangular leaf and a large eatable fruit.*

28. Mesembryanthemum (*Bicolorum*) foliis fubulatis lævibus punctatis distinctis caule frutefcente corollis bicoloribus. Lin. Sp. Plant. 695. *Mefembryanthemum with awl-shaped smooth leaves, which have different spots, a shrubby stalk, and the flower of two colours.* Ficoides Capenfis frutefcens, folio tereti punctato, petalis luteis. Brad. Suec. 1. p. 8. tab. 7. *Shrubby Fig Marygold of the Cape, with a taper leaf having punctures, and yellow petals.*

29. Mesembryanthemum (*Acinaciforme*) foliis acinaciformibus impunctatis connatis, angulo carinali fcabris, petalis lanceolatis. Lin. Sp. 695. *Mefembryanthemum with sharp, three-cornered, unspotted leaves, joined at their base, whose keel are rough, and spear-shaped petals of the flower.* Ficoides Africana folio longo triangulari incurvo, caule purpureo. Tourn. Act. Par. 1705. *African Fig Marygold with a long triangular leaf, which is incurved, and a purple stalk.*

30. Mesembryanthemum (*Loreum*) foliis femicylindricis recurvis congeftis bafi interiore gibbis connatis, caule pendulo. Lin. Sp. 694. *Mefembryanthemum with cylindrical recurved leaves, whose base are clustered and join, and a pendulous stalk.* Mefembryanthemum loreum. Hort. Elth. tab. 200.

31. Mesembryanthemum (*Serratum*) foliis fubulatis triquetris punctatis distinctis angulo carinali retrorfum ferratis. Lin. Sp. 696. *Mefembryanthemum with awl-shaped leaves having distinct spots, and the angle of the keel sawed.* Mefembryanthemum ferratum flore acetabuliformi luteo. Hort. Elth. tab. 192.

32. Mesembryanthemum (*Tuberculatum*) acaule foliis femicylindricis connatis externè tuberculatis. Hort. Cliff. 219. *Mefembryanthemum without a stalk, and cylindrical leaves which have tubercles on their outsides, and are joined at their base.* Ficoides Afra, folio triangulari, longo, fucculento, caulibus rubris. Boerh. Ind. alt. 290. *African Fig Marygold with a long, triangular, succulent leaf, and red stalks.*

33. Mesembryanthemum (*Veruculatum*) foliis triquetro-cylindricis acutis connatis arcuatis impunctatis distinctis. Hort. Cliff. 220. *Mefembryanthemum with three-cornered cylindrical leaves which are connected at their base, bowed and smooth.* Ficoides Afra arborefcens, folio tereti glauco, apice purpureo craffo. Boerh. Ind. alt. 291. *African Tree Fig Marygold, with a taper gray leaf, having a thick purple top.*

34. Mesembryanthemum (*Glaucum*) foliis triquetris acutis, punctatis distinctis calycinis foliolis ovatocordatis. Lin. Sp. 696. *Mefembryanthemum with acute three-cornered leaves marked with punctures, and oval heart-shaped empalements.* Ficoides Afra caule lignofo, erecta, folio triangulari enfiformi fcabro, flore luteo magno. Boerh. Ind. alt. 289. *African Fig Marygold with an erect ligneous stalk, a triangular, cimeter-shaped, rough leaf, and a large yellow flower.*

35. Mesembryanthemum (*Corniculatum*) foliis triquetro-femicylindricis fcabrido-punctatis, fupra bafin linea elevatis connatis. Lin. Sp. 697. *Stalky Mefembryanthemum with three-cornered, femicylindrical, rough, spotted leaves, which are connected at their base.* Ficoides Afra triangulari longiffimo, marginibus obtufioribus, flore amplo, intus pallidè luteo, extus lineâ rubrâ longâ picto. Boerh. Ind. alt. 289. *African Fig Mary-*

gold *with a long triangular leaf, obtufer borders, and a large flower of a pale yellow within, and marked with a long red streak on the outside.*

36. Mesembryanthemum (*Expanfum*) foliis planiufculis lanceolatis impunctatis patentibus distinctis oppoficis alternatifque remotis. Lin. Sp. 697. *Mefembryanthemum with plain, spear-shaped, unspotted leaves, which spread distinctly, and are opposite and alternate at a distance.* Ficoides Africana humifufa, folio triangulari longiore glauco, flore flavefcente. Tourn. Acad. R. Par. 1705. *Trailing African Fig Marygold, with a longer, gray, triangular leaf, and a yellowish flower.*

37. Mesembryanthemum (*Micans*) foliis fubulatis triquetris punctatis distinctis, caule fcabro. Lin. Sp. 696. *Mefembryanthemum with three-cornered awl-shaped leaves, which are distinctly spotted, and a rough stalk.* Mefembryanthemum micans, flore Phœnicio, filamentris atris. Hort. Elth. tab. 215.

38. Mesembryanthemum (*Tortuofum*) foliis planiufculis oblongo-ovatis fubpapillofis confertis connatis, calycibus tryphyllis bicornibus. Lin. Sp. 697. *Mefembryanthemum with plain, oblong, oval leaves joining at their base, and a three-leaved empalement with two horns.* Ficoides Capenfis procumbens aleæ folio, flore albo medio croceo. Brad. Suec. Dec. 2. p. 7. tab. 16. *Trailing Fig Marygold of the Cape, with an Olive leaf, and a white flower of a Saffron colour in the middle.*

39 Mesembryanthemum (*Ringens*) fubacaule, foliis ciliato-dentatis. Lin. Hort. Cliff. 218. *Mefembryanthemum with a short stalk, and leaves having hairy indentures.* Ficoides Capenfis humilis, folio triangulari prope fumitatem dentato, flore luteo. Brad. Suec. Dec. 2. p. 8. tab. 17. *Low Fig Marygold of the Cape, with a triangular leaf indented toward the top, and a yellow flower, commonly called Dogs Chap Ficoides.*

40. Mesembryanthemum (*Roftratum*) acaule, foliis femicylindricis connatis externe tuberculatis. Lin. Sp. 696. *Mefembryanthemum without a stalk, having cylindrical leaves joined at their base, and tubercles on the outside.* Ficoides Afra folio triangulari, enfiformi craffo brevi, ad margines laterales multis majoribus fpinis aculeato. Martyn. Cent. 30. tab. 30. *African Fig Marygold, with a triangular, cimeter-shaped, short, thick leaf, whose side borders have many large spines, commonly called Cats Chap Ficoides.*

41. Mesembryanthemum (*Dolabriforme*) foliis dolabriformibus punctatis. Hort. Cliff. 219. *Mefembryanthemum with ax-shaped spotted leaves.* Ficoides Capenfis humilis foliis cornua cervi referentibus, punctatis luteis, noctiflora. Brad. Suec. 1. p. 11. tab. 10. *Low Fig Marygold of the Cape, with leaves like a stag's horn, yellow petals, and a flower opening at night.*

42. Mesembryanthemum (*Difforme*) foliis difformibus punctatis connatis. Prod. Leyd. 287. *Mefembryanthemum with deformed leaves.* Ficoides Afra foliis latiffimis craffimis lucidis, difformibus. Boerh. Ind. alt. 292. *African Fig Marygold, with very broad, thick, shining, deformed leaves.*

43. Mesembryanthemum (*Lucidnm*) acaule foliis linguiformibus lucidis imarginatis. *Mefembryanthemum without a stalk, and tongue-shaped lucid leaves, indented at the top.* Ficoides Afra acaulos, foliis latiffimis craffis lucidis conjugatis, flore aureo ampliffimo. Tourn. Acad. R. Scien. 1705. *African Fig Marygold without a stalk, broad, thick, shining leaves growing by pairs, and a very large yellow flower.*

44. Mesembryanthemum (*Linguiforme*) acaule foliis linguiformibus altero margine craffioribus impunctatis. Lin. Sp. 699. *Mefembryanthemum without a stalk, very broad tongue-shaped leaves, one edge being thicker than the other, and without spots.* Ficoides Afra acaulos, foliis latiffimis craffiffimis, lucidis conjugatis, flore aureo amplo, pedunculo brevi. Boerh. Ind. alt. 292. *African Fig Marygold having no stalk, very broad, thick, shining leaves placed by pairs, and a large golden flower with a short foot-stalk.*

45. Mesembryanthemum (*Albidum*) acaule foliis triquetris. *Mefembryanthemum having no stalk, and gray, entire, three-cornered leaves.* Mefembryanthemum foliis robuftis albicantibus. Hort. Elth. 243. *Mefembryanthemum with strong whitish leaves.*

46. MESEMBRYANTHEMUM (*Pugioniforme*) foliis alternis fubularis triquetris longiffimis impunctatis. Hort. Cliff. 216. *Mefembryanthemum with alternate, awl-fhaped, three-cornered leaves, which are very long, without fpots.* Ficoides Capenfis, caryophylli folio, flore aureo fpeciofo. Brad. Succ. Dec. 2. p. 5. tab. 14. *Fig Marygold of the Cape, with a Clove Gilliflower leaf, and a beautiful golden-coloured flower.*

Thefe plants are moft of them natives of the Cape of Good Hope, from whence their feeds were firft brought to Holland, and the plants raifed in many of their curious gardens, and have fince been communicated to moft parts of Europe; thefe were at firft titled Chryfanthemum by the old botanifts, but afterward they were titled Ficoides by Herman and Tournefort, from their capfules being fhaped like little Figs; afterward they had this title of Mefembryanthemum applied to them, which fignifies a flower opening in the middle of the day, which is what moft of the fpecies do; there are three or four of them which open in the evening, and are clofed all the day; thefe have been feparated from the others by fome, and have had the title of Nycterianthemum applied to them, from their flowers being expanded in the night; but as they all agree in the characters which diftinguifh the genus, they fhould by no means be feparated.

Moft of the plants of this genus have beautiful flowers, which appear at different feafons of the year; fome of them flower early in the fpring, others in fummer, fome in the autumn; and there are others which flower in winter; and many of them produce their flowers in fuch quantity, as that when they are expanded, the plants are entirely covered with them; they have all of them thick fucculent leaves, but fome of the fpecies are much more fo than others, and the figures of their leaves vary fo much in the feveral fpecies, that they afford an agreeable variety when they are not in flower.

To defcribe all the fpecies which are here mentioned, would fwell this work too much, and as their titles are fhort defcriptions of the fpecies, I fhall not enlarge more on that head, but proceed to their culture. All the forts here mentioned are perennial plants except the two firft, which are annual. The perennial forts are eafily propagated by cuttings during any of the fummer months; fuch of them as have fhrubby ftalks and branches, very readily take root when planted in a bed of light foil, and covered either with mats or glaffes, but when they are covered with the latter, they muft be fhaded every day when the fun is warm; thefe cuttings of the fhrubby forts need not be cut from the plant more than five or fix days before they are planted, during which time they fhould be laid in a dry room, not too much expofed to the fun, that the part which was feparated from the old plants may heal over and dry before they are planted, otherwife they are apt to rot; thefe may be planted at about three inches diftance from each other, and the earth preffed clofe to them, but none of their leaves fhould be buried in the ground, for as they abound with moifture, fo if they are covered with the earth, it will caufe them to rot, and that often deftroys the cuttings; therefore when the cuttings are taken from the old plants, they fhould be divefted of their lower leaves, fo far as may be neceffary, to allow a naked ftalk of fufficient length for planting.

When the cuttings are planted, it will be neceffary to give them a little water, to fettle the ground about them, but it fhould be done with caution, for too much wet will fpoil them; if thefe are fhaded every day from nine or ten o'clock till three or four, when the fun is warm, it will prevent the ground from drying too faft, fo that the cuttings need not be watered oftener than once in a week; but if there fhould happen fome gentle fhowers of rain, it will be proper to take off their covers, and let them receive it, but they fhould be fcreened from hard rains. The cuttings thus managed will have put out good roots in about fix weeks, when they fhould be carefully taken up, and each planted in a feparate fmall pot filled with light fandy earth, and then placed in a fhady fituation, giving them a little water to fettle the earth to their roots; in this place they may remain about ten days or a fortnight, by which time they will have taken good root, and may be removed to a fheltered place, where they may have more fun, in which they may remain till autumn; during the fummer months, thefe may be watered twice, or in very hot weather, three times a week, but it muft not be given them in too great plenty; but as the fun declines in autumn, they fhould not have it oftener than once a week, for if they are often fupplied with it, the plants will grow luxuriant; their leaves and branches will be fo replete with moifture, that the early frofts in the autumn will deftroy them; whereas when they are kept dry, their growth will be ftinted, fo that they will be hardy enough to refift fmall frofts, but there muft be care taken that they do not fhoot their roots through the holes of the pots into the ground, for when they do, the plants will grow very luxuriant; and when the pots are removed, and thofe roots are torn off, their leaves and branches will fhrink, fo will not recover it in a long time, if ever; to prevent which, the pots fhould be removed every fortnight, and where the roots are beginning to come through the pots, they fhould be cut off. The forts which grow very freely fhould be fhifted three times in the fummer, to pare off their roots, and keep them within compafs, and thefe fhould never be planted in rich earth for the reafons before given; for if the earth is frefh, there will require no dung or other compoft, unlefs it is ftrong, in which cafe fea fand, or lime rubbifh, will be a good mixture; the quantity of either muft be in proportion to the ftiffnefs of the ground, always being careful to render it fo light, as that the wet may eafily pafs off.

We next proceed to treat of thofe forts, whofe ftalks and leaves are very fucculent. The cuttings of thefe fhould be taken from the plants ten days or a fortnight before they are planted, that they may have time for their wounded part to heal over and dry; the lower leaves of thefe fhould alfo be ftripped off, that their naked ftalks may be of a fufficient length for planting. As thefe are moftly plants of humble growth, fo if their ftalks are divefted of their leaves an inch and a half, it will be fufficient. The cuttings of thefe forts require to be covered with glaffes, to keep off the wet; they muft alfo have lefs water than the other, but in other particulars require the fame treatment. The roots of thefe do not fpread and extend fo much as thofe of the other, fo will not require to be fhifted oftener than twice a year at moft; they muft alfo be kept in fmall pots to confine their roots; the earth in which they are planted fhould be rather light and not rich. During the fummer feafon they muft not have too much wet, and in the winter they muft have but little water. If thefe fucculent forts are placed in an open airy glafs-cafe in winter, where they may have free air admitted to them in plenty in mild weather, and fcreened from the froft, they will thrive much better than when they are more tenderly treated. The other fhrubby kinds may be fheltered in winter under a common frame, where, if they are protected from froft and wet, it is all they require; for the hardier thefe are treated, the greater quantity of flowers they will produce: and fome of the forts are fo hardy, as to live abroad when planted clofe to a good afpected wall, and in a poor dry foil; fo that where there is room to difpofe them againft a wall, and the border is raifed with lime rubbifh to prevent their rooting deep and growing luxuriant, they may be preferved through the winter with very little fhelter, and thefe will flower much better than thofe under cover.

The firft fort grows naturally in Egypt, where they cut up the plants, and burn them for pot-afh; and this is efteemed as the beft fort for making hard fope, and the beft fort of glafs.

                                    This

This is an annual plant, which does not perfect feeds in England; for when it is placed in the stove, or kept in the hot-bed, their stalks grow long and slender, so are not productive of flowers; and those which are raised in hot-beds, and afterward exposed in the open air, will flower pretty freely, but do not perfect their seeds. As this plant will thrive in South Carolina as well as in its native soil, so it might turn to the advantage of that colony, and likewise become beneficial to the public, if the inhabitants could be prevailed on to cultivate this plant.

The second sort is annual; this is a native at the Cape of Good Hope. It is propagated for the oddness of its leaves and stalks, which are closely covered over with pellucid pimples full of moisture, which, when the sun shines on the plants, they reflect the light, and appear like small bubbles of ice; from whence some have called it the Ice Plant, and others have named it the Diamond Plant, or Diamond Ficoides.

This sort is propagated by feeds, which must be sown on a hot-bed early in the spring; and when the plants come up, they must be planted on a fresh hotbed to bring them forward; after they have taken root in the hot-bed, they should have but little wet, for moisture will rot them. When they are grown large enough to transplant again, they should be each planted into a small pot, filled with light fresh earth, but not rich, and plunged into a hot-bed of tan, observing to shade them in the heat of the day until they have taken new root; then they should have plenty of fresh air admitted to them every day in warm weather, to prevent their drawing weak. In the latter end of June, some of the plants may be inured to bear the open air, and afterward they may be turned out of the pots, and planted into a warm border, where they will thrive, and spread their branches to a great distance upon the ground; but these plants will not be very productive of flowers, therefore some of them must be continued in the small pots, and may at the same time, when the others are planted out, be removed into the stove or glass-case, placing them upon the shelves, that the roots may not get out from the bottom of the pots, so that they may be confined, which will cause them to flower plentifully, and from these good seeds may every year be obtained.

MESPILUS [Μεσπιλος, Gr.] Tourn. Inst. R. H. 641. tab. 410. Lin. Gen. Plant. 549. The Medlar.

The CHARACTERS are,
The empalement of the flower is permanent, of one leaf, cut into five spreading concave segments. The flower is composed of five roundish concave petals, which are inserted in the empalement. The number of stamina are different in the several species, from ten to twenty or more; these are also inserted in the empalement, and are terminated by single summits. The germen is situated under the flower, and supports an uncertain number of styles from three to five, which are crowned by headed stigmas. The germen afterward becomes a roundish or oval berry, carrying the empalement on its top, and inclosing four or five hard seeds.

This genus of plants is ranged in the fourth section of Linnæus's twelfth class, which includes the plants whose flowers have twenty stamina inserted to the em palement, and five styles.

The SPECIES are,
1. MESPILUS (Sylvestris) inermis, foliis lanceolatis dentatis acuminatis, subtus tomentosis, calycibus acuminatis. Smooth Medlar, with spear-shaped, acute-pointed, indented leaves, woolly on their under side, and acute-pointed empalements. Mespilus folio laurino major, fructu minori, rariori substantiâ. Hort. Cath. Greater Medlar with a Bay-tree leaf, and a smaller less substantial fruit.

2. MESPILUS (Germanica) inermis foliis lanceolatis integerrimis subtus tomentosis, calycibus acuminatis. Hort. Cliff. 189. Unarmed Medlar with spear-shaped entire leaves, which are downy on their under side, and acute-pointed empalements. Mespilus Germanica, folio laurino, non serrato, five Mespilus sylvestris. C. B.

P. 453. German Medlar with a Bay-tree leaf which is not sawed, or wild Medlar.

3. MESPILUS (Pyracantha) spinosa, foliis lanceolato-ovatis crenatis, calycibus fructûs obtusis. Hort. Cliff. 189. Prickly Medlar, with spear-shaped, oval, crenated leaves, and obtuse empalements to the fruit. Mespilus aculeata, amygdali folio. Tourn. Inst. 642. Prickly Medlar with an Almond leaf, called Pyracantha.

4. MESPILUS (Cordato) foliis cordata-ovatis acuminatis, acutè serratis, ramis spinosis. Fig. Plant. tab. 179. Medlar with heart-shaped, oval, acute-pointed leaves, which are sharply sawed, and prickly branches.

5. MESPILUS (Amelanchier) inermis, foliis ovalibus serratis, cauliculis hirsutis. Lin. Sp. Plant. 478. Medlar without thorns, having oval sawed leaves, and hairy stalks. Mespilus folio rotundiori, fructu nigro subdulci. Tourn. Inst. 642. Medlar with a rounder leaf and a black sweetish fruit, commonly called Amelanchier.

6. MESPILUS (Canadensis) foliis ovato-oblongis glabris serratis, caule inermi. Lin. Sp. Plant. 478. Medlar with oval, oblong, smooth, sawed leaves, and branches without thorns. Mespilus inermis, foliis subtus glabris obversè-ovatis. Flor. Virg. 54. Medlar without thorns, and obverse oval leaves, which are smooth on their under side.

7. MESPILUS (Cotoneaster) foliis ovatis integerrimis. Hort. Cliff. 189. Medlar with oval entire leaves. Mespilus folio subrotundo, fructu rubro. Tourn. Inst. R. H. 642. Medlar with a roundish leaf and a red fruit, commonly called Dwarf Quince.

8. MESPILUS (Chamæmespilus) inermis, foliis ovalibus serratis glabris, floribus capitatis, bracteis deciduis linearibus. Lin. Sp. Plant. 479. Medlar without thorns, having smooth, oval, sawed leaves, headed flowers, and linear bracteæ which fall off. Cotoneaster folio oblongo serrato. C. B. P. 452. Bastard Quince with an oblong sawed leaf.

9. MESPILUS (Orientalis) foliis ovatis crassis integerrimis, subtus tomentosis, floribus umbellatis axillaribus. Medlar with oval, thick, entire leaves, which are woolly on their under side, and flowers growing in umbels from the wings of the stalk. Chamæcrasus Idæa. Alp. Exot. 5. Dwarf Cherry of Mount Ida.

10. MESPILUS (Arbutifolia) inermis, foliis lanceolatis crenatis subtus tomentosis. Hort. Cliff. 189. Virginia Medlar with an Arbutus leaf. Mespilus Virginiana, folio arbuti. H. L. 578.

11. MESPILUS (Virginiana) inermis, foliis oblongo-ovatis, subtus tomentosis, fructu ovato, pedunculis longissimis. Smooth Virginia Medlar, with oblong oval leaves, downy on their under side, and oval fruit on long footstalks.

The first sort grows naturally in Sicily, where it becomes a large tree; this rises with a straiter stem, and the branches grow more upright than those of the Dutch Medlar; the leaves are narrower and not sawed on their edges; the flowers are smaller than those of the Dutch Medlar, and the fruit is shaped like a Pear.

The second sort is generally called the Dutch Medlar; this never rises with an upright stalk, but sends out crooked deformed branches at a small height from the ground; the leaves of this are very large, entire, and downy on their under side. The flowers are very large, as are also the fruit, which are rounder, and approach nearer to the shape of an Apple. This being the largest fruit, is now generally cultivated in the gardens; but there is one with smaller fruit, which is called the Nottingham Medlar, of a much quicker and more poignant taste than this; which is, I suppose, only a variety, so I have not enumerated it as a distinct species.

The fifth sort grows naturally in Austria, Italy, and France, particularly near Fontainebleau; this rises with many slender stalks about three or four feet high, which put out small side branches, covered with a dark purple bark, having no thorns, closely garnished with oval leaves, about three quarters of an inch long, and half an inch broad, slightly sawed on their edges; the small side branches which sustain the flowers,

flowers, are very hairy and woolly, as are also the foot-ftalks, and the under fide of the leaves, but their upper fides are fmooth and green. The flowers come out in bunches at the end of the fhoots, which have five long narrow petals, and about ten ftamina in each. The flowers are fucceeded by fmall fruit, which, when ripe, are black; the gardeners call this New England Quince; there is one of this kind which grows naturally in North America, but the leaves of that are wedge-fhaped and not fawed on the edges, fo I take it to be a different fpecies.

The fixth fort grows naturally in Canada; this is alfo a low fhrub, feldom rifing more than five feet high, dividing into feveral fmooth branches, covered with a purplifh bark. The leaves grow upon long flender foot-ftalks; they are one inch and a half long, and an inch broad, fmooth on both fides, and a little fawed on their edges. The flowers come out in fmall bunches at the end of the branches; they are about the fize of thofe of the common Hawthorn, and are fucceeded.by fmall fruit of a purplifh colour when ripe.

The feventh fort grows naturally on the Pyrenean mountains, and in other cold parts of Europe; this rifes with a fmooth fhrubby ftalk about four feet high, dividing into a few fmall branches, which are covered with a purple bark, and garnifhed with oval entire leaves, little more than one inch long, and about three quarters of an inch broad, having very fhort foot-ftalks. The flowers come out from the fide of the ftalks, two or three together; they are fmall, of a purplifh colour, and fit clofe to the ftalks; thefe appear in May, and are fucceeded by fmall roundifh fruit, which are of a bright red colour when ripe.

The eighth fort grows naturally in the northern parts of Europe; this hath a fmooth ftalk, rifing about four or five feet high, fending out flender branches, which are covered with a purplifh bark, and garnifhed with oval fmooth leaves about two inches long, and one inch and a half broad, fawed on their edges, but the teeth point upward; they have pretty long flender foot-ftalks, and are of a yellowifh green on both fides. The flowers come out from the wings of the ftalk, four or five joined together in a clofe head, of a purplifh colour; between the flowers come out long narrow braɛtea, which are purplifh, and fall off as the flowers begin to decay. The fruit is fmall, and red when ripe.

The ninth fort grows naturally upon mount Ida, in Crete, where the poor fhepherds feed upon the fruit when ripe; this hath a fmooth ftalk about eight feet high, dividing into many fmooth branches, garnifh-ed with oval leaves two inches and a half long, and near two inches broad, of a thick fubftance, and a dark green on their upper fide, but downy on their under, ftanding upon fhort foot-ftalks. The flowers come out from the fide of the ftalk upon fhort fmall branches, five or fix growing upon each in a clofe bunch; they are of a purple colour, the petals being but little longer than the empalement, which is woolly, and cut into five obtufe fegments. The fruit is large, roundifh, and of a fine red colour when ripe.

The tenth fort grows naturally in North America, where it rarely rifes more than five feet high, fending out a few upright branches, garnifhed with fpear-fhaped leaves whofe edges are crenated, and their under fide downy; the flowers are produced in fmall bunches on the fide, and at the extremity of the branches, which are fucceeded by fmall roundifh fruit a little comprefſed, of a purple colour when ripe.

The eleventh fort is an inhabitant of the fame country with the former; this rifes fix or eight feet high, fending out fide branches, garnifhed with oblong, oval, entire leaves, downy on their under fide; the flowers are produced in fmall bunches, ftanding on long foot-ftalks, having each five narrow white pe-tals which are contraɛted at their bafe, and are fuc-ceeded by oval fruit of a blue colour when ripe, and

are by fome of the inhabitants of America eaten in a fcarcity of other forts of fruit, but are not very palatable.

All thefe forts are hardy enough to thrive in the open air in England, and fome of them are very ornamen-tal plants for gardens, where, during the feafon of their flowering, they will make a fine appearance; and again, in autumn, when their fruit are ripe, they will afford an agreeable variety, and their fruit will be food for the deer and birds; fo that if clumps of each fort are planted in different parts of the garden, nothing can be more ornamental.

The American kinds are ufually propagated in the nurferies, by grafting or budding them upon the com-mon White Thorn, but the plants fo propagated will never grow to half the fize of thofe which are propa-gated by feeds; fo that thofe plants fhould always be chofen which have not been grafted or budded, but are upon their own roots.

But there are many who objeɛt to this method of raifing the plants from feeds, on account of their feeds not growing the firft year, as alfo from the te-diousnefs of the plant's growth after; but where a per-fon can furnifh himfelf with the fruit in autumn, and take out their feeds foon after they are ripe, putting them into the ground immediately, the plants will come up the following fpring, if they are kept clean from weeds, and in very dry weather fupplied with water, they will make good progrefs; but if they are planted in the places where they are to remain, after two years growth from feeds, they will fucceed much better than when the plants are of greater age; the ground fhould be well trenched, and cleanfed from the roots of all bad weeds. The beft time to tranf-plant them is in autumn, when their leaves fall off; thefe fhould be conftantly kept clean from weeds, and if the ground between the plants is dug every winter, it will greatly encourage the growth of the plants, fo that if they are cleaned three or four times in the fummer, it will be fufficient.

All the forts of Mefpilus and Cratægus will take; by budding or grafting upon each other; they will alfo take upon the Quince, or Pear ftocks, and both thefe will take upon the Medlars; fo that thefe have great affinity with each other, and might be with more propriety brought together under the fame ge-nus, than the Pear and Apple, which will not take upon each other; but although the Pear will take upon the White Thorn, yet it is not advifeable to make ufe of thefe ftocks, becaufe they generally caufe the fruit to be fmall and often to crack, and renders their flefh ftony; fo unlefs it is the very foft melting kinds of Pears which are upon thefe ftocks, the fruit will not be good.

METHONICA. See GLORIOSA.

MEUM. See ATHAMANTA.

MEZEREON. See THYMELÆA.

MICROPUS. Lin. Gen. Plant. 892. Gnaphalo-des. Tourn. Inft. R. H. 439. tab. 261. Baftard Cudweed.

The CHARACTERS are,

It hath hermaphrodite and female flowers, which are in-cluded in the fame double empalement; there are ten her-maphrodite flowers which compofe the difk; thefe have one petal, are funnel-fhaped, erect, and cut into five parts at the top, and have five fhort briftly ftamina, terminated by cylindrical fummits, with an obfolete germen fupporting a fhort flender ftyle, crowned by an obfolete ftigma. In the fame empalement are five female flowers in the circum-ference, which have each an oval germen which is com-prefſed, hid under the fcales of the interior empalement, each having a ftyle by their fide, which is briftly, turning toward the hermaphrodite flowers, crowned by flender acute-pointed ftigmas, divided in two parts. The female flowers have each a fingle oval feed fucceeding them, in-cluded in the fmall leaves of the empalement, but the her-maphrodite flowers are barren.

This genus of plants is ranged in the fourth feɛtion of Linnæus's nineteenth clafs, which includes thofe plants whofe flowers are compofed of female fruitful flowers

flowers in the border, and barren hermaphrodite flowers in the middle.

We have but one Species of this genus in the English gardens, viz.

Micropus (*Supinus*) caule proftrato, foliis geminis. Hort. Upfal. 275. Prod. Leyd. 145. *Micropus, or Baftard Gnaphalium, with a trailing ftalk.* Gnaphalodes Lufitanica. Tourn. Inft. R.H. 439. *Portugal Baftard Cudweed.* This is an annual plant, which grows naturally in Portugal, near the fea. The roots fend out feveral trailing ftalks about fix or eight inches long, garnifhed with fmall, oval, filvery leaves, whofe bafe embrace the ftalks. The flowers come out from the wings of the ftalks in fmall clufters; they are very fmall, white, and fit in a double empalement, the interior being fo large, as to almoft hide the flowers. It flowers in June and July, and the feeds ripen in autumn; this is frequently preferred in gardens for the beauty of its filvery leaves: if the feeds are fown in autumn, or are permitted to fcatter, the plants will come up in the fpring, and will require no other care but to keep them clean from weeds, and thin them where they are too clofe. When the feeds of this plant are fown in the fpring, they feldom grow the firft year.

MICROSCOPE, a dioptrical inftrument, by means of which very minute or fmall objects are reprefented very large, and capable of being viewed very diftinctly, according to the laws of refraction.

This inftrument may be of fingular ufe to a curious enquirer into the operation of vegetative nature, by viewing nicely the feveral minute veffels and parts of vegetables, in order to difcover their various ufes, and how the bufinefs of vegetation is carried on, as alfo to examine the minute parts of flowers, which are not obvious to the naked eye.

MILDEW is a difeafe that happens to plants, and is fuppofed to be caufed by a dewy moifture which falls on them, and continuing, for want of the fun's heat to draw it up, and by its acrimony corrodes, gnaws, and fpoils the inmoft fubftance of the plant, and hinders the circulation of the nutritive fap, upon which the leaves begin to fade, and the bloffoms and fruit are much prejudiced: but Mildew is rather a concrete fubftance, which exfudes through the pores of the leaves.

However, what the gardeners commonly call Mildew, is an infect, which is frequently found in great plenty, preying upon this exfudation.

Others fay, That Mildew is a thick clammy vapour, exhaled in the fpring and fummer from plants, bloffoms, and even the earth itfelf, in clofe ftill weather, where there is neither fun enough to draw it upwards to any confiderable height, nor wind of force ftrong enough to difperfe it, and that, hanging in the lower regions, when the cold of the evening comes on, it condenfes, and falls on plants, and with its thick clammy fubftance ftops the pores, and by that means prevents perfpiration, and hinders the fap from afcending to nourifh the flowers, fhoots, &c.

Some fay, That Mildew is a corrofive or nipping dew, proceeding from the vapours that are exhaled by the earth, which, being drawn up, and falling down again on the tender opening buds, infects them by its acrimony, and hinders the circulation of the nutritious fap in the proper veffels, upon which the leaves begin to fade, and the bloffoms and fruit receive a very great prejudice.

There are others who make this obfervation, That the places moft liable to Mildew are inclofed grounds and valleys, efpecially thofe that lie tending to the eaft; and the reafons that they give why thofe grounds which lie from the horizon to the eaft, are moft fubject to Mildew and blaftings, may be by the fun's attracting thofe vapours towards it, after the manner that a great fire in a room draws the air to it; fo the fun having fet thefe in motion, and not having ftrength enough to draw them into the middle region, to form them into a cloud, he does yet draw them till he be below the horizon, and then thefe dews tend to the

earth, from whence they were exhaled, and in motion to the weft, do, as it were, fall upon the ground which lies eaftward at right angles, and therefore is moft offenfive to them.

But I take the true caufe of the Mildew appearing moft upon plants which are expofed to the eaft, to proceed from a dry temperature in the air when the wind blows from that point, which ftops the pores of plants, and prevents their perfpiration, whereby the juices of the plants are concreted upon the furface of their leaves, which being of a fweetifh nature, infects are incited thereto, where, finding proper nutriment, they depofit their eggs, and multiply fo faft as to cover the whole furface of plants, and by their corroding the veffels, prevent the motions of their fap; and it is very probable, that the excrements of thefe infects may enter the veffels of plants, and by mixing with their juices, may fpread the infection all over them; for it is obfervable, whenever a tree has been greatly affected by this Mildew, it feldom recovers it in two or three years, and many times is never entirely clear from it after.

Others fuppofe, That the reafon why valleys afford more moifture than hills is, becaufe of the dew which is attracted from the earth and herbs as before, and that they afford more moifture than hills (they fay) is often feen by the mifts, which are more frequent on them than on hills; this being drawn by the fun in the day time, and wanting wind to affift its motion, hangs in the lower region, and when the fun fets, it falls upon the plants with its thick clammy fubftance, and hinders the fap of the plant or tree from afcending to nourifh its flowers or fhoots, in thofe whofe bark is tender and young, and the pores open with the heat of the feafon.

This dew has been obferved in the great leaved Cherries, fuch as the Black Heart, the White Heart, &c. to fall upon them at the top, juft at the beginning of the Midfummer fhoot, which has fo ftopped the fhoot that it has fhot forth in other places below, and on the top of thefe fhoots there have been many fmall flies feeding on this dew, which may plainly be feen and tafted on the leaves of Oak and Maple.

Some are of opinion, that Mildews and blights are the fame thing; but others again, that Mildew is quite another thing than blaftings. They fay Mildews are caufed from the condenfation of a fat and moift exhalation in a hot and dry fummer, from the bloffoms and vegetables, and alfo from the earth itfelf, which is condenfed into a fat glutinous matter by the coolnefs and ferenity of the air, and falls down on the earth again, part of which refts upon the leaves of the Oak and other trees, whofe leaves are fmooth, and for that reafon do not fo eafily admit the moifture into them, as the Elm, and other rougher leaves do.

Other parts of Mildew reft upon the ears and ftalks of Wheat, befpotting the fame with a different colour from what is natural, being of a glutinous fubftance, by the heat of the fun, and it binds up fo clofe the tender ears of Wheat, that it prevents the growth, and occafions it to be very light in the harveft.

Some are of opinion, that Mildews are the principal food of bees, it being fweet, and eafily converted into honey.

MILIUM. Tourn. Inft. R.H. 514. tab. 298. Lin. Gen. Plant. 73. [fo called of Mille, *Lat.* a thoufand, becaufe of the multitude of its grains.] Millet.

The Characters are,

It is of the Corn or Grafs tribe, with one flower in each chaff, the chaff opening with two oval acute-pointed valves. The petal of the flower is bivalve, and fmaller than the empalement. It hath three very fhort hairy ftamina, terminated by oblong fummits, and a roundifh germen with two hairy ftyles, crowned by brufh-fhaped ftigmas. The germen afterward turns to a roundifh feed, covered by the petal of the flower.

     This

This genus of plants is ranged in the second section of Linnæus's third class, which includes those plants whose flowers have three stamina and two styles.

The SPECIES are,

1. MILIUM (*Paniculum*) paniculâ laxâ flaccidâ, foliorum vaginis pubescentibus. *Millet with a loose hanging panicle, and the sheaths of the leaves hairy.* Milium semine luteo. C. B. P. 26. *Millet with a yellow seed.* Panicum Miliaceum. Lin. Sp.

2. MILIUM (*Sparsum*) paniculâ sparsâ erectâ, glumis aristatis. *Millet with a loose erect panicle, and bearded chaff.* Milium paniculâ amplâ erectâ sparsâ. Houst. MSS. *Millet with a large, erect, sparsed panicle.*

3. MILIUM (*Effusum*) floribus paniculatis dispersis. Flor. Suec. 55. *Millet with dispersed flowers.* Gramen sylvaticum paniculâ miliaceâ sparsâ. C. B. P. 3. *Wood Grass with a sparsed Millet-like panicle.*

4. MILIUM (*Confertum*) floribus paniculatis confertis. Prod. Leyd. 57. *Millet with panicles of flowers growing in clusters.* Gramen paniculatum Alpinum, latifolium, paniculâ miliaceâ sparsâ. Scheu. Gr. 34. *Broad-leaved, Alpine, Panicle Grass, with a sparsed Millet-like panicle.*

The first sort grows naturally in India, but is now cultivated in many parts of Europe as an esculent grain; this rises with a Reed-like stalk from three to four feet high, and is channelled; at every joint there is one Reed-like leaf, which is joined on the top of the sheath, which embraces and covers that joint of the stalk below the leaf; this sheath is closely covered with soft hairs, but the leaf which is expanded has none; that has several small longitudinal furrows running parallel to the midrib. The top of the stalk is terminated by a large loose panicle, which hangs on one side, having a chaffy flower, which is succeeded by a small round seed, which is often made into puddings, &c. There are two varieties of this, one with white, and the other hath black seeds, but do not differ in any other particular.

This plant is ranged under the title of Panicum, by Linnæus, but as it is more generally known by its former appellation, so I chuse to continue it.

The second sort was discovered growing naturally at La Vera Cruz; this has a slenderer stalk than the former, which rises about three feet high. The sheaths which surround it have no hairs, but are channelled. The leaves are shorter than those of the former. The panicle stands erect, and the chaff has shorter awns, or beards.

The other two sorts grow naturally in woods, and are never cultivated in the fields, so do not require any farther description.

The common Millet was originally brought from the Eastern countries, where it is still greatly cultivated, from whence we are furnished annually with this grain, which is by many persons greatly esteemed for puddings, &c. but is seldom cultivated in England in quantity, but by way of curiosity in small gardens, for feeding of poultry; but the seeds generally ripen very well.

They must be sown the beginning of April, upon a warm dry soil, but not too thick, because these plants divide into several branches, and should have much room; and when they come up, they should be cleared from weeds, after which they will, in a short time, get the better of them, and prevent their future growth. In August these seeds will ripen, when it must be cut down, and beaten out, as is practised for other grain; but when it begins to ripen, if it be not protected from birds, they will soon devour it.

MILLEFOLIUM. See ACHILLEA.

MILLERIA. Houst. Gen. Nov. Martyn. Cent. 4. Lin. Gen. Plant. 881.

The CHARACTERS are,

This hath a compound flower, composed of several florets, and one half floret, which are included in one common empalement of one leaf, which is cut into three parts, and is permanent. The hermaphrodite florets have one tubulous petal, which is erect, and indented at the brim in five parts; *these have five hairy stamina, with erect linear summits connected in their middle, to the side, and are the length of the petal, and an oblong narrow germen, supporting a slender style, crowned by two narrow, obtuse, spreading stigmas; these florets are barren. The female half florets is of one leaf, stretched out on one side like a tongue, and is indented at the top; this hath a large three-cornered germen, supporting a slender style, crowned by two long bristly stigmas. The germen afterward turns to an oblong, three-cornered, obtuse seed, inclosed in the empalement.*

This genus of plants is ranged in the fourth section of Linnæus's nineteenth class, which includes those plants with compound flowers, whose hermaphrodite flowers are barren, and the female flowers are fruitful.

The SPECIES are,

1. MILLERIA (*Quinqueflora*) foliis cordatis, pedunculis dichotomis. Hort. Cliff. 426. *Milleria with heart-shaped leaves, and forked stalks.* Milleria annua, erecta, major, foliis conjugatis, floribus spicatis luteis. Houst. MSS. *Greater, upright, annual Milleria, with leaves growing by pairs, and yellow spiked flowers.*

2. MILLERIA (*Maculata*) foliis infimis cordato-ovatis acutis rugosis, caulinis lanceolato-ovatis, acuminatis. *Milleria whose lower leaves are oval, heart-shaped, acute-pointed, and rough, and the upper ones oval, spear-shaped, and pointed.* Milleria annua erecta ramosior, foliis maculatis, profundiùs serratis. Martyn. Dec. 5. *Upright, annual, branching Milleria, with spotted leaves deeply sawed.*

3. MILLERIA (*Biflora*) foliis ovatis, pedunculis simplicissimis. Hort. Cliff. 425. *Milleria with oval leaves, and single foot-stalks.* Milleria annua erecta minor, foliis parietariæ, floribus ex foliorum alis. Houst. MSS. *Smaller, upright, annual Milleria, with a Pellitory leaf, and flowers proceeding from the wings of the leaves.*

4. MILLERIA (*Triflora*) foliis ovato-lanceolatis acuminatis trinerviis, pedunculis alaribus trifloris. *Milleria with oval, spear-shaped, acute-pointed leaves, having three veins, and foot-stalks proceeding from the wings of the leaves, with three flowers.* Milleria annua erecta, foliis parietariæ longioribus, floribus ex foliorum alis. Edit. Prior. *Annual erect Milleria, with a longer Pellitory leaf, and flowers proceeding from the wings of the leaves.*

The first sort was discovered by the late Dr. William Houstoun, at Campeachy, in the year 1731, from whence he sent the seeds to Europe; and as the characters which distinguish the genus, were different from all the other genera of the class to which it belongs, so he constituted a new genus with this title. This rises with an herbaceous branching stalk from four to five or six feet high, garnished with heart-shaped leaves about four inches long, and three inches broad toward their base, drawing to a point at the end, which are slightly sawed on their edges, having two veins on each side the midrib, which diverge and join to it near the base, meeting again at the point, which generally is oblique to the foot-stalk. The leaves are of a light green, and hairy, standing opposite; their foot-stalks are about an inch long, and have a part of the leaf running on each side like wings. The stalks divide upward into forks, and the foot-stalks of the flowers come out at the divisions; these branch again by pairs, and terminate in loose spikes of yellow flowers, composed of four or five hermaphrodite florets, which are barren, and one female half floret, which is succeeded by a single, oblong, angular seed, wrapped in the empalement of the flower. It flowers in July and August, and the seeds ripen in autumn.

The second sort was discovered by Mr. Robert Millar, at Campeachy, in the year 1734; this approaches near to the first sort, but the stalks rise six or seven feet high, branching out very wide. The leaves are seven inches long, and four inches and a half broad toward their base, ending in long acute points; they are deeper sawed on their edges, and have several

large

large black spots scattered over them; their surface is rougher, and they are of a darker green than those of the first. The upper leaves are long and spear-shaped; the foot-stalks of the flowers branch out wider, and the spikes of flowers are shorter than those of the first.

The third sort was discovered at Campeachy by the late Dr. Houstoun; this is also an annual plant, which rises with an herbaceous stalk upward of two feet high, branching out at a small distance from the root into three or four slender stalks, which are naked almost to the top, where they have two oval spear-shaped leaves placed opposite, which are about two inches long, and three quarters of an inch broad near their base, ending in points; they are hairy, and stand upon naked foot-stalks near an inch long, and are rough, having three longitudinal veins, and are slightly indented on their edges. The flowers come out at the foot-stalks of the leaves, in small clusters; the common empalement is composed of three orbicular leaves, which are compressed together; in each of these are situated two hermaphrodite florets, which are barren, and one female half floret, which is fruitful, being succeeded by a roundish angular seed, inclosed in the empalement. This flowers and perfects seeds about the same time with the former.

The fourth sort was discovered by the late Mr. Robert Millar, at Campeachy; this is an annual plant, which rises with an upright stalk three or four feet high, garnished the whole length with oval spear-shaped leaves near four inches long, and almost two broad near their base; they have three longitudinal veins, and toward the top there are two more which diverge from the midrib, but join again at the point. The upper side of the leaves are of a dark green and smooth, their under sides are of a pale green, and indented on their edges. The flowers grow from the wings of the leaves in small clusters, having three hermaphrodite and one female flower in each, standing upon short foot-stalks; these have empalements like the former, but they are much smaller. This flowers and seeds later in the year than either of the former, so that unless the plants are brought forward in the spring, they will not ripen their seeds in England.

The seeds of these plants should be sown early in the spring, on a moderate hot-bed; and when the plants are come up about two inches high, they should be each transplanted into a separate pot filled with light rich earth, and plunged into a moderate hot-bed of tanners bark, being careful to shade them from the sun until they have taken root, as also to water them frequently. After the plants are rooted, they should have a large share of free air admitted to them, by raising of the glasses of the hot-bed every day when the weather is warm, and in hot weather must be duly watered, for they are very thirsty plants. With this management, the plants will, in a month after transplanting, rise to a considerable height; therefore they should be shifted into larger pots, and placed in the stove, plunging them into the bark-bed, where they may have room to grow, especially the first and second sorts, which usually grow high and branch out where they are well managed. But the other sorts seldom rise above three or four feet high, and do not spread their branches very far, so these may be allowed less room.

In the middle of July these plants will begin to flower, and the seeds will be ripe about a month or six weeks after; therefore they must be gathered when they begin to change of a dark brown colour, otherwise they will soon fall off, especially those of the two large kinds, which will drop on the least touch when they are ripe. These plants will continue flowering till Michaelmas, or later, if the season proves favourable; but when the cold of the autumn comes on, they will soon decay.

MIMOSA. Tourn. Inst. R. H. 605. tab. 375. Lin. Gen. Plant. 597. The Sensitive Plant.

The CHARACTERS are,

The empalement of the flower is small, of one leaf, indented in five parts at the top: the flower has one funnel-shaped petal, which hath five points. It hath many long hairy stamina, terminated by prostrate summits, and an oblong germen supporting a short slender style, crowned by a truncated stigma. The germen afterward turns to a long jointed pod with several transverse partitions, inclosing compressed seeds of various forms, and there are many male, female, and hermaphrodite flowers mixed in some of the species.

This genus of plants Dr. Linnæus has joined to the Acacia of Tournefort, and the Inga of Plumier, and places it in the first section of his twenty-third class, which includes those plants which have male, female, and hermaphrodite flowers on the same plant, which have many stamina and one style.

The SPECIES are,

1. MIMOSA (Punctata) inermis, foliis bipinnatis, spicis decandris, inferioribus castratis corollatis caule erecto tereti. Lin. Sp. 1502. Sensitive Plant without spines, double winged leaves, having ten stamina, and the lower without stamina, and an erect taper stalk. Mimosa Jamaicensis. Zan. Hist. 144. Sensitive Plant of Jamaica.

2. MIMOSA (Plena) inermis, foliis bipinnatis, spicis pentandris, inferioribus plenis. Hort. Upsal. 145. Smooth Sensitive Plant with double winged leaves, the spikes with five stamina, and the under one double. Mimosa non spinosa, palustris & herbacea, procumbens, flore luteo pleno. Houst. MSS. Herbaceous, marsh, trailing Sensitive Plant without spines, and a double yellow flower.

3. MIMOSA (Pernambucana) inermis decumbens, foliis bipinnatis, spicis cernuis, pentandris, inferioribus castratis. Hort. Upsal. 145. Smooth Sensitive Plant with inclining stalks, double winged leaves, nodding spikes of flowers having five stamina, but the under ones without any. Mimosa spuria de Pernambuque, dicta mimosa Italica. Zan. Hist. 142. Spurious Sensitive Plant of Pernambuque, called Italian Sensitive Plant.

4. MIMOSA (Pudica) aculeata, foliis pinnatis. Prickly Sensitive Plant with winged leaves. Mimosa herbacea procumbens, & spinosa, caule tereti & villoso, siliquis articulatis. Houst. MSS. Trailing herbaceous Sensitive Plant having spines, with a taper and hairy stalk, and jointed pods.

5. MIMOSA (Pudica) foliis subdigitatis pinnatis, caule aculeata, hispido. Lin. Sp. 1501. Sensitive Plant with winged-headed leaves, a prickly declining stalk, and small pods growing in clusters, with prickly coverings. Mimosa humilis frutescens & spinosa, siliquis conglobatis. Plum. Cat. Low shrubby and prickly Sensitive Plant with clustered pods, commonly called the Humble Plant.

6. MIMOSA (Quadrivalvis) aculeata, foliis bipinnatis, caule quadrangulo, aculeis recurvis, leguminibus quadrivalvibus. Lin. Sp. Plant. 1508. Prickly Sensitive Plant with double winged leaves, a four-cornered stalk, recurved spines, and pods having four valves. Mimosa herbacea procumbens, & spinosa, caule quadrangulo, siliquis quadrivalvibus. Houst. MSS. Trailing and prickly herbaceous Sensitive Plant, with a quadrangular stalk, and pods having four valves.

7. MIMOSA (Sensitiva) foliis conjugatis pinnatis, partialibus bijugis, intimis minimis, caule aculeato. Lin. Sp. Plant. 1501. Sensitive Plant with conjugated winged leaves, whose wings have two pair of lobes, the inner of which are the least, and a prickly stalk. Mimosa spinosa prima, sive Brasiliana latifolia, siliquis, radiatis. Breyn. Cent. 1. 31. The first prickly, or broad-leaved Sensitive Plant of the Brazils, with radiated pods.

8. MIMOSA (Asperata) caule fruticoso, foliis bipinnatis, aculeatis, aculeis geminis, siliquis radiatis hirsutis. Fig. Plant. tab. 183. fol. 3. Sensitive Plant with a shrubby stalk, double winged prickly leaves, whose spines grow in pairs, and hairy radiated pods. Æschynomene spinosa quarta, sive foliolis Acaciæ angustioribus, frondibus validissimas spinas habentibus. Breyn. Cent. 1. 43. The fourth prickly Sensitive Plant,

Plant, with narrow Acacia leaves, armed with strong spine:.

9. MIMOSA (*Viva*) inermis, foliis conjugatis pinnatis, partialibus quadrijugis subrotundis, caule inermi herbaceo. Lin. Sp. 1500. *Sensitive Plant with a creeping, herbaceous, unarmed stalk, conjugated winged leaves, and globular flowers proceeding from the wings of the stalks.* Mimosa herbacea, non spinosa, minima, repens. Sloan. Hist. Jam. 2. p. 58. *The least creeping herbaceous Sensitive Plant, having no spines.*

10. MIMOSA (*Nilotica*) spinis stipularibus patentibus, foliis bipinnatis, partialibus extimis glandula interstinctis, spicis globosis pedunculatis. Haffelq. It. 475. *Acacia with double winged leaves, and globular spikes of flowers having foot-stalks.* Acacia Ægyptica. Hern. Mex. 866. *True Egyptian Acacia.*

11. MIMOSA (*Farnesiana*) spinis stipularibus distinctis, foliis bipinnatis, partialibus octojugis, spicis globosis sessilibus. Hort. Upsal. 146. Acacia Indica foliis, scorpioidis leguminosæ, siliquis fuscis teretibus resinosis. H. L. *Indian Acacia with taper resinous pods.*

12. MIMOSA (*Cornigera*) spinis stipularibus geminis connatis, foliis bipinnatis. Hort. Cliff. 208. *Acacia with two spines joined at their base, and doubly winged leaves.* Acacia similis Mexicoana, spinis cornu similibus. *The great horned Acacia.*

13. MIMOSA (*Unguis cati*) spinosa, foliis bigeminis obtusis. Hort. Cliff. 207. *Prickly Acacia with four obtuse leaves.* Acacia quodammodo accedens, five Ceratia & Acacia media Jamaicensis spinosa, bigeminatis foliis, flosculis staminets, atronitente fructu, siliquis intortis. Pluk. Phyt. *Acacia with branching leaves and twisted pods.*

14. MIMOSA (*Arborea*) inermis, foliis bipinnatis, pinnis dimidiatis acutis, caule arboreo. Lin. Sp. 1503. *Tree Acacia without thorns, doubly winged leaves, whose pinnæ are acute.* Acacia arborea maxima non spinoso, pinnis majoribus flore albo, siliqua contorta coccinea verticosa elegantissima. Sloan. Jam. 157.

15. MIMOSA (*Purpurea*) inermis, foliis conjugatis pinnatis, foliis intimis minoribus. Lin. Sp. 1500. *Purple Acacia without spines, conjugated winged leaves which are smallest below.* Acacia Americana frutescens non aculeata, flore purpurascente. Plum. Cat. *Shrubby American Acacia with thorns, and a purplish flower.*

16. MIMOSA (*Houstoniana*) inermis, foliis bipinnatis glabris, pinnis tenuissimis, siliquis latis villosis. Fig. Pl. 5. *Acacia without thorns, doubly winged smooth leaves, whose pinnæ are very narrow, and broad hairy pods.* Acacia Americana, non spinosa, flore purpureo, staminibus longissimis, siliquis planis villosis, pinnis foliorum tenuissimis. Houst. MSS. *American Acacia without thorns, having purple flowers, with very long filaments, flat hairy pods, and very narrow leaves.*

17. MIMOSA (*Lutea*) aculeata, foliis bipinnatis glabris, floribus globosis pedunculatis, aculeis longissimis. *Prickly Acacia with smooth doubly winged leaves, globular flowers having foot-stalks, and very long spines.* Acacia spinosa, foliorum pinnis tenuissimis glabris, floribus globosis lutea, spinis longissimis. Houst. MSS. *Prickly Acacia with very narrow smooth leaves, round yellow flowers, and very long thorns.*

18. MIMOSA (*Glauca*) inermis, foliis bipinnatis, partialibus sejugis, pinnis plurimis, glandula inter infima. Lin. Sp. Plant. 1502. *Acacia without thorns, doubly winged leaves, whose wings are separated, and have small glands between them.* Acacia non spinosa, flore albo, foliorum pinnis latiusculis glabris, siliquis longis planis. Houst. MSS. *White flowering Acacia without thorns, having broad smooth leaves, and long flat pods.*

19. MIMOSA (*Angustissima*) inermis, foliis bipinnatis, pinnis angustissimis glabris, leguminibus tumidis. *Narrow-leaved Acacia, with doubly winged smooth leaves, and jointed pods.* Acacia non spinosa, floribus globosis albis foliorum pinnis tenuissimis glabris, siliquis ad singula grana tumidis. Houst. MSS. *Acacia without thorns, having round white flowers, with very narrow smooth leaves, and jointed pods.*

20. MIMOSA (*Campeachiana*) spinosa, foliis bipinnatis, pinnis angustis, spinis singulis cornu bovinum per longitudinem fissum referentibus. *Acacia with doubly winged leaves having narrow pinnæ, and single spines like ox's horns split their length.* Acacia spinosa tenuifolia, spinis singulis cornu bovinum per longitudinem fissum referentibus. Houst. Cat. *Acacia with single thorns shaped like those of an ox's horn, and seem as if split thro' their length.*

21. MIMOSA (*Cinerea*) spinis solitariis, foliis bipinnatis, floribus spicatis. Flor. Zeyl. 215. *Acacia with single spines, doubly winged leaves, and spiked flowers.* Acacia spinosa tenuifolia, siliquis latis, spinis minimis recurvis solitariis. Houst. Cat. *Prickly narrow-leaved Acacia with broad pods, and small recurved spines, which come out single.*

22. MIMOSA (*Latifolia*) inermis, foliis conjugatis, pinnis terminalibus oppositis, lateralibus alternis. Lin. Sp. 1499. *Broad-leaved Acacia without thorns, conjugated leaves whose upper pinnæ are opposite, but the side ones are alternate.* Acacia non spinosa, juglandis folio, flore purpurascente. Plum. Sp. 17. *Acacia without thorns, Walnut-tree leaves, and a purple flower.*

23. MIMOSA (*Circinalis*) aculeata, foliis conjugatis pinnatis, pinnis æqualibus, stipulis spinosis. Lin. Sp. 1499. *Prickly Acacia with conjugated winged leaves, which are equal, and prickly stipulæ.* Acacia foliis amplioribus, siliquis circinatis. Plum. Sp. 17. *Acacia with broad leaves and twisted pods.*

24. MIMOSA (*Fagifolia*) inermis, foliis pinnatis bijugis petiolo marginato. Lin. Sp. 1498. *Broad-leaved Acacia without spines, whose wings have four lobes, and running foot-stalks.* Arbor siliquosa, faginis foliis, Americana, floribus comosis. Pluk. Phyt. tab. 141. fol. 2.

The first sort grows naturally in most of the islands in the West-Indies, and it has been found growing in some warm moist spots, as far north as Virginia. This rises with upright branching stalks six or seven feet high, which become ligneous toward the root, but are not perennial (at least they are not so here in any situation, the plants always decaying in winter;) these are smooth, and garnished with double winged leaves, composed of four or five pair of long winged lobes, which have about twenty pair of small leaves ranged along the midrib; they are smooth and rounded at their points, of a full green on their upper side, but pale on their under. These small leaves contract themselves together on their being touched, but the foot-stalks do not decline at the same time, as those do which are titled Humble Plants, so this is called the Sensitive Plant by way of distinction. The flowers are produced upon long foot-stalks, which come out from the wings of the leaves, and are disposed in globular heads which nod downward; they are yellow, and all those which have petals have ten stamina in each, but those situated round the border have neither petals or stamina; those on the upper part of the spike are succeeded by pods an inch and a half long, and a quarter of an inch broad, which change to a dark brown when ripe, inclosing three or four compressed, shining, black seeds.

The second sort was discovered by the late Dr. Houstoun at La Vera Cruz, growing in stagnant waters, where the stalks were very broad and flat, and floated on the surface, in the same way as the pond weeds do; but in those places where the water was dried up the stalks grew upright and were round, which is always the case when the plants are cultivated in gardens, so that they might easily pass for different plants, to those who never saw them growing in both situations. When this sort is cultivated in gardens, it has great resemblance to the first, but the stalks of this never grow so erect, the wings of the leaves are longer, and stand more horizontal; the heads of flowers are much larger, the stamina are longer, and the flowers on the under side of the spike which have no stamina are double: the pods of this sort are shorter, and much broader than those of the first sort. This is also an annual plant in this country. This sort was since discovered by a friend of mine, growing naturally

naturally in a marfhy fpot of land in the ifland of Barbuda, from whence he fent me the feeds, with a large
branch of the plant, in a glafs filled with a lixivium,
which preferved it in the ftate it was gathered, with
the flowers and pods upon it.

The third fort grows naturally in all the iflands of the
Weft-Indies, where it is titled the flothful Senfitive
Plant, becaufe the leaves do not contract on their being touched. The ftalks of this fort feldom rife more
than two feet and a half high, they are fmooth, and
garnifhed with double-winged leaves, compofed of
three or four pair of wings which are fhorter, and the
fmall leaves are much narrower than thofe of the two
former forts; the heads of flowers are fmaller, and
the pods are longer and narrower than thofe of the
other. This fort will live through the winter in a
moderate warm air.

The fourth fort was difcovered by the late Dr.
Houftoun, growing naturally at La Vera Cruz. This
hath ligneous ftalks which decline to the ground,
fpreading out two or three feet from the root, and
fend out feveral fide branches, which are armed with
fhort yellowifh fpines under the foot-ftalks of the
leaves, and are their whole length clofely covered
with briftly ftinging hairs; the foot-ftalks of the
leaves are three inches long, and at the top fuftain
four fingle winged leaves, whofe bafe meet in a point,
but fpread above like the fingers of an open hand.
Thefe wings are about three inches long, and are
clofely garnifhed with fmall narrow lobes, fet by
pairs along the midrib, which is alfo covered on the
under fide with the like briftly hairs as the ftalk.
The flowers come out from the wings of the leaves
upon pretty long foot-ftalks; they are collected into
globular heads, and are of a pale yellowifh colour;
thefe are fucceeded by fmall jointed pods, containing
two or three fhining black feeds.

The fifth fort is the moft common of any in the iflands
of the Weft-Indies, as alfo in the Englifh gardens;
the feeds of this fort are frequently fold in the feed-
fhops, by the title of Humble Plant. The roots of
this are compofed of a great number of hairy fibres,
which mat clofe together, from which come out feveral ligneous ftalks which naturally decline toward
the ground, unlefs they are fupported; they are armed with fhort recurved fpines, and garnifhed with
winged leaves, compofed of four, and fometimes five
wings, whofe bafe join at a point, where they are inferted to the foot-ftalk, fpreading upward like the
fingers of a hand; thefe wings are fhorter than thofe
of the former fort, and the ftalks are not hairy. The
flowers come out from the wings of the ftalks, upon
fhort foot-ftalks; they are collected in fmall globular heads, are yellow, and are fucceeded by fhort,
flat, jointed pods, which have two or three orbicular,
bordered, compreffed feeds in each: thefe pods are
in clofe clufters, almoft covered with ftinging hairy
covers.

The fixth fort grows naturally at La Vera Cruz, from
whence the late Dr. Houftoun fent the feeds. This
hath a perennial creeping root, which fpreads and
multiplies greatly in the lands, where it grows wild;
the ftalks are flender, and have four acute angles, armed with fhort recurved fpines pretty clofely; the
leaves ftand upon long prickly foot-ftalks, which are
thinly placed on the branches; they are compofed of
two pair of wings, ftanding about an inch afunder;
the wings are fhort, and the fmall leaves are narrow,
and not placed fo clofe together, as in many of the
other fpecies. The foot-ftalks of the flowers come
out from the wings of the leaves, fuftaining a fmall
globular head of purple flowers; thefe are fucceeded
by four-cornered pods about two inches long, which
have four cells, opening with four valves, containing
feveral angular feeds in each.

This fort fpreads fo much at the root, as to
render it not fo productive of flowers and feeds
as moft of the others; and the plants which are
propagated by parting of the roots, are always
weak, fo that the belt way is to propagate them

by feeds, when they can be obtained. This is one of
the forts, whofe foot-ftalks fall on being touched.

The feventh fort grows naturally at La Vera Cruz,
from whence the late Dr. Houftoun fent the feeds.
This rifes with a flender ligneous ftalk feven or eight
feet high, armed with fhort recurved thorns. The
leaves grow upon long foot-ftalks which are prickly,
each fuftaining two pair of wings; the exterior pair
have two lobes which join at their bafe, and are
rounded on their outfide, but ftrait on their inner
edges, very much fhaped like a pair of thofe fhears
ufed for fhearing of fheep; thefe two outer pair of
lobes are much larger than the inner; they are almoft
two inches long, and one broad in the middle. From
the place where thefe are inferted to the ftalk, come
out fmall branches which have three or four globular
heads of pale purple flowers coming out from the
fide, upon fhort foot-ftalks, and the principal ftalk
has many of thofe heads of flowers on the upper part
for more than a foot in length; and this, as alfo the
branches, are terminated by the like heads of flowers:
thefe are fucceeded by broad, flat, jointed pods,
which open with two valves, fome having but one,
others two, and fome have three orbicular compreffed
feeds. The leaves of this fort move but flowly when
they are touched, but the foot-ftalks fall when they
are preffed pretty hard.

The eighth fort was alfo found by the fame gentleman, growing naturally at La Vera Cruz. This hath
a fhrubby erect ftalk about five feet high, which is
hairy, and armed with fhort, broad, ftrong thorns,
which are white, ftanding on each fide fometimes almoft oppofite, and at others alternately. The leaves
are compofed of five or fix pair of wings, which are
ranged oppofite along a ftrong midrib, and between
each pair are placed two fhort ftrong fpines, pointing
out each way. The fmall leaves which compofe thefe
wings are extremely narrow, and ftand very clofe to
each other. Toward the upper part of the ftalk, the
flowers are produced from the fides, upon fhort foot-
ftalks; they are collected into globular heads, and
are of a bright purple colour; the ftalks are alfo terminated by fmaller heads of the like flowers. Thefe
are fucceeded by flat jointed pods about two inches
long, and a quarter of an inch broad, which fpread
open like rays, there being commonly five or fix of
thefe joined together at their bafe to the foot-ftalk.
Thefe pods feparate at each articulation, leaving the
two fide membranes or borders ftanding; and the
feeds which are compreffed and fquare, drop out from
the joints of the pods; thefe pods are hairy at firft,
but as they ripen become fmooth.

This is a perennial plant, which may be preferved
through the winter in a warm ftove, by which method the feeds may be obtained, for they feldom flower
the firft year. The foot-ftalks of this fort do not fall
on being touched, but the fmall leaves on the wings
clofe up.

The ninth fort grows naturally in Jamaica; this hath
trailing herbaceous ftalks, which put out roots at
every joint, which faften in the ground and fpread to
a great diftance, as they will alfo do here, when placed
in a bed of tanners bark. I have had a fingle plant
in one fummer, which has fpread near three feet
fquare, whofe branches were clofely joined, fo as to
cover the furface of the bed; but when they are thus
permitted to grow, they feldom produce flowers.
Thefe ftalks have no thorns, but are garnifhed with
winged leaves compofed of two pair of fhort wings,
whofe fmall leaves or lobes are narrow; thefe ftand
upon fhort foot-ftalks, which are fmooth. The
leaves of this fort contract and fall down upon the
leaft touch, fo that where the plant is extended to a
diftance, a perfon may draw any figure with a ftick
upon the leaves, which will be very vifible till the
leaves recover again. The flowers come out from
the wings of the leaves, upon naked foot-ftalks
about an inch in length; they are of a pale yellowifh colour, and are collected into fmall globular
heads; thefe are fucceeded by fhort, flat, jointed
pods,

pods, containing three or four compreſſed roundiſh ſeeds.

Theſe plants are all of them propagated by ſeeds, which ſhould be ſown early in the ſpring, upon a good hot-bed. If the ſeeds are good, the plants will appear in a fortnight or three weeks, when they will require to be treated with care, for they muſt not have much wet till they have acquired ſtrength; nor ſhould they be drawn too weak, ſo that freſh air ſhould be admitted to them at all times when the air is temperate. In about a fortnight or three weeks after the plants come up, they will be fit to tranſplant, eſpecially if the bed in which they were ſown, continues in a proper degree of heat; then there ſhould be a freſh hot-bed prepared to receive them, which ſhould be made a week before the plants are removed into it, that the violent heat may be abated before the earth is laid upon the dung, and the earth ſhould have time to warm before the plants are planted into it. Then the plants muſt be carefully raiſed up from the bed to preſerve the roots entire, and immediately planted in the new bed, at about three or four inches diſtance, preſſing the earth gently to their roots; then they ſhould be gently ſprinkled over with water, to ſettle the earth to their roots; after this they muſt be ſhaded from the ſun till they have taken new root, and the glaſſes of the hot-bed ſhould be covered every night to keep up the heat of the bed. When the plants are eſtabliſhed in their new bed, they muſt have frequent, but gentle waterings; and every day they muſt have free air admitted to them, in proportion to the warmth of the ſeaſon, to prevent their being drawn up weak; but they muſt be conſtantly kept in a moderate degree of heat, otherwiſe they will not thrive. In about a month after the plant will be ſtrong enough to remove again, when they ſhould be carefully taken up, preſerving as much earth to their roots as poſſible, and each planted in a ſeparate ſmall pot, filled with good kitchen-garden earth, and plunged into a hot-bed of tan, carefully ſhading them from the ſun till they have taken new root; then they muſt be treated in the ſame manner as other tender exotic plants from very warm countries.

The ſorts which grow upright and tall, will ſoon riſe high enough to reach the glaſſes of the hot-bed, eſpecially if they thrive well; therefore they ſhould be ſhifted into larger pots, and removed into the ſtove, and if they are plunged into the tan-bed there, it will greatly forward them. The firſt ſort will often flower here, if the plants are raiſed early in the ſpring, and brought forward by their removal from one hot-bed to another; and two or three times I have had their ſeeds ripen, but this can only be expected in very warm ſeaſons.

The perennial ſorts will live through the winter, if they are preſerved in a warm ſtove, and the following ſummer they will produce flowers and ripen their ſeeds. Some of theſe may be propagated by laying down their branches, which will put out roots, and then may be ſeparated from the old plants; and I have ſometimes propagated them by cuttings, but the plants which riſe from ſeeds are preferable to either of theſe.

There is no particular management which theſe plants require, different from others of the ſame warm countries; the great care muſt be to keep them in a proper temperature of heat, and not to give them too much water, eſpecially in cool weather; nor ſhould they be kept too dry, for many of the ſorts require frequent waterings, as they naturally grow in moiſt places. There ſhould alſo be care taken that they do not root into the tan-bed, for they ſoon put out their roots through the holes at the bottom of the pots, which, when they ſtrike into the tan, will cauſe the plants to grow very luxuriant; but when they are removed, and their roots are cut or broken off, the plants ſeldom ſurvive it; therefore the pots ſhould be frequently drawn out of the tan, and if any of the roots are beginning to get through the holes at the bottom, they ſhould be cut off cloſe; and when the

roots are very cloſely matted together, they ſhould be turned out of the pots, and pared round to reduce them, and then potted again, either in pots of the ſame ſize, or if the plants require, in pots one ſize larger; but they muſt not be over-potted, for then the plants will not thrive.

Some of thoſe ſorts whoſe ſtalks ſpread near the ground, may be turned out of the pots in the middle of June, and planted in a very warm border, where, if they are covered with bell or hand-glaſſes, they will live through the ſummer; but theſe will not grow very large, and upon the approach of cold in the autumn, they are ſoon deſtroyed: however, thoſe who have not conveniency of ſtoves or tan-beds, may raiſe the plants on common hot-beds in the ſpring; and when they have acquired ſtrength, they may be treated in this manner, whereby they will have the pleaſure of theſe plants in ſummer, though not in ſo great perfection, as thoſe who have the advantages beforementioned: but theſe plants will not thrive in the open air in this country, nor will they retain their ſenſibility when they are fully expoſed to the air.

It would be to little purpoſe to trouble the reader with the ſeveral idle ſtories related of theſe plants by travellers, nor to inſert what has been ſaid by others, who have attempted to account for the motion of the leaves of theſe plants on their being touched, ſince there has not been any thing wrote on this ſubject, worthy of being noticed, that I have yet ſeen; I ſhall therefore only mention what I have myſelf obſerved in theſe plants, for more than forty years that I have cultivated them.

The firſt is, that they are more or leſs ſuſceptible of the touch or preſſure, according to the warmth of the air in which they grow; for thoſe plants which are kept in a warm ſtove, contract their leaves immediately on being touched, either with the hand, a ſtick, or any other thing, or by the wind blowing upon them: thoſe of the ſorts only contract their ſmall leaves, which are placed along the midrib; others not only contract their ſmall leaves, but the foot-ſtalk alſo declines downward on being touched: the firſt are called Senſitive, and the ſecond Humble Plants; but when theſe plants are placed in a cooler ſituation, they do not move ſo ſoon, nor contract ſo cloſely, as thoſe which are in a greater warmth; and thoſe which are entirely expoſed to the open air, have very little motion, but remain in one ſtate, neither expanded nor cloſed, but between both, eſpecially in cool weather; nor do theſe ſhut themſelves at night, as thoſe do which are in a warm temperature of air.

The ſecond is, that it is not the light which cauſes them to expand, as ſome have affirmed, who have had no experience of theſe things; for in the longeſt days of ſummer, they are generally contracted by five or ſix in the evening, when the ſun remains above the horizon two or three hours longer; and although the glaſſes of the ſtove in which they are placed, is covered cloſe with ſhutters to exclude the light in the middle of the day, yet if the air of the ſtove is warm, the leaves of the plants will continue fully expanded, as I have ſeveral times obſerved. Nor do theſe plants continue ſhut till the ſun riſes in the morning, for I have frequently found their leaves fully expanded by the break of day in the morning; ſo that it is plain the light is not the cauſe of their expanſion, nor the want of it that of their contraction.

I have alſo obſerved, that thoſe plants which are placed in the greateſt warmth in winter, continue vigorous, and retain their faculty of contracting on being touched; but thoſe which are in a moderate warmth, have little or no motion.

When any of the upper leaves of theſe plants are touched, if they fall down and touch thoſe which are below them, it will occaſion their contracting and falling, ſo that by one touching another, they will continue falling for ſome time. When the air of the ſtove in which theſe plants ſtand, is in a proper temperature of warmth, the plants will recover themſelves, and their leaves will be fully expanded in about eight

or

or ten minutes. I have frequently watched them as they have been recovering, and have always found it has been by a vibratory motion, like the index of a clock.

Some of the forts are fo fufceptible of the touch, that the fmalleft drop of water falling on their leaves will caufe them to contract, but others do not move without a much greater preffure.

The roots of all the forts have a very ftrong difagreeable odour, almoft like that of a common fewer. I have met with fome accounts of thefe plants, in which it is mentioned, that the leaves and branches have a poifonous quality, and that the Indians extract a poifon from them, which kills by flow degrees, and that the root of the plant is the only remedy to expel it ; but how far this is true I cannot fay, having never made any experiments on the qualities of thefe plants; but if thefe plants are endowed with fo deadly a quality as related, this fenfibility with which they are endued, may be defigned by providence to caution perfons from being too free with it ; and as many of them are ftrongly armed with thorns, fo that is a guard againft their being eaten by animals; for in all the enquiries which I have made of thofe perfons who have refided in the countries where they naturally grow, I could never learn that any animal will browfe upon them.

Thefe plants are all of them natives of America, fo were unknown to the other parts of the world till that was difcovered, for I have not heard of any of them being found in any other country : and a few years ago I fent fome of the feeds of thefe plants to China, which fucceeded, and occafioned great admiration in all who faw the plants.

The Acacias are fo nearly allied to the Mimofas in their characters, that Linnæus has joined them in the fame genus ; and as his fyftem is now generally followed, fo in compliance with that I have done the fame.

The tenth fort of Acacia is the tree from whence the true Succus Acaciæ is taken, and the Gum Arabic exfudes from the branches of the fame; which, though mentioned as a native of Egypt, yet it is alfo found in divers parts of America, from whence the feed of this tree have been fent into England, and there raifed in feveral gardens near London.

This tree arrives to a large fize in the countries where it grows, but in England is rarely feen more than eight or ten feet high. It frequently flowers in autumn, but never produces any feeds.

The eleventh fort is the moft common kind in Jamaica and Barbadoes, and the other warm parts of America; and, for the fweetnefs of its flowers, has been difperfed through moft parts of Europe ; and though a native of the warmer parts of the Indies, it hath been made familiar to the Italian gardens, and is cultivated likewife in great plenty in Portugal and Spain.

The Italian gardeners, who bring over Orange-trees, &c. every year, generally bring alfo many young plants of this fort to England, under the title of Gazia ; but as they are too tender to live in a common green-houfe in England, fo few of thofe which are purchafed of them fucceed.

I have had fome plants of this fort upwards of fixteen feet high, which have produced great numbers of flowers in July and Auguft, but thefe were kept in a ftove in winter, and in glafs-cafes in fummer, to fcreen them from wet and the cold, for they will not flower in the open air in this country. The flowers are of a bright yellow colour, and fmell fweet; in the Weft-Indies it is called Sponge-tree.

The twelfth fort is at prefent very rare in England, and only to be found in fome curious gardens. This tree produces its fpines by pairs, which are extreme large and crooked, and of a whitifh colour; but I do not remember ever to have feen this flower.

In England, from the dried famples, however, which I have received from Campeachy, with many flowers upon them, there appears but little beauty in them ; nor do the trees in their native foil make a better ap-

pearance, their branches always growing deformed, and being but thinly garnifhed with leaves, when in their greateft vigour; but for feveral months they are deftitute of leaves, fo that the only thing remarkable in this tree is, the uncommon wreathed fpines with which the trunk and branches are fully befet. Thefe have the refemblance of animal horns, and are varioufly twifted and contorted.

The twenty-third fort was brought from the Bahama Iflands by Mr. Catefby, anno 1726. The feeds of this plant (which are flat, and one half of a beautiful red colour, the other half of a deep black) grow in long twifted pods, opening when the feeds are ripe, on one fide, and letting them out, which hanging by a fmall thread for fome time out of the pods, make a very agreeable appearance ; the leaves of this tree branch out and divide into many ramifications : the lobes are roundifh, and placed in a very regular order. The flowers have not as yet appeared in England, but from a painting done from the plant in the country, they feem to be very beautiful.

The thirteenth fort was brought from Jamaica, and is growing in the phyfic-garden at Chelfea ; this hath four large lobes to each leaf ; the fpines are fhort, ftiff, and crooked, and the feeds grow in twifted pods like the former. This plant is well defcribed in Sir Hans Sloane's Natural Hiftory of Jamaica. By the inhabitants of America it is called Doctor Long, under which name the feeds are frequently brought to England.

Moft of the other forts here mentioned, were collected by the late ingenious Dr. William Houftoun, in Jamaica, at Vera Cruz and Campeachy, who fent the feeds of moft of them into Europe, many of which are now growing in the phyfic-garden at Chelfea, where fome of them have produced flowers and plenty of feeds.

Thefe being all tender, are to be placed in ftoves in the winter, and in fummer muft be but a fhort time expofed to the open air, and have a warm fituation. They are propagated by fowing their feeds on a hotbed in the fpring of the year, which will in a fhort time appear above ground, and in about five or fix weeks after, be fit to tranfplant, when a frefh hot-bed is to be prepared for them, and fhould be pretty warm; the next thing to be provided is a quantity of fmall halfpenny pots, which are to be filled with frefh, light, fandy earth ; thefe fhould be plunged into the hot-bed, but not into dung ; for if thefe beds are made with warm horfe dung, they ought to be covered with earth as deep as the pots, whofe bottoms fhould reft upon the dung, for otherwife the roots of the plants may fuffer by too much heat ; but beds of tanners bark feldom heat fo violently. As foon as the earth in the pots is warm, which will be in two or three days, you fhould carefully take up the young plants out of the firft hot-bed, planting four or five plants into each of thefe pots, giving them a gentle watering to fettle the earth to their roots, and fcreening them with mats over the glaffes from the heat of the fun, until they have taken root; after which time you muft give them air, by raifing the glaffes in proportion to the heat of the weather, or to the conftitution of the plants.

The tenth, eleventh, and twelfth, forts are very tender, efpecially while young, therefore fhould have a hot-bed of tanners bark ; and as they increafe in bulk, fhould be fhifted into bigger pots. The earth for thefe fhould be a little lighter, and more inclined to a fand, than for the other forts ; but never plant them in pots that are too large, which is full as bad to thefe as to Orange-trees; neither give them too much water, efpecially in winter. The tenth fort being the hardieft of the three, will, when grown to be woody, ftand in a common ftove, which fhould be kept to the point of temperate heat in winter ; and in the fummer time, in warm weather, may enjoy the open free air : but the eleventh and twelfth forts muft have a bark-ftove in winter; nor fhould they be expofed to the open air in fummer, at leaft for four or five years, until they are grown very woody, for they are very tender, and with great difficulty preserved in this climate. The stove in which these should be placed in winter, must be kept above the temperate point, as marked in the botanical thermometers. These should have very little water in winter, but in summer time will require frequent refreshings, though at that season it should not be given them in great quantities at one time. The eleventh sort is a very beautiful tree. The twelfth sheds its leaves just before the new ones come on, so that it is naked of leaves about a month or six weeks in the spring of the year, which has occasioned some people to throw them away as dead, when, if they had let them remain, they would have come out fresh again. This I thought proper to mention, in order to caution people not to be too hasty in throwing out trees for dead, but preserve them through the succeeding summer, to see if they will shoot again; for I have known several plants, which, after having been given over by unskilful persons for dead, have the July following shot out vigorously again; and others, which have died to the surface of the earth, have risen again from the root.

The three sorts of horned Acacias are very often destitute of leaves for two or three months, appearing to have no life; but they will put out fresh leaves towards autumn, which is commonly the season when they are most vigorous. These should be exposed in the summer season for about two months, to clear them from insects, which greatly infest them, in a place defended from strong winds; and in the winter they require a moderate degree of warmth.

All the other sorts here mentioned are propagated by seeds, which, seldom ripening in this country, must be procured from America, particularly at Campeachy, where there is great variety of this tree, many sorts of which have been hitherto unknown to botanical writers. In bringing over the seeds of these trees, they should be taken out of the pods when gathered, and put up in papers, and ought to have Tobacco, or some other noxious herb, put between the papers, to keep off insects, otherwise the seeds will be eaten and destroyed before they arrive in England. For the insects deposit their eggs in small punctures which they make in the pods; and as these are soon hatched, so they immediately attack the seeds for food, and eat holes through them, by which they are spoiled from growing. This has often happened to seeds which have been sent me from America.

There are several of these Acacias, which are very tender while they are young; but, after two or three years growth, become hardy enough to bear the open air in summer, though scarce any of them will live through the winter in a green-house, unless they have some warmth in very cold weather.

Acacia Germanorum. See PRUNUS SYLVESTRIS.
Acacia Virginiana. See ROBINIA.
Acacia, the Three-thorned. See GLEDITSIA.

MIMULUS. Lin. Gen. Plant. 761. Cynorrhynchium. Mitch. 3.

The CHARACTERS are,

The flower hath an oblong, prismatical, permanent empalement of one leaf; it is of the lip or ringent kind, having one petal, whose tube is the length of the empalement, and the brim is divided into two lips. The upper lip is erect, divided at the top into two parts, which are reflexed on their side; the lower lip is broad and trifid, the middle segment is the least; the palate is convex and bifid. It has four slender stamina, two longer than the other, terminated by bifid kidney-shaped summits, and a conical german supporting a slender style, crowned by an oval, bifid, compressed stigma. The german afterward turns to an oval capsule with two cells, filled with small seeds.

This genus of plants is ranged in the second section of Linnæus's fourteenth class, which includes those plants whose flowers have two long and two short stamina, and their seeds are included in the capsule.

We know but one SPECIES of this genus at present in England, viz.

MIMULUS (*Ringens*) erectus, foliis oblongis linearibus sessilibus. Hort. Upsal. 176. tab. 2. *Upright Mimulus with oblong linear leaves sitting close to the stalk.* Digitalis perfoliata glabra, flore violaceo minore. Mor. Hist. 2. p. 479. *Smooth perfoliated Foxglove, with a small Violet flower.*

This plant grows naturally in North America in moist ground. It has a perennial root and an annual stalk, which decays in the autumn; the stalk is square, and rises a foot and a half high, garnished at each joint with two oblong smooth leaves, which are broadest at their base, where they almost join round the stalk, but end in acute points. The lower part of the stalk sends out two or three short branches, and the upper part is adorned with two flowers at each joint, coming from the bosom of the leaves on each side the stalk; these have an oblong curved empalement with five angles, indented at the top into five parts, out of which arises the flower, with a long curved tube, spreading open at the top into two lips, the upper lip standing erect, which is slightly cut into two parts at the top; the under lip turns downward, and is cut into three slight segments. The flowers are of a Violet colour, but have no scent. These appear in July, and are succeeded by oblong capsules with two cells, filled with small seeds, which in warm seasons ripen in the autumn.

This plant is very hardy in respect to cold, but should have a loamy soft soil, rather moist than dry, and not too much exposed to the sun. It may be propagated by parting of the roots in the autumn, but the slips should not be divided too small; it may also be propagated by seeds, which should be sown in autumn, soon after they are ripe, for those which are sown in the spring seldom grow the same year: these may be sown on a border exposed to the morning sun, and the plants may be afterward planted in the flower-garden.

MINT. See MENTHA.

MIRABILIS. Lin. Gen. Plant. 215. Jalapa. Tourn. Inst. R. H. 129. tab. 50. Marvel of Peru, or Four o'Clock Flower.

The CHARACTERS are,

The empalement of the flower has five, oval, spear-shaped, small leaves, and is erect, swelling, and permanent. The flower has one funnel-shaped petal, with a slender tube sitting upon the nectarium, which spreads open above, and is cut into five obtuse segments. It hath five slender stamina, which adhere to the petal, which are unequal and inclined, terminated by roundish summits, with a roundish germen within the nectarium, supporting a slender style, crowned by a globular stigma. The germen afterward becomes an oval five-cornered nut, inclosing one seed.

This genus of plants is ranged in the first section of Linnæus's fifth class, which includes those plants whose flowers have five stamina and one style.

The SPECIES are,

1. MIRABILIS (*Jalapa*) floribus congestis terminalibus erectis. Lin. Sp. Plant. 252. *Marvel of Peru, with bunches of flowers erect, terminating the stalk.* Admirabilis Peruviana. Cluf. Hist. 2. p. 87.

2. MIRABILIS (*Dichotoma*) floribus sessilibus axillaribus erectis solitariis. Amœn. Acad. 4. p. 267. *Marvel of Peru, with an erect single flower sitting close to the wings of the branches.* Jalapa officinarum. Mart. Cent. 1. t. 1. *The then supposed Jalap of the shops.*

3. MIRABILIS (*Longiflora*) floribus congestis terminalibus longissimis nutantibus, foliis subvillosis. Act. Holmenf. 1756. p. 176. *Long-flowered Marvel of Peru, whose flowers are in bunches, terminating the stalks and nodding, with hairy leaves.* Mirabilis Mexicana. Hem. Mex. 170. f. 2.

The first sort is the Marvel of Peru, which has been many years cultivated in the English gardens for ornament; of this there are several varieties, which differ in the colour of their flowers; two of these retain their difference, one of them has purple and white flowers, which are variable, some of them are plain purple, others are plain white, but most of them are variegated with the two colours; and all these varieties

ties are frequently upon the same plant, and at others on different plants; the other has red and yellow flowers, which are generally mixed in the same flowers, but are often with plain flowers of both colours on the same plant, intermixed with those which are variegated; but some plants have only plain flowers; and I have never found that the seeds of the purple and white sort, ever produced the yellow and red, nor the latter ever vary to the former, and I have constantly cultivated both more than forty years; but although these do not change from one to the other, yet as there is no other difference between them than in the colour of their flowers, I have not enumerated them as distinct species.

The second sort is very common in all the islands of the West-Indies, where the inhabitants call it the Four o'Clock Flower, from the flowers opening at that time of the day. Of this sort I have never seen any with variable flowers; they are of a purplish red colour, and not much more than half the size of the other. The stalks of this sort have thick swollen joints; the leaves are smaller, and the fruit is very rough, so there can be no doubt of their being distinct species, for I have never seen any alteration in this from seed, and I have cultivated it many years. Tournefort was informed by Father Plumier, that the root of this plant was the officinal Jalap, upon which he constituted the genus, and gave that title to it; but the late Dr. Houstoun was fully informed in the Spanish West-Indies of the contrary, and brought over a drawing of the plant which was made by a Spaniard at Halapa, and he carried two or three of the plants to Jamaica, where he planted them in a garden, but after he left the island they were destroyed by hogs: however, he was fully satisfied of its being a Convolvulus, which Mr. Ray had many years before given the Jalap the title of, but upon what authority it does not at present appear. Some few years after I received three seeds of the Jalap from the Spanish West-Indies, one of which grew, and became a large plant, having a bulbous root, as large as those of the Jalap which are imported, but the plant produced no flowers in the three years it lived; and in the winter 1739-40 it died, since when I have not been able to procure any seeds; however, I am fully satisfied that the Jalap is a species of Convolvulus: indeed the roots of the Marvel of Peru are purgative, and when given in a double quantity for a dose, will answer the purpose of Jalap.

The third sort was sent from Mexico a few years since. The seeds of this were first sent me from Paris, by Dr. Monier, of the Royal Academy of Sciences, and afterward I had some sent me from Madrid, by Dr. Hortega. The stalks of this sort fall on the ground, if they are not supported; these grow about three feet long, and divide into several branches, which are garnished with heart-shaped leaves, placed opposite; these, as also the stalks, are hairy and viscous, sticking to the fingers of those that handle them. The flowers come out at the end of the branches; they are white, and have very long slender tubes, and a faint musky odour; these are like the other sorts, closely shut all the day, but expand every evening when the sun declines. The seeds of this sort are larger than those of any other species, and are as rough as those of the second sort.

The two varieties of the first sort are very ornamental plants in gardens, during the months of July, August, and September; and if the season continues mild, they often last till near the end of October. The flowers do not open till toward the evening, while the weather continues warm, but in moderate cool weather, when the sun is obscured, they continue open almost the whole day. The flowers are so plentifully produced at the ends of the branches, as that when they are open, the plants seem entirely covered with them, and there being some plain, and others variegated on the same plants, they make a fine appearance. The plants are propagated by seeds, in the choice of which there should be care taken not to save any

from those plants whose flowers are plain; and those who are desirous of having only the variegated kinds, are careful to pull off all the plain flowers from those plants which they intend for seeds, to prevent them from bearing any seeds; by this method they rarely have any plants with plain flowers.

The seeds should be sown on a moderate hot-bed in March, and when the plants come up, they should have plenty of air admitted to them, when the weather is mild, to prevent their being drawn up weak; and when they are about two inches high, they should be transplanted on another very moderate hot-bed; or if they are each planted in a small pot filled with light earth, and plunged into a moderate hot-bed, it will be a more secure way, for then there will be no danger in shaking them out of the pots, when they are to be planted in the borders, so as to preserve all the earth to their roots; by this method, they will not require to be shaded, whereas those that are to be transplanted from the second hot-bed to the borders, often rise with little earth to their roots, so must be carefully shaded, otherwise they often miscarry.

When they are in the second hot-bed, they should be shaded till they have taken fresh root, after which they must have plenty of free air admitted to them to prevent their being drawn up weak, and in May they must be gradually inured to the open air. The beginning of June, if the season is favourable, they should be transplanted into the borders of the pleasure-garden, giving them proper room, and after they have taken new root, they will require no further care. If these seeds are sown in a warm border the beginning of April, they will grow very well, but the plants will be late in the season before they flower.

As the seeds of these plants ripen very well every year, so there are not many who are at the trouble of preserving their roots; but if these are taken out of the ground in autumn, and laid in dry sand all the winter, secured from frost, and planted again in the spring, they will grow much larger, and flower earlier than the seedling plants: or if the roots are covered in winter with tanners bark to keep out the frost, they may remain in the borders, provided the soil be dry. If the roots which are taken out of the ground, are planted the following spring in large pots, and plunged into a hot-bed, under a deep frame, they may be brought forward, and raised to the height of four or five feet, as I have frequently practised; and these plants have come earlier in the season to flower, so have been intermixed with other ornamental plants, to decorate halls and shady courts, where they have appeared very beautiful.

The other two species require the same treatment, but the second sort is not quite so hardy as the other two, so unless the plants are brought forward in the spring, they will not flower till very late, so their seeds will not ripen.

MISLETOE. See VISCUM.

MITELLA. Tourn. Inst. R. H. 241. tab. 126. Lin. Gen. Plant. 496. [so called of Mitella, Lat. a little mitre, because the seed-vessel of this plant resembles a bishop's mitre.] Bastard American Sanicle.

The CHARACTERS are,

The flower has a bell-shaped empalement of one leaf, cut into five points, which is permanent. It hath five petals, ending in many hairy points, and are inserted in the empalement, as are also the ten awl-shaped stamina, which are shorter than the petals, and terminated by roundish summits. It hath a roundish germen, which is bifid, with scarce any style, crowned by two obtuse stigmas. The empalement afterward becomes an oval capsule with one cell, opening with two valves, filled with small seeds.

This genus of plants is ranged in the second section of Linnæus's tenth class, which contains those plants whose flowers have ten stamina and two styles or stigmas.

The SPECIES are,

1. MITELLA (*Diphylla*) scapo diphyllo. Lin. Gen. Nov. 29. *Mitella with flower-stalks having two leaves.* Mitella

416

tella Americana, florum petalis fimbriatis. Tourn. Inft. 242. *American Mitella with fringed petals to the flowers.*

2. MITELLA (*Nuda*) fcapo nudo. Amœn. Acad. 2. p. 252. *Mitella with a naked ftalk.*

The firft fort grows naturally in the woods, in moft parts of North America. It has a perennial root, from which come out many heart-fhaped angular leaves, fome of which are obtufe, and others end in acute points; they are indented on their edges, and of a lucid green, a little hairy, and ftand upon pretty long foot-ftalks. The flower-ftalks arife immediately from the root, having two or three angular leaves toward the bottom, and about the middle of the ftalk come out two fmall leaves with acute angles, placed oppofite. The ftalks rife eight or nine inches high, and are terminated by a loofe fpike of fmall whitifh flowers, whofe petals are fringed on their edges; thefe appear the beginning of June, and are fucceeded by roundifh capfules filled with fmall feeds.

The fecond fort grows naturally in the northern parts of Afia; this is of a humbler growth than the firft, feldom rifing more than five or fix inches high. The leaves are not fo angular as thofe of the firft fort, and the flower-ftalks are always naked, having no leaves. The fpikes of flowers are fhorter, and more compact. Both thefe are propagated by parting of their roots; the beft time for this is in autumn: they fhould be planted in a fhady fituation, and they love a foft loamy foil.

MITELLA MAXIMA. See BIXA.

MOLDAVICA. See DRACOCEPHALUM.

MOLLE. See SCHINUS.

MOLLUGO. Lin. Gen. Plant. 99.

The CHARACTERS are,

The empalement of the flower is compofed of five oblong fmall leaves, which are coloured on their infide, and is permanent. The flower has five oval petals, which are fhorter than the empalement, and three briftly ftamina, which ftand near the ftyle, and are terminated by fingle fummits, with an oval germen having three furrows, fupporting three very fhort ftyles, crowned by obtufe ftigmas. The germen afterward becomes an oval capfule with three cells, filled with fmall kidney-fhaped feeds.

This genus of plants is ranged in the third fection of Linnæus's third clafs, which includes thofe plants whofe flowers have three ftamina and three ftyles.

The SPECIES are,

1. MOLLUGO (*Verticillata*) foliis verticillatis cuneiformibus acutis, caule fubdivifo decumbente, pedunculis unifloris. Hort. Upfal. 24. *Mollugo with acute wedge-fhaped leaves, growing in whorls, a trailing divided ftalk, and foot-ftalks bearing a fingle flower.* Alfine procumbens, galii facie Africana. Hort. Lugd. *Trailing African Chickweed, with the appearance of Ladies Bedftraw.*

2. MOLLUGO (*Quadrifolia*) foliis quaternis obovatis, paniculâ dichotomâ. Hort. Cliff. 28. *Mollugo with four leaves at each joint, which are almoft oval, and a panicle arifing at the divifion of the branches.* Herniaria alfines folio. Tourn. Inft. 507. *Rupturewort with a Moufe Ear leaf.*

There are two or three fpecies of this genus, which are rarely admitted into gardens, fo I have not enumerated them here.

Both thefe forts are annual; the firft is a native of warm countries, fo is lefs hardy than the fecond; they are both trailing plants, whofe ftalks lie flat on the ground; the firft fpreads out eight or nine inches every way, and at each joint is garnifhed with fix or feven fmall leaves fpread out in form of a ftar. The flowers are fmall, like thofe of Chickweed, one ftanding upon each foot-ftalk; thefe are fucceeded by oval capfules filled with fmall feeds, which, if permitted to fcatter, the plants will come up the following fpring without any care; but when the feeds happen to fall upon earth which is thrown upon a hot-bed, the plants will be forwarder and ftronger than thofe in the open air. This is preferved in fome gardens for the fake of variety, but has no great beauty.

MOLUCCELLA. Lin. Gen. Plant. 643. Molucca. Tourn. Inft. R. H. 187. tab. 88. [This plant takes its name from the Molucca Iflands, becaufe it was found there.] Molucca Balm.

The CHARACTERS are,

The flower hath a large permanent empalement of one leaf, which is deeply indented at the brim, where it fpreads open. The flower is of the lip kind, with a fhort tube and chaps. The upper lip is erect, concave, and entire. The under lip is trifid, the middle fegment being longer than the other. It has four ftamina fituated under the upper lip, two of which are fhorter than the other, crowned by fingle fummits, and a germen with four parts, fupporting a ftyle fituated with the ftamina, crowned by a bifid ftigma. The germen afterward turns to four angular convex feeds, fitting in the empalement.

This genus of plants is ranged in the firft fection of Linnæus's fourteenth clafs, which includes thofe plants whofe flowers have two long and two fhort ftamina, and are fucceeded by naked feeds in the empalement.

The SPECIES are,

1. MOLUCCELLA (*Lævis*) calycibus campaniformibus fubquinquedentatis, denticulis æqualibus. Lin. Sp. 821. *Molucca Balm with bell-fhaped empalements, indented in five equal parts.* Molucca lævis. Dod. Pempt. 92. *Smooth Molucca Balm.*

2. MOLUCCELLA (*Spinofa*) calycibus ringentibus octodentatis. Lin. Sp. 821. *Molucca Balm whofe empalements are ringent, indented in eight parts.* Molucca fpinofa. Dod. Pempt. 92. *Prickly Molucca Balm.*

The firft fort rifes with a fquare ftalk three feet high, fpreading out into many branches, which are fmooth, and come out by pairs, garnifhed with roundifh leaves, which are deeply notched on their edges, ftanding upon long foot-ftalks placed oppofite; they are fmooth, of a light green on both fides, and at the bafe of their foot-ftalks the flowers come out in whorls; thefe have very large fpreading empalements, which are indented in five parts, and immediately under them come out two bunches of pretty long fpines, one on each fide the ftalk, each bunch confifting of five or fix fpines arifing from the fame point. The flowers are fmall, and being fituated at the bottom of the large empalements, are not vifible at a diftance; they are white, with a caft of purple, and fhaped like thofe of the other lip flowers, having the upper lip entire, and hollowed like a fpoon, and the under lip is cut into three fegments, the middle one being the longeft. After the flower is paft, the germen turn to four club-fhaped angular feeds inclofed in the empalement. It flowers in July, but unlefs the feafon proves warm and dry, the feeds do not ripen in England. The fmell of this plant is to fome perfons very difagreeable, and to others very pleafant.

The fecond fort hath fquare fmooth ftalks, of a purplifh colour, which rife four feet high, and branch out in the fame manner. The leaves are fmaller, and ftand upon fhorter foot-ftalks; they are deeper, and more acutely indented on their edges. The empalements of the flowers are not fo large, and are cut into eight fegments, each being terminated by an acute fpine. The flowers are like thofe of the former fpecies, as are alfo the feeds; this is not fo hardy as the firft fort.

The firft grows naturally in feveral parts of Syria, and the fecond is a native of the Molucca Iflands, from whence this genus received its title. They are both annual plants, which decay foon after their feeds are ripe, and being natives of warm countries, they feldom perfect their feeds in England, when they are fown in the fpring; therefore the beft way is to raife the plants in autumn, and plant them in fmall pots; thefe fhould be placed under a hot-bed frame in winter, where they may have free air in mild weather, by taking off the glaffes, but covered in frofty weather, obferving to keep them pretty dry, otherwife they are very fubject to rot, when they are clofely covered in frofty weather. In the fpring the plants may be turned out of the pots, with all the earth about their roots, and planted in a warm border, defended from

from ftrong winds, giving them a little water to fettle the earth to their roots ; after this they will require no other care but to keep them clean from
weeds, and to fupport them with ftakes, to prevent
their being broken by the winds. The plants thus
preferved through the winter, will flower the latter
end of June, fo from thefe good feeds may be expected.

MOLY. See ALLIUM.

MOMORDICA. Tourn. Inft. R. H. 103. tab. 29,
30. Lin. Gen. Plant. 1090. Male Balfam Apple ; in
French, *Pomine de Marveille.*

The CHARACTERS are,

*It hath male and female flowers upon the fame plant.
The male flowers have a fpreading empalement of one leaf.
The flower hath one petal, which adheres to the empalement. It has three fhort awl-fhaped ftamina ; in two
of the ftamina the fummits are bifid, and eared on both
fides ; the third has a fingle eared fummit ; thefe are compreffed in a body. The female flowers have the fame empalement and petal as the male, but fit upon the germen ;
thefe have three fhort filaments without fummits. The
germen fupports one taper trifid ftyle, crowned by three oblong gibbous ftigmas. The germen afterward turns to an
oblong fruit, opening with an elafticity, having three membranaceous cells, filled with compreffed feeds.*

This genus of plants is ranged in the tenth fection of
Linnæus's twenty-firft clafs, which contains the
plants with male and female flowers on the fame
plant, whofe ftamina coalefce together.

The SPECIES are,

1. MOMORDICA (*Balfamina*) pomis angulatis tuberculatis, foliis glabris patenti-palmatis. Hort. Cliff. 451.
*Male Balfam Apple with angular warted fruit, and fmooth
open-handed leaves.* Momordica vulgaris. Tourn. Inft.
R. H. 103. *Common male Balfam Apple.*

2. MOMORDICA (*Charantia*) pomis angulatis tuberculatis, foliis villofis, longitudinaliter palmatis. Hort.
Cliff. 451. *Male Balfam Apple with angular warted
fruit, and hairy leaves, which are longitudinally hand-
fhaped.* Momordica Zeylanica, pampineâ fronde,
fructu longiori. Tourn. Inft. R. H. 103. *Male Balfam Apple of Ceylon, with a Vine leaf and a longer
fruit.*

3. MOMORDICA (*Zeylanica*) pomis ovatis acuminatis
tuberculatis, foliis glabris palmatis ferratis. *Male
Balfam Apple with an oval, acute-pointed, warted fruit,
and fmooth hand-fhaped leaves, which are fawed.* Momordica Zeylanica, pampineâ fronde, fructu breviori. Tourn. Inft. 103. *Male Balfam Apple of Ceylon,
with a Vine leaf and a fhorter fruit.*

4. MOMORDICA (*Elaterium*) pomis hifpidis, cirrhis nul-
lis. Lin. Sp. Plant. 1010. *Male Balfam Apple with a
prickly fruit, and no tendrils to the Vines.* Cucumis
fylveftris afininus dictus. C. B. P. 314. *Wild Cucumber, called Affes Cucumber, and the Elaterium of Boerhaave.*

The firft fort grows naturally in Afia, the fecond and
third in the ifland of Ceylon ; they are annual plants,
which perifh foon after they have ripened their fruit ;
thefe have trailing ftalks like thofe of the Cucumber
and Melon, which extend three or four feet in length,
fending out many fide branches which have tendrils,
bv which they faften themfelves to any neighbouring
plants, to fecure themfelves from being toffed and
blown about by the winds, and are garnifhed with
leaves fhaped like thofe of the Vine. The leaves of
the firft and third forts are fmooth, and deeply cut
into feveral fegments, and fpread open like a hand ;
but thofe of the fecond fort are extended more in
length, and are hairy. The fruit of the firft fpecies
is oval, ending in acute points, having feveral deep
angles, which have fharp tubercles placed on their
edges ; it changes to a red or purplifh colour when
ripe, opening with an elafticity, and throwing out
its feeds.

The fruit of the fecond fort is much longer than
that of the firft, and not fo deeply channelled. The
tubercles are fcattered all over the furface, and are
not fharp like thofe of the other ; this fruit is yel-

low, when ripe, and cafts out its feeds with an elafticity.

The fruit of the third fort is fhort and pointed like
that of the firft, but does not fwell fo large in the
middle. The angles of this are not deep, and the
whole furface is clofely fet with fharp tubercles ; this
changes to a deep Orange colour when ripe, and cafts
out its feeds in the like manner.

The fourth fort is commonly called Wild or Spurting
Cucumber, from its cafting out its feeds, together
with the vifcid juice in which the feeds are lodged,
with a violent force, if touched when ripe ; and from
hence it has fometimes the appellation of Noli me
tangere, or *touch me not.* This plant grows naturally in fome of the warm parts of Europe, but in
England it is cultivated in gardens for the fruit,
which is ufed in medicine, or rather the fæcula of
the juice of the fruit, which is the Elaterium of the
fhops.

This plant hath a large flefhy root fomewhat like that
of Briony, from which come forth every fpring feveral thick, rough, trailing ftalks, which divide into
many branches, and extend every way two or three
feet ; thefe are garnifhed with thick, rough, almoft
heart-fhaped leaves, of a gray colour, ftanding upon
long foot-ftalks. The flowers come out from the
wings of the ftalk, thefe are male and female, growing at different places on the fame plant, like thofe
of the common Cucumber, but they are much lefs,
of a pale yellow colour, with a greenifh bottom :
the male flowers ftand on fhort thick foot-ftalks, but
the female flowers fit upon the young fruit, which,
after the flower is faded, grows to be an inch and a
half long, and fwelling like a Cucumber, of a gray
colour like the leaves, and covered over with fhort
prickles. Thefe do not change their colour when
ripe, like moft of the other fruit of this clafs ; but
if attempted to be gathered, they quit the foot-
ftalk, and caft out the feeds and juice with great violence ; fo that where any plants are growing, and
the fruit permitted to ftand till it is ripe, the feeds
will be fcattered all round to a great diftance, and
there will be plenty of the plants produced the following fpring.

But when the fruit is defigned for ufe, it fhould always be gathered before it is ripe, otherwife the
greateft part of the juice will be loft, which is the
only valuable part ; for the juice which is expreffed,
with part of the parenchyma of the fruit, is not to
be compared with the other for its virtues ; for the
Elaterium which is made from clear juice of the
fruit, is much whiter, and will retain its virtues much
longer, than that which is extracted by preffure.

The three firft forts are annual ; their feeds muft be
fown on a hot-bed the beginning of March, and
when the plants come up, they fhould be tranfplanted out into a frefh hot-bed, after the manner of Cucumbers or Melons, putting two plants of the fame
kind under each light, and the plants watered and
fhaded until they have taken root ; after which they
muft be treated as Cucumbers, permitting their
branches to extend upon the ground in the fame manner, and obferve to keep them clear from weeds.

With this management (provided you do not let them
have too much wet, or expofe them too much to the
open air) they will produce their fruit in July, and
their feeds will ripen in Auguft and September, when
you muft obferve to gather it as foon as you fee the
fruit open, otherwife it will be caft abroad, and with
difficulty gathered up again.

Thefe plants are preferved in curious gardens for the
oddnefs of their fruit ; but as they take up a great
deal of room in the hot-beds, requiring frequent attendance, and being of little beauty or ufe, fo they
are not much cultivated in England, except in botanic gardens for variety.

There are fome perfons who put thefe plants in pots,
and faften them up to ftakes, to fupport the Vines
from trailing on the ground, and place the pots in
ftoves ; where, when they are fkilfully managed, they
will

will produce their fruit tolerably well; and in this way they make a better appearance, than when the Vines spread on the ground like Cucumbers and Melons. But when the plants spread on the ground, which is their natural way of growing, they thrive much better, and produce more fruit, than when they are supported; for though these plants have clafpers, yet these are not formed for climbing, but merely to fasten themselves about any neighbouring support, to secure them from being raised by the wind and broken; which would often happen, where they grow in the open air and are fully exposed, were it not for this security.

The fourth fort is easily propagated by seeds, which (as was before mentioned) if permitted to scatter, there will be a fupply of plants come up the following spring; or if the feeds are sown upon a bed of light earth, the plants will come up in about a month after, and may be tranfplanted to an open spot of ground, in rows at three or four feet diftance, and almost as far afunder in the rows; if these are carefully tranfplanted while young, there will be little hazard of their growing; and after they have taken new root, they will require no further care, but to keep them clear from weeds. If the ground is dry in which they are planted, the roots will continue three or four years, unlefs the winter fhould prove very fevere, which will kill them.

MONARDA. Lin. Gen. Plant. 34. Leonurus. Tourn. Inft. R. H. 187. tab. 87.

The CHARACTERS are,

The flower has a tubulous cylindrical empalement of one leaf, which is channelled, and cut into five equal parts at the brim. The flower hath one petal, and is of the lip kind, having a cylindrical tube longer than the empalement, divided at the top into two lips. The upper lip is narrow, entire, and erect; the under lip is broad, trifid, and reflexed; the middle fegment being long and narrow, those on the fide are obtuse. It hath two briftly ftamina the length of the upper lip, in which it is involved, terminated by comprefsed erect fummits. In the bottom of the tube is fituated a four-pointed germen, fupporting a flender ftyle involved with the ftamina, and crowned by an acute bifid ftigma. The germen afterward turns to four naked feeds, inclofed in the empalement.

This genus of plants is ranged in the firft fection of Linnæus's second clafs, which includes the plants whofe flowers have two ftamina and one ftyle.

The SPECIES are,

1. MONARDA (*Fiftulofa*) capitulis terminalibus, caule obtuf-angulo. Hort. Upfal. 12. *Monarda with heads of flowers terminating the ftalks, which have obtufe angles.* Leonurus Canadenfis, origani folio. Tourn. Inft. R. H. 187. *Canada Lion's Tail, with an Origanum leaf.*

2. MONARDA (*Didyma*) floribus capitatis, fub-didyma-mis, caule acutangulo. Lin. Sp. Plant. 32. *Monarda with headed flowers, whofe ftamina are almoft in two bodies, and an acute angular ftalk.* Monarda floribus capitatis verticillatifque, caule acutangulo, foliis lanceolato-ferratis glabris. Butt. Cun. 226. *Monarda with flowers collected in heads and whorls, an acute-angular ftalk, and fmooth, fawed, fpear-fhaped leaves, commonly called Ofwego Tea.*

3. MONARDA (*Punctata*) floribus verticillatis, corollis punctatis. Hort. Upfal. 12. *Monarda with flowers growing in whorls, whofe petals are fpotted.* Clinopodium Virginianum, anguftifolium, floribus amplis luteis, purpurâ maculâ notatis, cujus caulis fub quovis verticillo decem vel duodecim foliolis rubentibus eft circumcinctis. Banift. Raii Sup. 300. *Narrow-leaved Field Bafil of Virginia, with large yellow flowers fpotted with purple, whofe ftalks bear ten or twelve reddifh leaves under each whorl of flowers.*

The firft fort grows naturally in Canada, and many other parts of North America. It hath a perennial root, compofed of many ftrong fibres, which fpread far on every fide. The ftalks rife near three feet high, which are hairy, and have obtufe angles; thefe fend out two or four fmall fide branches toward the top,

garnifhed with oblong leaves, broad at their bafe, but terminate in acute points; they are hairy, a little indented on their edges, ftanding on fhort hairy foot-ftalks, and are placed oppofite. The ftalk and branches are terminated by heads of purple flowers, which have a long involucrum, compofed of five acute-pointed leaves. The flowers have each two ftamina which are longer than the petal, with a ftyle of the fame length, crowned by a bifid ftigma. The flowers appear in July, and are fucceeded by feeds which ripen in the autumn.

The fecond fort grows naturally in North America, where the inhabitants frequently ufe the leaves for tea, fo it is commonly called Ofwego Tea, by which title it was brought to England. This hath a perennial root and an annual ftalk, which decays every autumn. The ftalks of this fort are fmooth, having four acute angles; they rife about two feet high, and are garnifhed with fmooth, oval, fpear-fhaped leaves, which are indented on their edges, and ftand oppofite on very fhort foot-ftalks; thefe when bruifed, emit a very grateful refrefhing odour; the ftalks fend out toward their top two or four fmall fide branches, which are garnifhed with fmall leaves of the fame fhape with the other. The flowers are produced in large heads or whorls at the top of the ftalk, and there is often a fmaller whorl of flowers, growing round the ftalk at a joint below the head; and out of the head arifes a naked foot-ftalk, fuftaining a fmall head or whorl of flowers: the flowers are of a bright red colour; they have two lips, the upper lip is long, narrow, and entire, the under lip is cut into three parts; they have each two ftamina which are longer than the petal, terminated by comprefsed fummits, and many of them have two fhorter ftamina, without fummits. The plant flowers in July, but in a moift feafon, or when the plants are in a moift foil, they will continue in flower till the middle or latter end of September.

Both thefe forts may be propagated by parting of their roots; the firft does not multiply fo faft as the fecond, but as that produces plenty of feeds, fo it may be eafily propagated that way. If the feeds are fown in the autumn foon after they are ripe, the plants will come up the following fpring; but if they are not fown till fpring, the plants feldom rife till the next year. When the plants are come up and are fit to remove, they fhould be tranfplanted into a fhady border about nine inches diftance, and when they have taken new root, they will require no other care but to keep them clean from weeds till the autumn, when they fhould be tranfplanted into the borders where they are to remain. The following fummer they will flower and produce ripe feeds, but the roots will continue feveral years, and may be parted every other year to increafe them. This loves a foft loamy foil, and a fituation not too much expofed to the fun.

The fecond fort feldom ripens feeds in England, but it increafes faft enough by its creeping roots, as alfo by flips or cuttings, which, if planted in a fhady border in May, will take root in the fame manner as Mint or Balm; but as the roots multiply fo faft, there is feldom occafion to ufe any other method to propagate them.

This fort loves a moift light foil, and in a fituation where the plants have only the morning fun, they will continue longer in flower than thofe which are expofed to the full fun. This is a very ornamental plant in gardens, and the fcent of the leaves is very refrefhing and agreeable to moft people, and fome are very fond of the tea made with the young leaves.

The third fort grows naturally in North America; this is a biennial plant, and probably in its native country may be an annual, for the roots perifh after the plants have perfected their feeds. This hath fquare ftalks which rife about two feet high, branching out from the bottom to the top, and are garnifhed with fpear-fhaped leaves, which come out in clufters at each joint, where there are two larger leaves placed

placed oppofite, and feveral fmaller come out on each fide the ftalk ; the larger leaves are about two inches and a half long, and three quarters of an inch broad, and are flightly indented on their edges. Toward the upper part of their ftalk the flowers come out in large whorls, having to each whorl an involucrum, compofed of ten or twelve fmall fpear-fhaped leaves, of a purplifh red colour on their upper fide ; the flowers are pretty large, of the fame form with thofe of the other forts, of a dirty yellow colour fpotted with purple ; they have each two long ftamina fituated under the upper lip, which are terminated by bifid compreffed fummits, and are fucceeded by four naked feeds inclofed in the empalement. It flowers in July, and if the fummer proves favourable, the feeds fometimes ripen in the autumn.

This plant is propagated by feeds, which, if fown on a border of light earth expofed to the eaft, the plants will rife very freely ; when they are fit to remove, they may be tranfplanted into a fhady border, in the fame manner as hath been directed for the firft fort ; and if, they fhould fhoot up ftalks to flower, they fhould be cut down to ftrengthen the roots, that they may put out lateral buds, for when they are permitted to flower the firft year, the roots feldom live through the winter, therefore they fhould be prevented : in the autumn the plants may be removed, and planted in the open borders of the pleafure-garden, where they will flower the following fummer ; and if the feafon fhould prove dry, they fhould be duly watered, otherwife they will not be near fo beautiful, nor will the plants produce good feeds.

MONBIN. See SPONDIAS.

MONTIA. See HELIOCARPUS.

MORÆA. Lin. Gen. Plant. 60.

The CHARACTERS are,

The fheath of the flower has two valves ; the flower is compofed of fix petals, the three upper are erect and bifid, the three under fpread open ; it hath three fhort ftamina, terminated by oblong fummits. The germen is fituated below the flower, fupporting a fingle ftyle, crowned by a trifid erect ftigma. The germen afterward becomes a three-cornered capfule, having three furrows, with three cells, containing feveral round feeds.

This genus of plants is ranged in the firft fection of Linnæus's third clafs, intitled Triandria Monogynia, the flower having three ftamina and one ftyle.

The SPECIES are,

1. MORÆA (*Vegeta*) fpatha uniflora, foliis gladiolatis. *Morea with one flower in each fheath, and fword-fhaped leaves.* Moræa foliis canaliculatis. Lin. Sp. 59. *Morea with channelled leaves.*

2. MORÆA (*Juncea*) fpatha biflora, foliis fubulatis. *Morea with two flowers in each fheath, and awl-fhaped leaves.* Moræa foliis fubulatis. Lin. Sp. 59. *Morea with awl-fhaped leaves.*

Thefe plants are both natives of the Cape of Good Hope, from whence I received their feeds, which have fucceeded in the Chelfea garden, where the plants have feveral times produced their flowers, which differing from all the other genera of plants in the fame clafs, I have taken the liberty of titling it Morea, in honour of Robert More, Efq; of Shrewfbury, who is well fkilled in the fcience of botany, and alfo in other parts of natural hiftory.

The firft fort has fibrous roots like thofe of the Flag-leaved Iris, from whence arife many fmall fword-fhaped leaves, five or fix inches long, and half an inch broad in the middle, diminifhing toward both ends, of a deep green colour, lying over each other at their bafe, in the fame manner as the Iris ; the flower-ftalk arifes between the leaves from the root, about eight inches high, having one fmall leaf at each joint, and is terminated by one flower, which is covered with a fpatha (or fheath) having two valves ; the flower is of a dirty white, each petal having a blufh of purple toward their upper part ; and a pretty broad fpot of yellow toward their tails ; within are three flender ftamina terminated by oblong fummits, and one ftyle crowned by a trifid ftigma. The flow-

ers appear in June, and the feeds ripen the end of July.

The fecond fort hath a fmall bulbous root, a little compreffed on the fides, with a fmooth dark-coloured fkin, from which arife three or four awl-fhaped leaves of a pale green, fome of which are five inches long, and others are feven or eight, and about half an inch broad, terminating with three angles ; the foot-ftalks of the flowers rife about fix inches high, and generally bend at their lower joint ; thefe are garnifhed with a fmall leaf at each joint, whofe bafe almoft furrounds the ftalk, which is terminated by two flowers, encompaffed with a withered fheath ; the flowers are of an Orange colour ; the petals are pretty broad upward, but are connected at their bafe. Thefe appear in June, and the feeds ripen the end of July.

The plants are propagated either by feeds, or from offsets of the fecond fort, and by parting or dividing the roots of the firft ; the beft time for tranfplanting of them, and feparating the offsets of the fecond fort, and parting the roots of the firft, is in Auguft, that they may put out new fibres before winter ; and that is alfo the right feafon for fowing of the feeds, for when they are fown at this time of the year in fmall pots, and plunged into a bed of old tanners bark, under a common frame in winter, there is little danger of thefe feeds mifcarrying. The plants will alfo require this fort of fhelter in winter, for as they are too tender to thrive in the open air in England, and if they are placed in a green-houfe, they are apt to draw up weak, therefore when they are fheltered under a frame, fo as to enjoy the free open air in winter when the weather is warm, and fecured from froft and hard rains, they will flower and ripen their feeds better than with any other management : in fummer they fhould be fully expofed to the open air till October, when they fhould be removed into fhelter.

MORINA. Tourn. Cor. 48. tab. 480. Lin. Gen. Plant. 39. Diototheca. Vaill. Mem. Acad. 1722.

The CHARACTERS are,

It hath a double empalement ; that under the fruit is tubulous, cylindrical, of one leaf, indented at the brim, and permanent ; that of the flower is tubulous, bifid, of one leaf, and permanent. The flower hath one petal, with a long tube enlarged upward, and a little incurved. The top is divided into two lips ; the upper lip is fmall and bifid, the under lip is cut into three equal obtufe fegments, the middle one being extended beyond the other. It hath two brifly ftamina fituated near the ftyle, terminated by heart-fhaped erect fummits. The globular germen is fituated under the flower, fupporting a flender ftyle which is longer than the ftamina, crowned by a target-fhaped ftigma ; the germen afterward becomes a fingle feed, crowned by the empalement of the flower.

This genus of plants is ranged in the firft fection of Linnæus's fecond clafs, which contains thofe plants whofe flowers have two ftamina and one ftyle.

There is but one SPECIES of this genus at prefent known, which is,

MORINA (*Orientalis.*) Hort. Cliff. 14. Morina Orientalis, carlinæ folio. Tourn. Cor. *Eaftern Morina, with a Carline Thiftle leaf.*

This plant was difcovered by Dr. Tournefort, in his travels in the Levant, who gave it this name in honour of Dr. Morin, a phyfician at Paris.

It grows naturally near Erzeron in Perfia, and was in the Englifh gardens before the fevere winter in 1740, which killed all the plants that were here, alfo thofe in the garden at Paris; fo the only plant remaining was in the garden of Monfieur du Hamel. The root of this plant is taper and thick, running deep into the ground, fending out feveral thick ftrong fibres as large as a finger; the ftalk rifes near three feet high ; it is fmooth, of a purplifh colour toward the bottom, but hairy and green at the top, garnifhed at each joint by three or four prickly leaves like thofe of the Carline Thiftle ; they are four or five inches long, and an inch and a half broad, of a lucid green on their upper fide, but of a pale green on their under, and a little hairy, armed on their edges with fpines. The flowers come

out

out from the wings of the leaves on each fide the ftalk ; thefe have very long tubes, which are flender at the bottom, but are enlarged upward, and are a little incurved ; the brim fpreads open with two large lips, the upper lip is indented at the top and rounded, the lower lip is cut into three obtufe fegments ; under the lip are fituated two briftly ftamina which are crooked, and crowned with yellow fummits. Thefe flowers appear in July, but I never had any feeds fucceed them. Some of the flowers are white, and others of a purplifh red on the fame plant.

This plant is propagated by feed, which fhould be fown foon after it is ripe in the autumn, otherwife the plants will not come up the following fummer ; for I have feveral times obferved, where the feeds have been fown in the fpring, they have remained in the ground fourteen or fifteen months before the plants have appeared. Thefe feeds fhould be fown in the places where the plants are to remain, becaufe they fend forth tap-roots, which run very deep into the ground ; and when thefe are broken or injured in tranfplanting, the plants feldom thrive after. They may be fown in open beds or borders of frefh light earth, being careful to mark the places, that the ground may not be difturbed ; for it frequently happens, that the feeds do not come up the firft year, when they are fown in autumn ; but when they are fown in the fpring, they never come up the fame year. The ground where the feeds are fown muft be kept clear from weeds, which is all that is neceffary to be done, until the plants come up ; where they are too clofe together, they fhould be thinned while young, fo as to leave them near eighteen inches apart ; after which time, they will require no other culture but to keep them conftantly clear from weeds ; and in the fpring, juft before the plants put out new leaves, to dig the ground gently between them, and lay a little frefh earth over the furface of the bed to encourage them.

In autumn thefe plants decay to the ground, and fend forth new leaves the following fpring, but it will be three years from the time of the plants firft coming up to their flowering, though after that time they will flower every feafon ; and the roots will continue many years, provided they are not difturbed, or killed by very fevere froft.

MORUS. Tourn. Inft. R. H. 589. tab. 363. Lin. Gen. Plant. 936. [of μαυρὸς, black, becaufe its fruit is ordinarily fo.] The Mulberry-tree ; in French, *Murier*.

The CHARACTERS are,

It hath male flowers growing at feparate diftances from the female on the fame tree. The male flowers are collected in long taper ropes or katkins ; thefe have no petals, but have four awl-fhaped erect ftamina, which are longer than the empalement, terminated by fingle fummits. The female flowers are collected into roundifh heads ; thefe have no petals, but a heart-fhaped germen, fupporting two long, rough, reflexed ftyles, crowned by fingle ftigmas. The empalement of thefe afterward become large, flefhy, fucculent fruit, compofed of feveral protuberances, in each of which is lodged one oval feed.

This genus is of the fourth fection of Linnæus's twenty-firft clafs, which contains thofe plants which have male and female flowers at feparate diftances on the fame plant, and the male flowers have four ftamina.

The SPECIES are,

1. MORUS (*Nigra*) foliis cordatis. Hort. Cliff. 441. *Mulberry with rough heart-fhaped leaves.* Morus fructu nigro. C. B. P. 459. *Mulberry with a black fruit, or the common Mulberry.*

2. MORUS (*Laciniatis*) foliis palmatis hirfutis. *Mulberry with hand-fhaped hairy leaves.* Morus fructu nigro minori foliis eleganter laciniatis. Tourn. Inft. R. H. 589. *Smaller black Mulberry with elegant cut leaves.*

3. MORUS (*Rubra*) foliis cordatis fubtus villofis, amentis cylindricis. Lin. Sp. Plant. 986. *Mulberry with heart-fhaped leaves which are hairy on their under fide, and cylindrical katkins.* Morus Virginienfis arbor, loti arbo-

ris inftar ramofa, foliis ampliffimis. Pluk. Phyt. tab. 246. fol. 4. *Virginia Mulberry branching like the Nettle-tree, having very large leaves.*

4. MORUS (*Alba*) foliis oblique cordatis lævibus. Hort. Cliff. 441. *Mulberry with oblique, fmooth, heart-fhaped leaves.* Morus fructu albo. C. B. P. 459. *Mulberry with a white fruit.*

5. MORUS (*Tinctoria*) foliis oblique cordatis acuminatis hirfutis. *Mulberry with oblique, heart-fhaped, acute-pointed, hairy leaves.* Morus fructu viridi, ligno fulphureo tinctorio. Sloan. Hift. Jam. 2. p. 3. *Mulberry with a green fruit, whofe wood dyes a fulphur colour, or Fuftick wood.*

6. MORUS (*Papyrifera*) foliis palmatis, fructibus hifpidis. Lin. Sp. Plant. 986. *Mulberry with hand-fhaped leaves and prickly fruit.* Morus fativa, foliis urticæ mortuæ, cortice papyrifera. Kæmp. Amœn. 471. *Cultivated Mulberry with leaves like Dead Nettle, and of whofe bark paper is made.*

7. MORUS (*Tatarica*) foliis ovato-oblongis, utrinque æqualibus, inæqualiter ferratis. Flor. Zeyl. 337. *Mulberry with oval oblong leaves, which are equal on both fides, but unequally fawed.* Tinda-parua. Hort. Mal. 1. p. 87. fol. 49.

8. MORUS (*Zanthoxylum*) foliis ovato-oblongis acuminatis obliquis, ramis aculeatis. *Mulberry with oval, oblong, acute-pointed leaves, which are oblique to the foot-ftalk, and prickly branches.* Zanthoxylum aculeatum, carpini foliis, Americanum, cortice cinereo. Pluk. Phyt. 239. fol. 3. *Prickly Zanthoxylum of America, with Hornbeam leaves and an Afh-coloured bark.*

The firft fort is the common black Mulberry-tree, which is cultivated for the delicacy of its fruit. This tree grows naturally in Perfia, from whence it was firft brought to the fouthern parts of Europe, but is now become common in every part of Europe, where the winters are not very fevere ; for in the northern parts of Sweden, thefe trees will not live in the open air ; and in feveral parts of Germany they are planted againft walls, and treated in the fame way as Peach, and other tender fruits are here.

Thefe trees are generally of both fexes, having male flowers or katkins on the fame tree with the fruit ; but it often happens, that fome of the trees which are raifed from feeds, have generally male flowers, and produce no fruit ; fo that thofe who plant thefe trees for their fruit, fhould never make choice of fuch as have been propagated by feeds, unlefs they have feen them produce fruit in the nurfery. It is alfo the fureft way to mark fuch trees as are fruitful in the nurfery, at the time when their fruit is upon them, becaufe thofe trees which are propagated by layers, are fometimes of the male fort ; for I have feveral times obferved, that fome of the large branches of thefe trees have produced only katkins, when the other parts of the trees have been very fruitful ; fo that unlefs care is taken in the choice of the branches for making the layers, there is the fame hazard as in feedling trees : nor fhould the fhoots which come out near the roots of old trees be ever laid down, for thefe rarely produce fruit until they have been planted many years, although the trees from which thefe were produced might be very fruitful. I have obferved fome trees which produced only katkins for many years after they were planted, and afterward have become fruitful ; the fame I have obferved in Walnut-trees, and my honoured friend the Chevalier Rathgeb, has informed me, that he has obferved the fame in the Lentifk and Turpentine-trees.

The old Mulberry-trees are not only more fruitful than the young, but their fruit are much larger and better flavoured ; fo that where there are any of thefe old trees, it is the beft way to propagate from them, and to make choice of thofe branches which are moft fruitful. The ufual method of propagating thefe trees, is by laying down their branches, which will take root in one year, and are then feparated from the old trees ; but as the moft fruitful branches are often fo far from the ground as not be layed, unlefs by raifing of boxes or bafkets of earth upon fupports
for

for this purpose, so the better way is to propagate them by cuttings, which, if rightly chosen and skilfully managed, will take root very well; and in this method there will be no difficulty in having them from trees at a distance, and from the most fruitful branches. These cuttings should be the shoots of the former year, with one joint of the two years wood to their bottom; the cuttings should not be shortened, but planted their full length, leaving two or three buds above ground. The best season for planting them is in March, after the danger of hard frost is over; they should be planted in light rich earth, pressing the ground pretty close about them; and if they are covered with glasses, it will forward their putting out roots; but where there is not such conveniency, the ground about them should be covered with mofs, to prevent its drying; and where this is carefully done, the cuttings will require but little water, and will succeed much better than with having much wet. If the cuttings succeed well and make good shoots, they may be transplanted the following spring into a nursery, where they should be regularly trained to stems, by fixing down stakes by each, to which the principal shoots should be fastened; and most of the lateral branches should be closely pruned off, leaving only two or three of the weakest to detain the sap, for the augmentation of the stem; for when they are quite divested of their side shoots, the sap is mounted to the top, so that the heads of the trees grow too fast for the stems, and become too weighty for their support. In about four years growth in the nursery, they will be fit to transplant where they are to remain; for these trees are transplanted with greater safety while young, than when they are of a large size.

If the cuttings are planted in a bed fully exposed to the fun; it will be proper to arch the bed over with hoops, that they may be shaded with mats in the heat of the day during the spring, till they have put out roots; after which, the more they are exposed to the fun, the better they will succeed, provided the ground is covered with mofs or mulch to prevent its drying, for the fun will harden the shoots, and thereby they will be in less danger of suffering by the early frosts in autumn; for when these are in a shady situation, they are apt to grow vigorously in summer, so will be replete with moisture, and the early frosts in October frequently kill their tops; and if the following winter proves severe, they are often killed to their roots, and sometimes are entirely destroyed. I have two or three times made trial of planting the cuttings of Mulberries on a hot-bed, and have found them succeed extremely well. This I was led to by observing some sticks of Mulberry-trees which were cut for forks, and thrust into the hot-bed to fasten down the Vines of Cucumbers; which, although they had been cut from the tree a considerable time, yet many of them put out roots and shot out branches; so that where any person is in haste to propagate these trees, if the cuttings are planted on a moderate hot-bed, they will take root much sooner than in the common ground.

This tree delights to grow in rich light earth, such as is in most of the old kitchen-gardens about London, where there is also a great depth of earth; for in some of those gardens there are trees of a very great age, which are very healthy and fruitful, and their fruit is larger and better flavoured than those of younger trees. I have never yet seen any of these trees which were planted in a very stiff soil, or on shallow ground, either upon clay, chalk, or gravel, which have been healthy or fruitful, but their stems and branches are covered with mofs, so that the little fruit which they sometimes produce are small, ill tasted, and late before they ripen.

If these trees are planted in a situation where they are defended from the strong south and north-west winds, it will preserve their fruit from being blown off; but this shelter, whether it be trees or buildings, should be

at such a distance as not to keep off the fun; for where the fruit has not the benefit of his rays to dissipate the morning dews early, they will turn mouldy and rot upon the trees. There is never any occasion for pruning these trees, more than to cut off any of the branches which may grow across others, so as to rub and wound their bark, by their motion occasioned by the wind; for their shoots should never be shortened, because the fruit is produced on the young wood.

The second sort grows naturally in Sicily, from whence I received a parcel of the seeds, and raised a good number of the plants; all these were totally different in their leaves from the common Mulberry, so that I am certain of its being a distinct species. It is also a tree of humbler growth, but the fruit is small and has no flavour, so is not worth propagating; some of the trees produced fruit two or three years in the Chelsea garden.

The white Mulberry is commonly cultivated for its leaves to feed silk-worms in France, Italy, &c. though the Persians generally make use of the common black Mulberry for that purpose; and I have been assured by a gentleman of honour, who has made trial of both sorts of leaves, that the worms fed with those of the black sort produce much better silk than those fed with the white; but he observes that the leaves of the black sort should never be given to the worms after they have eaten for some time of the white, left the worms should burst, which is often the case when they are thus treated.

The trees which are designed to feed silk-worms, should never be suffered to grow tall, but rather kept in a sort of hedge; and instead of pulling off the leaves singly, they should be sheared off together with their young branches, which is much sooner done, and not so injurious to the tree.

This white sort may be propagated either from seeds or layers, as the black Mulberry, and is equally hardy; but the most expeditious method of raising these trees in quantity, is from the seeds, which may be procured in plenty from the south of France or Italy: the best way to sow these seeds in England, is to make a moderate hot-bed, which should be arched over with hoops, and covered with mats; upon this bed the seeds should be sown in the end of March, and covered over with light earth about a quarter of an inch deep: in very dry weather the bed must be frequently watered, and in the heat of the day shaded with mats, and also covered in the nights when they are cold; with this management the plants will come up in five or six weeks, and as they are tender when they first appear, so they must be guarded against frosty mornings, which often happen in May, and destroy such tender plants; during the summer they must be kept clean from weeds, which is all the culture they require: but there must be care taken of them the first winter, especially to cover them in autumn, when the first frosts come, which will kill the tender plants to the ground, if they are not protected; the following March these plants should be transplanted into the nursery to get strength, where they may remain two or three years, and then should be removed where they are to continue.

There are two or three varieties of this tree, which differ in the shape of their leaves, size, and colour of their fruit; but as they are of no other use than for their leaves, the strongest shooting and the largest leaved should be preferred.

The third sort, which is the large-leaved Virginian Mulberry with black shoots, is more uncommon than either of the former; there is a large tree of this growing in the gardens of the Bishop of London at Fulham, which has been several years an inhabitant of that garden, but has never produced any fruit that I could learn, but hath some years a great number of katkins, much like those of the Hazel-nut, which occasioned Mr. Ray to give it the name of Corylus; but it may be one of the male trees which do not produce fruit, as it sometimes happens in the common

sorts

forts of Mulberries; the leaves of this are somewhat like those of the common Mulberry-tree, but are rougher.

This tree has not been propagated yet in this country, for though it has been budded and grafted upon both the black and white Mulberries, yet I cannot hear that it hath succeeded upon either, so that I suspect it is not of this genus; and the tree being pretty tall, cannot be laid down, which is the most likely method to propagate it. This is very hardy, and will endure the cold of our climate in the open air very well, and is coveted as a curiosity by such as delight in a variety of trees and shrubs.

The fifth sort is the tree whose wood is used by the dyers, and is better known by the title of Fustick, which is given to the wood, than by its fruit, which is of no estimation. This grows naturally in most of the islands in the West-Indies, but in much greater plenty at Campeachy, where it abounds greatly. This wood is one of the commodities exported from Jamaica, where it grows in greater plenty than in any other of the British islands.

This tree in the countries where it grows naturally, rises to the height of sixty feet or upward; it has a light brown bark, which hath some shallow furrows; the wood is firm, solid, and of a bright yellow colour. It sends out many branches on every side, covered with a white bark, and are garnished with leaves about four inches long, which are broad at their base, indented at the foot-stalk, where they are rounded, but one side is broader than the other, so that they are oblique to the foot-stalk; these diminish gradually, and end in acute points; they are rough like those of the common Mulberry, of a dark green, and stand upon short foot-stalks. Toward the end of the young branches come out short katkins of a pale herbaceous colour, and in other parts of the same branches the fruit is produced, growing upon short foot-stalks; they are as large as nutmegs, of a roundish form, full of protuberances like the common Mulberry, green within, and also on the outside, of a luscious sweet taste when ripe.

It is too tender to thrive in this country, unless preserved in a warm stove. There are several of the plants now growing in the Chelsea garden, which were raised from seeds sent from Jamaica, by William Williams, Esq; with many other curious sorts, which are natives of that island. The seeds of this plant come up freely on a hot-bed, and when the plants are fit to remove, they should be each planted in a separate small pot filled with fresh light earth, and plunged into a hot-bed of tanners bark, and shaded from the sun till they have taken new root; then they should be treated in the same way as other plants from those hot countries, always keeping them in the tan-bed in the stove, where they will make good progress. These plants retain their leaves great part of the year in the stove.

The sixth sort grows naturally in China and Japan; it also grows naturally in South Carolina, from whence I have received the seeds; the inhabitants of Japan make paper of the bark; they cultivate the trees for that purpose on the hills and mountains, much after the same manner as Osiers are cultivated here, cutting down the young shoots in autumn for their bark. There were several of these trees raised from seeds a few years past, in the gardens of his Grace the Duke of Northumberland, who was so good as to favour me with one of the plants, which thrives very well in the open air without any shelter, as many of the trees and plants of those countries will do, if they grow on the mountains. This plant makes very strong vigorous shoots, but seems not to be of tall growth, for it sends out many lateral branches from the root upward. The leaves are large, some of them are entire, others are deeply cut into three, and some into five lobes, especially while the trees are young, dividing in form of a hand; they are of a dark green, and rough to the touch, but of a pale green, and somewhat hairy on their under side, falling

off on the first approach of frost in autumn, as do those of the common Mulberry. The description which Kæmpfer gives of the fruit is, that they are a little larger than Peas, surrounded with long purple hairs, are composed of acini, or protuberances, and when ripe, change to a black purple colour, and are full of sweet juice.

This tree may be propagated by laying down the branches, in the same way as is practised for the common Mulberry; or it may be multiplied by planting the cuttings, in the same manner as before directed for the common sort.

The seventh sort grows naturally in India, where it becomes a large tree. It hath soft, thick, yellowish bark, with a milky juice like the Fig, which is astringent. The branches come out on every side, which are garnished with oblong oval leaves, standing upon short foot-stalks; both sides of these leaves are equal, but their edges are unequally sawed; they are rough, of a dark green on their upper side, but pale on their under, standing alternately on the branches. The flowers come out in round heads at the foot-stalks of the leaves, on each side the branches; they are of an herbaceous white colour; the male flowers have four stamina; the female flowers are succeeded by roundish fruit, which are first green, afterwards white, and when ripe turn to a dark red colour. I received the seeds of this plant from Bombay, which succeeded in the Chelsea garden. The plants are too tender to live out of a stove in this country; for as I raised a good number of the plants, so when they had obtained strength, I placed some of them in different situations, where they were defended from the frost, but not any of them survived the winter, but those which were in the bark-stove, where they are constantly kept, and treated in the same manner as other tender plants, giving them but little water in winter, with which management the plants thrive, and retain their leaves all the year.

The eighth sort grows naturally in Jamaica, and also in the Bahama Islands, from both which places I have received the seeds. The wood of this tree is cut, and sold for the same uses as the fifth, from which this tree has not been well distinguished by the botanists: this does not grow to so great a size as the fifth; the branches are slenderer, the leaves are narrower, and are rounded at their base, sawed on their edges, and end in acute points. At the foot-stalk of each leaf comes out two sharp thorns, which, in the older branches grow to the length of two inches. The fruit is shaped like that of the fifth sort, but is smaller.

MOSCHATELLINA. See ADOXA.

MOSS. See MUSCUS.

MOTHERWORT. See CARDIACA.

MOULD, or earth, the goodness of which may be known by the sight, smell, and touch.

First, by the sight: those Moulds that are of a bright Chesnut, or hazelly colour, are counted the best; of this colour are the best loams, and also the best natural earth, and this will be the better yet, if it cuts like butter, and does not stick obstinately, but is short, tolerably light, breaking into small clods, is sweet, will be tempered without crusting or chapping, in dry weather, or turning to mortar in wet.

The next to that, the dark gray and russet Moulds are accounted the best, the light and dark Ash-colour are reckoned the worst; such as are usually found on common, or heathy ground; the clear tawny is by no means to be approved, but that of a yellowish red colour is accounted the worst of all; this is commonly found in wild and waste parts of the country, and for the most part produce nothing but Furz and Fern, according as their bottoms are more or less of a light and sandy, or of a spewy gravel, or clayey nature.

Secondly, by the smell: all lands that are good and wholesome, will, after rain, or breaking up by the spade, emit a good smell.

Thirdly, by the touch: by this means we may discover whether it consists of substances entirely arenaceous, or clammy; or, according as it is expressed by

Mr.

Mr. Evelyn, whether it be tender, fatty, deterfive, or flippery, or more harfh, gritty, porous, or friable. That being always the beft that is between the two extremes, and does not contain the two different qualities of foft and hard mixed, of moift and dry, of churlifh and mild, that is neither too unctuous or too lean, but fuch as will diffolve, of a juft confiftence, between fand and clay, and fuch as will not ftick to the fpade or fingers upon every flafh of rain.

A loam, or brick Mould, is not to be difapproved, as requiring little help or improvement but the fpade, and is efteemed both by the gardener and florift.

MUCILAGE is a vifcous clammy fubftance about feeds, &c.

MUCILAGINOUS fignifies, endowed with a clammy vifcous matter.

MULBERRY. See Morus.

MULLEIN. See Verbascum.

MULTISILIQUOUS plants are fuch as have after each flower, many diftinct, long, flender, and, oftentimes, crooked cafes, or filiquæ, in which their feed is contained, and, which, when they ripen, open of themfelves, and let the feeds drop. Of this kind is the Bear's-foot, Columbines, common Houfe-leek, Navelwort, Orpine, &c.

MUMMY, a fort of grafting wax, made of one pound of common black pitch, and a quarter of a pound of common turpentine, put into an earthen pot, and fet on the fire in the open air ; in doing this you ought to hold a cover in your hand, ready to cover it, in order to quench it, by putting it thereon, which is to be done feveral times, fetting it on the fire again, that the nitrous and volatile parts may be evaporated. The way to know when it is enough, is by pouring a little of it on a pewter plate, and if it be fo, it will coagulate prefently ; then this melted pitch is to be poured into another pot, and a little common wax is to be added to it, mixing them well together, and then to be kept for ufe.

Dr. Agricola directs the ufing this Mummy as follows :

When you would drefs roots with this wax, you muft melt it, and afterwards let it cool a little ; then dip in the ends of the roots you would plant (for he propofes it for the planting pieces of roots of trees, &c.) one after the other, but not too deep, and afterwards to put them in water, and to plant them in the earth, the fmall end downwards, fo that the larger end may appear a little way out thereof, and have the benefit of the air, and then to prefs the earth very hard down about them, that they may not receive too much wet, becaufe that would rot them.

Mummy for exotic plants ; the fame author directs the making it as follows :

Take half a pound of gum copal, beat it very fine, and fearce it ; take three pounds of Venice turpentine, and melt it over a flow fire in a ftrong earthen pot ; when the turpentine is melted and liquidated, put the fifted gum into it, keep it continually ftirring with a little ftick, augmenting the fire gradually, and it will all diffolve infenfibly ; afterwards let the turpentine evaporate well, and it will thicken ; and when it is become of a fufficient confiftence, you may make it up into little rolls, like fealing-wax, and keep it for ufe.

This Mummy, he fays, is an excellent vulnerary for plants, it being fubject to no corruption, as other gummy things are ; it hinders any rottennefs between the ftock and the root, by means of which the callus is formed the fooner, and fpreads over all the parts, and the ftock becomes entirely connected with the root. It alfo gives ftrength and vigour to the root, and likewife facilitates it.

Vegetable Mummy ; the fame author directs the making of this as follows :

Fill a large kettle, or earthen pot, about a third part full of common black pitch, and add to it a little fine refin, or fulphurated pitch, and a little yellow wax ; melt thefe together till they become liquid, then take them off the fire, and let them ftand till they have done fmoking, and, when cool, you

may, with a brufh, plafter the incifions which are made for the inoculation, grafting, &c.

Garden or Foreft Mummy ; the fame author directs the making it as follows :

Take three pounds of common turpentine, and four pounds of common pitch ; melt the turpentine over the fire, and, having beaten the pitch to a powder, throw it in ; when they are well mixed together, and grown pretty thick, take it off, and keep it for ufe. This compofition may be either made up into little fticks, like thofe of fealing-wax, to be made ufe of on little trees, or it may be kept in little pots, and melted over a flow fire, when there is occafion to ufe it, and, dipping a little brufh in it, you may plafter the graft.

The Noble Mummy, or grafting wax ; to make this the fame author directs :

Take two pounds of pure pitch, fuch as is called at Ratifbon virgin pitch, and add to it half a pound of good turpentine ; put them together in an earthen pot, and fet them over the fire, that the volatile part of the turpentine may evaporate, otherwife it would be very prejudicial to trees and roots. Prove it as you did the former, to know when it is enough ; then add to it half a pound of virgin wax, and half an ounce of pounded Myrrh and Aloes ; when thefe are well mixed, make it up into little rolls or plafters, or elfe it may be kept in gallipots.

The time he directs when the operation of the roots is to be performed, is in the month of September, October, and November ; though it may fucceed well at any time of the year, yet thofe months are the moft proper feafons for it. The only difference he fays, is, what is planted in the fpring, will fhoot out in June or July, and what is planted in autumn comes not forth till the month of April.

The aforefaid author mentions great performances by ufing thefe Mummies ; thofe who have a mind to be fatisfied, may perufe his treatife.

MUNTINGIA. Plum. Gen. Nov. 41. tab. 6. Lin. Gen. Plant. 575.

The Characters are,

The empalement of the flower is cut into five fegments to the bottom. The flower hath five heart-fhaped petals, narrow at their bafe, which are inferted in the empalement, and fpread open like a Rofe. It has a great number of ftamina, which are terminated by roundifh fummits. In the center is fituated a roundifh germen, having no ftyle, but is crowned by a ftigma divided into many parts. The germen afterward turns to a foft fruit, with one cell, crowned by the ftigma, like a navel, and filled with fmall feeds.

This genus of plants is ranged in the firft fection of Linnæus's thirteenth clafs, which includes thofe plants whofe flowers have many ftamina and one ftigma. According to Tournefort's fyftem, it muft be ranged in the eighth fection of his twenty-firft clafs, which contains the trees and fhrubs with a Rofe flower, whofe empalement becomes a fruit, having hard feeds.

We know but one Species of this genus, viz.

Muntingia (Calabura.) Jacq. Hift. tab. 107. Muntingia folio fericeo molli, fructu majori. Plum. Nov. Gen. 41. *Muntingia with a foft filky leaf, and a larger fruit.*

The title of this genus was given to it by Father Plumier, in honour of Dr Muntingius, who was profeffor of botany at Groningen in Holland, who publifhed a folio book of botany, entitled, Phytographia Curiofa, in which there are many figures of plants exhibited, engraven on copper-plates ; he alfo publifhed two books of plants in quarto, one of which is entitled, Aloidarum, in which the figures of feveral forts of Aloes are exhibited ; the title of the other is, De Herba Britannica Antiquorum.

This plant is figured and defcribed by Sir Hans Sloane, in his Hiftory of Jamaica, by the title of Loti arboris folio anguftiore, rubi flore, fructu polyfpermo umbilicato, 2. p. 80. This rifes to the height of thirty feet or more in its native foil, fending out many

many branches toward the top, which are covered with a fmooth, dark, purple bark, garnifhed with leaves about three inches long, and three quarters broad at their bafe, where they are rounded to a heart-fhape at the foot-ftalk, but end in acute points, are very woolly on their under fide, but fmooth above, and of a lucid green ; they are flightly fawed on their edges, and are placed alternately. The flowers come out from the wings of the ftalks, ftanding upon long foot-ftalks, compofed of five heart-fhaped petals, which are white, and fpread open, refembling thofe of the Bramble, having many ftamina about half the length of the petals, terminated by globular fum-mits, and in the center is fituated a roundifh ger-men, crowned by a many-pointed ftigma. The ger-men afterward turns to a pulpy umbilicated fruit, as large as the fruit of the Cockfpur Hawthorn, and, when ripe, of a dark purple colour, inclofing many fmall, hard, angular feeds; this fort has produced flowers and fruit in England.

The feeds of this plant were fent by Mr. Robert Millar from Jamaica, which fucceeded in fome of the Englifh gardens.

The plants are propagated by feeds, which fhould be fown in pots filled with light rich earth, and plunged into a moderate hot-bed of tanners bark, and in warm weather the glaffes fhould be raifed to admit frefh air. Thefe feeds will often remain in the ground a whole year before the plants will appear ; in which cafe the pots muft be kept conftantly clear from weeds, and fhould remain in the hot-bed till after Michaelmas, when they may be removed into the ftove, and plunged into the bark-bed, between other pots of tall plants, where they may remain during the winter feafon. Thefe pots fhould be now and then watered, when the earth appears dry, and in the beginning of March the pots fhould be removed out of the ftove, and placed into a frefh bark-bed under frames, which will bring up the plants foon after.

When the plants are come up about two inches high, they fhould be carefully taken out of the pots, and each planted into a feparate fmall pot filled with light rich earth, and then plunged into the hot-bed again, obferving to fhade them from the fun until they have taken new root, after which time they fhould be duly watered, and in warm weather they muft have a large fhare of frefh air. In this hot-bed the plants may remain until autumn, when the nights begin to be cold; at which time they fhould be removed into the ftove, and plunged into the bark-bed. During the winter feafon thefe plants muft be kept warm, efpecially while they are young, and fre-quently refrefhed with water; but it muft not be given to them in large quantities, left it rot the ten-der fibres of their roots. It will be proper to continue thefe plants in the ftove all the year, but in warm wea-ther they fhould have a large fhare of frefh air; but as the plants grow in ftrength, they will be more hardy, and may be expofed in fummer for two or three months, and in winter will live in a dry ftove, if kept in a moderate degree of heat.

MURUCUIA. See PASSIFLORA.

MUSA. Plum. Nov. Gen. 24. tab. 34. Lin. Gen. Plant. 1010. The Plantain-tree.

The CHARACTERS are,

It hath male and female flowers upon the fame foot-ftalk, fome of which are hermaphrodite ; thefe are produced on a fingle ftalk (or fpadix;) the male flowers are fituated on the upper part of the fpike, and the female below ; thefe are in bunches, each bunch having a fheath, or cover, which falls off. The flowers are of the lip kind. The petals conftitute the upper lip, and the nectarium the un-der ; they have fix awl-fhaped ftamina, five of which are fituated in the petal, and the fixth in the nectarium ; this is double the length of the other, terminated by a linear fummit ; the others have none. The germen is fituated under the flower, is long, having three obtufe angles, fupporting an erect cylindrical ftyle, crowned by a roundifh ftigma. The germen afterward turns to an ob-

long, three-cornered, flefhy fruit, covered with a thick rind, divided into three parts.

This genus of plants is ranged in the firft fection of Linnæus's twenty-third clafs, which includes thofe plants with male and female flowers, which have hermaphrodite flowers on the fame ftalk. Plumier ranges it in Tournefort's clafs, with the anomalous flowers of feveral petals ; and Garçin places it among the plants with a Lily flower.

The SPECIES are,

1. MUSA (*Paradifiaca*) fpadice nutante floribus mafcu-lis perfiftentibus. Lin. Sp. 1477. *Mufa with a nod-ding fpike, and nodding male flowers.* Mufa fructu cucumerino longiorio. Plum. Nov. Gen. 24. *Mufa with a longer Cucumber-fhaped fruit, commonly called Plantain-tree.*

2. MUSA (*Sapientum*) fpadice nutante floribus mafculis deciduis. Lin. Sp. 1477. *Mufa with a nodding fpike, and deciduous male flowers.* Mufa fructu cucumerino, breviore. Plum. Nov. Gen. 24. *Mufa with a fhorter Cucumber-fhaped fruit, commonly called Bonana.*

The firft fort is cultivated in all the iflands of the Weft-Indies, where the fruit generally ferves the ne-groes for bread, and fome of the white people alfo prefer it to moft other forts, efpecially to the Yams, and Caffada bread.

This plant rifes with a foft herbaceous ftalk fifteen or twenty feet high, and upward ; the lower part of the ftalk is often as large as a man's thigh, diminifhing gradually to the top, where the leaves come out on every fide, which are often more than fix feet long, and near two feet broad, with a ftrong flefhy mid-rib, and a great number of tranfverfe veins running from the midrib to the borders. The leaves are thin and tender, fo that where they are expofed to the open air, they are generally torn by the wind ; for as they are large, the wind has great power againft them : thefe leaves come out from the fide of the prin-cipal ftalk, inclofing it with their bafe ; they are rolled up at their firft appearance, but when they are ad-vanced above the ftalk, they expand quite flat, and turn backward ; as thefe leaves come up rolled in the manner before mentioned, their advance upward is fo quick, that their growth may be almoft difcerned by the naked eye ; and if a line is drawn acrofs, le-vel with the top of the leaf, in an hour's time the leaf will be near an inch above it. When the plant is grown to its full height, the fpike of flowers will appear from the center of the leaves, which is often near four feet in length, and nods on one fide. The flowers come out in bunches, thofe on the lower part of the fpike being the largeft ; the others diminifh in their fize upward ; each of thefe bunches is co-vered with a fpathæ or fheath, of a fine purple colour within, which drops off when the flowers open. The upper part of the fpike is made up of male or barren flowers, which are not fucceeded by fruit, but thofe of the fecond fort fall off with their covers. The fruit of this is eight or nine inches long, and above an inch diameter, a little incurved, and has three angles ; it is at firft green, but, when ripe, of a pale yellow colour. The fkin is tough, and within is a foft pulp of a lufcious fweet flavour. The fpikes of fruit are often fo large as to weigh upwards of forty pounds.

The fruit of the firft fort is generally cut before it is ripe, and roafted in the embers, then it is eaten in-ftead of bread. The leaves are ufed for napkins and table cloths, and are food for hogs.

The fecond fort, which is commonly called Bonana, differs from the firft, in having its ftalks marked with dark purple ftripes and fpots. The fruit is fhorter, ftraiter, and rounder, and the male flowers drop off ; the pulp is fofter, and of a more lufcious tafte, fo is generally eaten by way of defert, and feldom ufed in the fame way as the Plantain, therefore is not culti-vated in fuch plenty.

Both thefe plants were carried to the Weft-Indies from the Canary Iflands, to which place it is believed they

they were carried from Guinea, where they grow naturally : thefe plants are alſo cultivated in Egypt, and in moſt other hot countries, where they grow to perfeƈtion in about ten months, from their firſt planting, to the ripening of their fruit; when their ſtalks are cut down, ſeveral ſuckers come up from the root; they will alſo produce fruit in ten months after, ſo that by cutting down the ſtalks at different times, there is a conſtant ſucceſſion of fruit all the year.

In Europe there are ſome of theſe plants preſerved in the gardens of curious perſons, who have hot-houſes capacious enough for their reception, in many of which they have ripened their fruit very well; but as they grow very tall and their leaves are large, they require more room in the ſtove than moſt people care to allow them : they are propagated by ſuckers, which come from the roots of thoſe plants which have fruited; and many times the younger plants, when they are ſtinted in growth, will put out ſuckers ; theſe ſhould be carefully taken off, preſerving ſome fibres to their roots, and planted in pots filled with light rich earth, and plunged into the tan-bed in the ſtove : theſe may be taken off any time in ſummer, and it is beſt to take them off when young, becauſe if their roots are grown large, they do not put out new fibres ſo ſoon, and when the thick part of the root is cut in taking off, the plants often rot.

During the ſummer ſeaſon theſe plants muſt be plentifully watered, for the ſurface of their leaves being large, there is a great conſumption of moiſture, by perſpiration in hot weather, but in the winter they muſt be watered more ſparingly; though at that ſeaſon they muſt be often refreſhed, but it muſt not be given them in ſuch quantities.

The pots in which theſe plants are placed, ſhould be large in proportion to the ſize of the plants, for their roots generally extend pretty far, and the earth ſhould be rich and light. The degree of heat with which theſe plants thrive beſt, is much the ſame with the Anana, or Pine Apple, in which I have had many of theſe plants produce their fruit in perfeƈtion, and they were near twenty feet high.

The moſt ſure method to have theſe plants fruit in England is, after they have grown for ſome time in pots, ſo as to have made good roots, to ſhake them out of the pots with the ball of earth to their roots, and plant them into the tan-bed in the ſtove, obſerving to lay a little old tan near their roots for their fibres to ſtrike into, and in a few months the roots of theſe plants will extend themſelves many feet each way in the bark ; and theſe plants will thrive a great deal faſter than thoſe which are confined in pots, or tubs. When the bark-bed wants to be renewed with freſh tan, there ſhould be great care taken of the roots of theſe plants, not to cut or break them, as alſo to leave a large quantity of the old tan about them, becauſe if the new tan is laid too near them, it will ſcorch their roots, and injure them : theſe plants muſt be plentifully ſupplied with water, otherwiſe they will not thrive; in winter they ſhould be watered twice a week, giving at leaſt two quarts to each plant, but in ſummer they muſt be watered every other day, and double the quantity given to them each time. If the plants puſh out their flower-ſtems in the ſpring, there will be hopes of their perfeƈting their fruit ; but when they come out late in the year, the plants will ſometimes decay before the fruit is ripe. The ſtoves in which theſe plants are placed ſhould be at leaſt twenty feet in height, otherwiſe there will not be room for their leaves to expand ; for when the plants are in vigour, the leaves are often eight feet in length, and two feet broad : ſo that if the ſtems grow to be fourteen feet to the diviſion of the leaves, and the houſe is not twenty feet high, the leaves will be cramped, which will retard the growth of the plants ; beſides, when the leaves are bent againſt the glaſs, there will be danger of their breaking them, when they are growing vigorouſly ; for I have had in one night the ſtems of

ſuch bent leaves force through the glaſs, and by the next morning advanced two or three inches above the glaſs.

I have ſeen ſome bunches of fruit of the firſt ſort, which were upwards of forty pounds weight, and perfeƈtly ripe in England ; but this is not ſo good a fruit, as to tempt any perſon to be at the expence of raiſing them in England. The ſecond ſort is preferred to the firſt, for the flavour of its fruit, in all thoſe hot countries where theſe plants abound : the bunches of theſe are not near ſo large as thoſe of the firſt ſort, nor are the ſingle fruit near ſo long; theſe change to a deeper yellow colour as they ripen, but their taſte is ſomewhat like that of meally Figs. Some perſons who have reſided in the Weſt-Indies, having eaten ſome of theſe fruit which were produced in England, and thought them little inferior to thoſe which grew in America ; and I imagine, that the inhabitants of thoſe countries would not eſteem theſe fruits ſo much, had they variety of other ſorts; but, for want of better, they eat many kinds of fruit, which would not be valued in Europe, could they be obtained in perfeƈtion.

MUSCARI. Tourn. Inſt. R. H. 347. tab. 180. Muſk, or Grape Hyacinth, vulgò.

The CHARACTERS are,

The flower has no empalement. It hath one oval pitcher-ſhaped petal, which is reflexed at the brim. It hath three neƈtariums on the top of the germen, and ſix awl-ſhaped ſtamina which are ſhorter than the petal, whoſe ſummits join together, and in the center is ſituated a roundiſh three-cornered germen, ſupporting a ſingle ſtyle, crowned by an obtuſe ſtigma. The germen afterward turns to a roundiſh three-cornered capſule, having three cells, filled with roundiſh ſeeds.

Dr. Linnæus has joined this genus to the Hyacinth, which is placed in the firſt ſeƈtion of his ſixth claſs, which contains the plants whoſe flowers have ſix ſtamina and one ſtyle.

The SPECIES are,

1. MUSCARI (*Botryoide*) corollis globoſis uniformibus, foliis canaliculato-cylindricis ſtriƈtis. *Muſcari with uniform globular petals, and cylindrical gutter-ſhaped leaves.* Muſcari arvenſe, juncifolium, cæruleum, minus. Tourn. Inſt. 348. *Smaller blue Field Muſcary, with Ruſh leaves, commonly called Grape Hyacinth.*

2. MUSCARI (*Comoſis*) corollis angulato-cylindricis, ſummis ſterilibus longiùs pedicellatis. *Muſcari with angular cylindrical petals, which on the top of the ſpike are barren, and have longer foot-ſtalks.* Muſcari arvenſe, latifolium, purpuraſcens. Tourn. Inſt. 347. *Broadleaved, purple, Field Muſcari, commonly called Fair-haired Hyacinth.*

3. MUSCARI (*Racemoſus*) corollis ovatis, ſummis ſeſſilibus foliis laxis. *Muſcari with oval petals.* Muſcari obſoletiore flore. Cluſ. Hiſt. 1. p. 178. *Muſcari with an obſolete flower, commonly called Muſk Hyacinth.*

4. MUSCARI (*Monſtroſus*) corollis ſubovatis. *Muſcari with almoſt oval corolla.* Hyacinthus paniculâ cæruleâ. C. B. P. 42. *Blue paniculated Hyacinth, called Feathered Hyacinth.*

5. MUSCARI (*Orchioide*) corollis ſexpartitis, petalis tribus exterioribus brevioribus. *Muſcari with petals which are cut into ſix parts.* Hyacinthus orchioides Africanus major bifolius maculatus, flore ſulphureo, obſoleto majore. Breyn. Prod. 3. 24. *Greater African Hyacinth, reſembling Orchis, with two ſpotted leaves, and a larger, obſolete, ſulphur-coloured flower.*

The firſt ſort grows naturally in the vineyards and arable fields in France, Italy, and Germany, and where it is once planted in a garden, it is not eaſily rooted out, for the roots multiply greatly, and if they are permitted to ſcatter their ſeeds, the ground will be filled with the roots. There are three varieties of this, one with blue, another with white, and a third with Aſh-coloured flowers : the firſt ſort hath a ſmall, round, bulbous root, from which come out many leaves about ſix inches long, which are narrow, and their edges are incurved, ſo as to be ſhaped like a gutter : between theſe ariſe the flower-ſtalk, which

is

is naked, and toward the top garnished with a close spike of blue flowers, shaped like pitchers, sitting very close to the stalk; these smell like fresh starch, or the stones of Plumbs which are fresh. They flower in April, and the seeds ripen the latter end of June.

The second sort grows naturally in Spain and Portugal, from whence I have received both roots and seeds; this hath a bulbous root as large as a middling Onion, from which come out five or six leaves a foot long, and three quarters of an inch broad at their base, diminishing gradually to a point. The flowerstalk rises about a foot high, the lower half naked, but the upper is garnished with cylindrical, angular, purple flowers, standing upon foot-stalks half an inch long; these grow horizontally, but the stalk is terminated by a tuft of flowers whose petals are oval, and have neither germen or style, so are barren. This sort flowers the latter end of April, or the beginning of May; there is a variety of this with white, and another with blue flowers, but the purple is the most common.

The third sort hath pretty large, oval, bulbous roots, from which arise several leaves, which are about eight or nine inches long, and half an inch broad; they are incurved a little on their sides, and end in obtuse points; these embrace each other at their base; out of the middle of these, the stalk which sustains the flowers arises; they are naked below, but their upper parts are garnished with small flowers growing in a spike; these have oval pitcher-shaped petals, which are reflexed at their brim, and are of an Ash-coloured purple, or obsolete colour, seeming as if faded, but have an agreeable musky scent: these stalks do not rise more than six inches high, so the flowers make no great appearance; but where they are in some quantity, they will perfume the air to a considerable distance. This sort flowers in April, and the seeds ripen in July.

Of this there are two varieties, one of which has the same coloured flowers with this here enumerated, on the lower part of the spike, but they are larger, and have more of the purple cast, but the flowers on the upper part of the spike are yellow, and have a very grateful odour. The Dutch gardeners title it Tibcadi Muscari. As this is supposed to be only a seminal variety of the third, I have not enumerated it as distinct. There is another variety of this with very large yellow flowers, that has been lately raised from seeds in Holland, which the florists there sell for a guinea a root.

The fourth sort hath a large bulbous root, from which come out several plain leaves a foot long, and about half an inch broad at their base; they are smooth, and end in obtuse points. The flower-stalks rise near a foot and a half high; they are naked at the bottom for about seven or eight inches, above which the panicles of flowers begin, and terminate the stalks. The flowers stand upon foot-stalks which are more than an inch long, each sustaining three, four, or five flowers, whose petals are cut into slender filaments like hairs; they are of a purplish blue colour, and have neither stamina or germen, so do never produce seeds. It flowers in May, and, after the flowers are past, the stalks and leaves decay to the root, and new ones arise the following spring.

The fifth sort grows naturally at the Cape of Good Hope, from whence I received the seeds, which succeeded in the Chelsea garden, where the plants have flowered for several years past; this hath a small, white, bulbous root, about the size of a Hazel nut, from which comes out generally but two, (though sometimes when the roots are strong) three leaves, which are five or six inches long, and one inch and a half broad in the middle, ending in obtuse points; these are of a lucid green, and have many spots, or protuberances on their upper surface. The flower-stalk rises between them to the height of six or seven inches; it is round, smooth, and naked for three inches

high or more, and is terminated by a spike of flowers, which are of a pale sulphur colour; these have no foot-stalks; they have one petal, which is of an irregular figure, and cut at the top into six parts. The stamina are almost equal with the petal, and stand round the style, which is of the same length. The flowers appear in March, but are seldom succeeded by good seeds here.

The four first sorts are very hardy, so will thrive in the open air, and require no other culture than any other hardy bulbous-rooted flower; which is, to take up their roots every second or third year to separate their bulbs, for as some of the sorts multiply pretty fast, so when they are become large bunches, they do not flower so strong as when they are single: the best time to take them out of the ground, is soon after their stalks and leaves are decayed; then they should be spread on a mat, in a dry shady room for a fortnight to dry, after which they may be kept in boxes like other bulbous roots, till Michaelmas, when they may be planted again in the borders of the flower-garden, and treated in the same way as the common hardy kinds of Hyacinths.

The first sort should not be admitted into the flower-garden, because the roots will propagate so fast, as to become a troublesome weed there.

The second sort has but little beauty, so a few of these only should be allowed a place merely for the sake of variety; this is so hardy, as to thrive in any soil or situation.

The third sort merits a place for the extreme sweetness of its flowers, but especially that variety of it with yellow flowers, called Tibcady.

The fourth sort may also be allowed to have place in the common borders of the pleasure-garden, where they will add to the variety, and are by no means to be despised.

They are all easily propagated by offsets, which most of their roots send out in pretty great plenty, so that there is little occasion for sowing of their seeds, unless it be to gain some new varieties.

The fifth sort is too tender to thrive in the open air in England, so the roots must be planted in small pots, filled with light rich earth; and in the autumn they should be placed under a hot bed-frame, where they may be protected from frost, but should have as much free air as possible in mild weather; for when these are placed in a green-house, their leaves are drawn long and narrow, and the flower-stalks are generally weak, so never flower so well as when they have plenty of free air. These flowers will continue a month where they are not drawn, but will decay in half that time in a green-house.

These roots should be transplanted in July, when their stalks and leaves are decayed, and should be placed in the open air during the summer season, but should have very little water when their leaves are decayed.

MUSCIPULA. See SILENE.

MUSCOSE, MUSCOSUS, Mossy, or abounding with Moss.

MUSCOSITY, Mossiness.

MUSCUS, Moss.

These, though formerly supposed to be only excrescences produced from the earth, trees, &c. yet are no less perfect plants than those of greater magnitude, having roots, branches, flowers, and seeds, but yet cannot be propagated from the latter by any art.

The botanists distinguish these into several genera, under each of which are several species; but as they are plants of no use or beauty, it would be to little purpose to enumerate them in this place.

These plants chiefly flourish in cold countries, and in the winter season, and are many times very injurious to fruit-trees, which grow upon cold barren soils, or where they are so close planted as to exclude the free access of air. The only remedy in such cases is to cut down part of the trees, and plough up the ground between those left remaining: and in the

spring

spring of the year, in moist weather, you should, with an iron instrument made a little hollow, the better to surround the branches of the trees, scrape off the Moss, carrying it off the place; and by two or three times thus cleansing them, together with carefully stirring the ground, it may be entirely destroyed from the trees; but if you do not cut down part of the trees, and stir the ground well, the rubbing off the Moss will signify little; for the cause not being removed, the effect will not cease, but the Moss will in a short time be as troublesome as ever.

MUSHROOMS are, by many persons, supposed to be produced from the putrefaction of the dung, earth, &c. in which they are found; but notwithstanding this notion is pretty generally received amongst the unthinking part of mankind, yet by the curious naturalists, they are esteemed perfect plants, though their flowers and seeds have not as yet been perfectly discovered. But since they may, and are annually propagated by the gardeners near London, and are (the esculent sort of them) greatly esteemed by most curious palates, I shall briefly set down the method practised by the gardeners who cultivate them for sale.

But first, it will not be improper to give a short description of the true eatable kind, since there are several unwholesome sorts, which have been by unskilful persons gathered for the table.

The true Champignon, or Mushroom, appears at first of a roundish form, like a button; the upper part of which, as also the stalk, is very white; but being opened, the under part is of a livid flesh colour, but the fleshy part when broken is very white; when these are suffered to remain undisturbed, they will grow to a large size, and explicate themselves almost to a flatness, and the red part underneath will change to a dark colour.

In order to cultivate them, if you have no beds in your own, or in neighbouring gardens, which produce them, you should look abroad in rich pastures, during the months of August and September, until you find them (that being the season when they are naturally produced;) then you should open the ground about the roots of the Mushrooms, where you will find the earth, very often, full of small white knobs, which are the offsets, or young Mushrooms; these should be carefully gathered, preserving them in lumps with the earth about them: but as this spawn cannot be found in the pasture, except at the season when the Mushrooms are naturally produced, you may probably find some in old dunghills, especially where there has been much litter amongst it, and the wet hath not penetrated it to rot it; as likewise, by searching old hot-beds, it may be often found; for this spawn has the appearance of a white mould, shooting out in long strings, by which it may be easily known wherever it is met with: or this may be procured by mixing some long dung from the stable, which has not been thrown on a heap to ferment; which being mixed with strong earth, and put under cover to prevent wet getting to it, the more the air is excluded from it, the sooner the spawn will appear; but this must not be laid so close together as to heat, for that will destroy the spawn: in about two months after the spawn will appear, especially if the heap is closely covered with old thatch, or such litter as hath lain long abroad, so as not to ferment, then the beds may be prepared to receive the spawn: these beds should be made of dung, in which there is good store of litter, but this should not be thrown on a heap to ferment; that dung which hath lain spread abroad for a month or longer, is best. These beds should be made on dry ground, and the dung laid upon the surface; the width of these beds at bottom should be about two feet and a half or three feet, the length in proportion to the quantity of Mushrooms desired; then lay the dung about a foot thick, covering it about four inches with strong earth. Upon this lay more dung, about ten inches thick; then another layer of earth, still drawing in the sides of the bed, so

as to form it like the ridge of a house, which may be done by three layers of dung and as many of earth. When the bed is finished it should be covered with litter or old thatch, to keep out wet, as also to prevent its drying; in this situation it may remain eight or ten days, by which time the bed will be in a proper temperature of warmth to receive the spawn; for there should be only a moderate warmth in it, great heat destroying the spawn, as will also wet; therefore when the spawn is found, it should always be kept dry until it is used, for the drier it is; the better it will take in the bed; for I had a parcel of this spawn, which had lain near the oven of a stove upward of four months, and was become so dry, that I despaired of its success; but I never have yet seen any which produced so soon, nor in so great quantity as this.

The bed being in a proper temperature for the spawn, the covering of litter should be taken off, and the sides of the bed smoothed; then a covering of light rich earth about an inch thick should be laid all over the bed, but this should not be wet; upon this the spawn should be thrust, laying the lumps four or five inches asunder; then gently cover this with the same light earth above half an inch thick, and put the covering of litter over the bed, laying it so thick as to keep out wet, and prevent the bed from drying: when these beds are made in the spring or autumn, as the weather is in those seasons temperate, so the spawn will then take much sooner, and the Mushrooms will appear perhaps in a month after making; but those beds which are made in summer, when the season is hot, or in winter, when the weather is cold, are much longer before they produce.

The great skill in managing of these beds is, that of keeping them in a proper temperature of moisture, never suffering them to receive too much wet: during the summer season the beds may be uncovered, to receive gentle showers of rain at proper times; and in long dry seasons the beds should be now and then gently watered, but by no means suffer much wet to come to them; during the winter season they must be kept as dry as possible, and so closely covered as to keep out cold. In frosty or very cold weather, if some warm litter shaken out of a dung heap is laid on, it will promote the growth of the Mushrooms; but this must not be laid next the bed, but a covering of dry litter between the bed and this warm litter; and as often as the litter is found to decay, it should be renewed with fresh; and as the cold increases, the covering should be laid so much thicker. If these things are observed, there may be plenty of Mushrooms produced all the year; and these produced in beds, are much better for the table than any of those which are gathered in the fields.

A bed thus managed, if the spawn takes kindly, will continue good for several months, and produce great quantities of Mushrooms; from these beds when they are destroyed, you should take the spawn for a fresh supply, which may be laid up in a dry place until the proper season of using it, which should not be sooner than five or six weeks, that the spawn may have time to dry before it is put into the bed, otherwise it will not succeed well.

Sometimes it happens, that beds thus made do not produce any Mushrooms till they have lain five or six months, so that these beds should not be destroyed, though they should not at first answer expectation; for I have frequently known these to have produced great quantities of Mushrooms afterward, and have continued a long time in perfection.

MUSTARD. See SINAPI.

MYAGRUM. Tourn. Inst. R. H. 211. tab. 99. Lin. Gen. Plant. 713. Gold of Pleasure.

The CHARACTERS are,

The empalement of the flower is composed of four oblong, oval, coloured leaves, which fall off. The flower hath four roundish obtuse petals, placed in form of a cross. It hath six stamina the length of the petals, four of which are a little longer than the other, terminated by single summits.

mits. In the center is situated an oval germen, supporting slender style, crowned by an obtuse stigma. The germen afterward becomes a turbinated, heart-shaped, short pod, having two valves with a rigid style on the top, inclosing roundish seeds.

This genus of plants is ranged in the first section of Linnæus's fifteenth class, which contains the plants whose flowers have four long and two shorter stamina, and the seeds are inclosed in short small pods.

The Species are,

1. Myagrum (*Sativum*) siliculis ovatis, pedunculatis polyspermis. Hort. Cliff. 328. *Myagrum with oval pods having foot-stalks, inclosing several seeds.* Alysson segetum foliis auriculatis acutis. Tourn. Inst. R. H. *Corn Madwort with eared acute-pointed leaves, commonly called Gold of Pleasure.*

2. Myagrum (*Alyssum*) siliculis cordatis pedunculatis polyspermis, foliis denticulatis obtusis. *Myagrum with heart-shaped pods standing upon foot-stalks, having many seeds and indented leaves.* Alysson segetum foliis auriculatis acutis fructu majori. Tourn. Inst. 217. *Corn Madwort, with acute-eared leaves and a larger fruit.*

3. Myagrum (*Rugosum*) siliculis globosis compressis punctato-rugosis. Hort. Cliff. 328. *Myagrum with globular, compressed, small pods, having rough punctures.* Rapistrum arvense, folio auriculato acuto. Tourn. Inst. 211. *Field Charlock with an acute-eared leaf.*

4. Myagrum (*Perenne*) siliculis biarticulatis dispermis, foliis extrorsum sinuatis denticulatis. Hort. Upsal. 182. *Myagrum with short pods, having two joints and two seeds, and outer leaves which are sinuated and indented.* Rapistrum monospermum. C. B. P. 95. *One-seeded Charlock.*

5. Myagrum (*Perfoliatum*) siliculis obcordatis subsessilibus, foliis amplexicaulibus. Hort. Upsal. 182. *Myagrum with small heart-shaped pods sitting close to the stalk, and the leaves embracing it.* Myagrum monospermum latifolium. C. B. P. 109. *Broad-leaved Myagrum having one seed in a pod.*

The first sort grows naturally in Corn fields in the south of France and Italy; I have also found it growing in the Corn in Easthamsted-park, the seat of William Trumbull, Esq; but it is not common in this country. It is an annual plant, with an upright stalk about a foot and a half high, sending out two or four side branches toward the top, which grow erect; they are smooth, and have a fungous pith; the lower leaves are from three to four inches long, of a pale or yellowish green, and are eared at their base; those upon the stalks diminish in their size all the way up, and are entire, and almost embrace the stalks with their base. The flowers grow in loose spikes at the end of the branches, standing upon foot-stalks an inch long; they are composed of four small yellowish petals, placed in form of a cross; these are succeeded by oval capsules, which are bordered, and crowned at the top with the style of the flower, having two cells, which are filled with red seeds.

The second sort is also an annual plant, and differs from the first in having a taller stalk; the leaves are much longer, narrower, and are regularly indented on their edges, ending in obtuse points. The flowers are larger, but of the same form and colour; the capsules are much larger, and are shaped like a heart. Both these plants flower in June and July, and their seeds ripen in September.

The third sort grows naturally on the borders of arable fields, in the south of France and Italy. This is an annual plant, whose lower leaves are five or six inches long; they are hairy and succulent; their base is eared, and they end in acute points. The stalks rise a foot and a half high, they are brittle and hairy, branching out toward the top like the two former, and are terminated by short loose spikes of small pale flowers, which are succeeded by small, rough, roundish capsules, compressed at the top. It flowers in July, and the seeds ripen in autumn.

The fourth sort grows naturally amongst the Corn, in France and Germany. This is also an annual

plant; the lower leaves are large, jagged, and hairy; the stalks branch out from the bottom, and are garnished with leaves about four inches long and two broad; they are hairy, and unequally jagged. The stalks are terminated by very long loose spikes of yellow flowers, which are succeeded by short pods with two joints, each including one roundish seed. It flowers about the same time with the former.

The fifth sort grows naturally in the south of France and Italy; this hath a smooth branching stalk upward of two feet high; the lower leaves are five or six inches long, smooth, succulent, and a little indented; the upper leaves almost embrace the stalks with their base. The flowers are produced in long loose spikes, which are yellow, and sit close to the stalk; these are succeeded by heart-shaped compressed pods, divided into two cells by a longitudinal partition, each containing one roundish seed. It flowers at the same time with the former.

If the seeds of all these plants are permitted to scatter in the autumn, the plants will rise without any care, and only require to be thinned and kept clean from weeds. These autumnal plants will always ripen their seeds, whereas those which are sown in the spring sometimes fail.

MYOSOTIS. Dill. Gen. 3. Lin. Gen. 180. Mouse-ear.

The Characters are,

The flower hath an oblong, erect, permanent empalement, cut into five points; the flower is salver-shaped, having a short cylindrical tube, cut into five obtuse segments at the brim; the chaps are closed by five small scales which join, and are prominent. It hath five short stamina in the neck of the tube, terminated by small summits; and four germen supporting a slender style the length of the tube, crowned by an obtuse stigma; the germina afterward become four oval seeds inclosed in the empalement.

This genus of plants is ranged in the first section of Linnæus's fifth class, intitled Pentandria Monogynia, the flower having five stamina and one style.

The Species are,

1. Myosotis (*Virginica*) seminibus aculeatis glochidibus, foliis ovato-oblongis, ramis divaricatis. Lin. Sp. 189. *Mouse-ear with prickly seeds, oblong oval leaves, and divaricated branches.* Cynoglossum Virginianum, flore & fructu minimo. Mor. Hist. 3. tab. 30. fol. 9. *Virginian Hound's-tongue, with small flowers and seeds.*

2. Myosotis (*Lappula*) seminibus aculeis glochidibus, foliis lanceolatis pilosis. Flor. Suec. 150. *Mouse-ear with prickly seeds, and hairy spear-shaped leaves.* Cynoglossum minus. C. B. P. 257. *Smaller Hound's-tongue.*

3. Myosotis (*Apula*) seminibus nudis, foliis hispidis, racemis foliolis. Lin. Sp. 189. *Mouse-ear with naked seeds, stinging leaves, and leafy branches.* Echium luteum minimum. C. B. P. 254. *The least yellow Viper's Bugloss.*

There are one or two other species of this genus which grow naturally in England, so are rarely admitted into gardens, therefore are omitted here: and those here enumerated are seldom cultivated except in botanic gardens, being plants of little beauty or use. Those persons who are desirous of keeping them, should sow their seeds in the autumn, upon an open bed or border of light earth, and in the spring thin the plants where they are too close, and keep them clean from weeds, which is all the culture they require; and if their seeds are permitted to scatter, the plants will rise without farther trouble.

MYOSURUS, Mouse-tail.

This plant is very a-kin to the Ranunculus, in which genus it is ranged by some botanists; the flowers are extremely small, and are succeeded by long slender spikes of seeds, resembling the tail of a mouse, from whence it had the name. It grows wild upon moist grounds in divers parts of England, where it flowers the latter end of April; and the seeds ripen in a month after, when the plants decay, being annual. It is rarely cultivated in gardens, so I shall not trouble the reader with any further account of it.

MYRICA.

MYRICA. Lin. Gen. Plant. 981. Gale. Tourn. Act. Reg. Scien. 1706. The Candleberry Myrtle, Gale, or Sweet Willow; by some Myrtus Brabantica, or Dutch Myrtle; in French, *Piment Royal.*

The CHARACTERS are,

The male flowers are upon different plants from the female; the male flowers are produced in a loose, oblong, oval katkin, imbricated on every side; under each scale is situated one moon-shaped flower, having no petal, but hath four or six short slender stamina, terminated by large twin summits, whose lobes are bifid. The female flowers have neither petal or stamina, but an oval germen supporting two slender styles, crowned by single stigmas. The germen afterward becomes a berry with one cell, inclosing a single seed.

This genus of plants is ranged in the fourth section of Linnæus's twenty-second class, which includes the plants whose male flowers have four stamina, and are upon different plants from the fruit.

The SPECIES are,

1. MYRICA (*Gale*) foliis lanceolatis subserratis, caule fruticoso. Lin. Sp. Plant. 1024. *Myrica with spear-shaped sawed leaves and a shrubby stalk.* Gale frutex odoratus septentrionalium. J. B. 1. p. 2. 225. *Northern, shrubby, sweet Gale, sweet Willow, Dutch Myrtle, or Gale.*

2. MYRICA (*Cerifera*) foliis lanceolatis subserratis, caule arborescente. Kalm. *Myrica with spear-shaped leaves, and a shrubby stalk.* Myrtus Brabanticæ similis Caroliniensis baccifera, fructu racemoso sessili monopyreno. Pluk Phyt. tab. 48. fol. 9. *Carolina Myrtle like that of the Dutch, with berries growing in bunches, and sitting close to the stalks, commonly called Candleberry Myrtle.*

3. MYRICA (*Caroliniensis*) foliis lanceolatis serratis, caule suffruticosa. *Myrica with spear-shaped sawed leaves, and a shrubby stalk.* Myrtus Brabanticæ similis Caroliniensis humilior, foliis latioribus & magis serratis. Catesb. Car. vol. i. p. 13. *Lower Carolina Myrtle, or Candleberry-tree resembling that of Brabant, having broader leaves which are more sawed.*

4. MYRICA (*Asplenifolia*) foliis oblongis alternatim sinuatis. Hort. Cliff. 456. *Myrica with oblong oval leaves, which are alternately sinuated.* Gale Mariana Asplenii folio. Pet. Muf. 773. *Maryland Gale with a Spleenwort leaf.*

5. MYRICA (*Quercifolia*) foliis oblongis oppositè sinuatis glabris. *Myrica with oblong smooth leaves, which are oppositely sinuated.* Laurus Africana minor, folio querciûs. Hort. Amst. 2. p. 161. *Smaller African Bay with an Oak leaf.*

6. MYRICA (*Hirfuta*) foliis oblongis oppositè sinuatis hirsutis. *Myrica with oblong hairy leaves, which are oppositely sinuated.*

7. MYRICA (*Cordifolia*) foliis subcordatis serratis sessilibus. Hort. Cliff. 456. *Myrica with sawed leaves which are almost heart-shaped, and fit close to the stalk.* Gale Capensis, ilicis cocciferæ folio. Pet. Muf. 774. *Gale from the Cape, with a leaf like the Kermes Oak.*

The first sort grows naturally upon bogs in many parts of England, particularly in the northern and western counties, as also in Windsor-park, and near Tunbridge-wells. This rises with many shrubby stalks near four feet high, garnished with stiff spear-shaped slender branches, garnished with stiff spear-shaped leaves, about an inch and a half long, and half an inch broad in the middle; they are of a light or yellowish green, smooth, and a little sawed at their points, and emit a fragrant odour when bruised; they are placed alternately on their branches. The male flowers or katkins are produced from the side of the branches, growing upon separate plants from the female, which are succeeded by clusters of small berries, each having a single seed. It flowers in July, and the seeds ripen in autumn.

The leaves of this shrub has been by some persons gathered and used for Tea, but it is generally supposed to be hurtful to the brain; but from this use of it, a learned physician a few years since, wrote a treatise to prove this to be the true Tea, in which

he has only shewn his want of knowledge in these things.

It grows naturally in bogs, so cannot be made to thrive on dry land, for which reason it is seldom preserved in gardens.

The second sort grows naturally in North America, where the inhabitants get a sort of green wax from the berries, which they make into candles. The method of collecting and preparing this, is described by Mr. Catesby, in his History of Carolina.

This grows naturally in bogs and swampy lands, where it rises with many strong shrubby stalks eight or ten feet high, sending out several branches, garnished with stiff spear-shaped leaves near three inches long, and one broad in the middle; they are smooth and entire, having scarce any foot-stalks, of a yellowish lucid green on their upper side, but paler on their under, standing alternately, and pretty close to the branches; these have a very grateful odour when bruised. The katkins come out upon different plants from the berries; these are about an inch long, standing erect. The female flowers come out on the side of the branches in longish bunches, which are succeeded by small roundish berries, covered with a sort of meal. This shrub delights in a moist soft soil, in which it thrives extremely well, and lives in the open air without any protection.

The third sort grows naturally in Carolina; this doth not rise so high as the former, the branches are not so strong, and they have a grayish bark; the leaves are shorter, broader, and are sawed on their edges, but in other respects is like the second sort; the berries of this are also collected for the same purpose.

These sorts are propagated by seeds, which should be sown in the autumn, and then the plants will come up the following spring; but if the seeds are kept out of the ground till the spring, they seldom grow till the year after. These plants will require water in dry weather, and should be screened from frosts while young, but when they have obtained strength, they will resist the cold of this country very well.

The fourth sort grows naturally in Philadelphia, from whence many of the plants have been brought to England, and those which have been planted on a moist soil have thriven very well; some of these creep at their roots, and send up suckers plentifully, in the same manner as in their native soil.

This rises with slender shrubby stalks near three feet high, which are hairy, and divide into several slender branches, which are garnished with leaves from three to four inches long, and half an inch broad; they are alternately indented almost to the midrib, and have a great resemblance to those of Spleenwort; they are of a dark green, hairy on their under side, and sit close to the stalks. The male flowers or katkins come out on the side of the branches between the leaves; these are oval, and stand erect. I have not seen any of these plants in fruit, so I can give no description of it.

This sort may be propagated by suckers, which are sent out from the roots when it is planted in a loose moist soil, and will endure the cold full as well as the two former sorts.

The fifth and sixth sorts grow naturally at the Cape of Good Hope; these only differ from each other, in one having very smooth shining leaves, and those of the other hairy. I do not know if they are really different species, but as I received them from Holland as such, and the plants still retaining their difference, so I have enumerated them both.

These rise with shrubby slender stalks about four feet high, which divide into smaller branches, which in one sort are smooth, and in the other they are hairy; these are closely garnished with leaves about an inch and a half long, and almost an inch broad; some having two, others three, deep indentures on their sides, which are opposite; in one sort they are smooth and shining, and in the other they are hairy, and of a darker green; they fit close to the branches, and end

end in obtufe points which are indented : between the leaves come out fome oval katkins, which drop off, fo that all the plants which I have feen have been male, therefore I can give no account of the fruit, Thefe retain their leaves all the year, but are too tender to live through the winter in the open air in England, fo muft be placed in the green-houfe in winter. As thefe do not produce feeds here, fo they are propagated by layers, but they do not take root very freely, fo that the plants are not very common in Europe at prefent ; for I do not find that the cuttings of thefe plants will eafily take root, having made feveral trials of them in all the different methods ; nor have the Dutch gardeners had better fuccefs, fo that the plants are as fcarce there as in England.

When the layers are laid down, that part of the fhoot which is laid fhould be tongued at a joint, as is practifed in laying of Carnations ; and the young fhoots only fhould be chofen for this purpofe, for the old branches will not put out roots. Thefe layers are often two years before they will have taken root enough to tranfplant, for they fhould not be feparated from the old plants till they have made good roots, becaufe they are very fubject to mifcarry if they are not well rooted.

When they are taken off from the old plants, they fhould be each put into a feparate fmall pot, filled with foft, rich, loamy earth ; and if they are placed under a common frame, fhading them from the fun in the middle of the day, it will forward their taking new root ; then they may be placed in a fheltered fituation during the fummer, and in the autumn re-'moved into the green-houfe, and treated in the fame way as other plants from the fame country. The beft feafon for laying down the branches, I have obferved to be in July, and by the fame time the following year they have been fit to remove.

The feventh fort is a native of the Cape of Good Hope ; this hath a weak fhrubby ftalk which rifes five or fix feet high, fending out many long flender branches, which are 'clofely garnifhed their whole length with fmall heart-fhaped leaves, which fit clofe to the branches, and are flightly indented and waved on their edges. The flowers come out between the leaves in roundifh bunches ; thefe are male in all the the plants I have yet feen ; they have an uncertain number of ftamina, and are all included in one common fcaly involucrum or cover. Thefe flowers appear in July, but make no great appearance ; the leaves of this fort continue all the year green.

This is propagated in the fame way `as the two former forts, and is difficult to increafe, fo is not common in the European gardens. It requires the fame treatment as the two former forts.

MYRRHIS. See CHÆROPHYLLUM, SCANDIX, SISON.

MYRTUS. Tourn. Inft. R. H. 640. tab. 409. Lin. Gen. Plant. 543. Myrtle ; in French, Mirte.

The CHARACTERS are,

The empalement of the flower is of one leaf, cut into five acute points at the top, is permanent, and fits on the germen. The flower has five large oval petals which are inferted in the empalement, and a great number of fmall ftamina which are alfo inferted in the empalement, terminated by fmall fummits. The germen is fituated under the flower, fupporting a flender ftyle, crowned by an obtufe ftigma. The germen afterward turns to an oval berry with three cells, crowned by the empalement, each cell containing one or two kidney-fhaped feeds.

This genus of plants is ranged in the firft fection of Linnæus's twelfth clafs, in which is contained thofe plants whofe flowers have about twenty ftamina and one ftyle.

The SPECIES are,

1. MYRTUS (Communis) foliis ovatis, pedunculis longioribus. Myrtle with oval leaves, and longer foot-ftalks to the flowers. Myrtus latifolia Romana. C. B. P. 468. Broad-leaved Roman Myrtle, or common broad-leaved Myrtle.

2. MYRTUS (Belgica) foliis lanceolatis acuminatis. Myrtle with fpear-fhaped acute-pointed leaves. Myrtus la-

tifolia Belgica. C. B. P. 469. Broad-leaved Dutch Myrtle.

3. MYRTUS (Acuta) lanceolato-ovatis acutis. Myrtle with fpear-fhaped, oval, acute-pointed leaves. Myrtus fylveftris, foliis acutiffimis. C. B. P. 469. Wild Myrtle with very acute-pointed leaves.

4. MYRTUS (Bætica) foliis ovato-lanceolatis confertis. Myrtle with oval fpear-fhaped leaves growing in clufters. Myrtus latifolia Bœtica 2 vel foliis laurinus, confertim nafcentibus. C. B. P. 469. Second broad-leaved Spanifh Myrtle, with Bay leaves growing in clufters, commonly called Orange-leaved Myrtle.

5. MYRTUS (Italica) foliis ovato-lanceolatis acutis, ramis erectioribus. Myrtle with oval, acute-pointed, fpear-fhaped leaves, and erect branches. Myrtus communis Italica. C. B. P. 468. Common Italian Myrtle, called upright Myrtle.

6. MYRTUS (Tarentina) foliis ovatis, baccis rotundioribus. Myrtle with oval leaves and rounder berries. Myrtus minor vulgaris. C. B. P. 469. Common fmaller Myrtle, called the Box-leaved Myrtle.

7. MYRTUS (Minima) foliis lineari-lanceolatis acuminatis. Myrtle with linear, fpear-fhaped, acute-pointed leaves. Myrtus foliis minimis & mucronatis. C. B. P. 469. Myrtle with the fmalleft fharp-pointed leaves, commonly called Rofemary-leaved Myrtle.

8. MYRTUS (Zeylanica) pedunculis multifloris, foliis ovatis fubpetiolatis. Lin. Sp. Plant. 472. Myrtle with many flowers on each foot-ftalk, and oval leaves having fhort foot-ftalks. Myrtus Zeylanica odoratiffima, baccis niveis monococcis. H. L. 434. Sweet fmelling Myrtle of Ceylon, with fnow white berries containing one feed. The firft fort is the common broad-leaved Myrtle, which is one of the hardieft kinds we have. The leaves of this are an inch and a half long, and one inch broad, of a lucid green, ftanding upon fhort foot-ftalks. The flowers are larger than thofe of the other forts, and come out from the fide of the branches, on pretty long foot-ftalks ; thefe are fucceeded by oval berries of a dark purple colour, inclofing three or four hard kidney-fhaped feeds. It flowers in July and Auguft, and the berries ripen in winter. This fort is by fome called the flowering Myrtle, becaufe it generally has a greater quantity of flowers, and thofe are larger than of any other fort.

The fecond fort has leaves much lefs than thofe of the former, and are more pointed, ftanding clofer together on the branches ; the midrib on the under fide of the leaves is of a purple colour, they are of a darker green, and fit clofer to the branches. The flowers are fmaller, and have fhorter foot-ftalks than thofe of the firft fort ; this flowers a little later in the fummer, and feldom ripens its berries here.

The double flowering Myrtle I take to be a variety of this, for the leaves and growth of the plant, the fize of the flowers, and the time of flowering, agree better with this than any of the other forts.

The third fort grows naturally in the fouth of France and in Italy ; the leaves of this are much fmaller than thofe of the fecond, being lefs than an inch long, and not more than half an inch broad, of an oval fpear-fhape, ending in acute points, of a dull green, and fet pretty clofe on the branches. The flowers are fmaller than either of the former, and come out from the wings of the leaves toward the end of the branches ; the berries are fmall and oval.

The fourth fort hath a ftronger ftalk and branches than either of the former forts, and rifes to a greater height ; the leaves are oval, fpear-fhaped, and are placed in clufters round the branches ; thefe are of a dark green. The flowers are of a middling fize, and come out fparingly from between the leaves ; the berries are oval, and fmaller than thofe of the firft fort, but feldom ripens in England. The gardeners call this the Orange-leaved Myrtle, and by fome it is ftiled the Bay-leaved Myrtle. This fort is not fo hardy as the former.

The fifth fort is the common Italian Myrtle ; this hath oval fpear-fhaped leaves, ending in acute points ; the branches of this grow more erect than thofe of either

ther of the former forts, as do also the leaves, from whence it is called by the gardeners upright Myrtle. The flowers of this fort are not large, and the petals are marked with purple at their points, while they remain closed; the berries are small, oval, and of a purple colour. There is a variety of this with white berries, in which it only differs from this; and I believe the Nutmeg Myrtle is only a variety of this, for I have raised several of the plants from feed, many of which were so like the Italian Myrtle, as not to be diftinguished from it.

The fixth fort is commonly called the Box-leaved Myrtle; the leaves of this are oval, small, and fit close on the branches; they are of a lucid green, ending in obtuse points; the branches are weak, and frequently hang downward, when they are permitted to grow without fhortening, and have a grayish bark. The flowers are small, and come late in the summer, the berries are small and round.

The seventh fort is called the Rosemary-leaved Myrtle, and by some it is called the Thyme-leaved Myrtle. The branches of this grow pretty erect; the leaves are placed close on the branches; they are small, narrow, and end in acute points; they are of a lucid green, and have a fragrant odour when bruised. The flowers of this are small, and come late in the season, and are but seldom succeeded by berries here.

There are some other varieties of thefe Myrtles, which are propagated in the gardens for sale; but as their difference has been occafioned by culture, so it would be multiplying their titles to little purpose. Those which are here enumerated I believe to be really diftinct, for I have raised most of them from feeds, and have not found them change from one to another, though there has been other small variations among the plants.

The eighth fort is a native of the Island of Ceylon: this is much tenderer than either of the former forts, fo cannot be kept through the winter in England, without some artificial heat. This hath a ftrong upright ftalk, covered with a fmooth gray bark, dividing upward into many flender ftiff branches, garnifhed with oval leaves placed opposite, which are near two inches long, and an inch and a quarter broad, ending in points; they are of a lucid green, and have very fhort foot-ftalks. The flowers come out at the ends of the branches, feveral of them being fuftained upon one common foot-ftalk, which branches out, and each flower ftands on a very flender diftinct foot-ftalk; they are very like the flowers of Italian Myrtle, but always appear in December and January, and are never succeeded by berries here.

I fhall firft treat of the method of cultivating and propagating the common forts of Myrtle, as they all require nearly the fame management, and fhall afterward take notice of that of the laft mentioned, which require a different treatment; but as the varieties of the common forts of Myrtle are cultivated in the gardens for sale, I fhall juft mention the titles by which they are known, that the curious may be informed how many there are.

Two forts of Nutmeg Myrtles, one with a broader leaf than the other.

The Bird's Neft Myrtle, the ftriped Nutmeg Myrtle, the ftriped upright Myrtle, the ftriped Rosemary-leaved Myrtle, the ftriped Box-leaved Myrtle, and the ftriped broad-leaved Myrtle.

These plants may be all propagated from cuttings, the beft season for which is in the beginning of July, when you fhould make choice of some of the ftraiteft and moft vigorous young fhoots, which fhould be about fix or eight inches long, and the leaves on the lower part muft be ftripped off about two or three inches high, and the part twifted which is to be placed in the ground; then having filled a parcel of pots (in proportion to the quantity of cuttings defigned) with light rich earth, you fhould plant the cuttings therein, at about two inches diftance from each other, obferving to clofe the earth faft about them, and give them fome water to fettle it to the cuttings; then place the

pots under a common hot-bed frame, plunging them either into fome old dung, or tanners bark, which will prevent the earth from drying too faft; but you muft carefully fhade them with mats in the heat of the day, and give them air in proportion to the warmth of the feafon, not forgetting to water them every two or three days, as you fhall find the earth in the pots require it. With this management, in about fix weeks, the cuttings will be rooted, and begin to fhoot, when you muft inure them to the open air by degrees, into which they fhould be removed towards the latter end of Auguft, or the beginning of September, placing them in a fituation where they may be fheltered from cold winds, in which place they may remain till the middle or latter end of October, when the pots fhould be removed into the green-houfe, but fhould be placed in the coolest part thereof, that they may have air given to them whenever the weather is mild, for they require only to be protected from fevere cold, except the Orange-leaved, and the ftriped Nutmeg Myrtles, which are fomewhat tenderer than the reft, and fhould have a warmer fituation.

During the winter feafon, they muft be frequently, but gently watered; and, if any decayed leaves appear, they fhould be conftantly picked off, as alfo the pots kept clear from weeds, which, if permitted to grow, will foon overfpread the young plants, and deftroy them.

If thefe pots are placed under a common hot-bed frame in winter, where they may be fcreened from froft, and have the free air in mild weather, the young plants will fucceed better than in a green-houfe, provided they do not receive too much wet, and are not kept clofely covered, which will occafion their growing mouldy, and dropping their leaves.

The fpring following thefe plants fhould be taken out of the pots very carefully, preferving a ball of earth to the roots of each of them, and every one fhould be placed into a feparate fmall pot filled with rich light earth, obferving to water them well to fettle the earth to their roots, and place them under a frame until they have taken root; after which they fhould be inured to the open air, and in May they muft be placed abroad for the fummer, in a fheltered fituation, where they may be defended from ftrong winds.

During the fummer feafon they will require to be plentifully watered, efpecially being in fuch fmall pots, which in that feafon foon dry; therefore you fhould obferve to place them where they fhould receive the morning fun, for when they are too much expofed to the fun in the heat of the day, the moifture contained in the earth of thefe fmall pots will foon be exhaled, and the plants greatly retarded in their growth thereby.

In Auguft following you fhould examine your pots, to fee if the roots of the plants have not made way out through the hole in the bottom of the pots, which if you obferve, you muft then fhift them into pots a fize larger, filling them up with the like rich earth, and obferve to trim the roots which were matted to the fide of the pots, as alfo to loofen the earth from the outfide of the ball with your hands, fome of which fhould be taken off, that the roots may the eafier find paffage into the frefh earth; then you muft water them well, and place the pots in a fituation where they may be defended from ftrong winds; and at this time you may trim the plants, in order to reduce them to a regular figure; and if they are inclinable to make crooked ftems, you fhould thruft down a flender ftrait ftick clofe by them, to which their ftems fhould be faftened, fo as to bring them upright.

If care be taken to train them thus while they are young, the ftems afterward, when they have acquired ftrength, will continue ftrait without any fupport, and their branches may be pruned, fo as to form either balls or pyramids, which for fuch plants as are preferved in the green-houfe, and require to be kept in fmall

fmall compafs, is the beft method to have them handfome; but then thefe fheered plants will not produce any flowers, for which reafon that fort with double flowers fhould not be clipped, becaufe the chief beauty of that confifts in its flowers; but it will be neceffary to fuffer a plant or two of each kind to grow rude, for the ufe of their branches in nofegays, &c. for it will greatly deface thofe which have been conftantly fheered to cut off their branches.

As thefe plants advance in ftature, they fhould annually be removed into larger pots, according to the fize of their roots; but you muft be careful not to put them into pots too large, which will caufe them to fhoot weak, and many times prove the deftruction of them; therefore when they are taken out of the former pots, the earth about their roots fhould be pared off, and that within fide the ball muft be gently loofened, that the roots may not be too clofely confined; and then place them into the fame pots again, provided they are not too fmall, filling up the fides and bottom of them with frefh rich earth, and giving them plenty of water to fettle the earth to their roots; which fhould be frequently repeated, for they require to be often watered both in winter and fummer, but in hot weather they muft have it in plenty.

The beft feafon for fhifting thefe plants is either in April or Auguft, for if it be done much fooner in the fpring, the plants are then in a flow growing ftate, and fo not capable to ftrike out frefh roots again very foon; and if it be done later in autumn, the cold weather coming on will prevent their taking root; nor is it adviſeable to do it in the great heat of fummer, becaufe they will require to be very often watered, and alfo to be placed in the fhade, otherwife they will be liable to droop for a confiderable time; and that being the feafon when thefe plants fhould be placed amongft other exotics, to adorn the feveral parts of the garden, thefe plants, being then removed, fhould not be expofed until they have taken root again, which, at that time (if the feafon be hot and dry) will be three weeks or a month.

In October, when the nights begin to be frofty, you fhould remove the plants into the green-houfe; but if the weather proves favourable in autumn (as it often happens) they may remain abroad until the beginning of November; for if they are carried into the green-houfe too foon, and the autumn fhould prove warm, they will make frefh fhoots at that feafon, which will be weak, and often grow mouldy in winter, if the weather fhould be fo fevere as to require the windows to be kept clofely fhut, whereby they will be greatly defaced; for which reafon they fhould always be kept as long abroad as the feafon will permit, and removed out again in the fpring before they fhoot out; and during the winter feafon that they are in the green-houfe, they fhould have as much free air as poffible when the weather is mild.

The three firft-mentioned forts I have feen planted abroad in warm fituations, and upon a dry foil, where they have endured the cold of our winters for feveral years very well, with being only covered in very hard frofts with two or three mats, and the furface of the ground about their roots covered with a little mulch to prevent the froft from entering the ground; but in Cornwall and Devonfhire, where the winters are more favourable than in moft other parts of England, there are large hedges of Myrtle which have been planted feveral years, and are very thriving and vigorous, fome of which are upward of fix feet high; and I believe, if the double flowering kind were planted

abroad, it would endure the cold as well as any of the other forts, it being a native of the fouthern parts of France. This, and the Orange-leaved kind, are the moft difficult to take root from cuttings; but if they are planted toward the latter end of June, making choice of only fuch fhoots as are tender, and the pots are plunged into an old bed of tanners bark which has loft moft of its heat, and the glaffes fhaded every day, they will take root extremely well, as I have more than once experienced. The Orange-leaved fort, and thofe with variegated leaves, are fomewhat tenderer than the ordinary forts, and fhould be houfed a little fooner in autumn, and placed farther from the windows of the green-houfe.

The eighth fort is at prefent rare in Europe, fo is in very few gardens. This fort was by Dr. Linnæus feparated from the Myrtles in the former editions of his works, and had the title of Myrfine applied to it; but in his Species of Plants, he has joined it to that genus again, to which, according to his fyftem, it properly belongs; for the number of petals, ftamina, and ftyle, do agree with thofe of the Myrtle, but it differs in fructification, this having but one feed in each fruit, and the Myrtle has four or five.

This plant is with difficulty propagated, which occafions its prefent fcarcity, for as it does not produce ripe feeds in Europe, it can only be increafed by layers or cuttings. By the former method the layers are commonly two years before they take root, and the cuttings frequently fail, though the latter is preferred, when performed at a proper feafon and in a right method; the beft time to plant the cuttings is in May: in the choice of them, it fhould be the fhoots of the former year, with a fmall piece of the two years wood at bottom; thefe fhould be planted in fmall pots, filled with foft loamy earth, for fmall pots are to be preferred to large ones for this purpofe, and they fhould be plunged into a very moderate hot-bed of tanners bark; and if the pots are each covered with fmall bell or hand-glaffes, fuch as have been ufed for blowing of Carnations to exclude the air, it will be of great fervice to promote the cuttings putting out roots, though they are covered with the glaffes of the hot-bed above them; the cuttings fhould be fhaded from the fun in the heat of the day, and gently refrefhed with water, as the earth in the pots is found to dry, but they fhould by no means have too much wet; thofe cuttings which fucceed, will have taken root by July, when they fhould be gradually inured to bear the open air, into which it will be proper to remove them about the middle of that month, that they may be ftrengthened before winter, but it will not be proper to tranfplant the cuttings till fpring; the pots muft be removed into a temperate ftove in autumn, and during the winter the cuttings muft be gently refrefhed with water. In the fpring they fhould be carefully taken up, and each planted in a fmall pot filled with light earth from a kitchen-garden, and plunged into a moderate hotbed to forward their taking frefh root; then they fhould be gradually hardened, and in July placed in the open air in a fheltered fituation, where they may remain till the end of September, and then be removed into the ftove.

This plant will not live through the winter in England in a green-houfe, but if it is placed in a moderate degree of warmth, it will flower well in winter; and in July, Auguft, and September, the plants fhould be placed abroad in a fheltered fituation.

MYRTUS BRABANTICA. See MYRICA.

N.

NAPELLUS. See ACONITUM.
NAPUS. See BRASSICA and RAPA.
NAPÆA. Lin. Gen. Plant. 748. Malva. H. L.

The CHARACTERS are,
It hath male and hermaphrodite flowers in distinct plants. The male flowers have pitcher-shaped empalements of one leaf, which are permanent, and cut at the top into five segments. The flowers have five oblong petals, which are connected at their base, but spread open, and are divided at the top; they have many hairy stamina, which are joined at the bottom into a sort of a cylindrical column, terminated by roundish compressed summits. The hermaphrodite flowers have the like empalement, petals, and stamina, as the male, and have a conical germen, supporting a cylindrical style, divided at the top into ten parts, crowned by single stigmas. The germen afterward turns to an oval fruit, inclosed in the empalement, divided into ten cells, each containing one kidney-shaped seed.

This genus of plants is ranged in the third section of Linnæus's sixteenth class, which includes the plants whose flowers have many stamina, which are joined at their base to the style, and together form a column. As the plants of this genus have male and hermaphrodite flowers on distinct plants, so they differ from all the tribe of malvaceous plants, to which they properly belong, the flowers being monopetalous, the stamina and styles being joined at their base, forming a column, which are the essential characters of that class.

The SPECIES are,

1. NAPÆA (*Dioica*) pedunculis involucratis angulatis foliis scabris, floribus dioicis. Flor. Virg. 102. *Napæa with angular foot-stalks, rough leaves, and male and hermaphrodite flowers on different plants.* Abutilon folio profundè dissecto, pedunculis multifloris mas & fœmina. Ehret. Pict. 7 & 8. *Abutilon with a deeply divided leaf, and foot-stalks having many flowers, which are both male and female.*

2. NAPÆA (*Hermaphrodita*) pedunculis nudis lævibus, foliis glabris, floribus hermaphroditis. *Napæa with naked foot-stalks, smooth leaves and hermaphrodite flowers.* Althæa Ricini folio Virginiana. H. L. *Virginia Marshmallow with a Ricinus leaf.*

The first sort has perennial roots, which are composed of many thick fleshy fibres, which strike deep into the ground, and are connected at the top into a large head, from which come out a great number of rough hairy leaves, near a foot diameter each way, which are deeply cut into six or seven lobes, which are irregularly indented on their edges, each lobe having a strong midrib, which all meet in a center at the foot-stalk. The foot-stalks are large and long, arising immediately from the root, and spread out on every side. The flower-stalks rise seven or eight feet high, and divide into smaller branches, garnished at each joint with one leaf, of the same form as those below, but diminish in their size toward the top, where they seldom have more than three lobes, which are divided to the foot-stalk; toward the upper part of the stalk come out from the side at each joint a long foot-stalk, which branches out toward the top, sustaining several white flowers, which are tubulous at bottom, where the segments of the petal are connected, but they spread open above, and are divided into five ob-

tuse segments; in the center arises the column, to which the stamina are joined at their base, but spread open above, and in the hermaphrodite flowers the style is connected to the same column. The hermaphrodite flowers are succeeded by compressed orbicular fruit, inclosed in the empalement, and divided into five cells, each containing a kidney-shaped seed, but the male plants are barren. It flowers in July and the seeds ripen in autumn, soon after which the stalk decays, but the roots will live many years.

The second sort hath also a perennial root, which frequently creeps in the ground; this sends up smooth stalks, which rise about four feet high, garnished with smooth leaves, placed alternately, standing upon pretty long slender foot-stalks; they are deeply cut into three lobes, which end in acute points, and are irregularly sawed on their edges; those on the lower part of the stalk are near four inches long, and almost as much in breadth, but they diminish gradually toward the top of the stalk. At the base of the leaf comes out the foot-stalk of the flower, which is about three inches long, dividing at the top into three smaller, each sustaining one white flower of the same form with those of the first sort, but are smaller, and the column of stamina is longer, their summits standing out beyond the petal.

Both these plants grow naturally in Virginia, and other parts of North America; from the bark of these plants might be procured a sort of hemp, which many of the malvaceous tribe afford; and in some of the sorts which grow naturally in India, the fibres of the bark are so fine, as to spin into very fine threads, of which there might be woven very fine cloth.

These plants are easily propagated by seeds, which if sown on a bed of common earth in the spring, the plants will rise very freely, and will require no other care but to keep them clear from weeds till autumn, when they may be transplanted into the places where they are to remain; they delight in a rich moist soil, in which they will grow very luxuriantly, so they must be allowed room. The second sort may be propagated by its creeping roots, which may be parted in autumn; but as these plants have no great beauty, so one or two of each sort in a garden, for the sake of variety, will be enough.

NARCISSO LEUCOIUM. See GALANTHUS.

NARCISSUS. Lin. Gen. Plant. 364. [takes its name of ναρκὸς, or νάρκη, a torpidness, or deep sleep, because the smell of this flower is said to cause a heaviness of the head, and a stupidity. Plutarch tells us, this plant was sacred to the infernal gods. The poets tell us, that Narcissus was the son of Cephisus, and the nymph Lyriope; a youth of such excellent beauty, that once upon a time coming to a fountain to drink, and seeing his beauteous image in the water, he grew so enamoured with it that he pined away with desire, and was transformed into a flower of his name.] The Daffodil.

The CHARACTERS are,
The flowers are included in an oblong compressed spatha (or sheath) which tears open on the side, and withers. The flowers have a cylindrical funnel-shaped empalement of one leaf, which is spread open at the brim; they have six oval petals on the outside of the nectarium, which are inserted above their base, and fix awl-shaped stamina fixed

to

to the tube of the nectarium, terminated by oblong sum-mits ; they have a three-tornered, roundish, obtuse ger-men, situated below the flower, supporting a long slender style, crowned by a trifid stigma. The germen afterward turns to an obtuse, roundish, three-cornered capsule, with three cells, filled with globular seeds.

This genus of plants is ranged in the firft fection of Linnæus's fixth clafs, which contains thofe plants whofe flowers have fix ftamina and one ftyle.

The Species are,

1. Narcissus (*Pfeudonarciffus*) fpathâ uniflorâ, nectario campanulato erecto, crifpo æquante petala ovata. Lin. Sp. Plant. 414. *Daffodil with one flower in each sheath, whofe nectarium is erect, bell-shaped, and equal with the petals, which are oval.* Narciffus fylveftris pallidus, calyce luteo. C. B. P. 52. *Pale wild Daffo-dil with a yellow cup, or common Englifh Daffodil.*

2. Narcissus (*Poëticus*) fpathâ uniflorâ, nectario rotato breviffimo, fcariofo crenulato. Hort. Upfal. 74. *Daf-fodil with one flower in a sheath, having a very short robel-shaped nectarium indented on the edge.* Narciffus albus, circulo purpureo. C. B. P. 48. *White Daffodil with a purple circle in the middle.*

3. Narcissus (*Incomparibilis*) fpathâ uniflorâ, nectario campanulato erecto, petalo dimidio breviore. *Daffo-dil with one flower in a sheath, having an erect bell-shaped empalement half the length of the petal.* Nar-ciffus incomparibilis, flore pleno, partim flavo, par-tim croceo. H. R. Par. *The Incomparable Daffodil with a double flower, partly yellow, and partly Saffron-coloured.*

4. Narcissus (*Medio-luteus*) fpathâ biflorâ, nectarii campanulato, breviffimo, floribus nutantibus. *Daffo-dil with two flowers in a sheath, a short bell-shaped nec-tarium, and nodding flowers.* Narciffus medio luteus vulgaris. Park. *Common Daffodil with a yellow middle, called Primrofe Peerlefs.*

5. Narcissus (*Albus*) fpathâ uniflorâ, nectario campa-nulato breviffimo, petalis reflexis. *Daffodil with one flower in a sheath, having a very short bell-shaped necta-rium, and reflexed petals.* Narciffus albus, foliis re-flexis, calyce brevi aureo. H. R. Par. *Daffodil with white flowers, having reflexed petals, and a short golden cup.*

6. Narcissus (*Bulbocodium*) fpathâ uniflorâ, nectario turbinato petalis majore, genitalibus declinatis. Lin. Sp. Plant. 417. *Rufh-leaved Daffodil with one flower in each fheath, a turbinated nectarium larger than the petal, and declining ftamina.* Pfeudonarciffus juncifolius flavo flore. Cluf. Hift. 166. *Commonly called Hoop-petticoat Narciffus.*

7. Narcissus (*Serotinus*) fpathâ uniflorâ, nectario bre-viffimo fex-partito. Loefl. Lin. Sp. Plant. 290. *Daf-fodil with one flower in a sheath, having a very short nectarium, which is cut into fix parts.* Narciffus au-tumnalis minor. Cluf. Hifp. 251. *Smaller autumnal Daffodil.*

8. Narcissus (*Tazetta*) fpathâ multiflorâ, nectario campanulato, foliis planis. Hort. Upfal. 74. *Daffo-dil with many flowers in a sheath, having a bell-shaped nectarium, and plain leaves.* Narciffus luteus polyan-thos Lufitanicus. C. B. P. 50. *Yellow Portugal Daffo-dil with many flowers, commonly called Polyanthus Nar-ciffus.*

9. Narcissus (*Jonquilla*) fpathâ multiflorâ, nectario cam-panulato brevi, foliis fubulatis. Hort. Upfal. 75. *Daf-fodil with many flowers in a sheath, a short bell-shaped nectarium, and awl-shaped leaves.* Narciffus juncifolius luteus minor. C. B. P. 51. *Smaller yellow Rufh-leaved Daffodil, called Jonquil.*

The forts here enumerated, are all the real fpecies which I have met with in the Englifh gardens, though there is a great variety of other fpecies, which differ fo much from one another, as to render it very diffi-cult to afcertain the fpecies to which they belong ; in order to find out, as well as I could, from what fpe-cies many of thofe varieties have been raifed, I en-deavoured to degenerate as many of the double flower-ing, and others of the beft kinds, fo far as I could, by which I have obferved their feveral changes, and

fhall here mention under each fpecies, the varieties I have obferved.

The firft fort is the common Englifh Daffodil, which grows naturally by the borders of woods and fields in many parts of England ; this hath a large bulbous root, from which comes out five or fix flat leaves, about a foot long, and an inch broad, of a grayifh colour, and a little hollowed in the middle like the keel of a boat. The ftalk rifes a foot and a half high, having two fharp longitudinal angles ; at the top comes out a fingle flower, inclofed in a thin fpa-tha (or fheath), which is torn open on one fide, to make way for the flower to come out, and then wi-thers and remains on the top of the ftalk. The flower is of one petal or leaf, being connected at the bafe, but is cut into fix parts almoft to the bottom, which expand ; in the middle of this is fituated a bell-shaped nectarium, called by the gardeners a cup, which is equal in length to the petal, and ftands erect. The flower nods on the fide of the ftalk. The petal is of a pale brimftone colour, and the nectarium yellow. It flowers the beginning of April, and after the flowers are paft, the germen turns to a roundifh capfule, with three cells filled with roundifh black feeds, which ripen in July. This fort propagates very faft by offsets from the root.

The varieties of this are,

One with white petals, and a pale yellow cup.

One with yellow petals, and a golden cup.

The common double yellow Daffodil.

Another double Daffodil, with three or four cups within each other.

And, I believe, John Tradefcant's Daffodil may be referred to this fpecies.

The fecond fort grows naturally in the fouth of France and in Italy ; this hath a fmaller and rounder bulbous root than the former. The leaves are long-er, narrower, and flatter than thofe of that fort. The ftalks do not rife higher than the leaves, which are of a gray colour : at the top of the ftalk comes out one flower from the fheath, which nods on one fide. The petal of this is cut into fix fegments, which are rounded at their points ; they are of a fnow white, and fpread open flat. In the center is fituated a very fhort nectarium or cup, which is fringed on the border with a bright purple circle. The flowers have an agreeable odour. This flowers in May, but feldom produces feeds, however it increafes faft enough by offsets.

The double white Narciffus is the only variety of this which I have obferved, though there is mentioned in fome books feveral other.

The third fort grows naturally in Spain and Portu-gal, from whence I have received the roots. The bulbs of this fort are very like thofe of the firft. The leaves are longer, of a darker green, and the flower-ftalks rife higher. The fegments of the petal are rounder, and fpread open, flatter than thofe of the firft fort. The nectarium, or cup, in the middle, is about half the length of the petal, and is edged with a gold-coloured fringe. It flowers in April, but feldom pro-duces feeds here. This fort fports and varies more than any of the other : the following variations I have traced in the fame roots.

The roots of thefe, the firft year, produced very dou-ble flowers, of the fort which is commonly called the Incomparable Daffodil. The fix outer fegments of the petal were longer than either of the others, and white ; the middle was very full of fhorter petals, fome of which were white, others yellow, and col-lected into a globular figure : fome of thefe roots, the following year, produced flowers lefs double than be-fore, with no white petals in them, but the larger pe-tals were of a fulphur colour, and the others yellow ; from this they afterward degenerated to half double flowers, and at laft to fingle flowers, with a cup half the length of the petal, in which manner they have continued to flower many years ; fo that we may con-clude, that thofe varieties were firft obtained from the feeds of this fingle flower.

The

The fourth fort grows naturally in the south of France and in Italy, and has been found growing in the fields in some parts of England, but it is likely to have been from some roots which have been thrown out of gardens with rubbish. The roots of this fort are not so large as those of the first, and are rounder ; the leaves are long, of a gray colour, and smoother than those of the first ; the flower-stalks are of the same length with the leaves, and have commonly but one flower in a sheath, but sometimes when the roots are strong, they have two. The flower nods downward, the segments of the petal are a little waved on their edges, the nectarium or cup is short, and bordered with yellow ; it flowers in May. The scent of these flowers is not very agreeable, and as they are not very beautiful, so they are seldom cultivated in gardens, since the finer forts have been plenty. There is no variety of this so far as I have been able to trace, for I could never observe any variation in the flowers.

The fifth fort has some resemblance of the fourth, but the flowers are whiter, the segments of the petal are reflexed, and the border of the nectarium or cup is of a gold yellow colour ; this has some affinity to the second fort.

The sixth fort grows naturally in Portugal, from whence I have received the roots. The bulbs of this kind are small, the leaves are very narrow, having some resemblance to those of the Rush, but are a little compressed, and have a longitudinal furrow on one side ; these are seldom more than eight or nine inches long. The flower-stalk is slender, taper, and about six inches long, sustaining at the top one flower, which is at first inclosed in a sheath ; the petal is scarce half an inch long, and is cut into six acute segments ; the nectarium or cup is more than two inches long, very broad at the brim, lessening gradually to the base, being somewhat formed like the ladies hoop petticoats, from whence the flower is so called. It flowers in April, but does not produce seeds here. There are no varieties of this fort.

The seventh fort grows naturally in Spain ; this hath a small bulbous root ; the leaves are but few in number, and are narrow ; the stalk is jointed, and rises about nine inches high, sustaining at the top one flower, which at first is inclosed in the spatha, or sheath ; the flower is cut into six narrow segments, which are white ; the nectarium, or cup, is yellow. It flowers late in the autumn, and the roots are tender, so are often killed by hard frosts in England, which renders it scarce here.

The eighth fort grows naturally in Portugal, and in the islands of the Archipelago ; as of this there are a greater variety than of all the other species ; for as the flowers are very ornamental, and come early in the spring, so the florists in Holland, Flanders, and France, have taken great pains in cultivating and improving them ; so that at present the catalogues printed by the Dutch florists, contain more than thirty varieties, the principal of which are these hereafter mentioned.

These have yellow petals, with Orange, yellow, or sulphur-coloured cups, or nectariums.

The Great Algiers.	The Most Beautiful.
The Ladies Nosegay.	The Golden Star.
The Greater Bell.	The Mignon.
The Golden Royal.	The Zeylander.
The Golden Scepter.	The Madouse.
The Triumphant.	The Golden Sun.

The following have white petals, with yellow or sulphur-coloured cups or nectariums.

The Archdutchess.	The Greater Bozelman.
The Triumphant Nosegay.	The Czarina.
The New Dorothy.	The Grand Monarque.
The Passe Bozelman.	The Czar of Muscovy.
The Superb.	The Surpassante.

There are some with white petals and white cups, but these are not so much esteemed as the others,

though there are two or three varieties with large bunches of small white flowers, which have a very agreeable odour, so are as valuable as any of the other, and are later in flower than most of the other forts. There is also one with very double flowers, whose outer petals are white, and those in the middle are some white, and others of an Orange-colour, which have a very agreeable scent, and is the earliest in flowering ; it is generally called the Cyprus Narcissus, and seems to be a distinct species from the others. This, like most other double flowers, never produces any seeds, so is only propagated by offsets, and is the most beautiful of all the Narcissus, when blown upon glasses of water in a room ; but when it is planted in the ground, if the bed in which they are planted is not covered with mats in frosty weather, to prevent their flower-buds from being destroyed, they seldom flower ; for the leaves begin to shoot early in the autumn, and the flower-buds appear about Christmas, which are tender, so that if hard frost happen when they are coming out of the ground, it generally kills them ; but if they are properly screened from frost, they will flower in February, and in mild seasons often in January.

The ninth fort is the Jonquil, a flower so well known as to need no description ; of this there is the great and small Jonquil with single flowers, and the common fort with double flowers, which is most esteemed.

I shall first treat of the method for raising the fine forts of Polyanthus Narcissus from seeds, which is the way to obtain new varieties.

The not practising this has occasioned our sending abroad annually for great quantities of flower-roots, which have been kept up to a high price, on account of the great demand for them in England ; whereas if we were as industrious to propagate them as our neighbours, we might soon vie with them, if not out-do them, in most forts of flowers ; as may be seen, by the vast variety of Carnations, Auriculas, Ranunculas, &c. which have been produced from seeds in England, and exceed most of those kinds in any part of Europe.

You must be very careful in saving your seeds, to gather none but from such flowers as have good properties, and particularly from such only as have many flowers upon a stalk, that flower tall, and have beautiful cups to their flowers ; from such you may expect to have good flowers produced ; but if you sow ordinary seed, it is only putting yourself to trouble and expence to no purpose, since from such seeds there can be no hopes of procuring any valuable flowers.

Having provided yourself with good seeds, you must procure either some shallow cases or flat pans, made on purpose for the raising of seedlings, which should have holes in their bottoms, to let the moisture pass off ; these must be filled with fresh, light, sandy earth about the beginning of August (that being the season for sowing the seeds of most bulbous-rooted flowers ;) the earth in these must be levelled very even ; then sow the seeds thereon pretty thick, covering them over with fine sifted light earth about half an inch thick, and place the cases or pans in a situation where they may have only the morning sun till about ten o'clock, where they should remain until the beginning of October, when they must be removed into a warmer situation, placing them upon bricks, that the air may freely pass under the cases, which will preserve them from being too moist.

They should also be exposed to the full sun, but screened from the north and east winds ; and if the frost should be severe, they must be covered, otherwise there will be danger of their being destroyed ; in this situation they may remain until the beginning of April, by which time the plants will be up, when you must carefully clear them from weeds ; and if the season should prove dry, they must be frequently watered : the cases should also now be removed into their former shady position, or shaded in the middle of the day, for the heat of the noon-day sun will be too great for the young plants.

The latter end of June, when the leaves of the plants are decayed, you should take off the upper surface of the earth in the cases (which by that time will have contracted a mossiness, and, if suffered to remain, will greatly injure the young roots) observing not to take it so deep as to touch the roots; then sift some fresh light earth over the surface, about half an inch thick, which will greatly strengthen the roots; the same should also be repeated in October, when the cases are moved again into the sun.

During the summer season, if the weather should prove very wet, you must remove them into the sun till the earth be dry again; for if the roots receive much wet during the time they are inactive, it very often rots them; therefore you must never give them any water after their leaves are decayed, but only place them in the shade, as was before directed.

Thus you should manage them the two first seasons, till their leaves are decayed; but the second summer after sowing, you should carefully take up the roots; which may be done, by lifting the earth in the cases through a fine sieve, whereby the roots will be easily separated from the earth; then having prepared a bed or two of good fresh light earth, in proportion to the quantity of your roots, you should plant them therein, at about three inches distance every way, and about three inches deep in the ground.

These beds should be raised above the level of the ground, in proportion to the moisture of the soil, which if dry, three inches will be enough; but if it be wet, they must be raised six or eight inches high, and laid a little rounding, to shoot off the wet.

If these beds are made in July, which is the best time to transplant the roots, the weeds will soon appear very thick; therefore you should gently hoe the surface of the ground to destroy them, being very careful not to cut so deep as to touch any of the roots; and this should be repeated as often as may be found necessary, by the growth of the weeds, observing always to do it in dry weather, that they may be effectually destroyed; and toward the latter end of October, after having entirely cleared the beds from weeds, you should sift a little rich light earth over them, about an inch thick; the goodness of which will be washed down to the roots by the winter's rain, which will greatly encourage their shooting in the spring.

If the cold should be very severe in winter, you should cover the beds either with old tan or sea coal ashes, or in want of these with Pease-haulm, or some such light covering, to prevent the frost from penetrating the ground to the roots, which might greatly injure them while they are so young.

In the spring, when the plants begin to appear above ground, you must gently stir the surface of the ground, clearing it from weeds, &c. in doing of which, you should be very careful not to injure the plants; and if the season should prove dry, you should now and then gently refresh them with water, which will strengthen the roots.

When their leaves are decayed, you should clear the beds from weeds, and sift a little earth over them (as was before directed) which must also be repeated in October, in like manner; but the roots should not remain longer in these beds than two years, by which time they will have grown so large as to require more room; therefore they should be taken up as soon as their leaves are decayed, and planted into fresh beds, which should be dug deep, and a little very rotten dung buried in the bottom, for the fibres of the roots to strike into. Then the roots should be planted at six inches distance, and the same depth in the ground.

In the autumn, before the frost comes on, if some rotten tan is laid over the beds, it will keep out the frost, and greatly encourage the roots; and if the winter should prove severe, it will be proper to lay a greater thickness of tan over the beds, and also in the alleys, to keep out frost, or to cover them over with Straw, or Pease-haulm, otherwise they may be all destroyed by the cold. In the spring these coverings should be removed, as soon as the danger of hard frosts is over, and the beds must be kept clean from weeds the following summer: at Michaelmas they should have some fresh earth laid over the beds, and covered again with tan, and so every year continued till the roots flower, which is generally in five years from seed, when you should mark all such as promise well, which should be taken up as soon as their leaves decay, and planted at a greater distance in new prepared beds; but those which do not flower, or those you do not greatly esteem, should be permitted to remain in the same bed; therefore, in taking up those roots which you marked, you must be careful not to disturb the roots of those left, and also to level the earth again, and sift some fresh earth over the beds (as before) to encourage the roots; for it often happens in the seedlings of these flowers, that at their first time of blowing, their flowers seldom appear half so beautiful as they do the second year; for which reason none of them should be rejected until they have flowered two or three times, that so you may be assured of their worth.

Thus having laid down directions for the sowing and managing these roots, until they are strong enough to flower, I shall proceed to give some instructions for planting and managing the roots afterwards, so as to cause them to produce large fair flowers.

All the sorts of Narcissus which produce many flowers upon a stalk, should have a situation defended from cold and strong winds, otherwise they will be subject to be injured by the cold in winter, and their stems broken down when in flower; for notwithstanding their stalks are generally pretty strong, yet the number of flowers upon each renders their heads weighty, especially after rain, which lodges in the flowers, and, if succeeded by strong winds, very often destroys their beauty, if they are exposed thereto; so that a border under a hedge, which is open to the south-east, is preferable to any other position for these flowers.

The morning sun rising upon them will dry off the moisture which had lodged upon them the preceding night, and cause them to expand fairer than when they are planted in a shady situation; and if they are too much exposed to the afternoon sun, they will be hurried out of their beauty very soon; and the strong winds usually coming from the west and south-west points, they will be exposed to the fury of them, which frequently is very injurious to them.

Having made choice of a proper situation, you must then proceed to prepare the earth necessary to plant them in; for if the natural soil of the place be very strong or poor, it will be proper to make the border of new earth, removing the former soil away about three feet deep. The best earth for these flowers is a fresh, light, hazel loam, mixed with a little very rotten neats dung: this should be well mixed together, and often turned over, in order to sweeten it; then having removed away the old earth to the fore-mentioned depth, you should put a layer of rotten dung or tan in the bottom, about four or five inches thick, upon which you must lay some of the prepared earth about eighteen or twenty inches thick, making it exactly level; then having marked out by line the exact distances at which the roots are to be planted (which should not be less than six or eight inches square) you must place the roots accordingly, observing to set them upright; then you must cover them over with the before-mentioned earth about eight inches deep, being very careful in doing it, not to displace the roots; when this is done, you must make the surface of the border even, and make up the side straight, which will appear handsome.

The best time for planting these roots is in the end of August, or beginning of September; for if they are kept too long out of the ground, it will cause their flowers to be weak. You should also observe the nature of the soil where they are planted, and whether

ther the fituation be wet or dry, according to which you fhould adapt the frefh earth, and order the beds ; for if the foil be very ftrong and the fituation moift, you fhould then make choice of a light earth, and raife the beds fix or eight inches, or a foot, above the level of the ground, otherwife the roots will be in danger of perifhing by too much wet ; but if the fituation be dry and the foil naturally light, you fhould then allow the earth to be a little ftronger, and the beds fhould not be raifed above three or four inches high ; for if they are made too high, the roots will fuffer very much, if the fpring fhould prove dry, nor would the flowers be near fo fair. As alfo in very fevere winters, thofe beds which are raifed much above the level of the ground, will be more expofed to the cold than thofe which are lower, unlefs the alleys are filled up with rotten tan or litter.

During the fummer, the only culture thefe flowers require is, to keep them free from weeds ; and when their leaves are entirely decayed, they fhould be raked off, and the beds made clean : but by no means cut off their leaves till they are quite decayed, as is by fome practifed, for that greatly weakens the roots.

Towards the middle of October, if the weeds have grown upon the beds, you fhould in a dry day gently hoe the furface of the ground to deftroy them, obferving to rake it over fmooth again ; and before the frofts come on, the beds fhould be covered over two inches thick with rotten tan, to keep out the froft ; after which they will require no farther care till the fpring, when their leaves will appear above ground ; at which time you fhould gently ftir the furface of the earth with a fmall trowel, being very careful not to injure the leaves of the plants, and rake it fmooth with your hands, clearing off all weeds, &c. which, if fuffered to remain at that feafon, will foon grow fo faft as to appear unfightly, and will exhauft the nourifhment from the earth. With this management thefe roots will flower very ftrong, fome of which will appear in March, and the others in April ; which, if fuffered to remain, will continue in beauty a full month, and are, at that feafon, very great ornaments to a flower-garden.

After the flowers are paft, and the leaves decayed, you fhould ftir the furface of the ground, to prevent the weeds from growing, and if at the fame time you lay a little very rotten dung over the furface of the beds, the rain will wafh down the falts thereof, which will greatly encourage the roots the fucceeding year.

During the fummer feafon they will require no farther care, but to keep them clear from weeds till October, when the furface of the beds fhould be again ftirred, raking off all weeds, &c. and laying fome good frefh earth over the beds about an inch deep, which will make good the lofs fuftained by weeding, &c. and in the fpring you muft manage as was directed for the preceding year.

Thefe roots fhould not be tranfplanted oftener than every third year, if they are expected to flower ftrong and make a great increafe ; becaufe the firft year after removing, they never flower fo ftrong as they do the fecond and third ; nor will the roots increafe fo faft, when they are often tranfplanted ; but if you let them remain longer than three years unremoved, the number of offsets which by that time will be produced, will weaken the large bulbs, and caufe them to produce very weak flowers ; therefore at the time of tranfplanting them, all the fmall offsets fhould be taken off, and planted in a nurfery-bed by themfelves, but the large bulbs may be planted again for flowering. If you plant them in the fame bed where they grew before, you muft take out all the earth two feet deep, and fill it up again with frefh, in the manner before directed, which will be equal to removing them into another place : this is the conftant practice of the gardeners in Holland, who have but little room to change their roots ; therefore they every year remove the earth of their beds, and put in frefh, fo that the

fame place is conftantly occupied by the like flowers. But thofe people take up their roots every year, for as they cultivate them for fale, the rounder their roots are, the more valuable they will be : the way to have them fo is, to take their offsets from them annually ; for when their roots are left two or three years unremoved, the offsets will have grown large, and thefe preffing againft each other, will caufe their fides to be flatted ; fo that where the roots are propagated for fale, they fhould be annually taken up as foon as their leaves decay ; and the large bulbs may be kept out of the ground till the middle or end of October, but the offsets fhould be planted the beginning of September or fooner, that they may get ftrength, fo as to become blowing roots the following year : but where they are defigned for ornament, they fhould not be removed oftener than every third year, for then the roots will be in large bunches, and a number of ftalks with flowers coming from each bunch, they will make a much better appearance than where a fingle ftalk rifes from each root, which will be the cafe when the roots are annually removed.

The common forts of Daffodil are generally planted in large borders of the pleafure-garden, where, being intermixed with other bulbous-rooted flowers, they afford an agreeable variety in their feafons of flowering. Thefe roots are very hardy, and will thrive in almoft any foil or fituation, which renders them very proper for rural gardens, where, being planted under the fhade of trees, they will thrive for feveral years without tranfplanting, and produce annually in the fpring great quantities of flowers, which will make a good appearance before the trees come out in leaf.

The Jonquils fhould be planted in beds or borders, feparate from other roots, becaufe thefe require to be tranfplanted at leaft every year, otherwife their roots are apt to grow long and flender, and feldom flower well after ; which is alfo the cafe, if they are continued many years in the fame foil ; wherefore the roots fhould be often removed from one part of the garden to another, or at leaft, the earth fhould be often renewed, which is the moft probable method to preferve their flowers in perfection.

The foil in which thefe flowers fucceed beft, is an hazel loam, neither too light nor over ftiff ; it muft be frefh, and free from roots of trees or noxious weeds, but fhould not be dunged ; for it is very remarkable, that where the ground is made rich, they feldom continue good very long, but are fubject to fhoot downwards, and form long flender roots.

Thefe flowers are greatly efteemed by many people for their ftrong fweet fcent, though there be very few ladies that can bear the fmell of them ; fo powerful is it, that many times it overcomes their fpirits, efpecially if confined in a room ; for which reafon, they fhould never be planted too clofe to a habitation, left they become offenfive ; nor fhould the flowers be placed in fuch rooms where company is entertained.

NASTURTIUM. See LEPIDIUM.

NASTURTIUM INDICUM. See TROPÆOLUM.

NATURAL is belonging to, or proceeding from nature.

NATURE is a term varioufly ufed ; and Mr. Boyle, in a treatife of the vulgarly received notion of Nature, gives us eight principal ones.

1. Nature is ufed for the fyftem of the world, the machine of the univerfe, or the affemblage of all created beings.

In this fenfe we fay, the author of Nature, meaning GOD ; and fpeaking of the fun, call him the father of Nature, becaufe he warms the earth, and makes it fruitful ; and the eye of Nature, becaufe he illuminates the univerfe ; and of a phœnix, a unicorn, a griffin, a fatyr, that there are no fuch things in Nature.

2. Nature, in a more confined fenfe, comprehends the feveral kinds of beings, created and uncreated, corporeal and fpiritual : thus we fay, human Nature, i. e. all men who poffefs the fame rational fouls ; angelical Nature, divine Nature.

3. Nature,

3. Nature, in a ftill more reftrained fenfe, is ufed for the effence of a thing, or that attribute that makes a thing what it is; as, it is the Nature of the foul to think.

4. Nature is particularly ufed for the eftablifhed order and courfe of material things, the feries of the fecond caufes, or the laws that God has impofed on the motions imprefied by him. In this fenfe we fay, the day and night, by Nature, fucceed one another; phyfic is the ftudy of Nature; refpiration is by Nature neceffary to life.

5. Nature is alfo ufed to fignify an aggregate of powers, which belong to any body, efpecially a living one. Thus we fay, Nature is ftrong, Nature is weak, Nature is fpent, &c.

6. Nature is alfo more ftrictly ufed for the action of providence, the principle of all things, or that fpiritual being which is diffufed throughout the creation, and moves and acts in all bodies, and gives them certain properties, and procures certain effects. In this fenfe, Nature fignifies the qualities or virtues that God has given to his creatures, animal, vegetable, &c. In fpeaking of the action of Nature, no more is to be underftood, but that bodies act on one another in a manner agreeable to the general laws of motion which the Creator has eftablifhed.

NEBULOSE, or NEBULOUS, fignifies cloudy, mifty, foggy, hazy.

NECTARINE [properly fo called of nectar, the poetical drink of the Gods] Nectarine.

This fruit fhould have been placed under the article of Peaches, to which it properly belongs, differing from them in nothing more than in having a fmooth rind, and the flefh being firmer. Thefe the French diftinguifh by the name of Brugnon, as they do thofe Peaches which adhere to the ftone, by the name of Pavies, retaining the name of Péfche to only fuch as part from the ftone; but fince the writers in gardening have diftinguifhed this fruit by the name of Nectarine from the Peaches, fo I fhall follow their example, left by endeavouring to rectify their miftakes, I fhould render myfelf lefs intelligible to the reader. I fhall therefore mention the feveral varieties of this fruit, which have come to my knowledge :

1. Fairchild's early Nectarine. This is one of the earlieft ripe Nectarines we have; it is a fmall round fruit, about the fize of the Nutmeg Peach, of a beautiful red colour, and well flavoured; it ripens the end of July.

2. Elruge Nectarine : the tree has fawed leaves; the flowers are fmall; it is a middle-fized fruit, of a dark red or purple colour next the fun, but of a pale yellow or greenifh colour towards the wall; it parts from the ftone, and has a foft melting juice : this ripens in the beginning of Auguft.

3. Newington Nectarine : the tree has fawed leaves; the flowers are large and open; it is a fair large fruit, (when planted on a good foil) of a beautiful red colour next the fun, but of a bright yellow towards the wall; it has an excellent rich juice; the pulp adheres clofely to the ftone, where it is of a deep red colour : this ripens the latter end of Auguft, and is the beft flavoured of all the forts, or perhaps of any known fruit in the world.

4. Scarlet Nectarine is fomewhat lefs than the laft, of a fine red or fcarlet colour next the fun, but lofes itfelf in paler red towards the wall : this ripens in the end of Auguft.

5. Brugnon or Italian Nectarine, has fmooth leaves; the flowers are fmall; it is a fair large fruit, of a deep red colour next the fun, but of a foft yellow towards the wall; the pulp is firm, of a rich flavour, and clofely adheres to the ftone, where it is very red : this ripens in the end of Auguft.

6. Roman Red Nectarine has fmooth leaves, and large flowers; it is a large fair fruit, of a deep red or purple colour towards the fun, but has a yellowifh caft next the wall; the flefh is firm, of an excellent flavour, clofely adhering to the ftone, where it is very red : this ripens in September.

7. Murry Nectarine is a middle fized fruit, of a dirty red colour on the fide next the fun, but of a yellowifh green towards the wall, the pulp is tolerably well flavoured : this ripens the beginning of September.

8. Golden Nectarine is a fair handfome fruit, of a foft red colour next the fun, but of a bright yellow next the wall; the pulp is very yellow, of a rich flavour, and clofely adheres to the ftone, where it is of a faint red colour : this ripens the middle of September.

9. Temple's Nectarine is a middle-fized fruit, of a foft red colour next the fun, of a yellowifh green toward the wall : the pulp is melting, of a white colour towards the ftone, from which it parts, and has a fine poignant flavour; this ripens the end of September.

10. Peterborough, or late green Nectarine, is a middle fized fruit, of a pale green colour on the outfide next the fun, but of a whitifh green towards the wall; the flefh is firm, and, in a good feafon, tolerably well flavoured; this ripens the middle of October. There are fome perfons who pretend to have more varieties than I have here enumerated, but I much doubt whether they are different, there being fo near a refemblance between the fruits of this kind, that it requires a very clofe attention to diftinguifh them well, efpecially if the trees grow in different foils and afpects, which many times alters the fame fruit fo much, as hardly to be diftinguifhed by perfons who are very converfant with them; therefore, in order to be thoroughly acquainted with their differences, it is neceffary to confider the fhape and fize of their leaves, the fize of their flowers, their manner of fhooting, &c. which is many times very helpful in knowing of thefe fruits.

The culture of this fruit differing in nothing from that of the Peach, I fhall forbear mentioning any thing on that head in this place, to avoid repetition, but only wifh thofe perfons who propagate this fruit, will take their buds from bearing trees, and not from young nurfery trees, as is too often practifed; however, I fhall refer the reader to the article PERSICA, where there is an ample account of their planting, pruning, &c.

NEMORAL fignifies belonging to a wood or grove.

NEPETA. Lin. Gen. Plant. 629. Cataria. Tourn. Inft. R. H. 202. tab. 95. Catmint, or Nep; in French, *Herbes aux Chats.*

The CHARACTERS are,

The empalement of the flower is tubulous and cylindrical, indented into five acute parts at the top. The flower is of the lip kind, with one petal, having an incurved cylindrical tube, gaping at the top. The upper lip is erect, roundifh, and indented at the point. The under lip is large, concave, entire, and fawed on the edge. It hath four awl-fhaped ftamina fituated under the upper lip, two of which are fhorter than the other, terminated by incumbent fummits. In the bottom of the tube is fituated the quadrifid germen, fupporting a flender ftyle, crowned by a bifid acute ftigma. The germen afterward turns to four oval feeds, fitting in the empalement.

This genus of plants is ranged in the firft fection of Linnæus's fourteenth clafs, which includes thofe plants whofe flowers have two long and two fhorter ftamina, and are fucceeded by naked feeds fitting in the empalement.

The SPECIES are,

1. NEPETA (*Cataria*) floribus fpicatis, verticillis fubpedicellatis, foliis petiolatis cordatis dentato-ferratis. Lin. Sp. Plant. 796. *Catmint with fpiked flowers, whofe whorls have very fhort foot-ftalks, and heart-fhaped leaves growing on foot-ftalks, which are indented like the teeth of a faw.* Cataria major vulgaris. Tourn. Inft. R. H. 202. *Common greater Catmint.*

2. NEPETA (*Minor*) floribus fpicatis, fpicis interruptis, verticillis pedicellatis, foliis fubcordatis ferratis petiolatis. Cataria minor vulgaris. *Catmint with fpikes of flowers, with interrupted whorls ftanding on foot-ftalks, and fawed leaves, with foot-ftalks almoft heart-fhaped.* Cataria minor vulgaris.

garis. Tourn. Inſt. R. H. 202. *Smaller common Cat-*
mint.

3. NEPETA (*Anguſtifolia*) floribus ſpicatis, verticillis ſubſeſſilibus, foliis cordato-oblongis ſerratis ſeſſilibus.
Catmint with ſpiked flowers, whoſe whorls grow almoſt
cloſe to the ſtalks, and oblong, ſawed, heart-ſhaped leaves,
ſitting cloſe. Cataria anguſtifolia major. Tourn. Inſt.
R. H. 202. *Greater narrow-leaved Catmint.*

4. NEPETA (*Paniculata*) floribus paniculatis, foliis oblongo cordatis acutis ſerratis ſeſſilibus. *Catmint with*
panicled flowers, and oblong, heart-ſhaped, acute, ſawed
leaves, ſitting cloſe to the ſtalks. Cataria quæ nepeta
minor, folio meliſſæ Turcicæ. Boerh. Ind. alt. 1. 174.
Smaller Catmint with a Turkey Balm leaf.

5. NEPETA (*Italica*) floribus ſeſſilibus verticillato-ſpica-
tis, bracteis lanceolatis longitudine calycis, foliis petiolatis. Lin. Sp. Plant. 798. *Catmint whoſe flowers*
grow in whorled ſpikes, ſitting cloſe to the ſtalk, having
ſpear-ſhaped bractea the length of the empalement, with
leaves growing upon the foot-ſtalks. Cataria minor
Alpina. Tourn. Inſt. R. H. 202. *Smaller Alpine*
Catmint.

6. NEPETA (*Violacea*) verticillis pedunculatis corymboſis, foliis petiolatis cordato-oblongis dentatis. Lin.
Sp. Plant. 797. *Catmint with roundiſh whorls ſtanding*
upon foot-ſtalks, and oblong, heart-ſhaped, indented leaves.
Cataria Hiſpanica, betonicæ folio anguſtiore flore cæruleo. Tourn. Inſt. R. H. 202. *Spaniſh Catmint with*
a narrow Betony leaf, and a blue flower.

7. NEPETA (*Tuberoſa*) ſpicis ſeſſilibus, bracteis ovatis
coloratis, foliis ſummis ſeſſilibus. Hort. Cliff. 311.
Catmint with ſpiked flowers ſitting cloſe to the ſtalks, oval
coloured bractea, and the upper leaves ſitting cloſe to the
ſtalks. Cataria Hiſpanica, ſupina, betonicæ folio,
tuberoſa radice. Tourn. Inſt. R. H. 202. *Spaniſh Cat-*
mint with a declining ſtalk, a Betony leaf, and a tube-
rous root.

8. NEPETA (*Hirſuta*) floribus ſeſſilibus verticillato-ſpi-
catis, verticillis tomento obvolutis. Hort. Cliff. 311.
Catmint with flowers growing in whorled ſpikes ſitting
cloſe to the ſtalk, and the whorls covered with down.
Horminum ſpicatum lavendulæ flore & odore. Bocc.
Plant. Sic. 48. tab. 25. *Spiked Clary with a Lavender*
ſmell and flower.

9. NEPETA (*Virginica*) foliis lanceolatis, capitulis terminalibus, ſtaminibus flore longioribus. Lin. Sp.
Plant. 571. *Catmint with ſpear-ſhaped leaves, ſtalks ter-*
minated by flowers growing in heads, and ſtamina longer
than the flower. Clinopodium æmaraci folio, floribus
albis. Pluk. Alm. 110. *Field Baſil with a Marjoram*
leaf, and a white flower.

10. NEPETA (*Orientalis*) floribus ſpicatis, verticillis craſſioribus, foliis cordatis obtuſè dentatis petiolatis. *Cat-*
mint with ſpiked flowers, whoſe whorls are very thick,
and heart-ſhaped leaves which are obtuſely indented, and
ſtand upon foot-ſtalks. Cataria Orientalis, teucrii folio,
lavendulæ odore, verticillis florum craſſiſſimis. Tourn.
Cor. Inſt. 13. *Eaſtern Catmint with a Tree Germander*
leaf ſmelling like Lavender, and very thick whorls to the
flowers.

11. NEPETA (*Procumbens*) floribus verticillatis, bracteis
ovatis hirſutis, foliis cordato-ovatis crenatis, caule
procumbente. *Catmint with whorled flowers, having*
oval hairy bractea, oval heart-ſhaped leaves, which are
crenated, and a trailing ſtalk.

The firſt ſort is the common Nep, or Catmint, which
grows naturally on the ſide of banks and hedges in
many parts of England; this has a perennial root,
from which ariſe many branching ſtalks, which are
four-cornered, about two feet high, garniſhed at each
joint by two heart-ſhaped leaves ſtanding oppoſite,
upon pretty long foot-ſtalks; they are ſawed on their
edges, and are hoary on their under ſide. The flowers grow in ſpikes at the top of the ſtalks, and below
the ſpikes are two or three whorls of flowers, which
have very ſhort foot-ſtalks. The flowers are white,
and have two lips; the upper lip ſtands erect, and
the lower is a little reflexed, and indented at the
point; theſe are each ſucceeded by four oval black
ſeeds, which ripen in the empalement.

The whole plant has a ſtrong ſcent between Mint and
Penny Royal; it is called Catmint, becauſe the cats
are very fond of it, eſpecially when it is withered, for
then they will roll themſelves on it, and tear it to
pieces, chewing it in their mouths with great pleaſure. Mr. Ray mentions his having tranſplanted
ſome of the plants of this ſort from the fields, into
his garden, which were ſoon deſtroyed by the cats,
but the plants which came up from ſeeds in his garden eſcaped, which verifies the old proverb, viz. " If
" you let it the cats will eat it, if you ſow it the cats
" will not know it." I have frequently made trial of
this, and have always found it true; for I have tranſplanted one of the plants from another part of the
garden, within two feet of ſome plants which came
up from ſeeds, the latter has remained unhurt, when
the former has been torn to pieces and deſtroyed by
the cats; but I have always obſerved, where there is
a large quantity of the herb growing together, they
will not meddle with it. This flowers in June and
July, and the ſeeds ripen in autumn. It is uſed in
medicine.

The ſecond ſort grows naturally in Italy, and the
ſouth of France; the ſtalks of this are ſlendere, their
joints farther aſunder, the leaves are narrower, and
the whole plant whiter than the firſt. The ſpikes of
flowers are divided into whorls; the lower of theſe
are two inches apart, others are an inch, and the upper half an inch, and theſe differences are permanent, for I have always found the ſeeds produce the
ſame kind.

The ſtalks of the third ſort do not branch ſo much as
either of the former; they are ſlenderer, and their
joints farther aſunder; the leaves are ſmall, narrow,
and almoſt heart-ſhaped, ſawed on their edges, hoary,
and ſtand upon ſhort foot-ſtalks. The ſpikes of flowers
are more broken, or interrupted than thoſe of the ſecond, and the whorls ſtand upon foot-ſtalks. It grows
naturally in Italy.

The fourth ſort grows naturally in Sicily; this riſes
with a ſtrong four-cornered ſtalk near three feet
high; the lower joints are four or five inches aſunder.
The leaves are long, narrow, and heart-ſhaped, deeply
ſawed on their edges, and ſet pretty cloſe to the ſtalk.
The flowers grow in panicles along the ſtalks, and are
of a pale purpliſh colour. It flowers about the ſame
time with the other ſorts.

The fifth ſort grows naturally upon the Alps; the
ſtalks of this ſeldom riſe more than a foot and a half
high, ſending out very few branches. The whorls of
flowers which form the ſpike, are diſtant from each
other, and ſet cloſe to the ſtalk. The leaves are ſhort,
oval, heart-ſhaped, and ſtand upon foot-ſtalks; the
plant is hoary, and ſtrong ſcented.

The ſixth ſort grows naturally in Spain; the ſtalks of
this riſe about two feet high, and have a few ſlender
branches coming out from the ſides. The leaves are
heart-ſhaped, and indented on their edges. The
flowers grow in roundiſh whorls, upon foot-ſtalks,
and are blue; there is alſo a variety of this with white
flowers.

The ſeventh ſort grows naturally in Portugal; this
has a thick knobbed root, from which comes out one
or two ſtalks, which often decline to the ground;
they are about two feet and a half long, and ſend out
two ſide branches oppoſite. The leaves are oblong,
crenated on their edges, and ſit cloſe to the ſtalks,
and are of a deep green. The upper part of the ſtalk,
for more than a foot in length, is garniſhed with
whorls of flowers, the lower being two inches aſunder,
but are nearer all the way upward; theſe ſit very cloſe
to the ſtalks, and are guarded by oval, ſmall, coloured
leaves, or bracteæ. The flowers are blue, and ſhaped like thoſe of the other ſpecies; there is one of this
ſort with an erect ſtalk, which is the only difference
between them.

The eighth ſort grows naturally in Sicily. The ſtalks
of this grow about two feet high; the branches come
out toward the bottom; they are heart-ſhaped, obtuſe, and but little indented, ſtanding upon pretty

     long

long foot-ftalks. The ftalks are terminated by long fpikes of whorled flowers, which are feparated, and fit clofe to them; thefe are wrapped in a hoary down. The flowers are white, and appear in July.

The ninth fort grows naturally in North America; this hath a perennial root, from which arife feveral four-cornered ftalks two feet high, which are garnifhed with hairy leaves, fomewhat like thofe of Marjoram, but are larger. The flowers grow in whorls round the ftalks, and alfo at the extremity of the ftalk, in a large roundifh whorl or head; they are of a pale flefh colour, and their ftamina is longer than the petal. It flowers in July.

The tenth fort grows naturally in the Levant, from whence the feeds were fent to Paris, by Dr. Tournefort. The ftalks of this are ftrong, and rife near three feet high. The leaves are heart-fhaped, and have blunt indentures on their edges, ftanding upon fhort foot-ftalks. The flowers grow in whorled fpikes at the top of the ftalks; the whorls are very thick, and fet clofe together, terminating in an obtufe point. The flowers are of a pale flefh colour; the whole plant is hoary, and has a ftrong fcent.

The eleventh fort grows naturally among the rocks in Candia, where it is ufed as Water Germander by the inhabitants; this hath four-cornered ftalks a foot long, which trail upon the ground, fending out fome flender branches from the fide. The leaves are very like thofe of the round-leaved Mentaftrum, fitting clofe to the ftalk. The flowers grow in thick roundifh whorls, which fit clofe to the ftalk, and are furrounded by oval hairy leaves, or bractea. The flowers are white, and juft peep out of their empalements. The roots of this fort feldom continue longer than two years, but as the feeds ripen well, fo if they are permitted to fcatter, the plants will come up the following fpring.

All the forts are very hardy, fo are not injured by froft: they are eafily propagated by feeds, for if they are permitted to fall, the plants will rife without trouble; or if the feeds are fown, either in the fpring or autumn, the plants will come up, and require no other culture but to thin them where they are too clofe, and keep them clean from weeds. If thefe plants are fown upon a poor dry foil, they will not grow too rank, but will continue much longer, and appear handfomer than in rich ground, where they grow too luxuriant, and have not fo ftrong a fcent.

NERIUM. Lin. Gen. Plant. 262. Nerion. Tourn. Inft. R. H. 604. tab. 374. The Oleander, or Rofe Bay; in French, *Laurier Rofe.*

The CHARACTERS are,

The empalement of the flower is permanent, and cut into five acute fegments. The flower has one funnel-fhaped petal. The tube is cylindrical; the border is large, and cut into five broad obtufe fegments, which are oblique. It hath a nectarium terminating the tube, which are torn into hairy fegments. It hath five fhort awl-fhaped ftamina within the tube, with arrow-pointed fummits joining together, terminated by a long thread. It hath an oblong germen, which is bifid, with fcarce any ftyle, crowned by fingle ftigma. The germen afterward turns to two long, taper, acute-pointed pods, filled with oblong feeds, lying over each other like the fcales of fifh, and crowned with down.

This genus of plants is ranged in the firft fection of Linnæus's fifth clafs, which contains thofe plants whofe flowers have five ftamina and one ftyle.

The SPECIES are,

1. NERIUM (*Oleander*) foliis lineari-lanceolatis ternis. Hort. Cliff. 76. *Oleander, or Rofe Bay, with linear fpear-fhaped leaves, which are placed by threes round the ftalk.* Nerion floribus rubefcentibus. C. B. P. 464. *Oleander with red flowers.*

2. NERIUM (*Indicum*) foliis linearibus rigidis. *Oleander, or Rofe Bay, with linear rigid leaves.* Nerium Indicum, anguftifolium, floribus odoratis fimplicibus.

H. L. *Narrow-leaved Indian Rofe Bay, with fingle fweet-fcented flowers.*

3. NERIUM (*Latifolium*) foliis lanceolatis longioribus flaccidis. *Rofe Bay with longer, fpear-fhaped, flaccid leaves.* Nerium Indicum latifolium, floribus odoratis plenis. H. L. *Broad-leaved Indian Rofe Bay with double fweet flowers, commonly called the double Oleander.*

The firft fort grows naturally in Greece, and in feveral countries near the Mediterranean fea, generally by the fides of rivers and brooks: there are two varieties of this, one with white, the other with red flowers, but feem to have no other difference, fo may properly be placed together as one fpecies, though that with white flowers is rarely found growing wild in any place but the ifland of Crete.

Thefe rife with feveral ftalks to the height of eight or ten feet. The branches come out by threes round the principal ftalks, and have a fmooth bark, which in the red flowering is of a purplifh colour, but the white fort hath a light green bark. The leaves for the moft part ftand by threes round the ftalks, upon very fhort foot-ftalks, and point upward; they are about three or four inches long, and three quarters of an inch broad in the middle, of a dark green, very ftiff, and end in acute points. The flowers come out at the end of the branches, in large loofe bunches, which are in one of a bright purple, or crimfon colour, and in the other they are of a dirty white; they have fhort tubes, and fpread open at the top, where they are deeply cut into five obtufe fegments, which are twifted at bottom, fo are oblique to the tube. At the mouth of the tube, the torn capillary nectarium is fituated, and within the tube are the five ftamina, with the germen at bottom, which afterward turns to a brown, taper, double pod, about four inches long, which opens longitudinally on one fide, and is filled with oblong feeds, crowned with long hairy down, lying over each other like the fcales of fifh. This plant flowers in July and Auguft, and in warm feafons they are fucceeded by pods, but the feeds feldom ripen well here.

When the fummers are warm and dry, thefe plants make a fine appearance, for then they open and flower in great plenty; but, in cold moift feafons, the flowers often decay without expanding, and the fort with white flowers is more tender than the red; fo that unlefs the weather is warm and dry at the time the flowers appear, they rot, and make no figure, unlefs they are placed under glaffes to fcreen them.

The fecond fort grows naturally in India; this rifes with fhrubby ftalks fix or feven feet high, which are covered with a brown bark, and garnifhed with ftiff leaves from three to four inches long, and not more than a quarter of an inch broad; they are of a light green, and their edges are reflexed; thefe are placed fometimes oppofite, at others they are alternate, and fometimes by threes round the branches. The flowers are produced in loofe bunches at the end of the branches; they are of a pale red, and have an agreeable mufky fcent. It flowers at the fame time with the former, but thefe flowers feldom open here in the open air, fo that unlefs the plants are placed in an airy glafs-cafe, where they are defended from wet and cold, they feldom flower well.

The third fort grows naturally in both Indies; this plant was firft introduced to the Britifh Iflands in America, from the Spanifh Main, and is called by the inhabitants of thofe iflands South Sea Rofe; the beauty and fweetnefs of its flowers engaged the inhabitants of the iflands to cultivate the plants, fo that in many places they were planted to form hedges; but the cattle browzing upon them, when there was fcarcity of food, were many of them killed, which has occafioned their being deftroyed in places expofed to cattle; fo that now they are only preferved in gardens, where they make a fine appearance great part of the year, for in thofe warm countries they are feldom

dom deſtitute of flowers. This has been by ſome perſons, who have only a ſuperficial knowledge of plants, thought only a variety of the common ſort, but thoſe who have cultivated both, know better; for the firſt will live through the winter in the open air, in a warm ſituation, but this is too tender to thrive in England, unleſs preſerved in a warm green-houſe; nor will the plants flower without the aſſiſtance of a glaſs-caſe in ſummer. The third ſort was not known here till the beginning of laſt century, being a ſtranger in Europe, but the former has been in the Engliſh gardens near two centuries: nor has the ſeeds of the firſt ever produced plants of the third ſort, though this has been poſitively aſſerted by perſons of no ſkill.

The leaves of this ſort are ſix inches long, and one inch broad in the middle, of a much thinner texture than thoſe of the firſt, and their ends are generally reflexed; they are of a light green, and irregularly placed on the branches; ſometimes they are by pairs, at others alternate, and ſometimes by threes round the branches. The flowers are produced in very large bunches at the end of the branches, ſtanding upon long foot-ſtalks; they have three or four ſeries of petals within each other, ſo are more or leſs double. The flowers are much larger than thoſe of the common ſort, and ſmell like the flowers of Hawthorn. The plain flowers are of a ſoft red, or Peach colour; but in moſt they are beautifully variegated with a deeper red, and make a fine appearance. Their uſual time of flowering is in July and Auguſt, but if they are placed in a warm ſtove, they will continue in flower till Michaelmas. As the flowers of this are double, they are not ſucceeded by ſeeds; and at preſent we are unacquainted with the ſingle flowering of this kind, for the ſecond is undoubtedly a diſtinct ſpecies.

All the ſpecies of the Roſe Bay are ſuppoſed to have a poiſonous quality; the young branches, when cut or broken, have a milky ſap or juice, and the larger branches, when burnt, emit a very diſagreeable odour, ſo there is great reaſon to believe the plants have ſome noxious quality; but this genus of plants has been confounded by many of the writers on botany with the Chamærhododendros of Tournefort, and many of the noxious qualities with which the latter abounds, have been applied to the Nerium, but particularly that of the honey, about Trebiſond, which is reckoned very unwholſome, which has been ſuppoſed to be occaſioned by the bees ſucking it from the flowers of the Nerium; whereas it is from the flowers of the Chamærhododendros, as Tournefort has fully informed us; but the affinity of their names in the Greek language has occaſioned theſe two plants to be often confounded.

Theſe plants are generally propagated by layers in this country, for although they will ſometimes take root from cuttings, yet that being an uncertain method, the other is generally purſued; and as the plants are very apt to produce ſuckers, or ſhoots from their roots, thoſe are beſt adapted for laying, for the old branches will not put out roots; when theſe are laid down, they ſhould be ſlit at a joint, in the ſame manner as is practiſed in laying of Carnations, which will greatly facilitate their taking root: if theſe branches are laid down in autumn, and are properly ſupplied with water, they will have taken root by that time twelvemonth, when they ſhould be carefully raiſed up with a trowel; and if they have taken good root, they ſhould be cut off from the old plant, and each planted in a ſeparate ſmall pot, filled with ſoft loamy earth; thoſe of the common ſort will require no other care, but to be placed in a ſhady ſituation, and gently watered as the ſeaſon may require, till they have taken new root; but the two other ſpecies ſhould be plunged into a very moderate hot-bed, to forward their taking root, obſerving to ſhade them from the ſun in the heat of the day; after the common ſort has taken new root, the plants may be placed in a ſheltered ſituation with other hardy exo-

tics, where they may remain till the end of October, when they ſhould either be removed into the green-houſe, or placed under a hot-bed frame, where they may be protected from froſt in winter, but enjoy the free air at all times when the weather is mild.

This ſort is ſo hardy as to live abroad in mild winters, if planted in a warm ſituation; but as they are liable to be deſtroyed in ſevere froſt, the beſt way is to keep the plants in pots, or if they are very large in tubs, that they be ſheltered in winter, and in the ſummer removed abroad, placing them in a warm ſheltered ſituation. In the winter they may be placed with Myrtles, and other of the hardier kinds of exotic plants, in a place where they may have as much free air as poſſible in mild weather, but ſcreened from ſevere froſt; for if theſe are kept too warm in winter, they will not flower ſtrong, and when the air is excluded from them, the ends of their ſhoots will become mouldy; ſo that the hardier they are treated, provided they are not expoſed to hard froſts, the better they will thrive.

The other two ſorts require a different treatment, otherwiſe they will not make any appearance; therefore the young plants when they have taken new root, ſhould be gradually inured to bear the open air, into which they ſhould be removed in July, where they may remain till October, provided the weather continues mild; but during this time, they ſhould be placed in a ſheltered ſituation; and upon the firſt approach of froſt, they ſhould be removed into ſhelter, for if their leaves are injured by froſt, they will change to a pale yellow, and will not recover their uſual colour till the following autumn. Theſe ſorts may be preſerved in a good green-houſe through the winter, and the plants will be ſtronger than thoſe which are more tenderly treated; but in May, when the flower-buds begin to appear, the plants ſhould be placed in an open glaſs-caſe, where they may be defended from the inclemency of the weather; but when it is warm weather, the air ſhould at all times be admitted to them in plenty. With this management the flowers will expand, and continue long in beauty; and during that time, there are few plants which are equal to them, either to the eye or noſe, for their ſcent is very like that of the flowers of the White Thorn; and the bunches of flowers will be very large, if the plants are ſtrong.

NERVES are long tough ſtrings, which run either acroſs, or lengthways, in the leaves of plants.

NICOTIANA. Tourn. Inſt. R. H. 117. tab. 41. Lin. Gen. Plant. 220. [This plant takes its name from James Nicotius, counſellor to Francis II. King of France, who in the year 1560, being ambaſſador to the court of Portugal, bought the ſeeds of this plant of a Dutchman, who brought them from America, and ſent them to Queen Catharine de Medicis in France; where, being ſown, they produced ſeeds: the Indian inhabitants call it Tabac, becauſe it grew in an iſland called Tabaco, or Tobago. The leſſer ſort is by ſome called Hyoſcyamus, becauſe it agrees in ſome of its characters with this plant; it is alſo called Priapeia.] Tobacco; in French, Nicotiane ou Tabac.

The CHARACTERS are,

The empalement of the flower is permanent, of one leaf, cut into five acute ſegments. The flower has one funnel-ſhaped petal, with a long tub ſpread open at the brim, and ending in five acute points. It hath five awl-ſhaped ſtamina which are the length of the tube, a little inclined, and terminated by oblong ſummits; and an oval germen ſupporting a ſlender ſtyle, crowned by an indented ſtigma. The germen afterward turns to an oval capſule, with a furrow on each ſide, having two cells which open at the top, and are filled with rough ſeeds faſtened to the partition.

This genus of plants is ranged in the firſt ſection of Linnæus's fifth claſs, which contains thoſe plants whoſe flowers have five ſtem na and one ſtyle.

The

The SPECIES are,

1. NICOTIANA (*Latiffima*) foliis ovato-lanceolatis rugofis, femiamplexicaulibus. *Tobacco with oval, fpear-
fhaped, rough leaves, which half embrace the ftalks.*
Hyofcyamus Peruvianus. Ger. 357. *Tobacco, or Henbane of Peru.*

2. NICOTIANA (*Tabacum*) foliis lanceolato-ovatis decurrentibus, floribus acutis. Lin. Sp. Plant. 258. *Tobacco with oval, fpear-fhaped, running leaves, fitting clofe
to the ftalks.* Nicotiana major latifolia. C. B. P. 169.
Greater broad-leaved Tobacco.

3. NICOTIANA (*Anguftifolia*) foliis lanceolatis acutis, feffilibus, calycibus acutis, tubo floris longiffimo. Plat.
185. *Tobacco with acute fpear-fhaped leaves fitting clofe
to the ftalks, fharp-pointed empalements, and a very long
tube to the flower.* Nicotiana major anguftifolia. C.
B. P. 170. *Greater narrow-leaved Tobacco.*

4. NICOTIANA (*Fruticofa*) foliis lineari-lanceolatis acuminatis femiamplexicaulibus, caule-fruticofo. *Tobacco
with linear, fpear-fhaped, acute-pointed leaves, half embracing the ftalks, and a fhrubly ftalk.* Nicotiana major
anguftiffimo folio perennis. Juff. *Narroweft-leaved,
greater, perennial Tobacco.*

5. NICOTIANA (*Alba*) foliis ovatis acuminatis femiamplexicaulibus, capfulis ovatis obtufis. *Tobacco with
oval acute-pointed leaves half embracing the ftalk, and
oval obtufe feed-veffels.* Nicotiana major latifolia, floribus albis, vafculo brevi. Martyn. Dec. 5. *Greater
broad-leaved Tobacco with white flowers, and a fhort
feed-veffel.*

6. NICOTIANA (*Ruftica*) foliis petiolatis ovatis integerrimis, floribus obtufis. Lin. Sp. 258. *Tobacco with
oval entire leaves, and obtufe flowers.* Nicotiana minor.
C. B. P. 170. *Smaller Tobacco, commonly called Englifh
Tobacco.*

7. NICOTIANA (*Rugofa*) foliis ovatis rugofis petiolatis.
Tobacco with oval rough leaves, having foot-ftalks.
Nicotiana minor, foliis rugofioribus amplioribus.
Vaill. *Smaller Tobacco with larger and rougher leaves.*

8. NICOTIANA (*Paniculata*) foliis petiolatis cordatis integerrimis, floribus paniculatis obtufis clavatis. Lin.
Sp. Plant. 259. *Tobacco with heart-fhaped leaves, paniculated flowers, and club-fhaped tubes.* Nicotiana minor, folio cordiformi tubo floris prælongis. Feuill.
Obf. 1. p. 717. tab. 10. *Smaller Tobacco with a heart-
fhaped leaf, and a very long tube to the flower.*

9. NICOTIANA (*Glutinofa*) foliis petiolatis cordatis integerrimis, racemofis floribus fecundis ringentibus, calycibus inæqualibus. Lin. Sp. Plant. 259. *Tobacco
with heart-fhaped leaves, having foot-ftalks, branching
ringent petals, and unequal empalements.*

10. NICOTIANA (*Humilis*) foliis ovato-lanceolatis obtufis
rugofis, calycibus breviffimis. Plat. 185. *Tobacco with
oval, fpear-fhaped, obtufe, rough leaves, and a very
fhort empalement.* Nicotiana humilis, primulæ veris
folio. Houft. MSS. *Dwarf Tobacco with a Primrofe
leaf.*

The firft fort was formerly the moft common Tobacco which was fown in England, and which has been
generally taken for the common broad-leaved Tobacco of Cafpar Bauhin, and others, but is greatly different from it. The leaves of this fort are more than
a foot and a half long, and a foot broad, their furfaces very rough and glutinous: when thefe plants
are in a rich moift foil, they will grow more than ten
feet high; the bafe of the leaves half embrace the
ftalks; the upper part of the ftalk divides into finaller branches, which are terminated by loofe bunches
of flowers ftanding erect; they have pretty long tubes,
and are of a pale purplifh colour. It flowers in July
and Auguft, and the feeds ripen in the autumn.
This is the fort of Tabacco which is commonly
brought to the markets in pots to adorn the fhops
and balconies of London, and by fome is called Oroo-
noko Tobacco.

The fecond fort is the broad-leaved Tobacco of Caf-
per Bauhin; the ftalks of this feldom rife more than
five or fix feet high, and divide into more branches
than the firft. The leaves are about ten inches long,
and three and a half broad, finooth, and end in acute

points, fitting clofe to the ftalks; the flowers of this
are rather larger, and of a brighter purple colour
than thofe of the firft. It flowers and perfects feeds
at the fame time; this is by fome called fweet-fcented
Tobacco.

The third fort rifes with an upright branching ftalk
four or five feet high; the lower leaves are a foot
long, and three or four inches broad; thofe on the
ftalks are much narrower, leffening to the top, and
end in very acute points, fitting clofe to the ftalks;
they are very glutinous. The flowers grow in loofe
bunches at the top of the ftalks, they have long tubes,
and are of a bright purple or red colour. Thefe appear at the fame time with the former forts, and their
feeds ripen in the autumn.

The fourth fort rifes with very branching ftalks about
five feet high; the leaves on the lower part of the
ftalks are a foot and a half long, broad at the bafe,
where they half embrace the ftalks, and are about
three inches broad in the middle, terminating in long
acute points; the ftalks divide into many finaller
branches, which are terminated by loofe bunches of
flowers, of a bright purple colour, and are fucceeded
by acute-pointed feed-veffels. This flowers about
the fame time with the former, but if the plants are
placed in a warm green-houfe, they will live through
the winter. The feeds of this fort were fent me for
Brazil Tobacco.

The fifth fort grows naturally in the woods in the
ifland of Tobago, from whence the feeds were fent
me by the late Mr. Robert Millar. This rifes about
five feet high; the ftalk does not branch fo much as
thofe of the former; the leaves are large and oval,
about fifteen inches long and two broad in the middle,
but diminifh gradually in their fize to the top of the
ftalk, and with their bafe half embrace it. The
flowers grow in clofer bunches than thofe of the former, and are white; thefe are fucceeded by fhort,
oval, obtufe feed-veffels. It flowers and perfects feeds
about the fame time with the former.

The fixth fort is commonly called Englifh Tobacco,
from its having been the firft which was introduced
here, and being much more hardy than the other
forts. The feeds ripen very freely, and fcattering in
the autumn, the plants have come up without care,
wherever any of the plants have been fuffered to run
to feed, fo that it has been a weed in many places;
but it came originally from America, by the title of
Petum. Dodonæus, Tabernemontanus, and others,
have titled it Hyofcyamus luteus, from the affinity
there is between this plant and the Henbane; but the
flowers of this are tubulous, and not ringent, as are
thofe of the Henbane; nor do the feed-veffels of this
open with a lid on the top, as that of Henbane. The
ftalks of this feldom rife more than three feet high;
the leaves are placed alternately on the ftalks, ftanding upon fhort foot-ftalks; they are oval and fmooth.
The flowers grow in fmall loofe bunches on the
top of the ftalks; they have fhort tubes, which
fpread open at the top, and are cut into five obtufe
fegments, of an herbaceous yellow colour, appearing
in July, and are fucceeded by roundifh capfules, filled
with finall feeds, which ripen in the autumn.

The feventh fort rifes with a ftrong ftalk near four
feet high; the leaves of this are fhaped like thofe of
the former, but are greatly furrowed on their furface
and near twice the fize, of a darker green, and have
longer foot-ftalks. The flowers are larger than thofe
of the former, and of the fame fhape. This is undoubtedly a diftinct plant from the former, for I have
fown the feeds more than thirty years, and have never
found any of the plants vary.

The eighth fort was found growing naturally in the
valley of Lima, by Pere Feuille, in the year 1710;
and of late years the feeds of it were fent from Peru,
by the younger de Juffieu, to Paris. The ftalk of
this fort rifes more than three feet high, dividing upward into many fmaller panicled branches, which are
round and a little hairy; the leaves are heart-fhaped,
about four inches long, and three broad, ftanding
upon

upon pretty long foot-ſtalks: The flowers are produced in looſe panicles at the end of the branches; theſe have tubes about an inch long, ſhaped like a club; the brim is ſlightly cut into nine obtuſe ſegments, which are reflexed; they are of a yellowiſh green colour, and are ſucceeded by roundiſh capſules, filled with very ſmall ſeeds. It flowers about the ſame time with the other ſorts.

The ſeeds of the ninth ſort were ſent from Peru with thoſe of the former, by the younger de Juſſieu; the ſtalk of this is round, and riſes near four feet high, ſending out two or three branches from the lower part; the leaves are large, heart-ſhaped, and a little waved; they are very clammy, ſtanding upon long foot-ſtalks. The flowers grow in looſe ſpikes at the top of the ſtalk, having ſhort open tubes, which are curved almoſt like the lip flowers; they are of a dull purple colour; the empalement is unequally cut, one of the ſegments being twice the ſize of the other. The tenth ſort was diſcovered by the late Dr. Houſtoun at La Vera Cruz, who ſent the ſeeds to England. This hath a pretty thick taper root, which ſtrikes deep in the ground; at the top comes out ſix or ſeven oval ſpear-ſhaped leaves, which ſpread on the ſurface of the ground; they are about the ſize of thoſe of the common Primroſe, but are of a deeper green; the ſtalk riſes about a foot high, branching into three or four diviſions, at each of theſe is placed one ſmall leaf; the branches are terminated by a looſe ſpike of flowers, which are ſmall, tubulous, and of a yellowiſh green colour, having very ſhort empalements, which are cut at the brim into five acute ſegments. The ſeed-veſſel is ſmall, oval, and divided into two cells, which are full of ſmall ſeeds.

All the ſorts except the ſixth, ſeventh, and eighth, require the ſame culture, and are too tender to grow from ſeeds ſown in the full ground, to any degree of perfection in this country, ſo require to be raiſed in a hot-bed, after the following manner:

The ſeeds muſt be ſown upon a moderate hot-bed in March, and when the plants come up fit to remove, they ſhould be tranſplanted into a new hot-bed of a moderate warmth, about four inches aſunder each way, obſerving to water and ſhade them until they have taken root; after which you muſt let them have air in proportion to the warmth of the ſeaſon, otherwiſe they will draw up very weak, and be thereby leſs capable of enduring the open air: you muſt alſo obſerve to water them frequently, but while they are very young, it ſhould not be given to them in too great quantities; though when they are pretty ſtrong, they will require to have it often, and in plenty.

In this bed the plants ſhould remain until the middle of May, by which time (if they have ſucceeded well) they will touch each other, therefore they ſhould be inured to bear the open air gradually; after which they muſt be taken up carefully, preſerving a large ball of earth to each root, and planted into a rich light ſoil, in rows four feet aſunder, and the plants three feet diſtance in the rows, obſerving to water them until they have taken root; after which they will require no farther care (but only to keep them clean from weeds) until the plants begin to ſhew their flower-ſtems; at which time you ſhould cut off the tops of them, that their leaves may be the better nouriſhed, whereby they will be rendered larger, and of a thicker ſubſtance. In Auguſt they will be full grown, when they ſhould be cut for uſe; for if they are permitted to ſtand longer, their under leaves will begin to decay. This is to be underſtood for ſuch plants as are propagated for uſe, but thoſe plants which are deſigned for ornament, ſhould be planted in the borders of the pleaſure-garden, and permitted to grow their full height, where they will continue flowering from July, till the froſt puts a ſtop to them.

The three ſmaller ſorts of Tobacco are preſerved in botanic gardens for variety, but are ſeldom propagated for uſe. The firſt ſort is found growing upon dunghills in divers parts of England. The ſixth and ſeventh are very hardy, and may be propagated by ſowing their ſeeds in March, upon a bed of light earth, where they will come up, and may be tranſplanted into any part of the garden, where they will thrive without farther care.

The laſt ſort being ſomewhat tenderer than the other, ſhould be ſown early in the ſpring on a hot-bed; and when the plants come up, they ſhould be tranſplanted on another moderate hot-bed, where they muſt be duly watered, and ſhould have a large ſhare of free air in warm weather; and when the plants have obtained a good ſhare of ſtrength, they ſhould be tranſplanted into ſeparate pots, and plunged into a moderate hot-bed to bring them forward. About the middle of June ſome of the plants may be ſhaken out of the pots, and planted into beds of rich earth; but it will be proper to keep one or two plants in pots, which may be placed in the ſtove (in caſe the ſeaſon ſhould prove bad,) that they may ripen their ſeeds, ſo that the ſpecies may be preferred.

NIGELLA. Tourn. Inſt. R. H. 258. tab. 134. Lin. Gen. Plant. 606. [ſo called, as though Nigrella, from the colour of its ſeed, becauſe the ſeeds of this plant are, for the moſt part, black. It is alſo called Melanthium, of μίλας, black, and ἄνθος, a flower, q. d. black flower, although the flower is not black: it is alſo called Melaſpermum, of μίλας, black, and σπίρμα, ſeed.] Fennel-flower, or Devil in a buſh.

The CHARACTERS are,

The flower has no empalement, but a leafy periantbium. It hath five oval, obtuſe, plain petals, which ſpread open, and are contracted at their baſe, and eight very ſhort nectariums ſituated in a circle, each having two lips; the exterior being larger, the inferior bifid, plain, and convex; the interior is ſhorter, narrower, from an oval terminating in a line. It hath a great number of awl-ſhaped ſtamina, which are ſhorter than the petals, terminated by obtuſe, compreſſed, erect ſummits; and in ſome five, in others ten, oblong, convex, erect germen, ending in awl-ſhaped ſtyles, which are long, revolved, and permanent, having ſtigmas faſtened longitudinally to them. The germen afterward become ſo many oblong compreſſed capſules, divided by a furrow, but connected within, filled with rough angular ſeeds.

This genus of plants is ranged in the fifth ſection of Linnæus's thirteenth claſs, which includes thoſe plants whoſe flowers have many ſtamina and five ſtyles.

The SPECIES are,

1. NIGELLA (*Arvenſis*) piſtillis quinis, petalis integris, capſulis turbinatis. Lin. Sp. Plant. 534. *Fennel-flower having five pointals, entire petals, and turbinated ſeed-veſſels.* Nigella arvenſis cornuta. C. B. P. *Field horned Fennel-flower.*

2. NIGELLA (*Damaſcena*) floribus involucro folioſo cinctis. Hort. Cliff. 215. *Fennel-flower whoſe flowers are encompaſſed with a leafy involucrum.* Nigella anguſtifolia, flore majore cæruleo. C. B. P. 145. *Narrow-leaved Fennel-flower, having a larger, ſingle, blue flower.*

3. NIGELLA (*Sativa*) piſtillis quinis, capſulis muricatis ſubrotundis, foliis ſubpiloſis. Hort. Upſal. 154. *Fennel-flower with five pointals which are prickly, and leaves ſomewhat hairy.* Nigella flore minore ſimplici candido. C. B. P. 145. *Fennel-flower with a ſmaller, ſingle, white flower.*

4. NIGELLA (*Cretica*) piſtillis quinis, corolla-longioribus, petalis integris. *Fennel-flower with five pointals longer than the petals, which are entire.* Nigella Cretica latifolia odorata. Park. Theat. 1376. *Broad-leaved ſweet-ſmelling Fennel-flower of Crete.*

5. NIGELLA (*Latifolia*) piſtillis denis corolla brevioribus. *Fennel-flower with ten pointals which are ſhorter than the petals.* Nigella alba ſimplici flore. Alp. Exot. 261. *Fennel-flower with a ſingle white flower.*

6. NIGELLA (*Hiſpanica*) piſtillis denis corollam æquantibus. Hort. Upſal. 154. *Fennel-flower with ten pointals equalling the petal.* Nigella latifolia flore majore ſimplici cæruleo. C. B. P. 145. *Broad-leaved Fennel-flower with a large, ſingle, blue flower.*

7. NIGELLA (*Orientalis*) piſtillis denis corollâ longioribus. Hort. Cliff. 215. *Fennel-flower with ten pointals
which are longer than the petals.* Nigella Orientalis,
flore fuaveſcente, femine alato plano. Tourn. Cor. 19.
*Fennel-flower of the Eaſt, with a yellowiſh flower, and
a plain winged feed.*

The firſt ſort grows naturally among the Corn, in
France, Italy, and Germany, ſo is ſeldom propagated
in gardens; this riſes with ſlender ſtalks near a foot
high, which ſometimes branch out at the bottom, and
at others they are ſingle, garniſhed with a few very fine
cut leaves, ſomewhat like thoſe of Dill; each ſtalk is
terminated by one ſtar-pointed flower of five petals,
which are of a pale blue-colour, and have no leafy involucrum under them; theſe are ſucceeded by capſules, having five ſhort horns, which incline different
ways at the top, and are filled with rough black feeds;
there is a variety of this with white flowers, and another with double flowers.

The ſecond ſort grows naturally in Spain and Italy,
among the Corn; this riſes with an upright branching
ſtalk a foot and a half high, garniſhed with leaves
much longer and finer than thoſe of the firſt. The
flowers are large, of a pale blue, and have a long
leafy involucrum under each: theſe are ſucceeded by
larger ſwelling feed-veſſels, with horns at the top; of
this there is one with ſingle white flowers, and another
with double flowers, which is ſown in gardens for
ornament.

The third ſort grows naturally in Crete; this riſes
about the ſame height as the former. The leaves are
not ſo finely cut as thoſe of the ſecond, and are a little
hairy. At the top of each ſtalk is one flower, compoſed of five white petals, which are ſlightly cut at
their end into three points; theſe are ſucceeded by
oblong ſwelling feed-veſſels, with five horns at the
top, filled with ſmall pale-coloured feeds.

The fourth ſort grows naturally in Crete; this riſes
with branching ſtalks about a foot high, garniſhed
with ſhorter and broader leaves than either of the
other ſpecies. At the top of each branch is one
flower, having no involucrum; they are compoſed
of five oval petals, and have five pointals longer
than the petals; the feed-veſſel is not much ſwollen,
and has five ſlender horns at the top; the feeds are
of a light yellowiſh brown colour.

The fifth ſort is alſo a native of Crete; this riſes
with a branching ſtalk a foot high, garniſhed with
leaves like thoſe of Larkſpur. The flowers have five
large oval petals, which are entire, and ten pointals
which are ſhorter than the petals, and a great number of green ſtamina with blue chives; the feed-
veſſels are like thoſe of the laſt ſort.

The ſixth ſort riſes a foot and a half high; the lower
leaves are finely cut, but thoſe on the ſtalks are cut
into broader ſegments. The flowers are larger than
thoſe of the other ſpecies, and are of a fine blue colour: the pointals of this are of equal length with the
petals; the feed-veſſel has five horns, and is of a
firmer texture than any of the other. This grows naturally in the ſouth of France and Spain; there is a
variety of this with double flowers.

The ſeventh ſort grows naturally in the Corn-fields
about Aleppo; this riſes with a branching ſtalk a
foot and a half high, garniſhed with pretty long leaves,
which are finely divided. The flowers are produced
at the end of the branches; they are compoſed of five
yellowiſh leaves or petals; at the baſe of theſe are
placed eight nectariums, between which ariſe a great
number of ſtamina, with an unequal number of germen, ſome having but five, others have eight or nine;
they are oblong and compreſſed; theſe afterward become ſo many oblong compreſſed feed-veſſels, joined
together on their inner ſide, terminating with horns,
and open longitudinally, containing many thin compreſſed feeds, having borders round them.

The varieties of theſe with double flowers, are chiefly
propagated in gardens for ornament; but thoſe with
ſingle flowers are rarely admitted into any but botanic

gardens, where they are preſerved for the ſake of
variety.

All theſe plants may be propagated by ſowing their
feeds upon a bed of light earth, where they are to remain (for they ſeldom ſucceed well if tranſplanted;)
therefore, in order to have them intermixed amongſt
other annual flowers in the borders of the flower-garden, the feeds ſhould be ſown in patches at proper
diſtances; and when the plants come up, you muſt
pull up thoſe which grow too cloſe, leaving but three
or four of them in each patch, obſerving alſo to keep
them clear from weeds, which is all the culture they
require. In July they will produce their flowers, and
their feeds will ripen in Auguſt, when they ſhould be
gathered and dried; then rub out each ſort ſeparately, and preſerve them in a dry place.

The ſeaſon for ſowing theſe feeds is in March; but
if you ſow ſome of them in Auguſt, ſoon after they
are ripe, upon a dry ſoil and in a warm ſituation, they
will abide through the winter, and flower ſtrong the
ſucceeding year; ſo by ſowing the feeds at different
times, they may be continued in beauty moſt part of
the ſummer.

They are all annual plants, which periſh ſoon after
they have perfected their feeds; which, if permitted
to ſcatter upon the borders, will come up without any
farther care.

NIGELLASTRUM. See AGROSTEMMA.

NIGHTSHADE. See SOLANUM.

NIGHTSHADE, the Deadly. See BELLADONNA.

NIL. See ANIL.

NISSOLIA. See LATHYRUS.

NITRE is a kind of ſalt, impregnated with abundance of ſpirits out of the air, which renders it volatile.

Monſieur Le Clerc gives us the following account of it:
In Egypt they make a great quantity of it, but it is
not ſo good, for it is duſky, and full of knots and
ſtones.

It is made almoſt in the manner that ſalt is made,
but only that they uſe ſea-water in their ſalt-works,
and the water of Nile about their Nitre.

When the Nile retires, their Nitre-pits ſtand ſoaking
for forty days together; but as the Nitre is grown
firm, they are in haſte to carry it off, leſt it ſhould
melt again in the pits. They pile it up in heaps, and
it keeps very well.

The Memphian Nitre grows ſtrong, and there are ſeveral pits of ſtone thereabouts; out of theſe they
make veſſels, and ſome they melt down with ſulphur
among their coals.

This ſame Nitre they uſe alſo about ſuch things as
they would have to laſt a long time.

The proof of the goodneſs of Nitre is, that it be very
light, very friable, and very near of a purple colour.
There is but very little difference between the natural
and artificial Nitre; but that the one refines itſelf, and
the other is refined by art, as ſalt; and, indeed, all
Nitre is a kind of ſalt, and hardly differs from ſalt,
properly ſo-called, farther than in theſe reſpects,
That well refined Nitre is more acid and light than
ſalt, and eaſily takes fire.

The reaſon of which difference, he ſays, ſeems to
be;

1. That the angles at both ends of the oblong particles of Nitre are ſhorter than the angles of the ſaline
particles.

2. That the particles of Nitre are finer and fuller of
pores; which, when the particles of fire get in, they
ſoon put the nitrous particles into a hurry, till they
break to pieces, and turn to flame.

3. Nitre exceeds ſalt in lightneſs, becauſe the ſaline
particles contain more homogeneous matter in the
ſame compaſs, than the nitrous do.

Dr. Liſter tells us, he viewed the particles of Nitre
through a microſcope, and found them to have ſix
angles, parallelogram ſides, and pointed like a pyramid at one end.

Some

Some authors are of opinion, that the nitrous salts seem to be assigned by nature chiefly for the growth of plants.

Others differ from them in opinion, and say, that when Nitre is contiguous to plants, it rather destroys than nourishes them; but yet they allow, that Nitre and other salts do certainly loosen the earth, and separate the concreted parts of it, and by that means, fit and dispose them to be assumed by water, and carried up into the seed or plant, for its formation and augment.

It is observable, how all salts are wrought upon by moisture, how easily they liquidate and run with it; and when these are drawn off, and have deserted the lumps wherewith they were incorporated, those must moulder immediately, and fall asunder of course.

The hardest stone, if it has any salt mixed with the sand of which it consists, upon being exposed to a humid air, in a short time dissolves and crumbles all to pieces; and much more will clodded earth and clay, which is not of near so compact and solid a constitution as stone is.

If the earth be never so good and fit for the production of vegetables, little will come of it, unless the parts of it be separated and loose; and for this reason, is the ground digged, ploughed, and harrowed, and the clods broken; and it is this way that Nitre, sea-salt, and other salts, promote vegetation.

A certain gentleman has given a relation, That he dwelling in the country near a petre-house, where such saltpetre as is brought from abroad, is boiled and refined, to make gunpowder, this being so near as to communicate the steam of the Nitre to the greatest part of the orchard and garden; and, though some were of opinion that it injured his trees and plants, yet he found, that it had a contrary influence upon his orchard, &c. in that it never failed to bring him a plentiful crop of fruit every year, although those about him had but very little, or scarce any; notwithstanding his orchard, &c. was not less exposed to blighting winds by its natural situation, than the other orchards in the same town. From whence he judged, that the nitrous vapour which mixes with the air that surrounds his orchard, prevents blights, and is noxious to the caterpillars.

The Lord Bacon, in his Natural History, commends the use of Nitre, for the preservation of health in human bodies; and many skilful husbandmen have given it no less a character for the preservation of vegetables, if its quantity be rightly proportioned.

That the atmosphere does abound with saline particles, is most certain; for being filled continually with effluvia from earth and sea, it must needs have from both a great quantity of saline corpuscles; and the salt will be of different kinds, according to the variety of those salts from whence they are derived.

NOLANA. Royen. Lin. Gen. Plant. 193.

The CHARACTERS are,

The empalement of the flower is of one leaf, turbinated at the base, divided into five acute heart-shaped segments, and is permanent. The flower is bell-shaped, plaited, spread open, and is twice as large as the empalement; it hath five awl-shaped erect stamina, which are terminated by arrow-pointed summits, and five roundish germen surrounding a cylindrical erect style, crowned by a headed stigma. The succulent interior base of the receptacle becomes four cells, in which the seeds are inclosed.

This genus of plants is ranged in the first section of Linnæus's fifth class, which includes the plants having five stamina and one style.

We know but one SPECIES of this genus at present viz.

NOLANA (*Prostrata.*) Lin. Sp. 202. Dec. 1. tab. 2. *Trailing Nolana.* Atropa foliis geminatis, calycibus polycarpis, caule humifusa. Gouan. Monsp. 82. *Deadly Nightshade with two leaves at each joint, flower-cups with several seeds, and a trailing stalk.*

This plant grows naturally in Egypt, from whence I received the seeds, which were sent by Mr. Forschal,

one of the persons who were sent by the late king of Denmark, to make discoveries in the East.

It is an annual plant, with trailing stalks which lie prostrate on the ground, and divide into several branches, which are garnished with oval, spear-shaped, smooth leaves, having short foot-stalks; these come out single at some joints, by pairs at others, and frequently three or four at the upper joints: the flowers are produced singly from the forks of the branches, upon pretty long foot-stalks; they are shaped like those of the Winter Cherry, having short tubes, which spread open above, and are of a fine blue colour; these are succeeded by four naked seeds, sitting in the empalement of the flower. This plant flowers in July, and the seeds ripen in the beginning of September.

The seeds of this plant must be sown on a hot-bed in March, and when the plants come up and are fit to remove, they should be each transplanted into a small pot filled with light earth, and plunged into a fresh hot-bed to bring the plants forward, otherwise they will not ripen their seeds in this country; but when their flowers open in July, they should have a large share of air admitted to them when the weather is warm, to prevent their flowers falling away without producing seeds: with this management the plants will continue flowering till the early frost destroys them, and their flowers will produce ripe seeds the beginning of September.

NOLI ME TANGERE. See IMPATIENS.

NONSUCH, or FLOWER of BRISTOL. See LYCHNIS.

NORTHERN ASPECT is the least favourable of any in England, as having very little benefit from the sun, even in the height of summer, therefore can be of little use, whatever may have been advanced to the contrary; for although many sorts of fruit-trees will thrive and produce fruit in such positions, yet such fruit can be of little worth, since they are deprived of the kindly warmth of the sun to correct their crude juices, and render them well tasted and wholsome; therefore it is to little purpose to plant fruit-trees against such walls, except it be those which are intended for baking, &c. where the fire will ripen, and render those juices wholsome, which, for want of sun, could not be performed while growing. You may also plant Morello Cherries for preserving; and white and red Currants, to come late, after those which are exposed to the sun are gone; and if the soil be warm and dry, some sorts of summer Pears will do tolerably well on such an exposure, and will continue longer in eating, than if they were more exposed to the sun. But you should by no means plant Winter Pears in such an aspect, as hath been practised by many ignorant persons, since we find, that the best south walls, in some bad years, are barely warm enough to ripen those fruits.

Duke Cherries planted against walls exposed to the North, will ripen much later in the season, and, if the soil is warm, they will be well flavoured, so that hereby this fruit may be continued a month later than is usual.

NUCIFEROUS TREES, are such which produce nuts.

NUMMULARIA, See LYSIMACHIA.

NURSERY, or Nursery-garden, is a piece of land set apart for the raising and propagating all sorts of trees and plants to supply the garden, and other plantations. Of this sort there are a great number in the different parts of this kingdom, but particularly in the neighbourhood of London, which are occupied by the gardeners, whose business it is to raise trees, plants, and flowers for sale; and in many of these there is at present a much greater variety of trees and plants cultivated, than can be found in any other part of Europe. In France, their Nurseries, (which are but few, when compared with those in England) are chiefly confined to the propagation of fruit-trees, from whence they have the appellation of Pepinier. For there is scarce any of those gardens, where a person can be supplied

either

either with evergreens, flowering-shrubs, or forest-trees: and in Holland their Nurseries are principally for flowers; some few of them, indeed, propagate tender exotic plants. But those Nurseries in the neighbourhood of London do, several of them, include all these, and from hence most of the curious persons abroad are supplied with furniture for their gardens. But I do not propose in this place, to treat of these extensive Nurseries, or to give a description of them, therefore shall confine myself to treat of such Nurseries only as are absolutely necessary for all lovers of planting, to have upon the spot where they design to make their plantation. For if these are large, the expence of carrying a great number of trees, if the distance is great, will be no small article, beside the hazard of their growing; which, when the plants have been trained up in good land, and removed to an indifferent one, is very great. Therefore it is of the utmost consequence to every planter, to begin by making a Nursery. But in this article I must beg leave to observe, that a Nursery should not be fixed to any particular spot: I mean by this, that it would be wrong to continue the raising of trees any number of years upon the same spot of ground, because hereby the ground will be so much exhausted by the trees, as to render it unfit for the same purpose. Therefore all good Nursery gardeners shift and change their land from time to time, for when they have drawn off the trees from a a spot of ground, they either plant kitchen herbs, or other things, upon the ground for a year or two, by which time, as also by dunging and trenching the land, it is recovered, and made fit to receive other trees. But this they are obliged to from necessity, being confined to the same land; which is not the case with those gentlemen, who have large extent of ground in the country. Therefore all such persons I would advise to make Nurseries upon the ground which is intended for planting, where a sufficient number of the trees may be left standing, after the others have been drawn out to plant in other places; which, for all large growing trees, but particularly such as are cultivated for timber, will be found by much the most advantageous method; for all those trees which come up from the seed, or which are transplanted very young into the places where they are designed to remain, will make a much greater progress, and become larger trees, than any of those which are transplanted at a greater age. Therefore the Nurseries should be thinned early, by removing all those trees which are intended for other plantations while they are young, because hereby the expence and trouble of staking, tering, &c. will be saved, and the trees will succeed much better. But in exposed situations, where there are Nurseries made, it will be necessary to permit the trees, to stand much longer; that, by growing close together, they may shelter each other, and draw themselves up; and these should be thinned gradually, as the trees advance; for, by taking away too many at first, the cold will check the growth of the remaining trees. But then those trees which are taken out from these Nurseries, after a certain age, should not be depended on for planting; and it will be prudence rather to consign them for fuel, than by attempting to remove them large, whereby, in endeavouring to get them up with good roots, the roots of the standing trees will be often much injured.

What has been here proposed, must be understood for all large plantations in parks, woods, &c. but those Nurseries which are only intended for the raising of evergreens, flowering shrubs, or plants which are designed to embellish gardens, may be confined to one spot, because a small compass of ground will be sufficient for this purpose. Two or three acres of land employed this way, will be sufficient for the most extensive designs, and one acre will be full enough for those of moderate extent. And such a spot of ground may be always employed for sowing the seeds of foreign trees and plants, as also for raising many sorts of biennial and perennial flowers, to transplant into

the borders of the pleasure-garden, and for raising many kinds of bulbous-rooted flowers from seeds, whereby a variety of new sorts may be obtained annually, which will recompense for the trouble and expence, and will moreover be an agreeable diversion to all those persons who delight in the amusements of gardening.

Such a Nursery as this should be conveniently situated for water; for where that is wanting, there must be an expence attending the carriage of water in dry weather. It should also be as near the house as it can with conveniency be admitted, in order to render it easy to visit at all times of the year, because it is absolutely necessary that it should be under the inspection of the master, for unless he delights in it, there will be little hopes of success. The soil of this Nursery should also be good, and not too heavy and stiff, for such land will be very improper for sowing most sorts of seeds; because as this will detain the moisture in the spring and winter, the seeds of most tender things, especially of flowers, will rot in the ground, if sown early; therefore where persons are confined to such land, there should be a good quantity of sand, ashes, and other light manures buried, in order to separate the parts, and pulverize the ground; and if it is thrown up in ridges, to receive the frost in winter, it will be of great use to it, as will also the frequent forking, or stirring of the ground, both before and after it is planted.

The many advantages which attend the having such a Nursery, are so obvious to every person who has turned his thoughts in the least to this subject, that it is needless for me to mention them here; and therefore I shall only beg leave to repeat here what I have so frequently recommended, which is, the carefully keeping the ground always clean from weeds; for if these are permitted to grow, they will rob the young trees of their nourishment. Another principal business is, to dig the ground between the young plants at least once every year, to loosen it for the roots to strike out; but if the ground is stiff, it will be better if it is repeated twice a year, viz. in October and March, which will greatly promote the growth of the plants, and prepare their roots for transplanting.

But as there may be some persons who may have the curiosity to raise their own fruit-trees, which is what I would recommend to every one who is a lover of good fruit, because the uncertainty in procuring the intended kinds of each fruit is very great, when taken from common Nursery-gardens, so that most gentlemen who have planted many, have constantly complained of this disappointment; but beside this, there is another inconvenience, which, for want of skill, is scarce taken notice of, which is, the taking the buds or grafts from young trees in the Nurseries which have not borne fruit; this having been frequently repeated, renders the trees so raised as luxuriant as Willows, making shoots to the top of the walls in two or three years, and are rarely after fruitful with the most skilful management: I shall therefore treat of the proper method to make a Nursery of these trees.

In the doing of which you must observe the following rules:

1. That the soil in which you make the Nursery be not better than that where the trees are to be planted out for good; the not observing this is the reason that trees are often at a stand, or make but little progress for three or four years after they come from the Nursery, as it commonly happens to such trees as are raised near London, and carried into the northern parts of England, where, being planted in a poor soil and a much colder situation, the trees seldom succeed well; therefore it is by far the better method (when you have obtained the sorts you would propagate) to raise a Nursery of the several sorts of stocks proper for the various kinds of fruit, upon which you may bud or graft them; and those trees which are thus raised upon the soil, and in the same degree of warmth, where they are to be planted, will succeed much better than those

those brought from a greater distance and from a richer soil.

2. This ground ought to be fresh, and not such as has been already worn out by trees, or other large growing plants, for in such soil your stocks will not make any progress.

3. It ought not to be too wet, nor over dry, but rather of a middling nature; though of the two extremes, dry is to be preferred, because in such soils (though the trees do not make so great a progress as in moist, yet) they are generally sounder, and more disposed to fruitfulness.

4. You must also observe to inclose it, that cattle and vermin may not come in, for these will make sad havock with young trees, especially in winter, when the ground is covered with snow, that they have little other food which they can come at. The most mischievous of these animals are hares and rabbets, which are great destroyers of young trees at that season, by eating off all their bark; therefore you must carefully guard your Nursery against these enemies.

The ground being inclosed, should be carefully trenched about eighteen inches, or two feet deep, provided it will allow it; this should be done in August or September, that it may be ready to receive young stocks at the season for planting, which is commonly in the middle or end of October. In trenching the ground, you must be very careful to cleanse it from the roots of all noxious weeds, such as Couch-grass, Docks, &c. which, if left in the ground, will get in among the roots of the trees, so as not to be gotten out afterwards, and will spread and over-run the ground, to the great prejudice of your young stocks.

After having dug the ground, and the season being come for planting, you must level down the trenches as equal as possible, and then lay out the ground into quarters, proportionable to the size thereof, and those quarters may be laid out in beds, for the sowing of seeds or the stones of fruit.

The best sort of stocks for Peaches, Nectarines, &c. are such as are raised from the stones of the Muscle and white Pear Plumb, but you should never plant suckers of these (which is what some people practise) for these seldom make so good stocks, nor are ever well-rooted plants; besides, they are very subject to produce great quantities of suckers from their roots, which are very troublesome in the borders, or walks of a garden, and greatly injure the tree; so that you should annually, or at least every other year, sow a few stones of each, that you may never be at a loss for stocks.

For Pears, you should have such stocks as have been raised from the kernels of the fruit where perry hath been made, or else preserve the seeds of some sorts of summer Pears, which generally shoot strong and vigorous, as the Cuisse Madame, Windsor, &c. but when this is intended, the fruit should be suffered to hang upon the trees till they drop, and afterward permitted to rot; then take out the kernels and put them in sand, being careful to keep them from vermin, as also to place them where they may not be too damp, which will cause them to grow mouldy. These you should sow for stocks early in the spring, upon a bed of good light fresh earth, where they will come up in about six weeks, and, if kept clear from weeds, will be strong enough to transplant the October following. But for many sorts of summer and autumn Pears, Quince stocks are preferable to these (i. e. Pear) stocks; these are generally used for all the sorts of soft-melting Pears, but they are not so good for the breaking Pears, being apt to render those fruits which are grafted upon them stony; these are very often propagated from suckers, which are generally produced in plenty from the roots of old trees; but those are not near so good as such as are propagated from cuttings or layers, which have always much better roots, and are not so subject to produce suckers as the other, which is a very desirable quality, since these suckers do not only rob the trees of part of

their nourishment, but are very troublesome in a garden.

Apples are grafted or budded upon stocks raised from seeds which come from the cyder-press, or upon Crab stocks, the latter of which are esteemed for their durableness, especially for large standard trees; these should be raised from seeds, as the Pear stock, and must be treated in the same manner, for those procured from suckers, &c. are not near so good; but for small gardens, the Paradise stock hath been for some years past greatly esteemed, it being of very humble growth, causeth the fruit-trees grafted or budded thereon to bear very soon, and they may be kept in small compass; but these are only proper for very small gardens, or by way of curiosity, since the trees thus raised are but of short duration, and seldom arise to any size to produce fruit in quantities, unless the graft or bud be buried in planting, so that they put forth roots, and then they will be equal to trees grafted upon free stocks, since they receive but small advantage from the stock.

For Cherries, you should make use of stocks raised from the stones of the common Black, or the wild Honey Cherry, both of which are strong free growers, and produce the cleanest stocks.

For Plumbs, you may use the stones of most free-growing forts, which will also do very well for Apricots, these being not so difficult to take as Peaches or Nectarines; but (as I said before) these should not be raised from suckers for the reason there assigned, but rather from stones.

There are some persons who recommend the Almond stock for several sorts of tender Peaches, upon which they will take much better than upon Plumb stocks; but these being tender in their roots, and apt to shoot early in the spring, and being of short duration, are by many people rejected; but such tender sorts of Peaches which will not take upon Plumb stocks, should be budded upon Apricots, upon which they will take very well; and all sorts of Peaches which are planted upon dry soils, will continue much longer, and not be so subject to blight, if they are upon Apricots; for it is observed, that upon such soils where Peaches seldom do well, Apricots will thrive exceedingly, which may be owing to the strength and compactness of the vessels in the Apricots, which render it more capable of assimilating, or drawing its nourishment from the Plumb stock, which in dry soils seldom afford it in great plenty to the bud; and the Peach-tree being of a loose spongy nature, is not so capable to draw its nourishment therefrom, which occasions that weakness which is commonly observed in those trees, when planted on a dry soil; therefore it is the common practice of the Nursery-gardeners, to bud the Plumb stocks either with Apricots, or some free growing Peach; and after these have grown a year, they bud the tender sorts of Peaches upon these shoots, by which method many sorts succeed well, which in the common way will not thrive, or scarce keep alive; and these the gardeners term double worked Peaches.

There are some people who of late have budded and grafted Cherries upon stocks of the Cornish, and others on the Morello Cherry, which, they say, will render the trees more fruitful, and less luxuriant in growth, so that they may be kept in less compass; these stocks having the same effect upon Cherries, as the Paradise stock hath on Apples.

Having provided yourself with young stocks of all these different sorts, which should be raised in the seminary the preceding year, you should proceed to transplanting them in October (as was before directed) into the Nursery. The distance which they should be planted, if designed for standards, should be three feet and a half or four feet, row from row, and a foot and a half distant in the rows; but if for dwarfs, three feet row from row, and one foot in the rows, will be a sufficient distance.

In taking these stocks out of the seed-beds, you must raise the ground with a spade, in order to preserve

the roots as entire as poffible; then with your knife
you fhould prune off all the very fmall fibres; and
if there are any which have a tendency to root downright, fuch roots fhould be fhortened; then having
thus prepared the plants, you fhould draw a line
acrofs the ground intended to be planted, and with
your fpade open a trench thereby exactly ftrait, into
which you fhould place them at the diftance before-
mentioned, fetting them exactly upright; and then
put the earth in clofe to them, filling up the trench,
and with your foot prefs the earth gently to the
roots of them, obferving not to difplace them fo as
to make the rows crooked, which will render them
unfightly; thefe plants fhould by no means be headed, or pruned at top, which will weaken them, and
caufe them to produce lateral branches, and thereby
fpoil them.

If the winter fhould prove very cold, it will be of
great fervice to your young ftocks, to lay fome mulch
upon the furface of the ground near their roots, which
will prevent the froft from penetrating the ground, fo
as to hurt the tender fibres which were produced after planting; but you fhould be careful not to let it
lie too thick near the ftems of the plants, nor remain
too long, left the moifture fhould be prevented from
penetrating to the roots of the plants, which it often
does, where there is not due care taken to remove it
away as foon as the froft is over.

In the fummer feafon you muft always obferve, to
hoe and deftroy the weeds, which, if permitted to remain in the Nurfery, will greatly weaken and retard
the growth of your ftocks; and, the fucceeding years,
you fhould obferve to dig up the ground every fpring
between the rows, which will loofen it fo, as that the
fibres may eafily ftrike out on each fide, and the
weeds will thereby be deftroyed; you fhould alfo obferve, where any of the ftocks have fhot out lateral
branches, to prune them off, that they may be encouraged to grow upright and fmooth.

The fecond year after planting, fuch of the ftocks as
are defigned for dwarf trees will be fit to bud, but
thofe which are defigned for ftandards, fhould be fuffered to grow fix or feven feet high before they are
budded or grafted. The manner of budding and
grafting being fully defcribed under their refpective
heads, I fhall not repeat them in this place, nor need
I fay any thing more of treating thefe trees after budding, that being alfo treated of under the feveral articles of fruits; I fhall only add, that thofe ftocks
which were budded in the fummer, and have failed,
may be grafted the following fpring, but Peaches and
Nectarines never take well from grafts, thefe fhould
therefore be always budded.

The ground you intend for the Flower-nurfery fhould
be well fituated to the fun, but defended from ftrong
winds, by plantations of trees or buildings, and the
foil fhould be light and dry; which muft always be
obferved, efpecially for bulbous-rooted flowers, which
are defigned to be planted therein, the particulars
of which are exhibited under the feveral articles of
flowers.

In this Nurfery fhould be planted the offsets of all
your bulbous-rooted flowers, where they are to remain until they become blowing roots, when they
fhould be removed into the pleafure-garden, and
planted either in beds or borders, according to the
goodnefs of the flowers, or the management which
they require.

You may alfo in this ground raife the feveral forts of
bulbous-rooted flowers from feed, by which means
new varieties may be obtained; but moft people are
difcouraged from fetting about this work, from the
length of time before the feedlings will come to
flower: however, after a perfon hath once begun, and
conftantly continued fowing every year, after the parcel firft fown has flowered, the regular fucceffion of
them coming annually to flower, will not render this
method fo tedious as it at firft appeared.

The feedling Auriculas, Polyanthufes, Ranunculufes,
Anemonies, Carnations, &c. fhould be raifed in this

Nurfery, where they fhould be preferved until they
have flowered, when you fhould mark all fuch as are
worthy of being tranfplanted into the flower-garden,
which fhould be done in their proper feafons; for it
is not fo well to have all thefe feedling flowers expofed to public view in the flower-garden, becaufe
it always happens, that there are great numbers of
ordinary flowers produced amongft them, which will
make but an indifferent appearance in the pleafure-
garden.

NUX AVELLANA. See CORYLUS.
NUX JUGLANS. See JUGLANS.
NUX VESICARIA. See STAPHYLODENDRON.
NYCTANTHES. Lin. Gen. Plant. 16. Jafmi-
num. Raii Meth. Plant. Arabian Jafmine.

The CHARACTERS are,
The empalement of the flower is cylindrical, permanent, and
of one leaf, cut into eight or ten acute fegments. The flower
is of the falver-fhape, of one leaf, with a cylindrical tube
longer than the empalement, cut into eight or ten fegments at
the top, which fpread open. It hath two fmall awl-fhaped
ftamina, fituated at the bottom of the tube, terminated by
erect fummits, and one roundifh depreffed germen, fupporting a fingle ftyle the length of the tube, crowned by a bifid
erect ftigma. The germen afterward becomes a roundifh
berry with two cells, each containing a large roundifh feed.
This genus of plants is ranged in the firft fection of
Linnæus's fecond clafs, which includes thofe plants
whofe flowers have two ftamina and one ftyle.

The SPECIES are,
1. NYCTANTHES (Sambac) caule volubili, foliis fubovatis acutis. Hort. Upfal. 4. Nyctanthes with a winding
ftalk and acute leaves. Jafminum Arabicum. Cluf. Cur.
3. The Arabian Jafmine.
2. NYCTANTHES (Hirfuta) petiolis pedunculifque villofis. Lin. Sp. Plant. 6. Nyctanthes with the foot-ftalks of
the leaves and flowers hairy. Jafminum Indicum bacciferum, flore albo majore, noctu olente. Com. Hort.
Mal. Indian berry-bearing Jafmine, with a larger white
flower, fmelling by night.

The firft fort grows naturally in India, from whence it
has been formerly brought to the iflands in America,
where the plants are cultivated for ornament; this
rifes with a winding ftalk to the height of fifteen or
twenty feet, fending out many fmall branches, garnifhed with oval fmooth leaves near three inches long,
and almoft two broad, of a light green, ftanding op-
fite on fhort foot-ftalks, ending in acute points. The
flowers are produced at the end of the branches, and
alfo upon the fide fhoots, upon fhort foot-ftalks; each
generally fuftain three flowers, the two lower being oppofite, and the middle ones longer: thefe have cylindrical empalements, which are fhort, and are cut almoft
to the bottom into eight narrow fegments. The tube of
the flower is narrow, about half an inch long, and is
cut at the top into eight obtufe fegments, which expand quite flat; they are of a pure white, and have
a moft agreeable odour, fomewhat like the Orange-
flower, but fweeter; thefe flowers, when fully blown,
drop out of their cups upon being fhaken, and frequently fall in the night, fo that when the plants are
in full flower, the place under them is often covered
with flowers in the morning, which foon change to a
purplifh colour. The plants continue flowering great
part of the year, when they are kept in a proper temperature of warmth.

There is a variety of this fort with very large double
flowers, having a moft agreeable odour; which grows
naturally at Malabar, where the women ftring the
flowers to hang round their necks, and by way of
ornament. This fort was, fome years paft, growing
in the gardens at Hampton-Court, but was afterward loft, with many other rare plants, by the ignorance of the gardener; and, for feveral years paft,
was only known to grow in the gardens of the Duke
of Tufcany in Europe, who kept a conftant guard
over the plants, fo that neither cuttings or layers
might be taken from them, fo as to be propagated;
but I have lately received a plant of this fort, which
was brought from the Malabar coaft, with feveral other
rare

rare plants, by Captain Quick; and this is at prefent in fo flourifhing a ftate of health, that I hope foon to increafe the number of plants, which will be a great acquifition to the Englifh gardens.

Linnæus has fuppofed that fort of Jafmine, to which the title of Gardenia has been given, to be the fame with this; but as my plant has flowered here, fo it appears plainly to be an accidental variety of this Nyctanthes, the flowers changing to a purple colour before they drop off, whereas the plant titled Gardenia changes to a buff colour; befide, this Nyctanthes is a twining plant, whereas the other is of upright growth: he is likewife as much miftaken in fuppofing it to be the fame with Rumphius's plant, for it differs in many refpects from that, as alfo from Burman's figure; therefore if he had looked upon the figure, and attended to the defcription given of this plant in the Pifa Garden, he could not have fuppofed thefe two to be the fame plant.

The fecond fort grows naturally in India, where it rifes to the height of a tree, dividing into many branches, garnifhed with large, oval, fmooth leaves, of a lucid green, with hairy foot-ftalks; thefe come out on every fide the branches without order. The flowers are produced on the fide of the branches from the wings of the leaves, upon long hairy foot-ftalks, each fuftaining feven or eight flowers, which are of a pure white, and very fragrant, but have longer tubes than thofe of the former fort. The flowers of this plant open in the evening, and drop off in the morning, which has occafioned fome to give it the title of Arbor Triftis, or the Sorrowful-tree, from its cafting the flowers in the morning; this is very rare in Europe at prefent.

The plants of the firft fort are frequently brought from Italy by the Italian gardeners, who bring Orange-trees here for fale; but thofe plants are always grafted upon ftocks of the common Jafmine, which do not keep pace in their growth with the graft, fo become very unfightly, when the plants are grown to any fize; befides, the ftocks are very fubject to fhoot from the bottom, and if thefe fhoots are not conftantly rubbed off, they will draw the nourifhment from the graft and ftarve it: therefore the beft method to obtain the plants, is to propagate them by layers or cuttings; the former is the fureft method, for unlefs the cuttings are very carefully managed, they will not take root; and as the ftalks of this fort are pliable, they may be eafily brought down, and laid in pots filled with a foft loamy foil, which fhould be plunged into a hotbed of tan: if the branches are laid down in the fpring and carefully watered, they will put out roots by autumn, when they may be cut from the old plants, and each tranfplanted into a feparate fmall pot, and then plunged into the tan-bed, where they fhould be fhaded from the fun till they have taken new root.

If thefe plants are propagated by cuttings, they fhould be planted from May to Auguft, into pots filled with the before-mentioned earth, and plunged into a moderate hot-bed of tanners bark. The pots fhould be pretty large, and there may be ten or twelve cuttings planted in each; if thefe pots are clofely covered with bell or hand-glaffes to exclude the air, it will greatly promote their taking root; they muft alfo be fhaded from the fun in the heat of the day, and gently refrefhed with water when the earth is dry; with this management the cuttings will have taken root by Auguft, when they may be tranfplanted into feparate pots, and treated in the fame way as the layers.

Thefe plants may be preferved in a moderate degree of warmth, but if they are plunged into the tan-bed of the bark-ftove, they will thrive much better, and produce a greater quantity of flowers; and as the leaves continue all the year, the plants will make a fine appearance in the ftove at all feafons, and produce flowers great part of the year.

The fecond fort requires the fame treatment, but is much more difficult to propagate, fo is very rarely found in the European gardens; there were two or three of thefe plants brought from Florence a few years fince, but they were put into the hands of unfkilful perfons, fo were loft.

NYMPHÆA: Tourn. Inft. R. H. 260. tab. 137, 138. Lin. Gen. Plant. 579. [is fo called, becaufe it grows in water, which the poets feign to be the refidence of the nymphs.] The Water Lily; in French, *Nenufar.*

The CHARACTERS are,

The empalement of the flower is compofed of four or five coloured leaves, and is permanent. The flower hath many petals which are fmaller than the empalement, fitting on the fide of the germen, for the moft part in a fingle feries. It hath a great number of fhort, plain, incurved ftamina, with oblong fummits, like threads, growing to their borders. It hath a large oval germen, but no ftyle, with an orbicular, plain, target-fhaped ftigma, fitting clofe, whofe border is crenated and is permanent. The germen afterward becomes a hard, oval, flefhy fruit, with a rude narrow neck, crowned at the top, and divided into ten or fifteen cells full of pulp, with many roundifh feeds.

This genus of plants is ranged in the firft fection of Linnæus's thirteenth clafs, which contains thofe plants whofe flowers have many male parts and but one female.

The SPECIES are,

1. NYMPHÆA (*Lutea*) foliis cordatis integerrimis, calyce petalis majore pentaphyllo. Flor. Lap. 218. *Water Lily with entire heart-fhaped leaves, whofe empalement confifts of five leaves larger than the petals.* Nymphæa lutea major. C. B. P. 193. *Greater yellow Water Lily.*

2. NYMPHÆA (*Alba*) foliis cordatis integerrimis, calyce quadrifido. Lin. Sp. Plant. 510. *Water Lily with heart-fhaped entire leaves, and a four-pointed empalement.* Nymphæa alba major. C. B. P. 193. *Greater white Water Lily.*

There are fome other fpecies of this genus which are natives of warm countries, but as they cannot without great difficulty be cultivated here, fo I fhall not enumerate them; for unlefs there is a contrivance for ftanding water in the ftove, in which the plants may be planted, they will not grow; and fuch a place would be injurious to moft other plants in the ftove, by occafioning damps; fo that unlefs a ftove was contrived on purpofe for fome of thefe aquatic plants, it would be imprudent to attempt their cultivation.

The two forts here mentioned, grow naturally in ftanding waters in many parts of England; they have large roots, which are faftened in the ground, from which arife the ftalks to the furface of the water, where the leaves expand and float; they are large, roundifh, and heart-fhaped. The flowers arife between the leaves, and fwim upon the furface of the water. The white fort has a faint fweet fcent; thefe appear in July, and are fucceeded by large roundifh feed-veffels, filled with fhining black feeds, which ripen toward the end of Auguft, when they fink to the bottom of the water.

The beft method to propagate thefe plants is, to procure fome of their feed-veffels juft as they are ripe and ready to open; thefe fhould be thrown into canals, or large ditches of ftanding water, where the feeds will fink to the bottom, and the following fpring the plants will appear floating upon the furface of the water, and in June and July will produce their beautiful large flowers. When they are once fixed to the place, they will multiply exceedingly, fo as to cover the whole furface of the water in a few years.

In fome fmall gardens I have feen the plants cultivated in large troughs of water, where they have flourifhed very well, and have annually produced great quantities of flowers; but as the expence of thefe troughs is pretty great (their infides requiring to be limed with lead, to preferve them) there are but few people who care to be at that charge.

O.

O C Y

OAK. See QUERCUS.
OBELISCOTHEÇA. See RUD-
BECKIA.
OCHRUS. See PISUM.
OCULUS CHRISTI. See HORMINUM SYL-
VESTRE.
OCYMUM. Tourn. Inſt. R. H. 203. tab. 96. Lin.
Gen. Plant. 651. Baſil; in French, *Baſilic*.

The CHARACTERS are,
The empalement of the flower is ſhort, permanent, of one
leaf, divided into two lips ; the upper lip is plain, bifid,
and heart-ſhaped ; the under is cut into four acute ſegments.
The flower is of the lip kind, of one petal inverted. It
has a ſhort ſpreading tube ; the riſing lip is broad, and
cut into four obtuſe equal parts ; the reflexed lip is long,
narrow, and ſawed. It hath four ſtamina in the lower
lip, which are deflexed, two of which are a little longer
than the other, terminated by half-moon-ſhaped ſummits.
The germen is divided into four parts, ſupporting a ſlen-
der ſtyle, ſituated with the ſtamina, crowned by a bifid
ſtigma. The germen afterward become four naked ſeeds
incloſed in the empalement.

This genus of plants is ranged in the firſt ſection of
Linnæus's fourteenth claſs, which contains thoſe
plants whoſe flowers have two long and two ſhorter
ſtamina, and their ſeeds have no covering.

The SPECIES are,
1. OCYMUM (*Baſilicum*) foliis ovatis glabris, calycibus
ciliatis. Hort. Cliff. 315. *Baſil with oval ſmooth leaves,*
and hairy empalements. Ocymum caryophyllatum
majus. C. B. P. 226. *Greater Clove-ſcented, or common*
Baſil.
2. OCYMUM (*Minimum*) foliis ovatis integerrimis. Hort.
Upſal. 169. *Baſil with oval entire leaves.* Ocymum
minimum. C. B. P. 226. *The leaſt Baſil, commonly*
called Buſh Baſil.
3. OCYMUM (*Medium*) hirſutum, foliis ovato-lanceolatis
acuminatis dentatis. *Hairy Baſil with oval ſpear-ſhaped*
leaves which are indented, and in acute points. Ocymum medium vulgatius & nigrum. J. B. 3. p. 2.
247. *Common middle black Baſil.*
4. OCYMUM (*Americanum*) foliis ovato-oblongis ſerratis,
bracteis cordatis reflexis concavis ſpicis filiformibus.
Lin. Sp. Plant. 833. *Baſil with oval, oblong, ſawed*
leaves, and heart-ſhaped, concave, reflexed bractea.
5. OCYMUM (*Campechianum*) foliis lanceolatis ſubtus incanis, petiolis longiſſimis villoſis floribus pedunculatis. *Baſil with ſpear-ſhaped leaves, which are hoary on*
their under ſide, and very long hairy foot-ſtalks to the
flowers. Ocymum Campechianum odoratiſſimum.
Houſt. MSS. *The ſweeteſt-ſcented Baſil of Campeachy.*
6. OCYMUM (*Frutescens*) racemis ſecundis lateralibus,
caule erecto, Lin. Sp. Plant. 832. *Baſil with fruitful*
ſpikes of flowers on the ſide of the ſtalk, which are erect.
Ocymum Zeylanicum; perenne, odoratiſſimum latifolium. Burm. Zeyl. 174. tab. 80. fol 1. *Sweet-ſcented*
perennial Baſil of Ceylon, with broad leaves.

The three firſt ſorts grow naturally in India and Per-
ſia ; of theſe there are a great variety, which differ in
the ſize, ſhape, and colour of their leaves, as alſo in
their odour; but as theſe differences are accidental,
ſo I have not enumerated them, being convinced from
repeated experiments, that the ſeeds of one plant will
produce many varieties.
The firſt ſort riſes with a branching ſtalk a foot and a
half high; the leaves are large, oval, and ſmooth;

O C Y

the ſtalk is hairy, and four-cornered ; the leaves are
placed by pairs oppoſite, and the branches alſo come
out in the ſame manner; the ſtalk is terminated by a
whorled ſpike of flowers, which is five or ſix inches
long, and the branches are alſo terminated by ſhort
ſpikes of flowers of the ſame ſort; the whole plant
has a ſtrong ſcent of Cloves.
Of this there are the following varieties :
1. The fringed-leaved Baſil with purple leaves.
2. The green fringed-leaved Baſil.
3. The green Baſil with ſtudded leaves.
4. The large-leaved Baſil.
The ſecond ſort is a low buſhy plant, which ſeldom
riſes more than ſix inches high, ſpreading out into
branches from the bottom, forming an orbicular
head; the leaves are ſmall, oval, and ſmooth, ſtanding oppoſite on ſhort foot-ſtalks. The flowers are
produced in whorls toward the top of the branches;
they are ſmaller than thoſe of the former ſort, and are
ſeldom ſucceeded by ripe ſeeds in England.
Of this there are ſome varieties, as
1. The ſmalleſt Baſil with black purple leaves.
2. The ſmalleſt Baſil with variable leaves.
The third ſort is the common Baſil which is uſed in
medicine, and alſo in the kitchen, particularly by the
French cooks, who make great uſe of it in their ſoups
and ſauces. This riſes about ten inches high, ſending out branches by pairs oppoſite, from the bottom;
the ſtalks and branches are four-cornered ; the leaves
are oval, ſpear-ſhaped, ending in acute points, and
are indented on their edges ; the whole plant is hairy,
and has a ſtrong ſcent of Cloves, too powerful for
moſt perſons, but to ſome it is very agreeable: the
whole plant is an ingredient in the compound Briony-
water.
There are ſome varieties of this ſpecies, viz.
1. Common Baſil with very dark green leaves, and
a Violet-coloured flower.
2. Curled-leaved Baſil with ſhort ſpikes of flowers.
3. Narrow-leaved Baſil ſmelling like Fennel.
4. Middle Baſil with a ſcent of Citron.
5. Baſil with ſtudded leaves.
6. Baſil with leaves of three colours.
The fourth ſort grows naturally in India; this riſes
with a branching ſtalk a foot and a half high, which
is taper, and of a purpliſh colour; the leaves are
ſhort and hairy; they are of an oval oblong figure,
ending in obtuſe points, and are ſawed on their edges,
ſtanding upon pretty long foot-ſtalks. The ſtalks
are terminated by three ſpikes of flowers, that in the
middle being longer than the other two ; the ſpikes
are narrow, and the flower have ſhort foot-ſtalks;
under each whorl of flowers are two ſmall leaves (or
bractea) placed oppoſite, which are heart-ſhaped, concave, and reflexed. The flowers are ſmall, and in
ſome plants are of a purpliſh colour, but in general
they are white; their empalements are ſmooth, and
cut into five parts at the top; the ſtyle of the flower
is longer than the petal, and the whole plant has a
ſtrong, ſweet, aromatic odour.
The fifth ſort riſes with an upright ſtalk near two feet
high, ſending out ſometimes two, and at others four
branches towards the top, oppoſite, garniſhed with
ſpear-ſhaped leaves about three inches long, and one
broad in the middle, leſſening at both ends to a point ;
their foot-ſtalks are two inches long, and are hairy.
The

The flowers grow in whorled fpikes at the top of. the ftalks, the flowers ftanding upon foot-ftalks, each fuf-taining three flowers; thefe are about the fize of thofe of the common Bafil, and are white ; the whole plant has a ftrong aromatic odour. It grows naturally at Campeachy.

The fixth fort grows naturally in the ifland of Cey-lon ; this rifes with a fquare ftalk two feet high, which is hairy, and divides into three branches at the top ; the lower leaves are roundifh, ending in points; they are hairy, and crenated on their edges, ftanding upon flender foot-ftalks; the leaves on the ftalks are narrower and fhorter, and have foot-ftalks an inch long ; the ftalks are terminated by three fpikes of flowers in whorls, that in the middle being the longeft. The flowers are reflexed and hang down-ward, they are white, and larger than thofe of the common fort. This plant has lefs odour than the other forts.

Thefe plants being moft of them annual, are propa-gared from feeds, which fhould be fown in March, upon a moderate hot-bed ; and when the plants are come up, they fhould be tranfplanted into another moderate hot-bed, obferving to water and fhade them until they have taken root; after which they fhould have plenty of air in mild weather, otherwife they will draw up very weak ; you muft alfo water them frequently, for they love moifture. In May they fhould be taken up with a ball of earth to their roots, and tranfplanted either into pots or borders, obferv-ing to fhade them until they have taken root; after which they will require no farther care but to clear them from weeds, and refrefh them with water in dry weather. Though thefe plants are only propa-gared from feeds, yet if you have any particular fort which may arife from feeds, which you are defirous to increafe, you may take off cuttings any time in May, and plant them on a moderate hot-bed, ob-ferving to water and fhade them for about ten days ; in which time they will take root, and in three weeks time be fit to remove, either into pots or borders, with the feedling plants. In September thefe plants will perfect their feeds, when thofe forts which ap-pear the moftdiftinct, fhould have their feeds preferved feparate, for fowing the following fpring.

The feeds of thefe plants are ufually brought from the fouth of France or Italy every fpring, becaufe fome of them feldom ripen their feeds in this country in the open air. But whoever is curious to preferve the feeds of any of the varieties, fhould place them in an airy glafs-cafe or ftove in the autumn, when the weather begins to be cold or wet; and by fupplying them with water, and letting them have free air every day in mild weather, they will perfect their feeds very well in this country.

The fifth fort is more tender than any of the other ; this was difcovered growing wild at Campeachy, by the late Dr. William Houftoun, who fent the feeds to England. This fhould be fown on a hot-bed early in the fpring, and when the plants are come up, they fhould be tranfplanted on another very tempe-rate hot-bed to bring them forward ; and when they have obtained ftrength, they fhould be each tranf-planted into a feparate pot, and placed either in the ftove, or on a moderate hot-bed, where they may have a large fhare of air in warm weather ; but by being fheltered from the cold and wet, the plants will perfect their feeds very well in England.

The fixth fort grows to be fhrubby, and if placed in a moderate warmth in winter, may be preferved two years ; but this will ripen its feeds the firft year, if the plants are brought forward in the fpring ; but if this fhould. fail, the plants may be placed in the ftove, where they may be kept through the winter, and the following feafon they will perfect their feeds. In the fummer the plants fhould be placed in the open air in a fheltered fituation, and in warm weather they fhould have plenty of water.

There have been many fictitious ftories handed down through feveral generations, of fcorpions being bred

in the brain of perfons who frequently fmelled this plant ; and others have afferted, that fcorpions com-monly breed under the plants, but thefe ftories are without foundation : but it is certain, that the odour of thefe plants is too ftrong for moft perfons, efpeci-ally in a room, or if near them ; for which reafon they fhould not be placed too near the habitation, becaufe if they are in any quantity, the odour will extend at times to moft of the apartments when the windows are open.

ŒNANTHE. Tourn. Inft. R. H. 312. tab. 166. Lin. Gen. Plant. 314. [Oἰνανϑη, of Oἶνη, a Vine, and Ἀνϑ⊙, a flower. The ancients called any plant Œnanthe that flowered at the fame time with the Vine, or whofe flowers had the fame odour.] Water Dropwort.

The CHARACTERS are,
It is a plant with an umbelliferous flower ; the principal umbel has but few rays, but the particular umbels have many fhort ones. The principal involucrum is compofed of many fingle leaves, which are fhorter than the umbel ; the fmaller umbels have many fmall leaves ; the rays of the principal umbel are different. Thofe flowers in the difk are hermaphrodite, and are compofed of five heart-fhaped inflexed petals, which are almoft equal; thofe of the rays are male, and have five large unequal petals which are bifid ;' they have five fingle ftamina terminated by roundifh fummits. The germen is fituated under the flower, fupporting two awl-fhaped permanent ftyles, crowned by obtufe ftigmas. The germen afterward becomes an oval fruit, divided into two parts, containing two almoft oval feeds, convex on one fide and plain on the other.

This genus of plants is ranged in the fecond fection of Linnæus's fifth clafs, which contains thofe plants whofe flowers have five ftamina and two ftyles.

The SPECIES are;
1. ŒNANTHE (*Crocata*) foliis omnibus multifidis obtufis fubæqualibus. Hort. Cliff. 99. *Water Dropwort, whofe leaves all end in many obtufe points, and are almoft equal.* Œnanthe fucco virofo, cicutæ facie lobelii. J. B. 3. p. 2. 193. *Hemlock Dropwort:*

2. ŒNANTHE (*Fiftulofa*) ftolonifera, foliis caulinis pin-natis filiformibus fiftulofis. Lin. Sp. Plant. 254. *Water Dropwort, with flender, fiftular, winged leaves growing on the ftalks.* Œnanthe aquatica. C. B. P. 162. *Wa-ter Dropwort.*

3. ŒNANTHE (*Pimpinelloides*) foliolis radicalibus cunea-tis fiffis, caulinis integris linearibus longiffimis cana-liculatis. Hort. Cliff. 99. *Water Dropwort whofe lower leaves are oval and cut, but thofe on the ftalks entire, narrow, and channelled.* Œnanthe apii folio. C. B. P. 162. *Water Dropwort with a Smallage leaf.*

4. ŒNANTHE (*Prolifera*) umbellularum pedunculis marginalibus longioribus ramofis mafculis. Hort. Upfal. 63. *Water Dropwort whofe foot-ftalks on the borders of the umbels are longer, branching; and bear male flowers.* Œnanthe prolifera Apula. C. B. P. 163. *Childing Water Dropwort of Apulia.*

5. ŒNANTHE (*Globulofa*) fructibus globofis. Hort. Cliff. 99. *Water Dropwort with globular fruit.* Œnanthe Lufitanica, femine craffiore globofo. Tourn. Inft. 313. *Portugal Water Dropwort, with a thicker globu-lar feed.*

The firft of thofe here mentioned, is very common by the fides of the Thames on each fide London, as alfo by the fides of large ditches and rivers in divers parts of England: this plant commonly grows four or five feet high with ftrong jointed ftalks, which, being broken, emit a yellowifh fœtid juice ; the leaves are fomewhat like thofe of the common Hemlock, bur are of a lighter green colour : the roots divide into four or five large taper ones, which, when fepa-rated, have fome refemblance to Parfneps; for which fome ignorant perfons have boiled them, whereby themfelves and family have been poifoned.

This plant is one of the moft poifonous we know ; the juice which is at firft like milk, turns afterward to a Saffron colour: if a perfon fhould fwallow ever fo little of this juice, it will fo contract every part it touches, that there will immediately follow a terrible inflammation and gangrene: and what is worfe, there has not yet been found an antidote againft it; for which reafon, we ought to be very careful to know this plant, in order to avoid it, for fear we fhould take it for any other like it, which would cer-. tainly prove fatal.

The poifonous quality of this plant, had led fome perfons to believe it to be the Cicuta of the ancients; but according to Wepfer, the Sium alterum olufatri facie of Lobel, is what the ancients called Cicuta, as may be feen at large in Wepfer's book De Cicuta.

The fecond fort is very common in moift foils, and by the fides of rivers in divers parts of England: this is not fuppofed to be near fo ftrong as the firft, but is of a poifonous quality.

All the forts of thefe plants naturally grow in moift places, fo that whoever hath a mind to cultivate them, fhould fow their feeds foon after they are ripe in autumn, upon a moift foil, where they will come up, and thrive exceedingly the following fummer, and require no farther care but to clear them from weeds.

ŒNOTHERA. Lin. Gen. Plant. 424. Onagra. Tourn. Inft. R. H. 302. tab. 156. Tree Primrofe.

The CHARACTERS are,

The empalement of the flower is of one leaf, having a long cylindrical tube, cut into four fegments at the brim, which turn backward. The flower has four heart-fhaped petals, which are lengthways inferted in the divifions of the empalement. It hath eight awl-fhaped incurved fla- mina, which are inferted in the tube of the empalement, and are terminated by oblong proftrate fummits. The cy- lindrical germen is fituated under the tube of the empale- ment, fupporting a flender ftyle, crowned by a thick qua- drifid, obtufe, reflexed ftigma. The germen afterward becomes a four-cornered cylindrical capfule having four cells, which are filled with fmall angular feeds.

This genus of plants is ranged in the firft fection of Linnæus's eighth clafs, which includes thofe plants whofe flowers have eight ftamina and one ftyle.

The SPECIES are,

1. ŒNOTHERA (*Biennis*) foliis ovato-lanceolatis planis, caule muricato fubvillofo Vir. Cliff. 33. *Tree Prim- rofe, with plain, oval, fpear-fhaped leaves, and a rough hairy ftalk.* Onagra latifolia. Tourn. Inft. 302. *Broad- leaved Tree Primrofe.*

2. ŒNOTHERA (*Anguftifolia*) foliis lanceolatis dentatis, caule hifpido. *Tree Primrofe with fpear-fhaped indented leaves, and a prickly ftalk.* Onagra anguftifolia, caule rubro, flore minore. Tourn. Inft. R. H. 302. *Nar- row-leaved Tree Primrofe, with a red ftalk and a fmaller flower.*

3. ŒNOTHERA (*Glabra*) foliis lanceolatis planis, caule glabro. *Tree Primrofe with plain fpear-fhaped leaves, and a fmooth ftalk.*

4. ŒNOTHERA (*Mollifima*) foliis lanceolatis undulatis. Vir. Cliff. 33. *Tree Primrofe with waved fpear-fhaped leaves.* Onagra Bonarienfis villofa, flore mutabili. Hort. Elth. 297. *Hairy Tree Primrofe of Buenos Ayres, with a changeable flower.*

5. ŒNOTHERA (*Pumila*) foliis radicalibus ovatis, cauli- nis lanceolatis obtufis, capfulis ovatis fulcatis. Tab. 188. *Tree Primrofe with oval leaves at the root, thofe on the ftalks fpear-fhaped, blunt-pointed, and oval fur- rowed feed-veffels.*

The other fpecies which have been formerly placed in this genus, are now under JUSSIÆA and LUDWIGIA, to which the reader is defired to turn.

The three firft forts grow naturally in Virginia, and in other parts of North America, from whence their feeds were brought to Europe in the beginning of the fixteenth century; but they are now become fo com- mon in many parts of Europe, as to be taken for na- tives. The firft hath a long, thick, taper root, which runs deep into the ground, from which arife many obtufe leaves which fpread flat on the ground; be- tween thefe the ftalks come out, which rife between three and four feet high, and is of a pale green colour, a little hairy, and about the thicknefs of a

finger, full of pith; this is garnifhed with long nar- row leaves fet clofe to the ftalk, without order. The flowers are produced all along the ftalk from the wings of the leaves, the germen fitting clofe to the ftalk, from the top of which arifes the tube of the flower, which is narrow, more than two inches long; at the top is the empalement, which is cut into four acute fegments, which are reflexed downward. The petal of the flower is cut into four large obtufe fegments, which in the evening are expanded quite flat, but are fhut in the day; thefe are of a bright yellow colour. From the flower opening in the evening, many per- fons call it the Night Primrofe. The plants begin to flower about Midfummer, and as the ftalks advance in height, fo other flowers are produced, whereby there is a fucceffion of flowers on the fame plant till autumn.

The fecond fort hath red ftalks, which are fet with rough protuberances: it does not rife fo high as the firft, the leaves are narrower, and the flowers are fmaller.

The third fort differs from the firft, in having fhort- er ftalks, narrower leaves, and fmaller flowers; and from the fecond, in having fmooth ftalks, which are of a pale green colour. Thefe differences are perma- nent, fo they are undoubtedly different fpecies.

The fourth fort grows naturally at Buenos Ayres; this hath a fhrubby ftalk more than two feet high, hairy, garnifhed with narrow fpear-fhaped leaves ending in acute points; thefe fit clofe to the ftalks, being a little waved on their edges. The flowers come out from the wings of the leaves along the ftalks, like the other forts; they are firft of a pale yellow, but as they decay change to an Orange colour; they are fmaller than thofe of either of the former forts, and expand only in the evening; the feed-veffels are flen- der, taper, and hairy. This flowers at the fame time with the former.

The fifth fort grows naturally in Canada, from whence the feeds were brought to Paris a few years paft. This is a perennial plant; the root is fibrous; the lower leaves are oval and fmall, fitting clofe to the ground; the ftalk is flender, near a foot high, and is garnifhed with fmall fpear-fhaped leaves, of a light green, ending in blunt points, fitting clofe to the ftalks. The flowers come out from the wings of the leaves like the other fpecies; thefe are fmall, of a bright yellow colour, and appear at the fame time as the former, and are fucceeded by fhort, oval, fur- rowed feed-veffels, filled with fmall feeds.

The three firft forts are very hardy plants, and if once brought into a garden, and the feeds permitted to fcatter, there will be a fupply of plants without any care. They are biennial, and perifh after they have perfected their feeds. The feeds of thefe plants fhould be fown in the autumn, for thofe which are fown in the fpring feldom rife the fame year: when the plants come up, they fhould be thinned and kept clean from weeds, which is all the care they require till the autumn, when they fhould be tranf- planted to the places where they are defigned to flower; but as the roots of thefe plants ftrike deep in the ground, fo there fhould be care taken not to cut or break them in removing. The plants will thrive in almoft any foil or fituation, and will flower in London in fmall gardens, better than moft other plants.

The fourth fort is now become pretty common in the Englifh gardens, for if the feeds of this are per- mitted to fcatter, the plants will come up the follow- ing fpring, and require no other care but to keep them clean from weeds, and thin them where they grow too clofe. If thefe plants are kept in pots, and placed in a green-houfe in the autumn, they will live through the winter; but as they produce flowers and feeds in the open air, the plants are feldom preferved longer.

The fifth fort is perennial, and may be propagated either by parting of the roots, or by feeds: if it is by the former, the beft time for doing it is in the fpring; but

but if they are propagated by feeds, thefe fhould be fown in the autumn; and the fureft way is to fow the feeds in pots, and place them under a hot-bed frame in winter : in the fpring the plants will appear, and when they are fit to remove, a few of them may be planted in fmall pots, to be fheltered under a common frame in the winter; and the others may be planted in a fheltered border, where they will endure the cold of our ordinary winters very well, and the following fummer they will produce flowers and feeds in plenty; fo there will be little occafion for parting of their roots, becaufe the feedling plants will be much ftronger and flower better, than thofe propagated by offsets.

OLDENLANDIA. Plum. Nov. Gen. 42. tab. 36. Lin. Gen. Plant. 143.

The CHARACTERS are,

The empalement of the flower is permanent, fitting upon the germen, and is cut into five parts. The flower has four oval petals which fpread open, and are double the length of the empalement, and four ftamina terminated by fmall fummits. It hath a roundifh germen fituated under the flower, fupporting a fingle ftyle, crowned by an indented ftigma. The germen afterward turns to a globular capfule with two cells, filled with fmall feeds.

This genus of plants is ranged in the firft fection of Linnæus's fourth clafs, which includes thofe plants whofe flowers have four ftamina and one ftyle.

We have but one SPECIES of this genus in the Englifh gardens, which is,

OLDENLANDIA (*Corymbofa*) pedunculis multifloris, foliis lineari-lanceolatis. Lin. Sp. Plant. 119. *Oldenlandia with many flowers on a foot ftalk, and linear fpear-fhaped leaves.* Oldenlandia humilis hyffopifolia. Plum. Nov. Gen. *Dwarf Oldenlandia having a Hyffop leaf.*

This plant was difcovered in America by Father Plumier, who gave this name to it in honour of Henry Bernard Oldenland, a German, who was difciple of Dr. Herman at Leyden, and was a very curious botanift.

The feeds of this plant were fent into England by Mr. Robert Millar, who gathered them in Jamaica. It is a low annual plant, which feldom rifes above three or four inches high, and divides into many branches which fpread near the ground. Thefe branches are furnifhed with long narrow leaves, which are placed oppofite. From the wings of the leaves arifes the flower-ftalk, which grows about an inch, or a little more in length, and divides into three or four fmaller foot-ftalks; on the top of each of thefe, ftands one fmall white flower.

The feeds of this plant fhould be fown early in the fpring on a hot-bed, and when the plants are come up, they fhould be tranfplanted on another hot-bed, or into fmall pots, and plunged into a moderate hot-bed of tanners bark, obferving to water and fhade them until they have taken root; after which time they muft have a large fhare of free air in warm weather, and fhould be frequently refrefhed with water. With this management the plants will flower in June, and their feeds will ripen in July, fo that the feeds muft be gathered from time to time as they ripen; for as the branches grow larger, fo there will be frefh flowers produced until autumn, when the plants will perifh; but if the feeds are permitted to fcatter in the pots, the plants will foon after appear, which will live through the winter, provided they are placed in the ftove, and will flower early the following fpring.

OLEA. Tourn. Inft. R. H. 598. tab. 370. Lin. Gen. Plant. 20. [of Ἐλαία,] the Olive; in French, *Olivier.*

The CHARACTERS are,

It has a fmall tubulous empalement of one leaf, cut into four fegments at the top. The flower confifts of one petal which is tubulous, cut at the brim into four fegments which fpread open. It has two fhort ftamina terminated by erect fummits, and a roundifh germen fupporting a fhort ftyle, crowned by a thick bifid ftigma. The germen after-

ward turns to an oval fmooth fruit (or berry) with one cell, inclofing an oblong oval nut.

This genus of plants is ranged in the firft fection of Linnæus's fecond clafs, which contains thofe plants whofe flowers have two ftamina and one ftyle.

The SPECIES are,

1. OLEA (*Gallica*) foliis lineari-lanceolatis fubtus incanis. *Olive with linear fpear-fhaped leaves, which are hoary on their under fide.* Olea fructu oblongo minori. Tourn. Inft. R. H. 599. *Olive with a fmaller oblong fruit, commonly called Provence Olive.*

2. OLEA (*Hifpanica*) foliis lanceolatis, fructu ovato. *Olive with fpear-fhaped leaves, and an egg-fhaped fruit.* Olea fructu maximo. Tourn. Inft. R. H. 599. *Olive with the largeft fruit, called the Spanifh Olive.*

3. OLEA (*Sylveftris*) foliis lanceolatis obtufis rigidis, fubtus incanis. *Olive with fpear-fhaped, obtufe, rigid leaves, which are hoary on their under fide.* Olea fylveftris, folio duro, fubtus incano. C. B. P. 472. *The wild Olive with a hard leaf, and hoary on its under fide.*

4. OLEA (*Africana*) foliis lanceolatis lucidis, ramis teretibus. *Olive with fpear-fhaped fhining leaves, and taper branches.* Olea Afra, folio longo, lato, fupra atroviridi fplendente, infra pallidè viridi. Boer. Ind. alt. 2. 218. *African Olive, with a long, broad, fhining leaf, of a greenifh black above, and pale on its under fide.*

5. OLEA (*Buxifolia*) foliis ovatis rigidis feffilibus. *Olive with oval ftiff leaves, fitting clofe to the branches.* Olea Afra, folio buxi craffo atroviridi, lucido, cortice albo fcabro. Boerh. Ind. alt. 2. 218. *African Olive, with a thick, dark, fhining Box leaf, and a rough white bark, commonly called Box-leaved Olive.*

The firft fort is what the inhabitants of the fouth of France chiefly cultivate, becaufe from this fpecies the beft oil is made, which is a great branch of trade in Provence and Languedoc; and it is the fruit of this fort which is moft efteemed when pickled : of this there are fome varieties; the firft is called Olive Picholine; there is another with dark green fruit, one with white fruit, and another with fmaller and rounder fruit; but as thefe are fuppofed to be only accidental varieties which have rifen from the fame feeds, I have not enumerated them.

The Olive feldom rifes to be a large tree, and is rarely feen with a fingle ftein, but frequently two or three ftems rife from the fame root; thefe grow from twenty to thirty feet high, putting out branches from the fides almoft their whole length, which are covered with a gray bark, and garnifhed with ftiff leaves about two inches and a half long, and half an inch broad in the middle, gradually diminifhing to both ends; they are of a lively green on their upper fide, and hoary on their under, ftanding oppofite. The flowers are produced in fmall bunches from the wings of the leaves; they are fmall, white, and have fhort tubes, fpreading open at the top; thefe are fucceeded by oval fruit, which, in warm countries, ripen in the autumn.

The fecond fort is chiefly cultivated in Spain, where the trees grow to a much larger fize than the former fort; the leaves are much larger, and not fo white on their under fide; and the fruit is near twice the fize of thofe of the Provence Olive, but are of a ftrong rank flavour, and the oil made from thefe, is too ftrong for moft Englifh palates.

The third fort is the wild Olive, which grows naturally in woods, in the fouth of France, Spain, and Italy, fo is never cultivated; the leaves of this fort are much fhorter and ftiffer than thofe of the other; the branches are frequently armed with thorns, and the fruit is fmall and of no value.

The fourth and fifth forts grow naturally at the Cape of Good Hope; the fourth rifes to the height of the firft, to which it bears fome refemblance, but the bark is rougher; the leaves are not fo long, and are of a lucid green on their upper fide; but as this does not produce fruit in Europe, I can give no account of it.

The

OLE   **OLE**

The fifth fort is of humbler growth, feldom rifing more than four or five feet high, fending out branches from the root upward, forming a bufhy fhrub ; the branches are taper, and covered with a gray bark ; the leaves are oval, very ftiff, and fmaller than thofe of the other fpecies. This has not produced any fruit in England.

All thefe forts are preferved in the gardens of the curious, but they are rather too tender to thrive in the open air, in the neighbourhood of London, where they are fometimes planted againft walls, and with a little protection in very fevere froft, they are maintained pretty well ; but in Devonfhire there are fome of thefe trees, which have grown in the open air many years, and are feldom injured by the froft, but the fummers are not warm enough to bring the fruit to maturity. There were feveral of thefe trees planted againft a warm wall at Cambden-houfe near Kenfington, which fucceeded very well, till their tops were advanced above the wall ; after which they were generally killed in winter, fo far down as to the top of the wall. Thefe in 1719 produced a good number of fruit, which grew fo large as to be fit for pickling ; but fince that time, their fruit has feldom grown to any fize.

The Olive was, by the ancients, confidered as a maritime tree, and they fuppofed it would not thrive at any diftance from the fea ; but by experience, we find they will fucceed very well in any country, where the air is of a proper temperature of heat, though the trees are found to bear the fpray of the fea better than moft other forts.

In Languedoc and Provence, where the Olive-tree is greatly cultivated, they propagate it by truncheons fplit from the roots of the trees ; for as thefe trees are frequently hurt by hard frofts in winter, fo when their tops are killed, they fend up feveral ftalks from the root ; and when thefe are grown pretty ftrong, they feparate them with an ax from the root, in the doing of which they are careful to preferve a few roots to the truncheons ; thefe are cut off in the fpring, after the danger of froft is over, and planted about two feet deep in the ground, covering the furface with litter or mulch, to prevent the fun and wind from penetrating and drying of the ground ; when the plants have taken new root, they are careful to ftir the ground and deftroy the weeds.

This tree will grow in almoft any foil, but when it is planted in rich moift ground, they grow larger and make a finer appearance, than in poor land ; but the fruit is of lefs efteem, becaufe the oil made from it is not fo good as that which is produced in a leaner foil. The chalky ground is efteemed the beft for thefe trees, and the oil which is made from the trees growing in that fort of land is much finer, and will keep longer than the other.

In the countries where the inhabitants are curious in the making of their oil, they are frequently obliged to get truncheons of the ordinary forts of Olives to plant ; but after they have taken good root, they graft them with the fort of Olive which they prefer, to the others. In Languedoc they chiefly propagate the Cormeau, the Ampoulan, and Moureau, which are three varieties of the firft fpecies : but in Spain the fecond fort is generally cultivated, where they have more regard to the fize of the fruit, and the quantity of oil they will produce, than to their quality. If the culture of thefe trees was well underftood by the inhabitants of Carolina, and properly purfued, it might become a valuable branch of trade to them ; for there is no reafon to doubt of their fucceeding, the fummers there being hot enough to ripen the fruit to its utmoft perfection.

In this country the plants are only preferved by way of curiofity, and are placed in winter in the greenhoufe for variety, fo I fhall next give an account of the method by which they are here propagated, with their manner of treatment.

Thefe plants may be propagated by laying down their tender branches (in the manner practifed for other trees,) which fhould remain undifturbed two years ; in which time they will have put out roots, and may then be taken off from the old plants, and tranfplanted either into pots filled with frefh light earth, or into the open ground in a warm fituation. The beft feafon for tranfplanting is the beginning of April, when you fhould, if poffible, take the opportunity of a moift feafon ; and thofe which are planted in pots, fhould be placed in a fhady part of the green-houfe until they have taken root ; but thofe planted in the ground fhould have mulch laid about their roots, to prevent the earth from drying too faft, and now and then refrefhed with water ; but you muft by no means let them have too much moifture, which will rot the tender fibres of their roots, and deftroy the trees. When the plants have taken frefh root, thofe in the pots may be expofed to the open air, with other hardy exotics, with which they fhould be houfed in winter, and treated as Myrtles, and other lefs tender trees and fhrubs ; but thofe in the open air will require no farther care until the winter following, when you fhould mulch the ground about their roots, to prevent the froft from penetrating deep into it ; and if the froft fhould prove very fevere, you fhould cover them with mats, which will defend them from being injured thereby ; but you muft be cautious not to let the mats continue over them after the froft is paft, left by keeping them too clofe, their leaves and tender branches fhould turn mouldy for want of free air ; which will be of as bad confequence to the trees, as if they had been expofed to the froft, and many times worfe ; for it feldom happens, if they have taken much of this mould, or have been long covered, fo that it has entered the bark, that they are ever recoverable again ; whereas it often happens, that the froft only deftroys the tender fhoots ; but the body and larger branches remaining unhurt, put out again the fucceeding fpring.

Thefe trees are generally brought over from Italy every fpring, by the perfons who import Orangetrees, Jafmines, &c. from whom they may be procured pretty reafonable ; which is a better method than to raife them from layers in this country, that being too tedious ; and thofe which are thus brought over, have many times very large ftems, to which fize young plants in this country would not arrive in ten or twelve years. When you firft procure thefe ftems, you fhould (after having foaked their roots twenty-four hours in water, and cleaned them from the filth they have contracted in their paffage) plant them in pots filled with frefh light fandy earth, and plunge them into a moderate hot-bed, obferving to fcreen them from the violence of the fun in the heat of the day, and alfo to refrefh them with water, as you fhall find the earth in the pots dry. In this fituation they will begin to fhoot in fix weeks or two months after, when you fhould let them have air in proportion to the warmth of the feafon ; and after they have made pretty good fhoots, you fhould inure them to the open air by degrees, into which they fhould be removed, placing them in a fituation where they may be defended from ftrong winds ; in this place they fhould remain till October following, when they muft be removed into the green-houfe, as was before directed. Having thus managed thefe plants until they have acquired ftrong roots, and made tolerable good heads, you may draw them out of the pots, preferving the earth to their roots, and plant them in the open air in a warm fituation, where you muft manage them as was before directed for the young ones ; and thefe will in two or three years produce flowers, and in very warm feafons fome fruit, provided they do well. The Lucca and Box-leaved Olives are the hardieft, for which reafon they fhould be preferred to plant in the open air, but the firft fort will grow to be the largeft trees.

OMPHA-

OMPHALODES. See CYNOGLOSSUM.

ONAGRA. See ŒNOTHERA.

ONIONS. See CEPA.

ONOBRYCHIS. See HEDYSARUM.

ONONIS. Lin. Gen. Plant. 772. Anonis. Tourn. Inst. R. H. 408. tab. 229. Reft-harrow, Cammock, Pettywin ; in French, *Arrête-beuf.*

The CHARACTERS are,

The empalement of the flower is cut into five narrow segments, which end in acute points, the upper being a little raised and arched, the lower bending under the keel. The flower is of the butterfly kind. The standard is heart-shaped, depressed on the sides, and larger than the wings. The wings are oval and short ; the keel is pointed, and longer than the wings. It hath ten stamina joined together, terminated by single summits, and an oblong hairy germen, supporting a single style, crowned by an obtuse stigma. The germen afterward becomes a turgid pod with one cell, inclosing kidney-shaped seeds.

This genus of plants is ranged in the third section of Linnæus's seventeenth class, which includes those plants whose flowers have ten stamina joined in two bodies.

The SPECIES are,

1. ONONIS (*Spinosa*) floribus subsessilibus, solitariis lateralibus, caule spinoso. Hort. Cliff. 389. *Rest-harrow with single flowers sitting close to the sides of the branches, and a prickly stalk.* Anonis spinosa flore purpureo. C. B. P. 389. *Prickly Rest-harrow with a purple flower, sometimes called Cammock, or Petty-win, and in some countries, French Furze.*

2. ONONIS (*Mitis*) floribus subsessilibus solitariis lateralibus, ramis inermibus. Hort. Cliff. 359. *Rest-harrow with single flowers sitting close to the stalks, and branches without spines.* Anonis spinis carens purpurea. C. B. P. 389. *Purple Rest-harrow having no spines.*

3. ONONIS (*Repens*) caulibus diffusis, ramis erectis, foliis superioribus solitariis stipulis ovatis. Lin. Sp. 1006. *Rest-harrow with diffused stalks, which are erect, the upper leaves single, and oval stipulæ.* Anonis maritima procumbens, foliis hirsutis pubescentibus. Pluk. Alm. 33. *Trailing maritime Rest-harrow with hairy leaves.*

4. ONONIS (*Tridentata*) foliis ternatis carnosis sublinearibus tridentatis, fruticosa pedunculis bifloris. Lin. Sp Plant. 718. *Shrubby Rest-harrow, with trifoliate fleshy leaves which are narrow, and have three indentures.* Anonis Hispanica, frutescens, folio tridentato carnoso. Tourn. Inst. 408. *Shrubby Spanish Rest-harrow with a fleshy leaf, having three indentures.*

5. ONONIS (*Fruticosa*) fruticosa floribus paniculatis, pedunculis subtrifloris, stipulis vaginalibus, foliis ternatis lanceolatis serratis. Hort. Cliff. 358. *Rest-harrow with paniculated flowers growing three upon a foot-stalk, sheath-like stipulæ, and trifoliate leaves.* Anonis purpurea verna præcox frutescens, flore rubro amplo. Mor. Hist. 2. p. 170. *Early spring, purple, shrubby Rest-harrow, with a large red flower.*

6. ONONIS (*Natrix*) pedunculis unifloris aristatis foliis terminatis ovatis, stipulis integerrimis. Hort. Cliff. 358. *Rest-harrow with one flower on a foot-stalk terminated by a thread, and oval trifoliate leaves.* Anonis viscosa spinis carens lutea major. C. B. P. 389. *Glutinous Rest-harrow without spines, having a large yellow flower.*

7. ONONIS (*Viscosa*) pedunculis unifloris aristatis, foliis simplicibus inimis ternatis. Lin. Sp. 1009. *Rest-harrow with one flower on each foot-stalk terminated by a thread, whose lower leaves are trifoliate.* Anonis annua erectior, latifolia glutinosa Lusitanica. Tourn. Inst. 409. *Annual broad-leaved, glutinous, erect Rest-harrow of Portugal.*

8. ONONIS (*Minutissima*) floribus subsessilibus lateralibus, foliis ternatis glabris, stipulis setaceis, calycibus aristis corolla longioribus. Lin. Sp. Plant. 1007. *Rest-harrow with flowers sitting close to the sides of the stalks, trifoliate leaves, bristly stipulæ, and the beard of the calyx longer than the corolla.* Anonis flore luteo parvo. H. R. Par. *Rest-harrow with a small yellow flower.*

9. ONONIS (*Cristata*) pedunculis unifloris prælongis, ramis inermibus, foliis ternatis glabris, vaginis acutè dentatis. *Rest-harrow with one flower growing on a long foot-stalk, branches without spines, smooth trifoliate leaves, and sheaths which are sharply indented.* Anonis glabra inermis, pedunculis unifloris prælongis vaginis cristatis. Allion. *Smooth Rest-harrow without spines, having one flower on a long foot-stalk, with a crested sheath.*

10. ONONIS (*Ornithopodoides*) pedunculis bifloris aristatis, leguminibus linearibus cernuis. Prod. Leyd. 376. *Rest-harrow with two flowers on a foot-stalk terminated by a thread, and narrow nodding pods.* Anonis siliquis ornithopodii. Boerh. Ind. alt. 2. 34. *Rest-harrow with pods like those of the Bird's-foot.*

11. ONONIS (*Rotundifolia*) fruticosa pedunculis trifloris, calycibus triphyllo-bracteatis foliis ternatis subrotundis. Hort. Cliff. 358. *Rest-harrow with foot-stalks proceeding from the side of the branches, sustaining three flowers, and trifoliate roundish leaves.* Cicer sylvestre latifolium triphyllum. C. B. P. 347. *Broad three-leaved wild Chich.*

12. ONONIS (*Mitissima*) floribus sessilibus spicatis, bracteis stipularibus, ovatis ventricosis scariosis imbricatis. Lin. Sp. 1007. *Rest-harrow with spiked flowers sitting close, and oval stipulæ to the flowers.* Anonis alopecuroides, mitis annua purpurascens. Hort. Elth. 28. tab. 24. *Smooth, annual, purplish, Fox-tail Rest-harrow.*

13. ONONIS (*Alopecuroides*) spicis foliosis simplicibus ovatis obtusis stipulis dilatis. Lin. Sp. Plant. 1008. *Rest-harrow with leafy spikes, and single obtuse leaves.* Anonis sicula alopecuroides. Tourn. Inst. 408. *Fox-tail Rest-harrow of Sicily.*

14. ONONIS (*Amil*) foliis ternatis ovatis, petiolis longissimis, leguminibus hirsutis. *Rest-harrow with oval trifoliate leaves growing on very long foot-stalks, and hairy pods.* Anonis Americana, folio latiori subrotundo. Tourn. Inst. R. H. 409. *American Rest-harrow with a broader roundish leaf.*

15. ONONIS (*Decumbens*) foliis ternatis lineari-lanceolatis, caule decumbente, floribus spica is alaribus, leguminibus glabris. *Rest-harrow with trifoliate, narrow, spear-shaped leaves, a trailing stalk, flowers growing in spikes from the wings of the stalk, and smooth pods.* Anonis Americana, angustifolia, humilior & minus hirsuta. Houst. MSS. *Lower narrow-leaved American Rest-harrow, which is less hairy.*

The first sort is a common weed in most parts of England, so is rarely admitted into gardens. It has a strong creeping root, which spreads far in the ground, and is with great difficulty eradicated ; the stalks rise a foot and a half high, they are slender, purple, and hairy, sending out small branches on their side, which are armed with sharp prickles. The flowers come out singly from the side of the branches ; they are of the butterfly kind, and of a purple colour, which are succeeded by small pods, containing one or two kidney-shaped seeds. It flowers great part of summer, and the seeds ripen in the autumn. The root of this is one of the five opening roots ; the cortical part of it is esteemed a good medicine for stoppage of urine, and to open the obstructions of the liver and spleen ; there is a variety of this with white flowers.

The second sort grows naturally in many parts of England, and has been by some supposed to be only a variety of the first ; but I have cultivated both by seeds, and have always found the plants retain their difference ; the stalks of this sort are hairy, and more diffused than those of the first ; the leaves are broader, and sit closer on the branches ; the stalks do not grow so upright, and have no spines ; the flowers and pods are like those of the first. There is also a variety of this with white flowers.

The third sort grows naturally on the borders of the sea in several parts of England ; this hath a creeping root, from which arise many hairy stalks which are near two feet long, spreading on every side upon the ground, garnished with trifoliate hairy leaves, those on the lower part of the stalks being pretty large and oval,

oval, but the upper are fmaller and narrower. The flowers are like thofe of the firft in fhape, coming out fingly from the fide of the ftalks, but are of a brighter purple colour; the pods are fhort; containing two or three feeds in each. It flowers in July, and the feeds ripen in autumn.

The fourth fort grows naturally in Spain and Portugal; this rifes with fhrubby ftalks a foot and a half high, dividing into flender branches very full of joints, garnifhed with narrow, trifoliate, thick, flefhy leaves, ftanding upon fhort foot-ftalks. The flowers are produced at the end of the branches in loofe panicles, fome of the foot-ftalks fuftaining two, and others but one flower; they are of a fine purple colour, and appear in June; the feeds ripen in September.

The fifth fort grows naturally on the Alps: this is a very beautiful low fhrub; it rifes with flender fhrubby ftalks about two feet high, dividing into many branches, which are garnifhed with narrow trifoliate leaves fawed on their edges, fitting clofe to the branches. The flowers come out in panicles at the end of the branches upon long foot-ftalks, which for the moft part fuftain three large purple flowers; the ftipula is a kind of fheath, embracing the foot-ftalk of the flower. It flowers the end of May and the beginning of June, and the flowers are fucceeded by turgid pods about an inch long, which are hairy, inclofing three or four kidney-fhaped feeds, which ripen in Auguft.

The fixth fort grows naturally in the fouth of France and in Spain; this hath a perennial root and an annual ftalk, which rifes near two feet high, fending out fhort branches from the fide on the lower part of the plants, garnifhed with trifoliate oblong leaves, which are hairy and clammy. The flowers grow in loofe fpikes at the end of the ftalks; they are large, and of a bright yellow colour, ftanding upon pretty long foot-ftalks, which are extended beyond the leaves, the flowers hanging downward from the middle of the foot-ftalk. The flowers appear the latter end of June, which are fucceeded by turgid pods an inch long, containing three or four brown kidney-fhaped feeds, which ripen in September.

The feventh fort grows naturally in Portugal, from whence the feeds were fent to me. This is an annual plant, with a ftrong, herbaceous, hairy ftalk, rifing a foot and a half high, fending out branches the whole length, clofely garnifhed with trifoliate leaves; the middle lobe being large and oval, the two fide lobes long and narrow, rounded at their points and indented on their edges; they are very clammy. The foot-ftalks of the flowers come out from the wings of the ftalks fingly, each fuftaining one pale yellow flower, ftanding erect in the middle of the foot-ftalk, which is extended beyond the flower. This plant flowers in July, and the feeds ripen in autumn.

The eighth fort grows naturally in the fouth of France and Italy; this is an annual plant; the ftalks rife about nine inches high, fending out one or two fide branches toward the bottom; the leaves are fmall, trifoliate, and oval, ftanding upon pretty long foot-ftalks, and are indented on their edges. The flowers come out fingly at the wings of the ftalk; they are fmall, yellow, and fit very clofe to the ftalk, having a fharp briftly ftipula under the empalement; the pods are very fhort and turgid, containing two or three kidney-fhaped feeds. It flowers in July, and the feeds ripen in the autumn.

The ninth fort grows naturally on the Alps; this hath a perennial root, from which come out feveral flender trailing ftalks about fix inches long, garnifhed with fmall, trifoliate, oval leaves, indented on their edges, ftanding upon pretty fhort foot-ftalks. The flowers come out fingly toward the top of the ftalk, upon pretty flender foot-ftalks, arifing from the wings of the leaves, each fuftaining one yellow flower; the fheath embracing the bafe of the foot-ftalk, is fharply indented. This flowers in June, and the feeds ripen in the autumn.

The tenth fort grows naturally in Sicily, and is an annual plant; the ftalks rife about nine inches high, fending out one or two branches toward the bottom, garnifhed with fmall trifoliate leaves, which ftand on fhort foot-ftalks. The flowers come out from the fide of the branches upon fhort foot-ftalks, each fuftaining two fmall yellow flowers, which are fucceeded by jointed compreffed pods like thofe of Bird's-foot, having four or five kidney-fhaped feeds in each. This fort flowers in July, and the feeds ripen in the autumn.

The eleventh fort grows naturally on the Alps and Helvetian mountains; this rifes with a fingle jointed ftalk a foot and a half high, garnifhed with oval, indented, trifoliate leaves, ftanding on pretty long foot-ftalks. The foot-ftalks of the flowers come out from the wings of the leaves; they are long, flender, each fuftains three pale yellow flowers, which are fucceeded by fhort turgid pods, containing two or three feeds in each. It flowers in June, and the feeds ripen in September.

The twelfth fort came up in earth which was brought from Barbadoes, but it does not feem to be a native of that country, for it rifes eafily from feeds in the open air here, and perfects its feeds in the autumn, nor will it thrive in greater warmth. This hath an upright ftalk a foot and a half high, fending out fmall fide branches, which are garnifhed with roundifh trifoliate leaves fawed on their edges, ftanding upon fhort foot-ftalks. The flowers grow in fhort leafy fpikes at the end of the branches; they are fmall, and of a pale purple colour, appearing in July, and are fucceeded by fhort turgid pods, containing two or three kidney-fhaped feeds, which ripen in the autumn.

The thirteenth fort grows naturally in Portugal, Spain, and Italy. This is an annual plant, rifing with upright branching ftalks a foot high, garnifhed with fingle leaves fitting clofe to the ftalks; the larger leaves are oval, about one inch long and three quarters of an inch broad; the upper leaves are narrow, ending in obtufe points, and are flightly indented at their ends. The flowers grow in leafy fpikes at the end of the ftalks fet clofe together, having hairy empalements; they are pretty large, of a purple colour, and appear in July: thefe are fucceeded by taper pods about an inch long, inclofing four or five kidney-fhaped feeds. This plant has feveral titles, in the different books of botany.

The fourteenth fort grows naturally in the American iflands; this is an annual plant, rifing with a branching ftalk two feet high, garnifhed with trifoliate leaves, whofe lobes are oval, ftanding upon very long foot-ftalks, which are hairy. The flowers grow in loofe fpikes at the end of the branches; they are large, and of a purplifh yellow colour, and are fucceeded by very turgid hairy pods, each containing five or fix large kidney-fhaped feeds. This fort flowers in July and Auguft, and the feeds ripen in the autumn. From this plant Indigo was formerly made, which, I fuppofe, was of lefs value than that which is made of Anil, fo has not been for many years paft cultivated in any of the iflands.

The fifteenth fort was difcovered by the late Dr. Houftoun, growing naturally at La Vera Cruz in New Spain, from whence he fent the feeds to England. This is a perennial plant, from whofe roots come out feveral pretty ftrong branches, which fpread and incline toward the ground; thefe are garnifhed with narrow trifoliate leaves, very little hairy. The flowers come out in loofe panicles at the end of the branches; they are yellow, and are fucceeded by fmooth turgid pods about half an inch long, each containing two or three kidney-fhaped feeds. This flowers in July, and the feeds fometimes ripen here in the autumn.

The three firft forts are never cultivated in gardens, being very troublefome weeds whenever they get into the fields; for the roots fpread and multiply greatly in the ground, and are fo tough and ftrong, that the plough will fcarcely cut through them, fo are with great difficulty eradicated when they have once gotten poffeffion.

The

The fourth and fifth forts are low fhrubby plants, which are propagated by feeds. The fourth is too tender to thrive in the open air in England, unlefs it is planted in a warm fituation, and in very fevere froft covered to protect it. If the feeds of both thefe forts are fown upon a bed of light earth in April, the plants will come up in May, when they muft be kept clean from weeds; and if they are too clofe, fome of them fhould be carefully drawn up in moift weather, and tranfplanted at four or five inches diftance : thofe of the fourth fort upon a warm fheltered border, but the fifth may be planted in a fhady border, where they will thrive very well; after thefe have taken root, the plants will thrive very well, but muft be kept clean from weeds till the following autumn, when they may be tranfplanted to the places where they are to remain; thofe plants which were left growing in the bed where they were fown, muft alfo be treated in the fame way. Thefe plants will not thrive in pots, therefore fhould always be planted in the full ground, where the fixth fort will flourifh greatly, and frequently fend up many plants from their roots, but the other is more impatient of cold. Thefe plants will flower the fecond year, and make a fine appearance during the continuance of their flowers, and the fifth fort will produce feeds in plenty.

The fixth fort is propagated by feeds, which fhould be fown thin in drills upon a bed of light earth; and when the plants come up, they muft be kept clean from weeds till the autumn, when they fhould be carefully taken up, and tranfplanted into the borders of the pleafure-garden, where they are to remain; the fecond year they will flower and produce ripe feeds, but the roots will continue feveral years, and are very hardy.

The feventh, eighth, and eleventh forts are hardy annual plants; thefe are propagated by feeds, which fhould be fown in the places where the plants are to remain, and will require no other care but to thin them where they are too clofe, and keep them clean from weeds.

The ninth fort is a hardy perennial plant, but as it makes but little appearance, fo it is rarely preferved, unlefs in botanic gardens for the fake of variety; it rifes yearly from feed, and will thrive in any foil or fituation.

The fourteenth fort is an annual plant; the feeds of this muft be fown upon a moderate hot-bed in the fpring, and, when the plants are fit to remove, they fhould be tranfplanted to another moderate hot-bed to bring the plants forward, treating them in the fame way as the African and French Marygold. In June they fhould be taken up with balls of earth to their roots, and tranfplanted into the open borders, where, if they are fhaded till they have taken root, they will thrive and flower the following month, and perfect their feeds in autumn.

The eighteenth fort is a tender plant. The feeds of this fhould be fown upon a good hot-bed in the fpring, and when the plants are fit to remove, they fhould be each planted in a fmall pot filled with light loamy earth, and plunged into a hot-bed of tanners bark, obferving to fhade them from the fun till they have taken new root, after which they muft be treated in the fame way as other tender plants from the fame countries. In autumn they fhould be removed into the bark-ftove; the fummer following they will produce flowers, but they do not often perfect feeds in England.

ONOPORDUM. Lin. Gen. Plant. 834. Vaill. Act. Par. 1718. Carduus. Tourn. Inft. R. H. 440. tab. 253. Woolly Thiftle; in French, Chardon.

The CHARACTERS are,

The common empalement is roundifh, bellied, and imbricated, compofed of numerous fcales terminated by fpines. The flower is compofed of many hermaphrodite florets, which are funnel-fhaped, equal, and uniform, having narrow tubes fwelling at the brim, cut into five points; they have five fhort hairy ftamina, terminated by cylindrical fummits, and an oval germen crowned with down,

fupporting a flender ftyle terminated by a crowned ftigma. The germen becomes a fingle feed crowned with down, fitting in the empalement.

This genus of plants is ranged in the firft fection of Linnæus's nineteenth clafs, which includes thofe plants with compound flowers, whofe florets are all hermaphrodite and fruitful.

The SPECIES are,

1. ONOPORDUM (*Acanthium*) calycibus fquarrofis, foliis ovato-oblongis finuatis. Lin. Sp. Plant. 827. *Woolly Thiftle with rough empalements, and oblong, oval, finnated leaves.* Carduus tomentofus, acanthi folio, vulgaris. Tourn. Inft. R. H. 441. *Common Woolly Thiftle with a Bearfbreech leaf.*

2. ONOPORDUM (*Illyricum*) calycibus fquarrofis, fpinis foliis lanceolatis pinnatifidis. Lin. Sp. Plant. 1158. *Woolly Thiftle with rough empalements, and narrow leaves ending in many points.* Carduus tomentofus, acanthi folio anguftiori. Tourn. Inft. R. H. 441. *Woolly Thiftle with a narrower Bearfbreech leaf.*

3. ONOPORDUM (*Arabicum*) calycibus imbricatis. Hort. Upfal. 249. *Woolly Thiftle with imbricated empalements.* Carduus tomentofus, acanthi folio altiffimus, Lufitanicus. Tourn. Inft. 441. *Talloft woolly Thiftle of Portugal, with a Bearfbreech leaf.*

4. ONOPORDUM (*Orientale*) calycibus fquarrofis, foliis oblongis pinnato-finuatis decurrentibus, capite magno. *Woolly Thiftle with rough empalements, oblong, finuated, wing-pointed leaves running along the ftalk, and a large head.* Carduus tomentofus, acanthi folio Aleppicus, magno flore. Tourn. Inft. R. H. 441. *Woolly Thiftle of Aleppo with a Bearfbreech leaf, and a large flower.*

5. ONOPORDUM (*Acaulon*) fubacaule. Lin. Sp. 1159. *Woolly Thiftle with a head fitting clofe to the ground.* Onopordon acaulon ferme flore albicante. D. Juffieu. Vaill. Mem. 1718. *Woolly Thiftle without a ftalk, and having a whitifh flower.*

There are fome other fpecies of this genus, which are preferved in botanic gardens, and alfo feveral varieties differing in the colours of their flowers; but as thefe plants are rarely admitted into other gardens, fo it would be to little purpofe to enumerate them here.

The firft fort grows naturally on uncultivated places in moft parts of England. It is a biennial plant; the firft year it puts out many large downy leaves, which are finuated on their edges, and are prickly; thefe fpread on the ground, and continue the following winter, and in the fpring arifes the ftalk in the middle of the leaves, which, upon dunghills, or good ground, grows five or fix feet high, dividing upward into many branches, which have leafy borders running along them, indented, and each indenture is terminated by a fpine. The ftalks are terminated by fcaly heads of purple flowers, which appear in June, and to thefe fucceed oblong angular feeds crowned with a hairy down, which affift their fpreading about to a great diftance by the wind, fo that where the plants are permitted to ripen their feeds, they often become troublefome weeds.

The fecond fort grows naturally in Spain, Portugal, and the Levant; this rifes with a taller ftalk than the former, the leaves are much longer and narrower, and the indentures on their fides are regular, ending in fharp fpines. The heads of flowers are larger, and the fpines of the empalement are longer than thofe of the firft fort.

The third fort grows to the height of nine or ten feet; the ftalks divide into many branches; the leaves are longer than any of the other fpecies; the heads of flowers are large and of a purple colour; the empalement hath the fcales lying over each other like the fcales of fifh. This grows naturally in Spain and Portugal.

The fourth fort grows naturally about Aleppo; this rifes with an upright branching ftalk feven or eight feet high; the leaves are long and are regularly finuated on their borders, like wing-pointed leaves; the heads of the flowers are very large, and the empalement is very rough and prickly.

The

The fifth fort hath feveral oblong, oval, woolly leaves, which fpread on the ground ; between thefe comes out the head of flowers fitting clofe to the ground ; thefe heads are fmaller than any of the other, and the flowers are white. Some of thefe plants have been formerly cultivated for the table, but it was before the Englifh gardens were well fupplied with other efculent plants, for at prefent they are rarely eaten here. They require no culture, for if the feeds are permitted to fall, the plants will come up faft enough.

ONOSMA. Lin. Gen. 187.

The CHARACTERS are,

The flower hath a permanent empalement of one leaf, which is erect, and cut into five fegments ; the corolla is bellſhaped, of one petal, having a ſhort tube, with a fwelling top, the brim cut into five parts, and naked pervious chaps ; it hath five ſhort awl-ſhaped ſtamina, terminated by arrow-ſhaped ſummits, which are the length of the corolla, and a germen of four parts, ſupporting a ſlender ſtyle, crowned by an obtuſe ſtigma ; the germen afterward becomes four feeds fitting in the empalement.

This genus of plants is ranged in the firſt ſection of Linnæus's fifth claſs, intitled Pentandria Monogynia, the flowers having five ſtamina and one ſtyle.

The SPECIES are,

1. ONOSMA (*Simpliciſſima*) foliis confertiſſimis lanceolato-linearibus pilofis. Lin. Sp. 196. *Onoſma with hairy, linear, ſpear-ſhaped leaves growing in cluſters.* Echium Creticum. Alp. Exot. 130. *Cretan Viper's Buglofs.*

2. ONOSMA (*Orientalis*) foliis lanceolatis hifpidis, fructibus pendulis. Lin. Sp. 196. *Onoſma with hiſpid ſpear-ſhaped leaves, and hanging fruit.* Cerinthe Orientalis. Amœn. Acad. 4. p. 267. *Eaſtern Honeywort.*

3. ONOSMA (*Echioides*) foliis lanceolatis hifpidis, fructibus erectis. Lin. Sp. 196. *Onoſma with hiſpid ſpearſhaped leaves and erect fruit.* Anchuſa lutea minor. C. B. P. 255. *Smaller yellow Buglofs.*.

The firſt and ſecond forts are generally biennial plants, which perifh foon after they have perfected feeds ; though fometimes when they happen to grow out of the joints of walls, or the fiſſures of rocks, they will abide three or four years ; for in fuch fituations the plants are ſtinted in their growth, fo are lefs replete with moiſture, and more compact, whereby they are in lefs danger of ſuffering from froft in winter. Therefore, if all the three forts can be cultivated on a wall or in rubbifh, where their feeds may ſcatter, they may be maintained much better than in good ground. In order to have the plants grow in fuch fituations, it will be proper to fow their feeds foon after they are ripe, either on the joints of old walls, or in rubbifh, laying the ſtalks of the plants over the places where their feeds are fown, which will fhade them from the fun, and thereby greatly forward the vegetation of the feeds ; and when the plants are well eſtablifhed in their fituation, if they are permitted to ſcatter their feeds, they will maintain themſelves very well afterwards.

As thefe plants are feldom cultivated unlefs in botanic gardens, fo it will be unneceſſary to enlarge farther about them ; they flower early in the fpring, and their feeds ripen in June.

OPHIOGLOSSUM, Adder's-tongue.

This plant grows naturally in moift meadows, and is not eafily brought to thrive long in gardens, fo is rarely attempted.

OPHRYS. Tourn. Inſt. R. H. 437. tab. 250. Lin. Gen. Plant. 902. Twyblade.

The CHARACTERS are,

It has a ſingle ſtalk with a vague ſpatha (or ſheath.) The flower hath no empalement ; it conſiſts of five oblong petals which aſcend, and join fo as to form a helmet, and the under one is bifid. The nectarium is dependent, and keel-ſhaped behind, it hath two ſhort ſtamina fitting on the pointal, with erect ſummits faſtened to the interior border of the nectarium, and an oblong contorted germen ſituated under the flower, with a ſtyle adhering to the inner border of the nectarium, crowned by an obfolete ſtigma. The germen afterward turns to an oval, three-cor-

nered, obtuſe capſule, with one cell opening with three valves, and filled with ſmall feeds like duſt.

This genus of plants is ranged in the firſt ſection of Linnæus's twentieth claſs, which contains the plants whofe flowers have two ſtamina, which are joined to the ſtyle ; he has joined to this genus feveral fpecies of Orchis.

The SPECIES are,

1. OPHRYS (*Nidus avis*) bulbis fibroſo-faſciculatis caule vaginato, nectarii labio bifido. Lin. Sp. Plant. 1339. *Twyblade with a fibrous root bundled, and a bifid lip to the nectarium.* Ophrys bifolia. C. B. P. 87. *Common Twyblade, or Twayblade.*

2. OPHRYS (*Cordato*) bulbo fibroſo, caule bifolio, foliis cordatis. Lin. Sp. Plant. 946. *Twyblade with a fibrous root, and two heart-ſhaped leaves on the ſtalk.* Ophrys minima. C. B. P. 87. *Smalleſt Twyblade.*

3. OPHRYS (*Spiralis*) bulbis aggregatis oblongis, caule fubfoliofo, floribus fecundis, nectarii labio indivifo. Act. Upfal. 1740. *Twyblade with oblong cluſtered bulbs, a leafy ſtalk, fruitful flowers, and an undivided lip to the nectarium.* Orchis fpiralis alba odorata. J. B. 2. 769. *White, ſweet-ſcented, ſpiral Orchis, called Triple Ladies Traces.*

4. OPHRYS (*Monorchis*) bulbo globofo, caule nudo, nectarii labio trifido. Act. Upfal. 1740. *Twyblade with a globular bulb, a naked ſtalk, and a trifid lip to the nectarium.* Orchis odorata moſchata, five monorchis. C. B. P. 84. *Yellow, ſweet, or Muſk Orchis.*

5. OPHRYS (*Anthropophora*) bulbis fubrotundis, ſcapo foliofo, nectarii labio lineari tripartito, medio elongato bifido. Lin. Sp. Plant. 948. *Twyblade with roundiſh bulbs, a leafy ſtalk, and a narrow three-pointed lip to the nectarium, the middle ſegment of which is ſtretched out and bifid.* Orchis flore nudi hominis effigiem repræſentans fœmina. C. B. P. 82. *Man Orchis.*

6. OPHRYS (*Inſectifera*) bulbis fubrotundis, ſcapo foliofo, nectarii labio fubquinquelobo. Lin. Sp. Plant. 948. *Twyblade with roundiſh bulbs, a leafy ſtalk, and the lip of the nectarium divided almoſt into five lobes.* Orchis mufcam referens major. C. B. P. 83. *Greater Fly Orchis.*

7. OPHRYS (*Adrachnites*) bulbis fubrotundis, caule foliofo, nectarii labio trifido. *Twyblade with roundiſh bulbs, a leafy ſtalk, and a trifid lip to the nectarium.* Orchis fucum referens major, foliolis fuperioribus candidis, aut purpurafcentibus. C. B. P. 83. *The common Humble Bee Orchis.*

8. OPHRYS (*Sphegodes*) bulbis fubrotundis, caule fubfoliofo, nectarii labio trifido hirfuto. *Twyblade with roundiſh bulbs, a leafy ſtalk, and a hairy trifid lip to the nectarium.* Orchis five teſticulusfphegodes hirfutoflore. J. B. 2. 727. *Humble Bee Satyrion with green wings.*

The firſt fort grows naturally in woods, and fometimes in moift paftures in feveral parts of England. The root is compofed of many ſtrong fibres, from which arife two oval veined leaves three inches long, and two broad, joined at their bafe ; between thefe arifes a naked ſtalk about eight inches high, terminated by a loofe fpike of herbaceous flowers, refembling gnats, compofed of five petals, with a long bifid lip to the nectarium, with a creft or ſtandard above, and two wings on the fide. The flowers fit upon an angular germen, which afterward fwells to a capfule, opening when ripe in fix parts, and filled with ſmall duſty feeds. This plant refufes culture, but may be tranfplanted from the places where it grows naturally, into a fhady part of the garden, where, if the roots are not difturbed, they will continue feveral years, and flower in May, but they do not increafe in gardens. The beſt time to remove the roots is in July or Auguft, when the leaves are decaying, for it will be difficult to find the roots after the leaves are gone.

The fecond fort is found in fome of the northern counties in England, but is feldom feen growing in the fouth. This hath a ſmall bulb with many ſtrong fibres to the root, and fends out two ſmall, ribbed, fibres to the root, and fends out two ſmall, heart-ſhaped leaves at bottom. The ſtalk rifes about four inches high, and is terminated by a fpike of ſmall herbaceous flowers fhaped like thofe of the firſt fort.

The

The third fort grows upon chalky hills in feveral parts of England; this hath an oblong, cluftered, bulbous root, from which arifes a fingle ftalk fix inches high, having two oblong leaves at bottom, and rarely any above; the flowers are fmall, of a white colour, growing in a loofe fpike on the top of the ftalk; they have a mufky fcent. This flowers in Auguft.

This fort grows naturally in moift paftures in the northern parts of England; I have alfo found it in great plenty on Enfield Chace, not far from the town.

The fourth and fifth forts grow upon the chalk-hills near Northfleet in Kent, and alfo upon Caufham-hills near Reading; they have roundifh bulbous roots, from which come out a few oblong leaves; the ftalks rife a foot and a half high, garnifhed with a few narrower leaves; the flowers grow in a loofe fpike on the top of the ftalk; they are in one of a rufty iron colour, and the other hath herbaceous flowers. The lip of the nectarium is divided into three parts, the middle fegment being ftretched out much longer than the other, and is divided into two; the upper part of the flower being hooded, the whole bears fome refemblance to a naked man. They flower in June.

The eighth fort grows naturally in dry paftures in feveral parts of England, and is commonly called the Humble Bee Orchis; of this there are two or three varieties found wild in England, and feveral more in Spain and Portugal. This hath a roundifh bulbous root; the leaves are like thofe of the narrow-leaved Plantain. The ftalk rifes fix or feven inches high, having two or three fheath-fhaped leaves embracing it, which are erect; at the top of the ftalk come out two or three flowers without fpurs, having purplifh crefts and wings. The nectarium is large, fhaped like the body of a humble bee, of a dark footy colour, with two or three lines running acrofs it of a darker or lighter colour, which appear brighter or duller according to the pofition of the flower to the fun. It flowers early in June. There are fome varieties of this fort, which differ in the colour and fize of their flowers.

All thefe forts may be preferved in gardens, though not propagated there. The beft time to remove the roots from the places where they naturally grow, is juft before the ftalks fall, for at that time the roots may be eafily difcovered, and then they are beginning to reft, fo that the bulb will be fully formed for flowering the following year, and will not fhrink; but when they are removed at a time of the year when they are in action, the bulb defigned for flowering the following year, not being fully ripened, will fhrink, and frequently perifh; or if they furvive their removal, do not recover their former ftrength in lefs time than two years.

When thefe are removed into a garden, the foil fhould be adapted to the forts. Such of them as grow naturally in moift paftures, fhould be planted in fhady moift borders; thofe which are inhabitants of woods may be planted under trees in wilderneffes, but fuch as grow upon chalk-hills fhould have a bed of chalk prepared for them in an open fituation, and when the plants are fixed in their feveral places, they fhould not be difturbed after; for if they are kept clean from weeds, the lefs the ground is difturbed, the better the plants will thrive, and the longer they will continue.

OPUNTIA. Tourn. Inft. R. H. 239. tab. 122. Tuna. Hort. Elth. 295. Cactus. Lin. Gen. Plant. 539. [This plant is called Opuntia, becaufe Theophraftus writes, that it grows about Opuntium.] The Indian Fig, or prickly Pear; in French, Raquette.

The CHARACTERS are,

The flower is compofed of feveral petals, which are obtufe, concave, and placed in a circular order, fitting upon the germen. It has a great number of awl-fhaped ftamina, which are inferted in the germen, are fhorter than the petals; and terminated by oblong erect fummits. The germen, which is fituated under the flower, fupports a cylindrical ftyle the length of the ftamina, crowned by a multifid ftigma. The germen afterward turns to a flefhy

imbilicated fruit with one cell, inclofing many roundifh feeds.

This genus of plants is ranged in the fecond fection of Tournefort's fixth clafs, which includes the herbs with a Rofe flower, whofe pointal or empalement becomes a fruit with one capfule. Dr. Linnæus places it in the firft fection of his twelfth clafs, in which he ranges thofe plants whofe flowers have more than nineteen ftamina, which are inferted either into the empalement, or petals of the flower.

The SPECIES are,

1. OPUNTIA (*Vulgaris*, articulis ovatis compreffis, fpinis fetaceis. *Indian Fig with oval compreffed joints, and briftly fpines*. Opuntia vulgò herbariorum. J. B. 1. 154. *The common Opuntia, or Indian Fig.*

2. OPUNTIA (*Ficus Indica*) articulis ovato-oblongis, fpinis fetaceis. *Indian Fig with oblong oval joints, and briftly fpines.* Opuntia folio oblongo media. Tourn. Inft. R. H. 239. *Middle Indian Fig with oblong leaves.*

3. OPUNTIA (*Tuna*) articulis ovato-oblongis, fpinis fubulatis. *Indian Fig with oblong oval joints, and awl-fhaped fpines.* Opuntia major, validiffimis fpinis munita. Tourn. Inft. R. H. 239. *Greater Indian Fig with very ftrong fpines.*

4. OPUNTIA (*Elatior*) articulis ovato-oblongis, fpinis longiffimis nigricantibus. *Indian Fig with oblong oval joints, and very long black fpines.* Tuna elatior fpinis validis nigricantibus. Hort. Elth. tab. 194. *Taller Indian Fig with ftrong black fpines.*

5. OPUNTIA (*Maxima*) articulis ovato-oblongis craffiffimis, fpinis inæqualibus. *Indian Fig with oblong, oval, thick joints, and unequal fpines.* Opuntia maxima, folio fpinofo, latiffimo & longiffimo. Tourn. Inft. 240. *Greateft Indian Fig, with the longeft and broadeft prickly branches.*

6. OPUNTIA (*Cochinelifera*) articulis ovato-oblongis fubinermibus. *Indian Fig with oblong oval joints, almoft without fpines.* Opuntia maxima, folio oblongo-rotundo majore, fpinulis mollibus & innocentibus obfito, flore ftriis rubris variegato. Sloan. Cat. Jam. 194. *Greateft Indian Fig, with a larger, oblong, round leaf, armed with foft, innocent, fmall fpines, and a flower variegated with red ftripes, commonly called the Cochineal Fig.*

7. OPUNTIA (*Curaffavica*) articulis cylindrico-ventricofis, compreffis, fpinis fetaceis. *Indian Fig with compreffed, cylindrical, bellied joints, and briftly fpines.* Ficus Indica, feu Opuntia Curaffavica minima. Hort. Amft. 1. 107. *Indian Fig, or the leaft Opuntia of Curaffoa, frequently titled Pinpillou.*

8. OPUNTIA (*Spinofiffima*) articulis longiffimis tenuibus compreffis, fpinis longiffimis confertiffimis, gracilibus albicantibus armatis. Houft. MSS. *Stalky Indian Fig, with large, narrow, compreffed leaves, armed with the longeft, narroweft, white fpines, growing in clufters; this is by the gardeners called, Robinfon Crufoe's Coat.*

9. OPUNTIA (*Phyllanthus*) prolifer enfiformi-compreffus ferrato-repandus. *Indian Fig with compreffed fword-fhaped joints, whofe indentures turn backward.* Cereus fcolopendri folio brachiato. Hort. Elth. 73. tab. 64. *Torch Thiftle with a branching Spleenwort leaf.*

Thefe plants are all of them natives of America, though the firft fort is found growing wild on the fides of the roads about Naples, in Sicily, and Spain, but it is probable that the plants may have been brought from America thither at firft. This fort has been long in the Englifh gardens; the joints or branches of this are oval, or roundifh, compreffed on their two fides flat, and have fmall leaves coming out in knots on their furface, as alfo on their upper edges, which fall off in a fhort time; and at the fame knots there are three or four fhort briftly fpines, which do not appear unlefs they are clofely viewed; but on being handled, they enter the flefh, and feparate from the plant, fo are troublefome, and often very difficult to get out of the flefh. The branches of this fort fpread near the ground, and frequently trail upon it, putting out new roots, fo are extended to a confiderable diftance, and never rife in height; thefe are flefhy and herbaceous while they are young,

but

but as they grow old become drier, of a tough con-texture, and have ligneous fibres. The flowers come out on the upper edges of the branches, generally, though fometimes they are produced on their fides; thefe fit upon the embryo of their fruit, and are compofed of feveral roundifh concave petals, which fpread open; they are of a pale yellow colour, and within arife a great number of ftamina, faftened to the embryo of the fruit, which are terminated by ob-long fummits; and in the center is fituated the ftyle, crowned by a many-pointed ftigma; after the flowers are paft, the embryo fwells to an oblong fruit, whofe fkin, or cover, is fet with fmall fpines in clufters, and the infide is flefhy, of a purple, or red colour, in which are lodged many black feeds. This plant flow-ers here in July and Auguft, but unlefs the feafon is very warm, the fruit will not ripen in England.

I received fome branches of this fort from Mr. Peter Collinfon, F. R. S. who affured me they were fent him from Newfoundland, where the plants grow naturally, which is much farther to the north than it was before known to grow; and how it endures the cold of that country is inconceivable, for though the plants will live abroad in England, in a warm fitua-tion and a dry foil, yet, in fevere winters, they are generally deftroyed, if they are not protected from the froft.

The fecond fort hath oblong, oval, compreffed branches, which grow more erect than thofe of the firft, armed with long briftly fpines, which come out in clufters from a point on each of the compreffed fides, fpreading open like the rays of a ftar. The flowers grow upon the embryo of the fruit, which come out from the upper edges of the leaves like the firft, but are larger, and of a brighter yellow colour. The fruit is alfo larger, and of a deeper purple co-lour, the outer fkin is alfo armed with longer fpines; this is the moft common fort in Jamaica, and upon the fruit of this the wild fort of cochineal feeds, which is called Sylvefter. I had fome of the plants fent me with the live infects upon them from Jamaica, by the late Dr. Houftoun, who was writing a hiftory of thefe infects, at the time when he was taken ill and died; thefe infects kept alive upon the plants here for three or four months, but afterward perifhed. If the fruit of this plant is eaten, it will dye the urine of a bloody colour.

The third fort hath ftronger branches than the fecond, which are armed with larger thorns, of an awl-fhape; they are whitifh, and come out in clufters like thofe of the other fort. The flowers are large, of a bright yellow colour, and the fruit is fhaped like that of the fecond fort.

The fourth fort grows taller than either of the for-mer; the branches are larger, thicker, and of a deep-er green, and are armed with ftrong black fpines, which come out in clufters like thofe of the other forts, but the clufters are farther afunder. The flow-ers are produced from the upper edges of the branches; they are fmaller than thofe of the other forts, and are of a purplifh colour, as are alfo the ftamina; the fruit is of the fame form as thofe of the firft, but do do not ripen here.

The fifth fort is the largeft of all the forts yet known. The joints of thefe are more than a foot long, and eight inches broad; they are very thick, of a deep green colour, and armed with a few fhort briftly fpines; the older branches of this often become al-moft taper, and are very ftrong. The flowers of this fort I have never yet feen; for although I have had many of the plants more than ten feet high, none of them has produced any flowers.

The fixth fort has been always fuppofed to be the plant, upon which the cochineal infects feed; this hath oblong, fmooth, green branches, which grow erect, and rife to the height of eight or ten feet, hav-ing fcarce any fpines on them and thofe few which are, can fcarce be difcerned at a diftance, and are fo foft as not to be troublefome when handled. The flowers of this fort are fmall, and of a purple colour,

ftanding upon the embryo of the fruit, in the fame manner as thofe of the other fort, but do not expand open like them. The flowers of this appear late in the autumn, and the fruit drop off in winter, without coming to any perfection here; this fort is cultivated in the fields of New Spain, for the increafe of the in-fects, but it grows naturally in Jamaica, where it is probable the true cochineal might be difcovered, if perfons of fkill were to fearch after the infects.

The feventh fort is faid to grow naturally at Curaf-fao; this hath cylindrical fwelling joints, which are clofely armed with flender white fpines. The branches fpread out on every fide, and where they have no fupport, fall to the ground, very often feparating at the joints from the plants, and as they lie upon the ground, put out roots, fo form new plants; this fort very rarely produces flowers in England. In the Weft-Indies it is called Pinpillow, from the appear-ance which the branches have to a pin-cufhion ftuck full of pins.

The eighth fort was fent me from Jamaica by the late Dr. Houftoun, who found it growing naturally there in great plenty, but could never obferve either fruit or flower upon any of the plants, nor have any of them produced either in England. The branches of this fort have much longer joints than any of the other; they are narrower, and more compreffed. The fpines of this are very long, flender, and of a yellowifh brown colour, coming out in clufters all over the furface of the branches, croffing each other, fo as to render it dangerous to handle; for upon being touched, the fpines adhere to the hand and quit the branches, and penetrate into the flefh, fo become very troublefome.

The ninth fort grows naturally in the Brafils; this hath very thin branches, which are indented regularly on their edges, like Spleenwort; they are of a light green, and fhaped like a broad fword; thefe are fmooth, having no fpines. The flowers come out from the fide, and at the end of the branches, fit-ting on the embryos in the fame way as the other forts; they are of a pale yellow colour. The fruit is fhaped like thofe of the firft fort, but rarely ripen in England.

All thefe forts (except the firft) are too tender to thrive in the open air in England; nor can many of them be preferved through the winter here, unlefs they have artificial heat; for when they are placed in a green-houfe, they turn to a pale yellow colour, their branches fhrink, and frequently rot on the firft ap-proach of warm weather in the fpring.

Thefe plants may be all propagated by cutting off their branches at the joints, during any of the fum-mer months, which fhould be laid in a warm dry place for a fortnight, that the wounded part may be healed over, otherwife they will rot with the moifture which they imbibe at that part, as is the cafe with moft other fucculent plants. The foil in which thefe plants muft be planted, fhould be compofed after the following manner, viz. one third of light frefh earth from a pafture, a third part fea fand, and the other part fhould be one half rotten tan, and the other half lime rubbifh; thefe fhould be well mixed, and laid in a heap three or four months before it is ufed, ob-ferving to turn it over at leaft once a month, that the feveral parts may be well united; then you fhould pafs it through a rough fcreen, in order to feparate the largeft ftones and clods, but by no means fift it too fine, which is a very common fault; then you fhould referve fome of the fmaller ftones and rubbifh to lay at the bottom of the pots, in order to keep an open paffage for the moifture to drain off; which is what muft be obferved for all fucculent plants, for if the moifture be detained in the pots, it will rot their roots and deftroy the plants.

When you plant any of the branches of thefe plants (except the firft fort) you fhould plunge the pots into a moderate hot-bed, which will greatly facilitate their taking root; you fhould alfo refrefh them now and then with a little water, but be very careful not to let
them

them have too much, or be too often watered, especially before they are rooted. When the plants begin to shoot, you must give them a large share of air, by raising the glasses, otherwise their shoots will draw up so weak, as not to be able to support themselves; and after they have taken strong root, you should inure them to the air by degrees, and then remove them into the stove where they should remain, placing them near the glasses, which should always be opened in warm weather; so that they may have the advantage of a free air, and yet be protected from wet and cold.

During the summer season these plants will require to be often refreshed with water, but it must not be given to them in large quantities left it rot them, and in winter this should be proportioned to the warmth of the stove; for if the air be very warm they will require to be often refreshed, otherwise their branches will shrink; but if the house be kept in a moderate degree of warmth, they should have but little, for moisture at that season will rot them very soon. The heat in which these plants thrive best, is the temperate point, as marked on botanical thermometers, for if they are kept too warm in winter, it causes their shoots to be very tender, weak, and unsightly. Those sorts which are inclinable to grow upright, should have their branches supported with stakes, otherwise their weight is so great, that it will break them down.

These plants are by most people exposed to the open air in the summer season, but they thrive much better if they are continued in the stoves, provided the glasses be kept open, so that they may have free air; for when they are set abroad, the great rains which generally fall in summer, together with the unsettled temperature of the air in our climate, greatly diminish their beauty, by retarding their growth; and sometimes in wet summers they are so replete with moisture, as to rot in the succeeding winter; nor will those plants which are set abroad (I mean the tender sorts) produce their flowers and fruit in such plenty, as those which are constantly preserved in the house.

ORANGE. See AURANTIUM.

ORCHARD. In planting of an Orchard, great care should be had to the nature of the soil; and such sorts of fruits only should be chosen, as are best adapted to the ground designed for planting, otherwise there can be little hopes of their succeeding; and it is for want of rightly observing this method, that we see in many countries Orchards planted, which never arrive to any tolerable degree of perfection, the trees starving; and their bodies are either covered with Moss, or the bark cracks and divides, both which are evident signs of the weakness of the trees; whereas, if instead of Apples the Orchard had been planted with Pears, Cherries, or any other sort of fruit better adapted to the soil, the trees might have grown very well, and produced great quantities of fruit.

As to the position of the Orchard, (if you are at full liberty to chuse) a rising ground, open to the southeast, is to be preferred; but I would by no means advise planting upon the side of a hill, where the declivity is very great; for in such places the great rains commonly wash down the better part of the ground, whereby the trees would be deprived of proper nourishment; but where the rise is gentle, it is of great advantage to the trees, by admitting the sun and air between them, better than it can upon an entire level; which is an exceeding benefit to the fruit, by dissipating fogs and drying up the damps, which, when detained amongst the trees, mix with the air and render it rancid: if it be defended from the west, north, and east winds, it will also render the situation still more advantageous, for it is chiefly from those quarters that fruit-trees receive the greatest injury; therefore, if the place be not naturally defended from these by rising hills (which is always to be preferred,) then you

should plant large growing timber-trees at some distance from the Orchard, to answer this purpose.

You should also have a great regard to the distance of planting the trees, which is what few people have rightly considered; for if you plant them too close, they will be liable to blights; the air being hereby pent in amongst them, will also cause the fruit to be ill tasted, having a great quantity of damp vapours from the perspiration of the trees, and the exhalations from the earth mixed with it, which will be imbibed by the fruit, and render their juices crude and unwholsome.

Wherefore I cannot but recommend the method which has been lately practised by some particular gentlemen with very good success, and that is, to plant the trees fourscore feet asunder, but not in regular rows. The ground between the trees they plough and sow with Wheat and other crops, in the same manner as if it were clear from trees; and they observe their crops to be full as good as those quite exposed, except just under each tree, until they are grown large, and afford a great shade; and by thus ploughing and tilling the ground, the trees are rendered more vigorous and healthy, scarcely ever having any Moss, or other marks of poverty, and will abide much longer and produce better fruit.

If the ground in which you intend to plant an Orchard has been pasture for some years, then you should plough in the green sward the spring before you plant the trees; and if you will permit it to lie a summer fallow, it will greatly mend it, provided you stir it two or three times, to rot the sward of Grass, and prevent weeds growing thereon.

At Michaelmas you should plough it pretty deep, in order to make it loose for the roots of the trees, which should be planted thereon in October, provided the soil is dry; but if it be moist, the beginning of March will be a better season. The distance, if designed for a close Orchard, must not be less than forty feet, but the trees planted twice that distance will succeed better.

When you have finished planting the trees, you should provide some stakes to support them, otherwise the wind will blow them out of the ground; which will do them much injury, especially after they have been planted some time; for the ground in the autumn being warm, and for the most part moist, the trees will very soon push out a great number of young fibres; which, if broken off by their being displaced, will greatly retard the growth of the trees.

In the spring following, if the season should prove dry, you should cut a quantity of green sward, which must be laid upon the surface of the ground about their roots, turning the Grass downward, which will prevent the sun and wind from drying the ground, whereby a great expence of watering will be saved; and after the first year they will be out of danger, provided they have taken well.

Whenever you plough the ground betwixt these trees, you must be careful not to go too deep amongst their roots, left you should cut them off, which would greatly damage the trees; but if you do it cautiously, the stirring the surface of the ground will be of great benefit to them; though you should observe, never to sow too near the trees, nor suffer any great rooting weeds to grow about them, which would exhaust the goodness of the soil, and starve them.

If after the turf which was laid round the trees be rotted, you dig it in gently about the roots, it will greatly encourage them.

There are some persons who plant many sorts of fruit together in the same Orchard, mixing the trees alternately; but this is a method which should always be avoided, for hereby there will be a great difference in the growth of the trees, which will not only render them unsightly, but also the fruit upon the lower trees ill tasted, by the tall ones overshadowing them; so that if you are determined to plant several sorts of fruit on the same spot, you should observe to
place

place the largeſt growing trees backward, and ſo proceed to thoſe of leſs growth, continuing the ſame method quite through the whole plantation ; whereby it will appear at a diſtance in a regular ſlope, and the ſun and air will more equally paſs throughout the whole Orchard, that every tree may have an equal benefit therefrom ; but this can only be praĉtiſed upon good ground, in which moſt ſorts of fruit-trees will thrive.

The ſoil of your Orchard ſhould alſo be mended once in two or three years with dung, or other manure, which will alſo be abſolutely neceſſary for the crops ſown between ; ſo that where perſons are not inclinable to help their Orchards, where the expence of manure is pretty great, yet, as there is a crop expeĉted from the ground beſides the fruit, they will the more readily be at the charge upon that account.

In making choice of trees for an Orchard, you ſhould always obſerve to procure them from a ſoil nearly a-kin to that where they are to be planted, or rather poorer ; for if you have them from a very rich ſoil, and that wherein you plant them is but indifferent, they will not thrive well, eſpecially for four or five years after planting ; ſo that it is a very wrong praĉtice to make the nurſery where young trees are raiſed very rich, when the trees are deſigned for a middling or poor ſoil. The trees ſhould be alſo young and thriving, for whatever ſome perſons may adviſe to the contrary, yet it has always been obſerved, that though large trees may grow and produce fruit after being removed, they never make ſo good trees, nor are ſo long lived, as thoſe which are planted while young.

Theſe trees, after they are planted out, will require no other pruning, but only to cut out dead branches, or ſuch as croſs each other, which render their heads confuſed and unſightly : the pruning them too often, or ſhortening their branches, is very injurious ; eſpecially to Cherries and ſtone-fruit, which will gum prodigiouſly, and decay in ſuch places where they are cut ; and the Apples and Pears which are not of ſo nice a nature, will produce a greater quantity of lateral branches, which will fill the heads of the trees with weak ſhoots, whenever their branches are thus ſhortened ; and many times the fruit is hereby cut off, which, on many ſorts of fruit-trees, is firſt produced at the extremity of their ſhoots.

It may, perhaps, ſeem ſtrange to ſome perſons, that I ſhould recommend the allowing ſo much diſtance to the trees in an Orchard, becauſe a ſmall piece of ground will admit of very few trees when planted in this method ; but if they will pleaſe to obſerve, that when the trees are grown up, they will produce a great deal more fruit, than twice the number when planted cloſe, and will be vaſtly better taſted ; the trees when placed at a large diſtance, being never ſo much in danger of blighting as in cloſe plantations, as hath been obſerved in Herefordſhire, the great county for Orchards, where they find, that when Orchards are ſo planted or ſituated, that the air is pent up amongſt the trees, the vapours which ariſe from the damp of the ground, and the perſpiration of the trees, collect the heat of the ſun, and reflect it in ſtreams ſo as to cauſe what they call a fire-blaſt, which is the moſt hurtful to their fruits ; and this is moſt frequent where the Orchards are open to the ſouth ſun. But as Orchards ſhould never be planted, unleſs where large quantities of fruit are deſired, ſo it will be the ſame thing to allow twice or three times the quantity of ground ; ſince there may be a crop of grain of any ſort upon the ſame place (as was before ſaid,) ſo that there is no loſs of ground ; and for a family only it is hardly worth while to plant an Orchard, ſince a kitchen-garden well planted with eſpaliers, will afford more fruit than can be eaten while good, eſpecially if the kitchen-garden be proportioned to the largeneſs of the family ; and if cyder be required, there may be a large avenue of Apple-trees extended croſs a neighbouring field, which will render it pleaſant, and produce a great quantity of fruit ; or there

may be ſome ſingle rows of trees planted to ſurround fields, &c. which will fully anſwer the ſame purpoſe, and be leſs liable to the fire-blaſts before-mentioned.

ORCHIS. Tourn. Inſt. R. H. 431. tab. 248, 249. Lin. Gen. Plant. 900. [of ὄρχις, a teſticle, becauſe the root of this plant reſembles the teſticles of a man ; or of ὀρίγω, to have an appetite after, on account of its being a provocative to venery : it is alſo called κυνοσόρχις, of κυνός, a dog, and ὄρχις, a teſticle.] Satyrion, or Fool-ſtones.

The CHARACTERS are,

It hath a ſingle ſtalk with a vague ſheath ; it has no empalement. The flower hath five petals, three without and two within, which riſe and join in a ſtandard. The nectarium is of one leaf, fixed to the ſide of the receptacle, between the diviſion of the petals. The upper lip is ſhort and erect, the under large, broad, and ſpreading ; the tube is pendulous, horn-ſhaped, and prominent behind. It hath two ſhort ſlender ſtamina ſitting upon the point-al, with oval erect ſummits fixed to the upper lip of the nectarium. It hath an oblong contorted germen under the flower, with a ſhort ſtyle faſtened to the upper lip of the nectarium, crowned by an obtuſe compreſſed ſtigma. The germen afterward turns to an oblong capſule with one cell, having three keel-ſhaped valves, opening on the three ſides, but joined at top and bottom, filled with ſmall ſeeds like duſt.

This genus of plants is ranged in the firſt ſection of Linnæus's twentieth claſs, which contains thoſe plants whoſe flowers have two ſtamina, which are connected with, or fixed to the ſtyle.

The SPECIES are,

1. ORCHIS (*Morio*) bulbis indiviſis, nectarii labio quadrifido crenulato, cornu obtuſo. Act. Upſal. 1740. *Orchis with undivided bulbs, the lip of the nectarium cut into four points which are ſlightly indented, and an obtuſe horn.* Orchis morio fœmina. C. B. P. 82. *Common female Orchis.*

2. ORCHIS (*Maſcula*) bulbis indiviſis, nectarii labio quadrilobo crenulato, cornu obtuſo, petalis dorſalibus reflexis. Flor. Suec. 795. *Orchis with undivided bulbs, the lip of the nectarium having four lobes and an obtuſe horn, and the backs of the petals reflexed.* Orchis motio mas, foliis maculatis. C. B. P. 81. *The male Orchis with ſpotted leaves.*

3. ORCHIS (*Bifolia*) bulbis indiviſis, nectarii labio lanceolato integerrimo, cornu longiſſimo, petalis patentibus. Act. Upſal. 1740. *Orchis with undivided bulbs, the lip of the nectarium entire and ſpear-ſhaped, a very long horn, and petals ſpreading very wide.* Orchis alba bifolia minor, calcari oblongo. C. B. P. 83. *Smaller, white two-leaved Orchis, with an oblong ſpur, or Butterfly Orchis.*

4. ORCHIS (*Militaris*) bulbis indiviſis, nectarii labio quinquefido punctis ſcabro, cornu obtuſo, petalis confluentibus. Act. Upſal. 1740. *Orchis with undivided bulbs, a five-pointed lip to the nectarium, having rough ſpots, an obtuſe horn, and petals running together.* Orchis latifolia, hiante cucullo major. Tourn. Inſt. R. H. 432. *The Man Orchis.*

5. ORCHIS (*Pyramidalis*) bulbis indiviſis, nectarii labio trifido æquali integerrimo, cornu longo, petalis ſublanceolatis. Act. Upſal. 1740. *Orchis with undivided bulbs, an equal trifid lip to the nectarium, with a long horn, and ſpear-ſhaped petals.* Orchis militaris, montana, ſpicâ rubente, conglomeratâ. Tourn. Inſt. R. H. 432. *Mountain military Orchis, with a reddiſh conglomerated ſpike.*

6. ORCHIS (*Latifolia*) bulbis ſubpalmatis rectis, nectarii cornu conico, labio trilobo, lateralibus reflexo, bracteis flore longioribus. Act. Upſal. 1740. *Orchis with ſtrait, palmated, bulbous roots, a conical horn to the nectarium, the lip cut into three lobes, which are reflexed on the ſides, and bractea longer than the flowers.* Orchis palmata pratenſis, latifolia, longis calcaribus. C. B. P. 85. *Broad-leaved, Meadow, handed Orchis, having a long ſpur.*

7. ORCHIS (*Maculata*) bulbis palmatis patentibus, nectarii cornu germinibus breviore, labio plano petalis dorſalibus patulis. Act. Upſal. 1740. *Orchis with handed*

handed spreading bulbs, the horn of the nectarium shorter than the germen, a plain lip, and the hinder part of the petals spreading. Orchis palmata pratensis, maculata. C. B. P. 85. *Meadow handed Orchis, with spotted leaves.*

8. Orchis (*Cornopica*) bulbis palmatis, nectarii cornu, setaceo germinibus longiore, labio trifido, petalis duobus patentissimis. Act. Upsal. 1740. *Orchis with palmated bulbs, a bristly horn to the nectarium, which is longer than the germen, and a trifid lip.* Orchis palmata minor, calcaribus oblongis. C. B. P. 85. *Smaller palmated Orchis, with an oblong spur to the flower.*

9. Orchis (*Abortiva*) bulbis fasciculatis filiformibus, nectarii labio ovato integerrimo. Act. Upsal. 1740. *Orchis with thread-like bulbs growing in bunches, and the lip of the nectarium oval and entire.* Limidorum Austriacum. Clus. Pan. 241. *Purple Bird's-nest.*

The first sort grows naturally in pastures in most parts of England. This hath a double bulbous root, with some fibres coming out from the top; it has four or six oblong leaves lying on the ground, which are reflexed. The stalk rises nine or ten inches high, having four or six leaves which embrace it; this is terminated by a short loose spike of flowers, having a four-pointed indented lip to the nectarium, and an obtuse horn. The flowers are of a pale purple colour, marked with deeper purple spots; it flowers in May.

The second sort grows naturally in woods and shady places in many parts of England; this hath a double bulbous root, which is about the size and shape of middling Olives; it hath six or seven long broad leaves, shaped like those of Lilies, which have several black spots on their upper side; the stalk is round, and a foot high, having one or two smaller leaves embracing it. The flowers are disposed in a long spike on the top of the stalk; they are of a purple colour, marked with deep purple spots, and have an agreeable scent. It flowers the latter end of April.

The third sort grows naturally under the bushes by the side of pastures, in many parts of England. This hath a root composed of two oblong Pear-shaped bulbs, from which come out three or four Lily-shaped leaves, of a pale green, with a few faint spots; the stalk rises near a foot high, it is slender, furrowed, and has a very few small leaves which embrace it; this is terminated by a loose spike of white flowers, smelling sweet, which resemble a butterfly with expanded wings. This flowers in June.

The fourth sort is found growing naturally on Cawsham-hills, and in other places where the soil is chalk. The roots of this sort are composed of two bulbs, from which come out four or five oblong leaves; the stalk is about nine inches high, sustaining a loose spike of sweet-smelling flowers, each hanging on a pretty long foot-stalk; they have a short obtuse horn, a crest and wings, of an Ash-colour without, reddish within, and striped with deeper lines; the lip is oblong, divided into five parts, having rough spots. This flowers in June.

The fifth sort grows naturally on chalk-hills in several parts of England; the root of this is composed of two oblong bulbs, from which arise three or four narrow oblong leaves; the stalk rises a foot high, having three or four narrow erect leaves which embrace it. The flowers are produced in a thick roundish spike at the top; they are of a reddish colour, having long spurs, and the wings are acute-pointed. It flowers in June.

The sixth sort grows naturally in moist meadows in many parts of England; the root of this is composed of two fleshy bulbs, which are divided into four or five fingers, so as to resemble an open hand; the stalk rises from nine inches to a foot high, garnished with leaves the whole length, which are three or four inches long and one broad, embracing the stalk with their base; these are not spotted, and end in acute points. The flowers are disposed in a spike on the top of the stalk, with small narrow leaves (called bractea) between them, which are longer than the flowers. The spur is half an inch long, extended backward; the lip of the nectarium is broad, divided into three lobes, two side ones being reflexed; the flowers and bractea are of a purplish colour, having deep purple spots. It flowers in May. There are two varieties of this, differing in the colour of their flowers, and one with a narrower leaf.

The seventh sort grows naturally in moist meadows in several parts of England; the root of this is composed of two broad fleshy bulbs, both of which are divided into four fingers, which spread asunder. The stalk rises a foot and a half high, and is very strong, inclining to a purple colour; it is garnished with leaves the whole length; those on the lower part of the stalk are six inches long, and an inch and a half broad, embracing it with their base. The flowers are collected in a close spike at the top of the stalk; they are of a pale purple colour; the spur is about a third part of an inch long; the beard of the nectarium is plain, and divided into three parts, which is marked with deep purple spots; under each foot-stalk is placed a narrow leaf (or bractea) of a purplish colour. The leaves and stalks of the plant have many dark spots. It flowers in June. There are two or three varieties of this, which differ in the colour of their flowers.

The eighth sort grows naturally in moist meadows in several parts of England; this hath a double-handed root, that which sustains the stalk being wasting and decaying, but the other is full, succulent, and plump; the finger-like bulbs which compose the root are long, and spread asunder; the lower leaves are six or seven inches long, they are narrow, of a pale green, and have no spots. The stalk rises a foot high, it is garnished with a few narrow short leaves, which embrace it like sheaths; it is terminated by a beautiful spike of red flowers six inches long; the flowers are not marked with any spots; they have long, slender, bristly spurs like birds claws, being crooked; the lip of the nectarium is indented on the edge. It flowers in June.

The ninth sort grows naturally in shady woods in several parts of England, but particularly in Sussex and Hampshire, in both which counties I have several times found it. The root of this plant is composed of many thick, oblique, long fibres, which are fleshy; the stalk rises near two feet high, wrapped round with leaves like sheaths; they are of a purple colour. The flowers are disposed in a loose thyrse at the top of the stalk, and are of a purple colour, having an oval entire lip to the nectarium, the crest terminating in a horn. It flowers in June.

All these sorts of Orchis grow wild in several parts of England, but, for the extreme oddness and beauty of their flowers, deserve a place in every good garden; and the reason for their not being cultivated in gardens, proceeds from their difficulty to be transplanted; though this, I believe, may be easily overcome, where a person has an opportunity of marking their roots in their time of flowering, and letting them remain until their leaves are decayed, when they may be transplanted with safety; for it is the same with most sorts of bulbous or fleshy-rooted plants, which, if transplanted before their leaves decay, seldom live, notwithstanding you preserve a large ball of earth about them; for the extreme parts of their fibres extend to a great depth in the ground, from whence they receive their nourishment; which, if broken or damaged by taking up their roots, seldom thrive after; for though they may sometimes remain alive a year or two, yet they grow weaker until they quite decay; which is also the case with Tulips, Fritillarias, and other bulbous roots, when removed, after they have made shoots; so that whoever would cultivate them, should search them out in their season of flowering, and mark them; and when their leaves are decayed, or just as they are going off, the roots should be taken up, and planted in a soil or situation as nearly resembling that wherein they naturally grow, as possible, otherwise they will not thrive, so that they cannot be placed all in the same bed; for some are only found upon chalky hills, others in moist meadows, and some in shady woods, or under trees; but if their soil and situation be adapted to their various forts, they will thrive and continue several years, and, during their season of flowering, will afford as great varieties as any flowers which are at present cultivated.

The other sorts not here enumerated, may be found under the following articles, OPHRYS, SATYRIUM, SERAPIAS.

OREOSELINUM. See ATHAMANTA.

ORIGANUM. Lin. Gen. Plant. 645. Tourn. Inst. R. H. 198. tab. 94. [of Ὀρίγανον, of ὄρος, a mountain, and γάνυμαι, to rejoice, q. d. a plant that delights to grow upon mountains.] Origany or Pot Marjoram; in French, *Origan.*

The CHARACTERS are,

The flower is of the lip kind, having a cylindrical compressed tube; the upper lip is plain, erect, obtuse, and indented; the under lip is trifid, the segments being nearly equal. These are disposed in spikes composed of oval coloured leaves, placed over each other like the scales of fish. The flowers have four slender stamina, two being as long as the petal, the other two are longer, terminated by simple summits; they have a four-cornered germen, supporting a slender style inclining to the upper lip, crowned by a bifid stigma. The germen afterward turns to four seeds shut up in the empalement of the flower.

This genus of plants is ranged in the first section of Linnæus's fourteenth class, which includes the plants whose flowers have two long and two shorter stamina, and are succeeded by naked seeds. To this genus he has added the Majorana of Tournefort, and the Dictamnus of Boerhaave. The first has its flowers disposed in four-cornered scaly heads, the other has the flowers disposed in loose scaly heads, coming out from between the leaves.

The SPECIES are,

1. ORIGANUM (*Vulgare*) spicis subrotundis paniculatis conglomeratis, bracteis calyce longioribus ovatis. Lin. Sp. Plant. 590. *Pot Marjoram with roundish paniculated spikes gathered in clusters, and oval bractea which are longer than the empalement.* Origanum vulgare spontaneum. I. B. 2. 236. *Common Wild Origany.*

2. ORIGANUM (*Heracleoticum*) spicis longis pedunculis aggregatis, bracteis longitudine calycum. Lin. Gen. Plant. 589. *Origany with long spikes growing in bunches, and bractea as long as the empalement.* Origanum heracleoticum, culina Gallinacea Plinii. C. B. P. 223. *Winter Sweet Marjoram.*

3. ORIGANUM (*Latifolium*) spicis oblongis paniculatis conglomeratis, foliis ovatis glabris. *Origany with oblong spikes of flowers growing in clustered panicles, and oval smooth leaves.* Origanum humilius latifolium glabrum. Tourn. Inst. R. H. 199. *Low, broad-leaved, smooth Origany.*

4. ORIGANUM (*Humile*) caule repente, spicis oblongis conglomeratis, bracteis florum longioribus. *Origany with a creeping stalk, and oblong spikes of flowers growing in clusters, with bractea longer than the flower.* Origanum sylvestre, humile. C. B. P. 223. Prod. 109. *Low wild Origany.*

5. ORIGANUM (*Orientale*) caule erecto ramoso, foliis ovatis rugosis, spicis subrotundis conglomeratis, bracteis calycum brevioribus. *Origany with an erect branching stalk, oval rough leaves, roundish spikes of flowers growing in clusters, with bractea shorter than the empalement.* Origanum Orientale prunellæ folio glauco, flore purpureo. Buerh. Ind. alt. t. 179. *Eastern Origany with a gray Self-heal leaf, and a purple flower.*

6. ORIGANUM (*Creticum*) spicis aggregatis longis prismaticis rectis, bracteis membranaceis, calyce duplo longioribus. Lin. Sp. Plant. 589. *Origany with long, upright, prismatical spikes growing in clusters, and membranous bractea twice the length of the empalement.* Origanum Creticum. C. B. P. 223. *Origany of Crete.*

7. ORIGANUM (*Majorana*) foliis ovalibus obtusis, spicis subrotundis compactis pubescentibus. Hort. Cliff. 304.

Origany with oval obtuse leaves, and roundish, compact, hairy spikes. Majorana vulgaris. C. B. P. 224. *Common, or Sweet Marjoram.*

8. ORIGANUM (*Ægyptiacum*) foliis carnosis tomentosis, spicis nudis. Lin. Sp. Plant. 822. *Origany with fleshy woolly leaves.* Majorana rotundifolia, scutellata, exotica. H. R. Par. *Round-leaved foreign Marjoram with a spoon-shaped leaf.*

9. ORIGANUM (*Smyrnæum*) foliis ovatis acutè serratis, spicis congestis umbellatim fastigiatis. Hort. Cliff. 304. *Origany with oval leaves acutely sawed, and spikes of flowers disposed in umbellated bunches.* Origanum Smyrnæum. Wheel. Raii Hist. 450. *Origany of Smyrna.*

10. ORIGANUM (*Dictamnus*) foliis omnibus tomentosis, spicis nutantibus. *Origany with all the leaves woolly, and nodding spikes of flowers.* Dictamnus Creticus. C. B. P. 222. *The Dittany of Crete.*

11. ORIGANUM (*Sipyleum*) foliis omnibus glabris, spicis nutantibus. Hort. Cliff. 304. *Origany with all the leaves smooth, and nodding spikes of flowers.* Dictamnus montis Sipyli origani foliis. Flor. Bat. 2. 72. *Dittany of Mount Sipylus with an Origany leaf.*

12. ORIGANUM (*Hybridinum*) foliis inferioribus tomentosis, spicis nutantibus. Hort. Cliff. 304. *Origany with the under leaves hoary, and nodding spikes of flowers.* Origanum Dictamni Cretici facie, folio crasso, nunc villoso, nunc glabro. Tourn. Cor. 13. *Origany with the appearance of Dittany of Crete, and thick leaves sometimes hairy, at others smooth.*

13. ORIGANUM (*Onites*) spicis oblongis aggregatis hirsutis, foliis cordatis tomentosis. Lin. Sp. Plant. 590. *Origany with oblong hairy spikes growing in bunches, and heart-shaped woolly leaves.* Origanum lignosum Syracusanum perenne, umbellà amplissimâ brevi, lato & nervoso folio. Boerc. Muf. 2. p. 43. tab. 38. *Ligneous perennial Origany of Syracuse, with a short ample umbel, and a broad-veined leaf.*

The first sort grows naturally in thickets, and among bushes in several parts of England; the root is perennial, composed of many small ligneous fibres. The stalks are square, and rise near two feet high; they are ligneous, and garnished with oval leaves placed by pairs, and from the wings of these come out three or four smaller leaves on each side, which resemble those of Marjoram, sitting close to the stalk; they have an aromatic scent: the flowers are produced in roundish spikes growing in panicles at the top of the stalks, many of the spikes being gathered together; the flowers are of a flesh colour, and peep out of their scaly covering. Their upper lip is cut into two, standing erect, and the lower lip or beard is divided into three parts, and hangs downward the stamina stand out a little beyond the petals, and are of a purplish colour. It flowers in June and July, and the seeds ripen in the autumn. This sort is sometimes cultivated in gardens, and is by some called Pot Marjoram; it is generally used in soups.

It will rise plentifully from scattered seeds, or it may be propagated by parting the roots; the best time for doing this is in autumn, and the roots may be planted in any soil not over moist, and will thrive in any situation, so requires no other care but to keep them clear from weeds. There is a variety of this with white flowers and light green stalks, and another with variegated leaves.

The second sort is now commonly known by the title of Winter Sweet Marjoram, though it was formerly stiled Pot Marjoram. This hath a perennial root, from which arise many branching four-cornered stalks a foot and a half high, which are hairy, and inclining to a purplish colour, garnished with oval, obtuse, hairy leaves, resembling greatly those of Sweet Marjoram, standing by pairs on short foot-stalks; the flowers are disposed in spikes about two inches long, several arising together from the divisions of the stalk. The flowers are small, white, and peep out of their scaly covers; these appear in July, and the seeds ripen in autumn. It grows naturally in Greece and the warm parts of Europe, but is hardy enough to thrive in the

the open air in England, and is chiefly cultivated for nofegays, as it comes fooner to flower than Sweet Marjoram, fo it is ufed for the fame purpofes, till the other comes to maturity. There is a variety of this with variegated leaves. This is generally propagated by parting the roots in autumn, and fhould have a dry foil, where it will thrive, requiring no other culture than the firft fort.

The third fort grows naturally in France and Italy; this hath a perennial root, from which arife feveral flender bending ftalks near a foot high, garnifhed with oval fmooth leaves ftanding on pretty long footftalks. The flowers are produced in oblong fpikes, which grow in cluftered panicles; they are fmall, of a purplifh colour, peeping out of their fcaly coverings. It flowers in June, and may be propagated by parting the roots in the fame way as the former.

The fourth fort grows plentifully about Orleans; this hath a perennial root, from which arife feveral fourcornered ftalks about fix inches high, which frequently bend to the ground, and put out roots; they are garnifhed with oblong hairy leaves fitting clofe to the ftalk. The flowers grow in oblong cluftered fpikes at the top of the ftalks, having long coloured bracteæ between each; the flowers are fome whitifh, others purple in the fame fpikes; they are fmall, and peep out of their fcaly covers. This flowers in June, and may be propagated in the fame way as the former.

The fifth fort grows naturally in the Levant; it is a perennial plant. The ftalks rife two feet high, and branch out their whole length; they are purple, and garnifhed with oval rough leaves, fomewhat like thofe of Self-heal, but fmaller. The flowers grow in roundifh cluftered fpikes, having fhort bracteæ; they are purple, and appear in June, but are not fucceeded by feeds here. It is propagated by parting of the heads in the fame way as the former, and muft have a dry foil.

The fixth fort is the Origany of Crete, which is directed to be ufed in medicine, but there has been great confufion among botanifts in diftinguifhing the fpecies. This rifes with four-cornered ftalks a foot and half high, garnifhed with oval hoary leaves of a ftrong aromatic fcent. The flowers grow in long, crect, bunched fpikes at the top of the ftalks, having membraneous bracteæ between, which are twice the length of the empalement; the flowers are fmall and white, like thofe of the common Origany. It flowers in July, but feldom perfects feeds in England. It is propagated by parting the roots as the former, but muft have a dry foil and a warm fituation, otherwife it will not live through the winter here.

The feventh fort is the common Sweet Marjoram, which is fo well known as to need no defcription. With us in England it is efteemed an annual plant, though the roots often live through the winter in mild feafons, or if they are fheltered in a green-houfe; but in warm countries, I believe, it is only biennial. This is propagated by feeds, which are generally imported from the fouth of France or Italy, for they feldom ripen in England. Thefe are fown on a warm border toward the end of March, and when the plants are come about an inch high, they fhould be tranfplanted into beds of rich earth, at fix inches diftance every way, obferving to water them duly till they have taken new root; after which, they will require no other care but to keep them clean from weeds. The plants will fpread and cover the ground; in July they will begin to flower, at which time it is cut for ufe, and is then called Knotted Marjoram, from the flowers being collected into roundifh clofe heads like knots.

The eighth fort grows naturally in Africa; this is a perennial plant with a low fhrubby ftalk, feldom rifing more than a foot and half high, dividing into branches, which are garnifhed with roundifh, thick, woolly leaves, and hollowed like a ladle; they are like thofe of the common Marjoram, but are of a thicker fubftance and woolly, and have much the fame fcent.

The flowers are produced in roundifh fpikes, clofely joined together at the top of the ftalks, and, at the end of the fmall fide branches they are of a pale flefh colour, peeping out of their fcaly coverings. This fort flowers in July and Auguft, but does not ripen feeds in England.

It is propagated by flips or cuttings, which if planted in a border of good earth during any of the fummer months, and fhaded from the fun and duly watered, will take root freely; and afterward the plants may be taken up, and planted in fmall pots filled with light kitchen-garden earth, and placed in the fhade till they have taken new root, when they may be removed into an open fituation, where they may remain till the end of October, when they muft be placed under fhelter, for they will not thrive through the winter in the open air here; but if they are put under a hot-bed frame, where they may be protected from hard froft, and have as much free air as poffible in mild weather, they will thrive better than if they are more tenderly treated.

The tenth fort is the Dittany of Crete, which is ufed in medicine; this grows naturally upon Mount Ida, in Candia; it is a perennial plant. The ftalks are hairy, and rife about nine inches high, of a purplifh colour, and fend out fmall branches from their fides by pairs; they are garnifhed with round, thick, woolly leaves, which are very white; the whole plant has a piercing aromatic fcent, and biting tafte: the flowers are collected in loofe leafy heads of a purple colour, which nod downward; they are fmall, and of a purple colour; the ftamina ftands out beyond the petal, two of them being much longer than the other. It flowers in June and July, and in warm feafons the feeds fometimes ripen in autumn.

This is propagated eafily by planting cuttings or flips during any of the fummer months. Thefe fhould be planted either in pots or a fhady border, covering them clofe with a bell or hand-glafs to exclude the air, and now and then refrefhing them with water, but they muft not have too much wet. When thefe have taken root, they fhould be carefully taken up, and each planted into a feparate fmall pot filled with light earth, and placed in the fhade till they have taken new root, when they fhould be removed into an open fituation, where they may continue till autumn, and then placed under a hot-bed frame to fcreen them from the froft, but they fhould enjoy the free air at all times in mild weather. The following fpring fome of the plants may be fhaken out of the pots, and planted in a warm border near a good affected wall, and in a dry foil, where the plants will live through the common winters without any other fhelter; but as they are liable to be killed by fevere froft, it will be proper to keep a few plants in pots, to be fheltered in winter to preferve the kind.

The eleventh fort grows naturally on Mount Sipylus near Magnefia, where it was difcovered by Sir George Wheeler, who fent the feeds to the Oxford Garden, where the plants were raifed; this hath a perennial root, but an annual ftalk. The root is compofed of many flender ligneous fibres; the leaves are oval, fmooth, and of a grayifh colour; the ftalks are flender, of a purplifh colour, four-cornered, and fmooth; they rife near two feet high, fending out flender branches oppofite, which are terminated by flender oblong fpikes of purplifh flowers, which peep out of their fcaly covers; the flowers are fmall, but fhaded like thofe of the tenth fort; their ftamina are extended out of the petal to a confiderable length. The leaves, on the lower part of the ftalk, are almoft as large as the common Origany, but thofe on the upper part of the ftalk and branches are very fmall, and fit clofe to the ftalk. It flowers in June and July, and in warm feafons the feeds ripen here in autumn. It is propagated by cuttings or flips, in the fame way as the Cretan Dittany, and the plants require the fame treatment.

The twelfth fort is undoubtedly a variety, which has been produced from the intermixing of the farina

of

of the Cretan Dittany with that of Mount Sipylus; for the plants now in the Chelſea Garden were accidentally produced from the ſeeds of one ſpecies, where both ſorts ſtood near each other in the garden of John Browning, Eſq; of Lincoln's-Inn; the ſeeds were dropped from the plant into the border between the two ſorts, ſo that it is uncertain from which ſpecies; but as the ſtalks and heads of ſuch flowers bear a greater reſemblance to the Dittany of Mount Sipylus, we may ſuppoſe it aroſe from the ſeeds of that, which had been impregnated by the farina of the Cretan Dittany, which grew near it; for the°under leaves of this are round, of a thick texture and woolly, ſo nearly reſembling thoſe of the Cretan Dittany, as not to be diſtinguiſhed from it; but the ſtalks riſe full as high as thoſe of the Dittany of Sipylus, but branch out more their whole length; they are of a purple colour and hairy. The lower leaves on the ſtalks are much larger than thoſe of Mount Sipylus, and are hairy, approaching to thoſe of the Cretan Dittany, but are not ſo thick or woolly; the upper leaves are ſmooth, and approach to thoſe of the other ſort, but are larger, as are alſo the ſpikes of flowers, and the ſcaly leaves which cover the flowers are larger and of a deeper purple colour.

I have alſo dried ſamples of another variety, which aroſe from ſeeds in the Leyden Garden; the ſeeds were ſent from Paris, by the title which Tournefort gave to that which he found in the Levant, which I have joined to the variety before-mentioned. The leaves of this are as large as thoſe of the Dittany of Crete, but are not ſo thick or woolly; the ſtalks riſe more like thoſe of the Dittany of Mount Sipylus, but branch out wider at the top; the flowers grow in cloſer cluſters, and do not nod downward; they are ſmall, and ſhaped like thoſe of the former ſort, flowering at the ſame time.

By the title which Dr. Linnæus has given to the Cretan Dittany, it may be ſuppoſed he has not ſeen the true ſort, for his title better ſuits the variety to which I have applied it; for all the leaves of the true Dittany are very thick and woolly, even thoſe which are ſituated immediately below the flowers, whereas the lower leaves only are ſo in this title.

The thirteenth ſort grows at Syracuſe; this hath perennial ligneous ſtalks which riſe a foot and a half high, dividing into many ſmall branches, which are garniſhed with ſmall heart-ſhaped leaves a little larger than thoſe of Marjoram, which are woolly. The flowers grow in oblong tufted ſpikes which are hairy; they are ſmall, white, and peep out of their ſcaly covers; they appear in July, but ſeldom perfect ſeeds in England. This is propagated by cuttings or ſlips, in the ſame way as the tenth ſort, and the plants require the ſame treatment.

The firſt and ſixth ſorts are uſed in medicine, but the firſt being a native of this country, is frequently ſubſtituted for the other, which is pretty rare in England, and is now ſeldom imported here. When the firſt ſort is uſed, thoſe plants which grow upon dry barren ground are to be preferred, as they are much ſtronger and have greater virtue than thoſe which grow on good land, or are cultivated in gardens.

The Dittany of Crete is alſo uſed in medicine, but the dried herb is generally imported into England, which, by being cloſely packed, and the voyage being long, it loſes much of its virtue; ſo that if the plants of Engliſh growth are uſed, they would be found much better.

ORNITHOGALUM. Tourn. Inſt. R. H. 378. tab. 203. Lin. Gen. Plant. 377. ['Oρνιθόγαλον, of ὄρνις, a bird, and γάλα, milk, i. e. a plant whoſe flowers are as white as the white plumes of feathered animals.] Star of Bethlehem.

The CHARACTERS are,

The flower has no empalement. It is compoſed of ſix petals, whoſe under parts are erect, but ſpread open above, and are permanent. It hath ſix erect ſtamina about half the length of the petals, crowned by ſingle ſummits, with an angular germen, ſupporting an awl-ſhaped ſtyle which is

permanent, terminated by an obtuſe ſtigma. The germen afterward turns to a roundiſh angular capſule with three cells, filled with roundiſh ſeeds.

This genus of plants is ranged in the firſt ſection of Linnæus's ſixth claſs, in which are contained thoſe plants whoſe flowers have ſix ſtamina and one ſtyle.

The SPECIES are,

1. ORNITHOGALUM (*Pyrenaicum*) racemo longiſſimo, filamentis lanceolatis, pedunculis floriferis patentibus æqualibus, fructiferis ſcapo approximatis. Lin. Sp. Plant. 440. *Star-flower with a very long ſpike of flowers, ſpear-ſhaped filaments, and foot-ſtalks to the flowers equal, ſpreading, and thoſe of the fruit approaching to the ſtalk.* Ornithogalum anguſtifolium majus, floribus ex albo vireſcentibus. C. B. P. 70. *Greater narrow-leaved Star-flower, with whitiſh green flowers.*

2. ORNITHOGALUM (*Pyramidale*) racemo conico, floribus numeroſis adſcendentibus. Prod. Leyd. 32. *Star-flower with a conical ſpike, having numerous flowers riſing above each other.* Ornithogalum anguſtifolium, ſpicatum, maximum. C. B. P. 70. *Largeſt ſpiked Star-flower with a narrow leaf.*

3. ORNITHOGALUM (*Latifolium*) racemo longiſſimo, foliis lanceolato-enſiformibus. Lin. Sp. Plant. 307. *Star-flower with the longeſt ſpike, and ſpear-ſhaped leaves.* Ornithogalum latifolium & maximum. C. B. P. 70. *Greateſt broad-leaved Star-flower, called the Star-flower of Alexandria.*

4. ORNITHOGALUM (*Nutans*) floribus ſecundis pendulis, nectario ſtamineo campaniformi. Lin. Sp. Plant. 308. *Star-flower with fruitful hanging flowers, and a bell-ſhaped nectarium.* Ornithogalum Neapolitanum. Cluſ. App. 2. p. 9. *Star-flower of Naples.*

5. ORNITHOGALUM (*Luteum*) ſcapo angulato diphyllo, pedunculis umbellatis ſimplicibus. Flor. Suec. 270. *Star-flower with an angular ſtalk having two leaves, and ſingle umbellated foot-ſtalks.* Ornithogalum luteum. C. B. P. 71. *Yellow Star-flower.*

6. ORNITHOGALUM (*Minimum*) ſcapo angulato diphyllo, pedunculis umbellatis ramoſis. Flor. Suec. 271. *Star-flower with an angular ſtalk bearing two leaves, and branching foot-ſtalks having umbels.* Ornithogalum luteum minus. C. B. P. 71. *Smaller yellow Star-flower.*

7. ORNITHOGALUM (*Umbellatum*) floribus corymboſis, pedunculis ſcapo altioribus, filamentis emarginatis. Hort. Cliff. 124. *Star-flower with flowers growing in a corymbus, whoſe foot-ſtalks are taller than the ſtalk, and indented filaments.* Ornithogalum umbellatum medium anguſtifolium. C. B. P. 70. *Middle umbellated Star-flower having narrow leaves.*

8. ORNITHOGALUM (*Arabicum*) floribus corymboſis, pedunculis ſcapo humilioribus, filamentis emarginatis. Prod. Leyd. 32. *Star-flower with flowers growing in a corymbus, foot-ſtalks lower than the ſtalk, and indented filaments.* Ornithogalum Arabicum. Cluſ. Hiſt. 11. p. 186. *Star-flower of Arabia.*

9. ORNITHOGALUM (*Capenſe*) foliis cordatis ovatis. Prod. Leyd. 31. *Star-flower with oval heart-ſhaped leaves.* Ornithogalum Africanum plantaginis roſeæ folio, radice tuberoſâ. Hort. Amſt. 2. p. 175. *African Star-flower, with a Roſe Plantain leaf and a tuberous root.*

10. ORNITHOGALUM (*Tuberoſum*) racemo breviſſimo, foliis teretibus fiſtuloſis. *Star-flower with a very ſhort ſpike, and taper fiſtular leaves.* Ornithogalum Africanum, luteum odoratum, foliis cepaceis, radice tuberoſâ. H. L. *African Star-flower having yellow ſweet flowers, leaves reſembling thoſe of the Onion, and a tuberous root.*

The firſt ſort grows naturally near Briſtol, and alſo near Chicheſter in Suſſex, and ſome other parts of England. This hath a pretty large bulbous root, from which come out ſeveral long keel-ſhaped leaves, which ſpread on the ground; between theſe come out a ſingle naked ſtalk about two feet long, ſuſtaining a long looſe ſpike of flowers of a yellowiſh green colour, ſtanding upon pretty long foot-ſtalks, which ſpread wide from the principal ſtalk; the petals of the flowers are narrow, making but little appearance. The flowers have an agreeable ſcent; they appear in May, and when the ſeed-veſſels are formed, the foot-
ſtalks

ftalks which fuftain them become erect, and approach near the ftalk. The feeds ripen in Auguft.

The fecond fort grows naturally upon the hills in Portugal and Spain, but has been long cultivated in the Englifh gardens by the title of the Star of Bethlehem. This hath a very large, oval, bulbous root, from which arife feveral long keel-fhaped leaves of a dark green colour, in the middle of which come out a naked ftalk which rifes near three feet high, terminated by a long conical fpike of white flowers, ftanding upon pretty long foot-ftalks, rifing one above another in an upright fpike. Thefe appear in June, and are fucceeded by roundifh feed-veffels, having three cells filled with roundifh feeds, which ripen in Auguft.

The third fort grows naturally in Arabia ; this hath a very large bulbous root, from which come out feveral broad fword-fhaped leaves, which fpread on the ground ; the ftalk is thick and ftrong, rifing between two and three feet high, bearing a long fpike of large white flowers, ftanding upon long foot-ftalks. They are compofed of fix petals which fpread open in form of a ftar, and appear in June, but do not ripen their feeds in England.

The fourth fort grows in great abundance naturally in the kingdom of Naples, and is now become almoft as common in England, for the roots propagate fo faft by offsets and feeds, as to become troublefome weeds in gardens ; and in many places where the roots have been thrown out of gardens, they have grown upon dunghills and in wafte places as plentifully as weeds. This hath a pretty large, compreffed, bulbous root, from which come out many long, narrow, keel-fhaped leaves, of a dark green colour. The ftalks are very thick and fucculent, rifing about a foot high, fuftaining ten or twelve flowers in a loofe fpike, each hanging on a foot-ftalk an inch long ; they are compofed of fix petals, which are white within, but of a grayifh green on their outfide, having no fcent ; within the petals is fituated the bell-fhaped nectarium, compofed of fix leaves, out of which arife the fix ftamina, terminated by yellow fummits. The flowers appear in April, and are fucceeded by large, roundifh, three-cornered capfules, which are filled with roundifh feeds ; as the capfules grow large, they are fo heavy as to weigh the ftalk to the ground.

The fixth fort hath fmall bulbous roots not larger than Peas, from which arife one or two narrow keel-fhaped leaves about five inches long, of a grayifh colour ; the ftalk is angular, and rifes about four inches high, having two narrow keel-fhaped leaves juft below the flowers, which are difpofed in an umbel upon branching foot-ftalks ; thefe are yellow within, but of a purplifh green on their outfide. They appear in May, and are fucceeded by fmall triangular capfules, filled with reddifh uneven feeds. It grows on the borders of cultivated fields in France and Germany.

The feventh fort grows naturally in moft parts of Europe, and is fuppofed to do fo in England, though it is feldom found here, unlefs in orchards or grounds where the roots may have been planted, or thrown out of gardens with rubbifh. This hath a bulb as large as a fmall Onion, to which adhere many fmall offsets : the leaves are long, narrow, and keel-fhaped, fpreading on the ground, and have a longitudinal white line through the hollow. The ftalk rifes about fix inches high, fuftaining an umbel of flowers which are white within, but have broad green ftripes on the outfide of the petals ; thefe ftand upon long foot-ftalks, which rife above the principal ftalk. It flowers in April and May, and is fucceeded by roundifh three-cornered capfules filled with angular feeds, which ripen in July.

The eighth fort grows naturally in Arabia ; this hath a large bulbous root, from which arife many long keel-fhaped leaves, which embrace each other with their bafe ; they are of a deep green, and ftand erect. The flowers of this kind I have never yet feen, though I have tried many ways to procure them : the roots multiply exceedingly, and are never injured by froft,

although the leaves are put out before winter. Thefe roots are frequently brought over from Italy for fale; but I have not heard of any having flowered ; and Clufius fays, he never faw but one root flower, and that came from Conftantinople.

The ninth fort grows naturally at the Cape of Good Hope ; this hath an irregular tuberous root, varying greatly in form and fize, covered with a dark brown fkin, from which arife feveral oval heart-fhaped leaves, upon pretty long foot-ftalks ; they have feveral longitudinal veins like Ribwort Plantain. The flower-ftalks are flender, naked, and rife about a foot high, fuftaining feveral fmall, greenifh, white flowers, ftanding upon a loofe fpike, ftanding upon long flender foot-ftalks. They come out in November, making but little appearance, and are not fucceeded by feeds in England.

The tenth fort grows naturally on the dry rocks at the Cape of Good Hope ; this hath a large, depreffed, bulbous root, as big as a man's fift, covered with an uneven brown fkin, putting out feveral taper hollow leaves nine or ten inches long, between which comes forth a naked ftalk near a foot high, terminated by a loofe fpike of yellow flowers, of an agreeable fweet fcent. It flowers in May, but does produce feeds in England.

The three forts firft mentioned, are cultivated for ornament in the Englifh gardens. Thefe are propagated by offsets, which their roots commonly produce in great plenty. The beft time to tranfplant their roots is in July or Auguft, when their leaves are decayed ; for if they are removed late in autumn, their fibres will be fhot out, when they will be very apt to fuffer if difturbed. They fhould have a light fandy foil, but it muft not be over dunged. They may be intermixed with other bulbous-rooted flowers in the borders of the pleafure-garden, where they will afford an agreeable variety. Their roots need not be tranfplanted oftener than every other year, for if they are taken up every year, they will not increafe fo faft ; but when they are fuffered to remain too long unremoved, they will have fo many offsets about them as to weaken their blowing roots. Thefe may alfo be propagated from feeds, which fhould be fown and managed as moft other bulbous-rooted flowers, and will produce their flowers three or four years after fowing.

The fourth fort is fcarce worthy of a place in gardens, but as it will thrive in any fituation or under trees, fo a few plants may be admitted in obfcure places for the fake of variety.

The fifth fort has not much beauty, therefore a few roots of it will be enough for variety, as alfo of the fixth and feventh forts ; the two laft will thrive in fhade, but the fifth fhould have an open fituation.

The eighth fort multiplies fo faft by offsets from the roots as to become troublefome weeds in a garden, for every fmall root will grow, and in two years produce twenty or thirty more ; fo that unlefs the large roots are taken up every year and divefted of their offsets, the borders will be over-run with them.

The ninth fort is too tender to thrive in the open air in England, fo the roots of this fhould be planted in pots filled with light earth, and in the autumn placed under a hot-bed frame, where they may be fcreened from froft, and in mild weather enjoy the free air. The leaves of this appear in the autumn, and continue growing all the winter, fo muft not be expofed to froft ; nor fhould they be drawn up weak, for then the flowers will be few on a ftalk, and not large. If the pots do now and then receive a gentle fhower of rain in winter it will be fufficient, for they fhould not have much wet during that feafon. Toward the beginning of July the leaves and ftalks decay, and then the roots may be taken up, laying them in a dry cool place till the end of Auguft, when they muft be planted again.

The other fpecies which were included in this genus, are now removed to Scilla.

ORNITHOPUS. Lin. Gen. Plant. 790. Ornithopodium. Tourn. Inft. R. H. 400. tab. 224. Bird's-foot ; in French, *Pié-d'oifeau.*

The CHARACTERS are,

The empalement of the flower is permanent, of one leaf, tubulous, and indented in five equal fegments at the brim. The flower is of the butterfly kind, the ftandard is heart-ſhaped and entire; the wings are oval, erett, and almoſt as large as the ftandard; the keel is ſmall and com-preffed. It hath ten ftamina, nine of which are joined, and one ſtands feparate, terminated by fingle ſummits. The germen is narrow, fupporting a briſtly afcending ſtyle, terminated by a punŭtured ſtigma. The germen afterward becomes a taper incurved pod, having many joints con-nected together, but when ripe ſeparate, each containing one oblong ſeed.

This genus of plants is ranged in the third ſection of Linnæus's feventeenth claſs, which includes the plants whofe flowers have ten ſtamina joined in two bodies.

The SPECIES are,

1. ORNITHOPUS (*Perpufillus*) foliis pinnatis, leguminibus compreffis fubarcuatis. Hort. Upfal. 234. *Bird's-foot with winged leaves, and compreſſed pods a little arched.* Ornithopodium majus. C. B. P. 350. *Greater Bird's-foot.*

2. ORNITHOPUS (*Nodofa*) foliis pinnatis, leguminibus confertis pedunculatis. *Bird's-foot with winged leaves, and pods growing in cluſters upon foot-ſtalks.* Ornithopodium radice tuberculis nodosâ. C. B. P. 350. *Bird's-foot with knobbed tubercular roots.*

3. ORNITHOPUS (*Compreffus*) foliis pinnatis, pinnis leguminibus compreffis rugoſus. Hort. Cliff. 364. *Bird's-foot with linear winged leaves, and compreſſed pods grow-ing in pairs.* Ornithopodium Scorpoides, filiquâ com-preſsâ. Tourn. Inft. 400. *Bird's-foot with the appear-ance of Caterpillar, and flat pods.*

4. ORNITHOPUS (*Scorpioides*) foliis ternatis fubfeffilibus impari maximo. Hort. Cliff. 364. *Bird's-foot with tri-foliate leaves fitting cloſe to the ſtalk, and the middle lobe very large.* Ornithopodium Portulacæ folio. Tourn. Inft. 400. *Bird's-foot with a Purſlane leaf.*

The firft fort grows naturally in the fouth of France, in Spain and Italy. It is an annual plant, having many trailing ftalks a foot and a half long, from which come out a few fide branches, garniſhed with long winged leaves, compofed of about eighteen pair of ſmall oval lobes, terminated by an odd one; thefe lobes ftand fometimes oppoſite, and at others they are alternate and hairy. The flowers are produced in ſmall clufters at the top of foot-ftalks, which arife from the wings of the ftalks, and are near three inches long, having a ſmall winged leaf, part of which is below, and the other part above the flowers, fo that they feem to come from the midrib of the leaf; the flowers are of a deep gold colour, and fhaped like a butterfly. Thefe appear in July, and are fucceeded by flat nar-row pods about three inches long, which turn inward at the top like a bird's claw. They are jointed, and a little hairy, containing a fingle ſeed in each joint, which ripens in autumn, when the joints feparate and fall afunder.

The fecond fort grows naturally on dry commons and heaths in moſt parts of England. The root of this fort is compofed of two or three ftrong fibres, to which hang feveral ſmall tubercles or knobs like grains. There are many ſlender ftalks come out from the root, and fpread on the ground, from four to eight inches long, garniſhed with ſmall, winged, hairy leaves, compofed of fix or feven pair of narrow lobes, terminated by an odd one. The flowers ftand upon long ſlender foot-ftalks, which come out at every joint of the ftalk; they are ſmall, of a yellow colour, and are fucceeded by clufters of ſhort pods, which are a little incurved at the top. It flowers and feeds about the fame time as the former. The third fort grows plentifully about Meffina and Naples. The root of this fort runs deep into the ground, fending out a few ſmall fibres on the fide; the ftalks are about fix inches long, and do not lie flat on the ground like the other; the leaves are hairy, compofed of ten or twelve pair of narrow lobes placed

along the midrib, terminated by an odd one. The flowers grow in ſmall bunches on the top of the branches; they are yellow, and are generally fuc-ceeded by two flat pods not much more than an inch long, turned inward like a bird's claw. This flowers and feeds about the fame time with the former.

The fourth fort grows naturally among the Corn in Spain and Italy; this hath many ſmooth branching ftalks, which rife near two feet high, garniſhed toward their top with trifoliate oval leaves fitting cloſe, hav-ing two ſmall appendages. The lower leaves are often fingle, and of a grayiſh colour, the middle lobe being twice the fize of the two fide ones. The flowers ftand upon ſlender foot-ftalks, are yellow, and fuc-ceeded by taper pods, which are two inches long, ſhaped like a bird's claw. This flowers and feeds about the fame time with the former.

Thefe plants are propagated by fowing their feeds in the fpring upon a bed of light freſh earth, where they are to remain (for they feldom do well when they are tranfplanted;) when the plants come up, they muft be carefully cleared from weeds; and where they are too cloſe, fome of the plants ſhould be pulled out, fo as to leave the remaining ones about ten inches afun-der. In June thefe plants will flower, and the feeds will ripen in Auguſt. There is no great beauty in them, but for the variety of their jointed pods, they are preferved by thofe who are curious perfons in their plea-fure-gardens; where, if their feeds are fown in patches in the borders, each fort diftinctly by itſelf, and the plants thinned, leaving only two at each patch, they will require no farther care, and will add to the vari-ety, efpecially where the Snail and Caterpillar plants are preferved, which are very proper to intermix with them. They are all annual plants, which periſh foon after the feeds are ripe.

OROBANCHE, or Broom Rape.

There are fix or feven fpecies of this genus at prefent known, two of which grow naturally on dry grounds in feveral parts of England; but as all the forts do not agree with culture, fo they are not admitted into gardens. They are ranged in the fecond ſection of Linnæus's fourteenth claſs, intitled Didynamia An-giofpermia, the flowers having two long and two ſhorter ftamina, and their feeds being included in a capfule.

OROBUS. Tourn. Inft. R. H. 393. tab. 214. Lin. Gen. Plant. 780. [ὀροῦ☉, of ὀροῦντι, to cat, βῶς, an ox, q. d. an herb with which oxen are fed, becauſe the ancients uſed to fatten their oxen with a like herb.] Bitter Vetch; in French, *Orobe.*

The CHARACTERS are,

The empaleuent of the flower is tubulous, of one leaf, with an obtuſe baſe; the brim is oblique and indented in five parts, the three lower acute, the two upper ſhorter and ob-tuſe. The flower is of the butterfly kind; the ftandard is heart-ſhaped; the two wings are almoſt as long as the ftandard, and join together; the keel is bifid, acute-pointed, and rifing upwards; the borders are compreſſed, and the body ſwollen. It hath ten ftamina, nine are joined, and one ſeparate; thefe are rifing, and terminated by roundiſh ſummits. It hath a cylindrical compreſſed germen, ſup-porting a crooked rifing ſtyle, crowned by a narrow downy ſtigma, faſtened by the inner edge in the middle to the point of the ſtyle. The germen afterward becomes a long taper pod ending in an acute point, having one cell, contain-ing ſeveral roundiſh ſeeds.

This genus of plants is ranged in the third ſection of Linnæus's feventeenth claſs, which contains thofe plants whofe flowers have ten ſtamina joined in two bodies.

The SPECIES are,

1. OROBUS (*Vernus*) foliis pinnatis ovatis, ſtipulis femi-fagittatis integerrimis, caule fimplici. Lin. Sp. Plant. 728. *Bitter Vetch with oval winged leaves, entire ſtipulæ half arrow-pointed, and a ſingle ſtalk.* Orobus ſylvati-cus purpureus vernus. C. B. P. 351. *Purple, vernal, wood Bitter Vetch.*

2. OROBUS (*Tuberofus*) foliis pinnatis lanceolatis, ſtipulis femifagittatis, caule fimplici. Lin. Sp. Plant. 728.

Bitter

Bitter Vetch with spear-shaped winged leaves, entire half arrow-pointed stipulæ, and a single stalk. Orobus sylvaticus foliis oblongis glabris. Tourn. Inst. R. H. *i.* 393. *Wood Bitter Vetch with oblong smooth leaves.*

3. OROBUS (*Sylvaticus*) caulibus decumbentibus hirsutis ramosis. Cent. pl. 67. Flor. Angl. 275. *Bitter Vetch with hairy, branching, decumbent stalks.* Orobus sylvaticus nostras. Raii Syn. 324. *Wood Bitter Vetch.*

4. OROBUS (*Niger*) caule ramoso, foliis sexjugis ovatooblongis. Hort. Cliff. 366. *Bitter Vetch with a branching stalk, and leaves composed of six pair of oblong oval lobes.* Orobus sylvaticus foliis viciæ. C. B. P. 352. *Wood Bitter Vetch with a Vetch leaf.*

5. OROBUS (*Pyrenaicus*) caule ramoso, foliis bijugis lanceolatis nervosis, stipulis subspinosis. Lin. Sp. 1029. *Bitter Vetch with a branching stalk, and leaves composed of two pair of nervous spear-shaped lobes.* Orobus Pyrenaicus, foliis nervosis. Tourn. Inst. 393. *Bitter Vetch of the Pyrenees with nervous leaves.*

6. OROBUS (*Lathyroides*) foliis conjugatis subsessilibus, stipulis dentatis. Hort. Upsal. 220. *Bitter Vetch with leaves placed by couples close to the stalks, and indented stipulæ.* Lathyroides erecta, folio ovato acuminato, cæruleis viciæ floribus & siliquis, Sibirica. Amman. Ruth. 151. *Siberian, upright, Bastard Lathyrus, with an oval acute-pointed leaf, blue flowers, and pods like those of the Vetch.*

7. OROBUS (*Luteus*) foliis pinnatis ovato-oblongis, stipulis rotundato-lunatis dentatis, caule simplici. Lin. Sp. Plant. 728. *Bitter Vetch with oval, oblong, winged leaves, roundish, moon-shaped, indented stipulæ, and a single stalk.* Orobus Sibericus perenne. Gmel. *Perennial Siberian Bitter Vetch.*

8. OROBUS (*Venetis*) foliis pinnatis ovatis acutis, quatuor-jugatis, caule simplici. Tab. 193. fol. 2. *Bitter Vetch with oval, acute-pointed, winged leaves, having four pair of lobes and a single stalk.* Orobus Venetus. Cluf. Hist. 232. *Venetian Bitter Vetch.*

9. OROBUS (*Americanus*) foliis pinnatis lineari-lanceolatis infernè tomentosis, caule ramosissimo frutescente. *Bitter Vetch with linear, spear-shaped, winged leaves, which are woolly on their under side, and a very branching shrubby stalk.* Orobus Americanus erectus, foliorum pinnis angustioribus & subtus incanis, siliquis glabris. Houst. MSS. *Upright American Bitter Vetch, with very narrow lobes to the leaves, hoary on their under side, and having smooth pods.*

10. OROBUS (*Argentus*) foliis pinnatis oblongo-ovatis infernè sericeis, caule erecto tomentoso, floribus spicatis terminalibus. *Bitter Vetch with oblong, oval, winged leaves, which are silky on their under side, and have an upright woolly stalk, terminated by a spike of flowers.* Orobus Americanus, latifolius, argenteus, flore purpureo. Houst. MSS. *Broad-leaved, silvery, American Bitter Vetch, with a purple flower.*

11. OROBUS (*Procumbens*) foliis pinnatis, foliolis exterioribus majoribus tomentosis, caule procumbente. *Bitter Vetch with winged leaves, whose outer lobes are woolly, and a trailing stalk.* Orobus Americanus procumbens & hirsutus, flore purpureo. Houst. MSS. *Trailing, hairy, American Bitter Vetch, with a purple flower.*

12. OROBUS (*Coccineus*) foliis pinnatis, foliis linearibus villosis, caule procumbente floribus alaribus & terminalibus. *Bitter Vetch with winged leaves, having hairy linear lobes, a trailing stalk, and flowers growing on the sides and at the ends of the branches.* Orobus Americanus procumbens minimus, flore coccineo. Houst. MSS. *The least trailing American Bitter Vetch, having a scarlet flower.*

The first sort grows naturally in the forests of Germany and Switzerland. The root of this is perennial, composed of many strong fibres; the stalks rise a foot high, and are garnished with winged leaves, composed of two pair of oval acute-pointed lobes, and at the base of the foot-stalk is situated a stipula, (or small leaf,) shaped like the point of an arrow cut through the middle. This embraces the stalk. The lobes of the leaves are about an inch and an half long, and near an inch broad, ending in acute points,

The flowers stand upon foot-stalks, which arise from the wings of the stalk ; they are about three inches long, sustaining six or seven flowers ranged in a spike, which are of the butterfly kind. These are at first of a purple colour, but afterward change blue ; they appear early in the spring, and are succeeded by slender taper pods an inch and a half long, having one cell, in which are lodged four or five oblong bitter seeds, which ripen in June. There is a variety of this with pale flowers, which is preserved in some gardens. The second sort grows naturally in woods and shady places in most parts of England. This hath a perennial creeping root, from which arise angular stalks nine or ten inches long, garnished at each joint by one winged leaf, composed of four pair of smooth spear-shaped lobes, and, at the base of each, is situated a stipula like that of the first sort; and from the wings of the stalks arise the foot-stalks of the flowers, which are about four inches long, each sustaining two or three purplish red flowers, which turn to a deep purple before they fade. They appear in April, and are succeeded by long taper pods, containing six or seven roundish seeds, which ripen the beginning of June. These are called Wood or Heath Peas.

The third sort grows naturally in Cumberland and Wales. The root is perennial and ligneous, from which arise several hairy stalks a foot and a half high, garnished at each joint with one winged leaf, composed of ten or eleven pair of narrow lobes ranged close together along the midrib; at the base of which is situated an acute stipula embracing the stalk. The flowers are disposed in a close spike, standing upon foot-stalks three inches long, which arise from the wings of the leaves ; they are of a purple colour, and are succeeded by short flat pods, containing two or three seeds. It flowers the beginning of June, and the seeds ripen in July.

The fourth sort grows naturally on the mountains in Germany and Switzerland. This hath a strong, ligneous, perennial root, from which arise many branching stalks two feet high, garnished at each joint by one winged leaf, composed of five or six small, oblong, oval lobes ranged along the midrib. The flowers stand upon very long foot-stalks, which arise from the wings of the stalk ; these sustain at their top four, five, or six purple flowers, which appear in May, and are succeeded by compressed pods an inch and a half long, containing four or five oblong seeds, which ripen the beginning of July. The stalks decay in autumn, and new ones arise in the spring.

The fifth sort grows naturally on the Pyrenean mountains ; this ,hath a perennial root, from which arise several smooth branching stalks a foot and a half high, garnished with winged leaves composed of four pair of spear-shaped lobes, which have three longitudinal veins; at the base of the leaves is situated a stipula embracing the stalk, in the same manner as the first. The flowers stand upon long foot-stalks, arising from the wings of the leaves ; toward the upper part of the stalk they are ranged in a loose spike, are of a purple colour, appearing in May, and are succeeded by compressed pods about two inches long, containing three or four seeds, which ripen in July.

The sixth sort grows naturally in Siberia ; this hath a perennial root, from which arise three or four branching stalks about a foot high. The leaves stand by pairs opposite along the stalks, to which they sit close, having an indented stipula at their base ; the leaves are smooth, stiff, and of a lucid green. The flowers grow in close spikes upon short foot-stalks, which rise from the wings of the leaves at the top of the stalks, where are generally three or four of these spikes standing together. The flowers are of a fine blue colour, so make a pretty appearance. These appear in June, and are succeeded by short flattish pods, containing two or three seeds in each, which ripen in August.

The

The feventh fort grows naturally in Siberia ; this hath a perennial root, from which arife feveral herbaceous ftalks a foot and a half high, garnifhed with winged leaves, compofed of four or five pair of oval oblong lobes, having at their bafe a roundifh moon-fhaped ftipula embracing the ftalk. The flowers come out from the wings of the leaves upon fhort foot-ftalks ; they are large and of a purple colour, appearing in April, and are fucceeded by fwelling pods near two inches long, containing four or five feeds, which ripen in June.

The eighth fort grows naturally in Italy ; this hath a perennial root, from which arife feveral ftalks about a foot high, garnifhed with winged leaves, compofed of four pair of oval lobes, ending in acute points ; they are fmooth and of a pale green colour, placed pretty far diftant on the midrib. The flowers come out upon flender foot-ftalks, which arife from the wings of the leaves, four or five ftanding at the top ; they are of a purple colour, and appear in March. Thefe are fucceeded by fwelling pods an inch and a half long, each containing three or four roundifh feeds, which ripen in May.

The ninth fort grows naturally in Jamaica, from whence the late Dr. Houftoun fent the feeds in 1731. This rifes with a very branching ftalk about three feet high, which is ligneous ; the branches are garnifhed with winged leaves, compofed of five or fix pair of narrow fpear-fhaped lobes, which are woolly on their under fide. The flowers grow in loofe fpikes at the end of the branches, are of a pale purple colour, and are fucceeded by fmooth compreffed pods an inch and a half long, each containing five or fix roundifh feeds.

The tenth fort was difcovered by the late Dr. Houftoun at La Vera Cruz, from whence he fent the feeds to England. This rifes with a fhrubby ftalk five or fix feet high, dividing into many flender branches, which are covered with a brown woolly bark, and garnifhed with foft, fatteny, winged leaves ; thofe on the young branches are compofed of four pair of oval obtufe lobes, of a brownifh green colour, hairy on their upper fide, but of a filvery filky hue on their under. The leaves on the upper branches are compofed of feven or eight pair of oblong oval lobes, of the fame colour and confiftence as the lower. The flowers are produced in long erect fpikes at the end of the branches ; they are of a deep purple colour, and are fucceeded by long, woolly, compreffed pods, each conraining four or five feeds.

The eleventh fort was difcovered by Dr. Houftoun at La Vera Cruz, who fent it to England in 1730. This is a low plant, whofe ftalks bend to the ground, and are feldom more than fix or eight inches long, from which come out a few fhort fide branches ; they are garnifhed with winged leaves, compofed of four or five pair of fmall, oblong, oval, woolly lobes, terminated by an odd one, the upper lobes being much larger than the lower. The flowers come out in fmall bunches, ftanding upon fhort foot-ftalks, which arife from the wings of the ftalk ; they are fmall, and of a bright purple colour ; thefe are fucceeded by compreffed pods near two inches long, each having fix or feven roundifh compreffed feeds.

The twelfth fort was difcovered at the fame time, growing naturally in the fame country as the former, by the fame gentleman. This hath a pretty thick ligneous root, which fends out many flender ftalks a foot and a half long, trailing upon the ground, garnifhed with winged leaves, compofed of three or four pair of narrow hoary lobes, about half an inch long. The flowers come out from the fide and at the end of the ftalks, three or four ftanding upon a fhort foot-ftalk ; they are fmall and of a fcarlet colour, and are fucceeded by fhort taper pods, each containing three or four fmall roundifh feeds.

The eight forts which are firft mentioned, have perennial roots but annual ftalks, which decay every autumn ; feveral of thefe may be propagated by parting their roots ; the beft time for doing this is in the

autumn, that the plants may be well eftablifhed before the fpring ; for as feveral of them begin to put out their ftalks very early in the fpring, fo if they are then difturbed, it will either prevent their flowering, or caufe their flowers to be very weak. Moft of thefe plants delight in a fhady fituation, and love a loamy foil.

They are alfo propagated by feeds, but thefe fhould be fown in the autumn, for if they are kept out of the ground till fpring, many of the forts will never grow, and thofe which do, feldom vegetate the fame year ; and the fourth fort I could never raife from feeds fown in the fpring, though I have made the trial in different fituations many times ; but the feeds which have fcattered in the fummer, have come up well the following fpring, as have alfo thofe which were fown in September. When the plants come up they muft be kept clean from weeds, and where they are too clofe together they fhould be thinned, fo as they may have room to grow till the autumn, when they fhould be tranfplanted into the places where they are defigned to remain. If the roots are ftrong, they will flower very well the following fpring, but thofe which are weak will not flower till the fecond year ; therefore fuch may be planted in a fhady border at four or five inches diftance, where they may grow one year to get ftrength, and then may be removed to the places where they are to remain. The farther care of them is only to dig the ground between them in winter, and in fummer to keep them clean from weeds.

The four laft mentioned forts being natives of warm countries are tender, fo muft be preferved in ftoves, otherwife they will not live in England. Thefe are propagated by feeds, which fhould be fown early in the fpring, in fmall pots filled with light rich earth, and plunged into a hot-bed of tanners bark, obferving frequently to moiften the earth, otherwife the feeds will not grow. When the plants come up, they fhould be carefully taken out of the pots, and each tranfplanted into feparate fmall pots filled with rich earth, and then plunged again into the tan-bed, obferving to fhade them until they have taken root ; after which time they fhould have frefh air admitted to them every day in warm weather, and muft be frequently watered. With this management the plants will make a great progrefs. When any of the plants are grown too tall to remain in the hot-bed, they fhould be taken out, and plunged into the bark-bed in the ftove, where they may have room to grow, efpecially the ninth and tenth forts ; but the other two being of humbler growth, may be kept in the hot-bed until Michaelmas, when the nights begin to be cold ; at which time they fhould be removed into the ftove, and plunged into the bark-bed, where they muft be treated as other tender exotic plants ; by which method they may be preferred through the winter, and the following fummer they will produce flowers. Thefe plants are perennial, fo that if they fhould not perfect their feeds, the plants may be maintained for feveral years.

ORTEGIA HISPANICA.

This is called by Clufius, Juncaria Salmantica ; it is a low trailing plant, with Rufh-like ftalks, producing at the joints a few fmall almoft invifible flowers, therefore the plant is feldom cultivated except in botanic gardens for variety.

ORYZA. Tourn. Inft. R. H. 513. tab. 296. Rice ; in French, Ris.

The CHARACTERS are,

The chaff is fmall, acute-pointed, having two valves nearly equal, inclofing a fingle flower. The petal has two valves, which are hollow, compreffed, and boat-fhaped, ending in a beard or awn. It has a two-leaved nectarium, and fix hairy ftamina the length of the petal, terminated by fummits whofe bafe are bifid, and a turbinated germen, fupporting two reflexed hairy ftyles, crowned by feathered ftigmas. The germen afterward becomes one large, oblong, compreffed feed, having two channels on each fide, fitting on the petal of the flower.

This

This genus of plants is ranged in the second section of Linnæus's sixth class, which contains those plants whose flowers have six stamina and two styles.

We have but one Species of this plant, viz.

ORYZA (Sativa.) Matth. 403. Rice.

This grain is greatly cultivated in most of the eastern countries, where it is the chief support of the inhabitants ; and great quantities of it are brought into England and other European countries every year, where it is in great esteem for puddings, &c. it being too tender to be produced in these northern countries, without the assistance of artificial heat ; but from some seeds which were formerly sent to South Carolina, there have been great quantities produced ; and it is found to succeed as well there as in its native country, which is a very great improvement to our American settlements.

This plant grows upon moist soils, where the ground can be flowed over with water after it is come up ; so that whoever would cultivate it in England for curiosity, should sow the seeds upon a hot-bed ; and when the plants are come up, they should be transplanted into pots filled with rich light earth, and placed into pans of water, which should be plunged into a hot-bed ; and as the water wastes, so it must, from time to time, be renewed again, still preserving the water in the pans, otherwise they will not thrive, and keeping them in a stove all the summer ; and toward the latter end of August, they will produce their grain, which will ripen tolerably well, provided the autumn proves favourable.

OSIER. See SALIX.

OSMUNDA, the Osmund Royal, or flowering Fern.

This is one of the kinds of Fern which is distinguished from the other sorts, by its producing flowers on the top of the leaves ; whereas the others, for the most part, produce them on the back of their leaves.

There is but one kind of this plant, which grows wild in England, but there are several sorts of them which grow in America ; but as they are seldom kept in gardens, I shall not enumerate their species.

The common sort grows on bogs in several parts of England, therefore whoever hath an inclination to transplant it into gardens, should place it in a moist shady situation, otherwise it will not thrive.

OSTEOSPERMUM. Lin. Gen. Plant. 887. Monilifera. Vaill. Act. Par. 1720. Chrysanthemoides. Tourn. Act. Par. 1705. Hard-seeded Chrysanthemum.

The CHARACTERS are,

The flower hath an hemispherical empalement, which is single, and cut into many segments. The flower is composed of several hermaphrodite florets in the disk, which are tubulous, and cut at the brim into five parts. These are surrounded by several female florets, which are radiated, each having a long narrow tongue, which is cut into three parts at the top. The hermaphrodite florets have each five slender short stamina, terminated by cylindrical summits, with a small germen supporting a slender style, crowned by an obsolete stigma ; these are barren. The female florets have each a globular germen supporting a slender style, crowned by an indented stigma ; the germen afterward becomes one single hard seed.

This genus of plants is ranged in the fourth section of Linnæus's nineteenth class, intitled Syngenesia Polygamia Necessaria, the flowers being composed of hermaphrodite florets in the disk, which are barren, and female florets which are fruitful.

The SPECIES are,

1. OSTEOSPERMUM (Moniliferum) foliis ovalibus serratis petiolatis subdecurrentibus. Lin. Hort. Cliff. 424. Hard-seeded Chrysanthemum, with oval sawed leaves on running foot-stalks. Chrysanthemoides Afrum populi albæ foliis. Hort. Elth. 80. tab. 68. Hard-seeded African Chrysanthemum, with leaves like those of the white Poplar.

2. OSTEOSPERMUM (Pisiferum) foliis lanceolatis acutè dentatis, caule fruticoso. Tab. 194. fig. 1. Hard-seeded Chrysanthemum, with spear-shaped leaves which are acutely indented, and a shrubby stalk.

3. OSTEOSPERMUM (Spinosum) spinis ramosis. Lin. Hort. Cliff. 424. Hard-seeded Chrysanthemum, with branching spines. Chrysanthemoides Osteospermum Africanum odoratum, spinosum & viscosum. Hort. Amst. 2. p. 85. Hard-seeded Chrysanthemum of Africa, which is prickly, viscous, and sweet.

4. OSTEOSPERMUM (Polygaloides) foliis lanceolatis imbricatis sessilibus. Flor. Leyd. Prod. 179. Hard-seeded Chrysanthemum, with spear-shaped leaves sitting close to the stalks, and lying over each other like the scales of a fish. Monilifera poligoni foliis. Vaill. Act. Par. 1720. Monilifera with Knot Grass leaves.

The first sort grows naturally at the Cape of Good Hope, but has been several years an inhabitant in the English gardens. This rises with a shrubby stalk seven or eight feet high, covered with a smooth gray bark, and divides into several branches, garnished with oval leaves, which are unequally indented on their edges ; they are placed alternately, and are of a thick consistence, covered with a hoary down, which goes off from the older leaves. The flowers are produced in clusters at the end of the branches, six or eight coming out together, upon foot-stalks an inch and a half long ; these are yellow, and shaped like those of Ragwort. The border or rays are composed of about ten half florets, which spread open ; the disk or middle is composed of tubulous florets, which are cut into five parts at the brim ; these are barren, but the half florets round the border, have one hard seed succeeding each of them. This plant flowers but seldom here ; the time of its flowering is in July or August.

The second sort grows like the first, but the leaves are more pointed, of a green colour, and acutely sawed on the edges ; the foot-stalks of the leaves are bordered, and the leaves are deeply veined. This produces tufts of yellow flowers at the extremity of the shoots from spring to autumn, and frequently ripens seeds.

The third sort is a low shrubby plant, which seldom rises above three feet high, and divides into many branches ; the ends of the shoots are beset with green branching spines ; the leaves are very clammy, especially in warm weather ; these are long and narrow, and set on without any order. The flowers are produced singly at the ends of the shoots, which are yellow, and appear in July and August.

These three sorts are too tender to live in the open air in England, so are placed in the green-house in October, and may be treated in the same manner as Myrtles, and other hardy green-house plants, which require a large share of air in mild weather ; and in the beginning of May the plants may be removed into the open air, and placed in a sheltered situation during the summer season. The second and third sorts must have plenty of water, being very thirsty plants.

These plants are propagated by cuttings, which may be planted in any of the summer months, upon a bed of light earth, and should be watered and shaded until they have taken root, which they will be in five or six weeks, when they must be taken up and planted in pots ; for if they are suffered to stand long, they will make strong vigorous shoots, and will be difficult to transplant afterward, especially the first and second sorts ; but there is not so much danger of the third, which is not so vigorous, nor so easy in taking root as the other. During the summer season the pots should be frequently removed, to prevent the plants from rooting through the holes in the bottom of the pots into the ground, which they are very apt to do when they continue long undisturbed, and then they shoot very luxuriantly ; and, on their being removed, these shoots, and sometimes the whole plants, will decay.

The fourth sort grows naturally at the Cape of Good Hope ; this hath a shrubby stalk about four feet high, which divides into many small branches, garnished with small oblong leaves which sit close to them, and in some of the upper branches they lie over each other like the scales of fish. The flowers come out at the end of the branches, ſtanding ſingly upon foot-ſtalks, which are about an inch long ; the half florets which compoſe the border or rays, are acute-pointed and ſpread open ; 'the diſk is compoſed of florets which are barren. This ſort is propagated by cut-tings, in the ſame manner as the other ſorts, and muſt be treated in the ſame way.

OSYRIS. Lin. Gen. Plant. 978. Caſia. Tourn. Inſt. R. H. 664. tab. 488. Poets Caſia.

The CHARACTERS are,

It is male and female in different plants ; the empalement of the flower is of one leaf, which is divided into three acute ſegments. The flower hath no petals, but thoſe on the male plants have three ſhort ſtamina ; the female have a germen, which afterward changes to a globular berry, having a ſingle ſeed.

We know but one SPECIES of this plant, viz.

OSYRIS (*Alba*) fruteſcens bacciſera. C. B. P. *Shrubby berry-bearing Poets Caſia ; and by ſome, red-berried ſhrubby Caſia.*

This is a very low ſhrub, ſeldom riſing above two feet high, having ligneous branches, which are gar-niſhed with long narrow leaves, of a bright colour. The flowers appear in June, which are of a yellowiſh colour, and are ſucceeded by berries, which at firſt are green, and afterward turn to a bright red colour, ſomewhat like thoſe of Aſparagus.

This plant grows wild in the ſouth of France, in Spain, and ſome parts of Italy, by the ſide of roads, as alſo between the rocks, but is with great difficulty tranſplanted into gardens ; nor does it thrive after being removed, ſo that the only method to obtain this plant is, to ſow the berries where they are to re-main. Theſe berries commonly remain a year in the ground before the plants appear, and ſometimes they will lie two or three years, ſo that the ground ſhould not be diſturbed under three years, if the plants do not come up ſooner. Theſe ſeeds muſt be procured from the places where the plants naturally grow, for thoſe which have been brought into gardens never produce any, and it is with great difficulty they are preſerved alive.

OTHONNA. Lin. Gen. Plant. 888. Doria. Raii Meth Plant. 33. Jacobæa. Tourn. Inſt. R. H. 485. tab. 276. Ragwort.

The CHARACTERS are,

It hath a radiated flower, compoſed of hermaphrodite flo-rets which form the diſk, and female half florets which form the rays or border ; theſe are included in one com-mon ſingle empalement of one leaf, cut into eight or ten ſegments. The hermaphrodite flowers are tubulous, in-dented at the top in five parts ; the female half florets are ſtretched out like a tongue, and the point has three in-dentures which are reflexed. The hermaphrodite florets have ſhort hairy ſtamina, terminated by cylindrical ſum-mits, and an oblong germen ſupporting a ſlender ſtyle, crowned by a ſingle ſtigma. The female half florets have oblong germen with a ſlender ſtyle, crowned by a large bi-fid reflexed ſtigma. The hermaphrodite florets are ſeldom fruitful, but the female half florets have an oblong ſeed, which is ſometimes naked, and at others crowned with down ; theſe fit in the permanent empalement.

This genus of plants is ranged in the fourth ſection of Linnæus's nineteenth claſs, which includes the plants with compound flowers, whoſe female flowers are fruitful and the hermaphrodite barren.

The SPECIES are,

1. OTHONNA (*Coronopifolia*) foliis infimis lanceolatis in-tegerrimis, ſuperioribus ſinuato-dentatis. Hort. Cliff. 419. *Othonna with ſpear-ſhaped lower leaves which are entire, and the upper ones indented in ſinuſes.* Jacobæa Africana fruteſcens coronopi folio. Hort. Amſt. 2. p. 139. *Shrubby African Ragwort, with a Hartſhorn leaf.*

2. OTHONNA (*Calthoides*) foliis cuneiformibus integer-rimis ſeſſilibus, caule fruticoſo procumbente, pedun-culis longiſſimis. *Othonna with entire wedge-ſhaped leaves ſitting cloſe, a ſhrubby trailing ſtalk, and very long foot-ſtalks to the flowers.* Calthoides Africana, glaſti folio. Juſſ. *African Baſtard Marygold, with a Woad leaf.*

3. OTHONNA (*Pectinata*) foliis pinnatifidis, laciniis line-

aribus parallelis. Hort. Cliff. 419. *Othonna with wing-pointed leaves, whoſe ſegments are narrow and parallel.* Jacobæa Africana fruteſcens, foliis abſinthii umbelli-feri incanis. Hort. Amſt. 2. p. 137. tab. 69. *Shrubby African Ragwort, with hoary leaves like thoſe of the umbelliferous Wormwood.*

4. OTHONNA (*Abrotanifolia*) foliis multifido-pinnatis li-nearibus. Flor. Leyd. Prod. 380. *Othonna with very narrow leaves, ending in many winged points.* Jacobæa Africana fruteſcens, foliis abrotani, ſc. crithmi major & minor. Volk. Norim. 225. *Shrubby African Rag-wort, with a Southernwood or Samphire leaf.*

5. OTHONNA (*Bulboſa*) foliis ovato-cuneiformibus den-tatis. Lin. Sp. Plant. 926. *Othonna with oval, wedge-ſhaped, indented leaves.* Solidago foliis oblongis den-tatis glabris, floribus magnis umbellatis. Burm Afr. 164. tab. 59. *Woundwort with oblong, indented, ſmooth leaves, and large flowers growing in umbels.*

The firſt ſort grows naturally in Æthiopia. This riſes with a ſhrubby ſtalk four or five feet high, di-viding into ſeveral branches, garniſhed with grayiſh leaves placed without order, thoſe on their lower part being narrow and entire, but the others are indented on the edges after the manner of Hartſhorn. The flowers are produced in looſe umbels at the end of the branches ; they are yellow, and are ſucceeded by downy ſeeds.

The ſecond ſort was diſcovered by the late Dr. Shaw, growing naturally near Tunis in Africa, from whence he brought the ſeeds. This ſends out many ligne-ous ſtalks from the root, which ſpreads out on every ſide, declining toward the ground, garniſhed with grayiſh leaves, which are narrow at their baſe, en-larging upward, and are broad at their points, where they are rounded ; theſe fit cloſe to the ſtalks. The flowers are produced upon long, thick, ſucculent foot-ſtalks at the end of the branches ; they are yellow ; the rays are ſharp-pointed, and not much longer than the empalement ; the diſk is large, and the florets are as long as the empalement ; the ſeeds are crowned with a long down.

The third ſort grows naturally at the Cape of Good Hope, from whence the ſeeds were brought to Hol-land, and the plants were raiſed in the Amſterdam Garden in 1699. This riſes with a ſhrubby ſtalk about the thickneſs of a man's thumb, two or three feet high, which divide into many branches, covered with a hoary down, and garniſhed with hoary leaves about three inches long and one broad, cut into many nar-row ſegments almoſt to the midrib ; theſe ſegments are equal and parallel, and are indented at their ends into two or three points. The flowers are produced on long foot-ſtalks which ariſe from the wings of the ſtalks ; toward the end of the branches they have large yellow rays, or borders, with a diſk of florets, and are ſucceeded by oblong purple ſeeds crowned with down.

The fourth ſort grows naturally on the hills near the Cape of Good Hope, and was raiſed from ſeed in the Amſterdam Garden. This hath a low, ſhrubby, branching ſtalk ; the leaves are thick like thoſe of Samphire, and are cut into many narrow ſegments. The flowers are produced on ſhort foot-ſtalks at the end of the branches ; they are yellow, and ſhaped like the other ſpecies of this genus, and are ſucceeded by brown ſeeds crowned with ſoft down.

The fifth ſort grows naturally at the Cape of Good Hope. This hath a thick ſhrubby ſtalk, dividing into ſeveral branches which riſe five or ſix feet high ; the leaves come out in cluſters from one point, ſpread on every ſide ; they are ſmooth, narrow at their baſe, en-larging gradually to their points, which are rounded ; their edges are acutely indented like thoſe of the Holly. From the center of the leaves ariſe the foot-ſtalks of the flowers, which are five or ſix inches long, branch-ing out into ſeveral ſmaller, each ſuſtaining one yel-low radiated flower, ſhaped like the former ; theſe are ſucceeded by ſlender ſeeds crowned with down.

The firſt, ſecond, third, fourth and fifth ſorts, are preſerved in green-houſes through the winter, but require

quire no artificial warmth; if thefe are protected from the froft it is fufficient, and in mild weather they muft have a large fhare of free air. In the fummer they muft be placed abroad in a fheltered fituation, among other hardy exotic plants, where they will add to the variety, and flower great part of the feafon. Thefe may be all propagated by cuttings during the fummer months, which fhould be planted upon an old hot-bed, and covered with glaffes, fhading them from the fun in the heat of the day. When thefe have taken root, they fhould be planted each into a feparate pot filled with foft loamy earth, placing them in the fhade till they have taken new root; then they may be removed to a fheltered fituation, where they may remain till autumn, treating them in the fame way as the old plants.

The fecond fort will live in the open air if it is planted in a warm fituation and a dry foil. Some of thefe plants have endured the open air for more than twenty years in the Chelfea Garden, without protection. This is eafily propagated by cuttings, in the fame way as the former.

OXALIS. Lin. Gen. Plant. 515. Oxys. Tourn. Inft. R. H. 88. tab. 19. Wood-forrel.

The CHARACTERS are,

The empalement of the flower is fhort, permanent, and cut into five acute fegments. The flower is of one petal, cut into five obtufe indented fegments almoft to the bottom; it hath ten erect hairy ftamina, terminated by roundifh furrowed fummits, and a germen with five angles, fupporting five flender ftyles, crowned by obtufe ftigmas. The germen afterward becomes a five-cornered capfule with five cells, which open longitudinally at the angles, containing roundifh feeds, which are thrown out with an elafticity on the touch when ripe.

This genus of plants is ranged in the fifth fection of Linnæus's tenth clafs, which includes thofe plants whofe flowers have ten ftamina and five ftyles.

The SPECIES are,

1. OXALIS (*Acetofella*) fcapo unifloro, foliis ternatis, radice fquamofo-articulata. Hort. Cliff. 175. *Wood-forrel with one flower on a foot-ftalk, trifoliate leaves, and a fcaly jointed root.* Oxys flore albo. Tourn. Inft. 88. *Wood-forrel with a white flower.*

2. OXALIS (*Corniculata*) caule ramofo diffufo, pedunculis umbelliferis. Hort. Cliff. 175. *Wood-forrel with a branching diffufed ftalk, and umbellated foot-ftalks.* Oxys lutea. J. B. *Yellow Wood-forrel.*

3. OXALIS (*Stricta*) caule ramofo erecto, pedunculis umbelliferis. Flor. Virg. 161. *Wood-forrel with a branching upright ftalk, and umbellated foot-ftalks.* Oxys lutea, Americana, erectior. Tourn. Inft. R. H. 88. *Upright, yellow, American Wood-forrel.*

4. OXALIS (*Incarnata*) caule fubramofo bulbifero, pedunculis unifloris, foliis paffim verticillatis foliolis obcordatis. Lin. Sp. 622. *Wood-forrel with branching ftalks bearing bulbs, the leaves generally in whorls, and the fmall leaves heart-fhaped.* Oxys bulbofa Æthiopica minor, folio cordato, flore ex albido purpurafcente. Tourn. Inft. 89. *Smaller bulbous Ethiopian Wood-forrel, with a heart-fhaped leaf, and a purplifh white flower.*

5. OXALIS (*Purpurea*) fcapo unifloro, foliis ternatis, radice bulbofa. Hort. Cliff. 175. *Wood-forrel with a foot-ftalk fupporting one flower, trifoliate leaves, and a bulbous root.* Oxys bulbofa Africana, rotundifolia, caulibus & floribus purpureis amplis. Hort. Amft. 1. p. 41. tab. 21. *African bulbous Wood-forrel, having a round leaf, and large purple ftalks and flowers.*

6. OXALIS (*Pes-capræ*) fcapo umbellifero, foliis ternatis bipartitis. Lin. Sp. Plant. 434. *Wood-forrel with an umbelliferous ftalk, and trifoliate leaves divided in two parts.* Oxalis bulbofa pentaphylla & hexaphylla, floribus magnis luteis & copiofis. Burm. Afr. 80. tab. 29. *Bulbous Wood-forrel with five or fix leaves, and large yellow flowers in abundance.*

7. OXALIS (*Frutefcens*) caule erecto fruticofo, foliis ternatis, impari maximo. *Wood-forrel with an upright fhrubby ftalk, and trifoliate leaves, the middle one being very large.* Oxys lutea frutefcens, trifolii bituminofi facie. Plum. Cat. 2. *Yellow fhrubby Wood-forrel, with the appearance of bituminous Trefoil.*

8. OXALIS (*Barreleri*) caule ramofo erecto, pedunculis bifidis racemiferis. Lin. Sp. 624. *Wood-forrel with an erect branching ftalk, and branching bifid foot-ftalks.* Trifolium acetofum Americanum, rubro flore. Barrel. Rar. 64. *Three-leaved American Wood-forrel, with a red flower.*

The firft fort grows naturally in moift fhady woods, and clofe to hedges in moft parts of England, fo is but feldom admitted into gardens; though whoever is fond of acid herbs in fallads, can fcarce find a more grateful acid in any other plant. The roots of this fort are compofed of many fcaly joints, which propagate in great plenty. The leaves arife immediately from the roots upon fingle long foot-ftalks, are compofed of three heart-fhaped lobes, which meet in a center, where they join the foot-ftalk; they are of a pale green and hairy; between thefe come out the flowers upon pretty long foot-ftalks, each fuftaining one large white flower of the open bell fhape. Thefe appear in April and May, and are fucceeded by five-cornered oblong feed-veffels having five cells, inclofing fmall brownifh feeds; when thefe are ripe, the feed-veffels burft open at the leaft touch, and caft out the feeds to a confiderable diftance. This is the fort which is directed for medicinal ufe in the difpenfaries; but thofe people who fupply the market with herbs, generally bring the third fort, which is now become common in the gardens; but this hath very little acid, fo is unfit for the purpofes of the other; but as it rifes with an upright branching ftalk, fo it is foon gathered and tied up in bunches; whereas the leaves of the firft grow fingly from the root, and require more time in gathering. There is a variety of the firft fort with a purplifh flower, which grows naturally in the North of England, but, as it does not differ from it in any other refpect, I have not enumerated it.

The fecond fort is an annual plant, which grows naturally in woods and fhady places in Italy and Sicily. The root of this is long, flender, and fibrous; the ftalks trail upon the ground, fpreading out eight or nine inches wide on every fide, dividing into fmall branches; the leaves ftand upon pretty long foot-ftalks, and are compofed of three heart-fhaped lobes, which have deeper indentures at their points than thofe of the firft fort. The flowers are yellow, growing in form of an umbel, upon pretty long flender foot-ftalks, arifing from the fide of the branches. Thefe appear in June and July, and are fucceeded by feed-veffels near an inch long, which open with an elafticity, and caft out the feeds.

The third fort grows naturally in Virginia and other parts of North America, from whence the feeds were formerly brought to Europe; but wherever this plant has been once introduced and fuffered to ripen feeds, it has become a common weed. This is an annual plant, rifing with a branching herbaceous ftalk eight or nine inches high; the leaves ftand upon very long foot-ftalks, and are fhaped like thofe of the fecond fort. The flowers are yellow, ftanding in a fort of umbel, upon long, flender, erect foot-ftalks; the feed-veffels and feeds are like thofe of the fecond fort.

Thefe three forts require no particular culture; if the roots of the firft fort are taken up and tranfplanted in a fhady moift border, they will thrive and multiply exceedingly; and if they are kept clean from weeds, will require no other care. If the feeds of the other two forts are fown in an open border, the plants will rife freely, and require no care; for if they are permitted to fcatter their feeds, there will be a plentiful fupply of the plants.

The fourth fort hath a roundifh bulbous root, from which come out flender ftalks about fix inches high, which divide into branches by pairs, and from the divifions come out the foot-ftalks of the leaves; thefe are long, flender, and fuftain a trifoliate leaf compofed of three fmall, roundifh, heart-fhaped lobes. The foot-ftalks of the flowers are long, flender, and arife from the divifion of the ftalks, each fuftaining one purplifh flower about the fame fize and fhape as thofe of the firft fort. This flowers in May, June, and July, and fometimes produces ripe feeds in England. It grows naturally at the Cape of Good Hope, fo is too tender

to

to live through the winter in the open air in England ; but if it is sheltered from hard frost under a common hot-bed frame in winter, it will require no other protection. It propagates in plenty by offsets from the root, as also by bulbs, which come out from the side of the stalks.

The fifth sort grows naturally at the Cape of Good Hope in such plenty, that the earth which came from thence, in which some plants were brought to England, was full of it. This hath a roundish bulbous root, covered with a brown skin, sending out strong fibres which strike deep into the ground ; the leaves are trifoliate, composed of three roundish, large, hairy lobes, which are but little indented at the top; these stand upon long slender foot-stalks, which arise from a thick short stalk, which adheres to the root. The foot-stalks of the flowers arise between the leaves from the stalk, each supporting one large purple flower ; these appear in January and February, but are rarely succeeded by seeds here, but the roots put out offsets in great plenty, whereby it is propagated. This sort will not thrive in winter in the open air here, so the roots should be planted in pots, which may be sheltered under a common frame in winter, where it may have as much free air as possible in mild weather, otherwise the leaves will draw up weak ; for the leaves of this plant come out in October, and continue growing till May, when they begin to wither and decay. The roots may be transplanted any time after the leaves decay, till they begin to push out again.

The sixth sort is a native of the same country as the fifth ; the roots of this are bulbous ; the leaves stand upon long slender foot-stalks, which arise from a short stalk or head ; they are composed of three lobes, which are for the most part divided into two parts almost to their base. The foot-stalks of the flowers are five or six inches long, sustaining several large yellow flowers ranged in form of an umbel. These appear in March, and are sometimes succeeded by seeds here. This sort requires the same treatment as the fifth.

The seventh sort was discovered by Plumier in some of the French colonies in America, and was since found growing plentifully at La Vera Cruz by the late Dr. Houstoun, who sent it to England. This rises with a shrubby stalk a foot and a half high, sending out several slender branches, which are garnished with trifoliate small leaves, composed of three oval lobes, the middle one being twice as large as the side ones. These are placed by pairs opposite, and sometimes by threes round the stalk, standing upon short foot-stalks. The foot-stalks of the flowers arise from the wings of the stalks, are near two inches long, each sustaining four or five yellow flowers, whose petals are not much longer than the empalement; each of these have a smaller foot-stalk which is crooked, so that the flowers hang downward.

This sort is much tenderer than either of the former, so requires to be placed in a stove kept to a moderate degree of warmth in winter. It is propagated by seeds, which must be sown in pots, and plunged into a moderate hot-bed ; and when the plants come up, they should be each planted into a separate pot filled with light sandy earth, and plunged into a fresh hot-bed, shading them from the sun till they have taken new root; after which they must be treated in the same manner as other tender plants from the same country.

The eighth sort grows naturally in the Brazils; for in a tub of earth which came from thence, the plants came up in plenty. This seldom rises more than three or four inches high, having upright stalks; the leaves arec composed of three pretty large hairy lobes, standing on long foot-stalks. The flowers rise immediately from the root, having foot-stalks the same length with those of the leaves ; they are bifid, supporting two pretty large red flowers, which are succeeded by oblong capsules filled with brown seeds. This sort may be propagated by offsets from the root, or by seeds, and requires the same protection as the sixth sort.

O X-E Y E. See BUPHTHALMUM.
O X Y A C A N T H A. See BERBERIS.
O X Y S. See OXALIS.

P.

P A D

PADUS. Lin. Gen. Edit. prior. 476. Edit. 5. Prunus. 546. Cerasus & Laurocerasus. Tourn. Inst. R. H. 625, 627. tab. 401, 403. The Bird-cherry, or Cherry Laurel.

The CHARACTERS are,

The empalement of the flower is bell-shaped, of one leaf, indented in five parts at the brim, which spread open. The flower hath five large roundish petals, which spread open, and are inserted in the empalement. It hath from twenty to thirty awl-shaped stamina, which are inserted in the empalement, terminated by roundish summits, and a roundish germen supporting a slender style, crowned by an entire obtuse stigma. The germen afterward becomes a roundish fruit, inclosing an oval-pointed nut having rough furrows.

This genus of plants was by Dr. Linnæus, in the former editions of his Method, separated from the Cherries, to which they had been before joined, because the furrows of the nuts in this genus were obtuse, whereas those of the Cherries are acute ; but there is a more obvious distinction between them, which is, the flowers of the Padus are ranged in a long bunch (or racemus) and those of the Cherry have their foot-stalks arising from one joint ; but in the last edition of his Method, he has joined this genus, the Cherry and Apricot, to the Plumb, making them only species of

P A D

the same genus ; in which, I think, he has exceeded the boundaries of nature ; for although the Padus and Cerasus may with propriety be joined in the same genus, yet these ought by no means to be joined to the Prunus ; for it is well known, that the Cherry will not grow by grafting or budding upon the Plumb stock, nor the Plumb upon Cherry stocks, though there are no instances of two trees of the same genus, which will not grow upon each other, however different their exterior appearance may be.

It is ranged in the first section of Linnæus's twelfth class, which includes those plants whose flowers have from twenty to thirty stamina, which are either inserted in the empalement or petals of the flower, and but one style.

The SPECIES are,

1. PADUS (*Avium*) glandulis duobus, basi foliorum subjectis. Hort. Cliff. 185. *Bird-cherry with two glands at the base of the leaves.* Cerasus racemosa, sylvestris, fructu non eduli. C. B. P. 451. *Branching wild Cherry with a fruit not eatable.*

2. PADUS (*Rubra*) foliis lanceolato-ovatis deciduus, petiolis biglandulosis. tab. 196. fol. 2. *Bird-cherry with spear-shaped, oval, deciduous leaves, whose foot-stalks have two glands.* Cerasus racemosa sylvestris, fructu non
eduli

eduli rubro. H. R. Par. *Branching wild Bird-cherry with a red fruit, which is not eatable, and commonly called by the gardeners, Cornish Cherry.*

3. PADUS (*Virginiana*) foliis oblongo-ovatis ferratis acuminatis deciduis, bafi antice glandulofis. *Bird-cherry with oblong, oval, fawed, acute-pointed, deciduous leaves, and glands on the fore part of the foot-stalk.* Cerafi similis arbufcula Mariana, padi folio, flore albo parvo racemofo. Pluk. Mant. 43. Catefb. Car. 1. p. 28. *American Bird-cherry.*

4. PADUS (*Laurocerafus*) foliis fempervirentibus lanceolato-ovatis. Hort. Cliff. 42. *Bird-cherry with evergreen, fpear-fhaped, oval leaves.* Laurocerafus. Cluf. Hift. 1. p. 4. *The common Laurel.*

5. PADUS (*Lufitanica*) foliis oblongo-ovatis fempervirentibus eglandulofis. *Bird-cherry with oblong, oval, evergreen leaves, having glands.* Laurocerafus Lufitanica minor. Tourn. Inft. 628. *Smaller Portugal Laurel, called Afavero by the Portuguefe.*

6. PADUS (*Caroliniana*) foliis lanceolatis acutè denticulatis fempervirentibus. *Evergreen Bird-cherry with fpear-fhaped leaves, having fmall acute indentures, called in America Baftard Mahogany.*

The firft fort grows naturally in the hedges in Yorkfhire, and many of the northern counties in England, as alfo in fome few places near London, but it is propagated as a flowering-fhrub in the nurfery-gardens for fale. This rifes with feveral woody ftalks to the height of ten or twelve feet, which will grow to have ftems nine or ten inches diameter, if they are permitted to ftand; but as the fafhions of gardens have been frequently altering for fifty or fixty years paft, fo there are few places where any of the ornamental flowering trees have been fuffered to remain. The branches of this tree grow wide and fcattering; they are covered with a purplifh bark, and garnifhed with oval fpear-fhaped leaves placed alternate, which are flightly fawed on their edges, and have two fmall protuberances or glands at their bafe. The flowers are produced in long loofe bunches from the fide of the branches; they have five roundifh white petals, which are much fmaller than thofe of the Cherry, and are inferted in the border of the empalement; and within thefe are a great number of ftamina, which alfo are inferted in the empalement. The flowers ftand each upon a fhort foot-ftalk, and are ranged alternately along the principal foot-ftalk; they have a ftrong fcent, which is very difagreeable to moft perfons. Thefe flowers appear in May, and are fucceeded by fmall roundifh fruit, which are firft green, afterward turn red, and when ripe, are black, inclofing a roundifh furrowed ftone or nut, which ripens in Auguft.

The fecond fort grows naturally in Armenia, from whence I have received the feeds; but it has been many years ago propagated in the nurfery-gardens about London, where it is generally called Cornifh-cherry. This fort has been often confounded with the firft; many of the late writers in botany have fuppofed it was the fame fpecies, but I have raifed both forts from feeds, and have always found the young plants to retain their difference. This rifes with a ftrait upright ftem more than twenty feet high; the branches are fhorter, and grow clofer together than thofe of the firft, fo naturally form regular heads; the leaves of this are fhorter and broader than thofe of the other, and are not fo rough; the flowers grow in clofer fhorter fpikes, which ftand more erect; the fruit is larger, and red when ripe. This flowers a little after the firft fort.

The third fort grows naturally in Virginia, and other parts of North America. This rifes with a thick ftem from ten to thirty feet high, dividing into many branches, which have a dark purple bark, and are garnifhed with oval leaves placed alternately on fhort foot-ftalks; they are of a lucid green, and flightly fawed on their edges, continuing in verdure as late in the autumn as any of the deciduous trees. The flowers come out in bunches like thofe of the fecond fort, and are fucceeded by larger fruit, which is black when ripe, and is foon devoured by the birds. The

wood of this tree is beautifully veined with black and white, and will polifh very fmooth, fo is frequently ufed for cabinet work; as is alfo the wood of the firft fort, which is much ufed in France, where it is called, *Bois de Sainte-Lucie.*

The fourth fort is the common Laurel, which is now fo well known as to need no defcription. This grows naturally about Trebifond, near the Black Sea, and was brought to Europe about the year 1576, but is now become very common, efpecially in the warmer parts of Europe.

The fifth fort was brought to England from Portugal, but whether it is a native of that country, or was introduced there from fome other country, is hard to determine. The Portuguefe call it Aferaro, or Azerero. This was fuppofed to have been but a low evergreen fhrub, but by experience we find, that when it is in a proper foil, it will grow to a large fize. There are at prefent fome of thefe trees whofe trunks are more than a foot diameter, and twelve or fixteen feet high, which are not of many years ftanding, and are well furnifhed with branches, which when young have a reddifh bark; the leaves are fhorter than thofe of the common Laurel, approaching nearer to an oval form; they are of the fame confiftence, and of a lucid green, which mixing with the red branches, make a beautiful appearance. The flowers are produced in long loofe fpikes from the fide of the branches; they are white, and fhaped like thofe of the common Laurel, appearing in June, and are fucceeded by oval berries fmaller than thofe of the common Laurel; they are firft green, afterward red, and when ripe are black, inclofing a ftone like the Cherry.

The feeds of the fixth fort were fent from Carolina, by the title of Baftard Mahogany, from the colour of the wood, which is fomewhat like Mahogony. This feems to be little more than a fhrub, if we may judge from its growth here; the ftalk does not rife more than three feet high, but fends out lateral branches, which fpreaon every fide, covered with a brown bark, and garnifhed with fpear-fhaped leaves near two inches long, and three quarters of an inch broad, with fmall acute indentures on the edges; they ftand alternately upon very fhort foot-ftalks, and are of a lucid green, continuing their verdure all the year. This has not as yet flowered in England, fo I can give no account of it; but by the feeds and defcription which I received of its flowers, it belongs to this genus.

This plant will live in the open air here, if it is planted in a warm fituation, and fheltered in fevere froft, to which, if they are expofed, often deftroys them, efpecially while the plants are young; but when they have acquired ftrength, there is no doubt of their thriving very well in the open ground in fheltered fituations. It may be propagated in the fame manner as the Portugal Laurel from the berries; and if the branches are laid down they will take root, but the cuttings will not grow, fo far as I have experienced.

The three firft forts are eafily propagated, either by the feeds or layers; when they are propagated by the feeds they fhould be fown in the autumn, for if they are kept out of the ground till fpring, they feldom grow till the fecond year. Thefe may be fown upon a bed or border of good ground, in the fame way as the Cherry-ftones which are defigned for ftocks; and the young plants may be treated in the fame manner, planting them out in a nurfery, where they may ftand two years to get ftrength, and then they may be tranfplanted to the places where they are to remain. They are ufually intermixed with other flowering fhrubs, in wildernefs work, where they add to the variety.

If they are propagated by layers, the young fhoots fhould be laid down in the autumn, which will have good roots by that time twelvemonth, when they may be feparated from the old plants, and tranfplanted into a nurfery for a year or two to get ftrength, and may then be removed to the places where they are to grow.

The third fort will grow to be a very large tree when it is planted in a moift foil, but in dry ground it rarely rifes to be more than twenty feet high. There have been fome plants of late years raifed from feeds which came from Carolina, which have all the appearance of the third fort, but are of much humbler growth ; whether this may proceed from their being brought from a warmer climate, fo do not agree with the cold of our winters fo well as that, or whether they are a different fpecies from that, I cannot yet determine, as they have not produced fruit here.

The Laurel may be eafily propagated by planting of the cuttings; the beft time for doing this is in September, as foon as the autumnal rains fall to moiften the ground ; the cuttings muft be the fame year's fhoots, and if they have a fmall part of the former year's wood to their bottom, they will more certainly fucceed, and form better roots. Thefe fhould be planted in a foft loamy foil about fix inches deep, preffing the earth clofe to them. If thefe are properly planted, and the ground is good, there will few of the cuttings fail ; and if they are kept clean from weeds the following fummer, they will have made good fhoots by the following autumn, when they may be tranfplanted into a nurfery, where they may grow two years to get ftrength, and then fhould be removed to the places where they are to remain. Thefe plants were formerly kept in pots and tubs, and preferved in green-houfes in winter ; but afterward they were planted againft warm walls, to preferve them, being frequently injured by fevere froft. After this the plants were trained into pyramids and globes, and conftantly kept fheered ; by which the broad leaves were generally cut in the middle, which rendered the plants very unfightly. Of late years they have been more properly difpofed in gardens, by planting them to border woods, and the fides of wildernefs quarters; for which purpofe we have but few plants fo well adapted, for it will grow under the drip of trees, in fhade or fun ; and the branches will fpread to the ground, fo as to form a thicket ; and the leaves being large, and having a fine gloffy green colour, they fet off the woods and other plantations in winter, when the other trees have caft their leaves ; and in fummer they make a good contraft with the green of the other trees. Thefe trees are fometimes injured in very fevere winters, efpecially where they ftand fingle and are much expofed ; but where they grow in thickets, and are fcreened by other trees, they are feldom much hurt ; for in thofe places it is only the young tender fhoots which are injured, and there will be new fhoots produced immediately below thefe to fupply their place, fo that in one year the damage will be repaired. But whenever fuch fevere winters happen, thefe trees fhould not be cut or pruned till after the following Midfummer ; by which time it will appear what branches are dead, which may then be cut away, to the places where the new fhoots are produced ; for by haftily cutting thefe trees in the fpring, the drying winds have free ingrefs to the branches, whereby the fhoots fuffer as much, if not more, than they had done by the froft.

Thefe trees are alfo very ornamental, when they are mixed with other evergreen trees, in forming of thickets, or to fhut out the appearance of difagreeable objects ; for the leaves being very large, make a very good blind, and are equally ufeful for fcreening from winds ; fo that when they are planted between flowering-fhrubs, they may be trained fo as to fill up the vacancies in the middle of fuch plantations ; and will anfwer the purpofe of fcreening in the winter, and fhutting out the view through the fhrubs in all feafons : there are alfo many other purpofes to which this tree may be applied, fo as to render it very ornamental.

In warmer countries this tree will grow to a large fize, fo that in fome parts of Italy there are large woods of them ; but we cannot hope to have them grow to fo large ftems in England ; for fhould thefe trees be pruned up, in order to form them into ftems,

the froft would then become much more hurtful to them than in the manner they ufually grow, with their branches to the ground : however, if the trees are planted pretty clofe together in large thickets, and permitted to grow rude, they will defend each other from the froft, and they will grow to a confiderable height : an inftance of which is now in that noble plantation of evergreen trees, made by his Grace the Duke of Bedford at Wooburn-abbey, where there is a confiderable hill covered entirely with Laurels ; and in the other parts of the fame plantation, there are great numbers of thefe intermixed with the other evergreen trees, where they are already grown to a confiderable fize, and make a noble appearance.

There are fome perfons who propagate thefe trees from their berries, which is certainly the beft way to obtain good plants ; for thofe which come from feeds have a difpofition to an upright growth, whereas almoft all thofe which are raifed from cuttings or layers, incline more to an horizontal growth, and produce a greater number of lateral branches. When any perfon is defirous to propagate this tree by feeds, the berries muft be guarded from the birds, otherwife they will devour them before they are perfectly ripe, which is feldom earlier than the latter end of September, or the beginning of October, for they fhould hang until the outer pulp is quite black. When thefe berries are gathered, they fhould be fown foon after ; for when they are kept out of the ground till fpring, they frequently mifcarry ; and there will be no hazard in fowing them in the autumn, provided they are put in a dry foil ; and if the winter fhould prove fevere, the bed in which they are fown fhould be covered with rotten tan, ftraw, Peas-haulm, or any light covering, to prevent the froft from penetrating of the ground. The beft way will be to fow the berries in rows at about fix inches diftance, and one inch afunder in the rows ; if drills are made about three inches deep, and the berries fcattered in them, and the earth drawn over them, it will be a very good method. The following fpring the plants will appear, when they fhould be kept clean from weeds ; and if the feafon fhould prove dry, if they are duly watered, the plants will make fo good progrefs as to be fit for tranfplanting the following autumn, when they fhould be carefully taken up, and planted in a nurfery, placing them in rows at three feet afunder, and the plants one foot diftance in the rows. In this nurfery they may remain two years, by which time they will be fit to tranfplant where they are defigned to remain.

The beft feafon for tranfplanting thefe plants is in the autumn, as foon as the rain has prepared the ground for planting ; for although they often grow when removed in the fpring, yet thofe do not take fo well, nor make fo good progrefs as thofe which are removed in the autumn, efpecially if the plants are taken from a light foil, which generally falls away from their roots ; but if they are taken up with balls of earth to their roots, and removed but a fmall diftance, there will be no danger of tranfplanting them in the fpring, provided it is done before they begin to fhoot ; for as the plants will fhoot very early in the fpring, fo if they are removed after thay have fhot, the fhoots will decay, and many times the plants entirely fail.

There are fome perfons who, of late, have banifhed thefe plants from their gardens, as fuppofing them poffeffed of a poifonous quality, becaufe the diftilled water has proved fo in many inftances ; but however the diftilled water may have been found deftructive to. animals, yet from numberlefs experiments which have been made both of the leaves and fruit, it hath not appeared that there is the leaft hurtful quality in either ; fo that the whole muft be owing to the oil, which may be carried over in diftillation.

The berries have been long ufed to put into brandy, to make a fort of ratafia, and the leaves have alfo been put into cuftards, to give them an agreeable flavour ; and although thefe have been for many years much ufed, yet there hath been no one inftance of

their

their having done the leaft injury ; and as to the berries, I have known them eaten in great quantities without prejudice.

There are fome perfons who have grafted the Laurel upon Cherry ftocks, with defign to enlarge the trees, but although they will take very well upon each other, yet they feldom make much progrefs when either the Laurel is grafted on the Cherry, or the Cherry upon the Laurel ; fo that it is only a thing of curiofity, attended with no real ufe : and I would recommend to perfons who have this curiofity, to graft the Laurel upon the Cornifh Cherry, rather than any other fort of ftock, becaufe the graft will unite better with this ; and as it is a regular tree and grows large, fo it will better anfwer the purpofe of producing large trees.

The Portugal Laurel may be propagated in the fame way as the common Laurel, either by cuttings, layers, or feeds. If the cuttings are planted at the fame feafon, and in the fame way as hath been directed for the common Laurel, they will take root very freely ; or if the young branches are laid in the autumn, they will take root in one year, and may then be removed into a nurfery, where they may grow a year or two get ftrength, and then tranfplanted where they are to remain.

But although both thefe methods are very expeditious for the propagating thefe plants, yet I would recommend the raifing them from the berries, efpecially where they are defigned for tall ftandards ; for the plants which are propagated by cuttings and layers, put out more lateral branches and become bufhy, but are not fo well inclined to grow upright, as thofe which come from feeds : and as there are now many trees in the Englifh gardens which produce plenty of berries every year, fo if they are guarded from birds till they are ripe, there may be a fupply of them fufficient to raife plants enough without propagating them any other way. Thefe berries muft be fown in the autumn, and treated in the fame way as the common Laurel.

This tree delights in a gentle loamy foil, which is not too wet nor over dry, though it will grow upon almoft any foil : but the plants do not make fo great progrefs, nor appear fo beautiful, when planted in a very dry foil, or in ground that is too wet. The time of tranfplanting this, is the fame as for the common Laurel.

This tree is much hardier than the common Laurel, for in the fevere froft of the year 1740, when great numbers of Laurels were entirely killed, and moft of them loft their verdure, this remained unhurt in perfect verdure, which renders it more valuable ; and as by the appearance of fome trees now growing in the gardens, they feem as if they will grow to a large fize, fo it is likely to be one of the moft ornamental evergreens we have.

PÆONIA. Tourn. Inft. R. H. 273. tab. 146. Lin. Gen. Plant. 600. [fo called from Pæon the phyfician, becaufe he is faid to have cured Pluto, when wounded by Hercules, with this herb.] The Peony ; in French, *Pivoine*.

The CHARACTERS are,

The flower has a permanent empalement, compofed of five concave reflexed leaves, unequal in fize and pofition. The flower hath five large, roundifh, concave petals which fpread open, and a great number of fhort hairy ftamina, terminated by large, oblong, four-cornered fummits, with two, three, or four oval, erect, hairy germen in the center, having no ftyles, but have oblong, comprefled, obtufe, coloured ftigmas. The germen afterward become fo many oval, oblong, reflexed, hairy capfules, having one cell, open longitudinally, containing feveral oval, fhining, coloured feeds, fixed to the furrow.

This genus of plants is ranged in the fecond fection of Linnæus's thirteenth clafs, which contains thofe plants whofe flowers have many ftamina and two germen or ftyles.

The SPECIES are,

1. PÆONIA (*Mafcula*) foliis lobatis ex ovato-lanceolatis. Haller. Helv. 311. *Peony with lobated leaves which are*

oval and fpear-fhaped. Pæonia folio nigricante fplendido, quæ mas. C. B. P. 323. *Peony with dark fhining leaves, otherwife male Peony.*

2. PÆONIA (*Fæminea*) foliis difformiter lobatis. Haller. Helvet. 311. *Peony with difformed lobated leaves.* Pæonia communis, vel fœmina. C. B. P. 323. *Common or female Peony.*

3. PÆONIA (*Peregrina*) foliis difformiter lobatis, lobis incifis, petalis florum rotundioribus. *Peony with difformed lobated leaves which are cut, and rounder petals to the flower.* Pæonia peregrina, flore faturatè rubente. C. B. P. 324. *Foreign Peony with a deep red flower.*

4. PÆONIA (*Hirfuta*) foliis lobatis, lobis lanceolatis integerrimis. *Peony with lobated leaves, whofe lobes are fpear-fhaped and entire.* Pæonia fœmina flore pleno rubro majore. C. B. P. 324. *Female Peony with a larger double red flower.*

5. PÆONIA (*Tartarica*) foliis difformiter lobatis pubefcentibus. Tab. 199. *Peony with difformed lobated leaves, which are downy.*

6. PÆONIA (*Lufitanica*) foliis lobatis, lobis ovatis infernè incanis. *Peony with lobated leaves, whofe lobes are oval and hoary on their under fide.* Pæonia Lufitanica, flore fimplici odoro. Juff. *Peony of Portugal with a fingle fweet flower.*

The firft fort here enumerated, is the common male Peony, which grows naturally in the woods on the Helvetian mountains. The root of this is compofed of feveral oblong knobs, fhaped like the dugs of a cow, which hang by ftrings, faftened to the main head ; the ftalks rife about two feet and a half high, which are garnifhed with leaves compofed of feveral oval lobes, fome of which are cut into two or three fegments ; they are of a lucid green on their upper fide, but are hoary on their under. The ftalks are terminated by large fingle flowers, compofed of five or fix large roundifh red petals, inclofing a great number of ftamina, terminated by oblong yellow fummits. In the center is fituated two, three, or fometimes five germen, which join together at their bafe ; they are covered with a whitifh hairy down ; thefe afterward fpread afunder, and open longitudinally, expofing the roundifh feeds, which are firft red, then purple, and when perfectly ripe turn black. The flowers appear in May, and the feeds ripen in the autumn.

There is one variety of this with pale, and another with white flowers, as alfo one whofe leaves have larger lobes; but as thefe are generally fuppofed to be only feminal variations, fo I have not enumerated them here.

The fecond fort is called the female Peony ; the roots of this are compofed of feveral roundifh thick knobs or tubers, which hang below each other, faftened with ftrings ; the ftalks are green, and rife about the fame height as the former ; thefe are garnifhed with leaves, compofed of feveral unequal lobes, which are varioufly cut into many fegments ; they are of a paler green than thofe of the firft, and are hairy on their under fide ; the flowers are fmaller, and of a deeper purple colour. It flowers at the fame time as the firft.

There are feveral varieties of this fort with double flowers, which are cultivated in the Englifh gardens ; thefe differ in the fize and colour of their flowers, but are fuppofed to have been accidentally obtained from feeds.

The third fort grows naturally in the Levant ; the roots of this are compofed of roundifh knobs like thofe of the fecond fort, as are alfo the leaves, but are of a thicker fubftance ; the ftalks do not rife fo high, and the flowers have a greater number of petals. This flowers a little after the other. The large double purple Peony, I fufpect is a variety of this fort.

The fourth fort hath roots like the fecond ; the ftalks are taller, and of a purplifh colour ; the leaves are much longer, the lobes are fpear-fhaped and entire ; the flowers are large, and of a deep red colour. This flowers at the fame time as the two firft forts.

The

The feeds of the fifth fort were brought from the Levant, and from them there were plants raifed, which produced fingle, and others with double flowers, of the fame fhape, fize, and colour. The roots of thefe are compofed of oblong flefhy tubers or knobs; they are of a pale colour, and hang by ftrings like the other fpecies. The ftalks rife about two feet high, which are of a pale green, and are garnifhed with leaves compofed of feveral lobes, which are irregular in fhape and fize, fome of them having but fix, and others have eight or ten fpear-fhaped lobes; thefe are fome cut into two, fome three fegments, and others are entire; they are of a pale green, and are downy on their under fide. The ftalks are terminated by one flower of a bright red colour, a little lefs than that of the female Peony, and have fewer petals; they have a great number of ftamina, and fometimes two, at others three germen, like thofe of the female Peony, but fhorter and whiter. This flowers a little later than the common Peony.

The feeds of the fixth fort were fent to the Chelfea Garden by Dr. de Juffieu, who brought them from Portugal, where the plants grow naturally. The root of this fort is not compofed of roundifh tubers or knobs, but hath two or three long, taper, forked fangs like fingers. The ftalk rifes little more than a foot high, and is garnifhed with leaves compofed of three or four oval lobes, of a pale colour on their upper fide, and hoary on their under; the ftalk is terminated by a fingle flower, which is of a bright red colour, fmaller than either of the former, and an agreeable fweet fcent. This flowers about the fame time with the common fort.

The firft of thefe forts is chiefly propagated for the roots, which are ufed in medicine; for the flowers being fingle, do not afford near fo much pleafure as thofe with double flowers, nor will they abide near fo long in beauty.

All the forts with double flowers are preferved in curious gardens for the beauty of their flowers, which, when intermixed with other large growing plants in the borders of large gardens, will add to the variety; and the flowers are very ornamental in bafons or flower-pots, when placed in rooms.

They are all extremely hardy, and will grow in almoft any foil or fituation, which renders them more valuable; for they will thrive under the fhade of trees, and in fuch places they will continue much longer in beauty.

They are propagated by parting their roots, which multiply very faft. The beft feafon for tranfplanting them is toward the latter end of Auguft, or the beginning of September; for if they are removed after their roots have fhot out new fibres, they feldom flower ftrong the fucceeding fummer.

In parting thefe roots, you fhould always obferve to preferve a bud upon the crown of each offset, otherwife they will come to nothing; nor fhould you divide the roots too fmall (efpecially if you have regard to their blowing the following year) for when their offsets are weak, they many times do not flower the fucceeding fummer, or at leaft produce but one flower upon each root: but where you would multiply them in quantities, you may divide them as fmall as you pleafe, provided there be a bud to each offset; but then they fhould be planted in a nurfery-bed for a feafon or two to get ftrength, before they are placed in the flower-garden.

The fingle forts may be propagated from feeds (which they generally produce in large quantities, where the flowers are permitted to remain) which fhould be fown in the autumn foon after they are ripe, upon a bed of light frefh earth, covering them over about half an inch thick with the fame light earth. The fpring following the plants will come up, when they fhould be carefully cleared from weeds, and in very dry weather refrefhed with water, which will greatly forward their growth. In this bed they fhould remain two years before they are tranfplanted, obferving in autumn, when the leaves are decayed, to fpread

fome frefh rich earth over the beds about an inch thick, and conftantly to keep them clear from weeds. When you tranfplant them; (which fhould be done in September) you muft prepare fome beds of frefh light earth, which fhould be dug, and well cleaned from the roots of all noxious weeds; then plant the roots therein fix inches afunder, and about three inches deep. In thefe beds they may remain until they flower, after which they may be tranfplanted where you defign they fhould grow. It is very probable there may be fome varieties obtained from the feeds of thefe plants, as is common in moft other flowers; fo that thofe which produce beautiful flowers, may be placed in the flower-garden, but fuch as continue fingle or ill coloured, may be planted in beds to propagate for medicinal ufe.

The Portugal Peony may alfo be propagated either by feeds, or parting the roots, in the fame manner as the other forts, but fhould have a lighter foil and a warmer fituation. The flowers of this kind are fingle, but fmell very fweet, which renders it worthy of a place in every good garden.

PALIURUS. Tourn. Inft. R. H. 616. tab. 387. Rhamnus. Lin. Gen. Plant. 235. Chrift's Thorn.

The CHARACTERS are,

The flower has no empalement. It hath five petals which are ranged circularly, and end in acute points. It hath five ftamina, which are inferted in the fcales under the petals, terminated by fmall fummits, and a roundifh trifid germen, fupporting three fhort ftyles, crowned by obtufe ftigmas. The germen afterward becomes a buckler-fhaped nut divided into three cells, each containing one feed.

This genus of plants is by Dr. Linnæus joined to the Rhamnus, which is ranged in the firft fection of his fifth clafs, in which are placed thofe plants whofe flowers have five ftamina and one ftyle; but as the flowers of this have three ftyles, fo it fhould be ranged in his third fection.

We know but one SPECIES of this genus, viz.

PALIURUS (*Spina Chrifti.*) Dod. Pempt. 848. *Chrift's Thorn.* Rhamnus aculeis geminatis, inferiore reflexo, floribus trigynis. Hort. Cliff. 69. *Prickly Buckthorn with double thorns, the under ones of which are reflexed, and flowers containing three germina.*

This plant grows naturally in the hedges in Paleftine; it rifes with a pliant fhrubby ftalk to the height of eight or ten feet, fending out many weak flender branches, garnifhed with oval leaves placed alternately, ftanding upon foot-ftalks near one inch long; thefe have three longitudinal veins, and are of a pale green. The flowers come out at the wings of the ftalk in clufters, almoft the length of the young branches; they are of a greenifh yellow colour, and appear in June, and are fucceeded by broad, roundifh, buckler-fhaped feed-veffels, which have borders like the brims of a hat, the foot-ftalks being faftened to the middle; thefe have three cells, each containing one feed.

This is by many perfons fuppofed to be the plant, from which the crown of thorns which was put upon the head of our Saviour, was compofed; the truth of which is fupported by many travellers of credit, who affirm that this is one of the moft common fhrubs in the country of Judæa; and from the pliablenefs of its branches, which may eafily be wrought into any figure, it may afford a probability.

This fhrub grows wild in moft parts of the Levant, as alfo in Italy, Spain, Portugal, and the fouth of France, efpecially near Montpelier, from whence their feeds may be procured, for they do not ripen in England. Thefe feeds fhould be fown as foon as poffible after they arrive, on a bed of light earth, and the plants will come up the following fpring; but when the feeds are kept out of the ground till fpring, they will not come up till the next year, and very often fail; therefore it is much the beft way to fow them in the autumn. Thefe feedling plants may be tranfplanted the following feafon into a nurfery to get ftrength, before they are planted out for good.

It

It may alſo be propagated by laying down its tender branches in the ſpring of the year, which if carefully ſupplied with water in dry weather, will take
root in a year's time, and may then be taken off
from the old plant, and tranſplanted where they are
to remain.

The beſt time for tranſplanting this plant is in autumn, ſoon after the leaves decay, or the beginning
of April, juſt before it begins to ſhoot, obſerving to
lay ſome mulch upon the ground about their roots to
prevent them from drying, as alſo to refreſh them
now and then with a little water until they have taken
freſh root, after which they will require but very little
care. They are very hardy, and will grow to be ten
or twelve feet high, if planted in a dry ſoil and a
warm ſituation. There is little beauty in this plant,
but it is kept in gardens as a curioſity.

PALMA. Plum. Gen. 1. Raii Meth. Plant. 135.
The Palm-tree.

The CHARACTERS are,

*It hath male and female flowers in ſome ſpecies on the
ſame plant, and in others on different plants ; the empalement of the male flowers are divided into three parts.
The flowers of ſome ſpecies have three petals, and ſix
ſtamina terminated by oblong ſummits, with an obſolete
germen, ſupporting three ſhort ſtyles, crowned by acute
ſtigmas ; theſe are barren. The female flowers have a
common ſheath, but no empalement ; they have ſix ſhort
petals, and an oval germen ſitting upon an awl-ſhaped
ſtyle, crowned by a trifid ſtigma. The germen afterward
becomes a fruit· of various forms and ſizes in different
ſpecies.*

Mr. Ray ranges this genus in the front of his trees
and ſhrubs, which have male flowers at remote diſtances from the fruit, ſometimes on the ſame, and at
others on different trees. Dr. Linnæus has ſeparated
the ſpecies under the following genera, Chamærops,
Boraſſus, Corypha, Cocos, Phœnix, Areca, and
Elate, ranging them in his Appendix.

The SPECIES are,

1. PALMA (Dactylifera) frondibus pinnatis, foliolis anguſtioribus aculeis terminalibus. *Palm-tree with winged leaves, whoſe lobes are narrow, terminated by ſpines.*
Palma major. C. B. P. 506. *The greater Palm or Date-
tree.*

2. PALMA (Cocos) frondibus pinnatis, foliolis replicatis,
ſpadicibus alaribus, fructu maximo anguloſo. *Palm-
tree with winged leaves, whoſe lobes are folded back,
foot-ſtalks proceeding from the ſides of the branches, and a
large angular fruit.* Palma Indica, coccifera, angu-
loſa. C. B. P. 502. *Indian Palm-tree having an angular
fruit, commonly called Cocoa-nut.*

3. PALMA (Spinoſa) frondibus pinnatis, ubique aculeatis, aculeis nigricantibus fructu majore. *Palm-tree
with winged leaves, which are every where armed with
black ſpines, and bearing a larger fruit.* Palma to-
ta ſpinoſa major, fructu pruniformi. Sloan. Cat.
Jam. 177. *Greater Palm-tree which is all over prickly,
and a Plum-ſhaped fruit, commonly called great Macaw-tree.*

4. PALMA (Altiſſima) frondibus pinnatis, caudice æquali, fructu minore. *Palm-tree with winged leaves, an
equal trunk, and a ſmaller fruit.* Palma altiſſima non
ſpinoſa, fructu pruniformi minore racemoſo ſparſo.
Sloan. Cat. Jam. 176. *The talleſt Palm-tree having no
ſpines, and a ſmaller Plum-ſhaped fruit, growing in
long bunches ſcatteringly, commonly called the Cabbage-
tree.*

5. PALMA (Gracili) frondibus pinnatis, caudice tereti
aculeato, fructu minore. *Palm-tree with winged leaves,
a taper prickly ſtalk, and a ſmaller fruit.* Palma ſpinoſa
minor, caudice gracili, fructu pruniformi, minimo
rubro. Sloan. Cat. Jam. 178. *Smaller prickly Palm-tree
with a ſlender ſtalk, and the leaſt, red, Plum-ſhaped fruit,
called Prickly Pole.*

6. PALMA (Oleoſa) frondibus pinnatis, foliolis linearibus planis, ſtipitibus ſpinoſis. *Palm-tree with winged
leaves, having narrow plain lobes, and prickly midribs.*
Palma foliorum pediculis ſpinoſis, fructu pruniformi
luteo oleoſo. Sloan. Cat. Jam. 175. *Palm-tree with*

prickly foot-ſtalks to the leaves, and a yellow, Plum-
ſhaped, oily fruit, commonly called oily Palm-tree.

7. PALMA (Prunifera) frondibus pinnato-palmatis plicatis, caudice ſquamato. *Palm-tree with hand-ſhaped
winged leaves which are plaited, and a ſcaly ſtalk.* Palma Braſilienſis prunifera, folio plicatili ſeu flabel-
liformi, caudici ſquamato. Raii Hiſt. 1368. *Plum-
bearing Palm-tree of the Braſils, with a plaited or
fan-ſhaped leaf, and a ſcaly ſtalk, called Palmetto or
Thatch.*

8. PALMA (Polypodifolia) frondibus pinnatis, foliolis lineari-lanceolatis, petiolis ſpinoſis. Hort. Cliff. 482.
*Palm-tree with winged leaves, whoſe lobes are linearly
ſpear-ſhaped, and prickly foot-ſtalks.* Palma Japonica,
ſpinoſis pediculis, polypodii folio. Boerh. Ind. alt. 2.
170. *Palm-tree of Japan with prickly foot-ſtalks, and a
Polypody leaf, or the Sago-tree.*

9. PALMA (Pumila) fructu clavato polypyreno. Trew.
Dec. tab. 26. *Palm-tree with a club-ſhaped fruit containing many ſeeds.* Palma Americana foliis polygo-
nati brevioribus, læviter ſerratis, & nonnihil ſpinoſis,
trunco craſſo. Pluk. Phyt. tab. 103. fig. 2. & tab.
309. fig. 5. *American Palm-tree, with ſhorter Solomon's
Seal leaves which are lightly ſawed and ſomewhat
prickly, with a thick trunk.*

10. PALMA (Americana) frondibus pinnatis, foliolis lanceolatis plicatis geminatis ſparſis. *Palm-tree with winged leaves, whoſe lobes are ſpear-ſhaped, plaited, and come
out by pairs from one point ; ſtanding thinly along the midrib.* Palma altiſſima, non ſpinoſa, fructu oblongo.
Houſt. MSS. *Talleſt Palm-tree having no prickles, and
bearing an oblong fruit.*

11. PALMA (Draco) foliis ſimplicibus enſiformibus integerrimis flaccidis. *Palm-tree with ſingle, ſword-ſhaped,
entire flaccid leaves.* Palma prunifera foliis yuccæ,
fructu in racemis congeſtis ceraſi formi, duro, cinereo, piſi magnitudine, cujus lacryma ſanguis draco-
nis eſt dicta. Com. Cat. Amſt. *Plum-bearing Palm-
tree, with leaves like thoſe of the Yucca, and fruit gathered in long bunches, which are Cherry-ſhaped, Aſh-
coloured, hard, and the ſize of Peas, whoſe tears are
called Dragons Blood, commonly called Dragon-tree.*

The firſt ſort here mentioned, is the common Date-
tree, which grows plentifully in Africa, and ſome of
the eaſtern countries, from whence the fruit is brought
to England. This riſes to a great height in the warm
countries ; the ſtalks are generally full of rugged
knots, which are the veſtiges of the decayed leaves,
for the trunks of theſe trees are not ſolid like other
trees, but the center is filled with pith, round which
is a tough bark full of ſtrong fibres while young, but
as the trees grow old, ſo this bark hardens and becomes ligneous ; to this bark the leaves are cloſely
joined, which in the center riſe erect, being cloſely
folded or plaited together, but after they are advanced above the vagina which ſurrounds them, they expand very wide on every ſide the ſtem, and, as the
older leaves decay, the ſtalk advances in height. The
leaves of theſe trees, when grown to a ſize for bearing fruit, are ſix or eight feet long, and may be termed branches ; (for the trees have no other) theſe have
narrow long leaves (or pinnæ) ſet on alternately their
whole length. The ſmall leaves or lobes are toward
the baſe three feet long, and little more than one
inch broad ; they are cloſely folded together when
they firſt appear, and are wrapped round by brown
fibres or threads, which fall off as the leaves advance,
making way for them to expand ; theſe never open
flat, but are hollow like the keel of a boat, with a
ſharp ridge on their backſide ; they are very ſtiff,
and, when young, of a bright green, ending with a
ſharp black ſpine. Theſe trees have male flowers
on different plants from thoſe which produce the fruit,
and there is a neceſſity for ſome of the male trees to
grow near the female trees to render them fruitful ;
or, at leaſt, to impregnate the ovary of the ſeed,
without which the ſtones, which are taken out of the
fruit, will not grow. Moſt of the old authors, who
have mentioned theſe trees, affirm, that unleſs the
female or fruit-bearing Palm-trees have the aſſiſtance

9 T   of

of the male, they are barren; therefore in such places where there are no male trees near the female, the inhabitants cut off the bunches of male flowers when they are just opened, and carry them to the female trees, placing them on the branches near the female flowers to impregnate them; which, they all agree, has the desired effect, rendering the trees fruitful, which would otherwise have been barren. Pere Labat in his account of America, mentions a single tree of this kind, growing near a convent in the island of Martinico, which produced a great quantity of fruit, which came to maturity enough for eating; but, as there was no other tree of this kind in the island they were desirous to propagate it, and accordinly planted great numbers of the stones for several years, but not one of them grew; therefore after having made several trials without success, they were obliged to send to Africa, where these plants grew in plenty, for some of the fruit; the stones of which they planted, and raised many of the plants. He then conjectures, that the single tree before-mentioned, might be probably so far impregnated by some neighbouring Palm-trees of other species, as to render it capable of ripening the fruit, but not sufficient to make the seeds prolific, as is the case when animals of different kinds copulate.

The flowers of both sexes come out in very long bunches from the trunk between the leaves, and are covered with a spatha, (or sheath) which opens and withers; those of the male have six short stamina, with narrow four-cornered summits filled with farina. The female flowers have no stamina, but have a roundish germen, which afterward becomes an oval berry, with a thick pulp inclosing a hard oblong stone, with a deep furrow running longitudinally. The bunches of fruit are sometimes very large.

This species of Palm is by Dr. Linnæus titled Phœnix, which is the Greek name of it, and he makes it a distinct genus. There are some varieties, if not different species of this tree, in the warm countries; but as we cannot expect to see the trees in perfection in our country, it is not likely we shall come to any certainty how they differ from each other.

These plants may be easily produced from the seeds taken out of the fruit, (provided they are fresh) which should be sown in pots filled with light rich earth, and plunged into a moderate hot-bed of tanners bark, which should be kept in a moderate temperature of heat, and the earth frequently refreshed with water.

When the plants are come up, they should be each planted into a separate small pot filled with the same light rich earth, and plunged into a hot-bed again, observing to refresh them with water, as also to let them have air in proportion to the warmth of the season, and the bed in which they are placed. During the summer time they should remain in the same hot-bed, but in the beginning of August you should let them have a great share of air to harden them against the approach of winter; for if they are too much forced, they will be so tender as not to be preserved through the winter without much difficulty, especially if you have not the conveniency of a bark-stove to keep them in.

The beginning of October you must remove the plants into the stove, placing them where they may have a moderate share of heat (these being somewhat tenderer, while young, than after they have acquired some strength;) though indeed they may be sometimes preserved alive in a cooler situation, yet their progress would be so much retarded; as not to recover their vigour the succeeding summer. Nor is it worth the trouble of raising these plants from seeds, where a person has not the conveniency of a stove to forward their growth; for where this is wanting, they will not grow to any tolerable size in twenty years. Whenever these plants are removed, (which should be done once a year) you must be very careful not to cut or injure their large roots, which is very hurtful to them; but you should clear off all the small fibres

which are inclinable to mouldiness, for if these are left on, they will in time decay, and hinder the fresh fibres from coming out, which will greatly retard the growth of the plants.

The soil in which these plants should be placed, must be composed in the following manner, viz. half of light fresh earth taken from a pasture ground, the other half sea-sand, and rotten dung or tanners bark, in equal proportion; these should be carefully mixed, and laid in a heap three or four months at least before it is used, but should be often turned over to prevent the growth of weeds and to sweeten the earth.

You should also observe to allow them pots proportionable to the sizes of the plants; but you must never let them be too large, which is of worse consequence than if they are too small. During the summer season they should be frequently refreshed with water, but you must be careful not to give it in too great quantities; and in winter they must be now and then refreshed, especially if they are placed in a warm stove, otherwise they will require very little water at that season.

These plants are very slow growers, even in their native countries, notwithstanding they arrive to a great magnitude; for it has been often observed by several of the old inhabitants of those countries, that the plants of some of these kinds have not advanced two feet in height in ten years; so that when they are brought into these countries, it cannot be expected they should advance very fast, especially where there is not due care taken to preserve them warm in winter. But however slow of growth these plants are in their native countries, yet they may be with us greatly forwarded, by placing the pots into a hot-bed of tanners bark, which should be renewed as often as is necessary, and the plants always preserved therein both winter and summer, observing to shift them into larger pots as they advance in growth, as also to supply them with water properly, with which management I have had several of them come on very fast; for I observe the roots of these plants are very apt to root into the bark, if their pots remain a considerable time without shifting, where they meet with a gentle warmth, and the moisture arising from the fermentation of the bark doth preserve their fibres plump and vigorous; but although the leaves grow tall in a few years with this management, yet it is long before the plants come to have any stems. There are plants now in the Chelsea Garden, whose leaves are seven feet long, which were raised from seeds more than twenty years ago, and their stems are not two feet high, some of which have produced small bunches of male flowers.

The second sort here mentioned, is the Cocoa-nut, whose fruit are frequently brought to England, some of which are of a large size. The branches of this tree are winged like those of the former, but the small leaves or lobes are three times as broad; they open flat, their borders fold backward, and are of a lighter green than those of the first sort. The whole leaf (or branch) is often twelve or fourteen feet long; the male flowers grow in different parts of the same tree with the fruit, proceeding from the trunk between the leaves; they are disposed in long bunches, as are also the female, the nuts growing in very large clusters, which are covered with a thick fibrous coat adhering closely to them. The nuts are large, oval, and have three holes in the shell at the top; the kernel is firm, white within, and the shell contains a quantity of pale juice, which is called the milk.

The Cocoa-nut is cultivated in most of the inhabited parts of the East and West-Indies, but is supposed a native of the Maldives, and the desert islands of the East-Indies, from whence it is supposed it hath been transported to all the warm parts of America; for it is not found in any of the inland parts, nor any where far distant from settlements. It is one of the most useful trees to the inhabitants of America, who have many of the common necessaries of life from it. The bark of the tree is made into cordage, the shell of the nut

nut into drinking bowls, the kernel of the nut affords them a wholfome food, and the milk contained in the fhell a cooling liquor. The leaves of the trees are ufed for thatching their houfes, and are alfo wrought into bafkets, and moft other things which are made of Ofiers in Europe.

This tree is propagated by planting of the nuts, which in fix weeks or two months after planting will come up, provided they are frefh and thoroughly ripe, which is what few of them are which are brought to England ; for they always gather them before they are ripe, that they may keep during their paffage ; fo that the beft way to bring nuts into England for planting, would be to take fuch of them as are fully ripe, and put them in dry fand in a tub, where the vermin may not come to them ; and thefe will often fprout in their paffage, which will be an advantage, becaufe then they may be immediately planted into pots of earth, and plunged into the bark-bed.

Thefe plants, in the hot iflands of America, make confiderable progrefs in their growth, in which places there are fome trees of very great magnitude ; but in Europe it is of much flower growth, being many years before it advances to any confiderable height ; but as the young leaves of this plant are pretty large, they make a good appearance amongft other tender exotic plants in two or three years time. This plant is pre-ferved in fome curious gardens in England for variety, where it muft be placed in the bark-ftove, and ma-naged as hath been directed for the other kind of Palm ; obferving, as often as they are tranfplanted, not to cut their ftrong roots, which is generally death to moft of the Palm kind. Thefe plants muft not be too much confined in their roots, for if they are, they will make but little progrefs ; therefore, when the young plants have filled the pots with their roots, they fhould be fhifted into tubs of a moderate fize, that their roots may have room to extend ; but thefe tubs muft be kept conftantly plunged into the bark-bed, otherwife the plants will not thrive. The me-thod of raifing thefe plants from the nuts, when they are planted before they have fprouted, is fully de-fcribed under the article of raifing exotic feeds ; to which the reader is defired to turn, to avoid repetition.

The third fort is commonly called Macaw-tree by the inhabitants of the Britifh Iflands in America ; this rifes to the height of thirty or forty feet. The ftem is generally larger toward the top than at bottom ; the branches (or rather the leaves) are winged ; the fmall leaves or lobes are long and very broad ; the ftalk and leaves are ftrongly armed with black fpines of various fizes in every part ; the male and female flowers are on the fame tree, coming out in the fame manner as the Cocoa-nut. The fruit is about the fize of a middling Apple, and is inclofed in a very hard fhell.

The Macaw-tree is very common in the Caribbee Iflands, where the negroes pierce the tender fruit, from whence flows out a pleafant liquor, of which they are very fond ; and the body of the tree affords a folid timber, with which they make javelins, arrows, &c. and is by fome fuppofed to be a fort of Ebony. This tree grows very flow, and requires to be kept warm in winter.

The fourth fort is commonly called Cabbage-tree in the Weft-Indies ; this rifes to a very great height in the countries where it grows naturally. Ligon in his Hiftory of Barbadoes fays, there were then fome of thefe growing there, which were more than two hun-dred feet high, and that he was informed they were a hundred years growing to maturity, fo as to pro-duce feeds. The ftalks of thefe trees are feldom larger than a man's thigh ; they are fmoother than thofe of moft other forts, for the leaves naturally fall off entire from them, and only leave the veftigia or marks where they have grown. Thefe leaves (or branches) are twelve or fourteen feet long ; the fmall leaves or lobes are about a foot long, and half an inch broad, with feveral longitudinal plaits or furrows end-ing in foft acute points ; thefe are not fo ftiff as thofe

of the firft fort, and are placed alternately. The flowers come out in long loofe bunches below the leaves ; thefe branch out into many loofe ftrings, and are near four feet long, upon which the flowers are thinly placed. The female flowers are fucceeded by fruit about the fize of a Hazel nut, having a yellow-ifh fkin, fitting clofe to the ftrings of the principal foot-ftalk.

As the inner leaves of this encompafs the future buds more remarkably than moft of the other fpecies, fo it is diftinguifhed by this appellation of Cabbage-tree ; for the center fhoots, before they are expofed to the air, are white and very tender, like moft other plants which are blanched ; and this is the part which is cut out and eaten by the inhabitants, and is frequently pickled and fent to England by the title of Cabbage ; but whenever thefe fhoots are cut out, the plants de-cay, and never after thrive ; fo that it deftroys the plants, which is the reafon that few of the trees are now to be found in any of the iflands near fettlements, and thofe are left for ornament.

The fifth fort is commonly called Prickly Pole in Jamaica, where it naturally grows. Thefe trees are commonly found in thickets, where a great number of them are clofe together. Their ftalks are flender, feldom more than five or fix inches diameter, but rife to the height of forty feet, and are clofely armed with long thorns. The leaves are placed circularly on the top, (as in moft of the fpecies.) Thefe are winged, but the lobes are fhorter and greener than thofe of the other forts, and are clofely armed with thorns. The flowers come out in the fame manner as thofe of the Cocoa-nut, upon long branching foot-ftalks ; they are larger than the largeft gray Peas, flatted at the top, and are covered with a red fkin. The inha-bitants of Jamaica make rammers and rods for fcower-ing of guns, of the ftems of thefe trees, which are very tough and pliable ; but there is no ufe made of any other part, fo far as I can learn.

The fixth fort is called in the Weft-Indies the Oily Palm, and by fome Negroes Oil, for the fruit of this tree was firft carried from Africa to America by the negroes. It grows in great plenty on the coaft of Guinea, and alfo in the Cape de Verd Iflands, but was not in any of our American colonies till it was carried there ; but now the trees are in plenty in moft of the iflands, where the negroes are careful to propa-gate them.

The branches, (or rather the leaves) of this tree, are winged ; the fmall leaves or lobes, are long, narrow, and not fo ftiff as moft of the other forts ; the foot-ftalks of the leaves are broad at their bafe, where they embrace the ftem, diminifhing gradually upward, and are armed with ftrong, blunt, yellowifh thorns, which are largeft at their bafe. The flowers come out at the top of the ftem between the leaves ; fome bunches have only male flowers, others have female ; and the lat-ter are fucceeded by oval berries, bigger than thofe of the largeft Spanifh Olives, but of the fame fhape ; thefe grow in very large bunches, and when ripe are of a yellowifh colour.

From the fruit the inhabitants draw an oil, in the fame way as the oil is drawn from Olives ; from the body of the tree they extract a liquor, which, when ferment-ed, has a vinous quality, and will inebriate. The leaves of the tree are wrought into mats by the negroes, on which they lie.

The feventh fort is called Palmetto-tree, or Thatch, by the inhabitants of Jamaica, where this tree grows upon all the honey-comb rocks in great plenty. It rifes with a flender ftalk ten or twelve feet high, which is naked and fmooth, and at the top garnifh-ed with many fan-fhaped leaves placed circularly ; thefe have foot-ftalks two or three feet long, which are armed with a few ftrong, green, crooked fpines ; the pinnæ, or lobes, do all meet in one center, where they join the foot-ftalk, and are joined together a third part of their length from their bafe ; they are at firft clofely folded into plaits, but afterward fpread out like a fan ; their ends being pliant often hang downward,

downward, and between these pinnæ hang down long threads. The flowers and fruit come out from between the leaves; the fruit is of the shape and size of the small Lucca Olives. The leaves of this tree are used for thatch all over the West-Indies.

The eighth sort grows naturally in Japan, and also upon rocky dry mountains at Malabar. This in time rises with a strait trunk about forty feet high, which has many circles round it the whole length, which are occasioned by the vestigia of the leaves, which are placed circularly round the stem; so as these separate entirely and fall off, the circles remain where their base embraced the stalk. The stalks are terminated by an obtuse cone, just below which the leaves are placed; these on the large trees are eight or nine feet long, but those of the small plants are much less; the largest I have seen were not more than two feet long. The base of the foot-stalk, which partly embraces the trunk, is broad and three-cornered, and is armed on each side with short spines to the place where the leaves, or small leaves, begin. These pinnæ or lobes, are long, narrow, and entire, of a lucid green on their upper side, standing by pairs opposite along the midrib, very close together. The flowers and fruit are produced in large bunches at the foot-stalks of the leaves; the fruit is oval, about the size of a large Plum, and nearly of the same shape; the skin, or covering, changes first yellow, and afterward red when ripe, of a sweet taste, under which is a hard brown shell, inclosing a white nut, which is in taste like the Chestnut.

From the pith of the trunk of this tree is made the sago; this is first pulverized, then it is made into a paste, and afterward granulated.

The ninth sort was discovered by the late Dr. Houstoun, growing naturally in the sands near Old Vera Cruz in America. This hath a thick stem, which seldom rises more than two feet high. The leaves come out round the upper part of the stem, standing upon foot-stalks which are a foot and a half long; they are winged; the lobes or small leaves are about five inches long, and one and a half broad in the middle, drawing to a point at both ends; they are stiff, smooth, and entire, having a few small indentures at their points, and are placed alternate, of a pale green colour; there are fourteen or fifteen of these lobes ranged along the midrib, or stalk. The fruit rises up from the side of the stem, upon a short thick foot-stalk, standing upright, and shaped like a club, having many red seeds about the size of large Peas, standing in separate cells round the central foot-stalk, to which they adhere. These plants have their male flowers on separate plants from the fruit, for all those plants which have flowered in England are of the male kind. These plants lose their leaves before the fruit is ripe annually. The first time when Dr. Houstoun saw these plants growing at La Vera Cruz, they were in full leaf, but on his return to the same place three months after, the fruit was then ripe, and all the leaves were fallen off; and this he afterwards observed the following season.

The tenth sort was discovered by the late Dr. Houstoun in the Spanish West-Indies. This rises with a very tall naked trunk, garnished at the top with long winged branches or leaves, whose lobes are spearshaped and plaited; they are of a softer texture than any of the other sorts, and for the most part come out two from the same point, so stand by pairs on the same side of the midrib; they have two lobes on a side a little above each other, but there is a great space between every four lobes. The flowers come out in long bunches from between the leaves, the male flowers hanging on long tender strings; but the fruit, which is about the size of a middling Plum, is collected into large bunches.

The eleventh sort grows naturally in the Cape Verd Islands, from whence I had one of the plants brought me, as also in the Madeira, from whence I have received the seeds. This is called Dragon-tree, because the inspissated juice of the plants becomes a red powder, very like the eastern Dragons Blood, and is frequently used instead of it in the shops; but the tree, from whence the true Dragons Blood is taken, is of a very different genus from this. Dr. Van Royen, in the Prodromus of the Leyden Garden, has ranged this among the Yuccas, I suppose, from the similitude of the plant to those of that genus; for, as the fruit of this is a berry not unlike those of the Bay-tree, and the seeds of the Yucca grow in capsules with three cells, they cannot be of the same genus; nor have we any good account of the real characters of this plant, so as absolutely to determine the genus. Dr. Linnæus has, upon the information of his pupil Loefling, ranged it in his genus of Asparagus, to which it seems to have little affinity; therefore, as it has by several modern authors been ranged under this title, I have continued it there. This rises with a thick trunk nearly equal in size the whole length, the inner part of which is pithy; next to this is a circle of strong fibres, and the outside is soft. The stalk or trunk rises twelve or fourteen feet high, and is nearly of the same diameter the whole length, which is rarely more than eight or ten inches; there are the circular marks or rings left the whole length, where the leaves are fallen off; for as these half embrace the stalk with their base, so when they fall away, the vestigia where they grew remain. The top of the stalk sustains a large head of leaves, which come out singly all round it; they are shaped like those of the common Iris, but are much longer, being often four or five feet long, and an inch and a half broad at their base, where they embrace the stalk, and lessen gradually to the end, where they terminate in a point. These leaves are pliable, and hang down all round the stem; they are entire, and of a deep green, smooth on both surfaces, and greatly resemble those of the common yellow Iris. As this plant has not flowered in England, I can give no account of its flowers; but so far as I can judge from the berries which I have received, it may properly enough be ranged in this genus.

All these sorts of Palms are propagated by seeds, which should be sown in the same way as hath been directed for the first sort, and the plants should afterward be treated in the same manner; with this difference, that such of them as are natives of very warm countries, will require to be kept in a warmer air. The second, third, fourth, fifth, sixth, seventh, eighth, and ninth sorts should be constantly kept in the bark-bed in the stove, otherwise they will not make great progress in England; and when they do thrive, they grow in about twenty years too tall for most of the stoves which are at present built here, nor can we hope to see many of them produce their fruit in England; so the plants are preferred by the curious for their foliage, which being so singular and different from that of the European trees, renders them worthy of care.

The other sorts may be kept in a dry stove in winter in a moderate temperature of air, and in the heat of summer they may be exposed to the open air in a warm sheltered situation for about three months, but they should be removed into the stove before the morning frosts come on in the autumn. When these plants are kept in a moderate degree of warmth, they should have but little water during the winter season; and in the summer, when they are exposed in the open air, they must not be often watered, unless the season is remarkably dry and warm, for too much moisture will soon destroy them. The other management of them is nearly the same as for the Date Palms, which is not to cut their principal roots when they are shifted from one pot to another, nor to confine their roots too much; but as the plants grow in size, they should annually be removed into pots a size larger than those they were in the former year. The earth in which they are planted, should be light, so as to let the moisture easily pass off; for if it is strong, and detains the moisture, the tender fibres of the roots will rot.

PANAX.

PANAX. Lin. Gen. Plant. 1031. Panacea. Mitch. Gen. 26. Araliaftrum. Vaill. 6. Ginfeng or Ninfeng.

The CHARACTERS are,

It hath male and hermaphrodite flowers on diftinct plants; the male have fimple globular umbels, compofed of feveral coloured rays which are equal. The involucrum on the outfide, confifts of the fame number of fmall fpear-fhaped leaves. The flower has five narrow, oblong, blunt petals, which are reflexed, fitting on the empalement, and five oblong flender ftamina inferted in the empalement, terminated by fingle fummits. The hermaphrodite umbels are fimple, equal, and cluftered; the involucrum is fmall, permanent, and compofed of feveral awl-fhaped leaves; the empalement is fmall and permanent. The flowers have five oblong equal petals, which are recurved, and five fhort ftamina terminated by fingle fummits which fall off, with a roundifh germen under the empalement, fupporting two fmall erect ftyles, crowned by fingle ftigmas. The germen afterward becomes an umbilicated berry with two cells, each containing a fingle, heart-fhaped, convex, plain feed.

This genus of plants is ranged in the fecond fection of Linnæus's twenty-third clafs, which includes the plants whofe male flowers are upon diftinct parts from the female or hermaphrodite flowers.

The SPECIES are,

1. PANAX (*Quinquefolium*) foliis ternis quinatis. Flor. Virg. 147. *Panax with trifoliate Cinquefoil leaves.* Araliaftrum quinquefolii folio, majus, Ninzin vocatum. D. Sarrafin. Vaill. Gen. 43. *Greater five-leaved Baftard Aralia, called Ninzin.*

2. PANAX (*Trifolium*) foliis ternis ternatis. Flor. Virg. 35. *Panax with three trifoliate leaves.* Araliaftrum fragariæ folio minus. Vaill. Gen. 43. *Smaller Baftard Aralia with a Strawberry leaf.*

Both thefe plants grow naturally in North America; the firft is generally believed to be the fame as the Tartarian Ginfeng, the figures and defcriptions of that plant, which have been fent to Europe by the miffionaries, agreeing perfectly with the American plant. This hath a flefhy taper root as large as a man's finger, which is jointed, and frequently divided into two fmaller fibres downward. The ftalk rifes near a foot and a half high, naked at the bafe, where it generally divides into three fmaller foot-ftalks, each fuftaining a leaf compofed of five fpear-fhaped lobes, which are fawed on their edges; they are of a pale green, and a little hairy. The flowers grow on a flender foot-ftalk, juft at the divifion of the foot-ftalks, which fuftain the leaves, and are formed into a fmall umbel at the top; they are of an herbaceous yellow colour, compofed of five fmall petals which are recurved. Thefe appear the beginning of June, and are fucceeded by compreffed heart-fhaped berries, which are firft green, but afterward turn red, inclofing two hard, compreffed, heart-fhaped feeds, which ripen the beginning of Auguft.

The Chinefe hold this plant in great efteem, according to the accounts which have been tranfmitted to Europe by the miffionaries. Father Jartoux in his Letters fays, that the moft eminent phyficians in China have written whole volumes upon the virtues of this plant, and make it an ingredient in almoft all remedies which they give to their nobility, for it is of too high price for the common people. They affirm, that it is a fovereign remedy for all weaknefs occafioned by exceffive fatigues either of body or mind; that it cures weaknefs of the lungs, and the pleurify; that it ftops vomitings; that it ftrengthens the ftomach, and helps the appetite; that it ftrengthens the vital fpirits, and increafes lymph in the blood; in fhort, that it is good againft dizzinefs of the head and dimnefs of fight, and that it prolongs life in old age.

This father alfo fays, he has made trials of the root of this plant himfelf, and has, in an hour after taking half one of the roots, found himfelf greatly recovered from wearinefs and fatigue, and much more vigorous, and could bear labour with greater eafe than before.

He likewife mentions the emperor's having employed ten thoufand Tartars in the year 1709, to gather this plant in the defarts, where it naturally grows; thefe were attended by a guard of mandarines, who encamp with their tents in fuch places as are proper for the fubfiftence of their horfes, and from time to time fend their orders to the refpective troops under their care; and when they have completed their collection of roots, they return with their cargo to the city. The roots of this plant which have been gathered in America and brought to England, have been fent to China, where, at the beginning, there was a good market for them; but the quantities which were afterward fent, did not anfwer fo well, the market being overftocked with that commodity.

This plant has been introduced to the Englifh gardens from America, and where it has been planted in a fhady fituation and a light foil, the plants have thriven and produced flowers, and ripened their feeds annually, but not one of thefe feeds have grown; for I have feveral years fown them foon after they were ripe, without any fuccefs; I have alfo fown of the feeds which were fent me from America feveral times in various fituations, and have not raifed a fingle plant from either; and by the accounts which the miffionaries have fent from China, it appears, they have had no better fuccefs with the feeds of this plant, which they fay they have frequently fown in the gardens in China, but could not raife one plant; fo that I believe there is a neceffity for the hermaphrodite plants to have fome male plants ftand near them, to render the feeds prolific; for all thofe plants which I have feen, or faved the feeds from, were fuch as had hermaphrodite flowers; and though the feeds feemed to ripen perfectly, yet their not growing, though I have waited three years without difturbing of the ground, confirms me in this opinion.

The fecond fort grows naturally in the fame countries, but whether it is poffeffed of the fame qualities as the firft I cannot fay; I have feen but one plant of this fort in England, which was fent me a few years ago from Maryland, and did not live over the firft fummer, which was remarkably dry, and being planted in a dry foil, was the occafion of its death; the ftalk of this was fingle, and did not rife more than five inches high, dividing into three foot-ftalks, each fuftaining a trifoliate leaf, whofe lobes were longer, narrower, and deeper indented on their edges, than thofe of the former. The flower-ftalk rofe from the divifions of the foot-ftalk of the leaves, but before the flowers opened, the plant decayed, fo I can give no farther account of it.

PANCRATIUM. Dill. Hort. Elth. 221. fol. 289. Lin. Gen. Plant. 365. Narciffus. Tourn. Inft. R. H. 353. tab. 185. Sea Daffodil.

The CHARACTERS are,

The flowers are inclofed in an oblong fpatha or fheath, which tears open on the fide and withers. The flowers have a funnel-fhaped cylindrical nectarium of one leaf, fpreading open at the top, and fix fpear-fhaped petals, which are inferted on the outfide of the nectarium above its bafe, with fix long ftamina inferted in the brim of the nectarium; terminated by oblong proftrate fummits. They have a three-cornered obtufe germen fituated under the flower, fupporting a long flender ftyle, crowned by an obtufe ftigma. The germen afterward becomes a roundifh three-cornered capfule with three cells, filled with globular feeds.

This genus of plants is ranged in the firft fection of Linnæus's fixth clafs, which includes thofe plants whofe flowers have fix ftamina and one ftyle.

The SPECIES are,

1. PANCRATIUM (*Maritimum*) fpathâ multiflorâ, petalis planis, foliis lingulatis. Lin. Sp. Plant. 291. *Pancratium with a fheath containing many flowers, having plain petals, and tongue-fhaped leaves.* Narciffus maritimus. C. B. P. 540. *The Sea Daffodil.*

2. PANCRATIUM (*Illyricum*) fpathâ multiflorâ, foliis enfiformibus, ftaminibus nectario longioribus. Flor. Leyd. Prod. 34. *Pancratium with many flowers in a*

9 U   *fheath,*

sheath, sword-shaped leaves, and stamina longer than the nectarium. Narcissus Illyricus liliaceus. C. B. P. 55. *Lily Daffodil of Sclavonia.*

3. PANCRATIUM (*Zeylanicum*) spathâ uniflorâ, petalis reflexis. Flor. Zeyl. 126. *Pancratium with one flower in a sheath, whose petals are reflexed.* Narcissus Zeylanicus, flore albo hexagono odorato. H. L. 691. *Daffodil of Ceylon, with a white hexagonal sweet flower.*

4. PANCRATIUM (*Carribæum*) spathâ biflorâ. Hort. Cliff. 133. *Pancratium with two flowers in a sheath.* Pancratium Mexicanum, flore gemello candido. Hort. Elth. 299. tab. 222. *Mexican Pancratium, with two white flowers.*

5. PANCRATIUM (*Amboinense*) spathâ multiflorâ, foliis ovatis nervosis. Lin. Sp. Plant. 291. *Pancratium with many flowers in a sheath, and oval veined leaves.* Narcissus Amboinensis, folio latissimo subrotundo. Hort. Amst. 1. p. 77. tab. 39. *Narcissus of Amboyna, with the broadest roundish leaf.*

6. PANCRATIUM (*Carolinianum*) spathâ multiflorâ, foliis linearibus, staminibus nectarii longitudine. Lin. Sp. Plant. 291. *Pancratium with many flowers in a sheath, narrow leaves, and stamina the length of the nectarium.* Lilio-Narcissus polyanthos, flore albo. Catesb. Car. 3. p. 5. *The Lily Narcissus bearing many white flowers.*

7. PANCRATIUM (*Americanum*) spathâ multiflorâ, foliis carinatis angustioribus. *Pancratium with many flowers in a sheath, and narrow keel-shaped leaves.* Narcissus Americanus, flore multiplici, albo, odore balsami Peruviani. Tourn. Inst. R. H. 358. *American Narcissus with many white flowers, smelling like Balsam of Peru.*

8. PANCRATIUM (*Latifolium*) spathâ multiflorâ, foliis carinatis latioribus. *Pancratium with many flowers in a sheath, and broader keel-shaped leaves.* Narcissus totus albus, latifolius, polianthos, major odoratus, staminibus sex è tubi ampli margine extantibus. Sloan. Cat. Jam. 115. *Broad-leaved Daffodil, with many larger sweet flowers which are very white, and a large tube, out of whose border proceed six stamina.*

The first sort grows naturally on the sea-coast in Spain, and the south of France. This hath a large, coated, bulbous root, of an oblong form, covered with a dark skin ; the leaves are shaped like a tongue; they are more than a foot long, and one inch broad, of a deep green, six or seven of them rising together from the same root, encompassed at bottom with a vagina or sheath ; between these arise the stalk, which is a foot and a half long, naked, sustaining at the top six or eight white flowers, inclosed in a sheath, which withers and opens on the side, to make way for the flowers to come out. The germen are situated close to the top of the stalk, from these arise the tube of the flowers, which are three inches long; they are very narrow, swelling at the top, where the cup or nectarium is situated, on the outside of which is fastened the six segments or petals of the flower ; these are narrow, and extend a great length beyond the nectarium ; from the border of the nectarium arise six long slender stamina, terminated by oblong summits which are prostrate, and in the center arises a style the length of the stamina, terminated by an obtuse stigma. The flowers of this sort do not appear in England till the latter end of August, so are not succeeded by seeds here. The leaves of this sort are green all the winter, and decay in the spring, so the roots should be transplanted in June, after the leaves are decayed. This must be planted in a very warm border, and screened from severe frost, otherwise it will not live through the winter in England.

The second sort grows naturally in Sclavonia, and also in Sicily; this hath a large, coated, bulbous root, covered with a dark skin, sending out many thick strong fibres, which strike deep in the ground ; the leaves are sword-shaped, a foot and a half long and two inches broad, of a grayish colour. The stalks are thick, succulent, and rise near two feet high, sustaining at the top six or seven white flowers shaped like those of the first sort, but the tube is shorter and the stamina are much longer. This

flowers in June, and frequently produces seeds which ripen in September.

This sort is hardy, and will live through the winter in the full ground, being never injured but in very severe winters ; and if, in such seasons, the surface of the ground is covered with tanners bark, sea-coal ashes, straw, or Peas-haulm, to keep out the frost, there will be no danger of the roots suffering. It is propagated either by offsets from the roots, or from seeds ; the former is the more expeditious method, for the offsets will flower very strong the second year ; whereas those which are raised from seeds, seldom flower in less than five years.

The roots of this plant should not be removed oftener than every third year, if they are expected to flower strong ; the best time to transpant them is in the beginning of October, soon after their leaves decay : they should not be kept long out of the ground, for as they do not lose their fibres every year, so if these are dried by long keeping out of the ground, it greatly weakens the roots. It loves a light sandy soil, and a sheltered situation ; the roots should be planted nine inches or a foot asunder every way, and five inches deep in the ground.

If the plants are propagated by seeds, they should be sown in pots filled with light earth soon after they are ripe ; these pots should be placed under a hot-bed frame in winter to screen them from frost, but the glasses must be taken off every day in mild weather. The other management being the same as for the Narcissus, I need not repeat it here ; so shall only mention, that the young roots will require a little protection in winter, till they have obtained strength.

The third sort grows naturally at Ceylon ; this hath a pretty large bulbous root, the leaves are long and narrow, of a grayish colour, and pretty thick, standing upright ; the stalk rises between them a foot and a half high, naked, sustaining one flower at the top, whose petals are reflexed backward ; the nectarium is large, and cut at the brim into many acute segments ; the stamina are long, and turn toward each other at their points, in which it differs from the other species. The flower has a very agreeable scent, but is of short duration ; this is very rare in the gardens at present.

The fourth sort grows naturally at La Vera Cruz, from whence the late Dr. Houstoun brought some of the roots. The leaves of this sort are about a foot long and two inches broad, having three longitudinal furrows. The stalk rises about a foot high, then divides like a fork into two small foot-stalks, or rather tubes, which are narrow, green, and at first are encompassed by a thin spatha (or sheath) which withers, and opens to give way to the flowers, which are white, and shaped like those of the other species, but have no scent.

The fifth sort grows naturally at Amboyna, and also in the American islands. The root of this sort is oblong, white, and sends out several thick fleshy fibres, which strike downward ; the leaves stand upon very long foot-stalks, some of them are oval, and others heart-shaped, about seven inches long, and five broad, ending in points, having many deep longitudinal furrows ; they are of a light green, and their borders turn inward. The stalk is thick, round, and succulent, rising near two feet high, sustaining at the top several white flowers, shaped like the other species, but the petals are broader, the tube is shorter, and the stamina are not so long as the petals. These flowers have a thin sheath or covering, which splits open longitudinally, to make way for the flowers.

The sixth sort grows naturally in moist boggy soils in Georgia, where Mr. Catesby discovered it. This hath a roundish bulbous root, covered with a light brown skin, from which arise several narrow dark green leaves, about a foot long ; between these come out a thick stalk about nine inches high, sustaining six or seven white flowers, with very narrow petals, having large bell-shaped nectariums or cups, which are deeply indented on their brims ; the stamina do not rise far

above

above the nectarium, and are terminated by yellow summits.

The seventh sort grows naturally in the islands of the West-Indies, where it is called white Lily. This hath a pretty large bulbous root, a little flatted at the top, covered with a brown skin; the leaves are near a foot and a half long, and little more than one inch broad, of a dark green, and hollowed in the middle like the keel of a boat. The stalks rise near two feet high, which are thick, succulent, and naked, sustaining at the top eight or ten white flowers, shaped like those of the first sort, but are of a purer white, and have a strong sweet odour, like that of Balsam of Peru. The stamina of this are very long, spreading out wide each way; the pointal is of the same length, standing in the middle of the nectarium. These flowers are of short duration, seldom continuing longer in beauty than three or four days, and in very hot weather not so long; when these fade, the germen, which are situated at the bottom of the tubes, turn to so many oblong bulbs, which are irregular in form, and when ripe, drop off in the ground, where they put out fibres and become plants.

These foreign species are most, if not all of them, of this kind, bearing bulbs; whereas the two first have seed-vessels with three cells, inclosing many roundish black seeds, so that though they agree in the characters of their flowers, yet in this particular they differ greatly.

The eighth sort grows naturally in the West-Indies, where it is not distinguished from the former; but as I have frequently propagated both by their bulbs which succeed the flowers, and have always found the plants so raised continue their difference, I make no doubt of their being distinct species. This differs from the former, in the leaves being much longer and broader than that; for these are near two feet long, and more than three inches broad, and are hollowed like the keel of a boat. The flowers are larger, the petals longer, and the scent is not so strong as that of the former, and the roots flower in every season of the year. This seems to be the sort figured by Dr. Trew, in the twenty-seventh table of his Decades of Rare Plants, but if it is, the leaves in his figure are too flat.

These six sorts last mentioned are tender, so will not thrive in England, unless they are placed in a warm stove. The best way to have these plants in perfection, is to plunge the pots into the bark-bed in the stove, where they will thrive and flower exceeding well; for though they may be preserved in a dry stove, yet those will not thrive so well, nor will their flowers be so strong, as when they are plunged in the tan-bed, nor will they flower oftener than once a year; whereas when they are in the tan-bed, the same roots will often flower two or three times in a year. I have had several of the species in flower at all seasons of the year, so there has not been a month when some of them were not in flower.

They are propagated by offsets from the roots, as also by the bulbs which succeed the flowers; if the latter are planted in small pots filled with light earth from a kitchen-garden, and plunged into a moderate hot-bed, they will soon put out roots and leaves, and with proper management, will become blowing roots in one year, so that they may be easily propagated; and if they are constantly kept in the tan-bed in the stove, they will put out offsets from their roots, and thrive as well as in their native countries.

PANICLE. A Panicle is a stalk diffused into several pedicles or foot-stalks, sustaining the flowers or fruits, as in Oats, &c.

PANICUM. Tourn. Inst. R. H. 515. tab. 298. Lin. Gen. Plant. 70. Panic; in French, Panis.

The CHARACTERS are,

There is one flower in each chaff; the chaff opens with three valves which are oval, ending in acute points. The petals open with two oval acute-pointed valves. The flowers have three short hair-like stamina, terminated by oblong summits, and a roundish germen supporting two hair-like styles, crowned by feathered stigmas. The ger-

men afterward becomes a roundish seed, fastened to the withered petals.

This genus of plants is ranged in the second section of Linnæus's third class, which includes the plants whose flowers have three stamina and two styles.

The SPECIES are,

1. PANICUM (*Germanicum*) spicâ simplici cernuâ, setis brevioribus pedunculo hirsuto. *Panic with a single nodding spike, short awns, and a hairy foot-stalk.* Panicum Germanicum, sive panicula minore. C. B. P. 27. *German Panic with a smaller panicle.*

2. PANICUM (*Italicum*) spicâ compositâ, spiculis glomeratis, setis immixtis, pedunculo hirsuto. Lin. Sp. Plant. 56. *Panic with a compounded spike, whose smaller spikes grow in clusters intermixed with awns, and a hairy foot-stalk.* Panicum Italicum sive paniculâ majore. C. B. P. 27. *Italian Panic with a larger spike.*

3. PANICUM (*Indicum*) spicâ simplici longissimâ, setis hispidis, pedunculo hirsuto. *Panic with the longest single spike, prickly awns, and a hairy foot-stalk.* Panicum Indicum, spicâ longissimâ. C. B. P. 27. *Indian Panic with the longest spike.*

4. PANICUM (*Alopecuroedem*) spicâ tereti, involucellis bifloris fasciculato-pilosis. Flor. Zeyl. 44. *Panic with a taper spike having two flowers in each cover, and hairs growing in clusters.* Panicum Indicum altissimum, spicâ simplicibus mollibus, in foliorum alis longissimis pediculis insidentibus. Tourn. Inst. 515. *Tallest Indian Panic, with the soft single spikes proceeding from the wings of the leaves, and sitting upon very long foot-stalks.*

5. PANICUM (*Caeruleum*) spicâ simplici æquali, pedunculis bifloris. Prod. Leyd. 54. *Panic with an equal single spike, and two flowers growing on each foot-stalk.* Panicum Indicum, spicâ obtusâ cæruleâ. C. B. P. 7. *Indian Panic, with an obtuse blue spike.*

There are several other species of this genus than are here enumerated, some of which grow naturally in England; but as they are not cultivated, so it would be swelling this work too much if they were inserted here.

The first sort grows naturally in Germany and Hungary; of this there are three varieties, one with yellow grain, another with white, and the third has purple grains. This hath been formerly cultivated for bread, in some of the northern countries. It rises with a jointed Reed-like stalk about three feet high, and about the size of the common Reed, garnished at each joint with one Grass-like leaf a foot and a half long, and about an inch broad at the base where broadest, ending in acute points; they are rough to the touch, embracing the stalk at their base, and turn downward about half their length. The stalks are terminated by compact spikes, which are about the thickness of a man's finger at their base, growing taper toward their points, and are eight or nine inches long, closely set with small roundish grain like that of Millet. This is an annual plant, which perishes soon after the seeds are ripe.

The second sort is frequently cultivated in Italy, and other warm countries. This rises with a Reed-like stalk near four feet high, which is much thicker than that of the former; the leaves are also broader, but of the same shape. The spikes are a foot long, and twice the thickness of those of the former, but not so compact, being composed of several roundish clustered spikes; the grain is also larger, but of the same form. There are two or three varieties of this, which differ only in the colour of their grain; this is also annual. The third sort grows naturally in both Indies; this hath a Reed-like stalk as large as a man's thumb, rising upward of five feet high; the leaves are two inches broad, and more than two feet long, of the same form with those of the former sort; the spikes at the top are a foot and a half long, very compact, and thicker than a man's thumb at the base, growing taper toward the top. The seeds are much larger than those of the other sorts, and are in some white and in others yellow.

The

The fourth fort grows naturally in both Indies; this hath a ſtrong Reed-like ſtalk, which riſes ſix or ſeven feet high, garniſhed with leaves more than three feet long; they are near three inches broad at their baſe, leſſening to a point at the end, having a ſmooth ſurface; the ſpikes ariſe at the wings of the ſtalk; they are ſingle, but not ſo compact as thoſe of the former, having ſoft awns or beards; they are about ſix inches long, and ſtand upon very long foot-ſtalks; the grain of this is pretty large.

The fifth ſort grows naturally in Peru; this riſes with a Reed-like ſtalk ſix feet high, which ſends out two or three branches from the ſides, and is garniſhed with long leaves two inches broad at their baſe; the ſtalks are of a purple colour, the leaves are alſo inclining to the ſame. The ſpikes come out from the wings of the ſtalks, and at the end of the branches; they are about four or five inches long, thicker than a man's thumb, and almoſt equal at the point with the baſe. They are of a pale blue colour, having pretty long awns or beards of the ſame colour, as are alſo the ſeeds, which are larger and rounder than thoſe of the other ſorts.

The two firſt ſorts are ſown in ſeveral parts of Europe in the fields, as Corn, for the ſuſtenance of the inhabitants, but it is reckoned not to afford ſo good nouriſhment as Millet; however, it is frequently uſed in ſome parts of Germany and Italy, to make cakes and bread, but the German is not ſo much eſteemed as the Italian ſort; but as it will ripen better in cold countries than that, it is generally cultivated where a better ſort of grain will not ſucceed.

The ſeeds of this ſort may be ſown in the ſpring, at the ſame time as Barley is ſown, and may be managed exactly in the ſame way; but this ſhould not be ſown too thick, for theſe ſeeds are very ſmall, and the plants grow ſtronger, therefore require more room. The German ſort doth not grow above three feet high, unleſs it is ſown on very rich land, in which caſe it will riſe to be four feet high; but the leaves and ſtems of this Corn are very large, ſo require to ſtand four or five inches apart, otherwiſe they will grow up weak and come to little. Theſe large growing Corns ſhould be ſown in drills at about eighteen inches apart, ſo that the ground may be hoed between the rows of Corn, to keep them clear from weeds, and the ſtirring of the ground will greatly improve the Corn. In Auguſt the Corn will ripen, when it may be cut down and dried, and then ſhould be houſed.

The Italian Panic grows much larger than the German, and produces much larger ſpikes; ſo this ſhould be allowed more room to grow, otherwiſe it will come to little. This is alſo later before it ripens, ſo it is not very proper for cold countries.

The other ſorts are natives of very warm countries, where they are uſed by the inhabitants to make bread. Theſe grow very large, and require a good ſummer, otherwiſe they will not ripen in this country. The ſeeds of this kind ſhould be ſown the latter end of March or the beginning of April, on a moderate hot-bed, and the plants ſhould be planted out when grown to a proper ſize, upon a bed of light rich earth, in a warm ſituation. They ſhould be planted in rows about three feet aſunder, and the plants muſt be kept clear from weeds. When the plants are grown pretty tall, they ſhould be ſupported by ſtakes, otherwiſe the winds will break them down; and when the Corn begins to ripen, the birds muſt be kept from it, otherwiſe they will ſoon deſtroy it. Theſe ſorts are preſerved in ſome curious gardens for the ſake of variety, but they are not worth cultivating for uſe in England. The two laſt ſorts ſeldom ripen here.

PANSIE'S. See VIOLA TRICOLOR.

PAPAVER. Tourn. Inſt. R. H. 2. tab. 119. Lin. Gen. Plant. 573. Poppy; in French, Pavot.

The CHARACTERS are,

The empalement of the flower is oval, indented, and compoſed of two almoſt oval, concave, obtuſe leaves, which fall off. The flower has four large roundiſh petals which ſpread open, with a great number of hair-like ſtamina, terminated by oblong, compreſſed, erect ſummits. In the center is placed a large roundiſh germen having no ſtyle, but is crowned by a plain, radiated, target-ſhaped ſtigma. The germen afterward becomes a large capſule, crowned by the plain ſtigma, having one cell, opening in many places at the top under the crown, and is filled with ſmall ſeeds.

This genus of plants is ranged in the firſt ſection of Linnæus's thirteenth claſs, which includes thoſe plants whoſe flowers have many ſtamina and one germen.

The SPECIES are,

1. PAPAVER (Rhœas) capſulis glabris globoſis, caule piloſo multifloro, foliis pinnatifidis inciſis. Lin. Sp. Plant. 507. *Poppy with ſmooth globular heads, a hairy ſtalk with many flowers, and wing-pointed cut leaves.* Papaver erraticum, rubrum, campeſtre. J. B. 3. 395. *Common red field Poppy.*

2. PAPAVER (Hybridum) capſulis ſubgloboſis toroſis hiſpidis, caule folioſo multifloro. Lin. Sp. Plant. 506. *Poppy with globular capſules which are furrowed and prickly, and a leafy ſtalk bearing many flowers.* Argemone capitulo breviore hiſpido. J. B. 3. 396. *Argemone with a ſhorter prickly head.*

3. PAPAVER (Argemone) capſulis clavatis hiſpidis, caule folioſo multifloro. Lin. Sp. Plant. 506. *Poppy with nail-ſhaped prickly heads, and a leafy ſtalk bearing many flowers.* Papaver erraticum, capite longiore hiſpido. Tourn. Inſt. 238. *Field Poppy with a longer prickly head.*

4. PAPAVER (Alpinum) capſulā hiſpidā, ſcapo unifloro nudo hiſpido, foliis bipinnatis. Lin. Sp. Plant. 507. *Poppy with prickly heads, and a naked prickly ſtalk bearing one flower, and double winged leaves.* Argemone Alpina coriandri folio. C. B. P. 172. *Alpine Argemone with a Coriander leaf.*

5. PAPAVER (Cambricum) capſulis glabris oblongis, caule multifloro lævi, foliis pinnatis inciſis. Lin. Sp. Plant. 508. *Poppy with oblong ſmooth heads, a ſmooth ſtalk bearing many flowers, and cut winged leaves.* Papaver luteum perenne, laciniato folio, Cambrobritannicum. Raii Syn. Ed. 3. p. 309. *Yellow, Welch, perennial Poppy, with a cut leaf.*

6. PAPAVER (Nudicaule) capſulis hiſpidis, ſcapo unifloro nudo hiſpido, foliis ſimplicibus pinnato-ſinuatis. Hort. Upſal. 136. *Poppy with prickly heads, a naked rough ſtalk having one flower, and ſingle leaves which are wingedly ſinuated.* Papaver erraticum, luteo flore, capite oblongo hiſpido. Amman. Ruth. 61. *Field Poppy with a yellow flower, and an oblong prickly head.*

7. PAPAVER (Orientale) capſulis glabris, caulibus unifloris, ſcabris, foliis pinnatis ſerratis. Hort. Upſal. 136. *Poppy with ſmooth heads, rough leafy ſtalks having one flower, and ſawed winged leaves.* Papaver Orientale hirſutiſſimum flore magno. Tourn. Cor. 17. *Moſt hairy eaſtern Poppy with a large flower.*

8. PAPAVER (Somniferum) calycibus capſuliſque glabris, foliis amplexicaulibus inciſis. Lin. Sp. Plant. 508. *Poppy with ſmooth capſules and empalements, and cut leaves embracing the ſtalks.* Papaver hortenſe nigro ſemine, ſylveſtre Dioſcoridis, nigrum Plinii. C. B. P. 170. *Garden Poppy with black ſeeds.*

9. PAPAVER (Album) capſulis ovatis glabris, foliis latioribus amplexicaulibus marginibus inciſo-ſerratis. *Poppy with oval ſmooth heads, and broader leaves embracing the ſtalks, which are cut on their edges like the teeth of a ſaw.* Papaver hortenſe, ſemine albo, ſativum Dioſcoridis, album Plinii. C. B. P. 170. *Garden Poppy with white ſeeds, commonly called white Poppy.*

The firſt ſort is the common red Poppy, which grows naturally on arable land in moſt parts of England; from the flowers of this ſort is drawn a ſimple water, a tincture, a ſyrup and conſerve for medicinal uſe. It is an annual plant; from the roots riſe ſeveral rough branching ſtalks a foot and a half high, garniſhed with hairy leaves five or ſix inches long, deeply jagged almoſt to the midrib, thoſe on the lower part of the leaves being the deepeſt; theſe jags are oppoſite and regular, like thoſe of the winged leaves. At the top of each ſtalk ſtand the flowers, which have oval hairy empalements, opening with

two

two valves, and foon fall away. The flowers are compofed of four large roundifh petals, which are narrow at their bafe, but fpread out into a circular order; they are of a beautiful fcarlet colour, and foon fall off. Thefe appear in June, and are fucceeded by oblong fmooth heads, crowned by the flat target-fhaped ftigma, and perforated in feveral places at the top, filled with fmall purplifh-coloured feeds. There are feveral varieties of this with double flowers, cultivated in gardens; fome of them have white flowers, others have red flowers bordered with white, and fome have variegated flowers; but as thefe varieties have been produced by culture from the feeds of the common fort, they fhould be included in that fpecies. The fecond fort grows naturally among the Corn in many parts of England; the leaves of this fort are much fmaller than thofe of the firft, and are cut into much finer fegments; the ftalks are flender, a little more than a foot high, not fo branching as the former. The flowers are not fo large, and of a deep purple colour, very foon lafting away, feldom lafting more than a whole day; thefe are fucceeded by oblong prickly heads, filled with fmall black feeds. It flowers in June.

The third fort grows naturally among Corn in fome parts of England, but not in fo great plenty as either of the former. The leaves of this are finer cut and fmaller than thofe of the firft fort, but are not fo fine as thofe of the fecond; the ftalks do not rife fo high as either of the former, and feldom have many branches. The flowers are not half fo large as either of the former, and are of a copper colour, falling away in a few hours. Thefe appear in May, and are fucceeded by long, flender, prickly heads, which are channelled, filled with fmall, black, fhrivelled feeds.

The fourth fort grows naturally on the Alps, among the rocks. The leaves of this are fmooth and doubly winged, the fegments are finely cut; the ftalks rife about a foot high, fuftaining one fmall yellow, or copper-coloured flower, which is fucceeded by roundifh prickly heads, filled with fmall feeds. This flowers abour the fame time as the former fort.

The fifth fort has a perennial root; it grows naturally in Wales, and alfo in fome of the northern counties in England. I found it growing plentifully near Kirby-Lonfdale in Weftmoreland. Tournefort alfo found this plant upon the Pyrenean mountains. The leaves of this fort are winged; the lobes are deeply cut on their edges. The ftalks rife a foot high; they are fmooth, and are garnifhed with a few fmall leaves of the fame fhape as the lower. The upper part of the ftalk is naked, fuftaining one large yellow flower. Thefe appear in June, and are fucceeded by oblong fmooth capfules, filled with fmall purplifh feeds.

The fixth fort grows naturally on the confines of Ruffia, near Tartary. The leaves of this fort are fingle, and finuated almoft to the midrib in form of a winged leaf; they are rough and hairy. The ftalk rifes near two feet high; it is flender, naked, fuftaining one flower at the top, which is compofed of four roundifh petals of a pale yellow colour, each having a dark bottom or tail. The flowers have an agreeable fcent, but are of fhort duration. They come out in June, and are fucceeded by long rough capfules, filled with fmall feeds.

The feventh fort grows naturally in Armenia, from whence Dr. Tournefort fent the feeds to the royal gardens at Paris, where they fucceeded, and were afterward communicated to the curious gardens in England and Holland. The root of this plant is compofed of two or three ftrong fibres as thick as a man's little finger, which are a foot and a half long, of a dark brown on their outfide, and full of a milky juice, which is very bitter and acrid. The leaves are winged, and fawed on their edges; they are a foot long, clofely covered with briftly white hairs. The ftalks rife two feet and a half high; they are very rough and hairy, garnifhed below with leaves like thofe at bottom, but fmaller; the upper part is

naked, fuftaining at the top one very large flower, of the fame colour with the common red Poppy. Thefe appear in May, and are fucceeded by oval fmooth capfules, filled with purplifh feeds.

There are two or three varieties of this which differ only in the colour of their flowers; and I have been informed; there is a double flower of this kind, but I have not feen it. Tournefort fays, the Turks eat the green heads of this Poppy, although they are very bitter and acrid.

The eighth fort is the common black Poppy, the feeds of which are fold in the fhops by the title of Maw-feed. The fort with fingle flowers grows in the warm parts of Europe naturally; this is annual; the ftalks rife three feet high; they are fmooth, and divide into feveral branches, and are garnifhed with large leaves, which are fmooth, and deeply cut or jagged on their edges, embracing the ftalks with their bafe. The flowers grow on the top of the ftalks; they are compofed of four large roundifh petals of a purplifh colour, with dark bottoms, and are fucceeded by oval fmooth capfules filled with black feeds. It flowers in June, and the feeds ripen the latter end of Auguft.

There are great varieties in the flowers of this fort, fome having very large double flowers, which are variegated of feveral colours; fome are red and white, others purple and white, and fome are finely fpotted like Carnations; fo that during their fhort continuance in flower, there are few plants whofe flowers appear fo beautiful; but having an offenfive fcent, and being of fhort duration, they are not much regarded. The leaves of this fort are ufed as an ingredient in cooling ointments; and the heads of this were an ingredient in the fyrupus e Melonio, but in the late Difpenfaries they have been left out.

The ninth fort is the common white Poppy; this is cultivated in gardens for the heads, which are ufed in medicine. The ftalks of this are large, fmooth, and rife to the height of five or fix feet; they branch out into feveral fmaller, garnifhed with large grayifh leaves, whofe bafe embraces the ftalks; they are jagged irregularly on their fides. The flowers terminate the ftalks; thefe, when inclofed in the empalement, nod downward, but before the flowers open they are erect. The empalement of the flower is compofed of two large oval leaves, of the fame grayifh colour as the other; thefe feparate and foon drop off. The flower is compofed of four large, roundifh, white petals, which are of fhort duration, and are fucceeded by large roundifh heads as big as Oranges, flatted at both ends, having indented crowns, and are filled with fmall white feeds. This flowers in June, and the feeds ripen in Auguft.

There are feveral varieties of this fort, which differ in the colour of their flowers and multiplicity of petals; thofe with beautiful flowers are preferved in gardens for ornament, but that with the fingle flowers only is cultivated for ufe. The feeds of this fort are ufed in emulfions, being cooling, and good in fevers and inflammatory diftempers, as alfo for the ftrangury and heat of the urine. Of the dry heads infufed and boiled in water, is made the diacodium of the fhops.

It has been generally fuppofed, that from the heads of this fort of Poppy the opium is extracted; but one of the heads which I have by me, from which opium had been extracted in Turkey, is of a different fhape from thofe of this fort.

All the forts of Poppy are propagated by feeds, but the fifth and feventh forts, which have perennial roots, may be alfo propagated by offsets. The beft time for fowing the feeds is in September, when they will more certainly grow than thofe which are fown in the fpring; and thofe forts which are annual will make larger plants, and flower better than when they are fown in the fpring. The beft way is to fow the feeds of the annual kinds in the places where they are to remain, and to thin the plants where they are too clofe; thofe of the large kinds fhould not be left nearer to each other than a foot and a half, and the fmaller forts may be allowed about half that space. The culture they will require after this, is only to keep them clean from weeds.

Those who are curious to have fine Poppies in their gardens, carefully look over their plants when they begin to flower, and cut up all those plants whose flowers are not very double and well marked, before they open their flowers, to prevent their farina mixing with their finer flowers, which would degenerate them; and it is the not being careful of this, that causes the flowers to degenerate so frequently in many places, which is often supposed to be occasioned by the ground.

The yellow Welsh Poppy requires a cool shady situation, where the plants will thrive, and produce plenty of seeds annually. If these seeds are permitted to scatter, the plants will come up better than when sown by hand; but if they are sown, it should be always in the autumn; for the seeds of this, which are sown in the spring, rarely succeed.

The best time to transplant and part the roots of this sort is in the autumn, that the plants may be well established in their new quarters, before the dry weather comes on in the spring.

The eastern Poppy will thrive either in sun or shade, for I have several of these plants growing under trees, where they have thriven many years, and flower full as well as those in an open situation, but came later in the season. This will propagate very fast by its roots, so there is no necessity for sowing the seeds, unless to procure new varieties. This sort should be transplanted at the same season as the former; and if the seeds are sown, it should be at the same time, for the reasons before given.

PAPAVER CORNICULATUM. See GLAU-CIUM.

PAPAVER SPINOSUM. See AGREMONE.

PAPAYA. See CARICA.

PAPILIONACEOUS. A papilionaceous (or Pea-bloom) flower is so called, because in some measure it resembles a butterfly with its wings expanded. It always consists of these parts; the vexillum or standard, which is a large erect segment or petal; the alæ, or two wings, which compose the sides, and the carina, or keel, which is a concave petal or segment, resembling the lower part of a boat: this keel is sometimes entire, and sometimes it consists of two petals or segments adhering pretty close together. Of this tribe are Peas, Beans, Kidney-beans, Vetches, and other leguminous plants.

PAPPOSE PLANTS are such as have their seeds covered with a down, which adheres to the upper part of the seed, and are of use to spread them when ripe, by sustaining them in the air, so that they may be conveyed to a great distance. Of this kind are the Sow-thistles, Hawkweeds, Dandelion, Starworts, &c.

PARASITICAL PLANTS are such as are produced out of the trunk or branches of other plants, from whence they receive their nourishment, and will not grow upon the ground, as the Misleto, &c.

PARIETARIA. Tourn. Inst. R. H. 509. tab. 289. Lin. Gen. Plant. 1020. so called from Paries, *Lat.* a wall, because it grows on old walls.] Pellitory; in French, *Parietaire.*

The CHARACTERS are,

It hath hermaphrodite and female flowers upon the same plant. There are two hermaphrodite flowers contained in a six-leaved involucrum; these have a quadrifid plain empalement of one leaf, half the size of the involucrum. They have no petals, but four permanent awl-shaped stamina longer than the empalement, terminated by twin summits, with an oval germen supporting a slender coloured style, crowned by a pencil-shaped stigma. The germen afterward turns to an oval seed wrapped up in the empalement. The female flowers have no stamina, but in other respects are the same as the hermaphrodite.

This genus of plants is ranged in the first section of Linnæus's twenty-third class, which contains those plants which have hermaphrodite and female flowers on the same plant.

The SPECIES are,

1. PARIETARIA (*Officinalis*) foliis lanceolato-ovatis alternis. Hort. Upsal. 38. *Pellitory with oval spear-shaped leaves, placed alternately.* Parietaria officinarum & Dioscoridis. C. B. P. 121. *The officinal Pellitory of Dioscorides.*

2. PARIETARIA (*Judiaca*) foliis ovatis caulibus erectiusculis, calycibus trifloris, corollis hermaphroditis, defloratis elongato-cylindricis. Lin. Sp. 1492. *Pellitory with oval leaves, an erect stalk, and three flowers in each cup, which are hermaphrodite.* Parietaria minor Ocimi folio. C. B. P. 121. *Smaller Pellitory with a Basil leaf.*

The first sort grows naturally in Germany and Holland, but was not in England till the year 1727, when I brought it here. This is supposed to be the true sort which is recommended by the ancients to be used in medicine; it hath a thick perennial root, composed of fleshy reddish fibres, from which arise many stalks a foot and a half high, garnished with hairy, oval, spear-shaped leaves, about two inches long, and one broad in the middle, having several veins. The flowers come out in small clusters on the side of the stalks; they are small, of an herbaceous colour, so make no figure. These appear in succession all the summer months, and the seeds ripen accordingly, which are cast out to a distance with an elasticity when ripe.

The second sort grows plentifully on old walls, and the sides of dry banks in most parts of England; this differs from the former in having shorter stalks, and smaller oval leaves. The flowers are also less, and are in smaller clusters; in other respects they are the same.

They may be propagated in plenty from a single plant, which, if permitted to scatter its seeds, will fill the ground about it with young plants, for the seeds are very difficult to collect, as they are thrown out of their covers as soon as they are ripe.

There are three or four other species of this genus, but as they have little beauty and are of no use, so are not cultivated in gardens.

PARIS. Lin. Gen. Plant. 449. Herba Paris. Tourn. Inst. R. H. 233. tab. 117. True-love, or One-berry.

The CHARACTERS are,

The empalement of the flower is permanent, and composed of four leaves, which expand in form of a cross. The flower also hath four leaves, which spread open in the same manner, and are permanent. In the center of the flower is situated a roundish four-cornered germen, supporting four spreading styles, crowned by single summits. This is attended by eight stamina, each having an oblong summit, fastened by threads on each side to the stamina. The germen afterward changes to a roundish berry, having four cells which are filled with seeds.

This genus of plants is ranged in the fourth section of Linnæus's eighth class, which includes the plants whose flowers have eight stamina and four styles.

We know but one SPECIES of this genus, viz.

PARIS (*Quadrifolia*) foliis quaternis. Flor. Lapp. 155. *Herb Paris, True-love, or One-berry.*

This plant grows wild in moist shady woods in divers parts of England, but especially in the northern counties, and it is with great difficulty preserved in gardens. The only method to procure it, is to take up the plants from the places where they grow wild, preserving good balls of earth to their roots, and plant them in a shady moist border, where they may remain undisturbed, in which situation they will live some years; but as it is a plant of little beauty, it is rarely preserved in gardens.

PARKINSONIA. Plum. Nov. Gen. 25. tab. 3. Lin. Gen. Plant. 460.

The CHARACTERS are,

The empalement of the flower spreads open; it is of one leaf, indented in five parts at the top. The flower has five almost equal petals placed circularly; the four upper are oval, the under is kidney-shaped. It has ten declining stamina terminated by oblong summits, and a long taper germen with scarce any style, crowned by an obtuse stigma.

The

The germen afterward becomes a long taper pod with swelling joints, in each of which is lodged one oblong seed.

This genus of plants is ranged in the first section of Linnæus's tenth class, which includes those plants whose flowers have ten stamina and one style.

We know but one SPECIES of this genus, viz.

PARKINSONIA (*Aculeata.*) Parkinsonia. Hort. Cliff. 57. Parkinsonia aculeata, foliis minutis, uni costæ adnexis. Plum. Nov. Gen. 25. *Prickly Parkinsonia with very small leaves, which are fastened to one middle rib.*

This plant was discovered by Father Plumier in America, who gave it this name in honour of Mr. John Parkinson, who published an Universal History of Plants in English, in the year 1640.

It is very common in the Spanish West-Indies, but of late years it has been introduced into the English settlements in America, for the beauty and sweetness of its flowers. This, in the countries where it grows naturally, rises to be a tree of twenty feet high or more, and bears long slender bunches of yellow flowers, which hang down after the same manner as the Laburnum. These flowers have a most agreeable sweet scent, so as to perfume the air to a considerable distance round about the trees; for which reason, the inhabitants of the West-Indies plant them near their habitations. And though this plant has not been introduced many years into the English settlements, yet it is now become so common in all the islands, that but few houses are without some of the trees near it; for it produces flowers and seeds in plenty in about two years from seed, so that it may soon be made common in all hot countries; but in Europe it requires a stove, otherwise it will not live through the winter.

This plant is propagated by seeds, which should be sown in small pots filled with light fresh earth early in the spring, and the pots must be plunged into a hot-bed of tanners bark, where, in about three weeks or a month's time, the plants will come up, when they should be kept clear from weeds, and frequently refreshed with a little water. In a little time these plants will be fit to transplant, which should be done very carefully, so as not to injure their roots. They must be each planted into a separate halfpenny pot filled with light fresh earth, and then plunged into the hot-bed again, observing to stir up the tan; and if it hath lost its heat, there should be some fresh tan added to renew it again. Then shade the plants from the heat of the sun, until they have taken new root; after which time they should have fresh air admitted to them every day, in proportion to the warmth of the season. With this management the plants will grow so fast, as to fill the pots with their roots by the beginning of July, at which time they should be shifted into pots a little larger than the former, and plunged again into the bark-bed to forward their taking new root; after which it will be the best way to inure the plants by degrees to bear the open air, that they may be hardened before winter; for if they are kept too warm in winter, the plants will decay before the next spring. The only method by which I have succeeded in keeping this plant through the winter, was by hardening them in July and August to bear the open air; and in September I placed them on shelves in the dry stove, at the greatest distance from the fire, so that they were in a very temperate warmth; and there they retained their leaves all the winter, and continued in health, when those which were placed in a warmer situation, as also those in the green-house, were entirely destroyed, but these seldom survived the second winter.

PARNASSIA. Tourn. Inst. R. H. 246. tab. 127. Lin. Gen. Plant. 345. Grass of Parnassus.

The CHARACTERS are,

The flower hath a permanent spreading empalement, cut into five parts. The flower has five roundish, concave, spreading petals, which have five heart-shaped nectariums, and five stamina terminated by depressed summits, with a large oval germen having no style, but four obtuse permanent stigmas in their place. The germen afterward turns

to an oval four-cornered capsule with one cell, containing several oblong seeds.

This genus of plants is ranged in the fourth section of Linnæus's fifth class, which includes the plants whose flowers have five stamina and four styles.

The SPECIES are,

1. PARNASSIA (*Palustris.*) Parnassus Grass. Parnassia palustris & vulgaris. Inst. R. H. *Common Marsh Grass of Parnassus.*

2. PARNASSIA (*Pleno flore*) vulgaris flore pleno. *Common Grass of Parnassus, with a double flower.*

The former of these sorts grows wild in moist meadows in several parts of England, but particularly in the north; but it doth not grow in the neighbourhood of London, any nearer than on the other side of Watford, in the low meadows by Cassioberry, where it is in pretty great plenty.

The other sort is an accidental variety of the former, which has been discovered wild, and transplanted into gardens. This is but rarely to be found, being in very few gardens at present.

These plants may be taken up from the natural places of their growth, with balls of earth to their roots, and planted into pots filled with pretty strong, fresh, undunged earth, and placed in a shady situation, where, if they are constantly watered in dry weather, they will thrive very well, and flower every summer; but if the plants are planted in the full ground, it should be in a very moist shady border, otherwise they will not live; and these should be as duly watered as those in the pots in dry weather, to make them produce strong flowers.

They may be propagated by parting their roots, which should be done in March, before they put out new leaves; but the roots should not be divided too small, for that will prevent their flowering the following summer. These roots should always be planted in pretty strong fresh earth, for they will not thrive in a light rich soil. In the spring they must be constantly watered, if the season should prove dry, otherwise they will not flower; nor should they be parted oftener than every third year, to have them strong. These plants flower in July, and their seeds are ripe the latter end of August.

It is called Parnassus, from Mount Parnassus, on which it was supposed to grow; and from the cattle feeding on it, it was called a Grass, though the plant has no resemblance to any of the Grass kind, but is more like the Ranunculus in flower, and the leaves are pretty broad, oblong, and smooth.

PARONYCHIA. See ILLECEBRUM.

PARSLEY. See APIUM.

PARSNEP. See PASTINACA.

PARTERRE is a level division of ground, which, for the most part, faces the south and best front of a house, and is generally furnished with greens, flowers, &c.

There are several sorts of Parterres, as plain Grass with borders, and Parterres of embroidery, &c.

Plain Parterres are more beautiful in England than in any other countries, by reason of the excellency of our turf, and that decency and unaffected simplicity that it affords to the eye of the spectator.

Others are cut into shell and scroll-work, with sand-alleys between them, which are the finest Parterre works esteemed in France.

As to the general proportion of Parterres, an oblong or long square is accounted the most proper figure for a Parterre; because by the rules of perspective, or the natural declension of the visual rays in optics, a long square sinks almost to a square, and an exact square appears much less than it really is, therefore a Parterre should not be less than twice as long as it is broad; twice and a half is accounted a very good proportion, and it is very rare that three times is exceeded.

As to the breadth of a Parterre, it is to take its dimensions from the breadth of the front of the house. If the front of the house is one hundred feet long, the breadth of the Parterre should be one hundred and fifty

fifty feet; and if the front of the houfe be two hundred feet, the Parterre fhould be fifty feet broader; but where the front of the houfe exceeds the breadth of the Parterre, it will be a good proportion to make the Parterre of the fame dimenfions with the front.

Some do not approve of making Parterres very broad, becaufe it makes them appear too fhort; when nothing is more pleafing to the eye, than a contracted regular conduct and view, as foon as the perfon goes out of a houfe or building; and a forward direct view is the beft, whether it be either Parterre or lawn, or any other open fpace, either two, three, or fourfold in the width; and for that reafon, thofe defigns may juftly be difapproved, by which the noblenefs of the view is marred at the immediate entrance into the garden, the angle of light being broken and confufed.

The making of Parterres too large caufes a great expence, and at the fame time occafions a diminution of wood, which is the moft valuable part of a garden. As to the adorning and furnifhing thefe Parterres, whether it be plain or with embroidery, that depends much upon the form of them, and therefore muft be left to the judgment and fancy of the defigner.

PARTHENIUM. Lin. Gen. Plant. 939. Partheniaftrum. Niffol. Act. Par. 1711. Dill. Gen. 13. Baftard Feverfew.

The CHARACTERS are,

It hath a flower compofed of hermaphrodite florets and female half florets, which are inclofed in a common fiveleaved fpreading empalement. The hermaphrodite flowers which form the difk, have one tubulous petal cut into five parts at the brim; they have five hair-like ftamina the length of the tube, terminated by thick fummits. The germen is fituated below the floret, and is fcarce vifible, fupporting a flender ftyle having no ftigma; thefe florets are barren. The female florets which compofe the rays or border, are ftretched out on one fide like a tongue; thefe have a large, heart-fhaped, compreffed germen, with a flender ftyle crowned by two long fpreading ftigmas. Thefe are fucceeded by one heart-fhaped compreffed feed.

This genus of plants is ranged in the fifth fection of Linnæus's twenty-firft clafs, which includes thofe plants which have male and female, or hermaphrodite flowers in the fame plants, whofe male or hermaphrodite flowers have five ftamina.

The SPECIES are,

1. PARTHENIUM (*Hyfterophorus*) foliis compofito-multifidis. Lin. Hort. Cliff. 442. *Parthenium with many-pointed compound leaves.* Partheniaftrum artemifiæ folio, flore albo. Hort. Chelf. 152. *Baftard Feverfew, with a Mugwort leaf.*

2. PARTHENIUM (*Integrifolium*) foliis ovatis crenatis. Lin. Hort. Cliff. 442. *Parthenium with oval crenated leaves.* Partheniaftrum helenii folio. Hort. Elth. 302. tab. 225. *Baftard Feverfew with an Elecampane leaf.*

The firft fort grows wild in great plenty in the ifland of Jamaica, and in fome other of the Englifh fettlements in the Weft-Indies, where it is called wild Wormwood, and is ufed by the inhabitants as a vulnerary herb.

The fecond fort grows plentifully in feveral parts of the Spanifh Weft-Indies, from whence the feeds have been brought to Europe.

The firft is an annual plant, which may be propagated by fowing the feeds on a hot-bed early in the fpring; and when the plants come up, they fhould be tranfplanted on another hot-bed, at about five or fix inches diftance, obferving to water and fhade them until they have taken new root; after which time they muft have a pretty large fhare of frefh air in warm weather, by raifing the glaffes of the hot-bed every day, and they muft be duly watered every other day at leaft. When the plants have grown fo as to meet each other, they fhould be carefully taken up, preferving a ball of earth to their roots, and each planted into a feparate pot filled with light rich earth; and if they are plunged into a moderate hot-bed, it will greatly facilitate their taking frefh root; but where this conveniency is wanting, the plants

fhould be removed to a warm fheltered fituation, where they muft be fhaded from the fun until they have taken new root; after which time they may be expofed, with other hardy annual plants in a warm fituation, where they will flower in July, and their feeds will ripen in September. But if the feafon fhould prove cold and wet, it will be proper to have a plant or two in fhelter, either in the ftove, or under tall frames, in order to have good feeds, if thofe plants which are expofed fhould fail, whereby the fpecies may be preferved.

The fecond fort is a perennial plant, which dies to the ground every autumn, and fhoots up again the following fpring. The feeds of this fort were fent me by my good friend Dr. Thomas Dale, from South Carolina, where the plants grow wild. This may be propagated by parting the roots in autumn, and may be planted in the full ground, where it will abide the cold of our ordinary winters very well. This fort flowers in July, but feldom produces good feeds in England.

Thefe plants make no great appearance, fo are feldom cultivated but for the fake of variety.

PASQUE-FLOWER. See PULSATILLA.

PASSERINA. Lin. Gen. Plant. 440. Thymelæa. Tourn. Inft. R. H. 594. Pluk. Sanamunda. Cluf. Sparrow-wort.

The CHARACTERS are,

The flower has no empalement; it has one withered petal, having a flender cylindrical tube fwelling below the middle, and divided into four parts at the top, which fpread open. It hath eight brifly ftamina fitting on the top of the tube, terminated by erect fummits almoft oval. It has an oval germen under the tube, having a flender ftyle rifing on one fide of the top of the germen, crowned by a beaded ftigma, fet with prickly hairs on every fide. The germen afterward turns to an oval feed pointed at both ends, inclofed in a thick oval capfule of one cell.

This genus of plants is ranged in the firft fection of Linnæus's eighth clafs, which includes thofe plants whofe flowers have eight ftamina and one ftyle.

The SPECIES are,

1. PASSERINA (*Filiformis*) foliis linearibus convexis quadrifariàm imbricatis, ramis tomentofis. Lin. Sp. Plant. 559. *Sparrow-wort with linear convex leaves imbricated four ways, and downy branches.* Thymelæa Ethiopica, pafferinæ foliis. Breyn. Cent. 10. fig. 6. *Ethiopian Spurge Laurel, with Sparrow-wort leaves.*

2. PASSERINA (*Hirfuta*) foliis carnofis extus glabris, caulibus tomentofis. Lin. Sp. Plant. 559. *Sparrow-wort with flefhy leaves, which are fmooth on their outfide, and downy ftalks.* Sanamunda 3. Cluf. Hift. 1. p. 89. *The third Sanamunda of Clufius.*

3. PASSERINA (*Ciliata*) foliis lanceolatis fubciliatis erectis, ramis nudis. Lin. Sp. Plant. 559. *Sparrow-wort with fpear-fhaped erect leaves having fmall hairs and naked branches.* Sanamunda 1. Cluf. Hift. 88. *The firft Sanamunda of Clufius.*

4. PASSERINA (*Uniflora*) foliis linearibus oppofitis, floribus terminalibus folitariis, ramis glabris. Lin. Sp. Plant. 560. *Sparrow-wort with linear leaves placed oppofite, fingle flowers terminating the branches, and fmooth ftalks.* Thymelæa ramofa, linearibus foliis anguftis, flore folitario. Burm. Afr. 131. tab. 48. fig. 1. *Branching Spurge Laurel, with narrow linear leaves and a fingle flower.*

The firft fort grows naturally at the Cape of Good Hope, from whence it was firft brought to the gardens in Holland. This rifes with a fhrubby ftalk five or fix feet high, fending out branches the whole length, which, when young, grow erect, but as they advance in length, they incline toward an horizontal pofition; but more fo, when the fmall fhoots toward the end are full of flowers and feed-veffels, which weigh down the weak branches from their upright pofition. The branches are covered with a white down like meal, and are clofely garnifhed with very narrow leaves which are convex, and lie over each other in four rows like the fcales of fifh, fo as that the young branches feem as if they were four-cornered.

The

The flowers come out at the extremity of the young branches, from between the leaves on every fide; they are fmall and white, fo make but little appearance, and are fucceeded by fmall feed-veffels, which feem withered and dry. The flowers come out in June and July, and the feeds ripen in the autumn.

This plant may be propagated by cuttings during the fummer months, which fhould be planted in a bed of loamy earth, and clofely covered with a bell or handglafs to exclude the air, fhading them every day from the fun, and refrefhing them now and then with water. With this treatment the cuttings will have taken root in about two months, when they may be taken up, and each planted in a fmall pot filled with foft loamy earth, placing them in the fhade till they have taken new root; then they may be removed into a fheltered fituation, where they may remain till October, when they muft be placed in the green-houfe, for they will not live in the open air through the winter in England; but they require no other treatment, than Myrtles and other hardy green-houfe plants, which is to fcreen them from froft. As this plant retains its verdure all the year, fo it makes a pretty variety in the green-houfe in winter.

It may alfo be propagated by feeds, which if fown in the autumn foon after they are ripe, will more certainly fucceed, than at any other feafon of the year. The feeds fhould be fown in fmall pots filled with light earth, and if they are plunged into an old bed of tanners bark, under a common frame in winter; the plants will come up in the fpring, and fhould then be treated in the fame manner as thofe raifed from cuttings; but the feedling plants will grow more erect, and appear handfomer than thofe propagated by cuttings.

The fecond fort grows naturally in Spain and Portugal; this hath fhrubby ftalks, which rife to a greater height than the former; the branches grow more diffufed, and are covered with a meally down, garnifhed with fhort, thick, fucculent leaves, lying over each other like the fcales of fifh; they are fmooth and green on their outfide, but downy on their inner. The flowers are fmall and white, like thofe of the former, and appear about the fame time. This plant will live abroad in ordinary winters, if it is planted in a dry foil and a warm fituation; but in hard frofts the plants are frequently deftroyed, therefore one or two plants fhould be kept in pots, and fheltered in winter to preferve the fpecies. This may be propagated by cuttings, in the fame way as the former fort. The third fort grows naturally in Spain and Portugal, as alfo at the Cape of Good Hope. This hath a fhrubby ftalk rifing five or fix feet high, fending out many branches which are naked to their ends, where they are garnifhed with oblong leaves ftanding erect, which have hairy points. The flowers are fmall, white, and come out between the leaves at the end of the branches; they appear in June, but are not fucceeded by feeds in England. This may be propagated by cuttings as the two former, and requires the fame treatment.

The fourth fort grows naturally at the Cape of Good Hope; it hath a low fhrubby ftalk, which feldom rifes more than a foot high, dividing into many flender branches, which are fmooth, and fpread out on every fide, garnifhed with very narrow leaves placed oppofite; they are of a dark green, and have the appearance of thofe of the Fir-tree, but are narrower. The flowers come out fingly at the end of the branches, which are larger than thofe of the former, and the upper part of the petals is fpread open almoft flat; they are of a purple colour, and appear about the fame time as the former. This may be propagated by cuttings as the other forts, and the plants muft be treated as the firft fort.

PASSIFLORA. Lin. Gen. Plant. 910. Granadilla. Tourn. Inft. R. H. 240. tab. 124. Paffion-flower; in French, Fleur de la Paffion.

The CHARACTERS are,

The flower has a plain coloured empalement of five leaves, and five half fpear-fhaped petals, which are large, plain and obtufe. *The nectarium hath a triple crown; the outer, which is longer, is faftened to the infide of the petal, but is larger and compreffed above. It has five oval-fhaped ftamina, faftened at their bafe to the column of the ftyle annexed to the germen, fpreading out horizontally, and terminated by oblong, obtufe, incumbent fummits. The ftyle is an erect cylindrical column, upon whofe top fits an oval germen, with three fmaller ftyles which fpread out, crowned by headed ftigmas. The germen afterward becomes an oval flefhy fruit with one cell, fitting at the end of the ftyle, filled with oval feeds, faftened longitudinally to the fkin or fhell.*

This genus of plants is ranged in the fourth fection of Linnæus's twentieth clafs, which includes thofe plants whofe male and female parts are joined together, and their flowers have five ftamina.

The SPECIES are,

1. PASSIFLORA (*Incarnata*) foliis trilobis ferratis. Amœn. Acad. vol. i. p. 230. *Paffion-flower with leaves having three fawed lobes.* Granadilla Hifpanis, flos paffionis Italis. Hern. Mex. 888. *The Granadilla of the Spaniards, and the Paffion-flower of the Italians, commonly called three-leaved Paffion-flower.*

2. PASSIFLORA (*Cærulea*) foliis palmatis integerrimis. Amœn. Acad. vol. i. p. 231. *Paffion-flower with hand-fhaped entire leaves.* Granadilla pentaphyllos, flore cæruleo magno. Boerh. Ind. alt. 2. p. 81. *Five-leaved Paffion-flower, with a large blue flower, or the moft common Paffion-flower.*

3. PASSIFLORA (*Lutea*) foliis trilobis cordatis æqualibus obtufis glabris integerrimis. Amœn. Acad. vol. i. p. 224. *Paffion-flower with heart-fhaped leaves having three equal lobes, which are fmooth, obtufe, and entire.* Granadilla folio tricufpidi, flore parvo flavefcente. Tourn. Inft. R. H. 240. *Paffion-flower with a three-pointed leaf, and a fmall yellowifh flower.*

4. PASSIFLORA (*Glabra*) foliis trilobis integerrimis, lobis fublanceolatis, intermedio productiore. Amœn. Acad. vol. i. p. 229. *Paffion-flower with leaves having three entire lobes, which are fomewhat fpear-fhaped, and have the middle one longer than the others.* Flos paffionis minor, folio in tres lacinias non ferratis profundius divifo, flore luteo. Sloan. Cat. Jam. 104. *Smaller Paffion-flower, with a leaf deeply divided into three fegments which are not fawed, and a yellow flower.*

5. PASSIFLORA (*Suberofa*) foliis trilobis integerrimis glabris, cortice fuberofo. Amœn. Acad. 1. 226. *Paffion-flower with leaves having three entire fmooth lobes, and a Cork-like bark.* Flos paffionis Curaffavicus, folio glabro, trilobato, & angufto, flore flavefcente omnium minimo. Par. Bat. Pluk. Alm. 282. *Paffion-flower of Curaffao, with a fmooth leaf having three lobes, and the leaft yellow flower.*

6. PASSIFLORA (*Oliveforma*) foliis haftatis glabris, petalis florum anguftioribus. *Paffion-flower with halbert-pointed fmooth leaves, and narrow petals to the flowers.* Granadilla folio amplo tricufpidi, fructu olivæforma. Tourn. Inft. R. H. 240. *Paffion-flower with a large three-pointed leaf, and an Olive-fhaped fruit.*

7. PASSIFLORA (*Fœtida*) foliis trilobis cordatis pilofis, involucris multifido-capillaribus. Amœn. Acad. 1. p. 228. *Paffion-flower with leaves having three hairy lobes, and the involucrum of the flower compofed of many pointed hairs.* Granadilla fœtida, folio tricufpidi villofo, flore albo. Tourn. Inft. R. H. 240. *Stinking Paffion-flower with a hairy three-pointed leaf, and a white flower.*

8. PASSIFLORA (*Variegata*) foliis haftatis pilofis amplioribus, involucris multifido capillaribus. *Paffion-flower with the largeft halbert-pointed hairy leaves, and empalements compofed of many-pointed hairs.* Granadilla fœtida, folio tricufpidi villofo, flore purpureo variegato. Tourn. Inft. R. H. 241. *Stinking Paffion-flower with a hairy three-pointed leaf, and a flower variegated with purple.*

9. PASSIFLORA (*Holofericea*) foliis trilobis, bafi utrinque denticulo reflexo. Amœn. Acad. 1. p. 229. *Paffion-flower with leaves having three lobes, a little indented on each fide the bafe, which is reflexed.* Granadilla folio haftato holoferico, petalis candicantibus, fimbriis ex purpureo & luteo variis. Martyn. Dec. 51. *Paffion-flower with a filky halbert-pointed leaf, and flowers having*   *white*

white petals, which are variegated with a purple and yellow colour.

10. PASSIFLORA (*Capfularis*) foliis bilobis cordatis oblongis petiolatis. Lin. Sp. Plant. 957. *Paffion-flower with oblong heart-fhaped leaves, having two lobes ftanding upon foot-ftalks.* Granadilla flore fuaverubente folio bicorni. Tourn. Inft. R. H. 241. *Paffion-flower with a foft red flower, and a leaf ending with two horns.*

11. PASSIFLORA (*Vefpertillio*) foliis bilobis, bafi rotundatis biglandulofis, lobis acutis divaricatis, fubtus punctatis. Amœn. Acad. 1. 223. *Paffion-flower having two lobes, and two glands at the bafe of their leaves, whofe lobes are acute, fpread from each other, and fpotted on their under fide.* Granadilla bicornis, flore candido, filamentis intortis. Hort. Elth. 164. tab. 137. *Paffion-flower with a two-horned leaf, a white flower, and intorted filaments.*

12. PASSIFLORA (*Normalia*) foliis bilobis, bafi emarginatis, lobis linearibus obtufis divaricatis, intermedio obfoleto mucronato. Amœn. Acad. 5. 248. *Paffion-flower with leaves having two obtufe lobes, which are indented at the bafe, and have foot-ftalks.* Granadilla quæ Coanenepilli feu Contrayerva. Hernand. *Paffion-flower, called Coanenepilli or Contrayerva, by Hernandes.*

13. PASSIFLORA (*Bicorna*) foliis bilobis glabris rigidis, bafi indivifis. *Paffion-flower with ftiff fmooth leaves having two lobes, which are undivided at their bafe.* Granadilla folio bicorni, glabro rigido, flore albo. Houft. MSS. *Paffion-flower with a fmooth two-horned leaf, and a white flower.*

14. PASSIFLORA (*Murucuia*) foliis bilobis tranfverfis amplexicaulibus. Amœn. Acad. 1. p. 222. *Paffion-flower with tranfverfe leaves, having two lobes embracing the ftalk.* Murucuia folio lunato. Tourn. Inft. R. H. 251. *Murucuia with a moon-fhaped leaf.*

15. PASSIFLORA (*Maliformis*) foliis indivifis cordato-oblongis integerrimis, petiolis biglandulofis involucris integerrimis. Amœn. Acad. 1. p. 220. *Paffion-flower with undivided, heart-fhaped, oblong, entire leaves, foot-ftalks with two glands, and entire covers to the flowers.* Granadilla latifolia, fructu maliformi. Tourn. Inft. R. H. 241. *Broad-leaved Paffion-flower with an Apple-fhaped fruit, commonly called Granadilla in the Weft-Indies.*

16. PASSIFLORA (*Laurifolia*) foliis indivifis ovatis, integerrimis, petiolis biglandulofis involucris dentatis. Amœn. Acad. 1. p. 220. *Paffion-flower with oval entire leaves, foot-ftalks with two glands, and the covers of the flowers indented.* Granadilla fructu citriformi, foliis oblongis. Tourn. Inft. R. H. 241. *Paffion-flower with a Citron-fhaped fruit, and oblong leaves, commonly called Water Lemon in the Weft-Indies.*

17. PASSIFLORA (*Cupræa*) foliis indivifis ovatis integerrimis, petiolis æqualibus. Amœn. Acad. vol. 1. p. 219. *Paffion-flower with undivided, oval, entire leaves, and equal foot-ftalks.* Granadilla Americana, fructu fubrotundo, corolla floris erecta, petalis amœne fulvis, foliis integris. Martyn. Cent. 1. 37. *American Paffion-flower with a roundifh fruit, an erect corolla to the flower, the petals of a fine copper colour, and entire leaves.*

18. PASSIFLORA (*Serratifolia*) foliis indivifis ferratis. Amœn. Acad. 1. p. 217. *Paffion-flower with undivided fawed leaves.* Granadilla Americana, folio oblongo læviter ferrato, petalis ex viridi rubefcentibus. Mart. Cent. 1. p. 36. *American Paffion-flower, with oblong leaves which are flightly fawed, and petals to the flower of a greenifh red colour.*

19. PASSIFLORA (*Multiflora*) foliis indivifis oblongis integerrimis, floribus confertis. Amœn. Acad. 1. p. 221. *Paffion-flower with undivided, oblong, entire leaves, and flowers growing in clufters.* Clematis Indica, polyanthos odoratiffima. Plum. Pl. Amer. 75. tab. 90. *Indian Climber having many fweet flowers.*

20. PASSIFLORA (*Quadrangularis*) foliis indivifis fubcordatis integerrimis, petiolis fexglandulofis, caule membranaceo tetragono. Lin. Sp. Plant. 1356. *Paffion-flower with heart-fhaped entire leaves, whofe foot-ftalks have fix glands, and a four-cornered membranaceous ftalk.* Paffiflora foliis amplioribus cordatis, petiolis glandulis fex, caule quadrangulo alato. Brown. Jam. 327. *Paffion-*

flower with ample heart-fhaped leaves, whofe foot-ftalk; have fix glands, and a fquare winged ftalk.

The firft fort grows naturally in Virginia and other parts of North America; this was the firft known in Europe of all the fpecies, but was not very common in the Englifh gardens till of late years. The root of this plant is perennial, but the ftalk is annual in North America, dying to the ground every winter, as it alfo does in England, unlefs it is placed in a ftove. The ftalks of this are flender, rifing about four or five feet high, having tendrils or clafpers at each joint, which faften themfelves about whatever plant ftand near them, whereby the ftalk is fupported. At each joint comes out one leaf upon a fhort foot-ftalk; thefe have for the moft part three oblong lobes, which join at their bafe, but the two fide lobes are fometimes divided part of their length into two narrow fegments, fo as to refemble a two-lobed leaf; they are thin, of a light green, and flightly fawed on their edges. The flowers are produced from the joints of the ftalk at the foot-ftalks of the leaves; thefe have long flender foot-ftalks fucceeding each other, as the ftalks advance in height, during the fummer months. The involucrum of the flower is compofed of five oblong blunt-pointed leaves, of a pale green; thefe open and difclofe five more leaves or petals, which are white, having a fringe or circle of rays of a double order round the ftyle, of a purple colour, the lower row being the longeft. In the center of this arifes the pillar-like ftyle, with the roundifh germen at the top, furrounded at the bottom, where it adheres to the ftyle, with five flattifh ftamina which fpread out every way, and fuftain each of them an oblong fummit which hang downward, and on their under fide are covered with a yellow farina. The flowers have an agreeable fcent, but are of fhort duration, opening in the morning, and fade away in the evening, never opening again, but are fucceeded by frefh flowers, which come out at the joints of the ftalk above them. When the flowers fade, the roundifh germen fwells to a fruit as large as a middling Apple, which changes to a pale Orange colour when ripe, inclofing many oblong rough feeds inclofed in a fweetifh pulp. This fort is ufually propagated by feeds which are brought from America, for the feeds do not often ripen in England; though I have fometimes had feveral fruit perfectly ripe on plants, which were plunged in a tan-bed under a deep frame; but thofe plants which are expofed to the open air, do not produce fruit here. The feeds fhould be fown upon a moderate hot-bed, which will bring up the plants much fooner than when they are fown in the open air, fo they will have more time to get ftrength before winter. When the plants are come up two or three inches high, they fhould be carefully taken up, and each planted in a feparate fmall pot filled with good kitchen-garden earth, and plunged into a moderate hot-bed to forward their taking new root; after which they fhould be gradually inured to bear the open air, to which they fhould be expofed in fummer, but in the autumn they muft be placed under a garden-frame to fcreen them from the froft; but they fhould have the free air at all times in mild weather. The fpring following fome of thefe plants may be turned out of the pots, and planted in a warm border, where, if they are covered with tanners bark every winter to keep out the froft, they will live feveral years, their ftalks decaying in the autumn, and new ones arife in the fpring, which in warm feafons will flower very well. If thofe plants which are continued in pots, are plunged into a tan-bed, fome of them may produce fruit; and, if the ftalks of thefe are laid down in the beginning of June, into pots of earth plunged near them, they will take root by the end of Auguft, fo that the plants may be eafily propagated this way.

The fecond fort has not been many years in England, nor is now the moft common. This grows naturally in the Brafils, yet is hardy enough to thrive in the open air here, and is feldom injured except in very fevere winters, which commonly kills the branches to the ground, and fometimes deftroys the roots; this

rifes

rifes in a few years to a great height, if they have proper fupport. I have feen fome of thefe plants, whofe branches were trained up more than forty feet high. The ftalks will grow almoft as large as a man's arm, and are covered with a purplifh bark, but do not become very woody. The fhoots from thefe ftalks are often twelve or fifteen feet long in one fummer; they are very flender, fo muft be fupported, otherwife they will hang to the ground, intermix with each other, and appear very unfightly. Thefe ftee garnifhed at each joint with one hand-fhaped leaf, compofed of five fmooth entire lobes, the middle one, which is the longeft, being almoft four inches long, and one broad in the middle, the other are gradually fhorter, and the two outer lobes are frequently divided on their outer fide into two fmaller lobes or fegments. Their foot-ftalks are near two inches long, and have two fmall leaves or ears embracing the ftalks at their bafe, and from the fame point comes out a long clafper, which twifts round the neighbouring plants, whereby the ftalks are fupported. The flowers come out at the fame joint as the leaves; thefe have foot-ftalks almoft three inches long. The flowers have an outer cover, compofed of three concave oval leaves, of a paler green than the leaves of the plant, which are little more than half the length of the empalement, which is compofed of five oblong blunt leaves, of a very pale green; within thefe are five petals, nearly of the fame fhape and fize with the empalement, ftanding alternately between them. In the center of the flower arifes a thick club-like column about an inch long, on the top of which fits an oval germen, from whofe bafe fpreads out five awlfhaped horizontal ftamina, which are terminated by oblong broad fummits faftened in the middle of the ftamina, hanging downward; thefe may be moved round without feparating from the ftamina, and their under furface is charged with yellow farina; on the fide of the germen arife three flender purplifh ftyles near an inch long, fpreading from each other, terminated by obtufe ftigmas. Round the bottom of the column are two orders of rays; the inner, which is the fhorteft, inclines toward the column; the outer, which is near half the length of the petals, fpread open flat upon them; thefe rays are compofed of a great number of thread-like filaments, of a purple colour at bottom, but are blue on the outfide. The flowers have a faint fcent, and continue but one day; after they fade, the germen on the top of the column fwells to a large oval fruit about the fize and fhape of the Mogul Plum, and when ripe is of the fame pale yellow colour, inclofing a fweetifh difagreeable pulp, in which are lodged oblong feeds. This plant begins to flower early in July, and there is a fucceffion of flowers daily, till the froft in autumn puts a ftop to them.

It may be propagated by feeds, which fhould be fown in the fame manner as thofe of the firft fort, and the plants treated in the fame way till the following fpring, when they fhould be turned out of the pots, and planted againft a good afpected wall, where they may have height for their fhoots to extend, otherwife they will hang about and entangle with each other, fo make but an indifferent appearance; but where buildings are to be covered, this plant is very proper for the purpofe. After they have taken good root in their new quarters, the only care they will require, is to train their fhoots up againft the wall, as they extend in length, to prevent their hanging about, and if the winter proves fevere, the furface of the ground about their roots fhould be covered with mulch to keep the froft from penetrating of the ground; and if the ftalks and branches are covered with mats, Peashaulm, ftraw, or any fuch light covering, it will protect them in winter againft fevere frofts; but this covering muft be taken off in mild weather, otherwife it will caufe the branches to grow mouldy, which will be more injurious to them than the cold. In the fpring the plants fhould be trimmed, when all the fmall weak fhoots fhould be entirely cut off, and the ftrong ones fhortened to about four or five feet long,

which will caufe them to put out ftrong fhoots for flowering the following year.

This plant is alfo propagated by laying down the branches, which in one year will be well rooted; fo may be taken off from the old plants, and tranfplanted, where they are defigned to remain. The cuttings of this will alfo take root, if they are planted in a loamy foil not too ftiff, in the fpring, before they begin to fhoot. If thefe are covered with bell or hand-glaffes to exclude the air, they will fucceed much better than when they are otherwife treated; but when the cuttings put out fhoots, the air fhould be admitted to them, otherwife they will draw up weak and fpoil, and they muft be afterwards treated as the layers. Thofe plants which are propagated by layers or cuttings, do not produce fruit fo plentifully as the feedling plants; and I have found the plants which have been propagated two or three times, either by layers or cuttings, feldom produce fruit, which is common to many other plants.

If in very fevere winters the ftalks of thefe plants are killed to the ground, the roots often put out new ftalks the following fummer, therefore they fhould not be difturbed; and where there is mulch laid on the ground about their roots, there will be little danger of their being killed, although all the ftalks fhould be deftroyed.

There is a variety of this; the lobes of the leaves are much narrower, and are divided almoft to the bottom. The flowers come later in the fummer; the petals of the flowers are narrower, and of a purer white, but I believe it is only a feminal variation of the other, fo not worthy of being enumerated.

The third fort grows naturally in Virginia, and alfo in Jamaica; this hath a perennial creeping root, fending up many weak ftalks about three or four feet high, which are garnifhed with leaves fhaped very like thofe of Ivy, and are almoft as large, but of a pale green and very thin confiftence. The flowers come out from the wings of the ftalk upon flender foot-ftalks an inch and a half long, and at their bafe arife very flender tendrils, which clafp round any neighbouring fupport. The flowers are of a dirty yellow colour, and not larger than a fix-pence when expanded, fo make no great appearance. This may be propagated by its creeping roots, which may be parted in April, and planted where they are to remain. This fort will live in a warm border, if treated in the fame way as is directed for the firft fort. Some of thefe plants lived many years in the Chelfea Garden in a border to a fouth-weft afpect, but in the year 1740 they were killed by the froft.

The fourth fort grows naturally in Jamaica; this hath a perennial root, from which arife feveral flender ftalks four or five feet high, which have joints four or five inches afunder; at each of thefe come out one leaf, a tendril, and a flower. The leaves have three lobes; the middle one is three inches long, and almoft an inch broad in the middle; the two fide lobes are about two inches long, and three quarters of an inch broad, of a light green colour, and thin. The flowers are fmaller than thofe of the laft mentioned, and are of a greenifh colour; thefe are fucceeded by oval fruit, about the fize of fmall Olives, which turn purple when they are ripe.

The fifth fort grows naturally in moft of the Weft-India iflands; this rifes with a weak ftalk to the height of twenty feet. As the ftalks grow old, they have a thick fungous bark like that of the Cork-tree, which cracks and fplits. The fmaller branches are covered with a fmooth bark, and garnifhed with fmooth leaves at each joint, fitting upon very fhort foot-ftalks; thefe have three lobes, the middle one being much longer than thofe on the fides, fo that the whole leaf has the form of the point of thofe halberts ufed by the yeomen of the guards. The flowers are fmall, of a greenifh yellow colour, and are fucceeded by fmall oval fruit of a dark purple colour when ripe.

The fixth fort grows naturally in the Weft-Indies; this hath a perennial root, from which arife feveral flender

flender ftalks, which rife eight or ten feet high, garnifhed with fmooth green leaves ftanding upon flénder foot-ftalks. Thefe are but flightly indented into three lobes, which end in acute points, and are fhaped like the points of halberts, the middle one ftanding obliquely to the foot-ftalk. The flowers come out from the wings of the leaves on very fhort foot-ftalks; they are of a pale yellow. The petals of the flowers are very narrow, and longer than thofe of the two former forts; the fruit is fmaller and of an oval form, changing to a dark purple when ripe.

The feventh fort grows naturally in moft of the iflands in the Weft-Indies, where the inhabitants of the Britifh iflands call it Love in a Mift. The root of this is annual; the ftalks rife five or fix feet high when they are fupported; they are channelled and hairy. The leaves are heart-fhaped, divided into three lobes, the middle lobe being three inches long, and one and a half broad; the two fide lobes are fhort but broad; they are covered with fhort brown hairs. The tendrils come out at the fame place as the leaves, as do alfo the flowers, whofe foot-ftalks are two inches long, hairy, and pretty ftrong. The empalement of the flower is compofed of flender hairy filaments, which are wrought like a net; thefe are longer than the petals of the flower, and turn up round them, fo that the flowers are not very confpicuous at a diftance. Thefe are white, and of fhort duration; their ftructure is the fame with the other forts, and they are fucceeded by roundifh oval fruit about the fize of an ordinary Golden Pippin, of a yellowifh green colour, inclofed with a netted empalement. This plant is propagated by feeds, which fhould be fown upon a hot-bed early in the fpring, and when the plants are fit to remove, they fhould be each tranfplanted into a fmall pot filled with light kitchen-garden earth, and plunged again into a hot-bed, obferving to fhade them from the fun till they have taken new root; after which time they muft be treated in the fame way as other plants from the fame country, fhifting them into larger pots as their roots increafe; and when the plants are too tall to remain under the glaffes of the hot-bed, they fhould be removed into an airy glafs-cafe, where they fhould have the free air admitted to them in warm weather, but fcreened from the cold. In this fituation the plants will flower in July, and their feeds will ripen in the autumn. The whole plant has a difagreeable fcent when touched.

There is a variety of this, if it is not a diftinct fpecies, with hairy leaves not fo broad as thofe of the former. The whole leaf is fhaped more like the point of a halbert, and thofe leaves which grow toward the upper part of the ftalks, have very fmall indentures, fo approach near to fimple leaves without lobes. The flowers are alfo fmaller, but of the fame form, and the roots are of a fhorter duration, fo that I am inclined to believe it is a diftinct fpecies.

The eighth fort has fome appearance of the feventh, fo that many perfons have fuppofed it was only an accidental variety of it, but there can be no doubt of its being a different fpecies. The ftalks of this rife upward of twenty feet high, and will continue two or three years; the leaves are larger, but of the fame fhape, and hairy; the tendrils of this fort are very long, as are alfo the foot-ftalks of the flowers, which are fmooth, not hairy as the former; the empalement of the flowers is netted, but not fo long as in the former fort; the flowers are larger, and the rays are of a light blue colour; the fruit is much lefs and rounder than thofe of the other, and when ripe changes to a deep yellow colour.

The ninth fort was difcovered by the late Dr. Houftoun growing naturally at La Vera Cruz; this a perennial plant. The ftalks rife twenty feet high, dividing into many flender branches, which are covered with a foft hairy down. The leaves are fhaped like the point of a halbert; they are three inches long, and one inch and a half at their bafe, of a light green, foft and filky to the touch, ftanding obliquely to the foot-ftalks. The flowers come out at the wings of the leaves like the other fpecies; thefe are not half fo large as thofe

of the fecond fort, but are of the fame form. The petals are white, and the rays or filaments are purple, with a mixture of yellow. The fruit of this is fmall, roundifh, and yellow when ripe.

The tenth fort grows naturally in Jamaica, from whence the late Dr. Houftoun fent the feeds to England; this is a perennial plant. The ftalks are flender, and rife to twenty feet high when they are fupported, and divide into many weak branches; the leaves, flowers, and tendrils come out at each joint. The leaves are four inches long, and three broad, rounded at their bafe in form of a heart, but end at their points with two horns, which in fome leaves are more acute than in others, feveral of them appearing as if they were cut a little hollow at the top, like the leaves of the Tulip-tree. They have three longitudinal veins, which join at the bafe of the leaf to the foot-ftalk, but the two outer diverge toward the borders of the leaf in the middle, drawing inward again at the top. The leaves are of a deep green on their upper fide, but are pale on their under, and ftand upon fhort foot-ftalks; the foot-ftalks of the flowers are very flender, of a purplifh colour, about an inch and a half long. The flowers are fhaped like thofe of the other fpecies, but when expanded are not more than an inch and a half diameter, of a foft red colour, and little fcent. The fruit is fmall, oval, and when ripe, changes to a purple colour.

The eleventh fort was difcovered by the late Mr. Robert Millar, growing naturally near Carthagena in New Spain. This hath flender ftriated ftalks of a brownifh red colour, dividing into many flender branches, which are garnifhed with leaves fhaped like the wings of a bat when extended; they are about feven inches in length, meafuring from the two extended points, which may rather be termed the breadth, for from the bafe to the top they are not more than two inches and a half. The foot-ftalk is fet half an inch from the bafe of the leaf, from which come out three ribs or veins; two of them extend each way to the two narrow points of the leaf, the other rifes upright to the top, where is the greateft length of the leaf, if it may be fo termed. The figure of this leaf is the moft fingular of any I have yet feen. The flowers come out at the joints of the ftalk like the others, upon fhort flender foot-ftalks; they are about three inches diameter when expanded. The petals and rays are white; the rays are twifted and flender, extending beyond the petals. The fruit of this I have not feen entire.

The twelfth fort was difcovered by the late Dr. Houftoun, growing naturally at La Vera Cruz in New Spain. This hath flender angular ftalks which rife twenty feet high, fending out many branches, which are garnifhed with moon-fhaped leaves, and have two blunt lobes, fpreading afunder each way, fo as to have the appearance of a half moon. The flowers and tendrils come out from the fame joints of the ftalks. The flowers are of a pale colour and fmall, but fhaped like thofe of the other forts; thefe are fucceeded by oval fruit of a purple colour, about the fize of fmall oval Grapes.

The thirteenth fort has fome refemblance of the twelfth, but the ftalks are rounder and become ligneous. The leaves are almoft as ftiff as thofe of the Bay-tree, and are not fo deeply divided as thofe of the former. The flowers ftand upon long foot-ftalks, which are horizontal; they are fmall, white, and fhaped like thofe of the other fort. The fruit is oval, fmall, and of a purple colour, fitting clofe to the petals of the flowers, which are permanent. This was difcovered by the late Dr. Houftoun growing naturally at Carthagena in New Spain.

The fourteenth fort grows naturally in moft of the iflands in the Weft-Indies; this is by Tournefort feparated from this genus, and titled by him Murucuia, which is the Brafilian name for this, and fome of the other fpecies. This hath flender climbing ftalks, which are channelled, putting out tendrils at the joints, which faften themfelves about the neighbouring plants for fupport, and climb to the height of ten or twelve feet; they are garnished with leaves which are cut into two lobes at their base, but at the top are only a little hollowed at a distance from each point, rising again in the middle opposite the foot-stalk. The base of the two lobes spread and meet, so that they appear as if they embraced the stalk; but when they are viewed near, they are found divided to the short crooked foot-stalk, which does scarcely appear. There are two purplish veins arising from the foot-stalk, which extend each way to the points of the lobes. The leaves are of a lucid green on their upper surface, but pale on their under; the tendrils, which come out with the leaves, are very long, tough, and of a purple colour. The flowers are produced toward the end of the branches, coming out by pairs on each side the branches; these have purple foot-stalks an inch and a half long, sustaining one flower at the top, whose empalement is composed of five purple leaves, which form a kind of tube, and within are five very narrow purple petals. The column in the center of the flower is of the same length as the petals, but the stamina are extended an inch above. When the flowers fade, the germen swells to an oval purple fruit, the size of the small red Gooseberry, inclosing a soft pulp, in which are lodged the seeds.

The fifteenth sort grows naturally in the West-Indies, where the inhabitants call it Granadilla; the fruit of this sort is commonly eaten there, being served up to their table in deserts. This hath a thick, climbing, herbaceous, triangular stalk, sending out slender tendrils at each joint, which fasten to the bushes and hedges for support, rising to the height of fifteen or twenty feet, garnished at each joint with one large, oval, heart-shaped leaf, six inches long, and four broad in the middle, indented at the base, where the short foot-stalk is fastened to the branches, round at the top, having an acute point. There are two large stipulæ or ears joined to the stalks, which encompass the foot-stalks of the flowers and leaves, as also the base of the tendril. The leaves are of a lively green and thin texture, having one strong nerve or midrib running longitudinally, from which arise several small veins, which diverge to the sides, and incurve again toward the top. The flowers stand upon pretty long foot-stalks, which have two small glandules in the middle; the cover of the flower is composed of three soft velvety leaves, of a pale red, with some stripes of a lively red colour; the petals of the flower are white, and the rays are blue. These flowers are large, so make a fine appearance during their continuance; but they are like the other species, of short duration, but there is a succession of flowers for some time on the same plants. After the flowers are past, the germen swells to a roundish fruit, the size of a large Apple, of a yellow colour when ripe, having a thicker rind than any of the other sorts, inclosing a sweetish pulp, in which are lodged many oblong flat seeds, of a brownish colour, a little rough to the touch.

The sixteenth sort grows naturally in the islands of the West-Indies; this hath climbing rough stalks, which put out claspers at every joint like the others, which fasten to the neighbouring trees and hedges for support, and rise upward of twenty feet high, sending out many side branches. The leaves are four or five inches long, and two broad, of a pretty thick consistence, and of a bright green on their upper side, but pale on their under. The flowers come out at the joints of the stalks, upon foot-stalks an inch and a half long; the buds of the flowers are as large as pigeons eggs before they begin to expand. The cover of the flower is composed of three large, oval, green leaves, which are indented on their edges, and hollowed like a spoon: within these is the empalement of the flower, which is composed of five oblong leaves, of a pale green on their outside, but whitish within; these are about an inch and a half long, and half an inch broad. The petals of the flower are white, and stand alternately with those of the empalement, but are not more than half their breadth, and are marked

with several small, brownish, red spots. The rays of the flower are of a Violet colour; the column in the center is yellowish, as is also the round germen at the top, but the three styles are of a purple colour. These flowers have an agreeable odour, and when they fade, the germen swells to the size of a pullet's egg, and nearly of the same shape, which turns yellow when ripe. The rind is soft and thick; the pulp has an agreeable acid flavour, which quenches thirst, abates the heat of the stomach, gives an appetite, and recruits the spirits, so is commonly given in fevers. The seeds are heart-shaped and brownish.

The seventeenth sort grows naturally in the Bahama Islands, from whence the late Mr. Catesby sent the seeds to England; this hath slender, climbing, three-cornered stalks, which send out tendrils at each joint, fastening themselves to any neighbouring support. The stalks climb to the height of twelve or fourteen feet, and are garnished with oblong oval leaves about two inches long, and one broad, of a light green, and entire. Their foot-stalks are slender, and an inch long, from which arise three longitudinal veins, one running through the middle of the leaf, the other two diverge to the sides, drawing toward each other again at the point. The flowers come out from the wings of the stalk, upon slender foot-stalks an inch long; the empalement of the flower is composed of five oblong, narrow, purplish leaves, and within are five narrower petals of the same colour, which turn backward after they have been some time expanded. The column in the middle of the flower is very long and slender, supporting a round germen, from whose base spread out five slender stamina, terminated by oblong hanging summits, and from the top of the germen arise three slender styles, which spread asunder, and are crowned by roundish summits. When the flowers fade, the germen swells to an oval fruit about the size of sparrow's egg, which changes to a purple colour when ripe, filled with oblong seeds inclosed in a soft pulp.

The nineteenth sort was discovered by the late Dr. Houstoun at La Vera Cruz in New Spain, where it grows naturally, from whence he sent the seeds in 1731 to England, which succeeded in several gardens. This hath slender climbing stalks, sending out many small branches, which climb to the height of twenty-five or thirty feet, when they meet with neighbouring support, to which they fasten themselves by tendrils. The stalks by age become ligneous toward the bottom; their joints are not far asunder. The leaves stand upon short slender foot-stalks; they are three inches and a half long, and two broad in the middle, rounded at their base, but terminate in a point at the top; they are smooth, entire, and of a lively green colour. The flowers come out from the wings of the leaves, standing upon long foot-stalks; the empalement of the flower is composed of five oblong leaves, green on their outside, but whitish within. The flower has five oblong white petals, situated alternately to the leaves of the empalement, which spread open; the rays are of a bluish purple colour; inclining at bottom to red; the column in the center is short and thick; the germen on the top is oval, and, after the flowers fade, swells to the size of a pullet's egg, and changes to a pale yellow when ripe, having many oblong seeds inclosed in a soft pulp. The flowers of this kind have an agreeable odour, but are of short duration, seldom continuing twenty hours open; but there is a succession of flowers on the plants from June to September, and sometimes the fruit will ripen here.

The twentieth sort has much the appearance of the fifteenth, both in stalk and leaves; but the stalks of this have four angles, whereas those of the fifteenth have but three: the leaves also of that are not hollowed at their base, but those of twentieth sort are almost heart-shaped; the flower of it is much larger, though very like it in colour, and the fruit is near twice as large, and of a very agreeable flavour.

This requires the fame culture as the fifteenth, with which it will produce flowers, and often will ripen its fruit in England. By fome perfons this is confounded with the fifteenth fort, and paffes for the Granadilla.

All thefe perennial forts which are natives of the hot parts of America, require a ftove to preferve them here, without which they will not thrive; for although fome of the forts will live in the open air during the warm months in fummer, yet they make but little progrefs; nor will the plants produce many flowers, unlefs the pots in which they are planted are plunged into the tan-bed of the ftove, and their branches are trained againft an efpalier. The beft way to have them in perfection, is to make a border of earth on the back fide of the tan-bed, which may be feparated by planks to prevent the earth from mixing with the tan; and when the plants are ftrong enough, they fhould be turned out of the pots, and planted in this border; adjoining to which, fhould be a trelliage erected to the top of the ftove; againft this the ftalks of the plants muft be trained, and as they advance they will form a hedge to hide the wall of the ftove, and their leaves continuing green all the year, together with their flowers, which will be plentifully intermixed in fummer, will have a very agreeable effect.

As there will be only a plank partition between the earth and the tan, fo the earth will be kept warm by the tan-bed, which will be of great fervice to the roots of the plants. This border fhould not be lefs than two feet broad and three deep, which is the ufual depth of the pit for tan; fo that where thefe borders are intended, the pits fhould not be lefs than eight feet and a half, or nine feet and a half broad, that the bark-bed, exclufive of the border, may be fix and a half or feven feet wide. If the border is fenced off with ftrong fhip planks, they will laft fome years, efpecially if they are well painted over with a compofition of melted pitch, brick-duft and oil, which will preferve them found a long time; and the earth fhould be taken out carefully from between the roots of the plants, at leaft once a year, putting in frefh: with this management, I have feen thefe plants in great perfection. But where there has not been this conveniency, I have turned the plants out of the pots, and planted them into the tan-bed when it was half rotten, into which they have rooted exceedingly, and have thriven for two or three years as well as could be defired; but when their roots extended to a great diftance in the tan-bed, they have been injured by renewing of the bark; and when it has fermented pretty violently, the roots have been fcalded, and the plants have been killed, fo that the other method is more eligible.

Thefe plants are propagated by feeds, which fhould be fown upon a good hot-bed in the fpring, and when the plants are fit to remove, fhould be each planted in a fmall pot filled with good kitchen-garden earth, and plunged into a bed of tanners bark, obferving to fhade them from the fun till they have taken new root; then they muft be treated like other tender plants from the fame countries. When they are too high to remain under the glaffes of the hot-bed, they fhould be turned out of the pots and planted in the ftove, in the manner before mentioned.

As thefe forts do not often perfect their feeds here, fo they may be propagated by laying down their branches, which, if done in April, they will put out roots by the middle of Auguft, when they may be feparated from the old plants, and either planted in pots to get ftrength, or into the border of the ftove, where they are to remain.

Some of thefe forts may alfo be propagated by cuttings; thefe fhould be planted into pots about the middle or latter end of March, and plunged into a moderate hot-bed, obferving to fcreen them from the fun, and refrefh them with water gently, as often as the earth may require it; and in about two months or ten weeks, they will put out roots, and may then be treated as the feedling plants.

PASSION-FLOWER. See PASSIFLORA.

PASTINACA. Tourn. Inft. R. H. 319. tab. 170. Lin. Gen. Plant. 324. [of Paftus, Lat. fed; becaufe it it a plant whofe root is edible.] Parfnep; in French, Panais.

The CHARACTERS are,

It hath an umbellated flower; the principal umbel is compofed of many fmaller, and thefe are likewife compofed of feveral rays. They have no involucrum, and the empalement is fcarce vifible; the umbel is uniform. The flowers have five fpear-fhaped incurved petals, and five hair-like ftamina, terminated by roundifh fummits. The germen is fituated under the flower, fupporting two reflexed ftyles, crowned by obtufe ftigmas. The germen afterward becomes an elliptical, plain, compreffed fruit, dividing into two parts, having two bordered elliptical feeds.

This genus of plants is ranged in the fecond fection of Linnæus's fifth clafs, which contains thofe plants whofe flowers have five ftamina and two ftyles.

The SPECIES are,

1. PASTINACA (*Sylveftris*) foliis fimpliciter pinnatis hirfutis. *Parfnep with fingle, winged, hairy leaves.* Paftinaca fylveftris latifolia. C. B. P. 155. *Broad-leaved Wild Parfnep.*

2. PASTINACA (*Sativa*) foliis fimpliciter pinnatis glabris. *Parfnep with fingle winged fmooth leaves.* Paftinaca fativa, latifolia. C. B. P. 155. *Broad-leaved Garden Parfnep.*

3. PASTINACA (*Opopanax*) foliis decompofitis pinnatis. Hort. Cliff. 105. *Parfnep with decompounded winged leaves.* Paftinaca fylveftris altiffima. Tourn. Inft. 319. *Talleft wild Parfnep, by Cafpar Bauhin titled, Panax Coftinum.* Pin. 156.

The firft fort grows naturally on the fide of banks, and on dry land, in many parts of England. This is a biennial plant, the firft year fhooting out leaves which fpread on the furface of the ground; thefe are fingly winged, and the lobes are irregularly cut; the leaves are hairy. The following year the ftalks rife four or five feet high, which are channelled, hairy, and garnifhed with winged leaves like thofe at the bottom, but fmaller; the ftalk branches out toward the top, each branch being terminated by a large umbel of yellow flowers; thefe are fucceeded by compreffed fruit, having two flat bordered feeds. The plant flowers in June, and the feeds ripen in Auguft.

The root and feed of this fort is fometimes ufed in medicine, but it is feldom cultivated in gardens, the markets being fupplied from the fields; yet the druggifts commonly fell the feeds of the garden kind for it, which they may purchafe at an eafy price when it is too old to grow, but then the feeds can have no virtue left.

The fecond fort hath fmooth leaves, of a light or yellowifh green colour, in which this differs from the former; the ftalks alfo rife higher, and are deeper channelled; the foot-ftalks of the umbels are much longer, and the flowers are of a deeper yellow colour. Thefe two forts have been thought only varieties, the Garden Parfnep they have fuppofed to differ from the wild only by culture; but I have cultivated both many years, and have never found that either of the forts have varied; the feeds of each having conftantly produced the fame fort as they were taken from, fo that I am certain they are diftinct fpecies.

This fort is cultivated in kitchen-gardens, the roots of which are large, fweet, and accounted very nourifhing. They are propagated by feeds, which fhould be fown in February or March, in a rich mellow foil, which muft be well dug, that their roots may run downward, the greateft excellency being the length and bignefs of the roots. Thefe may be fown alone, or with Carrots, as is practifed by the kitchen-gardeners near London; fome of whom alfo mix Leeks, Onions, and Lettuce, with their Parfneps; but this I think very wrong, for it is not poffible, that fo many different forts can thrive well together, except they are allowed a confiderable diftance; and if fo, it will be equally the fame to fow the different forts feparate. However, Carrots and Parfneps may be fown together very well, efpecially where the Carrots are defigned to be drawn off very young ; becaufe the Parfneps generally fpread moft towards the latter end of the fummer, which is after the Carrots are gone, fo that there may be a double crop upon the fame ground.

When the plants are come up, you fhould hoe them out, leaving them about ten inches or a foot afunder ; obferving at the fame time to cut up all the weeds, which, if permitted to grow, would foon overbear the plants and choke them. This muft be repeated three or four times in the fpring, according as you find the weeds grow ; but in the latter part of fummer, when the plants are fo ftrong as to cover the ground, they will prevent the growth of weeds, fo that after that feafon they will require no farther care.

When the leaves begin to decay, the roots may be dug up for ufe, before which time they are feldom well tafted ; nor are they good for much in the fpring, after they are fhot out again ; fo that thofe who would preferve thefe roots for fpring ufe, fhould dig them up in the beginning of February, and bury them in fand, in a dry place, where they will remain good until the middle of April, or later.

If you intend to fave the feeds of this plant, you fhould make choice of fome of the longeft, ftraiteft, and largeft roots, which fhould be planted about two feet afunder, in fome place where they may be defended from the ftrong fouth and weft winds ; for the ftems of thefe plants commonly grow to a great height, and are very fubject to be broken by ftrong winds, if expofed thereto ; they fhould be conftantly kept clear from weeds, and if the feafon fhould prove very dry, if you give them fome water twice a week, it will caufe them to produce a greater quantity of feeds, which will be much ftronger than if they were wholly neglected. Toward the latter end of Auguft or the beginning of September, the feeds will be ripe ; at which time you fhould carefully cut off the umbels, and fpread them upon a coarfe cloth for two or three days to dry ; after which, the feeds fhould be beaten off, and put up for ufe ; but you muft never truft to thefe feeds after they are a year old, for they will feldom grow beyond that age.

The leaves of the Garden Parfnep are dangerous to handle, efpecially in a morning, while the dew remains upon them ; at which time, if they are handled by perfons who have a foft fkin, it will raife it in blifters. I have known fome gardeners, when they have been drawing up Carrots from among Parfneps in a morning, when their leaves were wet with dew, they have drawn the fleeves of their fhirts up to their fhoulders, to prevent their being wet ; by doing of which they have had their arms, fo far as they were bare, covered over with large blifters ; and thefe were full of a fcalding liquor, which has proved very troublefome for feveral days.

The third fort rifes with a green rough ftalk feven or eight feet high, garnifhed with large, decompounded, winged leaves, which are very rough to the touch, and of a dark green colour ; the juice is very yellow, which flows out where either the leaf or ftalk is broken ; the ftalks are divided upward into many horizontal branches, each being terminated by a large umbel of yellow flowers. Thefe appear in July, and are fucceeded by plain feeds which are bordered, and a little convex in the middle, which ripen in the autumn. The Opapanax of the fhops is thought to be the concrete juice of this plant.

PASTURE.

Pafture ground is of two forts : the one is low meadow land, which is often overflowed, and the other is upland, which lies high and dry. The firft of thefe will produce a much greater quantity of hay than the latter, and will not require manuring or dreffing fo often ; but then the hay produced on the upland is much preferable to the other, as is alfo the meat which is fed in the upland more valued than that which is fatted in rich meadows ; though the latter will make the fatter and larger cattle, as is feen by thofe which are brought from the low rich lands in Lincolnfhire. But where people are nice in their meat, they

will give a much larger price for fuch as hath been fed on the downs, or in fhort upland Pafture, than for the other, which is much larger. Befides this, dry Paftures have an advantage over the meadows, that they may be fed all the winter, and are not fo fubject to poach in wet weather ; nor will there be fo many bad weeds produced, which are great advantages, and do, in a great meafure, recompenfe for the fmallnefs of the crop.

I have already mentioned the advantages of meadow land, or fuch as is capable of being overflowed with water, and given directions for draining and improving low Pafture land, under the article of LAND ; therefore fhall not repeat what is there faid, but I fhall juft mention fome method for improving of upland Pafture.

The firft improvement of upland Pafture is, by fencing it, and dividing it into fmall fields of four, five, fix, eight, or ten acres each, planting timber trees in the hedge rows, which will fcreen the Grafs from the drying pinching winds of March; which prevents the Grafs from growing in large open lands ; fo that if April proves a cold dry month, the land produces very little hay ; whereas in the fheltered fields the Grafs will begin to grow early in March, and will foon after cover the ground, and prevent the fun from parching the roots of the Grafs, whereby it will keep growing, fo as to afford a tolerable crop, if the fpring fhould prove dry. But in fencing of land, it muft be obferved (as was before directed) not to make the inclofures too fmall, efpecially where the hedge rows are planted with trees ; becaufe when the trees are advanced to a confiderable height, they will fpread over the land ; and, where they are clofe, will render the Grafs four ; fo that inftead of being an advantage, it will greatly injure the Pafture.

The next improvement of upland Paftures is, to make the turf good, where, either from the badnefs of the foil, or want of proper care, the Grafs hath been deftroyed by Rufhes, bufhes, or mole-hills. Where the furface of the land is clayey and cold, it may be improved by paring it off, and burning it in the manner before directed under the article of LAND ; but if it is a hot fandy land, then chalk, lime, marle, or clay, are very proper manures to lay upon it ; but this fhould be laid in pretty good quantities, otherwife it will be of little fervice to the land.

If the ground is over-run with bufhes or Rufhes, it will be of great advantage to the land, to grub them up toward the latter part of the fummer, and after they are dried to burn them, and fpread the afhes over the ground juft before the autumnal rains ; at which time the furface of the land fhould be levelled, and fown with Grafs-feed, which, if done early in the autumn, will come up in a fhort time, and make good Grafs the following fpring. So alfo, where the land is full of mole-hills, thefe fhould be pared off, and either burnt for the afhes, or fpread immediately on the ground, when they are pared off, obferving to fow the bare patches with Grafs-feed, juft as the autumnal rains begin.

There are fome Pafture lands which are full of ant-hills, which are not only difagreeable to the fight, but where they are in any quantity, the Grafs cannot be mowed; therefore the turf which grows over them fhould be divided with an inftrument into three parts, and pared off each way ; then the middle or core of the hills fhould be dug out and fpread over the ground, leaving the holes open all the winter to deftroy the ants, and in the fpring the turf may be laid down again, and after the roots of the Grafs are fettled again in the ground, it fhould be rolled to fettle the furface, and make it even. If this is properly managed, it will be a great improvement to fuch land.

Where the land has been thus managed, it will be of great fervice to roll the turf in the months of February and March, with a heavy wood roller, always obferving to do it in moift weather, that the roll may make an impreffion : this will render the furface level, and make it much eafier to mow the Grafs, than

when

when the ground lies in hills; and will also cause the turf to thicken, so as to have what the people usually term a good bottom. The Grass likewise will be the sweeter for this husbandry, and it will be a great help to destroy bad weeds.

Another improvement of upland Pastures is the feeding them every other year; for where this is not practised, the land must be manured at least every third year; and where a farmer hath much arable land in his possession, he will not care to part with his manure to the Pasture. Therefore every farmer should endeavour to proportion his Pasture to his arable land, especially where manure is scarce, otherways he will soon find 'his error; for the Pasture is the foundation of all the profit, which may arise from the arable land. Whenever the upland Pastures are mended by manure, there should be a regard had to the nature of the soil, and a proper sort of manure applied: as for instance, all hot sandy lands should have a cool manure; neats dung and swines dung are very proper for such lands, as also marle and clay; but for cold lands, horse dung, ashes, or sand, and other warm manures, are proper. And when these are applied, it should be done in autumn, before the rains have soaked the ground, and rendered it too soft to cart on; and it should be carefully spread, breaking all the clods as small as possible, and early in the spring harrowed with bushes, to let it down to the roots of the Grass. When the manure is laid on at this season, the rains in winter will wash down the salts, so that the following spring the Grass will receive the advantage of it.

There should also be great care had to the destroying of weeds in the Pasture, every spring and autumn; for where this is not practised, the weeds will ripen their seeds, which will spread over the ground, and thereby fill it with such a crop of weeds as will soon over-bear the Grass, and render it very weak, if not destroy it; and it will be very difficult to root them out, after they have gotten such possession; especially Ragwort, Hawkweed, Dandelion, and such other weeds as have down adhering to their seeds.

These upland Pastures seldom degenerate the Grass which is sown on them, if the land is tolerably good; whereas the low meadows, which are overflowed in winter, in a few years turn to a harsh rushy Grass, but the upland will continue a fine sweet Grass for many years without renewing.

There is no part of husbandry, of which the farmers are in general more ignorant, than that of the Pasture; most of them suppose, that when the old Pasture is ploughed up, it can never be brought to have a good sward again; so their common method of managing their land after ploughing, and getting two or three crops of Corn is, to sow with their crop of Barley, some Grass-seeds, as they call them; that is, either the red Clover, which they intend to stand two years after the Corn is taken off the ground, or Rye-grass mixed with Trefoil; but as all these are at most but biennial plants, whose roots decay soon after their seeds are perfected, so the ground having no crop upon it, is again ploughed for Corn; and this is the constant round which the lands are employed in, by the better sort of farmers; for I never have met with one of them, who had the least notion of laying down their land to Grass for any longer continuance; therefore the seeds which they usually sow, are the best adapted for this purpose.

But whatever may have been the practice of these people, I hope to prove, that it is possible to lay down land, which has been in tillage, with Grass, in such manner as that the sward shall be as good, if not better, than any natural Grass, and of as long duration. But this is never to be expected, in the common method of sowing a crop of Corn with the Grass-seeds; for wherever this hath been practised, if the Corn has succeeded well, the Grass has been very poor and weak; so that if the land has not been very good, the Grass has scarcely been worth standing; for the following year it has produced but little hay, and

the year after the crop is worth little, either to mow or feed. Nor can it be expected it should be otherwise, for the ground cannot nourish two crops; and if there were no deficiency in the land, yet the Corn being the first, and most vigorous of growth, will keep the Grass from making any considerable progress; so that the plants will be extremely weak and but very thin, many of them which came up in the spring being destroyed by the Corn; for wherever there are roots of Corn, it cannot be expected there should be any Grass. Therefore the Grass must be thin, and, if the land is not in good heart to supply the Grass with nourishment, that the roots may branch out after the Corn is gone, there cannot be any considerable crop of Clover; and as these roots are biennial, many of the strongest plants will perish soon after they are cut; and the weak plants, which had made but little progress before, will be the principal part of the crop for the succeeding year, which is many times not worth standing.

Therefore, when ground is laid down for Grass, there should be no crop of any kind sown with the seeds; and the land should be well ploughed, and cleaned from weeds; otherwise the weeds will come up the first, and grow so strong, as to overbear the Grass, and if they are not pulled up, will entirely spoil it. The best season to sow the Grass seeds upon dry land is about the middle of August, if there is an appearance of rain; for the ground being then warm, if there happen some good showers of rain after the seed is sown, the Grass will soon make its appearance, and get sufficient rooting in the ground before winter, so will not be in danger of having the roots turned out of the ground by the frost, especially if the ground is well rolled before the frost comes on, which will press it down, and fix the earth close to the roots. Where this hath not been practised, the frost has often loosened the ground so much, as to let in the air to the roots of the Grass, and done it great damage; and this has been brought as an objection to the autumnal sowing of Grass; but it will be found to have no weight, if the above direction is practised; nor is there any hazard in sowing the Grass at this season, but that of dry weather after the seeds are sown; for if the Grass comes up well, and the ground is well rolled in the middle or end of October, and repeated the beginning of March, the sward will be closely joined at bottom, and a good crop of hay may be expected the same summer. In very open, exposed, cold lands, it is proper to sow the seeds earlier than is here mentioned, that the Grass may have time to get good rooting, before the cold season comes on to stop its growth; for in such situations, vegetation is over early in the autumn, so the Grass being weak, may be destroyed by frost: but if the seeds are sown in the beginning of August, and a few showers follow soon after to bring up the Grass, it will succeed much better than any which is sown in the spring, as I have several years experienced, on some places as much exposed as most in England. But where the ground cannot be prepared for sowing at that season, it may be performed the middle or latter end of March, according to the season's being early or late; for in backward springs and in cold land, I have often sowed the Grass in the middle of April with success; but there is danger in sowing late of dry weather, and especially if the land is light and dry; for I have seen many times the whole surface of the ground removed by strong winds at that season, so that the seeds have been driven in heaps to one side of the field. Therefore whenever the seeds are sown late in the spring, it will be proper to roll the ground well soon after the seeds are sown, to settle the surface, and prevent its being removed.

The sorts of seeds which are the best for this purpose, are the best sort of upland hay-seeds, taken from the cleanest Pastures, where there are no bad weeds; if this seed is sifted to clean it from rubbish, three, or at most four bushels, will be sufficient to sow an acre of land. The other sort is the Trifolium *pratense* pratenfe album, which is commonly known by the names of White Dutch Clover, or White Honey-fuckle Grafs. Eight pounds of this feed will be enough for one acre of land. The Grafs-feed fhould be fown firft, and then the Dutch Clover-feed may be afterward fown ; but they fhould not be mixed together, becaufe the Clover-feeds being the heavieft, will fall to the bottom, and confequently the ground will be unequally fown with them.

After the feeds are fown, the ground fhould be lightly harrowed to bury the feeds ; but this fhould be performed with a fhort-toothed harrow, otherwife the feeds will be buried too deep. Two or three days after fowing, if the furface of the ground is dry, it fhould be rolled with a Barley roller to break the clods and fmooth the ground, which will fettle it, and prevent the feeds from being removed by the wind. When the feeds are come up, if the land fhould produce many weeds, thefe fhould be drawn out before they grow fo tall as to overbear the Grafs ; for where this has been neglected, the weeds have taken fuch poffeffion of the ground, as to keep down the Grafs and ftarve it ; and when thefe weeds have been fuffered to remain until they have fhed their feeds, the land has been fo plentifully ftocked with them, as entirely to deftroy the Grafs ; therefore it is one. of the principal parts of hufbandry, never to fuffer weeds to grow on the land.

If the ground is rolled two or three times at proper diftances after the Grafs is up, it will prefs down the Grafs, and caufe it to make a thicker bottom ; for as the Dutch Clover will put out roots from every joint of the branches which are near the ground, fo by preffing down the ftalks, the roots will mat fo clofely together, as to form a fward fo thick as to cover the whole furface of the ground, and form a green carpet, which will better refift the drought. For if we do but examine the common Paftures in fummer (in moft of which there are patches of this White Honey-fuckle Grafs growing naturally) we fhall find thefe patches to be the only verdure remaining in the fields. And this the farmers in general acknowledge, is the fweeteft feed for all forts of cattle, yet never had any notion of propagating it by feeds till of late years. Nor has this been long practifed in England ; for till within a few years, that fome curious perfons imported the feed from Brabant, where it had been long cultivated, there was not any of the feeds faved in England ; though now there are feveral perfons who fave the feeds here, which fucceed full as well as any of the foreign feeds which are imported.

As this White Clover is an abiding plant, fo it is certainly the very beft fort to fow where Paftures are laid down to remain ; for as the hay-feeds which are taken from the beft Paftures, will be compofed of various forts of Grafs, fome of which may be but annual and others biennial, fo when thofe go off, there will be many and large patches of ground left bare and naked, if there is not a fufficient quantity of the White Clover to fpread over and cover the land. Therefore a good fward can never be expected where this is not fown ; for in moft of the natural Paftures, we find this plant makes no fmall fhare of the fward ; and it is equally good for wet and dry land, growing naturally upon gravel and clay in moft parts of England ; which is a plain indication how eafily this plant may be cultivated to great advantage, in moft forts of land throughout th's kingdom.

Therefore the true caufe why the land which is in tillage is not brought to a good turf again, in the ufual method of hufbandry is, from the farmers not diftinguifhing which Graffes are annual, from thofe which are perennial ; for if annual or biennial Graffes are fown, thefe will of courfe foon decay ; fo that unlefs where fome of their feeds may have ripened and fallen, nothing can be expected on the land but what will naturally come up. Therefore this, together with the covetous method of laying down the ground with a crop of Corn, has occafioned the general failure of increafing the Pafture in many parts of England,

where it is now much more valuable than any arable land.

After the ground has been fown in the manner before directed, and brought to a good fward, the way to preferve it good is, by conftantly rolling the ground with a heavy roller, every fpring and autumn, as hath been before directed. This piece of hufbandry is rarely practifed by farmers, but thofe who do, find their account in it, for it is of great benefit to the Grafs. Another thing fhould alfo be carefully performed, which is, to cut up Docks, Dandelion, Knapweed, and all fuch bad weeds, by their roots, every fpring and autumn ; this will increafe the quantity of good Grafs, and preferve the Paftures in beauty. Dreffing of thefe Paftures every third year, is alfo a good piece of hufbandry, for otherwife it cannot be expected the ground fhould continue to produce good crops. Befides this, it will be neceffary to change the feafons of mowing, and not to mow the fame ground every year, but to mow one feafon, and feed the next ; for where the ground is every year mown, it muft be conftantly dreffed, as moft of the Grafs grounds near London, otherwife the ground will be foon exhaufted.

Of late years there has been an emulation, efpecially among gentlemen, to improve their Paftures, by fowing feveral forts of Grafs-feeds ; and there have been fome perfons of little fkill in thefe matters, who have impofed on many ignorant people, by felling them feeds of fome foreign Grafs, recommending them for fome particular quality, but when tried have proved of little worth, whereby they have loft a feafon or two, and have had their work to begin again. Therefore I would advife every perfon, not to truft too much upon the faith of fuch practitioners, who, upon flight experiments, have ventured to recommend without judgment ; for of all the forts of Grafs-feeds which have been brought from America (of which I have, at various times, fown more than a hundred different fpecies) I have found none equal to the common Poa Grafs, which grows naturally in England, either for duration or verdure ; therefore that, and about fix or feven other forts, are the beft worth cultivating ; but the trouble of collecting thefe in quantity is fo great, as to deter moft people from attempting it ; and in the purchafing of hay-feeds, there is generally more feeds of weeds than Grafs, which will fill the ground ; therefore for fome years paft, I have recommended and fown only the White Dutch Clover-feeds, and have waited for the natural Grafs coming up amongft it, and have generally fucceeded better this way than by fowing hay-feed with it ; for if the Pafture is duly weeded, rolled, and dreffed, all bad weeds may be deftroyed, and a fine durable turf obtained : whereas the Burnet, and many other plants, which have been extolled as a good winter pabulum, are of fhort duration, fo very improper for improving land ; nor are there two better plants yet known for the purpofe of fodder, than the Lucern 'and Saint-foin ; for where thefe are properly fown upon right foils and duly cultivated, they will produce a much greater quantity of food, than can be procured from the fame quantity of land, fown with any other abiding plant : therefore I wifh thofe who are curious to have much fodder for their cattle, to apply themfelves to the culture of thefe, and not engage in uncertain experiments.

PAVIA. Boerh. Ind. alt. 2. p. 260. Efculus. Lin. Gen. Plant. 420. The fcarlet, flowering, Horfe Cheftnut.

The CHARACTERS are,

The flower has a fmall bellied empalement of one leaf, indented in five parts at the top. The flower has five roundifh petals, waved and plaited on their borders, and narrow at their bafe, where they are inferted in the empalement. It hath eight ftamina which are declined, and as long as the petals, terminated by rifing fummits ; and a roundifh germen fitting upon an awl-fhaped ftyle, crowned by an acuminated ftigma. The germen afterward becomes an oval, Pear-fhaped, leathery capfule with three cells,

PAV

in which is sometimes one, and at others two, almost globular seeds.

This genus of plants should be ranged in the first section of Linnæus's eighth class, which includes those plants whose flowers have eight stamina and one style; but he has joined this to the Horse Chestnut, under the title Esculus, and places it in his seventh class; but as the flowers of this have eight stamina, and those of the Horse Chestnut but seven; and the capsule of this is smooth, and that of the Horse Chestnut prickly, so they may be very well separated.

There is but one Species of this genus, viz.

Pavia (*Octandria.*) Boerh. Ind. alt. 2. p. 260. *The scarlet Horse Chestnut.* Dr. Linnæus titles it, Esculus floribus octandris. Sp. Plant. 344. *Esculus with flowers having eight stamina.*

This plant grows naturally in Carolina and the Brazils; from the first the seeds were brought to England, where the plants have been of late years much cultivated in the gardens. In Carolina it is but of humble growth, seldom rising more than eight or ten feet high; the stalk is pretty thick and woody, sending out several branches, which spread out on every side, which are garnished with hand-shaped leaves, composed of five or six spear-shaped lobes, which unite at their base where they join the foot-stalk; they are of a light green, having a rough surface, and are sawed on their edges; these have long foot-stalks, and stand opposite on the branches. The flowers are produced in loose spikes at the end of the branches, standing upon long naked foot-stalks, which sustain five or six tubulous flowers spread open at the top, where the petals are irregular in size and length, having an appearance of a lip flower; they are of a bright red colour, and have eight stamina the length of the petals. When the flowers fade, the germen swells to a Pear-shaped fruit, with a thick russet cover having three cells, one of which, and sometimes two, are pregnant with globular seeds. It flowers in July, and the seeds sometimes ripen here in autumn. It may be propagated by sowing the seeds in the spring, upon a moderate hot-bed covered with light sandy earth; and when the plants come up, they should be carefully cleared from weeds, but they must not be transplanted until the year following. But as these seedling plants are tender while they are young, so they should be covered with mats the following winter; and this should be carefully performed in autumn, when the early frosts begin; for as the tops of these young plants are very tender, so a small frost will pinch them; and when the tops are killed, they generally decay to the ground; and when this happens, they seldom make good plants after. Therefore this should be constantly observed for two or three years at least, by which time the plants will have gotten strength enough to resist the frost, when they should be removed just before they begin to shoot, and placed either in a nursery to be trained up, or otherwise where they are to remain; observing, if the season proves dry, to water them until they have taken root, as also to lay some mulch upon the surface of the ground, to prevent the sun and wind from drying it too fast; and as the plants advance, the lateral branches should be pruned off, in order to reduce them to regular stems.

You must also observe to dig the ground about their roots every spring, that it may be loose, to admit the fibres of the roots, which, while young, are too tender to penetrate the ground if it be very hard.

With this management the plants will greatly advance, and in four or five years will produce flowers and often fruits, which in warm seasons ripen enough to grow, so that the plants may be multiplied therefrom very fast.

This tree may also be propagated by budding or grafting it upon the common Horse Chestnut, which is the common method practised by the nurserymen; but the trees thus raised, seldom make a good appearance long, for the common Horse Chestnut will be more than twice the size of the other, and fre-

PAU

quently put out shoots below the graft, and sometimes the grafts are blown out of the stocks, after ten years growth; but these stocks render the trees hardy, and of a larger growth.

PAULLINIA. Lin. Gen. Plant. 446. Serjana. Plum. Nov. Gen. 34. tab. 35. Cururu. Plum. Nov. Gen. 34. tab. 35.

The Characters are,

The flower has a spreading permanent empalement, composed of four small oval leaves. It hath four oblong oval petals twice the size of the empalement, and eight short stamina, terminated by small summits, with a turbinated germen, having three obtuse corners, supporting three short slender styles, crowned by spreading stigmas. The germen afterward turns to a large three-cornered capsule with three cells, each containing one almost oval seed. The capsule of Plumier's Serjana has the seeds fastened to the base, and that of Cururu has the seeds growing to the top. This genus of plants is ranged in the third section of Linnæus's eighth class, which includes those plants whose flowers have eight stamina and three styles.

The Species are,

1. Paullinia (*Serjana*) foliis ternatis, petiolis teretiusculis, foliolis ovato-oblongis. Lin. Sp. Plant. 365. *Three-leaved Paullinia with taper foot-stalks, and oblong oval lobes to the leaves.* Serjana scandens, triphylla & racemosa. Plum. Nov. Gen. 34. *Climbing branching Serjana with three leaves.*

2. Paullinia (*Mexicana*) foliis biternatis, petiolis marginatis, foliis ovatis integris. Lin. Sp. Plant. 366. *Paullinia with nine lobes in each leaf, bordered foot-stalks, having oval entire lobes.* Serjana scandens enneaphylla & racemosa. Plum. Nov. Gen. 34. *Climbing branching Serjana with nine leaves.*

3. Paullinia (*Cururu*) foliis ternatis, foliolis cuneiformibus, obtusis subdentatis. Lin. Sp. Plant. 365. *Three-leaved Paullinia with trifoliate leaves having wedge-shaped lobes, which are obtuse and somewhat indented.* Cururu scandens triphylla. Plum. Nov. Gen. 34. *Climbing three-leaved Cururu.*

4. Paullinia (*Curassavica*) foliis biternatis, foliolis ovatis. Lin. Sp. Plant. 366. *Paullinia with double trifoliate leaves, having oval sinnated lobes.* Cururu scandens enneaphylla, fructu racemoso rubro. Plum. Nov. Gen. 34. *Climbing nine-leaved Cururu, with a red branching fruit.*

5. Paullinia (*Pinnata*) foliis pinnatis, foliolis incisis, petiolis marginatis. Hort. Cliff. 52. *Paullinia with winged leaves whose lobes are cut, and bordered foot-stalks.* Cururu scandens pentaphylla. Plum. Nov. Gen. 37. *Climbing five-leaved Cururu.*

6. Paullinia (*Tomentosa*) foliis pinnatis tomentosis, foliolis ovatis incisis, petiolis marginatis. *Paullinia with winged woolly leaves whose lobes are oval, cut on their edges, and bordered foot-stalks.* Cururu scandens, pentaphylla & villosa, fructu racemoso rubro. Houst. MSS. *Climbing Cururu with five leaves which are hairy, and a red fruit growing in long bunches.*

These plants all grow naturally in the West-Indies, where there are several other species which are not here enumerated. They have climbing stalks with tendrils at each joint, by which they fasten themselves to the neighbouring trees, and rise to the height of thirty or forty feet, garnished at each joint with one leaf, which in some species is composed of three lobes like Trefoil, in others of five lobes; some have nine, and others have many lobes. These are in some species entire, in others they are indented at the point, and some are cut on their edges; in some species their surface is smooth, in others they are woolly. The flowers come out in long bunches like those of Currants; they are small and white, so make no figure; these are succeeded by three-cornered capsules having three cells, which in the Cururu of Plumier, contain roundish seeds; but those of the Serjana have winged seeds like those of the Maple reversed, being fastened at the extremity of the wing to the capsule, the seed hanging downward.

As these plants are so tender as not to live through the winter in England, unless they are placed in a warm stove, ftove, and requiring a large fhare of room, they are feldom propagated in Europe, unlefs in botanic gardens for the fake of variety, for their flowers have very little beauty to recommend them.

They are propagated by feeds, which muft be obtained from the countries where they naturally grow, for they do not produce feeds in England. Thefe fhould be fown in fmall pots, filled with light earth, as foon as they arrive, and the pots fhould be plunged into a moderate hot-bed of tanners bark. If thefe feeds arrive in the autumn, the pots fhould be plunged into the bark-bed in the ftove, and then there will be a probability of the plants coming up the following fpring ; but thofe feeds which do not arrive here till fpring, will not come up the fame year, fo the pots in which they are fown, fhould be plunged into a moderate hot-bed under a frame, where they may be continued all the fummer, but in the autumn they fhould be removed into the ftove, where they fhould remain during the winter, and as the earth in the pots will be dry, fo they fhould be now and then watered, but it fhould be given fparingly. The following fpring the pots fhould be removed out of the ftove and plunged into a new hot-bed under a frame, which will bring up the plants in about fix weeks if the feeds are good. When the plants are fit to remove, they fhould be each planted in a fmall pot filled with light earth, and plunged into a hot-bed of tanners bark, obferving to fhade them every day from the fun till they have taken new root, after which they fhould have free air admitted to them daily, in proportion to the warmth of the feafon. In the autumn they muft be removed into the bark-ftove, where they fhould conftantly remain, and muft be treated in the fame way as other tender plants.

PEACH. See PERSICA.

PEAR. See PYRUS.

PEAS. See PISUM.

PEAS EVERLASTING. See LATHYRUS.

PEDICLE is that part of a ftalk which immediately fuftains the leaf, a flower, or a fruit, and is commonly called a foot-ftalk.

PEDICULARIS, Rattle, Cockfcomb, or Loufewort.

There are four different kinds of this plant, which grow wild in paftures in feveral parts of England, and in fome low meadows are very troublefome to the paftures, efpecially one fort with yellow flowers, which rifes to be a foot high, or more, and is often in fuch plenty, as to be the moft predominant plant ; but this is very bad food for cattle, and when it is mowed with the Grafs for hay, renders it of little value. The feeds of this plant are generally ripe by the time the Grafs is mowed, fo that whenever perfons take Grafs-feed for fowing, they fhould be very careful that none of this feed is mixed with it. As thefe plants are never cultivated, I fhall not trouble the reader with their feveral varieties.

PEGANUM. Lin. Gen. Plant. 530. Harmala. Tourn. Inft. R. H. 257. tab. 133. Wild Affyrian Rue.

The CHARACTERS are,

The flower has a permanent empalement, compofed of five narrow erect leaves the length of the petal. It has five oblong oval petals which fpread open, and fifteen awlfhaped ftamina about half the length of the petals, whofe bafes fpread into a nectarium under the germen, and are terminated by erect oblong fummits. It has a three-cornered roundifh germen, elevated at the bafe of the flower, with a three-cornered flender ftyle the length of the fummits, and three ftigmas which are longer than the ftyle. The germen afterward becomes a roundifh three-cornered capfule, having three cells, filled with oval acute-pointed feeds.

This genus of plants is ranged in the firft fection of Linnæus's eleventh clafs, which includes thofe plants whofe flowers have from eleven to nineteen ftamina, and one ftyle.

We have but one SPECIES in the Englifh gardens at prefent, viz.

PEGANUM (*Harmala*) foliis multifidis. Hort. Upfal. 144.

Peganum with many-pointed leaves. Harmala. Dod. Pempt. 121. Ruta fylveftris, flore magno albo. C.B.P. 336. *Wild Rue with a large white flower.*

This plant grows naturally in Spain and Syria ; it has a root as large as a man's little finger, which by age becomes woody. The ftalks decay every autumn, and new ones arife in the fpring ; thefe grow about a foot long, and divide into feveral fmall branches, which are garnifhed with oblong thick leaves cut into feveral narrow fegments ; they are of a dark green, and of a gummy bitterifh tafte. The flowers are produced at the end of the branches, fitting clofe between the leaves ; they are compofed of five roundifh white petals, which open like a Rofe, having fifteen awl-fhaped ftamina, terminated by oblong, yellow, erect fummits. In the center is fituated a roundifh three-cornered germen, having a three-cornered ftyle the length of the ftamina, with three ftigmas which are longer than the ftyle. The germen afterward becomes a roundifh three-cornered capfule, having three cells, which contain feveral oval acute-pointed feeds. It flowers in July, and in warm fummers the feeds will ripen here in the autumn.

It is propagated by feeds, which fhould be fown thinly on a bed of light earth the beginning of April, and when the plants come up, they muft be conftantly kept clean from weeds, which is all the culture they will require till the end of October, or the beginning of November, when their ftalks decay. At which time, if the bed is covered with tanners bark, afhes, faw-duft, or fuch like covering to keep out the froft, it will be a fecure way to preferve the roots, which when young are fomewhat tender. The following March the roots may be taken up, and tranfplanted into a warm fituation and a dry foil, where they will continue feveral years. This is fometimes ufed in medicine.

PELECINUS. See BISERRULA.

PELLITORY OF SPAIN. See ANTHEMIS.

PELLITORY OF THE WALL. See PARIETARIA.

PELTARIA. Jacq. Vind. 260. Lin. Gen. Plant. 806. Mountain Treacle Muftard.

The CHARACTERS are,

The empalement of the flower is compofed of four fmall, concave, coloured leaves which fall off ; the flower has four petals placed in form of a crofs, whofe necks are fhorter than the empalement, and fix awl-fhaped ftamina, two of which are fhorter than the empalement, terminated by fingle fummits, with a roundifh germen fupporting a fhort ftyle, crowned by an obtufe ftigma. The germen afterward becomes a roundifh compreffed pod with one cell, containing one roundifh feed.

This genus of plants is ranged in the firft fection of Linnæus's fifteenth clafs, intitled Tetradynamia Siliculofa, the flower having four long and two fhort ftamina, and the feeds being included in fhort pods.

We have but one SPECIES of this genus, viz.

PELTARIA (*Alliacea.*) Jacq. Vind. 260. Lin. Sp. Plant. 910. *Peltaria or Treacle Muftard.* Thlafpi montanum, glafti folio majus. C. B. P. 106. *Mountain Treacle Muftard with a Woad leaf.*

This plant grows naturally upon the mountains in Auftria and Iftria ; it is a biennial, fo generally dies foon after the feeds are perfected. It rifes with an upright branching ftalk about a foot high, garnifhed with heart-fhaped fmooth leaves, which embrace the ftalks with their bafe ; the ftalks are terminated by clufters of white flowers growing in form of umbels, each flower having four petals placed in form of a crofs ; thefe are fucceeded by roundifh compreffed pods, each containing one feed of the fame form. The plant flowers in May, and the feeds ripen in July. This is eafily propagated by feeds, which may be fown in fmall patches in the borders of the flowergarden the beginning of April, and when the plants are up, there fhould be four or five left in each patch ; the others fhould be pulled out, to give thefe room to grow ; after this, they will require no other culture but to keep them clean from weeds.

PENDU-

PENDULOUS HEADS OF FLOWERS are such as hang downward.

PENNATED. A pennated leaf (called in Latin *Folium Pennatum*) is a compound leaf, divided into several parts (each of which is called a lobe,) placed along the middle rib, either alternately, or by pairs. When the middle rib is terminated by an odd lobe, it is said to be unequally pennated, and equally pennated, when it is not terminated by an odd lobe. When the lobes are all nearly of the same form and bigness, it is called an uniform pennated leaf; when they are not so, it is said to be difform. Examples of pennated leaves are the Ash, Walnut, &c.

PENNY-ROYAL. See PULEGIUM.

PENTAPETALOUS FLOWERS are such as have five leaves.

PENTAPETES. Lin. Gen. Plant 757. Alcea. Raii Supp. 523.

The CHARACTERS are,

The flower has for the most part a double empalement, the outer being small and composed of three leaves, the inner is cut into five parts which are reflexed. It has five oblong petals which spread open, and fifteen narrow stamina joined in a tube at their base, with five long coloured summits, which are erect and barren; between each of these are three stamina, terminated by oblong erect summits. It has a roundish germen, with a cylindrical style the length of the stamina, crowned by a thick stigma. The germen afterward becomes an oval capsule with five cells, filled with oblong seeds.

This genus of plants is ranged in the third section of Linnæus's sixteenth class, which includes those plants whose flowers have many stamina which are connected with the style, forming together a column.

We have but one SPECIES of this genus at present in the English gardens, viz.

PENTAPETES (*Phœnicia*) foliis hastato-lanceolatis serratis. Lin. Sp. Plant. 698. *Pentapetes with halbert-pointed, spear-shaped, sawed leaves.* Alcea Indica lucido hastato folio, flore blattarie Phœnicio. Raii Supp. 523. *Indian Vervain Mallow with a lucid spear-shaped leaf, and a scarlet flower like Moth Mullein.*

This plant grows naturally in India, from whence I have several times received the seeds; it is an annual plant which dies in the autumn, soon after it has ripened the seeds. It hath an upright stalk from two to near three feet high, sending out side branches the whole length; those from the lower part of the stalks are the longest, the others gradually diminish, so as to form a sort of pyramid. These are garnished with leaves of different forms; the lower leaves, which are largest, are cut on their sides towards the base into two side lobes which are short, and the middle is extended two or three inches farther in length, so that the leaves greatly resemble the points of halberts in their shape; they are slightly sawed on their edges, and are of a lucid green on their upper side, but are paler on their under, standing upon pretty long foot-stalks. The leaves which are on the upper part of the branches are much narrower, and some of them have very small indentures on their sides; these sit closer to the stalks, and are placed alternately. From the wings of the stalks the flowers come out; they are for the most part single, but sometimes there are two arising at the same place from the sides of the footstalk of the leaves. The foot-stalk of the flower is short and slender. The exterior empalement of the flower is composed of three short leaves, which fall off soon; the interior is of one leaf, cut at the top into five acute segments, which spread open, and are almost as long as the petal. The flower is of one petal, cut into five obtuse segments almost to the bottom, but as they are joined and fall off in one piece, so the flower is monopetalous, according to Mr. Ray and Tournefort. In the center of the flower arises a short thick column, to which adhere fifteen short stamina, terminated by oblong erect summits, and between every third stamina is situated a larger stamina, with an oblong erect summit of a deep red colour; these

five large summits are barren, having no farina fœcundens upon them. Between the stamina is situated a roundish germen, supporting a style the length of the stamina, which is crowned by a thick stigma. These being all joined at their base into a sort of column, distinguish the tribe to which it belongs, which is the malvaceous; so that though the flower at first appearance greatly resembles the flowers of Moth Mullein, yet upon examination of its essential characters, it will be found to belong to the class here mentioned. The flowers are of a fine scarlet colour, appearing in July, and are succeeded by roundish capsules with five cells, which are a little woody, each cell inclosing three or four oblong seeds, which ripen in the autumn.

The seeds of this plant must be sown upon a good hot-bed early in March, and when the plants are fit to transplant, there should be a new hot-bed prepared to receive them, into which should be plunged some small pots filled with good kitchen-garden earth; in each of these should be one plant put, giving them a little water to settle the earth to their roots; they must also be shaded from the sun till they have taken new root, then they should be treated in the same way as other tender exotic plants, admitting the free air to them every day in proportion to the warmth of the season, and covering the glasses with mats every evening to keep them warm. When the plants are advanced in their growth so as to fill the pots with their roots, they should be shifted into larger pots, filled with the same sort of earth as before, and plunged into another hot-bed, where they may remain as long as they can stand under the glasses of the bed without being injured; and afterward they must be removed either into a stove or a glass-case, where they may be screened from the cold, and in warm weather have plenty of fresh air admitted to them. With this management the plants will begin to flower early in July, and there will be a succession of flowers continued till the end of September, during which time they will make a good appearance. The seeds ripen gradually after each other in the same succession as the flowers were produced, so they should be gathered as soon as their capsules begin to open at the top. These plants are sometimes turned out of the pots, when they are strong and planted in warm borders, where, if the seasons prove very warm, the plants will flower pretty well; but these very rarely perfect their seeds, so that in order to have them in perfection, they must be treated in the manner before directed.

PENTAPHYLLOIDES. See POTENTILLA.

PENTHORUM. Gronov. Virg. 51. Lin. Gen. Plant. 580.

The CHARACTERS are,

The flower hath a permanent empalement of one leaf, cut into five equal segments; the flower has sometimes five small narrow petals situated between the segments of the empalement, and ten equal bristly stamina twice the length of the empalement, which are permanent, terminated by roundish deciduous summits. It hath a coloured germen with five styles the length of the stamina, crowned by obtuse stigmas; and a single five-cornered conical capsule having five cells, filled with small compressed seeds.

This genus of plants is ranged in the fourth section of Linnæus's tenth class, intitled Decandria Pentagynia, which contains those plants whose flowers have ten stamina and five styles.

We have but one SPECIES of this genus, viz.

PENTHORUM (*Sedoides*.) Gron. Virg. 51. Lin. Sp. 620. *Penthorum like Houseleek.*

This is a biennial plant, which grows naturally in Virginia. The stalks rise about a foot high, garnished with oblong leaves placed alternately, and are terminated by clusters of greenish yellow flowers, which make little appearance; these are succeeded by five-cornered conical capsules, filled with small compressed seeds. The flowers appear the latter end of July, and the seeds ripen in the autumn.

Aa

As this plant makes but a mean appearance, so it is rarely cultivated, except in botanic gardens for the sake of variety; but such as are desirous to have it, should sow the seeds on a moist shady spot of ground, and when the plants come up, if they are thinned and kept clean from weeds, they will require no other culture.

PEONY. See PÆONIA.

PEPO. See CUCURBITA.

PERENNIAL PLANTS are such whose roots will abide many years, whether they retain their leaves in winter or not; those which retain their leaves are called Evergreens, but such as cast their leaves are called Deciduous or Perdifols. Some of these have annual stalks, which die to the root every autumn, and shoot up again in the spring; to which Jungius gives the title of Radix restibilis.

PERESKIA. Plum. Nov. Gen. 37. tab. 26. Cactus. Lin. Gen. Plant. 539. Gooseberry, vulgò.

The CHARACTERS are,

It hath a Rose-shaped flower consisting of several leaves, which are placed orbicularly, whose cup afterward becomes a soft, fleshy, globular fruit beset with leaves. In the middle of the fruit are many flat roundish seeds included in a mucilage.

We have but one SPECIES of this plant, viz.

PERESKIA (*Aculeata*) aculeata, flore albo, fructu flavascente. Plum. Nov. Gen. 37. *Prickly Pereskia with a white flower, and a yellowish fruit.* Cactus caule tereti arboreo spinoso, foliis lanceolato-ovatis. Lin. Hort. Upsal. 122. *Cactus with a taper, tree-like, prickly stalk, and spear-shaped oval leaves.*

This plant grows in some parts of the Spanish West-Indies, from whence it was brought to the English settlements in America, where it is called a Gooseberry, and by the Dutch it is called Blad Apple. It hath many slender branches which will not support themselves, so must be supported by stakes, otherwise they will trail on whatever plants grow near them. These branches, as also the stem of the plant, are beset with long whitish spines, which are produced in tufts. The leaves are roundish, very thick, and succulent, and the fruit is about the size of a Walnut, having tufts of small leaves on it, and hath a whitish mucilaginous pulp.

It may be propagated by planting of the cuttings during any of the summer months: these cuttings should be planted in pots filled with fresh light earth, and plunged into a moderate hot-bed of tanners bark, observing to shade them from the sun in the heat of the day, as also to refresh them every third or fourth day with water. In about two months the cuttings will have made good roots, when they may be carefully taken out of the pots, and each planted into a separate pot filled with fresh earth, and then plunged into the hot-bed again, where they may remain during the summer season; but at Michaelmas, when the nights begin to be cold, they should be removed into the stove, and plunged into the bark-bed. During the winter season the plants must be kept warm, and should be watered twice a week; but in cold weather it should not be given in large quantities. In summer they must have a large share of air, and must be more plentifully watered, but they should constantly remain in the stove; for though they will bear the open air in summer in a warm situation, yet they will make no progress if they are placed abroad; nor do they thrive near so well in the dry stove, as when they are plunged in the tan; so that the best way is to set them next a trellis, at the back of the tan-bed, to which their branches may be fastened, to prevent their trailing on other plants. This plant has not as yet produced either flowers or fruit in England, but as there are several plants pretty well grown in the gardens of the curious, we may expect some of them will flower in a short time.

PERICLYMENUM. Tourn. Inst. R. H. 608. tab. 578. Caprifolium. Tourn. Inst. R. H. 608. tab. 379 Lonicera. Lin. Gen. Plant. 210. Honeysuckle; in French, *Chevre fenille.*

The CHARACTERS are,

The empalement of the flower is small, and cut into five parts sitting upon the germen. The flower is of one petal, having an oblong tube, which is cut at the top into five segments which turn backward. It has five awl-shaped stamina almost the length of the petal, terminated by oblong summits, and a roundish germen situated below the flower, supported by a slender style, crowned by an obtuse stigma. The germen afterward becomes an umbilicated berry with two cells, each containing one roundish seed.

This genus of plants is by Dr. Linnæus placed in the first section of his fifth class, which includes those plants whose flowers have five stamina and one style, and joins it to the Lonicera of Plumier, and the Chamæcerasus of Tournefort; but as the flowers of this genus differ greatly in their form from either of those genera, so I have taken the liberty of separating it from them.

The SPECIES are,

1. PERICLYMENUM (*Sempervirens*) floribus capitatis terminalibus omnibus connatis sempervirentibus. *Honeysuckle with flowers growing in heads at the end of the branches, and evergreen leaves joined round the stalk.* Periclymenum perfoliatum Virginianum sempervirens & florens. H. L. *Perfoliate, evergreen, Virginia Honeysuckle which always flowers, commonly called Trumpet Honeysuckle.*

2. PERICLYMENUM (*Racemosum*) racemis lateralibus oppositis, floribus pendulis, foliis lanceolatis integerrimis. *Honeysuckle with flowers in long bunches growing opposite, hanging down, and entire spear-shaped leaves.* Periclymenum racemosum flore flavascente, fructu niveo. Hort. Elth. 306. tab. 228. *Honeysuckle with yellowish flowers growing in bunches, and a snowy fruit.*

3. PERICLYMENUM (*Verticillatum*) corymbis terminalibus, foliis ovatis verticillatis petiolatis. *Honeysuckle with round bunches of flowers at the end of the branches, and oval leaves growing in whorls, having foot-stalks.* Periclymenum aliud arborescens ramulis inflexis, flore corallino. Plum. Cat. 17. *Another tree-like Honeysuckle with inflexed branches, and a coral-coloured flower.*

4. PERICLYMENUM (*Germanicum*) capitulis ovatis imbricatis terminalibus, foliis omnibus distinctis. *Honeysuckle with oval imbricated heads terminating the stalks, and the leaves distinct.* Caprifolium Germanicum. Dod. p. 411. *The German Honeysuckle.*

5. PERICLYMENUM (*Italicum*) floribus verticillatis terminalibus sessilibus, foliis summis connato-perfoliatis. Hort. Cliff. 45. *Honeysuckle with whorls of flowers sitting close at the ends of the branches, and the upper leaves surrounding the stalk.* Caprifolium Italicum. Dod. p. 411. *Italian Honeysuckle.*

6. PERICLYMENUM (*Vulgare*) floribus corymbosis terminalibus, foliis hirsutis distinctis, viminibus tenuioribus. *Honeysuckle with a corymbus of flowers terminating the stalks, hairy leaves growing distinct, and very slender branches, commonly called English Honeysuckle, or Woodbine.*

7. PERICLYMENUM (*Americanum*) floribus verticillatis terminalibus sessilibus, foliis connato-perfoliatis sempervirentibus glabris. *Honeysuckle with whorled flowers fitting close, terminating the stalks, and smooth evergreen leaves surrounding the stalks.* Caprifolium perfoliatum sempervirens, floribus speciosis. Hort. Chelf. *The evergreen Honeysuckle, having beautiful flowers.*

The first sort grows naturally in Virginia, and many other parts of North America, but has been long cultivated in the English gardens by the title of Virginia Trumpet Honeysuckle. Of these there are two varieties, if not distinct species, one being much hardier than the other. The old sort, which came from Virginia, has stronger shoots; the leaves are of a brighter green; the bunches of flowers are larger, and deeper coloured than the other which came from Carolina. These plants have the appearance of the common Honeysuckle, but the shoots are weaker than any of those, except the wild sort called Woodbine; they are of a purplish red colour, and smooth. The leaves are of an oblong oval shape inverted, and closely clofely furround the ftalk; of a lucid green on their upper fide, but pale on their under. The flowers are produced in bunches at the end of the branches; thefe have long flender tubes, which are enlarged at the top, where they are cut into five almoft equal fegments. The outfide of the flower is of a bright fcarlet, and the infide yellow; they have great appearance of the Honeyfuckle, but are not fo deeply divided, nor are the fegments reflexed. They have no odour, but for the beauty of their flowers, and their long continuance, together with their leaves being evergreen, they are preferved in moft curious gardens.

Thefe plants fhould be planted againft walls or pales, to which their branches fhould be trained for fupport, otherwife they will fall to the ground; for they cannot be reduced to heads like many of the Honeyfuckles, becaufe their branches are too weak and rambling, and are liable to be killed in fevere winters; therefore they fhould be planted to a warm afpect, where they will begin to flower the latter end of June, and there will be a fucceffion of flowers till the autumn. Thefe are propagated by laying down their young branches, which will eafily take root, and may be afterward treated like the Honeyfuckle.

The fecond fort grows naturally in Jamaica; this hath many flender branches which cannot fupport themfelves, but trail upon any neighbouring bufhes. They grow eight or ten feet long, are covered with a brown bark, and garnifhed with fpear-fhaped leaves about two inches and a half long, and one broad in the middle; of a lucid green on their upper fide, but pale on their under, ftanding by pairs oppofite. The flowers come out from the fide of the branches at each joint; they are ranged on each fide the foot-ftalk in long bunches like Currants. The bunches come out oppofite; they are three or four inches long. The flowers are fmall, of a yellowifh green, and are fucceeded by fmall berries of a fnow white colour, from whence the plant is called Snowberry-bufh in America.

The third fort grows naturally in fome of the iflands in the Weft-Indies; this rifes with a fhrubby ftalk ten or twelve feet high, fending out many flender branches, covered with a light brown bark, garnifhed with oval leaves near two inches long, and an inch and a quarter broad, four of them coming out at each joint in whorls round the ftalk; they ftand upon fhort foot-ftalks, and have one ftrong midrib, with feveral veins running from the midrib to the fides. The flowers come out in round bunches at the end of the branches; they are of a deep coral colour on their outfide, but of a pale red within. This was found growing in Jamaica by the late Dr. Houftoun, who brought it to England.

Thefe two forts are too tender to thrive in this country without artificial heat; they are propagated by feeds, which muft be procured from the countries where they naturally grow, for they do not ripen feeds here. Thefe fhould be fown in pots, and plunged into a moderate hot-bed, where they may remain till the autumn, for the plants rarely come up the firft year; fo the pots fhould be removed into the ftove for the winter feafon, and the following fpring placed on a frefh hot-bed, which will bring up the plants; and when they are fit to remove, they fhould be each planted in a feparate fmall pot filled with light earth, and plunged into a frefh hot-bed, fhading them from the fun till they have taken new root, after which they muft be treated in the manner as other tender plants from thofe countries. As the plants obtain ftrength, they fhould be more hardily treated, by placing them abroad in a fheltered fituation for two months or ten weeks, in the warmeft part of the fummer, and in the winter they may be placed in a dry ftove, kept to a moderate temperature of warmth, where they will thrive, and produce their flowers in the autumn.

The fourth fort is the common Dutch or German Honeyfuckle, which has been generally fuppofed the

fame with the Englifh wild fort called Woodbine, but is undoubtedly a very different fpecies, for the fhoots of this are much ftronger. The plants may be trained with ftems, and formed into heads, which the wild fort cannot, their branches being too weak and trailing for this purpofe. The branches of this are fmooth, of a purplifh colour, garnifhed with oblong oval leaves three inches long, and an inch and three quarters broad, of a lucid green on their upper fide, but pale on their under, having very fhort foot-ftalks; they are placed by pairs, but are not joined at their bafe. The flowers are produced in bunches at the end of the branches, each flower arifing out of a fcaly cover, which cover, after the flowers fade, forms an oval head, whofe fcales lie over each other like thofe outfide, and yellowifh within, of a very agreeable of fifh. The flowers are of a reddifh colour on their odour. This fort flowers in June, July, and Auguft. There are two other varieties of this fpecies, one is called the long blowing, and the other the late red Honeyfuckle.

The fifth fort is commonly called the Italian Honeyfuckle; of this there are two or three varieties, the early white Honeyfuckle is one; this is the firft which flowers, always appearing in May. The branches of this are flender, covered with a light green bark, and garnifhed with oval leaves of a thin texture, placed by pairs, fitting clofe to the branches, but thofe which are fituated toward the end of the branches, join at their bafe, fo that the ftalk feems as if it came through the leaves. The flowers are produced in whorled bunches at the end of the branches; they are white, and have a very fragrant odour, but are of fhort duration, fo that in about a fortnight they are entirely over; and foon after the leaves appear as if blighted and fickly, making an indifferent appearance the whole fummer, which has rendered them lefs valued than the others. The other variety is the yellow Italian Honeyfuckle, which is the next in fucceffion to the white. The fhoots of this are much like thofe of the former, but have a darker bark; the leaves are alfo of a deeper green; the flowers are of a yellowifh red, and appear foon after the white; they are not of much longer duration, and are fucceeded by red berries, containing one hard feed inclofed in a foft pulp, which ripens in the autumn.

The fixth fort is the common wild Englifh Honeyfuckle or Woodbine; this grows naturally in the hedges in many parts of England. The branches are very flender and hairy, trailing over the neighbouring bufhes, and twining round the boughs of trees; the leaves are oblong, hairy, and diftinct, not joined at their bafe; they are placed oppofite; the flowers are produced in long bunches at the end of the branches. There are two varieties, one with white, and the other yellowifh red flowers. Thefe appear in July, and there is a fucceffion of flowers till the autumn.

There is alfo a variety of this with variegated leaves, and one with cut leaves fomewhat like the leaves of Oak, and one of thefe with variegated leaves; but, as thefe are accidental varieties, I have not enumerated them.

The feventh fort is fuppofed to grow naturally in North America; this hath ftrong branches, covered with a purple bark, which are garnifhed with lucid green leaves embracing the ftalks, which continue their verdure all the year. The flowers are produced in whorled bunches at the end of the branches; there are frequently two and fometimes three of thefe bunches rifing one out of another; they are of a bright red on their outfide, and yellow within, of a ftrong aromatic flavour. This fort begins to flower in June, and there is a fucceffion of flowers till the froft puts a ftop to them, fo that it is the moft valuable of all the forts.

All the forts of Honeyfuckles are propagated either by layers or cuttings: when they are propagated by layers, the young fhoots only fhould be chofen for that purpofe; they fhould be layed in the autumn, and

and by the following autumn they will have taken root, when they ſhould be cut off from the plants, and either planted where they are to remain, or into a nurſery to be trained up, either for ſtandards, which muſt be done by fixing down ſtakes to the ſtem of each plant, to which their principal ſtalk ſhould be faſtened, and all the other muſt be cut off; the principal ſtalk muſt be trained to the intended height of the ſtem, then it ſhould be ſhortened to force out lateral branches, and theſe ſhould be again ſtopped to prevent their growing too long; by the conſtant repeating this as the ſhoots are produced, they may be formed into a ſort of ſtandard; but if any regard is had to their flowering, they cannot be formed into regular heads, for by conſtantly ſhortening their branches, the flower-buds will be cut off, ſo that few flowers can be expected; and as it is an unnatural form for theſe trees, ſo there ſhould be but few of them reduced to it, for when they are planted near other buſhes, in whoſe branches the ſhoots of the Honeyſuckles may run and mix, they will flower much better, and have a finer appearance than when they are more regularly trained; therefore, when the plants are in the nurſery, if two or three of the principal ſhoots are trained up to the ſtakes, and the others are entirely cut off, they will be fit to tranſplant the following autumn, to the places where they are to remain; for though the roots may be tranſplanted of a greater age, yet they do not thrive ſo well as when they are removed while they are young. When theſe plants are propagated by cuttings, they ſhould be planted in September, as ſoon as the ground is moiſtened by rain. The cuttings ſhould have four joints, three of which ſhould be buried in the ground, and the fourth above the ſurface, from which the ſhoots ſhould be produced. Theſe may be planted in rows, at about a foot diſtance row from row, and four inches aſunder in the rows, treading the earth cloſe to them; and as the evergreen and late red Honeyſuckles, are a little more tender than the other ſorts, ſo if the ground between the rows where theſe are planted, is covered with tanners bark or other mulch to keep out the froſt in winter, and the drying winds of the ſpring, it will be of great advantage to the cuttings; and if the cuttings of theſe ſorts have a ſmall piece of the two years wood at their bottom, there will be no hazard of their taking root. The plants which are raiſed from cuttings, are preferable to thoſe which are propagated by layers, as they have generally better roots.

Theſe plants will grow in almoſt any ſoil or ſituation (except the laſt mentioned, which will not thrive where they are too much expoſed to the cold in winter) they thrive beſt in a ſoft ſandy loam, and will retain their leaves in greater verdure in ſuch ground than if planted in a dry gravelly ſoil, where in warm dry ſeaſons their leaves often ſhrink, and hang in a very diſagreeable manner; nor will thoſe ſorts which naturally flower late in the autumn, continue ſo long in beauty on a dry ground, unleſs the ſeaſon ſhould prove moiſt and cold, as thoſe in a gentle loam, not too ſtiff or wet.

There are few ſorts of ſhrubs which deſerve cultivation better than moſt of theſe, for their flowers are very beautiful, and perfume the air to a great diſtance with their odour, eſpecially in the mornings and evenings, and in cloudy weather, when the ſun does not exhale their odour, and raiſe it too high to be perceptible; ſo that in all retired walks, there cannot be too many of theſe intermixed with the other ſhrubs. I have ſeen theſe plants intermixed in hedges planted either with Alder or Laurel, where the branches have been artfully trained between thoſe of the hedge; from which the flowers have appeared diſperſed from the bottom of the hedge to the top, and being intermixed with the ſtrong green leaves of the plants which principally compoſe the hedge, they have made a fine appearance; but the beſt ſorts for this purpoſe, are the evergreen and long-blowing Honeyſuckles, be-

cauſe their flowers continue in ſucceſſion much longer than the other ſorts.

Theſe plants may be propagated by ſeeds, but unleſs they are ſown in the autumn ſoon after they are ripe, the plants will not come up the firſt year.

PERIPLOCA. Tourn. Inſt. R. H. 93. tab. 22. Lin. Gen. Plant. 267. [Περιπλοκη, of περι, about, and πλοκη, a knitting or plaiting, becauſe this plant entangles itſelf with itſelf, or any other neighbouring plants.] Virginian Silk.

The CHARACTERS are,

The flower hath a ſmall permanent empalement, cut into five points. The flower has one plain petal, cut into five narrow ſegments, which are indented at their points, with a ſmall nectarium going round the center of the petal, and the five incurved filaments which are not ſo long as the petal, and five ſhort ſtamina terminated by erect ſummits which join in a head. It has a ſmall bifid germen with ſcarce any ſtyle, crowned by two ſimple ſtigmas. The germen afterward becomes two oblong bellied capſules with one cell, filled with ſeeds crowned with down, lying over each other like the ſcales of fiſh.

This genus of plants is ranged in the ſecond ſection of Linnæus's fifth claſs, which includes thoſe plants whoſe flowers have five ſtamina and two ſtyles.

The SPECIES are,

1. PERIPLOCA (*Græca*) floribus internè hirſutis. Lin. Sp. Plant. 211. *Virginia Silk, with flowers hairy on their inſide.* Periploca foliis oblongis. Tourn. Init. R. H. 93. *Virginia Silk with oblong leaves.*

2. PERIPLOCA (*Africana*) caule hirſuto. Lin. Sp. Plant. 211. *Virginia Silk with a hairy ſtalk.* Apocynum ſcandens, Africanum, vincæ pervincæ folio ſubincanum. Com. Plant. Rar. 18. *Climbing African Dogſbane, with a hoary Periwinkle leaf.*

3. PERIPLOCA (*Fruticoſa*) foliis oblongo-cordatis pubeſcentibus, floribus alaribus, caule fruticoſo ſcandente. *Virginia Silk, with oblong heart-ſhaped leaves which are covered with ſoft hairs, and flowers proceeding from the ſides of the ſtalks, which are ſhrubby.* Periploca foliis cordatis holoſericeis, floribus parvis, albis, campaniformibus. Houſt. MSS. *Periploca with heart-ſhaped ſilky leaves, and ſmall, white, bell-ſhaped flowers.*

The firſt ſort grows naturally in Syria, but is hardy enough to thrive in the open air in England. It hath twining ſhrubby ſtalks, covered with a dark bark, which twiſt round any neighbouring ſupport, and will riſe more than forty feet high, ſending out ſlender branches from the ſide, which twine round each other, and are garniſhed with oval ſpear-ſhaped leaves near four inches long, and two broad in the middle, of a lucid green on their upper ſide, but pale on their under, ſtanding by pairs, upon ſhort foot-ſtalks. The flowers come out toward the end of the ſmall branches in bunches; they are of a purple colour, and hairy on their inſide, compoſed of one petal, cut into five ſegments almoſt to the bottom, which ſpread open in form of a ſtar, and within is ſituated a nectarium, which goes round the five ſhort ſtamina and germen, and is hairy. The germen afterward turns to a double long taper pod or capſule, filled with compreſſed ſeeds, lying over each other like the ſcales of fiſh, having a ſoft down fixed to their top. This plant flowers in July and Auguſt, but rarely ripens its ſeeds in England.

It is eaſily propagated by laying down of the branches, which will put out roots in one year, and may then be cut from the old plant, and planted where they are to remain. Theſe may be tranſplanted either in autumn, when the leaves begin to fall, or in the ſpring before they begin to ſhoot, and muſt be planted where they may have ſupport, otherwiſe they will trail on the ground, and faſten themſelves about whatever plants are near them.

The ſecond ſort grows naturally in Africa; this hath many ſlender ſtalks, which twine about each other, or any neighbouring ſupport, and will riſe near three feet high, putting out ſeveral ſmall ſide branches; theſe are hairy, as are alſo the leaves, which are oval, about

about three quarters of an inch long, and half an inch broad, ftanding by pairs upon very fhort foot-ftalks. The flowers come out in fmall bunches from the fide of the ftalks; they are fmall, and of a worn-out purplifh colour, and a fweet fcent, being cut into five narrow fegments almoft to the bottom. It flowers in the fummer months, but does not produce feeds here. There is a variety of this with fmooth leaves and ftalks, from the fame country.

The third fort was difcovered by the late Dr. Houftoun, growing naturally at La Vera Cruz in America. This rifes with a ftrong woody ftalk to the height of five or fix feet, covered with a gray bark, putting out many weak branches, which twift themfelves about any neighbouring fupport, and rife to the height of twenty feet; they are garnifhed with heart-fhaped leaves three inches long, and two broad near their bafe; they are of a yellowifh green, covered with filky hairs, which are foft to the touch; they ftand oppofite upon pretty long foot-ftalks. The flowers come out in fmall bunches from the wings of the leaves; they are fmall, white, and of the open bell fhape; thefe are fucceeded by fwelling taper pods, filled with feeds crowned with long feathery down.

The fecond fort is hardy enough to thrive in this country, with a little protection from the froft in winter. If the plants are fheltered under a common frame or placed in a green-houfe during the winter feafon, and placed abroad with other hardy exotic plants in fummer, they will thrive and flower very well; but as all the plants of this genus have a milky juice, fo they fhould not have much wet, efpecially in cold weather, left it rot them. They are eafily propagated by laying down of their branches, which in one year will have roots enough to tranfplant; thefe fhould be planted in a light fandy loam not rich, and the pots muft not be too large, for when they are over potted they will not thrive.

The third fort is tender, fo will not thrive in England, unlefs the plants are placed in a warm ftove. They may be propagated by laying down of their branches in the fame manner as the former; or from feeds, when they can be procured from the places where they naturally grow. Thefe fhould be fown upon a good hot-bed, and when the plants come up, they muft be treated in the fame manner as other tender exotic plants.

If thefe plants are conftantly kept plunged in the tanbed of the ftove, they will thrive and flower much better than in any other fituation, but the ftove fhould not be kept too warm in winter; and in the fummer the plants fhould have a large fhare of free air admitted to them; for when they are kept too clofe, their leaves will be covered with infects, and the plants will become fickly in a fhort time.

All the fpecies of this genus are fuppofed to be hurtful to animals, as the Dogfbanes in general are, and thefe are very near a-kin to them, both in their characters and qualities.

PERIWINCLE. See VINCA.

PERSEA. Plum. Nov. Gen. 44. tab. 20. Laurtis. Lin. Gen. Plant. 452. The Avocado, or Avogato Pear.

The CHARACTERS are,

The flower hath no empalement, but is compofed of fix petals ending in acute points, which fpread open. It hath fix ftamina which are about half the length of the petals, terminated by roundifh fummits, and a fhort ftyle, crowned by a pyramidal germen, which afterward becomes a large flefhy pyramidal fruit, inclofing an oval feed having two lobes.

This genus of plants Dr. Linnæus has joined to his genus of Laurus, which he places in the firft fection of his ninth clafs, which includes thofe plants whofe flowers have nine ftamina and one ftyle.

We have but one SPECIES of this plant, viz.

PERSEA (*Americana.*) Cluf. Hilt. *The Avocado, or Avogato Pear.*

This tree grows in great plenty in the Spanifh Weft-

Indies, as alfo in the ifland of Jamaica, and hath been tranfplanted into moft of the Englifh fettlements in the Weft-Indies on account of its fruit; which is not only efteemed by the inhabitants as a fruit to be eaten by way of defert, but is very neceffary for the fupport of life. The fruit of itfelf is very infipid, for which reafon they generally eat it with the juice of Lemons and fugar, to give it a piquancy. It is very nourifhing, and is reckoned a great incentive to venery. Some people eat this fruit with vinegar and Pepper.

In the warm countries where this is planted, it grows to the height of thirty feet or more, and has a trunk as large as our common Apple-trees; the bark is fmooth, and of an Afh colour; the brances are befet with pretty large, oblong, fmooth leaves, like thofe of Laurel, which are of a deep green colour, and continue on the tree throughout the year. The flowers and fruit are, for the moft part, produced toward the extremity of the branches. The fruit is as large as one of the largeft Pears, inclofing a large feed with two lobes, included in a thin fhell.

In Europe this plant is preferved as a curiofity, by thofe perfons who delight in collecting exotic plants; and though there is little hope of its producing fruit, yet for the beauty of its fhining green leaves, which continue through the winter, it deferves a place in every curious collection of plants.

It is propagated by feeds, which fhould be obtained as frefh as poffible from the countries of its growth; and if they are brought over in fand, will be more likely to grow, than fuch as are brought over dry. Thefe nuts or feeds fhould be planted in pots, filled with light rich earth, and plunged into a hot-bed of tanners bark, which fhould be kept pretty warm. The pots fhould be alfo frequently watered when the earth appears dry, which will greatly facilitate the vegetation of the feed, provided the water is not given in large quantities, which would rot them. In about five or fix weeks the plants will come up, when they muft be treated very tenderly, for the bed muft be kept in a due temperature for heat; and when the weather proves warm, the frefh air fhould be admitted to the plants, by raifing the glaffes a little. When they have grown about four inches high, they fhould be carefully tranfplanted; and where there are feveral plants in one pot, they muft be parted, being careful to preferve a ball of earth to the root of each, and planted into feparate fmall pots filled with light rich earth, and then plunged into a hot-bed of tanners bark, obferving to fhade them until they have taken new root; after which time they fhould have frefh air admitted to them, in proportion to the warmth of the feafon. Towards Michaelmas the plants muft be removed into the ftove, and plunged into the bark-bed, where, during the winter feafon, they fhould be kept in a moderate warmth, and muft be gently watered twice a week. In the fpring the plants fhould be fhifted into pots a fize larger than the former, and the bark-bed fhould be then renewed with frefh tan, which will fet the plants in a growing ftate early, whereby they will make a fine progrefs the following fummer. Thefe plants muft be conftantly kept in the ftove, for they are too tender to bear the open air in this country at any feafon, but in warm weather fhould have a large fhare of air admitted to them.

PERSICA. Tourn. Inft. R. H. 624. tab. 402. [fo called of Perfia in Afia, from whence this kind of plant was brought into our climate.] The Peach-tree. Amygdalus. Lin. Gen. 619.

The CHARACTERS are,

The flower has a tubulous empalement of one leaf, cut into five obtufe fegments which fpread open. It hath five oblong, oval, obtufe petals, which are inferted in the empalement, and about thirty erect flender ftamina which are fhorter than the petals, terminated by fingle fummits; thefe are alfo inferted in the empalement. It hath a roundifh hairy germen, fupporting a ftyle the length of the ftamina, crowned by a headed ftigma. The germen afterward

afterward becomes a roundish, woolly, large, esculent fruit, with a longitudinal furrow, inclosing an oval nut with a netted shell, having many punctures.

This genus of plants is ranged in the first section of Linnæus's twelfth class, which includes those plants whose flowers have from twenty to thirty stamina, which are inserted in the empalement of the flower, and one style.

There is a great variety of these trees, which are cultivated in the gardens of those who are curious in collecting the several sorts of fruit from the different parts of Europe: I shall therefore first beg leave to mention two or three sorts, which are cultivated for the beauty of their flowers; after which I shall enumerate the several varieties of good fruit which have come to my knowledge.

The SPECIES are,

1. PERSICA (*Vulgaris*) vulgaris, flore pleno. Tourn. Inst. R. H. 625. *Common Peach-tree with double flowers.*
2. PERSICA (*Nana*) Africana nana, flore incarnato simplici. Tourn. Inst. R. H. 625. *Dwarf Almond with single flowers*, vulgò.
3. PERSICA (*Amygdalus*) Africana nana flore incarnato pleno. Tourn. Inst. R. H. 925. *Double flowering Dwarf Almond*, vulgò.

The first of these trees is a very great ornament in a garden early in the spring, the flowers being very large, double, and of a beautiful red or purple colour. This may be planted in standards, and if intermixed with other flowering trees of the same growth, makes a very agreeable variety; or it may be planted against the walls of the pleasure-garden, where the beautiful appearance of its flowers early in the spring, will be more acceptable in such places than the choicest fruits, which must be exposed to servants, and others, so that they seldom can be preserved in large families until they are ripe. This tree may be propagated by budding it on the Almond or Plum stocks, in the same manner as the other sort of Peaches, and should be planted in a good fresh soil that is not over moist.

The other two sorts are of humbler growth, seldom rising above three or four feet high; these may be budded upon Almond stocks, or propagated by layers; they will also take upon Plum stocks, but they are very apt to canker, after they have stood four or five years upon those stocks, especially that with double flowers, which is tenderer than the other, which sends out suckers from the root, whereby it may be propagated in great plenty.

These shrubs make a very agreeable variety amongst low flowering trees, in small wilderness quarters. The single sort flowers in the beginning of April, and the double is commonly three weeks later.

I shall now proceed to mention the sorts of good Peaches which have come to my knowledge; and though perhaps a greater number of sorts may be found in some catalogues of fruits, yet I doubt whether many of them are not the same kinds called by different names; for, in order to determine the various kinds, it is necessary to observe the shape and size of the flowers, as well as the different parts of the fruit; for this does sometimes determine the kind, when the fruit alone is not sufficient; besides, there is a vast difference in the size and flavour of the same Peach, when planted on different soils and aspects; so, that it is almost impossible for a person who is very conversant with these fruits to distinguish them, when brought from various gardens.

The present confusion of the names of fruits, hath been many times owing to the bringing over trees from France; for the persons who are generally employed to bring over those trees for sale, are entirely ignorant of their various sorts, and do themselves take them upon trust, from the persons who make it their business to propagate great quantities, to supply the markets of France, whither they are brought in waggons, and sold out in parcels to those persons who bring them into England. It also happens many times, if they are received by right names, that these

in length of time are lost, or the trees come into the possession of other persons, who not knowing the true name of the fruit, do often give them new names, whereby there is such a confusion in the names of fruit, as is impossible to rectify; and hence some persons have supposed a much greater variety of Peaches than there is in reality, though as the greatest part of these have been obtained from seeds, so their varieties may be multiplied annually, until there be no end of the sorts. However, I shall content myself with enumerating the principal sorts now known in England, which are sufficient for any gentleman to make a collection to continue through the whole season of fruit.

1. The white Nutmeg (called by the French, L'Avant Péche Blanche:) this tree has sawed leaves, and generally shoots very weak, unless it is budded upon an Apricot stock; the flowers are large and open; the fruit is small and white, as is also the pulp at the stone, from which it separates; it is a little musky and sugary, but is only esteemed for its being the first sort ripe. It is in eating pretty early in July, and soon becomes mealy.

2. The red Nutmeg (called by the French, L'Avant Péche de Troyes:) this tree has sawed leaves, the flowers are large and open; the fruit is larger and rounder than the white Nutmeg, and is of a bright vermilion colour; the flesh is white, and very red at the stone; it has a rich musky flavour, and parts from the stone. This Peach is well esteemed, it ripens toward the end of July.

3. The early or small Mignon (called by the French, La Double de Troyes, or Mignonette:) this tree has small contracted flowers, the fruit is of a middling size, and round; it is very red on the side next the sun; the flesh is white, and separates from the stone, where it is red; the juice is vinous and rich. It is ripe the end of July, or beginning of August.

4. The yellow Alberge: this tree has smooth leaves; the flowers are small and contracted; the fruit is of a middling size, somewhat long; the flesh is yellow and dry; it is seldom well flavoured, but should be perfectly ripe before it is gathered, otherwise it is good for little. It is ripe early in August.

5. The white Magdalen: this tree has sawed leaves; the flowers are large and open; the wood is generally black at the pith; the fruit is round, of a middling size; the flesh is white to the stone, from which it separates; the juice is seldom high flavoured; the stone is very small. This ripens early in August.

6. The early purple (called by the French, La Pourprée hâtive:) this tree has smooth leaves; the flowers are large and open; the fruit is large, round, and of a fine red colour; the flesh is white, but very red at the stone; is very full of juice, which has a rich vinous flavour, and is by all good judges esteemed an excellent Peach. This is ripe before the middle of August.

7. The large or French Mignon: the leaves of this tree are smooth; the flowers are large and open; the fruit is a little oblong, and generally swelling on one side; it is of a fine colour; the juice is very sugary, and of a high flavour; the flesh is white, but very red at the stone, which is small. This is ripe in the middle of August, and is justly esteemed one of the best Peaches; this separates from the stone. This sort of Peach is tender, and will not thrive on a common stock, so is generally budded upon some vigorous shooting Peach, or an Apricot, by the nurserymen, which enhances the price of the trees. But the best method is to bud this Peach into some old healthy Apricot, which is planted to a south or south-east aspect, and to cut away the Apricot when the buds have taken, and made shoots: upon some trees which I have been thus managed, there has been a much greater quantity of fairer, and better flavoured fruit than I have ever observed elsewhere, and the trees have been much more healthy.

8. The Chevreuse, or Belle Chevreuse: this tree has smooth leaves; the flowers are small and contracted;

the

the fruit is of a middling fize, a little oblong, of a fine red colour; the flesh is white, but very red at the stone, from which it separates; it is very full of a rich sugary juice, and ripens toward the end of August. This is a very good bearer, and may be ranged with the good Peaches.

9. The red Magdalen (called by the French about Paris, Madeleine de Courson :) the leaves of this tree are deeply sawed; the flowers are large and open; the fruit is large and round, of a fine red colour; the flesh is white, but very red at the stone, from which it separates; the juice is very sugary, and of an exquisite flavour. The fruit is ripe the end of August; it is one of the best sort of Peaches.

10. The early Newington (or Smith's Newington :) this is very like, if not the same, with what the French call Le Pavie blanc. This tree has sawed leaves; the flowers are large and open; the fruit is of a middling size, is of a fine red on the side next the sun; the flesh is firm and white, but very red at the stone, to which it closely adheres. It hath a sugary juice, and is ripe the end of August.

11. The Montauban: this tree has sawed leaves; the flowers are large and open; the fruit is of a middling size, of a deep red, inclining to purple next the sun, but of a pale colour toward the wall; the flesh is melting and white to the stone, from which it separates; the juice is rich, and the tree is a good bearer. It ripens the middle of August, and is well esteemed.

12. The Malta (which is very like, if not the same, with the Italian Peach :) this tree has sawed leaves; the flowers are large and open; the fruit is of a middling size, of a fine red next the sun: the flesh is white and melting, but red at the stone, from which it separates; the stone is flat and pointed; the tree is a good bearer. This ripens the end of August.

13. The Noblest: this tree has sawed leaves; the flowers are large and open; the fruit is large, of a bright red next the sun; the flesh is white and melting, and separates from the stone, where it is of a faint red colour; the juice is very rich in a good season. It ripens the end of August.

14. The Chancellor: the leaves of this tree are smooth; the flowers are small and contracted; the fruit is shaped somewhat like the Belle Chevreuse, but is rounder; the flesh is white and melting, and separates from the stone, where it is of a fine red colour; the skin is very thin, and the juice is very rich. It ripens about the end of August, and is esteemed one of the best sort of Peaches. This tree is very tender, and will not succeed on common stocks, so is budded twice as the Mignon; and if budded on Apricots, as was directed for that sort, will thrive much better than in any other method.

15. The Bellegarde (or as the French call it, the Gallande :) this tree has smooth leaves; the flowers are small and contracted; the fruit is very large and round, of a deep purple colour on the side to the sun; the flesh is white, melting, and separates from the stone, where it is of a deep red colour; the juice is very rich. This ripens the beginning of September, and is an excellent Peach, but at present not common.

16. The Lisle (or as the French call it, La petite Violette hâtive :) this tree has smooth leaves; the flowers are small and contracted; the fruit is of a middling size, of a fine Violet colour toward the sun; the flesh is of a pale yellow and melting, but adheres to the stone, where it is very red; the juice is very vinous. This ripens the beginning of September.

17. The Bourdine: this tree has smooth leaves; the flowers are small and contracted; the fruit is large, round, and of a fine red colour next the sun; the flesh is white, melting, and separates from the stone, where it is of a fine red colour; the juice is vinous and rich; this ripens the beginning of September, and is greatly esteemed by the curious. The tree bears plentifully, and will produce fruit in standards very well.

18. The Rossanna: this tree has smooth leaves; the flowers are small and contracted; the fruit is large, a little longer than the Alberge; the flesh is yellow and separates from the stone, where it is red; the juice is rich and vinous. This ripens the beginning of September, and is esteemed a good Peach. This is the same with what some call the purple, and others the red Alberge, it being of a fine purple colour on the side next the sun.

19. The Admirable: this tree hath smooth leaves; the flowers are small and contracted; the fruit is large, round, and red on the side next the sun; the flesh is white, melting, and separates from the stone, where it is of a deep red colour; the juice is sugary and rich. This ripens the beginning of September. This is by some called the early Admirable, but is certainly what the French call L'Admirable, and they have no other of this name which ripens later.

20. The old Newington: this tree has sawed leaves; the flowers are large and open; the fruit is fair and large, of a beautiful red colour next the sun; the flesh is white, melting, and closely adheres to the stone, where it is of a deep red colour; the juice is very rich and vinous. This is esteemed one of the best sorts of Pavies. It ripens about the middle of September.

21. The Rambouillet (commonly called Rumbullion :) this tree has smooth leaves; the flowers are large and open; the fruit is of a middling size, rather round than long, deeply divided by a sulcus or furrow in the middle; it is of a fine red colour next the sun, but of a light yellow next the wall; the flesh is melting, of a bright yellow colour, and separates from the stone, where it is of a deep red colour; the juice is rich, and of a vinous flavour. This ripens the middle of September, and is a good bearer.

22. The Bellis (which I believe to be what the French call La Belle de Vitry :) the leaves of this tree are sawed; the flowers are small and contracted; the fruit is of a middle size, round, and of a pale red next the sun; the flesh is white and adheres to the stone, where it is red; the juice is vinous and rich. This ripens the middle of September.

23. The Portugal: this tree has smooth leaves; the flowers are large and open; the fruit is large, and of a beautiful red colour towards the sun, the skin generally spotted; the flesh is firm, white, and closely adheres to the stone, where it is of a faint red colour; the stone is small, but full of deep furrows; the juice is rich and vinous. This ripens the middle of September.

24. La Teton de Venus (or Venus's breast,) so called from its having a rising like a dug, or bubby : this tree has smooth leaves; the flowers are small and contracted; the fruit is of a middling size resembling the Admirable, of a pale red colour next the sun; the flesh is melting, white, and separates from the stone, where it is red; the juice is sugary and rich. This ripens late in September.

25. La Pourprée (or as the French call it Pourprée tardive, i. e. the late purple :) this tree has very large leaves which are sawed; the shoots are very strong; the flowers are small and contracted; the fruit is large, round, and of a fine purple colour; the flesh is white, melting, and separates from the stone, where it is red; the juice is sugary and rich. This ripens late in September.

26. The Nivette: this tree has sawed leaves; the flowers are small and contracted; the fruit is large, somewhat longer than round, of a bright red colour next the sun, and of a pale yellow on their other side; the flesh is melting, and full of rich juice, and is very red at the stone, from which it separates. This is esteemed one of the best Peaches; it ripens in the middle of September.

27. The Royal (La Royale:) this tree has smooth leaves; the flowers are small and contracted; the fruit is large, round, and of a deep red on the side next the sun, and of a paler colour on the other side; the flesh is white, melting, and full of a rich juice; it parts from the stone, where it is of a deep red colour.

lour. This ripens the middle of September, and, when the autumn is good, is an excellent Peach.

28. The Perfique: this tree has fawed leaves; the flowers are fmall and contracted; the fruit is large, oblong, and of a fine red colour next the fun; the flefh is melting, and full of a rich juice; it feparates from the ftone, where it is of a deep red colour. The ftalk has a fmall knot upon it; this makes a fine tree, and is a good bearer; it ripens the end of September. Many gardeners call this the Nivette.

29. The monftrous Pavy of Pomponne (called by the French, La Pavie rouge de Pomponne :) the leaves of this tree are fmooth; the flowers are large and open; the fruit is very large and round, many times fourteen inches in circumference; the flefh is white, melting, and clofely adheres to the ftone, where it is of a deep red colour; the outfide is a beautiful red next the fun, and of a pale flefh colour on the other fide. This ripens the end of October, and when the autumn is warm, is an excellent Peach.

30. The Catharine: this tree hath fmooth leaves; the flowers are fmall and contracted; the fruit is large, round, and of a dark red colour next the fun; the flefh is white, melting, and full of a rich juice. It clofely adheres to the ftone, where it is of a deep red colour; it ripens the beginning of October, and in very good feafons is an excellent Peach, but being fo very late ripe, there are not many fituations where it ripens well.

31. The Bloody Peach (called by the French, La Sanguinolle :) this Peach is of a middling fize, of a deep red next the fun; the flefh is of a deep red quite to the ftone, and from thence is by fome gardeners called the Mulberry Peach. This fruit rarely ripens in England, fo is not often planted, but it bakes and preferves excellently; for which, as alfo tho curiofity, one or two trees may be planted, where there is extent of walling.

There are fome other forts of Peaches which are kept in fome of the nurferies, but thofe which are here enumerated, are the forts moft worth planting, and in the lift, the choiceft only fhould be planted; but I fhall juft mention the names of thofe forts omitted, for the fatisfaction of the curious.

The Sion; the Bourdeaux; the Swalch or Dutch; the Carlifle; the Eaton; the Péche de Pau; yellow Admirable; the double Flower. This laft fort is generally planted more for the beauty of the flowers, than for the goodnefs of the fruit, of which fome years the ftandard trees produce great plenty; but they are late ripe, and have a cold, watery, infipid juice. The Dwarf Peach is alfo preferved in fome places as a curiofity. This is a very tender tree, making very weak fhoots, which are very full of flower-buds. The fruit is not fo large as a Nutmeg, and not good, nor will the tree laft any time, fo it is not worth cultivating.

And indeed, from thefe thirty-one above-named, there are not above ten of them which I would advife to be planted; becaufe, when a perfon can be furnifhed with thofe which are good, or has the beft of the feafon, it is not worth while to plant any which are middling or indifferent, for the fake of variety; therefore the forts which I fhould prefer, are thefe after-mentioned.

The early purple; the Groffe Mignon; Belle Chevreufe; red Magdalen; Chancellor; Bellegarde; Bourdine; Roffanna; Rambouillet, and Nivette. Thefe are the forts beft worth planting; and as they fucceed each other, they will furnifh the table thro' the feafon of Peaches; and, where there is room, and the fituation very warm, one or two trees of the Catharine Peach fhould have place, for in very warm feafons it is an excellent fruit.

As thefe eleven forts do follow each other in their time of ripening, fo unlefs there is extent of good afpected walls, thefe will be fufficient to furnifh any family during the feafon of this fruit: but as in fome feafons there will be fome forts of Peaches very good, which in other feafons often prove but indifferent; there-

fore when there is a fufficient extent of good walls, I would recommend the planting three or four other forts, which fome years are excellent, though in general are not fo good as thofe. before-mentioned. Thefe are the Montauban, the Lifle, the old Newington, La Teton de Venus, the Catharine, and the Perfique.

The French diftinguifh thofe we call Peaches into two forts, viz. Pavies and Peaches; thofe are called Peaches which quit the ftone, and thofe, whofe flefh clofely adheres to the ftone, are called Pavies. Thefe are much more efteemed in France than the Peaches, though in England the latter are preferred to the former by many perfons.

The French alfo diftinguifh them into male and female; the Pavies they make to be the male, and the Peaches the female; but this divifion is without foundation, fince the kernels of both forts will produce trees equally; for the flowers of Peach-trees are generally hermaphrodite, and have all the parts of generation in them, fo that there is no neceffity for fuppofing any of them to be entirely male or female: but it is likely, that this diftinction is of long ftanding, before perfons had a perfect notion of male and female in plants, or at leaft they did not know how to diftinguifh them afunder.

The Nectarines (as I have in another place faid) are by the French called Brugnons, which differ from the other two forts, in having a firm hard flefh, and the fkin quite fmooth, without any down upon them. The forts of thefe I have already mentioned under the article NECTARINES, to which the reader may readily turn, therefore I fhall not repeat them in this place.

I fhall now fet down the good qualities of Peaches, by which any perfon may judge of their worth.

A good Peach ought to have a firm flefh; the fkin fhould be thin, of a deep or bright red colour next the fun, and of a yellowifh caft next the wall. The flefh fhould be of a yellowifh colour, full of juice, which fhould be high-flavoured, the ftone fmall, and the pulp or flefh very thick. When a Peach hath all thefe qualities, it may be efteemed a valuable fruit.

All the different forts of Peaches have been originally obtained from the ftones, which, being planted produce new varieties, as do the feeds of all other fruits; fo that where perfons have garden enough to allow room for propagating thefe fruits from feeds, there is no doubt but many good forts may be obtained, which will be better adapted to our climate, than fuch as are brought from warmer countries; though it is true, that there will be many of them good for nothing, as is the cafe of moft fruits and flowers which are produced from feeds, amongft which there may be fome valuable kinds, fuperior to thofe from whence the feeds were taken, yet there is always a great number which are little worth; but if we can obtain only two or three valuable forts, it is fufficient to make amends for the trouble of raifing them; but where perfons are fo curious as to plant the ftones of thefe fruits, great regard fhould be had to the forts; and if the fruits were permitted to remain upon the trees until they dropped off, the kernels would be fitter for planting, and more likely to grow. The beft forts for fowing are thofe whofe flefh is firm, and cleaves to the ftone; and from amongft thefe you fhould chufe fuch as ripen pretty early, and have a rich vinous juice, from which forts fome good fruit may be expected.

Thefe ftones fhould be planted in autumn, on a bed of light dry earth, about three inches deep, and four inches afunder; and in the winter the beds fhould be covered to protect them from the froft, which, if permitted to enter deep into the ground, will deftroy them. In the fpring, when the plants come up, they fhould be carefully cleared from the weeds, which fhould alfo be obferved throughout the fummer; and if the fpring fhould prove very dry, if you refrefh them now and then with a little water, it will greatly promote their growth. In this bed they fhould remain

main

main until the following spring, when they should be carefully taken up, so as not to break their tender roots, and transplanted into a nursery in rows three feet asunder, and one foot distant plant from plant in the rows, observing to lay a little mulch upon the surface of the ground about their roots, to prevent its drying too fast; and if the spring should prove very dry, you should give them a little water once a week, until they have taken root; after which they should be constantly kept clear from weeds, and the ground between the rows carefully dug every spring to loosen it, so as that the tender fibres may strike out on every side.

In this nursery they may continue one or two years, according to the progress they make; after which they should be transplanted where they are to remain, to produce fruit.

In removing these trees, you should observe to prune their downright roots, if they have any, pretty short, and to cut off all bruised parts of the roots, as also all the small fibres, which generally dry, and when left upon the roots after planting again, grow mouldy and decay, so that they are injurious to the new fibres which are shot out from the roots, and very often prevent the growth of the trees; but you should by no means prune their heads, for the plants which are produced from stones, are generally of a more spongy texture, and so more liable to decay when cut, than those which are budded upon other stocks. Besides, as these trees are designed for standards (for it is not proper to plant them against walls, until you see the produce of the fruit, to shew which of them deserves to be cultivated,) they will never require any other pruning, but only to cut out decayed branches, or such as shoot out very irregular from the sides, for more than this is generally very injurious to them.

In planting these trees, it will be the better way to dispose them singly in the quarters of the kitchengarden, where they will thrive, and produce fruit much better than if they are planted near each other in rows; and, as they are thus singly disposed, they will not do much injury to the crops which grow under them.

When they have produced fruit, you will soon be a judge of their goodness, therefore such of them as you dislike may be destroyed; but those which are good; may be propagated by inoculating them upon other stocks, which is the common method now practised to propagate these fruits, therefore I shall now proceed to treat of that more particularly; in the doing of which, I shall set down the method now commonly practised by the nursery-gardeners, and then propose some few things of my own as an improvement thereon, for such persons who are very curious to have good fruit. But first,

You should be provided with stocks of the Muscle and white Pear Plums, which are generally esteemed the two best sorts of Plums for stocks to inoculate Peaches and Nectarines upon; as also some Almond and Apricot stocks, for some tender sorts of Peaches which will not grow upon Plum stocks. These should be all produced from the stone (as hath been already directed in the article NURSERY,) and not from suckers, for the reasons there laid down. These stocks should be transplanted, when they have had one year's growth in the seed-bed, for the younger they are transplanted, the better they will succeed, and hereby they will be prevented from sending taproots deep in the ground; for by shortening those roots which seem so disposed, it will cause them to put out horizontal roots. These stocks should be planted at the distance above-mentioned, viz. the rows three feet asunder, and one foot apart in the rows. This is wider than most nurserymen plant them, but I shall give my reasons hereafter for this.

When these stocks have grown in the nursery two years, they will be strong enough to bud; the season for which is commonly about Midsummer, or any time in July, when the rind will easily separate from

the wood, when you should make choice of some good cuttings of the sorts of fruit you intend to propagate, always observing to take them from healthy trees, and such as generally produce a good quantity of well-tasted fruit; for it is very certain, that any sort of fruit may be so far degenerated where this care is wanting, as not to be like the same kind. Besides, whenever a tree is unhealthy, the buds taken from that tree will always retain the distemper, in a greater or less degree, according as it hath imbibed a greater or less quantity of the distempered juice. Thus, for instance, where a Peach or Nectarine-tree hath been greatly blighted, so as that the shoots have grown bushed, and the leaves curled up to a great degree, that distemper is seldom recovered again by the greatest art, or at least not under several years management; for let the seasons prove ever so favourable, yet these trees will continually shew the same distemper, which many persons are so weak as to suppose a fresh blight, whereas in reality it is no other but the remains of the former sickness, which are spread and intermixed with all the juices of the tree; so that whatever buds are taken from such trees, will always retain a part of the distemper.

Upon the care which is taken in the choice of the buds, the whole success depends; therefore a person who is curious to have good fruit, cannot be too careful in this particular; for in general no more is regarded by those nurserymen who are the most careful in propagating the several sorts of fruit-trees, than the taking their buds or grafts from the true kinds of fruit-trees; but there is still more care required to have found healthy trees, especially in this of Peaches and Nectarines; for if the buds are taken from young plants in the nursery which have not produced fruit, the shoots of which are generally very strong and vigorous, these buds will have so vicious a habit, as rarely to be corrected and brought into good order; for they will shoot more like the Willow than the Peach, the joints being extended to a great distance from each other, the shoots very gross, and the wood pithy; therefore where the practice of taking the buds from nursery-trees is long continued, there can be little hopes of the trees so raised. I would therefore recommend it to every curious person, to procure their buds from such trees as have been long growing, whose fruit are well flavoured, and the trees perfectly found; as also never to make choice of the strongest or most luxuriant shoots of these trees, but such shoots as are well conditioned, and whose buds grow pretty close together. And although these do not make so strong shoots the following years, as those which are taken from luxuriant branches, yet they will be better disposed to bear fruit, and will make much better trees.

The cuttings with which you are thus to be provided, should always be taken from the trees either in a morning or evening, or else in a cloudy day; for if they are cut off when the sun is very hot, the shoots will perspire so freely, as to leave the buds destitute of moisture, which is often the cause of their miscarrying; and the sooner they are put into the stocks when cut from the trees, the better they will take. The manner of this operation being fully explained under the article of INOCULATION, I shall not repeat it in this place. The management of these trees, during their remaining time in the nursery, is likewise fully set down under that article. I shall therefore proceed to give some directions for the choice of these trees, when they are to be procured from a nursery. The first care should be to find out a person of character to deal with, on whose integrity you may depend, not only for having the trees of those kinds which you propose, but also for their buds being taken from bearing trees; and either see them taken up, or let some person you can confide in do it for you; because, as most of the nurserymen have dealings with each other, if the person applied to has not the sort of fruit desired in his own nursery, he procures them from another; and if the gardener from
whom

whom he gets them, is not as honeſt and careful as himſelf, it is a great chance if the trees prove to be of the right kinds.

The trees ſhould alſo be choſen in the autumn, before others have drawn out the beſt; for thoſe who go firſt to the nurſeries, if they have ſkill, will always draw the fineſt plants. In the choice of the trees, you ſhould obſerve the ſtocks upon which they have been budded, that they are of the right ſort, whether Plum or Apricot; that they are found and young, not ſuch as had been budded the preceding year and failed, nor thoſe which have been cut down. If the ſize of the ſtock is near that of a man's finger, it will be better than if they are larger; theſe ſhould be clear of moſs or canker. The buds ſhould be of one year's growth only, and not ſuch as have been cut down in the ſpring, and made a ſecond ſhoot; nor ſhould thoſe trees be choſen whoſe ſhoots are very ſtrong and luxuriant, but ſuch as have clean ſhoots, of a moderate ſize, whoſe joints are not too far aſunder; and thoſe trees which ſtand on the outſide rows, or near the ends of the rows, where they have moſt air, are generally ſuch; for, where they ſtand cloſe in the nurſery, their ſhoots are drawn up in length, their joints are much farther aſunder, and their buds or eyes are flat; for which reaſon, I have before adviſed the planting of the ſtocks at a greater diſtance than the nurſerymen generally allow them; and, if a careful diſcreet nurſeryman would be at the trouble and expence in the raiſing of his Peach-trees according to this method, he would better deſerve three ſhillings per tree, than one in the manner they are uſually raiſed; for every perſon who is at the expence of building walls for fruit, ſhould not think of ſaving a few ſhillings in the purchaſe of their trees; becauſe, if they are bad, or not of the right kinds, there is a great loſs of time and expence to no purpoſe, and the diſappointment will be ſo great, after waiting three or four years, as to diſcourage many from making farther trials, thinking themſelves liable to the ſame ill ſucceſs.

When the trees are choſen in the nurſery, the next care muſt be to have them carefully taken up out of the ground, ſo as not to break or tear their roots, nor injure their bark; for as theſe trees are very apt to gum in thoſe places where they are wounded, there cannot be too much care taken of this. If the trees are to be tranſported to a diſtant place, their roots ſhould be cloſely wrapped either with haybands, ſtraw, or Peas-haulm, and mats ſewed over theſe, to prevent the air from drying their roots and branches. If the leaves of the trees are not fallen when they are taken up, they ſhould be carefully ſtripped off, before the trees are packed up; for when there are many of theſe left, they are very apt to heat, if they are long in their paſſage, and often occaſion a mouldineſs very hurtful to the branches.

We come next to the preparing of the ground to receive the trees. The beſt earth for Peach-trees is ſuch as is taken from a paſture-ground, that is neither too ſtiff and moiſt, nor over dry, but of a middling nature, ſuch as is termed hazel loam. This ſhould be dug from the ſurface of the ground about ten inches deep, taking the turf with it, and ſhould be laid in heaps eight or ten months at leaſt; but that which is prepared one year or more is ſtill better before it be uſed, that it may have the winter's froſt, and ſummer's heat to mellow it; during which time it ſhould be often turned, to rot the turf and break the clods, whereby it will be rendered very light and eaſy to work; and about the beginning of September you ſhould carry it into the garden, and make the borders, which muſt be raiſed in height proportionable to the moiſture of the garden; but if the ground be very wet, it will be adviſeable to lay ſome rubbiſh in the bottom of the border to drain off the moiſture, alſo to prevent the roots of the trees from running downward; and in this caſe it will be proper to make ſome under-ground drains at the bottom of the border, to convey off the ſuperfluous moiſture; which, if

detained about the roots of the trees, will greatly prejudice them; then raiſe a border of earth at leaſt a foot, or in very wet land two feet above the level of the ground, ſo that the roots of the trees may always remain dry; but if the ground be pretty dry, the borders ſhould not be raiſed above ſix or eight inches higher than the ſurface, which will be ſufficient to allow for their ſinking,

As to the breadth of theſe borders, that cannot be too great; but they ſhould never be leſs than ſix or eight feet broad, where fruit-trees are planted, for when the borders are made very narrow, the roots of the trees will be ſo confined in four or five years time, that they will ſeldom thrive well after. The depth of theſe borders ſhould not be greater than two feet and a half; for when they are prepared to a great depth, it only entices the roots of the trees downward, which may be the cauſe of their future barrenneſs; for their roots being got down below the influences of the ſun and ſhowers, imbibe a great quantity of crude juices, which only add to the luxuriant growth of the trees, and deſtroy their fruitfulneſs; beſides, whatever fruit are produced from ſuch trees, are not near ſo well taſted as thoſe are which grow upon thoſe trees whoſe roots lie near the ſurface, and enjoy the kindly benefit of the ſun's heat, to correct and digeſt whatever crudities there may be in the earth.

Where the natural ſoil of the garden is ſhallow, and either chalk, clay, or gravel lies near the ſurface, theſe ſhould not be dug out to make pits to receive the earth for the border, as is by ſome practiſed, for this will be no better than planting the trees in tubs or caſes, for their roots will be confined to theſe pits; ſo that when they are extended to the ſides, and can get no farther, the trees will blight and decay; and if it is clay on the ſides, the wet will be detained as in a baſon; and the earth of the border will be like mud in very wet ſeaſons, ſo unfit for the roots of theſe trees. Therefore, whenever it ſo happens that the ground is of either of the ſorts before-mentioned, it will be the beſt way to raiſe the borders of a proper thickneſs of good earth over theſe, rather than to ſink down into them; for when the roots of the trees lie near the ſurface of the ground, they will extend to a great diſtance in ſearch of nouriſhment; but if they get below the ſtaple of the land, they can find nothing but four crude paſture very unfit for vegetation.

Your borders being thus prepared, ſhould lie about three weeks or a month to ſettle, by which time the ſeaſon for planting will be come, which ſhould be performed as ſoon as the leaves begin to decay, that the trees may put out new roots, before the froſt comes on to prevent them. Your ground being ready, and the trees brought carefully to the place, the next work is to prepare them for planting, which is to be performed in the following manner: you muſt ſhorten all the roots, and cut off ſmooth and broken or bruiſed roots, as alſo all the ſmall fibres ſhould be taken off, for the reaſons before given; and where any of the roots croſs each other, the worſt of them muſt be cut out, that they may not injure the other.

And having thus prepared your trees, you ſhould meaſure out their diſtance, which ought never to be leſs than twelve feet; but where the ground is very good, they ſhould be planted fourteen feet aſunder. This I doubt not, will be thought too great a diſtance by many perſons, eſpecially ſince it is contrary to the general practice at this time; but I am ſatisfied whoever ſhall try the experiment, will find it no more than is ſufficient for theſe trees where they are rightly managed; for if they take kindly to the ſoil, their branches may be ſo trained as to furniſh all the lower part of the wall in a few years, which is what ſhould be principally regarded, and not, as is too often the practice, run up the ſhoots in height, and leave all the lower part of the tree deſtitute of bearing wood, ſo that in a few years there will not be any fruit but upon the upper part of the tree, which alſo muſt be the caſe where they are planted too cloſe, becauſe there being no room to extend the branches on either ſide,

they

they are obliged to lead them upright, which produces the before-mentioned ill effect.

There may be also some persons, who may think this distance too small for these trees, because Plums, Cherries, and most other sorts of fruit-trees require much more room; but when it is considered, that Peach and Nectarine-trees produce their fruit only upon the former year's wood, and not upon spurs, as Cherries, Plums, and Pears do, so that the shoots of these trees must be annually shortened in every part of them to obtain bearing wood; therefore the trees may be kept in much less compass than those of any other sort of fruit, and thereby every part of the wall may be constantly supplied with bearing branches; for when the trees are planted at a great distance, the branches are often extended to such lengths as to leave the middle of the trees naked, for there are never any good shoots produced from the old branches of these trees.

And here I cannot help taking notice of another very great error in disposition of wall-fruit, which is the placing standard or half standard trees between the others, to cover the upper part of the wall, and to produce fruit, until the trees underneath are grown up sufficient to furnish the walls, when the standards are to be taken away. This is done, without considering that the greater number of trees which are planted in a small compass, the less nourishment they can receive, and so consequently must be the weaker, for the same space of ground cannot nourish twenty trees equally as well as it could ten; so that whatever strength the standard-trees may have, the dwarfs will be proportionably weaker; and it is a common observation, that most trees extend their roots as far under ground, as their branches spread above ground; so that there should always be the same allowance given to the wall-trees, if we would have them strong and vigorous; therefore the building very high walls for fruit, unless for Pears, is to no purpose, for a ten or twelve feet wall will be sufficient for most sorts of fruit. I have seen gardens planted with fruit-trees by persons of great esteem for their skill in this art, where Peach and Nectarine-trees have been placed against walls exposed to the east and west, but could never see any of the fruit on those trees come to perfection; for which reason I would caution every person never to follow such examples, because it is well known, that the best aspected walls do barely ripen many of the latter Peaches some years; therefore the only aspect to which these trees should be exposed, is south, or with a point or two to the east, and some sorts may do well if they are a point or two to the west.

In the disposition of the trees, it will not be amiss to plant those sorts of Peaches near each other, which ripen about the same time; for by so doing, the fruit may be the better guarded from men and insects, and this will save a great deal of trouble in gathering of the fruit; for if a person is obliged to go from one part of the garden to the other, or perhaps to look over all the walls of the garden every time the fruit is gathered, it is a great loss of time, which may be avoided by this first care in planting the trees.

But to return to planting; after you have marked out the places where each tree is to stand, you must with your spade make a hole wide enough to receive the roots of the tree; then you should place it down, observing to turn the bud outwards; that the wounded part of the stock may be hid from sight; and let the stem of the tree be placed about four or five inches from the wall, with its head inclining thereto; then fill in the earth with your hands, observing to break the clods, that the earth may fall in between the roots, so as no void spaces may be left about them. You should also gently shake the tree with your hands, to settle the earth down the better between the roots; then with your foot gently press down the earth about the stem, but do not tread it down too hard, which is many times a very great fault; for when the ground is inclinable to bind, the treading it close doth often

render the ground so hard, as that the tender fibres of the roots cannot strike into it, whereby the tree remains at a stand for some time; and if the earth be not loosened in time, it frequently dies; so that whenever you observe the earth of your borders to be bound, either by great rains, or from any other cause, you should dig or fork it, to loosen it again, observing always to do it in dry weather, if in winter or spring; but in summer it should be done in a moist season.

Although I have here given directions for the choice of trees from the nursery, after the usual method of planting these trees, which is that of taking such as have made one year's shoot, yet I would prefer those which were budded the preceding summer, and have made no shoot; for if the bud is found and plump, and the bark of the stock well closed where the bud is inserted, there will be no danger of its growing; and when the bud has made a shoot the following spring the length of five or six inches, if it is stopped by pinching off the top, it will put out lateral branches, which may be trained to the wall, and this will prevent any cutting off the head, as must be done to those trees which have had one year's growth in the nursery; for these trees do not care for those large amputations, especially some of the more tender sorts; so by this method of planting these trees in bud, no time will be lost, when it is considered that the trees which have shot must be cut down, and there is a hazard of their shooting again; therefore I am convinced from experience, that it is the best method.

After you have thus planted your trees, which have made their shoots in the nursery, you should fasten their heads to the wall, to prevent their being shaken by the wind, which would disturb their roots, and break off the tender fibres soon after they were produced, to the no small prejudice of the trees; you should also lay some mulch upon the surface of the ground about their roots, before the frost sets in, to prevent it from penetrating the ground, which would injure, if not destroy, the small fibres; but this mulch should not be laid upon the ground too early, lest it prevent the autumnal rains from penetrating to the roots.

These things being duly observed, they will require no farther care till the beginning or middle of March, according as the season is earlier or later; when you must cut off the heads of the new planted trees, leaving only four or five eyes above the bud; in doing of which, you must be very careful not to disturb their roots; to prevent which, you should place your foot down close to the stem of the tree, and take fast hold of that part of the stock below the bud with one hand, to hold it steady, while with the other hand you gently slope off the head of the tree with a sharp knife at the intended place, which should always be just above a bud; this should always be done in dry weather, for if there should be much rain soon after it is done, there will be some danger that the wet will enter the wounded part, and damage the tree; nor should it be done in frosty weather for the same reason, for that would enter the wounded part and prevent its healing over. After you have headed the trees, you should gently loosen the earth of the borders, to admit the fibres of the roots; but you must be very careful in doing of this, not to cut or bruise their new roots, which would also damage them; and if the mulch which was laid about their roots in autumn be rotten, you may dig it into the border at some distance from the roots of the trees; and when the dry weather comes on, you should pare off some turf from a pasture ground, which should be laid upon the surface of the border about the roots of the trees, turning the Grass downward, which will preserve a gentle moisture in the earth, better than any other sort of mulch; and this will not harbour insects, as most sorts of dung and litter do, to the no small detriment of the trees.

Those trees which are planted in bud, and have not made any shoots, should have their stocks cut down at this season just above the bud, for the buds will rarely shoot unless this is performed ; and the nearer they are cut to the bud, the sooner will the head of the stock be covered by the buds ; for although it may be necessary to leave a part of the stock above the bud, in those trees which are in the nursery, to which the shoots made by the buds may be fastened, to prevent their being broken by the wind ; yet as these are placed against the wall, to which the shoots may be fastened, there will be no want of any part of the stock.

In watering these new planted trees, which should not be done unless the spring proves very dry, you should observe to do it with a nossel upon the watering-pot, so as to let it out in drops ; for when it is hastily poured down, it causes the ground to bind ; and if you water over the head of the tree, it will be of great service to it. Your waterings should not be repeated too often, nor should they be given in great quantity, both which are very injurious to new planted trees.

In the middle or latter end of May, when these trees will have several shoots six or eight inches in length, you should nail them to the wall, observing to train them horizontally, rubbing off all fore-right shoots, or such as are weak, whereby those which are preferred will be much stronger ; but if there are not more than two shoots produced, and those very strong, you should at the same time nip off their tops, which will cause each of them to push out two or more shoots, whereby the wall will be better supplied with branches ; you must also continue to refresh them with water in dry weather, during the whole season, otherwise they will be apt to suffer ; for their roots having but little hold of the ground the first year after transplanting, if the season should prove very dry, it will greatly retard their growth, if due care be not taken to water them.

In the beginning of October, when you observe the trees have done shooting, you should prune them ; in doing of which, you must shorten the branches in proportion to the strength of the tree ; which, if strong, may be left eight inches long, but if weak, should be shortened to four or five ; then you should train them horizontally to the wall (as was before directed,) so that the middle of the trees may be void of branches, for that part of the tree will be easily furnished with wood afterwards ; whereas, if the shoots are trained perpendicularly to the wall, those which are the strongest, will draw the greatest share of the sap from the roots, and mount upwards ; so that the side branches will be deprived of their nourishment and grow weaker, until they many times decay ; and this is the reason that we see so many Peach-trees with one or two upright shoots in the middle, and the two sides wholly unfurnished with branches, whereby the middle of each tree cannot produce any fruit, that being filled with large wood, which never produces any bearing shoots. Nor can the two sides of the trees be regularly filled with fruitful branches, when this defect happens to them ; therefore this method should be carefully observed in the training up young trees, for when they are permitted to run into disorder at first, it will be impossible to reduce them into a regular healthful state afterwards, the wood of these trees being too soft and pithy to admit of being cut down (as may be practised on many other hardy fruit-trees, which will shoot out vigorously again ;) whereas these will gum at the places where they are wounded, and in a few years entirely decay.

The summer following, when the trees begin to shoot, you should carefully look over them, to rub off all fore-right buds, or such as are ill placed, and train those which are designed to remain horizontally to the wall, in their due order as they are produced, for this is the principal season when you can best order the trees as you would have them ; whereas, if they are neglected until Midsummer, as is the common practice, a great part of the nourishment will be exhausted by fore-right shoots, and other useless branches, which must afterwards be cut off ; and hereby the re-

maining shoots will be rendered very weak, and perhaps some part of the wall be entirely furnished with branches ; which might have been easily supplied in May, by stopping some of the stronger shoots in such parts of the tree where there is a necessity for more branches, which would cause each of them to shoot out two or more side branches below the ends of the shoots, which may be guided into the vacant parts of the tree as they are produced, so as that every part may be regularly furnished with proper wood, which is the greatest beauty and excellency of wall-trees ; but you should always forbear stopping the shoots in summer, where there is not a necessity for branches to fill the wall ; for there cannot be a greater fault committed, than that of multiplying the number of shoots, so as to cause a confusion, whereby the branches will be too weak to produce good fruit ; besides, when they are too close laid in against the wall, the air is excluded from the shoots by the great number of leaves, so that they are never duly ripened ; and consequently, what fruit is produced thereon, cannot be so well tasted, as those which are produced upon such trees where the shoots receive all the advantages of the sun and air to bring them to maturity.

Thus having set down the method of training up young trees, I shall now proceed to their pruning and future management ; which, being the same as with full grown trees, will serve for general directions how to manage these sorts of fruit.

In the pruning of Peach and Nectarine-trees (which require the same management) the two following rules should be strictly observed, viz. First, That every part of the tree be equally furnished with bearing wood ; and secondly, That the branches are not laid in too close to each other for the reasons before laid down (with some others which will be hereafter inserted.) As to the first, it must be observed, That Peach and Nectarine-trees produce their fruit upon the young wood, either of the preceding year, or at most, the two years shoots, after which age they do not bear ; therefore the branches should be shortened, so as to cause them to produce new shoots annually in every part of the tree ; which cannot be done in the ordinary method of pruning, where persons neglect their trees at the proper season when they are most capable of management, which is in April, May, and June ; at which time the luxuriant growth of branches may be checked by pinching, and new shoots produced where they are wanting, by stopping the neighbouring branches ; which shoots, being produced at that season, will have time enough to ripen and gain strength before the autumn comes on ; whereas all those shoots which are produced after the middle of June, will be crude and pithy ; and though they may sometimes produce a few blossoms, yet those rarely bring fruit ; nor are the future branches good which are produced from such wood, the vessels being too large to strain the juices, so that they easily admit of great quantities of crude nourishment to pass through them. Therefore those persons who only regard their wall-trees at two different seasons, viz. the winter and Midsummer pruning, cannot possibly have them in good order ; for when all the branches which were produced in the spring, are permitted to remain until the middle or latter end of June (as is the common practice) some of the most vigorous will draw the greatest part of the nourishment from the weaker branches, which, when the strong ones are taken off, will be too weak to produce fair fruit ; and hereby the strength of the tree is exhausted, to nourish the useless branches which are annually cut off again ; and thus are too many trees managed, and at the same time complaints made of their luxuriancy ; because two or three shoots, by drawing away the greatest share of the nourishment grow very strong and woody (whereas, if the nourishment had been equally distributed to a regular quantity of branches, there would be no sign of their too great strength) until by often cutting off these vigorous branches, the trees are either entirely destroyed, or at least rendered so weak as not to be

able

able to produce fruit; for although by thus weakening the branches, it is often the means to produce a good number of bloſſoms (as may many times be obſerved alſo upon autumnal ſhoots;) yet the utmoſt of their ſtrength is ſpent in expanding the flowers, ſo that they rarely produce fruit; and very often the greateſt part of the branches die ſoon after, which is ſuppoſed to be occaſioned by a blight (as I have elſewhere ſaid) when in reality it is nothing leſs than the fault of thoſe who have the management of the trees. It is therefore of the greateſt conſequence to wall-trees, eſpecially of theſe ſorts, to go over them two or three times in the months of April, May, and June, to rub off all irregular ſhoots, and to train in the branches that are left in due order to the wall, that each ſhoot may have an equal advantage of ſun and air, both of which are abſolutely neceſſary to ripen and prepare the wood for the next year's bearing; therefore the oftener the trees are looked over, to diveſt them of the uſeleſs branches, from the time they firſt begin to ſhoot in the ſpring till the autumn, the better will the wood be ripened for the ſucceeding year. And by duly obſerving this in ſummer, there will not be occaſion for ſo much cutting as is often practiſed on Peach-trees, to their great injury; for their wood branches are generally ſoft, tender, and pithy, which when greatly wounded, are not healed over again ſo ſoon as in many other ſorts of trees; and the wet inſinuating into the wounded parts, doth often cauſe the branches to canker and die; which may be entirely avoided by the gentle eaſy method of pinching and rubbing off the buds in the manner here directed, which makes no wounds on the tree; and hereby a vaſt deal of labour is ſaved, for one perſon who is ready at this buſineſs will go over a greater quantity of walling in one day, than three or four can when ſuffered to grow rude; ſo that if the trees are permitted to grow rude all the ſpring, they will require ſix times the labour to reduce them into order. Beſides, it is a great diſadvantage to the fruit, in permitting the branches of the trees to extend from the wall and ſhade them; and when they have grown under the ſhelter of theſe branches and leaves all the ſpring, until Midſummer, then by pruning off and ſhortening moſt of theſe ſhoots, and nailing the others cloſe to the wall, the fruit are ſuddenly expoſed to the ſun and air, whereby they receive a very great check, and are not only retarded in their growth, but often rendered ill-taſted, and have tough ſkins. The diſtance which the branches of theſe trees ſhould be allowed againſt the wall, muſt be proportioned to the ſize of the fruit or the length of the leaves; for if we obſerve how the branches of the trees are naturally diſpoſed to grow, we ſhall always find them placed at a greater or leſs diſtance, as their leaves are larger or ſmaller, as I have already obſerved under the article Leaves. And there is no ſurer guide to a curious artiſt than nature, from whence a gardener ſhould always be directed in every part of his profeſſion, ſince his buſineſs is to aid and aſſiſt nature, where ſhe is not capable of bringing her productions to maturity; or where there is room, to make conſiderable improvements by art; which cannot be any otherwiſe effected, than by gently aſſiſting her in her own way.

But to return to pruning theſe trees: the branches being carefully trained in, as before directed, in the ſpring and ſummer ſeaſons, we come now to treat of the winter pruning, which is commonly performed in February or March. But the beſt ſeaſon for this work is in October, when their leaves begin to fall, which will be early enough for their wounds to heal before the froſt comes on, ſo that there will be no danger of their being hurt hereby; and the branches of the trees being proportioned to the ſtrength of the roots at that ſeaſon, all the aſcending ſap in the ſpring will be employed to nouriſh only thoſe uſeful parts of the branches which are left; whereas, if they are left unpruned till February, the ſap in the branches being then in motion, as may be obſerved by the

ſwelling of the buds, the greateſt part of it will be drawn up to the extreme parts of the branches, to nouriſh ſuch bloſſoms as muſt be afterwards cut off; and this may be eaſily known by obſerving the ſtrongeſt ſhoots at that ſeaſon, when you will find the extreme buds to ſwell faſter than moſt of the lower ones; for there being no leaves then upon the branches to detain the ſap to nouriſh the lower buds, the upper ones will always draw from thoſe below.

But it is a conſtant practice amongſt gardeners, founded upon long experience, to prune weak trees early in the winter, and luxuriant trees late in the ſpring, in order to check their luxuriancy. Now it is evident, that this check does not proceed from any conſiderable loſs of ſap at the wounds of the pruned tree (excepting a few of the bleeding trees, when cut at that ſeaſon) but muſt ariſe from ſome other cauſe; for by ſeveral experiments made by the Rev. Dr. Hales, in fixing mercurial gages to the ſtems of freſh cut trees, he found thoſe wounds were conſtantly in an imbibing ſtate, except the Vine in the bleeding ſeaſon. Therefore when a weak tree is pruned early in the beginning of winter, the orifices of the ſap-veſſels are cloſed up long before the ſpring; and conſequently, when in the ſpring and ſummer, the warm weather advancing, the attracting force of the perſpiring leaves is not then weakened by many inlets from freſh wounds, but is wholly exerted in drawing ſap from the root; whereas, on the other hand, when a luxuriant tree is pruned late in the ſpring, the force of its leaves to attract ſap from the root, will be much ſpent and loſt at the ſeveral freſh cut inlets. Beſides, if it were no advantage to the trees to prune them at this ſeaſon, (which I think no one will have reaſon to doubt after making the trial) but that it only ſucceeds as well as the ſpring pruning, yet there is a great advantage in doing it at Michaelmas, for that being a much more leiſure ſeaſon with gardeners than the ſpring, they will have more time to perform it carefully; and then they will not have too many things come together, which may require to be immediately executed; for the ſpring being the principal ſeaſon for cropping their kitchen-gardens and attending their hot-beds, if they are diſengaged from the buſineſs of pruning at that time, it will be of great advantage, eſpecially where there is a great quantity of walling. And here is alſo another benefit in pruning at this ſeaſon, which is, the having the borders at liberty to dig and make clean before the ſpring, ſo that the garden may not appear in a litter at that ſeaſon.

Having ſaid thus much concerning the time of pruning, I ſhall now proceed to give ſome general directions how it is to be performed on Peach and Nectarine-trees, which require a very different management from moſt other ſorts of fruits.

In pruning theſe trees, you ſhould always obſerve where branches are ſhortened, to cut them behind a wood-bud, which may be eaſily diſtinguiſhed from the bloſſom-buds, which are ſhorter, rounder, and more turgid than the wood-buds; for if the ſhoot have not a leading bud where it is cut, it is very apt to die down to the next leading bud; ſo that what fruit may be produced above that, will come to nothing, there being always a neceſſity of a leading bud to attract the nouriſhment; for it is not ſufficient to have a leaf-bud, as ſome have imagined, ſince that will attract but a ſmall quantity of nouriſhment, the great uſe of the leaves being to perſpire away ſuch crude juices as are unfit to enter the fruit. The length you ſhould leave theſe branches, ſhould be proportioned to the ſtrength of the tree, which, in a healthy ſtrong tree, may be left ten or twelve inches, or more; but in a weak one, they ſhould not be more than ſix inches; however, in this you muſt be guided by the poſition of a leading bud; for it is better to leave a ſhoot three or four inches longer, or to cut it two or three inches ſhorter than might be proper to do, provided there be one of theſe buds, it being abſolutely neceſſary for the future welfare of the tree;
you

you fhould alfo cut out entirely all weak fhoots, tho' they may have many bloffom-buds upon them; for thefe have not ftrength enough to nourifh the fruit, but they will weaken the other parts of the tree.

In nailing the fhoots to the wall, you muft be careful to place them at as equal diftances as poffible, that their leaves, when come out, may have room to grow without fhading the branches too much; and you fhould never nail them upright if it can be avoided; for when they are thus trained, they are very fubject to fhoot from the uppermoft eyes, and the lower part of the fhoots will thereby become naked.

There is not any thing in the bufinefs of gardening, which has more exercifed the thoughts of the curious, than how to preferve their tender forts of fruit from being blighted in the fpring of the year, and yet there has been little written upon this fubject which is worth notice: fome have propofed mattreffes of ftraw or Reeds to be placed before the fruit-trees againft walls, to prevent their being blafted; others have directed the fixing horizontal fhelters in their walls, to prevent the perpendicular dew or rain from falling upon the bloffoms of the fruit-trees, which they fuppofed to be the chief caufe of their blighting; but both thefe contrivances have been far from anfwering the expectations of thofe perfons who have put them in practice, as I have elfewhere fhewn; therefore it may not be improper to repeat fome things in this place, which I have before mentioned in relation to this matter. And

Firft, I have already faid, that the blights which are fo often complained of, do not fo often proceed from any external caufe, or inclemency in the feafon, as from a diftemper or weaknefs in the trees; for if we obferve the trees at that feafon, where they are the moft fubject to what is called a blight, we fhall find the branches very fmall, weak, and not half ripened, as alfo trained in very clofe to each other; thefe branches are, for the moft part, full of bloffom-buds (which is chiefly occafioned by their want of ftrength.) Thefe buds do indeed open, and to perfons not fkilled in fruit-trees, fhew a great profpect of a plentiful crop of fruit; whereas the whole ftrength of the branches is fpent in nourifhing the flowers, and being unable to do any more, the bloffoms fall off, and the fmall efforts of the leaf-buds are checked, fo that many times great part of the branches die away, and this is called a great blight; whereas, at the fame time it may be often obferved, that fome trees of a different fort, nay, even fome of the fame fort, were ftronger and in health, though placed in the fame foil, expofed to the fame afpect, and fubject to the fame inclemency of air, have efcaped very well, when the weak trees have appeared to be almoft dead; which is a plain indication, that it proceeds from fome caufe within the tree, and not from any external blight. All this will therefore be remedied, by obferving the foregoing directions in the pruning and management of the trees, fo as never to over-burden them with branches, nor to fuffer any particular part of the trees to exhauft the whole nourifhment from the root, which will caufe the other parts to be very weak; but to diftribute the nourifhment equally to every fhoot, that there may be none too vigorous, at the fame time that others are too weak; and by continually rubbing off ufelefs or fore-right fhoots as they are produced, the ftrength of the trees will not be fpent, to nourifh fuch branches as muft be afterwards cut out; which is too often feen in the management of thefe trees. And

Secondly, It fometimes happens, that the roots of thefe trees are buried too deep in the ground, which, in a cold or moift foil, is one of the greateft difadvantages that can attend thefe tender fruits; for the fap which is contained in the branches, being by the warmth of the fun, put ftrongly into motion early in the fpring, is exhaufted in nourifhing the bloffoms; and a part of it is perfpired through the wood-branches, fo that its ftrength is loft before the warmth can reach to their roots, to put them into an equal motion in

fearch of frefh nourifhment, to fupply the expence of the branches; for want of which, the bloffoms fall off and decay, and the fhoots feem to be at a ftand, until the farther advance of the warmth penetrates to the roots, and fets them in motion; when fuddenly after, the trees, which before looked weak and decaying, make prodigious progrefs in their fhoots; and before the fummer is fpent, are furnifhed with much ftronger branches than thofe trees which have the full advantage of fun and fhowers, and are more fruitful and healthy; which muft certainly be owing to the caufe here mentioned, as alfo to their drawing in a great quantity of crude moifture, which, though productive of wood, is yet unkindly for fruit: if therefore this be the cafe, there is no way of helping it, but by raifing up the trees, if they are young; or if they are too old to remove, it is the better way to root them out and make new borders of frefh earth, and plant down young trees; for it is a great vexation to be at the trouble and expence of pruning and managing thefe trees, without having the pleafure of reaping any advantage from them, which will always be the cafe where the trees are thus injudicioufly planted. Or,

Thirdly, This may proceed from the trees wanting nourifhment, which is many times the cafe, where they are planted in a hard gravelly foil, in which it is the common practice to dig borders three or four feet wide, and three feet deep into the rock of gravel, which is filled with good frefh earth, into which the trees are planted, where they will thrive pretty well for two years, until their roots reach the gravel, where they are confined as if planted in a pot; and for want of proper nourifhment, the branches continually decay every year. This cannot be helped where the trees have been growing fome years, without taking them entirely up, or by digging away the gravel from their roots, and adding a large quantity of frefh earth, that may afford them a fupply of nourifhment a few years longer; but trees fo planted, cannot by any art be continued long in health.

But if the unfruitfulnefs of the trees does not proceed from any of the before-mentioned caufes, and is the effect of unkindly feafons, then the beft method yet known is, in dry weather, when little dew falls, to fprinkle the branches of the trees gently with water foon after the bloffoming feafon, and while the youngfet fruit is tender, which fhould always be done before noon, that the moifture may evaporate before the night comes on; and if in the night you carefully cover the trees with mats, canvas, or fome fuch light covering, it will be of great fervice to them: however, where the trees are ftrong and vigorous, they are not fo liable to fuffer by a fmall inclemency, as are thofe which are weak, fo that there will be few feafons in which there may not be hopes of a moderate quantity of fruit from them, though there fhould be no covering ufed; for where thefe coverings are ufed, if it is not performed with great care and diligence, it is much better to have no covering, but to truft to the clemency of the feafon; for if the coverings are kept too clofe, or continued too long, the trees will receive more injury hereby, than from being conftantly expofed; or, if after having been covered for fome time, and then incautioufly removed, fo as to expofe the trees too fuddenly to the open air, they will fuffer more thereby than if they had not been covered. However, I muft repeat in this place what has been before mentioned under another article, of a management which has been generally attended with fuccefs, which is, the putting up two feather-edge deal boards joined together over the top of the trees, fo as to form a pent-houfe to caft off perpendicular wet. Thefe fhould be fixed up when the trees begin to bloffom, and fhould remain till the fruit is well fet, when they fhould be taken down to admit the dew and rain to the leaves and branches of the trees, which muft not be longer kept off; and where the wall is long, and expofed to currents of wind, if at the diftance of forty feet from each other, are fixed fome crofs Reed-hedges

hedges, to projeft about ten feet from the wall, thefe will break the force of the wind, and prevent its deftroying of the bloffoms; and thefe may be removed away as foon as the danger is over. Where thefe things have been praftifed, they were generally attended with fuccefs; and as there will be no trouble of covering and uncovering in this method, after they are fixed up, there can be no danger of negleft, as very often is the cafe, when the trouble is great, or to be often repeated.

When your fruit is fet, and grown to the bignefs of a fmall nut, you fhould look over the trees and thin them, leaving them at leaft five or fix inches afunder; for when they are permitted to remain in bunches, as they are often produced, the nourifhment which fhould be employed wholly to the fruits defigned to ftand, will be equally fpent amongft the whole number, a great part of which muft be afterwards pulled off; fo that the fooner this is done, the better it will be for the remaining fruit; and if it fhould fometimes happen, that a part of thofe left, by any accident, fhould be deftroyed, yet the remaining ones will be much the larger and better tafted for it, and the trees will gain more ftrength, for a moderate quantity of fruit is always preferable to a great crop; the fruit when but few, will be much larger, better tafted, and the trees in a condition to bear well the fucceeding year; whereas when they are overcharged with fruit, it is always fmall, ill tafted, and the trees are generally fo much weakened thereby, as not to be in a condition for bearing well for two or three years after; fo that upon the whole, it is much better to have a leffer number of fruit than is commonly efteemed a crop, than to have too many, fince the fruit and alfo the trees are benefited thereby. The quantity of fruit to be left on large full-grown trees fhould never be greater than five dozen upon each; but on middling trees, three or four dozen will be enough.

If the feafon fhould prove hot and dry, it will be proper to draw up the earth round the ftem of each tree, to form a hollow bafon of about fix feet diameter, and cover the furface of the ground in this bafon with mulch; and once in a week or fortnight, according to the heat and drought of the feafon, pour down eight or ten gallons of water to the root of each tree; or where there is an engine which will difperfe the water in gentle eafy drops like rain, if the fame, or a larger quantity of water is fprinkled all over the branches of the trees, and this, foaking down to the roots, will keep the fruit conftantly growing, which will prevent their falling off the trees, as they generally do where this method is not praftifed; and the fruit being thus conftantly nourifhed, will be much better tafted, and hereby the trees will be maintained in vigour; fo that it is what I can from long experience recommend, as one of the moft neceffary things to be praftifed by all lovers of good fruit. But this fhould not be continued longer than while the fruit are growing, for afterward it will be hurtful to the trees and fruit, for a dry autumn ripens both wood and fruit better than a moift later feafon.

When the Peach-trees are carefully managed in the fpring of the year, according to the rules before laid down, all the nourifhment which the roots can fupply will be ufefully employed in nourifhing fuch fhoots only as are to be continued, as alfo the quantity of fruit which is proper for each tree, therefore both muft of confequence be rendered better; for where there is not this care, the trees foon grow ragged, and are not furnifhed properly with branches; and thofe fhoots which are produced, are fome of them very weak, and others very luxuriant, whereby the trees are rendered very unfightly, as alfo unhealthy, and never continues many years fruitful; and by thus training the branches to the wall as they are produced, the fruit will be always expofed to the fun and air; which in the common method of managing thefe trees, by letting their branches grow rude all the fpring, they are deprived from, and confequently do not receive the benefit from thefe equal to thofe

which are properly managed; and by the timely rubbing off ufelefs and luxuriant fhoots, it will fave much trouble, and prevent the ufe of the knife in fummer, which is very hurtful to thefe trees, for there will be no need to fhorten any of the fhoots in fummer.

When thefe rules are duly executed, there will be no occafion to pull off the leaves of the trees, to admit the fun to the fruit, which is often praftifed; for if we confider, that the leaves are abfolutely neceffary to cherifh the bloffom-buds, which are always formed at the foot-ftalks of the leaves, the pulling them off before they have performed the office affigned them by nature, is doing great injury to the trees, therefore I caution every one againft that praftice.

It is a common opinion which has for fome years prevailed, even amongft perfons of good underftanding, that Peach-trees are not long lived, therefore fhould be renewed every twenty years; but this is a great miftake, for I have eaten fome of the fineft Peaches of various kinds, which grew on trees which had been planted above fifty years: and I am convinced by experience, that when the trees are budded upon proper ftocks, and carefully planted and managed, they may be continued fruitful and healthy fixty years and upward; and the fruit produced on thefe old trees will be much better-flavoured, than any of thofe upon young trees; but I fuppofe the foundation of the above opinion was taken from the French, who generally bud their Peaches upon Almond ftocks, which are of fhort duration, thefe feldom lafting good more than twenty years; but this feldom being praftifed in England, the cafe is widely different; nor indeed fhould we fetch our examples from that nation, where the profeffors of the art of gardening are at leaft a century behind the Englifh; and from their prefent difpofition, feem unlikely to overtake them; for they depart from nature in almoft every part of gardening, and are more pleafed with introducing their little inventions of pruning and managing their fruit-trees, according to their own fancy, than they are careful to draw their inftruftions from nature, from whence the the true art is to be obtained; fo that in very few inftances gardeners fhould deviate from nature, unlefs it be in thofe particulars, where art may be praftifed to the greateft advantage, which is in the procuring many forts of efculent plants and fruits earlier and better flavoured than can be obtained without, in which the French are extremely deficient; and herein they truft too much to nature, and ufe too little art.

In one of the moft celebrated of their authors, who treats very particularly of fruit-trees, there are directions for planting of Peach-trees twelve feet afunder, and at the fame time he advifes the planting of Pear-trees but nine or ten feet diftance; and yet he fays, that a Pear-tree in health will fhoot three feet on each fide every year; therefore he does not allow room for thefe trees to grow more than two years, before they meet. There is alfo another thing pofitively laid down by the fame author, which is, never to lay any dung upon the borders where fruit-trees are growing, which, he fays, will render the fruit ill tafted; and this opinion has too generally prevailed in England; but this hath been exploded by one of his own countrymen, who affirms, that from upward of twenty years experience, thofe trees where the borders had been conftantly dunged, always produced the moft delicious fruit, and the trees were in the greateft vigour; and the fame gentleman mentions the praftice of the gardeners at Montreuil near Paris, who have for fome generations been famous for the culture of Peaches; and are as careful to dung the borders where their Peach-trees grow every other year, as the kitchen-gardeners are for their legumes.

And from a long experience it is, that I can fubfcribe to the truth of this; for in fome particular gardens, where the beft fruit grew that I have yet tafted, the ground was conftantly dunged every other year; therefore it is what I muft recommend to the praftice of every curious perfon, with this caution, always to ufe fuch dung for their borders as is well rotted, and to

dig

dig it into the borders in November, that the rain may wafh down the falts before the fpring comes on; and where the ground is very loofe or fandy, it will be the beft way to make ufe of neats dung, which is cooler than that of horfes, but for cold ftrong land the latter is to be preferred.

If the ground is well trenched every year about the roots, it will be of great fervice to them; and where the foil is fubjeft to bind very clofe, if it is forked two or three times in a year to loofen the furface, it will greatly help the trees. The borders fhould not be crouded with any large growing plants, which will draw away the nourifhment from the trees; therefore when any fort of kitchen herbs are planted on thefe borders, they fhould be only fuch as are of fmall growth, and which may be taken off early in the fpring; and if this is carefully obferved, the cultivating fmall things on thefe borders can do no harm, becaufe the ground will be ftirred the oftener, on account of thefe fmall crops, than perhaps it would have been, when no ufe was to be made of the borders. Thefe rules which are here laid down, if properly obferved, will direct any curious perfon how to have plenty of good fruit, as alfo to preferve the trees in vigour a great number of years.

PERVINCA. See VINCA.

PETALS are the fine coloured leaves which compofe the moft confpicuous parts of a flower; thefe are called in Latin Petala, to diftinguifh them from the leaves of plants, which are called Folia.

PETASITES. See TUSSILAGO.

PETIVERIA. Plum. Nov. Gen. 50. tab. 39. Lin. Gen. Plant. 417. Guinea Henweed.

The CHARACTERS are,

The flower hath a permanent empalement, compofed of five narrow obtufe leaves which are equal. It hath four fmall white petals, placed in form of a crofs, which foon fall off, and fix awl-fhaped erect ftamina terminated by fingle fummits. In the center is fituated an oblong compreffed germen, with four awl-fhaped ftyles, crowned by obtufe permanent ftigmas. The germen afterward becomes one oblong feed, narrow at the bottom and taper, but broad above, where it is compreffed and indented at the top, refembling an inverted fhield armed with the acute ftyle, which is reflexed.

This genus of plants is ranged in the fourth fection of Linnæus's fixth clafs, which includes thofe plants whofe flowers have fix ftamina and four ftyles.

The SPECIES are,

1. PETIVERIA (*Alliacea*) floribus hexandris. Hort. Cliff. 141. *Petiveria with fix ftamina in the flowers.* Verbena aut fcorodoniæ affinis anomala, flore albido calyce afpero, alii odore. Sloan. Hift. 1. p. 171. *commonly called Guinea Henweed.*

2. PETIVERIA (*Octandra*) floribus octandris. Lin. Sp. Plant. 486. *Petiveria with eight ftamina in the flowers.* Petiveria folani foliis, loculis fpinofis. Plum. Nov. Gen. 50.

The title of this genus was given to it by Father Plumier, who difcovered it in America, in honour of Mr. James Petiver, an apothecary of London, who was a curious botanift.

The firft is a very common plant in Jamaica, Barbadoes, and moft of the other iflands in the Weft-Indies, where it grows in fhady woods, and all the favannas, in fuch plenty, as to become a troublefome weed; and as this plant will endure a great deal of drought, it remains green when other plants are burned up, which occafions the cattle to browze on it; and having a moft unfavoury ftrong fcent, fomewhat like wild Garlick, it gives the cows milk the fame flavour, and the cattle which are killed foon after feeding on this plant, have a moft intolerable fcent, and their flefh is good for little. The roots are ftrong, and ftrike deep in the ground; the ftalks rife from two to three feet high; they are jointed and become ligneous at bottom, and are garnifhed with oblong leaves three inches long, and an inch and a half broad, of a deep green, and veined; thefe are placed alternately upon fhort foot-ftalks. The flow-

ers are produced in flender fpikes at the end of the branches; they are very fmall, fo make no figure. They appear in June, and are fucceeded by fhort feedveffels fhaped like an inverted fhield, containing one oblong feed which ripens in the autumn.

The fecond fort is very like the firft, from which it differs in having a fhorter and narrower ftalk, and the flowers having eight ftamina; but unlefs thefe marks are diftinguifhed by a nice obferver, they may both pafs for one plant.

In Europe, thefe plants are preferved in the gardens of thofe perfons who are curious in botany; but they have little beauty, and having fo ftrong rank fcent upon being handled, renders them lefs valuable. They are propagated by feeds, which muft be fown on a hot-bed early in the fpring, and when the plants are come up, they fhould be each tranfplanted into a feparate pot, and plunged into a moderate hot-bed to bring them forward. When the plants have obtained a good fhare of ftrength, they fhould be inured to bear the open air by degrees, into which they may be removed toward the latter end of June, placing them in a warm fituation, where they may remain till autumn, when they fhould be removed into the ftove, and in winter muft have a moderate degree of warmth, otherwife they will not live in this country. They will produce flowers and feeds every fummer, and will continue feveral years, remaining conftantly green throughout the year, and may be propagated by flips or cuttings.

PETREA. Houft. Gen. Nov. Lin. Gen. Plant. 682.

The CHARACTERS are,

The flower hath a bell-fhaped empalement of one leaf, cut into five large obtufe fegments almoft to the bottom, which are coloured, expanded and permanent. The flower hath one petal, having a fhort tube, but is cut above into five almoft equal fegments, which are expanded. It hath four fhort ftamina fituated in the tube, two of which are a little longer than the other, terminated by fingle fummits, and four germen fupporting a flender ftyle, crowned by an obtufe ftigma. The germen afterward become four feeds wrapped up in a fringed cover.

This genus of plants is ranged in the fecond fection of Linnæus's fourteenth clafs, which includes thofe plants whofe flowers have two long and two fhorter ftamina, and the feeds are inclofed in a cover.

The title of this genus was given to this plant by the late Dr. Houftoun, who difcovered it growing naturally at La Vera Cruz in New Spain, in honour of Lord Petre, who was a great encourager of botany, and was poffeffed of a noble collection of exotic plants.

We have but one SPECIES of this genus, viz.

PETREA (*Volubilis*) frutefcens foliis lanceolatis rigidis, flore racemofo pendulo. *Shrubby Petrea with ftiff fpear-fhaped leaves, and flowers growing in long hanging bunches.*

This plant was firft difcovered by the late Dr. Houftoun, growing naturally at La Vera Cruz in New-Spain, in 1731, fince which time it was fent me from the ifland Berbuda, where it alfo grows naturally. It rifes with a woody ftalk to the height of fifteen or fixteen feet, which is covered with a light gray bark, fending out feveral long branches; thefe have a whiter bark than the ftem, and are garnifhed with leaves at each joint, which on the lower part of the branches are placed by threes round them, but higher up they ftand by pairs; they are about five inches long, and two inches and a half broad in the middle, drawing to a point at each end; they are ftiff, and their furface rough, of a light green, having a ftrong dark midrib, with feveral tranfverfe veins running from the midrib to the borders, which are entire. The flowers are produced at the end of the branches growing in loofe bunches, which are nine or ten inches long, each flower ftanding upon a flender foot-ftalk about an inch long; the empalement of the flower is compofed of five narrow obtufe leaves about an inch long, which are of a fine blue colour, fo are much more confpicuous than the petals, which are white,

white, and not more than half the length of the empalement. After the flower is paft, the four germen in the center become fo many oblong feeds wrapped up in a fringed cover.

The Doctor found a variety of this with blue petals, of the fame bright colour with the empalement, which made a fine appearance, every branch being terminated by a long ftring of thefe flowers, fo that he has ranked this among the firft clafs of beautiful American trees.

So far as I have been able to difcover from the dried famples which the Doctor brought to England, it appears that there are male and female flowers either on different parts of the fame tree, or upon different trees; for one fpike of flowers feems to be entirely male, and the other fpikes are female, but the Doctor has not noticed this in his manufcript.

This is propagated by feeds, which muft be obtained from the places where the trees grow naturally, and thefe are very few good; for, from the feeds which the Doctor fent to England, there were but two plants raifed, though the feeds were diftributed to feveral perfons; and this is a fort of confirmation of the fpikes of flowers being of different fexes, and that the feeds gathered by the Doctor, were taken either from trees at fome diftance from the male, or fuch parts of the fame tree which were remote from the male flowers. The feeds muft be fown in a good hot-bed, and when the plants come up, they fhould be each planted in a feparate fmall pot filled with light loamy earth, and plunged into a hot-bed of tanners bark, and afterwards placed in the bark-bed in the ftove, where they fhould conftantly remain, and be treated like other plants of the fame country.

PETROSELINUM. See APIUM.

PEUCEDANUM. Tourn. Inft. R. H. 318. tab. 169. Lin. Gen. Plant. 302. Hogs-fennel, or Sulphur-wort.

The CHARACTERS are,

It hath an umbelliferous flower. The principal umbel is compofed of feveral long narrow umbels which fpread open. The cover of the large umbel is compofed of many linear reflexed leaves. The empalement of the flower is fmall and indented in five parts. The petals of the great umbel are uniform. The flower is compofed of five oblong incurved petals, which are equal and entire; they have each five b.... .... , terminated by fingle fummits, with a.. .. .. ermen fituated under the flower, fupporting two ..... ftyles, crowned by obtufe ftigmas. The germen afterward it... is an oval fruit channelled on each fide, fplitting in two parts, containing two feeds convex on one fide, comprefs... n: the other, with three raifed furrows, and a broad membranaceous border indented at the top.

This genus of plants is ranged in the fecond fection of Linnæus's fifth clafs, which includes the plants whofe flowers have five ftamina and two ftyles.

The SPECIES are,

1. PEUCEDANUM (Officinale) foliis quinquies tripartitis linearibus. Lin. Sp. Plant. 358. Hogs-fennel with leaves which are divided by fives, and thefe are again divided into three linear fegments. Peucedanum Germanicum. C. B. P. 149. German Hogs-fennel.

2. PEUCEDANUM (Italicum) foliis tripartitis filiformibus longioribus, umbellis difformibus. Hogs-fennel with leaves cut into three parts, which are longer, flender, and have irregular umbels. Peucedanum majus Italicum. C. B. P. 149. Greater Italian Hogs-fennel.

3. PEUCEDANUM (Alpeftre) foliolis linearibus ramofis. Hort. Cliff. 94. Hogs-fennel with leaves branching, which are very flender. Ferula foliis libanotidis brevioribus, alpeftris, umbellis ampliffimis. Boerh. Ind. alt. 1. p. 65.

4. PEUCEDANUM (Minus) foliis pinnatis, foliolis pinnatifidis, laciniis linearibus oppofitis, caule ramofiffimo patulo. Flor. Angl. 101. Hogs-fennel with winged leaves whofe cuts are linear and oppofite, with a fpreading branching ftalk.

5. PEUCEDANUM (Nodofum) foliolis alternatim multifidis. Hort. Cliff. 94. Hogs-fennel with many-pointed

leaves placed alternately. Silaum (quod ligufticum Creticum, foliis fœniculi caule nodofo. Tourn. Cor. 23.)

The firft fort is faid to grow naturally in England, but I have not been lucky enough to find it, though I have fearched the places where it is mentioned, but it grows in feveral parts of Germany in marfhy meadows. This hath a perennial root, which divides into many ftrong fibres running deep in the ground, from which arife the foot-ftalks of the leaves which are channelled; thefe are naked at bottom, but about four or five inches from the root branches into five fmaller foot-ftalks, and thefe again divide into three, and each of thefe divifions fuftain three narrow leaves, which when bruifed emit a ftrong fcent like fulphur. The ftalks rife near two feet high; they are channelled, and divide into two or three branches, each being terminated by a large regular umbel of yellow flowers, compofed of feveral fmall umbels which are circular. Thefe flowers appear in June, and are fucceeded by comprefled feeds, which are deeply furrowed, and ripen in the autumn.

The fecond fort grows naturally on the mountains, and alfo in the low valleys by the fides of rivers in Italy. The root of this is perennial, ftriking deep into the ground; the foot-ftalks of the leaves are large and furrowed, dividing into three fmall branches, which are again divided into three, and thefe end with three long narrow lobes or fmall leaves, which are much longer than thofe of the other fort. The ftalks which fuftain the umbels rife near three feet high, and divide toward the top into feveral fmall branches, each fuftaining an umbel compofed of feveral fmaller rays or umbels, which ftand upon very long foot-ftalks, that fpread out irregularly. The flowers of this are yellow, and fhaped like thofe of the former, but are much larger, as are alfo the feeds, but have the fame form as the other. It flowers and perfects feeds about the fame time as the former.

The third fort grows naturally in the foreft of Fontainbleau, and fome other parts of France; it hath a perennial root, from which come out leaves which branch into feveral divifions, that divide again into fmaller; each of thefe fmaller divifions are garnifhed with five fhort narrow leaves. The ftalks are round, and not fo deeply channelled as either of the former, fuftaining a large umbel of yellow flowers fhaped like thofe of the former forts; the feeds are fhorter, but of the fame fhape as thofe. It flowers in June, and the feeds ripen the beginning of September.

The fourth fort grows naturally on St. Vincent's rock near Briftol; this is a biennial plant, which perifhes foon after it has perfected its feeds. The leaves of this fort are fhort and very narrow, fpreading near the furface of the ground; the ftalks rife near a foot high, but are branched almoft from the bottom; thefe branches are almoft horizontal, and are garnifhed with a few narrow fhort leaves of a lucid green. Each ftalk is terminated by a fmall umbel of flowers, which are of an herbaceous yellow colour and fmall. Thefe are fucceeded by fmall channelled feeds.

The fifth fort grows naturally in Crete; it is not a plant of long duration in England, nor do the feeds ripen well here. The ftalks rife a foot and a half high, having pretty large knots at the joints, from which arifes a leaf cut into many divifions; the flowers terminate the ftalks in umbels, and appear the beginning of July, and in warm feafons the feeds will ripen in the autumn.

The firft fort ftands in the lift of medicinal plants, but is at prefent rarely ufed; the roots are the only part prefcribed. It is accounted good to clear the lungs of tough vifcid phlegm, and thereby to help old coughs and fhortnefs of breath; it likewife opens obftructions of the liver and fpleen, and helps the jaundice.

The other forts are preferved in botanic gardens for the fake of variety; they are all propagated by feeds, which fhould be fown in the autumn foon after they are ripe, for thofe which are fown in the fpring feldom

www.ingramcontent.com/pod-product-compliance
Lightning Source LLC
Chambersburg PA
CBHW032300280326
41932CB00009B/636